W9-BRI-818

## How to Use the Maps in *World Civilizations, 4th Edition*

Here are some basic map concepts that will help you to get the most out of the maps in this textbook.

- Always look at the scale, which allows you to determine the distance in miles or kilometers between locations on the map.
- Examine the legend carefully. It explains the colors and symbols used on the map.
- Note the locations of mountains, rivers, oceans, and other geographic features, and consider how these would affect such human activities as agriculture, commerce, travel, and warfare.
- Read the map caption thoroughly. It provides important information, sometimes not covered in the text itself.
- Many of the text's maps also carry a globe icon alongside the title, which indicates that the map appears in interactive form on the text's website: http://history.wadsworth.com/adler04/

ICELAND
NORWAY
SWEDEN
FINLAND
ESTONIA
LATVIA
LITHUANIA
UNITED KINGDOM
DENMARK
IRELAND
NETH.
POLAND
BELARUS
GERMANY
BELGIUM
LUX.
CZECH
SLOVAKIA
UKRAINE
LIECH.
AUST.
HUNGARY
MOLDOVA
FRANCE
SW.
SLO.
CRO.
BO.-HER.
YUGO.
ROMANIA
BULGARIA
ITALY
ALB.
MACE.
GREECE
PORTUGAL
SPAIN
MALTA
MOROCCO
TUNISIA
CYPRUS
LEB.
ISRAEL
SYRIA
GEORGIA
ARM.
AZER.
TURKEY
IRAQ
JORDAN
KUWAIT
IRAN
BAHRAIN
UNITED ARAB EMIR.
OMAN
SAUDI ARABIA
YEMEN
RUSSIA
KAZAKHSTAN
UZBEKISTAN
TURKMENISTAN
KYRGYZSTAN
TAJIKISTAN
AFGHAN-ISTAN
PAKISTAN
MONGOLIA
CHINA
N. KOREA
S. KOREA
JAPAN
NEPAL
BHUTAN
BANGLADESH
INDIA
MYANMAR
VIETNAM
LAOS
THAILAND
CAMBODIA
TAIWAN
PHILIPPINES
SRI LANKA
BRUNEI
MALAYSIA
I N D O N E S I A
PAPUA NEW GUINEA
PACIFIC OCEAN
INDIAN OCEAN
AUSTRALIA
W. SAHARA (Mor.)
ALGERIA
LIBYA
EGYPT
MAURITANIA
MALI
NIGER
CHAD
SUDAN
ERITREA
DJIBOUTI
SENEGAL
GUINEA
BURKINA FASO
BENIN
NIGERIA
IVORY COAST
LIBERIA
GHANA
TOGO
CENTRAL AFRICAN REP.
ETHIOPIA
SOMALIA
CAMEROON
EQUATORIAL GUINEA
GABON
CONGO REP.
CABINDA (Ang.)
RWANDA
DEM. REP. OF THE CONGO
UGANDA
KENYA
BURUNDI
TANZANIA
SEYCHELLES
COMOROS
MALAWI
ANGOLA
ZAMBIA
MOZAMBIQUE
MADAGASCAR
NAMIBIA
ZIMBABWE
BOTSWANA
MAURITIUS (Fr.)
REUNION (Fr.)
SWAZILAND
SOUTH AFRICA
LESOTHO
ANTIC OCEAN
ANTARCTICA

RUSSIA
ALASKA
(U.S.)
CANADA
GREENLAND
(Den.)
UNITED
STATES
ATLANTIC
OCEAN
BAHAMAS
MEXICO
CUBA
DOMINICAN REP.
Puerto Rico (U.S.)
HAWAII
(U.S.)
JAMAICA
HAITI
ST. KITTS
BELIZE
VIRGIN ISLANDS
ANTIGUA
GUATEMALA
HONDURAS
ST. LUCIA
DOMINICA
EL SALVADOR
BARBADOS
NICARAGUA
ST. VINCENT
GRENADA
TRINIDAD & TOBAGO
COSTA RICA
VENEZUELA
GUYANA
PANAMA
SURINAME
FR. GUIANA
PACIFIC
COLOMBIA
ECUADOR
OCEAN
PERU
BRAZIL
KIRIBATI
NAURU
TOKELAU
SOLOMON
ISLANDS
TUVALU
WEST.
SAMOA
AM.
SAMOA
VANUATU
FIJI
COOK
IS.
(N.Z.)
TONGA
NIUE
(N.Z.)
FRENCH
POLYNESIA
NEW
CALEDONIA
(Fr.)
BOLIVIA
PARAGUAY
PITCAIRN
(U.K.)
ARGENTINA
URUGUAY
CHILE
NEW
ZEALAND
FALKLAND IS.
(U.K.)

FOURTH EDITION

# WORLD CIVILIZATIONS

PHILIP J. ADLER ✠ RANDALL L. POUWELS

EAST CAROLINA UNIVERSITY ✠ UNIVERSITY OF CENTRAL ARKANSAS

Australia • Canada • Mexico • Singapore • Spain
United Kingdom • United States

*For Gracie, an historical event*
*—Philip Adler*

*To Claire Faye Haney Pouwels*
*in loving memory*
*—Randall Pouwels*

*Publisher:* Clark Baxter
*Senior Development Editor:* Sue Gleason
*Assistant Editor:* Paul Massicotte
*Editorial Assistants:* Lucinda Bingham, Emily Perkins
*Technology Project Manager:* Melinda Newfarmer
*Marketing Manager:* Lori Grebe Cook
*Advertising Project Manager:* Laurel Anderson
*Senior Project Manager, Editorial Production:* Kimberly Adams
*Executive Art Director:* Maria Epes
*Print/Media Buyer:* Karen Hunt
*Permissions Editor:* Joohee Lee
*Production Service:* Lachina Publishing Services
*Text Designer:* Gopa
*Photo Researcher:* Linda Sykes
*Copy Editor:* Ginjer Clarke
*Illustrator:* Pam Brossia
*Cover Designer:* Gopa
*Cover Image:* Kyoto bridge by moonlight, from the series "100 Views of Famous Places in Edo," pub. 1855 (color woodblock print), by Ando or Utagawa Hiroshige (1797–1858). Victoria & Albert Museum, London, UK/ Bridgeman Art Library
*Cover Printer:* Transcontinental Printing/Interglobe
*Compositor:* Lachina Publishing Services
*Printer:* Transcontinental Printing/Interglobe



Printed in Canada
2 3 4 5 6 7 09 08 07 06 05



Library of Congress Control Number: 2004111570

Student Edition: ISBN 0-534-59933-8
Instructor's Edition: ISBN 0-534-60635-0

**Thomson Higher Education**
**10 Davis Drive**
**Belmont, CA 94002-3098**
**USA**

**Asia (including India)**
Thomson Learning
5 Shenton Way
#01-01 UIC Building
Singapore 068808

**Australia/New Zealand**
Thomson Learning Australia
102 Dodds Street
Southbank, Victoria 3006
Australia

**Canada**
Thomson Nelson
1120 Birchmount Road
Toronto, Ontario M1K 5G4
Canada

**UK/Europe/Middle East/Africa**
Thomson Learning
High Holborn House
50–51 Bedford Row
London WC1R 4LR
United Kingdom

**Latin America**
Thomson Learning
Seneca, 53
Colonia Polanco
11560 Mexico
D.F. Mexico

# Brief Contents

## PART FIVE: REVOLUTIONS, IDEOLOGY, AND THE NEW IMPERIALISM, 1700–1920 408



## PART SIX: EQUILIBRIUM REESTABLISHED: THE TWENTIETH-CENTURY WORLD AND BEYOND, 1920–PRESENT 576

# Contents

# MAPS

# PREFACE

*WORLD CIVILIZATIONS* is a brief history of civilized life since its inceptions some 5,000 years ago. It is meant to be used in conjunction with a lecture course in world history at the introductory level. The authors, who bring more than fifty total years of classroom experience to its writing, have kept the needs and interests of freshman and sophomore students in two- and four-year colleges and universities constantly in mind.

*World Civilizations* deals with the history of civilization throughout the globe but attempts to walk a middle line between exhaustive detail and frustrating brevity. Its narrative embraces every major civilized epoch, but the treatment of topics is selective and follows definite patterns and hierarchies. It deliberately tilts toward social and cultural topics, as well as toward the long-term processes that affect the lives of the millions, rather than the acts of "the captains and the kings." The evolution of law and the formative powers of religion upon early government, for example, receive considerably more attention than wars and diplomatic arrangements. The rise of an industrial working class in European cities is accorded more space than the trade policies of European governments. Such selectivity, of course, is forced on any author of any text, but the firm intent to keep this a concise survey necessitated a particularly close review of the material. Dividing a brief narrative into fifty-six short chapters both gives the instructor considerable leeway for additional material or expansion of the topics and makes it likelier that students will read the assigned material. This approach has been relatively successful and has found sufficient favor among many teachers to justify the appearance of this fourth edition.

## CHANGES IN THIS EDITION

This has been a truly exhaustive revision, in both content and organization, reflected in part by the addition of a new coauthor, Randall L. Pouwels, a specialist in the Americas, Islam, and Africa. With the help of reviewers and editors, the authors scrutinized every line of this text with an eye toward a more comparative, global treatment of world history. The following points are among the many changes in this edition:

*Chapter 1* A new table on the evolution of the genus *Homo*. The idea of matriarchy in prehistoric human groups is introduced. New Evidence of the Past boxes on archaeological findings and the meaning of prehistoric art.

*Chapter 2* New sections on the economics of earning a living, on the status of women, and on sexuality and marriage in Mesopotamia. New map of Hammurabi's empire.

*Chapter 3* Contrasts between Mesopotamia and Egypt are more sharply delineated throughout the chapter. New Evidence of the Past box on the discovery of the tomb of Tutankhamen.

*Chapter 4* Expanded coverage of the role of women and marriage in Hebrew society. New Evidence of the Past box on the Dead Sea Scrolls.

*Chapter 5* New section on daily life and the position of women in early India. Added discussion of the Arthasastra.

*Chapter 6* Added material on Confucius's view of women.

*Chapter 7* Newly called out section on the role of geography in Greece's early political development.

*Chapter 8* Greek and Chinese philosophy compared and contrasted. New section on society and economy in Hellenic culture, including labor, education, slavery, and gender relations.

*Chapter 9* New section on society and economy in Hellenistic society, including the economy and the role of women.

*Chapter 10* A combination of the third edition's Chapters 11 and 12 into one chapter on Rome from Republic through Empire. New sections on Roman law and on society and economy, including slavery, gender relations, and education. An expanded section on Roman thought.

*Chapter 11* New map on the spread of Christianity.

*Chapter 12* This chapter was moved to the beginning of Part Three, to fall in better chronological order; coverage of the conquest was moved to the new Chapter 30. New material added on early land bridge migrations; Paleoindians and the Archaic Period; the Agricultural Revolution in the Americas; Teotihuacán; and North Americans. One new map of migrations and all new illustrations. New Evidence of the Past box on oral Native American corn myths.

*Chapter 13* This chapter was also moved for better chronological order. Now includes a new section on Songhay. New Evidence of the Past boxes on Ibn Khaldun's account of the decline of Ghana and the rise of Mali and Mansa Musa and on Ibn Battuta's visit to East Africa.

*Chapter 14* New coverage of the Kharijite Muslims and of the problems of expansion during the Umayyad Dynasty. New Evidence of the Past box from Ibn Ishaq's biography of Muhammad, collected from oral histories.

*Chapter 15* New section "The Further Development of Islamic Religious Thought," including coverage of Sufism. Expanded coverage of the status of women, including *purdah*. New Evidence of the Past box on the Sufi verses of Al Rumi.

*Chapter 16* Expanded coverage of Islam in India and the Delhi Sultanate.

*Chapter 17* Significance of the standardization of the Chinese written language and Confucianism's impact on education underscored.

*Chapter 18* The Chinese model for Japanese government underscored.

*Chapter 19* The significance of the crusades for Muslim–Christian relations underscored.

*Chapter 21* Section on family life and education moved to chapter end, for a more seamless telling of the political and artistic story of the Renaissance.

*Chapter 22* A largely new chapter, "The Mongol Intrusion," covering the Mongol conquests and the Yuan Dynasty in China. New chronology of the Great Khans; all new illustrations; new Law and Government box, "A Muslim Describes the Mongol Invasion."

*Chapter 27* Largely new chapter on the rise and fall of the Muslim empires, including the Ottomans, Safavids, and Mughals. New Evidence of the Past box on harem intrigue under Suleiman.

*Chapter 29* New Arts and Culture box on the origins and evolution of haiku. New map of Tokugawa Japan.

*Chapter 30* Chapter now covers from the conquest until before the independence movements. An expanded excerpt on debt peonage in the Society and Economy box. New Patterns of Belief box on religious festivals in Cuzco.

*Chapter 34* Old Chapters 38 and 39 combined, for more integrated coverage of the social impacts of industrialization.

*Chapter 37* A largely new chapter on the decline of the Muslim empires and the fundamentalist response prior to World War I. New Patterns of Belief box on a founder of Islamic fundamentalism.

*Chapter 38* Largely new chapter on Africa prior to 1880, including the slave trade as well as Muslim and European incursions. New map of Africa in the nineteenth century. New Law and Government box, a letter of King Affonso of Kongo.

*Chapter 39* New chapter on Latin America from independence to World War I. New Law and Government box on Juan Alberdi's plan for the political reorganization of Argentina. New Society and Economy box on the division of land in Mexico.

*Chapter 43* Background information on totalitarianism moved here from the chapter on Nazi Germany, in order to provide students with a better understanding of Italian fascism.

*Chapter 45* Chapter now focuses on Hitler and the Nazi state.

*Chapters 51–56* Updated to reflect events through 2004, including the war in Iraq, weapons of mass destruction, and global warming.

*Chapter 52* Now covers Africa from "the scramble for Africa" to the present.

*Chapter 54* New Law and Government box, the McMahon letter and the Balfour declaration.

## Organization of the Fourth Edition

The table of contents in this fourth edition contains a significantly increased amount of non-Western coverage—half the chapters in the book—and has been reorganized chronologically. In response to reviewer and adopter recommendations, the material from the last edition's "Ordinary Lives" chapters now appears in the appropriate chapters in particular eras, in order to provide a fuller, richer picture of those eras. And the split volumes available for two-term courses now divide at "to 1700" and "since 1500," to reflect the majority of world history courses. The split volumes now begin and end cleanly, at the beginning and end of major parts, so that each volume provides access to the necessary part pedagogical features.

The organization of *World Civilizations* is chronological. There are six parts, dealing with six chronological eras from ancient civilizations (3500–500 B.C.E.) to recent times (post-1920 C.E.). The parts have several binding threads of development in common, but the main point of reference is the relative degree of contact among civilizations. This ranges from near-perfect isolation, as, for example, in ancient China, to close and continual interaction, as in the late twentieth-century world.

The second organizing principle is the prioritization of certain topics and processes. We generally emphasize sociocultural and economic affairs, and keep the longer term in perspective, while deliberately minimizing some short-term phenomena. In terms of the space allotted, we emphasize the more recent epochs of history, in line with the recognition of growing global interdependence and cultural contact.

Although this text was, from its inception, meant as a world history and contains proportionately more material on non-Western peoples and cultures than many others currently in print, the Western nations receive attention consonant with their importance to the history of the globe. (In this respect, "Western" means not only European but also North American since the eighteenth century.) The treatment adopted in this book should allow any student to find an adequate explanation of the rise of the West to temporary dominion in modern times and the reasons for the reestablishment of worldwide cultural equilibrium in the latter half of the twentieth century.

After an introductory chapter on prehistory, we look first at Mesopotamia, Egypt, India, and China. In these river valley environments, humans were first successful in adapting nature to their needs on a large scale, a process that we call "civilization." Between about 2500 B.C.E. and about 1000 B.C.E., the river valley civilizations matured and developed a culture in most phases of life: a fashion of thinking and acting that would be a model for as long as that civilization was vital and capable of defending itself. Elsewhere, in Africa and in Mesoamerica, similar processes were under way. However, in two noteworthy respects these regions provided exceptions to the pattern by which people learned to produce food for themselves. In Africa's case, people of the Sahara region domesticated livestock, most likely cattle, before they learned to grow and depend on crops. Also unlike the patterns established in the Old World, early Native American farmers of the Western hemisphere developed forms of agriculture that did not depend on the flood waters of major rivers.

By 500 B.C.E., the Near Eastern civilizations centered in Egypt and Mesopotamia were in decline and had been replaced by Mediterranean-based ones, as well as new ones in Africa, Asia, and the New World, which drew on the older civilizations to some extent but also added some novel and distinctive features of their own. First the Greeks, then the Romans, succeeded in bringing much of the known world under their influence, culminating in the great Roman Empire reaching from Spain to Persia. For Europe, the greatest single addition to civilized life in this era was the combination of Jewish theology and Greco-Roman philosophy and science.

In the millennium between 500 B.C.E. and 500 C.E., the entire globe underwent important change. India's Hindu religion and philosophy had been challenged by Buddhism, while China recovered from political dismemberment to become the permanent chief factor in East Asian affairs. Japan emerged slowly from a prehistoric stage under Chinese tutelage, while the southeastern part of the Asian continent attained a high civilization created in part by Indian traders and Buddhist missionaries.

In the Mediterranean starting about 800, an amalgam of Greco-Roman, Germanic, and Jewish-Christian beliefs called Europe, or Western Christianity, had emerged after the collapse of Roman civilization. At the same time, the emergence of Islam created what many scholars believe was the first truly "world" civilization. Rivaling the great civilizations of Asia and considerably surpassing that of Europe, the great empire of the Abbasid caliphs in Baghdad (750–1258 C.E.) acted as a commercial and intellectual bridge that transcended regional barriers from China to Europe. Therefore, in the many lands and peoples bordering the Indian Ocean, the spread of Islam along the highways of commerce contributed to the emergence of sophisticated maritime civilizations in Southeast Asia, India, and East Africa. In West Africa, the great Sudanic civilizations of Mali and later Songhay likewise were based solidly on an Islamic foundation. Despite isolation, Native Americans of the New World created a series of highly sophisticated civilizations in the high Andes mountains of South America, in Mesoamerica, and in the southwestern and midwestern parts of what now is the United States.

By 1500, Western Christianity began to rise to a position of worldwide domination, marked by the voyages of discovery and ensuing colonization. In the next three centuries, the Europeans and their colonial outposts slowly wove a web of worldwide commercial and technological interests anchored on military force. Our book's treatment of the entire post-1500 age gives much attention to the impacts of Western culture and ideas on non-Western peoples, and vice versa. In particular, it looks at the African civilizations encountered by early European traders and what became of them, and at the Native American civilizations of North and Latin America and their fate under Spanish conquest and rule.

From 1700 through World War I, Europe led the world in practically every field of material human life, including military affairs, science, commerce, and living standards. This was the age of Europe's imperial control of the rest of the world. The Americas, much of Asia, Oceania, and coastal Africa all became formal or informal colonies at one time, and some remained under direct European control until the mid-twentieth century.

In the nineteenth and twentieth centuries, the pendulum of power swung steadily away from Europe and toward what had been the periphery: first, North America; then, Russia, Japan, and the non-Western peoples. As we enter a new millennium, the world not only has shrunk but has again been anchored on multiple power bases, Western and other. A degree of equilibrium is rapidly being restored, this time built on a foundation of Western science and technology that has been adopted throughout the globe.

Our periodization scheme, then, is a sixfold one:

- Ancient Civilizations, 3500–500 B.C.E.
- Classical Mediterranean Civilizations, 500 B.C.E.–800 C.E.
- Equilibrium among Polycentric Civilizations, 500–1500 C.E.
- Disequilibrium: The Western Encounter with the Non-Western World, 1500–1700 C.E.
- Revolutions, Ideology, and the New Imperialism, 1700–1920
- Equilibrium Reestablished: The Twentieth-Century World and Beyond, 1920–Present

## Pedagogy

An important feature of *World Civilizations* is its division into a number of short chapters. Each of its fifty-six chapters is meant to constitute a unit suitable in scope for a single lecture, short enough to allow easy digestion and with strong logical coherence. Each chapter offers the following features:

- Thematic boxes keyed to the five broad text themes: Society and Economy, Law and Government, Patterns of Belief, Science and Technology, and Arts and Culture. All chapters have one or more of these inserts, some of which are based on biography, many others on primary sources. To encourage readers to interact with the material as historians would and to compare themes across chapters, each boxed feature now concludes with "Analyze and Interpret" questions. And, to provide readers with access to additional readings, many document excerpts are keyed to the full document or related documents available in the free *HistoryNow* study system.
- A new boxed feature, Evidence of the Past, spotlights artifacts, material culture, and oral traditions as source materials for historical study. Once writing became common, of course, some materials that you will see in Evidence of the Past are written primary sources, but we will point out to you, where appropriate, their roots in oral traditions. We will also include some eyewitness accounts for your analysis.
- A chapter outline and a brief chapter chronology help readers focus on the key concepts in the material they are about to encounter.
- A chapter summary encapsulates the significance of the chapter's concepts.
- A "Test Your Knowledge" section at the end of the chapter provides a brief—and unique—self-test. Each test has been thoroughly accuracy-checked, revised, and expanded to include ten items with five choices each. Reviewers tell us that their students rely on these tests to assess their understanding of each chapter and to prepare for quizzes and exams.
- Key terms appear in boldface type and are repeated at chapter end in an "Identification Terms" quiz.
- Search terms for the InfoTrac College Edition® online database and a sampling of the documents available in the *HistoryNow* study system also appear at the end of each chapter.
- Color illustrations, many of them new, and abundant maps. We have added new "Worldview" maps that show global developments. Many maps are keyed with icons to indicate that there is an interactive version of the map on the text website. And strong map and photo captions encourage readers to think beyond the mere appearance of each visual and to make connections across chapters, regions, and concepts.
- A pullout world map in the front of the book, with a helpful key on "How to Read a Map."

Other features include the following:

- An end-of-book Glossary, now with a pronunciation guide, provides explanations of unfamiliar terms and pronunciation guidance for the more difficult among them.
- Each period opens with a brief part introduction and a Worldview map highlighting the major civilizations discussed in that part of the text. At the end of each part, there is a Worldview chart comparing the same civilizations, color-coded to the same groups in the part-opening map and affording a nutshell review of their accomplishments according to the text's five major themes.

## Supplements

The following supplements are available for the instructor:

- **Instructor's Resource CD-ROM for *World Civilizations* with Multimedia Manager and ExamView® Computerized Testing**

  This all-in-one multimedia resource includes the *Instructor's Manual,* the *Resource Integration Guide,* and Microsoft® PowerPoint® slides with lecture outlines. Most of the map acetates are incorporated into the presentations. Also included is ExamView, an easy-to-use assessment and tutorial system that allows instructors to create, deliver, and customize tests and study guides (both print and online) in minutes. ExamView offers both a Quick Test Wizard and an Online Test Wizard that guide users step by step through the process of creating tests—users can even see the test they are creating on the screen exactly as it will print or display online. Instructors can build tests with as many as 250 questions using up to 12 question types. Using ExamView's complete word-processing capabilities, instructors can add an unlimited number of new questions or edit existing questions.

- ***Instructor's Manual with Test Bank***
  Prepared by Janet Brantley, Texarkana College. One volume serves all three versions of the text. Includes the *Resource Integration Guide,* chapter outlines, lecture topics, definitions of terms to know, and student activities, including journal entry topics. The test bank includes over 2,500 multiple-choice, essay, and fill-in-the-blank questions. Multiple-choice questions now have five choices each. Also available on the Instructor's Resource CD-ROM.

- **Map Acetates with Commentary for World History**
  Includes over 100 four-color maps from the text and other sources. Packages are three-hole punched and shrinkwrapped. Map commentary is provided by James Harrison, Siena College.

- **Music CDs**
  Available to instructors upon request, these CDs include musical selections to enrich lectures, from Purcell through Ravi Shankar. A correlation guide is available in the *Resource Integration Guide* in the Instructor's Resource CD-ROM and the *Instructor's Manual with Test Bank.*

- **Sights and Sounds of History**
  Short, focused video clips, photos, artwork, animations, music, and dramatic readings are used to bring life to the historical topics and events that are most difficult for students to appreciate from a textbook alone. For example, students will experience the grandeur of Versailles and the defeat felt by a German soldier at Stalingrad. The video segments (averaging four minutes in length) are available on VHS and make excellent lecture launchers.

- **CNN Videos—World History**
  These compelling videos feature footage from CNN. Organized by topics covered in a typical course, the videos are divided into short segments—perfect for introducing key concepts in contexts relevant to students' lives. High-interest clips are followed by questions designed to spark class discussion.

- **JoinIn™ on *TurningPoint®* for *World Civilizations***
  This CD-ROM contains preloaded, book-specific Response System content (via our exclusive relationship with *TurningPoint®* software) designed to work seamlessly with Microsoft PowerPoint and the "clicker" hardware of the instructor's choice.

The following supplements are available for the student:

- ***HistoryNow***
  This free, web-based intelligent study system saves time for students and instructors by providing a complete package of diagnostic quizzes, a personalized study plan, integrated multimedia elements, learning modules, over 450 primary sources, and an instructor grade book.

- ***HistoryUnbound: Online Explorations in World History***
  This visually driven journey takes students on twenty-nine unique explorations into world history. Each exploration consists of a topical module complete with an overview of the topic, interactive maps and timelines, art images, primary and secondary source readings, a glossary, and questions. Allowing students to explore the past in a new way, *HistoryUnbound* comes with a printed book-specific Correlation Guide consisting of a brief description of each module, along with its list of readings, section questions, and module-level questions, as well as the one-time registration access code.

- **Wadsworth History Resource Center and Book Companion Website**
  http://history.wadsworth.com/adler04/
  Both instructors and students will enjoy the chapter-by-chapter resources for *World Civilizations,* with access to the Wadsworth History Resource Center at http://history.wadsworth.com. Text-specific content for students includes interactive maps, interactive timelines, tutorial quizzes, glossary, hyperlinks, InfoTrac College Edition exercises, Internet activities, and a full text Bibliography. Instructors also have access to the *Instructor's Manual* and PowerPoint slides (access code required). The newly enhanced Wadsworth History Resource Center features such resources as documents and links to online readings correlated to specific periods in world history, and photos that provide visual connections to events, places, and people covered in a world history course.

- ***Migration in Modern World History, 1500–2000,* CD-ROM (with User Guide)**
  Motivates students to challenge, assemble, and critique interactively interpretations of history. This media curriculum on CD-ROM was developed by Patrick Manning and the World History Center at Northeastern University. *Migration* goes beyond the mere chronicling of migratory paths. Over 400 primary source documents on the CD-ROM provide a springboard to exploring a wide range of global issues in social, cultural, economic, and political history during the period 1500–2000.

- ***The Journey of Civilization* CD-ROM**
  This exciting CD-ROM takes students on eighteen interactive journeys through history. Enhanced with QuickTime® movies, animations, sound clips, maps, and more, the journeys allow students to engage in history as active participants rather than as passive observers.

- ***HistoryUnbound WebTutor™ Advantage* for *World Civilizations* for WebCT™ or Blackboard®**
  *WebTutor Advantage's* preformatted content offers flexibility in assigning content and the ability to create and manage a custom course website. *WebTutor Advantage's* course management tool gives instructors the ability to provide virtual office hours, post syllabi, set up threaded discussions, track student progress with the quizzing material, and much more. For students, *WebTutor Advantage* offers real-time access to all of the modules from the *HistoryUnbound* product, which includes over 400 readings, numerous interactive maps, and end-of-section critical thinking questions that can be assigned and included in the gradebook. Instructors can access password-protected Instructor Resources for lectures and class preparation. WebTutor Advantage also provides robust communication tools, such as a course calendar, asynchronous discussion, real-time chat, a whiteboard, and an integrated e-mail system.

- ***World History Resource Center: The Modern World*— An Online Document Database**
  Gale's *History Resource Center: The Modern World* is the latest in our virtual library collection. The Modern World collection consists of Gale reference sources, full-text periodicals, and an extensive collection of primary source documents. Learn more about this innovative electronic reference and how it integrates such a diverse collection of resources to reflect students' natural research process by visiting http://www.gale.com/modernworld/. Access to this resource can be bundled with the text for a minimal charge.

- **InfoTrac College Edition**
  A Wadsworth exclusive. Students receive four months of access to InfoTrac College Edition's online database of continuously updated, full-length articles from more than 5,000 journals and periodicals—spanning more than twenty years. By doing a simple keyword search, users can generate a powerful list of related articles from thousands, then select relevant articles to explore or print out for reference or further study.

- **Map Workbooks**
  In two volumes. Feature approximately thirty map exercises that help students improve their geographic understanding of the world. *Not sold separately.*

- ***Magellan World History Atlas***
  Available to bundle with any world history text, the atlas contains forty-five full-color historical maps, including "The Vietnam War, 1964–1975" and "States of the World, 2001." *Not sold separately.*

- ***Sources in World History***
  This two-volume reader by Mark Kishlansky, Harvard University, is a collection of primary source documents designed to supplement any world history text.

- ***Exploring the European Past: Texts and Images***
  *Exploring the European Past (ETEP)* is a fully customizable, second-generation reader designed to bring to life the events, people, and concepts that define Western civilization, for the European portion of your course. As opposed to traditional readers, *ETEP* integrates written and visual materials into one product. Each reader is a unique combination of ancient and modern voices and timeless images chosen to enhance instruction and complement this text. The *ETEP* program consists of printed primary and secondary sources, plus online visual sources provided via our secure website. Our collection of readings and visual sources now features more than sixty historical themes, from antiquity through the twentieth century. To review the written sources currently available, visit http://www.textchoice.com (instructor site). If you would like to preview the *ETEP* visual sources, visit http://etep.thomsonlearning.com (student site). For more information, please call 800-355-9983.

## ACKNOWLEDGMENTS

The authors are happy to acknowledge the sustained aid given them by many individuals during the long incubation period of this text. Phil Adler's colleagues in the history department at East Carolina University, at the annual meetings of the test planners and graders of the Advanced Placement in European History, and in several professional organizations, notably the American Association for the Advancement of Slavic Studies, are particularly to be thanked.

In addition, the following reviewers of past editions were instrumental in the gradual transformation of a manuscript into a book; we remain indebted to all of them and to the students in HIST 1030–1031, who suffered through the early versions of the work.

William S. Arnett, *West Virginia University*
Kenneth C. Barnes, *University of Central Arkansas*
Marsha Beal, *Vincennes University*
Charmarie J. Blaisdell, *Northeastern University*
Laura Blunk, *Cuyahoga Community College*
William Brazill, *Wayne State University*
Alice Catherine Carls, *University of Tennessee–Martin*
Orazio A. Ciccarelli, *University of Southern Mississippi*
Robert Clouse, *Indiana State University*
Sara Crook, *Peru State University*
Sonny Davis, *Texas A&M University at Kingsville*
Joseph Dorinson, *Long Island University, Brooklyn Campus*
Arthur Durand, *Metropolitan Community College*
Frank N. Egerton, *University of Wisconsin–Parkside*
Ken Fenster, *DeKalb College*
Tom Fiddick, *University of Evansville*
David Fischer, *Midlands Technical College*
Jerry Gershenhorn, *North Carolina Central University*
Erwin Grieshaber, *Mankato State University*
Eric Haines, *Bellevue Community College*
Mary Headberg, *Saginaw Valley State University*
Daniel Heimmermann, *University of Northern Arizona*
Charles Holt, *Morehead State University*
Kirk A. Hoppe, *University of Illinois–Chicago*
Raymond Hylton, *Virginia Union University*
Fay Jensen, *DeKalb College–North Campus*
Aman Kabourou, *Dutchess Community College*
Louis Lucas, *West Virginia State College*
Ed Massey, *Bee County College*
Bob McGregor, *University of Illinois–Springfield*
John Mears, *Southern Methodist University*
Will Morris, *Midland College*
Gene Alan Müller, *El Paso Community College*
David T. Murphy, *Anderson University*
Tim Myers, *Butler County Community College*
Elsa A. Nystrom, *Kennesaw State University*
William Paquette, *Tidewater Community College*
Nancy Rachels, *Hillsborough Community College*
Enrique Ramirez, *Tyler Junior College*
Bolivar Ramos, *Mesa Community College*
Robin Rudoff, *East Texas State University*
Anthony R. Santoro, *Christopher Newport University*
Shapur Shahbazi, *Eastern Oregon State University*
John Simpson, *Pierce College*
John S. H. Smith, *Northern Nevada Community College*
Maureen Sowa, *Bristol Community College*
Irvin D. Talbott, *Glenville State College*
Maxine Taylor, *Northwestern State University*
Eugene T. Thompson, *Ricks College*
Susan Tindall, *Georgia State University*
Kate Transchel, *California State University, Chico*
Bill Warren, *Valley City State University*
Robert Welborn, *Clayton State College*
David Wilcox, *Houston Community College*
Steve Wiley, *Anoka-Ramsey Community College*
John Yarnevich, *Truckee Meadows Community College–Old Towne Mall Campus*
John M. Yaura, *University of Redlands*

Many thanks, too, to Lee Congdon, James Madison University; Maia Conrad, Christopher Newport University; Theron E. Corse, Fayetteville State University; Dennis Fiems, Oakland Community College, Highland Lakes; Lauren Heymeher, Texarkana College; Maria Iacullo, CUNY Brooklyn College; Rebecca C. Peterson, Graceland College; Donna Rahel, Peru State College; Thomas J. Roland, University of Wisconsin–Oshkosh; James Stewart, Western State College of Colorado; and Brian E. Strayer, Andrews University.

And this fourth edition, an especially thoroughgoing revision, had an especially perceptive group of reviewers. Our thanks to them for their comments and suggestions.

Patricia M. Ali, *Morris College*
Brian Bunk, *Central Connecticut State University*
Joseph Dorinson, *Long Island University*
Ali Gheissari, *San Diego University*
Samuel Hoff, *Delaware State University*
Ellen J. Jenkins, *Arkansas Technical University*
Aran S. MacKinnon, *University of West Georgia*
Thomas M. Ricks, *University of Pennsylvania*
Gary Scudder, *Champlain College*
Anthony J. Springer, *Dallas Christian College*
Kate Transchel, *California State University, Chico*
Lloyd Uglow, *Southwestern Assemblies of God University*
Peter von Sivers, *University of Utah*
Max E. White, *Piedmont College*
Michael D. Wilson, *Vanguard University*

But we would like to give special kudos to the following members of our Editorial Review Board, who stood by us throughout this edition's development process, approving every change and every new idea that you see in the text and package. Their involvement has been extraordinarily helpful and much appreciated. Janet Brantley in particular provided invaluable service accuracy-checking and rewriting the Test Your Knowledge questions, as well as preparing the new *Instructor's Manual with Test Bank*. And Werner Steger reviewed the Test Your Knowledge questions one final time, to assure their quality and accuracy.

Robin L. Anderson, *Arkansas State University*
Janet Brantley, *Texarkana College*
Stewart Brewer, *Dana College*
Janice Dinsmore, *Wayne State College*
Terrence Monroe, *Darton College*
Elsa Nystrom, *Kennesaw State University*
Thomas G. Smith, *Nichols College*
Werner Steger, *Dutchess Community College*

We would also like to acknowledge Clark Baxter's contribution as publisher; Sue Gleason's as senior development editor; Kim Adams's as senior project manager, editorial production; Ronn Jost's as project manager for Lachina Publishing Services.

And special thanks go to Joel B. Pouwels, Associate Professor of Spanish, University of Central Arkansas, for her important suggestions and contributions to the chapters on Latin American civilizations.

*Note:* Throughout the work, the pinyin orthography has been adopted for Chinese names. The older Wade-Giles system has been included in parentheses at the first mention and retained in a few cases where common usage demands it (Chiang Kai-shek, for example).

# About the Authors

PHILIP J. ADLER has taught college courses in world history to undergraduates for almost thirty years prior to his recent retirement. Dr. Adler took his Ph.D. at the University of Vienna following military service overseas in the 1950s. His dissertation was on the activity of the South Slav émigrés during World War I, and his academic specialty was the modern history of Eastern Europe and the Austro-Hungarian empire. His research has been supported by Fulbright and National Endowment for the Humanities grants. Adler has published widely in the historical journals of this country and German-speaking Europe. He is currently Professor Emeritus at East Carolina University, where he spent most of his teaching career.

RANDALL L. POUWELS earned his B.A. in history at the University of Wisconsin and his Ph.D. in history at UCLA in 1979. His Ph.D. dissertation was on the history of Islam in East Africa. His book *Horn and Crescent: Cultural Change and Traditional Islam on the East African Coast, 800–1900* (Cambridge, 1987) has become a standard work in African history. *The History of Islam in Africa* (Athens, Oxford, and Cape Town, 2000) was jointly edited with Nehemia Levtzion of Hebrew University, Jerusalem. Widely praised in reviews, it was selected by *Choice* as an Outstanding Academic Title for 2001 and was made a selection of the History Book Club. In addition, he has written numerous articles and reviews on East African history, the history of Islam in Africa, and historical methodologies. His other research interests include the history of the Middle East and the history and archaeology of Native Americans. Over the years, his work has been supported by grants and fellowships from Fulbright-Hays, the National Endowment for the Humanities, the Social Studies Research Council, the National Geographic Society, and the American Philosophical Society. He has taught African history for over twenty years at LaTrobe University in Melbourne, Australia, and at UCLA. He is presently Professor of African and Middle Eastern History at the University of Central Arkansas.

# Introduction to the Student: Why Is History Worth Studying?

Human actions tend to fall into broad patterns, whether they occurred yesterday or 5,000 years ago. Physical needs, such as the need for food, water, and breathable air, dictate some actions. Others stem from emotional and intellectual needs, such as religious belief or the search for immortality. Human action also results from desires, such as literary ambition or scientific curiosity, or the quest for political power over others, rather than from absolute needs.

History is the record of how people have tried to meet those needs or fulfill those desires. Many generations of our ancestors have found that familiarity with that record can be useful in guiding their own actions. The study of past human acts also encourages us to see our own present possibilities, both individual and collective. This may be history's greatest value.

Many people are naturally attracted to the study of history, but others find it difficult or (even worse) "irrelevant." Some students—perhaps yourself—dread history courses, saying that they can see no point in learning about the past. My life, they say, is here and now; leave the past to the past. What can be said in response to justify the study of history?

People who are ignorant of their past are also ignorant of much of their present, for the one grows directly out of the other. If we ignore or forget the experience of those who have lived before us, we are like an amnesia victim, constantly puzzled by what should be familiar, surprised by what should be predictable. Not only do we not know what we should know, but we cannot perceive our true possibilities, because we have nothing to measure them against. The nonhistorical mind does not know what it is missing—and, contrary to the old saying, what you don't know can definitely hurt you!

A word of caution here: this is not a question of "history repeats itself." This often-quoted cliché is clearly nonsense if taken literally. History does *not* repeat itself exactly, and the difference in details is always important. But history does exhibit general patterns, dictated by common human needs and desires. The French Revolution will not recur just as it did 215 years ago. But, as we know all too well, people still depose their leaders and rise up in arms to change the way they live. Some knowledge of and respect for those patterns has been a vital part of the mental equipment of all human societies.

But there is another, more personal reason to learn about the past. Adults who are historically unconscious are confined within a figurative wooden packing crate, into which they were put by the accident of birth at a given time and in a given place. The boards forming the box restrict their freedom and block their view in all directions. One board of the box might be the prosperity—or lack of it—into which they were born; another, their physical appearance, race, or ethnic group. Other boards could be their religion, whether they were born in a city slum or a small village, or whether they had a chance at formal education (about three-fourths of the world's children never go beyond the third year of school). These and many other boards form the boxes into which we are all born.

If we are to fully realize our potential as human beings, some of the boards must be removed so that we can see out, gain other vistas and visions, and have a chance to measure and compare our experiences with others outside. And the smaller our "global village" becomes, the more important it becomes to learn more about the world beyond the campus, city, state, and country in which we live. An introductory course in world history is an ideal way to learn about life outside the box.

As a good student, your best resource is your own sense of curiosity. Keep it active as you go through these pages. Remember, this and every other textbook is the *beginning,* not the end, of your search for useful knowledge. Good luck!

*P. J. A.*
*R. L. P.*

*Note:* Some of you may at first be confused by dates followed by B.C.E., meaning "before the common era," and C.E., meaning "common era." These terms are used to reflect a global perspective, and they correspond to the Western equivalents B.C. (before Christ) and A.D. *(anno Domini).* Also, a caution about the word *century* is in order: the phrase *seventeenth century* C.E. refers to the years 1601 to 1699 in the common era, and the phrase *first century* B.C.E. refers to the years 99 to 0 B.C.E. With a little practice, these terms become second nature and will increase your fluency in history.

# PART ONE

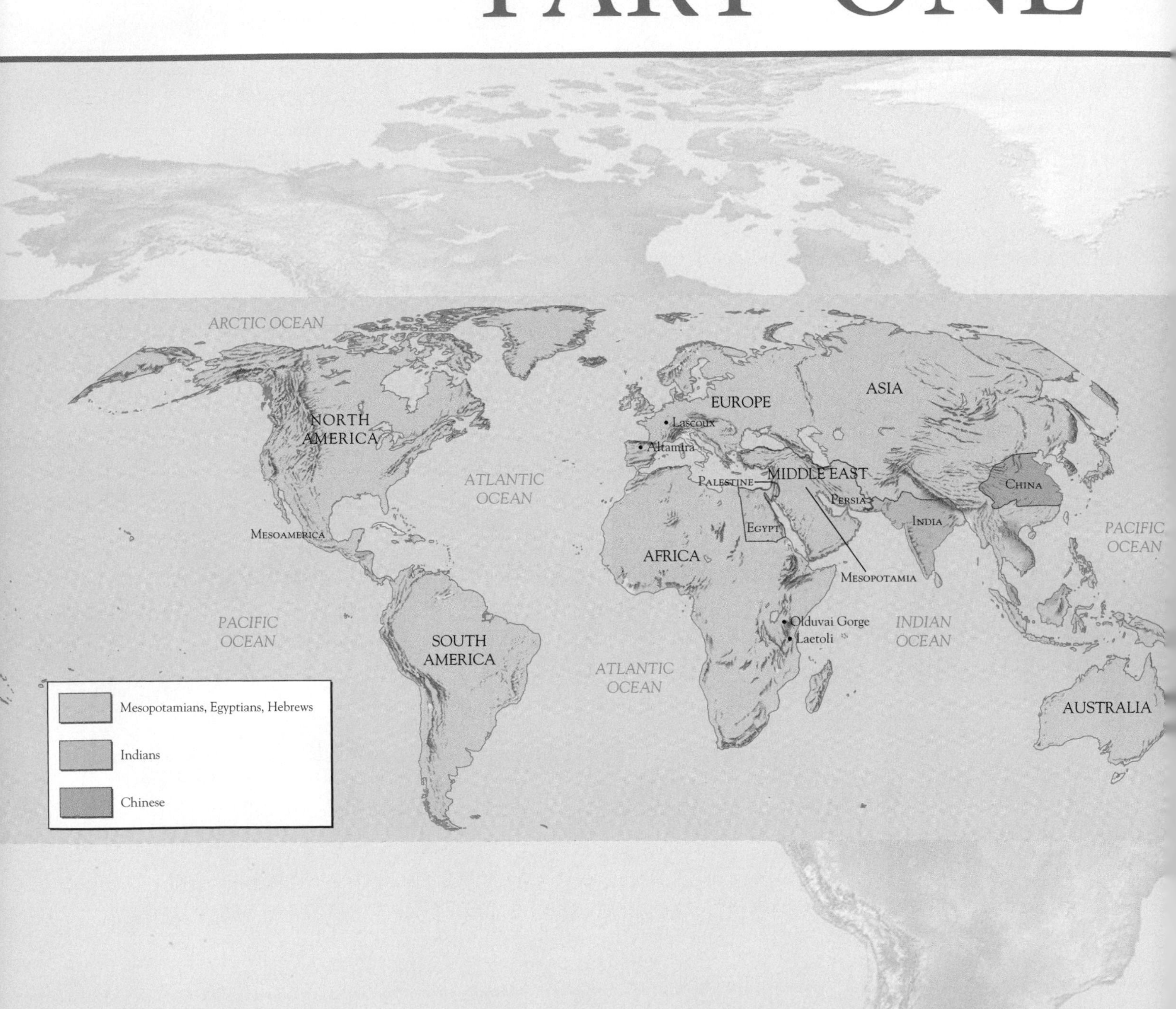
ARCTIC OCEAN
NORTH AMERICA
MESOAMERICA
ATLANTIC OCEAN
PACIFIC OCEAN
SOUTH AMERICA
EUROPE
Lascoux
Altamira
ASIA
MIDDLE EAST
PALESTINE
PERSIA
CHINA
INDIA
EGYPT
AFRICA
MESOPOTAMIA
PACIFIC OCEAN
Olduvai Gorge
Laetoli
INDIAN OCEAN
ATLANTIC OCEAN
AUSTRALIA
Mesopotamians, Egyptians, Hebrews
Indians
Chinese

# Ancient Civilizations, 3500–500 B.C.E.

How and when did civilization begin? To answer that question, the first six chapters of this book examine the growth of civilized life in four quite different areas of the globe before 500 B.C.E. The first chapter deals with the enormous stretch of time between the advent of *Homo sapiens* throughout much of the Earth and about 5000 B.C.E. We look at the general conditions of life and the achievements of human beings before history, or systematic written records of the past. These early breakthroughs are truly impressive, and it is a mark of their fundamental importance that we so rarely think about them. We cannot envision an existence in which they were unknown. Metalworking, writing, art, settled habitation, and religious belief are just a few of the triumphs of prehistoric humans' imagination and skill.

Most important of all, the commitment to growing—rather than chasing or gathering—food gradually took root among widely scattered groups in the late Neolithic Age (c. 8000–5000 B.C.E.). This Agricultural Revolution is one of the two epoch-making changes in human life to date, the other being the Industrial Revolution commencing in the late 18th century. Agriculture generated the material basis of *civilization* as that word is generally understood. Urban living, statutory law, government by officials, writing beyond mere record keeping, military forces, and socioeconomic classes are all indirect products of the adoption of food growing as the primary source of sustenance for a given group or tribe.

Chapters 2 through 6 examine the establishment and development of urban life in the river valleys of western Asia, northeast Africa, India, and China. First in chronology was probably Mesopotamia, but it was quickly rivaled by development in the Nile valley of Egypt. Both of these cultures began to take definite form about 3500 B.C.E. and reached their apex between about 1500 and 1200. Somewhat later, the plains of the Indus River in India's far west produced a highly organized and urban society that prospered until about the middle of the second millennium B.C.E., when it went into decline and was forgotten for many centuries. Simultaneous with the decline of the Indus valley civilization, the north-central region of China gave birth to a civilized state ruled by the Shang dynasties. Like the others, this society was founded on a mastery of irrigated farming. Unlike the Mesopotamians and the Indus peoples, both the Egyptians and the Chinese maintained the major elements of their early civilizations down to modern days.

Part One also provides brief accounts of a few of the other major contributors to world civilization before 500 B.C.E. Chapter 4 puts the warlike Assyrians and the first of the several Persian empires into perspective and examines the small but crucially important nation of the Jews and their religious convictions.

We open Part One and each of the other five parts in this book with a Worldview map that highlights the civilizations and cultures during the era covered by that part. This provides readers with a big-picture overview of the places and peoples discussed in the part, as a general frame of reference before they begin to study. At the end of each part, readers will find a Worldview chart, designed to provide a thumbnail comparison of the text's themes playing out across the various peoples of the part's epoch. The cultures in the Worldview maps are color-coded to those in the end-of-part charts.

*Civilization is a movement and not a condition, a voyage and not a harbor.*
Arnold J. Toynbee

# 1 Prehistory

Definition of Terms

The Evolving Past

The Paleolithic Age
Human Development During the Paleolithic

The Neolithic Age: Agriculture
Irrigation Civilizations

Metal and Its Uses

| | |
|---|---|
| c. 100,000–150,000 B.C.E. | *Homo sapiens* appear |
| c. 8000 B.C.E. | Neolithic Age commences |
| c. 7000 B.C.E. | Bronze Age begins |
| c. 3500 B.C.E. | Irrigation civilizations in Mesopotamia, Egypt |
| c. 1500 B.C.E. | Iron Age begins |

History, in the strictest sense, means a systematic written record of the human past. But most people don't use "history" in the strict sense. They define the word *history* as whatever has happened in the past to human beings, which, of course, is a much bigger proposition. Humans, however defined, have inhabited the Earth for a long time. Before history began, an extremely lengthy period of time elapsed during which human beings gradually mastered the various abilities of mind and body that together enabled their survival as a species on Earth. This period of human existence before any written record is called **prehistory.** By latest reckonings, it is several million years in extent. During this time, humans slowly and sporadically evolved from beings who were only slightly different from their genetic cousins among the great apes to creatures who have proven marvelously resourceful and adaptable. Tens of thousands of years before the beginning of the historical period, they populated the entire Earth (except Antarctica), developed religions, made tools, created art forms, mastered agriculture, and demonstrated many other talents and achievements.

By far the major portion of prehistory is and will remain unknown to us. From time to time, researchers are able to find some measurable remnants of ancient life amid the debris of the past, from which they might deduce informed guesses and even certainties regarding prehistoric humankind. Modern sciences, which do not depend on written evidence, are capable of occasionally penetrating the dark space of human development before history. Bones and pottery shards help us understand the material conditions of life among our distant ancestors. But the bulk of the human evolutionary record will necessarily remain closed to us, insofar as it was nonmaterial and did not leave such artifacts.

The development of human creatures from their earliest origins has become one of the most controversial of modern sciences. Every year, it seems, new evidence comes to light that purports to extend the age of the genus *Homo* farther back in time, and with a more tangled ancestry. Whereas until recently it was assumed that *Homo* evolved along a clear-cut and single-stemmed line, it is now generally accepted that human beings' family tree is more like a bush with many branches, of which almost all have died (see Table 1.1).

A humanlike creature, or **hominid,** was walking about in East Africa more than 5.5 million years ago, by latest reckoning. In the usage of contemporary science, the fundamental differences between humans and apes are certain deviations in bone structures of the foot and hand, the size of the brain, and the use of language. Because language necessarily could leave no traces until the invention of writing, physical anthropology depends primarily on skeletal remains to establish the age and

**TABLE 1.1 Evolution of the Genus *Homo***

| | |
|---|---|
| *Homo habilis* (Toolmakers) | 3.5 to 4 million years ago |
| *Homo erectus* (Bipedal walkers) | 1.5 to 1.8 million years ago |
| *Homo sapiens* (Neanderthals) | 100,000 years ago |
| *Homo sapiens sapiens* (Modern humans) | 30,000 years ago |

source of animal life, including humans. Bone fragments recovered at different sites in East Africa since the 1970s indicate that upright-walking (bipedal) animals possessing the essential anatomical attributes of modern humans were extant millions of years ago. A recent discovery shows bipedalism in a foot bone dating to more than 7 million years ago. This would put the creature it belonged to near the epoch when current anthropology places the genetic division between the genus *Homo* and its closest relations, the great apes.

*Homo,* we now know, subdivided into many species—a tree with many branches. Only one has survived to the present: the modern human being we see in our mirrors and all around us. Regardless of race or stature or any other physical characteristic, our fellow humans are all members of the species called *Homo sapiens* or, according to some authors, *Homo sapiens sapiens.* Both terms denote "thinking or skillful man" and a type of being that has populated Earth since roughly 100,000 years ago, at least, and that has outlasted its various predecessors among the hominids, such as Neanderthal Man, Cro-Magnon, *Australopithecus,* and myriad others whom we know only from the fossil evidence they occasionally left behind. All of these eventually disappeared for reasons that we may only guess at. In any case, the evolutionary tree proved to have many limbs that end in darkness. Only *Homo sapiens* and the great apes (that is, gorilla, orangutan, and chimpanzee) remain.

It is almost universally believed that *Homo sapiens* originated in Africa, probably in that continent's eastern regions, and migrated from there starting perhaps 40,000 years ago, first into the Middle East and then Europe. By perhaps 25,000 to 30,000 years ago, the sole surviving representative of the genus *Homo* was found on every continent but Antarctica and, possibly, the Americas. Worldview Map 1.1 shows the spread of *Homo sapiens* across the globe.

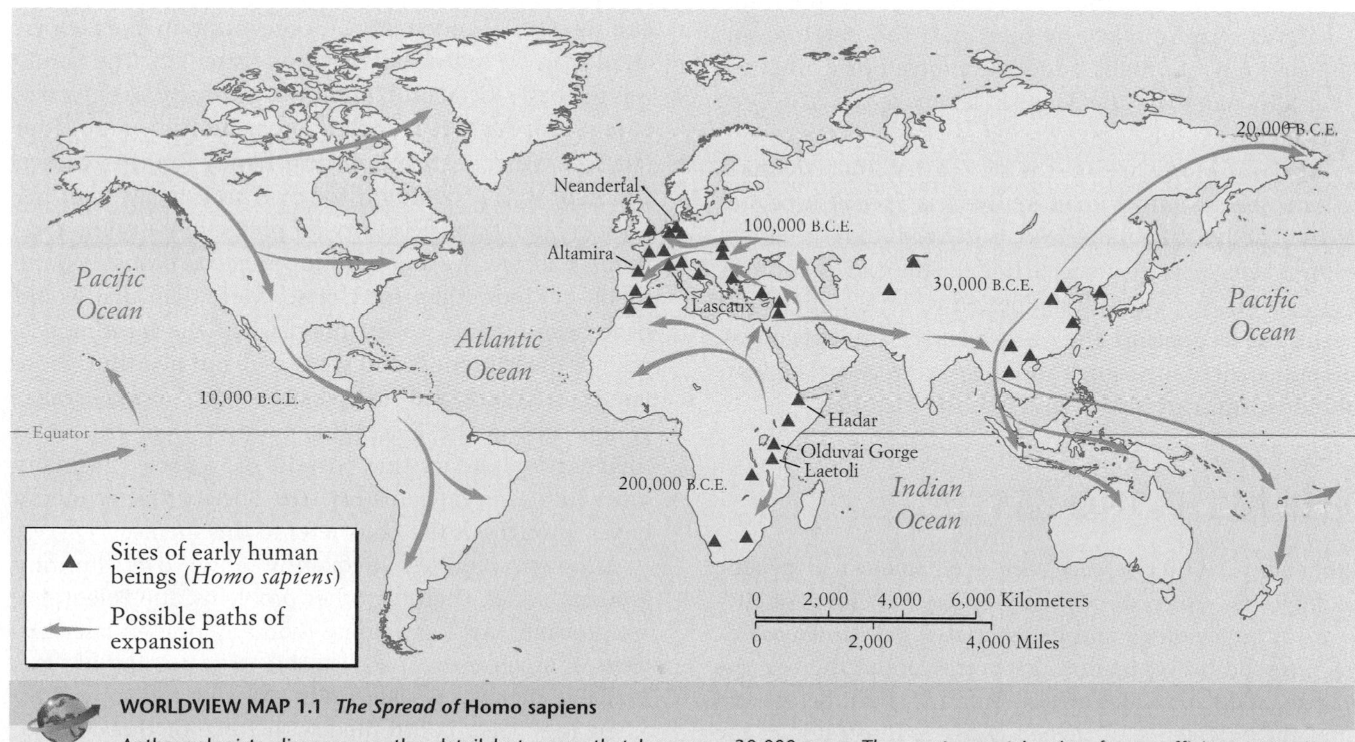


**WORLDVIEW MAP 1.1** *The Spread of* **Homo sapiens**

Anthropologists disagree on the detail but agree that human beings entirely similar to ourselves probably existed in every continent but Antarctica no later than 20,000 B.C.E. Their origin seems to have been in East Africa. From there, they expanded into southwest Asia and Europe, and into East Asia by perhaps 30,000 B.C.E. The most recent Ice Age froze sufficient water in the Pacific Basin to enable crossing by land into North America by about 20,000 B.C.E. The rapid ensuing migration southward carried *Homo sapiens* into South America by no later than 10,000 B.C.E.

## Definition of Terms

Let's start our exploration of the past with some definitions of certain key words and phrases:

- **History** is the systematic record of what people have done in the past. In this context, the past can mean 10,000 years ago or yesterday. History depends on memory; it is remembered activities. What has happened but been forgotten—which is, of course, the vast majority of what has happened—is technically not history.
- **Prehistory** is whatever happened to people in the period before writing.
- **Historiography** is the written form of history, as processed through an author's brain and bias working on the raw materials he or she has found.
- **Culture** is the human-created part of the environment, the "way of life" of a distinct group of humans interacting with one another. In prehistory, culture is often associated with and identified by particular tools.
- **Civilization** is a complex, developed culture usually associated with specific achievements such as agriculture, urban life, specialized labor, and a system of writing.
- **Archaeology** is the study of prehistoric and/or historical cultures through examination of their artifacts (anything made by humans). The name means "the study of origins," and like almost every other scientific name in the English language, it is derived from Greek.
- **Anthropology** refers to the science that studies humans as a species rather than studying a special aspect of their activity. Its name, too, is derived from Greek.

Archaeologists are crucial to the study of prehistoric humans. In that transitional period when writing is just beginning to develop, the *paleontologists* (students of fossils and ancient life forms) and the *paleographers* (students of old writing) are also essential to the historian.

## The Evolving Past

Probably no other science, not even nuclear or genetic biology, has evolved so swiftly in the past forty or fifty years as archaeology and its associated *paleoanthropology.* Each season brings its new discoveries about the age, the nature, and the locales of early humans, both before and after the emergence of *Homo sapiens,* as illustrated in the Evidence of the Past box. Throughout this book, in Evidence of the Past boxes, we will broaden the usual definition of *primary sources* (original documents of the time) to include objects, artifacts, and such nonwritten sources as the spoken word.

Tool-making ability is a primary indicator of the development of the hominids. Recently, the archaeological evidence we are discussing has been brought forward from southern Africa's Blombos cave complex to show that refined tools of both bone and stone were being made much earlier than previously thought, dating back well into the Paleolithic, some 70,000 years ago. Some of the stone materials bear regular markings that had no discernible functional purpose and must therefore have been made for decoration or the aesthetic pleasure of the maker. In other words, they were rudimentary art forms, and as such, they predate by many thousands of years the earliest previously dated art, found in the caves of Paleolithic France and Spain.

## The Paleolithic Age

The lengthy period extending from about the appearance of the first tool-making hominids to about 8,000 B.C.E. is known as the Paleolithic Age, or Old Stone Age, so called because tools were made of stone and were still quite crude (*paleo* = old; *lithos* = stone). By the end of the Paleolithic, humans inhabited all the continents except Antarctica. Paleolithic peoples were hunters and foragers, but life was not easy, and famine was always near at hand.

Paleolithic hunting and gathering was done in groups, and success depended more on organization and cooperation than on individual bravery or strength. The family was the basic social unit, but it was normally an extended family that included uncles, aunts, in-laws, and other relatives rather than the nuclear family (mother, father, children) that is common today. A unit larger than the nuclear family was necessary for protection. But the total number able to live and hunt together was probably quite small—no more than forty or so. More than that would have been difficult to maintain when the hunting was poor or the wild fruits and seeds were not plentiful. Close family relations and interchange with other, similar groups among the Paleolithic hunters were critical to their survival, a fact that we will see reflected in many other locales in later history. The Society and Economy boxes throughout the book refer to this theme.

Although conflicts frequently arose over hunting grounds, water, theft, or other problems, the Paleolithic era probably saw less warfare than any time in later history. So much open space capable of sustaining life was available that the weaker units probably just moved on when they were confronted with force or threats. Violence tempered and controlled by consensual authority was a constant factor in determining historical and prehistoric life. The Law and Government boxes throughout the book will help us follow this theme.

## *Human Development during the Paleolithic*

During the Paleolithic, both the physical appearance of humans and their vital capacity to reason and plan changed considerably. Because of the extensive work of anthropologists since World War II, we know that at least seventeen varieties of hominid evolved during this time. Much evidence uncovered in East Africa and the Near East as well as Europe indicates that all of these species of *Homo* came to an evolutionary dead end except for *Homo sapiens*. Some time between 50,000 and 10,000 years ago, *Homo sapiens* seems to have become the sole species of *Homo* to survive anywhere.

Why this is so is problematic. Some believe bloody warfare may have erupted between competing species of hominids; others posit a peaceable, gradual absorption by the more advanced species. A good example of the failed species is the famous **Neanderthal Man,** who flourished in western Germany about 30,000 years ago and then disappeared at about the same time that *Homo sapiens* appeared in Europe.

What happened to Neanderthal Man? Climatic changes probably affected and perhaps even caused this and other evolutionary developments. We know that the end of the last of several Ice Ages—almost 12,000 years ago—coincided with the appearance of *Homo sapiens* throughout the Northern Hemisphere. It is entirely possible that the pre–*Homo sapiens* inhabitants of Europe, such as Neanderthal Man, failed to adapt to the changed climate, in the same way that some zoologists believe that the dinosaurs failed to adapt much earlier.

During the Paleolithic, humans became more upright, and their skull changed shape to encompass a gradually

EVIDENCE OF THE PAST

### Unearthing Our Ancestors

**THE 1974 DISCOVERY** of the skeletal remains of a hominid nicknamed "Lucy" by an American team of researchers in Ethiopia was a key advance in modern anthropology. Lucy (named whimsically after the Beatles' song "Lucy in the Sky with Diamonds") is the first generally accepted example of *Australopithecus afarensis,* a bipedal creature who roamed eastern Africa's savanna more than 3 million years ago. The immediate ancestor of *Homo,* as opposed to hominid, Lucy and her small-boned fellows were a hybrid between modern humans and apes. A few years later, the fossil footprints of similar creatures were found in the volcanic ash of Laetoli, Tanzania, by the British Leakey family of anthropologists. These footprints showed a pair of individuals walking upright for several yards and were dated at about 3.5 million years ago. Since then, further discoveries around the globe have pushed the frontier between human and hominid even farther back in time.

It is currently thought that the decisive differentiation between humans and apes, genetically speaking, occurred 6 to 8 million years ago. This is based on DNA analysis of bone fragments from the skeletons of Lucy and other australopiths and on evidence of bipedal locomotion (standing and walking in an erect position). The oldest known exemplar of bipedal movement is *Ardepithecus ramidus,* discovered in Ethiopia in 2001. If it is accepted by the anthropologists as authentically dated at 5.5 million years of age, *Ardepithecus ramidus* approaches the earliest limits of the genus *Homo.*

Kenneth Garrett/National Geographic Image Collection/Getty Images

**FOOTPRINTS FROM 3.5 MILLION B.C.E.** These fossilized prints were found by the Leakeys in Laetoli, in present-day Tanzania in East Africa. The stride and distribution of weight on the foot indicate that these creatures were walking upright and were thus some of the earliest of the hominids.

#### *Analyze and Interpret*

Do you find it demeaning or humiliating that you (and all of your friends and family) are closely related as a species to the great apes? Does the extent of body hair or posture have any essential connection with the moral or cultural refinement of a given creature?

enlarging brain. Their bodies grew less hairy and their arms shorter. Hip structure changed to allow a more erect gait. Eyesight grew sharper and the sense of smell less so. All of these changes and many others were adaptations that reflected both humans' changed physical environment and their increasing mastery and manipulation of that environment.

The changed physical environment was reflected in the substitution of semipermanent shelter for the nomadism of an earlier day. By the late Paleolithic, groups were living in caves, lean-tos, and other shelters for long periods of time, perhaps several months. Whereas earlier a group rarely remained more than a few weeks at a given locale, now they could stay in one place several months to await the ripening of certain fruit or the migration of the animals. Even more important, humans' ability to master their physical environment was constantly increasing as they learned to make clothing for cold seasons, to kindle fire where and when it was needed, and to devise new tools for new tasks. The earliest human artwork came in the late Paleolithic. Certain caves of southern France (Lascaux) and Spain (Altamira) are world famous for their lifelike portraits of deer and other animals (see Evidence of the Past). Other human explorations of the aesthetic, whether in art, architecture, sculpture, music, or literature, are the subjects of Arts and Culture boxes throughout the text.

In such ways, humans began to bend the physical world to their will. As they developed an ability to plan and to remember what had been successful in the past, so they could repeat it. Humans in the late Paleolithic were making rapid strides toward civilization. They would reach the state of advanced mastery of tool making and innovative problem solving that we call the *Neolithic Age*.

## The Neolithic Age: Agriculture

Although the Paleolithic saw notable developments, it was in the Neolithic, or New Stone Age, that humans made the breakthrough to advanced culture and even-

EVIDENCE OF THE PAST

### Paleolithic Art

**Paleolithic art** in its most striking forms has been found in southern France and northern Spain, in caves that bear many marks of ancient human occupancy. The painting of horses here was found on one side of a large room in the recently discovered Chauvet Pont-d'arc cave in the southwest of France. This painting pushes back the time frame of European art by more than 15,000 years, to approximately 31,000 B.C.E. It is a section of a large mural depicting many different animals. The reasons why these paintings came into existence are much guessed at by modern researchers. Many believe that the prehistoric hunter was attempting to capture the spirit of the animal prey he sought in the coming hunts. Some believe that the animals pictured were the totemic protectors of the inhabitants of the caves, like the "medicine" of the Native Americans. And others think that, apart from any religious or magical qualities, the pictures display early humankind's strong aesthetic urge, much as men and women have done ever since by capturing lifelike representations of the living things around them.

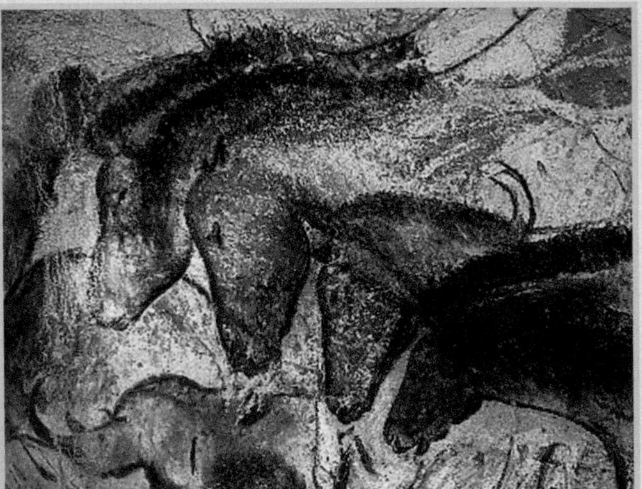



**Horses.** The Paleolithic artist demonstrates a mastery of his or her material that is the envy of any observer. These horses are a detail of a much larger fresco of animal sketches covering most of one side of a large room at the recently discovered Chauvet Pont-d'Arc cave in southern France. This painting pushes back the time framework of European art by more than 15,000 years, to approximately 31,000 B.C.E.

#### *Analyze and Interpret*

What do you believe might be the most persuasive argument for early artists' motivations?

tually civilization. As we saw, Paleolithic groups were essentially nomadic. They depended on either hunting and gathering or raising animals for food. Both the hunter-gatherers and the herders had a mobile life. The former moved with the seasons and the migration of the animals they hunted; the latter had to move with their animals when the grazing was exhausted. Both had no reason to attempt to settle down and every reason not to. In the Neolithic, this situation changed. The gradual adoption of agriculture demanded a *sedentary,* or settled, life.

Anthony Bannister, Gallo Images/Corbis

**MODERN HUNTER-GATHERERS.** The man is setting a guinea fowl trap to supplement his family's diet in Namibia, southern Africa. His Bushmen kin are some of the last of the world's hunting-gathering folk, who range the Kalahari Desert much as their ancient forebears did.

The beginnings of farming used to be called the **Agricultural Revolution.** Now, we know that if this was a revolution, it was a very slow one. Most peoples took about five to ten generations (200 to 400 years) to complete it. Gradually, hunting-herding as the primary way to gain food gave way to sowing and harvesting. Usually, agriculture went hand in hand with hunting for a long, long time. Some members of the group would hunt while others raised some form of grain from wild grasses, the usual form of agriculture. When agriculture became the primary way of getting something to eat, the Agricultural Revolution was complete for that group. Throughout this book, we will be watching traditional beliefs and lifestyles giving way, however grudgingly, to the challenges brought forth by changes in the natural or the manmade environments. The Agricultural Revolution of the Neolithic Era was one of the vastest of such changes. The Science and Technology boxes will provide a perspective on others.

With such a slow transition, is *revolution* an appropriate word to describe the adoption of the agricultural lifestyle? Yes, because such adoption did lead to revolutionary changes in the long run. First, it meant that people settled down permanently. To be near the cultivated area, people settled in villages and then in towns, where they lived and worked in many new, specialized occupations that were unknown to preagricultural society. These settlements could not depend on the luck of hunting or fishing or on sporadic harvests of wild seeds and berries to supply their daily needs. Only regularized farming could support the specialists who populated the towns, and only intensive agriculture could produce the dependable surplus of food that was necessary to allow the population to grow. Of course, occasional years of famine still occurred. But the lean years were far less frequent than when people depended on hunting-gathering for sustenance. Thus, one major result of agriculture was a steadily *expanding population* that lived in *permanent settlements.*

Second, agriculture was the force behind creating the concept of "mine versus thine"—that is, *privately owned property* in land. Until farming became common, there was no concept of private property; land, water, game, and fish belonged to all who needed them. But once a group had labored hard to establish a productive farm, they wanted permanent possession. After all, they had to clear the land, supply water at the right time, and organize labor for the harvest. Who would do that if they had no assurance that next year and the next the land would still be theirs?

Third, agriculture necessitated the development of *systematized regulation* to enforce the rights of one party over those of another when disputes arose over property. Codes of law, enforced by organized authority (or government officials), were important results of agriculture's introduction. The function of law is to govern relations between individuals and groups so that security is established and the welfare of all is promoted. Law and the exercise of lawful authority is one of the recurrent themes in this book, and we will look at it in the Law and Government boxes.

A fourth change was the increasing *specialization of labor.* It made no sense for a Neolithic farmer to try to be a soldier or carpenter as well as a food grower. Efforts were more productive for the entire community if people specialized; the same principle applied to the carpenter and the soldier, who were not expected to farm.

Agriculture also led to an *enlarged public role for women* in Neolithic society, apparently a direct result of the fact that the first farmers were probably women. There is even some evidence of **matriarchy** (female social and political dominance) in Neolithic China. The association of women with fertility, personified in a whole series of Earth Mother goddesses in various cultures, was also important in this development. As the persons who brought forth life, women were seen as the key to assuring that the Earth Mother would respond to the villagers' prayers for food from her womb. In many areas where agriculture became important, *female-centered religious cults* and female priestesses replaced male gods and priests. Changes in religious belief and practice carry the widest-ranging consequences for any society, ancient or modern. Often they have been manifested in the concepts of good and bad that dictated public and private behavior patterns, or morality. We will observe many such changes as we progress through this world history, and the Patterns of Belief boxes will reinforce the theme.

Alterations in lifestyle came about gradually, of course, as a group learned to depend on crop growing for its main food supply. When that change took place varied sharply from one continent or region to the next. In a few places, it has still not occurred. A few nomadic tribes or hunter-gatherer groups can still be found, although they are fast disappearing under the intrusions of modern communications and technology.

Where were the first agricultural societies? For many years, researchers believed that agriculture must have emerged first in the Near or Middle East and spread gradually from there into Asia and Africa. According to this **diffusion theory** of cultural accomplishment, knowledge of new techniques spreads through human contacts, as water might spread on blotting paper. But now it is known that as early as 7000 B.C.E., agriculture had developed in at least four separate areas independent of outside influences: the Near East, Central America, northern China, and West Africa. Slightly later, the first domesticated animals were being raised as a part of village life. The raising of pigs, sheep, cattle, and goats for food goes back at least as far as 4000 B.C.E. (The horse comes considerably later, as we shall see.) Worldview Map 1.2 shows where some common plant and animal species were first cultivated or domesticated.

## Irrigation Civilizations

Several of the earliest civilizations developed in the plains bordering on major rivers or in the valleys the rivers cre-

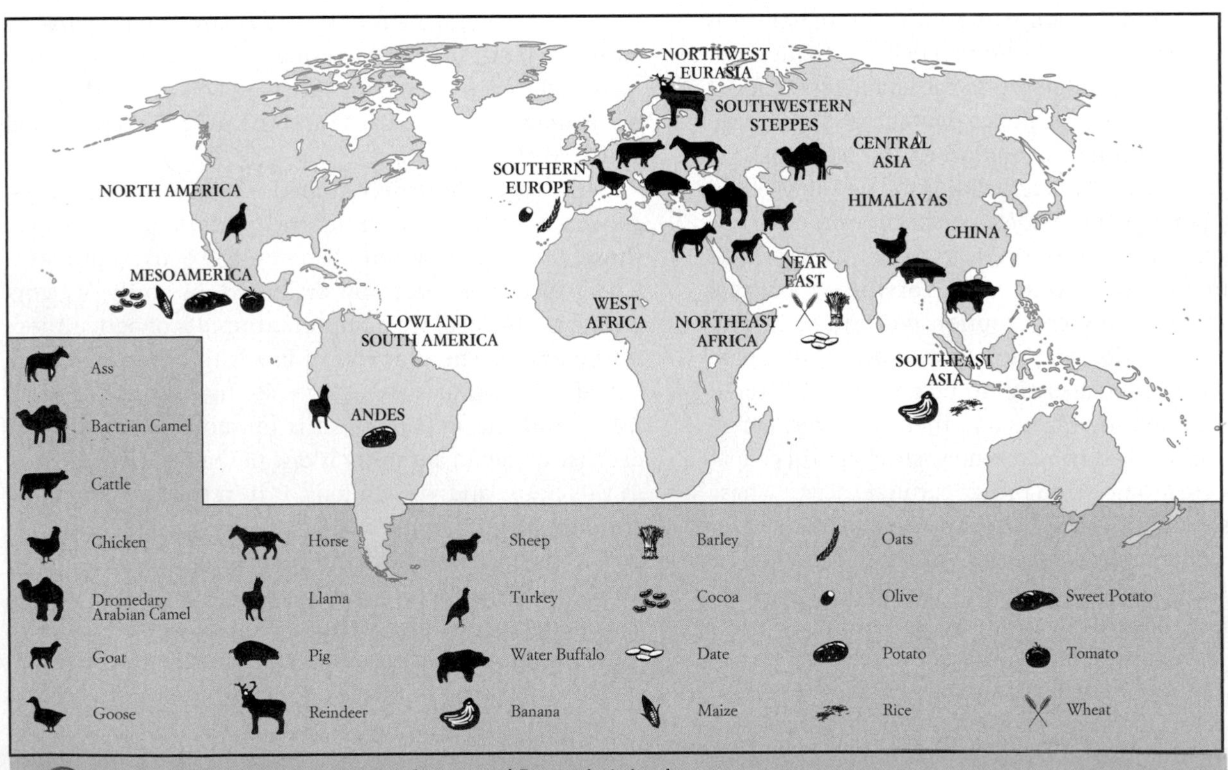


**WORLDVIEW MAP 1.2** ***Origin of Crops and Domestic Animals***

This map shows where particular plant and animal species were first cultivated or domesticated. Did these practices arise independently in different areas, or did they appear by diffusion? In the case of some species (for example, the pig), there seems to have been independent development in different areas. In most cases, however, the contact between neighboring cultures facilitated the rapid rise of plant and animal cultivation around the globe.

ated. Not coincidentally, four of the most important civilizations, which we examine in the next chapters, emerged in this way. The development of high civilization depended on intensive, productive agriculture, and the development of agriculture depended in turn on the excellent soil and regular supply of water provided by the river. In ancient Mesopotamia, the dual drainage of the Tigris and Euphrates rivers made the first urban civilization possible. In Egypt, the Nile—the world's longest river at more than 4,000 miles—was the life-giving source of everything the people needed and cherished. In India, the beginnings of civilization are traced to the extensive fields on both sides of the Indus River, which flows more than 2,000 miles from the slopes of the Himalayas to the ocean. In northern China, the valley of the Yellow River, which is about 2,700 miles long, was the cradle of the oldest continuous civilization in world history. Worldview Map 1.3 shows these four early civilizations. And, finally, present-day studies in the western valleys of the Andes in Peru also show an advanced, ceramic-making civilization that was previously unsuspected.

Naturhistorisches Museum, Vienna, Austria/Ali Meyer/ Bridgeman Art Library

**VENUS OF WILLEMSDORF.** Unearthed near the small Austrian village of Willemsdorf one hundred years ago, this is one of the better-known "Earth Mothers" found in excavations throughout central and eastern Europe. Its age is approximately 28,000 years. The emphasis on fertility aspects and the deemphasis of individual features tells us something of the value of women in Neolithic societies.

What else did the rivers provide besides good crops and essential water? They also offered a sure and generally easy form of transport and communication, allowing intervillage trade and encouraging central authorities to

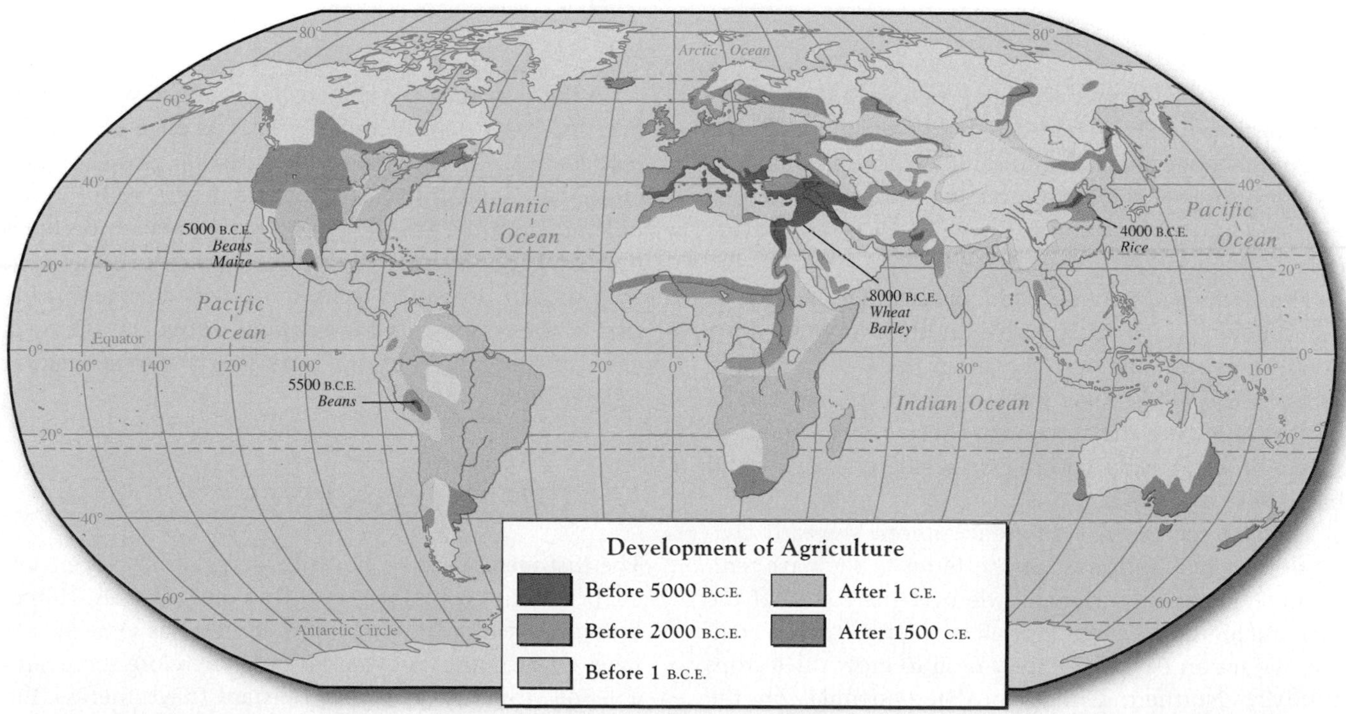

**WORLDVIEW MAP 1.3** *Early Agriculture*

Several of the earliest civilizations were centered around rivers, which provided good soil and water for agriculture. Ancient Mesopotamia grew up around the Tigris and Euphrates rivers. Egyptian civilization flourished along the Nile. Indian civilization began in fields along the Indus. The Yellow River supported early Chinese agrarian civilization. What do you suppose the new science of paleobotany might involve as its study, and how does it assist in dating early agriculture?

**Life in Prehistory.** In this movie reenactment of Neolithic hunters having a meal, we see a typical campfire. The refuse from such meals, piled generation after generation in the same campsites, provides modern archaeology with much of its research evidence.

extend their powers over a much greater area than would have been possible if they had only overland contacts. The interchange of goods and services between individuals or groups is a constant motivating force in human history, and we will look at this theme in differing contexts in later chapters.

The rivers had very different natures. The Tigris and the Yellow were as destructive in their unpredictable flooding as the Nile and the Indus were peaceful and friendly. The Yellow River was so ruinous at times that its ancient name was the "sorrow of China." But without its source of water, early farming in northern China would have been impossible.

Climate, too, made a difference among the early civilizations. Egypt and most of the Indus valley have temperate climates that change little over the course of the year and are suitable for crops all year long. It is not at all unusual for an Egyptian family farm to grow three crops annually. Northern China and Mesopotamia, on the other hand, experience much more severe changes of weather, not only from season to season but from day to day.

In the Near East, the climate has changed significantly over the past two millennia. What was once a relatively moderate place, with adequate rain for growing grain crops, has gradually become an arid desert, with intense heat much of the year. Present-day Iraq, which occupies the old Mesopotamia, is a difficult place to farm even with modern irrigation techniques. This change is a big part of the reason that Mesopotamia, after thousands of years of cultural leadership, sank slowly into stagnation in later days.

## Metal and Its Uses

The first metal used by humans seems to have been soft copper. When combined with lead and tin ores, copper becomes the more useful bronze. Bronze has some advantages over copper: it is harder (and therefore more suitable for weaponry) and more resistant to weathering. But it has several disadvantages when compared with other metals: it is relatively difficult to make, its weight is excessive for many uses, and it cannot keep a fine edge for tools and cutting weapons. Above all, bronze was difficult to obtain in the ancient world and expensive.

The period when bronze art objects and bronze weapons predominated in a given part of the world is called its *Bronze Age*. In western Asia, where civilizations first appeared, the Bronze Age extended from about 7000 B.C.E. to about 1500 B.C.E., when a major innovation in human technology made its first appearance: the smelting of iron.

The discovery of how to smelt and temper iron tools and weapons was a major turning point in the civilized development of every people, ushering in an *Iron Age*. Iron is the key metal of history. Wherever it has come into common use, certain advances have occurred. Iron plowshares open areas to cultivation that previously could not be tilled. Iron weapons and body armor give warfare a new look. Iron tools enable new technical progress and expanded production. Iron utensils are cheaper than other metals, last longer, resist fiery heat, and do not easily shatter or lose their edge.

Iron ore is one of the more common metallic ores, and it is often found on or near the Earth's surface (unlike copper and lead). It is easily segregated from the surrounding soils or rock. The crucial breakthrough was learning how to temper the ore—that is, how to purify it so that the iron could be formed and used without shattering. The Indo-European people known as Hittites, who lived in modern-day Turkey, were apparently the first to smelt and temper iron. By 1200 B.C.E., this knowledge was spreading rapidly among Middle Eastern and Egyptian peoples.

## Summary

The prehistory of the human race is immeasurably longer than the short period (5,000 years or so) of which we have historical knowledge. During the last 50,000 years of the prehistoric period, men and women became physically and mentally indistinguishable from ourselves and spread across the Earth. Developing agriculture to supplement hunting and gathering, humans slowly attained that advanced state we call civilization in the later part of the Neolithic Age, around 3000 B.C.E. Urban life was now possible, a system of government and record keeping evolved, and advanced weapons and tools of metal were invented.

In the next chapters, we examine the four earliest centers of advanced civilization, one by one, and look at the reasons that each of them became such a center. The similarities and contrasts among these civilizations gave each of them a particular character that would last for thousands of years and in some cases until the present day.

## Identification Terms

Test your knowledge of this chapter's key concepts by defining the following terms. If you can't recall the meaning of certain terms, refresh your memory by looking up the boldfaced term in the chapter, turning to the Glossary at the end of the book, or working with the flashcards that are available on the *World Civilizations* Companion Website: **http://history.wadsworth.com/adler04/**.

Agricultural Revolution
anthropology
archaeology
civilization
culture
diffusion theory
historiography
history
hominid
matriarchy
Neanderthal Man
prehistory

## Test Your Knowledge

Test your knowledge of this chapter by answering the following questions. Complete answers appear at the end of the book. You may also take this quiz interactively and find even more quiz questions on the *World Civilizations* Companion Website: **http://history.wadsworth.com/adler04/**.

1. One term that is used to denote "thinking or skillful man" is
   a. Cro-Magnon.
   b. *Homo sapiens sapiens.*
   c. Paleolithic.
   d. Neanderthal.
   e. *Australopithecus.*
2. The way of life of a people, or the imprint of humans on the environment, is known as
   a. civilization.
   b. anthropology.
   c. prehistory.
   d. paleoanthropology.
   e. culture.
3. Which of the following statements most aptly describes Paleolithic society?
   a. The hunt was the only way to obtain food regularly.
   b. There was constant fighting among families and clans.
   c. The individual was more important than the group.
   d. Cooperation was necessary for survival.
   e. Extended family units usually numbered about sixty.
4. The Agricultural Revolution occurred first during the
   a. Neolithic.
   b. Bronze Age.
   c. Paleolithic.
   d. Mesozoic.
   e. Iron Age.
5. Among the major changes that occur as a result of the adoption of agriculture by any group is
   a. the abandonment of traditional village life.
   b. a decrease in trading.
   c. an increase in population.
   d. a reduction in animal raising.
   e. an increase in the percentage of people living in rural areas.
6. The first farmers were probably
   a. Andean.
   b. nomads.
   c. women.
   d. Indian.
   e. hunter-gatherers.
7. Which of these factors was of decisive importance to Neolithic agriculture?
   a. Use of beasts of burden for plowing
   b. Mastery of irrigation techniques
   c. Development of natural insecticides
   d. Existence of large cities as marketplaces
   e. Development of heavy iron plows for cultivation
8. The increase in the number of humans during the Neolithic Age was primarily caused by
   a. the disappearance of epidemic disease.
   b. a surplus of food.
   c. decreased intergroup violence.
   d. a greater respect for the aged.
   e. increasing understanding of the use of herbs for medicinal purposes.
9. The site of the oldest known continuous civilization in world history was in
   a. southern Africa.
   b. western Africa.
   c. the Nile River valley.
   d. Mesopotamia.
   e. northern China.
10. The use of bronze as the primary metal for tools and weapons
    a. came after iron.
    b. was dictated by its ease of making.
    c. started about 7000 B.C.E. in western Asia.
    d. came after urban civilizations were established in the Near East.
    e. predated the use of copper.

## InfoTrac College Edition

Visit the source collections at

**http://infotrac.thomsonlearning.com**

and use the Search function with the following key terms:

antiquities Paleolithic Neolithic

## Wadsworth History Website Resources

Visit the World History Resource Center at **http://history.wadsworth.com/world** for a wealth of general resources and the *World Civilizations* Companion Website at **http://history.wadsworth.com/adler04/** for resources specific to this textbook.

## HistoryNow

Enter *HistoryNow* using the access card that is available for *World Civilizations. HistoryNow* will assist you in understanding the content in this chapter with lesson plans generated for your needs. For other chapters, you will be able to read many primary source documents online. Prehistory, of course, has no primary source documents.

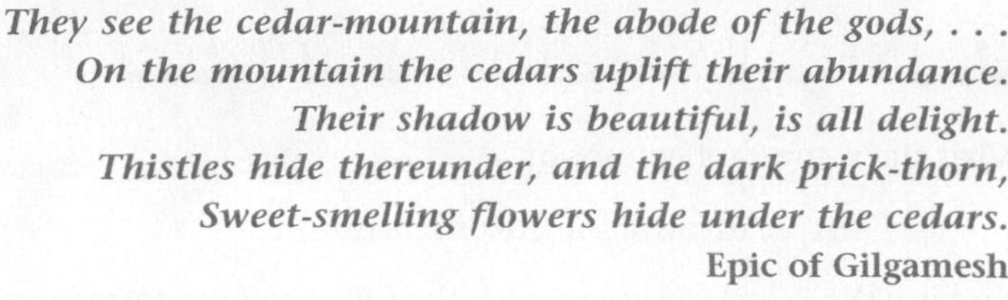

*They see the cedar-mountain, the abode of the gods, . . .*
*On the mountain the cedars uplift their abundance.*
*Their shadow is beautiful, is all delight.*
*Thistles hide thereunder, and the dark prick-thorn,*
*Sweet-smelling flowers hide under the cedars.*
Epic of Gilgamesh

# 2 Mesopotamia

Sumerian Civilization
Earning a Living
The Evolution of Writing
Mathematics and Chronology
Religion and the Afterlife
Law
Government and Social Structure
The Status of Women

Successors to Sumeria

The Decline of Mesopotamia in World History

| | |
|---|---|
| c. 5000 B.C.E. | Sumerians arrive in Mesopotamia |
| c. 3500 B.C.E. | Cuneiform writing |
| c. 3000 B.C.E. | Sumerian city-states develop |
| c. 2300 B.C.E. | Sargon of Akkad |
| 1700s B.C.E. | Hammurabi/Oldest surviving law code |
| c. 1500 B.C.E. | Hittites conquer Mesopotamia |
| c. 900 B.C.E. | Rise of Assyria |
| 539 B.C.E. | Conquest by Persia |

The population increase enabled by the Agricultural Revolution was first exemplified by the creation of farming villages, in which previously nomadic food gatherers settled to plant and tend their crops. Grains were the usual basis of early agriculture, and those areas with fertile soil, sufficient rain, and a temperate climate to support wild grains were the pioneers of village development. From the farming village slowly evolved the much more socially differentiated town, with its various economic divisions and occupational specialties. And from the town in some places grew the larger centers of governmental power, religious ritual, and cultural sophistication termed *cities*.

The earliest development of city life that we know of came about in southwestern Asia, in the land that the ancient Greeks called Mesopotamia ("land between the rivers")—now the southeastern portion of Iraq. The rivers, the Euphrates and the Tigris, originate in present-day Turkey and parallel each other for about 400 miles before joining together to flow into the head of the Persian Gulf (see Map 2.1). In the lower courses of the rivers, in the third millennium B.C.E., originated the first urban civilization of the world. This civilization was supported by extensive irrigation farming, pioneered by a people called **Sumerians,** who came into lower Mesopotamia from somewhere to the east about 5000 B.C.E. Gradually, the Sumerians created a series of small competing kingdoms, or city-states, each of which was centered on a good-sized town. Here they developed a series of ideas and techniques that would provide the foundation of a distinct and highly influential civilization.

## Sumerian Civilization

The Sumerians were the first people to do a number of highly significant things—all of them characteristics of what we call "civilization."

- They created the first large *cities,* as distinct from towns. The largest of these cities may have contained upward of 100,000 people (about the size of present-day Charleston, South Carolina; Kansas City, Kansas; or Reno, Nevada). All early civilizations had an advanced center such as this, which drew its necessities from a surrounding countryside subject to it. Most of these centers originated as a place of worship honoring one or more gods. Gradually, the ceremonial aspects of the shrine and its attendant priesthood were joined by

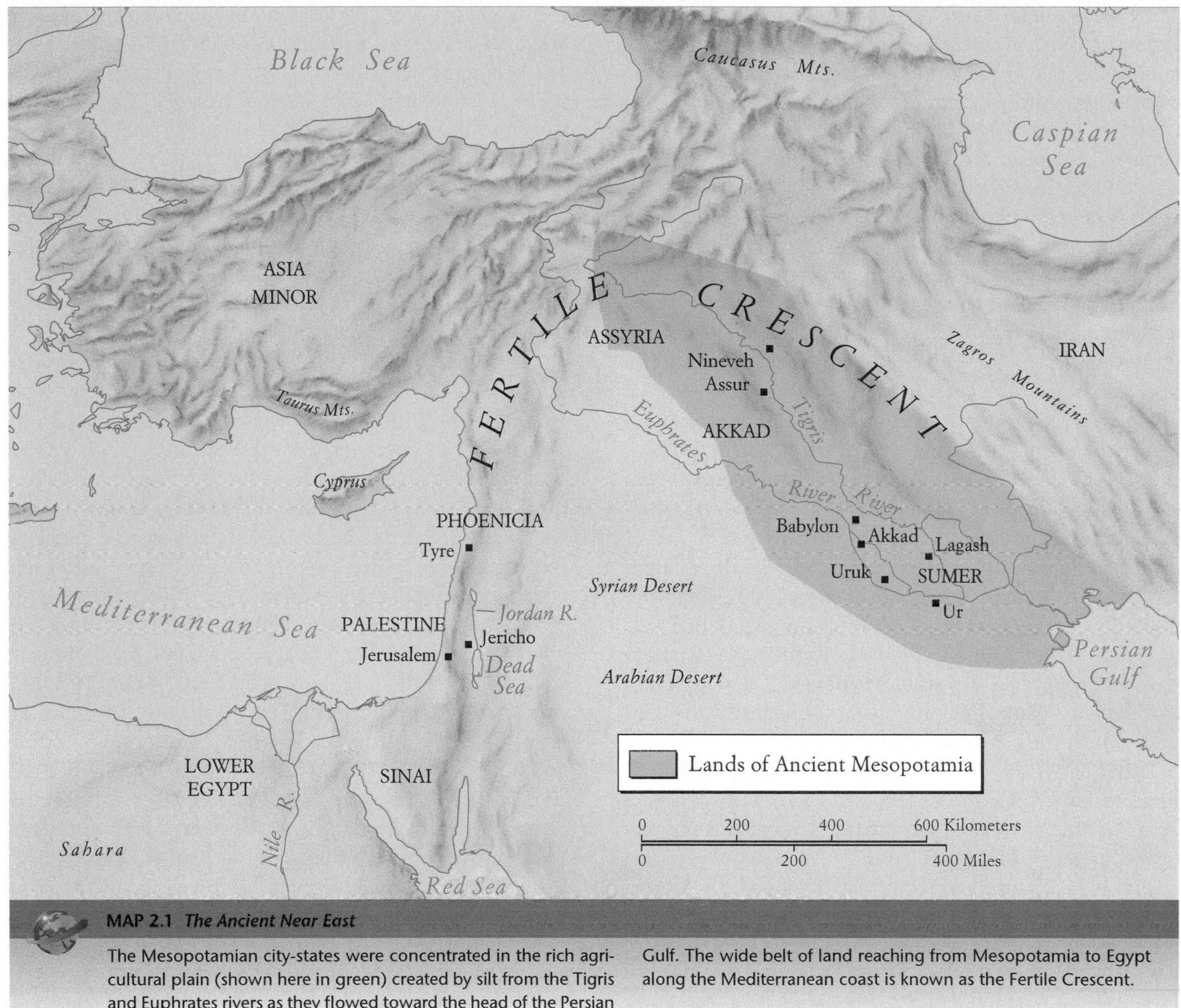


**MAP 2.1** *The Ancient Near East*

The Mesopotamian city-states were concentrated in the rich agricultural plain (shown here in green) created by silt from the Tigris and Euphrates rivers as they flowed toward the head of the Persian Gulf. The wide belt of land reaching from Mesopotamia to Egypt along the Mediterranean coast is known as the Fertile Crescent.

commercial and governmental pursuits, a place in which a growing population of labor-specialized people was supported by a sophisticated irrigation agriculture.

- They developed the first sophisticated system of *writing.*
- They built the first monumental buildings, using as the basic principle of support the post-and-lintel system (beams held up by columns, used today in structures as varied as monkey bars and bridges).
- They probably invented the wheel as a load-bearing transportation device and were the first to use bricks made from sun-baked clay.
- They were the first to design and build an irrigation system powered by the force of gravity.
- They were the first to use the plow and among the first to make bronze metal utensils and weaponry.

What we know of the Sumerians is extremely impressive. We know a good deal not only because they left extensive records and physical evidence of their own but also because they had enormous influence on their neighbors and rivals, such as the Akkadians and Egyptians, as well as their several conquering successors in Mesopotamia.

The Sumerians were not the only settlers of the broad plain on either side of the two rivers. In fact, they were not even the first people in those regions. Unlike most of their neighboring tribes, the Sumerians were not members of the **Semitic** language family. (*Note:* A language group or family is related by its grammar and sometimes by its vocabulary and alphabet. The Semitic family is one of the major language families in the world and includes both Hebrew and Arabic as well as many others.)

By somewhere about 3000 B.C.E., the Sumerians had extended their domain upriver into Semite-inhabited regions, as far as the future city of Babylon. Either by coercion or peaceably, no one knows which, they began to civilize these *barbarians* (a Greek word meaning simply people who speak a different language and are supposedly inferior). Large towns grew up, with neighborhoods of craftspeople, merchants, and laborers. Trade grew rapidly, not only between food-growing villages and the towns but also among the towns scattered for hundreds of miles along the banks of the rivers. Trade in the products both of agriculture and of handicrafts was vitally important to the rise of the Mesopotamian civilization. The Sumerian cities were close enough to the head of navigation in the Persian Gulf to maintain constant contact with peoples on either side of that extended bay of the Indian Ocean. Chief articles of export were woolen cloth and foodstuffs, while imports focused on luxury goods, timber, and metal.

The early history of Mesopotamia under the Sumerians is a tale of great technological and cultural advances, marred by strife, disunion, and unceasing warfare. Trade wars and disputes over water assured that no centralized governing power was possible. Whenever one city managed to seize control of substantial supplies of water and trade, the others upstream or downstream would band together against it, or its subjects would rebel. Conflicts seem to have been the order of the day, with city-state vying against city-state in a constant struggle for mastery over the precious irrigated lands.

Not until about 2300 B.C.E. was the land between the rivers brought under one effective rule, and that was imposed by a Semitic invader known as Sargon the Great, who conquered the entire plain. Sargon established his capital in the new town of Akkad, near modern-day Baghdad, capital of Iraq. Although the Akkadian Empire lasted less than a century, its influence was great, for it spread Sumerian culture and methods far and wide in the Near and Middle East, through that wide belt of land reaching from Mesopotamia to Egypt that is called the **Fertile Crescent** (see Map 2.1).

Although the separate Sumerian city-states never united until they were overwhelmed by outsiders, their cultural and religious achievements and beliefs would be picked up by their conquerors and essentially retained by all their successors in Mesopotamia.

## *Earning a Living*

Most Mesopotamians at this time drew their livelihood from the land either directly, as farmers and herders, or indirectly, as carters, wine pressers, millers, or any of the dozens of other occupations that transformed agrarian products into food and drink and delivered them to the consumer. For every person who lived in an urban setting and did not have to grow his or her own food, there were ten or twenty who lived in agrarian villages and who spent most of their labor in the fields or the pasture. As we know from both historical and archaeological evidence of many kinds and from many places, commerce was also primarily concerned with trade in foodstuffs, grain above all. It is easy for us to forget just how much of the time and energy of early civilizations went into the pursuit of sufficient caloric intake! Three square meals a day were often the exception, and the ordinary person rarely took them for granted.

Not all occupations involved farming or foodstuffs, however. A few of the many nonagrarian occupations required education and a degree of formal training: scribes, bookkeepers, and the priesthood, for example. Although each civilization had some learned occupations, they varied in prestige and in the number of persons who practiced them. Mesopotamian city dwellers seem to have been literate to an unusual degree and took writing for granted as a normal part of daily life. Many other occupations did not require literacy, but they did demand a lengthy period of apprenticeship. Most of these occupations were found in the towns. They included metalworking, leatherwork, jewelry making, all types of ceramics, fine and rough carpentry, masonry, and other building trades. Besides these skilled jobs, there were shopkeepers, their clerks and errand boys, casual laborers available for any type of manual task, and a large number of trades connected with the production of clothing and textiles. Many people were also involved in the preparation, distribution, and sale of food, whether in shops or eating places such as taverns and street booths. One crucial task, which we in the present-day United States rarely think about, was obtaining a regular supply of water. This was one of the most important tasks of women and children, and took great amounts of time and labor.

Some civilized centers employed more of one type of labor than others, but overall there was a rough parity. Most jobs were in very small-scale enterprises. These were usually family owned and staffed, with perhaps two or three paid or slave laborers. Slavery was less common in some places than others, but in all ancient societies except early Egypt and China, slaves made up a sizable portion of the working population. They sometimes performed much of the particularly unpleasant or dangerous work (mining and handling the dead, for example).

## *The Evolution of Writing*

Spoken language was one of the key achievements of early human beings, enabling an intensity and variety of communication that was previously unknown. We have no idea, of course, when this occurred among a given group of people, but it must have been very far back in prehistory, perhaps millions of years ago. Not until some time in the fourth millennium (4000–3000 B.C.E.), however, was oral language joined to a written form, so as to remain permanently accessible.

Perhaps the most important and lasting of all the Sumerian accomplishments was the gradual invention of a system of writing, which evolved from their need to keep good records for commercial and religious taxation, marital and inheritance contracts, and some other activities in which it was important to have a clear, mutually agreed-upon version of past events. Some type of marks on some type of medium (clay, paper, wood, stone) had been in use long, long before 3500 B.C.E. What did the Sumerians of that epoch do to justify the claim of having invented writing? Significantly, they moved beyond pictorial writing, or symbols derived from pictures, into a further phase of conveying meaning through abstract marks.

All writing derives originally from a simplified picture. This is called *pictography,* and it has been used from one end of the Earth to the other. Pictography had several obvious disadvantages, though. For one thing, it could not convey the meaning of abstractions (things that have no material, tangible existence). Nor could it communicate the tense of a verb, or the degree of an adjective or adverb, or many other things that language has to handle well.

The way that the Sumerians (and later peoples) got around these difficulties was to expand their pictorial writing gradually to a much more sophisticated level, so that it included special signs for abstractions, tenses, and so on—signs that had nothing to do with tangible objects. These are called *conventional signs* and may be invented for any meaning desired by their users. For example, if both of us agree that the signs "cc" stand for "the boy in the blue suit," then that is what they mean

Louvre, Paris/Erich Lessing/Art Resource, NY

**CUNEIFORM WRITING.** This example of cuneiform writing (8 × 8 × 2 cm) describes a gift of a house and a male slave with a list of witnesses on the last three lines. Note the dimensions, somewhat smaller than an average hand in length.

Scala/Art Resource, NY

**SUMERIAN SEALS.** These carved cylindrical seals of ivory were equivalent to signatures, identifying the authors of the clay tablet documents they marked. Some have been found as far away as India.

when we see them on a piece of paper, or a rock surface, or wherever. If we further agree that by adding the vertical stroke "!" we make a verb into a future tense, then it is future tense so far as we're concerned. Very slowly, the Sumerians expanded their pictographic vocabulary in this way, while simultaneously simplifying and standardizing their pictures, so that they could be written more rapidly and recognized more easily by strangers.

A big breakthrough came some time in the third millennium, when a series of clever scribes began to use written signs to indicate the sounds of the spoken language. This was the beginning of the *phonetic written language,* in which the signs had a direct connection with the oral language. Although the Sumerians did not progress as far as an alphabet, they started down the path that would culminate in one about 2,000 years later.

The basic format of the written language after about 3500 B.C.E. was a script written in wedge-shaped characters, the **cuneiform,** on clay tablets about the size of your hand. Tens of thousands of these tablets covered by cuneiform writings have been dug up in modern times. Most of them pertain to contracts between private parties or between a private party and officials. But other tablets contain prayers of all sorts, proclamations by officials, law codes and judgments, and some letters and poetry. Sumerian cuneiform remained the basic script of most Near and Middle Eastern languages until about 1000 B.C.E., when its use began to fade out.

## Mathematics and Chronology

After the invention of writing, perhaps the most dramatic advance made by these early inhabitants of Mesopotamia was in mathematics and chronology. Sumerian math was based on units of 60 and its divisors, and this, of course, is the reason that we still measure time in intervals of 60 seconds and 60 minutes. Much of our basic geometry and trigonometry, such as the 360 degrees of a circle, also stems from the Sumerians. Their calendar was based on the visible movement of the moon in the night skies, and was thus a lunar calendar, as were the calendars of most other ancient peoples. The year was based on the passage of seasons and the position of the stars. It was subdivided into lunar months, corresponding to the period between one full moon and the next. In calculating the year's length, the Sumerians arrived at a figure close to our own, although they were not quite as close as the Egyptians, employing their solar calendar. All in all, Sumerian math, including its further development by the Babylonians and Persians, has held up very well and has been influential in all later Western science, including that of the Greeks.

## Religion and the Afterlife

Our knowledge of the Sumerians' religion is sketchy and unsure. Apparently, they believed in a host of gods (**polytheism,** Greek for "many gods") of various ranks. There were many male and female deities, each with specific competencies in human affairs. The gods were much like superhumans, with all the faults and weaknesses of men and women. Some of them lived forever, but others died just as humans did. Some were immensely powerful; their will affected all the Sumerian settlements, and they were believed to rule over all human beings. In addition, each city-kingdom had its local powers, crucial to the prosper-

Georg Gerster/Photo Researchers

**ZIGGURAT.** The stepped pyramidal form for religious monuments has been used from one end of the Earth to the other. It combines an overpowering sense of mass and permanency with a mystical projection of divine superiority over earthbound humans. Pyramids like this Mesopotamian ziggurat can also be found in Egypt, Central America, and, in modified form, Southeast Asia. The Mesopotamian variety was constructed of earthen bricks, which demanded frequent renovation lest they dissolve into ruins through time's erosive force or an enemy's vandalism.

ity of its citizens, who had to be carefully placated by the mediating priests. The gods were thought to reside at times in the great temple complexes crowned and protected by the ***ziggurats,*** or stepped pyramids, where hundreds of priests and their dependents ritually worshipped them on behalf of the city's welfare. The best-known ziggurat was erected by the powerful city of **Babylon** long after the Sumerian Epoch. It was the Tower of Babel of biblical fame.

The gods were frequently cruel toward their human creatures and highly unpredictable. Men and women were the slaves of their god-creators, intended as the providers of the labors that the gods didn't wish to perform. There is no trace of a loving relationship between deities and men. Nor is there any trace of ethics in Mesopotamian religion. The demands of the gods had no intrinsic connection with doing good or avoiding evil on Earth. The gods often punished humans, but not for moral failings, or what we would call "sin." When comprehensible at all, the reasons for the punishment were petty and unworthy, but generally they were simply unknowable. The punishments often took the form of natural catastrophes, such as droughts or floods that harmed the entire community. To avert punishment, the gods had to be appeased with frequent, costly rituals and ceremonies, which were the responsibility of a hereditary priesthood. The priests used their power as interpreters of the will of the gods to create large and wealthy temple communities, supported by the offerings of the citizens. In some Sumerian cities, the priests seem to have been the true rulers for a time. This practice ended with the conquest by Sargon the Great, who made the royal throne, supported by a powerful army, the undisputed center of authority.

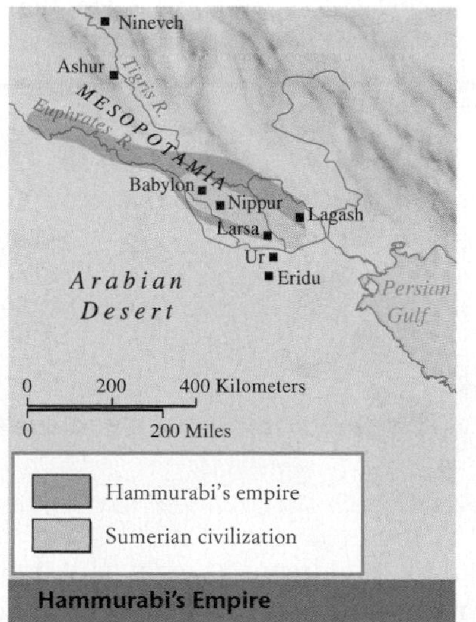

Hammurabi's Empire

The religion was certainly not an optimistic one, and it seems to have had no clear ideas on the nature of the afterlife or who, if anyone, could enjoy immortality. The best approach seemed to be to honor and obey the gods as well as you could, to appease them by making offerings through their powerful priests, and to hope for the best in the afterlife, if there was one. The concept of a heaven or a hell seems to have been very vague.

Much of what is known about Mesopotamian religious belief derives from their literature, in which several major myths of Western civilization, including the Flood and the Garden of Eden, find their first expression. Particularly important is the creation myth embraced in the ***Epic of Gilgamesh,*** the first epic poem in world literature. Gilgamesh is a man, a king of one of the city-states, who desires the secret of immortal life, but the gods, jealous of his power, defeat him. The excerpts in the Patterns of Belief box show the similarity between the flood stories in *Gilgamesh* and the Book of Genesis of the Judeo-Christian Scripture.

## Law

One of the earliest known complete codes of laws originated in post-Sumerian Mesopotamia in the 1700s B.C.E. during the reign of the emperor Hammurabi. He is the first of the historic lawgivers whose work has survived into our times. (His accomplishments are described in the Law and Government box.) His code certainly had predecessors that have been lost, because its legal concepts and vocabulary are much too sophisticated for it to have been a first effort.

The code is based on two distinctive principles: punishment depended on the social rank of the violator, and offenders were subjected to the same damages or injury that they caused to others. These ideas would be incorporated into many later codes over the next 2,000 years, although rejected by modern democratic theory. A commoner would get a different, more severe punishment than would a noble or official for the same offense. And a slave (of whom there were many) would be treated more harshly still. If in the same social class as the victim, the offender would have to give "an eye for an eye, a tooth for a tooth." Another basic principle of Mesopotamian law was that the government should act as an impartial referee among its subject citizens, seeing to it that the wronged party got satisfaction from the wrongdoer. The victim had the right to demand personal compensation from the person who had caused him grief—a legal concept that is being reintroduced into American criminal law.

People were not equal before the law: husbands had a great deal of power over wives, fathers over children, rich over poor, free citizens over slaves. Nevertheless, a definite attempt was made to protect the defenseless and to see that all received justice.

Much of Hammurabi's code dealt with social and family problems, such as the support of widows and orphans, illegitimacy, adultery, and rape. Clearly, the position of women was inferior to that of men, but they did have certain legal rights and were not just the property of their male relatives. A wife could divorce her husband, and if the husband was found to be at fault, the wife was entitled to the property she had brought into the marriage. Women could also enter

PATTERNS OF BELIEF

## The *Epic of Gilgamesh*

**The collection of stories** that is termed the *Epic of Gilgamesh* is one of the earliest approaches to analyzing the relations of gods and humans. It portrays a society in search of a religious basis for human action. Stories of the Flood occur in many ancient cultural traditions, such as the Noah story in the Old Testament of the Hebrews, the creation myths of the Hindus, and some of the North American Indian creation stories. In each case, the story tells of a disastrous flood that engulfed the entire Earth and nearly annihilated humanity.

In the Middle Eastern tradition, the narrative of the Flood is first found in the *Epic of Gilgamesh.* In this version, the main focus of the story is on the inevitability of death and the defeat of the hero as he attempts to achieve immortality. The Mesopotamian counterpart of the biblical Noah is Utnapishtim. Here his description of the flood is contrasted with the version recounted in Genesis:

### *Gilgamesh*

> The gods of the abyss rose up; Nergal pulled out the dams of the netherworld, Ninurta the war-lord threw down the dikes . . . a stupor of despair went up to heaven when the god of storms turned daylight into darkness, when he smashed the earth like a teacup. One whole day the tempest raged, gathering fury as it went, and it poured over the people like the tide of battle; a man could not see his brother nor could the people be seen from heaven. Even the gods were terrified at the flood, they fled to the highest heaven . . . they crouched against the walls, cowering . . . the gods of heaven and hell wept . . . for six days and six nights the winds blew, tempest and flood raged together like warring hosts. . . . I looked at the face of the earth, and all was silence, all mankind was turned into clay. . . . I bowed low, and I wept. . . .

### *Genesis*

> All the fountains of the great deep burst forth and the floodgates of the heavens were opened. And rain fell on the earth for forty days and forty nights. . . . The waters increased and bore up the ark, and it rose above the earth. The waters rose higher and higher, and increased greatly on the earth . . . the waters rose higher and higher, so that all the highest mountains everywhere under the heavens were covered. All flesh that moved on the earth died: birds, cattle, wild animals, all creatures that crawl upon the earth, and all men. Only Noah and those with him in the ark were saved.

*Gilgamesh* is a grim tale that speaks of death and the afterlife in pessimistic and fearful tones. Indicative is this description by Gilgamesh's companion Enkidu of a vivid dream he had had, foreshadowing his approaching death:

> I stood alone before an awful Being; his face was somber like the blackbird of the storm. He fell upon me with the talons of an eagle, and he held me fast, pinioned by his claws until I smothered; then he transformed me so that my arms became wings covered with feathers . . . and he led me away, to the house from which those who enter never return . . . whose people sit in darkness, dust their food and clay their meat. They are clothed like birds with wings for coverings, they see no light, they sit in darkness.

The epic ends with the failure of Gilgamesh's quest for the secret of immortal life. The somber funeral chant seems to underline the poet's sense of resignation and futility:

> The king has laid himself down, and will not rise again.
> The Lord of Kullab [that is, Gilgamesh] will not rise again,
> He overcame evil, but he will not rise again,
> Though he was strong of arm, he will not rise again,
> Possessing wisdom and a comely face, he will not rise again.

### *Analyze and Interpret*

What does the emphasis on defeat and death in the *Gilgamesh* story signify in terms of the beliefs of the peoples who created these myths? Read the full accounts of the flood in *Gilgamesh* and Genesis. What do you make of the differences?



**HistoryNow™**
***To read the entire* Epic of Gilgamesh, *point your browser to the documents area of* HistoryNow.**

into contracts and have custody over minor children under certain conditions—two rights that many later civilizations denied them.

### *Government and Social Structure*

Government in Mesopotamia can be divided into two types: the **theocracy** (rule by gods or their priests) of the early city-states of the Sumerians, and the kingdom-empires of their successors, starting with Sargon the Great of Akkad. The cities were ruled by a king, assisted by noble officials and priests. In Sumerian times, the kings were no more than figureheads for the priests, but later they exercised decisive power.

The city ruled by an elite headed by a king-emperor was quite different in its social subdivisions from the

LAW AND GOVERNMENT

## Hammurabi

**THE EMPEROR HAMMURABI,** who ruled Mesopotamia from about 1792 to about 1750 B.C.E., is best known for the code of laws that bears his name, one of the earliest law codes yet discovered. Hammurabi's empire stretched from the desolate mountains of Zagros in western Iran to the edge of the Arabian Desert. It was centered on the great city of Babylon in central Mesopotamia. Although nature has not been generous with this region, its ruler was successful in bringing prosperity and peace to most of his subjects.

Like all Middle Eastern kingdoms, the Amorite Hammurabi's empire was originally created by conquest. He formed coalitions with his Semite neighbors and won the loyalty of the smaller Amorite city-states that surrounded his own. Babylon emerged as a center of both manufacturing and trade, and its influence reached from the head of the Persian Gulf to the eastern shore of the Mediterranean.

The emperor's main concern, however, was to maintain order in this large region through authority, which answered what he perceived to be the needs of his people. To that effect, he gave his subjects a complex law code. Its 282 decrees, collectively termed the Code of Hammurabi, were inscribed on stone *stelae,* or columns, and erected in many public places. The one shown here was discovered in Persian Susa in the nineteenth century and is now in the Louvre in Paris.

The code dealt primarily with civil affairs such as marriage and inheritance, family relations, property rights, and business practices. Criminal offenses were punished with varying degrees of severity, depending on the social status of the offender and the victim. Clear distinctions were made between the rights of the upper classes and those of commoners. Payments were generally allowed as restitution for damage done to commoners by nobles. A commoner who caused damage to a noble, however, might have to pay with his head. Trial by ordeal, retribution by retaliatory action, and capital punishment were common practices. But judges distinguished between intentional and unintentional injuries, and monetary fines were normally used as punishment where no malicious intent was shown. The "eye for an eye" morality often associated with Hammurabi's code was relatively restricted in application and applied only to crimes committed against social equals.

The code made theft a serious crime and devoted great attention to crimes against property in general. Workers had to do an adequate job or be punished for negligence. Official fee tables were ordained for medical care, and woe to the doctor who was found guilty of malpractice! Although the code did not concern itself with religious belief or practice, it did accord considerable powers to the administering judges, who were often priests. In general, it established strict standards of justice and public morality.

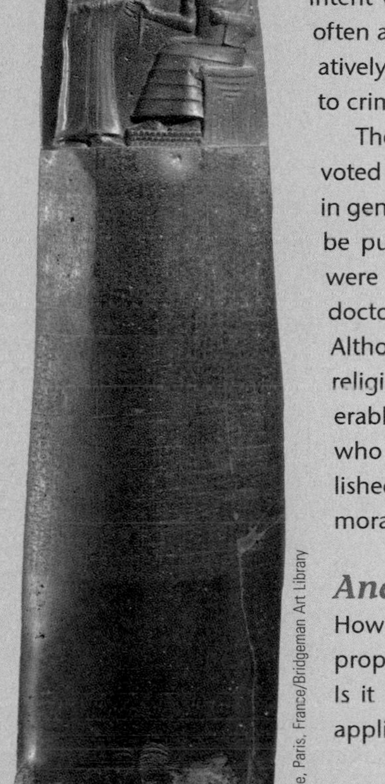



**STELA OF HAMMURABI.** The stela is about five feet high, showing the king receiving the code from Shamash, god of justice, at the top and the actual text of the 282 laws below.

### *Analyze and Interpret*

How does the Code of Hammurabi show that property rights were superior to human rights? Is it unusual to show class distinctions in the application of laws?

**HistoryNow™**

***To read the entire Code of Hammurabi, point your browser to the documents area of* HistoryNow.**

village. In the village, social equality was rarely challenged, and a leveling interdependency in everyday life was taken for granted. In the urban areas, on the contrary, distinctions among persons were essential and expected to be displayed in many fashions and activities. Above all, the lower classes supported the far less numerous upper ones through both labor and taxes.

The Mesopotamian civilization apparently had but three classes of people, the first of which being the small groups of priests and noble landlords (often two branches of a single group) who were great landlords and had a monopoly on the higher offices of the city. Behind the priesthood stood the immense power of the high gods of the Sumerians and their successors: the deities of earth, sky, fire, fresh water, salt water, and storm. The second group, the freemen, was the most numerous class. They did the bulk of the city's work and trading, and owned and worked most of the outlying farmlands. The relatively protected position of freemen is attested to by Hammurabi's code (see Law and Government box) and by the thousands of other documents recovered in the nineteenth and twentieth centuries from the ruins of Sumerian cities. Both priests and nobles depended on their skills and their labor, which was presumably given on a more or less voluntary basis.

Finally, the slaves, who at times were very numerous, often possessed considerable skills and were given some responsible positions. Freemen had some political rights, but slaves had none. As we will repeatedly see, slaves were common in most ancient societies, and enslavement was by no means the morally contemptible and personally humiliating condition it would frequently become later. Slavery had nothing much to do with race or ethnicity and everything to do with bad luck, such as being on the losing side of a war or falling into debt. Most slaves in Mesopotamia—and elsewhere—had run up debts that they could not otherwise repay. It was not at all uncommon to become someone's slave for a few years and then resume your freedom when you had paid off what you owed. Hereditary slavery was rare. Many owners routinely freed their slaves in their wills as a mark of piety and benevolence.

Maltreatment of slaves did occur, but mostly to field workers, miners, or criminals who had been enslaved as punishment and had had no personal contacts with their owner. On the other side, in all ancient societies many slaves engaged in business, many had advanced skills in the crafts, and some managed to accumulate enough money working on their own accounts that they could buy their freedom. The conditions of slaves in the ancient world varied so enormously that we cannot generalize about them with any accuracy except to say that slaves were politically and legally inferior to free citizens.

## The Status of Women

Historians generally agree on some categorical statements about the women of ancient Mesopotamia and Egypt:

- In the earliest stage of civilization, women shared more or less equally with men in social prestige and power.
- This egalitarianism was undermined and overturned by the coming of militarized society (armies), the heavy plow in agriculture, and the establishment of large-scale trade over long distances.
- The trend toward **patriarchy**—a society in which males have social and political dominance—proceeded at varying speeds in different societies but was impossible to reverse once it started.

Ancient law codes from Mesopotamia show a definite break between about 2000 and 1000 B.C.E., with Hammurabi's code being a transition. In the earliest contracts and rulings (and to a lesser degree in Hammurabi's code), the female enjoys extensive rights; by about 1200, she is an object ruled by men.

In Mesopotamia, most of the household and artisan occupations were open to women as well as to men. Women could engage in small-scale business in their own name (but normally under a male relative's supervision). A woman only rarely operated in affairs completely independently.

Adultery was always considered the worst of all possible offenses between husband and wife because it put the children's parentage under a cloud of doubt and thus undermined the family's continuity. Punishment for wifely adultery could be death, not only for her but also for her lover if he were caught. Note that, in Hammurabi's code, adultery as a legal concept was limited to the wife's acts. The husband's sexual activity with slave girls or freeborn concubines, as he might see fit, was taken for granted. The double standard has existed since the beginnings of history.

Divorce and lawsuits arising from it were frequent in Mesopotamia, as the tablets attest. Most divorces were initiated by husbands, who were disappointed by childless wives or were sexually attracted to another woman and did not wish to or could not support the first wife as well. The lawsuits resulted when the wife or her father protested the lack of provision made for her support or the husband's attempt to retain her dowry. Then as now, lawyers must have relied on divorce proceedings for a substantial part of their income.

***Sexual and Marital Life.*** Because children and the continuity of the family were the real reasons for marriage, the marital bed was an honorable and even sacred place, and what took place there was in no way shameful. But the male and female had desires that went beyond the creation of children, and these were also nothing to be ashamed of, for these desires were implanted in humans by the all-wise gods. Everywhere in the Near East, starting apparently with the Sumerians and long continuing, the rites of the Sacred Marriage between a god and his high priestess, celebrating the fertility of the earth and of all creatures on it, were central to religious practice. The result was a fundamentally different attitude toward sex than we commonly find in civilized society today. Whether sexual pleasure outside marriage was permissible, however, depended on the status of the individuals concerned.

Marriage was always arranged by the two families—something so important could never be left to chance attraction. A great many of the clay tablets dug up in Mesopotamian ruins deal with marital contracts. Some of them were made when the bride and groom were still babies. Such early arrangements were especially common for girls, who normally were considerably younger at marriage than their husbands.

Marriage usually involved the exchange of bride money and a dowry. Bride money was a payment by the groom's family to the bride's family as specified in the marital contract. The dowry was also specified in the contract and was paid by the bride's family to the groom when the couple began to live together. The dowry remained in the husband's control as long as the marriage lasted. When the wife died, the dowry was distributed among her children, if she had any.

Every ancient culture insisted that brides should be virgins. This was one of the reasons for the early marriage of women. Although many literary works and folktales describe the social condemnation that awaited a woman who lost her virginity before marriage, it is still quite clear that lovemaking between young unmarried persons was by no means unheard of and did not always result in shame. Loss of virginity was regarded as damage to the family's property rather than a moral offense. As such, it could be made good by the payment of a fine. Punishment for seducing a virgin was less severe than for adultery or rape. Some authorities believe that the early stages of civilization in all areas were more tolerant of nonvirginal marriage for women than were later ones. If premarital relations were followed by marriage, very little fuss was made.

## Successors to Sumeria

After the conquest by Sargon of Akkad, Mesopotamia was subjected to a long series of foreign invasions and conquests by nomadic peoples eager to enjoy the fruits of civilized life. These barbaric nomads generally adopted the beliefs and values of those they had conquered. After the Akkadians, the most important of them were as follows, in sequence:

1. The *Amorites,* or *Old Babylonians,* a Semitic people who conquered the plains under their great emperor Hammurabi in the 1700s B.C.E.
2. The **Hittites,** an Indo-European group of tribes who came out of southern Russia into modern-day Turkey and constructed an empire there that reached as far into the east and south as the Zagros Mountains and Palestine. The first people to smelt iron, the Hittites were a remarkable group who took over the river plain about 1500 B.C.E. They were skilled administrators and established the first example of a multiethnic state, which worked fairly well.
3. After the Hittites fell to unknown invaders about 1200, the *Assyrians* gradually rose to power around 900 B.C.E., operating from their northern Mesopotamian center at Nineveh. We will deal with the imperial Assyrian Period from about 800 to 600 B.C.E. in Chapter 4.
4. Finally, after a brief period under the *New Babylonians* (or *Chaldees,* as the Old Testament calls them), the plains fell to the mighty *Persian Empire* in the 500s B.C.E. and stayed under Persian (Iranian) rule for most of the next thousand years (see Chapter 4).

Lynn Abercrombie/National Geographic Image Collection/Getty Images

**Sumerian Art.** This golden bull's head adorns a lyre unearthed in the royal tombs of Ur, in southern Mesopotamia. It dates to roughly 2500 B.C.E.

## The Decline of Mesopotamia in World History

The valley of the Tigris and Euphrates rivers ceased to be of central importance in the ancient world after the Persian conquest. The Persians did not choose to make their capital there, nor did they adopt the ideas and the cultural models of their new province, as all previous conquerors had. The Persians were already far advanced beyond barbarism when they conquered Mesopotamia and perhaps were not so easily impressed.

Various problems contributed to the decline of Mesopotamia, but it is certain that it proceeded in part from one of the first known examples of long-term environmental degradation. Significantly, the cities' food supply declined as the irrigated farms of the lower plains no longer produced abundant harvests. Thanks to several thousand years of salt deposits from the evaporated waters of the canals and ditches, the fields—unrenewed by fertilizers and exposed to a gradually harshening climate of sandstorms and great heat—were simply not capable of producing as much as the population needed. The once-thriving city-states and rich fields were gradually abandoned, and the center of power and culture moved elsewhere.

Mesopotamia slowly receded into the background of civilized activities from the Persian conquest until the ninth century C.E., when for a time it became the political and spiritual center of the far-flung world of Islam. But it was not until the mid-twentieth century, with the rise of Muslim fundamentalism and the coming of the Oil Age, that the area again became a vital world center.

## Summary

The earliest of the mutually dependent agglomerations of agriculturalists and skilled trades that we call towns and cities were founded in fourth millennium B.C.E. Mesopotamia, when an Asian people called Sumerians created them. Headed originally by a theocratic priesthood and later by warrior-kings, the Sumerian city-states left their various successors a rich variety of new techniques and viewpoints, including the load-bearing wheel, the first sophisticated writing system, an accurate chronology and mathematics, and impressive architectural skills. Their religion seems harsh and pessimistic to us now, but it apparently reflected their perceptions of the dangerous world around them, in which natural and manmade disasters were common and the gods cared little for their human slaves.

## Identification Terms

Test your knowledge of this chapter's key concepts by defining the following terms. If you can't recall the meaning of certain terms, refresh your memory by looking up the boldfaced term in the chapter, turning to the Glossary at the end of the book, or working with the flashcards that are available on the *World Civilizations* Companion Website: **http://history.wadsworth.com/adler04/**.

Babylon
cuneiform
*Epic of Gilgamesh*
Fertile Crescent
Hittites
patriarchy
polytheism
Semitic
Sumerians
theocracy
*ziggurats*

## Test Your Knowledge

Test your knowledge of this chapter by answering the following questions. Complete answers appear at the end of the book. You may also take this quiz interactively and find even more quiz questions on the *World Civilizations* Companion Website: **http://history.wadsworth.com/adler04/**.

1. The founders of ancient Mesopotamian civilization were the
   a. Sumerians.
   b. Amorites.
   c. Semites.
   d. Babylonians.
   e. Hittites.
2. The Tigris and Euphrates rivers were important to Mesopotamians primarily because
   a. they kept out potential raiders.
   b. they made irrigation possible.
   c. they drained off the water from the frequent storms.
   d. they brought the people together.
   e. they provided transportation to the sea.
3. The Mesopotamian ziggurat was a
   a. military fort.
   b. temple of worship.
   c. household shrine.
   d. royal palace.
   e. burial tomb.
4. Pictographs are a form of writing that
   a. uses pictures and words.
   b. uses agreed-upon signs to make pictures.
   c. puts abstract ideas into pictorial form.
   d. uses pictures of material objects to form meanings.
   e. uses conventional signs to designate parts of speech.
5. Mesopotamians considered their gods to be
   a. about equal in power.
   b. the creators of people and the universe.
   c. responsive to human needs and wants.
   d. disembodied spirits.
   e. always concerned with the well-being of human beings.
6. The *Epic of Gilgamesh* deals with the
   a. struggle between good and evil.
   b. details of death and the afterlife.
   c. proof of the existence of gods.
   d. conflict between men and women.
   e. conflict between humans and the gods.
7. The law code of King Hammurabi
   a. ensured equal treatment for all offenders.
   b. was the first law code ever written.
   c. used fines and financial punishments exclusively.
   d. ordered punishments in accord with the social rank of the offender.
   e. dealt mainly with matters of business.
8. In Sumerian and later government in Mesopotamia,
   a. theocracy succeeded the rule of kings.
   b. a warrior aristocracy was the rule from the beginning.
   c. a monarchy succeeded the rule of priests.
   d. the common people always had the last word.
   e. kings and priests usually worked together to create laws.
9. Becoming enslaved in Mesopotamia was most often the result of which of the following causes?
   a. Commission of crime or personal violence
   b. Being a prisoner of war or in debt
   c. Blasphemy
   d. Rebellion
   e. Defiance of the gods
10. A major reason for the decline of Mesopotamia in importance after the Persian conquests seems to have been
   a. an environmental change.
   b. unceasing warfare among the Persians.
   c. the conquest of the area by barbarians.
   d. the technological lag from which the area had always suffered.
   e. an alteration in trade routes which drew people elsewhere.

## InfoTrac College Edition

Visit the source collections at

**http://infotrac.thomsonlearning.com**

and use the Search function with the following key terms:

Mesopotamia  Sumer or Sumerian  Babylonian

## Wadsworth History Website Resources

Visit the World History Resource Center at **http://history.wadsworth.com/world** for a wealth of general resources and the *World Civilizations* Companion Website at **http://history.wadsworth.com/adler04/** for resources specific to this textbook.

## HistoryNow

Enter *HistoryNow* using the access card that is available for *World Civilizations. HistoryNow* will assist you in understanding the content in this chapter with lesson plans generated for your needs. In addition, you can read the following documents, and many more, online:

*Epic of Gilgamesh*  Code of Hammurabi

*They [Egyptian priests] have told me that 341 generations separate the first King of Egypt from the last. Reckoning three generations as a century . . . a total of 11,340 years.*
Herodotus, *Histories*, Book II

# 3 Egypt

THE NATURAL ENVIRONMENT
Egypt's Protective Isolation
Egypt's Uniqueness

THE PHARAOH: EGYPT'S GOD-KING
Government Under the Pharaoh
The Old Kingdom, Middle Kingdom, and New Kingdom

CULTURAL ACHIEVEMENTS

RELIGION AND ETERNAL LIFE

EGYPT'S PEOPLE AND THEIR DAILY LIVES

EGYPT AND MESOPOTAMIA: CONTRASTS

| | |
|---|---|
| c. 3100–2200 B.C.E. | OLD KINGDOM |
| c. 2600–2100 B.C.E. | PYRAMID-BUILDING AGE |
| c. 2200–2100 B.C.E. | FIRST INTERMEDIATE PERIOD |
| c. 2100–1650 B.C.E. | MIDDLE KINGDOM |
| c. 1650–1570 B.C.E. | SECOND INTERMEDIATE PERIOD |
| 1500s B.C.E. | HYKSOS INVASION |
| c. 1550–700 B.C.E. | NEW KINGDOM |
| c. 1550–1250 B.C.E. | THE EMPIRE |
| 1300s B.C.E. | AKHNATON'S MONOTHEIST EXPERIMENT |
| | TUTANKHAMEN |
| 525 B.C.E. | PERSIAN CONQUEST |

IT WOULD BE HARD TO FIND two other ancient civilizations that present as sharp a contrast in some respects as Mesopotamia on one end of the Fertile Crescent and Egypt on the other. Much of the reason for this disparity had to do with geography. Mesopotamia lay open to destructive assault from several directions and was repeatedly conquered by alien forces. Egypt saw no such threats for millennia. Although their centers were only some 800 miles apart, over countryside that was relatively easy to cross, and although we know that Mesopotamia exercised considerable influence on Egypt's cultural development, the two societies evolved very different patterns of beliefs and values. Quite unlike Mesopotamia, Egypt became an island in time and space that enjoyed more than one thousand years of civilized living with little disturbance from the outside world. When that disturbance did come at last, Egypt's reaction proved too inflexible to allow it to survive in its uniqueness.

## The Natural Environment

Like Mesopotamia, Egypt depended on the waters of a great river system. Egypt is, and has always been, the valley of the Nile—a green strip averaging about thirty miles wide, with forbidding desert hills on either side. The 4,000-mile-long river—the world's longest—originates far to the south in the lakes of central Africa and flows north until it empties into the Mediterranean Sea at Alexandria.

Unlike the unpredictably flooding Tigris and Euphrates, the Nile is a benevolent river, and without it life in Egypt would have been unthinkable. In contrast to the Tigris, the Nile annually would swell gently in late summer until it overflowed its low banks and spread out over the valley floor, carrying with it a load of extremely fertile silt. Two or three weeks later, the flood would subside, depositing the silt to renew the valley with a fresh layer of good topsoil. The Egyptians trapped receding waters in a series of small reservoirs connected to an intricate system of gated ditches that would later convey the water into the surrounding fields for irrigation.

Not only the highly predictable watering, but also climatic advantages make Egypt an ideal area for intensive agriculture, and it has supported three crops per year for a very long time. The entire year is one long growing season in Egypt. The climate is moderate and constant, with few storms and no frosts ever. The sun shines in modern Egypt an average of 361 days per year, and there is no reason to think that it was any different 4,000 years ago. Rain is almost unknown, and the temperature is in the seventies year round. In Mesopotamia, by contrast, farmers have always had to cope with excessive heat, drought, sandstorms, occasional floods, and insect invasions.

## Egypt's Protective Isolation

But not only in agriculture was Egypt blessed by its environment. Unlike Mesopotamia, which had no defensible natural boundaries and was repeatedly invaded from all sides, Egypt was secure in its geographic isolation. The country was also protected against invasion by the deserts on the east and west of the valley and by the so-called cataracts (rapids) of the northerly flowing Nile, which prevented easy passage into Egypt from the south, where enemies (Nubians, Ethiopians) dwelled. On the north, the sea gave the Nile delta some protection from unwanted intruders, while still allowing the Egyptians to develop maritime operations. Only on the northeast, where the narrow Sinai peninsula links Egypt to Asia (see Map 3.1), was a land-based invasion possible, and most of Egypt's eventual invaders and conquerors arrived from this direction.

Egypt's natural walls kept it safe from external danger for a very long time, however. For about 2,500 years, a uniquely Egyptian civilization developed in almost unbroken safety. But this isolation also had its drawbacks. When serious external challenges finally did come, the Egyptian governing class and general society were not prepared to resist effectively and could not adequately respond to the new situation.

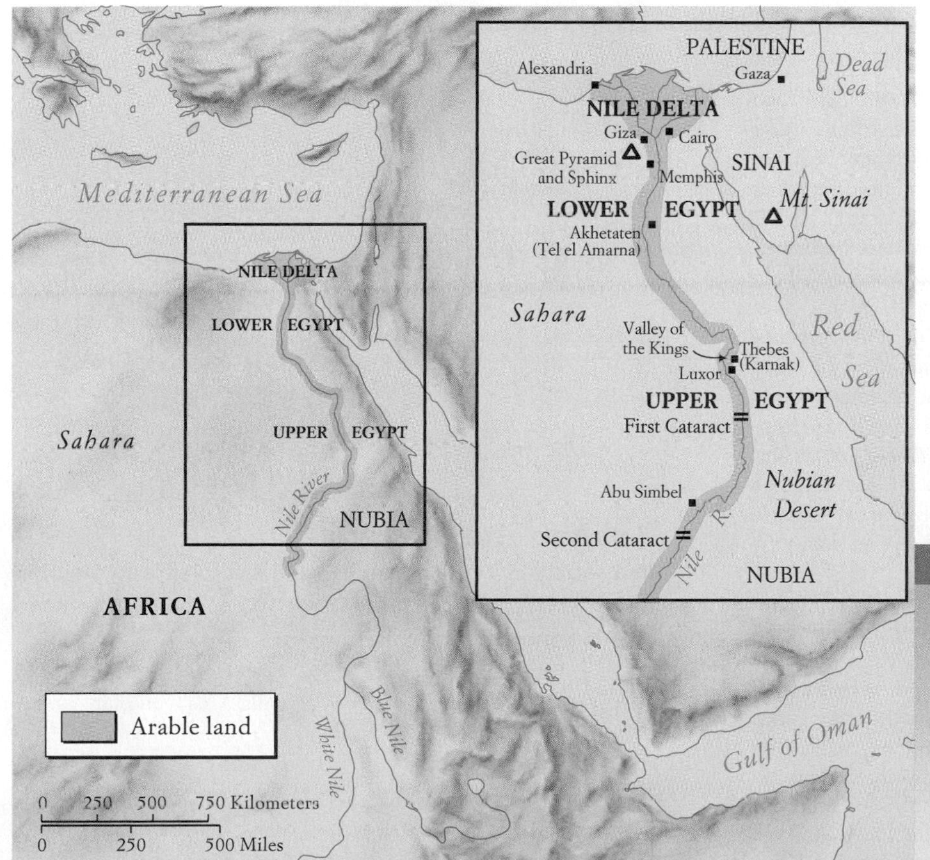


**MAP 3.1** *Ancient Egypt and the Nile*

The first tourist to leave an account of Egypt was the Greek Herodotus in the fifth century B.C.E. He called Egypt "the gift of the Nile," a phrase that still describes the relation of the river and the people. The arable portion of the Nile valley extended about 800 miles upriver in ancient times, but the Delta and the lower third of this section were the crucial food-growing area and the seat of most of the village populations.

## Egypt's Uniqueness

No other ancient civilization was so different as Egypt. The country possessed everything needed for a decent life: excellent agriculture, a skilled and numerous population, natural barriers against invasion, and great natural resources, including varied and exotic animal life. Together, they gave Egypt advantages that could only be envied. (See Evidence of the Past for an ancient account of Egyptian wildlife.)

In fact, over time the Egyptian educated class, especially the officials and priests, developed a sort of superiority complex toward foreigners that is rivaled in history only by that of the Chinese. The Egyptians were convinced that the gods smiled on them and their land, that they already possessed the best of all worlds in Egypt, and that they could learn nothing of significant value from others. When the king dealt with foreign traders, he could successfully pretend to his own people that the for-

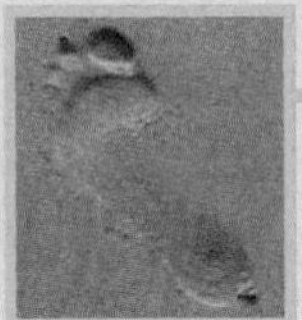

EVIDENCE OF THE PAST

### Egyptian Wildlife

**The fifth-century Greek historian and traveler Herodotus** was fascinated by Egypt and its inhabitants. How much of what he relates is attributable to firsthand information and how much to old wives' tales is a matter of debate. But Herodotus knew how to tell a good story, and his history therefore has been read avidly since his own time.

> The number of domestic animals in Egypt is very great, and would be greater still were it not for what befalls the cats. As the females, when they have kittened, no longer seek the company of the males, these last, to obtain once more their companionship practice a curious artifice. They seize the kittens, carry them off, and kill them, but do not eat them afterward. Upon this the females, being deprived of their young and longing to supply their place, seek the males once more. . . . On every occasion of a fire in Egypt the strangest prodigy occurs with the cats. The inhabitants allow the fire to rage as it pleases while they stand about at intervals and watch these animals, which slipping by the men or else leaping over them, rush headlong into the flames. When this happens the Egyptians are in deep sorrow. If a cat dies in a private house by a natural death, all the inmates of the house shave their eyebrows; on the death of a dog they shave the head and the whole body.
>
> The following are the peculiarities of the crocodile: during the four winter months they eat nothing. They are four-footed and live both on land and in water. The female lays and hatches her eggs ashore, passing the greater portion of the day on dry land, but at night retiring to the river. . . . Of all known animals this is the one which from the smallest size grows to be the greatest: for the egg of the crocodile is but little bigger that that of the goose, and the young crocodile is in proportion to the egg; yet when it is full grown, the animals measure frequently seventeen cubits and even more.

Louvre, Paris, France/Bridgeman Art Library

**Mummified Cat.** The high regard enjoyed by cats in Egypt can be seen from the tender care given this carefully stucceod and painted one, by the will, no doubt, of its deceased owner.

### Analyze and Interpret

In a society in which weapons were inaccessible to the ordinary person, what attitudes might be commonly found toward dangerous animals?

Source: Herodotus, *The Histories,* Book III, trans. A. de Sélincourt (Harmondsworth: Penguin, 1954).

**HistoryNow™**

***To read more of Herodotus's work, point your browser to the documents area of* HistoryNow.**

eigners had come to "give tribute," while the king showed his own generosity by showering "gifts" in return.

So secure were the Egyptians for so long that their security eventually turned into a weakness. Their self-sufficiency became a kind of mental cage, hemming in their imaginations and preventing the Egyptians from responding to change, even as such response became increasingly necessary. In short, they lost their ability to adapt effectively to external challenges. But this weakness took a very long time to show itself—about 2,000 years!

## The Pharaoh: Egypt's God-King

As is true of almost all early peoples, the Egyptians' religious beliefs reflected their environment to some extent, and the fully developed religion had an enormous impact on the nature of their government.

In contrast to Mesopotamia, Egypt was quickly and decisively unified. About 3100 B.C.E., all of the middle and lower reaches of the Nile valley came under one ruler. From the Mediterranean Sea southward to the Nubian Desert, the country and the numerous already-civilized villagers came under the control of a **pharaoh** (meaning "from the great house"). The first pharaoh was called Menes, but he appears to have been merely a legend—or if he existed in fact, we know nothing of him but his name.

The period from 3100 to about 2500 B.C.E. was Egypt's foundation period and the time of its greatest triumphs and cultural achievements. During these centuries, the land was ruled by an unbroken line of god-kings who apparently faced no serious threats either inside or outside their domain.

It is important to recognize that the pharaoh was not *like* a god. Instead, he *was* a god, a god who chose to live on Earth among his favored people for a time. From the moment that his days-long coronation ceremony was completed, he was no longer a mortal man. He had become immortal, a reincarnation of the great divinity **Horus.** The pharaoh's will was law, and his wisdom was all-knowing. What he desired was by definition correct and just. What he did was the will of the almighty gods, speaking through him as one of them. His regulations must be carried out without question. Otherwise, the gods might cease to smile on Egypt. His wife and family, especially his son who would succeed him, shared to some degree in this celestial glory, but only the reigning pharaoh was divine. Such powers in the monarch are rare in history, and Egypt's god-king was truly extraordinary in the prestige he enjoyed among his people.

### *Government Under the Pharaoh*

The pharaoh governed through a group of officials composed mainly of noble landowners who were responsible to him but were granted great local powers. When a weak pharaoh came to the throne, the prestige of the central authority could and occasionally did break down in the provinces, but its memory never disappeared entirely.

There were two short intervals in Egypt's long history when the pharaoh's powers were seriously diminished, in the so-called Intermediate Periods of 2200–2100 B.C.E. and 1650–1570 B.C.E. The causes of the first breakdown remain unclear, but it was not the result of invasion. The second of these periods is known to have been triggered by the invasion of the mysterious **Hyksos** people, who crossed the Sinai peninsula and conquered the Nile delta. In both cases, a new, native Egyptian dynasty appeared within a century and reestablished effective central government. The monarchy's grip on the loyalties of the people was sufficient that it could reform the government in the same style, with the same values and officials as before.

What enabled the pharaoh to retain such near-magical power over his subjects for so long? For almost 2,000 years, the belief in the divinity of the king (or queen—there were at least three female pharaohs) persisted, as did the conviction that Egypt was specially favored and protected by the gods. This was the result of the happy situation that Egypt enjoyed through climate and geography. Nature provided, as nowhere else, a perpetual agricultural abundance, making Egypt the only place in the known world at that time to be able to export grain surpluses. Furthermore, for 3,000 years of civilized life, until about 1000 B.C.E., Egypt was only rarely touched by war and foreign invasion. Until the Empire Period, no army—that great eater of taxes—was necessary.

### *The Old Kingdom, Middle Kingdom, and New Kingdom*

It has long been customary to divide Egypt's ancient history into *dynasties* (periods of monarchic rule by one family). In all there were thirty-one dynasties, beginning with the legendary Menes and ending with the dynasty that fell to the Persian invaders in 525 B.C.E. The greatest were those of the pyramid-building epoch and those of the Empire, about 1500–1300 B.C.E. The dynasties are traditionally grouped under three kingdoms: Old, Middle, and New.

***Old Kingdom.*** The **Old Kingdom** (3100–2200 B.C.E.), which extended from Menes to the *First Intermediate Period,* was ancient Egypt's most fertile and successful era.

During these 900 years, both form and content were perfected in most of those achievements that made Egypt remarkable: art and architecture, divine monarchy, religion, social and economic stability, and prosperity. The pharaohs of this epoch seem to have been unchallenged leaders who enjoyed the willing loyalty of their people. Later cultural and intellectual developments were almost always only a slight variation or a deterioration of the pattern established during the Old Kingdom.

***Middle Kingdom.*** The **Middle Kingdom** (2100–1650 B.C.E.) followed the First Intermediate Period with 500 years of political stability and the continued refinement of the arts and crafts. The country under pharaoh's rule was extended up the Nile to the south. Trade with neighbors, including Mesopotamia and Nubia (see Map 3.1), became more extensive. The condition of the laboring poor in the hundreds of Nile-side villages seems to have gradually worsened, however. Religion became more democratic in its view of who could enter the afterlife, and a small middle class of officials and merchants began to make itself apparent.

***New Kingdom.*** The **New Kingdom** (1550–700 B.C.E.) is also called the *Empire,* although the name really belongs only to its first three centuries (1550–1250). The New Kingdom began after the defeat of the Hyksos invaders in the 1500s (the *Second Intermediate Period*). It lasted through the years of imperial wars against the Hittites and others for control of Mesopotamia, which ended with Egyptian withdrawal. Then came long centuries of sporadic weakness and resurgence that ended with Egypt's permanent conquest by foreigners.

The Empire was an ambitious experiment in which the Egyptians, headed by aggressive pharaohs, attempted to convert their eastern neighbors to their lifestyle and government theory. The experiment did not work well, however. Apparently no one else was able to understand the Egyptian view of life or wanted it to be imposed on them. The Empire did not last because of both military reversals starting around the time of Pharaoh Akhnaton (1300s B.C.E.) and internal discontent. By 1100, the pharaoh again ruled only the Nile valley.

During their last 300 years of independent existence, the Egyptians were frequently subjected to foreign invasion, both over the Sinai Desert and from the south by way of the great river. Before the Persians arrived in 525, others such as the Kushites (Ethiopians) and the Nubians (Sudanese) had repeatedly invaded—a sure sign that the power of the god-king over his people was weakening (see Chapters 4 and 13). But even after the Persian conquest, which marked the real end of ancient Egypt's existence as an independent state (all the way until the twentieth century!), the life of ordinary people in the fields and orchards saw no marked change. Only the person to whom taxes and rents were paid was different. The cultural forms and beliefs of the inhabitants were by now so deeply rooted that no foreign overlord could alter them.

## Cultural Achievements

The wealth of the pharaoh and the willingness and skill of his people allowed the erection of the most stupendous monuments put up by any people or government anywhere: the pyramids and temples of the Old Kingdom. Visitors have marveled at these stone wonders ever since. The Great Pyramid of Khufu (Cheops), located a few miles outside present-day Cairo, is easily the largest and grandest commemorative edifice ever built. The pyramids (built between 2600 and 2100 B.C.E.) were designed as tombs for the living pharaoh and were built while he was still alive. They possessed immense—and still unknown—religious significance for the Egyptians. Much is still unknown about the pyramids' true purposes, but the perfection of their construction and the art of the burial chambers show Egyptian civilization at its most impressive.

The pyramids were not the only stone monuments erected along the Nile. In the period around 1300, several warrior-pharaohs celebrated the fame of their empire by erecting enormous statues of themselves and their favored gods, and even larger temples in which to put them. At the Nile sites of *Karnak* and *Tel el Amarna,* some of these still stand. Most losses of artistic and architectural wonders in Egypt have been caused not by time or erosion but by vandalism and organized tomb and treasure robbers over many centuries. All of the pharaohs' tombs discovered to date, except one, have long since been robbed of the burial treasure interred with the mummy of the dead god-king. The exception is that of the famous King Tutankhamen—King Tut—whose underground burial chamber was discovered in the early 1920s. **Tutankhamen** (ruled 1347–1339 B.C.E.) died at the age of eighteen without having done anything of consequence during his short reign. The world probably would never have noted him had not the British archaeologist Howard Carter stumbled on his grave 3,000 years later. (See Evidence of the Past.)

Egyptian monarchic statuary is distinguished by the peculiar combination of graceful and natural lines in association with great dignity and awesomeness. This awe is reinforced by the art and architecture that surround the great statues, which are designed to impress all onlookers with the permanence and power of the Egyptian monarchy. The Egyptians' mastery of stone is rivaled

Tibor Eognár/Corbis

**THE GREAT PYRAMIDS.** These three massive stone monuments lie just outside the modern city limits of Cairo. The center one is the pyramid of Khufu, or Cheops, the largest masonry construct of all time. Aside from serving as the pharaohs' tombs, the pyramids apparently held great religious significance for the Egyptians, who believed it to be an honor to contribute their labor and skill to their construction. The pyramids were replaced by underground tombs beginning in the Middle Kingdom, probably because of both the expense and the difficulty of keeping them safe from tomb robbers, who were little deterred by religious principles.

in Western civilization only by the artistry of the classical Greeks and Romans. And most of this art was apparently created by artists and architects who did not know the principle of the wheel and had only primitive tools and what we would consider very clumsy math and physics!

Other art forms in which Egypt excelled included fresco painting (tinting freshly laid plaster on interior walls), fine ceramics of all sorts and uses, imaginative and finely worked jewelry in both stones and metals, and miniature sculpture. When upper-class Egyptians died, hundreds of small statues would be buried with their mummified remains. The Egyptians believed that what had been precious to a person in earthly life would also be desired in the next (a belief shared by the people of Mesopotamia), so they interred statues and models representing the person's earthly family and friends, his or her interests and activities. Music and dance were also well developed, as we know from their lively portrayal in thousands of paintings and statuary groups depicting the life of the people of all ranks, from the nobles to the poorest peasants. Egypt's artistic heritage is exceeded by that of few, if any, other peoples.

Egyptian writing developed differently from that of Mesopotamia. **Hieroglyphics** (literally, "sacred carvings") were pictographs that could convey either an idea, such as "man," or a phonetic sound, by picturing an object that begins with a strong consonant sound. The word for *owl,* for example, began with the consonant "m" sound in spoken Egyptian, so a picture of an owl could be used to indicate that sound. This beginning of an alphabet was not fully developed, however. The use of hieroglyphics, which began as far back as 3000 B.C.E., was confined to a small group of educated persons and gradually faded out after Egypt lost its independence in the sixth century B.C.E. The complete repertory of 604 hieroglyphic symbols is now deciphered, enabling the reading of many thousands of ancient inscriptions.

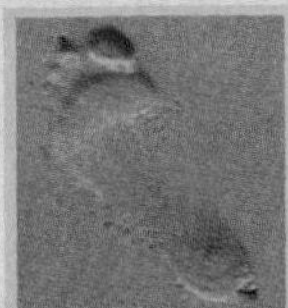

EVIDENCE OF THE PAST

## "Wonderful Things!"

**After several years of searching** the Valley of the Kings, Howard Carter had found the buried tomb of the pharaoh Tutankhamen. He describes the experience in his own words:

> The following day, November 26, was the day of days, the most wonderful I have ever lived through and certainly one whose like I can never hope to see again. . . . Slowly, desperately slowly, it seemed to us, the remains of the passage debris was removed, until at last we had the whole door before us. The decisive moment had arrived. With trembling hands I made a tiny breach in the upper left-hand corner. . . . Candle tests were applied as a precaution against foul gases and then, widening the hole a little, I inserted the candle and peered in. At first I could see nothing, the hot air escaping from the chamber causing the candle flame to flicker but presently, as my eyes grew accustomed to the light details of the room within emerged slowly from the mist; strange animals, statues and gold—everywhere the glint of gold. For the moment I was struck dumb with amazement, and when Lord Carnarvon [Carter's sponsor] unable to stand the suspense any longer, inquired anxiously, "Can you see anything?" it was all I could do to get out the words, "Yes, wonderful things!"

### *Analyze and Interpret*

How do contemporary archaeological digs in Egypt differ from those of eighty years ago in terms of leadership and ownership of what might be found?

Source: Christine Hobson, *The World of the Pharaohs* (New York: Thames & Hudson, 1987), p. 110.

Robert Holmes/Corbis

**The Golden Death Mask of King Tut.** The burial site of young King Tutankhamen became one of the most spectacular archaeological finds of the twentieth century. For eight years, British archaeologist Howard Carter salvaged its magnificent treasure, after his discovery of it in 1922, classifying and restoring more than 5,000 objects, including a beautiful golden death mask, a gilded throne, statues, vases, and hundreds of artifacts made of wood covered in gold leaf and decorated with gems. A magnificent stone sarcophagus held the luxurious coffin, richly wrought in pure gold. The treasure offered scholars and the public a glimpse of the wealth of the ancient Egyptians and their Nile kingdom.

## Religion and Eternal Life

Egypt's religion was almost infinitely polytheistic. At least 3,000 separate names of gods have been identified in Egyptian writings, many of them the same deities but with different names over the centuries. Chief among them were the gods of the sun, *Amon* and *Ra,* who were originally separate but later combined into one being. Other important deities included **Isis,** goddess of the Nile and of fertility; **Osiris,** ruler of the afterlife; their son, *Horus,* made visible as the ruling pharaoh; and *Ptah,* the god of all life on Earth.

The Egyptians believed firmly in the afterlife. Originally, it seems to have been viewed as a possibility only for the upper class, but gradually the afterlife was democratized. By about 1000 B.C.E., most Egyptians apparently believed in a scheme of eternal reward or punishment for their *ka,* which had to submit to a moral Last Judgment

British Museum, London, UK/Bridgeman Art Library

**EGYPTIAN HIEROGLYPHICS.** The Rosetta Stone was discovered by French scientists accompanying Napoleon's army during its occupation of Egypt in the 1790s. It contains three versions of the same priestly decree for the second century B.C.E.: hieroglyphic Egyptian, demotic (cursive) Egyptian, and Greek. By comparing the three, the brilliant linguist Jean François Champollion was able in 1822 to finally break the code of hieroglyphic symbols and commence the modern study of the Egyptian language.

by Osiris. ***Ka*** referred to the life-essence that could return to life, given the correct preparation, even after the death of the original physical body.

Mostly, it seems, Egyptians expected reward. They thought of eternity as a sort of endless procession by the deceased's *ka* through the heavens and the gods' abodes there. In the company of friends and family, watched over by the protective and benevolent gods, the individual would proceed in a stately circle around the sun forever. There was no need to work and no suffering. Such was heaven. The notion of hell as a place where the evil paid for their sins came along in Egypt only during the New Kingdom, when things had begun to go sour.

The priests played an important role in Egyptian culture, although they were not as prominent as in several other civilizations. At times, they seem to have been the power behind the throne, especially when the king had made himself unpopular or was unusually weak in character.

In the reign of the young and inexperienced **Akhnaton** (1367–1350 B.C.E.), the priests vehemently opposed a unique experiment: the pharaoh's attempt to change the basic polytheistic nature of Egyptian religion. Why the young Akhnaton (aided by his beautiful wife Nefertiti) chose to attempt to introduce a monotheistic ("one-god") cult of the sun god, newly renamed Aton, we can only guess. This attempt at **monotheism** was a great novelty in ancient civilization, and it was not to be heard of again until the emergence of Judaism five or six centuries later. The pharaoh announced that Aton was his heavenly father and that Aton alone was to be worshiped as the single and universal god of all creation. The priests naturally opposed this revolutionary change, and as soon as Akhnaton was dead (possibly by poison), they denounced his ideas and went back to the old ways under the boy-pharaoh Tutankhamen.

## EGYPT'S PEOPLE AND THEIR DAILY LIVES

The Egyptian population was composed overwhelmingly of peasants, who lived in the villages that crowded along the Nile. Most were free tenant farmers who worked on the estate of a large landholder or government official, who had been granted the land as payment for services to the crown. Each village followed a similar pattern: the huts were set close together within, and the fields lay outside. Several adults lived in each hut. Each day the

Roger Wood/Corbis

**EGYPTIAN FEMALE DEITY.** This figure of Selket, one of the many female deities in the Egyptian pantheon, was probably commissioned by a grateful devotee. Selket was the goddess who healed bites and wounds, and was thus held in particular reverence by common folk who worked in the fields and on the banks of the crocodile-infested Nile.

peasants would go out to work in the fields, care for the irrigation works, or tend the animals.

Besides farmers, many small merchants and craftspeople lived in the villages. But Egypt had no real cities as in Mesopotamia, where neighborhoods were filled with specialized wholesale and retail markets, and dozens of crafts were practiced in hundreds of workshops. Egypt's successive capital cities, such as Memphis, Tel el Amarna, and Thebes, were really royal palaces, shrines, and pleasure grounds for the wealthy, not commercial centers. The common people had nothing to do with the capitals except for occasional huge labor projects. Large-scale trade and commerce were of relatively minor importance in Egyptian history and for a very long period were treated as a monopoly belonging to the government's officials. A small middle class existed by consent of the government officialdom.

Archivo Iconografico, S.A./Corbis

**Egyptian Fresco.** The optimistic Egyptians' love of music and feasting is evident in this fresco from a New Kingdom noble's tomb near Thebes. The emphasis on the eyes of the female figures was one of the many conventions that the anonymous artists were obliged to follow.

As the centuries passed, daily life changed remarkably little. Slavery was originally rare but increased during the Empire, when professional soldiers became necessary and prisoners of war became common. As in Mesopotamia, slavery was most often the result of owing debts to a landlord or committing a serious crime. A kind of serfdom—lifelong restrictions on one's physical and social mobility—also came into existence in later Egypt. Free tenant families were gradually turned into serfs, probably because of debt, and then had to work the land in a system of sharecropping that ensured that they remained in their village.

All in all, however, the common people of Egypt were better off more of the time than the commoners in almost any other ancient society. They were usually free, had enough to eat, lived in one of the world's easiest and most healthful climates, did not have to pay heavy taxes until fairly late, and were usually ruled by a relatively just and effective government with honest officials. They even had hopes of pleasing the gods and attaining immortality. Compared with the fate of many others, that was not a bad prospect!

## Egypt and Mesopotamia: Contrasts

The two outstanding early centers of Near Eastern civilized life—Egypt and Mesopotamia—were situated fairly close to each other and experienced considerable cross-cultural stimuli at times. But their differences were notable and permanent. Egypt enjoyed enormous stability. Life was highly predictable: tomorrow was today and yesterday under unchanged or only slightly changed circumstances. Mesopotamia, on the contrary, was frequently subject to violent change. Not only were invasions or war commonplace, but the kings—who were men, not gods—were often challenged by rebels and curtailed in their power by angry gods or human rivals.

Egypt was protected from outsiders for a very long time by natural barriers and could pick and choose among the cultural influences it wanted to adopt. Mesopotamia was a crossroads between barbarism and civilization, as well as between barbarian and barbarian. New ideas, new techniques, and new beliefs were introduced by invasion, trade, and simple curiosity.

Egypt had been a unified nation as long as tradition taught or anyone could remember. The Egyptians viewed the world as consisting of the Egyptian people and the rest, whom they regarded as inferiors who had little to teach Egypt. This feeling persisted long after the time when it was clearly no longer true, and it contributed much to the Egyptians' eventual vulnerability to outside forces. As their ability to resist foreign invaders declined, the Egyptian governing class took refuge in a false sense of superiority in culture.

Mesopotamia, on the other hand, was a melting pot. Repeatedly, large groups of outsiders would arrive with sufficient military or economic power to establish their ideas and beliefs among the conquered people, at least for as long as they needed to strike roots and change some elements of the previous civilization. Stagnation behind a wall of security could not occur—challenge was on the daily menu. In Egypt, the sense of superiority seems to have eventually become a sort of "defense mechanism" that prevented the rulers from seeing the truth and choked off badly needed reform. They viewed change as subversive and successfully resisted it for a long time—so long as to make successful adjustment almost impossible.

Of these two early civilizations, however, Mesopotamia proved to be the major cradle of later Western traditions and beliefs. For all its long life and success, Egypt was something of an island in space and time, with relatively little permanent influence on its neighbors or on future generations. In the next chapter, we will look at some of those neighbors in the Near East, including two peoples who eventually conquered Egypt—the Assyrians and the Persians.

## Summary

The Nile valley produced a civilized society as early as any in the world, thanks to an unusual combination of favorable climate and geography. Even before the emergence of central government under a god-king called pharaoh, the farmers along the river had devised an intricate system of irrigated fields that gave Egypt an enviable surplus of food. The unification of the villages was accomplished about 3100 B.C.E., giving rise to the high civilization of the Old Kingdom and its awesome monuments celebrating the linkage of Egypt and the protective gods. Aside from the abnormal collapse of central government in the brief Intermediate Periods, the rulers of Egypt were uniquely successful, maintaining two thousand years of prosperity and isolation from contacts with others, except on their own terms. This success allowed the reigning group to assume a superiority that, although originally justified, gradually became a clinging to tradition for its own sake. When the misguided attempt at empire failed, Egypt faced the challenge of repeated foreign invasions after about 1000 B.C.E. The divine kings lost their stature, and the static civilization of the Nile fell under the sway of once disdained aliens from the east and south. The Persian conquest in 525 B.C.E. completed the decline of the pharaohs' state into dependency.

## Identification Terms

Test your knowledge of this chapter's key concepts by defining the following terms. If you can't recall the meaning of certain terms, refresh your memory by looking up the boldfaced term in the chapter, turning to the Glossary at the end of the book, or working with the flashcards that are available on the *World Civilizations* Companion Website: **http://history.wadsworth.com/adler04/**.

Akhnaton
hieroglyphics
Horus
Hyksos
Isis
*ka*
Middle Kingdom
monotheism
New Kingdom
Old Kingdom
Osiris
pharaoh
Tutankhamen

## Test Your Knowledge

Test your knowledge of this chapter by answering the following questions. Complete answers appear at the end of the book. You may also take this quiz interactively and find even more quiz questions on the *World Civilizations* Companion Website: **http://history.wadsworth.com/adler04/**.

1. Which of these adjectives would you *not* associate with ancient Egypt?
   a. Stable
   b. Predictable
   c. Poor
   d. Isolated
   e. Unique

2. The geographic status of Egypt destined the country to be
   a. vulnerable to repeated invasions.
   b. a crossroads of travelers through the ages.
   c. almost self-contained.
   d. divided into many different natural regions.
   e. left out of maritime expeditions.
3. The key element of Egypt's government was
   a. the pharaoh's efficient police.
   b. the code of royal law.
   c. popular respect for the god-king.
   d. a powerful military establishment.
   e. a nobility that was completely self-regulatory.
4. The Middle Kingdom was ended in Egypt by
   a. the coming of the Hyksos invaders.
   b. revolt against the pharaoh Akhnaton.
   c. invasion by the Nubians.
   d. the Persian conquest.
   e. a thirty-year drought.
5. Which of the following was *true* of Egypt's cultural achievements?
   a. The use of hieroglyphics eventually gave the Egyptians a complete alphabet.
   b. Most of early Egypt's architectural wonders have been destroyed by erosion.
   c. The use of the wheel aided the Egyptians' use of stone as art.
   d. The pyramids were constructed during the Middle Kingdom.
   e. Egypt's great statues were designed to illustrate the power and endurance of the pharaohs.
6. The key to understanding ancient Egyptian hieroglyphics was the
   a. conquest of Egypt by the Persians and their translations.
   b. discovery of the similarities between them and ancient Sumerian writing.
   c. translation of the Rosetta Stone.
   d. ability of modern linguists using computers to compare them with other languages.
   e. discovery and translation of a wall of writings in the tomb of King Tutankhamen.
7. Slavery in Egypt
   a. became rarer as the New Kingdom expanded Egypt's borders.
   b. was the result mainly of debt and crime.
   c. was quite different from that of Mesopotamia in nature and causes.
   d. was almost unknown.
   e. was most prevalent during the First Intermediate Period.
8. The pharaoh Akhnaton fostered a
   a. belief in a single god.
   b. return to traditional religious belief.
   c. major reform in landholding and agriculture.
   d. major change in government's nature.
   e. reverence for Egyptian ancestors.
9. Which of the following was least likely to have occurred in Egypt from 3000 to about 1000 B.C.E.?
   a. Social rebellion against the government
   b. Drastic change in the prestige of various Egyptian deities
   c. Invasion from outside Egypt
   d. Attempt to extend rule over non-Egyptians
   e. Extensive trade with outside peoples
10. A chief difference between Egypt and Mesopotamia lay in
    a. their relative dependence on irrigation farming.
    b. Egypt's more democratic government.
    c. Mesopotamia's superior artistic creativity.
    d. Egypt's acceptance of monotheism.
    e. the relative importance of city life and commerce.

## InfoTrac College Edition

Visit the source collections at

**http://infotrac.thomsonlearning.com**

and use the Search function with the following key terms:

Egypt history pharaoh Tutankhamen

## Wadsworth History Website Resources

Visit the World History Resource Center at **http://history.wadsworth.com/world** for a wealth of general resources and the *World Civilizations* Companion Website at **http://history.wadsworth.com/adler04/** for resources specific to this textbook.

## HistoryNow

Enter *HistoryNow* using the access card that is available for *World Civilizations*. *HistoryNow* will assist you in understanding the content in this chapter with lesson plans generated for your needs. In addition, you can read the following documents, and many more, online:

Herodotus, *The Histories*

*The Lord our God made a covenant, not only with our fathers, but with all of us living today. . . . The Lord said, "I am the Lord your God . . . Worship no God but me."*

The Bible

# 4 Warriors and Deities in the Near East: Persians and Jews



| | |
|---|---|
| 1900s B.C.E. | Hebrews leave Mesopotamia |
| c. 1250 B.C.E. | Hebrew Exodus from Egypt |
| c. 1000 B.C.E. | Hebrew Kingdom established; Phoenicians develop early alphabet |
| c. 800 B.C.E. | Assyrian Empire expands; Carthage founded by Phoenicians |
| 722 B.C.E. | Assyrians conquer Samaria |
| 612 B.C.E. | Fall of Nineveh/end of Assyrian Empire |
| 500s B.C.E. | Establishment and expansion of Persian Empire |
| 586–539 B.C.E. | Babylonian Captivity of Jews |

The Near East, that area between the Nile valley and the western borders of Iran, was from earliest times a region of cultural overlap and interchange. First one people and then another would take command of a portion of the region for a century or more, only to fall under the sway of the next onslaught of newcomers. Petty states and kingdoms arose whose very names are sometimes forgotten but whose contributions to the ascent of civilization in this region were collectively impressive. In this chapter, we look at three of the most important of these—briefly at the transitory glory of Assyria and Phoenicia, and in more detail at the much larger and longer-lived monarchy of Persia. Then we review the history of the Hebrews, a people whose historic achievement lay in their gradual working out of a unique vision of the nature of the Divinity and the relation of God and humans, a vision that passed on into the very heart of Western civilization.

## The Assyrian Empire

The Assyrians were a Semitic tribal group who emerged from nomadism in what is now northern Iraq in the twelfth century B.C.E., following the decline of the Hittite monarchy based in Turkey. They entered history about 900 B.C.E. as challengers to other Semites in the Tigris valley. Their chief town, **Nineveh,** lay in the upper valley of the Tigris, and their chief god was the fierce **Assur,** from whom the people derived their name. By 800 B.C.E., through their own ferocity and cunning in war, the Assyrian kings had conquered much of the Tigris–Euphrates region and were fighting the Babylonians for the southern portion (see Map 4.1). The Assyrians displayed great talent in military affairs. Their army was large and seemingly invincible, using new tactics to negate the traditional advantage of charioteers over foot soldiers.

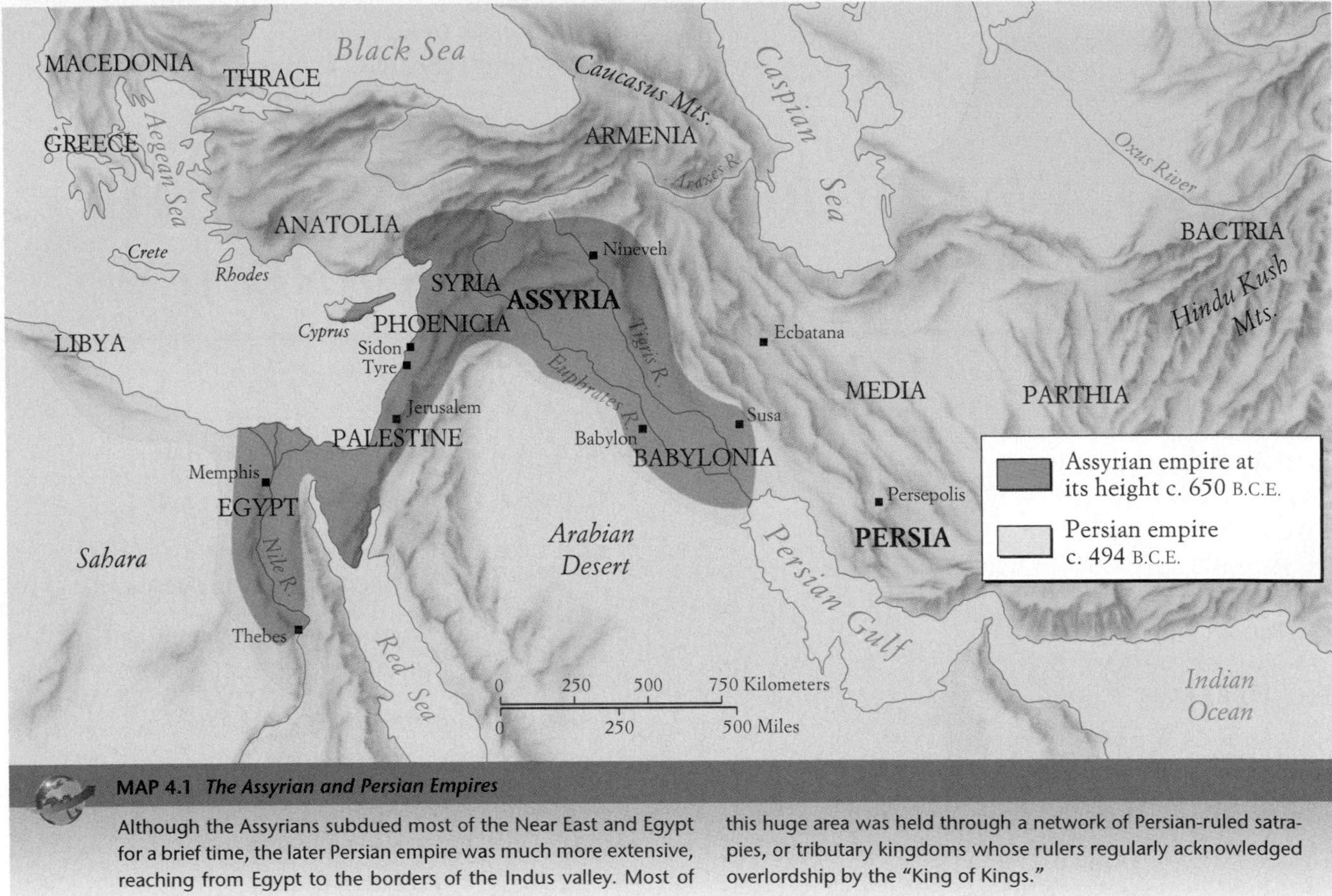


**MAP 4.1** ***The Assyrian and Persian Empires***

Although the Assyrians subdued most of the Near East and Egypt for a brief time, the later Persian empire was much more extensive, reaching from Egypt to the borders of the Indus valley. Most of this huge area was held through a network of Persian-ruled satrapies, or tributary kingdoms whose rulers regularly acknowledged overlordship by the "King of Kings."

By this epoch, the horse and the chariot were the chief force in warfare. (It is believed that the chariot was introduced to Near Eastern warfare by the Hyksos invaders of Egypt in the 1500s B.C.E.) For centuries, leather-clad warriors armed with short swords had fought from chariots drawn by two or three horses. The chariots would split the loose ranks of the enemy foot soldiers, and the momentum of the horses combined with the raised platform gave the swordsmen an almost irresistible advantage over opposing infantry. The early Assyrian kings took away this advantage, however, by fielding tight-knit infantry formations with long spears and swords, protected on the flanks by bands of horsemen who engaged the enemy charioteers while they were still far off. The infantry were heavily armored and so disciplined that they would stand up to a chariot charge without breaking. The Assyrians were also experts in siege warfare, and no enemy walled town or fort could hold for long against their artillery of stone-throwing catapults and rams.

Anyone who resisted the Assyrians and lost suffered a terrible fate: wholesale slavery, execution, pillage, and rape. Once conquered, the enemy was closely supervised, and any effort to spring free was immediately suppressed. The chronicles left by the Assyrians delight in telling of the huge piles of dead left by the triumphant armies of such kings as Tiglath-Pileser, who reigned in the seventh century B.C.E.:

> Like the Thunder, I crushed corpses of their warriors in the battle. I made their blood flow over into all the ravines and over the high places. I cut off their heads and piled them at the walls of their cities like heaps of grain. I carried off their booty, their goods, and their property beyond all reckoning. Six thousand, the remainder of their troops who had fled before my weapons and thrown themselves at my feet, I took away as prisoners and added to the peoples of my country [that is, slaves]. (From J. B. Pritchard, ed., *Ancient Near Eastern Texts,* 3d ed. Princeton, NJ: Princeton University Press, 1969.)

The Assyrians were perhaps the most hated conquerors in ancient history. Only their expertly calculated plans to "divide and conquer" and their mass deportations of subject peoples enabled them to remain in power as long as they did. At one point their empire reached from the upper Tigris to central Egypt. It was governed from Nineveh by a network of military commanders who had no mercy for rebels and held large numbers of hostages for the good behavior of the rest of their people.

But less than a century after its high point of power, Nineveh was in total ruins ("not a stone upon a stone," asserts the Old Testament), and the Assyrians were swept from the pages of history as though they had never existed. Their many enemies and rebellious subjects, led by the Chaldees of New Babylon, finally united against their oppressor and took full revenge for Assyrian atrocities. When they captured Nineveh in 612 B.C.E., the victors even salted the fertile irrigated lands that ringed the city, to prevent the site from ever being inhabited again. It was indeed forgotten until the middle of the nineteenth century, when Nineveh's ruins were unearthed by some of the earliest archaeological expeditions to the East.

With such determined erasure of their history, how can we know anything about the Assyrians' past? Remarkably, they combined their delight in slaughter with a sophisticated appreciation for all forms of pictorial and architectural art. Much of our knowledge about the Assyrians comes from their extensive portrayals of court life in bas relief sculpture, as well as from archaeological discoveries from their ruined cities. One of the last kings of the Assyrians, Assurbanipal, established the largest library known to the Near East in ancient times. More than 20,000 "books" of clay tablets have been recovered from the site in Nineveh since the nineteenth century.

**ASSURBANIPAL AT WAR.** This Assyrian bas relief shows King Assurbanipal charging the enemy in his war chariot, accompanied by picked spearmen who thrust away the hostile infantry as the monarch loads his bow. The Assyrian genius for portrayal of violent motion comes through strongly in these reliefs, which date from the 600s B.C.E.

## THE PHOENICIANS

Another small but significant Semitic people were the unwarlike Phoenicians, who originally inhabited a strip along the coast of what is now Lebanon. From their ports of Tyre and Sidon, they became the greatest maritime traders and colonizers of the ancient Near East. Their trade in luxury wares such as copper and dyes took them through the Mediterranean and into the Atlantic as far as the coast of Britain (Cornwall). Here they obtained the precious tin that could be mixed with copper and lead to form bronze, the main metallic resource before 1000 B.C.E. The Phoenicians also apparently spread the art of iron making from the Hittite settlements to the Greeks and westward into Africa. They established a whole series of colonies in the western Mediterranean. Some of these became important in their own right, and one of them, the rich city-state of Carthage, founded around 800 B.C.E., became the great rival to Rome until its final defeat around 200 B.C.E. The Phoenicians themselves were absorbed into the Assyrian and succeeding empires but remained the paramount Mediterranean traders and seafarers until the rise of Greece in the 600s B.C.E.

The Phoenicians' most notable contribution came in the linguistic field. They were the first to use a *phonetic alphabet,* a system of twenty-two written marks ("letters"), each of which corresponded to a specific consonant sound of the oral language. The Phoenicians' alphabet, which emerged about 1000 B.C.E., was a definite advance in simplicity and accessibility of written communication over both the cuneiforms of the Sumerians and the hieroglyphs of the Egyptians. The Greeks later improved the Phoenician alphabet; added signs for the vowels, which the Phoenicians did not employ; and thereby created essentially the same alphabet (although in a different letter form) that we use in Western scripts today.

## THE PERSIANS

Until the twentieth century, present-day Iran was called *Persia.* Its ruling group was for a millennium, 500 B.C.E. to 500 C.E., the most powerful of the many peoples in western Asia. Iran is mostly a high, arid plateau, surrounded on the north, west, and east by high mountains and on the south by the Indian Ocean (see Map 4.1). For a long time, the country has been a natural divide-point for travel from the eastern Mediterranean to China and India, and vice versa. Later, it became the great exchange point between the Arabic-Muslim world and the Indo-Hindu. Thanks to this strategic position, Iran and the Iranians have long been able to play a considerable role in world affairs.

The Persians were an Indo-European-speaking people who had migrated slowly south from the central Asian steppes into Iran. Actually, several related groups, collectively termed *Iranians,* moved south starting about 1000 B.C.E. At this epoch they were still nomadic and knew nothing of agriculture or other civilized crafts and techniques. They did, however, possess large numbers of horses, and their skill at cavalry tactics enabled them to gradually overcome their rivals for territorial mastery. Eventually, through both war and trading contacts with their Mesopotamian neighbors to the west, they learned the basics of agriculture and a sedentary, civilized life.

Persepolis, Iran/Bridgeman Art Library

**LION KILLING A BULL.** This vivid depiction of a lion bringing down a wild onager is taken from the palace ruins at Persepolis. This complex was started in the sixth century and was added to by various Iranian rulers until its destruction by the triumphant Alexander the Great in 330. The Persian court shared the Assyrian pleasure in hunting scenes.

## The Persian Empire

In the mid–sixth century B.C.E., the Persians united under a brilliant warrior-king, Cyrus the Great, and quickly overcame their Iranian cousins and neighbors, the Medes. In a remarkable series of campaigns between 559 and 530 B.C.E., Cyrus then extended his domains from the borders of India to the Mediterranean coast. By 525, his son and immediate successor, Cambyses, had broadened the empire to include part of Arabia and the lower Nile valley. The main Persian cities were at Susa, Persepolis, and Ecbatana in Iran, not in Mesopotamia. The gradual decline of Mesopotamia's importance can be dated to this time.

Cyrus had a concept of imperial rule that was quite different from that of the Assyrians. He realized that many of his new subjects—peoples as radically different as the Hebrews from the Egyptians—were more advanced in many ways than his own Persians and that he could learn from them. Accordingly, his government was a sort of umbrella, sheltering many different peoples and beliefs under the supervision of the "King of Kings" at Persepolis.

Giraudon/Art Resource, NY

**HALL OF A HUNDRED COLUMNS.** This is the great assembly and banquet hall erected by Darius I in Persepolis and burned to the ground by the triumphant conqueror Alexander. Its vast size was symbolic of the great powers exercised by the Persian emperor.

The Persian subjects were generally allowed to retain their own customs and laws. Their appointed Persian supervisors (*satraps*) only interfered when the central government's policies were threatened or disobeyed. In the provinces (**satrapies**), the local authorities were kept in power after conquest by Persia, so long as they swore obedience to the monarch, paid their (relatively light) taxes, provided soldiers, and gave aid and comfort to the Persians when called upon to do so. Religion was totally free, and all sorts of beliefs flourished under Persian rule, from the freed-from-Babylon Hebrews to the fire worshipers of the Indian borderlands. Most remarkably, the initial move toward an ethical religion seems to have come with the teaching of **Zarathustra,** as outlined in the Patterns of Belief box, "Zarathustra's Vision."

Darius I (522–486) was the third great Persian ruler, following Cyrus and Cambyses. During his reign, the empire reached its maximal extent (see Map 4.1). A stable

PATTERNS OF BELIEF

## Zarathustra's Vision

**We usually think of the connection** between religious belief and morality as intrinsic and logical: moral actions are the concrete manifestations of a belief in good and evil, ultimately determined by a supernatural code or by conscience. Yet in ancient times, people did not usually regard the supernatural gods as arbiters of human moral conduct. Rather, gods were seen as personifications of natural forces that made men their helpless playthings unless appeased by worship and sacrifice. This attitude was as prevalent among Iranians in the sixth century B.C.E. as any other people, but it would change radically when a prophet arose among them called Zarathustra, or Zoroaster.

About Zarathustra's life we know nothing except that he was a Persian and lived probably in the 500s B.C.E. His teaching, however, was written down long after his death, possibly as late as the third century C.E. This Zoroastrian scripture, known as the *Avesta,* tells in fragmentary fashion the beliefs of a man who founded a new type of religion, a faith that linked the gods and humans in a new fashion.

Zarathustra preached that two principles are in eternal conflict: good and evil, truth and lies. Good is incarnated in the impersonal deity Ahura-mazda and evil by its twin Ahriman (a close approximation of the Christian Lucifer). The two would struggle for the souls of men, and eventually Ahura-mazda would triumph. Humans, as the possessors of free will, could and must choose between the two gods, serving one and defying the other. In an afterlife, individuals would be made responsible for their choice. They would stand before a divine tribunal and have to answer for their lives on Earth. If the balance was found positive, they would enjoy heaven in eternity; if negative, hell awaited them.

The role of priests was very important, for they interpreted what was right and wrong conduct. The fire worship that had prevailed among Iranians before Zarathustra continued to play a significant role, and a sacred fire was at the heart of the worship of Ahura-mazda. For a time, the teachings of the Zoroastrians became the state cult of imperial Persia, and both Darius I and his son Xerxes were known to be sympathizers.

The similarities between Zarathustra's doctrines and Judaism and Christianity are not coincidental. The Last Judgment that all souls must undergo, the responsibility of the exercise of free will, the eternal bliss of heaven, and the torments of hell entered first Jewish and then Christian belief. Through Zoroastrian preaching and converts in the eastern Mediterranean, the image of an all-powerful God who allowed humans the supreme freedom of the choice between good and evil entered the mainsprings of Western religious culture. Zarathustra's teaching that Ahriman was closely bound up with the flesh, while Ahura-mazda was a noncorporeal entity, a spirit, would come to haunt Christianity for ages, and it appeared again and again in various sects. The most famous of these was medieval Manichaeism, which derived its beliefs from the Middle East and spread throughout Mediterranean Europe. It taught that the flesh is essentially evil, the province of the devil. Many people think that the puritanical element in Christianity is largely the product of this belated offshoot of the Zoroastrian creed.

What has become of the religion of Zarathustra? In Persia, it gradually declined into superstition and was almost extinguished in the wake of the Muslim conquest of Persia in the 600s C.E. The Parsees of the region around Bombay, India, are the center of the cult in modern times. Their scripture, the *Avesta,* remains one of the first attempts to unite *religion,* worship of the immortal gods, with *ethics,* a code of proper conduct for mortal men.

### *Analyze and Interpret*

How do Christianity and Zoroastrian beliefs converge, and how do they contrast in their treatment of the nature of sin? Why is the concept of free will a necessary precondition for a code of ethics and an ethical religion?

coinage in gold and silver and a calendar that was commonly used throughout the Near East were introduced. Darius's law code was also an advanced and refined distillation of earlier codes from Mesopotamia and Egypt. For the next century, the peoples of the empire flourished under enlightened Persian leadership.

## The Hebrews

What we know of the ancient Twelve Tribes of the Hebrews is derived in large part from the poetic history of the Old Testament. In recent years, the Old Testament's stories have been partially borne out by modern archaeological evidence. It is clear that many events and stories previously regarded as mythological have a strong basis in fact.

The Hebraic tradition of a certain Abraham leading his people out of the wilderness and into the land of Canaan refers to what is now generally accepted as historical fact: nomadic, primitive Semitic tribes departed from someplace in northern Mesopotamia in the twentieth century B.C.E. and wandered for a lengthy time through what is now Saudi Arabia. By the 1500s B.C.E., they were established in Canaan, the southern part of Palestine (see Map 4.2). Here they came under imperial Egyptian rule, and a good portion of the Twelve Tribes went off—perhaps voluntarily, perhaps as coerced slaves—to live in the Nile delta.

We know that, in the thirteenth century B.C.E., many semicivilized peoples were moving about the eastern Mediterranean region. The Hebrews' **Exodus** from Egypt under their legendary leader Moses occurred during that century. The exact reasons for the Exodus are not clear, but it is entirely possible that the Old Testament story of brutal treatment by the pharaoh is true. In any case, under Moses, the Hebrews resolved to return to the "land of milk and honey," the Promised Land of Canaan, whose memory had been kept alive by their leaders in Egypt.

Escaping the pharaoh's wrathful pursuit (told in the Old Testament story of Moses' parting the Red Sea), the Hebrews wandered across the Sinai peninsula until they encountered the Canaanites and the Philistines, who were already settled in coastal Palestine. At first the Philistines were able to hold the newcomers at bay. But by about 1000, the Hebrews had overcome the Canaanites and set up their own small kingdom, with Saul as the first king. Saul carried the war to the Philistines, and his work was carried on by his lieutenant and successor, David. David (the victor over the giant Goliath in the Old Testament) was a great warrior hero, and he was successful in conquering Jerusalem, which then became the Hebrews' capital.

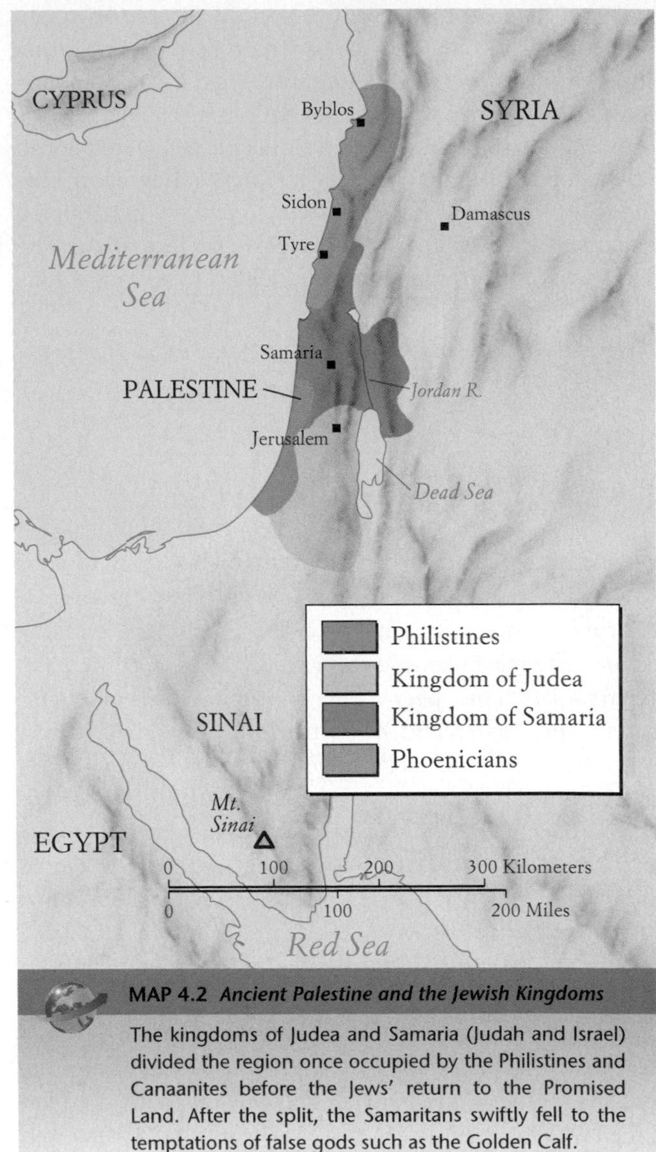


**MAP 4.2** *Ancient Palestine and the Jewish Kingdoms*

The kingdoms of Judea and Samaria (Judah and Israel) divided the region once occupied by the Philistines and Canaanites before the Jews' return to the Promised Land. After the split, the Samaritans swiftly fell to the temptations of false gods such as the Golden Calf.

David's son, **Solomon** (ruled 970–935 B.C.E.), was the most renowned king of the Hebrews. During his reign, the Hebrews briefly became an important factor in Near Eastern affairs, serving as trading intermediaries between Egypt and the Mesopotamians. The famous Temple of Jerusalem—which a triumphant Solomon constructed of stone and cedarwood, and decorated inside and out with gold—became a wonder of the ancient world. But many of his subjects hated Solomon because of his heavy taxes and luxurious living, as noted in Law and Government, "King Solomon." When he died, a revolt against his successor split the Hebrew Kingdom in two: Judea and Samaria, or, as they are sometimes called, Judah and Israel.

Although ethnically very close, the two kingdoms were hostile to each other. As time passed, Samaritans and Judeans (or Jews, as they came to be called) came to look

**The Landscape: A Promised Land?** The harshness of the present-day Israeli landscape stands in sharp contrast to the biblical "land flowing with milk and honey" that the early Hebrews pined for in their Egyptian exile. There is much evidence that climatic change has indeed made desert from what once was a reasonably fertile and well-watered soil.

Benjamin Rondel/Corbis

on one another as different peoples. Their differences arose primarily because of differing religious beliefs but also because Judea came under the shadow of a briefly revived Egyptian empire, while Samaria fell to the successive conquerors of Mesopotamia.

The kingdom of Samaria/Israel was ended in 722 by a failed rebellion against the Assyrian overlords, resulting in the scattering of the populace far and wide (the first **Diaspora,** or "scattering") and the eventual loss of them (the ten Lost Tribes of Jewish tradition) to Judaic belief. Judea, however, survived under the Assyrians until the defeat of the latter in 612. It then fell under Babylonian (Chaldean) overlordship. The ill-fated attempt to throw off this yoke led to the crushing defeat by King Nebuchadnezzar in 586 and the ensuing Babylonian Captivity (586–539 B.C.E.), when thousands of Jews were taken off to Babylon as hostages for the good behavior of the rest. The great temple of Solomon was demolished. Becoming one of the provinces of the Persian Empire after 539 B.C.E., the Judeans continued under Persian rule until Alexander the Great toppled the King of Kings in the 330s (see Chapter 9). They then lived under the successors of Alexander until the gradual extension of Roman power reached Palestine.

## Jewish Religious Belief and Its Evolution

From the time of the kingdom of Saul, a great god known as *Yahweh* (Jehovah) was established as the Hebrews' chief deity, but by no means the only one. In Samaria, Yahweh was eventually relegated to an inferior position. But in Judea, Yahweh's cult gradually triumphed over all rivals, and this god became the only deity of the Jews of Jerusalem.

This condition of having a single god was a distinct oddity among ancient peoples. *Monotheism* was so rare that we know of only one pre-Jewish experiment with it—that of Akhnaton in Egypt (see Chapter 3). Some of the Hebrews were living in Egypt during Akhnaton's reign, and it is possible that the pharaoh's doctrines penetrated into Jewish consciousness. Zarathustra's doctrine of dualism between two almost-equal deities who wrestled over the souls of men undoubtedly had much to do with the later forms of Hebrew belief, but just how they are related is a subject for argument.

By the 600s, the Judean Jews, under the influence of a whole series of great prophets, including Amos, Hosea, Ezekiel, and Isaiah, came to believe themselves bound to Yahweh by a sacred contract, the Covenant, given to Moses during the Exodus. The contract was understood to mean that, if the Jews remained constant in their worship of Yahweh and kept the faith he instilled in them, they would eventually triumph over all of their enemies and be a respected and lordly people on Earth. The faith that Yahweh desired was supported by a set of rigid rules given to Moses by Yahweh on Mount Sinai, from which eventually evolved a whole law code that governed every aspect of Hebrew daily life. Coming to be known to later Jews and Christians as the Ten Commandments, these moral regulations have been adapted to much different social circumstances.

The Jewish faith was one of the earliest attempts to formalize an ethical system and to link it with the worship

LAW AND GOVERNMENT

## King Solomon

**The story of King Solomon** is an illuminating example of how tradition can be consciously or unconsciously adapted to fit the needs of a people. The Old Testament tells us that Solomon ruled the united tribes of the Jews with wisdom and justice and that his people looked up to him as an exemplary ruler. In fact, Solomon's wisdom and justice often seemed conspicuous by their absence, and his kingdom did not long outlast his own life.

The son of King David and his fourth wife, Bathsheba, Solomon succeeded his father, despite the existence of an older surviving son. His mother, with the help of the prophet Nathan, persuaded the old king to recognize Solomon as his heir shortly before his death. Several years later, Solomon secured the throne by eliminating his rival on charges of plotting against him.

Ignoring Hebrew traditions that emphasized the collective nature of leadership and the collaboration of king and priest, the young ruler established an absolute monarchy. He adopted a style of living and governing that was foreign to previous Jewish kings and subordinated all else to enriching his court and its prestige. The Canaanites, defeated by David but long allowed to go their own way, were now reduced to slavery and forced to work for Solomon's projects. Under Solomon's hand, the city of Jerusalem grew in commercial importance in the Near East. He was able to extend his influence into Mesopotamia and northern Egypt by marrying foreign brides, including the daughter of the pharaoh.

In place of the simple quarters that had sufficed for David, Solomon constructed a large royal home which rivaled those of the Persians in size and fittings. The famous Temple of Jerusalem became a wonder of the ancient world. Visitors from many countries came to marvel and to ask Solomon for solutions to their problems, for the king was reputed to have great wisdom. The Twelve Tribes of Israelites, so long isolated and ignored, became commercially versatile and sophisticated. But the king's extravagances were much resented, and they exacerbated the split that was already developing between Judea and Samaria-Israel.

During Solomon's reign, Judea received commercial advantages and paid less taxes. The northern ten tribes became indignant, threatening to sever their relations with Jerusalem and Judea even before Solomon's death. When the king died in 935, the Hebrew tribes split and formed the two separate, rival kingdoms of Judea and Israel, lessening their ability to rule their satellite peoples and exposing themselves to foreign threats. The vassal kingdoms that David had painfully conquered were lost, and the trading empire that Solomon had labored for forty years to create was destroyed forever. "Vanity of vanities, all is vanity."

Private Collection/Christie's Images/Bridgeman Art Library

**The Wailing Wall, in Jerusalem.** In the center of old Jerusalem stands the last remnant of Solomon's temple, shown here in a late nineteenth-century watercolor, where devout Jews today pray to the god of their forebears. In the years following the Temple's destruction by the Babylonians, the Romans prohibited Jews from entering Jerusalem at all, so the customary place for mourning the Temple's loss was instead the Mount of Olives, to the east of and overlooking the Temple Mount.

### *Analyze and Interpret*

What might explain the Old Testament's admiring view of Solomon? Can you give a modern example of how national or regional tradition has been bent to fit the current need or desire of a people? What is meant in modern times by "the wisdom of Solomon"?

of supernatural deities. *Ethics* is the study of good and evil and determining what is right and wrong in human life and conduct. Yahweh's followers gradually came to regard him as an enforcer of correct ethical actions. Those who did evil on Earth would be made to suffer, if not in this world, then in the one to come. This belief was not unusual, for other religions had made at least some moves toward punishment of evildoers. The laws of Yahweh, however, also assured that the good would be rewarded—again, if not in this life, then in the eternal one to come.

How did people know whether they were doing good or evil? One way was by following the laws of Yahweh. Increasingly, though, they could also rely on the knowledge of what is right and what is wrong that Yahweh imprinted in every heart: conscience. The Ten Commandments were particularly the Jews' property, given to them as a mark of favor by their lord and protector Yahweh. But all men and women everywhere were believed to have been given conscience, and insofar as they followed conscience, they were doing the Lord's work and possibly gaining eternal salvation.

## Economic Change and Social Customs

Although their religious beliefs would have immense influence on Western civilization, the Jews were mostly minor players on the Near Eastern stage in economic affairs and politics. They had never been numerous, and the split between Israelites and Judeans weakened both groups. With the rise of Assyria, both Israel and Judea had to engage in numerous expensive wars and suffered economically. Both became relatively insignificant backwaters under the direct or indirect rule of powerful neighbors.

When the kingdom was founded under Saul, most Hebrews were still rural herders and peasants, living as Abraham had lived. Over the next half millennium, however, many Hebrews made the transition from rural to town life. As many people shifted from subsistence farming to wage earning, social tensions dividing rich and poor began to appear. The strong solidarity that had marked the Hebrews earlier broke down. The prophets of the eighth through fifth centuries called repeatedly for social justice and remind us that exploitation of widows and orphans and abuse of the weak by the strong were by no means limited to the despised Gentiles (all non-Jews).

More than most, the Jews divided all humanity into we and they. This was undoubtedly the result of their religious tradition, whereby they had been selected as the Chosen. Jews looked upon non-Jews as distinctly lesser breeds, whose main function in the divine plan was to act as tempters and obstacles that the pious must overcome. In their preoccupation with the finer points of the Law laid down by Moses and his successors, the Hebrews deliberately segregated themselves from other peoples. Intermarriage with nonbelievers was tantamount to treason and was punished by immediate expulsion from the community. Ancient Judaism was almost never open to converts.

The Judaic Yahweh was definitely a male lawgiver, speaking to other males in a society in which women counted only as the relatives and dependents of men. The nomadic background of the Twelve Tribes is evident here, exhibiting the universal tendency of nomadic people to subordinate females and consider them as the possessions of their men. In the Old Testament, even when a Jewish woman acts in self-assertive fashion, the point is to secure some advantage or distinction for a male, not on her own behalf. Judith slays Holofernes not to avenge herself for her sexual exploitation, but to secure the safety of her people. Marriage and divorce reflected the patriarchal values. The married state was strongly preferred, and in fact, bachelors were looked on as failures and shirkers of duty. Young men were supposed to marry by no later than age twenty-four and preferably by twenty. Girls were thought ready for marriage at puberty, roughly about age thirteen. A man could have several legal wives and an unlimited number of concubines, but as in other societies, only the wealthy could afford this practice. The wife married into the husband's family and moved into his house. The property she brought into the marriage remained hers, however, and could be removed again if her husband divorced her for any reason but unfaithfulness. Divorce was easy enough for the husband but very unusual for a wife to initiate. Women caught in adultery could be killed, but typically they were divorced and sent back to their father's home. Infidelity by the husband was a crime only if committed with a married woman.

As with almost all early peoples, children were the whole point of marriage. The continuation of the family was the primary duty of both husband and wife. The oldest male child received the lion's share of the inheritance, but the other boys were not shut out. The girls, on the other hand, received nothing beyond their dowries, because through marriage they would be joined to another family, which would care for them. The education of all children was carried on within the family circle and was religious in nature. Literacy was uncommon among the country folk but not so among the urbanites.

Jewish arts and sciences were relatively undeveloped compared with those of their more sophisticated and richer neighbors. Excepting the Old Testament's poetry, the Jews produced little of note in any of the art forms. The representation of living things was thought to be sacrilegious and was banned. There is no record of any important Jewish contributions to the sciences.

## A Changing Theology

In the centuries after the fall of the monarchies of Samaria and Judea, the Jews' conception of Yahweh changed in several significant ways, linked to their political relations with others. After losing their independence, the Jewish people went through a long spiritual crisis. Their hope for a triumph over their enemies was not realized. Indeed, quite the contrary happened: the *Babylonian Captivity* (586–539 B.C.E.) was a particular low point. Many Jews never returned, having been seduced by the "Great Whore" Babylon into the worship of false gods, as had their erstwhile co-believers in Samaria. Those who returned after release by the Persians under Cyrus were the "tried and true" who had been tested and, strong in their faith, had survived. They rebuilt the destroyed Temple and restructured their theology. Aided by new interpretations of the Covenant (the *Talmud*), the Jews reappraised and made precise the nature of God and their relation to him.

During this post-Captivity period, the image of Yahweh took on clearer lines. Not only was Yahweh the only god; he was the *universal* god of all. Whether or not the Gentiles worshiped him, he was their all-powerful judge and would reward or punish them (mostly the latter) as they conformed or not to the demands of conscience.

God was a *just* god, who would reward and punish according to ethical principles, but he was also a *merciful* god who would not turn a deaf ear to the earnest penitent. His ways were mysterious to men such as the sorely tried Job in the Old Testament, but they would someday be seen for what they were: righteous and just.

God was an *omnipotent* and *omniscient* (all powerful and all-knowing) master, who could do whatever he desired, always and everywhere. The Creator of nature, he stood outside his creation, transcending it. There were no other opposing forces (gods) that could frustrate his will, but in his wisdom, Yahweh had granted his creature Man free will and allowed the principle of evil to arise in the form of the fallen angel, Lucifer or Satan. Humankind could ignore conscience and the Law and choose evil, much as Zarathustra had taught. If they did, they would face a Last Judgment that would condemn them to eternal punishment and deprive them of the fate that Yahweh desired and offered: salvation in blessedness.

Finally, Yahweh gradually came to be a *personal* deity, in a way in which no other ancient god had been. He could be prayed to directly; he was observant of all that affected a man's or a woman's life. His actions were not impulsive or unpredictable. He wanted his people not as slaves but as friends. The relationship between God and Man is meant to be one of mutual love. In a sense, God needed Man to complete the work of creation.

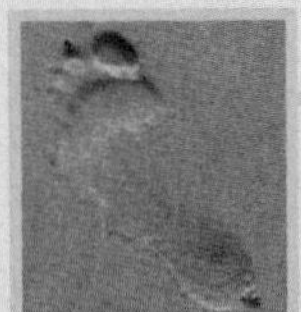

EVIDENCE OF THE PAST

## The Dead Sea Scrolls

**ARAB SHEPHERD BOYS ON WATCH** over their family sheep in the rocky hills over the Dead Sea made a dramatic discovery in 1947, when they brought the so-called Dead Sea Scrolls to light. After two thousand or more years resting at the bottom of a shaft-like cave, these copper, leather, and papyrus manuscripts—more than 600 all told—would substantially increase our knowledge of the Jewish people and their beliefs at the era of Christ's birth and earlier.

The scrolls are the assorted documents deemed most worthy of preservation by a religious brotherhood that chose to withdraw from participation in public life in Judea, in favor of a type of monastic community. Convinced of the impending end of the world and the coming of a Last Judgment, these individuals studied and fasted while awaiting the coming of a messiah. In the past forty years, extensive archaeological work shows that the brotherhood (there seem to have been no females) lived in hermit-like isolation in a barren country that now forms part of the Israel–Jordan border, near a place called Qumran. There they devoted their lives to a spiritual odyssey that they hoped would place them among the saved.

Authorities have now dated the writing to between the third century B.C.E. and the year 68 C.E. They make no mention anywhere of the life of Jesus of Nazareth, but in several other fashions confirm previous scholarly presumptions about the events of those years in Roman Palestine. The final entries in the scrolls coincide with the brutal campaign of the Roman general Vespasian against the Zealots, the Jewish rebels against Rome's rule who ignited the Jewish War and the second destruction of the Temple of Solomon. It is thought that the scrolls were hidden away to preserve them from Roman destruction.

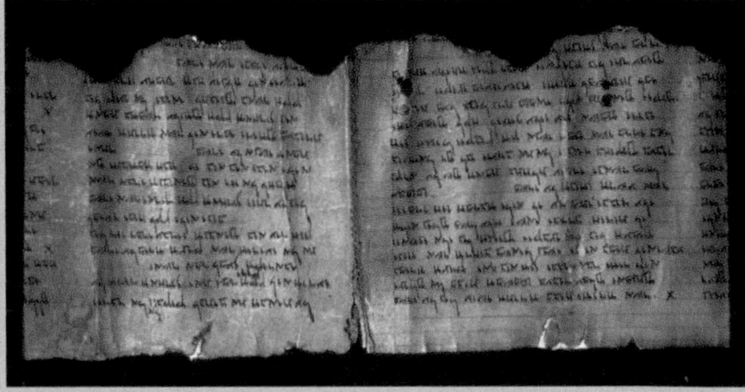



**THE DEAD SEA SCROLLS.** These historic documents were found in a cave above the Dead Sea in 1947. The scrolls have been largely deciphered in recent years and have proven a rich source of knowledge of Jewish society and customs around the first century C.E.

### *Analyze and Interpret*

How does the omission of any mention of Jesus in the scrolls affect the credibility of the New Testament? Would you expect that the life and message of Jesus would be well known to the Qumran brotherhood who wrote the scrolls? Would they necessarily accept him as the true Messiah?

The promise to preserve the Jews as a people that Yahweh had given Moses was what held the Judean Jews together after the Assyrian and Babylonian conquests. But inevitably some of them, including many of the learned men (rabbis), came to think of this promise as one aimed not at simple preservation but at counterconquest by the Jews of their enemies. Instead of being a contemptible minority in the empires of the mighty ones, the Hebrews would be the mighty and bend the others to their will.

In this way grew the hopes for a **messiah,** a redeemer who would take the Jews out of their humiliations and make them a people to be feared and respected (see Evidence of the Past). In this manner, the message of the Lord speaking through the great prophets was distorted into a promise of earthly grandeur rather than a promise of immortal salvation for those who believed. When a man named Jesus appeared, claiming to be the messiah and speaking of his kingdom "which was not of this earth," there was disappointment and disbelief among many of those who heard him.

By the time of the Roman conquest of the Near East, in the first century before Christ, some of the Jewish leaders had become fanatical, believing in the protection of mighty Yahweh against all odds. These **Zealots** were unwilling to bend before any nonbeliever, however powerful he might be. This would cause the tension between the Jewish nation and the Roman overlords that eventually resulted in war and the second Diaspora, the forced emigration of much of this small people from their ancestral home to all corners of the great Roman Empire.

Wherever the Jews went, they took their national badge of distinction with them: the unerring belief in their identity as the Chosen and their particular vision of the nature of God and his operations in the minds and hearts of humans. This was a vision of the relationship between the deity and his creations that no other people had: mutually dependent, ethical, and just, but also merciful on the Lord's side; submissive but not slavish on Man's side. It was the relationship between a stern but loving father and an independent, sinful, but dutiful child. The mold for the evolution of Christianity had been formed. All that was needed was the appearance of the long-rumored messiah who would fulfill the promise that the Chosen would enter glory, someday.

## SUMMARY

After the decline of Mesopotamia and Egypt in the first millennium B.C.E., several smaller peoples contributed their diverse talents to the spread of civilized life. The Assyrian Empire, founded on an efficient army, lasted only a brief time. After it was toppled in the seventh century B.C.E. by a coalition of enemies, most traces of it were wiped away in its Mesopotamian homeland. One of the Assyrians' conquests was Phoenicia, whose people are remembered for their maritime explorations and colonization, and for taking the first major steps toward a phonetic alphabet.

For more than 200 years after the conquests of Cyrus the Great, the Persian Empire brought relative peace and progress to much of the Near East. Learning from their more advanced subjects, the imperial governors allowed substantial freedom of worship, language, and custom, while upholding superior justice and efficient administration. Trade and crafts flourished throughout the immense empire. From the preachings of Zarathustra emerged a new, highly sophisticated ethics that was elevated to a state religion.

The contribution of the Jews to later history was of a different nature. The Twelve Tribes of the Hebrews wandered out of Mesopotamia and entered Palestine some time in the middle of the second millennium B.C.E. After a long duel with powerful neighbors, the Jews set up a monarchy that broke into two parts in the 900s. The larger segment, Samaria or Israel, gradually fell away from Judaism and was dispersed by Assyrian conquest. The smaller part, Judea with its capital Jerusalem, stayed true to Yahweh and survived as a province of other empires into Roman times.

What distinguished the Jews was their monotheistic religion and their linkage of a universal God with ethical standards in this life and immortal salvation in the next. Their gradually evolving vision of an omnipotent, just, and merciful Lord who would one day send a messiah to lead the Hebrews to glory would be the cement that held this small people together. It was a vision unique to them, and its power carried the Jews through a history of subjugation and torment.

## Identification Terms

Test your knowledge of this chapter's key concepts by defining the following terms. If you can't recall the meaning of certain terms, refresh your memory by looking up the boldfaced term in the chapter, turning to the Glossary at the end of the book, or working with the flashcards that are available on the *World Civilizations* Companion Website: **http://history.wadsworth.com/adler04/**.

Assur
Diaspora
Exodus
messiah
Nineveh
satrapies
Solomon
Zarathustra (Zoroaster)
Zealots

## Test Your Knowledge

Test your knowledge of this chapter by answering the following questions. Complete answers appear at the end of the book. You may also take this quiz interactively and find even more quiz questions on the *World Civilizations* Companion Website: **http://history.wadsworth.com/adler04/**.

1. The people who conquered the Semites of the Tigris valley in the eighth century B.C.E. were
   a. Babylonians.
   b. Assyrians.
   c. Phoenicians.
   d. Egyptians.
   e. Hittites.
2. The key to Assyrian success in empire building was
   a. cultural superiority.
   b. respectful treatment of conquered peoples.
   c. the bravery of the individual soldier.
   d. effective military organization.
   e. wholesale execution of their enemies.
3. The overthrow of the Assyrians was accomplished by
   a. an internal palace plot.
   b. a coalition of their enemies led by the Babylonians.
   c. the Egyptian and Hittite armies.
   d. a general rebellion of the slaves.
   e. the invasion of the Hyksos peoples.
4. The outstanding contribution of the Phoenicians to world history was the
   a. marine compass.
   b. phonetic alphabet.
   c. invention of coinage.
   d. gyroscope.
   e. chariot.
5. The creator of the Persian empire was
   a. Zoroaster.
   b. Xerxes.
   c. Cyrus.
   d. Ahura-mazda.
   e. Cambyses.
6. Which of the following is the correct chronological sequence of empires?
   a. Assyrian, Persian, Hittite, Sumerian
   b. Persian, Hittite, Sumerian, Assyrian
   c. Sumerian, Hittite, Assyrian, Persian
   d. Hittite, Assyrian, Sumerian, Persian
   e. Hittite, Persian, Sumerian, Assyrian
7. The first king of the Hebrew Kingdom founded after the Exodus was
   a. David.
   b. Saul.
   c. Solomon.
   d. Isaiah.
   e. Judah.
8. The Covenant of the Hebrews with their god Yahweh
   a. was given to Moses during the Exodus from Egypt.
   b. had nothing to do with individual conduct, only with group survival.
   c. was a contract that was allowed to lapse.
   d. guaranteed each believing Hebrew immortality.
   e. provided the basis for early Persian law.
9. Belief in the messiah among Jews of the first century B.C.E. was focused on
   a. hope for a statesman who would lead the Jews to a new homeland.
   b. expectation of a military leader who would help the Jews repel the Romans.
   c. finding a political leader who would assert Jewish supremacy.
   d. a hermit who rejected society, such as John the Baptist.
   e. having the Son of God come to Earth to bring eternal salvation.

10. The critical new factor in the Jews' vision of God that had developed by the first century C.E. was the
   a. link between the merciful deity and humans' ethical conduct on Earth.
   b. belief that God was all-powerful and that he controlled all human affairs.
   c. belief that God was supreme over all other deities.
   d. promise of an eternal life given by God to those whom he deemed worthy.
   e. belief in a messiah who would remove his people from their troubled lives on Earth.

## InfoTrac College Edition

Visit the source collections at

**http://infotrac.thomsonlearning.com**

and use the Search function with the following key terms:

Persia or Persian    Hebrew

## Wadsworth History Website Resources

Visit the World History Resource Center at **http://history.wadsworth.com/world** for a wealth of general resources and the *World Civilizations* Companion Website at **http://history.wadsworth.com/adler04/** for resources specific to this textbook.

## HistoryNow

Enter *HistoryNow* using the access card that is available for *World Civilizations*. *HistoryNow* will assist you in understanding the content in this chapter with lesson plans generated for your needs. In addition, you can read the following documents, and many more, online:

2 Kings 17:1-16    Psalm 137

*He who worships God must stand distinct from Him,*
*So only shall he know the joyful love of God.*
*For if he say that God and he are one,*
*That joy, that love, shall vanish instantly away.*
"Song of Tukaram"

# 5 India's Beginnings

Indus Valley Civilization
Mohenjo-Daro and Harappa

The Vedic Epoch
The Beginnings of the Caste System

Hinduism

Buddhism
Teachings of the Buddha

The Mauryan Dynasty

Daily Life and the Position of Women

Buddhism's Spread

| | |
|---|---|
| c. 2500–1900 B.C.E. | Mohenjo-Daro and Harappa flourish |
| c. 1500 B.C.E. | Invasion of Aryans |
| c. 1500–500 B.C.E. | The Vedic Epoch |
| 563–483 B.C.E. | Life of the Buddha |
| 326 B.C.E. | Invasion by Alexander the Great |
| 320–232 B.C.E. | Mauryan Dynasty |

How old are the most ancient civilizations? Is it possible that the oldest of all are yet to be discovered? Until fairly recently it was believed that the civilization of India had been founded only some 2,000 years ago, far later than China, Egypt, or Mesopotamia. But in the early twentieth century, archaeologists found that a highly advanced, urbanized civilization had existed since the middle of the third millennium B.C.E. in the valley of the Indus River in what is now Pakistan. The discovery of this chapter in world history is a dramatic story, and much of the detail is still being pieced together. Enough is known, however, to whet our appetite to know much more, especially about the possible contributions of this civilization to one of the world's leading religious beliefs, Hinduism.

## Indus Valley Civilization

As in Mesopotamia and Egypt, the earliest Indian civilization was located in the plain bordering a great stream. The Indus River flows south and west from the foothills of the Himalayan range, the world's loftiest and most forbidding mountains. The Himalayas are the highest of several ranges that separate India and Pakistan from Tajikistan and China (see Map 5.1).

In the 1850s, when India was still under British colonial rule, a railway was extended across the Indus. During the construction, the British engineers noticed that the local workers were bringing in large quantities of hewn stone and brick from somewhere nearby. When the engineers inquired, they learned that the local residents had long been accustomed to go to a certain site where huge piles of these materials were easily unearthed. The engineers notified the authorities, and the sites were put under archaeological supervision, which has continued ever since.

The major dig is at a place in modern Pakistan called **Mohenjo-Daro,** about 300 miles upstream from the mouth of the river. Some years later, another major site was located 400 miles farther up the river at Harappa. In between these large ruins are dozens of smaller sites being

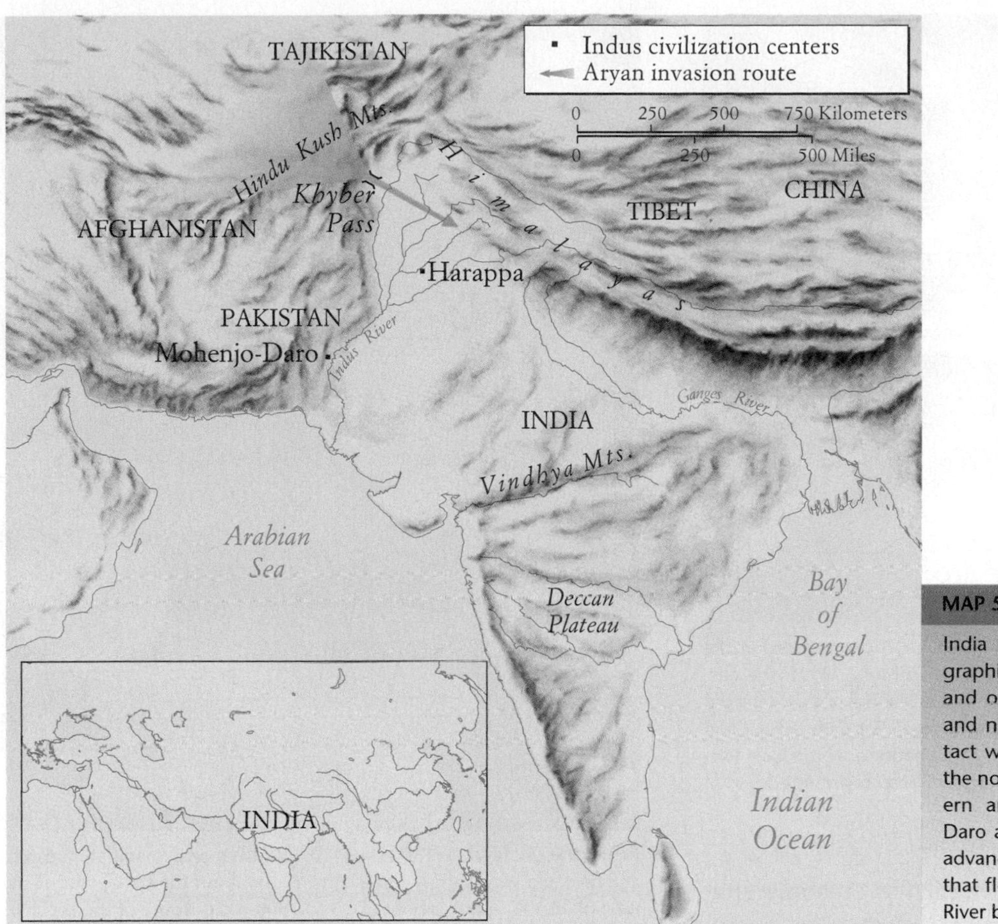


**MAP 5.1** ***The Indian Subcontinent***

India is a very large and diverse geographic entity, ringed by the Himalayas and other high mountains to the north and northeast. The usual routes of contact with other peoples have been from the northwest and by sea from both eastern and western directions. Mohenjo-Daro and Harappa were part of a highly advanced, urbanized ancient civilization that flourished in the valley of the Indus River before the Aryan invasions.

slowly uncovered, first by British and now by Pakistani experts. In terms of area covered, this is by far the largest ancient civilization ever found.

## Mohenjo-Daro and Harappa

What exactly is being uncovered? At Mohenjo-Daro, archaeologists have found the remnants of large, carefully constructed walls and the city they enclosed. The city was more than three miles across and probably housed more than 100,000 people at some time in the distant past. Now, little remains except the brick with which it was built, buried underground by the passage of time, storms, vandalism, and decay. Many smaller towns and villages have also been found under the dust of centuries, scattered along the Indus and its several tributaries in western India.

The cities and villages were built of fired brick and carefully planned. The streets ran at precise right angles, like William Penn's grid plan of Philadelphia, and they were of two widths. The main thoroughfares were thirty-four feet wide, large enough to allow two large carts to pass safely and still leave room for several pedestrians. The smaller avenues were nine feet wide. Many of the buildings had two or even three stories, which was unusual for residences in the ancient world. They were built of bricks that are almost always of two sizes, but only those two. The interior dimensions of the houses were almost identical. A sewage canal ran from each house to a larger canal in the street that carried off household wastes. Small statues of gods and goddesses, almost always of the same size and posture, are frequently found in the house foundations.

All this regularity suggests a government that was very powerful in the eyes of its subjects and probably gained its authority from religious belief. Some experts on Indus civilization believe that it was a *theocracy,* in which the priests ruled as representatives of the gods. In no other way, they think, could the government's power have been strong enough to command residential uniformity over a period of centuries, as happened in Mohenjo-Daro and Harappa.

**Ruins of Mohenjo-Daro.** Systematic excavation commenced in the ruins of Mohenjo-Daro in the late nineteenth century, under the auspices of the British colonial government. It continues today, directed by the Pakistani government. Shown here is the Great Bath, a pool and surrounding cells that clearly existed for ritual bathing. Some have suggested that the emphasis on purification by water in present-day Hinduism may go back to these origins.

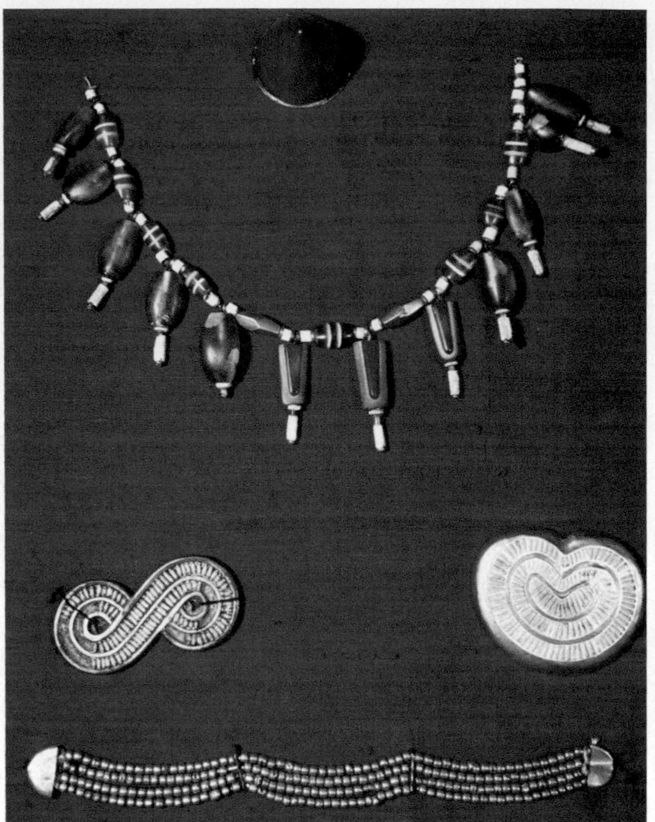


**Indus Valley Jewelry.** The fine workmanship and imagination exhibited here allow us to draw some conclusions about the state of Indus civilization at this epoch, about 2000 to 1800 B.C.E. Some of the precious stones in this jewelry had to have been brought from as far away as China.

Both cities also contain monumental buildings situated on a citadel, which were probably a communal granary and the temples of the local gods. Harappa differs from Mohenjo-Daro in building style and other details, but the similarities are strong enough that the two cities and the surrounding villages are believed to constitute one civilization, sometimes termed *Dravidian.*

For their food, the cities depended on the irrigated farms of the surrounding plain. Like the people of Egypt, the ordinary people apparently enjoyed a high standard of living for many generations. Objects found in the ruins indicate that trade was carried on with Mesopotamia at least as early as 2000 B.C.E. and also with the peoples of southern India and Afghanistan. Although a good many works of art and figurines have been found, the occasional writing has not yet been deciphered. Its 270-odd characters thus far discovered are different from all other known scripts and have no alphabet. Our inability to decipher the writing, as well as the long period when this civilization was forgotten, have hindered scholars' efforts to obtain a detailed knowledge of these people. We still know next to nothing about their religion, their government, the social divisions of the people, and their scientific and intellectual accomplishments. Much is still shrouded in mystery and perhaps always will be.

One thing now seems clear, however: the cities and villages were prosperous, expanding settlements from at least 2500 to about 1900 B.C.E. Around 1900, for reasons still only guessed at, they began a long decline, which ended with the abandonment of Mohenjo-Daro about 1200 B.C.E. and Harappa somewhat later. Some evidence indicates that landslides changed the course of the lower Indus and prevented the continuation of the intensive irrigation that had supported the cities. Some people think that the population may have fallen victim to malaria, as the blocked river created mosquito-ridden swamps nearby. Others think that the irrigated land gradually became alkaline and nonproductive, as happened in lower Mesopotamia. Whatever the role of natural disasters, it is certain that the decline of the Indus valley was accelerated by an invasion of nomads called *Aryans,* who descended into the valley from Afghanistan and Iran about 1500 B.C.E.

## The Vedic Epoch

The Aryans were one of the earliest horse-breeding people of ancient Asia, and their aggressive ways were the terror of other civilizations besides that of the Indus valley. It is thought that they overwhelmed the civilized Indians in the valley and set themselves up as a sort of master group, using the Indians as labor to do the farming and trading that the Aryan warriors despised as inferior. As we noted, their conquest of the more advanced peoples may have been aided by natural disasters that had severely weakened the economy.

Our knowledge of the Aryans comes largely from their **Vedas,** ancient oral epics that were written down only long after the Aryan invasion, so the pictures they present may be deceptive. We know that the Aryans were Indo-European speakers originally resident in central Asia, who worshiped gods of the sky and storm, and made impressive use of bronze weaponry and horse-drawn chariots in battle. (Apparently, the Indus valley people knew the horse only as a beast of burden and were at a disadvantage against the Aryan chariots.) The **Rigveda,** the oldest and most important Veda, paints a picture of a war-loving, violent folk, led by their *raja,* or chieftain, and their magic-working priests.

In time, the Aryans extended their rule across all of northern India to the Ganges valley. Gradually, they abandoned their nomadic ways and settled down as agriculturists and town dwellers. They never conquered the southern half of India, and as a result, the southern culture and religion still differ from those of the north in some respects.

### The Beginnings of the Caste System

The Vedas describe the beliefs of a warlike people who saw themselves as the natural masters of the inferior Indians and who underlined their difference by dividing society into four groups or classes. The two highest classes of priests and warriors were reserved for the Aryans and their pureblooded descendants. The priests were called **Brahmins** and originally were superior in status to the warriors, who were called *kshatrija* and evolved over time from warriors to the governing class. The third class, the *vaishya,* was probably the most numerous and included freemen, farmers, and traders. In the fourth and lowest group within the system were the unfree: the serfs or *shudra.*

Over the long course of the Vedic Epoch (over a thousand years, from 1500 to about 500 B.C.E.), these four classes evolved into something more complex by far: multiple social groups defined by birth, or **caste.** A caste is a social unit into which individuals are born and that dictates most aspects of daily life. It confers a status that cannot be changed. Each caste except the very lowest has special duties and privileges, some of which are economic in nature, whereas others are manifested by dietary and marital restrictions. A high-caste Indian normally has very little contact with lower castes and none at all with the outcastes, or *pariahs.* Perhaps a seventh of Indian society still falls into this last category—the untouchables—whose members until recently were treated worse than animals.

The stratification of Indian society begun by the Aryan conquest persists to the present day. The Aryans were gradually absorbed into the indigenous Indian peoples through intermarriage with high-status individuals, but the caste system took ever-stronger root. By the eighteenth century there were more than 3,000 separate subcastes, or *jati.* Although the number has probably declined since then, the belief that one is born into a group that is fixed by age-old traditions and allows no change is still strong among rural Indians.

Throughout Indian history, caste has had the effect of inhibiting any type of change, particularly social change. Why? Combined with the beliefs of Hinduism (see the next section), caste made it next to impossible for someone born into a low state to climb the ranks of social prestige and privilege. It also limited political power to the uppermost ranks, in much the same fashion as the exercise of government in medieval Europe was limited to the aristocracy. Caste discouraged or prohibited cultural innovation by those in the lower ranks (the vast majority of Indians). Meanwhile, those on top were very content to have things go on forever as they were. Under the Aryan-founded caste system, India became a highly stratified and immobile society.

## Hinduism

The religion of the overwhelming majority of Indians is Hinduism, the fourth largest in the world with about 900 million adherents. Hinduism is both more and less than a *religion* as the West understands that term: it is a way of life, a philosophical system, an inspiration for art, and the basis of all Indian political theory in the past. But it is not a rigid set of theological doctrines that must be believed to find truth or to be saved in eternity. And it possesses almost innumerable localized variations in manner and content.

The Hindu faith is a product of the slow mixing of the Aryan beliefs with those of the native Dravidian culture. Many of Hinduism's basic principles reflect the patriarchal and class-conscious society that the Aryan conquerors founded and that was strengthened in its stratification by the conquerors' beliefs. A revelatory glimpse at early Hinduism is given by the Laws of Manu, as excerpted in the Society and Economy box. Family relations are seen to be governed by social class, as is the relation of men to women and husbands to wives.

SOCIETY AND ECONOMY

## The Laws of Manu

**The Laws of Manu are an ancient compilation** of teachings from Hindu India. Manu was a being simultaneously human and divine, from whom devout Hindus could learn what was needed for perfection and the attainment of *moksha*. Manu's laws were the cornerstone of Hindu traditional opinion on the rights and duties of the sexes and of family members, as well as castes. These opinions and prejudices did not change substantially until recent times. The attitude of the Laws of Manu toward women and the lower castes are especially revealing. (*Note:* The *shudra* are the lowest of the original four castes of India established during the Aryan epoch.)

> That place where the shudra are very numerous . . . soon entirely perishes, afflicted by disease and famine.
>
> A Brahmin may confidently take the goods of his shudra, because the slave cannot have any possessions and the master may take his property.
>
> A Brahmin who takes a shudra to wife and to his bed will after death sink into Hell; if he begets a child with her, he will lose the rank of Brahmin. The son whom a Brahmin begets through lust upon a shudra female is, although alive, a corpse and hence called a living corpse. A shudra who has intercourse with a woman of a twice-born caste [that is, a Brahmin] shall be punished so: if she was unguarded he loses the offending part [his genitals] and all his property; if she was guarded, everything including his life.
>
> Women . . . give themselves to the handsome and the ugly. Through their passion for men, through their unstable temper, through their natural heartlessness they become disloyal toward their husbands, however carefully they may be guarded. Knowing their disposition, which the lord of creation laid upon them, to be so, every man should most strenuously exert himself to guard them. When creating them, Manu allotted to women a love of their bed, of their seat and of ornament, impure desire, wrath, dishonesty, malice, and bad conduct. . . .
>
> It is the nature of women to seduce men in this world; for that reason the wise are never unguarded in the company of females. For women are able to lead astray in this world not only the fool, but even a learned man, and make of him a slave of desire and wrath.

But the exhortations of Manu are not completely one-sided:

> Reprehensible is the father who gives not his daughter in marriage at the proper time [namely, puberty]; reprehensible is the husband who approaches not his wife in due season, and reprehensible is the son who does not protect his mother after her husband has died.
>
> Drinking spirituous liquors, associating with wicked ones, separation from the husband, rambling abroad, sleeping at unseasonable hours, and dwelling in houses of other men are the six causes of ruin in women.

### *Analyze and Interpret*

How do these laws differ, if at all, from the attitudes toward women reflected in the code of Hammurabi? Where did women find better protection and justice, by modern standards?

Source: D. Johnson, ed., *Sources of World Civilization,* Vol. 1. © 1994, Simon & Schuster.

**History Now™**

***To read more of the Laws of Manu, point your browser to the documents area of* HistoryNow.**

But Hinduism is different from the religions of the West in its insistence on the illusory nature of the tangible world and the acceptance of the individual's fate in earthly life. Its most basic principles and beliefs are as follows:

1. The nonmaterial, intangible world is the real and permanent one.
2. The soul must pass through a series of bodily existences, being reincarnated (*samsara*) each time in accord with its karma.
3. ***Karma*** is the tally of good and bad committed by an individual in a given life. Good karma results in birth into a higher caste in the next life; bad karma, into a lower one.
4. One must strive for good karma through following the code of morals prescribed for one's caste, called ***dharma,*** as closely as one can.

The gods *Brahman* (the impersonal life force), *Shiva* (the creator and destroyer), and *Vishnu* (the preserver) dominate an almost endless array of supernatural beings. Most Hindus are devotees of either Shiva or Vishnu as the foremost deity, but they worship them in a huge variety of rituals.

When a person has lived a life in perfect accord with his or her dharma, death will lead to final release from reincarnation and the great Wheel of Life. This release is ***moksha,*** and it is the end for which all good Hindus live. Moksha is sometimes compared with the heaven of the

Western world, but it differs in one all-important respect: moksha is the end of individuality, and the individual soul is submerged into the world-soul represented by Brahman. A classic analogy is a raindrop, which, after many transformations, finds its way back to the ocean that originated it and is dissolved therein.

Vedic Hinduism was highly ritualistic and exclusive in nature. The priestly caste—Brahmins—had power by virtue of their mastery of complex ceremonies and their semimagical knowledge of the gods. Gradually, the more educated people became alienated from this ritualism and sought other ways to explain the mystery of human fate. In the fifth century B.C.E., two new modes of thought gradually became established in India: *Jainism* and *Buddhism*.

Jainism is limited in its historical appeal. It is less a supernatural religion than a philosophy that emphasizes the sacredness of all life (see Chapter 16). In modern India, the Jains are a small number of high-caste people representing perhaps 2 percent of the total Indian population.

In contrast, Buddhism is and has long been one of the great religions of the world. It has adherents in all South and East Asian nations, and includes several sects. Buddhism today has the third largest membership of all faiths after Christianity and Islam.

Francis G. Mayer/Corbis

**SHIVA IN THE DANCE OF LIFE.** One of the great trinity of Hindu deities, Shiva is sometimes portrayed as a male, sometimes as a female. Shiva is the god who presides over becoming and destroying, representing the eternal flux of life.

# BUDDHISM

Buddhism began in India as an intellectual and emotional revolt against the emptiness of Vedic ritualism. Originally an earthly philosophy that rejected the idea of immortal life and the gods, it was turned into a supernatural belief system soon after the death of its founder, the Buddha.

**Siddhartha Gautama** (563–483 B.C.E.), an Indian aristocrat, was the Buddha, or Enlightened One, and his life is fairly well documented (see the Patterns of Belief box). As a young man, he wandered for several years through the north of India seeking more satisfying answers to the riddle of life. Only after intensive meditation was he finally able to come to terms with himself and human existence. He then became the teacher of a large and growing band of disciples, who spread his word gradually throughout the subcontinent and then into East Asia. Buddhism eventually came to be much more important in China and Japan than in India, where it was practically extinct by 1000 C.E.

## *Teachings of the Buddha*

What was the essence of the Buddha's teachings? The Buddha taught that everyone, regardless of caste, could attain ***nirvana,*** which is the Buddhist equivalent of Hindu moksha: release from human life and its woes. Nirvana is attained not through reincarnations and striving for better karma, but through the self-taught mastery of oneself: the gods have nothing to do with it, and priests are superfluous. The way to self-mastery lies through the **Four Noble Truths** and the **Eightfold Path,** which the Buddha laid out in his teachings.

Touched by a singular ray of enlightenment as a middle-aged seeker, the Buddha preached that the misery and disappointments of human life can be understood only in the light of the Four Noble Truths he had at last experienced:

1. All life is permeated by suffering.
2. All suffering is caused by desire.
3. Desire can only be finally overcome by reaching the state of nirvana.
4. The way to nirvana is guided by eight principles.

## The Buddha

**Siddhartha Gautama (c. 563–483 b.c.e.)** was the pampered son of a princely Indian family in the northern borderlands, near present-day Nepal. A member of the *kshatrija* caste of warrior-governors, the young man had every prospect of a conventionally happy and rewarding life as master of a handful of villages. Married young to a local aristocrat like himself, he dedicated himself to the usual pursuits—hunting, feasting, revelry—of his class and time.

But in his late twenties, a notable change occurred. According to a cherished Buddhist legend, on successive excursions he encountered an aged man, then a sick man, and finally a corpse by the roadside. These reminders of the common fate set the young man thinking about the nature of all human life, in a (for him) novel way. Finally, he abandoned home, wife, and family, and set out to find his own answers. In the already-traditional Indian fashion, he became a wandering ascetic, begging a handful of rice to stay alive while seeking truth in meditation.

Years went by as Siddhartha sought to answer his questions. But for long he found no convincing answers, neither in the extreme self-denial practiced by some nor in the mystical contemplation recommended by others. At last, as he sat under the bodhi tree (the tree of wisdom) through an agonizingly long night of intensive meditation, enlightenment reached him. He arose, confident in his new perceptions, and began to gather around him the beginnings of the community known as Buddhists ("the enlightened ones").

From that point on, the Buddha developed a philosophy that was a revision of the ruling Vedic Hindu faith of India and, in some important ways, a denial of it. By the Buddha's death, the new faith was firmly established, and some version of his teaching would gradually grow to be the majority viewpoint before being extinguished in the land of its birth.

In the original Buddhism, little attention was given to the role of the supernatural powers in human life or to reincarnation. The gods were thought to exist but to have minimal influence on an individual karma, or fate. Gods could not assist a person to find what Hindus call *moksha* and Buddhists *nirvana,* or the state of release from earthly life and its inherent suffering. But in time, this changed among the majority, or Mahayana Buddhists, who came to look on the Buddha and other *bodhisattvas* as divine immortals who could be called on for spiritual assistance.

How would this development have been received by the Buddha during his own lifetime? The answer is not hard to guess because his rejection of supernatural deities was well known. But it remains true that the very breadth of Buddhist doctrines and practices, which range from simple repetitive chants to the most refined intellectual exercise, have allowed a sizable proportion of humankind to identify with this creed in one or another of its forms.

Sheldan Collins/Corbis

**Reclining Buddha.** A so-called reclining Buddha, one of the frequent colossal representations of the Buddha on the island of Sri Lanka, the center of the Theravada school of the religion.

### *Analyze and Interpret*

Contrast the Buddhist emphasis on human beings' capability of finding their own way to serenity with the Zoroastrian convictions you read about in Chapter 4. Which seems more persuasive? Why?

The Eightfold Path to nirvana demands right (or righteous, we would say) ideas, right thought, right speech, right action, right living, right effort, right consciousness, and right meditation. The person who consistently follows these steps is assured of conquering desire and will therefore be released from suffering, which is the ultimate goal of human life.

The heart of the Buddha's message is that suffering and loss in this life are caused by the desire for an illusory power and happiness. Once the individual understands that power is not desirable and that such happiness is self-deception, the temptation to pursue them will gradually disappear. The individual will then find the serenity of soul and the harmony with nature and fellow human beings that constitute true fulfillment.

Buddhism quickly spread among Indians of all backgrounds and regions, carried forth by the Buddha's disciples during his lifetime. What made it so appealing? Much of the popularity of Buddhism stemmed from its *democracy of spirit*. Everyone, male and female, high and low, was able to discover the Four Truths and follow the Eightfold Path. No one was excluded because of caste restrictions or poverty.

Soon after the Buddha's death, his followers made him into a god with eternal life—a thought foreign to his own teaching. His movement also gradually split into two major branches: *Theravada* and *Mahayana* Buddhism.

**Theravada** (Hinayana), which means "the narrower vehicle," is the stricter version of the faith. Theravada Buddhism emphasizes the monastic life for both men and women, and takes a rather rigorous approach to what a good person who seeks nirvana must believe. It claims to be the pure form of the Buddha's teachings and rejects the idea of the reincarnation of the Master or other enlightened ones (*bodhisattva*) appearing on Earth. It is particularly strong in Sri Lanka and Cambodia.

**Mahayana** Buddhism is much more liberal in its beliefs, viewing the doctrines of the Buddha as a sort of initial step rather than as the ultimate word. The word *Mahayana* means "the larger vehicle," reflecting the belief that there are many ways to salvation. Its faithful believe that there are many buddhas, not just Siddhartha Gautama, and that many more will appear. Monastic life is a good thing for those who can assume it, but most Mahayana Buddhists will never do so and do not feel themselves disadvantaged thereby. Mahayana adherents far outnumber the others and are found in Vietnam, China, Japan, and Korea. Unlike the history of the Jewish, Christian, and Muslim sects, the two forms of Buddhism take a "live and let live" attitude toward each other, just as the various types of Hinduism do.

## The Mauryan Dynasty

For a century and a half after the Buddha's death, the philosophy he founded gained adherents steadily but remained a distinctly minority view in a land of Hindu believers. In the 330s B.C.E., however, the invasion of India by Alexander the Great (see Chapter 9) not only brought the first direct contact with Western ideas and art forms but also enabled a brief period of political unity under the Mauryan Dynasty, which moved into the vacuum left by Alexander's retreat. The founder of this first historical dynasty in India was Chandragupta Maurya, who succeeded in seizing supreme powers in northwestern India upon the withdrawal of the Greeks. His success is partly attributed to the advice of his associate, Kautilya, who insisted on the primacy of the end over the means in all things political. This advice is the core of the **Arthasastra,** a compilation of hard-bitten governmental policies supposedly written by Kautilya to guide his master, and one of the few literary sources of early India's history and culture. The rule of the dynasty was brief but important for India's future. The third and greatest of the Mauryan rulers, Ashoka (ruled 269–232 B.C.E.), is the outstanding native king of premodern times, admired by all Indians as the founding spirit of Indian unity and nationhood.

Ashoka's significance stems in large part from his role in spreading the Buddhist faith in India, thereby initiating the tradition of mutual tolerance between religions that is (or used to be) one of the subcontinent's cultural boasts. After a series of successful wars against the Mauryans' neighbors and rivals, Ashoka was shocked by the bloodshed at the battle of Kalinga at the midpoint of his reign. Influenced by Buddhist monks, the king became a devout Buddhist and pacifist. The last twenty years of his reign were marked by unprecedented internal prosperity and external peace. The monarch viewed himself as the responsible father of the people and exerted himself continually for their welfare. In so doing, he set a model of noble authority toward which later Indian rulers aspired but seldom reached. The inscriptions enunciating his decrees were placed on stone pillars scattered far and wide over his realm, and some of them survive today as the first examples of Indian written language. They, and the accounts of a few foreign travelers, are the means by which we know anything of Indian government in this early epoch.

After Ashoka's death, his weak successors soon gave up what he had gained, both in defense against invasion and in internal stability. Wave after wave of barbarian horsemen entered India through the gateway to Central Asia called the Khyber Pass (see Map 5.1). Most of them soon enough became sedentary in habit, adopted Indian civilization, and embraced the Buddhist faith. But the political unity established by the Mauryan rulers disintegrated. Four centuries passed before the Gupta Dynasty could reestablish it in the 300s C.E. We will revisit the turbulent course of Indian history in Chapter 16.

## Daily Life and the Position of Women

The almost entirely self-governing Indian villagers led lives controlled by the seasons, caste, and local tradition, punctuated by visits from the tax collector and by the birth and feast days of the deities. It was not, so far as we can see, a bitterly impoverished existence.

The abject rural misery often experienced in India's modern history is a relatively recent phenomenon—usually the product of a shortage of agricultural land—and until the last two or three centuries, shortages were almost unknown or limited to small areas. Although the material conditions of village life could not have been high by today's standards, the natives and the Aryan invaders had extensive areas of both irrigable and undeveloped land suitable to agriculture in various forms, and they brought these lands into production steadily for a millennium. What famines and hard times occurred were probably more the result of grasping landlords and destroying armies than the failings of nature and climate. When a shortage did threaten the food supply of large numbers or was seen as a menace, emigration to another, less crowded area was the usual, effective solution. Only in the recent past has the general sharp rise in populations around the globe made this type of movement not feasible.

As in the Near East, Indian tradition regarding the relative status of women shows an initial period of near equality or possibly matriarchy. But with the arrival of the Aryan nomads, female prestige began a descent that continued in the Vedic Hindu era. Manu, the legendary lawgiver, established the proper relation between the sexes once and for all (see box). Gradually, the ritual of widows' suicide (*sati*) and isolation from all nonfamily males (*purdah*) became established. Female subordination varied a bit according to caste, but the female's fundamental dharma in all castes was to obey and serve her husband and her sons.

Interestingly, in conjunction with this subordination went an emphasis on female sexuality. The female was often seen as being more sexually potent than the male. It is now sometimes argued that this attitude arose from men's fears about "the devouring woman," represented by the ferocious goddess of destruction, Kali. Some equivalent of the woman who is sexually insatiable and physically overpowering is found in several ancient religions whose rites were developed by men (as kings and priests). It is notably absent from those that arose during a period of female predominance (matriarchy) or when the sexes were more or less equal in public life. The tensions between the sexes are thus reflected from earliest times in differing views of the sexual instinct and its satisfaction.

Nimatallah/Art Resource, NY

**Kali.** The Indian goddess of destruction was frequently portrayed in a sexual context, but in this bronze representation (800–100 C.E.) from south India, she takes a Buddha-like position while extending her four arms with traditional household implements.

## Buddhism's Spread

Most of India's land connections with the outer world have been northwestward, across the same routes through the passes of Afghanistan and the Hindu Kush mountains that invaders followed again and again. From the northwest came the Aryans, then the Greco-Macedonians under Alexander, then the Persians in the early C.E. centuries, and eventually the Turks and Afghani Muslims.

Most of these intruders, even the savage horsemen from the Asian steppe, soon adopted civilized habits and enriched India's Hindu-Buddhist culture in one way or another. By sea, India's interchange with foreigners reached both the coast of east Africa and into the archipelagos of the Southwest Pacific, as well as the Southeast Asian mainland (see Chapter 16).

In contrast, early India had remarkably little cultural interchange with China, its sophisticated and powerful neighbor to the northeast. The main reason for this lack of contact was the extreme difficulty of crossing the Himalaya mountains and the fearsome terrain and sparse population of the Tibetan plateau behind them. The mountains ringing India to the north had no easy routes to the east, nor did the jungles of Burma allow passage in premodern days. There were, however, some exceptions to this mutual lack of contact. By far the most significant one was the export of the Buddhist faith from India to China. Starting in the first century C.E., the new doctrine, in its Mahayana form, penetrated across the mountains and entered deeply into Chinese cultural life. By the fifth or sixth century C.E., much of the Chinese educated class had taken up Buddhism to a greater or lesser degree, blending the new ideas with traditional Confucian practice and ethics.

In fact, the large-scale adoption of Mahayana Buddhism by the Chinese has been called the most far-reaching single cultural event in world history. The Chinese also passed on Buddhism to their satellites Korea and Vietnam, and through Korea, the faith entered Japan. In all of these places, Buddhism transformed the previous nature of cultural life. It had enormous impacts on East Asia between roughly 400 and 1000 C.E., by which time Buddhism in one of its variant sects was the primary faith of most of that huge region's populations.

**THE LIONS OF SARNATH.** Sarnath was the site where Siddhartha Gautama first preached. The Lions of Sarnath were created by King Ashoka to symbolize the proclamation of Buddhism to the world. The lions have been adopted by the modern republic of India as the official symbol of state.

Borromeo/Art Resource, NY

# SUMMARY

Civilized life is now known to have emerged in India much earlier than previously believed. By 2500 B.C.E., people of the Indus River valley had developed irrigated fields and good-sized towns that traded widely with both the surrounding villagers and distant neighbors to the west. These towns seem to have been governed by a priesthood, but information on their history is still sparse. The civilization was already in decline, possibly from natural causes, when it fell to Aryan nomads, who instituted the beginnings of the caste system.

In the thousand years after the Aryan conquest—the Vedic Epoch (1500–500 B.C.E.)—the Hindu religion was gradually constructed from a combination of Aryan belief and the Indus valley faith. When this ritualistic Hinduism was challenged by other, more ethically conscious doctrines such as Buddhism and Jainism, it gave way. Buddhism, in particular, became an international religion and philosophy, as several variants took root throughout East Asia.

Although arts and sciences flourished, the cultural and political unity of India was only sporadically enforced by a strong central government. Many invasions from the northwest kept India in a frequent state of political fragmentation. Religious belief, rather than government, was the cement that held its people together and gave the basis for their consciousness of being a nation.

## Identification Terms

Test your knowledge of this chapter's key concepts by defining the following terms. If you can't recall the meaning of certain terms, refresh your memory by looking up the boldfaced term in the chapter, turning to the Glossary at the end of the book, or working with the flashcards that are available on the *World Civilizations* Companion Website: **http://history.wadsworth.com/adler04/**.

| | | | |
|---|---|---|---|
| Arthasastra | Eightfold Path | Manu | Rigveda |
| Brahmin | Four Noble Truths | Mohenjo-Daro | Siddhartha Gautama |
| caste | *karma* | *moksha* | Theravada |
| *dharma* | Mahayana | *nirvana* | Vedas |

## Test Your Knowledge

Test your knowledge of this chapter by answering the following questions. Complete answers appear at the end of the book. You may also take this quiz interactively and find even more quiz questions on the *World Civilizations* Companion Website: **http://history.wadsworth.com/adler04/**.

1. The excavation of Mohenjo-Daro indicates that India's earliest civilization
   a. had a strong central government.
   b. was governed by merchants.
   c. had little if any commercial contacts with other civilized lands.
   d. had no dependence on irrigation agriculture.
   e. flourished despite the absence of any large building projects.
2. The evolution of Indian castes came about because of
   a. economic necessities.
   b. the application of Vedic beliefs to Indian realities.
   c. the teachings of the Buddhist monks.
   d. climate and geography.
   e. the need for major social reforms.
3. In Indian society after the Aryan conquest, the highest social group was that of the
   a. priests.
   b. warriors.
   c. tillers of the soil.
   d. educated.
   e. vaishya.
4. The Laws of Manu show a society in which
   a. there were no essential differences between male and female.
   b. there was a strong sense of social justice.
   c. children were not valued.
   d. women were considered a source of temptation.
   e. slaves were afforded some measure of protection.
5. *Karma* is a Sanskrit word meaning
   a. the soul.
   b. release from earthly cycles.
   c. the uppermost caste in Hindu society.
   d. the tally of good and bad acts in a person's life.
   e. the code of morals for one's caste.
6. Which of the following religions of India emphasizes above all the sacred nature of all life?
   a. Jainism
   b. Buddhism
   c. Hinduism
   d. Mithraism
   e. Zoroastrianism
7. The Buddha taught all but which one of the following?
   a. All persons are destined for immortal happiness in an afterlife.
   b. Sorrow is generated by desire.
   c. Every individual is capable of attaining nirvana.
   d. Gods are of little or no significance in attaining true happiness.
   e. Nirvana is achieved by successfully following the Noble Eightfold Path.
8. The first true dynasty in India was founded by
   a. Ashoka.
   b. Manu.
   c. Chandragupta Maurya.
   d. Kautilya.
   e. Siddhartha Gautama.
9. Women's status in India could best be described as
   a. improving during the Vedic Period.
   b. developing a true matriarchy as time passed.
   c. offering more choices to women of higher caste.
   d. supporting the role of mother, but rejecting the sexual side of marriage.
   e. entering into a period of decline after the Aryan invasion.

10. The most significant contribution of India to world history is probably
    a. the model of good government given by Ashoka.
    b. the development of higher mathematics.
    c. the passing of Buddhism to China.
    d. the spiritual precepts of the Vedas.
    e. its model of respect for women.

## InfoTrac College Edition

Visit the source collections at

**http://infotrac.thomsonlearning.com**

and use the Search function with the following key terms:

Vedas Hinduism Buddhism

## Wadsworth History Website Resources

Visit the World History Resource Center at **http://history.wadsworth.com/world** for a wealth of general resources and the *World Civilizations* Companion Website at **http://history.wadsworth.com/adler04/** for resources specific to this textbook.

## HistoryNow

Enter *HistoryNow* using the access card that is available for *World Civilizations*. *HistoryNow* will assist you in understanding the content in this chapter with lesson plans generated for your needs. In addition, you can read the following documents, and many more, online:

Laws of Manu

*The people of our race were created by Heaven*
*Having from the beginning distinctions and rules*
*Our people cling to customs*
*And what they admire is seemly behavior.*
*The Zhou Book of Songs*

# 6 Ancient China to 500 B.C.E.



| | |
|---|---|
| c. 1700–c. 1100 B.C.E. | Shang Dynasty |
| c. 1100–c. 750 B.C.E. | Zhou Dynasty: unified empire |
| c. 750–c. 400 B.C.E. | Later Zhou Dynasty |
| 551–479 B.C.E. | Life of Confucius |
| c. 400–225 B.C.E. | Era of the Warring States |

The most stable and in many ways the most successful civilization that history has known began in China in the second millennium B.C.E. It continued in its essentials through many changes in political leadership, meanwhile subjecting an enormous area and many different peoples to "the Chinese way." The Chinese educated classes, who considered themselves the hub of the universe, formed the most cohesive ruling group the world has ever seen. They combined scholarship and artistic sensitivity with great administrative abilities. Much of China's permanent culture was already firmly established by about 500 B.C.E., and it would change only very slowly.

## Earliest China: the Shang Era

Slightly before the Aryan invaders arrived in the Indus valley, the Neolithic farming villages along the central course of the Yellow River were drawn into an organized state for the first time (see Map 6.1 inset). This state was the product of military conquest by a people closely related to the villagers, the Shang. The **Shang Dynasty** replaced the villagers' earlier political overseers, but otherwise introduced little if any cultural change. The Shang Dynasty may have been preceded by another, the Hsia, which is mentioned in the ancient histories as the first of the Chinese ruling groups. Like the Shang, the existence of the Hsia has recently been confirmed by archaeological evidence, but our knowledge of it is still in a beginning stage.

Like other Chinese, the Shang and the people they conquered were members of the Sino-Tibetan language group and the Mongoloid or "yellow-skinned" race. Other members of these groups include the North American Indians and the Turks. The society the Shang took over was already well on the way to civilized life. There is much evidence of the development of agriculture as far back as the 7000s B.C.E. along the Yellow River, and by the time of the Shang, farming had long ago replaced hunting and gathering as the mainstay of the economy. The villagers had several types of domesticated animals and were growing wheat on the fertile soil that the north wind blows into the area from Mongolia. In later days, the vast plain on both sides of the river would be China's breadbasket, but life was never easy for the inhabitants. Unlike the floods of the Nile, the Yellow River's floods

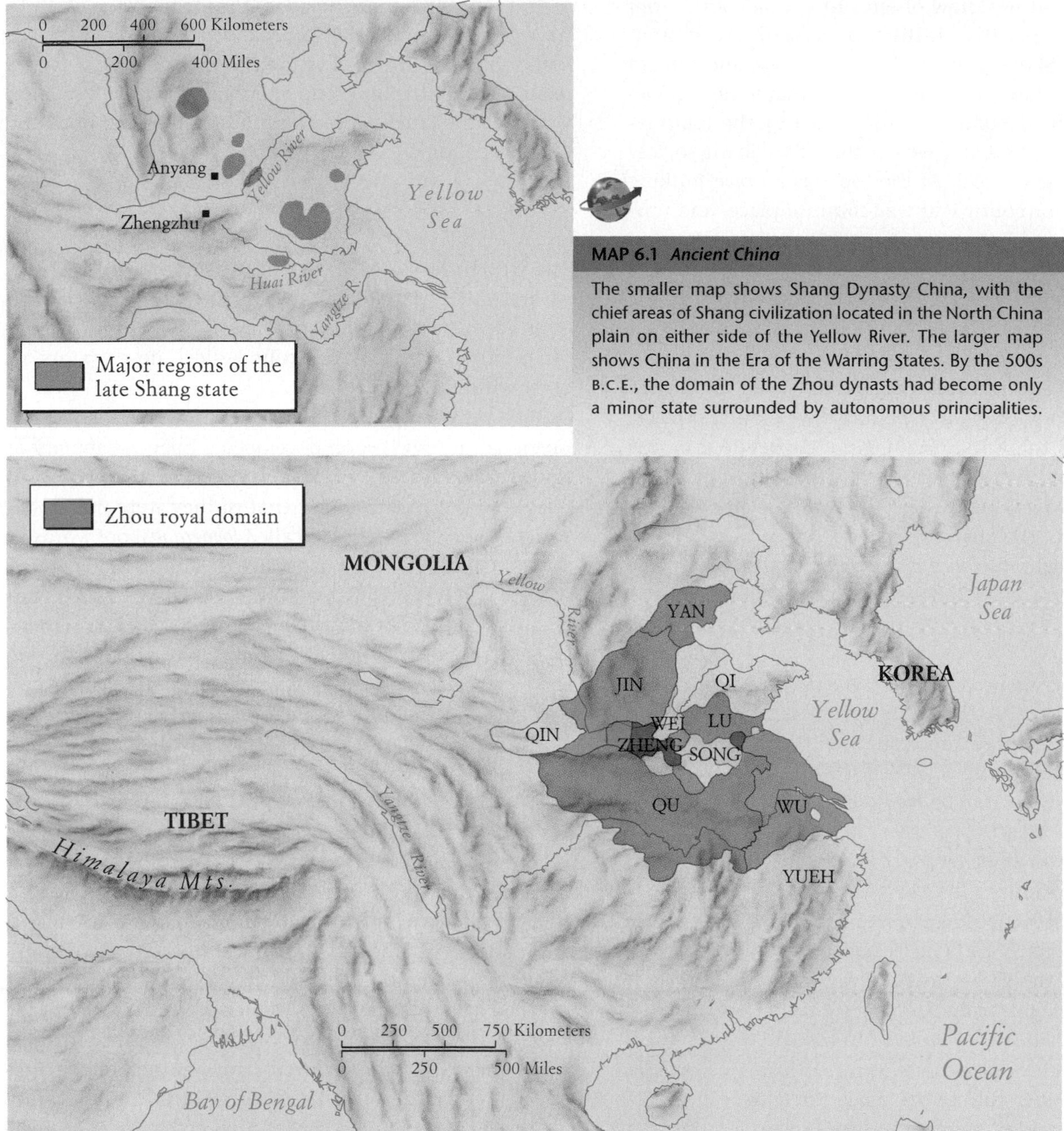


**MAP 6.1** *Ancient China*

The smaller map shows Shang Dynasty China, with the chief areas of Shang civilization located in the North China plain on either side of the Yellow River. The larger map shows China in the Era of the Warring States. By the 500s B.C.E., the domain of the Zhou dynasts had become only a minor state surrounded by autonomous principalities.

were tremendously damaging and had to be controlled by extensive levees, painfully erected and maintained.

The central valley of the Yellow River was the cradle of Chinese civilization, but another river would play almost as important a role in China's later history: the Yangtze. This great stream is much tamer than the Yellow and runs far to the south through a warmer and wetter landscape. By about the fifth century C.E., it was the center of China's rice culture. Eventually, the rice of the Yangtze became even more important to the Chinese food supply than the wheat of the Yellow River drainage. The plains along the two rivers and the coastal area between their deltas were—and still are—the most densely populated and most important regions of China.

Of all the ancient civilizations, China was the most isolated from outside influences, even more so than Egypt. Both agriculture and metalworking apparently originated independently in China. No connections with either Indian or Mesopotamian arts and sciences are known until much later, after the civilization along the Yellow and Yangtze rivers had developed its own characteristics and technology.

Most of what we know of ancient China comes from archaeology rather than history, because Shang writings were limited. Starting in the 1920s, Chinese and foreign archaeologists have been excavating many rich gravesites. From the elaborate order followed by the tomb remains and their contents, we can infer that Shang society was strictly hierarchical. At the top was a powerful king with his warrior court. War was commonplace, and warriors were favored in every way, much as in feudal Europe. On a level below the warriors were many skilled artisans and a growing class of small traders in the towns. In the countryside lived the great majority, the peasants in their villages. Scholars are not sure whether the early Chinese had a formal supernatural religion in which all participated or whether belief in the afterlife was commonplace. Many experts think that the upper class believed in one set of gods, while the majority worshiped another.

Several fundamental aspects of Chinese life were already visible in the Shang Epoch:

- *The supreme importance of the family.* More than any other culture, the Chinese rely on the family to serve as a model for public life and the source of all private virtue.
- *The reverence shown to ancestors and the aged by the young.* The Chinese believe that experience is far more important than theory and that the young must learn from the aged if harmony is to be preserved and progress achieved.
- *The emphasis on this world.* No other civilization of early times was so *secular* in orientation. Although the emperor was titled Son of Heaven, China never had a priestly caste, and the government always subordinated religious affairs to earthly, practical tasks.
- *The importance of education, particularly literacy.* No other culture has made the ability to read and write so critical for success. The ancient Chinese written language was extremely complex (it has since been simplified). Years of hard study were required to master it, but once it was acquired, it opened the doors to both wealth and power.

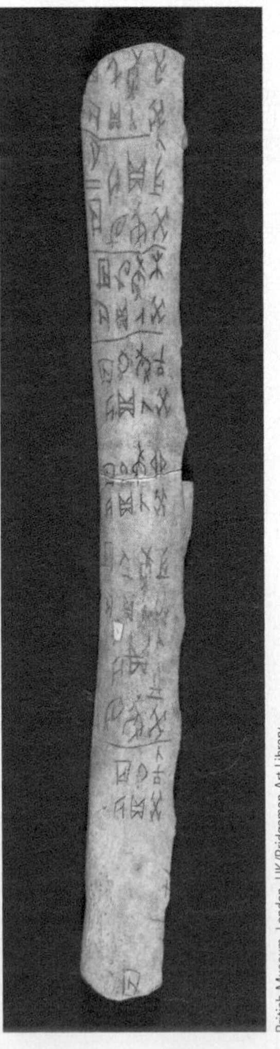

British Museum, London, UK/Bridgeman Art Library

**Oracle Bone.** On the flat surface of bones such as this, Shang sages incised the earliest surviving examples of Chinese ideographs. The messages are questions addressed to the gods, and the sages read the answers by examining the patterns of cracks in the bones after hot irons had been pressed against them.

In the twelfth century B.C.E., the Shang rulers seem to have faced internal conflicts that weakened the dynasty. Somewhat later they fell to the **Zhou** (Chou) **Dynasty,** a related but barbarian group from farther west. The Zhou would be the longest-lived and most influential of all the Chinese ruling dynasties.

## Writing

The written language was critically important in China. Its beginnings date to about 1500 B.C.E., and it is still in essentially the same format today. How did it differ from other written languages, and how did it develop (apparently without input from non-Chinese sources)?

Like most languages, written Chinese was originally pictographic, but it soon developed a huge vocabulary of signs that had no picture equivalents and were not at all related to the spoken word (that is, they were not alphabetic). These characters are called *logographs,* or "words in signs." Chinese spoken language is monosyllabic (each word has but one syllable), and a single logograph can take the place of as many as several words in other languages, conveying whole descriptions or actions in one sign. Some logographs were derived from certain common pictorial roots, but others were not connected in any way, which made learning them difficult. All in all, students had to memorize about 5,000 logographs to be considered literate. Understandably, literacy was rare, and those who knew how to read and write entered a kind of elite club that carried tremendous prestige.

Although writing emerged considerably later in China than in Mesopotamia or Egypt, it developed quickly and had a richer vocabulary and more conceptual refinement than any other written language before the first century C.E. The earliest writing beyond pictography is found on *oracle bones,* animal bones and shells that were used to divine the gods' wishes. By the end of the Shang Period, about 1100 B.C.E., histories and stories were being written, and some have been preserved.

The written language was immensely important in unifying the groups and subgroups who came to call themselves Chinese. China has dozens of spoken dialects, which are mutually unintelligible, but it has only one way of writing, which can be understood by all who can read.

### *Art and Architecture*

The greatest artistic achievement of the ancient Chinese was undoubtedly their bronze work. Craftsmen in the late Shang and early Zhou periods turned out drinking cups, vases, wine vessels, brooches, and medallions, whose technical excellence and artistic grace were stunning. Metal technology in general was advanced in early China. Besides bronze, cast iron and copper were widely used for both tools and weaponry.

The Shang buildings that have been partially unearthed by modern archaeologists are impressive in both size and design. The upper class built large palaces and strong forts around towns such as Anyang and Zhengzhou (Chengchu) in the middle reaches of the Yellow River plain. The distinctive Chinese architectural style, with pagoda-type roof lines and diminishing upper stories, was developed at this time, although it was carried out much more elaborately later. Most of the art forms of modern China had their roots in very early times.

## The Zhou Dynasty

During the 700 years that they ruled, at least in name, the Zhou greatly extended China's borders. Where the Shang had been content to rule a relatively restricted segment of north-central China on either side of the Yellow River, the Zhou reached out almost to the sea in the east and well into Inner Mongolia in the west. We know much more about the Zhou Era than the Shang because an extensive literature survives. Much history was written, and records of all types from tax rolls to lists of imports and exports have been found. The dynasty falls into two distinct phases: the unified empire, from about 1100 to about 750 B.C.E., and the Later Zhou, from about 750 to about 400 B.C.E. The earlier period was the more important. The Later Zhou Dynasty experienced a series of constant provincial revolts until, finally, the central government broke down altogether (see Map 6.1).

One of the novelties of the Zhou Period was the idea of the **mandate of heaven.** To justify their forcible overthrow of the Shang, the first Zhou rulers developed the idea that "heaven"—that is, the supernatural deities who oversaw all life—gave the chosen earthly ruler a mandate, or vote of confidence. So long as he ruled well and justly, he retained the mandate, but it would be taken from him if he betrayed the deities' trust. A ruler who failed to protect his people from invaders or failed to contain internal revolt had betrayed this trust. Thus, if a Chinese ruler fell to superior force or a successful conspiracy, it was a sign that he had "lost the mandate" and should be replaced. This marvelously self-serving theory (it was used to justify innumerable conspiracies and rebellions) was to be highly influential in Chinese history.

Patrick Aventurier/Liaison/Getty Images

**Warriors.** These clay statuettes of imperial warriors date from approximately the third century B.C.E., when they were a burial accompaniment for a lord of the Zhou Period. Their upraised hands once held spears and swords.

**Bronze Elephant.** The form of bronze casting known as *cir perdue* (lost wax) was widely used by the Zhou Dynasty artists. But the finest work was performed by using clay molds that locked tightly together before the liquid metal was poured into them. This enabled them to achieve a particularly fine detailing of the surface, as seen here.

The first Zhou kings were powerful rulers who depended mainly on their swords. The royal court employed hundreds of skilled administrators, and we see the faint beginning of a professional bureaucracy in the Zhou Era. China led the world in this development, as in so many others. As the centuries passed, however, power slipped from the monarch's hand and a feudal society developed, as the kings delegated more and more of their military and administrative duties to local aristocrats. These men stood to gain from the acquisition of new territory, and they did so at every chance. As a result, China expanded, but at the same time the control of the royal government weakened. By the 500s, the local aristocrats were in command of much of the empire, and by 400, the central power had broken down completely—one of the few times that has happened in China.

## Culture and Daily Life under the Zhou

Although the Zhou rulers eventually failed to keep the nation together, their era saw great advances in every area of arts and crafts. Silkworm cultivation and the weaving of silk have been demonstrated to be an important part of Zhou culture and trade with foreign states. The famous Silk Road, the caravan route to the Near East and the Black Sea, was already in existence. Bronze work, exemplified in all manner of weaponry, vessels, and statues, reached an apex of perfection. Much of it was produced using the lost wax method of casting into molds, a method that allowed great delicacy of form and design. Starting in the sixth century B.C.E., iron came into common use for tools and utensils, as well as weapons. The iron plowshare opened up huge areas of northern and central China to agriculture, enabling an unprecedented growth of population during the Zhou Era of perhaps 400 percent. It also provided for the supplying of the large towns of Anyang and Loyang, the capitals of the Zhou kings.

Wars between the contending aristocrats and against the nomads on China's northern borders were also common, and the use of the war chariot led to a technical breakthrough of the first rank: a horse harness or collar that allowed the horse to pull with the full strength of its shoulders and body without choking. This type of harness transformed the value of horses, not only in warfare but also as beasts of burden. Only much later did other civilizations recognize and copy this fundamental change.

As for living standards in Zhou China, the evidence we have suggests that peasants were moderately prosperous and rarely enslaved at this time. Although their life was undoubtedly difficult, it was not miserable. Zhou peasants were in more or less the same economic situation as Egyptian peasants: they were sharecropping tenants on the aristocracy's land, with some rights, and at least in the early Zhou years were usually protected from the worst excesses of grasping landlords by a powerful and respected government.

**Bronze Statue.** This figure of bronze and jade shows a boy with his pet birds. Such scenes from everyday life were unusual in Chinese art of the late Zhou Period, when this foot-high statue was made.

In the literary arts, most of the classics that have been taught to Chinese children ever since originated in the Zhou era. The earliest surviving books stem from the 800s B.C.E., much earlier than any that survive from other civilized centers. They were written either on strips of specially prepared bamboo, strung together with silken cord, or on silk scrolls. Professional historians, employed by the court, wrote chronicles of the rulers and their achievements. Poetry made its first appearance in Chinese letters during the early Zhou, beginning a tradition of sensitive, perceptive nature poetry that continues to the present day. The revered collection called *The Book of Songs* was produced by one or several hands at this period, remaining a mainstay of Chinese education ever since. Calligraphy also began at this time, and officials were expected to master this art form as a qualification for office.

## Confucius and the Confucian Philosophy

China's greatest single cultural force, the historical figure Kung Fu-tzu (551–479 B.C.E.), or **Confucius,** appeared toward the end of the Zhou Era. For twenty centuries, Confucius was the most respected name in China, the molder of Chinese patterns of education, and the authority on what a true Chinese should and should not do. (See his biography in the Law and Government box.)

Confucius's interests were practical, centered on the hierarchy of ethical and political relations between individuals, and especially between the citizenry and the governor. The great model for Confucius's politics was the Chinese family.

Among the Chinese, the *yin-yang principles* identified the female as the passive element and the male as the active, creative one. (See the Society and Economy box for more on Chinese family customs.) Although all civilizations we have thus far studied gave pride of place to the father, none applied this principle so systematically as the Chinese. In ancient China, the father was accorded absolute obedience by children and grandchildren, whereas the mother supposedly never raised her voice in contradiction to her husband. A widow owed the same obedience to her father and sons. This arrangement remained the ideal in modern China before the communist takeover, although one can question whether it was a reality. There is no scarcity of reports of independent Chinese wives within the four walls of the home in modern times. But without a doubt, the principle of male superiority and female inferiority was adhered to and implemented systematically throughout Chinese history. For Confucius, whose teachings formed the basis of Chinese education for 2,300 years, women scarcely existed. He mentions them rarely and only in the context of male activity. As late as the seventeenth century, Chinese philosophers debated whether the female was fully human.

In Confucius's view, the state should be like a harmonious family: the father was the undisputed head, each person had his or her special rights and duties, and the wisdom of the aged guided the young. The oldest male was responsible for protecting and guiding the others, who owed him absolute obedience even when he appeared to be wrong.

Confucius insisted on *gentility*—that is, courtesy, justice, and moderation—as the chief virtue of the public man. He taught that the rich and the strong should feel a sense of obligation toward the poor and the weak. A gentleman was made, not born. An aristocrat might not be a gentleman, whereas a lowborn person could learn to be one. The proper calling of a gentleman was government. He should advise the ruler and see to it that government policies were fair and promoted the general welfare. A ruler who followed the advice of his gentlemanly counselors would surely retain the mandate of heaven.

This philosophy of public service by scholarly, virtuous officials was to have enormous influence on China. Rulers came to be judged according to whether they used the Confucian prescriptions for good government. A corps of officials educated on Confucian principles, subscribing to his values, and believing him to be the Great Teacher came into existence. These **mandarins,** as the West later called them, were the actual governing class of China for 2,000 years.

An unfortunate result of this system was the tendency of most rulers to interpret Confucian moderation and distrust of violence as resistance to needed change. The rulers naturally tended to see, in Confucius's admonition that the state should resemble a well-run family, a condemnation of revolt for any reason. In time, many of the Confucian-trained bureaucrats not only agreed but came to believe that the status quo was the only natural and proper way of doing things. The insistence that harmony was the chief goal of politics and social policy sometimes was twisted into an excuse for stagnation. It led to a contempt for the new and a fear of change, however necessary. From time to time in China's long history, this resistance to change has led to acute problems.

## Rivals to Confucius

In the later Zhou Period, two especially persistent rival philosophies arose to challenge the Confucian view. Neither was as successful in capturing the permanent allegiance of the educated classes, but both were repeatedly seized upon as an alternative or a necessary addition to the Great Teacher.

# Confucius (551–479 B.C.E.)

**THE MOST REVERED** of all Chinese statesmen and philosophers was Master Kung, or Kung Fu-tzu, known in the West as Confucius. As a lasting influence on a nation, he has no equal in world history. During his long lifetime, he acquired a devoted group of followers who gave educated Chinese their moral and ethical landmarks for 2,000 years. Confucianism has, of course, evolved considerably over the centuries, and no one now knows precisely what the Master's original thoughts may have been. But by reading what his disciples said about him and about their own understanding of his message, we can appreciate his greatness and his importance in the life of the Chinese people. He established a tradition of cultural values that has changed, not in its essentials, but in its degree of acceptance.

Confucius was born into an impoverished but aristocratic family in the state of Lu at the time when the Zhou Empire was falling apart and the Era of the Warring States was beginning. Given a good education, the young man set out to find a suitable place for himself in the world. His ambition was to acquire a post in the government of his home state, which would allow him to exert a real influence for good and to assist the princely ruler in providing wise and benevolent rule.

Frustrated by the intrigues of his rivals in Lu, where he briefly obtained a post in the ministry of justice, Confucius was forced to seek a position elsewhere. But in the neighboring states, too, he was disappointed in his quest, never securing more than minor and temporary positions before running afoul of backbiting competitors or speaking his mind when that was a dangerous thing to do. He had to return to Lu to earn his living as a teacher, and for the rest of his life he subsisted modestly on the tuition fees of his wealthier students.

Bettmann/Corbis

**PORTRAIT OF CONFUCIUS.** This undated illustration, much like other depictions of Confucius after his death, was based on a relief from the stela in the Pei Lin de Sigan-fou.

Confucius accepted this fate with difficulty. For many years he continued to hope for appointment as an adviser to the prince and thus to translate his beliefs into government policy. Only gradually did he realize that by his teaching he could have more influence on the fate of his people than he might ever attain as a minister to a trivial and corrupt ruler. By the end of his life, his fame had already reached much of China's small educated class, and his students were going out to found schools of their own, reflecting the principles the Master had taught them.

Confucius taught that all human affairs, public and private, were structured by the Five Relationships: father and son, husband and wife, elder and younger brother, ruler and official, and friend and friend. The fact that three of these relationships are within the family circle shows the Confucian emphasis on the family. He believed it to be the model and building block of all other social or political arrangements. This emphasis continues in Chinese life to this day.

Confucius was not so much an original thinker as a great summarizer and rephraser of the truths already embraced by his people. He did not attempt a complete philosophical system and was not at all interested in theology or what is now called *metaphysics*. Rather, his focus was always on the relation of human being to human being, and especially on the relation of governor to governed. He was an eminently secular thinker, and this tradition, too, has continued among educated Chinese to the present.

Two of the sayings attributed to him in the collection of his sayings called the *Analects* give the flavor of his teaching:

> Tsi-guang [a disciple] asked about government. Confucius said: "Sufficient food, sufficient armament, and sufficient confidence of the people are the necessities."
>
> "Forced to give up one, which would you abandon first?"
>
> "I would abandon armament."
>
> "Forced to give up one of the remaining two, which would you abandon?"
>
> "I would abandon food. There has always been death from famine, but no state can exist without the confidence of its people."

The Master always emphasized the necessity of the ruler setting a good example:

> Replying to Chi Gang-tsi who had asked him about the nature of good government, Confucius said, "To govern is to rectify. If you lead the people by virtue of rectifying yourself, who will dare not be rectified by you?"

## *Analyze and Interpret*

After a generation of contemptuous treatment and proscription, the Chinese communist government has recently allowed the reintroduction of Confucian teaching and commentary in the schools. Why do you think this has happened? Do you think Confucius has anything to say to modern people?

**HistoryNow™**

*To read more from the* **Analects**, *point your browser to the documents area of* **HistoryNow.**

SOCIETY AND ECONOMY

## A Chinese Dilemma

**THE CHINESE PEOPLE** have had since time immemorial a peculiarly firm sense of social obligations and the proper relations among family members. Confucius took the well-regulated family as the model of the well-governed state, and of his Five Relationships, which he said formed the basis of all society, three of them were within the family. The following story helps us understand how important such relations were to the Chinese.

> In the sixth century B.C.E., when the armies of Wu invaded the state of Ch'u, its prince had to flee to a city ruled by one of his vassals. Now it happened that the father of this prince, coveting his possessions, had caused the father of the vassal to be put to death. The younger brother of the vassal wished to kill the prince to avenge his father, but the elder demurred. "Revenge," he declared, "can only be spoken of as between equals. . . . If not, then there could be no such thing as superiors and inferiors. . . . It may not be done." But his younger brother replied, "I cannot consider that; I am thinking of our father!" Because he feared for the safety of his prince, the elder brother helped him remove to another city. When the invasion was over and conditions had returned to normal, the prince rewarded both brothers, which caused great surprise. Rather, he was told, he should have rewarded the elder and put the younger to death. "No," he replied, "both of these men acted properly, the one toward his father, the other toward his ruler. Was it not just, then, to reward them both?"

### Analyze and Interpret

How do the prince's and the elder brother's acts exemplify the Confucian emphasis on social harmony and just distinction between authority and subject persons?

Source: From H. G. Creel, *The Birth of China: A Study of the Formative Period of Chinese Civilization* (New York: Ungar, 1967).

Boltin Picture Library

**EARLY ZHOU SCULPTURE.** The Chinese mastery of saying much with little in their arts is demonstrated here. What do these comic wood figures suggest about the male–female relationship in ancient China?

## *Daoism*

Daoism (Taoism) is a philosophy centered on nature and following the "Way" (*Dao*) it shows us. It was supposedly the product of a teacher-sage called **Lao Zi (Lao-tzu)**, who purportedly was a near-contemporary of Confucius but may be entirely legendary. The book attributed to him, the famous ***The Way of the Dao (Dao de Jing)***, was probably written by his followers much later.

Unlike Confucius, Daoism sees the best government as the least government, a minimum of correction and guidance for those who are *inherently unable and unwilling to govern themselves*. In so doing, the rulers should follow the Way of Nature, as it is perceived through meditation and observation. The intelligent man seeks a lifestyle that is in tune with the natural world, a harmony of parts in a serene whole. The excerpt from the *Dao de Jing* in the Patterns of Belief box shows this harmony through paradoxical examples drawn from everyday life. All extremes should be avoided, even those meant to be benevolent. The truly good ruler does little except *be;* excessive action is as bad as no corrective action at all.

Daoism has taken so many forms through the centuries that it is almost impossible to provide a single description

# *Dao de Jing* of Lao Zi

**CONFUCIAN PHILOSOPHY WAS** by no means universally accepted in ancient China. It had to overcome several rival points of view among the educated class and was only partly successful in doing so. Among the ordinary people, Daoism was always stronger because it lent itself more readily to personal interpretation and to the rampant superstitions of the illiterate. It drew many of its principles from close observation of nature, emphasizing the necessity of bringing one's life into harmony with nature. Rather than the illusions of well-bred Confucians or the brutality of the Legalists, the followers of the Way sought serenity through acceptance of what is.

The *Dao de Jing,* or *The Way of the Dao,* is a collection of sayings attributed to Lao Zi (Lao-tzu), who supposedly lived in the sixth century B.C.E. Like much Chinese philosophy, the essence of the *Dao de Jing* is the search for balance between opposites, between the *yin* and *yang* principles. Unlike Confucianism, Daoism puts little faith in reason and foresight as the way to happiness. Instead, it urges its followers to accept the mystery of life and stop striving for a false mastery. It delights in putting its truths as paradoxes.

**Chapter II**

It is because every one under Heaven recognizes beauty
as beauty, that the idea of ugliness exists.
And equally if every one recognized virtue as virtue, this
would merely create fresh conceptions of wickedness.
For truly Being and Not-Being grow out of one another;
Difficult and easy complete one another;
Long and short test one another;
High and low determine one another.
Pitch and mode give harmony to one another.
Front and back give sequence to one another.
Therefore the Sage relies on actionless activity,
Carries on wordless teaching. . . .

**Chapter IV**

The Way is like an empty vessel
That yet may be drawn from
Without ever needing to be filled.
It is bottomless; the very progenitor of all things in
the world.
In it all sharpness is blunted,
All tangles untied,
All glare tempered,
All dust smoothed.
It is like a deep pool that never dries.
Was it too the child of something else? We cannot tell.
But as a substanceless image it existed before the Ancestor.

**Chapter IX**

Stretch a bow to the very full,
And you will wish you had stopped in time;
Temper a sword–edge to its very sharpest,
And you will find it soon grows dull.
When bronze and jade fill your hall
It can no longer be guarded.
Wealth and place breed insolence
That brings ruin in its train.
When your work is done, then withdraw!
Such is Heaven's Way.

**Chapter XI**

We put thirty spokes together and call it a wheel;
But it is on the space where there is nothing that the
usefulness of the wheel depends.
We turn clay to make a vessel;
But it is on the space where there is nothing that the
usefulness of the vessel depends.
We pierce doors and windows to make a house;
But it is on these spaces where there is nothing that the
usefulness of the house depends.
Therefore, just as we take advantage of what is, we should
recognize the usefulness of what is not.

## *Analyze and Interpret*

What application of Daoist thought can you find in your own experiences? Does the paradox of saying that doors and windows can be appreciated only if one keeps in mind the house walls strike you as truthful? as memorable?

Source: *The Way and Its Power: A Study of the Dao de Qing,* ed. and trans. A. Waley. © 1934.

**History Now™**

***To read more from the* Dao de Jing*, point your browser to the documents area of* HistoryNow.**

of it. Originally, it was a philosophy of the educated classes, but it eventually degenerated into a superstition of the peasants. Yet for many centuries, it was a serious rival of Confucius's ideas and was often adopted by Chinese seeking harmony with the natural world and escape from earthly conflicts. This dichotomy was summed up in the saying that the educated classes were "Confucian by day, Daoist by night." In their rational, public lives, they abided by practical Confucian principles of conduct, but in the quiet of their beds, they sought immersion in mysterious, suprarational nature.

### Legalism

**Legalism** was more a philosophy of government than a philosophy of private life. It was popularized in the **Era of the Warring States** (c. 400–c. 225 B.C.E.) between the collapse of central Zhou dynastic authority (around 400 B.C.E.) and the rise of the Qin emperor in the 220s (see Chapter 17). The general breakdown of authority that characterized this period provided the motivation for Legalist ideas.

The Legalists were convinced that a government that allowed freedom to its subjects was asking for trouble. Legalism was a rationalized form of governmental manipulation. It was not so much a philosophy as a justification for applying force when persuasion had failed. The basis of Legalism was the conviction that most people are inclined to evil selfishness, and it is the task of government to restrain them and simultaneously guide them into doing good—that is, what the governors want. This task is to be accomplished by controlling people even before their evil nature has manifested itself in their acts. In other words, the Legalists advocated strict censorship, prescribed education (differing by class), and immediate crushing of any signs of independent thought or action that could upset the status quo.

In a later chapter, we shall investigate how the Chinese government and state were definitively formed in the second and first centuries B.C.E. But Chinese political culture, as distinct from the state, was already shaped by 500 B.C.E. and would not change much until the modern era. The emphasis on the family, the respect due to elders, the subordination of women to men, the focus on this life on Earth rather than on a life to come, and the lofty position of the educated were already deeply rooted in Chinese society long before the Romans had established their empire.

## SUMMARY

The civilization of China originated in the Neolithic villages of the northern plains near the Yellow River in the second millennium B.C.E. Under the first historical dynasties of the Shang and the Zhou, this agrarian civilization displayed certain characteristics that were to mark China for many centuries to come: reverence for ancestors, the tremendous importance of the family, and the prestige of the educated and of the written word. Fine arts and literature were cultivated in forms that persisted: bronzeware, ceramics, silk, historical literature, and nature poetry.

The Shang dynasts were a warrior aristocracy who took over the village folk as their subjects in the eighteenth century B.C.E. What we know of them is almost entirely through a smattering of oracular fragments and archaeology performed in recent times. They were succeeded after several centuries by another warrior group called the Zhou, which established perhaps the most influential of all Chinese dynasties in the realm of culture. The arts flourished, and the limits of the state expanded greatly. Gradually, however, power to hold this vast realm together escaped from the dynastic ruler's hands and flowed into those of the provincial aristocrats.

The breakdown of central government that ended the long Zhou Dynasty and introduced the Era of the Warring States demanded further definition of basic values. In response, three great schools of practical philosophy arose between 500 and 250 B.C.E.: Confucianism, Daoism, and Legalism. Of these, the most significant for later Chinese history was the secularist, rationalist, and pragmatic thought of Confucius, the Sage of China for the next 2,000 years.

## Identification Terms

Test your knowledge of this chapter's key concepts by defining the following terms. If you can't recall the meaning of certain terms, refresh your memory by looking up the boldfaced term in the chapter, turning to the Glossary at the end of the book, or working with the flashcards that are available on the *World Civilizations* Companion Website: **http://history.wadsworth.com/adler04/**.

Confucius
*The Way of the Dao* (*Dao de Jing*)
Era of the Warring States
Lao Zi (Lao-tzu)
Legalism
mandarins
mandate of heaven
Shang Dynasty
Zhou Dynasty

## Test Your Knowledge

Test your knowledge of this chapter by answering the following questions. Complete answers appear at the end of the book. You may also take this quiz interactively and find even more quiz questions on the *World Civilizations* Companion Website: **http://history.wadsworth.com/adler04/**.

1. China's geography
   a. isolated it from other civilizations.
   b. was semitropical.
   c. is much like that of Mesopotamia.
   d. made it a natural marketplace and exchange point.
   e. made the development of agriculture difficult.
2. The Shang Dynasty was established in northern China at roughly the same time as the
   a. rise of the Assyrians.
   b. Aryan conquest of northern India.
   c. beginnings of Sumerian civilization.
   d. first dynasty in Egypt.
   e. founding of the first civilization in the Yangtze River region.
3. Early Chinese religious thought is noteworthy for its
   a. insistence on the existence of only two gods.
   b. emphasis on devotion to the spirits of the ancestors.
   c. superstition about heaven and hell.
   d. clear and detailed theology.
   e. development of a priestly class.
4. A significant long-term advantage of the Chinese style of writing is its
   a. easiness to learn.
   b. independence of regional dialects.
   c. effective use of an alphabet.
   d. small vocabulary.
   e. use of simple pictographs.
5. After seizing power from the Shang, the Zhou rulers adopted a
   a. theory of government that justified their actions.
   b. militarized dictatorship.
   c. theocracy in which the priests had final powers.
   d. democracy.
   e. comprehensive bureaucracy.
6. Which one of the following products was undeveloped in ancient China?
   a. Iron weaponry
   b. Silken cloth
   c. Fine bronzeware
   d. Iron plowshares
   e. Porcelain tableware
7. Which one of the following statements is *contrary* to Confucian teaching?
   a. The family is the proper model for good government.
   b. The young should be constantly seeking new and more effective modes of action.
   c. The gentleman is made and not born.
   d. The interactions of social groups should be controlled by formalities and courtesy.
   e. Virtuous scholarly gentlemen should involve themselves in public service.
8. In many aspects of philosophy, Chinese thought generally aimed at
   a. attaining union with the immortal gods.
   b. inspiring loyalty and fear in the common people.
   c. teaching myths and magical formulas.
   d. attaining harmony and avoiding disorder on Earth.
   e. developing innovations in government and finance.
9. Daoist political views emphasized that people
   a. get the government they deserve.
   b. are naturally evil and government must restrain them.
   c. should be enslaved to ensure peace.
   d. should be left to their own devices as much as possible.
   e. should defer to their rulers, who are naturally much wiser.

10. Legalism could best be described as
   a. a form of government that recognized the worth of individuals.
   b. a justification for forcing people to do what their government said they should.
   c. supportive of societal freedom.
   d. an ethical system that supported the independent actions of the people.
   e. a way of encouraging people to develop constraints on their own behavior.

## InfoTrac College Edition

Visit the source collections at

**http://infotrac.thomsonlearning.com**

and use the Search function with the following key terms:

Confucius Confucian Taoism

## Wadsworth History Website Resources

Visit the World History Resource Center at **http://history.wadsworth.com/world** for a wealth of general resources and the *World Civilizations* Companion Website at **http://history.wadsworth.com/adler04/** for resources specific to this textbook.

## HistoryNow

Enter *HistoryNow* using the access card that is available for *World Civilizations*. *HistoryNow* will assist you in understanding the content in this chapter with lesson plans generated for your needs. In addition, you can read the following documents, and many more, online:

Confucius, *Analects* Lao Zi, *Dao de Jing*

# Worldview One

## Law and Government

## Society and Economy

### Mesopotamians, Egyptians, Hebrews

**Law and Government**

*Mesopotamia:* Early law is based on different treatment for differing classes. Property is better protected than people, but some care is shown for all persons' interests. Government is originally theocratic but becomes monarchic after c. 2000 B.C.E., when contesting city-states are conquered by an external invader and put under centralized rule.

*Egypt:* Law is the divine wisdom and justice of the pharaoh, administered by his officials. Government displays great stability under god-king until as late as 1000 B.C.E., when foreign invasions multiply after failed attempt at empire.

*Israel:* Law is based on Moses' Covenant with Yahweh, which provides a divinely ordained ethical foundation for Hebraic custom. The twelve tribes long for a messiah and king who will lead them to earthly dominion but are repeatedly disappointed after the collapse of Solomon's kingdom and its division into the hostile successor states of Israel and Samaria.

**Society and Economy**

Mesopotamia is active in commerce originating in large towns and cities, which are themselves dependent on intensive irrigation farming. Trade with the Indus valley, the Black Sea region, Egypt, and Persia is attested to by archaeology. Skilled craftsmen as well as priests and governors supply the export trade. Egypt is the most fertile part of the world and can export grain as well as copper to its neighbors, while remaining almost self-sufficient for millennia. Unlike Mesopotamia, no large urban areas are developed and relatively little contact is made with others throughout most of this epoch. The Hebrews sporadically play an intermediary role in the trade between the Nile and the eastern Mediterranean civilizations, but their economy is basically agrarian and pastoral throughout this period.

As elsewhere in the ancient world, patriarchy is the rule for Mesopotamians, Egyptians, and Hebrews. Most routine occupations are open to women as well as to men in all of the ancient societies, but women normally act under a male's supervision.

### Indians

**Law and Government**

Government is presumed to be a theocracy in the Indus valley civilization; no evidence as to its nature is available. Law remains customary and unwritten long after the Aryan invasion (c. 1500 B.C.E.). The brahmin priests retain their lawmaking position as the Aryan-Indian amalgam gradually produces Vedic Hinduism. Important concepts and customs are memorized by succeeding generations, dominated by the self-interest of the uppermost castes. The evolution of Aryan warrior-kings as partners of the brahmins brings a series of petty principalities in northern India and the extension of Aryan colonization from the Indus valley to the Ganges valley. By the end of the period the Aryans have been absorbed into the Indian mass.

**Society and Economy**

Indian and other South Asian cultures are overwhelmingly agrarian into modern times. Large towns exist from earliest times (Harappa, Mohenjo- Daro), but the large majority of people live in villages, with little contact outside their own region. Trade with Mesopotamia and Persia is active from the pre-Aryan period; later, maritime trade with both the eastern and western shores of the Indian Ocean is common and, by the end of the period, with the early Southeast Asian states as well.

The general position of women in the earliest Indian civilizations is unclear. According to Hindu tradition, however, the woman is intended to serve and obey the male. Gradually, the rituals of *sati* (widow's suicide) and *purdah* (isolation from all nonfamily males) become established, and female subordination is the rule.

### Chinese

**Law and Government**

China develops writing early and keeps extensive records from c. 1000 B.C.E. Chinese law, which is customary in this period, looks to the protection of property and maintenance of the clan/family as determining factors for justice. Government is monarchic and warrior-oriented, with Shang conquerors as models for the succeeding Zhou. Zhou dynasts lose their grip on outlying "warlords" by the end of the period, and the Era of Warring States opens.

**Society and Economy**

As in South Asia, most Chinese live in villages, raising grain and engaging in pastoral agriculture. A few large towns exist, but as yet play only a minor role in the economy. Trade with others is negligible in this era. China is still isolated from the rest of the world. Rice culture has not yet begun, as the south remains unconquered. Contact with India, Vietnam, and Japan is not yet undertaken.

Some evidence exists of a very early period of matriarchy in Neolithic China, but for the most part, the father is accorded absolute obedience in ancient China. The Chinese wife's lot is by far the hardest of those in all ancient civilizations, with wife beating and submissive loyalty the norm.

# Ancient Civilizations, 3500–500 B.C.E.

## Patterns of Belief

## Arts and Culture

## Science and Technology

Religious belief dictates the type of government in the earliest period, but gradually separates the king from the priest. Mesopotamia adopts a pessimistic view of the human-god relationship and the afterlife, elevating the powers of the priests.

Egypt had a uniquely optimistic view of the afterlife and the role of the protecting gods, which lasted more than 2,000 years, until the collapse of its empire and foreign invasions forced a reconsideration. Jews draw on Zoroastrian Persian traditions to pioneer monotheism and to elevate Yahweh into a universal lawgiver to all humanity, with a special relationship with his chosen people, based on mutual love and justice in a life to come.

Mesopotamians produce the first monumental architecture, first urban society, first sophisticated writing system, and much else. Arts flourish under priestly and royal patronage, but relatively little has survived time and wars.

Egypt's pyramids are the most impressive ancient construction of all; massive sculpture, interior fresco painting, and ceramics are other Egyptian strengths in art.

At the end of the period, Hebrews produce the Bible as literature and a history of the race.

Mesopotamians play a huge role in early science: chronology, calendar, math, physics, and astronomy are all highly developed by 2500 B.C.E. Technology (e.g., mudbrick construction, city sanitation, hydraulics for city and farming, and so on) also has a major place in the daily life of the city-states.

Egypt also develops considerable science but is not so consistently innovative. Medicine and pharmacy are strengths, as are skill in construction and stonework. A solar calendar is developed. Jews lag in both science and technology, remaining dependent on others throughout this period.

Religion of India is a mixture of Indus civilization belief and Aryan "sky gods." The Vedas brought by the Aryans become sacred scripture for emerging Vedic Hinduism by 1000 B.C.E. Brahmin priestly castes are co-rulers with the warriors who conquer North India and impose Aryan rule. South India is not conquered, but is strongly influenced by Vedic beliefs. At the end of the period, Buddhism begins to gain ground rapidly among all Indians and has an enormous impact on philosophy as well as theology.

South Asian art largely reflects the religious mythology, as it does elsewhere until modern times. Much has been lost to the climate. Some sculpture and minor arts survive from ruins of Indus valley towns. Stone temples and carvings survive in limited numbers; the extensive sacred literature is entirely oral into the first centuries C.E., when the Vedas, Upanishads, and other Hindu and Buddhist epics that date in oral form from 1700–500 B.C.E. are first written.

Indians master metalworking (weapons, utensils) early, progressing rapidly through the Bronze Age to the Iron Age by 1000 B.C.E. Mathematics are especially important, navigation arts are well developed, and engineering skills enable them to erect massive temples and fortresses. Lack of written data hinders detailed knowledge of Indian science in this era.

Chinese religion is conditioned by ancestral continuity; honor of lineage is all-important, with gods playing relatively minor roles. There is no state theology, but the emperor supposedly enjoys the "mandate of heaven" to rule and serves as high priest. At the end of the period, the Confucian ethical and philosophical system, which will be a substitute for supernatural religion for educated classes, is beginning. The peasant majority goes on with superstition-ridden Dao.

Chinese arts in several formats take on lasting features during the Zhou Dynasty: bronzes, landscape painting, nature poetry, ceramics, silk, and pagoda architecture. Language arts are highly developed, despite difficulties of ideographic language. Reverence for education and for the aged is already apparent. The supreme importance of the family is continually emphasized in this patriarchal society.

Metal technology is well advanced in China: the Bronze Age commences by 3000 B.C.E., and iron is introduced, probably from India, by the 600s. Shang bronzes are the finest ever cast, while the Zhou Dynasty sees major improvements in agricultural productivity and weaponry. Copper coins circulate; lacquerware and silk processing are major home industries.

# PART TWO

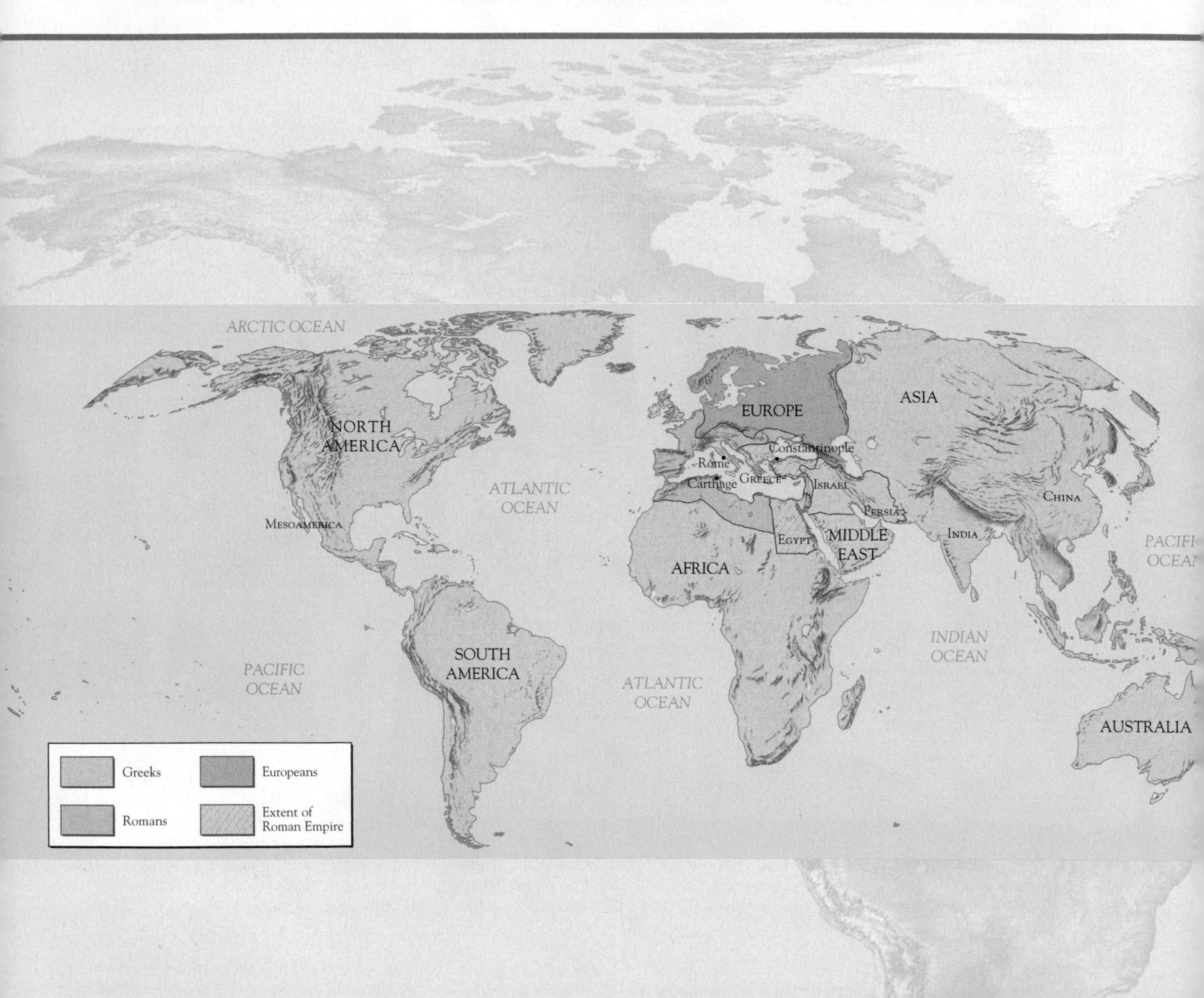
ARCTIC OCEAN
NORTH AMERICA
MESOAMERICA
ATLANTIC OCEAN
EUROPE
ASIA
Constantinople
Rome
Carthage
GREECE
ISRAEL
PERSIA
EGYPT
MIDDLE EAST
INDIA
CHINA
PACIFIC OCEAN
AFRICA
SOUTH AMERICA
PACIFIC OCEAN
ATLANTIC OCEAN
INDIAN OCEAN
AUSTRALIA
Greeks
Europeans
Romans
Extent of Roman Empire

# Classical Mediterranean Civilizations, 500 B.C.E.–800 C.E.

WHY DO WE use the word *classical* to identify the thousand-year epoch from 500 B.C.E. to roughly 800 C.E.? In the eastern Mediterranean and the East and South Asian river valley civilizations, this period saw an impressive cultural expansion and development, especially in philosophy, the arts, and language. The monuments and methodologies created then served as benchmarks for many centuries for the Mediterranean, Indian, and Chinese peoples. Some have even endured to the present day. For example, the use of the architrave and exterior columns to lend both dignity and accessibility to the facade of public buildings (such as the Parthenon shown in Chapter 8) has persisted through 2,500 years in Western architecture.

The two other early centers of civilization—Mesopotamia and the Nile valley—did not undergo similar expansion. In Egypt, the heritage of 2,000 years of cultural and political sovereignty was eroded by invaders from both Asia and Africa. After about 500 B.C.E., Egypt was under foreign masters and became ever more peripheral to the world's affairs. Somewhat similar was the fate of Mesopotamia, where ecological damage intensified the negative effects of the Persians' decision to locate their chief cities elsewhere. The once-blooming fields surrounding cities such as Uruk and Lagash have long since been reduced to stark desert.

A hallmark of the Classical Age was the larger territorial size of the civilized societies and their more pronounced cultural attractions for the nomadic barbarians on their fringes. Urban centers were both more numerous and more important. Economic sophistication was evident in the expanded long-distance trade for the more numerous upper classes and in the more refined instruments of payment and credit employed by the merchants. For example, the beginning of the letter of credit was introduced in China to facilitate merchants' exchanges. Social strata were more differentiated and more complex than in the ancient age, and social tensions more evident. Wars were fought on a much larger scale and provided the impetus for much development of government.

Knowledge of the natural world (that is, science) made great strides in certain fields, such as physics, but was paltry in many others, such as geology. Technology, on the other hand, remained primitive in an age of easy access to slave labor. Supernatural and salvationist religions, especially Christianity, came to play an ever-increasing part in daily life after about 300 C.E. in the Mediterranean basin.

In this part of our book, we look at the classical civilization of the Mediterranean and western Europe, established first by the Greeks and then expanded and modified by the Romans. (We will turn to the classical age in South and East Asia in Part Three.) Chapters 7, 8, and 9 outline the history of the Greeks. Although we note the Greeks' debts to their Mesopotamian and Egyptian predecessors, our emphasis is on the remarkable two centuries between 500 and 300 B.C.E. In Chapters 10 and 11 follows the story of the rise and accomplishments of the Roman Empire between about 500 B.C.E. and 200 C.E., as well as its decline and transformation, and the beginnings of medieval Europe, between about 200 and 800 C.E.

*The function of the ruler is to use his best endeavors to make his subjects happier.*
Socrates

# 7 The Greek Adventure

Geography and Political Development

The Mycenaean Civilization

Early Hellenic Civilization

Athens and Sparta
Early Athens
Athenian Democracy
Spartan Militarism

The Persian Wars

The Peloponnesian War

The Final Act in Classical Greece

| | |
|---|---|
| c. 2000–c. 1100 B.C.E. | Mycenaean Age |
| c. 1900–c. 1300 B.C.E. | Minoan civilization on Crete |
| c. 1100–c. 800 B.C.E. | Dark Age |
| c. 800–c. 300 B.C.E. | Hellenic civilization |
| c. 500–c. 325 B.C.E. | Classical Age in Greece |
| c. 300 B.C.E.–100 C.E. | Hellenistic civilization |

The small, rocky peninsula in the eastern Mediterranean Sea that is now called Greece proved to be the single most important source of later civilization in the Western world. In this unpromising landscape emerged a vigorous, imaginative people who gave later human beings a tradition of thought and values that is still very much alive.

The history of the ancient Greeks can be divided into three epochs:

1. The *Mycenaean Age* lasted from about 2000 B.C.E. to the conquest of the Greek peninsula by invaders in the 1100s.
2. The *Hellenic Period* extended from the time of Homer to the conquest of the Greek city-states by the Macedonians in the mid-300s. It includes the Classical Age, when Greek philosophical and artistic achievements were most impressive.
3. The *Hellenistic Age* was the final blossoming of Greek cultural innovation, lasting from about 300 B.C.E. to the first century C.E. During this age, emigrant Greeks interacted politically and intellectually with other peoples to produce a hybrid culture that was extraordinarily influential on the arts and science of both Western and Asian civilizations.

We will look now at the political and social aspects of the Mycenaean and Hellenic periods, and then we will focus on intellectual and artistic developments in Chapter 8. In Chapter 9 we will examine the Hellenistic era.

## Geography and Political Development

More than most societies, Greece was shaped by its geography. It is the tip of the European mainland that gradually sank beneath the Mediterranean many tens of thousands of years ago, leaving only the tops of a high mountain range as islands in the Aegean and eastern limits of the Mediterranean. Greece has little suitable land for large-scale farming, no broad river valleys, and no expansive level plains. No place in modern Greece is located more than eighty miles from the sea. Dozens of protected harbors and bays can be found all along the coast. From an early time, the Greeks became expert sailors, and ships and shipping have been a major part of their livelihood since ancient days. The mountains of the peninsula make overland travel there difficult, and it has almost always been easier to travel and trade by sea than by land.

This geography also encouraged political fragmentation. The people in each valley and river basin developed their own separate sense of community and identity, much as the people of the valleys of our own Appalachians did. Greeks grew up thinking of themselves first as residents of a given place or town and only secondarily as sharing a common culture and language with the other inhabitants of the peninsula. This would be a critical weakness in the development of a united Greek nation.

## The Mycenaean Civilization

The first Indo-European speakers to enter the peninsula came about 2000 B.C.E. as stock-raising nomads from the eastern European plains. By about 1600, they had become sedentary, and some of them lived in fair-sized towns, notably *Mycenae* on the eastern side of the Peloponnesus (see Map 7.1 inset). The people of this epoch are known as the **Mycenaeans,** and the first few hundred years of Greek civilization are called the Mycenaean Age.

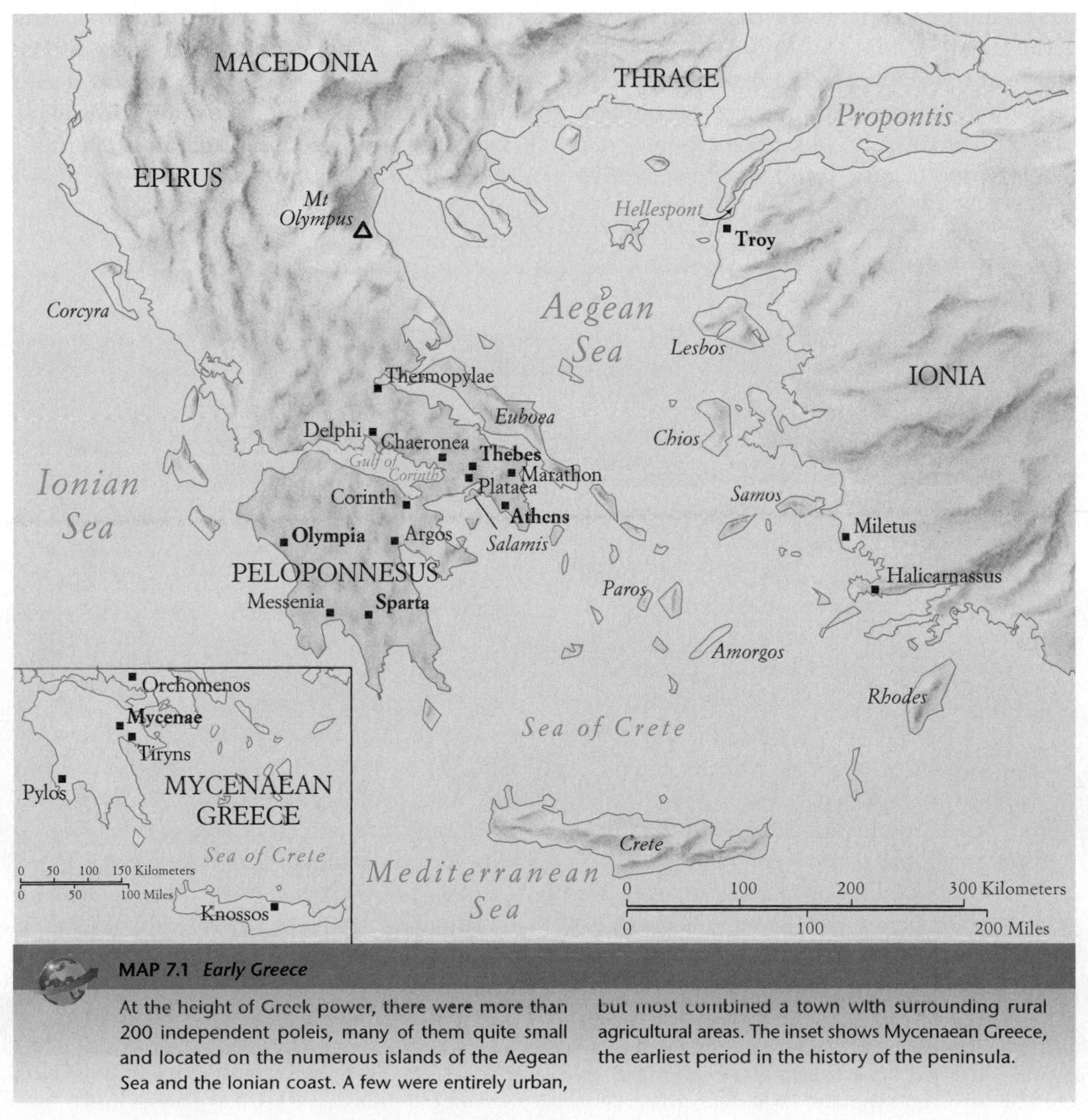


MAP 7.1 *Early Greece*

At the height of Greek power, there were more than 200 independent poleis, many of them quite small and located on the numerous islands of the Aegean Sea and the Ionian coast. A few were entirely urban, but most combined a town with surrounding rural agricultural areas. The inset shows Mycenaean Greece, the earliest period in the history of the peninsula.

Our knowledge of this period comes largely from archaeological excavations and from the ***Iliad*** and the ***Odyssey,*** two epics of ancient Greece written by the magnificent poet **Homer** in the eighth century B.C.E. The *Iliad* deals with the Mycenaeans' war against the powerful city-state of Troy, and the *Odyssey* tells of the adventures of the hero Odysseus (Ulysses) after the war (see Arts and Culture). For a long time, historians believed that the Trojan War was simply a fiction created by a great poet about his ancestors. But thanks to archaeology, we know that there actually was a Troy and that it was destroyed about the time that Homer indicates—about 1300 B.C.E. Whether it was destroyed by the Greeks or not, we do not know, but there is no reason not to believe so. Ancient Troy, now a great pile of rubble, was situated on a hill commanding the entrance into the straits called the Hellespont. Much evidence indicates that the Greek towns, led by Mycenae, were engaged in commercial rivalry with Troy throughout this period and may well have made war on their nearby enemy.

The Mycenaean civilization was guided by the model of one of its trading partners and rivals: Crete. This large island supported an urbanized civilization of its own, dating back to at least 1900 B.C.E. Historians and archaeologists call the Cretan culture **Minoan** after Minos, the mythical king of Crete. The Minoan towns, led by *Knossos* on the northern coast (see Map 7.1 inset), were masters of a wide-ranging maritime empire, including coastal Greece, by about 1600 and had much influence on the civilizing of the Greeks.

The Minoans taught their pupils too well in some ways, however, and about 1400 the warlike Mycenaeans turned on their teachers and destroyed much of the island settlements, aided by either volcanic explosions or earthquakes. By about 1300, the high Minoan civilization was in ashes, and the island of Crete ceased to play an important role in Mediterranean affairs.

The Mycenaeans themselves seem to have engaged in extensive internal warfare among the competing towns. These wars weakened them sufficiently that they fell to a new wave of nomads from the north, the *Dorians*. From about 1100 B.C.E. to about 800, the culture of the Greek peninsula declined, so much so that this period is called the *Dark Age*. Not only did arts and crafts decline, but even the ability to write seems to have been largely lost during these centuries. Were the Dorians to blame, or did the Mycenaeans simply fight one another to mutual exhaustion and destruction, as many experts think? The

Yann Arthus-Bertrand/Corbis

**Ruins of Troy.** This aerial view of the mound where ancient Troy once sat shows the partly reconstituted city walls and the stadium (lower center). Destroyed many times both before and after the Mycenaean Age, the rubble covers the entire hillside and in places is the hill itself.

ARTS AND CULTURE

## Odysseus and the Cyclops

**The Homeric hero** Odysseus (Ulysses) served as one of the chief role models for the ancient Greeks. He embodied in an epic work of literature, the *Odyssey,* the qualities of craftiness and effective action that the Greeks considered most commendable in a man.

One of Odysseus's most formidable challenges came when he and his shipboard companions found themselves at the mercy of the dreadful one-eyed giant, the Cyclops. The Cyclops invited the sailors to land on his island and then entertained himself by dismembering and devouring the Greeks two at a time. Then the sly Odysseus devised his counterblow:

I, holding in my hands an ivy bowl full of the dark wine stood close up to the Cyclops and spoke out:

"Here, Cyclops, have a drink of wine, now you have fed on human flesh, and see what kind of drink our ship carried. . . ."

Three times I brought it to him, and gave it him, three times he recklessly drained it, but when the wine had got into the brain of the Cyclops, then I spoke to him, and my words were full of beguilement.

[The Cyclops falls asleep.]

I shoved the sharp pointed beam underneath a bed of cinders, waiting for it to heat. . . . [W]hen the beam of olive-wood, green as it was, was nearly at the point of catching fire and glowed, terribly incandescent, then I brought it close up from the fire and my friends about me stood fast. . . .

They seized the beam of olive, sharp at the end, and leaned on it into the eye [of the now sleeping giant], while I from above, leaning my weight on it twirled it . . . and the blood boiled around the hot point, so that the blast and scorch of the burning ball singed all his eyebrows and eyelids, and the fire made the roots of his eye crackle. . . .

He gave a giant, horrid cry and the rocks rattled from the sound. . . .

[The now-blinded Cyclops attempts to capture the Greeks by feeling for them, but they escape his wrath by suspending themselves beneath sheep that walk past him to the waiting boat.]

When I was as far from the land as a voice shouting carries, I called aloud to the Cyclops, taunting him:

"Cyclops, in the end it was no weak man's companions you were to eat by violence and force in your hollow cave, and your evil deeds were to catch up with you, and be too strong for you, ugly creature, who dared to eat your own guests in your own house, so that Zeus and the rest of the gods have punished you."

### *Analyze and Interpret*

What qualities of character does this anecdote reveal as admired by the Greeks?



**History Now™**

***To read more from the* Odyssey, *point your browser to the documents area of* HistoryNow.**

answer is unclear. What is clear is that the formerly urban civilization reverted to a rural, much less sophisticated level during the Dark Age.

## Early Hellenic Civilization

Starting about 800 B.C.E., the Greek mainland slowly recovered the levels of civilization created during the Mycenaean Period and then went on to far greater heights.

During and after the Dark Age, the institution of the ***polis*** (plural, *poleis*) gradually developed. In Greek, *polis* means the community of adult free persons who make up a town or any inhabited place. In modern political vocabulary, the word is usually translated as "city-state." A polis could be almost any size. It is thought that Classical Athens, the largest and most powerful, had almost 300,000 inhabitants at its peak (about the size of our present-day Buffalo, New York), whereas the smallest were scarcely more than villages. At one time the Greek mainland and inhabitable islands (all told, about the size of Maryland) were the home to more than 200 poleis. Each thought of itself as a political and cultural unit, independent of every other. Yet each polis also thought of itself as part of that distinct and superior family of peoples calling themselves Greek.

The polis was much more than a political-territorial unit. It was the frame of reference for the entire public life of its citizens and for much private life as well. The mutual interdependence of the citizenry was exhibited in different ways. A sense of common life and shared destiny was promoted by governmental policies and tech-

**Mycenaean Gold Goblet.** This fifteenth-century B.C.E. vessel was used for ritual drinking at the banquets that were an important part of Greek noble society.

niques. The inherent superiority of the local format of governing for the public welfare was taken for granted, even when these ways might differ sharply from one polis to its nearest neighbor. Citizenship was greatly prized, and by no means was everyone who lived in a polis a full citizen. Women were entirely excluded from political life. There were many resident aliens, who were excluded from citizenship, as were the numerous slaves. Normally, only free males of twenty years of age or more possessed full civil rights. That meant that as much as 80 percent of the population might be excluded from political life because of their gender, age, or social status.

Each large polis had more or less the same economic and demographic design: a town of varying size, surrounded by farmland, pasture, and woods that supplied the town with food and other necessities. In the town lived artisans of all kinds, small traders and import–export merchants, intellectuals, philosophers, artists, and all the rest who make up a civilized society. Life was simpler in the countryside. Like all other peoples, most Greeks were peasants, woodcutters, ditch diggers, and all of those others of whom formal history knows little except that they existed.

## Athens and Sparta

The two poleis that dominated Greek life and politics in the Classical Age were Athens and Sparta. They were poles apart in their conceptions of the good life for their citizens. Athens was the center of Greek educational, artistic, and scientific activity as well as the birthplace of political democracy. Sparta was a militaristic, authoritarian society that held the arts and intellectual life in contempt and dreaded the extension of freedom to the individual or the community. Eventually, the two opposites came into conflict. Interestingly, it was the artistic, philosophical, and democratic Athenian polis that provoked the unnecessary war that ultimately ruined it.

In general, four types of government were known to the Greeks:

1. A **monarchy** is rule by a single person, a king or equivalent (either sex) who has the final word in law by right. Most of the poleis were monarchies at one time or another, and many of them apparently began and ended as such.
2. An **aristocracy** is rule by those who are born to the leading families and thereby are qualified to rule, whether or not they are particularly qualified in other ways. Aristocrats are born to the nobility, but not all nobles are born aristocrats.
3. An **oligarchy** is rule by a few, and almost always the few are the wealthiest members of society. Many poleis were ruled by an oligarchy of landlords whose land was worked by tenant farmers.
4. A **democracy** is rule by the people, almost always by means of majority vote on disputed issues. Voting rights in executive and legislative acts are limited to citizens, and in the Greek poleis, this meant freeborn adult males.

Additionally, the Greek word *tyranny* originally meant rule by a dictator who had illegally seized power. That person might be a good or bad ruler, a man or a woman.

### Early Athens

Athens went through all of these forms of government in the period after 750 B.C.E., when we begin to know something definite about its history. The original monarchy was gradually forced aside by the aristocrats, who ruled the polis in the seventh and early sixth centuries. The aristocrats gave way in the 500s to oligarchs, some of whom were nobly born and some of whom were rich commoners. The most important oligarch was Solon, who ruled in the early sixth century. When the polis faced a social and economic crisis generated by lack of agrarian land, the other oligarchs gave him supreme power to quell the discontent. Solon responded by establishing a constitution that struck an uneasy balance between the desires of the wealthy few and the demands of the impoverished and indebted masses. Neither group was satisfied, however, and the contest soon resumed.

Eventually, an aristocratic tyrant named Pisistratus succeeded in making himself the sole ruler and made certain important concessions to the common people to gain their support for his plan to start a new monarchic dynasty with his sons as his successors. But the sons were not nearly as clever as their father and were swept from power by rebellion in 510 B.C.E.

Courtesy of American School of Athens

**RECONSTRUCTED TRIREME.** This reconstruction was done by Greek university students in the 1980s after careful study of many contemporary vase paintings. Besides sails on two masts, it bears the three rows of oars that give the boat its name. These vessels were used for trade and piracy, indiscriminately.

The winner of the ensuing free-for-all was **Cleisthenes,** an aristocrat and the true founder of the Athenian democracy. Cleisthenes believed that the people should have the last word in their own government, both because it was just and because he believed it was the best way to keep civil peace.

## Athenian Democracy

Cleisthenes (ruled 508–494 B.C.E.) in effect gave away his tyrannical powers to a series of political bodies that were unprecedentedly democratic in character: the *ekklesia, boule,* and *deme.* The *ekklesia* was the general "town meeting" of all free male Athenians, called on an ad hoc basis to make critical decisions affecting the future of the polis. All could speak freely in an attempt to win over the others; all could be elected to any office; all could vote at the meetings of the ekklesia in the center plaza of Athens below the Acropolis hill.

The *boule* was a council of 500 citizens who were chosen by lot for one-year terms. It served as a day-to-day legislature and executive, making and implementing policy under the general supervision of the ekklesia. The boule and its officers supervised the civil and military affairs of the polis and carried out many of the functions of a modern city council. All male citizens could expect to serve at least one term on it.

The *deme* was the basic political subdivision of the polis. It was a territorial unit, something like a modern precinct or ward, but smaller in population. Each deme was entitled to select a certain number of boule members and was represented more or less equally in the officers of the polis.

To enforce the will of the majority without resort to bloodshed and possible civil war, Cleisthenes introduced the idea of *ostracism,* or the "pushing out" of a citizen who would not conform to the will of his neighbors. An ostracized person must go into exile and lost all rights of

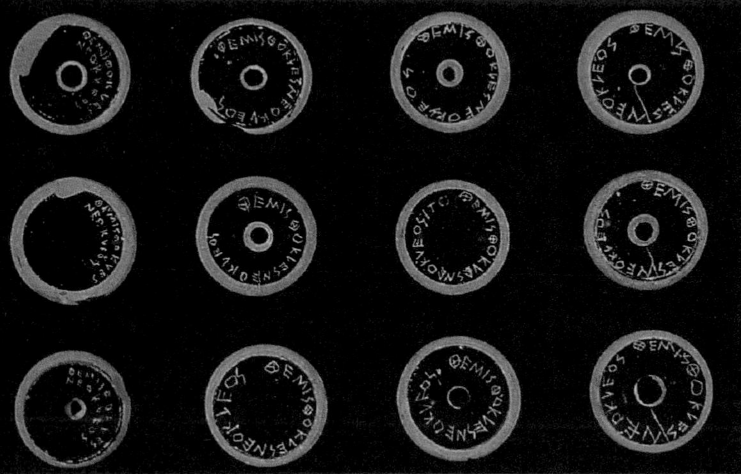

American School of Classical Studies at Athens: Agora Excavations

**Ostraka Shards.** Each year the citizenry of Athens was allowed to vote to ostracize any of their colleagues. The ballot was a ceramic token inscribed in advance with a name (top) or a piece of broken pottery (above). If someone received a predetermined number of votes, that person was expelled from the polis. How did this relate to the creation of a political democracy?

citizenship for a certain length of time, normally ten years. So attached were the Greeks to their poleis that some preferred to kill themselves rather than submit to ostracism.

Of all the Athenian political institutions, democracy has attracted the most attention from later history. Americans tend to think of political democracy as a natural and normal way to govern a state, but in actuality, until the twentieth century, democracy was a very abnormal system of government. It was talked about a good deal but was not put into practice outside the West and in only a limited way within it. A great many modern countries still give only lip service to the idea of democracy, and sometimes not even that. The idea that the ordinary man or woman was capable of governing wisely and efficiently was quite daring when first introduced. After the initial democracy failed in Athens, as it did after about a century, it was so discredited that after the fourth century B.C.E. it was not resurrected as a legitimate and practical system of government until the eighteenth century C.E.—2,200 years later!

How many other poleis became democracies at some time? The answer is not clear, but under the strong pressure of powerful Athens, probably quite a few adopted similar governments between 500 and 400 B.C.E. But even within Athens (as well as everywhere else), there was strong resistance to the idea that did not cease until democracy had been abandoned and condemned as "the rule of the mob." Ironically, it was the democratic leadership in Athens that created the conditions that allowed their opponents to win out.

## *Spartan Militarism*

By about 500 B.C.E., Sparta differed from Athens in almost every possible way, although the two were originally similar. The Spartan polis, located in the southern Peloponnesus about eighty miles from Athens, was a small city surrounded by pastoral villages. As the population grew in the 700s, the Spartans engaged in a bloody territorial war, the **Messenian Wars,** with their nearest Greek neighbor, Messenia, and finally won. The defeated people were reduced to a state of near slavery *(helotry)* to the Spartans, who from this point on became culturally different from most other Greeks. The most striking example of their divergence was their voluntary abdication of individual freedoms. During the 600s, the Messenians rebelled again and again, and as a result the Spartans made themselves into a nation of soldiers and helpers of soldiers so that they could maintain their endangered privileges.

Sparta's economic needs were largely met by the captive helots. They worked the fields and conducted the necessary crafts and commerce under close supervision. The Spartans themselves devoted their energies to the military arts. Male children entered a barracks at the age of seven and were allowed only sufficient free time thereafter to ensure that another generation of Spartan warriors would be born of Spartan mothers.

Unlike other Greeks, the Spartans held the arts in contempt and rejected individualism as being unworthy of them. Public life was expressed in total obedience to the state, which was headed by a group of elected officers called *ephors,* under the symbolic leadership of a dual monarchy. This strange combination seems to have worked satisfactorily into the 300s.

What did the other Greeks think of Sparta? One might think they would detest such a regime, but on the contrary, most Greeks admired the Spartan way of life, especially its undoubted self-discipline, courage, rigid obedience, and physical vigor. Even many Athenians thought the Spartan way was superior to their own and envied the single-minded patriotism displayed by the Spartans in all their public affairs.

Despite its military nature, Sparta was a conservative and nonaggressive state. The Spartan army was so large and so feared that after about 600, Sparta rarely had to use it in war. Sparta actually became a peaceable polis and directed all of its attention to keeping the political status quo within its own borders and, so far as possible, outside them.

## The Persian Wars

Throughout the early fifth century B.C.E., the foreign policy interests of Athens and Sparta more or less coincided. Both were primarily concerned with maintaining their independence in the face of foreign threats. These threats originated from imperial Persia, which had expanded rapidly in the 500s, as we described in Chapter 4. They took the form of two Greco-Persian wars.

The First Persian War ended with an Athenian victory. The Persian emperor Darius I was faced with spreading rebellion among some of his subjects, Greeks on the Turkish coast (Ionia). When he attempted to subdue them, Athens went to their aid. Determined to punish the Athenians for their boldness and wishing in any case to expand his domains still further, Darius sent an army across the Aegean Sea to the Greek mainland. Aided by brilliant generalship, the Athenians were waiting and defeated the Persian expedition at the battle of Marathon in 490.

Erich Lessing/Art Resource, NY

**GREEK VASE.** This vase shows a fight between a Greek hoplite (infantryman) and his Persian cavalry enemy. A product of the late fifth century B.C.E., it was probably a commemoration of the great Greek triumph over Darius's troops.

The Second Persian War (480–478 B.C.E.) was fought on both land and sea and resulted in an even more decisive Greek victory. Ten years passed before Darius's successor, Xerxes, could find time to take up the challenge. This time, not only Athens but several other Greek poleis assisted the defensive effort. Spartan troops lived up to their fame at the battle of Thermopylae in 480 and again at the decisive defeat of the Persian force at Platea in 479. The Athenian navy completely routed the larger Persian fleet at Salamis and established Athens as the premier naval force in the eastern Mediterranean.

By the end of these **Persian Wars,** the Greeks had decisively turned back the attempts of the Asian empire to establish a universal monarchy over the Mediterranean basin. It was in retrospect a crucial turning point for Western civilization. The idea that, at least in the long run, the common man was capable of perceiving the common good and of ruling wisely and effectively toward that end—the belief in democracy—would have been submerged, perhaps indefinitely, beneath the acquiescence to the rule of the privileged, for the privileged.

## The Peloponnesian War

The Greeks' victory in the Persian Wars did not lead to harmony among the Greek poleis, however. Athens used its new prestige and growing wealth to form a group of unwilling satellites (the Delian League) among the nearby poleis. The democrats, led by the great orator **Pericles,** were now in command and were responsible for bringing Athens into conflict with Corinth, one of Sparta's Peloponnesian allies. Corinth asked Sparta for help, and when the Spartans warned the Athenians to back down, Pericles responded with war. Athens was embarked on an imperial adventure, with the goal of extending its authority over not only Greece but the surrounding coasts as well. It turned out to be a fatal error, although Pericles did not live to realize it. (See Law and Government.)

With its strong navy, Athens believed that it could hold off the land-based Spartans indefinitely while building up its alliances. These allied forces would then be able to challenge the Spartan army on Sparta's home territory.

For most of its duration, the **Peloponnesian War** (431–404 B.C.E.) was an intermittently fought deadlock. Neither side was able to deal the other an effective blow, and long truces allowed the combatants to regain their strength. After Pericles died in 429, the Athenian democrats argued among themselves while the antidemocratic forces within the polis gained strength. An ambitious attempt to weaken Sparta by attacking its allies on Sicily went astray and turned into disaster. Finally, in 404 the Spartans obtained effective naval aid (from Persia!) and defeated the Athenians at sea. After that, it was a simple matter for their large army to lay siege to Athens and starve it into surrender.

The Peloponnesian War ended with a technical victory for Sparta, but actually it was a loss for all concerned. The Spartan leadership was not inclined or equipped to lead the squabbling Greeks into an effective central government. Defeated Athens was torn between the

LAW AND GOVERNMENT

# Pericles (c. 495–429 B.C.E.)

**ONE OF THE GREAT FIGURES** of democratic politics, the Greek general and democratic statesman Pericles (c. 495–429 B.C.E.) is also a prime example of the dangers of the imperial vision. Desiring originally to bring his fellow Greeks into a mutually supportive defensive alliance against Persia, by the end of his career he was viewed as the chief villain of an imperialist scheme to reduce all Greeks to Athenian subjects. The seduction of power granted by the democratic majority proved too much for him. Pericles was born into an aristocratic Athenian family and received a traditional education in rhetoric under Anaxagoras, a leading philosopher. Committing himself to the emergent democratic party in the hurly-burly of polis politics, he rose quickly to prominence. At the age of thirty-two, he became chief magistrate (the equivalent of mayor). For the next thirty-three years, Pericles was the leading political figure in Athens, a feat that speaks volumes not only about his abilities but also about his sensitivity to popular opinion in a city where every free male saw himself as a co-maker of policy.

**PERICLES.** This idealized bust of Pericles—here a Roman copy—was created just after his death.

In power, Pericles showed himself sincerely committed to the extension of democracy, although he was not above using a bit of demagoguery to retain his grip on popular affection. By appealing to the emotions of the populace, he reformed the political and judicial systems to allow greater participation by the ordinary citizen. He instituted a system of paying jurors and established new courts to hear criminal cases, thus lessening the powers of the aristocratic judges. He raised the payment citizens received for attending the great debates in the agora in the town's center where questions of policy were decided. By paying for jury duty and attendance at the assemblies, Pericles ensured that ordinary men could take time off from work to participate.

Pericles was a master orator, and his speeches were deemed masterpieces of effective rhetoric. Only one has come down to us: the famous Funeral Oration given near the end of his life to commemorate the Athenians who had fallen in the Peloponnesian War. Here is a sample:

> Our constitution is called democracy because power is in the hands not of a minority but of the whole people. . . . No one, so long as he has it in him to be of service to the state, is kept in political obscurity because of poverty. . . . [We] do not say that a man who takes no interest in politics is minding his own business; we say that he has no business here at all. . . .

Under Pericles, Athens became the center of the extraordinary intellectual and artistic life that is always associated with the term "Classical Age." But in relations with other Greek city-states, Pericles was not so fortunate. (It was he who transformed the Delian League from a defensive alliance against the Persians into an instrument of Athenian empire building.) It was he who spent the forced contributions of the other members of the Delian League on the beautification of Athens and the expansion of its navy, which was then used to blackmail the other Greeks into submission to the will of Athens. And, it was Pericles who refused to take the warnings of the Spartans seriously when they sought to protect their allies against Athenian aggression. This made war inevitable, and the Peloponnesian War wrecked all hopes of Greek unity. It ended in a decisive defeat for Athens and for the Periclean policy of expansion. The following epoch saw the beginning of the long decline of classical Greece, rendering the poleis into mere provinces of new and alien empires.

## *Analyze and Interpret*

The Peloponnesian War was originally popular among the Athenians. Although he had severe reservations, Pericles felt himself duty bound as democratic leader to follow their will. What does this tell you of the nature of democracy? What limits, if any, would you put on the exercise of authority in government by the majority?

**History Now™**

***To read all of Pericles' Funeral Oration, point your browser to the documents area of* HistoryNow.**

discredited democrats and the conservatives favored by Sparta.

## The Final Act in Classical Greece

After the war, the Greeks fought intermittently among themselves for political supremacy for two generations. Whenever a strong contender emerged, such as the major polis of Thebes, the others would band together against it. Once they had succeeded in defeating their rival, they would begin to quarrel among themselves, and the fragile unity would break down once again. The Greek passion for independence and individuality had degenerated into endless quarrels and maneuvering for power with no clear vision of what that power should create.

To the north of Greece were a people—the Macedonians—whom the Greeks regarded as savage and barbarian, although they were ethnically related. Philip of Macedonia, the ruler of this northern kingdom, had transformed it from a primitive society into an effectively governed, aggressive state. One by one he began to absorb the northern Greek poleis, until by the 340s he had made himself the master of much of the mainland.

After much delay, the Athenians finally awoke to the danger and convinced Thebes to join with them against the menace from the north. In the battle of Chaeronea in 338 B.C.E., however, Philip's forces defeated the allies. The former city-states became provinces in a rapidly forming Macedonian Empire. Chaeronea was the effective end of the era of polis independence and of the Classical Age. From the latter part of the fourth century B.C.E. onward, Greeks were to be almost always under the rule of foreigners to whom the daring ideas of polis democracy were unknown or inimical.

## Summary

The Greeks were an Indo-European nomadic group who entered the Greek peninsula around 2000 B.C.E. and were gradually civilized, in part through the agency of the Minoans on Crete. By 1200, the Greeks had developed to the point that they were able to conquer their former overlords and mount an expedition against Troy. Following the coming of the Dorian invaders, however, Greece entered a Dark Age of cultural regression. This period ended around 800, and the Greeks began their ascent to high civilization that culminated in the Classical Age from 500 to 325 B.C.E.

In the Classical Age, the democratically led polis of Athens became the most important of the more than 200 city-states. Athens evolved through the various types of Greek government to achieve a limited but real democracy in the early fifth century. Through its commercial and maritime supremacy, it became the richest and most culturally significant of the poleis.

Victory over the Persians in the two Persian Wars encouraged democratic and imperialist Athens to attempt dominion over many other city-states. Its main opponent was militaristic and conservative Sparta, and the two came to blows in the lengthy Peloponnesian War, which ended with a Spartan victory in 404. Seventy years later, the real winner, however, proved to be the semibarbaric Macedonians, whose king Philip took advantage of the continuing intra-Hellenic disharmony and warfare to impose his rule over all of Greece at the battle of Chaeronea.

## Identification Terms

Test your knowledge of this chapter's key concepts by defining the following terms. If you can't recall the meaning of certain terms, refresh your memory by looking up the boldfaced term in the chapter, turning to the Glossary at the end of the book, or working with the flashcards that are available on the *World Civilizations* Companion Website: **http://history.wadsworth.com/adler04/**.

| | | | |
|---|---|---|---|
| aristocracy | *Iliad* | Mycenaeans | Pericles |
| Cleisthenes | Messenian Wars | *Odyssey* | Persian Wars |
| democracy | Minoan | oligarchy | *polis* |
| Homer | monarchy | Peloponnesian War | |

## Test Your Knowledge

Test your knowledge of this chapter by answering the following questions. Complete answers appear at the end of the book. You may also take this quiz interactively and find even more quiz questions on the *World Civilizations* Companion Website: **http://history.wadsworth.com/adler04/**.

1. The Mycenaean period of Greek history
   a. preceded the Dark Age.
   b. followed the Dark Age.
   c. was the high point of Greek political culture.
   d. saw the Greeks ruling several other peoples.
   e. contributed a great deal to Dorian culture.
2. In Homer's poem, Odysseus (Ulysses) conquered the Cyclops by
   a. killing him in a duel.
   b. blinding him.
   c. tricking him to jump into the sea.
   d. tying him down while he was sleeping.
   e. convincing him to drink a poisonous concoction.
3. The polis was a
   a. warrior-king.
   b. community of citizens.
   c. commercial league of merchants.
   d. temple complex.
   e. barracks for military youth in Sparta.
4. Athenian women were
   a. secluded within the home after marriage.
   b. considered the collective sexual property of all free Greek males.
   c. excluded from any political role.
   d. viewed as the more talented of the two sexes.
   e. considered vital to the production of strong warrior offspring.
5. Which of the following was *not* a form of classical Greek government?
   a. Monarchy
   b. Hierarchy
   c. Oligarchy
   d. Democracy
   e. Aristocracy
6. In early Greece, a tyranny was rule by
   a. the professional military.
   b. a small group.
   c. a person who had illegally seized power.
   d. a person who was evil and vicious.
   e. groups of individuals born into leading families.
7. The founder of the Athenian democracy was
   a. Solon.
   b. Cleisthenes.
   c. Pisistratus.
   d. Plato.
   e. Homer.
8. The critical factor in transforming Sparta from an ordinary polis into a special one was
   a. the war against the neighboring Messenians.
   b. the invasions by the Persians.
   c. the war against Athens.
   d. its commercial rivalry with Athens.
   e. its use of slavery to advance its standing as a polis.
9. The battle of Marathon was fought during the
   a. Peloponnesian War.
   b. Second Persian War.
   c. Siege of Sparta.
   d. Athenian navy's rout of its enemy at Salamis.
   e. First Persian War.
10. The Peloponnesian War is best described as
   a. a struggle between Athens and the rest of Greece.
   b. the start of an era of Spartan dictatorship in Greece.
   c. the discrediting of the Athenian democracy as leader of Greece.
   d. the establishment of Persian influence in Greece.
   e. simply one more in a line of victories for Athens.

## InfoTrac College Edition

Visit the source collections at

**http://infotrac.thomsonlearning.com**

and use the Search function with the following key terms:

Greece history Peloponnesian War Sparta

## Wadsworth History Website Resources

Visit the World History Resource Center at **http://history.wadsworth.com/world** for a wealth of general resources and the *World Civilizations* Companion Website at **http://history.wadsworth.com/adler04/** for resources specific to this textbook.

## HistoryNow

Enter *HistoryNow* using the access card that is available for *World Civilizations*. *HistoryNow* will assist you in understanding the content in this chapter with lesson plans generated for your needs. In addition, you can read the following documents, and many more, online:

Pericles, Funeral Oration Homer, the *Odyssey*

*For we are lovers of the beautiful, yet simple in our tastes; we cultivate the mind without loss of manliness.*

The Funeral Oration of Pericles

# 8 Hellenic Culture



| | |
|---|---|
| 776 B.C.E. | First Olympic Games |
| c. 600–c. 500 B.C.E. | Pre-Socratic philosophers |
| c. 500–c. 300 B.C.E. | Classical Age |
| 470–399 B.C.E. | Socrates |
| c. 427–347 B.C.E. | Plato |
| 384–322 B.C.E. | Aristotle |

The Greek Contribution to the creation of Western civilization equals that of the Jews and the Christians. In addition to the concept of democratic government, the Greek achievement was exemplified most strikingly in the fine arts and in the search for wisdom, which the Greeks called *philosophy.* In both areas, the Greeks developed models and modes of thought that have remained appealing for twenty-five centuries and are still valid and inspiring today. The overall achievement of the Greeks during their great age is summed up in the term *Hellenic culture,* and we turn now to some of its specific aspects.

## Philosophy: The Love of Wisdom

The Greek word *philosophy* means "love of wisdom." The Greeks used it to mean examination of the entire spectrum of human knowledge and not just the narrower fields of inquiry, such as the rules of logic, to which it is conventionally limited today. The ancient Greeks can legitimately be called the originators of philosophy. Of course, other peoples before them had attempted to work out the nature and meaning of human existence, but none pursued their studies so systematically or with as much boldness and imagination as the Greeks, starting in the sixth century B.C.E.

As we know it, Greek philosophy can be divided into two periods: the Pre-Socratic period and the Classical Age. The first period extends from the earliest surviving philosophical writings around 600 B.C.E. to the life of Socrates (470–399 B.C.E.). The second period extends from Socrates through about 300 B.C.E.

### *Pre-Socratic Philosophy*

The Pre-Socratic philosophers devoted themselves mainly to investigating the origin and nature of the physical world. They were less concerned with truth or how to distinguish between good and evil than philosophers would be in the Classical Age and later. The first philosopher whose writings have survived (in fragmentary form) is Thales of Miletus, who lived in about 600. During the

**SOCRATES.** Plato tells us that his master Socrates was considered extraordinarily ugly, but his mastery of logic and beauty of expression made all those who heard him forget everything else about him.

Museo Archeologico Nazionale, Naples/Alinari/Bridgeman Art Library

500s, a group of thinkers attempted to analyze the physical nature of the world and make it intelligible. Some of their ideas have had a lively influence on philosophy ever since, and some of their general concepts, such as Democritus's vision of the atom as the fundamental building block of nature, have been proven correct in modern times.

The greatest contribution of the Pre-Socratics was the concept of law in the universe. Unlike any previous thinkers, these Greeks believed that what happened in the physical cosmos was the result of laws of causation and thus understandable and predictable on a purely natural level. They did not deny the gods or the powers of the gods, but they did not look to the gods as the normal and usual causes of phenomena. Instead, they conceived of what we now call *natural law*—a set of phenomena in nature that, when properly understood, explain why certain things occur.

Two of the greatest of the Pre-Socratics were Anaximander and Hippocrates. Anaximander was the father of the theory of natural evolution of species—long before Darwin ever dreamed of it. He also thought the physical universe had no limits. He conceived of it as boundless and constantly expanding, much as modern astronomers do. Hippocrates is best known as a founder of scientific medicine, but curing people was really only incidental to his intellectual interests. First and foremost, he wished to teach people to observe the life around them. He was the first great **empiricist** in the natural sciences, arriving at his general theories only after careful and prolonged observation of those aspects of the world that could be weighed and measured.

## *The Classical Age: Socrates, Plato, and Aristotle*

Socrates (470–399 B.C.E.) was the first philosopher to focus on the ethical and epistemological (truth-establishing) questions that have haunted the thoughtful since the dawn of creation. Like most of the Classical Age figures, he concentrated on human rationality rather than on physical nature. He was more interested in "How do I know?" than in "What is to be known?"

Systematic questioning is the essence of the *Socratic method,* which teachers have used ever since. Socrates believed that intellectual excellence could be acquired. He would systematically question his young disciples, allowing them to take nothing for granted. He challenged them to examine fearlessly and justify everything before taking it for truth.

Our knowledge of Socrates comes not from him directly but from the numerous works of his pupil and admirer, Plato (427–347 B.C.E.), who joined his master in Athens a few years before Socrates' suicide. Socrates, Plato tells us, was accused of poisoning the minds of the youth of Athens by his irreverent questions, which greatly irritated the conservative elders of the polis. Brought to trial, he was found guilty and given the choice of exile or suicide. A true Greek, Socrates chose suicide rather than being cast out of his chosen community.

Plato defended his teacher from the unjust accusation, but nevertheless he was a different thinker from his predecessor. Plato tried above all to solve the problem of how the mind can experience and recognize Truth and ultimate reality (see the description of his **metaphor of the cave** in the Patterns of Belief box). He concluded that it cannot, beyond a certain superficial point. He also ventured

## Plato's Metaphor of the Cave

**THE CLASSICAL GREEKS** were the ancient world's great pioneers into the question of how the mind works. Seeing Man as a part of the natural world, they wished to know as much as possible about him. Of the great trinity of Greek classical philosophers, Plato distinguished himself by wrestling with the eternal question: How does the human brain penetrate appearances to attain Reality? Our impressions of the outer world originally are entirely dependent on sensory data: what can be touched, or smelled, or seen and heard. How, then, can we formulate ideas that go beyond the specific detail of particular objects that the senses perceive? Or is there any idea, beyond the specific object? Could there be an abstract Idea of, say, a chair? Or only of *this* chair, with rounded legs and a straight back made of walnut wood? Most particularly, are there ideals of Truth, Beauty, and Goodness that lie behind the weak and unstable versions of those virtues that human experience can conceive of?

Plato thought that such abstractions existed and were far more perfect in their nature than any specific version of them that the senses might perceive. But he also believed that most people were unable to apprehend such Ideals in anything like their pure forms. Few men and women possessed the mental powers and the desire to allow them to penetrate beyond mere appearances into Truth and Reality.

Seeking to convey his meaning, Plato came to write the metaphor of the cave, which has remained one of the best-known philosophical anecdotes in history. Most people, he said, were like prisoners condemned to existence in a dark cave. They peered constantly through the dim light trying to make out what was happening around them:

> Imagine the condition of men living in a cavern underground, with an entrance open to the daylight and a long passage entering the cave. Here they have been since childhood, chained by the leg and by the neck, so that they cannot move and can see only what is directly in front of them. At some higher place in the cave, a fire burns, and between the prisoners and the fire is a track with a parapet built in front of it, like a screen at a puppet show which hides the performers while they show their puppets. . . .
>
> Now behind this parapet, imagine persons carrying along various artificial objects, including figures of men and of animals in wood or stone or other material which project above the parapet. . . . The prisoners, then, would recognize as reality nothing but the shadows of those artificial objects.

Our sense impressions, unenlightened by wisdom, deliver us into a prison of ignorance, where men mistake blurred shadows for reality.

Plato further says that if a prisoner were released and allowed to go out into the unaccustomed sunlight, he would, of course, be blinded by the light and utterly confused. But this would change as he became accustomed to his new condition; his ability to see this huge new world would gradually increase:

> He would need, then, to grow accustomed before he could see things in the upper world. At first, it would be easiest to make out shadows, and then the images of men and things reflected in water, and later on the things themselves. After that, it would be easier to watch the heavenly bodies and the skies by night, looking at the light of the moon and stars rather than the sun and the light of the sun in daytime.

Plato drew his conservative political and social conclusions from these beliefs about the nature of Reality and human ability to perceive it. He thought that relatively few people would ever be released from the cave of ignorance and shadow-play. Those who did attain to the upper world of Truth and slowly and with difficulty worked through the ever-higher, more accurate stages of Reality should be given the leadership positions. They deserved to be leaders not only because they merited power and prestige, but because they—and not the masses who remained in the cave—were able to make proper choices for the welfare of the whole society. Plato, who lived through the Peloponnesian War, remained a convinced antidemocrat all his life.

### *Analyze and Interpret*

Does the metaphor employed by Plato explain to you his point about the difference between Reality and appearances? In what way does this story link with Plato's contempt for democratic politics?

Source: F. M. Cornford translation, *The Republic of Plato* (Oxford: Oxford University Press, 1941). By permission of Oxford University Press.

**HistoryNow™**

***To read more of Plato's* Republic, *point your browser to the documents area of* HistoryNow.**

into an analysis of politics as it should be (in the *Republic*) and as it existed (in the *Laws*). Plato was an antidemocrat, and his arguments have often been used by conservatives and monarchists ever since. During his lifetime, Greece was in constant turmoil, which probably influenced his strongly conservative political views.

Aristotle (384–322 B.C.E.) was a pupil of Plato (who founded the first Academy in Athens), but he, too, differed sharply from his teacher. Aristotle is the nearest equivalent to a universal genius that Greece produced. His interests included practically every field of science yet known, as well as the formal analysis of thought and actions that we now know as philosophy.

Most of what Aristotle wrote has survived and can fill a whole shelf of books. His best-known works are the *Politics, Physics,* and *Metaphysics,* but he was also a first-rate mathematician, an astronomer, the founder of botany, and a student of medicine. So great was his renown in the medieval world that both European Christians and Arab Muslims referred to him simply as "the Master." The Christian scholars thought of him as a sort of pagan saint, who lacked only the light of the Revelation as outlined in their scripture. The learned Muslims thought of him as the greatest natural philosopher and man of science the world had yet produced.

Greek philosophy was marked at all times by the strong sense of self-confidence that the philosophers brought to it. The Greeks believed that humans were quite capable of understanding the cosmos and all that lived within it by use of reason and careful observation. In that sense, the Greeks were the world's first real scientists. They were not overawed by the gods but created the gods in their own image and never resorted to supernatural powers to explain what could be explained by law. The knowledge the Greeks sought in their "love of wisdom" was that which was reachable by the unaided human intellect.

## Greek Religion

Not all Greeks were able to find the truth they needed in philosophy. Probably the large majority of people were not exposed to or were unable to follow the complex reasonings of the philosophers. They turned instead to religion. Like most of the other peoples we have discussed, the Greeks were polytheistic. Their important gods included Zeus, the father figure; Hera, the wife of Zeus; Poseidon, god of the seas; Athena, goddess of wisdom and also of war; Apollo, god of the sun; and Demeter, goddess of fertility.

Yet Greek religion was rather different from the religions we discussed earlier, in at least two ways. First, from early times, the Greek gods were less threatening and less omnipotent than other peoples' gods. Second, the Greeks never created a priestly class or caste, but used their priests only as informal leaders of loosely organized services. After about 500 B.C.E., the priests and priestesses receded more and more into the background, and many of the gods themselves became mere symbolic figures. Even the great deities whom all Greeks recognized, such as Zeus, were not taken too seriously by the educated. They were certainly not feared in the way that the Sumerians feared their gods or the Jews feared Yahweh. The gods of the classical Greeks were creatures molded in their own image, with the foibles and strengths of men.

How did Greek religion compare with our modern ideas of religion? It differed in many ways. It was not revealed to humans by a supernatural authority. It did not stem from a holy book. It made no attempt to impose a system of moral conduct on the faithful. The Greeks never had a centralized ecclesiastical authority or a hierarchy of priests. Greek religion after the fifth century was largely a series of rituals, something like our American celebration of the Fourth of July. Participating in the rituals was an act of polis patriotism as much as worship and had little or nothing to do with the ethics and morality of private life.

As with the Chinese Confucians, it was *this world* that engaged the educated Greeks and provided the frame of reference for defining good and evil. Normally, the educated people did not speculate about the afterlife and saw no reason to fear it. By the opening of the Classical Era, most of them apparently no longer believed in immortality, if they ever had. For them, philosophy increasingly took the place once occupied by supernatural religion. The acts of the gods came to be viewed as myths, stories that served a useful moral purpose in educating the people to their duties and responsibilities as good citizens of the polis and as good Greeks.

In addition to the defining figures whom all Greeks recognized, each polis had its own local deities. For example, Athena was the patron goddess of the city of Athens as well as the goddess of war. The cults of these local gods were forms of civic celebrations in which everyone joined, even those who did not believe in supernatural forces or immortal life. The Greeks did not believe that the gods controlled human destiny in any detailed fashion. Behind and above the gods was an impersonal and unavoidable Fate, a force that could not be successfully defied by either humans or gods.

In Classical philosophy, the ideal of the **golden mean,** the middle ground between all extremes of thought and action, was a particular attraction. The Greeks distrusted radical measures and tried to find that which embraced the good without claiming to be the best. They believed that the person who claimed to have the perfect solution to a problem was being misled by **hubris,** a false overconfidence. The gods were "setting him up," as we might put it, and disaster was sure to follow. The wise person always kept this in mind and acted accordingly.

Adherence to the golden mean should by no means be seen as a sign of humility. The Greeks were not humble by nature but were quite willing to take chances and to stretch their intellectual powers to the utmost. They believed passionately in the human potential, but they did not defy Fate or the gods without expecting to be punished. The great tragedies written by Sophocles (c. 497–406 B.C.E.) are perhaps the most dramatically effective expressions of this expectation, particularly his trilogy about the doomed ***Oedipus Rex*** and his vain struggle to avoid the fate that lay in wait for him (see the Arts and Culture box).

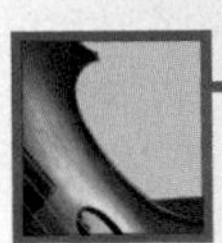

ARTS AND CULTURE

## *Oedipus Rex*

**GREEK CLASSICAL TRAGEDY** was built on the conviction that an inexorable Fate had the final word in the life of human beings. Fate might be evaded or even defied for a time, but sooner or later, its commands would be obeyed. In this view (which it seems all educated Greeks held), Man himself assured the punishments and retributions that descended on him by reason of his fatal moral shortcomings.

One of the most compelling renditions of this principle is told in the three plays of the fifth century B.C.E. Athenian playwright Sophocles that tell the story of Oedipus, whose hubris (false overconfidence) in believing that he could defy the destiny prescribed for him led him into ultimate tragedy. It is also a sharp departure from the classical Greek misogyny, in that the daughter of Oedipus is revealed as the source of true wisdom and a pillar of strength for her suffering father.

Oedipus was the son of King Laius of the city-state of Thebes. Because the oracle of Apollo had prophesied that this boy would one day kill his father and disgrace his mother, King Laius ordered his newborn son to be taken out to a hillside and left to die of exposure. Unknown to the sorrowing parents, a shepherd happened by and rescued the child, taking him to the court of Polybius, the king of neighboring Corinth, who was childless. Brought up as the heir to Corinth's throne, Oedipus was told of the prophecy one day and fled the city, as he loved Polybius and thought him to be his natural father. Wandering through Greece, Oedipus happened to encounter Laius on the road. As a result of a foolish argument over precedence, the hot-tempered Oedipus killed his true father. Some days later, he came to Theban territory and challenged the monster Sphinx who had terrorized the city for many months, devouring anyone who could not solve her riddle: "What goes on four feet in the morning, two at noon, and three in the evening?" Oedipus replied, correctly, "Man, in life's three stages."

As a prize for freeing the city, Oedipus was married to the widowed queen Jocasta, his own mother, thus fulfilling the prophecy of years ago. With Jocasta he raised two sons and two daughters before the awful secret was revealed. In horror and shame, Jocasta committed suicide. Oedipus in despair blinded himself and was driven from the palace by public outrage to a life of exile. Only his daughter Antigone accompanied him.

The story is told in the play *Oedipus Rex,* which was first produced in Athens about 429 B.C.E. at the height of the Peloponnesian War and the same year as the death of Pericles. The story of the unhappy ex-king is continued in Sophocles' *Oedipus at Colonus*. Colonus is a place near Athens where Antigone helps her father comprehend what has happened and prepare for death. Antigone is the protagonist of the final play in the cycle named after her, in which the heartbreaking tragedy of a man who thought he might triumph over Fate by his superior wisdom and willpower is brought to an end. The moral that Sophocles wished to teach is that intelligence and will alone are not sufficient for a good life. Compassion and consideration, qualities that Oedipus lacked until his last days, but then learned from his daughter, are more important. Antigone, the faithful daughter whose love overcomes her revulsion and alone of the children elects to share her father's misery, is the real heroine of the piece.

### *Analyze and Interpret*

Does Oedipus's end seem too harsh? Why do you think the Greeks, so much advanced in thought over earlier peoples regarding moral choices, retained their strong condemnation of incest? How does all-powerful Fate reveal itself in this story?

**History Now™**

***To read selections from* Oedipus Rex*, point your browser to the documents area of* HistoryNow.**

## THE ARTS AND LITERATURE

The classical Greeks gave at least three major art forms to Western civilization: (1) drama, a Greek invention that arose in the 600s, presumably in Athens, as a sort of pageant depicting scenes from the myths about the gods and their interventions in human affairs; (2) lyric poetry, originating in the pre-Classical Era and represented best by surviving fragments from the work of Sappho, a woman who lived on the island of Lesbos in the 600s; and (3) "classical" architecture, most notably the temples scattered about the shores of the Mediterranean by Greek colonists, as well as on the Acropolis in Athens and in many other poleis. Besides these forms, which they originated, the Greeks excelled in epic poetry (represented by the *Iliad* and *Odyssey*); magnificent sculpture of the human form and face at a level of skill not previously approached; dance, which was a particular passion for both men and women; fine ceramic wares of every sort; and painting, mainly on ceramic vessels and plaques.

The particular strengths of Greek pictorial and architectural art were the harmony and symmetry of the parts with the whole; the ability to depict the ideal beauty of the human form, while still maintaining recognizable realism in their portrayals; and the combination of grace and strength balanced in vital tension. The models established during the Classical Age have remained supremely important to artists of the West ever since. Most plastic forms of European art are derived from these models, at least until the twentieth century.

Most Hellenic art was anonymous. The artist worked as a member of the polis, contributing what he did best to the benefit of his fellow citizens, just as others contributed by paying taxes or working on the roads. We do know that the main Athenian temple, the **Parthenon,** was erected by order of Pericles during the Peloponnesian War as a shrine to Athena, the patron of the city. Within the Parthenon stood an enormous marble statue of Athena made by Phidias, the most famous of all the Athenian sculptors.

Greek literature took several distinct forms. Poetry of all types was very highly developed from the time of Homer (eighth century) onward. Much has been lost. The outstanding names besides Sappho are Hesiod, Euripides, Aeschylus, Sophocles, Aristophanes, and Pindar. Most of these were dramatists as well as poets. The great trio of

Acropolis, Athens, Greece/Alinari/Bridgeman Art Library

**THE PARTHENON.** Atop the hill in central Athens called the Acropolis, the Parthenon was designed to be the center of Athenian spiritual life and its most sacred temple. Constructed in the fifth century B.C.E., the now-empty interior once featured a massive statue of the patroness of the city, the goddess of both war and wisdom, Athena. It was then seriously damaged by an explosion of gunpowder during a seventeenth-century war between Turks and Italians. The style of its building has been praised and imitated throughout the world.

Euripides, Aeschylus, and Sophocles created the tragic form, while Aristophanes is the first noted comic playwright.

Drama was one of the Greeks' most popular arts, and the plays that have survived represent possibly one-hundredth of what was written in the fifth and fourth centuries. Playwrights and actors were originally amateurs, but they soon became professionals. Every citizen was expected to take part occasionally in the dramatic productions, which soon came to be a central element in the numerous civic celebrations that marked the life of the polis.

Dance and music were intensely cultivated by both professionals and amateurs. Greek literature of all types refers abundantly to both arts, and they are depicted as well in Greek painting and sculpture. The god Dionysius was particularly connected with orgiastic, out-of-doors dancing, accompanied by reed and string instruments, which celebrated the god's triumphant return from the dead. His cult was also instrumental in creating the first drama.

The ancient Greeks prized craftsmanship. They evidently learned much of their skill in ceramics and metalwork from the Egyptians and the Minoans, but they improved on their models. Greek ceramics were in great demand throughout the Mediterranean world, and Greek ships frequently set sail loaded with wine jugs, olive oil vessels, and other household utensils made from clay, as well as fine work. Much of the Athenian population evidently worked for the export trade, making objects of clay, metal, leather, and wood.

## Society and Economy

Greece was a country of small farmers, who labored long and hard to make a living from the stony, unrewarding soil. Many pastured a few goats and sheep as well. Both olives and wine grapes supplemented grain farming and inshore fishing.

The Greek polis was usually a small place (Athens was the exception), and its inhabitants were generally racially and culturally homogeneous. The center of the polis was a town of moderate size, with a population of 10,000 to 20,000 as a rough average. It supported all of the usual urban trades and crafts. Most urban adults debated about and participated in civic culture and politics, which were matters of wide concern.

The general level of education among the urban Greeks of the Classical Age was remarkably high and was not approximated again in the Western world until much later. Neither the Romans nor the medieval Europeans came close. Yet, like politics, education was also basically an urban phenomenon. Most of the country people must have been illiterate.

Educated and property-owning Greeks thought of manual labor as being beneath the dignity of the free, and assigned as much of it as possible to their slaves. But the majority could not afford to keep slaves and had to do the work themselves. Machinery of even primitive design was unknown. Most Greeks active in the labor force were free men and women, working for themselves or for a wage in small-scale enterprises.

### Slavery

It has frequently been remarked that Athenian democracy was built on and supported by a large population of slaves. This statement is true, but it may not be as damning as it seems at first. Certainly, slaves were numerous (perhaps 30 percent of the total population). Both Greeks and foreigners could be enslaved, usually as the result of debt. Slaves were normally not abused by their masters, and many slaves were prized workers and craftsmen who worked for pay but were not free to go off at will to other employment. Many of these men and women were employed directly by the state, and most of the rest were domestic servants of all types, rather than independently productive workers. The kind of plantation agriculture that depended on coerced labor was not found in Greece because of the unpromising terrain. The individual slaveholder usually did not own more than one or two men or women and used them more as servants and assistants than as laborers. Only in the polis-owned silver mines near Athens were slaves abused as a matter of course, and these slaves were normally criminals, not debtors. Still, slaves did not enjoy civil rights in politics, nor could they serve in the military.

The freeman and his family generally lived very simply. He made a modest income working for others or for the polis (all poleis usually had an ongoing public works program) or as an independent shopkeeper. His wife normally worked inside the home, performing the usual domestic duties.

### Gender Relations

The degree of freedom accorded to women in classical Greek society has been a topic of intense debate in recent years. Historians agree that women were generally excluded from any effective exercise of political and economic powers, and that the Greeks were the Western originators of *misogyny,* the distrust and dislike of women by men. An authority on Greek women says that they neither had nor sought political power but worked through their husbands or fathers or sons. Any women who took political action did so only under certain closely defined conditions, and unless they did so at least ostensibly on behalf of a male relative, they and those around them came "to a bad end." The great tragic heroines such as Electra, Antigone, and Medea and the mythological heroines such as Cassandra and Artemis are examples of women who met such a fate.

Greek males' treatment of the other sex exhibits some interesting variations. Another modern scholar notes that the antifemale prejudice exhibited in later Greek literature is not present in the Homeric period. The women of Sparta were free and equal with their menfolk. Spartan women allegedly shared the sexual favors of their men, regardless of marriage. The men were so frequently away in the field or in barracks that both they and the government saw this practice as essential to Sparta's survival. Because our knowledge of Sparta comes exclusively from non-Spartan literary sources, it is impossible to know whether this very unusual attitude was actual fact or another example of the antidemocratic Athenian authors' admiration for their powerful neighbor.

In contrast, we have a good deal of definite information about Athens. Respectable Athenian women were limited to the home and could make only rare public excursions under the guardianship of servants and slaves. Their work was closely prescribed for them: management of the household and supervision of children and servants. Within the four walls of the home, one or two rooms were reserved for their use. In multistoried houses, these rooms were normally upstairs, but in any house, they would be in the back, away from the street. This segregation was the Greek equivalent of the Muslim *harem* or the Hindu *purdah,* and it fulfilled the same purpose: keeping women, as the valuable possession of men, away from the prying eyes of nonfamily members and all sexual temptations. Poor urban women undoubtedly had more freedom to leave the home and enter the workplace unescorted, as did rural women, who had a great many essential tasks to perform daily, some of them outdoors.

Not only was the Athenian woman excluded from politics, but she was also legally and customarily inferior to men in terms of property holding, custody of children, marriage and divorce, and business enterprises. A freeborn, native Athenian woman was recognized as having some civic rights, but her citizenship was limited and very different from that enjoyed by males. Its main advantage was that Athenian citizenship could be passed on to (male) children through her.

Prostitution was common in classical Greece. The upper rank of women who engaged in it were equivalent to the geisha of modern Japan. They were the ***hetaerae***—well-educated, well-paid performers who amused their clients in many nonsexual fashions as well as the essential acts of their trade.

Homosexuality seems to have been relatively common, at least among the educated, and to have been looked on as a tolerable, although somewhat disreputable, practice.

**THE CONVERSATION.** This glimpse of ordinary affairs is unusual for Greek art in that it portrays females who have no visible connection to the more often depicted male life. It is a product of the third century B.C.E.

It was viewed as particularly disreputable for the older man, because he was sometimes led to ignore his family responsibilities by a younger lover. From the glancing attention paid to the subject in the surviving literature, it is impossible to know how common such relations were, what the nonhomosexual majority thought of them, or indeed much else regarding the sexual practices of the time.

Scala/Art Resource, NY

**DISCOBOLUS.** This Roman copy of a fifth-century Greek original by the great sculptor Myron is deservedly famous for its combination of manly strength and graceful control. The athlete prepares his body for an extreme effort at tossing the heavy stone disc, one of the feats at the original Olympic Games. Competition in the nude was the norm for both Greeks and Romans.

## SPORT

The Greeks were the first people to look on the nurture of the physique (the word itself is Greek) as an important part of human life. They admired a healthy body and thought it was a duty to cultivate its possibilities. As part of this effort, they organized the first athletic events open to all male citizens. The most important was the great pan-Hellenic festival known to us as the *Olympic Games*.

According to the records, the Olympics were first held in 776 B.C.E. and then every four years thereafter in the small polis of Olympia on the west coast of the Peloponnesian peninsula. The games were originally more a religious festival than a sports event but soon became both. The best Greek athletes competed for their hometowns in foot races, chariot drives, the discus throw, weightlifting, and several other contests. Prizes were limited to honors and a crown of laurel leaves.

The games lasted for about a week and were immensely popular. They served an important function as a sort of patriotic reunion for people from all over the Greek world. After the Macedonian conquest, the games declined and then ceased for twenty-three centuries until they were revived in the late nineteenth century.

## THE GREEK LEGACY

The dimensions and lasting importance of the Greeks' bequest to Western civilization cannot be overemphasized. When the poleis fell to the Macedonians, this bequest was retained, although in diluted forms. When the Greco-Macedonian world was then itself overtaken by the all-conquering Romans a couple of hundred years later, the new masters adopted much of the Greek heritage with great enthusiasm and made it their own. In this way, the Greek style and the content of their art, philosophy, science, and government gradually infiltrated much of Europe. In the process, though, parts were lost permanently, and much of it was radically altered by other views and conditions of life.

The mixture of Greek with non-Greek produced a peculiar form of civilization that spread through much of the Mediterranean and the Near East after the Macedonian conquest and during the Roman Era. We will look at this civilization in the following chapter and see that it was very different from Hellenic civilization in many ways, but it never severed all connections with the original Greek model.

## Summary

Hellenic culture represents a high point in the history of the world. The two or three centuries embraced by the Classical Age produced a series of remarkable achievements in the fine arts and in the systematic inquiry into humans and nature that we call philosophy. In some of these affairs, the Greeks built on foundations laid by others, including the Egyptians and the Phoenicians. In other, such as drama and lyric poetry, they were pioneers. In philosophy, the mighty trio of Socrates, Plato, and Aristotle defined most of the questions that the world would ask of the universe ever since. In drama, Aeschylus, Sophocles, and Euripides played the same pathbreaking role. Poets such as Sappho and Pindar, sculptors such as Phidias, and the mostly unknown architects of the Classical Age created monuments that remain models of excellence.

In all of their efforts, the Greeks' intellectual fearlessness and respect for the powers of reason are strikingly apparent. They believed, as they said, that "Man is the measure" and that what could not be analyzed by the educated mind was probably best left alone as being unworthy of their efforts. Their legacies in intellectual and artistic activities rank with those of their predecessors, the Hebrews, in religion and with their successors, the Romans, in government and law.

## Identification Terms

Test your knowledge of this chapter's key concepts by defining the following terms. If you can't recall the meaning of certain terms, refresh your memory by looking up the boldfaced term in the chapter, turning to the Glossary at the end of the book, or working with the flashcards that are available on the *World Civilizations* Companion Website: **http://history.wadsworth.com/adler04/**.

empiricist
golden mean
*hetaerae*
hubris
metaphor of the cave
*Oedipus Rex*
Parthenon

## Test Your Knowledge

Test your knowledge of this chapter by answering the following questions. Complete answers appear at the end of the book. You may also take this quiz interactively and find even more quiz questions on the *World Civilizations* Companion Website: **http://history.wadsworth.com/adler04/**.

1. The pre-Socratic philosophers sought most of all to explain the
   a. human capacity to reason.
   b. motion of the stars.
   c. composition and laws of the natural world.
   d. reasons for the existence of good and evil.
   e. creation of the world.
2. The cave metaphor in Plato's writings refers to
   a. the need of humans to have a place of refuge from their enemies.
   b. the ability of humans to form a community.
   c. the difference between reality and falsely understood images.
   d. the importance of a stable physical environment.
   e. the desire of humans to create a stable home environment.
3. Greek religion was
   a. controlled by a powerful priesthood.
   b. the same from one end of the country to the other.
   c. filled with gods created in man's image.
   d. dominated by fear of the afterlife.
   e. centered around an ethical system of high moral conduct.

4. Hubris meant to the Greeks
   a. an unjustified sense of proud self-confidence.
   b. an excellent command of physical strength.
   c. an apparent mastery of some talent that was deceptive in nature.
   d. an attempt to defy the gods' will.
   e. the ability to understand philosophy.
5. Sophocles and Euripides are best known as Greek
   a. dramatists.
   b. poets.
   c. sculptors.
   d. painters.
   e. architects.
6. In the Greek polis, the majority of urban adults
   a. spent some time each year working in the surrounding fields.
   b. owned between five and ten slaves.
   c. allowed women more freedom than they achieved in rural areas.
   d. rented slaves occasionally from the very wealthy.
   e. participated in civic affairs as a matter of course.
7. Slavery in classical Greece was
   a. common and harsh.
   b. nonexistent.
   c. rare.
   d. common and usually mild.
   e. used mostly for obtaining farm labor.
8. The Athenian women who had more opportunity to live life as they chose were the
   a. aristocrats.
   b. mothers.
   c. unmarried girls.
   d. entertainer-prostitutes.
   e. poor urban workers.
9. The classical Olympic Games shared all but which one of these features:
   a. They were open to all male citizens.
   b. They were aimed at establishing a "pecking order" of physical strength.
   c. They were held on a regular schedule.
   d. The visitors were rewarded with honors rather than prizes.
   e. They became both religious and sporting events.
10. Which adjective is *least* appropriate for the classical Greeks?
    a. Intimidated
    b. Rational
    c. Proud
    d. Curious
    e. Creative

## InfoTrac College Edition

Visit the source collections at

**http://infotrac.thomsonlearning.com**

and use the Search function with the following key terms:

Greek mythology    Greece history    Plato
Aristotle    Socrates

## Wadsworth History Website Resources

Visit the World History Resource Center at **http://history.wadsworth.com/world** for a wealth of general resources and the *World Civilizations* Companion Website at **http://history.wadsworth.com/adler04/** for resources specific to this textbook.

## History Now

Enter *HistoryNow* using the access card that is available for *World Civilizations*. *HistoryNow* will assist you in understanding the content in this chapter with lesson plans generated for your needs. In addition, you can read the following documents, and many more, online:

Plato, the *Republic*    Sophocles, *Oedipus Rex*

*To one who asked him the proper time for taking meals, he said, "If a rich man, when you will; if a poor man, when you can."*
Diogenes the Cynic

# 9 Hellenistic Civilization



| | |
|---|---|
| 336–323 B.C.E. | Alexander the Great's reign and campaigns |
| c. 300–50 B.C.E. | Hellenistic Age in eastern Mediterranean |

The new style of civilized community and art forms created by the Greeks of the Classical Age is called *Hellenism.* After the Greeks fell to the Macedonian barbarians in 338 B.C.E., Hellenism in a diluted and corrupted form was spread into the East and Egypt by the conquerors and their Greek associates. This altered form of Hellenism is known as *Hellenistic* culture or civilization. It retained some of the values and attitudes of the classical Greek polis, but it also gradually dropped many in favor of the very different values and attitudes of the Eastern kingdoms and empires.

## Alexander and the Creation of a World Empire

After the battle at Chaeronea, which brought him mastery of the former poleis of Greece, King Philip of Macedonia was assassinated, and his young son, Alexander, succeeded to the throne. In his thirteen-year reign (336–323 B.C.E.), Alexander conquered most of the world known to the Greeks and proved himself one of the most remarkable individuals in world history. His boldness and vigor became the stuff of legend among the Greeks who fought under him. Both traits are attested to by the story Plutarch tells in the anecdote in this chapter (see the box "Plutarch on Alexander"). Alexander's break with previous military tradition regarding the status of the conqueror is also memorable, as Society and Economy describes.

At the time of his death, Philip had been organizing a large combined Macedonian–Greek army with the announced purpose of invading the huge Persian Empire. After swiftly putting down a rebellion in Thebes, Alexander continued this plan and crossed the Dardanelles in 334 with an army of about 55,000 men (very large for the times). In three great battles fought in Asia Minor, the young general brought down the mightiest empire the world had yet seen, the empire of Darius III of Persia, who was slain by his own troops after the third and decisive loss at Gaugamela in present-day Iraq (see Map 9.1).

Conquering an unresisting Egypt, Alexander then invaded the Persian heartland and proceeded eastward into

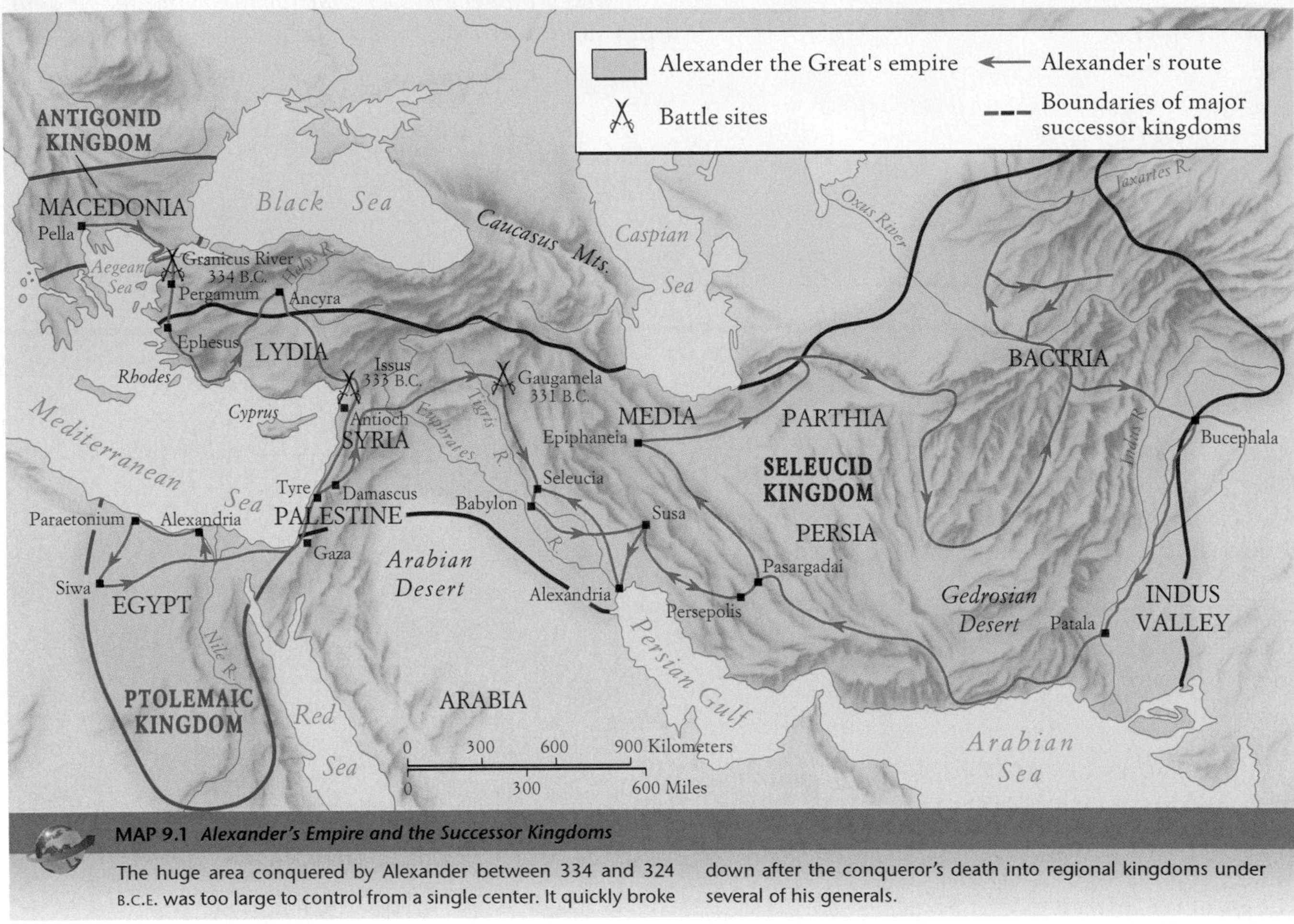


**MAP 9.1** *Alexander's Empire and the Successor Kingdoms*

The huge area conquered by Alexander between 334 and 324 B.C.E. was too large to control from a single center. It quickly broke down after the conqueror's death into regional kingdoms under several of his generals.

the unknown borderlands of India. After spending five years defeating the numerous tribal kingdoms of the Indus basin and the wild highlands to its north (present-day Pakistan and Afghanistan), his remaining troops finally mutinied and refused to go farther. In 324, Alexander led his exhausted men back to Persia. A year later, he died in Babylon at the age of thirty-three. The few years of his reign and his much-disputed view of the desirable form of imperial government would have a lasting effect on much of the world's history, as outlined in Law and Government.

## A Mixed Culture

Alexander the Great (as he was soon called) had founded the largest empire yet seen in history, but it began to disintegrate almost on the day of his death. He left an infant son by his last and favorite wife, Roxana, but the child became a mere pawn as Alexander's generals struggled to succeed him as sole ruler. (The son was eventually put to death at age sixteen by one of the contestants.) Finally, the exhausted combatants tired of the civil war and split up the vast territories conquered by Alexander into a series of kingdoms, each originally ruled by one of Alexander's generals. Collectively, these successor states in southwestern Asia and the eastern Mediterranean are called the **Hellenistic** kingdoms.

Everywhere Alexander led his armies, he founded new cities or towns, several of which bore his name. He then recruited Greeks from the homeland to come and establish themselves as a ruling group in the new cities. He encouraged them to follow his own example and intermarry with the locals. Tens of thousands of Greeks took up the invitation, leaving overcrowded, resource-poor Greece to make their names and fortunes in the countries now under Greco-Macedonian control. Inevitably, they brought with them the values they had cherished in their native land. As the conquerors, the Greeks could and did impose their ideas on the Asiatics and Egyptians with whom they had contact or intermarried.

The result was a mixed culture that blended Greek and Asiatic attitudes. A major example of this is the fate of the Greek civic community. The conquering Greeks first tried to reconstruct the polis mode of shared government and

SOCIETY AND ECONOMY

## Plutarch on Alexander: *Parallel Lives*

**Alexander of Macedonia** is known to us through several eyewitness accounts. The best biography of all, however, was written by a Greek citizen of the Roman Empire who lived several hundred years after Alexander. Plutarch wrote his *Parallel Lives* to provide the youth of Rome with examples of both Greek and Roman heroes for them to emulate. It has been a favorite ever since and includes this famous anecdote:

> Philonicus the Thessalian brought the horse Bucephalus to Philip, offering to sell him for thirteen talents of silver; but when they went into the field to try him they found him so very vicious and unmanageable that he reared up when they endeavored to mount him and would not suffer even the voices of Philip's attendants. Upon which, Alexander, who stood nearby, said, "What an excellent horse do they lose for want of boldness to manage him! . . . I could manage this horse better than the others do."

> Philip, who was a harsh father, challenged his son to prove his boast:

> Alexander immediately ran to the horse and taking hold of his bridle turned him directly toward the sun, having, it seems, observed that he was disturbed by and afraid of the motion of his own shadow. . . . Then, stroking him gently when he found him beginning to grow eager and fiery, with one nimble step he securely mounted him, and when he was seated by little and little drew in the bridle and curbed him so, without either striking or spurring him. Presently, when he found him free from all rebelliousness and only impatient for the course, he let him go at full speed, inciting him now with a commanding voice and urging him also with his heel. Philip and his friends looked on at first in silence and anxiety, till seeing him turn at the end of the course and come back rejoicing and triumphing for what he had performed, they all burst out into acclamations of applause; and his father, shedding tears of joy, kissed Alexander as he came down from the horse and in his exultation said, "O my son, look thee out for a kingdom equal to and worthy of thyself, for Macedonia is too little for thee!"

### *Analyze and Interpret*

Why might Plutarch, writing in the second century C.E., want to use Alexander as one of his *Parallel Lives* for the instruction and entertainment of Roman youth? Besides bravery and intelligence, what other characteristics of Alexander are hinted at here that would appeal to a patriotic Roman?

**History Now™**

***To read Plutarch's "Life of Alexander," point your browser to the documents area of* HistoryNow.**

interdependent community in their new homes but quickly found that this was impossible. The Easterners had no experience of the polis form of government and did not understand it. They had never governed themselves but had always had an all-powerful king who ruled through his appointed or hereditary officials and generals. Soon the ruling Greeks themselves adopted the monarchical form of government. Thus, instead of the small, tight-knit community of equal citizens that was typical of the polis of the Classical Age, a Hellenistic state was typically a large kingdom in which a bureaucracy governed at the king's command. The inhabitants, whether Greek or native, were no longer citizens but subjects—a very different concept.

Although Alexander never conquered India's heartland, the Greek invasion of the Indus plains also had lasting effects. It introduced the Indian Hindu/Buddhist world to the Western world, and from this time onward, there were direct trade contacts between India and the eastern end of the Mediterranean. The invasion also disrupted the existing political balance in northern India, opening a vacuum that paved the way for the conquering Mauryan dynasty, including the great Ashoka (see Chapter 5).

## *Greeks and Easterners in the Hellenistic Kingdoms*

The civil wars after Alexander's death resulted in the formation of three major successor kingdoms, each ruled by a former Greek general who had fought his way into that position (see Map 9.1):

1. The **Ptolemaic Kingdom of Egypt.** A general named Ptolemy succeeded in capturing Egypt, the richest of all the provinces of Alexander's empire. There he ruled as a divine king, just as the pharaohs once had. By the 100s B.C.E., the many immigrant Greeks and the Egyptian upper class had intermixed sufficiently to make Egypt a hybrid society. Many Greeks adopted the Egyptian way of life, which they found pleasant. Meanwhile, ordinary Egyptians remained exploited peasants or slaves.

LAW AND GOVERNMENT

# Alexander the Great (356–323 B.C.E.)

**ALEXANDER THE GREAT** was perhaps the most renowned of all the world's military heroes. His campaigns carried him to the farthest limits of the world known to the Greeks, and his underlings and soldiery introduced many peoples to the culture and ideas of the polis society. Of these facts there exists no substantive dispute among historians. But another side to the Alexandrine life story generates acute disagreements—namely, whether the conquering hero also had a soaring vision of human unity and equality under a single government headed, of course, by himself.

The outstanding early biographer of Alexander was the Roman Arrian, who wrote in the second century C.E. Arrian believed in a kind of divine mission begun and fulfilled in part by Alexander and then completed by Rome of his own day. His treatment of the hero was thus highly sympathetic, and he inspired many later biographers to portray Alexander as the creator of a new form of government: a tolerant community in which all citizens would share in the mutual benefits engendered by the vision of the central authority. Some think that he intended to create a world empire in which all peoples would be equal—a sort of world federation. This would have been a stunning break from previous military tradition, in which the conquerors occupy the highest rank for an indefinite period, and the conquered must abase themselves.

Pinacoteca Capitolina, Palazzo Conservatori, Rome, Italy/Index/Bridgeman Art Library

**ALEXANDER.** This marble bust of the conqueror is a Roman copy of a Greek original. It emphasizes Alexander's youthful beauty but may have been close to the reality of his appearance.

The most noted modern adherent of this view is William Tarn, whose biography of the hero was the defining one for generations of nineteenth- and twentieth-century students. Tarn saw Alexander as the political innovator of genius, anxious to overcome the tradition of brute force and exploitation in the manner of the Assyrians and replace it with a grand vision of equable treatment and opportunity for all. Other historians have seen little grounds, however, for such beliefs; because Alexander left no expression of his intents, it must remain an unresolved question.

In any case, Alexander was certainly an innovator in allowing at least the ruling families of the newly conquered peoples political and social equality with the Greco-Macedonians whom he led. This was a source of considerable dismay among them. When Alexander adopted some Asian customs, such as prostration in the presence of the ruler, his men protested so vehemently that the new ceremonies had to be dropped. There was also considerable resentment at the more or less forced mass marriages of the Greek soldiery to Asiatic women, in emulation of Alexander's own multiple marriages to the daughters of the conquered princes.

Both types of marriage were aimed at establishing lasting ties between subject and conquerors, and they were partially responsible for the Hellenizing of the East, as Alexander intended. But the emperor's own liaisons could not fulfill his hopes to establish an Alexandrine dynasty. The vast empire he had overrun in only twelve years collapsed just as quickly at his untimely death into warring fragments. After a lengthy period of manuevering for succession and dominance among the generals who had commanded Alexander's army, the all-conquering Romans gradually took over the Mediterranean portion of the empire and made clients of much of the rest. Like Arrian, they proudly saw themselves as the continuers and completers of the Alexandrine tradition.

## *Analyze and Interpret*

Why might the figure of Alexander have left so deep an impression on the non-Greek peoples he briefly ruled? And why would the Greeks themselves be less enthusiastic about his career and his legacies in government?

2. The **Seleucid Kingdom of Persia.** The Seleucid kingdom, which was the successor to most of the once-mighty empire of Darius III, reached from India's borders to the shores of the Mediterranean. It was founded by a former general named Seleucus, and, like Ptolemaic Egypt, it lasted until the Roman assault in the first century B.C.E. Many tens of thousands of Greek immigrants came here as officials, soldiers, or craftsmen, and the contact between the locals and Greeks was extensive in the western parts of the kingdom, especially Syria and Turkey. The kingdom was too large to govern effectively, however, and it began to lose pieces to rebels and petty kings on its borders as early as the 200s. By the time the Romans were invading the western areas, most of the east was already lost.
3. The **Antigonid Kingdom.** This kingdom was also founded by a general, who claimed the old Macedonian homeland and ruled part of what had been Greece as well. The rest of Greece was divided among several leagues of city-states, which vied with each other for political and economic supremacy, until both they and the Macedonians fell to the Romans in the middle 100s B.C.E.

## Society and Economy

During the Hellenistic Age, a true urban civilization, in which the towns and cities were far more important than the more numerous rural areas, came into existence for the first time since the decline of the Mesopotamian cities. Large cities—such as Alexandria in Egypt, Antioch in Syria, and Susa in Persia—dominated the life of the Hellenistic kingdoms. Like modern cities, Hellenistic towns were centers of commerce and learning with great museums, libraries, and amusement halls. One or two of them possibly had more than 500,000 inhabitants, drawn from a vast variety of ethnic backgrounds.

What was life in these cities like, and who populated them? Most of the people were free, but there were also many slaves. Lifelong slavery became more common in the Hellenistic era than it had been in the Classical Age—another example of the Eastern tradition coming to outweigh the Greek. For the first time, large groups of people were pulled into lifelong slave status, which was hereditary and passed on to their children. Even the free majority felt little sense of community, largely because they came from so many different social and ethnic groups.

Didyma, Turkey/Giraudon/Bridgeman Art Library

**Temple of Apollo at Didyma.** These massive steps led up to an even more massive hall, dedicated to Apollo by the grateful citizenry of Seleucid Ionia. Begun in the late fourth century B.C.E., the temple was not completed until the early Christian Era. Its ruins stand in modern Turkey.

On the contrary, the feeling of alienation, of being distanced from others in the psychic sense, seems to have been common. Many city people were peasants who had fled from the civil wars after Alexander's death. Many others were former prisoners of war who had been uprooted from their homes and forced into new surroundings. They had little in common with their neighbors except that they were all the subjects of the powerful rulers and their bureaucrats.

Originally, the Greeks were the governing class of the cities, but gradually they intermarried and were absorbed by the larger group that surrounded them. The Greek language remained the tongue of the cultured, but in most other respects, the Eastern way of life and thought became predominant.

### *The Hellenistic Economy*

As we have seen, Hellenistic civilization was much more urban than Greece had been during the Classical Age. The Hellenistic economy was characterized by large-scale, long-distance enterprises. Big cities like Pergamum, Alexandria, and Antioch required large-scale planning to ensure that they would be supplied with food and consumer necessities of all types. Manufacturing and commerce were common, sometimes on an impressively large scale.

Trade was carried on in all directions, even with China and Spain. The goods traded included ceramic and metal housewares, olive oil, wine, and, perhaps most commonly, grain. These items were carried by land and sea to all corners of the Near and Middle East and most of coastal Europe, as well as to India. One mercantile contract, written in what is now Somalia in Africa, has survived. It was signed by a Greek from Greece, a Carthaginian from North Africa, and a black from the African interior. In this era, the Greeks really came to the fore as tireless and daring mariners of the world's seas.

Trade with the East was carried on both through traditional overland routes and by sea. Silk now entered the Western world as the most valuable single item by weight in world commerce. The Chinese monopoly on fine silk production would not be broken until centuries later, and cloth equal to the Chinese would not be produced in the West until modern times. This and other luxury trade goods enabled the uppermost classes of the Hellenistic societies to become wealthy indeed.

Outside the cities and towns, the economy depended as ever on farming and related activities such as fruit growing, timber harvesting, beekeeping, and fishing. The plantation system of agriculture, based on large gangs of unfree labor, was introduced wherever it could flourish. In many places, small farmers were forced into debt, and the family farms that had been typical of earlier Greece, for example, gave way to some form of tenant bondage to a large landlord.

In Ptolemaic Egypt, the old system went on without change: small sharecroppers tilled the land for the great landlords, except now the lords were mostly Greeks, and the exploitation was more severe. Egypt was the wealthiest of all the successor kingdoms, and the Ptolemaic Dynasty, which ruled Egypt for three centuries until it fell to the Romans, was the envy of the other Hellenistic kings. Cleopatra, who died in 30 B.C.E., was the last of these Greek–Egyptian monarchs.

### *Social Relations*

Mainly on the basis of literary sources, historians generally agree that women's overall status gradually rose in the Hellenistic and Roman imperial eras. Of course, this statement applies more to the upper classes than to the lower ones. In the Hellenistic cities, upper-class women played an active role in business affairs, and the older prohibitions about leaving the family home seem to have faded. By the time of the Roman dominion, women in the East sometimes held positions of importance in politics, such as the queen Cleopatra. Priestesses such as the female oracles at Delphi were accorded semidivine status by their male adherents and fellow citizens. The rights of married women definitely increased. They were no longer regarded as the property of husbands and fathers, but as independent legal personages.

Women also had more opportunities for education in this age. The founder of the Epicurean philosophy (see "Philosophy: Three Hellenistic Varieties"), for example, admitted females to his school on the same criteria as males. Illiteracy was the rule for women outside the urban upper classes but was apparently somewhat reduced even there. Even physical exercise, always a justification for segregating males and females in classical Greece, was now opened to some females as well.

## Religion

In form and content, the Hellenistic religions that evolved after the conquests of Alexander were different from both the Greek religion of the Classical Age and the earlier religions of China and India. In form, the new religions were frequently modeled on Greek beliefs: worship was often conducted outdoors, and the priests played a relatively minor role and were accorded little prestige. In content, however, Eastern contributions far outweighed those of the Greeks. Despite the prestige of the conquering Greeks, the worship of the traditional

Greek gods such as Zeus and Athena soon died out completely in the East.

Why did this happen? Recall that participation in the cults of the traditional Greek gods did not imply a specific theology, or an ethical viewpoint, or even an emotional attachment to the gods. The rites were civic ceremonies of a homogeneous community rather than a moral guide to living well or a promise of salvation. As such, they held no appeal to non-Greeks, who neither understood the patriotic meaning of the ceremonies nor found in them any moral or emotional support.

As time passed, instead of the natives' adopting the Greek religion, the Greek immigrants turned more and more to the native cults, which were allowed full freedom under Greek rule. These religions *did* offer some promise of eternal life or earthly prosperity. They provided some concrete emotional support, and they also responded to human longing for security and a guide to right and wrong.

In the second century B.C.E., these Eastern religions became immensely popular among many of the Eastern Greeks, especially the lower classes. Three of the most important were the cults of Isis, goddess of the Nile and renewal; Mithra, god of eternal life; and Serapis, the Egyptian god of the underworld and the judge of souls. All three shared certain characteristics, which allow them to be grouped as **mystery religions;** that is, they demanded faith rather than reason as the ultimate justification for their teachings. To believers, who followed the instructions of the powerful priests, they promised eternal life. Life would overcome death, and the afterworld would be an infinitely more pleasant place than this one. These deities were universal gods who had final jurisdiction over all people everywhere, whether individuals recognized the god or not. The stage was thus being set for the triumph of the greatest of the mystery religions: Christianity.

## Philosophy: Three Hellenistic Varieties

The mystery religions were especially appealing to the less educated and the poor. These people were the most likely to suffer the alienation and desperation that were often part of life in the large, impersonal Hellenistic towns. For them, the promise of a better life in the next world would be the true reason for enduring the hardships of living at all.

Members of the better-educated upper class were more inclined to look askance at such "pie in the sky." They turned instead to philosophies that seemed more realistic and did not demand a difficult leap of faith. In addition, they sought a concept of human community that could satisfy them as the polis ideal faded.

Three philosophies in particular attracted the Hellenistic Greeks. The first to appear was **Cynicism,** which emerged as an organized school in the middle 300s but became more popular later. Its major figure was the famous Diogenes, who reportedly toured the streets of Athens with a lantern in full daylight, searching for an honest man. Cynicism has come to mean something very different from what it signified originally. Cynicism was the opposite of what is now called *materialism.* In his teachings, Diogenes called for a return to absolute simplicity and a rejection of artificial divisions, whether political or economic. Relatively few people could adapt to the rigid poverty and absence of egotism that the Cynics demanded, but the philosophy nevertheless had a great impact on Hellenistic civilized life, in much the same way that St. Francis would influence thirteenth-century Christianity.

Casa di Lucrezio Frontone, Pompeii, Italy/Roger-Viollet, Paris/Bridgeman Art Library

**Venus and Mars.** Frescoes humanizing the divinities were a favorite mode of art in the Hellenistic Age. This one shows the wedding of Venus and Mars, as the Romans called their epitomes of feminine beauty and virile manhood. It was painted on an interior wall in Pompeii, Italy.

The second philosophy was **Epicureanism,** named after its founder, Epicurus, who taught at his school in Athens during the early third century B.C.E. (After the Macedonian conquest, Athens continued to be the undisputed intellectual center of the Greek world for many years despite its loss of political importance.) Like *cynicism,* the word *epicurean* has undergone a major transformation of meaning. Epicurus taught that the principal good of life was pleasure, which he defined as the avoidance of pain. He was not talking about physical sensation so much as mental or spiritual pleasure and pain. He believed that inner peace was to be obtained only by consciously rejecting the values and prejudices of others and turning inward to discover what is important to you. Epicureanism resembles Buddhism in certain respects, and some think that this is no coincidence. Epicurus may have had knowledge of the Indian philosophy, which was spreading rapidly in the East during this period. Epicureanism led to political indifference and even withdrawal, because it said that political life led to delusive excitement and false passion: better to ignore the public affairs of the world, and focus on finding your own serenity.

The third philosophy, **Stoicism,** captured the largest following among the Hellenistic population. It was the product of a freed slave, a Phoenician named Zeno who had been brought to Athens around 300 B.C.E. The name *Stoicism* came about because Zeno taught at the *stoa,* a certain open place in the city's center. Zeno emphasized the brotherhood of all men and disdained the social conventions that falsely separated them. He taught that a good man was obliged to participate in public life to help the less fortunate as best he could. Whether he was successful or not was not so important as the fact that he had tried. The Stoics (again, the word has undergone a huge change in meaning from ancient times to the present) thought that it was not whether you won or lost but how you played the game that mattered. Virtue was, and had to be, its own reward.

The Stoics made popular the novel concept of an overarching natural law that governed all human affairs. One law for all, which was implanted in the brains and hearts of all humans by the fact of their humanity, was the Stoics' guiding principle. This concept was to gain a following among the Romans after they came into the eastern Hellenistic world. Stoicism eventually became the normal belief of the Roman ruling class. It was a philosophy of noble acts, guided by lofty ideals of what a human being could and should be. It strongly emphasized the necessity of service to one's fellows and the recognition that all are essentially equal under the skin.

## Science and the Arts

### *The Pursuit of Science*

The common belief that Greek science had its heyday during the Classical Age is erroneous. The pursuit of scientific knowledge did not really come into its own until the Hellenistic Period. The most important areas of inquiry were biology, astronomy, geography, physics, and math. The medical arts were particularly prominent during this period. The third and second centuries B.C.E. produced several major contributors to medical knowledge and theory. The biggest single center of science was in the great city of Alexandria, Egypt, where the rich Ptolemaic kings established and supported many research centers. The contemporary world's largest library and museum there were destroyed much later by fire and earthquake (see the Science and Technology box).

Why did science flourish in the Hellenistic period? For one, the Greek habit of rational and logical thought was especially useful in the sciences. Aristotle, who had tutored young Alexander, insisted on the necessity of careful observation of phenomena before attempting to explain their causes. His successors at the *Lyceum,* the famous school he founded in Athens, proceeded along those lines and obtained worthwhile results in several fields.

Another of the chief stimuli to scientific work was the new exposure of the Greeks to the Babylonian mathematicians and astronomers/astrologers, thanks to the conquests of Alexander. Now in the Hellenistic Age, the Greek world was brought for the first time into extensive contact with the cumulative knowledge of the Middle East. Scientists profited from the work done by Mesopotamian, and especially Babylonian, scholars during the previous three centuries.

The work in astronomy done at this time would stand without serious challenge until the sixteenth century C.E. Among the outstanding astronomers were Aristarchus of Samos (310–230 B.C.E.) and Hipparchus of Nicaea (260–190 B.C.E.). Aristarchus proposed a **heliocentric** model of the universe in which the Earth revolved around the sun. It was attacked by Hipparchus and others, however, and in the second century C.E., a later astronomer named Ptolemy picked up the theory of a **geocentric** universe (that is, centered on the Earth). The geocentric model became the standard wisdom of astronomy for the next 1,500 years, until Copernicus questioned it. The most important figures in geography were the Greek Eratosthenes (c. 276–c. 194 B.C.E.) and Strabo (c. 64 B.C.E.–c. 23 C.E.). Eratosthenes calculated the circumference of the

SCIENCE AND TECHNOLOGY

## Hellenistic Scientists

**EGYPTIAN ALEXANDRIA** under the dynasty of the Ptolemaic kings was the largest city of the Hellenistic world. Founded and named by the world conqueror in the late fourth century B.C.E., it grew steadily, fattened by the increasing trade of the Nile valley with the remainder of the Greco-Roman world. At some point in the third century B.C.E., a museum and library were established there, which quickly became the intellectual and scientific center of the Mediterranean region. A recent British historian of science tells us about the type of research carried on there, the nature of the museum, and three of the Hellenistic researchers. Quoting the Roman author Cicero, he says:

> Strato the physicist was of the opinion that all divine power resides in nature, which is a power without shape or capacity to feel, containing within itself all the causes of coming-to-be, of growth, and of decay. Final causes, such as Aristotle posited, are out; nor is there any place in Strato's world for divine providence. Further . . . it seems clear that Strato endeavored to solve his problems by means of experimentation [a much debated question in the history of science].
>
> [T]he second of our Hellenistic scientists, Philo of Byzantium, worked in Alexandria around 200 B.C. Philo's work was concerned with artillery, comprising mechanical arrow-firing catapults and stone-throwing ballistas. . . . The most important fact revealed by recent research is the indication of *repeated experiment* as a means of establishing a method and a formula to be incorporated in the specification for the construction of different types of missile launchers.
>
> While Philo's name is associated with a variety of writings on scientific subjects, that of Ktesibios is linked with an equally wide range of inventions, most of which are based on the application of the principles of hydraulics. . . . His inventions included, in addition to the twin-cylinder water pump, a water-clock, a pipe organ powered by an ingenious combination of water and compressed air, and an improved catapult which operated by bronze springs instead of twisted animal sinews. He is also credited with a considerable number of inventions designed for entertainment, the so-called automata. . . .
>
> It is an easy step from the most famous inventor of his day [that is, Philo] to the Museum with which he was associated. The House of the Muses [the Museum] was evidently a research organization, supported, like the Library, by a royal endowment. Traditional accounts . . . assume that the Library, which rapidly acquired a worldwide reputation, was separate from the Museum; but it is more likely that both were parts of what might be called a research institute, which provided facilities for workers in a wide variety of disciplines belonging to what we would now call the humanities and the sciences.
>
> Contrary to the commonly held opinion that under Rome the Museum and the Library suffered a rapid decline into total obscurity, we have evidence that both were still operating many centuries later, even if not as vigorously as in their heyday. . . . Medicine was in the most flourishing condition of all the sciences there, enjoying such a high reputation that the only qualification an intending practitioner needed to produce was a statement that he had received his training at Alexandria. The most important scientific advances seem to have been made in pure mathematics, mechanics, physics, geography, and medicine.

### *Analyze and Interpret*

Why do you think it was important whether scientists of this age employed experiments to determine factual knowledge? What might be a modern equivalent to the Alexandria institute?

Source: K. D. White, in *Hellenistic History and Culture*, ed. P. Green (Berkeley: University of California Press, 1991), p. 216f. Used by permission.

Earth accurately. His data provided the first reliable maps of the globe (see Worldview Map 9.2).

In physics, the outstanding researcher was Archimedes (c. 287–212 B.C.E.), who was equally important in mathematics. In the third century B.C.E., Euclid, an Egyptian Greek, produced the most influential math treatise ever written, the *Elements of Geometry.*

The Greeks in general were not interested in the practical aspects of science, which we now call technology. Most of Hellenistic science was not driven by the desire to ease people's burdens or to save labor. Many discoveries and experimental results were allowed to be forgotten because no one saw any need to transform these theoretical breakthroughs into practical applications for daily life. The physical experiments performed by the brilliant Archimedes are a good example; neither he nor his fellow scientists ever tried to apply his findings to ordinary work tasks.

Why were the Greeks so uninterested in practical applications? The reasons are not clear. One factor seems to have been that the Greeks' reverence for the intellect was coupled with a contempt for manual labor. They

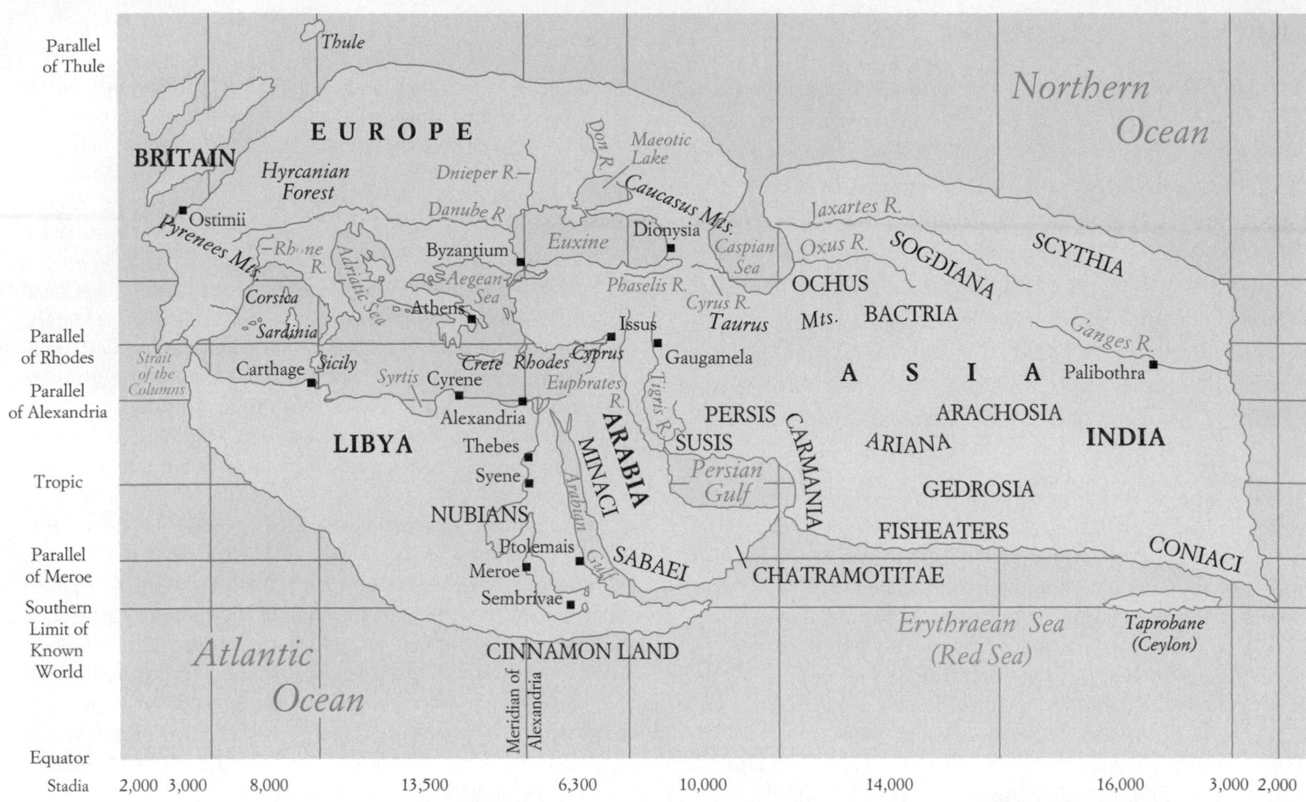

**WORLDVIEW MAP 9.2** ***The World According to Eratosthenes***

This is the first world map that bears substantial relation to the globe as modern people know it. It was drawn by the Greek geographer Eratosthenes in the third century B.C.E., relying on his own observations and on reports by mariners and other travelers.

seemed to think that hard labor was fitting only for beasts, not for intelligent human beings. Then, too, labor-saving devices were not much in demand in the Hellenistic Period. An abundance of labor was available for all tasks: slaves were much more numerous now than they had been earlier, and their situation could be only marginally affected, if at all, by technology.

By about 200 B.C.E., Hellenistic science had begun a slow decline. Astronomy was being replaced by astrology, and the initial advances in physics and math were not followed up. Only in medicine were some significant advances made, notably by the so-called **Empiricists,** doctors who were convinced that the answer to the ills of the body was to be found in the careful analysis of diseases and their physical causes. Building on the work of the great Hippocrates, these men identified much of the body's physiology, including the circulation of the blood and the functions of the nerves, the liver, and other vital organs. Medical knowledge would not reach so high a level again in the West until the end of the Middle Ages.

## *Art and Literature*

In the arts, a hybrid of classical Greek and traditional Eastern forms and content came into existence. Hellenic forms often became a thin veneer, covering the underlying Syrian, Egyptian, or Persian traditions. Some of the new forms were truly impressive in concept and excellent in execution, but later ages have deemed most of them a deterioration from what the Greeks had achieved during the Hellenic Period.

The fine arts were generally modeled on the art of the Hellenic Age but tended to be more realistic. They also lacked some of the creative vigor and imagination that had so marked Greek art in the earlier period, and they sometimes tended toward a love of display for its own sake—a sort of boastfulness and pretentiousness. In the Hellenistic Age, many individuals became immensely rich through trade or manufacturing, and they wanted to show off their new wealth. The newly rich indulged their desires by adorning their homes with works of art or sponsoring a piece of sculpture for the community.

A chief hallmark of Hellenistic art was the new emphasis on the individual artist as creator. In this epoch, for the first time, the name of the artist is almost always found on a work of art. We even hear of architects who took money for their plans, rather than being satisfied with the honor given by their associates or the community. This emphasis on the individual is another aspect of the decreased sense of community and the growing alienation that we noted earlier in this chapter.

Much more literature has survived from the Hellenistic Age than from the Classical Age. Unfortunately, the Hellenistic Age produced many second-rate but few first-rate talents. Both artistic inspiration and execution seem to have declined. There were many imitators but few original thinkers. The main centers of literature were in Alexandria, Rhodes, Pergamum, and other eastern areas rather than in Athens or Greece itself.

The same was generally true of the plastic arts. Great sculpture and buildings were more likely to be created in the East than in Greece, in large part because the richest cities of th Hellenistic Age were found there, along with the wealthiest inhabitants. In imagination and execution, much Hellenistic sculpture and architecture was extremely impressive. Indeed, it was much superior to the literary works of the time. The absolute mastery of stone that was already established by the artists of the Classical Age continued and developed even further. Such great works as *Laocoön, The Dying Gaul,* and *The Old Shepherdess* (see the photo) show an ability to "make the stone speak" that has been the envy of other ages. But even in sculpture, there was a great deal of copying of earlier forms and an abundance of second-class work.

Alinari/Art Resource, NY

**Old Shepherdess.** Hellenistic artists were often intent on both producing a realistic portrayal and demonstrating their technical mastery. Both intentions are fully achieved in this life-size statue of an old shepherdess. One can almost see movement in the detailed folds of the old woman's robe.

## Summary

The Hellenistic Age is a convenient although deceptively simple label for a widely varying mix of peoples and ideas. For about three centuries, from the death of Alexander to the Romans' coming into the East, the world affected by Greek ideas increased dramatically in physical extent, encompassing Mediterranean and western Asian cultures. This period also saw the first large-scale contacts between the civilization of the Mediterranean basin and those of East Asia, mainly India but also China.

The philosophies and religious thought of the Hellenistic world eventually became the basic lenses through which the entire European continent (and its North American offspring) would perceive the world of the spirit. Our cultural debts to these Greco-Eastern forebears are beyond easy measure. They include both science and Christianity.

Pagan and Christian Rome was also very much a part of the Hellenistic culture, and through it, the civilization of the Mediterranean was passed on to Europe in later years. In the next two chapters, we will see how the unimportant and provincial city of Rome became the inheritor of the Hellenistic East. We will also look at the way the Romans altered Hellenistic culture until it became a specifically Roman civilization.

## Identification Terms

Test your knowledge of this chapter's key concepts by defining the following terms. If you can't recall the meaning of certain terms, refresh your memory by looking up the boldfaced term in the chapter, turning to the Glossary at the end of the book, or working with the flashcards that are available on the *World Civilizations* Companion Website: **http://history.wadsworth.com/adler04/**.

Antigonid Kingdom
Cynicism
Empiricist
Epicureanism
geocentric
heliocentric
Hellenistic
mystery religions
Ptolemaic Kingdom of Egypt
Seleucid Kingdom of Persia
Stoicism

## Test Your Knowledge

Test your knowledge of this chapter by answering the following questions. Complete answers appear at the end of the book. You may also take this quiz interactively and find even more quiz questions on the *World Civilizations* Companion Website: **http://history.wadsworth.com/adler04/**.

1. *Hellenistic* refers to a
   a. blend of Greek and Eastern ideas and forms.
   b. blend of Greek and Roman ideas and forms.
   c. purely Greek style later transferred to Rome.
   d. mixed style limited in extent to Europe.
   e. blend of Greek, Roman, and Eastern style.
2. According to Plutarch, Alexander most impressed his father by
   a. slaying the giant Hercules.
   b. riding a wild horse.
   c. leading the Macedonian army.
   d. constructing a bridge over the Hellespont.
   e. invading the Persian Empire.
3. The Greek immigrants to Hellenistic Asia were usually
   a. resented and resisted by the local authorities.
   b. given favored official and financial positions.
   c. poverty-stricken workers and craftsmen.
   d. eager to mix with the native populations.
   e. discouraged from intermarrying with local people.
4. In the Hellenistic Period, the sociopolitical unit replacing the classical polis was the
   a. village.
   b. city.
   c. city-state.
   d. family.
   e. kingdom.
5. Which of these adjectives is the *least* appropriate description of Hellenistic society and customs discussed in this chapter?
   a. Alienated
   b. Stratified
   c. Urban
   d. Communal
   e. Diverse
6. Which of the following does *not* describe the Egypt of the Ptolemies?
   a. A backwater in the sciences
   b. A wealthy government
   c. One of the most important of the Hellenistic kingdoms
   d. A highly centralized political and economic authority
   e. An entity envied by other Hellenistic kings
7. In public affairs, the Epicureans insisted
   a. on active participation by their followers.
   b. that all politics and governments were equally corrupt.
   c. that democracy was superior to all other types of government.
   d. on indifference to government.
   e. that inner peace could be achieved through civic involvement.
8. Stoicists believed in
   a. the brotherhood of all men.
   b. the natural superiority of Greeks over all others.
   c. the quest for personal pleasure being the only meaning in life.
   d. the impossibility of finding an honest man or woman.
   e. the acceptance of one's lot in life.
9. The scientific interests of the Hellenistic Period
   a. were limited to math.
   b. led to an industrial revolution.
   c. were limited to agriculture.
   d. had little connection with technology.
   e. tended toward the practical application of knowledge.

10. The art of the Hellenistic Period
  a. flourished because of the many vibrant, creative minds involved.
  b. is noted for its emphasis on the community rather than the individual.
  c. was created by artists who desired only the honor of being identified publicly.
  d. surpassed in quality that of the earlier Greeks.
  e. was often used by the newly affluent to flaunt their wealth.

## InfoTrac College Edition

Visit the source collections at

**http://infotrac.thomsonlearning.com**

and use the Search function with the following key terms:

Greece history    Alexander the Great    Archimedes

## Wadsworth History Website Resources

Visit the World History Resource Center at **http://history.wadsworth.com/world** for a wealth of general resources and the *World Civilizations* Companion Website at **http://history.wadsworth.com/adler04/** for resources specific to this textbook.

## HistoryNow

Enter *HistoryNow* using the access card that is available for *World Civilizations*. *HistoryNow* will assist you in understanding the content in this chapter with lesson plans generated for your needs. In addition, you can read the following documents, and many more, online:

Plutarch, "Life of Alexander"

*It is the nature of a Roman to do, and to suffer bravely.*
Livy

# 10 Rome: City-State to Empire



| | |
|---|---|
| c. 750–509 B.C.E. | Etruscans rule Rome |
| c. 509–31 B.C.E. | Roman republic |
| 300s–200s B.C.E. | Conquest of Italy |
| 264–202 B.C.E. | The First and Second Punic Wars |
| 50s–30s B.C.E. | The two triumvirates |
| 27 B.C.E.–14 C.E. | Reign of Augustus |
| 31 B.C.E.–180 C.E. | Pax Romana |
| 14 C.E.–69 C.E. | Julio-Claudian emperors |
| 69 C.E.–96 C.E. | Flavian emperors |
| 161 C.E..–180 C.E. | Marcus Aurelius |

The successor to the Greek and Persian civilizations in the Mediterranean basin and the Near East was Rome, the Italian city-state that grew to be an empire and the dominant power in East and West alike. Although Rome is considered the successor to Hellenistic Greece, they actually overlapped in time, and Rome itself is in many ways a Hellenistic entity. In this chapter we will look at several centuries of Rome's growth from an insignificant Italian town dominated by a traditional upper class to an unusual combination of aristocracy and merit, subscribing to pseudo-democratic principles: the Roman *res publica,* or republic. Eventually, the disparity of civic means and ends generated by territorial expansion became too much, and from the ruins of this Roman republic then arose a vision of empire that has served the Western world as a model ever since. For two and a half centuries, Rome maintained peace and relative prosperity throughout most of Europe and the Mediterranean basin. Striking an uneasy but sustainable balance between the powers of a policy-making group in Rome and provincial officers drawn from many peoples, the system proved successful in a variety of circumstances, meeting needs both local and imperial.

## Roman Foundations

Rome is situated about halfway down the western coast of the Italian peninsula, where one of the country's few sizable rivers, the Tiber, flows through fertile plain before emptying into the sea (Map 10.1).

Very early Italy and the Italians are even more of a mystery than Greece and the Greeks. We do know that Indo-European peoples settled central and southern Italy at least as early as 1500 B.C.E. They developed farming villages but lagged seriously behind the peoples of the eastern Mediterranean and the Near East.

About 800 B.C.E., three peoples from the East began to enter Italy first as colonists and then as rulers of various segments of the peninsula: the Etruscans, the Greeks, and the Phoenicians. Each of these civilized groups contributed substantially to Italian development, and the first two had a decisive effect on Roman civilization's early forms.

The **Etruscans,** already highly civilized, came into Italy about 800, probably by following a route along the

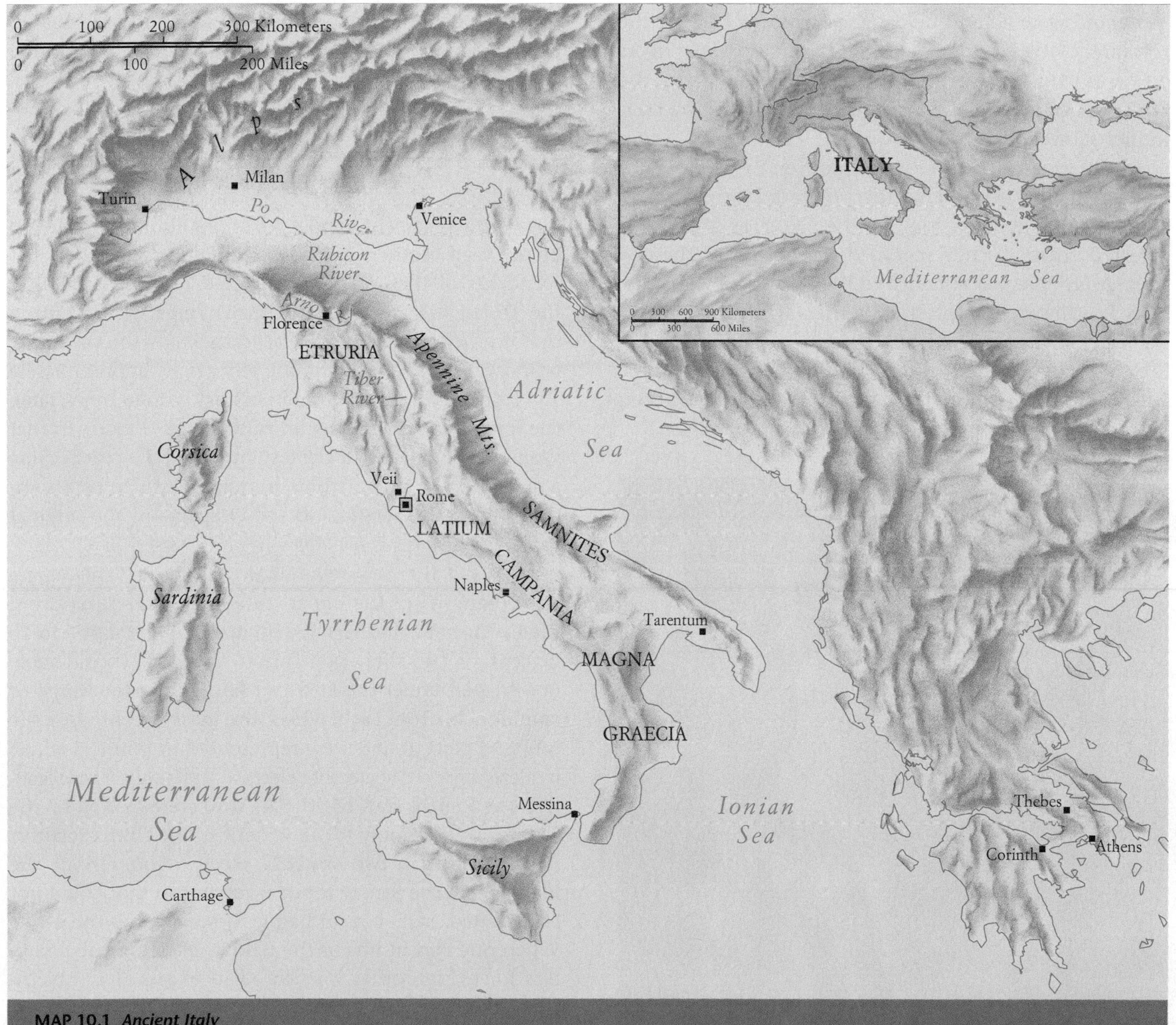


**MAP 10.1** *Ancient Italy*

The Italian peninsula was invaded innumerable times in history. The native Italic peoples of the north and center were taken over by the more civilized Etruscans in the tenth to eighth centuries B.C.E. Rome was probably founded by the uniting of several villages under a single government in the eighth century, as Roman legend states.

northern Adriatic Sea. They established a series of small city-states in the northern and central areas of the peninsula, ruling over the native Italic people by virtue of their superior weaponry and organization. They left a small amount of writing, but it has never been deciphered, so we have no historical record in the strict sense. We do know that a federation headed by Etruscan kings ruled over early Rome from about 750 to about 509 B.C.E. The pictorial record left by the Etruscans, mainly in recently rediscovered underground tombs, makes it clear that the early Romans derived much of their religious beliefs, art forms, and architecture from these peoples.

According to Roman sources that may be unreliable, the Romans eventually rebelled against the idea of monarchy and were able to defeat the Etruscans because the pleasure-loving Etruscans could not stand up to the rigors of war as long as their rivals. After the Roman victory, the Etruscans gradually fade from history, absorbed by their former subjects.

In the long run, the Greeks had even more influence on Roman attitudes and manners than did the Etruscans. Whereas the Romans viewed the latter as rivals and defeated enemies, they regarded the Greeks as the one alien group that was superior to them in some ways. The early Romans were impressed by the advanced culture of the Greek migrants who had settled in southern Italy during the 700s. Overcrowding at home had caused these Greek colonists to leave their homes in Corinth, Thebes, and other Greek cities and settle in foreign places. They soon transformed southern Italy into a prosperous and commercially advanced civilization but found they had to fight both the Etruscans and the Phoenicians to hold onto it. True to Greek tradition, they made the job much harder by fighting among themselves.

Museo Etrusco, Lazio, Rome, Italy/Bernard Cox/Bridgeman Art Library

**ETRUSCAN WINGED HORSES.** The vivid quality of Etruscan statuary is one of our few sources of knowledge about these people, who were the forerunners of and cultural models for the Romans in central Italy. The superb mastery of anatomy displayed here was a particular strength of Roman sculpture at a later date.

Phoenician influence on Italian events came through **Carthage.** This great trading city had become independent of its homeland, Phoenicia, by 700. During this epoch, Carthage was the most powerful force in the western Mediterranean, sending ships as far away as Britain and the North Sea, as well as up the Nile, and founding colonies of its own all over the coasts of Spain and France. The Carthaginians fought the Greek cities of southern Italy and Sicily to a draw until the Romans were able to take advantage of their mutual exhaustion to conquer both groups.

## REPUBLICAN GOVERNMENT

According to ancient Roman tradition, Rome was founded by the twin brothers Romulus and Remus, legendary descendants of the survivors who fled burning Troy after the Trojan War. Modern historians agree with tradition that the city-state of Rome was founded by the voluntary unification of seven agrarian villages at approximately 753 B.C.E. According to Roman history written much later, the town was under Etruscan rule until 509 B.C.E. In that year, a rebellion ousted the last king, and the city became a *res publica*—a state without a monarch, ruled by a combination of the Senate and the citizens—in the original Latin, the *Senatus et populus*.

How did the new republic govern itself? The Senate was composed of the upper class, the **patricians** (from the Latin *patres*, "fathers"), who made up perhaps 5 to 10 percent of the total population and had considerable power even under the Etruscan king. The **plebeians,** or commoners (from Latin *plebs*, "the mass"), composed the other 90 percent and were represented in political affairs by delegates to the elective General Assembly. The executive was a small staff of officials who were elected by the Senate and Assembly for short terms. The chief executive power resided in two **consuls,** elected from among the members of the Senate for one-year terms that could not be repeated. Each consul had veto power over the other. When one consul was in the field as leader of the republic's forces, the other was the head of the civil government at home. Below the consuls in authority were the **censors,** always drawn from the ranks of the senators. The censors (from *census*) were originally tax assessors, but later they came to have the power to supervise the conduct and morals of their fellow senators. The tiny Roman bureaucracy also included a few other offices, which were dominated by the patricians until a series of plebeian revolts or threats to revolt gradually opened them up to the commoners.

Originally, the General Assembly was intended to be as powerful as—perhaps more so than—the Senate, which had only advisory powers. But soon after the foundation of the republic, the Senate had obtained decisive power while the Assembly became a seldom-summoned rubber stamp. For two centuries, the plebeians made considerable progress in their struggle to attain equality.

By about 250, the Roman political structure offered to all appearances a nice balance between the aristocrats and the common people. The chief officers of the plebeians were the **tribunes.** There were about ten tribunes, and they had great power to speak and act in the name of the common Romans. At first, the tribunes were chosen from the common people and were their true representatives. Later, however, after about 200, the tribunes were offered membership in the Senate, and as they sought to become censors and consuls, they came to identify increasingly with the interests of the patricians and less with those of the plebeians. This development was to be fateful for the republic.

After the passage of the Hortensian Law (named after the consul of the day) in 287, plebeians and patricians had equal voting rights and supposedly equal access to office. But in practice, this nod toward democratic principles was not authentic. A combination of wealth and aristocratic birth retained control of the Senate. Democracy eventually would fail in Rome, just as it had in Athens.

## *Rome's Conquest of Italy*

Under this mixed government of aristocrats and commoners, the Roman city-state gradually and painfully became the master of the Italian peninsula. Down to about 340, the almost constant conflicts focused on a strip of land along the west coast. The Romans led a federation of tribes living in this plain of Latium, first against the Etruscans and then against other Italians (see Map 10.1).

Although Rome suffered a devastating invasion by Celtic tribes called Gauls in 390, the Romans and their Latin allies ruled most of central Italy by 340 or so. When the Latins then attempted to revolt against Roman overlordship, the Romans crushed them. Next they turned their attention to the Samnites, a group of Italic tribes in the south and east of the peninsula.

The war against the Samnites was lengthy and difficult. During this conflict the Romans perfected their military organization and created the myth of Roman invincibility.

The surrender of the Samnites in 282 B.C.E. brought the Romans a new neighbor and rival: the Greek city-states of southern Italy, which were supported by Pyrrhus, a powerful Greco-Macedonian general. After a couple of costly victories, Pyrrhus was defeated. Rome thus inserted itself into the ongoing struggle between the Greeks and the Carthaginians in Sicily. It would be only a matter of time before the two burgeoning powers of the western Mediterranean engaged in a contest for supremacy.

During these almost continuous conflicts, the Romans learned how to assure that yesterday's enemies became today's friends and allies. A pragmatic and flexible people, the Roman governing groups very soon realized that their original practice of humiliating and enslaving the conquered was counterproductive. Instead, they began to encourage the subject populations to become integrated with Rome—to become "good Romans" regardless of their ethnic or historical affiliations. The Romans gave partial citizenship rights to the conquered Italians as long as they did not rebel and agreed to supply troops when Rome called. This arrangement was advantageous to the conquered because it eased their tax burden, assured them of Roman assistance against their own enemies, and gave them wide-ranging powers of self-government.

Some of the conquered were eventually allowed to become full citizens, which meant they could run for office and vote in Roman elections, serve in the Roman army and bureaucracy, and have protection for property and other preferential legal rights that were not available to noncitizens.

The upper classes of the conquered Italians and Greeks were soon eager to latinize themselves and thus to qualify as full citizens. They achieved this status by intermarrying with Romans, adopting the Latin language, and accepting the basic elements of Roman custom and law.

## *The Punic Wars*

Although the Romans were nearly constantly at war between 500 and 275 B.C.E., these conflicts generally dealt with peoples who were similar to themselves and whose conquered lands were adjacent to Roman possessions. Not until the First **Punic War** (264–241 B.C.E.) did Rome more or less openly embark on imperial expansion. With that war, Rome started down the road to an *imperium* (empire), although it retained the laws and politics of a quasi-democratic city-state. This created internal tensions that ultimately could not be resolved.

The First Punic War broke out over the question of dominance in Sicily and ended twenty years later with the surrender of the important colonies of Sicily and Sardinia to Rome. Carthage, however, was far from completely subdued, and during the ensuing truce, it built up its forces and then invaded Italy. The brilliant Carthaginian general Hannibal won battle after battle against the desperate Romans but lost the war. Finally, after ravaging Italy for fifteen years in the Second Punic War (218–202), he was finally forced to return to Carthage to defend

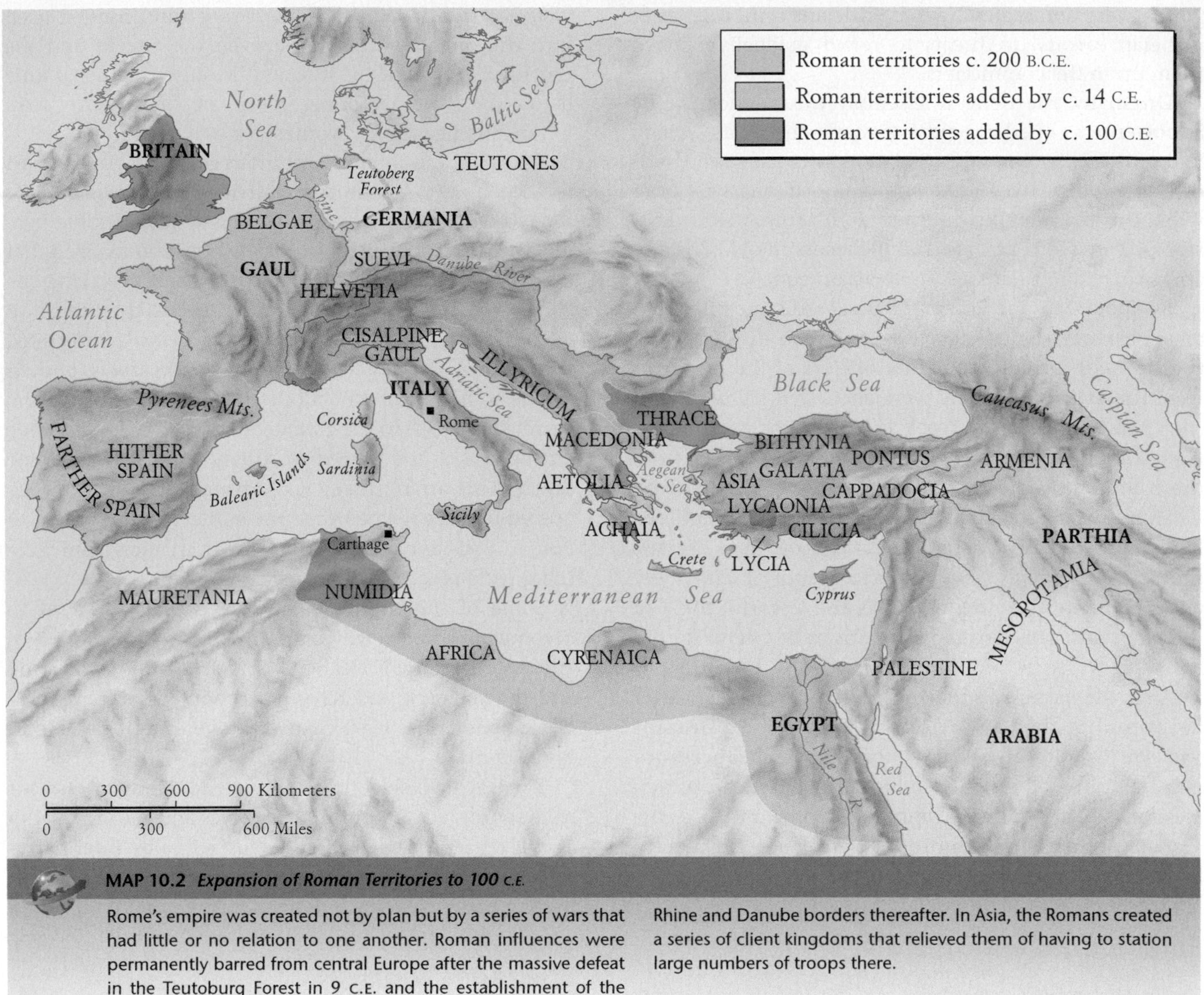


**MAP 10.2** ***Expansion of Roman Territories to 100 C.E.***

Rome's empire was created not by plan but by a series of wars that had little or no relation to one another. Roman influences were permanently barred from central Europe after the massive defeat in the Teutoburg Forest in 9 C.E. and the establishment of the Rhine and Danube borders thereafter. In Asia, the Romans created a series of client kingdoms that relieved them of having to station large numbers of troops there.

the city against a Roman counterinvasion. The decisive **battle of Zama** in 202 was a clear Roman victory, and Carthage was forced to give up most of its extensive holdings in Africa and Spain. These were made into new provinces of what by now was a rapidly growing empire (see Map 10.2). The Punic Wars determined that Roman, and not Carthaginian, culture and civilization would control the Mediterranean basin for the foreseeable future.

## The Conquest of the East

Victorious against Carthage, the Romans at once turned their eyes eastward. Until now they had tried to stay out of the continuous quarreling of the Hellenistic kingdoms. But in the 190s, immediately after the Punic Wars, ambitious consuls saw an opportunity to profit from the internal Greek struggle. Within a very short time, the Greco-Macedonian kingdom was under Rome's control.

Roman armies soon defeated the other Hellenistic kingdoms around the eastern edge of the Mediterranean. These petty kingdoms could have been at once made into Roman provinces. But some senators expressed strong opposition to this move, believing that the expansive, materialistic society being created by military conquests was far from what Roman traditions of thrifty living and modest ambition honored. A seesaw struggle between conservatives, who wished Rome to remain an ethnically homogeneous Italian city-state, and imperialists, who wanted expansion (and wealth!), went on for about a century (150–50 B.C.E.). The conservatives were fighting for a lost cause, however. By the latter date, the question had become which of the pro-imperialist groups would eventually seize supreme power.

The conquest of the East was executed by an outstanding military machine. It was composed mainly of infantry, which was recruited from all male citizens. In the

**ROMAN INFANTRYMAN.** This picture shows a bronze figure of a Roman legionary in full dress at the time of the empire in the second century C.E. The soldier's vest is constructed of overlapping metal bands that, although heavy and awkward, protected him effectively from enemy thrusts.

early republic, only property holders were allowed citizenship, and only citizens could bear arms. The commanders were all patricians, whereas the plebeians served in the ranks. Service was for an indefinite term, and as the wars multiplied in the fourth and third centuries B.C.E., many citizens were away from their homes for lengthy periods. The effects were ruinous for many simple peasant-soldiers, who could not tend their fields adequately and had no other source of income (because army service was considered an honor, soldiers were not paid).

As early as the mid-300s, military needs were urgent enough that a group of permanent commanders/governors called **proconsuls** was created. The custom of electing commanders annually fell into disuse, as it was clear that men of talent would be needed for more than a year. In this way, a group of men emerged who were both politically potent through their connections in the Senate and militarily potent through their command responsibilities. So long as they continued to regard the Senate and the consuls whom the Senate elected as their rightful superiors, all went well.

But it was inevitable that an ambitious commander would come along who would look first to personal advancement and only later or never to the welfare of the state. Such men began to appear regularly after the First Punic War, which created myriad opportunities to get rich in the new territories won from Carthage. These opportunities redoubled after the Second Punic War. By then, Rome was rapidly developing a volunteer, professional army that would look to its field commanders and not to a distant Senate as its legitimate director.

## *The Late Republic's Crisis*

All through this imperial expansion, Rome's government had remained technically that of an ethnically homogeneous city-state, with traditional powers allocated between the senatorial upper class and the masses. By the end of the second century, the real Rome had deviated far from this ideal, and the strains were beginning to show, as the Society and Economy box reveals.

Many poverty-stricken former farmers flocked into the city, seeking any kind of work and ready to listen to anyone promising them a better existence. Many of them had served in the army for years and were then discharged only to find that their lands had been seized for debt or confiscated through the maneuvers of wealthy speculators. The new landowners created great estates that were worked by the vast numbers of slaves that the Roman overseas conquests were bringing into Italy.

The members of this new urban **proletariat**—people without sources of income except the daily sale of their labor—were citizens with votes, and they were ready to sell those votes to the highest bidder. They were also ready to follow any general who promised them a decent living in his army of long-serving veterans. Men would serve out their time and then be given a good mustering-out pension or a bit of land to support themselves in old age. That land could easily enough be taken from the victims of new Roman-incited wars around the Mediterranean and in what is now western Europe. But in Italy itself, this "land problem"—the forcing of the peasant-soldiers off their ancestral land—proved insoluble.

Starting about 150 B.C.E., Roman public life thus became a complex struggle between those upper-class individuals who saw the growing need for social and political reform and those who rejected reform under the banner of sacred tradition. Among the former was a certain Marius. This former consul saw his chance for fame in a war against African rebels and had himself reelected consul for six terms—a first that was to become commonplace within a couple more decades. Marius also abolished the property qualification for his soldiers, thereby opening the way for an army composed of men who had nothing to lose by enlisting and would follow any leaders who made sure they got plunder and pensions. More and more, the Roman military was becoming a force for instability and the essential base for all who had political ambitions.

In 83 B.C.E. the harsh soldier-consul Sulla made himself dictator and packed the Senate with new men who would obey him. Sulla instituted several beneficial political reforms as well, but they were abolished as soon as he died in 78, and the government reverted immediately to open or covert warfare of wealthy senatorial groups against each other.

SOCIETY AND ECONOMY

## "Rape of the Sabine Women"

**From earliest times,** the Roman ruling class saw itself as ordained to be the proud culmination of civilization and the executors of the will of their gods.

A favorite story was told by the first-century writer Livy, the official historian of the city in the time when Rome was transforming itself into an empire. It deals with the manner in which the first settlers, led by the mythical Romulus, procured wives for themselves: the "Rape of the Sabine Women." The tale shows not only the Romans' admiration for the warrior but also their vision of the proper relations between male and female.

Having lured the neighboring Sabine people to come to join in watching an athletic contest, Romulus and his fellow Romans sprang their trap:

> The day for the spectacle arrived and while [the Sabines'] eyes and minds were intent on it, a prearranged free-for-all began, with the Roman men scattering at an agreed upon signal to seize the unmarried girls. . . . As the games broke up in confusion and fear, the grieving parents of the maidens ran off, accusing the Romans of violating their sacred obligations as hosts and invoking the god to whose festival and games they had been deceitfully invited contrary to religion and good faith. The abducted maidens had no better hopes than their parents, nor was their indignation less. But Romulus repeatedly went about in person to visit them, arguing that what had happened was due to the arrogance of their parents, who had refused intermarriage with their neighbors. Despite this, he promised that they would enjoy the full rights of a proper marriage, becoming partners in all the fortunes the couple might share, in Rome's citizenship, and in the begetting of children, the object dearest to every person's heart. So let them now abate their anger, let them give their hearts to those whom chance had given their bodies. . . .

To Romulus's entreaties the husbands added their own honeyed words, claiming that they had acted out of desire and love, an avowal calculated to appeal most to a woman's nature. While the Sabine women were thus soon soothed, their fathers and brothers were definitely not, and a fierce war between them and Rome quickly ensued. A great deal of slaughter seemed inevitable, but Livy goes on:

> [A]t this moment the Sabine women boldly interposed themselves amid the flying spears. Their misfortunes overcame womanish fear: with hair streaming and garments torn they made a mad rush from the sidelines, parting the battling armies and checking their angry strife. Appealing to fathers on one side and husbands on the other, they declared their kin by marriage should not defile themselves by impious carnage, nor leave the stain of blood upon their descendants, grandfathers upon grandsons, fathers upon children. "If you cannot abide the ties between you that our marriage has created turn your anger against us. We are the cause of this war, we the cause of husbands and fathers lying wounded and slain. Only one side can win this battle. As for us, it is better to die than to live, for we must do so as widows and orphans."

Their appeal moved both leaders and rank and file: silence and a sudden hush fell upon the field. The commanders then came forward to strike a treaty by which they not only made peace but united the two peoples in a single community.

### *Analyze and Interpret*

What does the story tell you of Roman notions of fair play? Can you defend this view, or does armed might never make moral right in human relationships?

Source: Livy, *The Histories*, trans. F. J. Luce (Oxford: Oxford University Press, 1998), p. 14f.

**History Now™**

***To read more of Livy's* Histories, *point your browser to the documents area of* HistoryNow.**

## *The Triumvirates*

The final collapse of the psuedo-democracy and the republican system was brought on by the patrician general and politician Julius Caesar (died 44 B.C.E.), who saw that it had become corrupt and was unsuited for governance of a far-flung empire. He conspired with others who were also discontented with the Senate leadership to form an alliance known as the *First Triumvirate* (rule of three). The other members were the wealthy speculator Crassus and the brilliant general Pompey.

During the 50s B.C.E., Caesar made his reputation by conquering the semicivilized Gauls in what is now France, which he turned into a Roman province of great potential. His ambitions fully awakened, he now wished to become consul and use that powerful office to make basic changes in the structure of government. He was opposed by his former ally Pompey and the large majority of the Senate, who viewed him as a dangerous radical. Emerging the victor after a difficult struggle, Caesar made himself dictator and fully intended to start a royal dynasty. He subordinated the Senate entirely to himself and initiated several major reforms of the existing system, including even the Roman calendar. But, in March 44, he was assassinated by conservative senators. His only surviving male relative was his adoptive son Octavian Caesar, whom he had made his political heir. But Octavian was only eighteen when Caesar died. He had little political experience and lacked military prowess, so it appeared unlikely that he would ever fill the office of his adoptive father.

When the senatorial assassins of Julius Caesar could not agree on what should be done to restore the republic, Octavian, the financier Lepidus, and the general Mark Antony formed an alliance known as the *Second Triumvirate.* The three allies crushed the assassins and then divided the empire: Antony took the East and Egypt; Octavian, Italy and the West; and Lepidus, Africa. Octavian soon showed himself a gifted politician, but he stood in the shadow of Mark Antony. (Lepidus had no independent political hopes and could be ignored.) Antony made himself unpopular in Rome by apparently succumbing to the charms of the queen of Egypt, Cleopatra, and maltreating his noble Roman wife and her influential family. Octavian cleverly built his political strength in Italy and acquired much experience in handling men. When the test came, he was ready. In 32 B.C.E., Octavian maneuvered Antony into declaring war against him. The victory of Octavian's forces at the decisive **battle of Actium** in 31 B.C.E. marked the effective beginning of the Roman Empire.

## The Augustan Age

Octavian's victory had made him master of the Roman world. The question was, how would he respond to this opportunity? Like his predecessor Julius Caesar, Octavian knew that basic reforms were necessary if the Roman state was to survive. But he also knew how resistant the Roman people were to innovations that challenged ancient custom.

### Augustus's Reforms

Octavian's response was to *retain the form, while changing the substance.* Mindful of the Romans' respect for tradition, Octavian pretended to be simply another elected consul, another *pontifex maximus* (high priest of the state religion), and another general of the Roman legions. In reality, he became consul for life, his priestly duties were crowned with semidivine status, and his military resources overshadowed all possible rivals. He enlarged the Senate, packing it with loyal supporters. He made a great show of working with the Senate, while giving it enough busywork to keep it out of mischief. Meanwhile, he made all real policy decisions. He cut the army's size by half, while retaining all key military posts under his direct control.

Early in his reign, Octavian accepted the title *Augustus* ("revered one") from a grateful Senate, and it is as "Augustus Caesar" that he is best known. He preferred to be called ***princeps*** ("first citizen"), and his rule is often called the Principate. It lasted from 27 B.C.E., when he was elected consul for life, until his natural death in 14 C.E. In those forty years, Augustus placed his mark on every aspect of public affairs. He was so successful overall that his system lasted for the next two and a half centuries without fundamental change. Augustus created a type of constitutional monarchy that was suited to contemporary Roman realities. To many people, it long remained the model of what effective and just imperial government should be.

### Imperial Government Policies

In government and constitutional matters, Augustus kept the republican institutions intact. Supposedly, the *Senatus et populus* together were still the sovereign power, with the consul simply their agent. In practice, however, Augustus had the final word in everything important through his control of the military and the Senate. His steadily increasing prestige with the commoners also helped him. Ordinary Romans were appalled by the rebellions, civil wars, and political assassinations that had become commonplace in the last decades of the republic. After 31 B.C.E., however, Augustus was strong enough to intimidate any would-be troublemakers. He became immensely popular among the common people as a result.

In social policy, Augustus recognized the problems presented by the numbers of propertyless, impoverished citizens, especially in the cities. He therefore provided the urban poor with basic food rations from the state treasury, supplemented by "gifts" from the consul, from his

Segovia, Spain/Ken Welsh/Bridgeman Art Library

**Roman Aqueduct in Spain.** This modern photo shows the enduring nature of Roman civic architecture all around the Mediterranean basin. This aqueduct might still be employed by the citizens of Segovia, Spain, to bring fresh water to them. Similar structures stand in southern France and in Turkey.

own resources. This annual dole of grain and oil became an important means of controlling public opinion for Augustus and his successors. He also instituted huge public works programs, both to provide employment and to glorify his government. Projects were carried out all over the empire, but especially in Rome. Many of the surviving Roman bridges, aqueducts, roads (the famous, enduring Roman roads), forts, and temples were constructed during his reign or were started by him and completed later.

Augustus also attempted to institute moral reform and end the love of luxury that had become characteristic of the aristocratic class during the late republic. In his own life with his wife Livia, he set an example of modest living. He also tried to discourage the influx of slaves because he believed that the vast number of slaves being imported into Italy represented luxury and, as such, threatened the traditional lifestyle. But none of these moral reform attempts proved successful over the long run. His imperial successors soon gave up the struggle.

Augustus also tried to revive the faith in the old gods and the state cult by conscientiously serving as high priest. Here, too, he was unsuccessful in the long run. The educated classes emulated the Greeks by turning from supernatural religion toward philosophy, and the masses sought something more satisfying emotionally than the barren ceremonies of the state cult. This they found in the mystery religions, with their promise of salvation.

In foreign policy, the northern frontiers in Germany and the Low Countries had long been a problem that Augustus was determined to solve by conquering the fierce tribes who lived there. This foray ended in spectacular failure: in 9 C.E., Germanic tribes ambushed and exterminated a Roman army that had pushed eastward into the Teutoburg forests. The entire Germania province was thereby lost, and the borders between Roman and non-Roman Europe were henceforth the Rhine and Danube rivers (see Map 10.2). After Augustus, Rome's only significant territorial acquisitions were in the British Isles and in present-day Romania.

To govern this vast empire of about 60 million, Augustus reformed its protection and administration. The outermost provinces, including Spain, Mesopotamia, and Egypt, were either put directly under his own control as "imperial" provinces or turned over to local rulers who were faithful satellites. Most of the army was stationed in the imperial provinces, enabling Augustus to keep the military under his surveillance and control.

Augustus initiated other reforms in military matters as well. The standing army had become increasingly large and unwieldy, as well as politically dangerous, so he reduced its size by more than half, to about 250,000 men. The army was made thoroughly professional and used extensively as an engineering force to build roads and public works all over the provinces. Twenty-eight legions, each with about 6,000 highly trained and disciplined infantry, were supported by cavalry and by a large number of auxiliaries, taken from the non-Roman populations of the provinces.

The volunteers who made up the legions served for twenty years and were given a mustering-out bonus sufficient to set them up as small landowners or businessmen.

The legionaries were highly mobile, and a common soldier often served in five or six different provinces before retirement. The auxiliaries served for twenty-five years and were normally given citizenship on retirement. In and around Rome, Augustus maintained his personal bodyguard and imperial garrison, the **Praetorian Guard.** Containing about 10,000 men, it was the only armed force allowed in Italy. Whoever controlled its loyalty had a potent lever for political power in his hand.

Augustus also reorganized the Roman navy and used it effectively to rid the major rivers and the Mediterranean of pirates, who had been disrupting shipping. For the next 200 years, the navy protected the provinces and Italy from waterborne threats. Not until recent times were the seas around Europe as safe as in the first and second centuries.

## *Peace and Prosperity*

The **Pax Romana,** the Roman peace from 31 B.C.E. until 180 C.E., was the greatest of Augustus's achievements. For nearly two and a half centuries, the Western world from Syria to Spain and from Bristol to Belgrade was unified and generally peaceful under a single central authority enjoined by common law. This record has not been approached since. With Augustus's reign, Rome entered six generations of peace and prosperity. Literature and the arts flourished, supported by generous subsidies from the state treasury and commissions from a new class of wealthy men who wished to celebrate their achievements. Augustus set the tone by encouraging the arts in public spaces and buildings of all sorts and providing personal financial support for many of the outstanding literary figures of his time.

How did the Pax Romana benefit people throughout the far-flung Roman Empire? It allowed, for example, Syrian merchants to move their textile goods safely from Damascus to Alexandria. From there, Egyptians would transport the goods through a peaceable sea to Gibraltar, and from there, the goods would go on to Cornwall in Britain, where they would be exchanged for tin ore, which would then be brought back to a bronze foundry in Damascus. Under the Pax Romana, people throughout the empire lived under a common concept of peaceful order, expressed and upheld through laws that were as valid in London as in Vienna or Barcelona (all cities founded by the Romans). The provinces were supervised by governors (proconsuls) appointed in Rome, but they were allowed considerable freedom of action in local affairs while being protected by Roman garrisons.

### The Succession Problem

One important problem that Augustus was unable to solve was that of succession to his office and powers. Having only a daughter (the scandalous Julia), he adopted her husband, Tiberius, as his son and co-ruler. He thus set an example that would be followed by most of his successors: a combination of *heredity,* meaning succession by blood, and co-option, meaning succession by designation of the ruler. But this method often resulted in chaos and was at times disregarded in favor of heredity alone.

Tiberius was an effective ruler, although by no means the equal of Augustus in popularity or ability to manipulate the Senate. Whereas Augustus had been deified (declared a god) by a grateful Senate almost immediately after his death, Tiberius was much resented. He was followed by other members of the family of Augustus (the Julio-Claudians) until 68 C.E., when the succession system experienced its first crisis. The last of the Julio-Claudians, the unpopular Nero, committed suicide in 69, and after some bloodstained manuevering was replaced by the Flavian emperors from 69 to 96. They based their right to rule simply on having imposing military force behind them. Even though these generals were effective and wise rulers, they set an ominous precedent of coerced selection that would come back to haunt Rome in the third century.

## Imperial Unification

The successors of Augustus continued his work of bringing together the very diverse peoples over whom they ruled. Gradually, the Latin language became the common denominator of higher culture in the western half of the empire, while Greek continued to serve that function in the East. The government used both languages equally in its dealings with its subjects.

The imperial government became increasingly centralized. The freedoms of the cities of the ancient East were curtailed by Roman directives and governors sent out from Italy or selected from the romanized locals. In the western half of the empire, the Roman authorities founded many ***municipia.*** These were towns with their surrounding countryside that formed governmental units similar in size and function to our own counties. The municipal authorities were partly appointed by Rome and partly elected from and by leading local families. The provincial governor (usually an Italian given the job as political patronage) was responsible for their good behavior. He was backed by a garrison commander, who had wide-ranging authority in matters both military and civil.

Everywhere, the government became open to non-Italians, as soon as they had romanized themselves sufficiently to become citizens. (Citizenship was eventually granted to all freemen by a popularity-seeking emperor in 212.) From the time of the emperor Hadrian (the 120s C.E.), half of the members of the Senate were of provincial origin. Men of talent could rise swiftly to the highest offices regardless of their ethnic background. Religious differences were ignored, so long as one was willing to make the undemanding ceremonial tributes to the official Roman gods (Jupiter, Neptune, and the like). Most individuals had no difficulty combining this state cult with the more intimate religions of their preference.

## Roman Culture

In general, the Romans borrowed heavily and willingly from the Greek heritage in philosophy, the sciences, and the arts, but that does not mean that they developed no native culture. Their own genius and inclinations lay more in the fields of law and administration than in the realm of imagination or the fine arts. In the practical aspects of public life, such as engineering, sanitation, finance, and a system of justice, the Romans had few equals. They were always willing to experiment until they found a winning combination or at least one that was acceptable to the majority of citizens. At the same time, they never failed to make elaborate bows to a sometimes fictional tradition and to insist that they were following in the footsteps of the hallowed past when, in fact, they were making changes demanded by new circumstances.

### Law

An indisputably great Roman achievement was the development of a system of law with the flexibility to meet the needs of subject peoples as diverse as the primitive Britons and the ultra-civilized Syrians. This law system and a government that combined effective central controls with wide local autonomy are perhaps the most valued Roman gifts to later civilized society. Many types of law originally existed within the borders of the empire, but these gradually gave way to the system that the Romans had hammered out by trial and error during the republic and that continued to be developed in the empire. The basic principles of this legal system were (1) the notion of *precedent* as coequal to the letter of the law, (2) the belief that *equity* (fairness) was the goal of all law, and (3) the importance of *interpretation* in applying the law to individual cases.

The Romans had various codes of law. One originally applied only to citizens, and another applied only to aliens and travelers on Roman territory. During the early empire, the law code that governed relations between citizens and non-Romans, known as the ***jus gentium*** ("law of peoples"), gradually came to be accepted as basic. The rights of citizens and noncitizens, of natives and aliens, came to be seen as worthy of protection by the Roman authorities. These rights were not equal, but they were recognized as existing. This concept paved the way for what we call "international law," and it gradually took Roman justice far beyond the usual concepts of "us against you" that other ancient peoples normally employed with foreigners.

Later, in the third and fourth centuries, the Romans evolved *natural law,* the idea that all humans, by virtue of their humanity, possess certain rights and duties that all courts must recognize. As the Romans adopted Christianity, this natural law came to be viewed as the product of a God-ordained order that had been put into the world with the creation of Adam.

Louvre, Paris, France/Lauros/Giraudon/Bridgeman Art Library

**A Roman Emperor.** The Roman preference for realism in their pictorial arts is shown by this bust of a man assumed to be Emperor Macrin. Although their techniques were generally dependent on classical Greek models, the Romans soon progressed beyond the desire merely to imitate.

## *The Arts*

Roman art forms varied sharply in development and imagination. The Latin language evolved rapidly as the republic expanded its contacts with others. Roman literature began in the third century B.C.E., when poetry of some excellence, historiography of a rather inferior sort, and drama modeled on that of the Greeks began to appear. During the republic's last century, Cicero, Julius Caesar, Terence, Polybius, Cato, and Lucretius were major contributors. The best days of Roman literature, however, were still ahead, in the early imperial epoch, when a brilliant constellation around the emperors Augustus and Tiberius created a memorable body of poetry and prose. Virgil's *Aeneid* became the official version of the founding of Rome by refugees from the burning Troy; Ovid, Horace, and Catullus established Latin poetry equal to yet different from its Greek models. In the hands of prose masters such as the historian Tacitus, the satirist Juvenal, and the storytellers Pliny, Petronius, and Suetonius, the Latin language became an extraordinary instrument capable of extreme directness and concision.

In the pictorial and plastic (three-dimensional) arts, the early Roman sculptors and architects worked from both Etruscan and Greek models without much elaboration of their own. With few exceptions, the "Greek" statues in the world's fine arts museums are Roman copies of originals that have long since disappeared. By the end of the republican era this was changing, and a specifically native style was emerging. One of its greatest strengths was portrait sculpture, especially the busts that were produced in large numbers. These are amazingly realistic and seem modern in a way that other ancient art generally does not.

The architectural style favored in the republic was strongly reminiscent of the Greek temple, but it also incorporated Hellenistic arches and circles, as in the frequent cupola roofs and semicircular altars, to a much greater degree. Roman skill in masonry work and affinity to the grand style combined to give magnificent expression to public works and buildings throughout the empire. The Forum and the Coliseum still stand in modern Rome, witnesses to the exceptional quality of Roman stone work.

## *Patterns of Belief*

"How best to live?" was a question that preoccupied imperial Romans. Perhaps the greatest of all the emperors after Augustus was Marcus Aurelius (ruled 161–180 C.E.), the last of the Five Good Emperors who ruled in the second century C.E. He left a small book of aphorisms called *Meditations,* which has been a best-seller ever since (see the Patterns of Belief box). Marcus settled on a pessimistic Stoicism as the most fitting cloak for a good man in a bad world, especially a man who had to exercise power. This was a common feeling among upper-class Romans, and it became ever more popular in the third and fourth centuries as civic difficulties multiplied. Like Marcus Aurelius, Roman Stoics often opposed Christianity because they rejected external prescriptions for morality. Instead, they insisted that each person is responsible for searching and following his own conscience. Seneca, another Stoic and the most persuasive of the Roman moralists, had a somewhat different way of looking at things. He introduced a new note of humane compassion, a belief that all shared in the divine spark and should be valued as fellow creatures.

The Roman character, insofar as one can sum up a heterogeneous people's character, leaned toward the pragmatic and the here and now. Romans admired the doer more than the thinker, the soldier more than the philosopher, and the artisan more than the artist. The educated class could and did appreciate "the finer things." They admired and cultivated art in many media and many forms and spent lavishly to obtain it for their own prestige and pleasure. But they did not, generally speaking, provide that sort of intense, sustained interest that led to superior aesthetic standards and to the inspiration of superior and original works of art, such as the

PATTERNS OF BELIEF

## The *Meditations* of Marcus Aurelius

**Marcus Aurelius** (121–180 C.E.) was perhaps the greatest of all the Roman rulers, in the sense of moral grandeur. As the last of the Five Good Emperors who ruled in the second century C.E., he inherited an empire that was still intact and at peace internally. But on its eastern borders, the first of the lethal challenges from the Germanic tribes materialized during his reign (161–180), and he had to spend much of his time organizing and leading the empire's defenses.

Even during his campaigns, his mind was attuned to the Stoic philosophy, which the Roman upper classes had acquired from the Greeks. In *Meditations,* he wrote a personal journal of the adventure of a life consciously lived. His book, which was never meant for publication, has lived on into our day because of its nobility of thought and expression. Some excerpts follow:

> Begin each day by reminding yourself: today I shall meet with meddlers, ingrates, insolence, disloyalty, ill-will and selfishness—all of them due to the offenders' ignorance of what is good and what evil. But I have long perceived the nature of good and its nobility, the nature of evil and its meanness, and also the nature of the culprit himself, who is my brother . . . therefore, none of those things can injure me, for no one can implicate me in what is degrading. . . .
>
> Never value the advantages derived from anything involving breach of faith, loss of self-respect, hatred, suspicion, or execration of others, insincerity, or the desire for something which has to be veiled or curtained. One whose chief regard is for his own mind, and for the divinity within him and the service of its goodness, will strike no poses, utter no complaints, and crave neither for solitude nor yet for the crowd. . . .
>
> Hour by hour resolve firmly, like a Roman and a man, to do what comes to hand with correct and natural dignity, and with humanity, independence, and justice. Allow your mind freedom from all other considerations. This you can do if you will approach each action as though it were your last, dismissing the wayward thought, the emotional recoil from the commands of reason, the desire to create an impression, the admiration of self, the discontent with your lot. See how little a man needs to master, for his days to flow on in quietness and piety; he has to observe but these few counsels, and the gods will ask nothing more.

### *Analyze and Interpret*

Of the various world religions encountered thus far in this book, which seems closest in its ethical principles to Marcus's *Meditations*? Can you see why the *Meditations* was a particular favorite with Christians after Constantine's time?

Source: Excerpt from Marcus Aurelius, *Meditations,* trans. Maxwell Staniforth, © 1964, Penguin Classics. Reprinted by permission of Penguin, Ltd.

**History Now™**

***To read more from Marcus Aurelius's* Meditations, *point your browser to the documents area of* HistoryNow.**

Greeks possessed in abundance. The early empire's successes in several fields were magnificent and long lasting, but they were not rooted in an original view of earthly life or a new conception of humans' duties and aspirations.

The religious convictions of the Romans centered on duty to the state and the family hearth. Toward the state, the Roman patricians felt a personalized attachment, a sense of duty, and a proud obedience to tradition handed down from generation to generation. Toward the patriarchal family and its symbol, the hearth, the Romans felt the same attachment as most ancient peoples, with the honor of the lineage being of the usual great importance to them.

Roman religion was a matter of mutual promises: on the gods' side, protection for the community and survival for the individual; on the human side, ceremonial worship and due respect. Priests and priestesses existed in Rome but had relatively little power and prestige among the people. It was a religion of state, rather than of individuals, and it was common for Romans to worship other gods besides those of the official cult. In the imperial period, many emperors were deified, and most of the mystery religions of the Hellenistic world eventually were taken up by Rome.

Chief among the many Roman gods was Jupiter, a father figure modeled on the Greek Zeus. Also important were Apollo, Neptune (Poseidon), Venus (Aphrodite), Minerva (Athena), and Mars (Ares). Like the rituals of the Greeks, the worship given to these deities was more like a present-day patriotic ceremony than a modern church service. Even less than among the Greeks did the Romans look to the civic gods for ethical guidance or to secure personal immortality by passing a last judgment. The Roman notion of an afterlife changed from person to person and from age to age during Rome's long history. In broad terms it resembled that of the educated Greeks: the existence of an afterlife was an open question, but if it did exist, one could know nothing about it or secure admission to it through the gods.

Ideally, and in their own musings about the good life, educated Romans generally affirmed Stoicism, believing that service to the state and the human community was the highest duty. They thought that the only way to ensure against the disappointments of earthly life was to renounce the pursuit of wealth and power and live a life of modest seclusion. But few Romans who had a choice did that! As a governing class, they were very much attuned to the delights of wealth and power and very much willing to make great efforts to get them. A people who made much of military virtue and unquestioning obedience, they also insisted on the autonomy of the individual's conscience. A people who were notably conscious of the concept of justice and the rule of law, they also had many moments of collective blind rage when they exerted sadistic power over others. Nobility of thought was sometimes marred by base actions and even baser motives.

## Society and Economy

In general, the Romans were successful in creating a single, unified vision of what life was about—and how it should best be lived—that was accepted from Britain to Egypt and from Spain to Romania. We have a great deal of information about the economic and cultural life in the first and second centuries C.E., when the empire was prospering.

Trade and manufacturing enjoyed a considerable boom. Trade was conducted mainly within the borders of the empire but also extended beyond them to India, Africa, and even China during the Han Dynasty, which closely paralleled the rise and fall of the Roman hegemony in Europe. Trade with China was focused on luxuries and was not direct but conducted through Asian intermediaries. Increasingly, the balance of trade within the empire shifted to favor the East (meaning the area from the Adriatic to Mesopotamia and Egypt). Italy became more and more dependent on imports from other parts of the empire, mainly from the East, where the levels of skills far exceeded those of the West. In the East lived the bulk of the population and the majority of the urbanites. Here, too, were the sophisticated, civilized traditions of the Hellenistic world. Even the skilled slave labor in Italy came almost exclusively from Eastern sources.

During Rome's imperial age, the methods by which the ordinary man made a living changed little from earlier days. Farming or herding animals remained the paramount occupation. At the same time, the urban population grew considerably, especially in the West. (See the Society and Economy box for details of what these people ate.) In the towns, the number of people—both men and women—engaged in skilled or semiskilled labor increased steadily. But the real growth of urban population came from the influx of country people who had lost their land and their livelihood. They came to town hoping for a better life, but many ended up as beggars.

Most Roman subjects, as always, worked the land. But much of this land was now owned either by the imperial government or by wealthy absentee landlords. Small free farmers were a declining species by the second century. They were replaced not so much by slaves as by sharecropper-tenants, who were still free in most of the empire but would not long remain so.

In the Italian and western European countryside, the land controlled by the *villa,* or country estate of the wealthy, was steadily gaining at the expense of the im-

SOCIETY AND ECONOMY

## The Roman Cuisine

**The differences between** the items on the Roman table and those we are accustomed to on our own were perhaps not so great as generally imagined, but there were indeed some:

> [T]he Romans had no coffee, tea, sugar, liquors, truffles, potatoes or beans; tomatoes were unknown, dried herbs rare and imported. Sweets were made with honey, and sometimes with honey and cheese. The only intoxicating drink was wine; even in bars (thermopolia), which, to judge from Pompeii, were as common then as now, hot wine was drunk. . . .
>
> The use of bread seems to have become general only at the beginning of the second century B.C. Besides special types of bread, like barley and spelt bread, there were three main grades: 1) black bread, of coarsely ground flour, 2) whiter, but still coarse, and 3) the best quality.
>
> The commonest vegetables were lentils and chickpeas, and among green vegetables lettuce, cabbage and leeks. . . . The Romans were great devotees of mushrooms, as is shown by many references, particularly in Martial. The olive, which we regard simply as a hors d'oeuvre, was much more highly esteemed. . . .
>
> The commonest fruits were those we still have: apples, pears, cherries, plums, grapes (fresh, dried or preserved), walnuts, almonds, and chestnuts. . . . The apricot was introduced from Armenia, and used in the preparation of certain dishes, for example chopped ham. Dates (imported from warmer countries) seem to have been very common.
>
> The animal world contributed to the Roman table a little more widely than it does to ours. Besides beef and pork the Romans ate venison, the flesh of wild asses (onager), and dormice, to the raising of which tremendous care was paid. . . . Animals which have disappeared from our table but were much prized by the Romans were the flamingo, of which the tongue was particularly esteemed, the stork, the crane and even the psittacus, a small talking bird of the parrot family. The peacock was an object of great gastronomic enthusiasm among the Romans.

### *Analyze and Interpret*

From your reading of this selection, why can you believe that obesity was not a common Roman health problem?

Source: Ugo Paoli, *Rome: Its People, Life, and Customs* (New York: Greenwood, 1963).

poverished small farmers. More and more people were tempted or coerced into giving up their independence to obtain regular income and protection against rapacious tax collectors. Another ominous trend in the empire was the increasing social stratification, particularly in the towns of Italy. The rich were more numerous than ever before, and the poor were both more numerous and more miserable. Wealth seems to have become the main qualification for public office.

### *Slave and Free*

The number of slaves climbed sharply in the first century B.C.E. Roman legions took over one province after another and made off with the human booty. The alien slaves were often more educated and better skilled than the native Italians, and slaves from Greece, in particular, brought high prices in the market. Augustus tried to protect the free citizens by banning the importation of additional slaves into Italy, but his measures were evaded and later revoked.

Roman slavery was harsher than had been the case earlier. The large merchant fleet and the navy depended on galley slaves. The extensive Roman mining industry also depended on slave labor, because this job was so dangerous that few freemen could be lured into it. Slave families were broken up and sold to the highest bidders. Slaves supposedly could own no property of their own, nor could they inherit or bequeath property. The children from a marriage of slaves were automatically the property of the parents' owners. Rape of another's slave was considered a damage to the slave owner, not to the slave, and was paid for accordingly. The rape of a slave by his or her owner was not an offense at all.

Despite such treatment, by the third and fourth centuries C.E., free persons were increasingly selling themselves into voluntary slavery, which promised them a better material life than freedom could. Sometimes, too, the self-sale was a dodge to avoid the tax, which a free person had to pay but a slave did not. It is not possible to know which motive predominated.

### *Gender Relations*

The earmark of female status was the far-reaching authority of the father over his daughter and, indeed, over all his *familia,* defined as wife, children, grandchildren, and household slaves. This ***patria potestas*** (literally, the "power of the father") extended even to life and death, although the exercise of the death penalty was rare.

All Roman law was concerned primarily with the protection of property, and the laws concerning women clearly

**A Roman Apartment House.** This model has been reconstructed from archaeological evidence found at Ostia, Rome's port. The building on the right is the home of a wealthy family, possibly the owners of the multistory tenement to the left. Although some tenements were solidly built, many were thrown up to maximize the income for the landlord and allowed to become filthy nests.

show that they were considered the property of the male head of the familia. It is worth noting that the father's powers exceeded those of the husband. For example, if a wife died without leaving a will, the property she left reverted not to her husband but to her father. A woman who passed from her father's control and was not under that of a husband was termed ***sui juris*** ("of his or her own law"). This status was quite unusual. Women who were neither married nor possessing sui juris had to be under tutelage—that is, a male relative was legally responsible for her.

Roman girls married young by our standards, and betrothal was often much earlier still. Marriage at age thirteen was not unusual. The girl's consent was not necessary. Unlike many other civilizations, the Roman widow was expected to remarry if she could, and she was normally then sui juris, legally equal to her new husband in terms of control over property.

Divorce of wives by husbands was common among the upper classes. Augustus, scandalized by the habits of some of his colleagues, decreed that a man catching his wife in adultery must divorce her or be considered her procurer and be punished himself. Divorce was much harder for a woman to obtain, and sexual impotence was one of the few grounds accepted. Because marriage was considered a consensual union rather than a legal obligation of the spouses, the lack of continued consent was itself grounds for its dissolution. This is the source of the modern divorce by "irreconcilable differences." Abortion was legal until the first century C.E., and when it was then declared a crime, it was because the act affected the property of the father of the fetus—a typical Roman viewpoint. Infanticide by exposure also continued, but no one knows how common it may have been or whether it favored the male over the female child, as is frequently assumed. A large proportion of slaves and prostitutes originated as girl babies picked up "from the trash heap," as the Roman saying went.

Women worked in all trades not requiring the heaviest labor. Textile trades were still the most common occupation for women of all classes, slave and free. Midwives, many physicians, scribes, and secretaries were female. Personal servants, hairdressers, nannies, and masseuses (a Roman passion) were always women. Entertainers of all sorts—acrobats, clowns, actresses, musicians, dancers—were in high demand. They were often female and frequently combined their stage talents with a bit of prostitution on the side. The tradition that female artistes are sexually available continues in Mediterranean folklore to the present day.

Like most peoples, Romans attempted to legislate morality. Rape and female adultery were two of the most serious offenses. Both were punishable by death, although actual prosecutions seem to have been few.

Homosexuality does not appear to have been as widespread in Rome as it had been in Greece, although it was certainly not unusual among the upper classes. Prostitution was not itself illegal, but it carried with it *infamia,* meaning disrepute and shame for the practitioners. Prostitutes were expected to register with the local authorities, and they paid heavy taxes on their earnings. Nevertheless, they were not criminals but were simply engaged in business and were so treated. Brothel keeping in Roman times, as earlier and later, was one of the more dependable sources of wealth for the (generally female) proprietors.

## Children and Education

The male child of patrician birth was important as the continuer of the familia, and much attention was devoted to his education, sometimes at a school, but more often by a live-in tutor. Strict demands for achievement were placed on him from the earliest years. Learning was acquired for a communal purpose: to advance the welfare of the state. Therefore, the most important subjects to master were law and the principles of government. All men of affairs were also taught rhetoric and philosophy. Science and the fine arts were of secondary importance and were viewed as personal matters, possibly important to the individual but only incidental to the community.

The segregation of the sexes that was so marked in classical Greece was largely overcome in Roman theory and, to some extent, in practice. Roman females gradually received increased freedom to enter the "great world" of male concerns. They could do this through advanced studies and larger political responsibilities. Hence, by the second century C.E., it was no longer absurd for a middle-class Roman girl to study mathematics or philosophy or to become an instructor in one of the arts—all careers that had been closed even to upper-class Greek females.

**Girl Reading.** This tender rendition of a young girl daydreaming over her studies is marked by a sentiment not often encountered in Roman painting.

# Summary

The peculiar balance of political power between aristocrats and commoners that the Roman republic established lasted as long as Rome remained a socially and ethnically homogeneous state and extended its rule only to Italy. This situation ended with Rome's hard-fought success in the Punic Wars of the third century B.C.E., when the city-state became in fact, but not yet in name, an empire.

The failure of the republic's pseudo-democratic political structure to adapt to the changed circumstances led to civil war and constant upheaval during the last century of its existence. Reformers attempted in vain to find a solution during these unstable years. Julius Caesar tried to establish a monarchy but was cut down by his conservative enemies. His adoptive son Octavian had better success, as the first emperor, Augustus Caesar. For more than 200 years, the Augustan reforms, continued by a series of able successors, enabled Rome to prosper in peace while creating a Mediterranean and west European hegemony.

Roman republican culture and art forms were originally based on Greek and Etruscan models, with the Greeks of the Hellenistic Age being particularly important. In form and content, philosophy and religious belief resembled the Greek originals from which they were largely derived. More innovation was shown during the late republican and imperial epoch, but the creative artistic imagination was generally not the Romans' strong point. In law and government and in the practical application of scientific knowledge to everyday problems of society, however, few surpassed them.

## Identification Terms

Test your knowledge of this chapter's key concepts by defining the following terms. If you can't recall the meaning of certain terms, refresh your memory by looking up the boldfaced term in the chapter, turning to the Glossary at the end of the book, or working with the flashcards that are available on the *World Civilizations* Companion Website: **http://history.wadsworth.com/adler04/**.

Actium, battle of
Carthage
censors
consuls
Etruscans
*jus gentium*
*municipia*
*patria potestas*
patricians
Pax Romana
plebeians
Praetorian Guard
*princeps*
proconsuls
proletariat
Punic War
*sui juris*
tribunes
Zama, battle of

## Test Your Knowledge

Test your knowledge of this chapter by answering the following questions. Complete answers appear at the end of the book. You may also take this quiz interactively and find even more quiz questions on the *World Civilizations* Companion Website: **http://history.wadsworth.com/adler04/**.

1. The peoples who exerted the greatest influence on early Rome were the
   a. Etruscans and Hittites.
   b. Greeks and Egyptians.
   c. Greeks and Etruscans.
   d. Egyptians and Etruscans.
   e. Etruscans and Phoenicians.
2. Chief executive authority in the Roman republic was exercised by
   a. a king.
   b. two consuls.
   c. four praetors.
   d. ten tribunes.
   e. three censors.
3. The first decisive change in the political nature of Rome from a homogeneous city-state to an empire came after the
   a. conquest of Greece.
   b. triumph of Octavian Caesar over his partners in the Second Triumvirate.
   c. attainment of supreme power by Julius Caesar.
   d. winning of the wars against Carthage.
   e. death of Julius Caesar.
4. The first province outside the Italian "boot" to be added to the Romans' sphere of government was
   a. Gaul.
   b. Greece.
   c. Sicily.
   d. Egypt.
   e. Carthage.
5. The group of Roman officials who came to govern the new provinces won from Carthage was
   a. the proconsuls.
   b. the censors.
   c. the triumvirates.
   d. the tribunes.
   e. the senators.
6. Roman law is notable for its
   a. egoism and arrogance.
   b. brutality and vengeance.
   c. gentleness and mercy.
   d. practicality and flexibility.
   e. rigidity and stagnation.
7. A chief strength of Roman arts was their
   a. portrait painting.
   b. dramatic tragedy.
   c. miniature goldwork.
   d. sculpted busts.
   e. well-developed historiography.
8. The Roman state religion consisted mainly of
   a. ritual and ceremony.
   b. prayer for personal salvation.
   c. theological discussions.
   d. emotion-charged public devotions.
   e. rejection of Greek polytheism.
9. Slavery after about 100 B.C.E. was usually
   a. harsher and more common than had been the case earlier.
   b. a temporary condition that was easily overcome.

c. a punishment reserved for serious crimes against the state.
d. reserved for non-Italians.
e. a hereditary condition.

10. For Roman women, divorce was
a. as easily obtained as for men.
b. an absolute impossibility because of patria potestas.
c. granted only for cases of homosexuality in the husband.
d. possible only when no children could be conceived.
e. difficult but obtainable on a few grounds.

## InfoTrac College Edition

Visit the source collections at

**http://infotrac.thomsonlearning.com**

and use the Search function with the following key terms:

Rome history
Roman republic
Julius (and Caesar)
Roman Empire
Roman law

## Wadsworth History Website Resources

Visit the World History Resource Center at **http://history.wadsworth.com/world** for a wealth of general resources and the *World Civilizations* Companion Website at **http://history.wadsworth.com/adler04/** for resources specific to this textbook.

## HistoryNow

Enter *HistoryNow* using the access card that is available for *World Civilizations*. *HistoryNow* will assist you in understanding the content in this chapter with lesson plans generated for your needs. In addition, you can read the following documents, and many more, online:

Livy, *Histories*

*They have no fixed abode, no home or law or settled manner of life, but wander.*

Ammianus Marcellinus (Roman historian, speaking of the German tribes)

# 11 Imperial Decline and the Birth of Christian Europe

Internal Upheavals and Invading Barbarians

Restructuring of the Empire

Christianity
- The Appeal of Christianity
- Christianity's Spread and Official Adoption
- Early Church Organization and Doctrine

Germanic Invaders

German Customs and Society
- Conversion to Christianity
- Germanic Law
- Female Status
- Beginnings of Feudalism
- The Dark Age

Charlemagne and the Holy Roman Empire
- Carolingian Renaissance
- Disintegration of the Carolingian Empire
- Renewed Invasions
- Development of Feudalism

The Byzantine Empire

| | |
|---|---|
| c. 6 B.C.E.–29 C.E. | Life of Jesus of Nazareth |
| 284–305 C.E. | Diocletian/Empire divided East and West |
| 313–337 C.E. | Constantine/Christianity tolerated |
| 381 C.E. | Theodosius makes Christianity official religion |
| late 300s–400s C.E. | Germanic invaders enter western empire |
| 527–565 C.E. | Justinian I/*Corpus Juris* |
| c. 500–800 | "Dark Age"/Germanic kingdoms |
| 768–814 | Charlemagne/Carolingian renaissance |
| 800s–900s | Rise of feudalism |

After Marcus Aurelius's reign (161–180 C.E.), Rome's power and its convictions of a mandate to rule began to decline. Several of the outer provinces were invaded briefly by Germanic tribes in the mid-200s, and the whole empire was wracked by internal strife that threatened to bring its traditional authority down entirely. At the beginning of the fourth century came an effort at renewal and realignment based in part on the official embrace of the formerly condemned Christianity and in part on absolute monarchy as the new style of rule. But this effort was doomed in the longer run. Germans increasingly forced their way into the empire's heartlands and imposed their own partially digested forms of Roman law and governmental technique on the populace at large. Only after the slow process of conversion to Christian belief had effected some softening of the Germanic warrior culture did the general regression in the art and craft of civilization become less apparent and this so-called Dark Age begin to lift. Charlemagne's interlude as reviver of Roman authority and belief, however bravely undertaken, proved to be a transitory moment.

## Internal Upheaval and Invading Barbarians

After the unfortunate reign (180–193) of the corrupt and incompetent Commodus, son of Marcus Aurelius, the central government fell into the hands of military usurpers for almost a century. Agriculture, which had always provided the livelihood of most Roman subjects, was increasingly dominated by large estates employing unfree labor. Cities declined in size and importance as civil wars among the generals reduced one urban center after another to ashes or strangled its commerce. Some of the provinces were relatively untouched by these conflicts, particularly in the East. This fact reinforced the ever-clearer political and economic dominance of the eastern half of the empire over the western.

In the half-century between 235 and 284, Rome had twenty emperors, eighteen of whom died by violence. This was the infamous age of the **Barracks Emperors.** An ambitious commander who had the momentary support of a legion or two might attempt to seize power in Rome or in one or another of the provinces. Those who had the allegiance of the Italian garrison, the Praetorian Guard, were the most powerful at any given moment, and the guard was easily bought with promises of booty.

Ordinary citizens were not involved in these struggles, of course, but they suffered the effects in many ways. Respect for imperial authority disappeared, the courts of law were overruled by force, and bribery and corruption of officials became commonplace. The long-distance trade that had sustained much of Roman prosperity was badly disrupted.

It was Rome's bad luck that the Barracks Emperors coincided with the first really serious challenges from the barbarian tribes beyond its borders. In the later third century, the "Wandering of the Peoples," the long-sustained nomadic migrations begun much earlier from Asia and eastern Europe, reached the outer provinces from the Low Countries all the way to the Balkans. When these tribal peoples reached the river frontiers (the Rhine and the Danube), they found large gaps in the defenses, caused by the army's dissolution into a series of quasi-private forces. Sometimes peaceably and sometimes by force, the newcomers crossed into the civilized areas in groups both small and large.

Almost miraculously, the last few general-emperors in the 270s were able to beat off the barbarian attacks and manipulate the various tribes and nations into fighting one another more than the Romans. Rome gained breathing space that was utilized by the last of the Barracks Emperors, Diocletian, to reorganize the badly wounded government.

## Restructuring of the Empire

Under Diocletian (ruled 284–305), a capable general who had fought his way to supreme power, the fiction created by Augustus Caesar that he was merely first among equals was finally buried. From now on, the emperor was clearly the absolute ruler of a subservient *Senatus et populus.* His bureaucrats were his instrument to effect his will, rather than agents of the Roman people. Diocletian brooked no opposition, not because he was a tyrant, but because he saw that if the empire was to survive, something new must be tried immediately.

To make the huge empire more governable, Diocletian divided it into western and eastern halves and underlined the dominance of the East by taking that half for his personal domain (see Map 11.1). The other he gave to a trusted associate to rule from Rome as his deputy. Each of the two co-emperors appointed an assistant, who was to follow him in office. This system, called the **Tetrarchy** (rule of four), was supposed to end the civil wars. It failed as soon as Diocletian retired (305 C.E.), but the reorganization of the empire into two halves remained.

Diocletian also attempted to revive the economy by lowering inflation, which had been rampant since the early Barracks Emperors. He issued the first governmental "price ceilings" on consumer goods in Western history (which failed, of course). He attempted to restore the badly damaged faith in the value of Roman coinage, whose gold and silver content had been steadily and surreptitiously reduced. He also increased the tax burden and insisted that the tax collectors were personally responsible for making up any arrearages in their districts. The net result was to make taxes more hated than ever and the tax collectors' posts almost unfillable.

Constantine the Great (ruled 313–337), Diocletian's successor to supreme power after an eight-year civil war, generally continued these policies and increased the restrictions on personal freedoms that the central government was steadily imposing. The measures were aimed especially at the free peasants, who were being forced into debt by the big landlords and who often ran away or sold themselves into slavery or were otherwise lost to the tax collector.

In the 330s, Constantine took the long-expected step of formally transferring the government to the East. Perched on the shore of the strait between Europe and Asia in a highly strategic location, the new capital city of Byzantium was well defensible from both land and sea. In time, the city of Constantine (Constantinople in Greek) became the largest city in the Christian world. Greek was the dominant language in the new capital, and Greeks were the dominant cultural force from the beginning.

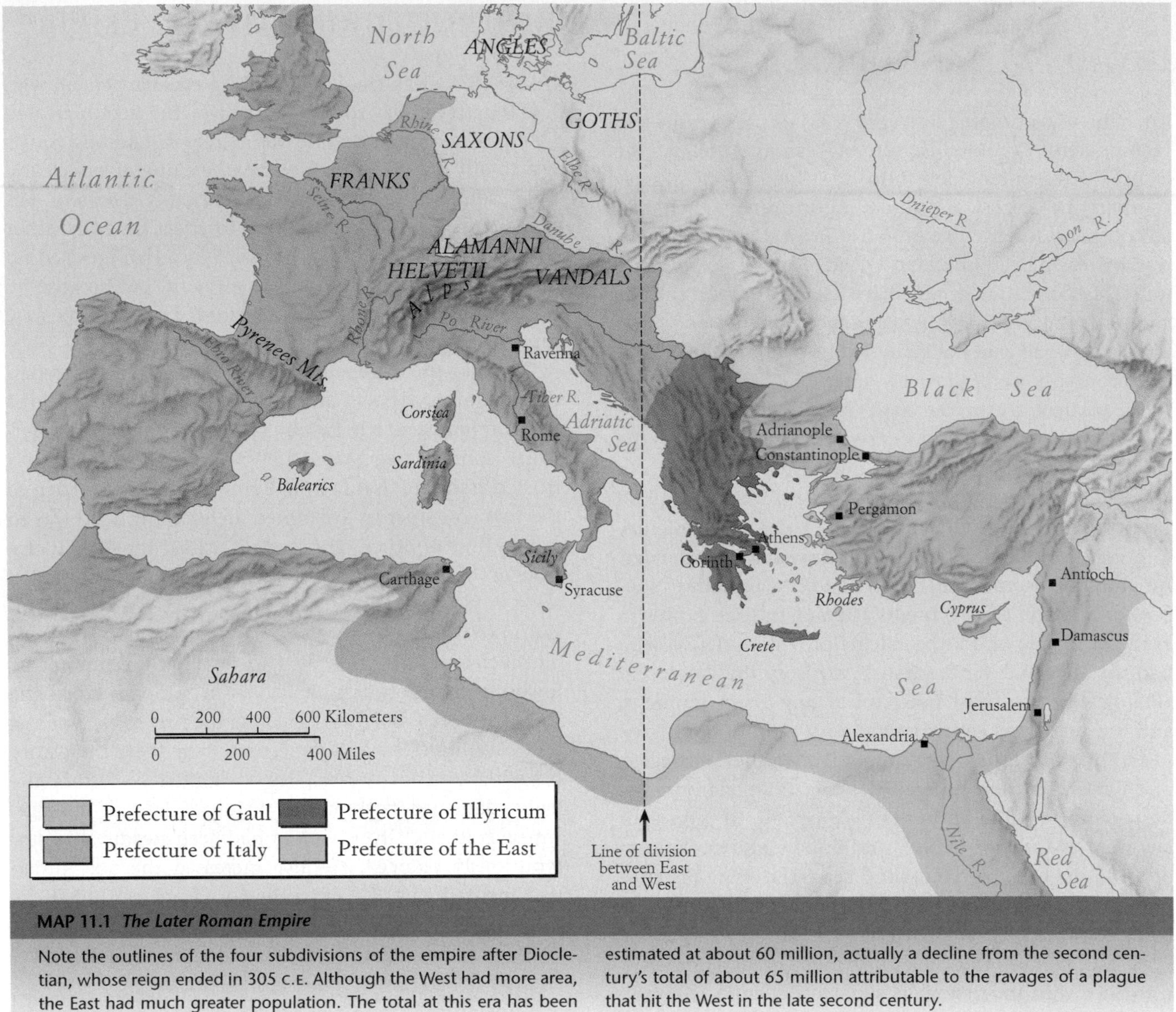


**MAP 11.1** ***The Later Roman Empire***

Note the outlines of the four subdivisions of the empire after Diocletian, whose reign ended in 305 C.E. Although the West had more area, the East had much greater population. The total at this era has been estimated at about 60 million, actually a decline from the second century's total of about 65 million attributable to the ravages of a plague that hit the West in the late second century.

What happened to the old Rome in the West? Although the deputy emperor maintained his government there for another century and a half, that city and surrounding Italy were in steady decline. Rome was ravaged by two Vandal raids (in 410 and 455) that left parts of it in permanent ruin. Finally, in 476, a German chieftain pushed aside the insignificant and powerless deputy of Constantinople and crowned himself king of Italy, an event conventionally taken as the end of the Roman Empire in the West.

## Christianity

While the Roman Empire weakened and crumbled, a new force—Christianity—developed within it. *Jesus of Nazareth* (c. 6 B.C.E.–29 C.E.), whom about one-third of the world's population assert to be the Son of God and Redeemer of Mankind, was born during the reign of Augustus Caesar, about a generation after Pompey had incorporated Judaea into the growing Roman Empire. We summarize his life and influence in the Patterns of Belief box.

During the last century B.C.E., the Hellenistic mystery religions (see Chapter 9) had become widely popular. Egyptian, Persian, Greek, and Italian cults promising power and immortality appealed to the lower ranks of a population that was steadily being divided into economic haves and have-nots. The Jews were not immune to this appeal and subdivided into several factions that held different views of the deliverer—the messiah promised to them long ago (see Chapter 4). None of these factions were receptive to the pacifist and provocative message of love and forgiveness that Jesus preached between 26 and 29 C.E. To the Sadducees and Pharisees, Jesus's admoni-

**The Walls of Constantinople.** After the move from Rome, the government devoted much money and energy to making the new capital impregnable from both sea and land. On the land side, a series of gigantic walls were erected, which protected Constantinople from all attacks until 1453, when the Ottoman Turks succeeded in capturing it by breaking down the walls with newly discovered gunpowder.

Scala/Art Resource, NY

tion to stop confusing the letter of the law with its spirit was an attempt to seduce the Jews, who had survived and remained a distinct nation only because of their unbending adherence to their Mosaic laws. Zealots wished to fight the Romans and had no empathy with a prophet who asked them to "render unto Caesar the things that are Caesar's"—that is, to accept the legitimate demands of their Roman overlords.

Meanwhile, the Roman administrators must have regarded Jesus as a special irritant among an already-difficult, religiously obsessed people. The Jews' religious doctrines were of no concern to the Romans, but Jesus's challenges to the traditionalist rabbis did create difficulties in governing. In the most literal sense, Jesus was "stirring things up." As a result, when the Jewish leaders demanded that the Roman procurator, Pontius Pilate, allow them to punish this disturber of the peace, he reluctantly agreed, and Jesus was crucified on Golgotha near Jerusalem.

For a couple of decades thereafter, the Christian cult spread slowly in Judaea and was nearly unknown outside it. This situation changed as a result of two developments. First, the educated Jew Saul of Tarsus (c. 6–67 C.E.), a Roman citizen and sophisticate, was miraculously converted to Christianity on the road to Damascus. As the apostle Paul, he insisted on preaching to the Gentiles (non-Jews). Second, the fanatical element among the Jews rebelled against the Roman overlords in the **Jewish War** (67–71 C.E.). After the Romans crushed it, they decided to punish this troublesome people by dispersing them in what came to be known as the *Diaspora* (actually, the second Diaspora: see Chapter 4). One result of this forced eviction from Judaea was the establishment of Jewish exile colonies that became breeding grounds for Christianity throughout the eastern Mediterranean basin and soon in Italy itself. Spurred by the strenuous efforts of the apostle Paul and his band of missionaries, the Christian doctrine was spreading steadily, if not spectacularly, among both ex-Jews and Gentiles by the end of the first century.

## The Appeal of Christianity

What was the appeal of the new religion? First, it distinguished itself from all of the other mystery religions by its *universality.* All persons were eligible: men and women, Jew and Gentile, rich and poor, Roman and non-Roman. Second, Christianity offered a message of *hope and optimism* in a Hellenistic cultural world that appeared increasingly grim for the aspirations of ordinary people. Not only were believers promised a blessed life to come, but the prospects for a better life on this Earth also appeared to be good. The Second Coming of the Lord and its accompanying Last Judgment, when the just would be rewarded and the evil punished according to their desserts, were thought to be not far off. Third, Christians were far ahead of their rivals in the *spirit of mutuality* that marked the early converts. To be a Christian was to accept an active obligation to assist your fellows in any way you might. It also meant you could count on their help and prayers when needed. Finally, Christianity featured an *appeal to idealism* that was much more powerful than anything its rivals offered. It emphasized charity and unselfish devotion in a way that had strong appeal to people

PATTERNS OF BELIEF

# Jesus of Nazareth (c. 6 B.C.E.–c. 29 C.E.)

**The life and works of Jesus** have affected more people more directly than those of any other individual in world history. With more than 2 billion formal adherents, Christianity is the world's most widespread faith. As with other important world religions, its founder's life is known only in sketchy outline.

In the centuries of Hellenistic civilization, several religions arose in the eastern Mediterranean that shared certain fundamental features. They insisted that there was a better life to come after the earthly existence and that some individuals had the potential to share in that life. They also maintained that it was necessary to follow the teaching of a mythic hero-prophet in order to realize that potential. These were the "mystery" religions, whose members depended on an act of faith by the believer, rather than mere attendance at a priestly ceremony.

**Christ and the Fishers of Souls.** This Ravenna, Italy, mosaic dating from the sixth century shows Christ calling to his disciples Peter and Andrew and telling them that henceforth they would be "fishers of souls." Fishing was a common mode of making a living in the Near East, in both fresh and salt waters. The mosaic was done, like many others, while Ravenna was the capital of the Byzantine government's attempt to regain Italy for the emperor.

San Apollinare Nuovo Ravenna/Dagli Orti/The Art Archive

Christianity was by far the most important of the mystery religions. Its founder was not a mythic hero, such as the Egyptian Osiris or the Greek Cybele, but a real historical person, Jesus of Nazareth, later called by his followers the *Christos,* or Messiah. Jesus was born in the newly romanized province of Judaea, the former kingdom of Judah and home of the two tribes of Israel that had stayed true to the Mosaic Law.

Of Jesus's early life until he embarked on his preaching career at about age thirty, we know next to nothing. The Christian disciples who wrote the books of the New Testament did not think it relevant to Jesus's work to tell us of his youth or the intellectual context in which he grew up.

It is reasonably sure that Jesus was born to a couple—Mary and Joseph—who were quite ordinary, practicing Jews. Their status was undistinguished before the miraculous selection of the young Virgin Mary as the mother of the Messiah. For many years thereafter, the family (Jesus may have had at least one half-brother, the apostle James) led an obscure life in the region of Galilee, probably in the town of Nazareth.

Around 26 C.E., Jesus was introduced to the teachings of John the Baptist, one of the numerous wandering sages of the day. In that same year, Pontius Pilate was appointed governor of Judaea. He was an average official, concerned mainly with making money out of his position and keeping the subject population sufficiently quiet so as not to create difficulties for his reputation back in Rome.

During the next few years, a group of lower-class Jews attached themselves to Jesus, seeing in him truly the Son of God and the long-awaited Messiah, as he claimed to be. Most of the time, Jesus followed the precepts of Jewish law and tradition quite closely, and he repeatedly said that he did not intend to found a new religion. But his bold insistence on the spirit, rather than the letter, of the law and his flat statement that, although he was the Messiah, his kingdom was not of this world, cast him in a dubious light among the tradition-bound rabbis. Before long, his message of faith in God, hope in his mercy to secure salvation, and love of one's fellow man was being seen by the high-placed as potentially revolutionary. They carried their complaints to Pontius Pilate and induced him to let them crucify Christ as an enemy of Roman rule as well as of the Mosaic Law.

The Sermon on the Mount gives us the most coherent and concise overview of Jesus's message. It is a message of tolerance, justice, and humility, of turning the other cheek and keeping the peace. Jesus thus differentiated himself and his doctrines from all other mystery religions, in which the prospect of eventually triumphing over enemies and reveling in the "good things" of the world was a major motivation for keeping the faith. Already by the Resurrection three days after his crucifixion, the small cadre of believers in Christ the Messiah felt they were the possessors of a sacred truth. Led by the apostles, they prepared to carry out their heavy responsibility to "make smooth the path of the Lord" on Earth.

## *Analyze and Interpret*

Why do you think the Bible has nothing to say of the early years of Jesus? What is meant by the spirit rather than the letter of the law being the crucial thing? How does the Sermon on the Mount exemplify the spirit of early Christianity?

**HistoryNow™**

***To read about Jesus's life in the Gospel according to Mark and about the work of the apostles, point your browser to the documents area of* HistoryNow.**

weary of a world that seemed to be dominated by the drive for wealth and power.

The Gospels ("good news") of the four evangelists, Mark, Luke, Matthew, and John, were the original doctrinal foundations of the faith. They were written and collected in the late first century C.E., along with the letters of St. Paul to the communities of Christians he had founded in the eastern Mediterranean. By the second century, a written New Testament had appeared that was accepted by all Christians and largely superseded the Old Testament of the Jews in their eyes.

## Christianity's Spread and Official Adoption

Slowly, Christian cells sprang up in the major towns all over the Mediterranean basin (see Map 11.2). The story of Peter the Apostle coming to Rome and dying a martyr's death shortly after the death of Christ may well be factual. Certainly several disciples, spurred on by Paul, left the strictly Jewish environment in which the religion had begun and "went out into the world" of Roman pagan culture. Paul himself is thought to have died a martyr in Rome under the persecution ordered by the emperor Nero.

By the early fourth century, it has been estimated that about 10 percent of the population of the East had become Christian and perhaps 5 percent of the West. In this situation, the emperor Constantine (whose mother Helena was a Christian) decided to end the persecution of Christians that had been going on at intervals since Nero's time. In 313 he issued the *Edict of Milan,* which announced the official toleration of Christianity and signaled that the new religion was favored at the imperial court. Constantine seemingly became a Christian only on his deathbed in 337, but from this time on, all emperors

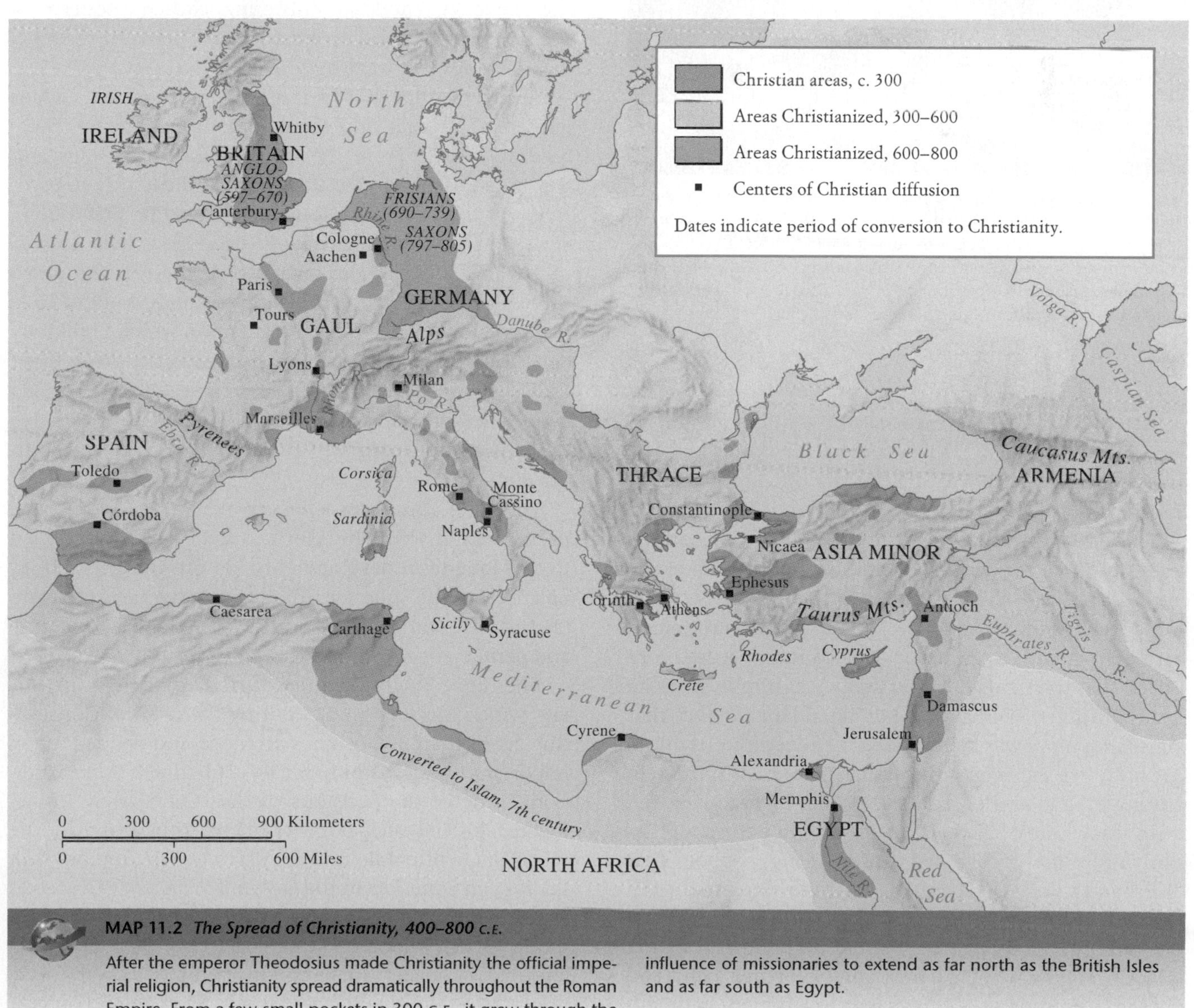


**MAP 11.2** ***The Spread of Christianity, 400–800 C.E.***

After the emperor Theodosius made Christianity the official imperial religion, Christianity spread dramatically throughout the Roman Empire. From a few small pockets in 300 C.E., it grew through the influence of missionaries to extend as far north as the British Isles and as far south as Egypt.

AKG London

**CHRIST IN BETHANIA.** This masterpiece of late Byzantine art shows Christ with his disciples at Bethany. It is a fresco in the Ascension church at Decani, in southern Serbia, painted in the mid-fourteenth century by an anonymous group of Greek and Serbian artists who had been trained in Byzantine technique. Note the use of curvature to focus the viewer's attention on the prostrate figure at the bottom.

in East and West, with the exception of Julian (361–363), were Christians. In 381, the emperor Theodosius took the final step of making Christianity the official religion of the empire.

Why did the suspicious and warlike Constantine decide to stake his own fate, and possibly the fate of the empire, on a new religion that had distinguished itself by its pacifism and its rejection of the traditional Roman state cult? As the story has it, Constantine became convinced that the Christian God had aided him in a crucial battle during the civil war, but historians suspect that something more was behind such a momentous decision. Probably, he expected this move would assist him in shoring up a wounded political system by gradually creating a new unity between governors and governed. Certainly, too, he recognized the growing support that Christianity was attracting among those who counted in Roman society.

Constantine's recognition would both aid and hinder the new religion. Giving Christianity a favored status and putting the resources of the secular government behind it spurred its growth. Soon Christians were a majority in the cities. (The countryside appears to have been much slower to adopt the new creed.) At the same time, Constantine's decision ensured that the Christian church would be linked with the state and the wishes of the state's governors. Church councils would soon find that civil questions would sometimes override purely religious considerations.

## *Early Church Organization and Doctrine*

Under Constantine, Christians came out into the open and organized their church on Roman civil models. In each community of any size, bishops were elected as heads of a diocese. They in turn appointed priests on the recommendation of the local faithful. The early Christian emperors made the fateful decision to allow the bishops to create their own courts and laws (*canon law*) for judging the clergy and administering church property—a decision that later led to great friction between revenue-seeking kings and wealthy bishops.

Several bishops of important eastern dioceses, such as Jerusalem, Antioch, and Alexandria, claimed direct office-holding descent from the twelve apostles of Jesus and therefore possessed special prestige and the title of *patriarch*. But the bishop of Rome claimed to be first among equals through the doctrine of *Petrine Succession*. According to this concept, the bishop of Rome was the direct successor of Peter, the first bishop of Rome, whom Christ had pronounced the "rock [*petros*] upon which I build my church." He therefore succeeded Peter as the preeminent leader of the church. This claim was stubbornly resisted by the patriarchs and other bishops until a pope was able to get it acknowledged by a church council in the sixth century.

The early church experienced many serious disputes in theology as well. The efforts to settle such disputes led to two long-term developments: (1) the council of bishops became the supreme arbiter in matters of faith, and (2) the civil and religious authorities established a close and permanent relationship.

The first council was the **Council of Nicaea,** in Turkey, which was held in 325 during the reign of Constantine. More than 300 bishops attended and defined many important questions of theology and church administration. Some of the decisions of the council were implemented by the secular government, thus bringing the second new principle into play. From this time onward, the Roman emperors in the East and West saw themselves as possessing executive powers within the Christian community—a development that led to conflict when the emperor and bishops had differing opinions on the civic implications of theological issues. Even after Emperor Theodosius, many educated Romans still could not bring themselves to adopt the new faith, which they regarded as a mixture of base superstition and a sort of cannibalism (the host, or Eucharist). The challenges that paganism presented to Christianity contributed to the rise of a school of Christian explainers of sacred doctrine, or *apologists,* in the 300s and 400s. The most important of these *Fathers of the Church,* as they are called, were Augustine and Ambrose, the bishops of Hippo (North Africa) and Milan, respectively. Their writings are the secondary foundation of the Christian faith, as the Gospels are the primary one. St. Augustine has been especially influential in molding belief. His *Confessions* and *The City of God* have been the most important repositories of Christian teaching after the Gospels.

By the early fifth century, the Christian faith was giving the tottering Roman Empire a new system of morality and ethics that challenged the old beliefs in myriad ways. After Theodosius's reign (378–395), the imperial government was a Christian entity, so Christians could actively support it and perhaps even defend it against its external enemies. But if this worldly empire fell, it was no tragedy. It was only the otherworldly kingdom of the Lord that should count in man's eyes. By thus shifting the focus to the next world, Christian doctrine made it easier to accept the sometimes painful ending of the western Roman Empire that was occurring at the hands of Germanic warriors.

Only slowly did many Christians acquiesce to the idea of blending Christian and pagan worldviews and realize that there was something to be learned from the Roman secular environment while they awaited the Last Judgment. By the time they had arrived at this realization, however, much of that secular world had already been hammered to pieces.

## Germanic Invaders

After the capital was moved to Constantinople, the western provinces were gradually sacrificed to the Germans, who by this time were being pushed from behind by various Asiatic peoples. The invasion of the Huns, Asian nomads who suddenly appeared in the 440s and pillaged their way through Italy, confirmed the Romans' decision to more or less abandon the West (see Map 11.3). The Huns dispersed after the death of their warrior leader, Attila, but the vulnerability of the West had been demonstrated, and the Germans would take full advantage of that fact.

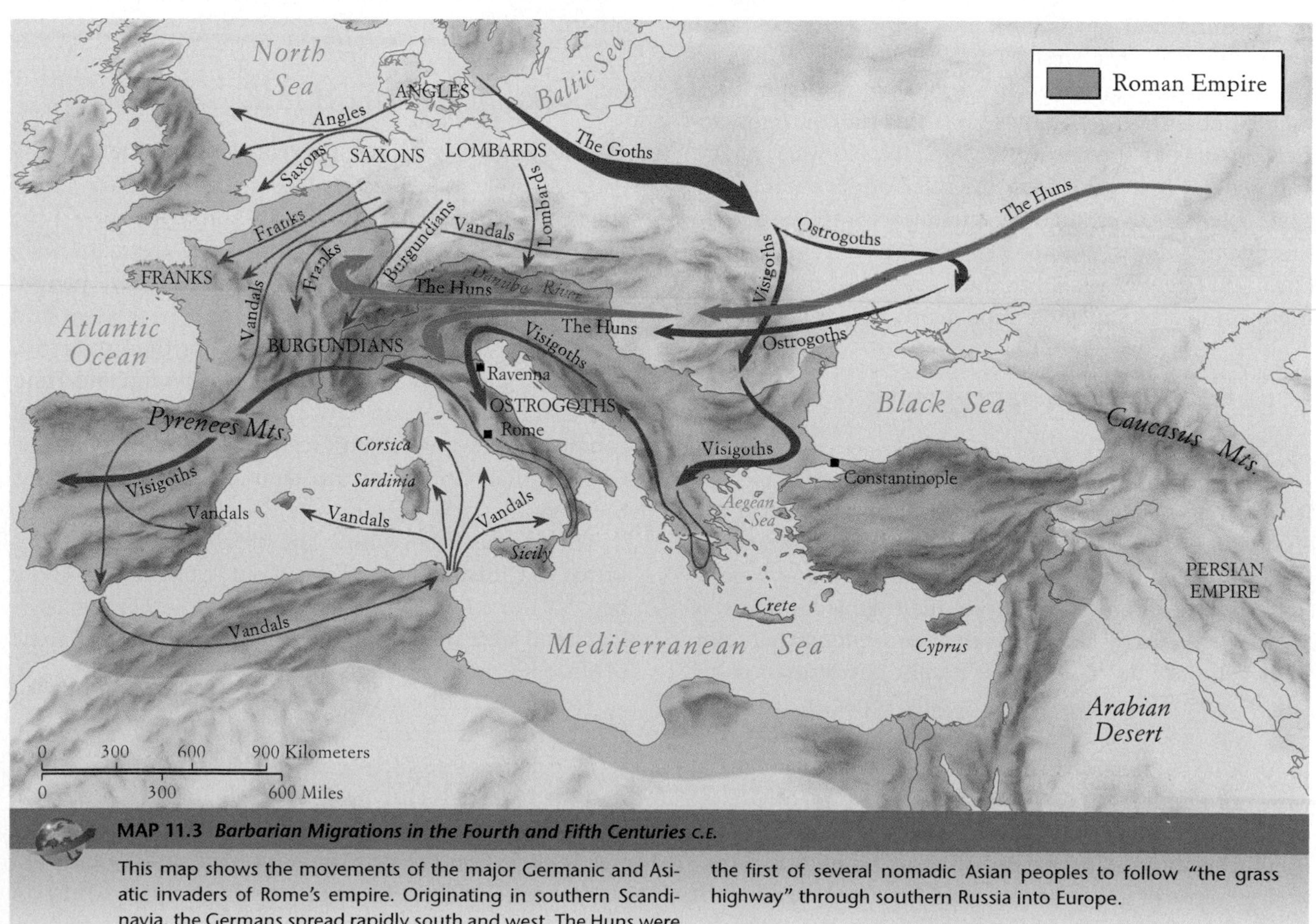


**MAP 11.3** ***Barbarian Migrations in the Fourth and Fifth Centuries*** C.E.

This map shows the movements of the major Germanic and Asiatic invaders of Rome's empire. Originating in southern Scandinavia, the Germans spread rapidly south and west. The Huns were the first of several nomadic Asian peoples to follow "the grass highway" through southern Russia into Europe.

What we know of the early Germanic people derives entirely from Roman sources, for they left no writings of their own and, in fact, had no written language until they learned Latin from the Romans. They spent much time fighting one another, and the Romans encouraged this behavior to keep the Germans weak. But once they learned to band together, the outer defenses of the Roman Empire came under frequent attack from a fierce and determined foe.

In the fourth and fifth centuries, the Germanic tribes roamed through the western provinces more or less at will (see Map 11.3). Replacing the demoralized Roman officials with their own men, the tribal war chiefs began to create rough-and-ready kingdoms:

1. The *Franks* established the core of the French kingdom in the fifth century.
2. The *Saxons* set up a kingdom in northern Germany from present-day Holland eastward.
3. The *Angles* and *Saxons* invaded and conquered England in the fifth century.
4. The *Vandals* invaded Roman North Africa, established a kingdom there, and from it made the raid on Rome (455), which gave their name to history.
5. The *West Goths (Visigoths)* took over Spain.
6. The *East Goths (Ostrogoths)* took over most of Italy after the Huns' raid.

By the 500s, the western half of the empire was an administrative and sometimes also a physical ruin. Germanic nobles had generally supplanted Italian or romanized officials as the authorities. Small-scale wars, piracy, and general insecurity were the rule. Under such conditions, Roman government and traditions and the Roman lifestyle gradually disappeared except in a handful of cities and larger towns. Even there, trade and manufacturing dwindled, as the population supporting them shrank.

## Germanic Customs and Society

It would take centuries for the two cultures—Roman and Germanic—to blend together to form the new culture that we call medieval European. The Germans were at first starkly differentiated from their subjects. Most of them wanted to be Roman, as they understood that term. They certainly did not hate or despise the Roman population or think themselves culturally superior. Intermarriage was practiced from the start. But they brought with them a large number of habits, beliefs, and values that were not at all like those of the conquered.

From the comments of the Romans who observed them, we know that the Germans had a highly personalized concept of government. Authority was exercised by an elected leader. He received the sworn loyalty of his warriors, but the leader's final authority applied only in time of war. In peacetime, the Germans remained essentially large families led by the oldest male, each of whom was a little king in his own right. If the war leader was defeated or the warriors were dissatisfied with his leadership, he could be deposed. There was no hierarchy below the chief and apparently no permanent offices of any sort.

For many years, the new Germanic leaders had no fixed residences but traveled continuously about their domains "showing the flag" of authority and acting as chief justices to resolve disputes. Gradually, this changed to the extent that the king had a favorite castle or a walled town named for him, where he might stay for part of each year.

Very slowly also, the idea made headway that the subject paid tribute and gave loyalty to the *office* of king, rather than to the individual holder of the crown. This last development resulted from Roman influence, and its contribution to peaceable transfer of power and stable government was so clear that all of the tribal leaders adopted it sooner or later. The Christian church authorities helped in this by preaching that the crown itself was a sacred object and that its holder was a sacred person, ordained by an all-wise God to exercise civil powers over others.

### Conversion to Christianity

The Germans had strong supernatural beliefs when they entered the Roman Empire, but we do not know much about their religion because it was thoroughly rooted out during the Christian Era. Originally, the Germans were *animists,* who saw spiritual powers in certain natural objects, such as trees. As with many other peoples around the globe (consider the Aryans in India or the Egyptians), their chief gods were sky deities, such as Wotan and Thor, who had no connection with either an afterlife or ethical conduct, but served as enforcers of the tribe's will. The Germans had no priests, no temples, and little, if any, theology.

The various tribes within the old Roman Empire converted to Christianity between about 450 and 700. Those beyond the empire's borders converted somewhat later. Last of all were the Scandinavians and Lithuanians, some of whom remained pagans as late as 1100.

The method of conversion was similar in all cases. A small group of priests, perhaps headed by a bishop, secured an invitation to go to the king and explain to him the Christian gospel. If they were fortunate (rarely!), conversion of the king, his queen, or important nobles was achieved on the first try. After baptism (the outward sign of joining the Christian world), the new Christian would exert pressure on family and cronies to join also, and they, in turn, would exhort their vassals and dependents. When much of the upper class was converted, at least in name, and some native priests were in place, the tribe or nation was considered Christian, a part of the growing family of ex-pagans who had adopted the new religion.

Why did the German authorities accept Christianity? Their reasons were almost always a combination of internal politics, desire for trade, and recognition of the advantages that Christian law could give the ruler in his efforts to create a stable dynasty. It generally took decades for the faith to filter down to the common people, even in a rudimentary sense. Centuries might pass before the villagers could be said to have much knowledge of church doctrine and before they would give up their most cherished pagan customs. Medieval Christianity was in fact a hodgepodge of pagan and Christian images and beliefs. Most priests were satisfied if their faithful achieved a limited understanding of sin, heaven and hell, and the coming Last Judgment. More could not be expected.

Réunion des Musées Nationaux/Art Resource, NY

**The Warrior Christ.** In the early medieval age, it was common to represent spiritual beings as literally engaged in battle for men's souls. In this sixth-century terra cotta relief, Christ is shown armed with sword and spear, treading on the hated symbol of primeval evil, the serpent Lucifer.

## Germanic Law

Germanic law was very different from Roman law and much more primitive. It derived from custom, which was unwritten and allowed for no fine points of interpretation. Law was the collective memory of the tribe or clan as to what had been done before in similar circumstances. It did not inquire into motivation but looked simply at the result.

The ultimate object of Germanic law was preventing or diminishing personal violence, which endangered the whole tribe's welfare. The guilty party, as determined by the assembly, was punished by the imposition of a money fine, or ***wergeld,*** which was paid to the victim as compensation. In this way, the blood feuds that would have eventually wrecked the tribe's ability to survive were avoided and the honor of the victim maintained.

The Germans used trial by fire and by water to determine guilt in criminal cases in which the evidence was not clear-cut. In some capital cases in which the two parties were of equal rank, they sometimes reverted to the extreme measure of trial by combat to get a verdict. As in ancient Mesopotamia, the object of a trial was to ascertain whether illicit damage had been done to an individual and, if so, how much compensation the victim was owed by the perpetrator. As in Hammurabi's code, the court, which was the general meeting of the elders of the clan or village, acted as a detached referee between the opposing parties. Also reminiscent of the older code, but not so overtly, justice was to a large extent modified by social status.

## Female Status

The status of women in pre-Christian Germanic society is a subject of much debate. According to some Roman sources, women who were married had considerable freedom and rights, more so than Roman matrons did. Although it was a warrior society, an extraordinary amount of attention seems to have been paid to the rights of mothers and wives, in both the legal and the social senses. In some cases, the widows of prominent men succeeded to their husband's position, a phenomenon the Romans found remarkable. After the Germans became Christian, there are many instances of queens and princesses exercising governmental power. The exercise of managerial powers by noble women was routine in their husband's death or absence.

The legal value (*wergeld*) of women of childbearing age was much higher than that of women who were too young or too old to have children. This reflects the view we have found in other ancient societies that women's chief asset was their ability to perpetuate the male family's name and honor. The Romans admired the Germans' sexual morality (although admittedly not to the point of adopting it themselves). Rape was a capital crime when committed against equals, as was adultery by a woman. Both concubinage and prostitution seem to have been unknown.

Musee Conde, Chantilly, France/Giraudon/Bridgeman Art Library

**THE FARMER'S TASKS.** Pastoral life in medieval Europe required the work of men, women, and children. This painting, from a *Book of Hours,* a compilation of sketches and devotions meant to guide the faithful in a Christian lifestyle, shows both the layout of a manor and its peasants at work.

## Beginnings of Feudalism

In the countryside, a process that had begun during the Barracks Emperors' rule accelerated dramatically. This was the establishment of large estates or **manors,** which were almost entirely self-sufficient and self-governing. The manor normally began as a villa, the country hideaway of a wealthy Roman official in quieter days. As order broke down and the province could ignore the central government, some of these officials became the equivalent of Chinese warlords, maintaining private armies to secure the peace in their own localities. Frequently extorting services and free labor from the villagers nearby, they evaded the central government's controls and taxes. These men grew ever more wealthy and powerful and began to acquire the peasants' lands through bribery, intimidation, and trade for the protection they offered.

When the invasions began, these strongmen simply took over the basic elements of government altogether. In return for physical protection and some assurance of order in their lives, the peasants would often offer part of their land and labor to the "lord" for some period, perhaps life. In this way was born both the later European nobility (or a large part of it) and the feudal system of agricultural estates worked by bound laborers. The serfs of later days were the descendants of these free men and women who were desperately seeking protection in a world of chaos and danger.

As the cities and towns declined, more and more of the population found itself in manorial villages, dependent on and loosely controlled by the Roman or German lord and his small band of armed henchmen. Economic life became much simpler, but it was more a daily struggle for survival than a civilized existence. The skills and contacts of Roman days fell into disuse, for there was little demand for them in this rough and sometimes brutal world. Trade in all but the barest necessities over the shortest distances became rare. Neither the roads nor the waters of western Europe were safe from marauders and pirates, and the Roman transport network fell to pieces.

## The Dark Age

So backward did much of society become that it was once usual to refer to the centuries between 500 and 800 as the Dark Age in Europe. Similarly to its namesake in ancient Greece, this term refers as much to the lack of documentation as to the ignorance of people living then. Not only have many documents perished through vandalism and neglect, but relatively few records were kept in the first place. Only the clergy had much need of writing, and many of the priests and monks in the seventh and eighth centuries did well to read or write more than their names. They were almost always illiterate in the official Latin language of the church and knew their church history and doctrines only by hearsay. Many a bishop could not write his sermon.

The venal and immoral conduct of some clergy gave rise to scandal. In many places church offices were bought and sold like so many pounds of butter. Rome was far away and could be easily ignored in church affairs, as it was in civil ones. Besides, the pope in this era was always an Italian nobleman who rarely gave much attention to things spiritual. This was particularly the case after 700.

In some countries, notably the German lands east of the Rhine, the bishops were more or less forced by the king to take on secular and even military duties as the king's lieutenants. The churchman was often the only educated person in the area and the only one who had some concept of administration and record keeping. The combination of civil and religious duties was, however, injurious to the religious. The bishop or abbot (the head of a monastery) often devoted more time and energy to his secular affairs than to his spiritual ones. All too frequently, important clergymen bribed their way into their position with the intention of using it as a means of obtaining wealth or influence in political matters. Their ecclesiastical duties played little or no role in these considerations. In the circumstances, it is more remarkable that some clergy *were* good and gentle men who tried to follow the rules than that many were not.

Having said all that, it is still true that the Christian church was the only imperial Roman institution that survived the Germanic onslaught more or less intact. The church was changed, usually for the worse, by German custom and concepts, but it did survive as recognizably the same institution that had won the religious allegiance of most Roman citizens in the fourth century. All of the education that was available in early medieval Europe was supplied by the church, which also operated whatever charitable and medical institutions existed. When the higher concepts of Roman law were recovered in Europe, the church adopted them first in its canon law and spread them to secular life by its teaching.

The *Age of Faith* had opened, and the church's teachings and preachings about the nature of humans and their relations with God were to have tremendous influence on every facet of human affairs, an influence that did not diminish noticeably for about a thousand years.

## Charlemagne and the Holy Roman Empire

The greatest of the Germanic kings by far was *Charlemagne* (Charles the Great), king of the Franks (768–800) and the first Holy Roman Emperor (800–814). The kingdom of the Franks had been in a favored position since its founder, Clovis, had been the first important German ruler to accept Roman Christianity, in or about 500. Charlemagne became king through the aggressive action of his father, a high official who seized royal power. An alliance with the pope in Rome did much to cement the new king's shaky legal position. Charlemagne earned the papacy's lasting gratitude by crushing the Lombards, a Germanic people who had settled in northern Italy and were pushing south, threatening Rome.

For more than thirty years (772–804), Charlemagne was at war with one or another pagan German neighbor. His persistence was rewarded by the establishment of by far the largest territory under one ruler since Roman times and by the granting of the title *emperor* by Pope Leo III. (See Map 11.4.)

Charles's new empire was an attempt to revive the Roman order in Europe, in close cooperation with the Christian church. According to medieval theory, the civil government and the ecclesiastical establishment were two arms of a single body, directed by one head: Christ. Charlemagne's coronation by Leo in the papal city on Christmas Day 800 was looked on as the culmination of that dream of proper governance and as the greatest event since the birth of Christ.

The emperor in Constantinople was not pleased, to put it mildly.

### Carolingian Renaissance

Charlemagne's claims to fame stem more from his brave attempts to restore learning and stable government to Europe than from his coronation as the first emperor.

He revived the Roman office of *comes,* or count, as the representative of the king in the provinces. He started the ***missi dominici,*** special officers who checked up on the counts and others and reported directly to the king. Knowing that most people were touched more directly by religion than by government, Charlemagne also concerned himself with the state of the church. Many of his most trusted officials were picked from the clergy, a practice that would lead to problems in later days.

Charles admired learning, although he had little himself (supposedly, he, too, could not sign his name!). From all parts of his domains and from England, he brought men to his court who could teach and train others. Notable among them was *Alcuin,* an Anglo-Saxon monk of great

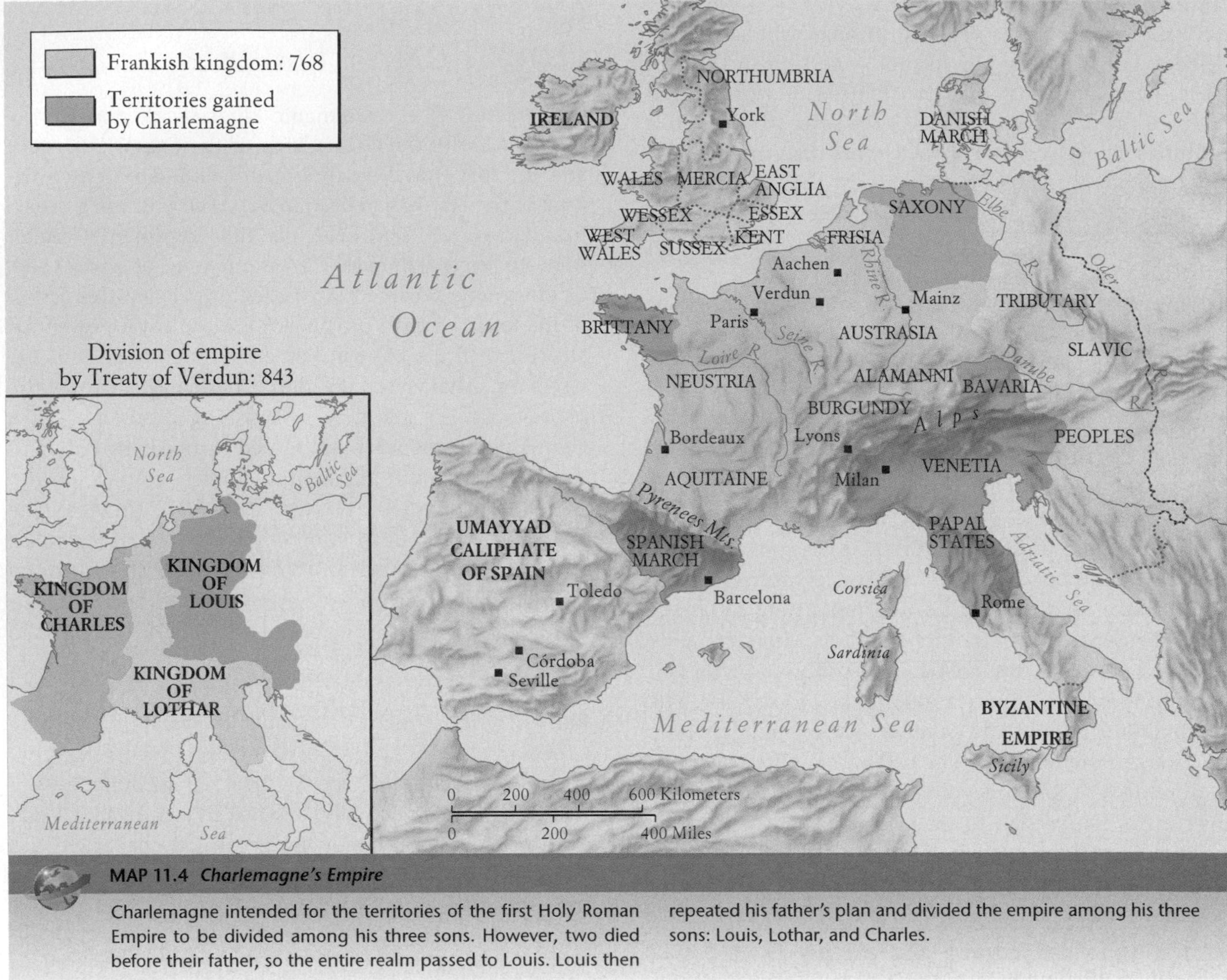


**MAP 11.4** *Charlemagne's Empire*

Charlemagne intended for the territories of the first Holy Roman Empire to be divided among his three sons. However, two died before their father, so the entire realm passed to Louis. Louis then repeated his father's plan and divided the empire among his three sons: Louis, Lothar, and Charles.

ability, who directed the palace school for clergy and officials set up by the king. For the first time since the 400s, something like higher education was available to a select few. Not overly pious himself, Charlemagne still respected and encouraged piety in others. At his orders, many new parishes were founded or given large new endowments, and these were reinforced by the establishment of many more monasteries.

But all Charlemagne's efforts were insufficient to turn the tide of disorder and violence. His "renaissance" was short lived, and his schools and governmental innovations were soon in ruins. The times were not ripe for them. In the first crises, they collapsed, and the darkness descended again.

## Disintegration of the Carolingian Empire

Charlemagne eventually bequeathed his empire to his only surviving son, Louis the Pious, a man who was unfit for the heavy responsibility. By Louis's will, the empire was divided among his three sons: Charles, Lothar, and Louis. Charles received France; Lothar, the midlands between France and Germany reaching down into Italy; and Louis, Germany. Fraternal war for supremacy immediately ensued. The *Treaty of Verdun* in 843, which established the peace, is one of the most important treaties in world history, for the general linguistic and cultural borders it established still exist today, 1,160 years later (see inset, Map 11.4). When Lothar died a few years later, the midlands were divided between the survivors, Charles and Louis. After a brief period, the title of Holy Roman Emperor was settled on the king of Germany, the successors of Louis, who retained it until the nineteenth century.

## Renewed Invasions

In the late ninth century, the center and western parts of Europe were attacked from three directions: the Vikings swept down from the north, the Magyars advanced from

SOCIETY AND ECONOMY

## Charlemagne

**THE MONK EINHARD** was a German. In the 790s, he went to join the school founded by Charlemagne and administered by Alcuin in the Carolingian capital at Aachen. After Charles's death, Einhard found time to write the most famous biography of the Christian Middle Age. He was particularly concerned with giving his readers a view of Charles as a human being. Very brief and easily read, the *Life of Charlemagne* is our chief source of information about the character of the first Holy Roman Emperor.

**Chapters 18 and 19: Private Life**

At his mother's request he married a daughter of the Lombard king Desiderius but repudiated her for unknown reasons after one year. Then he married Hildegard, who came from a noble Swabian family. With her he had three sons, Charles, Pepin, and Louis, and as many daughters. . . . [H]e had three more daughters with his third wife Fastrada. . . . When Fastrada died he took Liutgard to wife. . . . After her death he had four concubines. . . .

For the education of his children, Charles made the following provisions. . . . [A]s soon as the boys were old enough they had to learn how to ride, hunt, and handle weapons in Frankish style. The girls had to get used to carding wool and to the distaff and spindle. (To prevent their getting bored and lazy he gave orders for them to be taught to engage in these and in all other virtuous activities). . . . When his sons and daughter died, Charles reacted to their deaths with much less equanimity than might have been expected of so strong-minded a man. Because of his deep devotion to them he broke down in tears. . . . For Charles was by nature a man who had a great gift for friendship, who made friends easily and never wavered in his loyalty to them. Those whom he loved could rely on him absolutely.

He supervised the upbringing of his sons and daughters very carefully. . . . Although the girls were very beautiful and he loved them dearly it is odd that he did not permit any of them to get married, neither to a man of his own nation nor to a foreigner. Rather, he kept all of them with him until his death, saying he could not live without their company. And on account of this, he had to suffer a number of unpleasant experiences, however lucky he was in other respects. But he never let on that he had heard of any suspicions about their chastity or any rumors about them.

**Chapter 25: Studies**

Charles was a gifted speaker. He spoke fluently and expressed what he had to say with great clarity. Not only was he proficient in his mother tongue (Frankish) but he also took trouble to learn foreign languages. He spoke Latin as well as his own language, but Greek he understood better than he could speak it—He also tried his hand at writing, and to this end kept writing tablets and notebooks under his pillow in bed—But since he had only started late in life, he never became very accomplished in the art.

Musee Conde, Chantilly, France/Giraudon/Bridgeman Art Library

**THE POPE CROWNS CHARLEMAGNE, 800 C.E.** Legend states that the pope surprised Charlemagne with the offer of a crown. The Frankish king seems to have been less than impressed with the distinction, as he rarely if ever employed the new title.

### *Analyze and Interpret*

How does Charles's possessiveness toward his daughters make him more believable as a human being? What do you make of Einhard's statement that Charles "had to suffer a number of unpleasant experiences"? What do you think about the fact that this pillar of the church took at least four wives and concubines?

**HistoryNow™**

*To read more selections from Einhard's* **Life of Charlemagne,** *point your browser to the documents area of* **HistoryNow.**

the east, and the Muslims attacked from the Mediterranean. In the ensuing chaos, all that Charlemagne had been able to do was extinguished, and government reverted back to a primitive military contract between individuals for mutual defense.

The Vikings or Norsemen were the most serious threat and had the most extensive impact. Superbly gifted warriors, these Scandinavians came in swift boats to ravage the coastal communities and then flee before effective countermeasures could be taken. From their headquarters in Denmark and southern Sweden, every year after about 790 they sailed forth and soon discovered that the Franks, Angles, and Saxons were no match for them. In 834, a large band of Vikings sailed up the Seine and sacked Paris. Seventy years later, they advanced into the Mediterranean and sacked the great city of Seville in the heart of the Spanish caliphate.

By the late 800s, the Vikings were no longer content to raid. They came to conquer. Much of eastern England, Brittany and Normandy in France, Holland, and Iceland fell to them. In their new lands, they quickly learned to govern by intimidation rather than to plunder and burn, and taxes took the place of armed bands. They learned the advantages of literacy and eventually adopted Christianity in place of their northern gods. By about 1000, the Vikings had footholds ranging from the coast of the North Sea to the eastern Mediterranean. They had become one of the most capable of all the European peoples in government and administration, as well as the military arts.

The Magyars were a different proposition. They were the next-to-last version of the Asiatic invasions of western Europe, which had begun as far back as the Huns. This resemblance earned their descendants the name *Hungarians* in modern nomenclature. The Magyars arrived in Europe at the end of the ninth century and for fifty years fought the Christianized Germans for mastery. Finally, in a great battle in 955, the Magyars were defeated and retired to the Hungarian plains, where they gradually settled down. In 1000, their king and patron saint, Stephen, accepted Roman Christianity, and the Magyars joined the family of civilized nations.

The Muslims of the Mediterranean were descendants of North African peoples who had been harassing southern Europe as pirates and raiders ever since the 700s. In the late 800s, they wrested Sicily and part of southern Italy from the Italians and thereby posed a direct threat to Rome. But the Muslims were checked and soon settled down to join the heterogeneous group of immigrants who had been coming to southern Italy for a long time. The Muslims' highly civilized rule was finally disrupted by the attacks of the newly Christian Vikings, who began battling them for mastery in the eleventh century and eventually reconquered Sicily and the southern tip of the peninsula from them.

### *Development of Feudalism*

The invasions fragmented governmental authority, as the royal courts in France and Germany were unable to defend their territories successfully, particularly against the Viking attacks. It fell to local strongmen to defend their own areas as best they could. Men on horseback had great advantages in battle, and the demand for them rose steadily. Thus, the original **knights** were mercenaries, professional warriors-at-horse who sold their services to the highest bidder. What was bid normally was land and the labor of those who worked it. In this way, large tracts passed from the king, technically the owner of all land in his kingdom, to warriors who were the lords and masters of the commoners living on these estates.

The invasions thus greatly stimulated the arrival of the professional army and the feudal military system in northern Europe, which bore the brunt of the attacks. Any headway Charlemagne had made in restoring the idea of a central authority was soon eradicated. The noble, with control over one or more estates on which manorial agriculture was practiced with serf labor, now became a combined military and civil ruler for a whole locality. The king remained the object of special respect, and the sacred powers of the royal crown were acknowledged by all. But day-to-day administration, military defense, and justice were all carried out by the feudal nobles and their hired men-at-arms.

## The Byzantine Empire

The eastern half of the early Christian world is usually known as the **Byzantine Empire** (from *Byzantium,* the original Greek name for the town Constantine renamed for himself). It proved to be an extraordinarily resilient competitor among the several rivals for supremacy in the eastern Mediterranean.

In keeping with Eastern traditions, the nature of the imperial throne became even more autocratic than in Rome. The emperor became a semidivine figure, ruling through a large and efficient bureaucracy. Despite occasional religiously inspired revolts (notably the *Iconoclastic* uprising against the imperial decree forbidding worship of images), the government and the population were strongly bonded by Christianity and a belief in the emperor as Christ's deputy on Earth. In fact, this spiritual bond enabled the long life of the empire in the face of many trials, until its ultimate death at the hand of the Ottoman Turks in the fifteenth century.

Unlike the West, the East accepted the emperor as the dominant partner in affairs of church and state. He appointed his patriarchs, and he had the power to remove them. This *caesaro-papism* (the monarch as both head of state and head of church) was to sharply distinguish the Byzantine from the Latin world of faith. The founder of this tradition was the powerful emperor *Justinian* (ruled 527–565), who also put his stamp on the appearance of the capital through a huge program of public works. The most spectacular was the great central church of Constantinople, the **Hagia Sophia,** or Church of Holy Wisdom, which remains today as a magnificent reminder of past glories.

As already noted, after the transfer of imperial government to Constantinople, the western provinces became expendable. The heartlands, those areas that had been assigned to the eastern half as organized by Diocletian, were given the bulk of the army and received the major part of state expenditures (as it produced by far the greater amount of state taxes). Even after large regions has been lost to Slavic, Persian, and Asiatic invasions, the Christian Eastern Empire would remain the most potent political and military entity in the Mediterranean basin.

In the mid-500s, the ambitious Justinian made a concerted and initially successful effort to recover the lost Western provinces. The dream of re-creating the empire was ultimately a failure, however. Within just two generations, almost all of the reconquered areas (in Italy, Spain, and north Africa) had fallen to new invaders. The effort had exhausted the Byzantines and would never be attempted again.

From the early 600s, the empire was under more or less constant attack for two centuries. During this period, it lost not only the western reconquests but also most of its own eastern territories, first to Avars and Persians and then to Arabs and Slavs. The besieging Muslims nearly succeeded in taking Constantinople in 717, when the desperate defenders used "Greek fire," a combustible liquid, to beat them off at sea. While the imperial defenders were occupied, their tributary Slavic subjects in the Balkans (Bulgars, Serbs) established independent states that soon became powerful enough to threaten the Greeks from the north. Yet again and again the Constantinople authorities would somehow find the energy and skill to foil their opponents or set them against one another.

In the long term, perhaps the most outstanding achievement of the Byzantine rulers was the Christianization of eastern Europe. By the 700s, priests of the Western church, supported by the bishop of Rome, had made many converts among the Germanic tribes and kingdoms. But they had not yet ventured into eastern Europe, which had never been under Roman rule. Here, the field was open to the Byzantine missionaries.

The mission to the Slavic peoples was pursued with energy and devotion. Beginning in the 800s, Greek monks moved into the nearby Balkans and then to the coast of the Black Sea and into Russia. Their eventual success in bringing Christianity to these regions meant that the

Prado, Madrid, Spain/Bridgeman Art Library

**GREEK FIRE.** The secret weapon that saved Constantinople from Muslim invaders in 717 is thought to have been a combination of sulfur naphtha and quicklime set alight. "Greek fire" was emitted from bronze jets mounted on the prows of Byzantine galleys and on the city walls during the Muslim invasions.

inhabitants of the present-day states of Russia, Romania, Serbia, Bulgaria, and, of course, Greece would look for centuries to Constantinople rather than Rome. Constantinople molded their religious and cultural values, their laws and their literature, their styles of art and architecture, and, thanks to their ethnically organized churches, their very sense of nationhood.

The conversion of the Slavs to Greek-rite Christianity proved to be a crucial and permanent turning point in European history. The split that originated in the rivalry between the bishops of Rome and Constantinople gradually deepened. It was reflected in the cultural and religious differences between Greek and Latin. After many years of alternating friction and patched-up amity, the rift culminated in the division of Christianity between West and East. In 1054, a headstrong pope encountered a stubborn patriarch who refused to yield to the pope's demands for complete subordination in a matter of doctrine. The two leaders then excommunicated each other in a fit of theological egotism. Despite several efforts—most recently, Pope John Paul's visit to Orthodox Ukraine in 2001—their successors have not been able to overcome their differences.

One other enormously influential result of Byzantine initiative was the huge collection called the ***Corpus Juris.*** This sixth-century distillation of Roman law and practice was undertaken (once again!) at the emperor Justinian's command and passed on to posterity. It is the foundation for most Western medieval and early modern law codes, and its basic precepts (see Chapter 10) are operative in many Roman Catholic countries of Europe and Latin America to the present day.

## Summary

The Germanic invasions of the third and fourth centuries found a Roman society that was already sorely tried under the burdens of heavy taxes, declining productivity, population loss, and instability at the top. The demoralization was slowed but could not be stopped by the authoritarian reforms of Diocletian and Constantine. In the meantime, the new mystery religion named after Jesus Christ gathered strength within the Roman realm. Christianity spread rapidly after winning the favor of Constantine and his successors, but it could not halt the constellation of forces laying waste to the western provinces.

The Germanic tribes took note of Rome's weakness and acted accordingly. A regressive Dark Age of violence and ignorance ensued, from which relatively little documentation has survived. In time, the efforts of missionaries and the examples of civic organization demontrated by the romanized subject populace showed results, as the Germanic warriors set up royal or princely governments of a rough-and-ready sort. By the 700s in the former Roman provinces, these attempts had become stabilized and Christianized, at least in the governing classes.

The most important of the early medieval rulers was Charlemagne, the first Holy Roman Emperor as well as king of the Franks. His attempts to restore the ancient empire went astray almost as soon as he was dead, and the renaissance that he promoted also proved ephemeral. New invasions by Vikings, Magyars, and Muslims, and the chaotic conditions they created in Europe, were too much for the personal system of government that Charlemagne had established. It collapsed and was replaced by a highly decentralized administration based on agrarian manors and local military power in the hands of a self-appointed elite, the nobility.

In the eastern half of the old empire, a form of semidivine monarchy possessing great power continued for a thousand years after the collapse in the West. After the failed attempt of Justinian to recover the western provinces, attacks came from all sides. The most persistent and successful attackers were the Arab Muslims, who by the 700s had taken most of the former imperial lands of the eastern Mediterranean. The conversion of the Slavs and some other peoples to Greek-rite Christianity was an outstanding achievement, but the split with the Roman church that came in the eleventh century was to be fateful.

## Identification Terms

Test your knowledge of this chapter's key concepts by defining the following terms. If you can't recall the meaning of certain terms, refresh your memory by looking up the boldfaced term in the chapter, turning to the Glossary at the end of the book, or working with the flashcards that are available on the *World Civilizations* Companion Website: **http://history.wadsworth.com/adler04/**.

Barracks Emperors
Byzantine Empire
*Corpus Juris*
Council of Nicaea
Hagia Sophia
Jewish War
knights
manors
*missi dominici*
Tetrarchy
*wergeld*

## Test Your Knowledge

Test your knowledge of this chapter by answering the following questions. Complete answers appear at the end of the book. You may also take this quiz interactively and find even more quiz questions on the *World Civilizations* Companion Website: **http://history.wadsworth.com/adler04/**.

1. The reforming emperor who created the Tetrarchy was
   a. Commodus.
   b. Constantine.
   c. Diocletian.
   d. Augustus.
   e. Justinian.

2. Which of the following does *not* help explain the appeal of early Christianity?
   a. Encouragement of military valor
   b. Sense of supernatural mission
   c. Receptivity to all potential converts
   d. Promotion of a sense of community among its adherents
   e. Emphasis on moral behavior and concern for others
3. Christianity became a universal faith rather than a Jewish sect in large part due to the efforts of
   a. the Roman officials in Judaea.
   b. the apostle Paul.
   c. the apostle Peter.
   d. the Zealots.
   e. the emperor Constantine.
4. The emperor Theodosius is important to Christian history for
   a. his final persecution of Christians.
   b. making Christianity the official religion of the empire.
   c. beginning the practice of intervening in internal church affairs.
   d. moving the church headquarters to Constantinople.
   e. issuing the Edict of Milan, which was the first official acceptance of Christianity.
5. The first attempt to clarify matters of church administration was the
   a. Treaty of Verdun (843).
   b. Edict of Milan.
   c. Corpus Juris.
   d. Carolingian revival.
   e. Council of Nicaea.
6. The first Holy Roman Emperor was
   a. Pippin I.
   b. Richard the Lion-hearted.
   c. Charlemagne.
   d. Leo III.
   e. Diocletian.
7. The biographer of Charlemagne tells us that the king
   a. cared greatly about the manners of his courtiers.
   b. enjoyed the company of his daughters.
   c. despised physical exercise.
   d. read and wrote a great deal.
   e. encouraged his children to marry and bear him grandchildren.
8. The decisive advantage held by the Vikings in their raids on Europe was their
   a. overwhelming numbers.
   b. superior weapons.
   c. great courage under attack.
   d. use of naval tactics to strike swiftly.
   e. willingness to adopt the ways of those they conquered.
9. The Treaty of Verdun in 843
   a. divided Europe between Muslims and Christians.
   b. created the kingdom of the Franks.
   c. was a compromise between Eastern and Western Christianity.
   d. divided Charlemagne's empire into three states.
   e. provided for religious toleration within the Holy Roman Empire.
10. Which of the following was *not* accomplished by Justinian?
   a. Temporary reconquest of part of the western empire
   b. Construction of the Hagia Sophia
   c. Defeat of the Arab invaders
   d. Composition of a new code of law
   e. Establishment of the concept of the monarch serving as head of the church

## InfoTrac College Edition

Visit the source collections at

**http://infotrac.thomsonlearning.com**

and use the Search function with the following key terms:

Charlemagne    Byzantium    early Christianity

## Wadsworth History Website Resources

Visit the World History Resource Center at **http://history.wadsworth.com/world** for a wealth of general resources and the *World Civilizations* Companion Website at **http://history.wadsworth.com/adler04/** for resources specific to this textbook.

## HistoryNow

Enter *HistoryNow* using the access card that is available for *World Civilizations. HistoryNow* will assist you in understanding the content in this chapter with lesson plans generated for your needs. In addition, you can read the following documents, and many more, online:

Gospel According to Mark    Einhard, *Life of Charlemagne*

Marcus Aurelius, *Meditations*

# Worldview Two

## Law and Government

## Society and Economy

### Greeks

**Law and Government:** After the eclipse of the original Greek (Mycenean) civilization and the ensuing Dark Age, the evolution of written law and developed monarchy begins with the reforms of Draco and Solon in the sixth century B.C.E. Although property still outweighs personal rights, there is a noticeable shift toward the latter in lawgiving. Strong differences continue between slaves and freemen and between aliens and citizens in this wholly patriarchal society. Mass political activity within the framework of the polis is stimulated by the democratic reforms of the fifth century in Athens. Sparta emerges as the opposite pole to Athens; the ensuing Peloponnesian War leads to the "barbarian" Macedonian takeover. The polis ideals gradually die out under alien rule, first under Hellenistic monarchies, then under the conquering Romans.

**Society and Economy:** Small farms, home crafts, and maritime trade were at all times the backbone of the Classical Age economy. The absence of large fertile areas restricts the emergence of plantations and estates. Overpopulation becomes a major problem by the 600s but is solved by large-scale emigration and the establishment of colonies around the Mediterranean. Trade, both maritime and overland, becomes critical to the maintenance of home country prosperity. In the Hellenistic period (after 300 B.C.E.), large numbers of Greeks emigrate to the East as favored citizens. Massive urban development in the Hellenistic monarchies creates a new, socioeconomically stratified society. Slavery becomes commonplace, as does large-scale manufacturing and estate agriculture. Under Roman rule, the Greek homeland diminishes steadily in economic importance and becomes largely impoverished.

### Romans

**Law and Government:** The evolution of Roman law and government forms is particularly marked over this millennium. Beginning with usual class-based justice and oral law, the Roman republic produces written codes by the fifth century B.C.E. and the eventual balance of patrician–plebian powers. The Punic Wars and resultant imperial outreach corrupt this balance, however, and bring about social problems that cannot be solved peacefully. Augustus's administrative reforms answer the most pressing needs for civic peace and stability for the next two centuries, while law continues evolution on the basis of equity and precedent. The central government's authority is sharply weakened in the West by transfer to Constantinople and then destroyed by successive Germanic invaders after 370s C.E. Eastern provinces remain secure.

**Society and Economy:** Small peasants were the bulk of the original Roman citizenry but, after the Punic Wars, are increasingly overshadowed by hordes of slaves and unfree immigrants from Africa and the eastern Mediterranean. Italy becomes dependent on food imports. Plantations and estates replace farms, while the urban proletariat multiplies. After about 200 C.E., the western provinces lose ground to the richer, more populous East, a process hastened by the Germanic invasions. Socioeconomic reforms of Diocletian and Constantine (295–335 C.E.) do not stop declining productivity of western provinces and resultant vulnerability to invaders.

### Europeans

**Law and Government:** Roman institutions are transformed by Germanic admixtures; government evolves slowly from the imperial model through feudal decentralization to the monarchies of the late Medieval Age.

**Society and Economy:** Economic activity is increasingly mixed between agrarian and nonagrarian fields, but peasant farmers and pastors still make up the large majority.

# Classical Mediterranean Civilizations, 500 B.C.E.–800 C.E.

## Patterns of Belief

Greeks of the Classical Age are founders of philosophy as a rational exercise. They also explore most of the questions that have occupied Western philosophy in metaphysics, ethics, and epistemology. Religion is conceived of as a civic duty more than as a path to immortality. Lack of fear of the gods and of their priestly agents is particularly striking. Gods are seen as humans writ large, with faults and virtues of same. Theology and ethics are sharply separated; the educated class turns to philosophy as a guide to ethical action: "Man the measure." After about the second century B.C.E., the religion–philosophy divergence is ever stronger as masses turn to mystery religions from the East.

Romans adopt notions of the supernatural and immortality from the Etruscans and Greeks, modifying them to fit their own civic religion. In philosophy, the Roman adaptations of Greek Stoicism and Epicureanism become the most common beliefs of the educated classes. No connections are established between theology and ethics until the advent of mystery religions, including Christianity. Christianity is originally adopted by the government of Constantine to sustain faltering imperial rule in the fourth century, and it soon becomes the equal or even senior partner of the civil regime in the West. The Roman papacy assumes governmental powers for Italy when the empire's attempt to recover under Justinian eventually fails.

Roman papal Christianity is gradually superimposed on western and central Europe through missionary activity in the 500s to 800s.

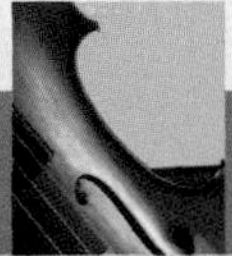

## Arts and Culture

The Classical Age brings a brilliant flowering of both literary and plastic arts, giving many models for later Western civilization. Particular mastery of sculpture, architecture, poetry of several formats, drama, and history is achieved. In the Hellenistic period, Roman overlords generally adopt Greek models for their own literature and sculpture, thus spreading them throughout western Europe. Greeks are patriarchal to the point of misogyny in their public and private culture. Large cities dominate the culture of the Hellenistic kingdoms and contribute to the continuing differentiation between rich and poor classes.

Art is of high technical quality but lacks creative imagination in contrast to Greeks and Egyptians. Artists are generally content to follow models from abroad in both plastic and literary forms. Exceptions are some minor literary genres, mosaic work, and architecture. Public life is not so patriarchal as that of Greece but is more affected by class divisions. Romans give great respect to tradition while demonstrating considerable flexibility in governance and social organization. Urban life is increasingly the dominant matrix of Roman culture as the empire matures, but it gives way in the western half as invasions begin.

Greco-Roman models are lost to northern and central Europe after the Roman collapse.

## Science and Technology

In the Classical Age, Greeks profit from their extensive contacts with Mesopotamia and Egypt. Physical science is generally subordinated to philosophy in the broad sense, of which it is considered a branch. In the Hellenistic period, physical sciences are selectively advanced, especially mathematics, physics, and medicine. At all times, little or no interest in technology was apparent. Scientific knowledge is pursued for its own sake rather than for possible application.

Roman science depends entirely on Hellenistic predecessors, which entered Italy from the East, particularly Egypt. As with the Classical Greeks, an abundance of slaves and other cheap labor argues against any search for labor-saving techniques. The only interest shown in technology is in the construction and engineering fields, which are a massively developed specialty in the empire. The novel use of brick and cement, construction of bridges, forts, aqueducts, hydrology systems, road building, and the like are extensive and sophisticated throughout the provinces as well as in Italy.

Natural sciences stagnate or worse until the late medieval period.

# PART THREE

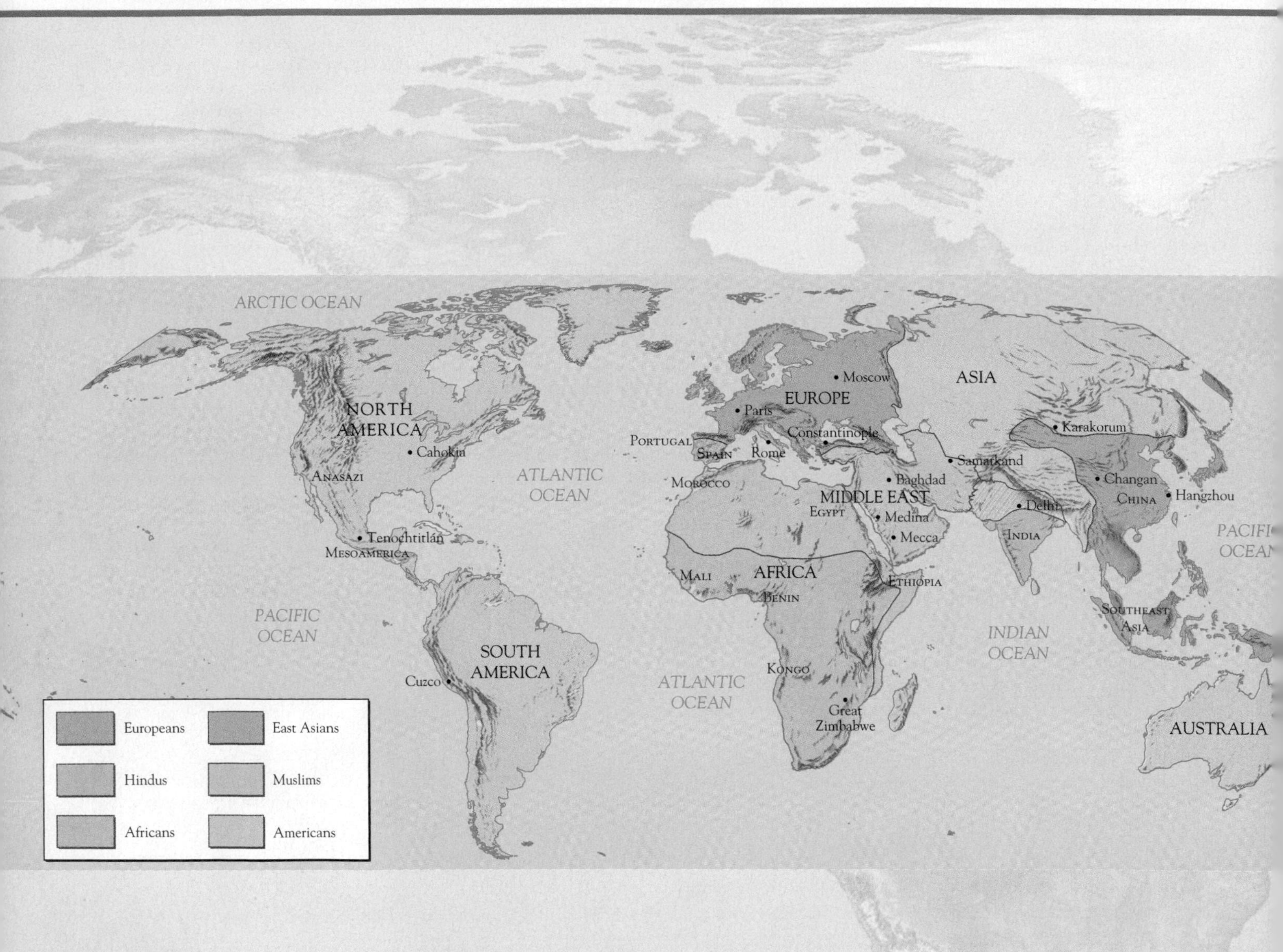
ARCTIC OCEAN
NORTH AMERICA
Cahokia
Anasazi
ATLANTIC OCEAN
Tenochtitlán
Mesoamerica
PACIFIC OCEAN
SOUTH AMERICA
Cuzco
Portugal
Spain
Morocco
Paris
Rome
Moscow
EUROPE
Constantinople
ASIA
Karakorum
Samarkand
Baghdad
MIDDLE EAST
Egypt
Medina
Mecca
Changan
China
Hangzhou
Delhi
India
Mali
AFRICA
Benin
Ethiopia
Kongo
Great Zimbabwe
ATLANTIC OCEAN
INDIAN OCEAN
Southeast Asia
PACIFIC OCEAN
AUSTRALIA
Europeans
East Asians
Hindus
Muslims
Africans
Americans

# Equilibrium among Polycentric Civilizations, 500–1500 C.E.

Before about 500 C.E., contacts among the centers of advanced civilized life were limited and tenuous. Usually, they were made through intermediate, less-developed societies. Rome, for example, had only the most sparing contacts with China, and they were all indirect. Its contacts with Hindu India were more direct but still very limited. For that matter, India and China had very little contact with one another despite their geographic proximity. Thanks to the mountain walls and the deserts that separated them, few Chinese and still fewer Indians dared make that journey. After 500, however, entirely new centers of civilization emerged, quite detached from the original West Asian and Mediterranean locales.

In still-isolated America, throughout this period a series of ever more skilled and more populous Indian societies arose in the middle latitudes of the continent and along its western fringe. They were mysteriously (to us) dispersed or overcome by later comers, until the most advanced and skilled of all fell prey to the Spanish conquistadors.

In sub-Saharan Africa, urban life and organized territorial states were emerging by about 500 C.E. About the same epoch, the Mesoamerican Indians and the Muslims of Asia and northern Africa had achieved a high degree of city-based civilization, the former developing independently of all other models and the latter building on the ancient base in western Asia. As one example, commercial relations between Mediterranean Christians and the Hindu/Buddhist regions became closer and more extensive. Both overland and by sea, the Muslims of the eastern fringe of the Mediterranean were the essential mediators between these distant centers and profited from the middleman role. At the end of the period, a reinvigorated Islam extended its conquests in both southern Europe and Africa. An observer would have been hard put to guess which of the two great contesting religions/polities—Christianity and Islam—would emerge as the determinant of world history in the next century.

In Asia, this millennium was an era of tremendous vitality and productivity—the South and East Asian Classical Age—which was briefly interrupted by the Mongol conquests of the thirteenth century. But the Mongols were soon assimilated or expelled by their Chinese/Turkic/Persian subjects.

In the West, the entire thousand-year epoch from 500 to 1500 C.E. carries the title Middle Age. But this term has no relevance to the rest of the civilized world, of course, and should be avoided when speaking of any culture other than the Christian Europeans. In Europe, the Middle Age began with the gradual collapse of the Roman West under the assaults of the Germanic tribes and ended with the triumph of the new secularism of the Renaissance.

Chapter 12 surveys the chief actors in the pageant of pre-Columbian America. Sub-Saharan Africa's immense variety is examined in Chapter 13, as parts of the continent emerge into historical light. Chapters 14 and 15 deal with the rise of Islam and its culture. The next several chapters look at the stable and technically advanced South and East Asian societies. The first of this series (Chapter 16) surveys India's flourishing Hindu and Buddhist cultures. The second (Chapter 17) looks at China in the great age of Confucian order and prosperity. Then comes Japan (Chapter 18) as it evolved from an adjunct of China and Korea into cultural and political sovereignty, along with the early histories of the islands and mainland of southeastern Asia. The focus returns to the West in Chapters 19 through 21, as we look at the European Middle Ages and the decline that followed, through the revival termed the European Renaissance. Finally, Chapter 22 deals with the Mongol eruption into the major civilizations of Asia. In the end, however, their conquests enabled the unification of lands and peoples on an unprecedented scale and brought both peace and prosperity to a large part of the Old World.

*And the man took an ear of corn and roasted it, and found it good.*
Frank Russell, *Myths of the Jicarilla Apaches*, 1898

# 12 THE AMERICAS BEFORE COLUMBUS



| | |
|---|---|
| c. 30,000–10,000 B.C.E. | ARRIVAL OF ANCESTRAL NATIVE AMERICANS |
| c. 9500–8900 B.C.E. | CLOVIS AND FOLSOM HUNTING CULTURES |
| c. 8000–2000 B.C.E. | ARCHAIC GATHERING CULTURES |
| c. 5500–2000 B.C.E. | AGRICULTURE BEGINS |
| c. 1500–300 B.C.E. | OLMEC CIVILIZATION |
| c. 800–400 B.C.E. | CHAVIN CULTURE |
| c. 600 B.C.E.–1300 C.E. | CAHOKIA |
| c. 400 B.C.E.–1300 C.E. | CLASSICAL MAYAN CIVILIZATION/ TEOTIHUACÁN |
| c. 400–800 C.E. | FIRST PUEBLOAN PIT HOUSE COMMUNITIES |
| c. 800–1150 C.E. | TOLTECS/CHACO CANYON |
| c. 1100–1500s | INCAN CIVILIZATION |
| c. 1300s–1521 | AZTEC CIVILIZATION |

LIKE AFRICA, THE AMERICAS exhibit a tremendous range of cultures and physical environments, from the Inuit Eskimos of northern Canada to the sophisticated city builders of Central America, from the deserts of the American Southwest to the jungles of the Amazon basin. The first Native Americans arrived in the New World much later than humans *(Homo sapiens sapiens)* had evolved and spread elsewhere in the world. Reliable linguistic, genetic, and dental studies suggest that they came in three distinct waves, probably between 30,000 and 10,000 B.C.E. The **Amerindians** were the first migrants to come, probably from northeast Asia. They were the ancestors of the numerous Native American peoples found throughout the Western Hemisphere today, from southern Canada to Tierra del Fuego at the southern tip of South America. Following them came a second group, from Central Asia, most of whose descendants today are located in western Canada, with the exception of the Navajo and Apache peoples, who migrated to the American Southwest between 1300 and 1500 C.E. The last group to arrive again came from northeastern Asia. Their modern descendants are the Inuit Eskimo peoples of northern Canada and Alaska.

Just how these varied peoples came to the New World is fiercely debated. The most widely accepted theory is that they arrived near the end of the Pleistocene era, the last Ice Age, by means of a "land bridge" that, because of lower sea levels, connected Northeast Asia and Alaska.

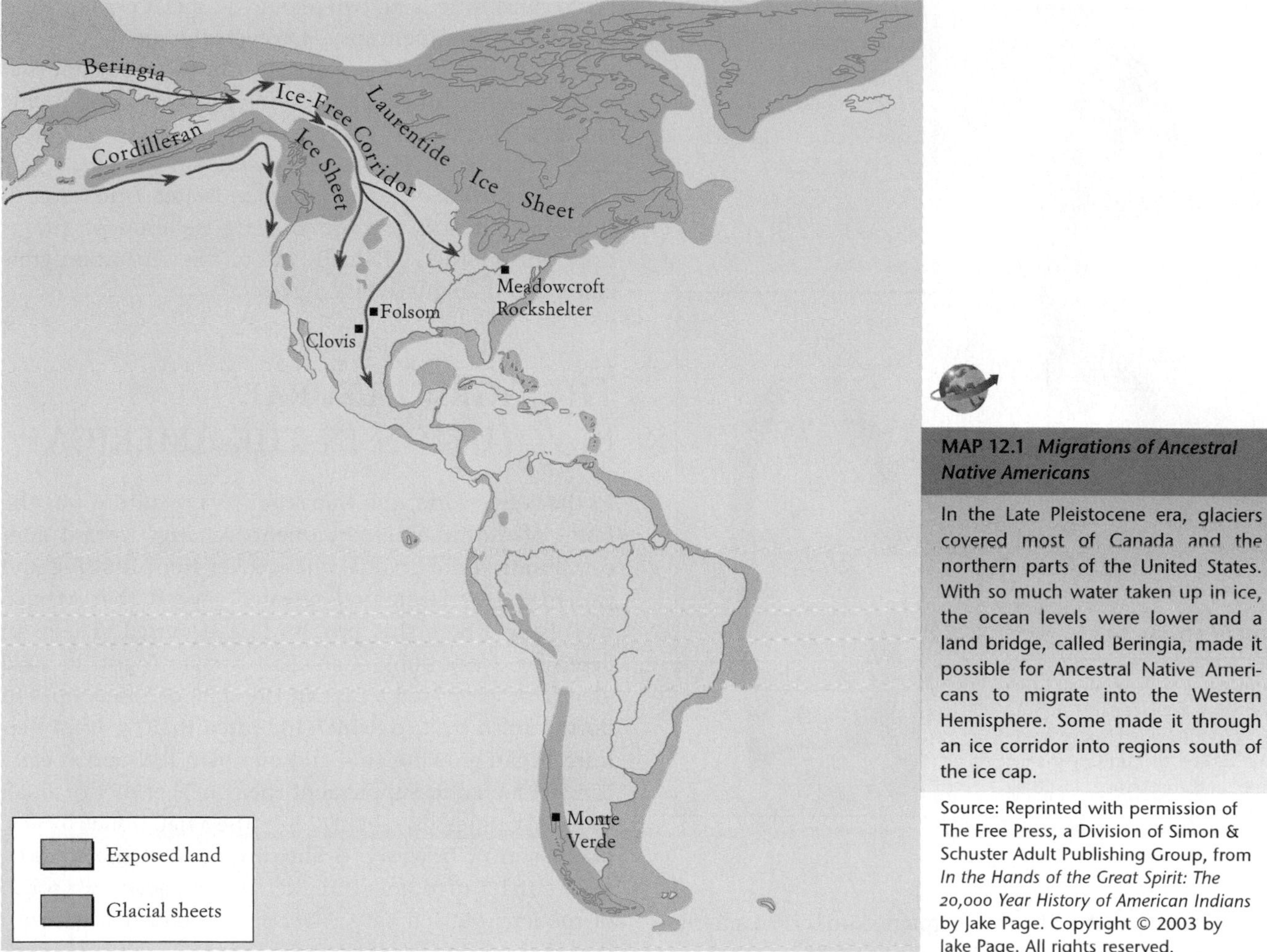


**MAP 12.1** ***Migrations of Ancestral Native Americans***

In the Late Pleistocene era, glaciers covered most of Canada and the northern parts of the United States. With so much water taken up in ice, the ocean levels were lower and a land bridge, called Beringia, made it possible for Ancestral Native Americans to migrate into the Western Hemisphere. Some made it through an ice corridor into regions south of the ice cap.

Source: Reprinted with permission of The Free Press, a Division of Simon & Schuster Adult Publishing Group, from *In the Hands of the Great Spirit: The 20,000 Year History of American Indians* by Jake Page. Copyright © 2003 by Jake Page. All rights reserved.

Archaeologists have named this land bridge **Beringia** because it covered what is now the Bering Strait (see Map 12.1). Although Canada at that time was covered by massive glaciers, these early immigrants made their way southward through an opening in the glacial sheets and along a Pacific coastal plain into what is now North and Central America. Eventually they populated the entire hemisphere. Where conditions were favorable, some eventually settled down to become farmers. For many centuries before this, however, from about 9500 to 8900 B.C.E., they lived as late Paleolithic hunters and gatherers during what is usually called the **Paleoindian Period.**

## Paleoindian America

Once south of the glaciers, the earliest ancestral Native Americans arrived in a North America whose climate was considerably cooler and moister than it is today. Here they found a world with abundant plant and wild animal life, which included many forms of megafauna; that is, giant, now extinct beasts such as the woolly mammoth, the giant sloth, and the giant bison. Not surprisingly, therefore, the earliest Native American cultures that archaeologists have uncovered were big-game hunters. The **Clovis culture** was the earliest-known hunting culture, dating between about 9500 and 8900 B.C.E. Associated with this archaeological culture in particular were large, deeply notched, leaf-shaped spearheads called "Clovis points," which early Native Americans of North America used to kill their megafauna prey.

After 8900, the climate gradually became drier, and the megafauna gradually died out. As this occurred, hunters turned increasingly to bison, elk, and deer as their prey, and fluted **Folsom points** replaced the larger Clovis spearheads. Wherever archaeologists have discovered Folsom sites, associated with these missile (spear, dart, and arrow) heads have been such items as hammer stones, used for breaking bones from which marrow was extracted; stone end scrapers that were used for scraping hides; and cutting tools and bone eye needles for preparing hides as clothing and containers. As these missile heads grew smaller, they were placed at the head of spear throwers

From Jake Page, *In the Hands of the Great Spirit* (New York: Free Press, 2003), p. 23.

**Clovis and Folsom Points.** Clovis points, like the one above, were used to hunt very large game, around 9500 B.C.E. Later, they were replaced by Folsom points (right), when Native Americans turned to hunting smaller game and gathering for their food supply.

called *atlatls*. (Bows and arrows remained unknown among many Native Americans until about 400 C.E.)

## The Archaic Period

As had happened with the Clovis culture, the Folsom complex disappeared as the climate continued changing. Conditions everywhere became warmer and drier, and in the American Southwest and in northern Mexico, where Native Americans were the first to turn to agriculture, desert conditions eventually replaced what once had been grasslands. Therefore, during what archaeologists call the **Archaic Period,** people were forced to rely more on gathering wild plants as their primary sources of food. In contrast to the specialized hunting implements of the Paleolithic period, Archaic tool kits were less specialized and included more equipment for processing plant foods, such as rice grass, goosefoot, and dropseed, as well as prickly pear cactus. Deer, elk, and mountain sheep continued to be hunted, although discoveries of snares, small traps, and smaller cutting tools among the bones of rabbits, desert mice, rats, squirrels, birds, snakes, and other reptiles imply that humans were forced to rely on much more humble daily fare.

Precious little is known about the social organization of these early Americans. However, the small size and temporary nature of most Archaic campsites suggest that most groups consisted of relatively few, highly mobile families. Such mobility seems to have been considerably more restricted than in the Paleoindian Period, largely due to the relative scarcity of groundwater. One result of this phenomenon was the growing isolation of groups from one another. Gradually out of this separation grew cultural and language differences.

## The Agricultural Revolution in the Americas

In the New World, the transition to agriculture was the result of continued environmental change toward drier conditions and a gradual changeover from hunting and gathering. Archaeological research reveals that Mexico was likely where this process first occurred. There, in desertlike conditions, Canadian archaeologist Richard MacNeish excavated a cave in the state of Tamaulipas in northeastern Mexico, which indicated that Native Americans began growing chili and pumpkin for food as early as 5500 B.C.E., to supplement their meager diet of small desert creatures. By about 2500, they had added beans. Maize (corn), however, eventually became the foundation of the Native American diet. At Tehuacan, just south of modern Mexico City, MacNeish uncovered evidence that suggests maize was gradually grown and domesticated between about 4000 and 2500 B.C.E.

Farming seems to have become general throughout Mexico, Central America, and the coastal plain of Peru in South America by 1500 B.C.E. By then, farmers were living in small villages, usually in structures called "pit houses." Although these varied somewhat in form, pit houses typically consisted of a framework of wood poles thatched with tree branches and leaves, built over a pit dug into the ground. Their technology remained Neolithic, but Mexican farmers were, archaeologists estimate, able to grow enough corn, beans, squash, and chili peppers in just eight to ten weeks to support a small family for up to an entire year. This level of productivity made it possible for the great civilizations of Mexico, Central America, and the Andean Mountain nations of South America to develop.

## First Civilizations

The earliest American civilizations did not locate in river valleys but on the elevated plateaus or the tropic lowlands inland from the Caribbean Sea.

## The Olmecs

The earliest civilization we now know about (through archaeology only) arose in what is now southern Mexico and bears the name **Olmec.** It existed between 1500 and about 300 B.C.E., when enemies from the north overwhelmed it and then quickly adopted many features of the civilization they had conquered.

The Olmec were the foundation of all other Amerindian cultures in Central America. Olmec pottery and decorative ceramics have been found throughout Mexico and as far south as Costa Rica (see Map 12.2). Their main sites thus far discovered, east of Mexico City and near the Caribbean port of Veracruz, consist of a central fortified complex of governmental halls and religious shrines. As with all succeeding pre-Columbian civilizations (those before Columbus), a pervasive religious faith centering on worship of gods in feline images was the inspiration for much of their art and architecture.

The enormous heads of basalt that they left behind most remarkably express the Olmecs' skill in stonework. Standing up to nine feet high and weighing up to twelve tons, these realistically modeled, flat-nosed, thick-lipped heads fulfilled unknown ceremonial functions for the Olmecs. Their Negroid features have given rise to speculation about the possible African origins of the earliest colonists. No evidence of this connection yet exists.

Olmec masonry skills also enabled them to build ceremonial stone pyramids, one of which reached 110 feet high. This Great Pyramid speaks of a degree of civilized organization and a ready supply of labor, suggesting that Olmec agriculture must have been sufficiently advanced to support a large population. The Olmec had a primitive form of writing and a number system, neither of which is understood but which enabled them to survey and build a large number of massive edifices. Surviving art (sculpture) indicates that a small, elite group centering on the priests of the official religion had great powers, and the ruler was probably a hereditary king/high priest. More than this is not known.

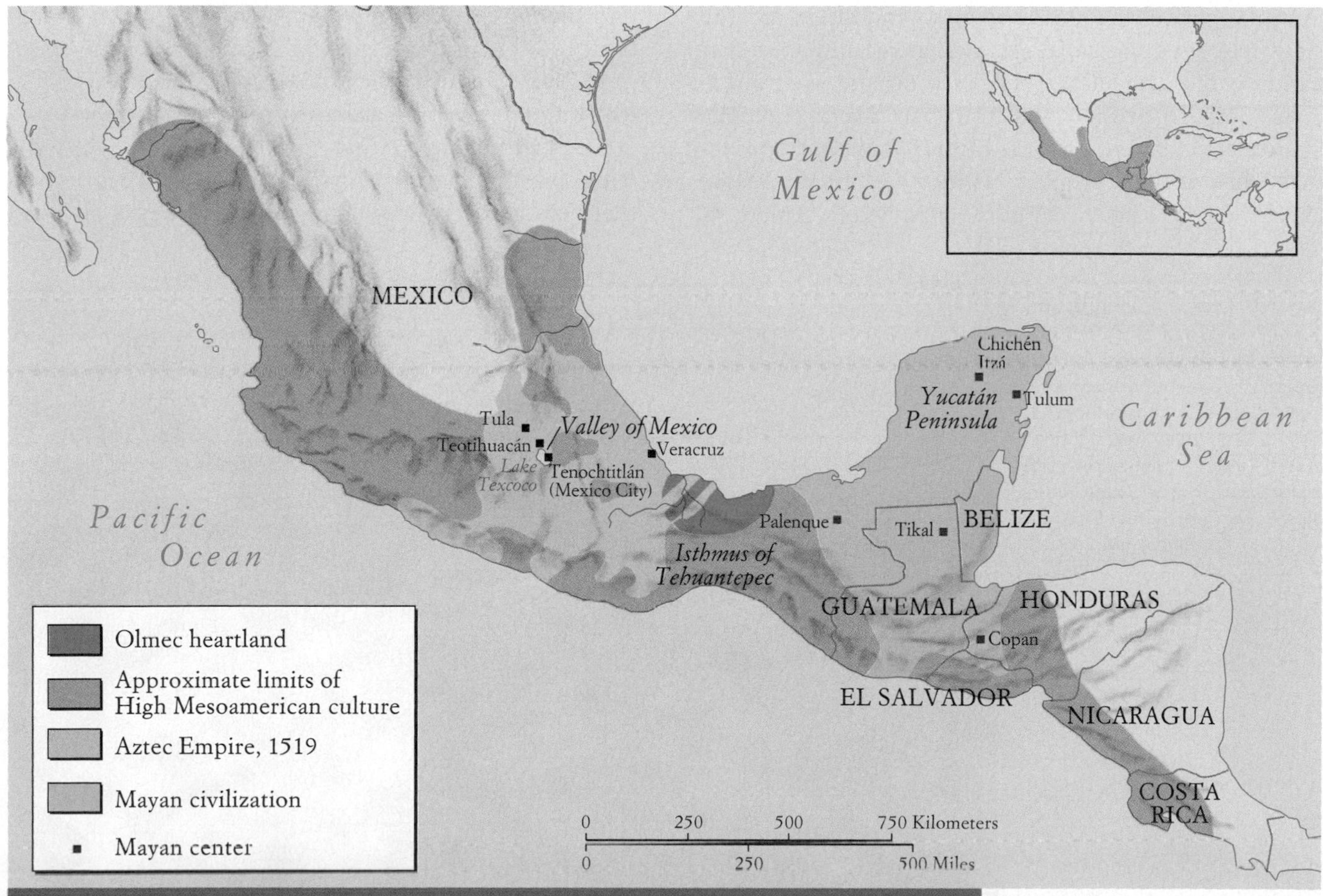


**MAP 12.2** ***Mesoamerican Civilizations***

The Aztec empire was at its height when the Spanish arrived. The Mayan cities of Palenque and Tikal were abandoned in the tenth century for unknown reasons, possibly failure of the food supply.

## The Chavin

In South America at the same epoch, the **Chavin** culture centered on the high valleys immediately inland from the Peruvian coast showed a comparable development. Between about 800 and 400 B.C.E., Native American people settled into a Neolithic agrarian lifestyle whose fragmentary material remnants are best known in the form of the clay and jade sculpture in which they excelled. Much goldware has also been found, at sites as high in the forbidding mountains as 11,000 feet. The triumph of the Chavin lay above all in the provision of adequate food for a dense population in such topographically difficult areas. This achievement has barely been reproduced aided by the technology of the late twentieth century in modern Peru.

## The Maya

Before or around 300 C.E., the Olmec civilization collapsed. Its place as civilized leader in coastal Mexico was taken by the **Maya,** who were the most advanced of all the pre-Columbian Amerindians. Their mysterious demise as organized states before the arrival of the Spaniards is a continuing problem for archaeologists and historians. The Maya had a written language, a calendar, and an understanding of mathematics that was far more advanced than European mathematics in the twelfth century. The recent decipherment of some of the Mayan written language has enabled scholars to more accurately reconstruct the events portrayed in the rich pictorial images of Mayan stonework, although much remains obscure. All in all, more is known about the life of the Mayan people than about any of the other Mesoamericans. They are the model for the classical image of Amerindian civilization.

The historical outline is by now fairly clear. From about 400 B.C.E., the southern tip of present-day Mexico and Guatemala (the Yucatán) were governed by a hierarchy of Mayan cities ruled by hereditary kings. Some cities contained several tens of thousands of people (see Map 12.2), but most of the population were peasant villagers who lived in satellite settlements on the cities' periphery. The whole population of the Mayan Empire or federation may have reached 14 million—far and away the largest state under one government outside Asia at that time.

Public buildings of truly amazing dimensions were the heart of the cities. Temples, palaces, and ball courts, many of them employing the blunt-tipped pyramid form, are so arranged as to construct a massive arena or assembly ground. To these forums at designated times would stream tens, perhaps hundreds, of thousands, to experience the priest-led worship ceremonies or the installation of a new monarch.

The cities seem to have been more religious and administrative centers than commercial and manufacturing centers. None of them approached the size of the Mesopotamian towns of a much earlier epoch. Trade was a relatively minor part of Mayan life.

The political and social power rested, as with the Olmec, in the hands of a hereditary elite. To judge from their costumes in surviving artwork, they were very

**MAYAN PALACE AT PALENQUE.** The Mayan civilization of present-day eastern Mexico was older than the Aztec civilization but showed some similarities. New gods responsible for rain and fertility were adopted, as well as the building of pyramids and palaces. This seventh-century palace was uncovered from the jungle in the nineteenth century.

wealthy. The common folk seem to have been divided into freemen, serfs, and slaves, as in much of the ancient world.

Religious belief was paramount in ordering the round of daily life. The ruling class included priests, who had magical powers given to them by the gods. They also had access to the underworld, which seems to have been as fearsome as that of Mesopotamia. In the Mayan cosmology there existed thirteen Heavens and nine Hells. No hint of ethical religion exists, however. The gods, like those of Sumeria, played multiple roles in human affairs, and in their persons they combined beastly and human traits. The jaguar—a species of great cat indigenous to the Americas—was particularly revered. Human sacrifices apparently were common and provided the rulers with companions on their journey to the next world.

Giraudon/Bridgeman Art Library

**Chichén Itzá.** This enormous construction is the so-called Temple of 1,000 Columns, erected between 1000 and 1200 C.E. by the late Mayan civilization. Its exact purpose is unknown, but it probably served as a royal palace.

For several centuries these cities and their satellite villages prospered. Then, for reasons unknown, they began to decline, and some had to be abandoned. A revival occurred about 1000 C.E. and lasted until about 1300, when the last Mayan site seems to have been finally abandoned. By the time Cortés arrived in the Valley of Mexico two hundred years later, the Mayan achievements had been forgotten.

Their memory has been revived by the nineteenth- and twentieth-century discoveries of giant basalt heads and whole figures scattered about in the southern Mexican jungle, along with the ruins of great stone pyramids and temples in the Yucatán peninsula. These sites have now become major tourist attractions, especially **Chichén Itzá,** where a vast complex of Mayan buildings has been excavated. The pyramid form was almost the same as that of Egypt and the mastery of stonework almost as complete. The Mayan ruins are an American version of Tel Amarna or Karnak, and it is not surprising that some anthropologists are convinced that a human link existed between ancient Egypt and Mexico.

The most notable accomplishment of the Maya in science was their astoundingly accurate astronomy, based on an equally refined mathematics. The Mayan calendar had two distinct numeration systems, allowing them to construct a chronology that could date events for a space of more than two thousand years. In literature, little survived the Spanish colonial censorship, but the Maya were the only pre-Columbian people who completed the transition to full literacy. The handful of codices (ancient documents) is supplemented by the extensive sculpted glyphs decorating the exterior and interior of the monuments the Maya left behind. Unfortunately, these materials tell us little to nothing of the political or social life of the era but are mostly concerned with the events in the reign of one or another monarch.

## Teotihuacán

During the same era when the Mayan surge was reaching its peak, another high culture was appearing in the Valley of Mexico some hundreds of miles west of Yucatán. The metropolis of **Teotihuacán** rose in the rich farmlands in the northern part of the valley around 200 B.C.E. Like the cities of the Olmecs and the classical Maya, Teotihuacán seems to have functioned primarily as a center of religious rituals and offerings to the gods of nature who were so crucial to settled agriculture. These cities centered on great religious monuments in the pyramidal form found all over Central America. Along the two-mile-long Avenue of the Dead, legions of priests managed the continual offerings demanded of them by their nature gods. Two of the pyramids, the Pyramids of the Sun and the Moon at Teotihuacán, are among the largest masonry structures ever built. The Pyramid of the Sun is actually larger in total volume than the Great Pyramid of Egypt.

Some scholars think Teotihuacán might have been the first true city of the Western Hemisphere. It grew to become the largest and most impressive of all the ancient pre-Columbian centers. Historians believe that its population may have reached as much as 125,000—far greater than that of any contemporary European city. And Teotihuacán was unusual in that its inhabitants included more than just the normal priests and rulers. Although the houses of the priests and nobles filled its center, it was laid out in *barrios,* or quarters, for the ordinary people who farmed the fields surrounding the city.

**Avenue of the Dead at Teotihuacán.** The ceremonial heart of the city, the Avenue of the Dead was lined with dozens of temples and pyramids, like the gigantic Pyramid of the Sun, shown at the upper left. Here, feather-clad priests carried out elaborate daily rituals and sacrifices to gods like Quetzalcoatl, who regulated such matters as fertility, rainfall, childbirth, and even the arts.

### *The Toltecs*

The **Toltecs** were a federation of nomads from the deserts of northern Mexico, who became famous among their successors, especially the Aztecs, as a race of heroes and founders. Their chief city was at **Tula,** located about thirty miles from Teotihuacán. In about 700, the Toltecs were severely defeated by barbarians from the southwest, and they marched south, through the Valley of Mexico. The city of Teotihuacán was destroyed, never to be rebuilt. Tula later replaced it, probably with enslaved captives from Teotihuacán, and the Toltecs managed to restore themselves to supremacy until the 1100s. Then they were finally overcome by new nomads, who eventually gave way themselves in the 1300s to the all-conquering Aztecs.

## Aztec Rule in Mexico

In the space of two hundred years, the **Aztec** people converted themselves from nomad barbarians to the elite of a huge state embracing many millions of Amerindians. It was governed from a city (**Tenochtitlán**) that was the largest in the New World and one of the largest anywhere. These achievements were based on the foundation provided by earlier Amerindian civilizations, but the Aztecs contributed some new characteristics.

The ruling group among the Aztecs was a militaristic clique of aristocrats, whose lives revolved around conquest. War was their reason for existence. It shaped their religion and imposed a social structure that was unique in America. The chief god was Huitzilopochtli, god of the sun at noon. To keep him in his proper place in the sky, thereby assuring that the crops would have the warmth they needed to grow, the sun had to be fed with human blood. Therefore, the Aztec religion featured frequent human sacrifices on altars in the middle of their great city. Some of these ceremonies—attested to not only by the horrified Spanish invaders but also by Aztec sources—were staggering in their bloodiness: thousands of victims, taken from other Indian tribes specifically for that purpose, were sacrificed at one time. Cannibalism was also a part of the ritual. The heart was cut out of a living victim's chest by priests wielding glasslike obsidian knives and then devoured by the Aztec nobility.

Researchers have suggested several more practical explanations for these mass sacrifices. The theory that commands the most support is that they were a form of rule by terror; that is, the Aztec elite tried to prevent rebellions by terrorizing the population into submission. The Aztecs were thus a sort of super-Assyrians, ruling their unfortunate neighbors by fear and random slaughter. How long would such a hateful rule have lasted if the Spanish had not arrived on the scene? That is an open question. We know from Aztec records that it had lasted about a century before the Europeans arrived in 1519. During that time, Aztec rule, originally limited to the marshy confines of Tenochtitlán, had steadily expanded until it encompassed the center of present-day Mexico from the Atlantic to the Pacific and reached down into the former Mayan lands in present-day Guatemala (see Map 12.3). The last emperor before the Spaniards came had greatly enlarged the domains he ruled.

**MAP 12.3** ***The Aztec, Incan, and Mayan Empires***

The relative size of the three best-known pre-Columbian states at their maximum extents is shown here. Given the vast extent of the Inca Empire, a road system was essential for maintaining communication, as well as political and economic cohesiveness.

## *Aztec Government and Society*

How was the Aztecs' militaristic society organized? We know a good deal about the Aztec state, thanks to their pictographic records, or *codices*. The Spanish preserved some of these records so they could learn more about their new subjects and control them more efficiently. More information came from the devoted efforts of a Franciscan monk who spent years interviewing Aztec survivors in the 1530s. The Society and Economy box gives more information.

At the top of the social hierarchy were the officials of the emperor, who governed like feudal lords in the provinces conquered by the Aztec armies. They had earned their positions by distinguishing themselves on the battlefield. The emperor rewarded them with great powers as judges, commanders, and administrators of a highly developed and complex provincial government.

Next came a class of warriors, who were continuously recruited from the ordinary freemen. They had to prove themselves in battle by taking at least four prisoners for sacrifice. If successful, they were allowed to share in the booty of the Aztecs' constant warfare. The great majority of the Aztecs fell into the next category: ordinary free people who did the usual work of any society. They tilled the fields, carried burdens, built the buildings and roads, and so on. They might also be called for military duty in a pinch and thus shared in the essential purpose of the state.

At the bottom were the serfs, whose rights and duties were similar to those of medieval European serfs, and the slaves, who had been captured from other Indians or were victims of debt. If the priests did not destine them for human sacrifice, Aztec slaves were often able to gain their freedom. Most of them actually did so, sooner or later.

The Aztecs also had a large and powerful group of priests. The highest served as advisers to the emperor in

SOCIETY AND ECONOMY

## Aztec Family Role Models

**In the mid-sixteenth century,** some thirty years after the Spanish conquest, a learned and industrious monk named Bernardino de Sahagun undertook a remarkable mission: to create an ethnographic portrait of the Aztecs as they lived before the European invasion. Sahagun held many interviews with Indians of all social classes and ages, to hear their own versions of their culture and beliefs. Included are several thumbnail summaries of what was expected of men and women, of family members, of the upper and lower strata of Aztec society, and even of some professions. A few examples follow:

> The Father: the father is the founder of lineage. He is diligent, compassionate, sympathetic, a careful administrator of his household. He is the educator, the model-giver, the teacher. He saves up for himself and for his dependents. He cares for his goods, and for the goods of others. . . . He is thrifty and cares for the future. He regulates and establishes good order. . . .
>
> The bad father is not compassionate, he is neglectful and not reliable. He is a poor worker and lazy. . . .
>
> The Mother: the mother has children and cares for them. She nurses them at her breast. She is sincere, agile, and a willing worker, diligent in her duties and watchful over others. She teaches, and is mindful of her dependents. She caresses and serves others, she is mindful of their needs. She is careful and thrifty, ever vigilant of others, and always at work.
>
> The bad mother is dull, stupid and lazy. She is a spendthrift and a thief, a deceiver and a cheat. She loses things through her neglect. She is frequently angry, and not heedful of others. She encourages disobedience in her children. . . .
>
> The Nobleman: the man who has noble lineage is exemplary in his life. He follows the good example of others. . . . He speaks eloquently, he is mild in speech, and virtuous . . . noble of heart and worthy of gratitude. He is discreet, gentle, well reared in manner. He is moderate, energetic, inquiring. . . . He provides nourishment for others, comfort. He sustains others. . . . He magnifies others and diminishes himself from modesty. He is a mourner for the dead, a doer of penances. . . .
>
> The bad nobleman is ungrateful, a debaser and disparager of others' property, he is contemptuous and arrogant. He creates disorder. . . .
>
> The Physician: the physician is knowledgeable of herbs and medicines from roots and plants; she is fully experienced in these things. She is a conductor of examinations, a woman of much experience, a counselor for the ill. The good physician is a restorer, a provider of health, one who makes the ill feel well. She cures people, she provides them with health again. She bleeds the sick . . . with an obsidian lancet she bleeds them and restores them.

### *Analyze and Interpret*

Do these descriptions of good and bad persons differ in substantial ways from modern ones? How do the expectations of men and of women differ in Aztec society, from these examples?

Source: Bernardino de Sahagún, *The General History of the Things of New Spain* (Santa Fe, NM: School of American Research, 1950).

his palace. The monarch was a quasi-divine person, who was selected by election from among the male members of the ruling family.

Although we have little information except the sketchy reports of an occasional missionary father or other European observer, upper-class Aztec women seem to have had some private rights and freedoms that many sixteenth-century European women might have envied, but the destruction of the Aztec written sources and the absence of others make it impossible to know for certain. Certainly, the Spanish witnesses in Mexico and Peru gave no indication of female governors or high officials, and the major deities that have been identified are male.

## The Inca

Another major Amerindian civilization existed far to the south of Mexico, almost certainly remaining in ignorance of the Aztec realm and its accomplishments. In present-day Peru, in the Andes Mountains that run from north to south through the country, an extraordinarily talented people—the **Inca**—had recently constructed a militaristic empire, just as the Aztecs had done in Mexico. (The title "Inca" really refers to the ruler of this empire, but it is also commonly used to refer to the tribal group that ruled the surrounding peoples and to the empire they created.)

This empire rested on a dramatically increased food supply made possible by agricultural advances. The Peruvian Indians gradually learned how to grow new crops and increase the yields of established crops by using fertilizer and metal tools. By so doing, they were capable of producing enough of a food surplus to support both a large army and a leisure class that devoted itself to government and religious duties. Like the Aztecs, their success in conquests kept the Inca under the constant pressure of keeping a large group of subjects under strict control.

Centered on the town of **Cuzco** in one of the high valleys that penetrate the massive wall of the Andes, the Inca started bringing their immediate neighbors under their rule in the 1200s. By the mid-1400s, they had created a state that rested on the forced labor of the conquered peoples, who are thought to have numbered as many as 8 million. If this number is accurate, the Inca, like the Aztecs, ruled over more people than any European state at the time. The critical breakthrough to empire, rather than merely regional dominance, came with the rule of Pachacuti Inca in the 1450s. Eighty years before the Spaniards came, he expanded his petty kingdom to boundaries that reached into present-day Argentina in the south and what is today central Ecuador to the north.

After conquering a new area, the Inca often deported the inhabitants, moving them from their native region to an alien place, where they would be entirely dependent on Cuzco's protection from resentful neighbors—a practice that is reminiscent of Assyrian (and early Roman) techniques of rule. Local chiefs were forced to take full responsibility for the obedience and good behavior of their people. The taxes were collected by an efficient administrative system. The Inca also established colonies among their subjects. The colonists helped encourage the conquered people to transfer their loyalty to their new masters and also ensured that a military force would be available if needed to suppress a rebellion.

The Inca's cultural impact on their subjects is evident from the linguistic changes that occurred. Along the west coast, the Incas' **Quechua,** now the official language of most Peruvians, along with Spanish, supplanted the variety of unwritten languages that previously had existed among the South American Indians. Unlike the Mesoamericans, however, the Inca did not develop a written language. Basic numerical data were calculated with a type of abacus using knotted strings.

To unify their lands, the Inca built great roads running north and south both along the coast and in the mountains. They constructed irrigation systems, dams, and canals, and built terraces on the steep hillsides so crops could be planted. The usage of metal was considerably more common in Incan lands than in Mexico. Copper jewelry and bronze tools are found among their gravesites. The llama, a member of the camel family, was used as a beast of burden in the highlands, giving the Inca another advantage over their contemporaries in Mesoamerica. The stone buildings of royal Cuzco are among the finest erected in the Americas, and fine textiles of both cotton and wool were commonplace possessions of the upper class.

One of the most magnificent achievements of Incan rule was **Machu Picchu,** a city in the clouds of the high Andes, whose ruins were discovered only in 1911. The Inca accomplished the awe-inspiring feat of moving thousands of huge stone blocks to build the walls of this fortress-city on a mountaintop, in the absence of almost all technology (probably even without the wheel). No one knows why the city was built or why it was abandoned.

### *Incan Government and Society*

Like most other ancient and pre-modern societies, Incan society exhibited sharp class divisions. A small elite of nobles was at the top, under their semi-divine king, the Inca, from whom all authority issued. A large army maintained obedience. Most rebellions against the Inca were, in fact, fraternal wars in which the rebel leader was a member of the imperial house. The Spaniards under Francisco Pizarro used one of these civil wars to great advantage when they arrived in 1533 to rob the gold of Cuzco.

The basic unit of both society and government was the ***ayllu,*** or clan. A village would normally possess two to four clans, headed by a male in the prime of life to whom all members of the clan owed absolute loyalty. He handled the clan's business dealings with outsiders. After conquering neighboring Indians, the Cuzco emperor broke up the old ayllus and replaced them with new ones based on place of residence, rather than common kinship. The head of the new ayllu was appointed by the emperor because of good service or demonstrated loyalty. He served the central government in about the same fashion as a feudal baron served the king of France. The ordinary people, organized in these new artificial clans, were his to do with as he liked, so long as they discharged their labor duty and paid any other tax demanded of them by the Inca in Cuzco.

Regimentation was a prominent feature of Incan government, but it also displayed a concern for social welfare that was unusual for early governments. In times of poor harvest, grain was distributed to the people from the government's enforced-collection granaries, as in China. Natural disasters, such as flooding mountain rivers, were common, and a system of central "relief funds" provided assistance for the areas affected. The central authorities also enforced a sort of pension system that provided for the destitute and the old. These features of the Incan regime have attracted much attention from modern historians, who see in them a tentative approach to the welfare state of the twentieth century.

## NORTH AMERICANS

Agriculture came to Native Americans more slowly than it did to those people in Central and South America. Corn and squash made their way into the mountainous parts of southern New Mexico sometime around 1500 B.C.E. and then quickly moved into other parts north of the Rio Grande River.

## The Ancestral Puebloan Civilization

By the early centuries of the Common Era, **Ancestral Puebloans** (sometimes called the **Anasazi**) were taking to more settled ways in the Four Corners area, where the states of Utah, Colorado, New Mexico, and Arizona meet today (see Map 12.4). Most continued their hunting and gathering ways, but their migratory routes had become noticeably more confined, and they appear to have spent longer periods in specific locations. They had begun growing corn and squash, and by 400 C.E., bows and arrows had replaced the atlatl, making hunting more efficient. (See Patterns of Belief for Native American oral traditions about the origins of corn.) Beans also had been added to their diet, making them less dependent on meat for protein. People had begun living in pit house villages, often for an entire growing season. The fact that they made baskets for both storage and cooking (using heated cooking stones in waterproof baskets) has led archaeologists to call the phase to about 700 C.E. the Basketmaker Period.

Beginning around 700, they started erecting rectangular, adobe houses above ground, beginning the so-called Pueblo I period. The Pueblo II (c. 800–1150) saw a dramatic increase in population as a result of noticeably higher rainfall and groundwater levels. Pueblo villages were both larger and more numerous across the American Southwest. However, the most remarkable development of this period was what is sometimes called the **Chaco phenomenon.** This refers to the construction of fourteen "Great Houses" in Chaco Canyon, located in northwestern New Mexico. The Great Houses were multistory stone-and-timber pueblos. The largest of these, Pueblo Bonito, numbered more than 600 rooms, contained more than 40 ritual enclosures called *kivas,* and possibly stood as high as five stories. Excavations have shown convincingly that it served a largely ceremonial function. Although few burials have been found in Pueblo Bonito and other Great Houses, archaeologists have unearthed large caches of rich ceremonial artifacts, such as turquoise-encrusted ceremonial beakers, the feathers and skeletal remains of macaws from Mexico, and seashells. Furthermore, scholars have discovered that Pueblo Bonito and other Chacoan Great Houses were aligned with such exactitude that they comprised a gigantic, highly precise structural assemblage for predicting the annual solar and eighteen-year lunar cycles, which rivaled in sophistication those of the Mesoamerican civilizations.

Chaco Canyon appears to have been the center of an extensive network of roads and "outlier" Great Houses. Questions have arisen, quite naturally, over the reason for the system of roads, constructed in almost perfectly straight lines for many miles in all directions. Clearly, both ritual and trade were factors, because all of these roads converged on Chaco Canyon, giving it the appearance of a regional center where people came to pay tribute and participate in the numerous *kivas* found in the Great Houses. The discovery of items that had to have been produced as far away as Mexico (macaws, copper bells), the Gulf of Mexico or the Gulf of California (seashells), the upper Rio Grande region (turquoise), and the

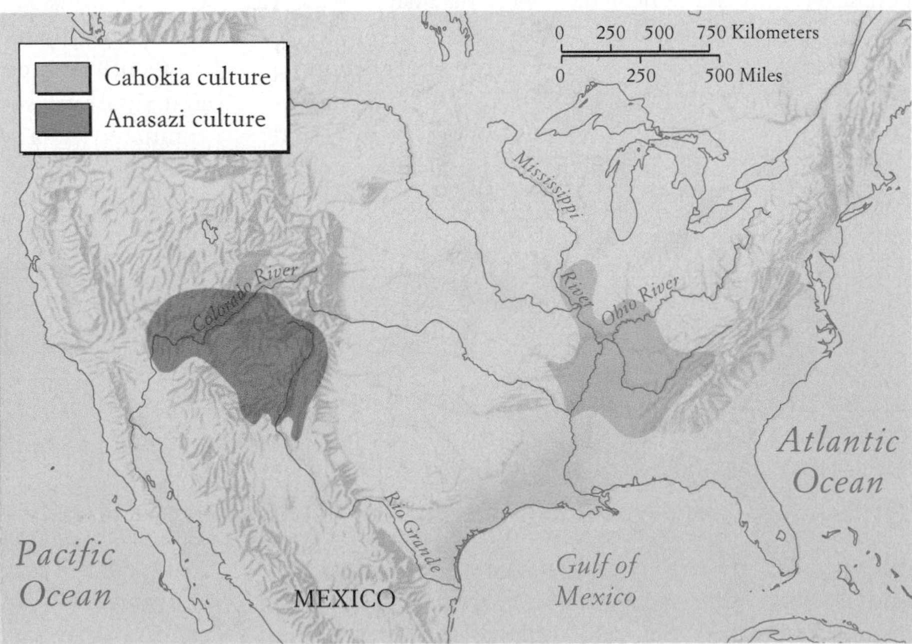


**MAP 12.4** ***Anasazi and Cahokia Cultures of North America***

Some time before 500 C.E., the nomads of the southwestern quarter of the present-day United States began to farm the riverine wetlands, raising maize, beans, and squash, which had been developed earlier in Mexico. Their success allowed the maintenance of cliffside pueblos of more than 200 individuals. Later, the Cahokia Indians of the midwestern Mississippi valley erected large burial mounds near their extensive agricultural villages.

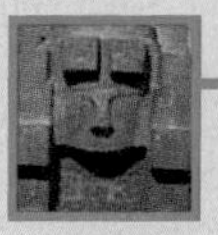

PATTERNS OF BELIEF

## Native American Corn Myths

**IN MANY NON-WESTERN SOCIETIES,** history and religious myth are not considered separate views of human existence. These two examples of Native American traditions provide explanations for the origins of corn (maize).

The first of these is a condensation of the *Popol Vuh,* a religious and philosophical tract than presents Mayan ideas about the structure of the universe and the world, as well as the nature of humanity. The *Popol Vuh* was a myth that would have been passed on orally from generation to generation, even acted out in ceremonies.

> [Speaking to Creator gods, Heart of Sky and Plumed Serpent]
>
> Fox: We bring you great news! We have found ears of yellow corn and white corn.
>
> Coyote: This is the ingredient you have been looking for to create human flesh!
>
> Parrot: The mountain we have just come from is thick with corn.
>
> Crow: Hundreds of plants grow there, strong and straight and tall. . . .
>
> Plumed Serpent: Let us grind the corn nine times!
>
> Narrator 2: And then the yellow corn was ground<br>
> And then the white corn.
>
> Heart of Sky: Let us add water!
>
> Narrator 2: The food came<br>
> With water to create strength,<br>
> And it became man's grease<br>
> And turned into his fat.
>
> Heart of Sky: The story of our beginnings will be told!
>
> Narrator 2: Only yellow corn<br>
> And white corn were their bodies.<br>
> Only food were the legs<br>
> And arms of man.<br>
> Those who were our first fathers<br>
> Were the four original men<br>
> Only food at the outset<br>
> Were their bodies.
>
> —Narine Polio

The following story is anthropologist Frank Waters's condensed version of the Hopi account of the relationships between the corn and the human race:

> With the pristine wisdom granted [the Hopi], they understood that the earth was a living entity like themselves. She was their mother; they were made from her flesh; they suckled at her breast. For her milk was the grass upon which all animals grazed and the corn which had been created specially to supply food for mankind. But the corn plant was also a living entity with a body similar to man's in many respects, and the people built its flesh into their own. Hence, corn was also their mother. Thus, they knew their mother in two aspects which were often synonymous—as Mother Earth and the Corn Mother.

### *Analyze and Interpret*

What do these traditional accounts seem to be saying about the relationship between humans and their food? Why do you suppose Native Americans relied on such stories rather than on more scientific explanations? How do such stories compare, for example, with the Book of Genesis in the Bible?

Sources: From website http://www.yale.edu/ynhti/curriculum/units/1999/2/99.02.09.x.html. Copyright © 1978–2004 by the Yale–New Haven Teachers Institute, all rights reserved, and Frank Waters, *Book of the Hopi. The First Revelation of the Hopi's Historical and Religious Worldview of Life* (New York: Penguin Books, 1963), p. 7.

**History Now™**

***To read the entire* Popol Vuh, *point your browser to the documents area of* HistoryNow.**

Chuska Mountains to the west (timber) support the theory of a regional trade center wielding great power.

The Pueblo II period of exceptionally clement weather for the Chacoans came to a rudely abrupt end around 1150, when a thirty-year drought forced the abandonment of the Great Houses and the thousands of smaller pueblos that were part of the Chacoan system. Many fled north to the Four Corners area. There they settled in what scholars call the "Great Pueblos," some of which were built in the alcoves of cliffs. Today, Mesa Verde National Park is where the most famous of these cliff dwellings can be found. Another long drought, from 1170 to 1300, caused the Ancestral Puebloans to finally abandon the Four Corners area completely.

From about 1300 to 1500, the Puebloan clans migrated westward, southward, and eastward. Their descendants today live in the Hopi, Zuni, Acoma, Laguna, and Upper Rio Grande Pueblos of Arizona and New Mexico. About the time they abandoned the Four Corners area, the ancestors of the Navajo and Apache peoples moved from their homelands in what is now western Canada into the lands abandoned by the Puebloans.

Richard A. Cooke/Corbis

**Pueblo Bonito.** Built in stages between 850 and 1150, Pueblo Bonito was the largest of the Chacoan Great Houses. It had more than 600 rooms, stood up to five stories tall, and contained more than forty ceremonial *kivas*. Despite their size, it is believed that the primary purpose of Great Houses like Pueblo Bonito was not for habitation, but ceremonial and, like Mesoamerican structures, astronomical.

## *The Mississippian and Cahokia Civilizations*

When knowledge of agriculture gradually altered people's life ways in the American Southwest, it was having similarly revolutionary effects on areas to the east. Mysterious mound-building cultures, based on hunting the abundant resources of the Ohio and Mississippi river valleys, appeared around 600 B.C.E. Scholars call these the Adena and Hopewell civilizations. By the early centuries C.E., another mound-building civilization had evolved out of these earlier ones. This one was based on farming and was far more sophisticated. With locations throughout much of the United States east of the Mississippi River, scholars have called this the Mississippian civilization.

The largest and most important mound-builder settlement of this period was at **Cahokia,** located near today's East St. Louis, Illinois. Although its exact relationship to other Mississippian locations is not yet archaeologically well-defined, it appears that the people who built Cahokia were Mississippians who had moved there from somewhere east of it around 600 C.E. With a peasant base capable of producing large surpluses of squash, beans, and maize, the Cahokian civilization might have had a social hierarchy from its inception. Ordinary Cahokians built their dwellings from simple materials like wood slats and mud, but nobles built their houses on the terraces of a large, pyramid-like mound, which today is called Monks Mound. Covering about eighteen acres and reaching nearly 100 feet at its highest point, Monks Mound was made entirely out of earth. It is the largest pyramid ever built in North America and the fourth largest in the entire world.

The entire Cahokia site included about eighty mounds of differing sizes and, apparently, purposes. Some, where excavators have found ceremonial objects, were meant simply as places for religious rituals. Others were evidently tombs, as they contained human remains. We know that human sacrifice was practiced, because in one instance, an especially important individual was buried amid copper sheets, baskets of mica, and 180 sacrificial victims from all ranks of Cahokian society.

Cahokia ended somewhat mysteriously around 1300. Archaeologists have suggested several explanations, such as environmental degradation, overpopulation, or climatic change, but nobody knows for sure why the site was abandoned.

## SUMMARY

The achievements of the Amerindian civilizations are imposing in some respects but paltry in others. When compared with the works of the Mesopotamian peoples, the Egyptians, or the Chinese, the relative absence of written documents and the small number of permanent monuments make it difficult to get a clear and comprehensive view of the Amerindians' abilities. Also, the physical isolation of the American continent from other centers of civilization assured that the Amerindians did not benefit from outside stimuli. What they produced came from their own mental and physical resources, so far as we can now tell. Yet the physical evidence that survives is certainly impressive. That the Inca could govern a huge empire without benefit of writing or the wheel seems to us almost a miracle. And yet it was done. That the Mayan pyramids in southern Mexico could soar upward of 300 feet without benefit of metal tools or any of the technological innovations of the Mesopotamians, Egyptians, and Hindus seems equally incredible. Yet it, too, was done.

The Amerindian civilizations are perhaps the most forceful argument against the diffusion theory of human progress. Most likely, the Amerindians created their own world through their own, unaided, intellectual efforts. What would have been an admirable achievement under any circumstances becomes astounding if the Amerindians did these things alone.

## IDENTIFICATION TERMS

Test your knowledge of this chapter's key concepts by defining the following terms. If you can't recall the meaning of certain terms, refresh your memory by looking up the boldfaced term in the chapter, turning to the Glossary at the end of the book, or working with the flashcards that are available on the *World Civilizations* Companion Website: **http://history.wadsworth.com/adler04/**.

Amerindians
Ancestral Puebloans (Anasazi)
Archaic Period
*ayllu*
Aztec
Beringia
Cahokia
Chaco phenomenon
Chavin
Chichén Itzá
Clovis culture
Cuzco
Folsom points
Inca
Machu Picchu
Maya
Olmec
Paleoindian Period
Quechua
Tenochtitlán
Teotihuacán
Toltec
Tula

## TEST YOUR KNOWLEDGE

Test your knowledge of this chapter by answering the following questions. Complete answers appear at the end of the book. You may also take this quiz interactively and find even more quiz questions on the *World Civilizations* Companion Website: **http://history.wadsworth.com/adler04/**.

1. Most archaeologists today accept the theory that the first inhabitants of the New World
   a. settled down to farming by 9500 B.C.E.
   b. brought "Clovis points" with them from Asia.
   c. developed *atlatls* hundreds of years before their arrival in North America.
   d. arrived on primitive ships from West Africa.
   e. crossed a land bridge from Asia into Alaska.

2. The most important factor leading to the gradual abandonment of hunting and gathering in favor of farming among Native Americans was
   a. increasing technological sophistication.
   b. political pressure exerted by chiefs.
   c. climatic change.
   d. growing trade and the need for surpluses.
   e. enforced settlement into towns by clan leaders.

3. The most advanced system of writing among the Amerindian civilizations was that of the
   a. Maya.
   b. Inca.
   c. Toltecs.
   d. Aztecs.
   e. Olmecs.
4. The overridingly important principle of Aztec society and government was
   a. cannibalism.
   b. war and its requirements.
   c. trade and the creation of wealth.
   d. art and excellence in its production.
   e. the establishment of great cities.
5. The Aztecs believed that human sacrifices were necessary for the
   a. sun god to continue to bless their crops.
   b. gods to give them victory against their enemies.
   c. moon to continue its orbit.
   d. rains to fall.
   e. birth of healthy children.
6. The Aztec society at the time of the Spaniards' arrival
   a. was disorganized, impoverished, and illiterate.
   b. existed without distinct social classes.
   c. was tolerant and peaceable.
   d. revolved around the emperor and war.
   e. operated within a steadily decreasing land area.
7. South America was home to which of these Amerindian civilizations?
   a. Aztecs
   b. Olmecs
   c. Maya
   d. Toltecs
   e. Inca
8. All of the following helped the Inca build and maintain their empire *except*
   a. the Quechua language.
   b. the reformed ayllu or clan organization.
   c. their excellent road system.
   d. wheeled transport.
   e. agricultural advances.
9. The Ancestral Puebloans ("Anasazi") were
   a. rivals to the Incan rulers in Peru.
   b. inhabitants of Mexico City before the Aztecs.
   c. the builders of "Great Houses."
   d. part of the Cahokia culture.
   e. some of the earliest mound builders.
10. The Cahokia civilization was
   a. related to the Mississippian civilization.
   b. derived from the Ancestral Puebloan civilization.
   c. founded by the Toltecs.
   d. based primarily on hunting and gathering.
   e. centered in the Four Corners region.

## InfoTrac College Edition

Visit the source collections at

**http://infotrac.thomsonlearning.com**

and use the Search function with the following key terms:

Inca or Incan     Aztec     Anasazi

## Wadsworth History Website Resources

Visit the World History Resource Center at **http://history.wadsworth.com/world** for a wealth of general resources and the *World Civilizations* Companion Website at **http://history.wadsworth.com/adler04/** for resources specific to this textbook.

## HistoryNow

Enter *HistoryNow* using the access card that is available for *World Civilizations. HistoryNow* will assist you in understanding the content in this chapter with lesson plans generated for your needs. In addition, you can read the following document, and many more, online:

*Popol Vuh*

*Not even God is wise enough.*
Yoruba Proverb

# 13 Africa from Kush to the Fifteenth Century



| | |
|---|---|
| 700s B.C.E.–350 C.E. | Kingdom of Kush |
| 300s–700s C.E. | Kingdom of Axum |
| c. 400–1100 C.E. | Kingdom of Ghana |
| 600s–700s C.E. | Arabs conquer Egypt and North Africa |
| 800s-1200s C.E. | Many Swahili city-states founded |
| c. 500s C.E. | Origins of Sudanese kingdoms/ trans-Saharan trade increases |
| c. 900s–c. 1400s C.E. | Great Zimbabwe flourishes |
| 1250 1450 C.E. | Kingdom of Mali flourishes |
| 1375–1591 C.E. | Songhay Kingdom flourishes |

The historiography of Africans has made impressive advances in the past fifty years. The greater part of the continent's people had no written language until relatively recent days or employed a language that has not been deciphered. Historiographic research in the usual literary sense was therefore difficult, but a combination of new methods of obtaining information about the past and new techniques for using that information have changed the situation radically. Now, archaeology, historical linguistics, art forms, and oral traditions have brought considerable illumination to Africa's past, and these sources are gradually revealing an extraordinary panorama of peoples and achievements.

Africa is a huge place—the second largest of the world's continents—and the chief characteristic of its history is its variety. Most of its several different climates and topographies have produced civilizations of various levels of sophistication. More even than elsewhere, Africa has repeatedly demonstrated that racial categorization has little meaning and even less relevance for explaining the successes or failures of peoples all over the world in their struggles to achieve better lives and more or less complex civilizations. Rather than race, the natural environment in which people live and their location on routes of trade and travel usually have proved to be the more decisive factors in their history.

## African Geography and Climates

Before the Europeans arrived during the fifteenth century C.E., many parts of Africa were isolated by their geography from other centers of human activity. The great exception was its Mediterranean coast and the northeastern portion, where both Egypt and the Horn of Africa (present-day Ethiopia and Somalia) were in continuous contact with the Near and Middle Eastern civilizations from at least as early as 2000 B.C.E.

The continent rises from the surrounding waters like an inverted saucer, with its coastal lowlands quickly giving way to deserts (in the north, northwest, and southwest) or to highlands and mountains (in the east and southeast) that dominate the vast interior (see Map 13.1). A coastal strip along the Mediterranean Sea quickly gives way to the Atlas mountains. South of these mountain ranges, the enormous Sahara Desert divides the continent into its North African and sub-Saharan components. The western coasts are marked by rain forest, which restricted travel to the rivers until recent times. Where the great rivers of the eastern interior break through the ring of mountains, tremendous waterfalls and rapids block human travel and transport. The fertile plateaus and rolling country until recently could be reached only after a dangerous and lengthy overland journey from the eastern coast. Long reaches of the continent's Atlantic coasts lack good harbors, and heavy surf makes the open beaches unusable by small craft almost everywhere except the Mediterranean. The coastal lands on the eastern side of the continent, those facing the Indian Ocean, however, have many excellent natural harbors that have served as places of trade and settlement for at least 2,000 years, as we shall see.

Although geography plays a major role, part of the reason for Africa's isolation is climatic. The continent is divided into five climatic and vegetative zones (see Map 13.1). Two of these, the desert and the rain forest, have been unsuited to sedentary life for any concentrated number of people, and a third, the Sahel or Sudan, is frequently afflicted with droughts of extreme nature. Perhaps 55 to 65 percent of the total area falls into one or another of these categories, in which sustenance for humans was (and is) difficult.

The five zones are as follows:

1. The *Mediterranean and extreme southern coasts,* with temperate weather and good soil
2. The *Sahel,* or the dry, mainly treeless steppes (semiarid grass-covered plains between the desert and the savanna) that cross Africa from the Atlantic to the Indian Oceans
3. The *deserts,* of which the enormous and growing Sahara is the chief but not the only one
4. The *rain forest,* which extends on either side of the equator in the west and center
5. The *savanna,* the grassland regions of the interior plateaus, mainly south of the Sahara Desert and in East and Central Africa

The various peoples of Africa developed sharply different ways of life depending on the zone where they lived. The Mediterranean coast was for most of its history closely linked to Europe and the Middle East. Egypt, as we have seen, was a land to itself in its isolated but benevolent Nile valley. In much of the center and west of the continent, the rain forest's unsuitability for grain agriculture inhibited large-scale development almost to the present. In the desert regions, nomadic pastoralism and small-scale oasis agriculture were the only possible lifestyles in historical times, and vast areas were left uninhabited. The dry Sahel also could support only a pastoral economy. Beyond the coastal strip, only the savannas of the west and the eastern plateaus and the equatorial forests had enough precipitation and reasonably good soil to sustain crop agriculture and dense village populations.

## Early Movements of Ideas and People

Like its climate, geography, and lifestyles, Africa's people are also diverse. In the coastal strip along the Mediterranean, the Nile valley, and the northern Sahara dwelled Egyptians and **Berbers**, later joined by Arabs after the Muslim expansion in the seventh century C.E. Along the northeastern coasts and upper Nile valley were Abyssinians (Ethiopians), Nubians, and Somalis. Various **Bantu**-speaking ethnic groups made up the large majority in the center and south by about 400 C.E. In the huge bulge of West Africa below the Sahara lived, and still live today, an assortment of peoples and language groups, mainly Bantu.

In the far south and southwest, the original settlers were the Khoisan, or "Bushmen," who still survive in much reduced numbers in a hunting-gathering culture in the Kalahari Desert. To the north of them in the center of the African forest belt live the Pygmies, also traditionally a hunting-gathering people. Today, hunting and gathering continue to supply the largest part of the daily diet in those few remaining regions of Africa that are blessed with more protein-bearing game than any other part of the globe.

In the forests and grassland savannas, many villages depended on either pastoralism or farming for their food supply. Many combined both of these subsistence activities in what scholars call "mixed farming." Hunting was often a subsidiary resource, especially in the grasslands where big game abounded. Traditionally, women performed most of the daily drudgery associated with farming: sowing, weeding, hoeing, and preparing the food. In

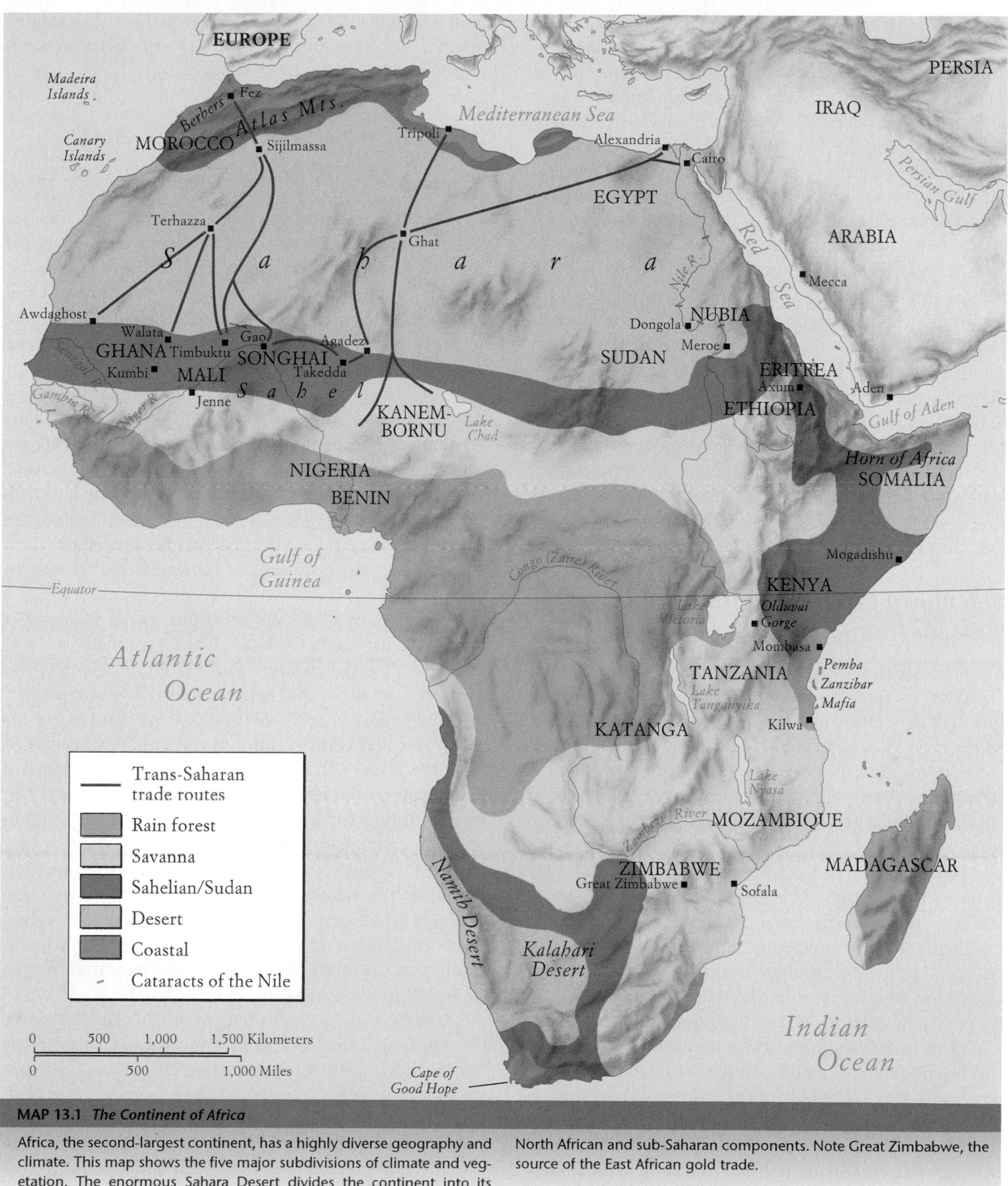


**MAP 13.1** ***The Continent of Africa***

Africa, the second-largest continent, has a highly diverse geography and climate. This map shows the five major subdivisions of climate and vegetation. The enormous Sahara Desert divides the continent into its North African and sub-Saharan components. Note Great Zimbabwe, the source of the East African gold trade.

some regions, such as present-day Kenya and Tanzania, the pastoral lifestyle predominated, and agriculture was limited. The same was true of the Sahel and the Sahara, where there was too little rainfall for agriculture. But in the more densely settled areas, farming supplied Africans, as all other peoples, with the essentials of life and represented the usual work.

As we saw in Chapter 1, the key element in the development of civilization normally is the availability of adequately watered agricultural land and iron tools. In Africa, these elements were closely associated, although tools such as hoes and even pottery continued to be made from stone during the early centuries of Africa's food-producing revolution. Most of the land suitable for intensive agriculture in pre-modern Africa was in the savanna south of the Sahara and in the Nile valley, with only bits and pieces elsewhere. The evidence provided by rock paintings and archaeology reveals that cattle pastoralism might have been practiced in the region of the Sahara during a wet phase that lasted from about 7500 to 2500 B.C.E. Once drier conditions began setting in, these Saharan herding peoples migrated north and south of the desert, largely confining their settlements to the banks of rivers and surviving lakes. Archaeologists have found evidence that demonstrates that, between about 4000 and 2500 B.C.E., the cultivation of native millet, sorghum, and rice began in the Nile River valley and the Niger River valley of West Africa. When agriculture spread south into the rain forests, conditions did not favor cereals. In these regions Africans learned to grow bananas and root crops such as yams, which could thrive in the humid climate and rain-drenched soils.

### *The Bantu Expansion into Subequatorial Africa*

Although stone tools continued to be in use for several centuries, the growing use of iron greatly facilitated the spread of agriculture into the southern half of Africa. The Bantu speakers, a large group of distantly related peoples, profited from their mastery of yam agriculture to begin a steady expansion south and east from the region of present-day Nigeria in West Africa through the rain forest some time well before 1000 B.C.E. Upon reaching the region to the west of Lake Victoria by 1000 B.C.E., they acquired iron technology and learned to breed livestock and grow the grain crops that did better than yams in the grasslands. These innovations helped them enlarge their numbers primarily through natural increase and the absorption of other peoples. By these means they established a series of small kingdoms stretching across eastern, central, and southern Africa until, by 400 C.E., they had reached the southern tip of the continent in present-day South Africa. The bulk of the Bantu-speaking inhabitants of central, eastern, and southern Africa are thought to be the descendants of these migrants. As the Bantu had no written language and built few monuments that have survived, most of what we know about this process has been inferred from archaeological and linguistic research. Only when they arrived on the coast of the Indian Ocean and built the port cities do we know much more than that they had created kingdoms dependent on agriculture and trade in the interior. Some of these states and kingdoms existed when the Portuguese arrived in the 1500s, and accounts of Portuguese travelers provide valuable additional information that supplements what archaeological and linguistic data provide.

## Social Organization and State Formation

In sub-Saharan Africa, the basic unit of society was not the nuclear family but the clan, or **lineage**, a much larger unit supposedly descended from a common ancestor. Within lineages, children took their names from and had specified status and rights through their lineage. Some societies seem to have followed **patrilineal descent** (descent and rights were determined by the father's lineage), but others followed **matrilineal descent** (names and rights were received from the mother's side). Clans lived together in compounds that grew in time to become villages or towns. People occasionally formed guild-like organizations to specialize in a certain craft, such as iron or copper smelting, pot making, basketry, salt-making, or even regional or long-distance trade. But most clans depended on either farming or herding activity to sustain them.

Several clans made up an ethnic group (sometimes called a "tribe"), and the local village was usually the keystone of all social organization and enforcement of the rules of daily life—what many would call "government." Because age was highly venerated, it was customary for the clan elders to make most of the important decisions for the village, although everyone usually had rights to participate in deliberations, and matters were usually discussed until a consensus opinion was reached. Religion and the maintenance of social order were closely linked, but we know little about the exact practices that were followed in the remote past. Religious sacrifices were demanded before any important action was taken. Excepting the Christian northeast, animism in a multiplicity of forms was universal before the influence of Islam began to be felt in the ninth century.

Arab travelers' accounts tell of the "shocking" freedom (to Muslims, at least) of women in African society in the tenth through thirteenth centuries. There was no attempt to seclude women or to restrict them from business dealings. Nevertheless, few women seem to have had equal access to political power. Male polygamy was the universal rule, and the number of wives a man had was taken as a sign of his wealth and social status. Taking additional wives as a man matured was considered a natural and desirable way of extending his kinship network. The offspring of these unions were considered the responsibility of the females, thus reinforcing the prevalent African custom of seeing the clan rather than the nuclear family as the primary unit of social life. When African people fell under the sway of Islam, women's personal and public lives were controlled more closely. Moreover, where matrilineal descent existed, it was usually replaced by patrilineal descent, and women's rights of inheritance were reduced to the general rule of Islamic law that restricted a woman's inheritance to only half that of a man.

Early European explorers/traders remarked on the existence of large numbers of people throughout sub-Saharan Africa who lived without any form of what they recognized as government. Perhaps as many as one-fourth of the African population, it has been estimated, lived in such apparently stateless societies at the advent of the Europeans. In making their judgment, the newcomers looked for the earmarks of government with which they were familiar in their European homelands: monarchs surrounded by subordinate officials, tax-collecting systems, defined frontiers, permanent military establishments, and, most important, written laws. They also assumed that the larger the state, the more advanced must be its civilization. These assumptions led most Europeans to conclude erroneously that Africans must be severely retarded in their political development, as some or most of these elements of the state were lacking in the sub-Saharan civilizations, especially where they did not have written language.

What can we say today about the early Europeans' assessment? In fact, the social controls necessary for the peace and security of any large group were always present but went unrecognized by the Westerners who came to Africa during the colonial era. In the absence of written laws, controls typically would have included conflict and dispute resolution by medicine men or women having spiritual access to clan and village ancestors; social rules and norms that regulated rights and duties between kin groups or lineages when one or more of their members were involved in dispute; and certain duties and privileges accorded to an age group. In all or several of these fashions, the village elders usually performed the functions that early Europeans normally expected a state and its officials to perform.

Where recognizable states did emerge, they typically were organized around the principle of divine kingship. Such state systems had no bureaucracies but did include large numbers of court functionaries who individually did not have the king's power, but whose collective will could negate that of the king if they believed his actions had exceeded the bounds of custom or propriety. Typically, these included such figures as the queen mother, a prime minister, the royal historian and praise-singer, royal drummers, commanders of the army, diviners, keepers of court protocol, and medicine men and women. The king was a member of a royal lineage that enjoyed great prestige or was thought to be sacred. He acted as intermediary between the living and the dead, and he was thought to be able to discern the wishes of the royal ancestors through divination of even spirit possession. Maintaining the ritual purity and strength of the king were thought to be essential to the welfare of the land and people, and a weak, sick or aged king threatened the state. He might be turned out or even killed. Usually, too, the divine king was surrounded by symbols of office, or regalia. These normally would have included ivory horns that were blown on ceremonial occasions, royal drums, ceremonial swords, umbrellas or fans, and a palanquin on which he was transported.

## Early States

Farther up the Nile from the lush irrigated ribbon that is Egypt, the river flows across a series of rapids (the famed cataracts) and makes a huge **S** turn through what is now one of the harshest deserts in the world. This area, which was never brought under the pharaoh's rule, despite numerous attempts, is modern southern Egypt and northern Sudan. In ancient terminology it was called *Nubia*. East and south of Nubia, across the Horn of Africa and reaching to the Red Sea, are present-day Eritrea, Ethiopia, and Somalia. These modern states are the successors to the ancient kingdoms of Kush and Axum. And these kingdoms were, in their turn, the successors of pharaonic Egypt as the centers of a flourishing high civilization.

### *Kush*

**Kush** was an African kingdom that emerged in the fifteenth century B.C.E. and prospered until its overthrow in the fourth century C.E. Its original capital was Kerma; then, after 900 B.C.E., the capital was located at Napata near the fourth cataract of the Nile. Archaeologists, who commenced work only about seventy years ago, are slowly unearthing the extensive ruins of its cities and especially its last capital at Meroe. The history of the kingdom in the strict, written sense is not available to us, as the Kushite script inscribed on many stone monuments is still undeciphered. Remarkably, it is alphabetic and thus rivals the achievement of the ancient Phoenicians.

Kush was at once the partner and the rival of the pharaohs in keeping open the busy maritime trade routes that spanned the Red Sea and the western reaches of the Indian Ocean. These routes connected the Mediterranean basin with southern Asia. They became increasingly profitable as the Hellenistic and Roman rulers of Egypt developed a taste for the luxury goods originating from East Africa, India, and China.

In its early history, when its capital was at Kerma, Kush was closely associated with Egypt and was strongly influenced by it in culture and religion. However, when the

Darrel Plowes

**Pyramids at Meroe.** Standing from 50 to 100 feet high, this roofless shrine and its surrounding pyramids are thought to be part of a royal tomb complex in the ancient capital of the Kushites.

Assyrians invaded Egypt in the eighth century B.C.E., the capital was moved a second time, farther up the Nile to Meroe. Once at Meroe, the kingdom cut most of its ties with Egypt and became increasingly African in character. From the sixth century B.C.E., Meroe was a major industrial center whose principal product was iron. Archaeologists have discovered numerous iron-smelting furnaces and large mounds of slag, an industrial by-product of iron making. By the third century B.C.E., Meroe was at its height. Its strength derived from its grip on the trade coming downriver from the African interior and on the perhaps more important trade with southern Arabia across the Red Sea. The most important commodities were gold and slaves, followed by such exotic luxury wares as animal hides, ostrich feathers, spices, ebony, and ivory, all of which were destined for the Mediterranean region or Arabia. Numerous records exist from Hellenistic Egypt detailing the results of commercial or diplomatic contacts with Kush, and in the Roman era such contacts continued for another three centuries.

## Axum

By the first century C.E., a rival power was rising on Kush's eastern flank. **Axum** in the Ethiopian highlands was the main city of a kingdom that had been established when immigrants from the southern reaches of Arabia arrived and intermarried with the local Africans during the last centuries B.C.E. After establishing its own Red Sea port, Axum became strong enough by the 300s to challenge Kush for control of the Red Sea trade and the upper Nile corridor. About 350 C.E., Axum made war on and conquered Kush. After this date, Kush rapidly descended into oblivion and was abandoned. The city's sparse ruins were not rediscovered until the late eighteenth century by the earliest European explorers.

The rise of Axum coincided with its conversion to Christianity by Byzantine missionaries. Only a generation after Constantine accepted the faith, the kings of Axum made the same choice. Thus began the extraordinary history of Christianity in Ethiopia, the modern name for Axum and its surrounding lands. It is the oldest and most distinctive version of that religion in all of Africa. In later centuries, the rugged mountains and physical isolation of much of the country enabled the Ethiopians to hold off repeated Muslim attempts to conquer it, both from the Nile valley and the Red Sea coasts. It also allowed the growth of a unique legend of royal descent, the Solomonic dynasty of Ethiopian Christian kings that commenced in biblical times and lasted until an army rebellion in 1970. According to this history, the royal line was descended from Menelik, son of the Hebrew king Solomon by the queen of Sheba.

Like its predecessor, Axum depended for its prosperity on its function as exchange depot for the Indian Ocean–Red Sea trade, as well as the Nile valley route. For a while in the sixth century, Axum was strong enough to cross the Red Sea and conquer a Jewish kingdom that had established itself in southwestern Arabia. However, the seventh-century Arab conquest of Egypt and South Arabia changed this situation dramatically, and within a century Christian Axum was driven from its Red Sea coast and under siege. Gradually, the city sank into the same forgetfulness that had claimed Kush nearly 500 years before. Its monuments and stelae fell down and were buried or forgotten by an impoverished remnant.

From the eighth century, Arab Muslims dominated the seaborne trade. Nubian society, which gradually had matured into the three small states of Noba, Makuria, and Alowa, took Axum's place along the Nile. Little is known about them except that they had converted to Christianity through Egyptian influence in the seventh and eighth centuries and managed to hold out against Muslim pressure until as late as the 1200s in some areas. Throughout this lengthy period from Axum's fall to the coming of Muslim hegemony in the upper Nile, a diminished commercial traffic along the great river bound Egypt with its southern borderlands in Nubia and the Sudan. But the level of urban, sedentary life reached by the Kushite and Axumite kingdoms was not again approached in northeastern Africa.

## The Sudanese Kingdoms

The Sudanese kingdoms were a series of states that were formed starting about 400 C.E. in the bulge of West Africa below the great Sahara Desert. Here, iron tools, good soils, and the transport afforded by the Niger River had enabled agriculture to advance and provide for a rapidly growing population and an active trade northward across the Sahara with the Berbers and Arabs. Two of these kingdoms are especially well known to modern historians: Ghana and Mali.

### Ghana

**Ghana**, the first of these kingdoms, endured for at least 500 years before it fell apart in the eleventh century as a result of a combination of events, including the onslaught of a Muslim *jihad*. Its exact origins are conjectural, but the Soninke people probably founded it some time in the first centuries C.E., perhaps as early as 400. Its kings established a monopoly of trade in gold obtained from a mining region to the southwest of Ghana on the Senegal River, so the kingdom grew and became a regional power after it began dealings with the Muslims to the north in the eighth century. The *ghana* was the title given to its divine king who ruled through a network of regional officials in an area that at one point reached the size of Texas. Kumbi Saleh, the capital town, was sufficiently impressive that the sophisticated Muslim geographer al-Bakri spent some time describing it in a well-known travel and sightseeing guide of the eleventh century.

The Muslims, both Arabic and Berber, were influential in Ghana and, for that matter, in most of the Sudanese West African kingdoms that followed. The peoples of the Sudan believed in the usual nature and ancestor spirits, but many experienced little difficulty converting to the monotheistic doctrines of Islam that were preached by Arab merchants and missionaries. Like the earlier Christians of Rome, the missionaries concentrated their efforts on the upper class, usually in the towns where trade flourished. By adopting the new doctrine, their African merchant partners quickly gained advantages: literacy; access to new commerce and financial connections; a written law code (the *Sharia*) that helped facilitate commerce; and access to trade networks that extended across the known world at that time. Soon non-Muslim villagers and Muslim urbanites coexisted in these states without apparent friction. The Muslims introduced their concepts of law and administration, as well as religious belief. Kings who chose to continue following their traditional religions often relied on Muslim advisers for political and administrative advice.

### Mali

Ghana's sources of gold dried up, which fatally weakened it when confronted by a Berber-led holy war in the eleventh century. Its regional segments warred with one another until one emerged under a semi-mythical king, Sundiata, who was powerful enough to subdue the region's neighbors around 1250 (see Evidence of the Past). This was the kingdom of **Mali**, which survived to about 1450. Mali was larger and better organized than Ghana, and the gold trade on which its kings depended, like those of the *ghanas* before them, seems to have come from a new region closer to the headwaters of the Niger River, which lay at the heart of the new kingdom (see Map 13.1). The original ruling clan, the Keitas, were nominally Muslims, but they ruled primarily as divine kings who governed with the help of their court officials and regional representatives. The adoption of stricter forms of Islam early in the fourteenth century by a new ruling clan, the Mansas, encouraged good relations with the trans-Saharan Berbers, whose trading activities were essential to the prosperity of the kingdom.

Like the earlier Kush and Axum, the Sudanese kingdoms were first and foremost the products of a strategic trading position. In this case, controlling movement along a lengthy stretch of the southern fringe of the Sahara allowed them to monitor the movements of trade goods from sub-Saharan to North Africa (and on to both Europe and the East). Both Ghana and Mali relied heavily on the taxes imposed on the Saharan traders in three vital commodities: gold, salt, and slaves. Although the king had other means of support for his extensive and expensive court and army, these taxes made the wheels go 'round, so to speak.

African gold was essential to Roman and medieval European commerce, as well as to the Muslim world. Gold ore was rare in Europe, but it was found in large quantities in

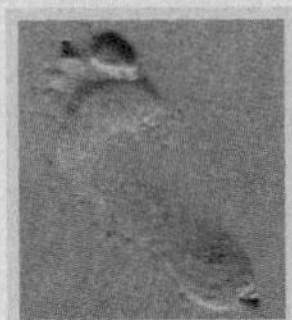

EVIDENCE OF THE PAST

## Ibn Khaldun's Account of the Decline of Ghana and the Rise of Mali and Mansa Musa

**Abu Zayd 'Abd ar-Rahman ibn Khaldun** is a well-known and highly regarded historian of the fourteenth century. He was born in Tunis in 1332 and died in 1406. The following selection is taken from the introduction of his great work of history and geography, *Kitab al-Ibar,* whose full title, loosely translated, is "The Book of Examples and the Register of the Origin and History of the Arabs, the Persians and the Berbers." Although he never traveled to the Sudan, as a secretary to various Moroccan rulers Khaldun would have had access to correspondence between Mali and Morocco, and he apparently used Malian oral historians (*griots*) as additional sources of information.

> When Ifriqiya and the Maghrib were conquered [by the Arabs] merchants penetrated the western part of the land of the Sudan and found among them no king greater than the king of Ghana. Ghana was bounded on the west by the Ocean. They were a very mighty people exercising vast authority. The seat of their authority was Ghana, a dual city on both banks of the [Niger River], one of the greatest and most populous cities in the world. . . .
>
> The neighbors of Ghana on the east, as chroniclers assert, were another people known as [Soso] . . . and beyond them another people known as Mali, and beyond them another known as . . . [Gao] . . . then beyond them another known as Takrur. . . . Later the authority of the people of Ghana waned and their prestige declined as that of the veiled people, their neighbors on the north next to the land of the Berbers, grew (as we have related). These extended their domination over the Sudan [black people], and pillaged, imposed tribute and poll tax, and converted many of them to Islam. Then the authority of the rulers of Ghana dwindled away and they were overcome by the [Soso], a neighboring people of the Sudan, who subjugated and absorbed them.
>
> Later the people of Mali outnumbered the peoples of the Sudan in their neighborhood and dominated the whole region. They vanquished the [Soso] and acquired all their possessions, both their ancient kingdom and that of Ghana as far as the Ocean on the west. They were Muslims. . . . Their greatest king, who overcame the [Soso], conquered their country, and seized the power from their hands, was named Mari Jata. Mari, in their language, means "ruler of the blood royal," and jata "lion." . . .
>
> Their rule reached from the Ocean and Ghana in the west to the land of Takrur in the east. Their authority became mighty and all the peoples of the Sudan stood in awe of them. Merchants from the Maghrib and Ifriqiya traveled to their country. Al-Hajj Yunus, the Takruri interpreter, said that the conqueror of [Gao] was Saghamanja, one of the generals of Mansa Musa. . . .
>
> Mansa Musa was an upright man and a great king, and his tales of justice are still told. He made the Pilgrimage [to Mecca] in 724/1324. . . .

### Analyze and Interpret

Why do you think the capital city of the king of Ghana is described as having been two cities? (*Hint:* It had to do with religion.) What role does religion seem to have played in the downfall of Ghana? At times the author uses the word *Sudan* to refer to a region and at other times to a people. What do you think *Sudan* means in Arabic?

Source: J. F. P. Hopkins (trans.) and N. Levtzion (ed. and ann.), *Corpus of Early Arabic Sources for West African History* (London: Cambridge University Press, 1981), pp. 332–334.

Robert Harding Picture Library

**Jenne Mosque.** Perhaps the largest building of earth construction in the world, this Grand Mosque dates from the fourteenth century in Mali. Its outer mud sheathing must be renewed yearly by the volunteer work of much of the Muslim population. What also suggests it is a work of art?

parts of sub-Saharan Africa that were controlled by western Sudanese merchants and those of Swahili city-states like Kilwa in East Africa.

Salt was almost as prized as gold in the ancient world. Although it was a necessity, supplies were limited in most areas except near the sea, and it was difficult to transport without large loss. This made salt highly valuable, and saltpans in oases like Taghaza and Tassili on the southern side of the Sahara were major sources.

Slaves were common in the African markets long before the Europeans began the Atlantic slave trade. European, African, and Muslim cultures had no scruples about slave trading or possession in this epoch. As in every other part of the ancient world, slavery was an accepted consequence of war, debt, and crime. Being captured in raids by hostile neighbors was reason enough for enslavement. Large numbers of slaves passed northward through Ghana and Mali, bound for collection points on the Mediterranean coast. From there they were traded all over the known world.

The kingdom of Mali expanded by military conquests in the thirteenth century, until it came to dominate much of West Africa. Early Africa's most noted ruler, the far-traveled *Mansa Musa,* ruled from 1307 to 1332. He extended the kingdom as far north as the Berber towns in Morocco and eastward to include the great mid-Saharan trading post of Timbuktu. Perhaps 8 million people lived under his rule—at a time when the population of England was about 4 million.

Like his immediate predecessors, Mansa Musa was a Muslim, and in 1324 he made the pilgrimage to the holy places in Arabia. His huge entourage, laden with gold staffs and plates, entered Cairo like a victory procession and made an impression that became folklore. Thanks to Mansa Musa's support, Islam gained much ground in West Africa during his lifetime. Thereafter, the religion gradually passed through the upper classes to the common people. Since then, the Muslim presence in sub-Saharan Africa has been growing slowly for many generations. It has had almost the same impact there as Christianity did in the Germanic kingdoms. Much African law, social organization, literature, and political institutions stem from it.

Mansa Musa and his successor, Mansa Sulayman, also especially encouraged scholarship, and Musa founded a *madrasa* (university) at the famous Sankore mosque in

**The King of Mali in the European Imagination.** This fourteenth-century European map shows a rather fanciful rendering of a king of Mali, often presumed to be Mansa Musa, holding a large nugget and a large gold scepter.

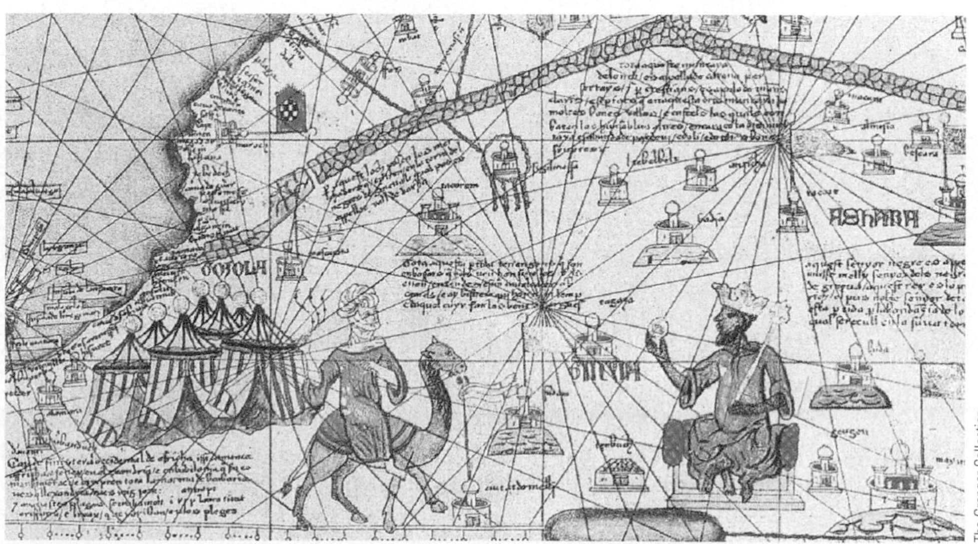

The Granger Collection

Timbuktu. The city gradually gained fame as a center of Islamic book production as well as trade.

### *Songhay*

The Niger River city of Gao was already the focus of central Sudanic trade at the time of Ghana's greatness in the western Sudan. It remained in the shadow of its more powerful western Sudanic neighbors through the centuries of Mali's greatness, and in fact, realizing its importance, Mansa Musa subjugated Gao in 1325. Its dominance of the Niger River trade and most of the major trans-Saharan routes to the east of Timbuktu enabled it to exercise great commercial and military power. This power was realized when its first great king, Sonni Ali (1464–1492), employed a strategy that combined coordinate attacks of a robust cavalry of armored warriors with a sturdy navy of river canoes to extend his conquests to create the core of what became the kingdom of **Songhay**. Under Sonni Ali and his successors, Songhay eventually became the mightiest of the great Sudanic states of West Africa.

Askia Muhammad (1493–1528) continued his predecessor, Ali's, expansionist ways. But, as important as his conquests were, Askia Muhammad's most lasting contribution to West African history lay in his support of Islam. Following the example of the great Malian emperors, Mansa Musa and Sulayman, Muhammad was an enthusiastic Muslim who gave Muslim scholars (*ulama*) important positions in his state apparatus; enforced orthodox practices among his subjects; built mosques; and subsidized book production and scholarship in the intellectual centers of Gao, Timbuktu, and Jenne.

Despite the works of Muhammad and his successors, simultaneous attacks by non-Muslim Mossi peoples from the south and Tuareg Berbers from the north gravely weakened the Songhay state during the 1500s. Its final overthrow came when Moroccan forces invaded it in 1591.

## The Swahili City-States

The East African city-states also had a large hand in the gradual commercial development of the continent. Well before the Common Era, Greek, Roman, and Egyptian ships that traveled down the Red Sea were trading with coastal ports of the Horn of Africa and "Azania," the name given to East Africa at that time. One account from the first century C.E., the *Periplus of the Erythraean Sea,* described Arab and Greco-Roman trade for ivory and tortoise shell with an East African town called Rhapta, for example. For many years archaeologists have searched unsuccessfully for this mysterious port. However, Roman coins and pottery have been found at locations as far south as the northern coastlands of what is now Mozambique.

An enormous expansion of this trade came after the seventh century, when the entire Indian Ocean became virtually an Islamic lake. Thereafter, Persian, Arab, and Indian traders arrived with the annual trade winds to trade with the local Bantu-speaking people, whom the Arabs called "the Zanj." Imports that were especially popular with these Zanj, known to us as the **Swahili**, were dates, glassware, Persian ceramics, Chinese porcelains and silks, Indian cotton fabrics, and glass beads. In return, they traded locally manufactured iron, timber, ivory, and sundry animal by-products such as hides, ambergris, rhinoceros horn, and tortoise shell. By the time the Portuguese arrived in the region in the late fifteenth century, Swahili ships also seem to have been making the reverse journey, building and sailing fully seaworthy ships of their own to ports of southern Arabia and India. Thus, the vast ocean separating Africa and Indonesia was well known to both African and Muslim travelers long before the arrival of the first Portuguese explorers.

Foreign Muslims and local, Bantu-speaking, coastal people steadily intermarried, and the children of these unions were raised as Muslims. Many coastal Africans opted to convert to Islam for many of the same reasons that West Africans did; however, the mixture of African and non-African peoples typically found in the major commercial entrepôts of the coast, like Kilwa and Mombasa, was probably even greater than what one typically would have encountered in the western Sudan. Islam served as the one binding thread. The greatest period of conversion seems to have been 1000 to 1500 C.E.

By the ninth century, a series of small city-states were established whose community life centered on manufacturing and trade. The earliest of these city-states, such as Mogadishu, Shanga, and Manda, were concentrated along the coasts of modern Somalia and Kenya. Once the gold from the coast of Mozambique, coming from Great Zimbabwe (see following section), began to dominate coastal trade, the great East African emporium of **Kilwa** became prominent. In most coastal centers, local Swahili controlled these sophisticated commercial states. In the late thirteenth century, however, the Mahdali clan from southwestern Arabia established an Arab Sultanate in Kilwa. Calling themselves the Abu'l-Mawahibs (loosely translated, "The Givers of Gifts"), their position was based on Islamic piety, claims of descent from the Prophet Muhammad, and a monopoly of Kilwa's gold trade with Great Zimbabwe. The Moroccan traveler, Ibn Battuta, visited the court of the reigning Abu'l-Mawahib in 1331 and provided one of the best accounts available from that period (see Evidence of the Past).

**The Palace of Husuni Kubwa.** Meaning "Great Palace" in Swahili, the Abu'l Mawahib sultans built this structure around the time Ibn Battuta visited Sultan Abu'l Mawahib Hasan al-Mahdali in 1331. The front part included rooms for the sultan's harem, as well as various audience courts and even an octagonal bathing pool. The large, open space at the rear appears to have been a warehouse area where trade goods were off-loaded from ships and stored. Archaeological excavation by H.N. Chittick in the early 1960s indicated that the palace was only lived in for a few decades and was abandoned by the late 14th century. Use of carved coral blocks and cupolas, as seen on the roof, were common features of medieval Swahili religious architecture.

Peter Garlake, *The Making of the Past: The Kingdoms of Africa* (Elsevier/Phaidon, 1990), p. 101.

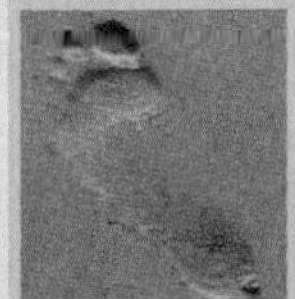

EVIDENCE OF THE PAST

## Ibn Battuta's Visit to East Africa

**The following is taken from** the account of the great fourteenth-century traveler from Morocco, Muhammad ibn Abdallah ibn Battuta (Ibn Battuta for short). Little is known about him aside from his account of his travels. He was born in Tangier in 1304 and died in 1377. He was in East Africa around 1331–1332, including the cities of Mogadishu, Mombasa, and Kilwa in his visit.

> Then I set off by sea from the town of Mogadishu for the land of the Swahili and the town of Kilwa, which is in the land of Zanj. We arrived at Mombasa, a large island. . . . The island is quite separate from the mainland. It grows bananas, lemons, and oranges. . . . The people [of the island] do not engage in agriculture, but import grain from the [people of the mainland, opposite the island]. The greater part of their diet is bananas and fish. They follow the Shafi'i [sect of Islam], and are devout, chaste, and virtuous. . . .
>
> We spent a night on the island and then set sail for Kilwa . . . the greater part of whose inhabitants are Zanj of very black complexion. . . .
>
> Kilwa is one of the most beautiful and well-constructed towns in the world. The whole of it is elegantly built. The roofs are built with mangrove pole. There is very much rain. The people are engaged in a holy war, for their country lies beside the pagan Zanj. Their chief qualities are devotion and piety: they follow the Shafi'i sect.
>
> When I arrived, the Sultan was Abu al-Muzaffar Hasan surnamed Abu al-Mawahib [loosely translated, "The Giver of Gifts"] . . . on account of his numerous charitable gifts. He frequently makes raids into the Zanj country [neighboring mainland], attacks them and carries off booty, of which he reserves a fifth, using it in the manner prescribed by the Koran [Qur'an]. That reserved for the kinsfolk of the Prophet [Muhammad] is kept separate in the Treasury, and when Sharifs [descendants of the Prophet] come to visit him, he gives it to them. They come to him from Iraq, the Hijaz, and other countries. I found several Sharifs from the Hijaz at his court. . . . This Sultan is very humble; he sits and eats with beggars, and venerates holy men and descendants of the Prophet.

### *Analyze and Interpret*

How credible do you think this source is? Do you know anything that suggests it might be accurate or inaccurate? What interesting things does the author say about the quality of Islamic practices in remote East Africa? Why do you think the Sultan of Kilwa and his descendants came to be called "The Giver of Gifts"?

Source: G. S. P. Freeman-Grenville, *The East African Coast, Select Documents* (London: Oxford University Press, 1962), pp. 31–32.

**History Now™**

***To read more from Ibn Battuta's* Travels*, point your browser to the documents area of* HistoryNow.**

## Great Zimbabwe

Southern Africa has a moderate climate and good soil, which encouraged settlement by Bantu-speaking farming peoples who reached it around the fourth century C.E. Later reports by shipwrecked Portuguese sailors indicate that, by the 1500s, Bantu-speaking mixed farmers and Khoisan-speaking hunter-gatherers and cattle pastoralists were living in agricultural villages, pastoralist communities, or hunter-gatherer camps all across the tip of the continent. Archaeology reveals that iron had come into use as early as the fourth century C.E. Nevertheless, the spread of mixed farming into areas that previously had been purely pastoralist or even hunting-gathering seems to have been slow.

The chief center of early settled life in southern Africa was not near the coast but far inland: **Great Zimbabwe**. Today the ruins of what was once a large capital city and fortress can be seen in the present-day nation of Zimbabwe inland from Mozambique. Great Zimbabwe was not discovered until 1871, and unfortunately, we know nothing of its history from written sources. Nevertheless, its massive walls and towers make it one of the most impressive monuments in Africa south of the pyramids. Apparently, the first stages of its construction were begun in the tenth and eleventh centuries by kings whose wealth and power rested, just as did that of the kings of Ghana and Mali, on the control of rich gold mines. Trade in gold and ivory passed down to the Swahili ports on the coast, while exotic imports such as glass beads and pottery passed hand to hand in the opposite direction to Zimbabwe.

The region flourished as a cultural and trading center. Additional stone structures continued to be built at the Great Zimbabwe site, and other *zimbabwes* (courts and burial places for royal clan members) were constructed until the fifteenth century, when the state broke apart and fell into decline for reasons that are not altogether known. Oral traditions suggest that internal dynastic disputes tore apart the political fabric of the land. We also know from early Portuguese sources that the supply of Zimbabwe's gold had begun to peter out by the early 1500s. As happened with other great world civilizations (for example, the Maya and the Ancestral Puebloans), the population might also have grown to the point that it tipped the delicate balance with the natural environment. In a sense, they might have become victims of their own success. The most likely explanation, however, as is usually the case in history, is that all of these factors combined caused the decline and abandonment of the site of Great Zimbabwe.

**Great Zimbabwe.** These stone walls are the only remnants of the once-important center of the gold trade in the south-central African interior. Europeans discovered them only in the late nineteenth century, and typical of attitudes of the time, believed they were built by some "white" race and not by the local Shona people.

## African Arts

In the absence of written languages, African art was necessarily visual and plastic, and the sculpture and inlay work of all parts of sub-Saharan Africa have lately aroused much interest and study in the Western world. Perhaps the most famous are the Benin bronzes from the West African kingdom of Benin, one of the successors to Mali. The highly stylized busts and full-length figures in bronze, gold, and combinations of metal and ebony are striking in their design and execution. They are obviously the product of a long tradition of excellence. Benin's enemies vandalized many of these pieces during the constant warfare that marred West African history. Many others were carried off as booty by the early Europeans and have since disappeared. Enough remain in museums, however, to give us some appreciation of the skill and imagination of the makers.

**BENIN BRONZE.** Made some time around the sixteenth century, this cast bronze plaque was made by the "lost wax" method of bronze casting, which involved making a clay mold over a wax core carved in the form of the image to be created. Once heated, melted wax is replaced by molten bronze and then cooled. This image depicts one of the *obas*, the divine kings of Benin.

The same is true of the wood sculptures of the Kanem and Bornu peoples of central Sudan, who assembled, between the twelfth and fifteenth centuries, a series of kingdoms in the vicinity of Lake Chad that lasted in one manifestation or another until the eighteenth century. The ivory and gold work of the Swahili city-states is also remarkable and much appreciated, especially by Middle Eastern buyers. Some Muslims looked on this infidel artwork depicting human figures as a mockery of Allah and destroyed much of it, either in place in Africa or later, in the countries to which it was transported.

The earthenware heads of the Nok people of prehistoric Nigeria, on the other hand, have come to light only in this century. Dating from roughly the first five centuries before the Christian era, these terra cotta portrait heads are the oldest examples yet found of African art. Their probable religious significance is not known.

## European Impressions

Unfortunately for the Africans' reputation, the fifteenth-century Europeans arrived on the African coast at about the same time that the most potent and most advanced of the sub-Saharan kingdoms collapsed or were in decline. In the absence of written sources, the causes of decline are not easily identified. They seem to have involved a lethal combination of internal quarrels among the nobility who served the king and conquest from outside, or sometimes by Muslims from Morocco.

As a result, the European explorer-traders perceived the kingdoms of Africa as subservient and backward. This impression was reinforced by the Africans' relative lack of knowledge in military and technological matters, and later by the readiness of some of the African kings and chieftains to allow the sale of competing or neighboring people into slavery—a practice that had been commonplace in Europe for a thousand years but that Christian and Jewish teaching had by that time effectively forbidden.

The Europeans (largely the Portuguese in the first century of contacts) concluded that the Africans were backward in their sensitivity and degree of civilization and that it would not be wrong to take advantage of them. Africans were perceived as not quite human, so what would have been a despicable sin against God and humanity if it had been done back home in Lisbon was quite forgivable—perhaps not worth a second thought—here. This callousness was undoubtedly reinforced by the desperate nature of business enterprise in the first centuries of the colonial era, when it is estimated that Europeans who went to the African coast had a 25 percent mortality rate per year. It was not an affair that encouraged second thoughts on the morality of what one was doing.

Other Europeans who came into contact as slavers with the West Africans shared the Portuguese attitude. Early attempts to convert the Africans to Christianity were quickly subordinated to business interests by the Portuguese and never attempted at all by their English, Dutch, and French successors until the nineteenth century. The tendency to see Africans as a source of profit rather than as fellow human beings was soon rationalized by everything from biblical quotations to Arab and Berber Muslim statements reflecting their own prejudices. The basis of European (and later American) racism directed against the dark-skinned peoples is to be found in these earliest contacts and the circumstances in which they were made.

## Summary

Africa is a continent of vast disparities in ethnic background, climate, and topography. Much of its interior remained shut off from the rest of the world until a century ago, and little was known of its history from either domestic or foreign sources. Only the Mediterranean coastal region and the Nile valley came to be included in the classical world, while the great Saharan desert long secluded the African heartland from northern penetration. In a prehistoric migration, the Bantu-speaking inhabitants of the western forest regions gradually came to occupy most of the continent in the early Christian era, aided by their mastery of iron and of advanced agriculture.

African state formation proceeded slowly and unevenly. The first were in the northeast, where ancient Egypt was followed by Kush and Axum as masters of the Indian Ocean–Mediterranean trade routes. Their decline followed upon Arab Muslim expansion in the eighth century. In the tenth and succeeding centuries, several large kingdoms arose in the western savanna lands, largely dependent on an active trade in gold and slaves across the desert to the northern Muslim regions. Ghana was the first of these commercially oriented kingdoms, followed by the larger and more permanent Mali and Songhay empires. A Muslim elite formed the governing class. In the Swahili city-states along the eastern coast, an Islamicized African population ruled, known as the Swahili. Islam, carried by proselytizing Arab merchants into the interior, was the prime force for political, legal, and administrative organization in much of pre-European Africa.

## Identification Terms

Test your knowledge of this chapter's key concepts by defining the following terms. If you can't recall the meaning of certain terms, refresh your memory by looking up the boldfaced term in the chapter, turning to the Glossary at the end of the book, or working with the flashcards that are available on the *World Civilizations* Companion Website: **http://history.wadsworth.com/adler04/**.

Axum
Bantu
Berbers
Ghana
Great Zimbabwe
Kilwa
Kush
lineage
Mali
matrilineal descent
patrilineal descent
Songhay
Swahili

## Test Your Knowledge

Test your knowledge of this chapter by answering the following questions. Complete answers appear at the end of the book. You may also take this quiz interactively and find even more quiz questions on the *World Civilizations* Companion Website: **http://history.wadsworth.com/adler04/**.

1. Pastoralism seems to have first appeared in Africa in the
   a. Mediterranean region.
   b. Sahara region.
   c. grassland savanna.
   d. Sahel.
   e. western Horn.

2. An important population movement in Africa was the
   a. drift of Bantu speakers from West Africa to the south and east.
   b. movement of the Pygmies from central to northern Africa.
   c. settlement of North Africa by the Tuaregs.
   d. coming of the Portuguese to colonize the coast.
   e. settlement of the Sahel by Arab traders.

3. The kingdom of Axum
   a. succeeded the kingdom of Kush in northeast Africa.
   b. was crushed by the Egyptians during the New Kingdom of Egypt.
   c. was the original home of the Bantus.
   d. was converted early to Islam.
   e. was ruled by Mansa Musa and his descendants.
4. By about the fifth century C.E., the population of the western Sudan had increased dramatically as a result of
   a. immigration from the eastern regions.
   b. changes in climate.
   c. increased food production.
   d. the practice of polygamy.
   e. large populations of slaves captured in battle.
5. Which factor has contributed to the greatest misunderstandings of Africans and their history?
   a. Religion
   b. Race
   c. Government
   d. Social organization
   e. Trade practices
6. The outside people having the greatest cultural influence on the kingdom of Ghana were the
   a. European colonists.
   b. Muslim Berbers and Arabs.
   c. Ethiopians.
   d. Egyptian Christians.
   e. Sudanese merchants.
7. Trade in slaves in both East and West Africa before the fifteenth century was
   a. commonplace.
   b. limited to extraordinary circumstances.
   c. controlled by the Muslims.
   d. rarely encountered.
   e. completely unknown.
8. The Swahili city-states were essentially populated by
   a. Arabs.
   b. Arabs, Persians, and Indians.
   c. Bantu animists.
   d. Bantu-speaking Muslims.
   e. refugees from Kush.
9. Mansa Musa was
   a. the outstanding Muslim geographer who described early Africa.
   b. the wealthy African king who journeyed to Arabia on pilgrimage.
   c. the founder of the kingdom of Mali.
   d. the Arab missionary who converted the king of Mali.
   e. the Moroccan traveler who visited Great Zimbabwe.
10. Which of the following, according to the text, was *not* a likely reason for the decline of Great Zimbabwe?
    a. Invasion by outsiders
    b. Dynastic quarrels
    c. Overpopulation of the land
    d. A decline in gold production
    e. Environmental upsets

## InfoTrac College Edition

Visit the source collections at

**http://infotrac.thomsonlearning.com**

and use the Search function with the following key terms:

Bantu Africa history

## Wadsworth History Website Resources

Visit the World History Resource Center at **http://history.wadsworth.com/world** for a wealth of general resources and the *World Civilizations* Companion Website at **http://history.wadsworth.com/adler04/** for resources specific to this textbook.

## HistoryNow

Enter *HistoryNow* using the access card that is available for *World Civilizations*. *HistoryNow* will assist you in understanding the content in this chapter with lesson plans generated for your needs. In addition, you can read the following documents, and many more, online:

Accounts of Meroe, Kush, and Axum, c. 430 B.C.E.–550 C.E.

Ibn Battuta, *Travels in Asia and Africa, 1325–1354*

*There is no god save God, and Muhammad is His Messenger.*
**Muslim profession of faith**

# 14 Islam

The Life of Muhammad the Prophet

Patterns of Belief in Islamic Doctrine

Arabia in Muhammad's Day

The Jihad

The Caliphate
The First Period, 632–661
The Umayyad Dynasty, 661–750
The Abbasid Dynasty, 750–1258

Conversion to Islam

Everyday Affairs

| | |
|---|---|
| c. 570–632 | Life of Muhammad |
| 640s | Conquest of Persian Empire and Egypt completed |
| 661–750 | Umayyad Dynasty at Damascus |
| 711–733 | Conquest of Spain/Muslims defeated at Tours |
| 750–1258 | Abbasid Dynasty at Baghdad |

In the Arabian town of Mecca, late in the sixth century, an individual was born who founded a religion that is now embraced by about one-fifth of the world's population. Muhammad created a faith that spread with incredible speed from his native land throughout the Near and Middle East. Carried on the strong swords of his followers, and later through conversions, Islam became a major rival to Christianity in the Mediterranean basin and to Hinduism and Buddhism in East and Southeast Asia. Like these faiths, Islam was far more than a supernatural religion; it also created a culture and a civilization.

## The Life of Muhammad the Prophet

The founder of Islam was born into a people about whom little documentary information exists prior to when he made them the spiritual and political center of a new civilization. Arabia is a large and sparsely settled peninsula extending from the Fertile Crescent in the north to well down the coast of Africa (see Map 14.1). Mecca, Muhammad's birthplace, was an important interchange where southern Asian and African goods coming across the Indian Ocean and the narrow Red Sea were transferred to caravans for shipment farther east. Considerable traffic also moved up and down the Red Sea to the ancient cities of the Near East and the Nile delta. For these reasons, the Mecca of Muhammad's time was a cosmopolitan place, with Egyptians, Jews, Greeks, and Africans living there, alongside the local Arab population. Long accustomed to trading and living with foreigners, the Arabs of towns like Mecca were using a written language and had well-developed systems of tribal and municipal governments. In such ways, the Arabs of the cities near the coast were far more advanced than the Bedouins (nomads) of the vast desert interior.

Several tribes or clans inhabited Mecca. The most important was the Quraysh, the clan into which Muhammad was born about 570. According to traditional Muslim accounts, the first forty years of his life were uneventful.

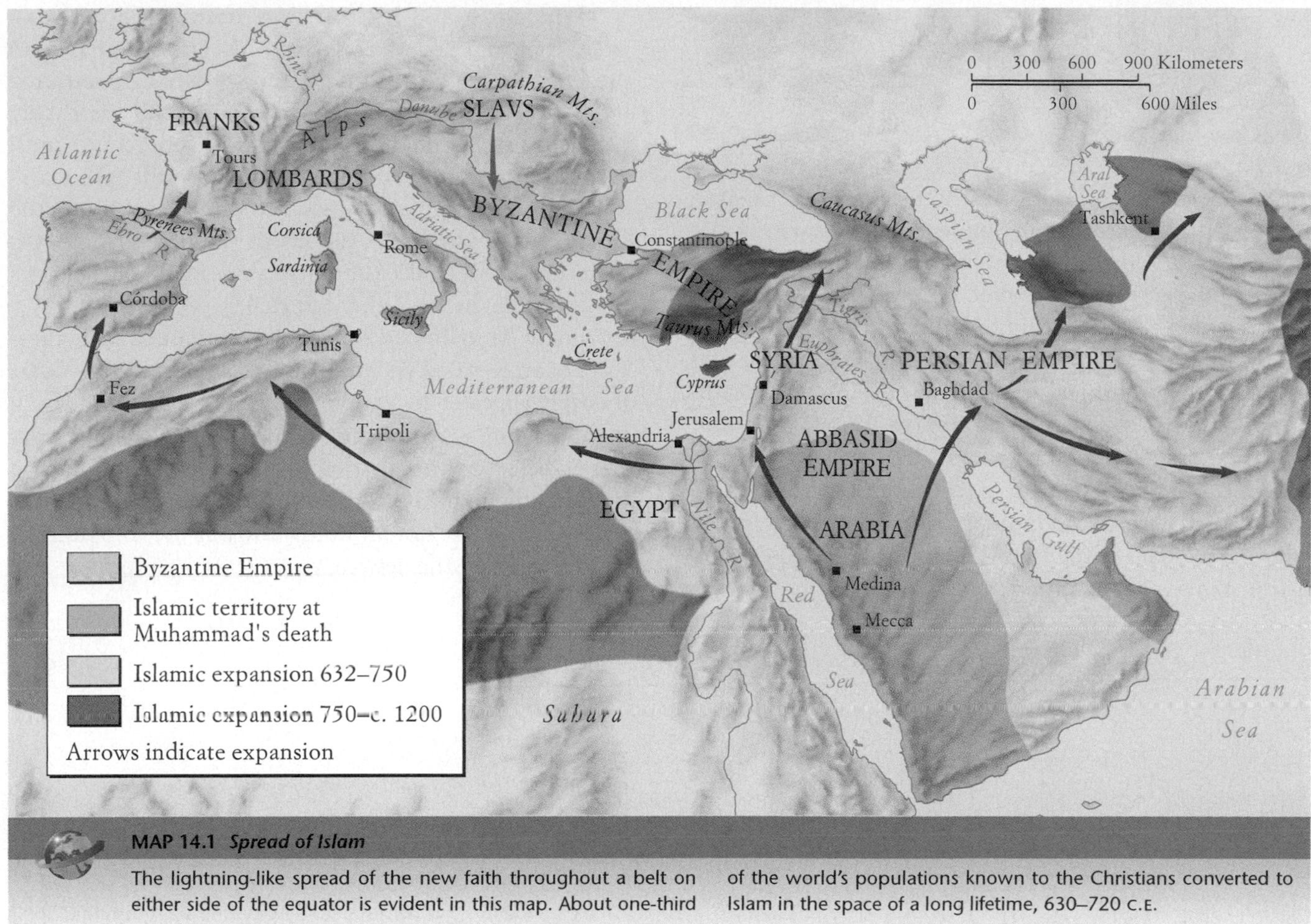


**MAP 14.1** ***Spread of Islam***

The lightning-like spread of the new faith throughout a belt on either side of the equator is evident in this map. About one-third of the world's populations known to the Christians converted to Islam in the space of a long lifetime, 630–720 C.E.

He was orphaned by the time he was six years old; his paternal uncle reared him and gave him the traditional protection of his clan. He married Khadija, a rich widow, and set himself up as a caravan trader of moderate means. The marriage produced six children, only one of whom survived, a daughter named Fatima.

Around 610 C.E., Muhammad began having mystical experiences that took the form of visits from a supernatural messenger. For days at a time he withdrew into the low mountains near Mecca, where long trances ensued in which the Archangel Gabriel began telling him of the One True God (**Allah**), and warning him of a coming Day of Judgment. For about three years he dared speak of these visions only to his immediate kin. (See Evidence of the Past.)

Finally, Muhammad began to preach about his visions in the street. Meccan authorities, however, supported a form of worship centered on nature deities and various cult objects, such as a Black Stone protected in a religious shrine called the ***Ka'ba***, which Muslims now believe God had once given to the Prophet Ibrahim (Abraham). Consequently, during his Meccan years, Muhammad's successful conversions were primarily (although not exclusively) among members of his own family, the Meccan poor, and some slaves. The deaths of his wife Khadija in 619 and of his uncle and protector in 620 produced a major crisis for Muhammad. Growing concerns for his and his followers' safety forced him to flee Mecca in 622, which came to be known as the year of the ***Hijra*** ("flight"). It became the first year of the Muslim calendar.

Muhammad fled to the rival city of Medina, where, despite the opposition of its three Jewish tribes to his claims of being God's prophet, he gradually gained the support he had vainly sought in Mecca. From 622 to 624, he gradually won over enough followers to begin a kind of trade war against the Meccan caravans and to force the city fathers there to negotiate with him on spiritual matters. He also won the support of nearby Bedouin tribes, and by 630 he was able to return to Mecca on pilgrimage to the Ka'ba at the head of a victorious community of converts. By the time of his death two years later, most of western Arabia was under Islamic control. A ***jihad***, a war of holy conquest in the name of Allah, was under way.

## Patterns of Belief in Islamic Doctrine

What message did Muhammad preach that found such ready acceptance? The doctrines of Islam (the word means "submission," in this case to God, or Allah) are the simplest and most readily understood of any of the world's major religions. They are laid out in written form in the **Qur'an**, the most sacred scriptures of the Muslim world, which the third caliph, Uthman (see the "Umayyad Dynasty" section), ordered to be collected from oral traditions twenty-three years after the Prophet's death. The basic ideas are expressed in the **Five Pillars of Islam**, which are described in the Patterns of Belief box. Without doubt, the simplicity of these teachings and their ritual requirements were important factors in winning many converts to Islam as the Islamic Empire expanded—in the first instance, through the sword.

Muhammad and his followers were able to achieve what they did for various reasons. First, Muhammad preached a straightforward doctrine of salvation, ensured by a God who never failed and whose will was clearly delineated in comprehensible principles and commands. Second, those who believed and tried to follow Muhammad's words (as gathered a few years after his death in the Qur'an) were assured of reward in the life to come. On the other hand, God's Messenger warned unbelievers of a fiery end that awaited them in Hell.

Finally, Muhammad's preaching contained large measures of an elevated yet attainable moral and ethical code. It deeply appealed to a population that wanted more than the purely ritualistic animist doctrine could give them but were repelled by the internal conflicts of Christendom or unsympathetic to the complexities of Judaism. His insistence that he was not an innovator, but the completer of the message of the Jewish and Christian prophets and

EVIDENCE OF THE PAST

### Muhammad Receives His First Revelation

Muhammad ibn Ishaq was the first person to write a biography of Muhammad, the Prophet of Islam. He lived a little more than a century (d. c. 768) after Muhammad and based his information on oral accounts he collected from the descendants of Muhammad's close associates. This is his account of the day, when Muhammad was about forty years old, of the Prophet's first visit by the Archangel Gabriel.

> "Relate to us, 'Ubayd, what the beginning of the Messenger of God's prophetic mission was like when Gabriel came to him." I was present as 'Ubayd related the following account to 'Abdallah b. al-Zubayr and those with him. He said, "The Messenger of God used to spend one month in every year in religious retreat on [Mount] Hira." . . .
>
> . . . feeding the poor who came to him. When he had completed this month of retreat the first thing which he would do on leaving, even before going home, was to circumambulate the Ka'bah seven times, or however many times God willed; then he would go home.
>
> When the month came in which God willed to ennoble him, in the year in which God made him his Messenger, this being the month of Ramadan, the Messenger of God went out as usual to Hira accompanied by his family. When the night came on which God ennobled him by making him his Messenger . . . Gabriel brought him the command of God. The Messenger of God said, 'Gabriel came to me as I was sleeping with a brocade cloth in which he was writing. He said, "Recite!" and I said, "I cannot recite." He pressed me tight and almost stifled me, until I thought that I should die. Then he let me go and said, "Recite!" I said, "What shall I recite?" only saying that in order to free myself from him, fearing that he might repeat what he had done to me. He said:
>
> Recite in the name of your Lord who creates! He creates man from a clot of blood. Recite: And your Lord is the most Bountiful, he who teaches by the pen, teaches man what he knew not.
>
> I recited it, and then he desisted and departed. I woke up, and it was as though these words had been written on my heart."

#### *Analyze and Interpret*

How accurate might this account be? What historical (not religious) reasons can you think of for believing or not believing this passage? How does this compare with the believability of similar passages about the prophets in the Old Testament and the accounts of Jesus in the New Testament of the Bible?

Source: From *The History of al-Tabari, Volume VI. Muhammad at Mecca.* Trans. W. Montgomery Watt and M.V. McDonald (Albany, NY: SUNY Press, 1988), pp. 70–71.

History Now™

***To read a selection from Ibn Ishaq's* Life of Muhammad, *point your browser to the documents area of* HistoryNow.**

PATTERNS OF BELIEF

## The Five Pillars of Islam

**From the outset,** Islam has rested on the Five Pillars taught by Muhammad. In more or less flexible forms, these beliefs are recognized and observed by all good Muslims, wherever and in whatever circumstances they may find themselves.

1. There is one God (whom Muslims call Allah), and Muhammad is His prophet. Islam is a thoroughly monotheistic faith. There are neither saints nor Trinity.
2. God demands prayer from His faithful five times daily: at daybreak, noon, in the mid-afternoon, twilight, and before retiring. Prayer is always done in the direction of Mecca. It is the outward sign of complete submission to the Lord.
3. Fasting and observance of dietary prohibitions are demanded of all who can. The month of Ramadan and some holy days are particularly important in this respect. Alcohol and all other mind-warping substances are forbidden, as insults to the handiwork of the perfect Creator.
4. Almsgiving toward the poor faithful is a command, enforced through the practice of tithing. Gifts and bequests to the deserving fellow Muslim are mandatory for those who would attain worldly distinction and the respect of their neighbor.
5. If possible, every Muslim must make the ***hajj*** ("pilgrimage") to the holy cities of Arabia at least once. In modern days this command has filled Mecca with upward of 2 million visitors at the height of the holy season.

Bibliothèque Nationale, Paris

**The Entry into Mecca by the Faithful.** In this thirteenth-century miniature from Baghdad, the *hajj*, or pilgrimage, is depicted in its glory. Supposedly devoted to pious purposes, the hajj was also an opportunity to display one's wealth.

### *Analyze and Interpret*

Considering this list of religious requirements, if you were a Muslim, and if your knowledge of your religion extended only to the performance of these duties, would Islam seem a spiritually satisfying religion to you? Why or why not? (*Hint:* Consult the next chapter's discussion of *Sufism* as a follow-up to this question.)

gospel writers was also of great significance in the success of his religion among the Eastern peoples.

## Arabia in Muhammad's Day

The Jews and Christians with whom Muhammad had contact in Mecca undoubtedly influenced the strict monotheism of Islam. Many other aspects of the Muslim faith also derive in some degree from other religions, such as the regulations against eating pork and using stimulants that alter the God-given nature of man. But the Muslim creed is not just a collection of other, previous beliefs by any means. It includes many elements that reflect the peculiar circumstances of Arabs and Arabia in the seventh century C.E.

At that time, much of the interior of the Arabian peninsula was barely inhabited except for scattered oases. The Bedouin tribes that passed from one oasis to the next with their herds were continually at war with one another for water and pasture. The virtues most respected in this society were those of the warrior: strict social and material equality, bravery, hardiness, loyalty, honor, and hospitality to strangers.

The Arabs' religion before Muhammad involved a series of animistic beliefs, such as the important one centering on the Ka'ba, a cubical stone shrine that contained the Black Stone. (Recall that *animism* means a conviction that objects such as rivers, trees, or stones possess spirits and spiritual qualities that have direct and potent impact on human lives.) In the coastal towns, these beliefs coexisted side by side with the monotheistic beliefs of Judaism, Christianity, and Zoroastrianism. There is evidence that belief in a principal, creator deity also existed in Arabia before Muhammad, although such evidence is vague and indirect.

**The Ka'ba in Mecca.** In this huge mosque courtyard assemble hundreds of thousands of worshipers during the Muslim holy days each year. The Ka'ba is the cubicle of stone in the center. It contains a piece of black meteorite worshipped by the Arabs before their conversion to Islam. During Muhammad's lifetime, it became the symbol of God's relationship to humanity and a symbol of Islamic unity.

Rulban Arikan/Photo Researchers, Inc.

In towns such as Mecca, commerce had bloomed to such an extent that many Arabs were seduced away from their traditional social equality by this newfound wealth. Traditions that underscored social and economic equality were being cast aside in favor of materialist values and social hierarchy. The cultural gap between town Arab and Bedouin had widened to such an extent that it threatened to become irrevocable. Worship at the Ka'ba shrine had become linked to trade for the merchants of Mecca, who profited greatly from the many thousands of Arabs from the interior who made annual processions there during the month of Ramadan to worship tribal and clan idols that were housed in the shrine.

From this standpoint, some scholars have interpreted Muhammad's religious message as the work of a reformer, a man who perceived many of the problems facing his people and responded to them. The verses of the Qur'an excerpted in the Patterns of Belief box contain many references to these problems and propose solutions. For example, the condition of women in pre-Muslim Arabia was apparently poor. A man could have as many wives as he wished, regardless of whether he could support them all. Women were practically powerless in legal matters, had no control over their dowries in marriage, and could not have custody over minor children after their husband's death, among other things. In his preaching, Muhammad took pains to change this situation and the attitude that lay behind it. In this way he was an innovator, reacting against a tradition that he believed to be ill founded. He imposed an absolute limit of four wives *per man,* although he made no restrictions on the number of a man's concubines. If additional wives could not be supported equally, they were not permitted. Although Muhammad denied that women were equal to men, he made it clear that women were not mere servants of men; that they had some inherent rights as persons, wives, and mothers; and that their honor and physical welfare needed protection by the men around them. The status of women in early Muslim teaching was relatively elevated. It might actually have been higher and more firmly recognized than the status accorded to women in the medieval West as well as in rural southern and eastern Asia.

## The Jihad

One of the unique aspects of Islam is the jihad, the effort or war for the establishment of God's law on Earth. Allah enjoined Muslims to fight against unbelief, both internal and external. The word *jihad* derives from the Arabic term *jahada,* which means "to strive," to exert oneself to eradicate disbelief. Disbelief can arise within oneself in the form of doubt, as well as in others. God commands the believer always to strive against doubt or the outright rejection of Him, so taking part in a jihad is a way of fighting Satan. To take up the Sword of God (*Sayf Allah*) is the

## The Qur'an

**THE QUR'AN IS NOT ONLY THE BIBLE** of the Muslims but also an elaborate and poetic code of daily conduct. It is a compilation, like the Christian and Jewish Bibles, formed in the memory of Muhammad's associates of his words and instructions after the Prophet's death. As the literal word of God, the holy book is held by all devout Muslims to be the unfailing source of wisdom, which, if adapted to the changing realities of daily life, can be as usable in the twenty-first century as it was in the seventh when it was written. Many of its verses have formed the basis of law in the Muslim countries. Now translated into every major language, the Qur'an was long available only in Arabic, one of the world's most poetic and subtle languages. This circumstance both helped and hindered the religion's eventual spread. Some excerpts follow:

**The Jihad**

Fight in the cause of God against those who fight against you, but do not begin hostilities. Surely, God loves not the aggressors. Once they start the fighting, kill them wherever you meet them, and drive them out from where they have driven you out; for aggression is more heinous than killing. But fight them until all aggression ceases and religion is professed for the pleasure of God alone. If they desist, then be mindful that no retaliation is permissible except against the aggressors.

Do not account those who are slain in the cause of God as dead. Indeed, they are living in the presence of their Lord and are provided for. They are jubilant . . . and rejoice for those who have not yet joined them. . . . They rejoice at the favor of God and His bounty, and at the realisation that God suffers not the reward of the faithful to be lost.

**Piety and Charity**

There is no piety in turning your faces toward the east or the west, but he is pious who believeth in God, and the last day, and the angels, and the scriptures, and the prophets; who for the love of God disburses his wealth to his kindred, and to the orphans, and the needy, and the wayfarer, and those who ask, and for ransoming. . . .

They who expend their wealth for the cause of God, and never follow what they have laid out with reproaches or harm, shall have their reward with the Lord; no fear shall come upon them, neither shall they be put to grief.

A kind speech and forgiveness is better than alms followed by injury. Give to the orphans their property; substitute not worthless things of your own for their valuable ones, and devour not their property after adding it to your own, for this is a great crime.

**Society and Economy**

Ye may divorce your wives twice. Keep them honorably, or put them away, with kindness. But it is not allowed you to appropriate to yourselves any of what you have once given them. . . . No blame shall attach to either of you for what the wife shall herself give for her redemption [from the marriage bond].

Men are superior to women on account of the qualities with which God hath gifted the one above the other, and on account of the outlay they make from their substance for them. Virtuous women are obedient, careful, during the husband's absence, because God hath of them been careful. But chide those for whose obstinacy you have cause to dread; remove them into beds apart, and whip them. But if they are obedient to you, then seek not occasion to abuse them.

**Christians and Jews**

Verily, they who believe and who follow the Jewish religion, and the Christians . . . whoever of these believeth in God and the Last Day, and does that which is right shall have their reward with the Lord. Fear shall not come upon them, neither shall they be grieved.

We believe in God and what has been sent down to us, and what was sent down to Abraham, Ishmael, Isaac, Jacob and their descendants, and what was given Moses, Jesus and the prophets by their Lord. We do not differentiate between them, and are committed to live at peace with Him.

### *Analyze and Interpret*

Does some of this excerpt remind you of the Laws of Manu? What similarities are most prominent? Note the fine line walked by the Qur'an between self-defense and aggressive war. What in the background of the Bedouin might have made this close distinction necessary and natural?

Source: From T. B. Irving, trans., *The Quran: Selections* (n.p.: Islamic Foundation, 1980).

**History Now™**

***To read more of the Qur'an, point your browser to the documents area of* HistoryNow.**

highest honor for a good Muslim. Dying in such an effort, whether through eradicating internal doubts or through external holy war, is a way of fulfilling one of God's commandments, so it assures one of a heavenly reward.

Aside from the salvation of one's soul, what was the earthly appeal of the jihad? It seems to have been based on several aspects of Arabic culture. The desert Bedouins were already a warlike people, accustomed to continual violence in the struggle for water and pasture. Much evidence also indicates that they faced an economic crisis at the time of Muhammad—namely, a severe overpopulation problem that overwhelmed the available sparse resources. Under such conditions, many people were willing to risk their lives for the possibility of a better future. It is likely that many of those who participated in the early conquests saw Muhammad as a successful war leader as much or as well as a religious prophet.

Once the jihad was under way, another factor favored its success: exhaustion and division among Islamic opponents. Both of the major opponents, the Byzantine Greeks in Constantinople and the Persians, had been fighting each other fiercely for the previous generation and were mutually exhausted. As a result, by 641, only nine years after the death of the Prophet, all of the huge Persian Empire had fallen to Arab armies, and much of the Byzantine territory in Asia (present-day Syria, Lebanon, and Turkey) had been taken as well (see Map 14.1). In place after place, the defenders of the Byzantine provinces put up only halfhearted resistance or none at all, as in Damascus. The religious differences within Christianity had become so acute in these lands that several sects of Christians preferred surrender to the Muslims to continuing to live under what they regarded as a high-handed, wrong-thinking emperor and his bishops. This was true not only in Syrian Damascus but also in several Christian centers in North Africa and Egypt, which were in religious revolt against the church leaders in Constantinople and Rome.

## THE CALIPHATE

The nature of Muslim leadership changed markedly from epoch to epoch in the 600 years between the founding of Islam in Arabia and 1260 C.E., when it passed from Arabic to Turco-Mongolian hands. While he had remained alive, Muhammad had been seen as a direct link to God for his little community. The ***Umma***, the Muslim community that he had founded, was unique in Arabia inasmuch as it was held together by belief and acted under the command of God, rather than being united by blood ties, as the clans and tribes had been. God took an interest in everything a Muslim did. There was no division between religious and secular affairs. Therefore, as God's mouthpiece and as the last of God's prophets, Muhammad was both a religious and a temporal ruler. His sudden death in 632 after a short illness, therefore, caused a crisis of leadership that has never been resolved to the satisfaction of all his followers to this day.

### *The First Period, 632–661*

Muhammad's unexpected death necessitated choosing another leader if the Muslim community was going to avoid falling apart. His closest followers at Medina argued over this choice, some believing the leadership should fall to a close family member, in particular his cousin and

Bridgeman Art Library

**THE DOME OF THE ROCK.** This great edifice, erected by Muslims in Jerusalem in the late seventh century, has been used by three religions as a sacred place of worship. Supposedly Muhammad ascended into heaven from this spot.

son-in-law, Ali, others thinking that it should be the "best qualified," the person who was closest to the Prophet and who best represented his teachings. They decided on Abu Bakr, Muhammad's closest friend, his father-in-law, and one of his first converts. Unsure what Abu Bakr's exact status was, most addressed him simply as *Khalifat ar-Rasul Allah,* Deputy of God's Messenger. Although the title was humble in origin and meaning, the term stuck as **caliph**.

Abu Bakr was elected by a committee of his closest associates, as were the next three caliphs. Soon after fighting a brief war to reunite the Muslims, Abu Bakr (632–634) died and was succeeded by a general, Omar (634–644), who ruled over Islam for ten years. Omar was the real founder of the early Muslim Empire. His Arab armies pushed deep into North Africa, conquering Egypt by 642. At the same time, he invaded Persia and the Byzantine territory in the eastern Mediterranean. By the time of Omar's death in 644, mounted Arab raiders were penetrating as far as western India.

With such rapid expansion, administration of this vast and growing empire had to be done on an ad hoc basis. The system Omar devised was brilliant at first but proved troublesome in the longer term. As the Arab tribesmen poured into one conquered land after another, the caliph created a system of rule called an "Arab Islamic theocracy." It was an Islamic theocracy because, in theory at least, God's commands, as preserved through the Qur'an, provided the principles by which the Caliph and his lieutenants ruled. Ethnically, it was Arab because the caliph kept the conquering Arabs segregated from the vanquished in fortified encampments. To maintain this system, the Caliph pensioned the Arab tribes out of booty taken in battle and from a special poll tax that was collected from non-Muslim subject peoples (jizya).

This stunningly rapid expansion came to a halt because of a civil war in 656 for mastery within the Muslim world, which brought Ali, husband of Fatima and Muhammad's son-in-law, to the fore. Ali was the last "orthodox" caliph for a long time. His assassination by a dissident in 661 marked the end of the first phase of Muslim expansion.

## *The Umayyad Dynasty, 661–750*

The first four caliphs had been elected, but three of the four died by murder. At this point, because the elective system had clearly failed, the system of succession became dynastic, although the elective outer form was preserved. From 661, two dynasties of caliphs came to rule the Islamic world: the Umayyads from 661 to 750, and then the Abbasids from 750 to 1258.

Following the murder of Ali, the governor of Syria, Muawiya, initiated the **Umayyad Dynasty**. This change from electing the caliph to dynastic succession proved fateful. Ali's supporters continued to believe that he possessed a special spiritual knowledge (*ilm*) that he had inherited from Muhammad's bloodline, and therefore that he had been the rightful caliph. These supporters of Ali came to be known as **Shi'ites**, and they formed a significant minority within Islam that continues to the present. They believed that only the lineal descendants of the Prophet through Ali and Muhammad's daughter, Fatima, were qualified to become caliphs, and they looked on the Umayyad dynasty as illegitimate usurpers. Another minority, called **Kharijites**, rejected the caliphs for another reason. They disallowed any form of dynastic succession, believing that only a Muslim free of all sin was fit to lead. Pointing to the increasingly secular lifestyles of the caliphs, as well as to their greater concerns for the secular aspects of ruling than for religious principles, this group frequently fought against the rule of the majority and of the caliphs.

The supporters of Muawiya and his successors were known as **Sunni**, and they constituted the large majority (currently, almost 90 percent) of Muslims at all times. They largely acquiesced to the legitimacy of the caliphal dynasties. Primarily out of concern for maintaining the unity of Allah's community of believers, they rejected the politically divisive claims of the radical Kharijites and of the Shi'ites that the family of Muhammad possessed some special enlightenment in spiritual matters. In any case, exactly the opposite situation came about: continual rivalries and battles between Shi'ite, Kharijite, and Sunni were to have decisive effects on the political unity of the Muslim world. Most members of these minorities came to be concentrated in Persia and the Near East, but they had support in many other areas and were always a counterweight to the policies of the Sunni central government. From their ranks came many of the later sects of Islam.

Muawiya proved to be a skillful organizer and statesman. He moved the capital from Medina (where Muhammad had established it) to his native Damascus, where he could be more fully in charge. He made the office of caliph more powerful than it had been before and also laid the foundation for the splendid imperial style that would characterize later caliphs, in great contrast to the austerity and simplicity of the first days. Muawiya made clear the dynastic quality of his rule by forcing the reluctant tribal leaders to accept his son as his successor. From that time on, the caliphs were normally the son or brother of the previous ruler.

The Umayyads continued the advances to east and west, although not quite so brilliantly and rapidly as before. To the east, Arab armies penetrated as far as western China before being checked, and they pushed deep into central Asia (to Tashkent in Uzbekistan). Afghanistan became a Muslim outpost. In the west, the outstanding achievement was the conquest of North Africa between 665 and 742, and of Christian Spain between 711 and 721. At least part of Spain would remain in Muslim hands until the time of Christopher Columbus. The Arab horsemen actually penetrated far beyond the Pyrenees, but they were defeated in 733 at Tours in central France by Charlemagne's predecessor, the Frankish leader Charles Martel, in one of the key battles of European history. This expedition proved to be the high-water mark of Arab Muslim penetration into Europe, and soon afterward they retreated behind the Pyrenees to set up a Spanish caliphate based in the city of Córdoba.

Expansion and time, however, brought unanticipated changes that spelled trouble for the regime. Partly out of religious conviction and, no doubt, partly too as a way of avoiding the poll tax (*jizya*), many non-Muslims started converting to Islam. The administration handled this situation by joining converts to existing Arab tribes as "clients" (*mawali*). However, they consigned these non-Arab converts to the status of second-class Muslims by requiring that they continue paying the burdensome *jizya*. This was necessary to maintain the pension system, but it caused widespread resentment of the caliphs and the privileged Arabs.

Dispersal of the Muslims during the conquests over a wide empire also fostered religious problems. Trouble began with the third caliph, Uthman. Fearing that diverse versions of the Qur'an were beginning to appear, in 655 the caliph ordered that an official edition be issued. Many accused him of setting the power of the state over religion. Later Umayyad caliphs also led notoriously secular lifestyles, so that many accused them of being indifferent Muslims and failing to provide religious leadership.

In the 740s, rebel armies, consisting largely of *mawali* demanding social and religious equality with Arab Muslims, overthrew the Umayyad dynasty. After a brief period of uncertainty, the Abbasid clan was able to take over as a new dynasty of caliphs. One of their first moves was to transfer the seat of government from unfriendly Damascus to the entirely new city of **Baghdad** in Iraq, which was built for that purpose. Their 500-year reign from the fabled capital of Baghdad was the golden age of Islamic civilization.

### *The Abbasid Dynasty, 750–1258*

The **Abbasid Dynasty** of caliphs claimed descent from Abbas, the uncle of Muhammad, and for that reason were initially more acceptable to the Shi'ite faction than the Umayyads had been. The Abbasids also differed from the Umayyads in another important way. Whereas the Umayyads had favored the Arabs in matters of taxation, social status, and religion, the Abbasids opened up the faith to all comers on an essentially equal basis. Such changes enabled Islam to develop into a true world religion during their long reign. Arab officials attempted to retain their monopoly on important posts in the central and provincial administration. But gradually, Persians, Greeks, Syrians, Berbers from North Africa and the Sahara, Spanish ex-Christians, and many others found their way into the inner circles of Muslim authority and prestige. In every area, experienced officials from the conquered peoples were retained in office, although supervised by Arabs.

Through these non-Arab officials, the Abbasid administration incorporated several foreign models of government. As time passed, and more conquered peoples chose to convert to Islam, other ethnic groups steadily diluted the Arab ruling group. These non-Arab converts to Islam made it into a highly cosmopolitan, multiethnic religion and civilization. Like the doctrines of Islam, the community of believers was soon marked by its eclecticism and heterogeneity.

Even with the cement of a common faith, the empire was simply too large and its peoples too diverse to hold together politically and administratively. Within little more than a century of the founding of the Abbasid caliphate, the powers of the central government underwent a gradual but cumulatively severe decline. Many segments of the Islamic world broke away from the political control of Baghdad. Spain became fully independent as the Caliphate of Córdoba. North Africa, Egypt, the eastern regions of Persia, and Afghanistan also freed themselves. But the Muslim faith was strong enough to bind this world together permanently in a religious and cultural sense. With the sole exception of Spain, where the Muslims were always a minority, those areas captured at one time or another by the Islamic forces after 629 remain mostly Muslim today. Those areas reach halfway around the globe, from Morocco to Indonesia.

## Conversion to Islam

Contrary to widespread Christian notions, Islam normally did not force conversion. In fact, after the first few years of conquest, the Arab leaders came to realize the disadvantages of mass conversion of the conquered and discouraged it. By the time of the Umayyads, conversion was looked on as a special allowance to deserving non-Muslims, especially those who had something to offer the conquerors in the way of talents, wealth, or domestic and international prestige.

No effort was made to convert the peasants or the urban masses. Life in the villages went on as before, with the peasants paying their rents and taxes or giving their labor to the new lords just as they had to their old rulers. When and if they converted, it was because of the genuine appeal of Islam as a faith, as well as specific local circumstances, rather than from pressure from above. Centuries passed before the peasants of Persia and Turkey accepted Islam. In Syria, Lebanon, and Egypt, whole villages remained loyal to their Christian beliefs during ten centuries of Muslim rule.

Intermarriage between Muslim and practicing non-Muslim was strictly prohibited. This restriction was a result of Qur'anic injunctions that Muslims marry Muslims. Moreover, Muslims had restricted social contact with non-Muslims, although the two groups did mix together in business transactions, administrative work, and even, at times, intellectual and cultural interchange (especially in Spain).

The Muslims did not view all non-Muslims the same way. Instead, they were categorized according to what the Qur'an and Arab tradition taught about their possession of spiritual truth. The Jews and the Christians were considered meritorious because both shared the same basic beliefs in the one God and His prophets (such as Abraham and Jesus of Nazareth), as did Islam. The Zoroastrians were viewed in much the same way. All three were classed as ***dhimmis***, or "Peoples of the Book," and were thought to have risen above what Muslims regarded as the superstitions of their many other subject peoples.

The dhimmis were not taxed as severely as pagans were, and they had legal and business rights that were denied to others. Restrictions on the dhimmis were generally not severe, and in many places evidence shows that they prospered. They could worship as they pleased, provided they observed limitations placed on public displays of belief and avoided proselytization, and they elected their own community leaders. Their position was normally better than that of Jews or Muslims under contemporary Christian rule, although there were instances of persecution in later centuries.

## Everyday Affairs

In the opening centuries of Muslim rule, the Muslims were a minority almost everywhere outside Arabia, so they had to accustom themselves to the habits and manners of their subjects, to some degree. Because the Bedouin pastoralists who formed the backbone of the early Islamic armies had little experience with administrative organization, manufacturing, or commerce and finance, they were willing to allow their more sophisticated subjects considerable leeway in such matters. Thus, Christian, Jewish, or pagan merchants and artisans were generally able to live and work as they were accustomed to doing, without severe disturbance. They managed routine government and economic affairs not only for themselves but also for the ruling Arabs. This gradually changed as the Bedouins settled into urban life and as converts to Islam became numerous, but in the meantime, the habit of using the conquered "infidels" to perform many of the ordinary tasks of life had become ingrained and was continued.

Similar patterns could be found in finance and administration: the conquered subjects were kept on in the middle and lower levels. Only Muslims could hold important political and military positions, however. The Muslim "aristocracy" maintained an advantage over the neo-Muslim converts as late as the ninth century, but Greek, Syrian, Persian, and other converts found their way into high posts in the central government in Baghdad under the Abbasids. And in the provinces, it was common to encounter neo-Muslims at the highest levels. With the native peoples playing such a large role in public affairs, it is not surprising that economic and administrative institutions came to be an amalgam of Arab and Greek, Persian, or Spanish customs.

Society in the Muslim world formed a definite social pyramid. During the Umayyad period, descendants of the old Bedouin clans were on top, followed by *mawali* converts from other religions. Once the Abbasids took power, this distinction ceased to exist. Below the Muslims came the dhimmis, then other non-Muslim freemen, and the slaves at the bottom. All five classes of society had their own rights and duties, and even the slaves had considerable legal protections. Normally, little friction existed between Muslims and non-Muslims, but the non-Muslims were always clearly second-class citizens, below every Muslim in dignity. Different courts of law had jurisdiction over legal disputes, depending on whether Muslims or non-Muslims were involved. All non-Muslims were taxed heavily, although, as we have seen, the burden on the dhimmis was less than on other non-Muslims.

As this discussion suggests, religion was truly the decisive factor in Muslim society. Like Christians and Jews, but even more so, good Muslims believed that a person's most essential characteristic was whether he or she adhered to the true faith—Islam. The fact that all three faiths—Christianity, Judaism, and Islam—believed in essentially the same patriarchal God was not enough to minimize the differences among them. Rather, in time those differences became magnified.

## Summary

The swords of the jihad armies propelled the surge of Islam outward from its native Arabia in the seventh century. But the attraction of the last of the Western world's major religions rested finally on its openness to all creeds and colors, its ease of understanding, and its assurance of heaven to those who followed its simple doctrines. The Prophet Muhammad saw himself as completing the works of Abraham and Jesus, as the final messenger of the one omnipotent God. Divisions among the Christians of the Near East assisted his work, by economic rewards to the Muslim conquerors and by the momentary exhaustion of both Byzantium and Persia. Already by the mid-600s, the new faith had reached Egypt and the borders of Hindustan. By the early 700s, the fall of Spain had given Islam a foothold in Europe. Not only was this the fastest spread of a creed in world history, but Islam would also go on spreading for many years to come.

The caliphs held the political leadership of the faith, at first through the Umayyad dynasty at Damascus, then through the Abbasids at their new capital at Baghdad. The unity of Islam was split as early as the first Umayyad caliph by the struggle between the Sunni majority and the Kharijite and Shi'ite minorities, the former of which insisted that a strict observance of religious principles mattered most in a caliph and the latter that a blood relationship with Muhammad was essential for the caliphate office.

The upshot of the Muslim explosion out of Arabia was the creation of a new civilization, which would span Iberia and a large part of the Afro-Asian world by the twelfth century and be carried deep into Christian eastern Europe in the fourteenth century. In the next chapter, we will look at the cultural aspects of this civilization in some detail.

## Identification Terms

Test your knowledge of this chapter's key concepts by defining the following terms. If you can't recall the meaning of certain terms, refresh your memory by looking up the boldfaced term in the chapter, turning to the Glossary at the end of the book, or working with the flashcards that are available on the *World Civilizations* Companion Website: **http://history.wadsworth.com/adler04/**.

Abbasid Dynasty
Allah
Baghdad
caliph
*dhimmis*
Five Pillars of Islam
*hajj*
*Hijra*
*jihad*
*Ka'ba*
Kharijites
Qur'an
Shi'ites
Sunni
Umayyad Dynasty
*Umma*

## Test Your Knowledge

Test your knowledge of this chapter by answering the following questions. Complete answers appear at the end of the book. You may also take this quiz interactively and find even more quiz questions on the *World Civilizations* Companion Website: **http://history.wadsworth.com/adler04/**.

1. Muhammad's religious awakening came
   a. as a result of a childhood experience.
   b. in his middle years, after a series of visions.
   c. in response to the Christian conquest of Mecca.
   d. after an encounter with a wandering holy man.
   e. after his rejection of the Jewish faith.

2. Muhammad began his mission to reform Arab beliefs because
   a. he was desperate for social prominence.
   b. he could not tolerate the evil behavior of his associates.
   c. the Archangel Gabriel convinced him he was chosen to do so.

d. he was inspired by the example of the early Christians.
e. he became angry over the interference of Meccan traders in religious matters.

3. Which of the following is *not* one of the Five Pillars of Islam?
   a. Frequent and regular prayer to Allah
   b. Fasting at prescribed times
   c. Almsgiving
   d. A pilgrimage to Mecca, if one is able
   e. Taking arms against the infidel
4. Which of the following statements about Islamic belief is *false?*
   a. A Last Judgment awaits all.
   b. The faithful will be guided by the Qur'an to salvation.
   c. Mortals must submit to the will of the one all-powerful Lord.
   d. The divinity of Jesus is beyond doubt.
   e. The Qur'an is the inspired word of Allah.
5. The farthest reach of Muslim expansion into western Europe was at
   a. Palermo.
   b. Tours.
   c. Córdoba.
   d. Gibraltar.
   e. the Pyrenees Mountains.
6. The conflicts between Sunni and Shi'ite Muslims centered on the
   a. divinity of Muhammad.
   b. authenticity of Muhammad's visions.
   c. location of the capital of the Islamic state.
   d. importance of blood kinship to Muhammad in choosing his successor.
   e. origin of the Qur'an.
7. The basis of all Muslim political theory is
   a. a person's religion.
   b. the wealth possessed by a given group of citizens.
   c. the social standing of an individual.
   d. the historical evolution of a given social group.
   e. the patriarchal family unit.
8. Which of the following areas had not fallen to Islam by the beginning of the Abbasid dynasty?
   a. Afghanistan
   b. Spain
   c. Iraq
   d. Syria
   e. Italy
9. Until 750, the social prestige and position of the Arab Bedouins
   a. varied according to their wealth.
   b. was sometimes below even that of slaves.
   c. was at the top of the pyramid.
   d. was above that of dhimmis but below that of converts.
   e. was lower than that of the dhimmis.
10. The dhimmis in early Muslim societies were
    a. Christians and Jews who had not converted to Islam.
    b. the merchants.
    c. the original Arabic believers in Islam.
    d. non-Arab converts to Islam.
    e. regarded by the Muslims as still mired in superstition.

## InfoTrac College Edition

Visit the source collections at

**http://infotrac.thomsonlearning.com**

and use the Search function with the following key terms:

Islam caliph or caliphate

## Wadsworth History Website Resources

Visit the World History Resource Center at **http://history.wadsworth.com/world** for a wealth of general resources and the *World Civilizations* Companion Website at **http://history.wadsworth.com/adler04/** for resources specific to this textbook.

## HistoryNow

Enter *HistoryNow* using the access card that is available for *World Civilizations. HistoryNow* will assist you in understanding the content in this chapter with lesson plans generated for your needs. In addition, you can read the following documents, and many more, online:

Ibn Ishaq, *Life of Muhammad* The Qur'an

*We believe in God and what has been sent down to us, and was sent down to Abraham, Ishmael, Isaac, Jacob, and their descendants, and what was given Moses, Jesus, and the prophets by their Lord.*

The Qur'an

# 15 Mature Islamic Society and Institutions

The Caliphate

The Further Development of Islamic Religious Thought

Literature and the Natural Sciences

The Arts in the Muslim World

Muslim Civilization at its Apex

Marriage and the Status of Women

The Decline of the Abbasids and the Coming of the Turks and Mongols

| | |
|---|---|
| 750 C.E. | Abbasid caliphate founded in Baghdad |
| 786–809 | Harun al-Rashid |
| 1055 | Seljuk Turks take power |
| 1258 | Mongols plunder Baghdad |

The consolidation of Islamic civilization took place during the period from the founding of the Abbasid Dynasty in 750 C.E. through the degeneration of that dynasty in the tenth century. In these 200 years, Islam created for its varied adherents a matrix of cultural characteristics that enabled it to survive both political and religious fragmentation, while still expanding eastward into Asia and southward into Africa. In the arts and sciences, the Muslim world now occupied the place once held by the classical Greeks and Romans, whose own accomplishments were largely preserved to a later age through Muslim solicitude.

Challenges to the caliphs' supremacy, not least from the Christian crusades to the Holy Land, temporarily checked the faith's expansion after about 900 C.E. A nearly complete breakdown of the Baghdad caliphate ensued in the eleventh and twelfth centuries, before first the all-conquering Mongols from the Central Asian deserts and then the Ottoman Turks took over the leadership of Islam and infused it with new vigor (see Chapters 22 and 27).

Even after all semblance of central governance of the vast empire had been destroyed, a clear unity was still visible in Islamic culture and lifestyle, whether in the Middle East, India, or Spain. Conflicts with other civilizations and cultures (African, Chinese, Hindu, Christian) only sharpened the Muslims' sense of what was proper and necessary for a life that was pleasing to God and rewarding to humans. How well such a sense was converted into actuality varied, of course, from country to country and time to time. But at its height, Islamic civilization was the envy of its Christian neighbors, with achievements in the sciences and arts that could rival even those of the Chinese.

## The Caliphate

We have seen how the Abbasid clan seized power from the Umayyads and transferred the capital to the new city of Baghdad in the 760s (see Chapter 14). This city quickly became one of the major cultural centers of the world, as the Abbasids adorned it with every form of art and encouraged its educational establishments with money and personal participation. They also further developed the Umayyad institutions of government.

The Abbasid caliphs had come to power on the promise to establish equality among all Muslims, regardless of their ethnicity. More important still, they had promised to provide more religious leadership. The Islamic community, as it had expanded into a vast empire and as Muslims had become widely scattered, started to show signs of sectarian division. Much of this centered on questions regarding the applicability of religion in people's everyday lives. With the sponsorship of the caliphs, religious scholars called the ***ulama*** operated to gradually bring into existence the ***Sharia***, or sacred law, based on the words of the Qur'an and the example, or ***Sunna***, set by the Prophet Muhammad in Muslim living. The Sharia involved far more than religious or doctrinal matters, strictly speaking. In the Muslim view, religion entered into virtually all spheres of what we consider civil and private life, so that the decisions of the ulama and the applications of the Sharia affected almost all aspects of public and private affairs.

Unlike the Western world, the Muslims' sacred book and the Sunna of the Prophet remained the twin bases of all holy law, and hence of all administration and government, to a very late date. The Qur'an was still the fount of all legal knowledge into modern times, and for some Islamic fundamentalists, it still is (for notable examples, in Afghanistan under the Taliban; in Iran since the revolution of 1979–1980; and in Libya and Saudi Arabia).

In Baghdad, an elaborate, mainly Persian bureaucracy exercised governing powers. The major institutions of the central government were the *diwan,* or state council, and the *qadis,* or judges who had jurisdiction in all disputes involving a Muslim. A **vizier**, a kind of prime minister for the caliphs who had enormous powers, headed this council. Many of the other officials were eunuchs (castrated male slaves), who were thought more likely to be devoted to the government because they could have no family interests of their own. In the provinces, the *emir,* or governor, was the key man. His tax-collecting responsibility was crucial to the well-being of the Baghdad government. Rebellions normally started in the provinces and were led by independent-minded emirs.

The Muslim army in the Abbasid era was international in composition. Many of the soldiers were slaves, taken from all the conquered peoples but especially from the Africans and Egyptians. They were well trained and equipped, and their commanders came to have increasing political power as the caliph became weaker. Some contemporary estimates of the army's size are incredibly large, running up to hundreds of thousands in the field at one time (which would have been a logistical impossibility for the time). Still, the Abbasid forces were undoubtedly the most impressive of the era and far overshadowed the Europeans' feudal levies and the Byzantines' professional soldiery. Abbasid raids into Afghanistan and western India established footholds that were gradually expanded by later Muslim regimes.

## The Further Development of Islamic Religious Thought

By the tenth century, the ulama had succeeded in systematizing the application of the Sharia to all spheres of Muslims' lives. This triumph was so complete that by then the ulama had succeeded in eclipsing even the caliphs as the primary source of authority on religious matters. While the caliphs remained the symbolic heads of the Islamic community, people turned to the ulama for religious guidance and education. Even more critical was the fact that the system and the sources of written law they had developed for seeking God's will in all things was considered to be complete, and therefore closed to further development. Known as the "Closing of the Gates," this closure effectively smothered all future independent thought and intellectual innovation after that time. From the tenth century on, the practice of religious law became utterly conservative, and the ulama exercised almost total control over defining acceptable, orthodox practices in God's eyes.

In the later Abbasid Dynasty, the tensions that had already manifested in the political and social spheres found expression also in the religious and philosophical aspects of Islam. A series of challenges to the orthodox interpretations of the Qur'an and its application to intellectual life was issued as early as the caliphate of al-Ma'mun (786–833) in the eighth century and later, which, although hotly rejected by the ulama authorities, could not be ignored.

Most noteworthy was the burgeoning success of the movements known collectively as Sufism. **Sufis** are, generally speaking, the equivalent of Christian and Buddhist mystics; they believe in a direct, personal path to the experience of God's presence. They rely as much on emotional connections to divine truth as on the workings of reason and the revealed word. Although they certainly revere the Qur'an, they do not necessarily see it as the sole path to God. They wish to bring the individual into the state of grace through his or her (Sufis were of both sexes) own commitment to the Divine. Sometimes this search for grace took the form of ecstatic dancing, which continued until the participants fell into a trance. One example was the Turkish Whirling Dervishes of the seventeenth and eighteenth century mentioned in accounts by Western travelers into the Muslim East. Many varieties of Sufism existed, among both Sunni and Shi'ite Muslims, and they were particularly active in mercantile circles. This practice assisted in the spread of the movement to all corners of Islam because of the Sufis' greater tolerance of local customs than most ulama were willing to allow.

Whether ecstatic dervish or reserved intellectual in his study, the relation between the Sufi and the ulama authorities was often strained to the point of mutual condemnation and even bloodshed. An Iranian Sufi, the great philosopher-theologian al-Ghazzali (1058–1111), managed to bring together the mystic enthusiasts and the conservative clerics into a fragile but lasting truce, with his profound synthesis of both points of view in the early twelfth century. Known as the "Renewer of Islam" because of his services, al-Ghazzali is one of the most important theologians of Islam. From Ghazzali's time, Sufism became very popular. Soon, other Sufi masters came forward and gathered circles of students and devotees around them. Some of these circles organized into religious associations, or *tariqas,* most of which were named after the Sufi master on whose teachings they were based. Such tariqas helped spread Islam into parts of Asia and Africa where it previously had only a weak hold at best. (See Evidence of the Past for an example of Sufi poetry.)

**WHIRLING DERVISHES.** This Persian miniature shows a group of Sufis, or dervishes, the members of popular Muslim religious associations called *tariqas,* which began forming in the century after the death of the great Sufi teacher, al-Ghazzali. In this particular tariqa, prolonged dancing was aimed at inducing a trance in which the faithful witnessed God's presence.

EVIDENCE OF THE PAST

## The Sufi Verses of Al Rumi

**FOLLOWING AL-GHAZZALI'S DEATH,** Sufism spread rapidly throughout the Islamic world. Many Sufis organized into associations, called ***tariqas,*** which functioned much like clubs or secret societies. Each of these had its own unique "way" (tariqa) of achieving spiritual ecstasy, as well as its own body of religious literature and lore, some of which took the form of music and spoken poetry. Here is an example of such Sufi poetry by the great thirteenth-century Persian mystic, Jalal al-Din al-Rumi:

> No joy have I found in the two worlds apart from thee, Beloved
> Many wonders have I seen: I have not seen a wonder like thee.
> They say that blazing fire is the infidel's portion:
> I have seen none, . . . excluded from thy fire.
> Often I have laid the spiritual ear at the window of the heart:
> Of a sudden didst thou lavish grace upon thy servant:
> I saw no cause for it save they infinite kindness.
> O chosen Cup-bearer, O apple of mine eyes, the like of thee
> Ne'er appeared in Persia, nor in Arabia have I found it.
> Pour out wine till I become a wanderer from myself;
> For in selfhood and existence I have felt only fatigue.
> O thou who art milk and sugar, O thou who art sun and moon,
> O thou who art mother and father, I have known no kin but thee.
> O indestructible Love, O divine Minstrel,
> Thou art both stay and refuge: a name equal to thee I have not found.
> We are pieces of steel, and thy love is the magnet:
> Thou art the source of all aspiration, in myself I have seen none.
> Silence, O brother! Put learning and culture away:
> Till Thou namedst culture, I knew no culture but Thee.

### *Analyze and Interpret*

Rumi uses the language of a suitor or lover: Whom is he actually addressing? Why does he choose this kind of language? Is it appropriate? Throughout the poem, he disavows all sense of earthly pleasure and even of himself. Why do you suppose he does this? What does it suggest about the method used by the religious mystic to achieve an ecstatic experience of God?

Source: Taken from *Selected Poems from the Diwani Shamsi Tabriz* (by Rumi), trans. by R.A. Nicholson (London: Cambridge University Press, 1898). Quoted in William H. McNeill and Marilyn R. Waldman, *The Islamic World* (Chicago: University of Chicago Press, 1973), pp. 243–244.

## Literature and the Natural Sciences

The Arabic language became an important source of unification in the Muslim world, spreading into its every part. Because the sacred book of the Qur'an could be written only in Arabic, every educated Muslim had to learn this language to some degree. The Arabs also came to possess a cheap and easily made writing medium—paper (picked up from the Chinese, as so much medieval technology would be). A paper factory was operating in Baghdad as early as 793, providing a great stimulus to making books and circulating ideas.

The university was also a Muslim creation. The world's oldest still-functioning higher educational institution is the Azhar Mosque University in Cairo, which was founded in the ninth century by Shi'ite ulama as a place of study in the religious sciences. (Today it is still considered one of the most prestigious mosque universities in the world, although the religious sciences taught there centuries ago became the "orthodox" Sunni sciences.) Long before the names of Aristotle and Plato were known in the Christian West, the Muslims of the Middle East had recognized the value of classical Greek learning and acted to preserve and expand it. Harun al-Rashid, one of the greatest of the Baghdad caliphs in the early ninth century, and his successors created a special bureau, called the "House of Wisdom," whose highest purpose was translating the great works of medicine, science, mathematics, astrology, alchemy, logic, and metaphysics from Greek and Sanskrit into Arabic. There, too, students of philosophy and the various sciences congregated and debated the writings of the Greek and Indian masters. The Muslims especially revered Aristotle, whom they regarded as the greatest teacher of all time. They passed on this esteem for Aristotle to their Christian subjects in Spain, who in turn transmitted it to the rest of Christian Europe in the twelfth and thirteenth centuries.

In the sciences, the Muslim contribution was selective but important. Unlike the Classical and Hellenistic civilizations, the contributions brought forth by Muslim scientists were often of substantial practical application. In the medical sciences, the four centuries between 800 and 1200 saw the world of Islam considerably ahead of any Western civilization. Pharmacology, physiology, anatomy, and, above all, ophthalmology and optical science were special strong points. In geography, Arabic and Persian writers and travelers were responsible for much new information about the known and the hitherto unknown world. In astronomy and astrology, the Muslims built on and expanded the traditions of careful observation they had inherited in the Near East. In mathematics they developed and rationalized the ancient Hindu system of numbers to make the Arabic numbers that are still in universal use. They also introduced the concepts of algebra and the decimal system to the West. One of the most important figures in Muslim science was Ibn Sina (Avicenna), a physician and scientist of great importance to medieval Europe and author of the famous handbook on clinical practice *The Canon of Medicine*. Other important individuals include the philosophers al-Kindi and Ibn Rushd (Averroës), and al-Zahrawi, a surgeon and medical innovator.

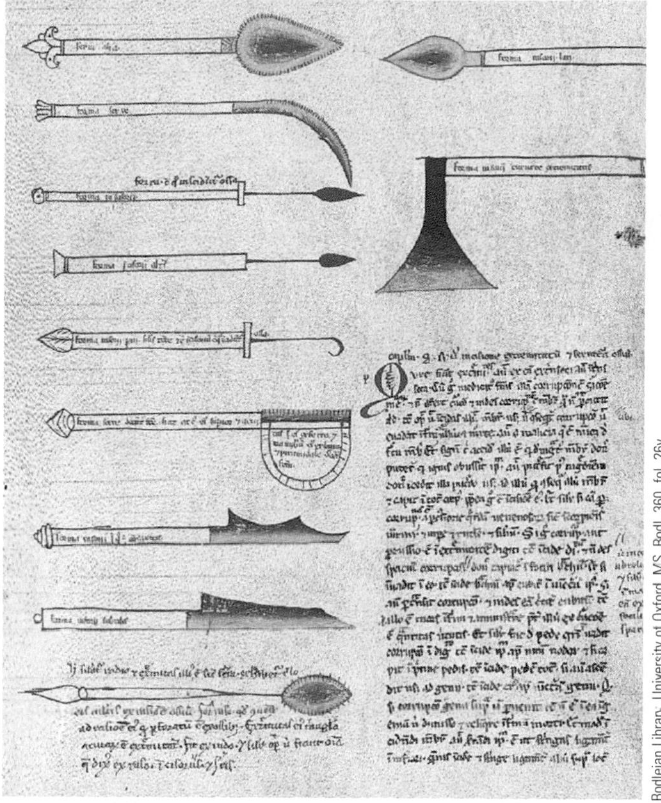

**SURGICAL INSTRUMENTS.** Islamic medicine was so far ahead of medieval European practice that, despite the enmity between Christianity and Islam, Arab doctors were frequently invited to spend time teaching in Europe. The Muslim practitioners were particularly adept at eye surgery and amputations.



## The Arts in the Muslim World

The Abbasid era was witness to an extraordinary flourishing of many of the arts—plastic, literary, and poetic. Some of them employed novel forms; others carried forth established tradition. Because the Qur'an prohibited the lifelike representation of the human figure as blasphemous to the creator, Allah, the Muslims had to turn to other motifs and developed an intricate, geometrically based format for the visual arts. The motifs of their painting, ceramics, mosaics, and inlay work—in all of which the Muslim world excelled—were based on garlands, plants, or geometric figures such as triangles, diamonds, and parallelograms. Because of the religious prohibition, the Muslims produced no sculpture beyond miniatures and, for a long time, no portrait painting.

In architecture, the Muslims, especially the Persians, developed a great deal of lastingly beautiful forms and executed them with great skill. The "most beautiful building in the world," the Taj Mahal in India, is a thoroughly Muslim creation (see the photo in Chapter 27). The use of reflecting pools and landscapes of great precision and intricate design was common in parks and public buildings. Great wealth and a love of luxury were earmarks of rulers throughout the world of Islam, and it was considered a mark of gentility and good manners for a ruler to spend lavishly on public and private adornments.

Calligraphy was a special strength of the Muslims, whose Arabic script is the product of aesthetic demands as much as the desire to communicate. As in ancient China, a beautiful script was considered to be as much a part of good breeding as beautiful clothing. Arabic lettering was incorporated into almost every form of art, generally as quotations from the Qur'an.

Giraudon/Art Resource, NY

**DECORATIVE TILES.** This magnificent tiled portal was the entry to the shrine of Imam Riza, in Mashad, Iran. Built in the early fifteenth century, it was a memorial to a shah from his widow.

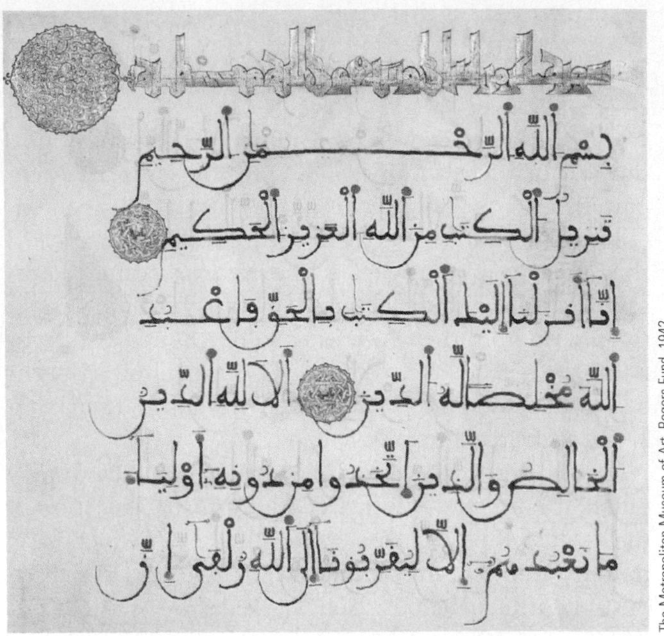

The Metropolitan Museum of Art, Rogers Fund, 1942

**ARABIC CALLIGRAPHY.** The beauty of written Arabic is rivaled only by the Oriental scripts. Several different styles evolved in different places and times, quite as distinct as the various alphabets of the Western world. Here is an eleventh-century Persian script.

In literature, the Persian language replaced Arabic as the preferred instrument of expression. The epic *Shah-Nama,* a prodigious collection of tales and anecdotes from the great poet Firdawsi, attempts to sum up Persia's history from the origins. Written in the early eleventh century, it is far better known and revered in the Muslim East than the *Rubaiyat* of Khayyam (see the Patterns of Belief box in Chapter 27).

Arabs developed storytelling to a high art and are generally credited with the invention of fiction—that is, stories told solely to entertain. The most famous book of stories in the history of the world is ***The 1001 Nights*** (also called ***The Arabian Nights***), which was supposedly created by a courtier at the court of Harun al-Rashid. Poetry was also a strongly cultivated and popular literary art form, especially among the Persian Muslims.

## MUSLIM CIVILIZATION AT ITS APEX

Muslim civilization flourished most brilliantly between about 900 and about 1200. At its height, Islam was the most lavish and innovative civilization of the world, rivaled only by China, with which it had extensive commercial and some intellectual contacts. The Muslim world at this time extended from the Atlantic to the Indian Ocean, and Muslim traders were found on every known continent and sea (see Map 15.1).

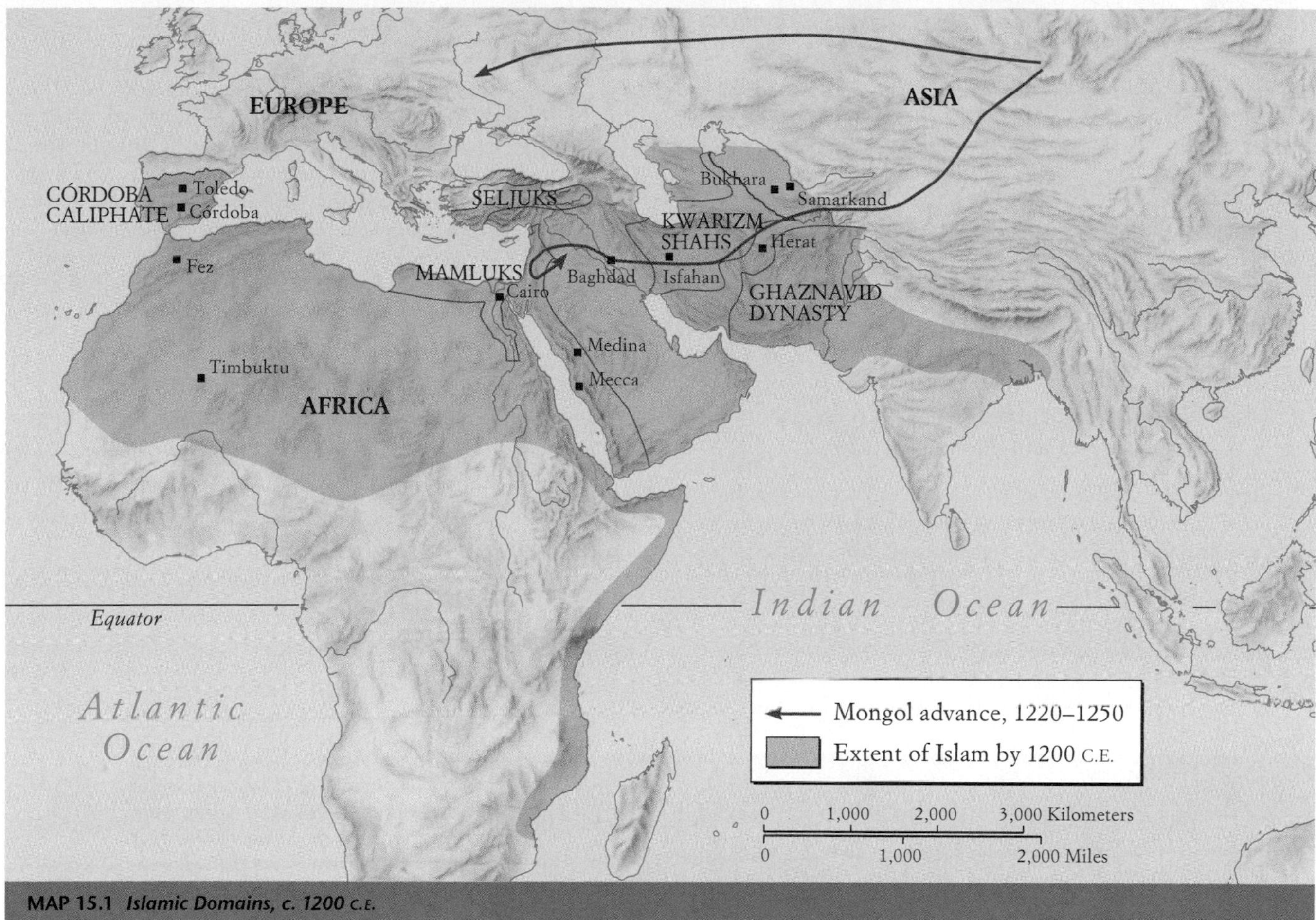


**MAP 15.1** *Islamic Domains, c. 1200 C.E.*

In this period, the Muslim world extended from the Atlantic to the Indian Ocean. By about 1200 C.E., the Baghdad caliph's hold on territories beyond Arabia and Iraq was minimal, if it existed at all. Persia and Egypt, as well as Spain and Afghanistan, were autonomous under their own shahs and caliphs. African Muslims had never had direct contact with Baghdad.

As we will see later in this chapter, the Mongol invasion commencing about 1230 was a huge shock to the Muslims of the Middle East. Until Mongols and, later, Turks had adopted Islam for themselves and spearheaded two more waves of military expansion in the fourteenth through sixteenth centuries, the Muslim civilization entered a period of retrenchment.

Islam provided a precise place for every person in its social scheme without severely limiting freedom of movement. Believers could move without hindrance all around a huge belt of settlements on either side of the equator, from Spain to the Philippines. Travelers could journey to distant lands, secure in the knowledge that they would be welcomed by their co-religionists and would find the same laws and religious values, the same literary language, and the same conceptions of justice and truth that they had known at home. Wherever they were, all Muslims knew they were members of a great community, the Muslim Umma.

The cities of this world were splendid and varied. Córdoba and Grenada were cities of perhaps a half million people in the tenth century; their ruling class was Muslim, from the North African Berber people, but their inhabitants included many Jews and Christians as well. Anything produced in the East or West could be purchased in the markets of Córdoba. The same was true of Baghdad, which had an even larger population and featured the most lavish imperial court of all under caliph Harun al-Rashid and his ninth-century successors.

Commerce was particularly well developed in the world of Islam, and the exhortation in the Qur'an to "honor the honest merchant" was generally observed. The Muslim faithful saw nothing wrong in getting rich. In contrast to both Christians and Buddhists, they considered a wealthy man to be the recipient of God's blessings for a good life. The rich had an obligation to share their wealth with the poor, however. Most schools, dormitories, hospitals, orphanages, and the like in Muslim areas are to this day the result of private donations and foundations, the ***waqf***, which are commonly included in Muslim wills (see the Society and Economy box).

SOCIETY AND ECONOMY

## Care of the Ill: Egypt in the Thirteenth Century

In the mid-thirteenth century, the Mamaluke governor of Egypt decided to ensure his soul's ascent to paradise by leaving a generous bequest to his subjects. In accord with imprecations frequently encountered in the pages of the Qur'an, the Emir Mansur ordained in his *waqf,* or testamentary gift, that a new hospital should be founded. It would contain not only a mosque but also a chapel for the Christian Copts; there would be separate buildings for male and female, as well as separate wards for several different diseases. There would be a library for the doctors and patients, and a pharmacy on premises.

The Mansur foundation would minister to as many as 8,000 people simultaneously, and the waqf stated that

> the hospital shall keep all patients, men and women, until they are completely recovered. All costs are to be borne by the hospital, whether the people come from afar or near, whether they are residents or foreigners, strong or weak, low or high, rich or poor, employed or unemployed, blind or sighted, physically or mentally ill, learned or illiterate. There are no conditions or consideration of payment; none is objected to even indirectly, for non-payment. The entire service is through the magnificence of Allah, the generous one.

Mansur's plan was put into effect at his death, and the hospital's lineal descendant exists today in Cairo.

### *Analyze and Interpret*

Why do you suppose a person would make such a bequest? From what you know about the Qur'an, what seems to have been the attitude of Muhammad toward the destitute? How does this belief compare with the attitudes of Christians and Jews?

Susan McCartney/Photo Researchers, Inc.

**Townscape of Grenada.** This striking view of one of the strongholds of the Moors (Muslims in Spain, from *moro,* "dark") shows the remnants of the medieval walls and the castle sitting on its hill below the high mountains of southern Spain.

## Marriage and the Status of Women

How did women fit into the social scheme of the Muslim world? The Qur'an openly states that men are superior to women and grants men the right to rule over them. On the other hand, the Qur'an also accorded women many protections from male abuse—far more than in pre-Islamic Arab society. How many of these beliefs were actually put into practice is difficult to know. As a generalization, the relatively elevated status of women in the early Islamic period appears to have undergone some decline in later centuries, as a result of expansion and the process of absorption of other cultures into Islam. Veiling and the seclusion of women, for example, were Indian practices in origin. Slave women were allowed more freedom than were the freeborn, but only because of and as a sign of their inferior position. Many were concubines.

The Qur'an allows but does not encourage a man to marry up to four wives if he can maintain them properly.

If additional wives cannot be supported properly, they are neither expected nor permitted. The marriages may be either serial or simultaneous. There is no limit on the number of concubines he can have. In practice, though, few Muslims had as many as four wives, and fewer still could afford concubines. The children of a concubine, if acknowledged by the father, were provided for in law and custom equally with those of a legal wife.

Many households kept at least one slave (sometimes the concubine). Slavery was common but usually not harsh. Most slaves worked in the household or shop, not in the fields or mines. It was common for slaves to be freed at any time for good behavior or because the owner wished to ensure Allah's blessing. Most people fell into slavery for the usual reasons: debts, wars, and bad luck. Muslims were not supposed to enslave other members of their faith, but this rule seems to have been frequently ignored or rationalized.

In theory at least, the household was ruled by the man, whose foremost duty toward it and himself was to maintain honor. Muslim society was dominated by honor and shame, and such notions often were tied up in social perceptions of how the women of a particular household behaved. Consequently, in most upper-class households, women's status was restricted the most. Here, women of reproductive age and children were restricted to the harem, the private areas of the house where they were kept in hiding (called ***purdah***) from the prying eyes of visitors and strangers. Visiting other women outside the home was permitted, although it was usually restricted to the evening and nighttime hours.

In practice, however, women's status was not always as limited as Islamic law and custom demanded. Although such rules of honor and behavior were common in well-to-do households in the Islamic heartlands, among the lower echelons of society, women often enjoyed considerably greater personal freedom. The same held true for Muslim women who lived in many parts of Asia and Africa. Sheer economic necessity, for example, usually made observing the rules of purdah impossible. Women were often occupied outside their households, fully participating in many breadwinning activities, as were male members of their homes and communities. Moreover, local traditions frequently overrode written law. Islamic "orthodoxy" made more allowance for local social traditions than called for by the written legal codes. Ample recent scholarship has shown that women in many Islamic societies exercised powers within the private sphere that sometimes exceeded those of male members. Houses, for example, sometimes actually belonged to the female members of a Muslim society, rather than to the males. Where divorces occurred, these women were left in possession of the house and the marriage goods, often ruling them as powerful matriarchs. Many such examples exist and deserve further exploration by interested students of history.

## The Decline of the Abbasids and the Coming of the Turks and Mongols

Despite all of their efforts, the Abbasids were unable to restore the political unity of the empire they had taken over in 750. Even great caliphs such as Harun al-Rashid, who was well known in the West, could not force the Spaniards and the North African emirates to submit to their rule. Gradually, during the 800s, almost all of the African and Arabian possessions broke away and became independent, leaving the Abbasids in control of only the Middle East. More and more, they came to depend on wild Turkish tribesmen, only some of whom had converted to Islam, for their protection against rebellion. It was inevitable that, as time passed and the caliphs became ever more dissolute, they would turn on their weak masters and make them into pawns.

In the mid-1000s C.E., a new group of Turks, known as **Seljuks**, surged out of Afghanistan into Iran and Iraq. In 1055, they entered Baghdad as victors. Keeping the Abbasid ruler on as a figurehead, the Seljuks took over the government for about a century, until they, too, fell prey to internal rivalries. The central government ceased to exist, and the Middle East became a series of large and small Muslim principalities, fighting one another for commercial and territorial advantage.

Into this disintegrated empire exploded a totally new force out of the East: Chinghis Khan (or Ghenghis Khan) and the **Mongols**. Chinghis started out as a minor tribal leader of the primitive Mongols, who inhabited the semi-desert steppes of northern Central Asia as nomadic pastoralists. In the late twelfth century, he was able to put together a series of victories over his rivals and set himself up as lord of his people. Leading an army of savage horsemen in a great campaign, he managed to conquer most of Central Asia and the Middle East before his death in the early 1200s.

Chinghis's immediate successor as Great Khan (the title means "lord") was victorious over Russians and ravaged about half of Europe before retiring in the 1230s. But a few years later, the Mongols felt ready to settle accounts with the Seljuks and other claimants to the Baghdad throne. They took Baghdad in an orgy of slaughter and rape—eyewitnesses claimed that some 800,000 people were killed! In this gory debacle, the Abbasid caliphate finally came to an end in 1258 and was replaced by the Mongol Khanate of Central Asia. This story continues in Chapter 22.

## Summary

Muslim civilization was an amalgam of the many civilizations that had preceded it. It was eclectic, taking from any forebear anything that seemed valuable or useful. In the opening centuries, the Arabs who had founded it by military conquest dominated the civilization, but it gradually opened up to all who professed the true faith of the Prophet and worshiped the one god, Allah. Much of the territory the Arabs conquered was already highly civilized, with well-developed religions. The Arabs therefore contented themselves with establishing a minority of rulers and traders and intermarrying with the natives as they converted to Islam. Based on the easy-to-understand principles of an all-embracing religious faith, Muslim civilization was a world into which many streams flowed to comprise a vast new sea.

## Identification Terms

Test your knowledge of this chapter's key concepts by defining the following terms. If you can't recall the meaning of certain terms, refresh your memory by looking up the boldfaced term in the chapter, turning to the Glossary at the end of the book, or working with the flashcards that are available on the *World Civilizations* Companion Website: **http://history.wadsworth.com/adler04/**.

Mongols
*purdah*
Seljuks
*Sharia*
Sufis
*Sunna*
*tariqas*
*The 1001 Nights (The Arabian Nights)*
*ulama*
vizier
*waqf*

## Test Your Knowledge

Test your knowledge of this chapter by answering the following questions. Complete answers appear at the end of the book. You may also take this quiz interactively and find even more quiz questions on the *World Civilizations* Companion Website: **http://history.wadsworth.com/adler04/**.

1. Which of the following cities was not a center of Muslim culture in this era?
   a. Cairo
   b. Constantinople
   c. Córdoba
   d. Baghdad
   e. Grenada
2. Sufism is the Islamic version of the intellectual phenomenon known in the West as
   a. communism.
   b. mysticism.
   c. individualism.
   d. feminism.
   e. agnosticism.
3. The common Muslim attitude toward trade and mercantile activity was
   a. that they were best left to the "infidel."
   b. reluctant acceptance of their necessity.
   c. that nothing was morally or ethically wrong with them.
   d. condemnation as temptations to evildoing.
   e. that only the upper class was to be involved.
4. Many Muslim scholars especially revered the work of
   a. Gautama Buddha.
   b. Aristotle.
   c. Confucius.
   d. Socrates.
   e. Harun al-Rashid.
5. Muslim knowledge significantly influenced the West in all of these areas except
   a. philosophy.
   b. law.
   c. medicine.
   d. mathematics.
   e. a written language.

6. The major area from which Muslim culture entered Christian Europe was
   a. Greece.
   b. Spain.
   c. Italy.
   d. Russia.
   e. Turkey.
7. The Canon of Medicine was the work of
   a. Aristotle.
   b. Harun al-Rashid.
   c. Avicenna.
   d. Averroës.
   e. al-Zahrawi.
8. The application and interpretation of Islamic law was largely in the hands of
   a. the caliphs.
   b. the Sharia.
   c. the ulama.
   d. Sufis.
   e. the viziers.
9. Before the time of al-Ghazzali, Sufism was
   a. organized into associations.
   b. highly unpopular.
   c. encouraged by the caliphs.
   d. discouraged by the ulama.
   e. popular only among slaves.
10. The concept of veiling and secluding women appears to have come from
   a. the Qur'an.
   b. Muhammad.
   c. Afghanistan.
   d. Avicenna.
   e. India.

## InfoTrac College Edition

Visit the source collections at

**http://infotrac.thomsonlearning.com**

and use the Search function with the following key terms:

caliph or caliphate Islam

## Wadsworth History Website Resources

Visit the World History Resource Center at **http://history.wadsworth.com/world** for a wealth of general resources and the *World Civilizations* Companion Website at **http://history.wadsworth.com/adler04/** for resources specific to this textbook.

## HistoryNow

Enter *HistoryNow* using the access card that is available for *World Civilizations*. *HistoryNow* will assist you in understanding the content in this chapter with lesson plans generated for your needs. In addition, you can read the following documents, and many more, online:

Ibn Sina (Avicenna), *On Medicine*

Harun al-Rashid, *The 1001 Nights*

*The people are numerous and happy. . . . if they want to go, they go; if they want to stay on, they stay. . . . Throughout the whole country the people do not kill any living creature.*
**Fa-Hsien**

# 16 Indian Civilization in its Golden Age



| | |
|---|---|
| c. 200–500 | Ajanta caves constructed and painted |
| 320–480 | Gupta Dynasty |
| c. 406 | Arrival of Fa-hsien in India |
| 480 | onward India divided between North and South |
| c. 500–c. 800 | Formative period of caste system |
| 711 | Muslims begin to invade northwestern India |
| c. 700–1000 | Hindu revival and decline of Buddhism in India |
| Late 1100s–1400s | Delhi sultanate in North India |

Under the Gupta Dynasty of kings (320–480 C.E.), India experienced a great flourishing of Hindu culture. At about the time that the Roman Empire was weakening, Hindu civilization stabilized. The caste system assured everyone of a definite place in society, and political affairs were in the hands of strong, effective rulers for a century and a half. Vedic Hindu religious belief responded to the challenge of Buddhism and reformed so effectively that it began to supplant Buddhism in the country. Indian merchants and emigrants carried Hindu theology and Sanskrit literature to Southeast Asia, where they merged with native religions and cultures. Long after the political unity under the Guptas ended, India continued to produce scientific advances and technological developments that are still not fully recognized in the West. The invasions of Muslim Turks and others from the northwest redivided India into political fragments, but the essential unity of its Hindu civilization carried on.

## The Gupta Dynasty

After the fall of the Mauryan Dynasty in the 200s B.C.E. (see Chapter 5), India reverted to a group of small principalities fighting one another for mastery. This was the usual political situation in India, where one invader after another succeeded in establishing only partial control, usually in the north, while Indian princes controlled the rest.

Not until 320 C.E. was another powerful native dynasty founded—that of the Gupta kings, who ruled from their base in the valley of the Ganges River on the east side of the subcontinent. They overcame their rivals to eventually create an empire over most of India, which lasted until about 500 C.E. when it was destroyed by a combination of internal dissension and external threats. The Gupta Dynasty was the last Indian-led unification of the country until the twentieth century. Long after the dynasty had disappeared, memories of its brilliance remained. As time wore on and India remained divided and subject to foreign invaders, the Guptas and their achievements became the standard by which other rulers were measured.

The Gupta Period is the first in Indian history for which more or less reliable firsthand accounts have survived. The most interesting is that of the Chinese Buddhist monk Fa-hsien, who visited India for a long period around 406 and left a diary of what he saw and did. According to his account, India was a stable society, well ruled by a king who was universally respected because he brought prosperity and order everywhere. Nevertheless, despite such sources, we know relatively little about Gupta India compared with what we know of other world civilizations of this date. Indians did not begin to keep historical records until very late, so, aside from works such as Fa-hsien's, the main written materials we have are religious poetry and folklore. Even these sources are sparse, for the tradition of both Hinduism and Buddhism was not literary but oral. What was important was memorized, generation after generation, but inevitably with some changes. It was not written down until much later, and then only in a much-altered version. For this reason historians have few definite records to work with in India until perhaps as late as 1500 C.E. and must depend heavily on both archaeology and travelers' reports, such as Fa-hsien's.

### *Economic and Cultural Progress*

In this classical age, the overwhelming majority of Indians continued to gain their daily sustenance from farming and herding, perhaps even more so than in other parts of the world. The agrarian villages, not the handful of towns and cities, were the vital center of Indian life. These villages changed little in activity or appearance over the centuries.

In the Gupta Period and for some time thereafter, India remained free from the problems of insufficient land and overpopulation in its rich river basins. The average villager seems to have been a landowner or tenant who worked a small plot that he had inherited and that he would pass on to an oldest son or sons.

In most of the subcontinent, rice was the chief crop, as it had become in most of South Asia. The huge demands this crop imposed on labor determined many aspects of life in the village: the cycle of rice planting, transplanting, and harvesting was the fundamental calendar. Water was crucial for rice growing, and control and distribution of water were the source of constant controversy and in some cases even wars between the numerous small principalities. In this respect and in its dependence on intensive, irrigation agriculture, India resembled both Mesopotamia and South China.

The arts flourished during the Gupta Period, and several models in architecture and sculpture were developed that remained the standards of beauty for a long time. The greatest of ancient India's playwrights, **Kalidasa,** wrote a series of works that remain popular today. He was a major contributor to the upsurge of Sanskrit literature at this time. Sanskrit, the language of the Aryans, was now formally adopted as a sacred literary script, but literacy remained exceptional.

The Gupta Period also produced notable achievements in the sciences. Mathematicians worked out the concept of zero, which enabled them to handle large numbers much more easily; zero is closely associated with the decimal system, which was probably also an Indian invention. The "Arabic" numbers that are used universally today also originated in Gupta India, so far as historians can determine. Indian astronomers also made several breakthroughs in explaining eclipses of the moon and in calculating geographic distances.

The medical sciences developed significantly during and after the Gupta Period. Pharmacy, surgery, and diagnosis of internal ills were Indian specialties, and wealthy Muslims from the West often came to Indian doctors for treatment. In this way began the active interchange between the Muslim and Hindu medical men that so profited the Muslims in the period after 850 C.E. and was eventually passed on to the backward Europeans.

## Political Fragmentation: South and North

After the demise of the Gupta Dynasty, India divided into political-cultural regions: South and North (see Map 16.1). Each of these regions further subdivided into several units ruled by hereditary or aristocratic leaders, but each region shared some common features distinguishing each from the other.

### *South: Hinduism and Buddhism*

Below the Deccan plateau, dark-skinned peoples whose languages came from the Dravidian and Pali families, quite different from those of the North, inhabited the South. The South's political history is almost unknown for several centuries, as it was never brought under direct Gupta rule, and few written records have survived. The invasions that perennially wracked the North had little effect on the South, whose contacts with foreigners were in the nature of peaceful commerce both east and west over the Indian Ocean. From the Gupta Period onward, little common political bond existed between the two regions for many centuries.

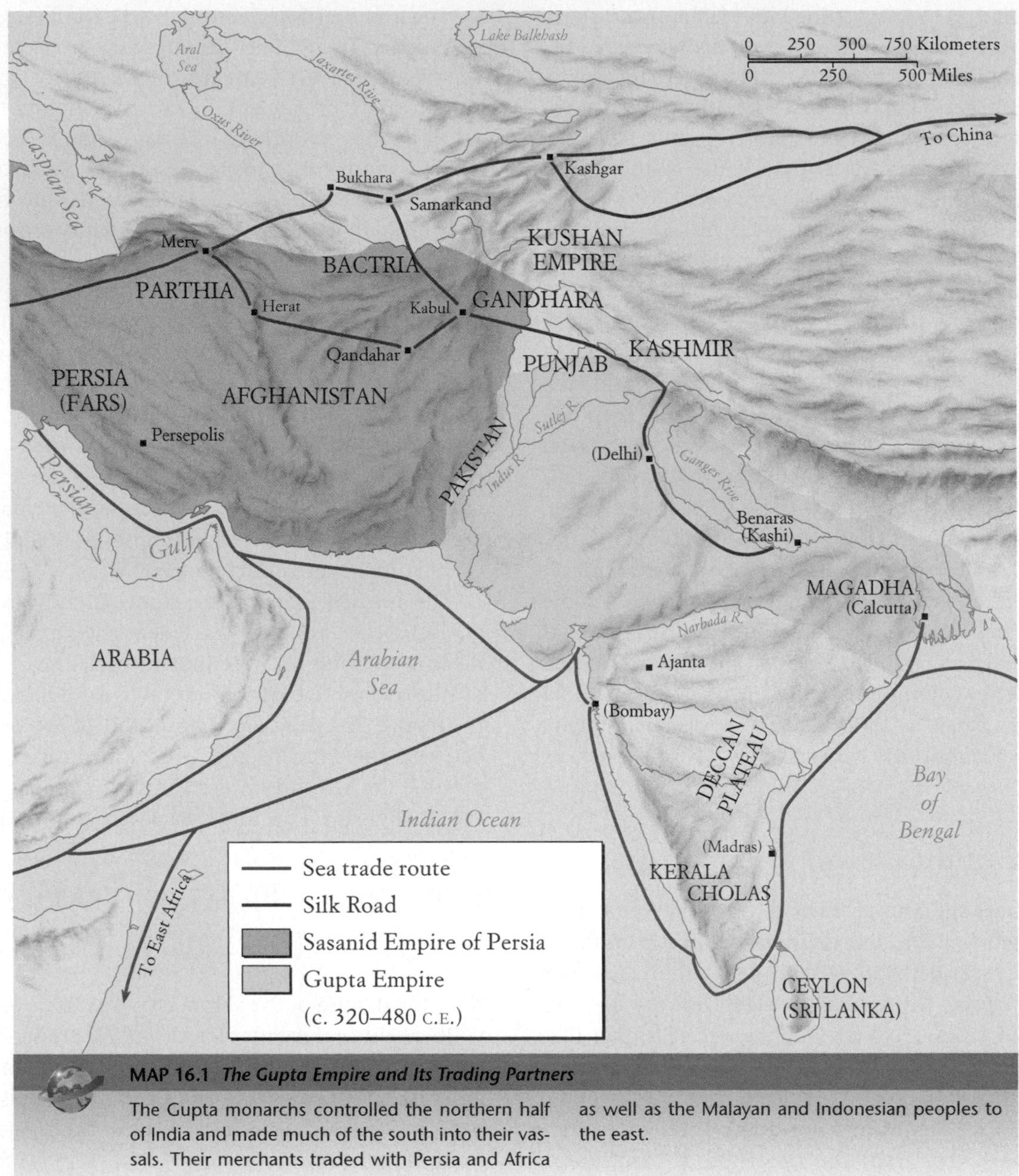


**MAP 16.1** ***The Gupta Empire and Its Trading Partners***

The Gupta monarchs controlled the northern half of India and made much of the south into their vassals. Their merchants traded with Persia and Africa as well as the Malayan and Indonesian peoples to the east.

The culture of the South was strongly influenced by varieties of Hinduism and particularly Buddhism, which differed from those of the North. The Theravada (Hinayana) form of Buddhism became dominant in the South, especially in Sri Lanka. Sri Lankan holy men and monasteries were instrumental in the conversion of much of Southeast Asia. The Theravada devotees tended to look down on the relatively flexible doctrines of the Mahayana adherents and rejected many as unworthy or inauthentic. This attitude contributed to the differentiation of South and North, which was already apparent in linguistic and ethnic spheres. Only the near extinction of Buddhism and the revival of Hinduism throughout the subcontinent allowed Indians to begin the slow development of a modern, politically expressed sense of nationhood.

The South saw a great flourishing of both Buddhist and Hindu architecture and sculpture between 300 and 700 C.E. Both religions encouraged the construction of massive stone *stupas,* rounded temples that stood in the midst of extensive complexes for both worship and living quarters. In the interiors stood statues of the gods and goddesses and all types of holy shrines. Sculpture, mainly in stone but also in bronze, seems to have been the art form of choice among Hindus during most of their history. Some of their life-size and larger-than-life-size works have survived to demonstrate the artists' skills. Even more

John Elk/Stock Boston

**STUPA RELIEFS.** The candid emphasis on sexual attributes in Hindu sculpture was considered to be justified recognition of a source of human pleasure. Throughout history, most peasant-based civilizations placed great importance on fertility; hence, sexuality was celebrated.

impressive are the many panels and figures that decorate the exteriors of the stupa temples and show us the vigor and life-affirming nature of Hindu art. Much of it was erotic and created a great deal of embarrassment among nineteenth-century British colonial observers. What would have been considered pornographic in a Western context apparently had no such connotations to Indians, either then or now.

Some painting has also survived, most notably in the **Ajanta Caves** in the South. Like most architecture and sculpture of India's Golden Age, all paintings were inspired by religious legends and stories, much as medieval European artworks were. The paintings portray gods good and bad and all sorts of quasi-divine demons taken from the rich religious folklore.

## North: Islam Comes to India

We have a good deal more political and military data from the North of India during the 700 years between the fall of the Gupta Dynasty and the erection of the Muslim sultanate in Delhi. The major question facing all North Indian rulers was how to defend themselves against the repeated and ever-fiercer assaults coming from Muslim forces out of Afghanistan on the northwestern frontier. From the eighth century onward, bands of Muslim raiders and would-be conquerors of the Hindu and Buddhist areas had harassed northwestern India.

The first wave of conquests of the seventh century had carried Islam only as far as northwestern India, reaching the Indus Valley and Multan in 711, and no farther. For another three centuries, Hindu dynasties in central India had proved sufficiently vigorous to discourage further invasion. By the early eleventh century, the military balance of power had shifted dramatically, however. A strong regime had been established in Afghanistan, whose military power rested on highly trained and mobile, professional slave troops of Turkish origins for whom the riches of India beckoned like ripe fruit. Between 1001 and 1030, their warlord, Mahmud al-Ghazni, launched powerful raids into northwestern India for the purpose not of empire building but of seizing booty. In one raid alone against the Temple of Shiva in Gujarat, Mahmud reportedly carried off nearly 3,000 pounds of gold. Yet the effects of these first raids hardly outlived Mahmud's death in 1030, and for another 165 years, Islamic rule languished. By the late 1100s, effective Islamic control had shrunk only to the region of the Punjab.

After a second wave of invasions beginning in 1192, Muslim commanders made their headquarters in the city of Delhi, which then became the capital of what came to be called the **Delhi sultanate**. Additional conquests were directed eastward as far as Bengal, until most of northern and central India fell to Muslim arms.

The sultanate lasted for another three centuries, and in that long span, the patterns of Muslim–Hindu relations were cast. Muslim intolerance of people they considered openly pagan meant that violence was the keynote of these relations from the beginning. Successful raids and victories frequently led to excessively high losses of life for Hindus and Buddhists defending their temples, monasteries, and homes. Mahmud's raid on the Temple of Shiva was followed by a slaughter of 50,000 Brahmins, or high-caste Hindus. Similar massacres occurred in Muslim attacks on the last remaining major Buddhist monastery.

Culturally speaking, the contacts between Islamic and Hindu/Buddhist civilizations were important. Beginning as early as the 800s, many Arab merchants visited the west coast of India. Some of their travel accounts survive and are important sources of Indian history. So many resident Muslims lived in some of the coastal towns as to justify building mosques. In addition to carrying cottons, silks, and fine steel swords from India to the world of Islam, these merchants, traders, and other Muslim visitors took back the Indians' knowledge of algebra and astronomy and other cultural achievements. Indian visitors came to Harun al-Rashid's Baghdad to train Islamic scholars at the request of the caliph. When Harun fell seriously ill, an Indian physician, who was then rewarded with the post of royal physician, cured him.

Muslim conquest brought on the final stage of the long decline of Buddhism in India. Buddhism was a proselytizing religion, like Islam, and the two competitors did not get along well. Whereas the Muslims were able to ignore or come to terms with Hinduism, they attacked Buddhism and its institutions, especially the few remaining monasteries that were the heart of the faith. Already weakened by a revitalized Hinduism, the Buddhist faith was now, in the twelfth century, wiped out in the land where it had originated. Its strong roots on the island of Sri Lanka, as well as in China, Korea, Japan, and much of Southeast Asia, guaranteed its continued existence, however.

## Hindu Doctrines in the Classical Age

The doctrines of Hinduism stem from a great mass of unwritten tradition but also from three written sources: the Vedas, the Upanishads, and the *Mahabharata*. The **Vedas** (see Chapter 5) are four lengthy epic poems that were originally brought to India by the Aryans and were then "nativized" over many centuries. Dealing with the relations between the many gods and their human subjects, they relate tales of the god-heroes who created the Earth and all that lies in it. The most significant is the **Rigveda**, which was written down in relatively modern times; it contains a great deal of information about the Aryan-Indian gods and their relations with humans. The chief deities are Indra and Varuna. Indra, the god of war and revelry, resembles the old Germanic god Thor in several ways. Varuna was the caretaker of proper order in the universe, the first hint of an ethical element in Indian religion. Vedic religion was one of ritual and sacrifice, with priests playing the leading role.

The **Upanishads** are a series of long and short philosophical speculations, apparently first produced in the eighth century B.C.E.; gradually, they were expanded to number more than 100 by a body of poems that deal with the human dilemma of being alive on Earth as a partial, incomplete being. The Upanishads are a long step forward from the relatively unsophisticated rituals and anecdotes

**Frescos at Ajanta Caves.** The Ajanta Caves complex was begun some time in the second century B.C.E. and completed in 478 C.E. Originally a Hindu project, it became a Buddhist retreat, and the hundreds of frescos and sculptures that grace it are mainly representative of Buddhist belief. The picture shows four seated bodhisattvas behind a row of amorous couples. Such a juxtapositioning of spirit and flesh is not unusual in Indian Buddhist art.

Vanni/Art Resource, NY

of the Vedas; with them begins the tradition of involved speculation that became a characteristic of later Hindu thought.

The supreme deities of all Hindus are Brahman, Vishnu, and Shiva. Although individuals may worship many gods, all Hindus believe in the paramount importance of these three. **Brahman** is the world-spirit, the source of all life and all objects in the universe—roughly equivalent to the Christian God the Father, but entirely impersonal. Hindus are generally subdivided into the devotees of either Vishnu or Shiva.

**Vishnu** is the Preserver, a sort of Christ figure without the ethical teachings. He (or sometimes, she; the Hindu deities are often bisexual) has appeared in nine incarnations thus far in world history, and there will be a tenth. The most popular of all Hindu gods, Vishnu is particularly beloved in the form of Krishna, the instructor and protector of all humans. The last of the Hindu trinity is **Shiva**, the Destroyer and also Creator. Shiva is best appreciated as the god of becoming, lord of both life and death. At times he or she is depicted as a beneficent bringer of joy; at other times he is the ruthless and irresistible destroyer, making way for new life to come.

Some of these beliefs, and particularly the position of the priests who interpreted them—the Brahmins—were challenged by the Buddhists and the Jains (see Chapter 5). By the first century C.E., Buddhism and Jainism had attracted the allegiance of a large part of the population (see the Patterns of Belief box). The old Vedic Hinduism proved unable to match the appeal of these religions to persons seeking an emotional and intellectually fulfilling experience.

Private collection/Ann & Bury Peerless Picture Library/Bridgeman Art Library

**HINDU GOD VISHNU.** Vishnu, the god of preservation (right), is depicted with his consort Lakshmi, riding the huge bird demon Garuda as it circles the cosmos in search of prey.

As Buddhism gradually evolved into a supernatural religion after its founder's death, Hinduism responded to the Buddhist challenge by developing a less formal and more speculative approach to the mysteries of eternal life and the gods who ordained human fate. The Upanishads and the *Mahabharata* are the embodiment of this response,

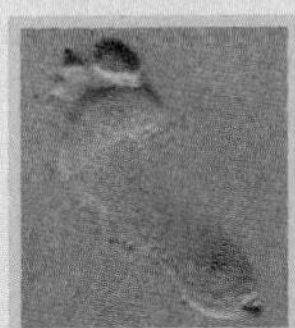

EVIDENCE OF THE PAST

## A Father's Lesson

**THE COMPLEXITIES OF HINDU** religious and philosophical speculations as they developed in the first millennium C.E. are often baffling to the reader. But occasionally help is forthcoming through one or another of the frequent Indian folk sayings that have evolved in the oral tradition:

> A learned father wished to instruct his son in the mysteries of the spirit that informs all earthly creatures but can never be apprehended by the senses.
>
> Father: Now you ask for that instruction by which we hear what cannot be heard, by which we perceive what cannot be perceived, by which we know what cannot be known.
>
> Son: What is that instruction, sir?
>
> F: Fetch me a fruit of the Nyagrodha tree.
>
> S: Here is one, sir.
>
> F: Break it.
>
> S: It is broken.
>
> F: What do you see?
>
> S: These seeds, almost infinitesimal.
>
> F: Break one.
>
> S: It is broken.
>
> F: What do you see there?
>
> S: Not anything, sir.
>
> F: My son, that subtle essence which you do not perceive there, of that very essence this great Nyagrodha tree exists.

### *Analyze and Interpret*

What is the meaning of this lesson?

Source: *Sacred Books of the East*, ed. F. Max Mueller (Oxford: Oxford University Press, 1999).

PATTERNS OF BELIEF

## Mahavira Vardhamana

Not all Indians are Hindus; here and there in that vast subcontinent live colonies of other believers, some of whom preceded the sixth-century arrival of the Christians in India by many centuries. Foremost among these are the Jains, who are concentrated in the province of Gujarat, particularly among the members of the mercantile castes. Although not numbering more than a few million, they have exercised an influence on Indian spiritual life that far exceeds their numbers.

The Jain religion owes its origins to the work of a sixth-century B.C.E. sage named Vardhamana, later given the title of *Mahavira,* or Great Hero. He lived from about 540 to 470 and was thus a contemporary of the Buddha, with whom he seems to have had some personal contact. Both men were members of the kshatriya caste and, like others of that warrior-governor grouping, resented the exclusive claims of the Brahmins to the priestly functions. Animal sacrifice played a major role in the Brahmins' Hinduism, and both the Buddha and Mahavira rejected it as inappropriate.

Mahavira later took this rejection to its ultimate form: he and his followers made every possible effort to avoid any form of violence to other creatures, even when that nonviolence represented death or danger to themselves. This doctrine of *ahimsa* was the outstanding characteristic of Jainism in Mahavira's day and remains so to the present.

Mahavira's background strongly resembles that of Siddhartha Gautama, the Buddha. He was born into a rich family but began to question the emptiness of his moral life when he was in his twenties. At age thirty, he abandoned his family to become a wandering seeker. Adopting an extreme asceticism (such as the Buddha tried and ultimately rejected), he even dispensed with clothing, preferring to wander naked through the world begging food and sleeping in the open.

After twelve years, he felt he had cleansed himself of worldly ambitions and was qualified to teach others. He preached the Five Great Vows: no killing under any circumstances, no untruth, no greed, total chastity, and no restrictive attachments to any person or object. Certainly, few could maintain these vows fully, but they were meant to be goals that one strived for and did not necessarily attain in one lifetime.

In the present day, Jains often wear gauze masks to avoid inadvertent intake of minute insects and constantly sweep their paths to avoid stepping on some tiny animal or plant. Bathing and moving about in the dark are avoided for the same reason. They set up hostels where they bring sick and aged animals, allowing them to die in peace. And they believe that voluntary starvation is the most admirable death once one has reached a state in which following the Great Vows is no longer possible.

Jainism strongly resembles the other great Eastern faiths in the absence of a Creator God from whom humans receive moral instruction or commands. Like Buddhism, Jainism accepts reincarnation and the concept of karma, with the accompanying striving for liberation from an earthly existence, moksha. The emphasis on ahimsa is its distinguishing mark, and through that pathway the teachings of Mahavira have had an important effect on Hindu and Buddhist belief. Mohandas Gandhi, the father of modern India and the teacher of worldwide nonviolent political action, is the outstanding modern example.

### *Analyze and Interpret*

Do you think the Jains' insistence on avoiding violence and coercion is practical in today's world? Could you imagine yourself living as a Jain?

**HistoryNow™**

***To read more about the Jain respect for life, point your browser to the documents area of* HistoryNow.**

which changed the old Vedic religion into something different. The ***Mahabharata*** *(Great Story)* is the world's longest poem. It contains about 200,000 lines, relating the exploits of the gods and some of their favored heroes on Earth. The most popular part, known by all Hindus, is the ***Bhagavad-Gita***, a segment in which the god Krishna instructs a warrior, Arjuna, in what is entailed in being a human being who strives to do good and avoid evil to his fellows. This new Hinduism was capable of arousing strong adherence among ordinary souls by giving them a meaningful guide to moral and ethical belief. In the second Patterns of Belief box, an excerpt from the *Mahabharata* gives a good example.

Both Buddhism and especially Hinduism in time evolved into many subdivisions, or sects, which worshiped somewhat differently and had different gods and prophets. All of these sects are notable for their tolerance toward others; in contrast to the historical Western religions and Islam, they do not assert that there is but one true path to heaven.

PATTERNS OF BELIEF

## An Excerpt from the *Bhagavad-Gita*

**Of the myriad Hindu sagas and poems,** the *Bhagavad-Gita* is the most popular and the best known among Westerners. Indian holy men and parents have also used it to teach moral behavior to succeeding generations. It is a part of the larger poem *Mahabharata*, a tale of the distant and mythical past, when two clans fought for supremacy in India. Just before the decisive struggle, one of the clan leaders, the warrior Arjuna, meditates on the meaning of life. His charioteer, who is the god Krishna in human disguise, answers his questions. Arjuna regrets having to kill his opponents whom he knows and respects, but Krishna tells him that his sorrow is misplaced because what Arjuna conceives of as the finality of death is not that:

You grieve for those beyond grief,
and you speak words of insight;
but learned men do not grieve
for the dead or for the living.
Never have I not existed,
nor you, nor these kings;
and never in the future
shall we cease to exist.
Just as the embattled self
enters childhood, youth, and old age,
so does it enter another body;
this does not confound a steadfast man . . .
Our bodies are known to end,
but the embodied Self is enduring,
indestructible, and immeasurable;
therefore, Arjuna, fight the battle!
He who thinks this Self a killer
and he who thinks it killed,
both fail to understand;
it does not kill, nor is it killed.
It is not born,
it does not die;
having been,
it will never not be;
unborn, enduring,
constant, and primordial,
it is not killed
when the body is killed.
Arjuna, when a man knows the Self
to be indestructible, enduring, unborn,
unchanging, how does he kill
or cause anyone to kill? . . .
Weapons do not cut it [the Self],
fire does not burn it,
waters do not wet it,
wind does not wither it.
It cannot be cut or burned;
it cannot be wet or withered,
it is enduring, all pervasive,
fixed, immobile, and timeless. . . .
The Self embodied in the body
of every being is indestructible;
you have no cause to grieve
for all these creatures, Arjuna!

### *Analyze and Interpret*

What does Krishna attempt to show Arjuna about the nature of his duty as a warrior? Is his counsel coldhearted or realistic, in your view? How could devout Hindus take comfort from this poem?



**History Now™**

*To read the* **Bhagavad-Gita,** *point your browser to the documents area of* **HistoryNow.**

## Development of the Caste System

By the end of the Gupta Period, the caste system founded by the Aryan conquerors reigned supreme. It had grown ever more refined in its applications and more complex in its structure as time passed. Subcastes had multiplied and were determined by geographic, ethnic, and kinship factors as well as the traditional social and economic categories. Along with the restructured Hindu belief, caste had become one of the two defining factors in the lives of all Indians. At the bottom were the outcastes or untouchables, who were condemned to a marginal existence as beggars, buriers of the dead, and dealers in animal products that were thought to be polluting. Above them were hundreds of varieties of farmers, craftsmen, and merchants, as well as laborers, each of which constituted a more or less closed grouping with its own (unwritten) rules of religious belief and social conduct (dharma).

Although caste members tended to belong to a distinct occupation, caste membership could also differ according to its territory or doctrines. For example, members of the

Ellora, Bombay, India/Bridgeman Art Library

**Ellora Cave Temples.** The immensity of these constructions can be gathered in this photo of one of the several courtyards dug out of the solid rock. The work is believed to have started around 600 C.E. Over the centuries, Hindu, Jain, and Buddhist artists and laborers contributed.

caste that specialized in credit and money lending in Calcutta were not members of the caste that dominated the same activity in Bombay or in Delhi. They could be seen as higher or lower in the intricate gradings of social prestige that caste imposed. Although it was possible to raise one's status by marriage with a higher-caste member, it was also possible to debase oneself by marriage to a lower one. It seems that impoverished members of the high-prestige castes who sought material advantage from marriage with a lower, but wealthy, individual attempted the usual rationalizations. All in all, such mixed marriages with their attendant changes of caste were rare in India, and the stratification of society, which commenced in Aryan times, grew ever stronger.

By about the ninth or tenth century C.E., the system had become so entrenched as to be a fundamental pillar of the revitalized Hindu culture. It was the cement holding the nation together, giving everyone a definite, easily

SOCIETY AND ECONOMY

## Caste and Diet

**Among the strongest ties** of Indian society since its history's beginnings is caste and the dictates of individual and group behavior that it enforces. The tradition that one's caste is the ultimate determinant of what can and cannot legitimately be done by an individual has been unshakable, even in contemporary India, where—at least in rural regions—it has resisted challenges and innovation with great tenacity. It was still more potent in early times, when the descendants of the Aryan invaders ruled. A recent summary of Indian social structure notes the following rules about diet and distance:

> An individual in a caste society lives in a hierarchical world. It is not only the people who are divided into higher and lower groups, but also the food they eat, the dress and ornaments they wear, and the customs and manners they practise. In India's dietetic hierarchy the highest castes are usually vegetarians and teetotallers. Even in meat there is a hierarchy: the highest non-vegetarian castes eschew chicken, pork, and beef. Wild pork is superior to domestic pork, since the village pig is a scavenger. Eating beef in rural India means eating carrion and it comes accordingly under a double ban. Liquor is prohibited to the high castes.
>
> Elaborate rules govern the acceptance of cooked food and water from another caste. Food cooked with ghee [a type of melted butter], milk, or butter is called pakka food and may be accepted from inferior castes. Kacca food, on the other hand, is food cooked in water and it may be accepted only from one's own or equivalent or superior castes. When two castes are contending for superiority, they stop accepting cooked food or water from each other. . . .
>
> Each caste has a culture which is to some extent autonomous: there are differences in dress, speech, manners, ritual and ways of life. . . . The concept of pollution plays a crucial part in maintaining the required distance between different castes. A high caste man may not touch a low caste man, let alone accept cooked food and water from him. Where the two castes involved belong to either extreme of the hierarchy, the lower caste man may be required to keep a minimum distance between himself and the high caste. In Kerala, a Nayadi had to keep 22 meters away from a Nambutri and 13 meters from a Tiyan, who himself had to keep 10 meters from a Nambutri.

### *Analyze and Interpret*

Can you think of certain advantages that being born into a caste society might afford even to low-caste people? Do you think India can develop a true democracy and stay wedded to a caste system in personal interrelations?

Source: N. K. Srinivas, *The Structure of Indian Society* (Delhi: Hindustan, 1980).

comprehended place in society. Yet at the same time, the caste system created permanent barriers among individuals—separations that persist today. The modern Indian constitution, adopted after independence in 1947, outlaws caste privilege and guarantees all Indians equality before the law. Yet the old categories persist, especially in the villages, where about 75 percent of Indians still live. (See Society and Economy for more on "Caste and Diet.")

## Social Customs

How did the Hindu masses organize their day-to-day lives? For Indians as for most early peoples, blood ties were the basis of social life. The extended family was universal: in-laws, cousins, and second and third generations all lived together under the same roof or in the same compound. The oldest competent male always exercised authority. Polygamy (the practice of having several wives) was common, as was concubinage for those who could not afford another wife. Children, especially the oldest boy, had an honored place and were often pampered.

Females were clearly and unequivocally subservient to the male. Women were expected to be good wives and mothers and to let the husband decide everything that pertained to affairs outside of the house. Marriage was arranged early in life by the parents of the bride and groom. As in most societies, marriage was primarily an economic and social affair, with the feelings of the individuals being distinctly secondary. Ideally, the girl was betrothed (formally engaged) immediately after coming into puberty, at about age thirteen or fourteen, and given into the care of her much older husband soon after. The reality usually differed, however, as many families began to betroth children as young as one to two years of age to ensure that they would have proper partners, always within their caste. The actual wedding did not take place until both parties were at least at the age of puberty, however. The wife was to be the faithful shadow of her husband and the bearer of children, preferably sons. A barren wife could expect that her husband would take additional wives to ensure the continuance of the family name, much as among the Chinese. Divorce was rare among the upper castes; we know little about the others.

Considerable evidence indicates that in early times, Hindu women, at least in the upper classes, had more freedoms than in other ancient societies. The Rigveda, for example, makes no mention of restricting women from public affairs, and women composed some of the numerous sacred texts, but later this freedom declined. In the *Mahabharata* epic, composed about 400 B.C.E., the female's status is generally inferior to that of any male. The veiling and strict social isolation of women among Hindus was reinforced with the Muslim conquests in the twelfth century. From that time onward, the Hindu population began a much stricter seclusion of respectable women and treated them as the property of fathers and husbands.The position of widows was especially pitiful. A widow was expected to be in permanent mourning and never to remarry. She was looked on with disdain, even by her relatives, and as the bringer of bad luck. It is no wonder that some women chose to follow their dead husbands into voluntary death through ***sati***, the ritual suicide of a wife after her husband's death, which was so shocking to Westerners. Actually, it seems, few widows, even in the priestly castes that were supposed to be a model to others, ever went so far in their devotion. But on occasion, a widow did fling herself into the flames of the cremation pyre, which was the usual way to dispose of bodies in India.

### *Sexuality*

One of the attributes of Hindu culture that is noted by almost all foreigners is its readiness to accept all forms of pleasure that the day might bring. In sharp contrast to Jewish and Christian suspicion of the senses' delights, Hinduism taught that human beings had a positive duty to seize pleasure where they might, so long as dharma was not violated. This was particularly the case in terms of sexual matters, which were given prominence in the famous *Kama Sutra,* composed some time before the first century C.E. as a treatise on one of the four spheres of Hindu life.

Prostitutes were as common in Indian life as elsewhere. Many were attached to the temples, where their services were offered to those who donated for the temples' support. Others were similar to the Greek *hetairae,* educated and artful women who served the upper class and held a position of general respect. Although the sacred texts denounced prostitution as being unworthy, the attitude of the ordinary man and woman was apparently more flexible. The Indian male's attitude toward women was marked by a strong duality: woman is both saint and strumpet, to be cherished and to be guarded against. The goddess Kali, who is sometimes pictured as a maternal guardian and sometimes as a demonic destroyer, is the classic example (see Chapter 5).

## India and East Asia

The culture and customs of Hinduism were rarely disseminated to other peoples. The Hindu faith was peculiarly interwoven with the historical experience and ancient beliefs of the peoples of the Indian subcontinent. Lacking a sacred book that defined a uniform dogma, Hindus normally showed little or no interest in converting others to the path of righteousness or initiating them into the mysteries of dharma. Most Hindus are, and have always been, residents of India.

There was, however, a major exception to this rule. In part of Southeast Asia, Indian colonies were gradually established during the sixth through the thirteenth centuries C.E. (see Chapter 18). Why this emigration started, why it continued, and who participated are questions that cannot be answered; historical records and other types of evidence are lacking. Clearly, though, these colonies must have been the result of invitation rather than conquest and were small in comparison with their host population. We know of but one example of Indian conquest in Southeast Asia over this lengthy period. Local rulers must have recognized the advanced civilization of the subcontinent as desirable in certain aspects for their own subjects. Precisely what the colonists offered is not certain and probably varied from place to place and situation to situation. It seems reasonable to assume that the Indian element functioned generally as teachers and administrators. Whether Brahmin priests, craftsmen, or artists of some type, the Asian hosts saw them as useful and nonthreatening instructors or models, and they allowed them to settle in numerous places. Indians seem always to have remained a small minority, and the relationship between hosts and guests was both peaceable and productive.

The Southeast Asians were highly selective in what they chose to adopt, however. They rejected major aspects of Hindu culture, notably the caste system, which never spread into Asia beyond India. The adoption of Indian custom by the host nation was normally limited to linguistic, commercial, and some artistic spheres. Certain elements of Hindu religious and philosophical belief were introduced into the native animisms. What eventually emerged was a mélange of the flexible Hindu theology and ceremonies with the native belief and practice. Southeast Asian religion remains to this day one of the outstanding examples of *syncretism* (mixed-source belief).

Buddhism succeeded Hinduism in India's cultural exports to the east. As their religion declined in India proper, thousands of Buddhist monks were encouraged to emigrate and establish their monasteries and temples among the peoples of the Asian islands and mainland. Eventually, by about the eleventh century, Buddhist practice completely supplanted Hinduism in Myanmar, Thailand, Cambodia, Laos, and Vietnam. The Hindu worldview seems to have depended largely on the peculiar traditions and conditions of the Indian peninsula for its flourishing, particularly on caste.

Not all of the Indo-Asian contacts were primarily religious or cultural. By about 1000 C.E., merchants and mariners from southern India were carrying on a lively trade in luxury items with Southeast Asian and South Pacific ports. Cinnamon, pepper, cloves, nutmeg, and Chinese silk were trans-shipped via South Indian ports across the western Indian Ocean and eventually to the Near East and the Mediterranean. Arab and other Muslim entrepreneurs carried on most of this lucrative trade, but the commercial colonies established in the islands were Indian.

In the large **Khmer** kingdom of Cambodia, both Hindu and Buddhist merchants, craftsmen, and artists found markets and patrons. The largest building in the world devoted to religion is the temple (***wat***) of **Anghor** in present-day northern Cambodia. It was built as a Hindu shrine under Indian inspiration and possible supervision

**ANGHOR WAT.** The enormous Buddhist temple at Anghor in Cambodia was the spiritual and political center of the ancient empire of the Khmer people. After the empire's fall, it was buried under jungle foliage for many centuries.

Tim Page/Corbis

in the tenth century. Somewhat later it was converted into a Buddhist temple. After the conquest of the Khmers by the neighboring Thais in the twelfth century, the great temple was neglected and forgotten for 700 years. Only since World War II has it been reclaimed from the surrounding jungle and become a major tourist attraction.

If the Khmers were the most notable partners of Indian cultural exchange on the mainland, the maritime empire of Srivijaya based on the island of Sumatra expanded Hinduism throughout the huge Indonesian archipelago. Originally a small city-state, Srivijaya had become a large state by the seventh century and remained so for 300 years. By about 1000 C.E., its power had sufficiently declined as to allow a successful piratical conquest by one of the south Indian principalities, Chola. For the next two centuries, Srivijaya served as the partner of Chola in organizing the commerce of the nearby islands and Malayan peninsula. The upper classes became Hindu and spread the religion widely. As in India, the absorptive Hindu belief took myriad forms in Southeast Asia, sometimes so merging with the local animisms or with Buddhism as to be almost unrecognizable to outsiders.

## Summary

India, in its golden or classical age (which was much longer than the classical age of the Greeks or most other peoples), saw the slow evolution of a civilization that was centered on the quest for understanding the relation between the earthly and the unearthly, between material reality and spiritual reality. Both Hindu and Buddhist beliefs evolved into forms quite different from their originals; in time, the revived Hinduism became again the faith of the vast majority. Written history is scarce until modern times because of the predominantly oral culture. We know that the Gupta Dynasty was a particular high point; after it collapsed in the fifth century C.E., the subcontinent broke up into political fragments, often ruled over by non-Indians in the North.

Beginning with the Islamic invasions stemming from Afghanistan in the eleventh century, North and South went their separate ways, though they remained linked by the Hindu faith. Priestly and commercial migrants from the South into Southeast Asia established colonies and a Hindu presence there among the upper classes. In the North, waves of Turkic peoples eventually were able to conquer the natives in the twelfth century and set up a Muslim sultanate at Delhi that ruled much of the subcontinent for the next several centuries.

Indian science, particularly mathematics, ranked near or on par with the world's most advanced types. In the temple ruins and the cave shrines that dot the peninsula, we can also obtain at least a minimal appreciation of the Indians' achievement in the arts.

## Identification Terms

Test your knowledge of this chapter's key concepts by defining the following terms. If you can't recall the meaning of certain terms, refresh your memory by looking up the boldfaced term in the chapter, turning to the Glossary at the end of the book, or working with the flashcards that are available on the *World Civilizations* Companion Website: **http://history.wadsworth.com/adler04.**

Ajanta Caves
Anghor Wat
*Bhagavad-Gita*
Brahman
Delhi sultanate
Kalidasa
Khmers
*Mahabharata*
Rigveda
*sati*
Shiva
Upanishads
Vedas
Vishnu

## Test Your Knowledge

Test your knowledge of this chapter by answering the following questions. Complete answers appear at the end of the book. You may also take this quiz interactively and find even more quiz questions on the *World Civilizations* Companion Website: **http://history.wadsworth.com/adler04.**

1. Hindus believe that the Vedas
   a. are sacred texts that introduced a caste system for society.
   b. are a remnant of the Aryan days that are no longer relevant.
   c. must be studied in old age.
   d. are forgeries by Westerners.
   e. were brought to their country from Afghanistan.
2. The best-known and most beloved Hindu scripture is the
   a. Rigveda.
   b. Upanishads.
   c. *Bhagavad-Gita.*
   d. Sangha.
   e. book of Vedas.
3. A peculiar facet of Indian civilization was its
   a. lack of interest in mathematics.
   b. avoidance of the pictorial arts.
   c. slowness in producing a literary culture.
   d. strong tendency toward political centralization.
   e. refusal to portray religious subjects in its art.
4. The major source of foreign troubles for India has been its
   a. sea frontiers to the east.
   b. borders with China.
   c. resident colonies of foreign traders.
   d. frontier with Afghanistan.
   e. lack of strong military leadership.
5. Southeast Asians experienced Hindu culture
   a. as a result of Indian conquests.
   b. in a selective and adapted fashion.
   c. mainly among the lower classes.
   d. both b and c.
   e. as one imposed on them arbitrarily.
6. The religion that suffered most severely from the Muslim Turks' invasion of India in the twelfth century was
   a. Christianity.
   b. Hinduism.
   c. Buddhism.
   d. Jainism.
   e. Sikhism.
7. The Jains are especially concerned to
   a. avoid killing any creature.
   b. avoid being shamed by others.
   c. spread their religion.
   d. be seen as superior to Hindus.
   e. reject animal sacrifices.
8. The last native dynasty to rule over the greater part of the Indian subcontinent was the
   a. Guptas.
   b. Afghans.
   c. Maurya.
   d. Delhi sultans.
   e. Ghaznivids.
9. Mahmud al-Ghazni and his troops were
   a. Persian.
   b. Arabs.
   c. Turks.
   d. Mongols.
   e. Afghans.
10. It is believed that the Arabic numerals used today originated in
   a. Saudi Arabia.
   b. western Afghanistan.
   c. Dravidian India.
   d. the Ajanta region.
   e. Gupta India.

## InfoTrac College Edition

Visit the source collections at

**http://infotrac.thomsonlearning.com**

and use the Search function with the following key terms:

Hinduism   Upanishad   Rigveda   *Mahabharata*

## Wadsworth History Website Resources

Visit the World History Resource Center at **http://history.wadsworth.com/world** for a wealth of general resources and the *World Civilizations* Companion Website at **http://history.wadsworth.com/adler04/** for resources specific to this textbook.

## HistoryNow

Enter *HistoryNow* using the access card that is available for *World Civilizations*. *HistoryNow* will assist you in understanding the content in this chapter with lesson plans generated for your needs. In addition, you can read the following documents, and many more, online:

The Jain Respect for Life   The *Bhagavad-Gita*

*Tzu-kung asked about the true gentleman. The Master said, "He does not preach what he practices until he has practiced what he preaches."*
The *Analects* of Confucius

# 17 EMPIRE OF THE MIDDLE: CHINA TO THE MONGOL CONQUEST



| | |
|---|---|
| 221–206 B.C.E. | QIN DYNASTY |
| 202 B.C.E.–220 C.E. | HAN DYNASTY |
| 220–580 C.E. | CHINA DIVIDED |
| 580–618 C.E. | SUI DYNASTY REUNIFIES CHINA |
| 618–907 C.E. | TANG DYNASTY |
| 960–1279 C.E. | SONG DYNASTY |

THE TREMENDOUS VITALITY and flexibility of Chinese civilization in the 1,500 years we examine in this chapter have no match in world history, anywhere. The longest-lived continuous political organism in the world, China was in these years able to combine the stability of an Egypt with the adaptability of a Japan. The government centered on the person of an emperor who, although by no means divine, was able to inspire the loyalty of a great many talented and ambitious servants in his bureaucracy—the world's first to be based more on merit than on birth. When the regime was at peace and working as designed, the life of the common people was about as good and secure as ever seen in the ancient world. Prosperity was widespread, and cities thrived while the villages were secure. When the regime broke down, however, the country fell into anarchy with cruel results for all. But for most of these 1,500 years, anarchy was held at bay, the emperor was seen by all to be the authentic Son of Heaven, and the arts and sciences prospered.

## THE QIN EMPEROR: FOUNDATION OF THE STATE

The last years of the Zhou Dynasty (see Chapter 6) were a sad tale of governmental collapse and warring feudal lords. By about 500 B.C.E., effective central government had become nonexistent, and a long period of intra-Chinese struggle known as the **Era of the Warring States** ensued until 220 B.C.E. It is significant that many of the outstanding philosophical contributions of Chinese thinkers—Confucian, Daoist, and Legalist—matured during this period. They aimed at either restoring proper order to a world gone astray or making it tolerable.

The relatively small northwestern state of Qin (Ch'in) adopted the Legalist doctrines wholeheartedly in the mid-200s (see Chapter 6). Guided by them, the Qin ruler managed to reunify the country by a combination of military force and administrative reorganization. The dynasty thus founded would have a short span, but the general

Bridgeman Art Library

**The Great Wall.** The golden light of sunset illumines a stretch of "the only earthly object visible from an orbiting space vehicle." The wall extends more than 1,800 miles in the present time, but much of its mainly mudbrick construction has been allowed to sink back into the surrounding terrain through lack of upkeep. Started on a more modest scale by the First Emperor in the 200s B.C.E., it was last renewed by the early Ching Qing dynasts in the 1600s.

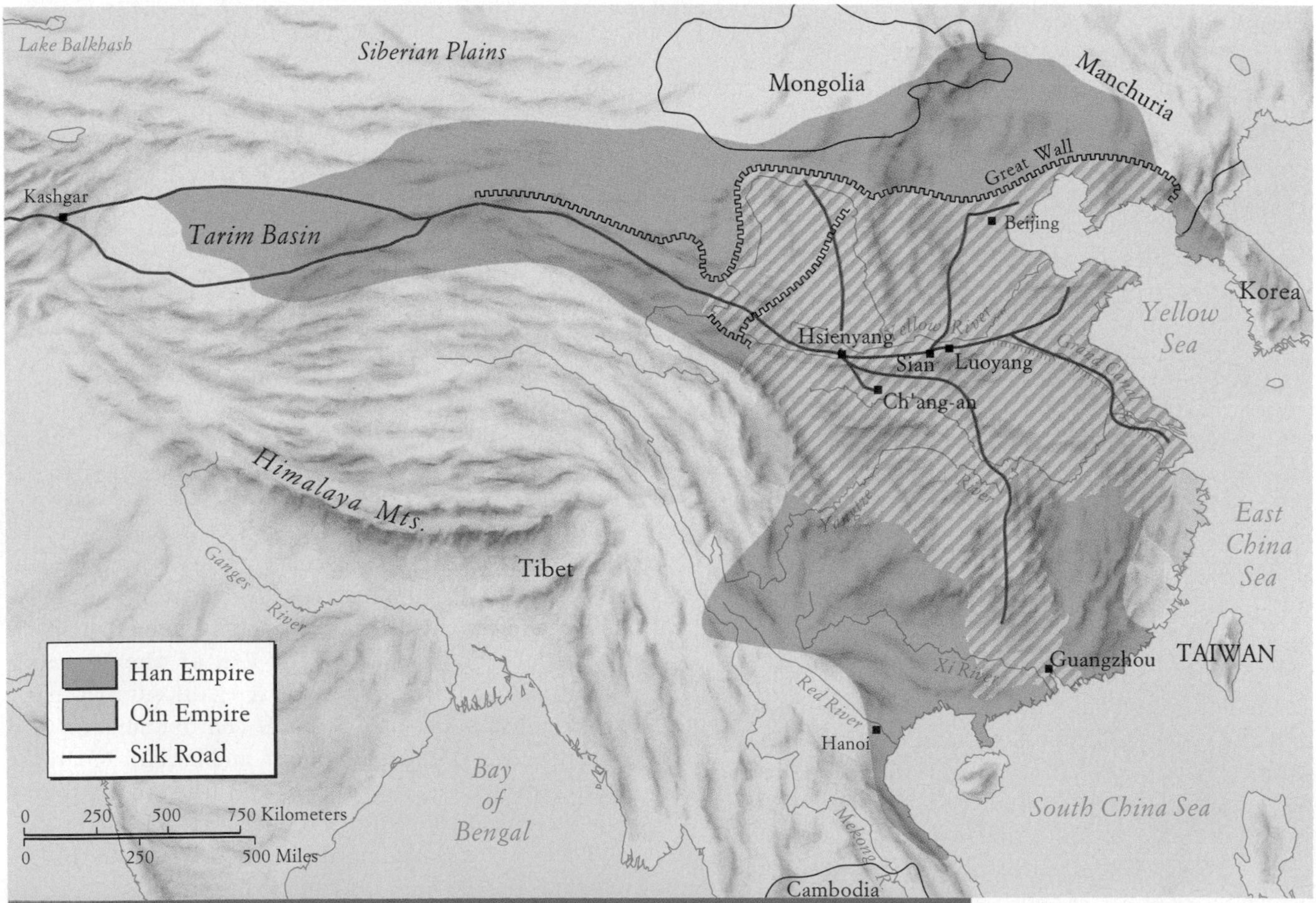

**MAP 17.1** *The Qin and Han Empires*

The Han Empire greatly expanded the borders established by the Qin emperor. By the mid-Han Period, China's extent westward reached well into central Asia.

Wolfgang Kaehler/Corbis

**Warriors from the First Emperor's Tomb.** The accidental discovery of the tomb of Shih Huang-di, the First Emperor, at Sian in 1974 revealed the terra cotta statues of more than 7,000 warriors buried with him. Armed with spears, swords, and bows, and presumably meant as a bodyguard in the next world, each of the life-sized warrior statues has individual facial features taken from living models.

principles that guided the Qin rule could still be traced in Chinese government until the twentieth century. Even the name of the country in Western languages comes from Qin. It was an awesome achievement.

The king of Qin (246–221 B.C.E.) and later **First Emperor** (221–210 B.C.E.) ruled all China only eleven years, but he made an imprint that was to last, as he boasted, "10,000 generations." Shih Huang-di, as he was called, was a man of tremendous administrative gifts and huge personality defects. Both were felt by his subjects. His generalship overwhelmed the rival Chinese states. In only nine years (230–221 B.C.E.), the six largest of them fell to Qin armies or surrendered. At once the process of centralization got under way along ruthless Legalist lines. Guided by the minister Li Si (Li Shu), the emperor set out to make his rule irresistible and to eliminate the entrenched feudal aristocracy. The country was divided into administrative units that persisted throughout later history. The emperor fixed weights and measures, made the size of the roads uniform so that all carts would fit the ruts, and introduced the first standard units of money. The system of writing was standardized so effectively that it is almost the same in the twenty-first century as it was then.

As a defense against the constant series of barbarian invaders from Mongolia, disconnected barriers that had been erected by various princes in the north and northwest were unified into the first version of the Great Wall (see Map 17.1). A whole list of other massive public works was started, including the tremendous imperial palace at Sian and the emperor's tomb in which more than 7,000 life-sized clay soldiers were buried with him. (They were discovered in 1974 and are now being restored.) Under Shih Huang-di, China expanded to both north and south. The region around Guangzhou (Canton) came under his control; it was to be China's premier port for many centuries to come. First contacts were made with the Vietnamese and with several other civilized and less civilized peoples to the west and south.

The First Emperor's reign also had its negative side. Convinced by his Legalist principles of the inherent evil of human nature, Shih Huang-di apparently became paranoid and engaged in torture and other harsh treatment of his subjects and officials. He especially hated the doctrines of Confucius, which he regarded as a menace to his style of autocratic rule, and ordered a **burning of the books** in a vain attempt to eradicate the Confucian philosophy from Chinese consciousness, an episode deeply resented by later generations. Shih Huang-di died of natural causes in 210, but the cruelties and heavy taxation that marked the First Emperor's reign assured that his son and weaker successor would not last long as ruler. The son's overthrow in 206 was followed by the establishment of one of the most successful of all the Chinese dynasties, the **Han Dynasty**, which lasted until 220 C.E.

## The Han Dynasty, 202 B.C.E.–220 C.E.

Han rule occurred almost simultaneously with the Roman heyday, and these two great empires of the East and West had other similarities as well. Both were basically urban in orientation, although the populations they ruled remained decidedly rural and peasant. Both depended on a nonhereditary officialdom to carry out the distant imperial court's will. Both taxed the peasants heavily, making themselves vulnerable to the loss of loyalty as the central government's power to enforce its will began to weaken. Both collapsed under the combined impact of invading barbarians and widespread regional revolts.

Why are the Han monarchs considered the primary shapers of China's national consciousness? Even more than Shih Huang-di, the Han rulers greatly expanded the Chinese frontiers west, north, and south. Under them, China took on more or less the geographic boundaries that it has retained ever since (except for the much later conquest of Tibet). These conquests brought the Chinese out of their isolation and into contact with the rest of the world for the first time. In the Han Period, the Chinese traded with Indians and even Romans, both directly and (mainly) through intermediaries. Chinese commercial contacts soon expanded into massive cultural influence on the Japanese, Koreans, and Vietnamese. Everywhere on the Asian mainland north of India and east of Cambodia, the "men of Han," as the Chinese called themselves, became the controlling factor in military, political, and commercial life.

The Han dynasts were not revolutionaries in any sense. They kept what the Qin had done to create the state and ensure its continued existence, while relaxing the strictness and brutality that had made the First Emperor hated. The restrictions against Confucianism were thrown out, and the Han rulers in fact adopted Confucius as the quasi-official philosopher of the regime.

This was a changed Confucianism, however, with more emphasis on the obedience owed by the children to the father—that is, by the people to the government. The person of the emperor was given a sacred aura by the renewed emphasis on the "mandate of Heaven," the theory that the gods approved and supported the emperor and all his actions until they showed otherwise. They showed otherwise by allowing the imperial armies to be defeated by the barbarians, by allowing rebels to succeed, or by permitting the provincial administration to break down. In that way, the path was opened to a new ruler or new dynasty, as the mandate of Heaven was being transferred to more competent hands. Using this logic, Chinese philosophers and political figures maintained the unbroken legitimacy of the central government, while recognizing and permitting the fairly frequent and violent overturns of individual rulers.

## *Arts and Sciences*

Under the Han rulers, arts and letters experienced a great upsurge in quality and quantity. History came into its own as a peculiarly congenial mode of understanding the world for the Chinese, who are perhaps the globe's most historically conscious people. Records were scrupulously kept, some of which have survived in the scripts of the noted historian Sima Qian (Ssu-ma Ch'ien) and the Pan family of scholars dating from the first century C.E. As a result, we know far more about ancient China than almost any other part of the civilized world insofar as official acts and personages are concerned. History for the Chinese, of course, was the record of what the uppermost 1 percent did and thought—the peasantry and other ordinary folk were beneath consideration as a historical force. (See the Law and Government box for anecdotes written by the great classical historian of China, Sima Qian.)

Mathematics, geography, and astronomy were points of strength in Han natural science, all of which led directly to technological innovations that were extremely useful to Chinese society. Some examples include the sternpost rudder and the magnetic compass, which together transformed the practice of navigation. The Han Period saw the invention of paper from wood pulp, truly one of the world's major inventions. By about the fifth century C.E., paper had become sufficiently cheap as to enter common usage, paving the way for the advent of wood-block printing.

Medicine was a particular interest of the Chinese, and Han doctors developed a pharmacology that was even more ambitious than the later Muslim one. Also, acupuncture first entered the historical record during the Han Period. Despite the persistence of superstition and folk medicine, a strong scientific tradition of healing through intensive knowledge of the parts of the body, the functions of internal organs, and the circulation of the blood was established during this period. This tradition has

**Two Equestriennes.** These ladies are mounted astride like men and control their mounts without benefit of stirrups. These are Han Dynasty clay statuettes. The fact that these women are mounted puts them into the tiny minority of females allowed to go abroad without male accompaniment.

LAW AND GOVERNMENT

## The Virtuous Officials

**THE GREATEST OF THE CLASSICAL HISTORIANS** of China, Sima Qian (c. 150–90 B.C.E.), wrote during the rule of the ambitious emperor Wu, who had expanded China's borders at the price of imposing a cruel, Legalist-inspired internal regime.

Sima Qian regretted the emperor's style of governance, but he could not, as court historian, openly oppose it. Instead, he indirectly criticized Wu by writing about the virtue of emperors and officials in the distant past, when Confucian principles guided the government and proper attention was paid to the welfare of the people. These appeals to traditional virtues were well understood by Sima's audience. Some anecdotes from these histories follow; the first deals with the capable minister Sun Shu-ao, the second with the righteous Kung-i Hsiu, and the third with the relentlessly logical Li Li. All three men served kings of the Zhou Dynasty.

> The people of Ch'u liked to use very low-slung carriages, but the king did not think that such carriages were good for the horses and wanted to issue an order forcing the people to use higher ones. Sun Shu-ao said, "If orders are issued too frequently to the people they will not know which ones to obey. It will not do to issue an order.
>
> "If your Majesty wishes the people to use high carriages, then I suggest that I instruct the officials to have the thresholds of the community gates made higher. Anyone who rides in a carriage must be a man of some social status, and a gentleman cannot be getting down from his carriage every time he has to pass through the community gate."
>
> The king gave his approval, and after half a year all the people had of their own accord made their carriages higher so that they could drive over the thresholds without difficulty. In this way, without instructing the people Sun Shu-ao led them to change their ways.
>
> Kung-i Hsiu was an erudite of Lu. Because of his outstanding ability he was made prime minister. . . .
>
> Once one of his retainers sent him a fish, but he refused to accept the gift. "I always heard that you were fond of fish," said another of his retainers. "Now that someone has sent you a fish, why don't you accept it?" "It is precisely because I am so fond of fish that I don't accept it," replied Kung-i Hsiu. "Now that I am minister I can afford to buy all the fish I want. But if I should accept this gift and lose my position as a result, who would ever provide me with a fish again?"
>
> Li Li was director of prisons under Duke Wen. Once, discovering that an innocent man had been executed because of an error in the investigation conducted by his office, he had himself bound and announced that he deserved the death penalty. Duke Wen said to him, "There are high officials and low officials, and there are light punishments and severe ones. Just because one of the petty clerks in your office made a mistake there is no reason why you should take the blame."
>
> But Li Li replied, "I occupy the position of head of this office and I have made no move to hand the post over. . . . I receive a large salary and I have not shared the profits with those under me. Now because of an error in the trial an innocent has been executed. I have never heard of a man in my position trying to shift the responsibility for such a crime to his subordinates!" Thus he declined to accept Duke Wen's suggestion.
>
> "If you insist that as a superior officer you yourself are to blame," said Duke Wen, "then do you mean that I, too, am to blame?" "The director of prisons," said Li Li, "must abide by the laws which govern his post. If he mistakenly condemns a man to punishment, he himself must suffer the punishment; if he mistakenly sentences a man to death, he himself must suffer death. Your Grace appointed me to this post precisely because you believed that I would be able to listen to difficult cases and decide doubtful points of law. But now since I have made a mistake in hearing a case and have executed an innocent, I naturally deserve to die for my offense." So in the end he refused to listen to the duke's arguments, but fell on his sword and died.

### *Analyze and Interpret*

How effective do you think Sima's critiques of his emperor would be, given the Chinese reverence for traditional virtues in their governors? What effect would such an approach have, do you think, in present-day American politics?

Source: Excerpted from *Records of the Grand Historian*, trans. Burton Watson (New York: Columbia University Press, 1961), vol. 2, pp. 413–418. Reprinted with permission from the publisher.

endured alongside the rather different approaches of the Western and Muslim medical practices and long ago made China one of the permanent centers of the healing arts.

In the fine arts, China continued to produce a variety of metallic and ceramic luxury items, which increasingly found their way into the Near East and even into Rome's eastern provinces. The production of silk was both an economic asset of the first rank and a fine art; for nearly 1,000 years, the Han and their successors in China maintained their monopoly, until the Byzantines were finally able to emulate them. Bronze work, jade figurines, and fine ceramics were particularly notable among the plastic arts, while poetry, landscape painting, and instrumental music figured prominently as part of the heritage of the Chinese educated class. The written language had become fully standardized by the end of the Han Period, and its adoption throughout the empire meant that educated citizens, regardless of their ethnic affiliation, could read and write the same way. This achievement was to be crucial for Chinese national unity.

## The Economy, Government, and Foreign Affairs

The Han Period also saw major advances in economic affairs. Canals were built, and the road system was extended to the south and west, improving communication and commerce. Large cities and numerous market towns came into existence. In the Chinese scale of values, merchants did not count for much: they were considered to be more or less parasites who lived off the work of the craftsmen and tillers of the land. They had none of the social prestige of the scholars or of the government officials and wealthy landowners. But they were still recognized as vital to the well-being of all and were seldom exploited as in some other civilizations. The urban markets were impressive: in both the variety of goods and the number of merchants, they seemed to have surpassed those of other contemporary civilizations, including Rome's.

Iron came into common use after about 500 B.C.E., greatly aiding the expansion of agriculture. The increased availability of iron allowed newly conquered lands in the north and northwest to be plowed. An improved horse harness was developed, enabling Chinese farmers to make much better use of the animal's strength. (This particular idea would not reach the West for another six centuries.) Animal fertilizer and crushed bones (phosphate) were applied to the land systematically. Through such methods, Chinese agriculture became the most productive in the world. The peasantry normally produced enough food for a steadily growing urban population, as well as themselves. The horrible famines that came to be common in Chinese history were a later occurrence.

Han government was more complex than anything seen earlier in China. The government functioned through the bureaucracy, whose members were chosen by a written examination on the principles of correct action in given situations. The examinees were expected to be thoroughly familiar with the Confucian texts and commentaries on them, and by this time Confucius had become the mainstay of the Chinese educational system. To be eligible to take the final examination in the capital, candidates had to pass several preliminary tests and be recommended by their teachers at all levels. This **meritocracy** was designed to bring the best talent to the service of the central government, regardless of social origin. Despite many individual interventions to ensure preference for sons and grandsons, a hereditary nobility was not allowed to develop. The **mandarins** (scholar-officials) of China were to give generally good service to their countrymen for most of the next 2,000 years.

Han China also achieved some notable successes in foreign affairs. Nomads such as the Toba, the White Huns, and others issuing out of the great reservoir of pastoral peoples in northern Asia (the present-day Siberian plains) were repeatedly successful in wresting a piece of the Han domain away, only to be rapidly integrated into Chinese civilization. Unlike India and the Middle East, China almost invariably absorbed and assimilated its nomadic invaders.

Peaceful contacts were made with India by traders and Buddhist monks; like the devout trader Fa-hsien (see Chapter 16), the Buddhists wished to learn more about the religion in the land of its birth. In the first century C.E., a Chinese trade mission was sent to make direct contact with the Romans in the Red Sea area. It reported back to the Han rulers that the Westerners' goods held little interest for China. The Chinese attitude that China had what the West wanted but the West had little to offer to the Middle Kingdom became steadily more rooted in the upper classes' mind as time wore on. Indeed, this belief was generally accurate, at least up to about 1500 C.E., but when it was no longer true, it proved difficult or impossible to change. It then turned into the sort of unimaginative defensiveness and worship of the past that would also handicap the Muslim world in the face of the aggressive European challenge.

The ambitious visions entertained by the Han rulers in time generated familiar problems. The enormous building projects started by the emperors or continued from the Qin Period, such as the building of the Great Wall and the grand mausoleums for the emperors, imposed heavy burdens on the common people. The bane of all Chinese governments, an exploited and rebellious peasantry, began to make itself heard from in the first century C.E. A reforming emperor, who in some ways resembled Rome's Augustus Caesar in his vision of the state, was killed before he could meet his goals. The result was an interval of chaos before order could be restored and the Later Han Dynasty established in 25 C.E.

## The End of the Dynasty

In time, following the inexorable cycle of Chinese dynasties, the Later Han broke down into anarchy, with warlords and peasant rebels ignoring the weakened or corrupt bureaucracy. For a time the Era of the Warring States was replicated. This time, though, only three contestants participated, and the anarchy lasted only 135 years instead of 250. Out of the conflict came two major political divisions: the North, which was dominated by the kingdom of Wei, and the South, where various princely dynasties took turns fighting one another for supreme power. The dividing line was the Yangtze River, which flows across almost the entire width of China (see Map 17.2).

During this partial breakdown, an immensely significant agrarian advance came about: the cultivation of rice

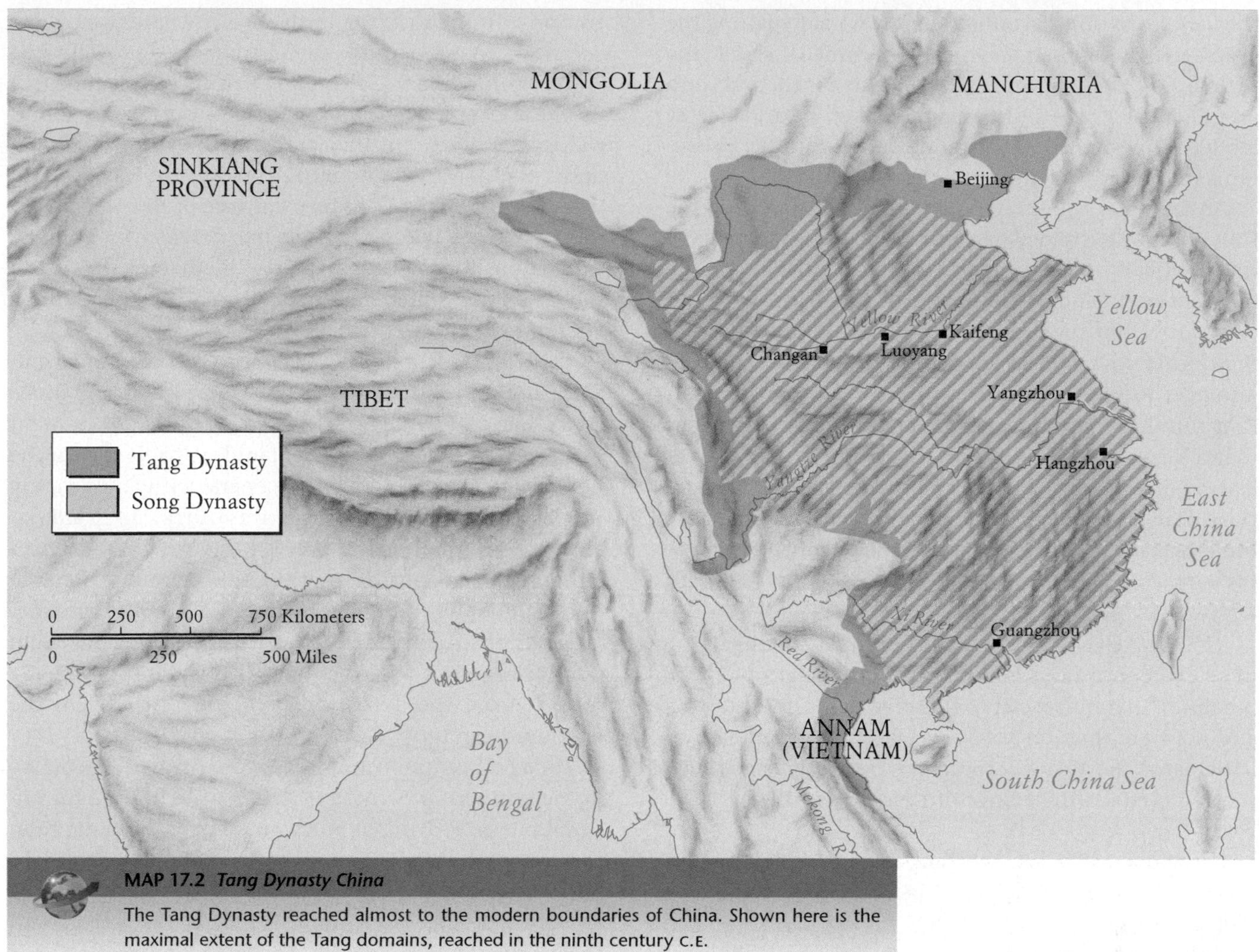


**MAP 17.2** *Tang Dynasty China*

The Tang Dynasty reached almost to the modern boundaries of China. Shown here is the maximal extent of the Tang domains, reached in the ninth century C.E.

in paddies (wet rice farming) gradually became entrenched in the South. This development was to be highly important for all later Chinese history, because the grain allowed the Chinese population to expand greatly without putting intolerable strains on the economy. A Vietnamese import into South China, rice requires a great deal of hand labor but produces more caloric energy per acre than any other grain crop. Rice enabled the population to grow and provided the work to keep the new hands busy. The South now began to rival the North in civilized development.

## The Tang Dynasty, 618–907

The brief Sui Dynasty (580–618) was followed by the line of the **Tang Dynasty** of emperors (618–907), who presided over one of the most brilliant epochs of China's long history. Like the Qin earlier, the two Sui rulers had reunified China and gone on to introduce unpopular but needed authoritarian reforms. Failed military expeditions against the northern nomads brought the Sui down in the course of a widespread rebellion. But their Tang successors continued their reforms while avoiding their military misadventures, thus paving the way for an economic advance that supported a rich cultural epoch.

The early Tang rulers' primary concern was to improve the state of the peasant tenants, who had recently fallen into much misery because of the rapacity of their landlords. The landlords had taken full advantage of the collapse of the Han government by shifting the burden of taxation to their tenants while increasing the rents charged them. The early Tang rulers adopted the *"equal field" system,* whereby the fertile land reverted to the state (that is, the imperial government) upon the death or old age of its peasant cultivator. It was then reassigned to another adult peasant in return for reasonable taxes and labor services. In this fashion, peasant needs and resources could be closely matched. For about a century there was a real improvement in the economic lives of the people.

The Tang re-created a generally efficient bureaucracy, which was firmly based, like the Han's, on Confucian ethics and the merit system. Although the wealthy and the families of officials often found ways of bypassing the exams or bribing their way into government service, the Tang open-examination system had so much to recommend it that it was still being employed in principle in modern times. Only the coming of democratic institutions in the early twentieth century ended its reign.

An imperial university originally created under the Han was now expanded to allow about 30,000 students to train annually for the demanding examinations. Only the very best candidates made it through this rigorous course to sit for the examinations that allocated posts at the central government level. Villagers would pool their resources to send a talented boy to a tutor and support him through the long years of preparation. They knew that if he were successful, he would bring back to the village far more than the cost to train him. Through Confucian ideals of family and the obligations of a gentleman, the official was made conscious of the debts he owed to his native place and would repay them over the rest of his active life.

The Tang also followed the Sui example in attempting to keep the mandarin officials loyal and incorruptible by ordaining that no official could serve in his home district and no more than once in any place. The Chinese thus anticipated the first European government to put such rules into effect (the France of King Louis XIV) by 1,000 years!

For about 150 years, the Tang dynasts were generally successful. From their capital Changan, they were active and aggressive in several directions. To the north and northwest, they managed either to win the barbarians' loyalties through judicious bribery or to defeat their incursions. To the east, the initial era of Chinese–Japanese cultural contacts opened, and the Japanese proved to be enthusiastic admirers of Chinese culture at this time (see the next chapter). Contact with the Korean kingdoms was more prickly, but this less numerous people still fell under the powerful magnetism of the splendid civilization to their south. The same was true of the Tibetans in the far west, who were just being touched by Chinese expeditions for the first time. The Vietnamese in the far south, on the other hand, steadfastly resisted Chinese attempts to colonize them.

In the mid-700s, the dynasty's successes ceased. An emperor fell under the sway of a beautiful and ambitious concubine and wholly neglected his duties; government was in effect turned over to her family. Unable to bear the humiliating situation longer, a general with a huge army rebelled, and the entire country was caught up in a devastating war from which the dynasty never recovered, although it did put down the rebels. Troubles on the northern borders mounted once again. Despite the brief intervals of strong rule in the early 800s, the Tang could not successfully quell the internal discontent that finally overwhelmed the dynasty with bloody anarchy in the later ninth century.

For a half-century China was again divided. Then, one of the northern provincial warlords made his bid for imperial power. Proving to be more adept as diplomat than as warrior, he was able to induce most of his rivals to join him voluntarily. The Chinese educated class always favored the idea of a single government center. Unlike Indians and the Middle Eastern peoples, educated Chinese regarded political fragmentation as an aberration, a throwback to

**Flight of the Emperor.** This painting dates from the Tang era and shows the artist's conception of the flight of emperor Ming Huan to safety from rebels who threatened his court. Note the primacy of the landscape over the human figures.

the time before civilization. They saw it as something to be avoided at all costs, even if unity entailed submission to an illegitimate, usurping ruler. When needed, the doctrine of the mandate of Heaven always provided a rationale for accepting new monarchs. Thus, they welcomed the coming of the **Song Dynasty**.

## The Song Dynasty, 960–1279

Armed with their newly discovered mandate, the successors to the Tang were able men. The Song rulers systematically promoted the many technical innovations that the Tang Period had produced and encouraged others. The most important of these was printing. At first printers used a separate carved wooden block for each page or column of ideographs, but by the eleventh century they had developed moveable wooden type, which sharply reduced the cost of printed material. Other labor-saving devices included the water pump and the spiral worm-drive for transport of liquids. Together, they revolutionized the use of irrigation, made mining less difficult and more efficient, and allowed the construction and use of locks, which made canal boats a more widespread and useful form of transport. Avenues of internal trade opened along the network of canals that linked the South with the North. These have been used ever since to move most of China's bulk goods.

Manufactures were much advanced by the invention of the waterwheel and the forge bellows. The abacus and the water clock enabled accurate measurement of quantity and of time. Perhaps the best known of all the Tang/Song inventions was gunpowder, which the Chinese used only for pyrotechnic entertainments for a long while but then adapted to warfare to a minor degree. Strong oceangoing vessels were armed with small rockets, for example, as defense against the frequent pirates. Gunpowder did not play a major role in Chinese military tactics until the 1200s, when it was used against the invading Mongols, who then carried it west to the Muslims and eventually the Europeans.

As in the Roman Empire and almost everywhere in the world, most people in Song China lived in villages, but the cities dictated the culture and defined the atmosphere of the empire. Along the canals in central and southern China sprang up several large cities, all with more than half a million in population. One of the largest was **Hangzhou**, whose delights and splendid vistas were described in wonder by the Venetian visitor Marco Polo (1254–1324) in the thirteenth century. (See the Society and Economy box for more details about Marco Polo.) Hangzhou was a port and grew in response to market forces and mercantile necessities rather than according to a government plan. Both Hangzhou and Kaifeng, the Song capital, are thought to have had more than a million inhabitants and contained all sorts of amusements and markets for rich and poor.

### Song Internal Policies

For the most part, the Song continued the government style and policies of the Tang Period. In the South, the bureaucracy they commanded worked well for an unusually long period of almost 300 years. Most decisions had to be made at the top in the capital, many by the emperor himself. By some estimates, only 30,000 officials were needed to govern this large empire (the size of all of Europe, with a much larger population). The habit of obedience and self-discipline was already deeply ingrained in the people, who were educated along Confucian lines and living for the most part in self-governing villages.

The generals of the large army were kept under tight control and were not allowed those liberties in the outermost provinces that had often degenerated into warlordism in the past. The rest of society looked down on the military; a popular saying held that soldiers were the lowest types of humans and that good men should not be turned into soldiers anymore than one would waste good iron to make nails. The military ranked even below the merchants, who gained somewhat in prestige during the Song Period but still occupied low rungs on the social ladder.

**Chinese Landscape.** The young court artist Wang Ximeng is credited with this panorama of an imaginary landscape set like a dream in vivid greens and blues. Wang lived in the early twelfth century under the Song Dynasty of emperors, but the techniques he employed date back to much earlier times.

The Palace Museum, Beijing

SOCIETY AND ECONOMY

## Marco's Millions

IN THE THIRTEENTH CENTURY, the Italian city-state of Venice was a notable power not only in the Mediterranean but also throughout Europe. Based entirely on its merchant navy, the tiny, aristocratically governed republic became rich from its carrying trade with the Byzantine Empire and the Muslim lands beyond. Venetian ships carried cargoes of silk, spices, precious stones and woods, ivory, jade, Chinese bronzes, and other luxury items for distribution throughout Europe. Their sailors returned with tales of wealth and wonders that awaited the venturesome in the vast Asian distances.

Among those who listened were Nicolo and Maffeo Polo, members of a merchant family. In 1261 they had journeyed as far as the Black Sea by ship and then overland along the Silk Road to China. The Italians stayed in the court of the Mongol emperor Kubilai Khan for a few years, then returned to Venice by sea. Several years later, they decided to repeat this strenuous journey, this time taking along Nicolo's seventeen-year-old son, Marco. After a tremendous series of difficulties, they succeeded in reaching Kubilai's capital at Beijing in 1275. Warmly received by the emperor, the Polos settled into a partly commercial, partly official life at the Mongol court.

Marco Polo, who quickly mastered Mongol and at least three other Asian languages, proved to be a particular asset. Enjoying the emperor's full confidence, he apparently traveled extensively as a government official, not only in China proper but also in other East Asian regions of the immense Mongol empire created by Chinghis Khan and his successors. These journeys gave Marco Polo opportunities to observe the customs, agriculture, commerce, and culture of several parts of Asia. For more than fifteen years, the Polos stayed on in Beijing. By this time the older men were anxious to return home, but the emperor was reluctant to part with them. In 1292, however, they persuaded him to allow them to depart, arriving in their hometown after a twenty-three-year absence in 1295.

Now a famous man, Marco Polo became an admiral in the Venetian navy. During a war with rival Genoa, he was captured and imprisoned briefly. His captors allowed him to pass the time by dictating his memoirs of his years in China, and these were published after Marco's release and return to Venice. The *Description of the World* by Marco Polo soon became a "best-seller" in several languages. It remained the most important source of European knowledge about Asia until the Portuguese explorers reached India in the early sixteenth century. Its detailed observations greatly expanded the sketchy data brought back by the occasional missionary or merchant who survived the hazards of a central Asian journey. Contemporary readers regarded much of the book, especially the sections on the richness and variety of Chinese urban life, as sheer lies and fantasies and referred to it satirically as "Marco's Millions." Not until the sixteenth century would his report be validated. A copy of the *Description of the World* accompanied Columbus on his first voyage.

### Analyze and Interpret

What does the ability of an Italian alien to rise to high position in the Mongol government tell you about the nature of the relation between the Mongols and the Chinese?

**HistoryNow™**

***To read Marco Polo's "Prologue to Travels," point your browser to the documents area of* HistoryNow.**

The Chinese economy reached an enviable state of smooth working and innovative production during this era. The final portion of the Grand Canal was completed in 611, an important link of the politically dominant North (the Yellow River plains) to the economically productive South (the Yangtze valley). A population estimated at more than 100 million by the end of the Song Period was supported in decent conditions. The introduction of a new hybrid rice from Annam (Vietnam) helped feed this large population. It was now possible to grow two crops per year in South China, doubling the land's productivity with little additional expenditure of energy or resources. The volume of domestic and foreign trade increased markedly, aided by the development and use of paper money and sophisticated banking and credit operations.

Silk was now joined by porcelain as a major luxury export article. Despite the risk of breakage, it was exported to many lands, including such distant places as the Arab colonies in East Africa. Large ships that used the magnetic compass and the sternpost rudder—both Chinese inventions—were built for the active trade with Japan and Southeast Asia. The itinerant Chinese traders as well as colonies of Chinese peoples throughout Asia have their ancestors in this (Song) period of prosperity.

## Foreign Affairs

Despite the triumphs and improvements in internal affairs under the Song Dynasty, China's control over its East Asian lands was drastically reduced from its high point during the Tang Dynasty. The emperors never succeeded in gaining firm control of the northern half of the country. Tibet and the far western province of Sinkiang were abandoned to the nomads who had continually contested the Han and Tang governments there. Fearful of the costs of reducing them to obedience, Vietnam and Korea were allowed to become autonomous regions, paying the Song a token tribute but effectively resisting any hints of Chinese sovereignty. The huge northeastern region of Manchuria, always a battleground between nomads and Chinese, broke away entirely.

These losses had a positive side, however. By giving up territories that were never firmly under China's hand, the Song were able to focus on the heartland, ruling the area between the Yellow and Yangtze rivers from their capital at Kaifeng. For two centuries the Song rulers and their large armies were able to repel the increasing pressures from the northern and western tribes, but in the twelfth century they weakened. Toward the end of the 1100s, they lost any semblance of control over the far west to the Mongols. By the mid-1200s, the Song had been defeated by the descendants of Chinghis Khan and formally gave up the north and center of traditional China to them. The Song were able to hold on for a brief time in the South, but in 1279 there, too, dominion passed into the hands of the Mongols under Kubilai Khan—the first and only time China has been conquered in its entirety by outsiders. The Mongol **Yuan Dynasty** thus began its century-long reign.

## Buddhism and Chinese Culture

The greatest single foreign cultural influence on China during the first millennium C.E.—and possibly ever—was the coming of Buddhism from its Indian birthplace. The Chinese proved responsive to the new faith, with all social and economic groups finding something in the doctrine that answered their needs. Buddhists believe in the essential equality of all. The enlightenment of the soul, which is the high point of a Buddhist life, is available to all who can find their way to it. Unlike Confucianism and Daoism, which are essentially philosophies of proper thought and conduct in this life and possess only incidental religious ideas, Buddhism, by the time it came to China, was a supernatural religion promising an afterlife of eternal bliss for the righteous. To the ordinary man and woman, this idea had far more appeal than any earthly philosophy. Another aspect of Buddhism's appeal was that the Mahayana version (see Chapter 5) adopted in China was very accommodating to existing beliefs—there was no conflict, for example, between traditional reverence toward the ancestors and the precepts of Buddhism in China.

The translation of Sanskrit texts into Chinese stimulated the literary qualities of the language, because the translators had to fashion ways of expressing difficult and complex ideas. Even more than prose, however, poetry benefited from the new religion and its ideals of serenity, self-mastery, and a peculiarly Chinese addition to classic Indian Buddhism—the appreciation of and joy in nature. Painting, sculpture, and architecture all show Buddhist influences, mostly traceable to India, but some original to China in their conceptions. From about the fourth century onward, China's high-culture arts were strongly molded by Buddhist belief. They not only portrayed themes from the life of the Buddha but also showed in many ways the religion's interpretation of what proper human life should be.

So widespread was Buddhism's appeal that inevitably a reaction set in against it. In part, this reaction was a political power phenomenon. In the 800s, the Tang Dynasty exploited nativist sentiment against the "foreign" religion to curb the worrisome autonomy of the wealthy and tax-resistant Buddhist monasteries. Most of their property was expropriated. But the reaction was also philosophical and intellectual in the form of Neo-Confucianism and a general revival of the Confucian credo.

The Neo-Confucians were philosophers who sought to change the world through emphasis on aspects of the master's thought most fully developed by his later disciple, Mencius (370–290 B.C.E.). In Neo-Confucianism, love and the responsibility of all to all were the great virtues. Unlike the Daoists and Buddhists, the Neo-Confucians insisted that all must partake of social life. Withdrawal and prolonged solitary meditation were impermissible. They also thought that formal education in morals and the arts and sciences was an absolute necessity for a decent life—it could not be left to the "enlightenment" of the individual seeker to discover what his fellow's welfare required. The Confucians' efforts to hold their own against their Buddhist competitors were a major reason that the Song Period was so fertile in all philosophical and artistic fields.

Tang and Song era formal culture was supremely literary in nature. The accomplished official was also expected to be a good poet, a calligrapher, and a philosopher able to expound his views by quoting the "scriptures" of Confucian and other systems of thought. Skills in painting and music were also considered part of the normal equipment of an educated and powerful man. This was the ideal of the mandarin, the man who held public responsibilities and proved himself worthy of them by virtue of his rich and deep culture. This ideal was often a reality in Tang and later dynastic history.

## Summary

The Chinese imperial style was molded once and for all by the ruthless Legalist known as the First Emperor in the third century B.C.E. The Qin Dynasty he founded quickly disappeared, but for four centuries his Han successors built on the foundations he left them to rule a greatly expanded China. Softening the brutal Qin policies to an acceptable level, the Han dynasts made Confucianism into a quasi-official philosophy.

After the Han's dissolution and a period of anarchy, the 500 years of the Tang and Song dynasties comprised the Golden Age of Chinese culture. Despite intermittent internal dissension, the imperial government promulgated and was supported by a vision of proper conduct that was Confucian in essence and widely subscribed to by the educated classes.

Internally, both the Tang and the Song saw a tremendous development of the economy and its capacity to maintain a rapidly growing and urbanizing population. Thanks in large part to advances in agriculture, few, if any, other civilizations could rival China's ability to supply all classes with the necessities of life. A series of technological inventions had immediate practical applications. It was also a period of extraordinary excellence in the fine arts and literature, which were supported by a large group of refined patrons and consumers in the persons of the landowning gentry and the mandarin officials. Buddhist influences were pervasive in both the popular and gentry cultures, rivaling but not overshadowing traditional Confucian thought.

In foreign affairs, the long seesaw struggle with the northern nomadic barbarians was finally lost when the Mongols of Kubilai Khan defeated the last Song rulers and established the Yuan Dynasty. All of China thus fell under alien rule for the first and only time. Also during the Song, China took on more or less its modern territorial outlines, with its withdrawals from Vietnam, Korea, and Mongolia. Cultural and commercial contacts with Japan were expanded, and there was extensive commercial intercourse with the Muslims to the west and the Indians to the south.

## Identification Terms

Test your knowledge of this chapter's key concepts by defining the following terms. If you can't recall the meaning of certain terms, refresh your memory by looking up the boldfaced term in the chapter, turning to the Glossary at the end of the book, or working with the flashcards that are available on the *World Civilizations* Companion Website: **http://history.wadsworth.com/adler04/**.

burning of the books
Era of the Warring States
First Emperor
Han Dynasty
Hangzhou
mandarins
meritocracy
Song Dynasty
Tang Dynasty
Yuan Dynasty

## Test Your Knowledge

Test your knowledge of this chapter by answering the following questions. Complete answers appear at the end of the book. You may also take this quiz interactively and find even more quiz questions on the *World Civilizations* Companion Website: **http://history.wadsworth.com/adler04/**.

1. The Qin First Emperor attained power by
   a. orchestrating a palace coup.
   b. playing on the superstitions of his people.
   c. assassinating the previous emperor.
   d. achieving triumph in battle.
   e. forging a political alliance with his strongest rival.
2. Which of the following was *not* a Chinese invention?
   a. The magnetic compass
   b The waterwheel
   c. Paper from wood
   d. Decimals
   e. Gunpowder

3. Which of the following was not formally a requirement for joining the Chinese bureaucracy?
   a. Single-minded dedication
   b. Extensive formalized education
   c. Connections with the higher social classes
   d. Passing of written examinations
   e. A high degree of intellectual ability
4. The Tang Dynasty was extremely influential in Chinese history as the
   a. developer of the mandarin system of scholar-officials.
   b. creator of the village democracy.
   c. reformer of the military.
   d. originator of the canal system.
   e. creator of an imperial university system.
5. The Song Dynasty was finally overturned by the
   a. Mongol conquerors.
   b. Korean invaders.
   c. Japanese pirates.
   d. Tang Dynasty.
   e. army of Shih Huang-di.
6. Marco Polo served as an official in the service of
   a. the Song emperor.
   b. the Mongol emperor.
   c. an Italian embassy to the Chinese government.
   d. Indian visitors to the Chinese court.
   e. an emperor of the Tang Dynasty.
7. Chinese Buddhism was different from the original conceptions of Siddhartha Gautama in
   a. the rigidity and uniformity of its doctrine.
   b. its insistence on the lifestyle of a hermit.
   c. its supernatural religious element.
   d. its appeal to only the upper classes.
   e. its emphasis on the study of religious works.
8. Buddhism found many sympathizers in China because it
   a. offered immortality to all social classes.
   b. was an import from Korea.
   c. came from a civilization that the Chinese regarded as superior to their own.
   d. demanded the rigorous intellectual effort that the Chinese so admired.
   e. echoed their long-held reverence for nature.
9. The burning of the books by the First Emperor was followed by the
   a. Song Dynasty.
   b. Sui Dynasty.
   c. Mongol Empire.
   d. Tang Dynasty.
   e. Han Dynasty.
10. The Grand Canal linked the Yellow River Plains to
   a. the South China Sea.
   b. the Korean peninsula.
   c. the Yangtze valley.
   d. the Great Wall.
   e. northern India.

## InfoTrac College Edition

Visit the source collections at

**http://infotrac.thomsonlearning.com**

and use the Search function with the following key terms:

| | | |
|---|---|---|
| Han Dynasty | Tang Dynasty | Song Dynasty |
| China history | China | Buddhism |

## Wadsworth History Website Resources

Visit the World History Resource Center at **http://history.wadsworth.com/world** for a wealth of general resources and the *World Civilizations* Companion Website at **http://history.wadsworth.com/adler04/** for resources specific to this textbook.

## HistoryNow

Enter *HistoryNow* using the access card that is available for *World Civilizations. HistoryNow* will assist you in understanding the content in this chapter with lesson plans generated for your needs. In addition, you can read the following documents, and many more, online:

Marco Polo, *Prologue to Travels*

*In life there is nothing more than life; in death nothing more than death; we are being born and are dying at every moment.*
**Dogen, Thirteenth-Century Zen Master**

# 18 Japan and Southeast Asia



| Japan | |
|---|---|
| 400s–500s | Yamato state formed |
| 604 | Shotoku's *Seventeen Point Constitution* |
| 710–794 | Nara Period |
| 794–1185 | Heian Period |
| 1185–1333 | Kamakura shogunate |
| 1336–1573 | Ashikaga shogunate |

| Southeast Asia | |
|---|---|
| c. 500 | Earliest mainland states founded |
| c. 900–1300 | Khmer, Burmese, Srivajayan empires flourish; Dai Viet Kingdom |
| 1250s–1280s | Mongol invasions; destruction of Malacca sultanate; Islam comes to Indonesia |
| 1400s | Anghor abandoned; rise of Thai Kingdom |

The island nation of Japan emerges from the mists of prehistory in the early centuries C.E., when Chinese travelers begin to report on their adventures there. Geography explains both Japan's receptivity to Chinese influence and its ability to reject that influence when it wished. Japan could adapt foreign ideas and values to its needs without having to suffer military or political domination from abroad. For the first thousand years of recorded Japanese history, until about 1500 C.E., the Japanese state was successful in this adaptation, fitting imported governmental and cultural institutions to existing customs and the requirements of the native society.

## Very Early Japan

The Japanese islands (the four main ones are Hokkaido, Honshu, Kyushu, and Shikoku) are situated off the Korean peninsula and Siberia, separated from the mainland by 120 to several hundred miles of open water (see Map 18.1). Together, these mountainous volcanic islands are about the size of California. Only about one-fifth of the surface area is suitable for agriculture, and Japan's climate ranges from sub-arctic in the extreme north to temperate on the main island of Honshu. The Japanese people are considered the most homogeneous in Asia, and this homogeneity has played a major role in the country's history right up to the present day. There has been no need to assimilate numerous immigrants, nor to make conscious concessions to other cultures. Where the original settlers came from is uncertain, but the Koreans and Japanese are much closer ethnically than the Chinese and Japanese. The native oral language of Japan is entirely different from Chinese. The written language, which originally borrowed heavily from written Chinese, is still different in many ways.

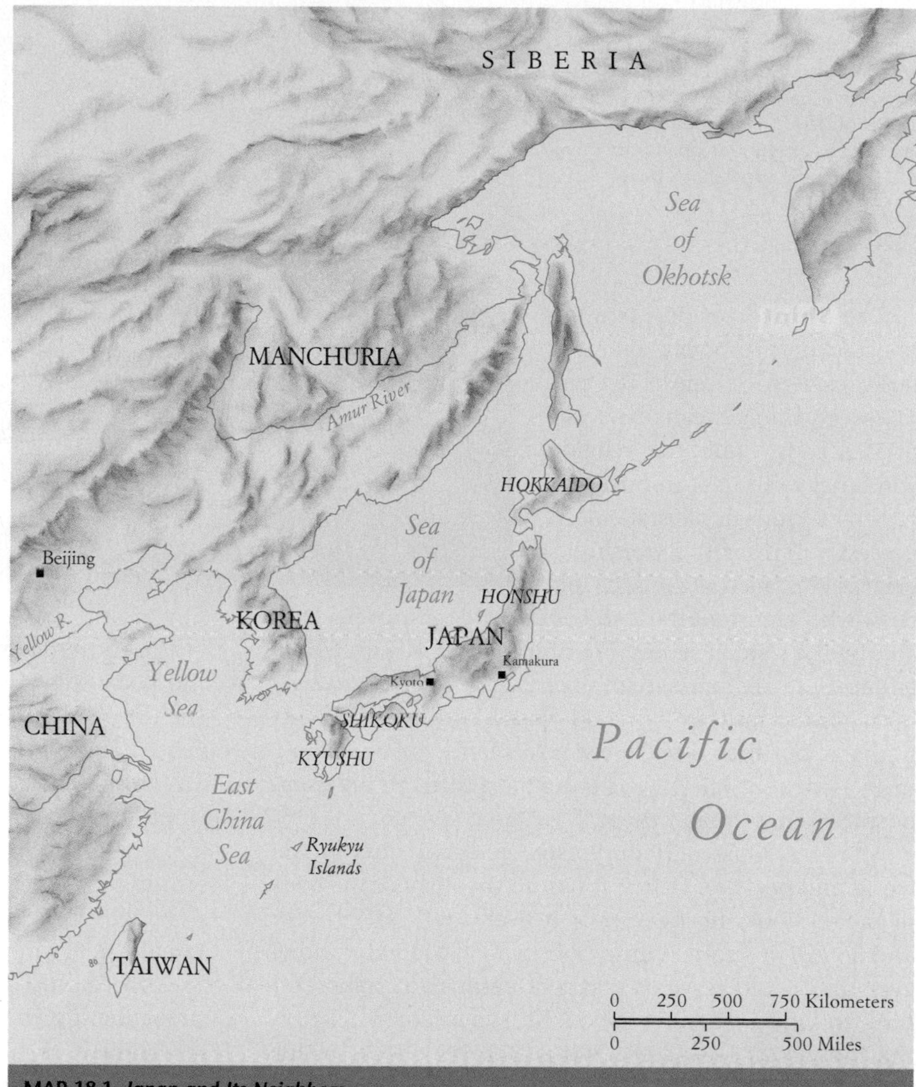


**MAP 18.1** ***Japan and Its Neighbors***

The hundred-mile interval between Japan and Korea was not difficult to cross even in ancient times, and Chinese cultural influences came into Japan via Korean intermediaries until direct contacts were established in the seventh century.

According to ancient Japanese legends, the Japanese people are the descendants of the Sun Goddess (Jimmu Tenno), who continues to have a special relationship with the country through the person of the emperor. For many centuries, the Japanese thought of the emperor as divine, a status that was only finally and formally rejected by terms of the Japanese peace treaty after World War II. Archaeological data reveal that as early as the middle of the first millennium B.C.E., a semicivilized society known as the Jomon people inhabited the southern island of Kyushu, burying their dead chieftains in elaborate mounds with many pottery figures. The Jomon became masters of wet-rice culture, the nutritional basis of all later Japanese civilization. Their success in adopting rice growing laid the foundations for the Yayoi culture a few centuries later, when these people (who seem to have been the ancestors of the present day Japanese) moved northward from their original home on Kyushu island. It was the Yayoi who eventually organized the first regional governments and produced the first Japanese state. The first written records do not appear until as late as the eighth century C.E., however; before that we must rely on archaeology and the occasional surviving travel reports of Chinese visitors.

## Buddhism and Shinto

The two major religious belief systems of both ancient and modern Japan are the import Buddhism and the native Shinto. Buddhism in Japan, as everywhere, proved capable of undergoing many mutations and adapting to local needs. The special Japanese versions are Zen, the Pure Land, and the Nichiren sects, which gradually developed after the introduction of the religion in the sixth century from Korea. Distinctions among the sects became clearer as time passed (see the discussion later in the chapter).

Buddhism gave Japanese religion a much broader and nobler intellectual content. Its insistence on ethical action and compassion for the weak and unfortunate was as beneficially transforming to Japanese life as it had been earlier in India and China. In Japan more than elsewhere in Asia, Buddhism emphasized meditation techniques. For the more intellectually demanding followers, Buddhist beliefs could be complex, but for most Japanese believers, the religion was relatively simple and joyful in its acceptance of things-as-they-are and in its anticipation of happiness in an eternal Heaven.

Calmann & King, London, UK/Bridgeman Art Library

**HORYU-JI PAGODA.** The massive Shinto temple is the world's oldest wooden building still in use. The 700-year-old structure stands in a park in the ancient Japanese capital of Nara. The pagoda style of architecture was brought to Japan from China and found new adaptations there.

The **Shinto** religion is a native Japanese product, but it is fairly close to Chinese Daoism. The word *Shinto* means "the way of the gods," and the religion combines a simple animism, in which all kinds of natural objects possess a spirit, with a worship of great deities, such as the Sun Goddess, who are immortal and benevolent but not perceivable by the human senses. The Shinto legends with which all Japanese are familiar speak of a time when all things, even stones and trees, could speak and interact with humans, but they were forced into silence later and now must evidence their powers to humans through the *kami,* or spirits, that inhabit them.

Shinto is a basically optimistic, guilt-free view of the world and personal ethics. It has no theology of the gods or sacred book, no heaven or hell or wrathful Yahweh, and no Fall of Adam. Shinto is supremely adaptable, however, and could serve as a sort of permanent underpinning to whatever more advanced, supernatural religion the individual Japanese might prefer. It persists to this day in that role.

## Government and Administration

For the most part, Japan has a mountainous and broken terrain, which, as in the Greek example, helps explain why the process of creating a central government with effective controls was peculiarly slow and subject to reverses. The beginning of organized large-scale government occurred in the Yamato Period in the fifth and sixth centuries C.E. At that time the term *Japan* indicated a collection of noble clans, who ruled over the commoners by a combination of military and economic power familiar to students of feudal Europe. The Yamato, the biggest and most potent of these clans, ruled over a good-sized arable area in central Honshu near what is now the city of Osaka. The Yamato claimed direct descent from the Sun Goddess and founded what was to become the imperial family of the Japanese state. This family, or more precisely the dynasty that began with the Yamato clan leaders, has never been overturned. The present-day emperor is considered the direct descendant from the earliest Yamato, although he is no longer seen as a divinity.

During this early period, the relationship between Japan and Korea was important for both countries (see below). There appear to have been invasions as well as much commerce in both directions, and many Koreans lived among the Japanese until well into the first millennium C.E. From Korea came several major cultural imports—most important, Buddhism, which arrived in Japan in the sixth century.

Buddhism soon became the favored viewpoint of the Yamato state's upper class, and by the beginning of the seventh century, it was used as the vehicle of a general strengthening and clarification of the role of the central government in Japan. In 604, Prince Shotoku, a Yamato leader and a devout Buddhist, offered the *Seventeen Point Constitution,* which is the founding document of the Japanese state. It was not really a constitution in the modern sense but rather a list inspired by Buddhist and Confucian doctrine of what a government and a loyal citizenry *ought* to do. It has had great influence on both the theory and practice of political science in Japan ever since.

The way of affairs in China was the general model for the Seventeen Points, so to put his constitution into effect, Shotoku sent selected youths to China for a period of study and training under teachers, artists, and officials. In the seventh century, thousands of Japanese were thus prepared for governmental responsibilities and were also trained in the arts and techniques of Tang China. The Chinese model was particularly apparent in government. The village was the foundational unit of all civic affairs. The state's territory was divided into administrative units similar to the Chinese provinces and districts. Tax money was now to be paid to the central government by the peasantry, thus weakening the local lords who had previously been the tax collectors. A ministry of eight officials was created to advise and assist the emperor, whose position was greatly strengthened by the official adoption of the Sun Goddess myth. In all, this was one of the earliest and most impressive examples of deliberate cultural transfer from one people to another in history.

The Chinese example had a powerful influence in most public and many private spheres, but it was not overwhelming. The Japanese soon showed they were confident of their own abilities to distinguish what was useful and what was not. For example, they adopted the Tang equal field system, in which land was frequently redistributed among the peasants to attempt to ensure equity, but the Japanese soon changed this system to allow an individual to have transferable (salable) rights to a parcel of productive land no matter who actually tilled it. Another example was the Japanese approach to bureaucracy. Although they admired the efficiency of the Chinese bureaucracy, they did not imitate it. The concept of competitive meritocracy was and remained alien to Japanese thinking. Having competitive exams open to all threatened deep-rooted Japanese social values. Government remained an aristocratic privilege in Japan; the lower classes were not allowed to attain high posts, regardless of their merit.

## The Nara and Heian Periods, 710–1185

For seventy years after the death of Prince Shotoku in 622, the reforms he advocated were continued by members of the Fujiwara clan, which had intermarried with the Yamato and were to be the leading actors in Japanese government for the next couple of centuries. The first capital, Nara, was established in central Honshu, in 710. Buddhism was especially popular among the Nara clans, and when a Buddhist monk named Dokyo attempted to use his following in the numerous monasteries to usurp political power, there was a strong reaction. Dokyo also allegedly used his position as chaplain to the empress to further his political ambitions. When the empress died, Dokyo was driven into exile. This experience may explain why in all the remainder of Japanese history there have been only two other female rulers.

The reaction against the Buddhist monks and monasteries did not mean a rejection of the religion. In the early ninth century, Japanese visitors to the mainland became acquainted with the Tendai and Shingon sects of Buddhism and took them back to Japan. These sects, in contrast to the earlier version, featured magical elements and promises of salvation to all, which made them highly popular, and they spread quickly. During this period, Buddhism in Japan started a steady transformation from a narrow preoccupation of the court aristocrats into a vehicle of popular devotion.

In 794, the imperial court was moved to a new town called Heian (modern **Kyoto**), where it remained until modern times. At this time, the aristocrats checked further Chinese influence by severing relations with the mainland—one of the several episodes of deliberate seclusion with which Japanese history is studded. For about a century, contacts with China and Korea were strictly limited, while the Japanese aristocracy devoted themselves to organizing the government and creating a cultural/artistic style that was uniquely their own. The process lasted several centuries and was more or less complete by about 1200.

Government during the Heian era quickly became a struggle—almost always concealed—between the Chinese model of an all-powerful emperor ruling through a bureaucracy and the kind of rough-and-ready decentralized feudalism that had marked the Yamato state before the reforms. The feudal aristocrats soon won out, as they proved more adept at securing the tax from rural peasant lands than the central government. Little by little, the emperors were reduced to ceremonial figures, accorded great respect but essentially without means of imposing their will. A series of provincial noble families—above all, the **Fujiwara clan**—were able to make themselves the real powers. The Fujiwara ruled from behind the throne by arranging marriages between their daughters and the children of the monarchs and then having themselves nominated as regents. They remained content to dominate indirectly and did not try to displace the ruler.

This system of disguised rule by powerful families at court was to become a recurrent part of Japanese life under the name of the **shogunate**. The true head of government was the *shogun,* or commander-in-chief of the imperial army. The shoguns stayed in the background but decided everything that mattered, while the divine emperors conducted the ceremonies.

After this system had worked fairly well for two centuries, it began to break down as rival clans finally found ways to break the Fujiwara monopoly. In the outlying provinces, and especially in eastern Japan, warriors known as *bushi* were experiencing a rise in power and prestige. The bushi, or **samurai**, as they are better known in the West, were the executors of the will of the large landholders and the enforcers of public order in a given locality. In their outlook, means of support, and demanding code of conduct (***bushido***), the bushi were similar to the medieval knights of western Europe. There were, however, some important differences: the samurai's code (see the Law and Government box) included no provision for chivalry toward women or for generosity toward a beaten opponent, who expected to die by ritual beheading. This made the samurai a more brutal and menacing figure to the ordinary man and woman.

Using their samurai effectively, the rival clans threw out the Fujiwara regents and then fought one another for supremacy. The house of Minamoto eventually won out and introduced the **Kamakura shogunate**.

LAW AND GOVERNMENT

## Samurai Honor

**The samurai warriors** were bound to a strict code of conduct that, among other things, told them that they were expected to die rather than surrender. Because it was commonplace for the victorious commander to order the execution of the captured enemy, the samurai usually had no choice in the matter. An expert in medieval Japanese affairs tells us:

> Those of the defeated who had not been killed in action often had recourse to suicide. We are in possession of many accounts of these suicides, whether the warrior cut open his abdomen with his dagger (*hari-kari* or *seppuku*), or threw himself onto his sword, or preferred to perish in his burning house with his most faithful servants and vassals (*junshi*, or collective suicide). When he was about to be taken prisoner, Yoshitsune "stabbed himself under the left breast, plunging the blade in so deeply it all but came out again in his back; then he made three further incisions, disemboweling himself and wiping the dagger on the sleeve of his robe." Thereupon his wife sought death at the hands of one of their vassals.

Some warriors' suicides were deliberately spectacular for the edification of their descendants:

> Yoshiteru climbed up on the watchtower of the second gate, from where he made sure that the Prince was now far away (for he had taken his place and his clothes in order to deceive the enemy and give his lord time to flee). When the time had come, he cut the handrail of the tower window so that he could be better seen, calling out his lord's name: "I am Son-un, prince of the blood of the first rank, Minister of Military Affairs and second son of Go-Daigo Tenno, ninety-fifth emperor since Jimmu Tenno. . . . Defeated by the rebels, I am taking my own life to avenge my wrongs in the Beyond.
>
> Learn from my example how a true warrior dies by his own hand when Fate plays him false!" Stripping off his armor, he threw it to the foot of the tower. Next he took off the jacket of his underdress with its tight fitting sleeves . . . and clad only in his brocaded breeches, he thrust a dagger into his white skin. He cut in a straight line from left to right, cast his entrails onto the handrail, placed the point of the sword in his mouth and flung himself headlong towards the ground.

Tower of London, London, UK/Bridgeman Art Library

**Samurai Armor.** The expenses entailed in properly outfitting a samurai were sometimes borne by the daimyo, who was his lord and to whom he was pledged for lifelong service, but the two swords carried by the warrior were always his personal property. By the end of the Kamakura era in the 1300s, the samurai were a separate class in Japanese society, a position retained until the late nineteenth century.

> This kind of death was admired by the samurai and deemed heroic and worthy of praise by generations to come. Many put an end to their life in this way.

### *Analyze and Interpret*

How did this suicidal concept of military honor influence the medieval history of Japan? What does the threat of Yoshiteru to "avenge my wrongs in the Beyond" seem to say about the nature of the life to come?

Source: From L. Frederic, *Daily Life in Japan at the Time of the Samurai* (New York: Praeger, 1972), p. 190f.

# The Kamakura Period, 1185–1333

The Kamakura Period of Japan's history (in most aspects, a Japanese version of European feudalism) was marked by the complete domination of the country by the samurai and their overlords in the clan aristocracy. The powers of the imperial court in Kyoto declined nearly to the vanishing point. Political leadership at any level depended on two factors: control of adequate numbers of fighting men and control of adequate *shoen* to support those fighting men.

The ***shoen*** were parcels of productive land, sometimes including villages. They had originally been created in the early Heian era as support for monasteries or rewards to servants of the emperor for outstanding service. Their critical feature was their exemption from the central government's taxing authority. Whereas most Japanese land was always considered the property of the emperor, lent out to his favored servants, the shoen and the rights to their use and income, called ***shiki***, were strictly private and remained outside normal laws.

A monastery or official who owned shoen would often convey them to a more powerful person, who would allow the original owner to continue as tenant under his protection. Thus, the ownership and use system became ever more complex and eventually resembled the European system of feudal vassalage. It was not unusual for a shoen to have three to five "lords" who each had some special rights (*shiki*) to the land and its produce. Shoen and shiki were thus the currency used by the aristocrats to pay their samurai. In this sense and others we noted earlier, the samurai closely resembled the European knights, but there were enough differences that some authorities see the samurai as quite different from the knights and reject the idea that Japanese society in this era was basically the same as medieval European.

One of the chief differences was the ***bakufu***, or military government under the shogun, which had no European equivalent. The shogun, always a member of the dominant clan controlling the emperor, was supposedly the executor of the emperor's will as head of the army. In fact, he was totally independent and the real ruler of Japan. The Kamakura Period derives its name from the small town of Kamakura where the shogun of the Minamoto clan resided—quite separate from the imperial court in Heian/Kyoto.

Perhaps the most dramatic demonstration of the way the shogun and his bakufu organization could lead the nation occurred in the late 1200s, when the feared Mongols under Kubilai Khan prepared to invade the islands (see Map 18.2). Having conquered China in its entirety and all of eastern Asia to Vietnam, the Mongols sought to do what the Chinese themselves had never attempted. Twice, the khan assembled armadas from his bases in Korea and landed on Kyushu, where his forces were met on the beach by the waiting samurai. The effectiveness of the Mongols' most potent weapon, their cavalry, was sharply limited by the terrain and by Japanese defenses, including a long wall along the coast that horses could not surmount. The Mongols called off the first invasion after fierce resistance led to a stalemate. The second attack in 1281 ended in a huge disaster when a typhoon (the *kamikaze*, or "divine wind") sank most of their ships and the 140,000 men on them. Mongol rule was thus never extended to the Japanese.

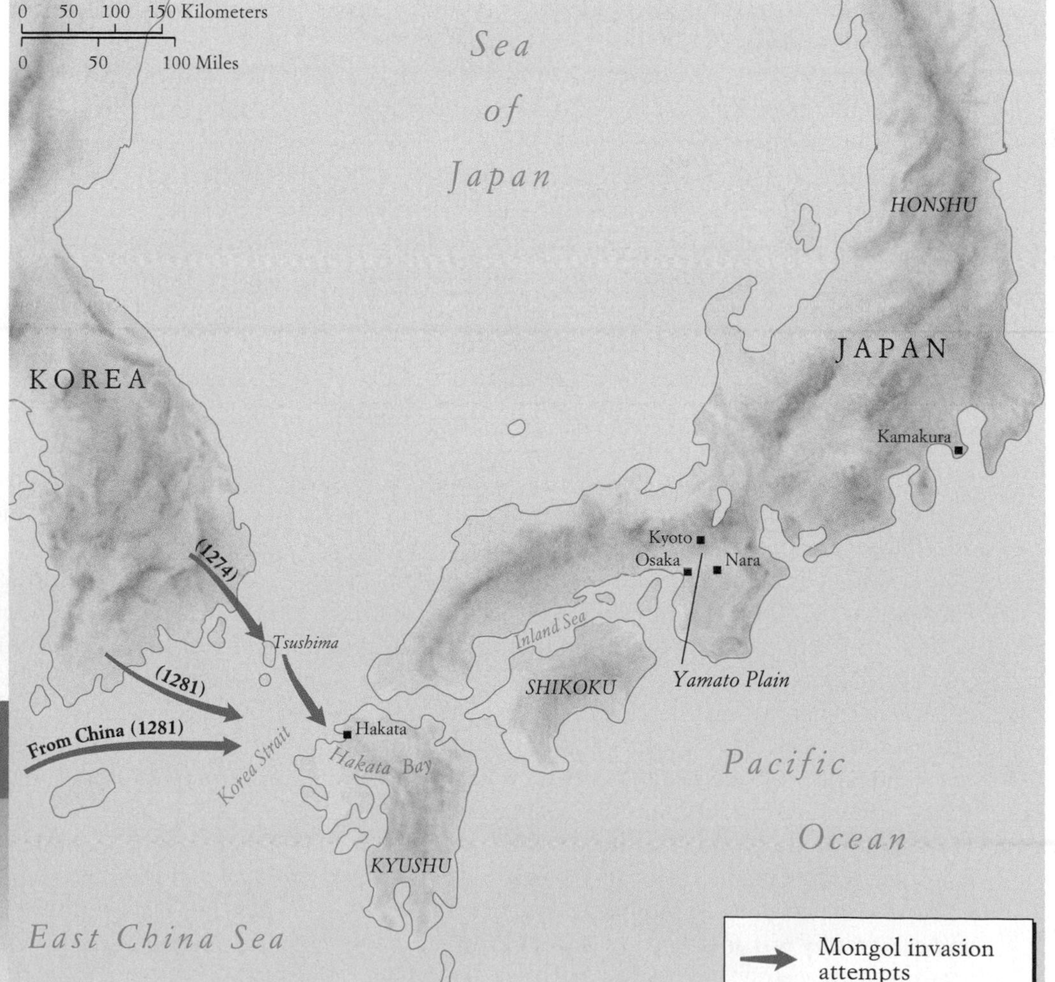


**MAP 18.2** ***Japan and the Mongol Invasion Routes in the Thirteenth Century***

From their bases in Korea and northern China, the Mongols mounted two invasion attempts against Japan within a seven-year period. Both were repulsed by the samurai gathered at Hakata Bay, aided by the kamikaze wind.

## The Arts and Culture in Medieval Japan

The partial severance of relations with China following the establishment of the capital in Heian allowed the Japanese full freedom to develop their own culture. Their language and literature show that they were vigorously imaginative. The Japanese and Chinese languages are radically different in both structure and vocabulary; the earliest Japanese writing was a close but necessarily clumsy adaptation of Chinese. This script was used in the eighth-century *Chronicles of Japan* (*Nihongi*) and the *Records of Ancient Matters* (*Kokiki*), the first Japanese books. In the Heian Period, the language was simplified and brought into closer conformity with oral Japanese. The gradual withdrawal from Chinese vocabulary and modes of expression forced the court authors to invent literary models and expressions of their own. Japanese writers thus evolved two *syllabaries,* written signs that were based on phonetics, rather than being ideographs or pictographs like Chinese, and could therefore be used to match the syllables of the spoken language—in other words, the beginnings of an alphabet.

The world's first novel, the famous ***Tale of Genji*** by the court lady Murasaki Shikibu (c. 976–1026), was written in the early eleventh century and tells us a great deal about the manners and customs of the Japanese aristocracy of the day (see the Arts and Culture box for an excerpt from Lady Murasaki). It reveals a culture of sensitive, perceptive people, who took intense pleasure in nature and in the company of other refined persons. The impressions left by the *Tale of Genji* are furthered by the other classic court tale of this era, Lady Sei Shonagon's *Pillow Book,* a collection of anecdotes and satirical essays centered on the art of love. Neither of these works owes anything to foreign models. The fact that their authors were women gives some indication of the high status of females among the educated class.

Poetry was the special strength of the early writers. Very early, the Japanese love of nature was evident. Prose was considered somewhat vulgar, and the domain of females, but poetry was for everyone—everyone, that is, in the tiny fraction of the population that partook of cultured recreations.

Japanese painting in the Heian era exhibited a marvelous sense of design and draftsmanship, following on the calligraphy practiced in the written word. Scenes from nature were preferred, but there was also a great deal of lively portraiture, much of it possessing the sense of amusement that marks many of Japan's arts. The well-born were expected to be proficient in dance and music, and calligraphy was as revered as it was in China.

Great attention was given to the cultivation of beauty in all its manifestations: literary, visual, plastic, and psychic. Men as well as women were expected to take pains with their appearance; both used cosmetics. (Blackened teeth were the rage among Heian court ladies!) A refined sense of color in dress was mandatory. Both sexes cried freely, and a sensitive sadness was cultivated. The Buddhist insistence on the transitory quality of all good things—the reminder that nothing is permanent—was at the heart of this aristocratic culture. Life was to be enjoyed, not to be worried about or reformed. The wise saw this instinctively and drew the proper conclusions. The Japanese would never have been so crude as to exclaim "Eat, drink, and be merry for tomorrow we die"; their message was more "Take pleasure now in the flight of the butterfly, for tomorrow neither it nor you will be with us."

### Buddhist Evolution

Two Buddhist sects, the Pure Land and the Nichiren, made many converts during the Kamakura Period. Both emphasized the salvationist aspect of the religion and the possibility of attaining nirvana through faith alone. The founder of the Pure Land sect, Honen (c. 1133–1212), insisted that the Buddha would save those souls who displayed their devotion to him by endlessly repeating his name. The Nichiren, who took their name from their thirteenth-century founder, held a similar belief in the mystical power of chanting devotional phrases and also emphasized the immortality of the soul. The Nichiren differed from all other Buddhists in being highly nationalistic and insisting that they alone had the power to lead the Japanese people on the righteous path.

Zen Buddhism, on the other hand, insisted on strenuous meditation exercises as the only way to purify the mind and prepare it for the experience of nirvana. Rising to prominence in the thirteenth century along with the Pure Land and Nichiren sects, Zen (derived from the Chinese *ch'an*) was to become the most influential of all forms of Buddhist worship in Japan. It was the preferred form for the samurai, who found that its emphases on self-reliance, rigorous discipline, and anti-intellectualism fit closely with their bushido code.

Interestingly, despite its popularity among warriors, Zen also underlay much of the Japanese interpretations of beauty and truth and remained a powerful influence on the visual arts. The famous rock gardens, for example, are a physical rendition of Zen principles of simplicity and restraint. Far outnumbered in adherents by both Pure Land and Nichiren, Zen became the favored belief among the upper class, and it has been the form of Buddhism peculiarly identified with Japan in foreign eyes.

ARTS AND CULTURE

## Lady Murasaki

**IN THE ELEVENTH CENTURY,** a Japanese noblewoman, whose name is uncertain, wrote the world's first work of literature that can be called a novel. The *Tale of Genji,* written between 1015 and 1025, is a long, fascinatingly detailed account of the life of a courtier at the Kyoto imperial palace and his relations with others there.

About the life of the author, we know only some fragments. She was born into an official's family, a member of the large and powerful Fujiwara clan that long occupied a major place in Japanese affairs. Shikibu, as she was named, probably received the minimal education customary for even high-class Japanese women.

Presumably, she did not know Chinese, which was the literary language of well-educated males in this epoch. She was married to another official at age twenty, but her husband died soon after, leaving his widow with a young daughter. For some years, Shikibu retired to a chaste widowhood in a provincial town. In 1004, her father received a long-sought appointment as governor of a province and used his influence to have his widowed daughter made lady-in-waiting to the empress Akiko in Kyoto.

From 1008 to 1010, Lady Murasaki (as she was now known at court) kept a diary, which was translated and published not long ago, but her major effort in her years with the empress in the extremely refined Kyoto palace was the *Tale of Genji.* In fifty-four books or chapters, which together are more than twice as long as Tolstoy's *War and Peace,* Lady Murasaki depicts the panorama of Japanese upper-class life in the ceremony-filled, ritualistic court of the emperor and his consort. She thus made a memorable, subtle outline of the traditions that guided the Japanese uppermost class and that would continue to be honored for most of the ensuing millennium.

Prince Genji (Shining One) is a fictional character but presumably was drawn closely on an actual one. Stricken by the death of his mother, to whom he was greatly attached, the young man comes to court to forget his sorrow. Popular with both sexes for his gallantry and charm, he engages in a series of love affairs with the court women, in which he displays both his amorous character and his artistic refinement. In a setting where manners are everything, Genji reigns supreme, but his escapades with the ladies lead to trouble with jealous husbands and suitors, and Genji is banished from the court. He soon obtains forgiveness and returns, only to fall deeply in love with the commoner Murasaki, whom he makes his wife. But she dies young and childless: heartbroken, Genji soon follows her in death.

The action now shifts to Genji's son and grandson by a former marriage. These two are in competition for the same girl, Ukifune, who feels committed to both in different ways. Depressed and ashamed, Ukifune attempts suicide but fails, and she decides to salvage her life by renouncing the world and entering a Buddhist monastery. The competing father and son are both deprived of what they want and are left in bewildered grief at their unconsummated love. The novel ends on a note of deep gloom.

The psychological intricacies of the story have fascinated Japanese readers for 900 years. The novel was first translated into English in the 1930s by Arthur Waley. Of Lady Murasaki's last years, we know nothing.

### *Analyze and Interpret*

Why do you think Murasaki chose this anything-but-happy ending to her novel? How much does it relate to what you understand as the ordinary lives of Japanese commoners in her day? Would that relationship be of concern to Lady Murasaki?

Private Collection/Bridgeman Art Library

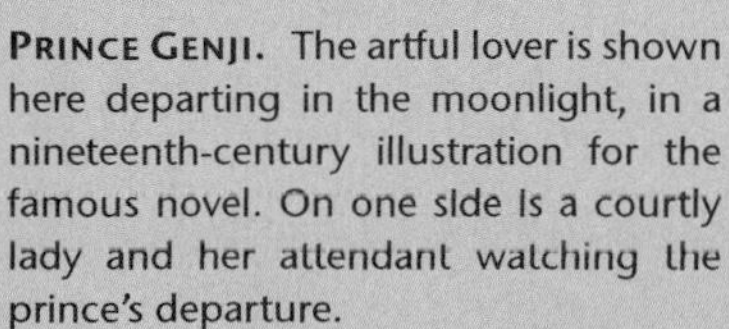

**PRINCE GENJI.** The artful lover is shown here departing in the moonlight, in a nineteenth-century illustration for the famous novel. On one side is a courtly lady and her attendant watching the prince's departure.

## THE ASHIKAGA SHOGUNATE, 1336–1573

The expenses of summoning a huge army to repel the Mongols in the 1280s proved fatal to the Minamoto clan. Despite their desperate efforts, they lost their hold on power. In 1336, the **Ashikaga clan** succeeded in establishing themselves in the shogunate, a position they continued to hold until the late sixteenth century.

The Ashikaga shoguns ruled from Kyoto as the head of an extended group of ***daimyo***, nobles who much resembled the dukes and counts of feudal Europe in their lifestyle and powers. Some daimyo were much more powerful than others, and at times they were practically independent of the shogun. The most trusted vassals of the reigning shogun were entrusted with the estates surrounding Kyoto, whereas the outer provinces were rife with rebellion and conflicts among the daimyo.

The Ashikaga Period is the culmination of Japanese feudalism, one long and bloody tale of wars among the nobility and between groups of nobles and the shogun. For long periods all semblance of central authority seemed to have broken down in Japan. The imperial court was shoved still further into the background and did not play an independent political role at all during this era. All concerned gave verbal respect and honor to the reigning emperor, but these phrases were not accompanied by any devolution of power to him.

In the period embraced by the Kamakura and Ashikaga shogunates, 1200–1500, Japanese art forms turned definitively away from the emulation of Chinese models and became fully rooted in Japanese experience. Cultural institutions also reflect the increasing attention given to the warrior (samurai) in this age of constant war. The new forms of popular Buddhist worship and the literature of the Kamakura epoch glorified the simple, straightforward virtues of the soldier, in sharp contrast to the subtleties and introspection of the earlier *Tale of Genji* and other stories of the court society.

### Contacts with China

Contacts with Song China were resumed and continued to be close throughout the Kamakura and Ashikaga shogunates, especially in trade. The Chinese especially desired the very fine Japanese steel for swords, which rivaled the "Damascus blades" for which European knights paid a fortune. Japan, in turn, received much from China, including the habit of tea drinking, which led to a whole subdivision of Japan's domestic culture, the tea ceremony. The coming of the Mongols briefly interrupted this commerce, but it soon resumed. Many goods were exchanged by force or illegally. Japanese pirates and smugglers gave the early Ming Dynasty (1378–1664) so much trouble that for a time, the Chinese rulers actually attempted to withdraw their coastal populations and make them live inland. Needless to say, this scheme was wholly impractical, and the smuggling went on unabated for another century, until Japan retired into voluntary seclusion (see Chapter 29).

**A JAPANESE LANDSCAPE.** Japanese painting strives for a harmonious balance between the works of humanity and Nature, and this balance is revealed in this sixteenth-century work. Although natural objects are given much space by the artist, the painting's focal point is the house and the human figure within it.

Chinese and Japanese Special Fund, courtesy of Museum of Fine Arts, Boston

### Korea

As mentioned earlier, much of the commerce in goods and ideas between Japan and China was mediated through Korea. That country had already been a civilized society for several hundred years by the time the Japanese were organizing the Yamoto state. Korea in turn had been strongly affected by its proximity to China and had fallen into the Chinese orbit during the later Han and the Tang dynastic periods. At this time, the Korean peninsula was divided between three contesting kingdoms, all of which became tributary states of China under the powerful Tang Dynasty. Confucian ethics were widely adopted by the upper class, and the Chinese style of centralized government by bureaucracy was imposed after the unification of the country in the tenth century by one of the three contestants, the kingdom of Silla.

The rulers of Silla imitated the Tang governors in China but were not completely successful in their political strivings to rule as the "Son of Heaven." A feudal division of power between king and local lords continued. Fortunately for the dynasty, the collapse of the Tang in Beijing, and the weakness of the Chinese thereafter, allowed the Koreans a large degree of autonomy for the next several centuries. It was during this era that Korean national culture received its most important monuments, and the amalgam of Buddhist faith with Confucian ethics was deeply and permanently embedded in the educated class.

Only with the coming of the conquering Mongols in the thirteenth century did Korea again fall under strict alien controls. As in China, and for the same reasons, the era of Mongol rule was painful for the Koreans, and the Korean king became a mere Mongol agent. When the Mongols were driven out of China, they were also forced out of Korea, and a new period of quasi-independence under a new dynasty began.

## The Early Southeast Asian States

The term *Southeast Asia* is a recent invention, not coming into wide usage until after World War II. It denotes an enormous and varied area ranging from Burma in the northwest to Indonesia's islands in the southeast. By general consensus Vietnam, Cambodia, Laos, Malaysia, Thailand, and the Philippine Islands are included in this region as well (see Map 18.3).

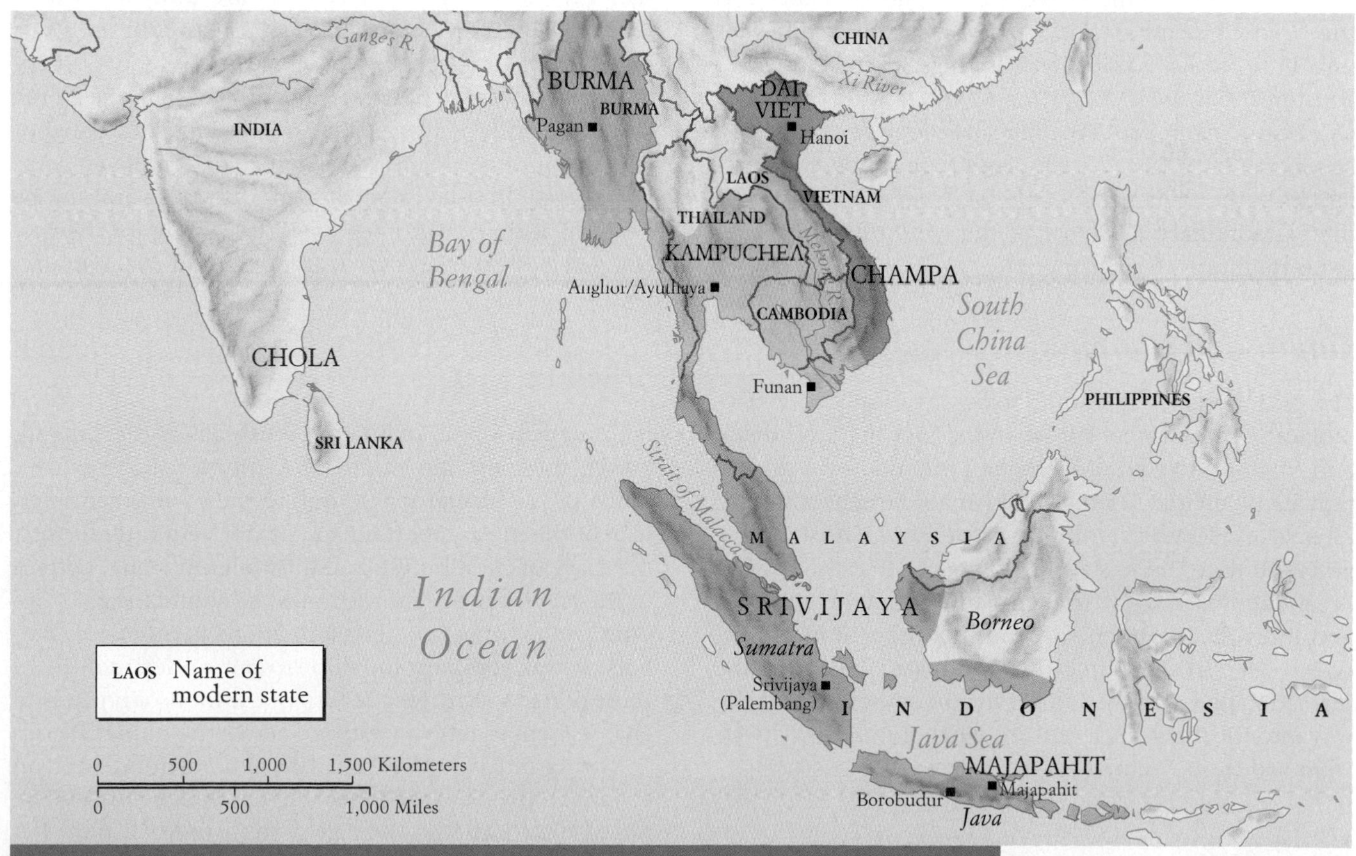


**MAP 18.3** *Southeast Asia, 500 C.E.–1200 C.E.*

Through the Strait of Malacca at the tip of the Malaysian peninsula passed the largest volume of maritime trade in the world during this epoch and later.

Although all of these states but Thailand entered modern times as colonial possessions of European states, they all had a lengthy history of independent political organization previously. Their history was very much a factor in defining and segregating one people from others despite strong ethnic similarity. Most of the mainland Southeast Asians are members of the Mongoloid (yellow-skinned) racial group, whereas most of the islanders are Malay or Australoid (brown-skinned) in background, with modern admixtures everywhere of Chinese and Indian immigrants. The original inhabitants of the mainland seem to have drifted slowly southward from southern China and eastward from India, whereas most of the islanders came apparently from the mainland at some later dates. Archaeology has shown Neolithic farming sites dating to the fifth millennium B.C.E. scattered throughout the region.

The earliest political-cultural units existed in the shadow of either imperial China or India, and these states were to have permanent influence on the Southeast Asians in many different spheres. As a general rule, China's influence was founded on military and diplomatic hegemony, whereas India's came via either a trading or a cultural-philosophical channel. The dividing line between the Chinese and the Indian spheres of culture was located in Vietnam, and there was little overlap.

Only in one Southeast Asian country—Vietnam—was the Chinese factor so powerful as to create at times an unwilling or coerced satellite. Elsewhere several influences conspired to make India the model and leading partner of Southeast Asia in cultural affairs: the activity of the Indians in the busy East–West Indian Ocean trade, the similarities in the Indian and Southeast Asian economies, and the extraordinary flexibility of the Hindu/Buddhist religious traditions (see Chapter 16).

## *Funan and Champa*

The earliest mainland entities to be historically or archaeologically proven were Funan, in the Mekong River delta, and Champa, in central Vietnam. Little is known for certain about ancient Champa and Funan. Both became empires of moderate extent during the early Christian era, and both were Hindu states, in the sense that the governing group was strongly influenced by Hindu Indian ideas and individuals. Funan succumbed to the Khmers (discussed later) in the sixth century and was wiped from the map. Champa managed to survive in some form all the way into the nineteenth century, when it was finally overwhelmed by its Vietnamese neighbors.

## *Kampuchea*

In the seventh century, the conquerors of Funan moved into the politically dominant role that they would continue to occupy for the next several hundred years. These conquerors were the **Khmers**, ancestors of the present-day Cambodians. They built the great civilization centered on the city of Anghor and its surrounding villages.

**Kampuchea**—the original (and current) name of the Khmer state otherwise known as Cambodia—was the greatest of the ancient Southeast Asian mainland kingdoms. It remained so until its slow decline and fall to the invading Thais. Its wealth was based on a wet-rice agrarian economy that supported perhaps a million people in and close to Anghor. The economy was based on hydrological engineering rivaling that of the Nile valley. These works modified the effects of the huge peaks and valleys of the monsoon weather pattern. They served some 12 million acres of paddies, which were capable of giving three harvests of rice per year.

Kampuchea began as another Hindu kingdom, with a semidivine king, but in the twelfth and thirteenth centuries Hindu belief was supplanted by Hinayana Buddhism (see Chapter 5), with its emphasis on the equality of men and rejection of monarchic divinity. Not even the immense temple at Anghor Wat, built as a king's funeral monument like the pyramids of Egypt, could reestablish the prestige of the throne. Perhaps the temple contributed to its decline because of the heavy taxation its construction necessitated—another similarity to the Egyptian experience. The steady chipping away of Khmer territories by the Champa state on its east and the Thais on its north and west seems to have been as much a consequence as a cause of the decline of royal powers. By the late fourteenth century, Thais were taking over Anghor and much of the Khmer kingdom. The temple-city was abandoned in the early fifteenth century, not to be heard of again until French explorers, acting for the new colonial power, rediscovered it after a half-millennium's lapse.

## *Srivijaya*

If Kampuchea was mainland Southeast Asia's primary power, the maritime empire of Srivijaya held sway over much of the insular region during these same centuries. One of the most important sources for very early history, the diary of the Chinese Buddhist pilgrim I Jing, written in the late seventh century, notes the abundance of shipping and mariners of all Asian nations in Srivijaya's harbors. It was common for ships to put up for months in these ports, waiting for the turn of the monsoon winds to enable them to return westward across the Indian Ocean.

Owing much to the initiatives and support of Indian colonists, the Sumatra-based Srivijayan kings gradually forced their way into the breach in intra-Asian trade left by the decline of Funan and Champa. Srivijaya sought little territory but focused instead on dominance in the busy straits of Malacca trade route, as well as supplying the South China ports with island spices and foodstuffs.

**THE CHINESE JUNK.** This form of naval architecture has served Chinese mariners for more than 700 years without change. It is extremely seaworthy, while allowing heavy cargo loads. A modern junk maneuvers in the harbor of Hong Kong here.

Bob Rowan/Corbis

It was a lucrative business, and the conquest of Srivijaya by the Chola buccaneers from India (see Chapter 16) did not impede it. On the contrary, Indian conquest brought a higher degree of organization and expansion to trade. Chinese recognition of the rights of Srivijaya to monopolize the north-south trade along the Chinese coasts and down to Malacca was also a huge asset. When this recognition was withdrawn because of Chinese rivalry, the empire began to decline in earnest.

## Majapahit

The final blows against Srivijaya were delivered by the **Majapahit** rulers, centered on eastern Java. They created the only indigenous (native to the area) empire to unify all of present-day Indonesia. Majapahit's success is supposedly attributable to the efforts of Indonesia's national hero, Gaja Mada, the first minister of the king for a generation (1331–1364).

Gaja Mada supervised the conquest of the entire archipelago and possibly (accounts vary) of a considerable part of the mainland as well. Like its insular predecessors, Majapahit's empire was a trading and commercial venture, with command of the sea being far more important than landed possessions. The glory lasted for less than a century, however, before other challengers arose, led by the new city of Malacca on the straits that bear the identical name (see Map 18.3).

Majapahit was the last great Hindu kingdom in Southeast Asia, and its demise in the fifteenth century was caused largely by the coming of an aggressive Islam, again spearheaded by immigrants from the Indian peninsula. Where Hinayana Buddhism had replaced original Hindu belief in most of the mainland, Islam now replaced it in most of the islands. By the time of the arrival of the Portuguese, who were the earliest Europeans in these latitudes, much of the population of the archipelago had been converted.

## Burma and Thailand

After the fall of the Khmers, the mainland was gradually divided among three principal entities. In the far west, the Burmese kingdom centered on the religious shrines at **Pagan**, which had been founded as far back as the ninth century. It had gradually spread south and east to embrace several minority groups related to the majority Burmans. Originally Hindu, thanks to the region's common borders with India, the governing class adopted the Hinayana Buddhism brought to them from the centers of that faith in Sri Lanka during the tenth and eleventh centuries.

In the 1280s, the Mongol conquerors of China sent armies to the south, where they severely ravaged several Southeast Asian states. Chief among these victims were the Burmans, who saw their capital city of Pagan utterly destroyed and their political dominion wrecked as well. Burma disintegrated into several rival principalities during the next three centuries.

To the east of Burma, the Thai people, with their religious and political center at **Ayuthaya**, took advantage of the opportunity afforded by Kampuchea's weakening and the Mongol destruction of the Pagan kingdom. Although the Mongols militarily overwhelmed the Thais in their expeditions of the 1280s, they later favored them as tributaries rather than objects of exploitation. The rise of Thai power was closely linked to this favoritism.

Three great monarchs in the thirteenth, fourteenth, and fifteenth centuries assured the Thai kingdom of central importance in mainland Asia throughout early modern times. Their contributions ranged from adoption of

Hinayana Buddhism, to a model land tenure system, an advanced and efficient code of law, and standardization of the language, both written and oral. Collectively, the Thai kings of the Chakri Dynasty created the most stable and most administratively advanced state in the area.

Thailand (the name is a recent replacement for *Siam*) became the successor-through-conquest of Kampuchea in the fourteenth and early fifteenth centuries. By the fifteenth century, less than a century after its founding, the capital Ayuthaya had a population estimated at 150,000. Its temples and public gardens rivaled those of Anghor in its heyday and quite overshadowed the now-ruined Pagan.

## Vietnam

Vietnam is the exception among the states we are now reviewing in its intense, love–hate relationship with China. For a thousand years, the Vietnamese were the oft-rebellious subjects of the emperor of the Middle Kingdom. When this "yoke" was finally thrown off in 939 C.E., the educated people had been sinicized (made Chinese) to an extent not otherwise experienced anywhere, even in Korea and Tibet.

*Nam viet* (land of the Viets) was made into a province of the Chinese empire by a Han ruler in 111 B.C.E. For the next thousand years, it was governed by imperial appointees who were schooled in Confucian principles and assisted by a cadre of Chinese officials. Mahayana Buddhism, similar to China's version, was brought to the country by Chinese missionary monks, soon becoming the dominant faith and remaining so when the rest of Southeast Asia had turned to the Hinayana version. The pre–twentieth century Vietnamese script was the only Southeast Asian form of writing based on Chinese ideographs. In many different ways, then, China was the tutelary deity of Viet culture.

Yet this closeness inevitably brought forth a mirror image of rejection and dislike. Heavy-handedness and the serene presumption of superiority that so marked China's upper classes in their contacts with foreigners left their scars on the Vietnamese as deeply as on anyone else. The national heroes are two sisters, Trung Trac and Trung Nhi, who as co-queens led an armed rebellion in 39 C.E. that resisted the Chinese for two years before being crushed. The sisters committed joint suicide and became the permanent focal point of anti-Chinese patriotism.

There followed 900 years of domination from the north, but the wish for independence never died out. After the weakening of the Tang Dynasty allowed successful revolt in 939, Vietnam (more precisely *Dai Viet,* the "kingdom of the Viets") became and remained a sovereign state for another millennium. Its relationship with its great neighbor to the north was always delicate, but the adoption of a tributary relationship, with certain advantages to both sides, allowed the Vietnamese effective sovereignty and maintained the peace. Even the Mongol conquerors of China came to accept the right of Dai Viet to exist as an independent entity. Their campaigns aimed at subduing the kingdom in both the 1250s and again in the 1280s were repelled by brilliantly led guerrilla warriors.

In the ensuing centuries, the Ly and the Tran dynasties ruled Dai Viet from the city eventually named Hanoi. They successfully expanded their territories against both the resurgent Champa kingdom to the south and the Khmers, later the Thais, to the west. In general, these dynasties followed the Chinese administrative style, backed up strongly by the official Confucian culture and the thorough sinicization of the educational system. The Le Dynasty was notably successful in organizing resistance against renewed Chinese invasion in the early 1400s, adding another chapter to the long Vietnamese saga of rejection of Chinese military hegemony coupled with admiration and pursuit of Chinese culture.

# Summary

The earliest period of Japan's history is shrouded in mist. The lack of written sources until the eighth century C.E. forces us to rely on archaeology and occasional references in Chinese travel accounts. Unlike many other peoples, the Japanese never experienced an alien military conquest that unified them under strong central control.

For most of Japanese history, the imperial court was essentially a symbol of national distinctiveness, based on religious mythology, rather than a government. Real power was exercised by feudal lords, organized loosely in clans, who dominated specific localities rather than nationally. In later times, the regent called the shogun was sometimes able to subdue these lords and create an effective military government parallel to that of the court.

Japan's relations with China and Korea were close through most of its early history but were punctuated with briefer periods of self-willed isolation. In the broadest senses, most of the models of Japanese culture can be traced to Chinese sources, which often came through Korea. Among Japan's notable borrowings from China were Buddhism, writing, and several art media and forms, but in each instance, the Japanese adapted these imports to create a peculiarly native product. They rejected entirely the Chinese style of imperial government and its accompanying bureaucracy, favoring instead a military feudalism.

The Southeast Asian societies experienced some type of extensive political organization beginning in the early Christian centuries, but little is known from historical sources until much later. The earliest mainland kingdoms seem to date from the fifth or sixth centuries C.E., and those in the islands a good deal later. The Burman Pagan kingdom was matched by the Khmers of Anghor and the later Thai kingdom centered on Ayuthaya as major cultural and political factors in the first 1,400 years of our era. Although they originally subscribed to Hindu viewpoints carried by Indian traders, all of these and other mainland countries converted in time to Hinayana Buddhism.

Unlike its neighbors, all of which were under strong Indian cultural influence, Vietnam looked to the north and emulated Chinese Confucian values and practice for a lengthy period without surrendering its insistence on political sovereignty. Some of the mainland entities extended their domains into Malaya and the archipelago of Indonesia, but generally speaking, the islands brought forth their own imperial centers that rose and fell depending on control of the lucrative maritime trading routes. At the end of the period under discussion, a militant and proselytizing Islam was replacing both Hindu and Buddhist religions in most of the islands.

## Identification Terms

Test your knowledge of this chapter's key concepts by defining the following terms. If you can't recall the meaning of certain terms, refresh your memory by looking up the boldfaced term in the chapter, turning to the Glossary at the end of the book, or working with the flashcards that are available on the *World Civilizations* Companion Website: **http://history.wadsworth.com/adler04.**

Ashikaga clan
Ayuthaya
*bakufu*
*bushido*
*daimyo*
Fujiwara clan
Kamakura shogunate
Kampuchea
Khmers
Kyoto
Majapahit
Pagan
samurai
*shiki*
Shinto
*shoen*
shogunate
*Tale of Genji*

## Test Your Knowledge

Test your knowledge of this chapter by answering the following questions. Complete answers appear at the end of the book. You may also take this quiz interactively and find even more quiz questions on the *World Civilizations* Companion Website: **http://history.wadsworth.com/adler04.**

1. Very early Japanese history is best summarized as
   a. a complete mystery until the Tang Dynasty in China.
   b. unknown except for sporadic Chinese reports.
   c. well-documented from native sources.
   d. dependent on the reports of Japan's early invaders.
   e. extensively documented in Japan's early written language.
2. The first Japanese government we know of was organized by the
   a. Yamato clan.
   b. Shinto monasteries.
   c. Buddhist monks.
   d. Heian emperors.
   e. Chinese conquerors.
3. Shinto is best defined as
   a. a belief in the infallibility of the emperor.
   b. the original capital city of Japan.
   c. the native religion of the Japanese.
   d. the most important of the Buddhist sects in Japan.
   e. a strongly ritualistic religion.
4. The chief original contribution of the Japanese to world literature was the
   a. novel.
   b. epic.

c. short story.
d. essay.
e. poem.

5. A shogun was
 a. the high priest of the Shinto temples.
 b. a samurai official.
 c. an illegal usurper of imperial authority.
 d. a general acting as political regent.
 e. a Japanese warrior.
6. In the Japanese feudal system, a shoen was
 a. an urban commercial concession.
 b. a property outside imperial taxation and controls.
 c. the preferred weapon of the samurai.
 d. land owned by a free peasant.
 e. land controlled by the state.
7. Which of the following best describes the relationship of China and Japan through 1400 C.E.?
 a. Japan was a willing student of Chinese culture.
 b. Japan selectively adopted Chinese models and ideas.
 c. Japan was forced to adopt Chinese models.
 d. Japan rejected Chinese pressures to conform.
 e. China made several cultural adjustments based on its interactions with Japan.
8. In Lady Murasaki's tale, Genji is
 a. a samurai warrior who has no time for love.
 b. a betrayed husband of a court beauty.
 c. a romantic lover of many court ladies.
 d. a wise peasant who avoids courtly snares.
 e. an elderly man recounting the adventures of his youth.
9. Which statement is correct about the early history of Southeast Asia?
 a. The mainland nations normally controlled the islands politically.
 b. The islands clung to their Hindu and animist beliefs throughout this period.
 c. The Hinayana Buddhists did not support the idea of divine kingship.
 d. The Khmer Empire was destroyed by the Chinese.
 e. When Portuguese merchants arrived in the region, most of its people were still Hindus.
10. Identify the false pairing of country/nation/empire with a geographic center:
 a. Kampuchea—Anghor
 b. Dai Viet—Hanoi
 c. Burma—Pagan
 d. Majapahit—Malacca
 e. Funan—Mekong River

## InfoTrac College Edition

Visit the source collections at

**http://infotrac.thomsonlearning.com**

and use the Search function with the following key terms:

Asia history  Japan history  Shinto

## Wadsworth History Website Resources

Visit the World History Resource Center at **http://history.wadsworth.com/world** for a wealth of general resources and the *World Civilizations* Companion Website at **http://history.wadsworth.com/adler04/** for resources specific to this textbook.

## HistoryNow

Enter *HistoryNow* using the access card that is available for *World Civilizations*. *HistoryNow* will assist you in understanding the content in this chapter with lesson plans generated for your needs. In addition, you can read the following documents, and many more, online:

Shotoku, *Seventeen-Point Constitution*
Ten Shinto Creation Stories

*Consider your origins: You were not born to live like brutes*
*but to follow virtue and knowledge.*
Dante

# 19 The European Middle Ages



| | |
|---|---|
| 500s | St. Benedict/Benedictine Rule |
| 1066 | William (the Conqueror) of Normandy conquers Anglo-Saxon England |
| c. 1075–1122 | Investiture Controversy |
| 1096 | First Crusade |
| 1100s | Gothic style begins |
| 1152–1190 | Emperor Frederick Barbarossa reigns |
| 1179–1223 | Philip II Augustus (France) |
| 1200 | University of Paris founded |
| 1212–1250 | Emperor Frederick II |

The feudal European community that emerged from the trials and troubles of the Dark Age was built on personal status. Feudal law and custom assigned everyone to a place on the social ladder, but their specific rung depended on whether their function was to fight, to pray, or to work. The great majority, of course, fell into the third category, but they could occasionally leave it by entering one of the others. The church was open to entry from below and grew steadily more powerful in both the spiritual and the civil spheres. Its claims in worldly matters brought it into increasing conflict with the kings and emperors, a conflict that hurt both sides. Despite the resistance of both church and nobles, the royal courts gained increasingly more prestige and power. The Middle Ages (c. 1000–1300 C.E.) saw the faint beginnings of the modern European state and society.

## The Workers

Most people were peasants who worked on and with the land. Perhaps 90 percent of the population in western Europe, and more in eastern Europe, worked the fields, orchards, and woodlots for a (generally hard) living. Their lives were filled with sweaty labor, but this work was far from continuous. For six months of the year or so in North Europe, they were restricted by climate and habit to their huts and villages. Then they spent a great deal of time on farm and household chores and literally "sitting about." Even during the growing season, from about April to the autumn harvest, many church-ordained holidays and village festivals interrupted the drudgery.

What the modern world calls labor discipline—that is, the custom of reporting to a given place at a given time daily, prepared to do a given job in a specified manner—was almost unknown. Work was largely a communal responsibility; people worked with others in a rhythm dictated by the needs of the community and ancient traditions. These traditions left much room for rest and recreation.

## The Feudal Serf

The work on the large manors, which (as we saw in Chapter 11) became dominant in western Europe, was performed by millions of serfs. By the year 1000, serfs had replaced slaves in most places in Europe. Slavery virtually disappeared because the Christian church was opposed to the enslavement of fellow Christians, and this viewpoint gradually prevailed. Because almost the entire continent had been converted to Christianity by 1100, few non-Christians were left who could be enslaved. Asiatics were sometimes encountered, and black slaves from Africa were occasionally purchased from Moorish traders, but they were so expensive that they were viewed as curiosities and kept in noble households rather than used for labor. In some places, particularly east of Germany, serfdom differed little from slavery in practice, and the following remarks apply more to the western region. Legally, however, a serf could not be bought or sold as a slave could, and no one questioned that a serf was a human being with God-given rights and a soul equal in the eyes of heaven to any other person.

Nevertheless, serfs were in important measure unfree. They were bound by law and tradition to a given place, normally a farm village, and to a given occupation, normally farmwork, under the loose supervision of their noble or clerical lord (*seigneur, Herr, suzerain*). The actual supervision was generally exercised by a steward or some other overseer appointed by the lord. Beyond this general statement, it is difficult to give a specific description of serfdom because conditions varied so much by time and place. Conditions in, say, tenth-century France were not the same as in eleventh-century Spain or England. In general, however, serfs were bound to perform labor services for their lord and to pay certain "dues" and taxes to the lord, which were set by tradition and by sporadic negotiations.

Only rarely were these conditions written. The labor took myriad forms, but usually included work on the **demesne,** the part of the agricultural land of the estate that belonged to the lord directly. The remainder of the estate's cultivable land (most of it, in most cases) was normally given out to the serfs for their own use (see Map 19.1). They did not own it outright, however, but had only a *usufruct* right (that is, a right to use the land, which was still owned by the lord). Serfs who fell into the lord's bad graces could lose their plots.

Serfdom usually became a hereditary condition. People usually had become serfs because they fell into debt or because they offered themselves and their land to a local strongman in exchange for his protection during a period of disorder. In bad times, it was always safer to be the ward of some powerful person than to try to stand alone.

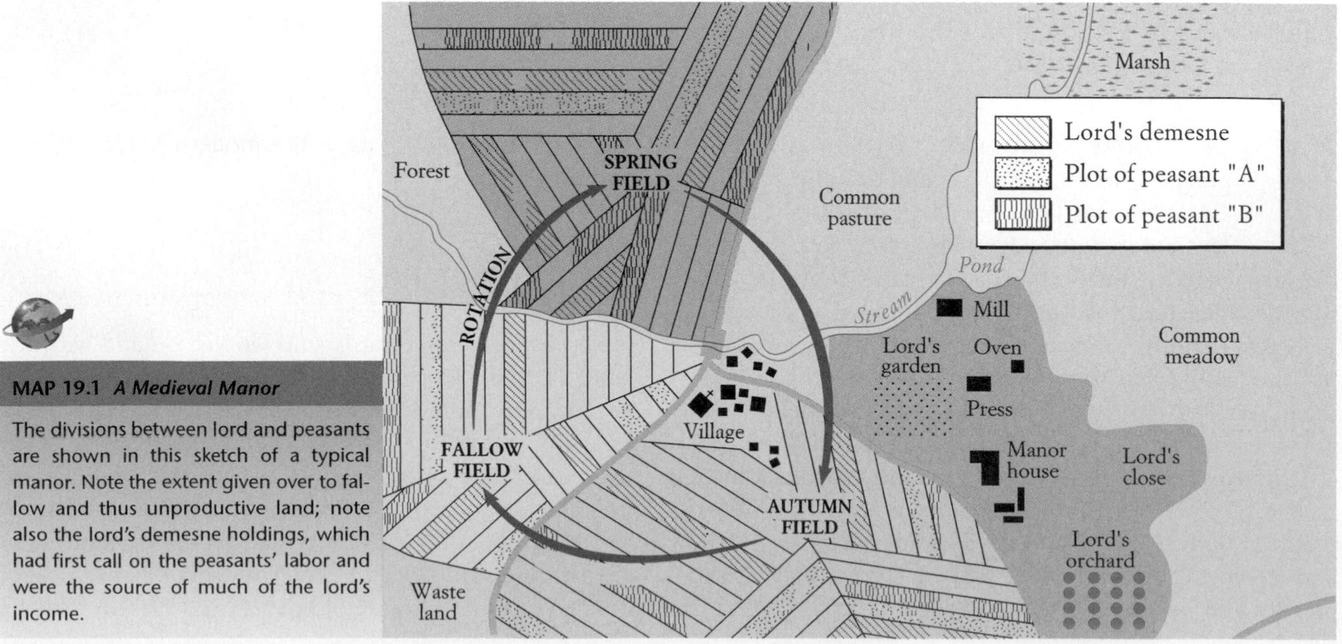


**MAP 19.1** ***A Medieval Manor***

The divisions between lord and peasants are shown in this sketch of a typical manor. Note the extent given over to fallow and thus unproductive land; note also the lord's demesne holdings, which had first call on the peasants' labor and were the source of much of the lord's income.

It was not unusual, however, for a serf to gain freedom. The most common way was simply to run away from the lord's manor and start a new life in freedom elsewhere, normally in a town. "Town air makes free" was an axiom of medieval lawyers. In western Europe, people who could prove they had resided in a town for a year and a day were considered legally free, whatever their previous condition may have been. Many other serfs gained their freedom with the lord's permission. Some were freed of further obligation by the lord's will; others were rewarded for good services; still others worked their way out of serfdom by paying off their debts. After the eleventh century, freedom could also be won by volunteering to open new lands, particularly in the Low Countries, where dikes were constructed and land was reclaimed from the sea, and in eastern Europe, where much uncultivated land still existed and lords were anxious to gain new labor.

After the tremendous loss of life during the Black Death (see Chapter 24), the serfs who survived were in a strengthened bargaining position with their masters, and serfdom in western Europe became less onerous. Peasant tenants still had to meet certain feudal dues and minor obligations, but the old hardships and treatment like slaves were over.

### *Medieval Agriculture*

Manorial agriculture made steady, although unspectacular progress during the Middle Ages. Productivity, which was formerly very low (perhaps a 3:1 ratio for return of grain from seed), improved with the invention and introduction of the iron-tipped plow in the twelfth century. Because it could till heavier soils, this implement opened up whole new regions to grain production. The introduction of the padded horse collar, which distributed the load so as to allow the horse to pull a much heavier burden, was another major advance. (It came almost a thousand years after its Chinese invention.) Horses were expensive and difficult to handle and keep fit, but they were so much more flexible and faster than oxen that their widespread use amounted to an agricultural innovation of the first importance—similar in impact to the introduction of tractors. The systematic use of animal manure as fertilizer also improved productivity, although this practice remained the exception.

The productivity of medieval agriculture was above all limited because one-third to one-half of the cultivated land was left **fallow** (unseeded) each year. This practice was necessary because it was the only way the land could recover its nutrients in the absence of fertilizer. Every farmer had a piece or a strip of land in both the cultivated and the fallow segments of the manor, which were rotated from year to year.

Famines were common in years when the harvest was poor; reserves were at best sufficient for one bad harvest, and the miserable state of transportation and roads made it difficult to move foodstuffs. It was not unusual for people to starve in one area, while others had a surplus 100 or 150 miles away.

### *Urban Workers*

The urban workers were not yet numerous and were sharply divided in income and social status. At the top were the craftsmen and shopkeepers. Some of them were highly skilled and enjoyed a solid economic livelihood; they could often afford to educate their children in the hope of advancing them still further. These people benefited from the guild system (see Chapter 24), which restricted competition and assured that their socioeconomic status would be secure.

Below these few fortunates were the semiskilled, unskilled, and casual laborers. These men and women worked for others and had few prospects of becoming independent. Many of them lived a hand-to-mouth existence that may have been harder than the lives of the bulk of the manorial peasants. They were often the victims of changed economic conditions (like a new trade route) or local famines. A great many oscillated between seasonal agrarian jobs and town occupations.

Finally, the towns were filled with marginal people who never had steady work. They begged or moved on to more promising places, "living on air" in the meantime. Historians have estimated that as many as one-fourth of the population of seventeenth-century Paris fell into this category.The number in medieval days was smaller, because the towns were still relatively small and residence rights were restricted, but there must have been many then, too.

## The Warriors

The European nobility of the Middle Ages constituted perhaps 2 to 3 percent of the population on average, although their numbers varied from country to country and region to region. Their rights stemmed generally from **patents of nobility**, royal documents that granted them or their ancestors the status of noble and certain privileges that went with that status.

What type of preferences did they enjoy? The privileges could be almost anything imaginable: economic, political, or social, but above all, they were social. The nobles were thought to be of a different nature than the commoners. They spoke mostly to one another, married other nobles, held exclusive gatherings, and enjoyed an altogether different lifestyle than ordinary people, be they well-off or poor.

Like serfdom, noble status was hereditary; nobles were generally born noble. Nobility was thus a caste that was more or less closed to outsiders. In medieval times, it was rarely possible to buy one's way into the nobility by purchase of a patent, although the practice became common later. Women were equally as noble as men, if they were born into the caste. They could not become noble by marriage, however, whereas men occasionally could. In any event, it was unusual for either male or female nobles to marry beneath their position.

Also like serfdom, nobility varied so much that it is impossible to generalize accurately beyond a few facts. Not all nobles were wealthy, although many were. The only type of wealth that was meaningful was land. By the 1300s, it was not so unusual to find impoverished nobles who were anxious to have their sons marry rich commoners' daughters. Many once-noble families sank out of sight, pulled down by their ineptitude in business, their mortgages, or their hugely wasteful lifestyle. Their places were taken by newcomers from below, who had obtained a patent for themselves in some way or another (perhaps as a reward for distinguished military service).

Nobles were always free; they could not be bound as an inferior to another, but they were also normally **vassals** of some person of superior rank to whom they owed feudal loyalty and specific duties. In the early Middle Ages, these duties were military in nature. Later, they often changed into some sort of service. The superior person to whom service was owed was called the vassal's **suzerain**. He (or she) gave something of value to the vassal in return, perhaps political advantage, protection, or administration of justice. The details of a medieval noble's life were dictated by this system of mutual obligations.

The nobility were not only free but were also the sole political factor in medieval life. The king depended on his nobility to run the government and administration. In some countries, churchmen who were not noble by birth also held some offices, but the secular nobles were everywhere the decisive factor in government at all levels, from the royal court to the village.

A noble's rank more or less determined his job; there were basically five ranks of nobility, ranging downward from duke to count to marquis to baron to knight. Each country had its variations on this scheme. The knights only were seminoble in that their status was solely for their own lifetimes; their sons might be ennobled by the king, but they had no claim to nobility by birth. Knights were by far the most numerous of the nobility and the least prestigious.

The nobles originally claimed their preferred status by virtue of being professional soldiers, guardians, and judges. They supposedly protected the other members of society, upheld justice, ensured that the weak were not abused by the strong, and guarded public morals. That, at least, was the nobles' story! In fact, nobles were often noble because they or their ancestors were successful brutes and pirates who possessed stronger arms than their neighbors and intimidated them into submission. Alternatively, they bought or fought their way into the king's favor or married their way upward.

In any case, the nobles considered themselves as the defenders of society through the command of both God and king and their own sense of honor. Honor was a particularly important aspect of their lives, and every person was supremely conscious of its obligations. Honor meant spending a year's income on the marriage of a daughter or on a proper costume for a court function. Honor meant fighting duels over alleged insults from other nobles and refusing to fight them with commoners. Honor meant living as a nobleman should: as though he had a huge income, while holding money in contempt.

How did noblewomen fit into this pattern? Female nobles frequently held positions of some power in public life. Queens were generally considered to be a political misfortune, but this did not prevent a few women from attaining that rank. More frequently, widows of royal husbands served as regents, as did Blanche of Castile (see the Law and Government box). The widows were usually expected to seek another husband and defer to his advice. Some did, and some did not.

In private life, many noblewomen exerted a strong influence on their husbands or ran the extensive and complex household themselves, as we know from many historical records. They were responsible for the day-to-day management of the estates; when their husband was absent, which was frequent, they moved into his shoes in matters of commerce and even warfare. There are records of duchesses and abbesses who did not hesitate to resort to arms to defend their rights.

First and foremost, however, like all medieval women outside the convents, a noblewoman was expected to produce legitimate children to ensure the continuity of the (male) family name and wealth. A barren noble wife was in a highly unenviable position; sterility was automatically attributed to the woman, but divorce was next to impossible because of the church's opposition. Hence, sonless fathers sometimes turned to concubines in their search for posterity. A bastard so produced would have only very limited rights, even if he was acknowledged, but for some desperate fathers this was better than nothing. The legal ramifications of bastardy, especially the ability to inherit titles and property, were a preoccupation of medieval lawyers.

LAW AND GOVERNMENT

## Blanche of Castile

**IN THE VIOLENT AND STRONGLY** patriarchal society of the Middle Ages, all women were under some constraints imposed by law and custom. Occasionally, an exception to the rule appeared, a woman who was in every way the equal of her male associates in terms of exercising public power. Blanche of Castile, queen of France, is a good example. She was also the medieval model of that perennial bugaboo of young wives, the possessive mother-in-law.

Blanche was a granddaughter of the most famous queen of the entire Middle Ages, Eleanor of Aquitaine, and the niece of the unfortunate John of England. Selected by her grandmother as a suitable match, she was married to the heir to the French throne, Louis, at the age of twelve. Her bridegroom was a ripe thirteen! This young age was not unusual for royal or noble marriages. The legal age of maturity was twelve for females, fourteen for males, conforming to current ideas on mental and moral development. For a time the wedded pair would live apart in their respective households. Such a marriage would not be consummated until later, when puberty had been reached at about sixteen for males, fourteen for females.

Blanche gave birth to her first child—of a total of twelve—when she was seventeen. Of the twelve, five lived to adulthood, which was a relatively high percentage for the time. The oldest surviving boy became King Louis IX, patron saint of the French kingdom. He and his mother remained extraordinarily close throughout their lives.

Blanche had a forceful temperament. At the age of twenty-eight, when her father-in-law, King Philip Augustus, refused to send money to her husband for one of the latter's feudal wars, Blanche swore that she would pawn her two children to get the needed cash. Philip decided to put up some funds after all.

Philip died in 1223, and Blanche's husband succeeded him as King Louis VIII. Only three years later, he also died, leaving his queen as regent and the guardian of his twelve-year-old heir, Louis IX. Blanche thus became not only queen but actual ruler. Although not unheard of in medieval Europe, it was unusual for a woman to exercise royal powers. Louis apparently knew and appreciated the qualities of his young wife; she did not disappoint his expectations.

Louis IX, a deeply pious person, was content to leave much of the task of governing to his mother even after he had attained his majority. Mother and son had a mutual appreciation that lasted until her death and was undisturbed by Louis's marriage in 1234. Blanche tried to make sure that this relationship would last by selecting Louis's bride, thirteen-year-old Marguerite of Provence. Joinville, Louis's contemporary biographer, tells us that despite Blanche's precautions, the mother-in-law was jealous of the young bride and took pains to assert her dominant position: "[Louis] acted on the advice of the good mother at his side, whose counsels he always followed."

Life at this court must have been difficult for young Marguerite, who found that the only way she could be with her husband without his mother was to accompany him on a crusade against the Muslims in the Holy Land in 1248. During the king's lengthy absence, Blanche again served as regent, and she was the reigning authority in France when she died, at age sixty-five, in 1252. Like her more famous grandmother Eleanor, she was a woman who knew how to handle the levers of power in a masculine age.

### *Analyze and Interpret*

Why was it considered to be a severe risk to the kingdom for a female to exercise actual governing duties? What might some of the positive, as well as negative, results be from marriage at the age of thirteen and fourteen into royal powers in the medieval age?

## THE WORSHIPERS

The men and women who worshiped were less numerous than the warriors, but they also filled a social niche that was just as important. In an age of faith, when no one doubted the reality of heaven, hell, or the Last Judgment, those who prayed for others were considered to be absolutely essential. They included both the parish clergy and the regular clergy, or monks, but because the monks were both more numerous and more important than the parish clergy, the following applies particularly to them.

The chief visible difference between monks and parish priests was that the monks lived somewhat apart from the world in communities called monasteries. The monastery has had a long history in the Christian world. The first ones were founded in the fourth century in Egypt, but the most important monastic institutions were those founded by the Italian St. Benedict in the sixth century. His **Benedictine Rule** for monastic life was the most widely observed, although several others were also in use during the Middle Ages (the Trappist and Cistercian rules, for example).

What was a Benedictine monastery like? The monks believed a mixture of manual and intellectual work was best for a pious and contemplative life. The monks operated extensive farms, which they sometimes leased out to peasants in part. They were also craftsmen, and the abbey house or main center of the monastery was a workshop filled with bustling activity, but the monks never forgot that their intercession with God on behalf of their fellows was at all times the center of their lives. From early morning to night, the Benedictines set aside hours for prayer and contemplation. They also usually ran schools for the more talented peasant youth, some of whom were invited to join them in the monastic life.

Monks and nuns (in the convents that were the close equivalent of the monasteries but designed for females) normally came from the aristocracy until the twelfth or thirteenth century, when they became increasingly middle class in origin. They were often the younger sons or daughters of a noble family, who had little hope of inheriting property sufficient to maintain them in proper style. Their parents therefore put them—with or without the agreement of the child—into a religious institution at the age of twelve or so. Sometimes, the child was miserable in the religious life and left it sooner or later without permission. More often, a compromise was arranged, and the unhappy monk or nun was allowed to leave without the scandal of an open rebellion.

The collective wealth of the monasteries was considerable. European Christians customarily remembered the church in their wills, if only to ensure that masses would be said for their souls in that waystation en route to heaven called purgatory. Noble sinners often tried to escape their just deserts at the Last Judgment by leaving the local monastery or convent a large bequest on their deathbed. Because most of the charitable institutions of the Middle Ages were connected with and run by the clergy, it was natural to leave money or income-producing property to the church. In these ways, the property controlled by the church, and above all by the numerous monasteries, grew to tremendous figures. Historians reckon that, as late as the fifteenth century, the property controlled by the church institutions in western Europe outvalued that controlled by the Crown and nobles together.

This involvement with the business world and large amounts of money often had deleterious effects on the spiritual life of the monks and the nuns. Too often, monastic policy was made by those who oversaw the investments and the rents, rather than the most pious and self-sacrificing individuals. The monasteries repeatedly fell into an atmosphere of corruption, fostered by the indifference of some of their leaders to religious affairs and their close attention to financial matters.

Despite this tendency, the monks and nuns did much good work and fulfilled the expectations of the rest of society by their devotions and their actions on behalf of the poor. We should remember that medieval government was primitive, and the social welfare services that we expect today from government did not exist. Instead, the church institutions—monasteries, convents, cathedrals, and parish churches—supplied most of the "welfare" for the aged, the poor, and the helpless. The clergy founded and managed the hospitals, orphanages, and hospices, asylums for the aged, and the shelters for the impoverished; provided scholarships for the deserving poor; and met a hundred other needs. In so doing, they were using funds contributed by the faithful or generated by the church business and rental income. Then as now, money was used for good ends as well as bad ones.

### *The New Clerical Orders*

In the thirteenth century, for various reasons **heresies** became more widespread in the church than ever before. Regular armed crusades were even mounted against them at times. These crusades meant to stamp out heresy by killing or suppressing the heretics. Brutal force was their hallmark. To a pair of saintly young priests, this was not the Christian way, and they sought a different approach.

St. Francis of Assisi was a young Italian who practiced a life of total poverty and total service to his fellows (see the Patterns of Belief box). St. Dominic, a contemporary of Francis of Assisi, was a young Spaniard who wanted to reform the clergy in a different way. He wanted especially to convert the heretics back to the true faith by showing them the error of their ways calmly and peaceably. The Dominican Order was therefore an intellectual group, specializing in lawyerly disputation and preaching. Dominicans were the outstanding professors of law and theology in the early universities of Europe, and they would later take the lead in the Inquisition in Spain against suspected heretics.

In their different ways, both Franciscans and Dominicans attempted to elevate the spiritual life of the clergy and, through them, the people of Europe. They attempted to bring about needed reforms in the church that the papal court was refusing to address. But their efforts were dulled with the passage of time and checked by a clerical hierarchy that did not want to hear of its failures and corruption or think about how to change.

## THE ECONOMIC REVIVAL

Starting in the eleventh century, the towns of Europe, so long stagnant or semideserted, began a strong revival. Some entirely new cities were founded, including Berlin, Moscow, and Munich. Mostly, however, the eleventh- and twelfth-century revival saw the renaissance of older sites under the influence of three related factors: (1) increased

PATTERNS OF BELIEF

## St. Francis of Assisi

**THE MAN CALLED FRANCIS OF ASSISI** has long been one of the most attractive of the medieval saints to modern eyes. His message was clear and simple: "Where there is hate, give love; where there is insult and wrongdoing, grant forgiveness and offer hope. Bestow happiness where there is sorrow, and give light where there is darkness." No one lived this high-minded creed better than its originator.

Francesco (Francis) de Bernadone was born the son of a wealthy cloth dealer in the prosperous town of Assisi in northern Italy. Although he apparently had no formal schooling, he was quick intellectually and was taken into his father's business early in life. He was a member of the "gilded youth" of the town, drinking heavily, getting involved with loose women, and generally enjoying himself as rich, carefree adolescents have always done. His life seems to have been an ongoing party.

But at age twenty, he opted to join the local freebooters (*condottieri*) and was taken prisoner during Assisi's squabble with the city-state of Perugia. He spent a year in captivity, which was surely a sobering experience. Two years later, ill with fever, he underwent a visionary experience that permanently changed his life. Faced with death, he came to believe that he had been spared for a purpose that he must discover. He renounced his family's wealth and began to dedicate his time to the service of God and the poor.

He visited the lepers and outcasts of the town and practiced a stringently simple life, begging his food. Wherever he was permitted, he preached to anyone who would listen a message of poverty, austerity, and, above all, love for every creature. Braving the inevitable ridicule, he called on his listeners to renounce their fortunes, sell their possessions, and give the proceeds to the poor around them. For his text, Francis took the word of Jesus to his apostles: "Take nothing for the journey, neither staff nor satchel, neither bread nor money." Trusting fully in the Lord, Francis demanded and practiced absolute poverty.

Some people were touched by the power and sincerity of his preaching and joined him. In a relatively brief time, he had a band of followers, the "Little Brothers of Francis," and came to the attention of Pope Innocent III. Although suspicious at first, Innocent eventually recognized Francis's sincerity and moral stature. His followers, called friars, were allowed to preach where they chose and to solicit the support of good Christians everywhere.

Francis died quite young, but not before he had almost single-handedly made substantial changes for the better in contemporary Christian practice. His example inspired many thousands to reject the materialism that had plagued the thirteenth-century clergy, especially the monastic orders. The Franciscans (who soon had a female auxiliary of nuns) always rejected the idea of the monastery, preferring to live and work among the people as helpmates and fellow sufferers.

Francis of Assisi felt a very strong bond between himself and all other beings. He addressed the birds and the beasts, the sun and the moon and the stars as his brothers and sisters. Once he preached a sermon to the birds, and the legend says that they responded by gathering around him. He did much to instill a love of God's natural world in his followers and should be called one of the Western world's first, and most attractive, ecologists.

### *Analyze and Interpret*

What effect on the Franciscan monks' attitude toward people might the founder's insistence that they beg for their food have? Do you know anyone whose lifestyle resembles that of Francis? What do you think of this person?

**HistoryNow™**

***To read more about St. Francis's life, point your browser to the documents area of* HistoryNow.**

trade, (2) a more peaceful environment, and (3) a higher degree of skills and entrepreneurial activity.

The basic reason for the resurgence of the towns was the rising volume of trade. After centuries of stagnation, Europe's merchants and moneylenders were again looking for new fields to conquer. The increasing ability of the royal governments to ensure a degree of law and order within their kingdoms was a key factor. Others included the steady rise in population, the ability of the townsmen to purchase their liberties from the feudal nobles (see the Society and Economy box), and the reappearance of clerical and professional people.

In western Europe, mercantile activity approached levels it had last reached a millennium earlier, in the fourth century. (In this context, "western" means Europe westward from midway across Germany, including Scandinavia and Italy.) Merchants found that a stable coinage and financial techniques such as letters of credit, which they learned from the Muslims, increased their commercial opportunities.

The obvious locations for markets were the strategic, protected places that had been market centers in Roman days. Old municipal centers, such as Cologne, Frankfurt, Innsbruck, Vienna, Lyon, and Paris, which had been almost

SOCIETY AND ECONOMY

## Liberties of Lorris

**IN THE TOWN CHARTER** of the small city of Lorris in northern France is the essence of the "liberties" that the medieval bourgeoisie gradually gained from a reluctant aristocracy, using the king as their protector. The charter of Lorris was granted by King Louis VII in 1155. By this time, the towns had fully recovered from the long centuries of decay and lawlessness after Rome's fall. Most of the rights deal with economic regulations and taxes because the feudal nobility were most likely to apply pressure in these areas. The eighteenth liberty is a good example of the rule that runaways would be free from serf status if they could remain in a town and out of trouble for a year and a day.

**The Charter of Lorris:**

2. Let no inhabitant of the parish of Lorris pay a duty of entry nor any tax for his food, and let him not pay any duty of measurement for the corn [grain] which his labor, or that of his animals may procure him, and let him pay no duty for the wine which he shall get from his vines.
3. Let none of them go on a [military] expedition, on foot or horseback, from which he cannot return home the same day! . . .
15. Let no man of Lorris do forced work for us, unless it be twice a year to take our wine to Orleans, and nowhere else . . .
18. Whoever shall remain a year and a day in the parish of Lorris without any claim having pursued him thither, and without the right [of remaining] having been forbidden him by us or by our provost [equivalent of sheriff], he shall remain there free and tranquil . . .
33. No man of Lorris shall pay any duty because of what he shall buy or sell for his own use on the territory of the parish, nor for what he shall buy on Wednesdays at the town market . . .

Given at Orleans, in the year of our Lord 1155.

### *Analyze and Interpret*

Who would be in the best position to take advantage of these liberties? Why would the local lords who fully controlled the peasants allow the townsmen these freedoms?

Source: As cited in O. Johnson, *World Civilization,* p. 364.

**History Now™**

***To read all of the Liberties of Lorris, point your browser to the documents area of* HistoryNow.**

abandoned in the sixth and seventh centuries, began to come back from the grave. They once again became what they had been under the Romans: commercial and crafts centers with some professionals and administrators, often in the employ of the church. Nevertheless, cities and towns were not yet large or numerous. By the twelfth century, for example, Cologne's population reached 30,000, which was a large city by medieval standards. The largest cities were Paris, Florence, and Venice, which had populations of somewhat less than 100,000 each in the twelfth century.

Several developments helped create a more peaceful setting for economic activity. One was the increased power of the church to enforce its condemnations of those who fought their fellow Europeans or engaged in random violence. As the church became a major property holder, it began to use its influence against those who destroyed property through war and plunder. The Peace of God and the Truce of God were now enforced across most of the continent. Under the Peace of God, noncombatants, such as women, merchants, peasants, and the clergy, were to be protected from violence. The Truce of God forbade fighting on Sundays and all holy feast days. Violators were subject to spiritual sanctions, including excommunication, and to civil penalties as well in most areas.

The **Crusades** also contributed to peace in Europe by giving ambitious young nobles an outlet to exercise their warlike impulses in a church-approved arena. Starting with the First Crusade in 1096, tens of thousands of aggressive younger sons of the nobility went off to Palestine or eastern Europe to fight the pagans, recover the long-lost Holy Land, and make their fortune (they hoped). Although the First Crusade was able to seize Jerusalem and briefly set up a Christian-ruled kingdom in Muslim Palestine, these exercises (there were eventually six, depending on how one counts) were usually destined to end in futility, or worse. One permanent effect was to refresh and deepen the animosity between Muslims and Christians, which had largely subsided since the Bedouin conquests had been completed centuries earlier. The terms *Crusade* and *crusader* have since then become the ultimate curse in Muslim countries, a counterweight to the jihad, directed by Satan rather than Allah.

The harmful aspects of the Crusades culminated in the fiasco of the Fourth Crusade (1204). In that, Western

Bibliothèque de L'Arsenal Paris, France/Bridgeman Art Library

**MEDIEVAL SHOPPING SCENE.** The bourgeoisie were generally occupied with buying and selling goods. This painting shows the commercial district of a French thirteenth-century town. From left to right, tailors, furriers, a barber, and a grocer are visible at work. Dogs were a constant sight in all medieval towns.

knights turned their belligerence and cupidity on their Greek hosts in Constantinople, rather than on the Muslims, and after much wanton plundering occupied the Christian city for the next sixty years. So great was the scandal that although several more attempts were made to organize feudal armies to regain the Holy Land for Christianity, none was successful and most were abortive. By the later 1200s, the Near East had reverted to uniform Muslim rule once again.

Finally, the renewed application of Roman law led to the use of legal procedures as a substitute for armed action in disputes. Interest in the corpus jurisprudentiae began in the law school founded at Bologna in the eleventh century. Roman law, which had always been retained to some slight degree in the church's administration of its internal matters, was now gradually reintroduced into secular affairs as well. The legal profession was already well-developed in the twelfth century.

In part, as a result of the first two factors, people began to develop greater skills and engage in more entrepreneurial activity. As trade and commerce increased and the threat of violence declined, it made sense for people to develop more skillful ways to make goods and provide services. As these skills became apparent to the potential users and buyers, entrepreneurs came into existence to bring the providers of skills and the users together. Along with entrepreneurs came real estate speculators (medieval towns were notoriously short on space), investment bankers (who usually started out as moneylenders), and a host of other commercial and financial occupations that we associate with doing business. Some of these people succeeded in becoming quite rich, and they displayed their success in fine townhouses and good living.

## *Bourgeoisie and Jews*

Many people in the towns were what we now call the upper middle class: doctors, lawyers, royal and clerical officeholders, and, first and foremost, merchants. These were the **bourgeoisie**, the educated, status-conscious people who lived within the *bourg* or *burg,* which was a walled settlement meant to protect life and property.

The towns and their inhabitants were by now becoming a major feature of the political and social landscape, particularly in northwestern Europe and northern Italy. In the thirteenth and fourteenth centuries, kings discovered that their surest allies against feudal rebels were the propertied townsmen. The towns were the source of a growing majority of the royal tax revenue, even though they contained only a small fraction (perhaps 10 percent) of the European population. Whereas the agrarian villagers' taxes disappeared into the pockets of the nobles and their agents, the towns paid their taxes directly to the royal treasury.

By now, the townspeople were no longer dependents of the local lord; having purchased a charter from the throne, they had the privilege of electing their own government officials and levying taxes for local needs. Their defense costs (town walls were costly to build and maintain) were borne by the citizenry, not put into the devious hands of the nobles. The towns often had the privilege of deciding citizens' cases in their own municipal courts; appeal went to the king's officials, not to the local nobleman.

The residents of these reviving towns were not all Christians. A small Jewish population had come to western Europe from the Mediterranean Jewish colonies of the Diaspora. They lived completely segregated from the Christian majority in small urban areas of a block or two called **ghettos**. Initially, Jews provided several of the elementary financial services in medieval cities and in the countryside, but by the thirteenth century they were being rivaled by Christians, who no longer paid much attention to the church's official distaste for usury, or the taking of

British Library/The Art Archive

**Moneylending.** This manuscript illustration from fourteenth-century Italy shows the moneylender and his clients. Note the monks and other church officials, as well as the women who avail themselves of these forerunners of banks.

money for the use of money (interest). Most places prohibited Jews from owning land or entering craft guilds, so they had little choice but to take up financial and mercantile pursuits.

Until the thirteenth century, outright attacks on the Jews were relatively rare, but in that century, the money-short kings of both England and France denounced and expelled the Jews on pretexts and seized their property, and the era of sporadic *pogroms,* or anti-Semitic mob actions, began. Fearful for their lives, the Jews began to migrate from western to eastern Europe. The eastern European states such as Poland and Hungary were more hospitable than the West at this juncture. These states, and especially their monarchic governments, badly needed the Jews' experience in trade and finance, which the native Christian populations were almost entirely lacking.

# Royal Kingdoms and the Formation of States

The revival of the towns and the growth of urban populations were important factors in the steady strengthening of the royal governments against the nobles' claims for autonomy and feudal fragmentation. The foundations of the modern states of England, France, and Germany can be traced back to the thirteenth and fourteenth centuries.

What is a **state**? A state is a definite territory with generally recognized boundaries and a sovereign government. It recognizes no superior sovereignty within its own borders. It suppresses violence and maintains order among its subjects in the name of law and defends those subjects from outside oppressors and internal criminals. The state exercises its powers through a group of elected or appointed officials, courts, police forces, and an army.

## *England and France*

England was a pioneer in creating a state. Since the fifth century, when the island was conquered by the barbarian Angles and Saxons, it had been divided among a series of tribal kingdoms that fought one another and the invading Vikings. The recently unified Anglo-Saxon kingdom of England had been invaded and conquered in 1066 by William (the Conqueror), the formidable duke of Normandy, who had a weak claim to the English throne that the English nobility had not recognized. By right of conquest of what he considered to be a collection of traitors, William proceeded to organize a new type of kingdom, in which the king alone was the source of final authority. Before this time, the kings of feudal Europe were always being reminded of their dependency on the voluntary collaboration of their nobles in national affairs. Now William could ignore these claims and establish a cadre of appointed noble officials who were all drawn from his supporters. A tangible sign of his power was the incredibly thorough and detailed **Domesday Book** (1086–1087), which was prepared as a royal census for tax purposes.

William's successors were not all so clever or determined as he, but by the middle of the twelfth century, the earmarks of a modern state were faintly visible in England. It had, among other things, a loyal corps of royal officials, a system of courts and laws that was more or less uniform from one end of the kingdom to the other, a royal army that looked only to the king, and a single national currency issued by the royal treasury.

France developed a little more slowly. In the early twelfth century, France was still a collection of nearly independent duchies and counties, whose feudal lords looked only reluctantly and occasionally to the king in

**A Prospect of Carcassonne.** The best-preserved walled medieval town in France, Carcassonne shows how important protection from enemy armies and marauders was in the Middle Ages. Most western European towns once possessed such walls but demolished them later to expand.

Paris. Some of the French lords, such as the count of Anjou and the duke of Normandy, could figuratively buy and sell the French king; the royal territory around Paris was a fraction of the size of their lands. Furthermore, the king had no royal army worthy of the name.

This situation began to change in the late twelfth century, when the ambitious Philip II Augustus (1179–1223) came to the throne and started the process of unifying and strengthening the country. By the end of the thirteenth century, the king had become stronger than any of his nobles and was sufficiently in control of taxation and the military that he could intimidate any of them or even a combination of them. The Crown would experience many ups and downs from this time onward in France, but the outlines of the French state were in place by 1300.

A major difference between the English and French systems of government was that the English crown relied on unpaid local officials, who were rewarded for their service by customary fees, social privileges, and legislative powers (in the Parliament created in the thirteenth century). The French, on the other hand, created a royal bureaucracy, staffed by highly trained and highly paid officials, who were responsible only to the king and kept clear of local ties. The English system allowed for a maximum of local variations in administration and justice, although the entire kingdom conformed to the common law that the kings had gradually imposed. Each English county, for example, had its own methods of tax assessment, types and rates of taxes, and voting rights, as did the associated kingdoms of Scotland and Wales. The French royal bureaucrats carried out the same duties in the same fashion from one end of France to the other, but they were not able to overcome the large linguistic and customary differences that distinguished Brittany from Normandy or Provence from Anjou. Until the Revolution of 1789, France remained more a series of adjoining semiautonomous countries than a single nation. Thus, England was held together by its national laws and the Parliament that made them, whereas France was unified by the Crown and its loyal hierarchy of officials.

## The German Empire

The modern state that we know as Germany was created only in the late nineteenth century. For many hundreds of years before that, its territory was an agglomeration of petty principalities, kingdoms, and free cities. This had not always been the case, however. In the Early Middle Ages, Germans had lived under one powerful government headed by an emperor who claimed descent from Charlemagne, but this state failed and broke up. In the eleventh century, the emperor and the pope in Rome became embroiled in a long, bitter struggle over who should have the right to "invest" bishops in Germany—that is, to select the bishops and install them in office. This **Investiture Controversy** (from about 1075 to 1122) ripped the empire apart, as one noble after another took the opportunity to pull clear of the central government's controls.

Another factor weakening the empire was that emperors succeeded to the throne through election. Prospective candidates engaged in all sorts of maneuvering and conspiracy and were even willing to barter away much of their monarchic power to gain votes. Civil wars among the nobility were common at the death of each emperor.

In 1152, the noble electors finally tired of this exhausting sport and agreed on a strong leader in Frederick Barbarossa, who tried his best to reunify the Germans. However, Barbarossa's claims to rule in northern Italy—a claim going back to Charlemagne's empire—brought him into conflict with the Italian city-states and the pope in Rome, and he threw away what he had accomplished toward German unity by his costly and vain military expeditions into Italy.

Later, in 1212, Barbarossa's grandson Frederick II became the Holy Roman Emperor of the German Nation (the official title of the German king) and opted to settle in Sicily, which he made into one of the leading states in contemporary Europe. In the process, he ignored his possessions across the Alps, and the Germans looked on him as almost a foreigner rather than their rightful king. By the time Frederick died in 1250, imperial authority in Germany was severely weakened and would not recover. Instead of becoming the dominant state of late medieval Europe as its geographic and demographic destiny suggested it would be, the land of the Germans gradually broke up into several dozen competing feudal domains and independent cities. Not until the middle of the nineteenth century did Germany make up the political ground it had lost in the thirteenth.

## Medieval Culture and Arts

What cultural changes accompanied this strengthening of central authority? The appearance of more effective central governments in parts of Europe during the twelfth century went hand in hand with the rising wealth of the urban population. Wealth meant a more lucrative base for taxes levied by the royal crown and by the church. To manage that wealth properly and to levy and collect the taxes, both institutions needed trained personnel who could plan and oversee the work of others. It is no accident that the first European universities appeared at this time.

### *The First Universities*

The first universities were established in Italy. In the towns of Bologna and Salerno, specialized academies devoted to law and medicine, respectively, gradually expanded and attracted students from all over Europe. Slightly later, in 1200, the University of Paris was founded by a royal charter; there students studied law, philosophy, and Christian theology.

Much of the university curriculum was devoted to commentaries on the semisacred books of the Greek Classical Age. Pagan authors such as Aristotle had long been forgotten in the Christian West, but they were now being recovered for study through the Muslims, especially in Spain, where the Christian majority had lived for centuries under Muslim rule. Unlike the West, the Muslims were quite aware of the value of the Greco-Roman classics and had preserved and studied them ever since conquering the Greek lands in the East (see Chapter 16).

The greatest Christian teacher of the twelfth and thirteenth centuries was St. Thomas Aquinas. In his *Summa Theologica,* he managed to use the arguments of Aristotle to prove the existence of God. Other great medieval teachers included Albertus Magnus and Peter Abelard, who used reason to teach the truths of faith in an age that was still ruled by universal belief in Christian doctrines.

The students at the universities were drawn from all strata of society, but most were apparently from the middle classes or the poor, who sacrificed much to pay their tuition charges (paid directly to the teachers, in this era). Many lived on the edge of starvation much of the time, but saw a university degree as a passport to a better social position and therefore worth the sacrifice. Many students supplemented their meager funds from home by serving as tutors to the children of the wealthy or as teachers in the "3 R" schools maintained in many towns.

Females were unknown in medieval universities, as either students or teachers. Tension between town and gown was common. Students frequently rioted in protest against the greed of their landlords or the restrictions imposed by town officials. The course of study for a degree in theology (one of the favorites) usually lasted five years, law the same, and medicine somewhat longer. Lectures were the standard approach to teaching, with stiff oral examinations administered when the student felt ready. (It is remarkable how little the basic methods of university education have changed over 700 years!)

### *Gothic Architecture*

The **Gothic style** of architecture and interior design came to be the norm in Europe during the thirteenth century. The first important example of Gothic architecture

Bibliothèque Nationale, Paris, France/Josse/The Art Archive

**CRAFTSMEN AND THEIR TOOLS.** This marvelously detailed miniature painting shows the crafts employed in sixteenth-century construction. Many of these techniques have not changed significantly since that time.

was the abbey church of St. Denis, which was built outside Paris in the mid-twelfth century. It was such an artistic success that the style spread rapidly throughout western Europe. The Gothic style's basic elements include a flood of illumination through windows and portals designed to throw the sunlight into every corner; an abundance of decoration, inside and out; and the use of arches, buttresses, and complex vaulting to support a sharply vertical, towering architecture.

The great Gothic cathedrals of the thirteenth and fourteenth centuries that were built from Italy north and west to England were expressions not only of building and artistic skills but also of the deep faith of those who constructed and used them. The cathedrals were also rich pictorial teaching devices, meant to instruct a still largely illiterate population in the mysteries and lessons of Christianity. Enormously expensive, they were built over generations of time with donations from all classes and the contributed labor of many hundreds of artisans. Each town strove to outdo its neighbors in the splendor of its cathedral. Many cathedrals were destroyed by fire at one time or another and were rebuilt. They could take 50 to 100 years to build or rebuild, and many were not completed until modern times.

## Vernacular Literature

Until the end of the thirteenth century, all serious writing between educated persons was normally conducted in Latin, the language of the church everywhere in western Europe and the most highly developed vocabulary and grammar of the day. In the fourteenth century, however, the common people's oral languages (the vernacular) began to be used for the first time as vehicles of literature, such as poems, plays, and elementary readers for children.

The most important of these early works was Dante Alighieri's *Divine Comedy;* written in Italian, it is one of the great poetic epics of world literature. Somewhat later came the first important work in English: Geoffrey Chaucer's *Canterbury Tales,* which presented a panorama of English society. In the ensuing years, authors writing in the German, French, and Spanish vernaculars also scored artistic breakthroughs in literature. By the end of the fourteenth century, Latin was no longer the automatic choice of the educated for communicating what they held important.

B II Ross/Corbis

**NOTRE DAME DE PARIS.** This triumphant realization of the possibilities of the Gothic style was begun in the thirteenth century in the heart of Paris by the river Seine. The cathedral has served as the seat of the archbishopric of Paris ever since and is revered as the epitome of French Catholicism's visible structure.

## Summary

The Middle Ages were a period of substantial advances for the Europeans, who came back from the long centuries of instability, violence, and ignorance that followed the fall of the western Roman Empire. Three segments of society were recognized: the workers, the warriors, and the worshipers. The first were by far the most numerous, but the other two had important roles to fill in government and society. Town life revived after 1000 C.E., especially in the western parts of the continent, where traders, bankers, and artisans of all types began to congregate in the former ghost towns left by the Romans. By the thirteenth century, towns and cities could be found with upward of 80,000 inhabitants. Cities such as Paris, Bologna, and Oxford had universities, and fine goods from the East were familiar, in part through the experiences of the crusaders, who sought to recover the Holy Land from its Muslim conquerors.

In the wake of growing population and increasing government stability, traders began to develop long-distance markets in basic goods. Peace was by no means universal, but the invasions had ceased and many of the riotous noblemen were diverted into the Crusades against the heathen in the Near East or in eastern Europe. The professions, particularly law, were also reviving, encouraged by the church and its strong interest in a law-abiding environment. Europe had finally emerged from the shadow of Rome's collapse and was developing a new culture. Noteworthy examples included the magnificent architecture and art of the Gothic style and the literary use of the vernacular languages.

## Identification Terms

Test your knowledge of this chapter's key concepts by defining the following terms. If you can't recall the meaning of certain terms, refresh your memory by looking up the boldfaced term in the chapter, turning to the Glossary at the end of the book, or working with the flashcards that are available on the *World Civilizations* Companion Website: **http://history.wadsworth.com/adler04**.

Benedictine Rule
bourgeoisie
Crusades
demesne
Domesday Book
fallow
ghettos
Gothic style
heresies
Investiture Controversy
patents of nobility
state
suzerain
vassals

## Test Your Knowledge

Test your knowledge of this chapter by answering the following questions. Complete answers appear at the end of the book. You may also take this quiz interactively and find even more quiz questions on the *World Civilizations* Companion Website: **http://history.wadsworth.com/adler04**.

1. A social group ignored by the original medieval divisions of humanity was the
   a. peasantry.
   b. merchants.
   c. monks.
   d. soldiers.
   e. nobles.
2. A basic distinction between European slaves and serfs was that slaves
   a. could be sold to another person.
   b. could be severely beaten.
   c. had to work much harder.
   d. could be judged and punished by their master.
   e. usually gained their freedom upon their master's death.
3. Which of the following statements about a medieval manor is *false*?
   a. It was normally an economically self-sufficient unit.
   b. It was normally headed by an official of the church or a noble.
   c. It was normally dependent on the labor rendered by unfree peasants.

d. It was normally a politically independent unit.
e. It normally had a large part of its land lying fallow.

4. Members of the medieval nobility
   a. did not have any special legal status.
   b. were uninterested in military affairs.
   c. generally inherited their position.
   d. were limited to males only.
   e. could not be bound to others as vassals.
5. Noblewomen in the Middle Ages
   a. were strictly confined to domestic duties.
   b. generally married men younger than themselves.
   c. often carried large managerial responsibilities.
   d. played no role in political life.
   e. were often divorced by their husbands if they failed to produce heirs.
6. The usual path to becoming a monk was to
   a. be handed over by one's parent to a monastery's care.
   b. retire to a monastery in middle age.
   c. enter a monastery after being widowed.
   d. be conscripted into an order from a quota of recruits.
   e. voluntarily enter a monastery at about the age of seventeen.
7. The Dominican Order concentrated most of its efforts on
   a. total service to their fellow man.
   b. rooting out heretics in the country of France.
   c. practicing lives of total poverty.
   d. reforming the Church officialdom.
   e. scholarly discourse and preaching.
8. Most Jews in medieval Europe
   a. were prohibited from owning land.
   b. found themselves welcomed into craft guilds because of their skills.
   c. refused to lend money to non-Jews, making them unwelcome in many places.
   d. became more numerous than Christians in many towns.
   e. eventually migrated from eastern to western Europe in large numbers.
9. A major difference between England and France was
   a. England's insistence on a strong royal government.
   b. France's royal dependency on officials who volunteered their duties.
   c. France's use of a corps of royally appointed officials in the provinces.
   d. England's attempts to hold the king responsible for the defense of the whole realm.
   e. France's issuance of a single national currency.
10. Which of the following was not a vital ingredient in the making of medieval European culture?
    a. The Greco-Roman artistic heritage
    b. The Roman pre-Christian cult
    c. Christian theology
    d. Germanic customs
    e. The development of universities

## InfoTrac College Edition

Visit the source collections at

**http://infotrac.thomsonlearning.com**

and use the Search function with the following key terms:

feudalism　feudal　cities and towns, medieval
medieval England

## Wadsworth History Website Resources

Visit the World History Resource Center at **http://history.wadsworth.com/world** for a wealth of general resources, and the *World Civilizations* Companion Website at **http://history.wadsworth.com/adler04** for resources specific to this textbook.

## History Now

Enter *HistoryNow* using the access card that is available for *World Civilizations. HistoryNow* will assist you in understanding the content in this chapter with lesson plans generated for your needs. In addition, you can read the following documents, and many more, online:

St. Benedict, *Rule*
Thomas of Celano, *First and Second Lives of Saint Francis*
Liberties of Lorris

*Man proposes, and God disposes.*
**Thomas A. Kempis**

# 20 Late Medieval Troubles



| | |
|---|---|
| 1198–1216 | Pope Innocent III |
| 1294–1303 | Pope Boniface VIII |
| 1305–1378 | Babylonian Captivity (papacy in Avignon) |
| 1337–1453 | Hundred Years' War |
| 1346–1350 | Black Death's first round |
| 1378–1417 | Great Schism |
| 1381 | English peasants' revolt/ Lollards and John Wyclif |
| 1414–1417 | Council of Constance |

Starting about 1000 C.E., European civilization was revitalized and flourished during several centuries of expansion and consolidation. In the fourteenth century, however, a series of unprecedented disasters sharply reduced the population and caused a decline in the economy that continued for about 150 years. The feudal governing system and the agriculturally based economy reeled under great blows: the Black Death, the Hundred Years' War, and the labor shortage these events created.

The leaders of the Christian church became embroiled in one scandalous affair after another: the shameful degradation of papal sovereignty during the Babylonian Captivity in France and then the Great Schism. Although the challenge to papal authority embodied in the Conciliar Movement was crushed, the popes never regained their previous moral authority, and the way was prepared for the eventual Protestant revolt against the Roman church.

## Disasters of the Fourteenth Century

The problems that manifested themselves in fourteenth-century Europe had their origins in earlier days. By 1300, the population had been growing steadily for two centuries, aided by the new land that had been put into production, several major technical breakthroughs in agriculture, and the unusually benevolent climate, which brought warmer temperatures and appropriate amounts of rain to most of western and southern Europe for a century or longer.

These happy circumstances came to an end in the early fourteenth century. Most good land was by now already being used, and the technology to exploit the marginal lands (swamps, marshes, hillsides, and the like) did not exist. The climate reverted to its long-term pattern, and no innovations appeared that would improve yields to feed the larger population.

As a result, local famines became commonplace in parts of Europe; those who did not starve were often physically weakened as a consequence of poor nutrition over many years. Europe had too many mouths to feed, and the balance was about to be restored through the natural disasters of famine and disease and the manmade disaster of war.

## *The Black Death*

The **Black Death** of the mid- and late fourteenth century is the most massive epidemic on record and by far the most lethal in European history. What was it, and why did it deal such a blow to Europe?

A form of bubonic plague common in the Asian steppes but previously unknown to Europeans was carried to the Mediterranean ports by Italian trading ships in 1346–1347. The plague bacillus was spread by fleas living on rats, and the rats were then (as now) found everywhere humans lived. Within two years, this usually fatal disease had spread all over western Europe; within two more, it had spread from Syria to Sweden and from Russia's western provinces to Spain (see Map 20.1). Millions of people died in the first years of the plague. To make matters worse, it came back again to some parts of Europe during the 1360s and 1370s, sometimes killing one-third or even one-half of the populations of towns and cities within a few weeks.

No one had any idea of how the disease was spread or what countermeasures should be taken. Fourteenth-century European medicine lagged behind the medical practices in several other parts of the world. Even if the

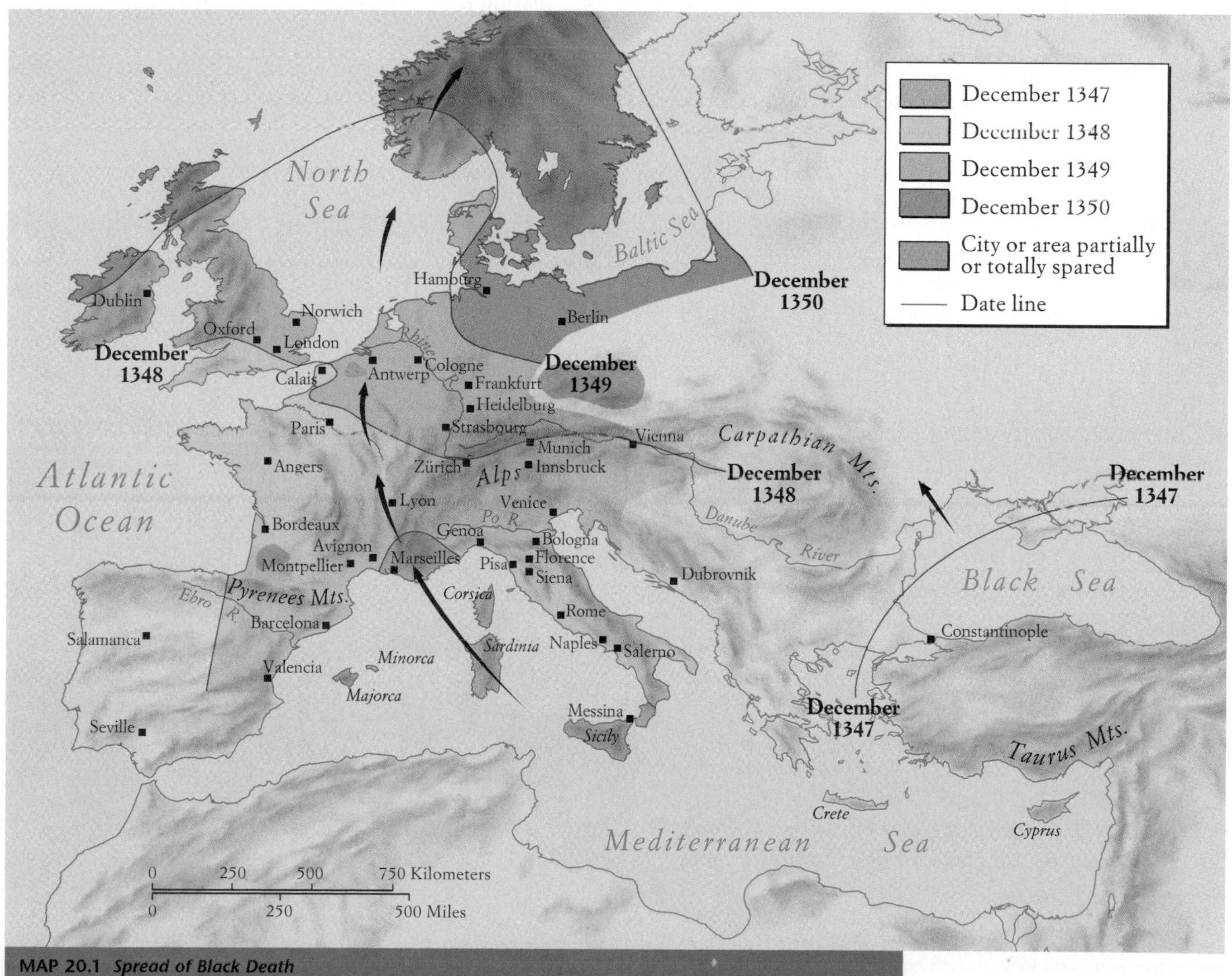


**MAP 20.1** *Spread of Black Death*

The original infections of plague were in Italy and spread rapidly north and west during the years 1346–1350. A pause ensued, but the plague returned on several occasions in parts of Europe until the 1380s.

Europeans had been on the same level as the Muslims or the Chinese, though, they would have been unable to halt the spread of the bacilli or prevent flea bites. Because Europeans lacked any immunity to the disease, a high death toll was virtually inevitable: death came in about two out of three cases, with the highest mortality rates in the old and the young. City dwellers died in vast numbers because crowded conditions aided the spread of the disease. Those who had some place of refuge fled into the countryside, often carrying the highly infectious disease with them.

Italy, England, and the Low Countries were the most savagely hit, because these were the most urbanized areas. Debate continues on just how many Europeans died from the plague, but historians believe that as much as one-fourth of the English population succumbed, over a period of a few years. Individual cities, such as Venice, Florence, and Antwerp, suffered even more; some cities were practically depopulated for a generation.

The economic consequences of the plague are not easily traced and do not lend themselves to generalizations. Government revenues were affected: with fewer taxpayers left alive, tax revenues declined sharply; public works such as the cathedrals had to be stopped for a generation or longer. Some places experienced a shortage of labor that was not relieved for at least two generations. In the towns, which had been overcrowded, the plague reduced the excess population, and the survivors enjoyed better health and work security. Wages for the surviving craftsmen and common laborers rose sharply despite vain attempts to impose wage and price controls. Merchants and traders found fewer consumers to buy their goods, however, and the volume of trade declined.

Peasants who were still bound in serfdom, those who had to pay high labor rents, and those who were otherwise dissatisfied with their lords took quick advantage of their strong bargaining position—or tried to. France, England, and Germany experienced peasant revolts against their lords. The peasants invariably lost these armed confrontations with the mounted and well-armed nobles, but in the longer run, the settlements made between lords and peasants favored the freedoms of the peasants. Serfdom of the near-slavery sort, which was already weak in western Europe, died as a result of the plague. The mobility of labor increased. Much land that had previously been worked had to be abandoned and reverted to waste.

What were the psychic consequences of the plague? These effects can be detected for the better part of a century after 1347. During the late fourteenth and fifteenth centuries, all types of European Christian art reveal a fascination with death. The figure of the Grim Reaper, the reminder of human mortality, and the waiting Last Judgment became major motifs in pictorial and sculptural art. The Dance of Death, a scene in which skeletons link arms with the living revelers, also appeared frequently. The grave is always present in the background, and morbidity is in the air.

Most Christians believed that a wrathful God had given earthly sinners a horrible warning about what awaited the world if morals and conduct were not improved. Many people joined penitential societies, and some engaged in flagellation (self-whipping). It was at this time that Christianity took on much of the burden of guilt and shame, the consciousness of sin, and its consequences that distinguishes it from other major religions.

**The Black Death.** A late medieval painter captures the dismay and despair of the victims of the plague. Note the swelling of the neck of the falling man, one of the most common signs of infection. Above, a devil and an angel battle in the sky, as St. Sebastian (with the arrow-pierced body) pleads for Christ's mercy on the sufferers.

*Saint Sebastian Interceding for the Plague Stricken* by Josse Lieferinxe, c. 1500. The Walters Art Museum, Baltimore 37.1995

## *The Hundred Years' War*

Even before the outbreak of the Black Death, another European disaster was under way: the Hundred Years' War. This conflict between England and France or, more accurately, between the kings and nobles of England and France, started because of a dynastic quarrel between the English Edward III and his French rival, Philip VI.

Recent interpretations of the causes of the war have stressed economic factors. English prosperity depended largely on trade with the towns of Flanders across the Channel, where most woolen cloth was produced using wool from English sheep. English control of the French duchy of Flanders would ensure the continuance of this prosperity and would be popular in both Flanders and England.

Questions of feudal allegiance also contributed to the conflict. The French kings had been trying for generations to increase their powers of taxation at the expense of their feudal vassals in the provinces. Many French nobles saw the English claim to Flanders as advantageous to themselves, because they thought an English king's control over the French provinces would inevitably be weaker than a French king's. So they fought with the English against their own monarch, saying that the English claim was better grounded in law than Philip's. The war turned out to be as much a civil war as a foreign invasion of France.

The course of the war was erratic. Several truces were signed, when one or both sides were exhausted. The conflict took place entirely on French soil, mostly in the provinces facing the English Channel or in the region of Paris. The major battles included **Crecy** in 1346, where the English archers used their new longbows effectively against the French (the English may have used a few of the just-introduced, gunpowder-charged cannon as well); Poitiers in 1356, where the English captured the French king and held him for ransom; and **Agincourt** in 1415, where the English routed the discouraged French a third time, but could not coerce a settlement.

By the 1420s, the war had long since lost its dynastic element. It had become a matter of national survival to the loyal French nobility, who were being pushed back to the walls of Paris (see Map 20.2). At this juncture appeared the patron saint of France, Joan of Arc. This peasant girl, who said she had been told by God to offer her services to the embattled (and ungrateful) Charles VII, routed the English and their French allies at Orleans in 1429 and changed the trend of the war, which now began to favor the French. In the ensuing twenty years, France recaptured almost all of the lands lost to the English invaders during the previous hundred. In 1453, the costly and sometimes bloody struggle finally ended with the English withdrawal from all of France except the port of Calais on the Channel.

***Consequences of the Hundred Years' War.*** Although originally popular among the English, the war eventually came to be seen as a bottomless pit swallowing up taxes and manpower. The costs of maintaining a large army of mercenaries in France for decades were enormous, and even the rich booty brought home from the captured French towns had not been enough to pay for the war. In addition, the war had disrupted England's commerce with continental markets.

The power and prestige of Parliament had increased, however. Since its origins in the thirteenth century, Parliament had met only sporadically. Now, in thirty-seven of the forty years between the beginning of the war in

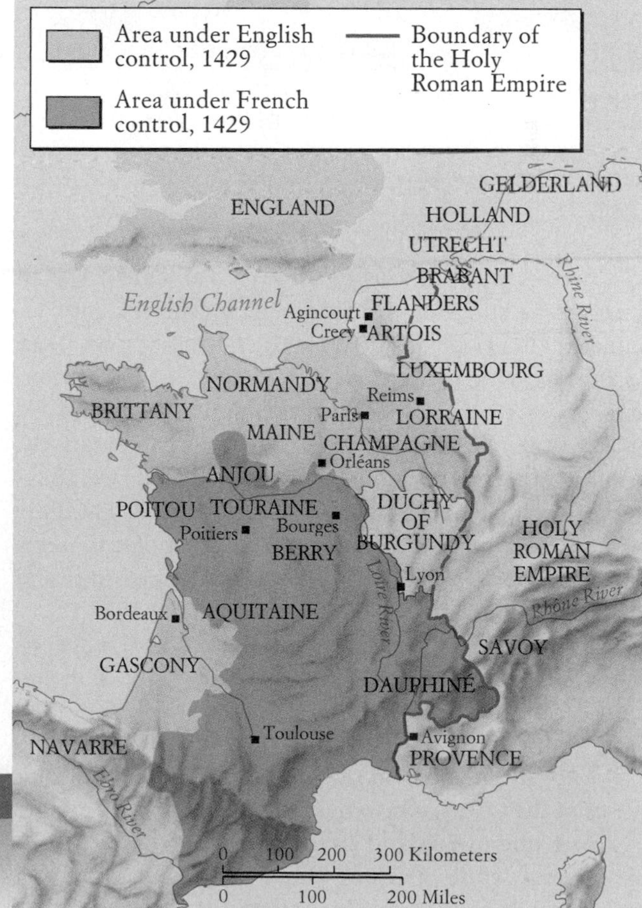

MAP 20.2 *The Hundred Years' War*

Much of northern and eastern France, especially the rich duchy of Burgundy, joined with the English invaders in the attempt to escape the reach of the monarchs based in Paris.

**Joan of Arc.** This miniature of the patron saint of France is one of the few contemporary renditions that has survived. A peasant dressed in armor, she was an extraordinary female figure in this age of male warriors drawn from the nobility.

1337 and Edward III's death in 1377, Parliament was in session. The king was always looking for money, and Parliament had to be consulted for the necessary new taxes. As a result, by the end of the war, Parliament was a determining voice in matters of taxation and other policy.

France did not experience a similar parliamentary development. The French kings allowed regional assemblies to meet in the major provinces, but they avoided holding a national assembly, which might have attempted to negotiate as equals with the Crown on national issues and policies.

This difference in parliamentary development between the two countries would become more significant and more visible as time wore on. France followed the path of most European monarchies in transferring power steadily *to* the royal officials and *away from* the nobles and burgesses of the towns, who would have been representatives to a parliament. England strengthened the powers of its parliament, while checking those of its king. In either case much depended on the personal traits of the king, the progress of wars, and sheer happenstance.

The Hundred Years' War effectively ended chivalric ideals of combat in Europe. The style of warfare changed dramatically during its course. No longer were the heavily armored horsemen the decisive weapon in battle. Cavalry would still play an important role in warfare for 400 years, but only as an auxiliary force, as it had been for the Romans. The infantry, supported by the earliest artillery and soon to be armed with muskets, were now what counted.

The longbow and cannon at Crecy had initiated a military revolution. With the introduction of gunpowder, war ceased to be a personal combat between equals. Now thanks to the cannon, you could kill your foe from a distance, even before you could see him plainly. The new tactics also proved to be great social levelers. Commoners armed with longbows could bring down mounted and armored knights. The noble horseman, who had been distinguished both physically (by being *above* the infantry) and economically (a horse was expensive to buy and maintain), was now brought down to the level of the infantryman, who could be equipped for a fraction of what it cost to equip a horseman. The infantryman could also be left to forage for himself at the expense of the local population as no horse could.

## Problems in the Church

The fourteenth century was also a disaster for the largest, most omnipresent institution in the Christian world: the Roman Catholic Church. Whether a devout Christian or not, every person's life was touched more or less directly by the church. The church was in every way the heart of the community throughout the Middle Age and into modern times. Whether in a village or a great city, the church was much more than a place of worship. Its bells rang out the news and announced emergencies. Popular festivities and the equivalents of town meetings were held there after the Mass. It was also an informal gathering point, a place for business dealings, and a social center. The three great events of ordinary lives were celebrated in the church: birth (baptism), marriage, and death (funeral).

Just as the church was the focal point of everyday life, the parish priest was an important man in the village community. Even if he was ignorant and illiterate, the priest was respected as the representative of an all-powerful, all-seeing lord and final judge. Few, indeed, would attempt to defy or even ignore him in the round of daily life. (For a look at the attractions of the nunnery for young medieval women, see the Society and Economy box on "Holy Maidenhood.")

The church courts determined whether marriages were legal and proper, who was a bastard, whether orphans had rights, whether contracts were legitimate, and whether sexual crimes had been committed. In the church, the

Archivo Iconografico, S.A./Corbis

**A Medieval Copyist at Work.** Thousands of monks labored at the tedious job of copying books for medieval libraries. This example comes from the thirteenth century.

chief judge was the pope, and the papal court in Rome handled thousands of cases that were appealed to it each year. Most of the lawyers of Europe from the twelfth through the fourteenth centuries were employed and trained by the church. As a result, the clergy came to have an increasingly legalistic, rather than a pedagogical or charitable, outlook.

Probably the greatest medieval pope, Innocent III, reigned from 1198 to 1216. He forced several kings of Europe to bow to his commands, including the unfortunate

SOCIETY AND ECONOMY

## Holy Maidenhood

**In the Middle Age,** literacy was still uncommon among the ordinary folk, so we cannot know much about their life at firsthand, but sometimes a beam of light illuminates the circumstance. A good example is *Holy Maidenhood,* by an anonymous author of the thirteenth century. Probably a cleric, he attempts to induce young women to enter the nunnery by arguing against marriage and all its consequences in this unhappy portrait of family relations:

> Look around, happy maiden, if the knot of wedlock be once knotted, let the man be idiot or cripple, be he whatever he may be, thou must keep to him. Thou sayest that a wife hath much comfort of her husband, when they are well consorted, and each is well content with the other. Yea; but 'tis rarely seen on earth. . . .
>
> [On childbearing]: Consider what joy ariseth when the offspring in thee quickeneth and groweth. How many miseries immediately wake up therewith, that work thee woe enough, fight against thy own flesh, and with many sorrows make war upon thy own nature. Thy ruddy face shall turn lean and grow green as grass. Thine eyes shall be dusky, and underneath grow pale; and by the giddiness of thy brain thy head shall ache sorely. Within thy belly, the uterus shall swell and strut out like a waterbag; thy bowels shall have pains, and there shall be stitches in thy flank. . . . All thy beauty is overthrown with withering.
>
> After all this, there cometh from the child thus born a crying and a weeping that must about midnight make thee to waken, or her that holds thy place, for whom thou must care [that is, a wet nurse]. And what of the cradle foulness, and the constant giving of the breast? to swaddle and feed the child at so many unhappy moments. . . . Little knoweth a maiden of all this trouble of wives' woes. . . .
>
> And what if I ask besides . . . how the wife stands that heareth when she comes in her child scream, sees the cat at the meat, and the hound at the hide? Her cake is burning on the stove, and her calf is sucking all the milk up, the pot is running into the fire, and the churl [manservant] is scolding. Though it be a silly tale, it ought, maiden, to deter thee more strongly from marriage, for it seems not silly to her that tries it.

### *Analyze and Interpret*

Aside from sheer technology, what part, if any, of these objections to the married state would now apply to discourage a prospective bride? What changes in the marital relationship has occurred in modern times to undermine the negative picture drawn here?

Source: Cited by Joseph and Frances Gies in *Women in the Middle Ages* (New York: Barnes & Noble, 1980).

John of England, Philip II Augustus of France, and Frederick II, the German emperor. But in behaving much like a secular king with his armies and his threats of war, Innocent sacrificed much of the moral authority he had derived from his position as successor to St. Peter and deputy of Christ on Earth.

Later thirteenth-century popes attempted to emulate Innocent with varying success, but all depended on their legal expertise or threat of armed force (the papal treasury assured the supply of mercenaries). Finally, Pope Boniface VIII (1294–1303) overreached badly when he attempted to assert that the clergy were exempt from royal taxes in both France and England. In the struggle of wills that followed, the kings of both countries were able to make Boniface back down: the clergy paid the royal taxes. It was a severe blow to papal prestige.

Some years later, the French monarch actually arrested the aged Boniface for a few days, dramatically demonstrating who held the whip hand if it should come to a showdown. Boniface died of humiliation, it was said, just days after his release. His successor was handpicked by Philip, the French king, who controlled the votes of the numerous French bishops.

## *The Babylonian Captivity*

The new pope was a French bishop who took the name Clement V. Rather than residing in Rome, he was induced to stay in the city of Avignon in what is now southern France. This was the first time since St. Peter that the head of the church had not resided in the Holy City of Christendom, and, to make matters worse, Clement's successors—mostly French bishops—stayed in Avignon as well. The **Babylonian Captivity**, as the popes' stay in Avignon came to be called, created a great scandal. Everyone except the French viewed the popes as captives of the French crown and unworthy to lead the universal church or decide questions of international justice.

In 1377, one of Clement's papal successors finally returned to Rome but died soon thereafter. In the ensuing election, great pressure was put on the attending bishops to elect an Italian, and the one duly elected took the name Urban VI. Urban was a well-intentioned reformer, but he went about his business in such an arrogant fashion that he had alienated all of his fellow bishops within weeks of his election. Declaring his election invalid because of pressures placed on them, the bishops elected another Frenchman, who took the name Clement VII. He immediately returned to Avignon and took up residence once more under the benevolent eye of the French king, but the bullheaded Urban refused to step down. There were thus two popes and doubt as to which, if either, was the legitimate one.

## *The Great Schism*

The final episode in this demeaning decline of papal authority now began. For forty years, Christians were treated to the spectacle of two popes denouncing each other as an impostor and the Anti-Christ. Europeans divided along national lines: the French, Scots, and Iberians supported Clement; the English and Germans preferred Urban (largely because his sentiments were anti-French). Neither side would give an inch, even after the two original contestants had died.

The **Great Schism** hastened the realization of an idea that had long been discussed among pious and concerned people: the calling of a council, a universal conclave of bishops to combat growing problems within the structure and doctrines of the church. The **Conciliar Movement** was a serious challenge to papal authority. Its supporters wished to enact some important reforms and thought that the papal government was far too committed to maintaining the status quo. Its adherents, therefore, argued that the entire church community, not the pope, had supreme powers of doctrinal definition. Such definition would be expressed in the meetings of a council, whose members should include laypersons and not just clerics. These ideas fell on fertile ground and were eventually picked up by other fourteenth-century figures, such as the English theologian John Wyclif.

Wyclif believed that the clergy had become corrupt and that individual Christians should be able to read and interpret the word of the Lord for themselves, rather than depending on a perhaps biased clergy. His doctrines were popular with the English poor and were emblazoned on the banners of the greatest popular uprising in English history, the revolt of 1381, which very nearly toppled the Crown. The rebels were called Wyclifites, or **Lollards**, and their ideas about the ability of ordinary people to interpret Scripture for themselves were to be spread to the Continent within a few years.

The scandal of the Schism aroused great resentment among Christians of all nations, and intense pressure was brought to bear on both papal courts to end their quarrel. Neither would, however, and finally a council was called at Pisa in Italy in 1409. The council declared both popes deposed and elected a new one, but neither of the deposed popes accepted the verdict, and so instead of two there were now three claimants!

A few years later, from 1414 to 1417, a bigger and more representative council met in the German city of Constance. The council had three objectives: (1) to end the Schism and return the papacy to Rome, (2) to condemn the Wyclifites and other heretics, and (3) to reform the church and clergy from top to bottom. The **Council of Constance** was successful in its first goal: a new pope was chosen, and the other three either stepped down voluntarily or were ignored. The council achieved some temporary success with its second goal of eliminating heresy, but the heresies it condemned simply went underground and emerged again a century later. As for the third objective, nothing was done; reforms were discussed, but the entrenched leaders made sure no real action was taken.

Additional councils were held over the next thirty years, but they achieved little or nothing in the vital areas of clerical corruption. The popes and other clerical officials who had resisted the whole idea of the council had triumphed, but their victory would come at a high price for their successors. The need for basic reform in the church continued to be ignored until the situation exploded with Martin Luther (see Chapter 24).

## Society and Work in Later Medieval Europe

As we have noted, an upsurge in peasant rebellions followed the Black Death. All of them were crushed. Nevertheless, in the long run, the peasants did succeed in obtaining more freedoms and security. The ***Jacquerie*** of 1358 in France shocked the nobility, as the peasants raped and looted, burned castles, and even destroyed chapels. The nobles took a heavy revenge, but the French and Flemish peasants were by no means through. Revolts occurred repeatedly throughout the 1300s and early 1400s in parts of France.

In England, the Lollard rebellion of 1381 was an equal jolt to the upper classes and the king. One of its leaders was the priest John Ball. His famous couplet would be shouted or mumbled from now on: "When Adam delved and Eva span/Who was then the gentleman?" (*Delved* means plowed, and *span* is old English for spun.) (See the Patterns of Belief box "John Ball's Preaching" for more discussion.)

The causes of the Lollard rebellion were complex and varied from place to place, but almost all of England was involved, and in an unusual development, the peasants were joined by many artisans and laborers in the towns. These urban workers had been impoverished by a rigid guild system that prevented newcomers from competing with the established shops and kept pay rates low for all but the workers at the top.

The **guilds** were medieval urban organizations that controlled what was made, for what price, and by whom. First formed in urban areas in the 1200s, the guilds were very strong by the fourteenth and fifteenth centuries. Their scheme, in which a worker advanced from apprentice to journeyman to master as his skills developed, was almost universal. Most journeymen never took the final step upward, however, because the guild restricted the number of masters who could practice their trade in a given area.

The guilds aimed at ensuring economic security for their members, not competitive advantage. The members fixed prices and established conditions of labor for employees, length of apprenticeships, pay scales, examinations for proving skills, and many other things. The labor shortages caused by the Black Death actually prolonged and strengthened the monopoly aspects of the guild system. In some European cities, the guilds, which abhorred the free market, were the chief determinants of economic activity until the nineteenth century.

Urban areas had been terribly overcrowded, at least until the Black Death. The reduced populations that followed the plague enabled many towns to engage in the first instances of urban planning. Many medieval towns emerged from the crisis with open spaces, parks, and suburbs that made them more attractive. (*Suburb* originally meant a settlement outside the walls of the town.) Again and again, a cramped city found it necessary to tear down the old walls and build new ones farther out. This expanding series of defensive earthwork and masonry walls is still perceptible in the maps of some modern European cities.

Inside the town walls or just outside, many types of skilled and semiskilled workers plied their trades, generally in home workshops employing one or two workers

**The Jacquerie.** This brilliant illustration exemplifies the usual end of a peasant rebellion in the fourteenth century; the nobles massacre their challengers and throw them into the river, cheered on by the ladies in the left background.

PATTERNS OF BELIEF

## John Ball's Preaching

**In the Lollard rebellion** in fourteenth-century England, the peasantry responded violently to the question "When Adam delved and Eva span, who was then the gentleman?" In his *Chronicles*, the medieval author Froissart tells us of what happened:

> A crazy priest in the county of Kent, called John Ball, who for his absurd preaching had thrice been confined to prison by the Archbishop of Canterbury, was greatly instrumental in exciting these rebellious ideas. Every Sunday after mass this John Ball was accustomed to assemble a crowd around him in the marketplace and preach to them. On such occasions he would say, "My good friends, matters cannot go on well in England until all things shall be in common; when there shall be neither vassals nor lords; when the lords shall be no more masters than ourselves. How ill they behave to us! For what reason do they thus hold us in bondage? Are we not all descended from the same parents, Adam and Eve? And what can they show, or what reason can they give, why they should be more masters than ourselves? They are clothed in velvet and rich stuffs, while we are forced to wear poor clothing. They have wines, spices, and fine bread, while we have only rye and the refuse of the straw; and when we drink, it must be water. They have handsome seats and manors, while we must brave the wind and rain in our labours in the field, and it is by our labour they have wherewithal to support their pomp. We are called slaves, and if we do not perform our service we are beaten, and we have no sovereign to whom we can complain or who would be willing to hear us. Let us go to the king and remonstrate with him; he is young, and from him we may obtain a favorable answer, and if not we must seek to amend our condition."
>
> Many in the city of London, envious of the rich and noble, having heard of John Ball's preaching, said among themselves that the country was badly governed, and that the nobility had seized upon all the gold and silver. These wicked Londoners began to assemble in parties and show signs of rebellion; they also invited all those who held like opinions in the adjoining counties to come to London: telling them that they would find the town open to them and the commonalty of the same way of thinking as themselves, and that they would so press the king, that there should no longer be a slave in England.

### Analyze and Interpret

What do you think was meant by the phrase "we must seek to amend our condition" in this statement? Why was it unusual that city dwellers would make common cause with the rural folk in something as dangerous as rebellion?

besides the family members. Factories, or mass employment places of production, were still in the distant future. Machines of any type independent of human or animal energy were unknown. Even water- and wind-powered mechanisms, such as waterwheels and windmills, were relatively rare. (The Society and Economy box relates more about medieval life, specifically that of an Italian family.)

## Late Medieval Art

Gothic cathedrals (see Chapter 19) remain the most impressive example of late medieval art forms. They combined architecture, painting, sculpture, inlay and carving, stained glass, and (in the church services) music and literature. The Gothic churches are some of the supreme examples of the ability to project a vision of life into concrete artistic format.

In the frescoes and altar screens created to decorate the churches' open places, the increasing refinement of

Strasbourg Cathedral, Strasbourg, Alsace, France/Peter Willi/ Bridgeman Art Library

**Strasbourg Cathedral Portal.** In the embrasures of this mighty stone portal are carved scenes from the Passion of Christ and the portraits of many prophets and Christian saints. They center on the Virgin and Child. The church used such sculpture and stonework as a teaching device for the many followers who could not read.

SOCIETY AND ECONOMY

## Margherita Datini (1360–1423)

**THE DISCOVERY OF HUNDREDS** of letters preserved by accident for 500 years in a residence in Prato, Italy, allows us to participate in many of the life events of a medieval Italian woman named Margherita Datini. She was the wife of a wealthy merchant, Francesco Datini, for more than thirty-five years, and during that time Francesco's frequent business trips made it necessary for the couple to communicate by letter.

The Datinis met in 1376, when he was almost forty and she was sixteen. Such an age difference was not uncommon in upper-class marriages of the period, although Datini was remarkable in not demanding a dowry from his bride's family. Margherita was an orphan, the daughter of a minor nobleman who had been executed in one of the incessant civil wars that wracked the northern Italian city-states. His property had been confiscated by the winners. Francesco was also an orphan, having lost both parents to the Black Plague, but he had been successful as a merchant in Avignon, serving the papacy of the Babylonian Captivity era. In 1382, the Datini household moved to the ancestral home in Prato, a textile town near Florence.

Datini decided to erect a real mansion on a lot he owned in the center of town, and he and Margherita lived out their long and generally happy lives there. The Datini house still stands. It is now a museum housing the archive they left. The Datinis experienced one great sadness: Margherita was unable to conceive, so they had no legitimate offspring. (Francesco had at least two illegitimate children and probably more.) Every classic remedy against barrenness was put into play, but nothing worked, not even the poultices of ghastly contents and the belts ornamented with prayers to St. Catherine.

Margherita's main tasks were the management of the large house and its several inhabitants. About eleven persons resided with the couple, four of whom were female slaves purchased at various times from Venetian merchants, who obtained them in Constantinople or in Venice's trading posts on the Black Sea. The others were servants, who were free to leave if they desired. All, slaves and servants, were treated well as members of the *famiglia,* the household. In addition to these live-in persons, several more servants came and went daily, so the lady of the house was constantly overseeing or instructing someone.

A few years after arriving back in Prato, Francesco's business as a cloth merchant and importer had grown so much that he opened a branch office in Pisa and a retail establishment in Florence. The separations these endeavors required persuaded Margherita to learn to read and write. In her frequent letters to her absent husband, she expresses many familiar concerns: he spends too much time away, he is probably unfaithful, and he gives his businesses more attention than his home. But good feeling is evidenced as well: Francesco clearly respected his wife's growing accomplishments as an educated woman; he was proud of her, while she was affectionate to him and wished she could see more of him. She even took care of his illegitimate daughter Ginevra as though the girl were her own.

When the plague returned in 1399, the Datinis pledged that they would endow a Prato charity if they survived. When Francesco died at the age of seventy-five in 1410, his wife was the executor of his will and followed his wishes by giving most of his large estate to the poor and orphans. The slaves were all freed and the servants well provided for, as were the surviving illegitimate children. Margherita survived thirteen more years, to age sixty-three, and is buried in Prato's St. Maria Novella churchyard, where the visitors to her former home can view her last resting place.

### *Analyze and Interpret*

What advantages can you see in an age difference so great as that of the Datinis at the time of marriage? Disadvantages? What do you think of the arrangement by which Margherita brought up the illegitimate daughter as her own, keeping in mind that she was childless and twenty-four years younger than her husband?

European painting is noteworthy, especially from the fourteenth century onward. Experimentation with perspective and more psychological realism in the portrayal of human faces is visible in Italian and Flemish work, particularly. Metalworking still lagged behind the achievements of the Chinese and the Muslims, but the gap was being narrowed and would be overcome by the fifteenth century.

A change in the sponsorship of artwork also gradually came about. The church or individual nobles and kings had directly commissioned most of the artwork of the High Middle Age. Most formal art was produced for the church as an institution or for individual clergy who had the wealth and the taste to indulge themselves while allegedly glorifying God.

Toward the end of the medieval period, members of the commercial class in the towns were at times wealthy enough to begin to play the role that had been monopolized by the nobility and clergy: patrons of the arts. In the fifteenth century, rich bankers or doctors began to commission portraits, although this practice was still not common. Most art was still the province of the two privileged classes, the churchmen and the warriors (nobles). Everyone in the medieval town may have contributed to the building of a new church, but the portrait sculpture over the main portal still depicted the bishop, and the front pew was reserved for the local baron.

## Medieval Sciences

In later medieval Europe, scientific studies improved somewhat from the elementary conditions of theory and practice in the earlier period. The introduction of Arabic numbers made doing math faster and easier. The Hindu/Arab invention of algebra was becoming known to Europeans. With it, they became much more adept at dealing with unknown quantities. Some faint beginnings of chemistry can be detected. These took the form of alchemy, the search (begun by the Muslims) for the magical substance that would transform base metal into gold and silver.

Geography made considerable progress, borrowing heavily from Muslim cartography and knowledge of the seas. Most educated people already believed the world was a sphere, for instance, before Portuguese voyages proved that it was. But except in anatomy, medicine and surgery made little headway beyond what the Muslims and Greeks already knew. (See the Science and Technology box for a sample of medieval medicine.) The main European medical center was at Salerno, which depended heavily on teachers from the Muslim countries. Physics and astronomy would only advance after the 1400s. Biological sciences were still in their infancy, the social sciences were not yet heard of, and botany and zoology were basically where the third-century Greeks had left them.

Part of the problem in the lagging development of the sciences was the insistence of the universities that were then multiplying throughout Europe that scientific knowledge was less important than the arts and humanities. In places such as Oxford, Paris, Salamanca, and Heidelberg, the majority of the teachers specialized in theology, classical languages, and rhetoric, rather than biology, physics, or mathematics. The science that the modern world takes for granted as a major source of truth did not yet exist.

Perhaps the most important advances in science in the later medieval period are to be found not in the answers but in the questions posed by such scholars as Albertus Magnus and Roger Bacon, of Paris and Oxford, respectively. Both were seeking new ways to collect data about the natural world and pioneered what we now call the "experimental method" of ascertaining truth.

As we observed in Chapter 19, the teachings of Aristotle held pride of place in the humanities and natural sciences. Now familiar to Christians from his Muslim admirers in Spain and Sicily, he became almost as important in European thought as he had been in Muslim studies. His theories about the form of the cosmos, the revolution of the planets, and the nature of matter were considered the last word on the subject, even though they sometimes clashed with what could be observed.

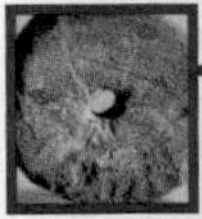

SCIENCE AND TECHNOLOGY

### Medieval Medicine

**Medieval medical lore often** sounds fantastic to modern audiences, but modern research has sometimes found that the folk medicine of Europe and other areas of the world has definite clinical value. A certain female physician of the eleventh or twelfth century named Trotula reportedly compiled the handbook from which the following interesting recipes were taken:

**Chapter 43: A Treatment for Lice**

For lice originating in the armpits and in the pubic hair, we mix ashes with oil and anoint those parts. For general lice around the eyes and head, we make an ointment sufficient strong to expel them: take of aloes one ounce, white lead five ounces, olibanum and bacon with its grease, the bacon finely chopped. Pulverize the other ingredients and make an ointment with the grease. . . .

**Chapter 55: Against Deafness**

For deafness take the cooked fat of fresh caught eels, juice of caprifolium, juice of Jove's beard [both are flowering weeds], and a handful of ant eggs. Grind, strain, and mix them with oil and cook. After cooking add vinegar or wine to make it more penetrating. Pour into the sound ear, and stop up the defective ear, letting the patient lie partly on the sound ear. In the morning he must be careful of drafts.

#### *Analyze and Interpret*

Unlike the medicine practiced by contemporary Arab/Muslim and Hindu doctors, medieval European practice was usually a concoction of fantasies and ignorance. The exceptions were limited to such matters as getting rid of body lice, which were a common nuisance. What do you make of such "medicine"?

This reverence for authority was characteristic of the Middle Ages and was sometimes a severe obstacle to the introduction of new knowledge.

The clash between new and old was especially clear in the branch of philosophy called metaphysics. In the thirteenth century, the learned Thomas Aquinas had bridged the chasm between classical and Christian doctrines in his *Summa Theologica (The Highest Theology).* This book became the standard work for Catholic theology into modern times. Its subtle and complex reasoning, however, was distorted by the "schoolmen," or *scholastics,* priests and university teachers who tried to ignore or undermine ideas that challenged tradition, especially church-approved tradition. Originally pioneers of a new rationalism that was very much needed in Western thought, the scholastics gradually became fossilized. By the 1400s, they had become a retarding force in education, committing themselves to verbal tricks and meaningless hairsplitting. By so doing they transformed the philosophy of the great Aquinas from the most subtle explanation of God's universe into an exercise for theology students.

## SUMMARY

The later Middle Age (fourteenth and fifteenth centuries) was a mixed scene of cultural advances, social violence, economic and military disasters, and religious strife. The fourteenth century was a particularly disastrous epoch. The Black Death carried off perhaps one-fourth of the population to an early death, thereby creating a shortage of labor that impeded Europe's recovery for generations. Peasants seized the chance to escape serfdom, sometimes to the extent of rebelling openly against their lords. Such revolts were put down mercilessly, but the days of serfdom in the old sense were over from Germany westward.

In the towns, the new bourgeoisie continued to gain prestige and wealth at the expense of the nobility, while having to defend their position against the rising discontent of the urban workers. The guilds, which were originally intended to protect the livelihood of the master artisans, increasingly became closed castes of privilege.

The Hundred Years' War dealt a heavy blow to the French monarchy, which was rescued from disintegration only through Joan of Arc. The war also ended the domination of the field of battle by noble horsemen and signaled the coming of modern gunpowder war. The Babylonian Captivity and the Great Schism marked the onset of a decline in the papacy that was not to be reversed until after Luther's challenge. The major weapon in the papal arsenal, the moral authority of the Vicar of Christ, was rapidly being dulled as pope after pope gave more attention to politics and power than to matters of faith.

## IDENTIFICATION TERMS

Test your knowledge of this chapter's key concepts by defining the following terms. If you can't recall the meaning of certain terms, refresh your memory by looking up the boldfaced term in the chapter, turning to the Glossary at the end of the book, or working with the flashcards that are available on the *World Civilizations* Companion Website: **http://history.wadsworth.com/adler04**.

Agincourt
Babylonian Captivity
Black Death
Conciliar Movement
Council of Constance
Crecy
Great Schism
guilds
*Jacquerie*
Lollards

## TEST YOUR KNOWLEDGE

Test your knowledge of this chapter by answering the following questions. Complete answers appear at the end of the book. You may also take this quiz interactively and find even more quiz questions on the *World Civilizations* Companion Website: **http://history.wadsworth.com/adler04**.

1. Which one of the following was *not* a consequence of the Black Death in European affairs?
   a. Severe labor shortage
   b. Preoccupation with death and guilt
   c. Heightened sensitivity to the natural world
   d. Increased readiness to rebel against the peasants' lords
   e. Declining tax revenues
2. Which of the following battles was a victory for the French in the Hundred Years' War?
   a. Crecy
   b. Orleans
   c. Agincourt
   d. Poitiers
   e. Calais
3. One consequence of the Hundred Years' War was
   a. an increase in the importance of France's parliament.
   b. an improvement in England's patterns of trade.
   c. an increasing acceptance of chivalry as a way of life.
   d. a more important role for the cavalry in battle.
   e. the development of a stronger parliament in England.
4. During the Babylonian Captivity, the pope became the satellite of the
   a. Holy Roman Emperor.
   b. Roman mob.
   c. French crown.
   d. German nobles.
   e. Swiss cantons.
5. One result of the Council of Constance was to
   a. elect a new pope in an attempt to end the Great Schism.
   b. end the idea of papal supremacy in the church.
   c. split the church into two halves.
   d. move the papacy from Rome to a new home in Avignon.
   e. initiate major reforms within the church.
6. The usual reaction of the nobles to peasant rebellions was to
   a. crush them and take bloody vengeance.
   b. blame the urban classes for inspiring them.
   c. negotiate a compromise at the expense of the Crown.
   d. free their remaining serfs and gain peace.
   e. hire German mercenaries to crush the rebellions for them.
7. John Ball was the leader of
   a. a movement to strip the English upper classes of their privileges.
   b. the movement to make church councils superior to the papacy in defining doctrine.
   c. the Jacquerie in France.
   d. an English army in France that introduced gunpowder to warfare.
   e. a group of artisans who pushed for greater recognition of the guild system.
8. Which of the following did Margherita Datini *not* experience in her lifetime?
   a. Raising the illegitimate daughter of her husband
   b. Losing her father by execution
   c. Being frequently separated from her husband by business
   d. Raising two healthy sons
   e. Managing her rather large, prosperous household
9. In the late medieval period, the apex of Gothic architecture could be seen in the
   a. universities.
   b. town squares.
   c. homes of the newly rich.
   d. government buildings.
   e. cathedrals.
10. A critically important figure for late medieval science was
   a. Aristotle.
   b. Euclid.
   c. Plato.
   d. Herodotus.
   e. Archimedes.

## InfoTrac College Edition

Visit the source collections at

**http://infotrac.thomsonlearning.com**

and use the Search function with the following key terms:

Middle Ages    Black Death    Hundred Years' War

## Wadsworth History Website Resources

Visit the World History Resource Center at **http://history.wadsworth.com/world** for a wealth of general resources, and the *World Civilizations* Companion Website at **http://history.wadsworth.com/adler04** for resources specific to this textbook.

## HistoryNow

Enter *HistoryNow* using the access card that is available for *World Civilizations. HistoryNow* will assist you in understanding the content in this chapter with lesson plans generated for your needs. In addition, you can read the following documents, and many more, online:

Boccacio, description of the Black Death

Jean Froissart, *The Battle of Crecy*

Jean Froissart, *The Jacquerie*

*Celui qui ne sait pas dissimuler ne sait pas regner.*
*(He who doesn't know how to deceive doesn't know how to rule.)*
Louis XI of France

# 21 The European Renaissance



| | |
|---|---|
| 1300s | Renaissance begins in Italy |
| 1400s | Renaissance spreads north of Alps |
| 1461–1483 | Reign of Louis XI of France |
| 1485–1509 | Reign of Henry VII Tudor of England |
| 1480 | Russians terminate Mongols' occupation |
| 1500s | New monarchies; new concept of state |
| 1511 | "Third Rome" idea broached in Russia |

Beginning in the fourteenth century, a new spirit manifested itself in Europe among the educated classes. Much later called the **Renaissance**, or "rebirth," it was mainly an urban phenomenon and restricted to the uppermost segments of society. There were in fact two distinct Renaissances: (1) a change in economic and social conditions and (2) an artistic and cultural movement that was founded on that change. The Renaissance also differed substantially south and north of the Alps. In the South (Italy), the intellectual spirit of the age was secular and anticlerical. In the North (German-speaking Europe), there was a more pronounced concern for religious reform and less emphasis on the assertion of individual excellence.

## The Italian City-States

The Renaissance began in the northern Italian city-states, such as Florence, Venice, Milan, and Pisa. By counterbalancing the governance claims of the papacy against those of the Holy Roman Emperor, these cities had gradually succeeded in becoming independent of both (see Map 21.1).

Why did the first stirrings of the rebirth manifest themselves in this place and in this time? These cities were rich because of both trade advantage and financial genius. Genoa and Venice dominated the Mediterranean trade routes with the East and Africa; Florence was the center of the skilled metal and leather trades and, with the Flemish, controlled the lucrative textile trade of much of Europe. In the fifteenth century, the huge wealth of the papal court made Rome once again—after a lapse of 1,000 years—a major center of culture and art.

But why specifically was Italy the leader? More and more in the late Middle Age, Italians were leading the way in innovations—scientific, artistic, and economic. Italians were the leading bankers, mariners, scientists, and engineers; the rest of Europe increasingly looked to Italy for what was new and sent their sons there to study. Even the devastation of the Black Death, which wracked the Italian cities, could not crush them. In a remarkably short time of two generations—by the early fifteenth century—

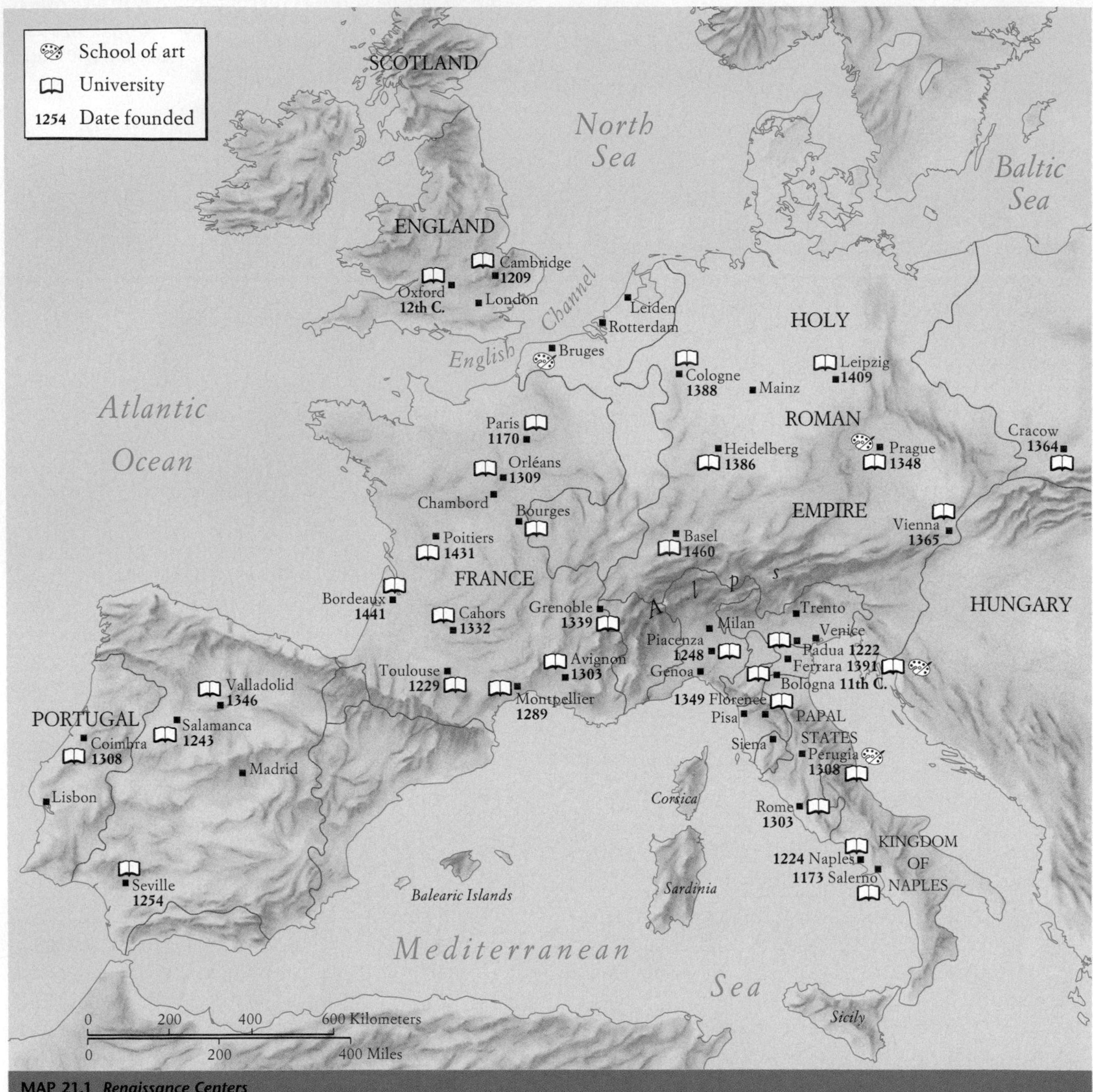


**MAP 21.1** ***Renaissance Centers***

The Renaissance was limited to the confines of the old Roman Empire and left stronger traces in Italy and northwest Europe than elsewhere. Like most cultural innovations after c. 1200, it was closely tied to the progress and prestige of the urban middle classes. Their absence in eastern Europe and weakness in the Iberian peninsula (Spain and Portugal) meant that the Renaissance was scarcely noticeable there.

they had returned to their prior prosperity and positions of leadership.

The city-states of the fourteenth and fifteenth centuries were princely *oligarchies.* In other words, a small group of wealthy aristocrats, headed by a prince with despotic power, ran the government. No commoners, whether urban workers or peasants outside the city gates, enjoyed even a hint of power. In fact, a huge gap existed between the ruling group of aristocrats, merchants, bankers, and traders and the rest of the population, who were regarded with a detached contempt. It was possible to rise into the ruling clique, but difficult. The key was money.

## The Renaissance Attitude

The wealthy in an Italian city were highly educated and very much aware of and proud of their good taste in the arts. Led by the prince, the members of the oligarchy spared no pains or money to assert their claims to glory and sophistication in the supreme art of living well. What did "living well" mean to these individuals? Certain elements recur:

- *Individualism.* Wealthy men and women of the Italian Renaissance believed that the age-old Christian emphasis on submerging one's fate within the general fate of the sons and daughters of Adam was wrong. They wished to set themselves apart from the masses and were supremely confident that they could. They despised Christian humility and encouraged a new pride in human potential. A thirst for fame and a strong desire to put their own imprint on the contemporary world were at the heart of their psychology.
- *Secularism.* Increasing **secularism** in Italy meant that the focus of the upper classes' attention shifted steadily away from the eternal to worldly affairs. The life to come receded into the background, and sometimes it was pushed offstage entirely. The here and now became the critical factor in determining acts and thoughts. The acquisitive instinct was sharpened, and few thought it wrong to pursue riches. Increasingly, people viewed life as an opportunity for glory and pleasure, rather than as a transitory stage on the way to eternal bliss or everlasting damnation. *Man was the measure*—the hoary Sophist motto—for what life had to offer.
- *Revival of classical values.* The ancient civilizations of the Greeks and especially the pagan Romans became the focus of artistic and cultural interest. Led by notable scholars such as Petrarch and Lorenzo Valla, the thinkers and writers of the fourteenth and fifteenth centuries looked back to pre-Christian Mediterranean culture for their values and standards. They were not anti-Christian so much as pro-pagan in their admiration for the achievements of Plato, Aristotle, Virgil, Terence, and countless other contributors to the pre-Christian intellectual world. The collection and careful editing of the ancient texts that had somehow survived (many through Muslim caretakers) became an obsession. What the modern world possesses of the Greco-Roman past is largely the work of the Renaissance.

There were, of course, variations of degree in these attitudes. Even in Italy, many people soberly upheld the medieval Christian viewpoint and insisted that humans were made for God and that the new emphasis on pleasure and self-fulfillment could lead only to disaster. Many of the scholars who paged through the Roman manuscripts were devout Christians, looking for holes in the arguments of their secular opponents or for proof of the earlier pagans' search for an all-knowing God.

In general, the Italian Renaissance was devoted to the *self*-realization of man as a being whose earthly life was the only sure one he had. It rejected the devotional Middle Ages (the term came into first usage at this time) as a dark interlude, which had lasted all too long, between the light of the Greco-Roman Classical Age and the rebirth now beginning.

## The Northern Renaissance

North of the Alps, the Renaissance was also a powerful force, but with a rather different character than in Italy. Carried to Germany and the Low Countries by students returning from study with the great Italian artists and writers, the new spirit underwent a sort of sea change as it came northward. It became more pietist and less pagan, more reformist, and less self-centered.

The term ***humanism*** is often applied to the northern Renaissance and its leading figures. The humanists were scholars who were painfully aware of the corruption of church and society and wished to remedy it by gradualist means, through reforms grounded in ancient Christian teachings. The Renaissance in this context meant an attempt to return the church and lay society in general to a purer state; it was an attempt to reawaken a sense of Christians' duties and responsibilities toward themselves and their fellow humans.

In the North as well as in Italy, scholars put great confidence in the powers of the intellect to find the truth and employ it to bring about necessary reform. The use of reason, rather than dogma, was an important article of faith for humanists everywhere. They believed that if people could be brought to see the good, they would pursue it. The trouble with the world was that the good was everywhere obscured by bad habits, ignorance, or malice.

How did the reformers propose to achieve their aims? The English Thomas More's ***Utopia*** is an excellent example. The book was meant as a satire and a lesson for society. The people of Utopia (Greek for "no place") do not seek wealth because they see no rewards in it. They put their neighbors' welfare ahead of their own. Their education continues throughout their entire lives rather than being limited to a few childhood years. All individuals are absolutely equal in powers and status, and they live by reason rather than passion and ignorance.

It was a radical message: More was saying that a corrupt and ignorant society, not the individual sinner, was responsible for the sorry state of the world. Adam's sin was not enough to explain humans' plight. The way people lived with one another must be reformed—and by humans themselves.

The best-known and most noble-minded of all the northern humanists was the Dutch Desiderius Erasmus, who lived in the late fifteenth and early sixteenth centuries; by his death, his works were being read throughout Europe. His *Praise of Folly* was a scorching indictment of the so-called wisdom of the world and a plea for a return to simple virtues. Even more influential was his

Francis G. Mayer/Corbis

**Thomas More.** The force of character of Sir Thomas More, English statesman and humanist, comes through strongly in this great portrait by Hans Holbein the Younger. The chain of office worn by More shows that the painting was made between 1529 and 1533, when he was the lord chancellor of King Henry VIII before being executed for resisting Henry's divorce and remarriage to Anne Boleyn.

new, carefully researched edition of the New Testament, with his commentaries and introduction.

Erasmus's work has two basic themes: the inner nature of Christianity and the importance of education. By the inner nature of Christianity, he meant that the true follower of Christ should emulate Christ's life, not what the theologians have tried to make out of his gospels. Erasmus condemned the empty formalism that was so common in the church of his day. In so doing, he was one of the most important forerunners of the Protestant Reformation, although he absolutely rejected Protestantism for himself and condemned Luther's arrogance (see Chapter 24).

Samuel H. Kress Collection, © 1995 Board of Trustees, National Gallery, Washington, D.C.

**Death and the Miser.** The Dutchman Hieronymous Bosch was the sixteenth-century master of the grotesque and the damned. Here he shows what happens to the treasure of a miser. As Death comes for him—and the angel implores him to put his faith in the crucified Christ—monsters and thieves make off with his money.

## The Political Economy of Renaissance Europe

The political theory of the Middle Ages was based on a strong centralizing monarchy, which was blessed and seconded by a powerful and respected clergy. The favorite image for government was a man wearing a crown and holding a cross in his left hand and a sword in his right. But in the Hundred Years' War and other late medieval conflicts, that image suffered serious damage. In country after country, the feudal nobility were able to reassert themselves and again decentralize political power. This decentralization was then reversed in the fifteenth and sixteenth centuries. The monarchs, now armed with a new theory of authority, effectively denied the nobles' claims of autonomy and subdued their frequent attempts to rebel. The new basis of royal authority was not church and king in partnership, but the king as executive of the state. What was new here was the idea of the *secular* state.

### The Theory of the State

The state in Renaissance thinking was an entity, a political organism that existed independently of the ruler or the subjects. It possessed three essential attributes: legitimacy, sovereignty, and territory.

- *Legitimacy* meant that the state possessed moral authority in the eyes of its subjects. It had a right to exist.
- *Sovereignty* meant that the state had an effective claim to equality with other states and that it acknowledged no higher earthly power over it.
- *Territory* is self-explanatory: the state possessed real estate that could be precisely bounded and contained certain human and material resources.

The royal personage was not the creator or owner, but only the servant, the executive agent, and protector of the state. He had every right and duty to use whatever means he deemed fit to ensure the state's welfare and expansion. In the fifteenth-century monarch's view, ensuring the welfare of the state was about the same as ensuring the welfare of the society in general. These so-called new monarchs were intent on one great goal: power. To be the proper servants of the state, they felt they must be the masters of all who might threaten it, and that meant being masters of intrigue, deceit, and intimidation. Renaissance politics was a rough game.

All of the Renaissance political theorists spent much time on the relationship between power and ethics, but none had the long-term impact of a young Italian with great ambitions, Niccoló Machiavelli. In his extraordinary treatise on politics entitled *The Prince* (1516), Machiavelli described power relations in government as he had experienced them—not as they *should* be, but as they were *in fact.* He thought that human beings are selfish by nature and must be restrained by the prince from doing evil to one another. In so doing, the prince could and should use all means open to him. He must be both the lion and the fox, the one who is feared and the one who is beloved. If it came to a choice between instilling fear and love, the wise prince will choose fear, which is more dependable (see the Law and Government box, which summarizes Machiavelli's position.)

### Royal Governments

What Machiavelli was preaching was already being followed by the more aggressive throne-holders of Europe. In the fifteenth century the powers and prestige of various royal governments increased significantly, especially in France, England, and Russia (see Map 21.2).

***France.*** France recovered much more rapidly than might have been expected from the devastation of the Hundred Years' War. The unpromising monarch who owed his throne to Joan of Arc's help, Charles VII (ruled 1422–1461), turned out to be one of the cleverest and most effective of kings. He created the first truly royal army and used it against those who tried to assert their independence. He also gained much stronger control over the French clergy, particularly the appointment of bishops.

Charles's policies were followed, with even greater cleverness, by his son Louis XI (ruled 1461–1483), the "Spider King," as he was called by his many enemies. Louis was especially effective at gaining middle-class support—and tax money—against the claims of the nobles. He also significantly expanded the size of the royal domain: that part of the country, centered on Paris, under the direct control of the Crown. Louis is credited with laying the foundation for the dimensions the French state attained under the great Bourbon kings of the seventeenth and eighteenth centuries.

***England.*** England took more time to establish a centralized monarchy than had France and never proceeded as far. The strong rule of the early Norman kings ended with weak or unlucky individuals such as John the First (and Last!). In 1215, John (ruled 1199–1216) had had to accept the *Magna Carta* from his rebellious nobles. Over the centuries, this Great Charter was gradually transformed from a statement of noble privilege against an unloved king to a doctrine that held that the monarch, like all others, was bound to obey the laws.

The Hundred Years' War further weakened the royal powers and strengthened Parliament, as we have noted. By the mid-fifteenth century, Parliament had become the

LAW AND GOVERNMENT

## Machiavelli's *The Prince*

**IN THE YEAR 1513,** the Florentine official and diplomat Niccoló Machiavelli (1469–1527) was arrested for treason and subjected to torture. Although he was soon released, his ambitions for power and wealth lay in ruins. Reluctantly retiring to his country estate, Machiavelli devoted much of his remaining life to writing a series of theoretical works on politics and the eventful history of his native Florence. But he is best remembered for his handbook on the art of governance, *The Prince,* the masterwork of Renaissance political literature. In it he elucidated a coldly realistic view—strongly reminiscent of the Chinese Legalists—of what law and lawgivers must do to preserve civic harmony.

Machiavelli's denial that common morality should influence a ruler's politics in any way and his insistence that violence and deceit can be justified in the name of good government have earned him a sinister reputation. To the present day, the adjective *Machiavellian* carries a cynical connotation. Yet the author, who had had every chance of observing what he wrote about, was just describing the actual practices of the Italian rulers of his day—and of many wielders of power since then.

> I say that every prince ought to wish to be considered kind rather than cruel. Nevertheless, he must take care to avoid misusing his kindness. Caesar Borgia* was considered cruel, yet his cruelty restored Romagna, uniting it in peace and loyalty. . . . A prince must be indifferent to the charge of cruelty if he is to keep his subjects loyal and united. . . . Disorders harm the entire citizenry, while the executions ordered by a prince harm only a few. Indeed, of all princes, the newly established one can least of all escape the charge of cruelty, for new states are encumbered with dangers.
>
> Here a question arises: whether it is better to be loved than feared, or the reverse. The answer is, of course, that it would be best to be both loved and feared. But since the two rarely come together, anyone compelled to choose will find greater security in being feared than in being loved. . . . Men are less concerned about offending someone they have cause to love than someone they have cause to fear. Love endures by a bond which men, being scoundrels, may break whenever it serves their advantage to do so; but fear is supported by the dread of pain, which is always present. . . .
>
> I conclude that since men will love what they themselves determine, but will fear as their ruler determines, a wise prince must rely upon what he, not others, can control. He need only strive to avoid being hated. Let the prince conquer his state, then, and preserve it; the methods employed will always be judged honorable, and everyone will praise him. For the mob of men is always impressed by appearances, and by results; and the world is composed of the mob.
>
> How praiseworthy it is, that a prince keeps his word and governs by candor, rather than craft, everyone knows . . . yet, those princes who had little regard for their word, and had the craft to turn men's minds, have accomplished great things, and in the end, they have overcome those who suited their actions to their pledges.

*Caesar Borgia was the illegitimate son of Pope Alexander VI and one of the most ruthless Italian noblemen of the day.

### *Analyze and Interpret*

Do you agree that the wise ruler will choose fear over love from his subjects? How do Machiavelli's precepts translate into present-day politics? Can you give some examples from the news this week?

Source: Niccoló Machiavelli, *The Prince,* trans. Luigi Ricci, as revised by E. A.Vincent (New York: Oxford University Press, 1935). Used by permission.

**History Now™**

***To read more of* The Prince, *point your browser to the documents area of* HistoryNow.**

preserve of semi-independent barons and earls, who held the tax purse strings and drove hard bargains with the king in the wake of the lost war. The nobility added to the turbulence by engaging in an obscure struggle over the succession to the throne. Called the **Wars of the Roses**, the conflict lasted fifteen years (1455–1471).

Three late-fifteenth-century kings (Edward IV, Richard III, and Henry VII) then gradually threw the balance of power in favor of the Crown. Of these, the most important was Henry VII (ruled 1485–1509), the founder of the Tudor Dynasty and a master of intimidation and intrigue. He enlisted the aid of the middle classes and the clergy, both of whom were exasperated by the squabbles of the nobles. Henry not only rebuilt the powers of the royal crown but also avoided foreign wars, which would have meant going back to the noble-dominated Parliament to beg for funds. By the time he died in 1509, the English royal government was in firm control of the state.

***The Holy Roman Empire (Germany).*** The great exception to the recovery of royal powers in the later fifteenth century was the German kingdom, technically still the Holy Roman Empire of the German Nation. Here there was no central power to recover; it had been utterly destroyed in the medieval struggles between emperor and pope and the struggles between emperor and nobles that then ensued.

**MAP 21.2** ***Europe, the Near East, and North Africa in the Renaissance***

The political divisions of the Mediterranean basin and Europe in the fifteenth century. Note the division of the former Abbasid caliphate, centered on Baghdad (not shown), into several independent sultanates and the Ottoman Empire.

Why couldn't the Germans recover from these eleventh- and twelfth-century troubles by the fifteenth century? The critical weakness of the monarchy was that the emperor was elected, rather than succeeding by hereditary right. The seven electors, who were all German princes and bishops, could and did negotiate with the various candidates to strike deals aimed at preserving noble autonomy. As a result, Germany had no centralized government in the fifteenth century. The emperor was only the first among equals, and sometimes not even that. He did not have a bureaucracy, a royal army, a national parliament, or the power to tax his subjects. The Holy Roman Empire was really a loose confederation of principalities, dukedoms, and even free cities, some of which were almost always squabbling among themselves. All real power was in the hands of the local aristocrats and the churchmen.

Among the candidates for this weak throne, the **Habsburg Dynasty** had most often been successful. This princely family had its home in Austria. In the late fifteenth and early sixteenth centuries, a series of extraordinary events propelled them into great international prominence for the first time. Thanks to a series of marriages and the unexpected deaths of rivals, by 1527 the Habsburg territories had trebled in Europe and also included the huge overseas empire being rapidly conquered by Spain, which was now under a Habsburg ruler. It appeared that for the first time since the twelfth century, the Holy Roman Emperor would be able to assert real authority, but the prospects of establishing strong royal rule in Germany were not realized: the burgeoning division in religious affairs between Catholics and Protestants frustrated all efforts to unify the nation until the late nineteenth century.

***Russia.*** Russia was a brand-new entrant—or rather a newly rediscovered entrant—on the European scene in the fifteenth century. The huge expanse of territory east of Christian Poland and Hungary was practically unknown to western Europeans after its conquest by the Mongols in the mid-1200s (see Chapters 14 and 17). Almost all cultural contacts between Russians and both the Latin and

Byzantine Christian worlds had been severed by the primitive Asiatic tribesmen. The latter's adoption of the Islamic faith in the fourteenth century deepened the chasm that separated them from their Russian subjects.

The "Mongol Yoke" that lay on Russia for almost two and a half centuries (1240–1480) caused a cultural retrogression of tremendous import. Before the Mongols came, the chief Russian state, the **Principality of Kiev**, had entertained close relations with Christian Europe and especially with the Orthodox Christian empire in Constantinople from which it had received its religion, literature, and law. Situated on the extreme eastern periphery of the Christian world, Russia had nevertheless felt itself and been considered a full member of the European family.

After the arrival of the Mongols, this situation changed radically. In an effort to escape the alien ruling group's taxes and cruelties, the clergy and people of Russia sought to isolate themselves and had become vulnerable to all of the ills that isolation entails. Ignorance and superstition became rife, even among the diminished number of the formally educated; the levels of technical and theoretical skills declined. Literacy all but disappeared among the laity.

In the absence of an independent Russian government, the Russian church came to play a particularly vital role in keeping the notion of a national community alive. The church of Rome had been rejected as heretical ever since the split in 1054. After the Turks seized Constantinople in 1453, the belief grew in Moscow that this had been God's punishment for the Greeks' waverings in defense of Orthodoxy. Now, Russia was to become the fortress of right belief: the **Third Rome**. As a Russian monk wrote to his ruler in 1511: "Two Romes [that is, the Christian Rome of the fourth century, and Constantinople] have fallen, but the Third [Moscow] stands and there will be no fourth." Russia's government and church saw themselves as the implements of divine providence that would bring the peoples of Europe back to the true faith and defeat the infidels, wherever they might be.

By the late fifteenth century, the Mongols had been so weakened by internal conflicts that their former partner, the prince of Moscow, defied them successfully in 1480 and asserted his independence. Already, Moscow had become the most powerful Russian principality by a combination of single-minded ambition and consistent good luck. Soon after the defeat of the Mongols, the prince of Moscow had extended his rule to all parts of the nation and had taken to calling himself *czar* ("Caesar" in Slavic) of Russia.

A czar had far more power than any other European ruler of the day. A czar's alleged powers were so impressive as to raise the question whether Russia was still a European state or whether, under the Mongols, it had become an Asiatic despotism in which the will of the ruler was automatically law of the land. Western European ambassadors and traders sent to Moscow in the sixteenth century felt that they had landed on truly foreign ground. They found themselves in a society that had no middle class and was untouched by the technical and psychological developments of the Renaissance. Its population's superstition and passivity were appalling, and its subservience toward its prince was striking to Western eyes.

## Art and Its Patrons

The most visible and historically appreciated form of Renaissance culture is its art, and Italy was the leader in every field. A tremendous creative outburst took place in Florence, Rome, Venice, Milan, and a dozen other city-states during the fifteenth and sixteenth centuries.

As in other widespread cultural phenomena, considerable variation existed from one locale to another. The spirit of North European painting and sculpture differed from that of the South. Northern art is more overtly religious and avoids the lush sensuousness that marks much Italian art. The outstanding exponents of the northern Renaissance in art were the Flemish portraitists of the fifteenth century, such as Van Eyck, Memmling, and Bosch. The Germans of the Rhine valley and Bavaria were also active in both painting and sculpture. Some of the most accomplished wood carvings of any age were produced in southern Germany and Austria during this era. These, too, display little of the delight in the flesh or the interest in experimentation of the Italians. In general, architecture followed the same pattern. Variations on the Gothic style continued to be the standard in the North, and northern architects made no effort to imitate the revived classicism that was so popular in Italy.

The spirit of this art, wherever produced, was quite different from that of medieval art. The latter attempted to portray concretely the collective belief of a community, the Christian community. It subordinated the individual and the particular to the group and the generic. Despite much technical innovation, medieval art was conservative and evolutionary in its spirit.

Renaissance art, in contrast, was intended to show the artist's mastery of technique and his newfound freedoms. It was experimental: new ideas were tried in all directions, and old ideas were put into new forms or media. The huge bronze doors of the Florentine cathedral cast by Ghiberti were something quite new: nothing like that had been attempted previously. With their twelve reliefs depicting the life of Christ, the doors were a brilliant success. Similarly, the enormous, architecturally unprecedented domes of the Florentine cathedral and St. Peter's in Rome were meant as a demonstration of what might be done by the bold human imagination, unfettered from its previous restrictions.

In painting, great talents such as Titian, da Vinci, Michelangelo, Botticelli, and Giotto led the way to an abundance of innovative compositions. All of them opened their studios to teach others, so that a wave of experimentation in the visual art forms swept across Italy and northward into Europe beyond the Alps. One of their great achievements was the mastery of perspective, which Giotto first accomplished in the early fourteenth century. He also led the way to a new realism in portraits.

In sculpture, the universal genius of Michelangelo was accompanied by Donatello, Cellini, and Bernini, to mention only some of the better-known names. Both Renaissance sculpture and painting broke sharply from their medieval forerunners. Artists now saw the human figure as a thing of superb animal beauty quite apart from its spiritual considerations or destiny.

Michelangelo was a leader in architecture as well. He designed much of the vast new St. Peter's Cathedral for one of the popes. Other leading architects included Bramante, da Vinci, and Brunelleschi. The basic architectural style of the Renaissance was an adaptation of the classical temple, with its balanced columns, magisterial domes, and lofty, symmetrical facades. The Gothic style was now dismissed as primitive and superstition-ridden in its striving toward a distant heaven.

The artist's position as a respected, powerful member of society was also a Renaissance novelty (one that has generally not been imitated since!). Several of the leading figures of the art world were well-rewarded in money and prestige. They could pick and choose among their patrons and did not hesitate to drive hard bargains for their talents. Leonardo da Vinci was one of the richest men of his time and lived accordingly. So did Michelangelo and Raphael, both of whom enjoyed papal esteem and commissions for the Vatican palaces and libraries.

Art was unashamedly used to display the wealth of the individual or group who had commissioned it, rather than their piety (as in medieval times). Artistic patronage was limited to a smaller group than had been true earlier. The princes and the oligarchies around them were a tiny fraction of Italian society, but they provided most of the artists' commissions. Only rarely would an artist work without a specific commission in the hope of finding a buyer later.

Artists dealt with their patrons as equals. It was not at all unusual for a secure artist to refuse a lucrative commission because of a disagreement. For the most part, the patrons respected talent and allowed the artists to execute their work much as they pleased. The idea of artistic genius came into currency at this time. Artists were thought to possess a "divine spark" or other quality that ordinary souls lacked, and therefore should be allowed to develop their talents without too much restriction.

Artists who were not good enough or sufficiently well-connected to secure commissions worked for others in their studios as anonymous helpers. Many of the great paintings of the Italian Renaissance were only sketched

Baptistery, Florence, Italy/Bridgeman Art Library

**Doors of Paradise.** The beauty of these bronze doors cast by Lorenzo Ghiberti for the cathedral in Florence was so overwhelming to his fellow citizens that they named them the Doors of Paradise. Ten panels show scenes from the Old Testament; the detail photo below shows the slaying of Goliath by David.

Baptistery, Florence, Italy/Bridgeman Art Library

Bettmann/Corbis

**MICHELANGELO'S CREATION OF ADAM.** This fresco was among many that the artist created for the Sistine Chapel in Rome between 1508 and 1512.

and outlined by the famous artist: unknown helpers finished out the brushwork.

## THE RENAISSANCE CHURCH

Much Renaissance literature satirizes the Christian clergy and focuses attention on the corruption and indifference that had become common in the higher ranks. These attacks are clearly directed at the personnel of the church, not its basic doctrines. At a time when increasing educational opportunity was giving birth to an urban group that was well-read in nonreligious literature, the open immorality of some clergy and the ignorance and selfishness of others generated continual scandal. Many village priests were still illiterate, and many monks had long since forgotten their vows of poverty and chastity. It was not at all unusual for a bishop never to set foot in his diocese because he preferred to live elsewhere. It was equally common for the abbot of a monastery to have produced a couple of illegitimate children with his "housekeeper." In any Italian town, the local clergy's political and financial interests often nullified their moral leadership. This embittered many of the leading figures of the Italian Renaissance and turned them into raging anticlerics.

The example came from the top. Some of the fifteenth- and sixteenth-century popes were distressingly ignorant of their religious duties and too mindful of their money and privileges. The Italian noble families who controlled the papacy and the papal court were involved in ongoing struggles for political domination of the peninsula and tended to treat the papacy and other high offices as their hereditary privilege. They regarded the increasing calls for reform as the mumblings of malcontents, which could be safely ignored. Only with the emergence of the Lutheran challenge would they slowly realize their error.

## FAMILY LIFE AND EDUCATION OF CHILDREN

Our knowledge of family life in the Renaissance comes largely from the upper classes, as is usual for premodern history. Men continued to marry quite late, in their thirties and forties, after securing their inheritances. Women were normally much younger at marriage, so there were many middle-aged widows. Marriage to a rich or moderately well-off widow who was still young enough to bear children was perceived as a desirable step for a man. Dowries were expected in every case, even among the poor in the countryside. A girl without a suitable dowry was practically unmarriageable.

Families were often large, especially among the well-to-do. The household might include children from a prior marriage, spinster sisters or elderly widows, servants, and perhaps the husband's illegitimate offspring. We know from surviving records that an Italian merchant's household might easily include as many as twenty persons, including servants. Wealthy households were of a similar size throughout most of the rest of Europe. (See the box on Margherita Datini in Chapter 20.)

The woman of such a house was expected to run this establishment with vigor and economy. If her husband was away (a business trip might last six months or longer), she was often entrusted with full authority. A woman had to be literate to handle these tasks, and all wealthy families had private tutors for their daughters as well as their sons.

In general, however, women did not fare well as a social group during the Renaissance. In fact, the position of upper-class women actually seems to have declined. They no longer enjoyed the political and economic liberties afforded to upper-class women during the Middle Age. Middle-class women, on the other hand, probably had greater responsibility for the management of household and business affairs and played a role almost equal to that of their husbands.

As in the medieval period, the wives of artisans and merchants were often essential partners of the males, whose work could not be performed without their wives. Of working-class women, we as usual know relatively little, but we can assume that the male-dominated, patriarchal society went on without essential change. A particular crisis was the Europe-wide obsession with witchcraft, which appeared in the sixteenth century and took most of its victims from among the female population (see the Society and Economy box).

SOCIETY AND ECONOMY

## Witchcraft

**A SPECIAL EXAMPLE OF THE RELATIVE** decline in the social status of females during the Renaissance and early modern eras is the witchcraft mania that raged throughout Europe in the late sixteenth and seventeenth centuries. Although witches could be of either sex, women were by far the more commonly accused of evil deeds. The following are excerpts from seventeenth-century German sources.

> The woman either hates or loves; there is no third way. When she cries, be careful. There's two kinds of feminine tears: one sort for true pain, the other for deceitfulness. . . . There are three other reasons for the fact that more women than men are superstitious: the first is that women are easily swayed, and the Devil seeks them out because he wishes to destroy their faith . . . the second is because Nature has created them from less stable material, and so they are more susceptible to the implantation of evil thoughts and diversions. The third reason is that their tongues are loose, and so when they have learned how to make evil have to share it with others of their own ilk, and attempt to gain revenge by witchcraft, as they don't have the strength of men.
>
> Women's physical weakness was already indicated by her creation from a bent rib [of Adam], thus an imperfect creature from the start.
>
> It is a fact that woman has only a weaker faith [in God], as the very etymology of her name states: the word *femina* comes from *fe* and *minus* (*fe* = fides, faith; *minus* = less; therefore *femina* = one with less faith). . . . Therefore, the female is evil by Nature, because she is more prone to doubts, and loses her faith more easily, which are the main requisites for witchcraft.

This view of the female nature had bloody consequences: near the German town of Thann, a witch hunt commenced in 1572 that went on at intervals until 1629. In that period 152 witches were put to death, generally by hanging, sometimes by burning. Of that number, only eight were males. Sometimes, five to eight women were put to death at one time. Three hundred six persons, mostly women, were executed as witches in only six years in villages near Trier. In two of the villages, only two women were left alive.

### *Analyze and Interpret*

Where do you think the argument that women "are more easily swayed" originated, in a male view? Does this reflect your own view of female nature? Are women also of "less stable material"?

Source: Cited in *Frauen in der Geschichte,* vol. 2, eds. Annette Kuhn and Jorn Rusen (Dusseldorf: Pädigogischer Verlag Schwann, 1982), pp. 114 and 122.

In both town and country, women had to do hard physical work as a matter of course. Spinning and weaving were the particular domain of the female, as well as care of rural livestock. In the towns, records show that women performed just about every task that men did: butchering, baking, metalwork, dyeing cloth, and performing all of the handwork trades that they had been doing throughout the medieval period. The separation of work by gender had not yet begun.

Education varied for the sexes, as had long been customary. In the towns, men were educated for an active career in commerce or a craft. Beginning at about age seven, they might attend a boarding school for a few years and then were apprenticed to an appropriate firm or craftsman. Literacy was common by this time among the urban population but still uncommon in the countryside, where most people lived. The peasant's son who received any education at all was still the exception, and the peasant bride who could spell out her name was a rare catch.

For girls of the upper and middle classes, education usually meant some study in the home under the supervision of a live-in or outside tutor, usually a seminary student who was trying to keep body and soul together until ordination. Their education focused on literacy in the vernacular with perhaps a bit of Latin, music making, and the domestic arts. Marriage was taken for granted as the fate of most young women. The alternative was a convent, which had little appeal, or spinsterhood, which had less. Intellectual women now had many more opportunities to express themselves in written forms, including history, poetry, religious tracts, and other formats, but their gender was still a severe obstacle to being taken seriously.

How were the earliest years passed? The treatment of young children was slowly changing among the upper classes, but not yet among the lower. Any family that could afford to do so—a minority, certainly—would send a newborn baby to a peasant wet nurse. She would keep the child until he or she was past the nursing stage—about two years (at times longer, and sometimes without any contact with the parents!). When the children returned to their parents' house, they were put under the exclusive care of the mother for the next several years. In wealthy homes, the father rarely had much to do with his children until they reached the "age of reason" (age seven), when he would take charge of their education.

The usual attitude among the upper classes was that very young children were of interest to adults only because they represented the continuation of the family line. After reaching age seven or so, they became more worthy of attention, not only because they had survived the most dangerous age but also because they were now becoming persons with recognizable traits and personalities. By the Renaissance epoch, beating and other severe punishments were applied less often than in earlier centuries but were still common enough, as we know from many diaries.

We know less for certain about the lower classes because of the usual absence of sources. Probably, babies and very young children continued to get little love and cherishing by modern standards for the sensible reason that the parents could expect that about half of their offspring would die before reaching their seventh year. After that age, they were treated somewhat better, if only because they represented potential labor and "social security" for the aged parent.

## SUMMARY

A rebirth of secular learning derived from classical authors began in fourteenth-century Italy and spread north across the Alps in ensuing years. Significant differences in mood and aims often existed between the two areas. The Renaissance produced the foundations of the modern state. That those foundations were laid along the lines of Machiavelli's *The Prince* rather than the lines of the northern Christian humanist tracts would prove fateful.

After the crisis of the Hundred Years' War had been surmounted, the fifteenth century saw a significant rise in monarchic powers and prestige. English and French kings fashioned effective controls over their unruly nobles. The Russian czar also emerged as a strong ruler, but in Germany and Italy no progress was made in the consolidation of central government.

Individualism and secularism made strong advances among the educated, whereas the moral prestige of the clergy, and particularly the Roman papacy, continued to sink. The arts flourished under the stimuli of new wealth in the cities and a governing class that placed great store on patronage and fame. Painting and architecture witnessed notable experiments and successful new talents.

## IDENTIFICATION TERMS

Test your knowledge of this chapter's key concepts by defining the following terms. If you can't recall the meaning of certain terms, refresh your memory by looking up the boldfaced term in the chapter, turning to the Glossary at the end of the book, or working with the flashcards that are available on the *World Civilizations* Companion Website: **http://history.wadsworth.com/adler04**.

Habsburg Dynasty
humanism
Principality of Kiev
Renaissance
secularism
Third Rome
*Utopia*
Wars of the Roses

## TEST YOUR KNOWLEDGE

Test your knowledge of this chapter by answering the following questions. Complete answers appear at the end of the book. You may also take this quiz interactively and find even more quiz questions on the *World Civilizations* Companion Website: **http://history.wadsworth.com/adler04**.

1. During the fifteenth century, the territory now called Italy was
   a. under the firm control of the Holy Roman Emperor.
   b. broken into several political units centered on cities.
   c. finally brought under the monopolistic control of the papacy.
   d. split in allegiance between Rome and Florence.
   e. mostly agricultural, with few people residing in urban areas.
2. Which of the following attributes *least* fits the Renaissance worldview?
   a. Ambition
   b. Arrogance
   c. Confidence
   d. Caution
   e. Worldliness

3. Which of the following statements about Renaissance secularism is *false*?
   a. It was vigorously opposed by Roman church leaders.
   b. It was partially a by-product of a changing economy.
   c. Most persons held to the basic tenets of Christian teaching.
   d. It encouraged the acquisition of material things.
   e. The upper class became more interested in worldly than spiritual matters.
4. The Renaissance in northern Europe differed from that of Italy by being
   a. less secular.
   b. more artistic.
   c. less serious.
   d. inferior in quality.
   e. less intellectually stimulating.
5. The basic message of More's *Utopia* is that
   a. personal wealth is the only sure path to social reforms.
   b. education cannot reduce human sinfulness.
   c. social institutions, not individuals, must be reformed first.
   d. people are inherently evil and cannot really be changed.
   e. to be happy, individuals must do what is best for their personal situations.
6. A new element in Renaissance city-state politics was
   a. the preference for using fear rather than piety as a basis of government.
   b. a professional army of mercenaries.
   c. an absolute monarchy.
   d. the organization of a taxation agency.
   e. the concept of a secular state that existed independently of both ruler and ruled.
7. One of the peculiar features of Russian Orthodoxy was the belief that
   a. Russians would be the political masters of all Europe.
   b. all Russians would be saved eternally.
   c. Moscow was destined to be the Third Rome.
   d. the state was nonexistent.
   e. the church should function independently of the state.
8. Titian and Van Eyck were both Renaissance
   a. architects.
   b. artists.
   c. political theorists.
   d. churchmen.
   e. writers.
9. Which of the following was *not* a cause for scandal in the Christian church of the sixteenth and seventeenth centuries?
   a. Illiteracy
   b. Immorality
   c. Thievery
   d. Unconcern
   e. Greed
10. The household of a wealthy sixteenth-century Italian could best be described as one in which
   a. women had no control over everyday affairs.
   b. husbands refused to travel outside the country because they did not trust their wives to run the households.
   c. widowed women were relegated to an inferior, almost superfluous existence.
   d. large numbers of variously related people sometimes resided together in one home.
   e. women, though deemed important to the running of the household, remained illiterate.

## InfoTrac College Edition

Visit the source collections at

**http://infotrac.thomsonlearning.com**

and use the Search function with the following key terms:

Renaissance Machiavelli humanism

## Wadsworth History Website Resources

Visit the World History Resource Center at **http://history.wadsworth.com/world** for a wealth of general resources, and the *World Civilizations* Companion Website at **http://history.wadsworth.com/adler04** for resources specific to this textbook.

## History Now

Enter *HistoryNow* using the access card that is available for *World Civilizations*. *HistoryNow* will assist you in understanding the content in this chapter with lesson plans generated for your needs. In addition, you can read the following documents, and many more, online:

Machiavelli, selections from *The Prince*

Two Tractates from Vittorino da Feltre and other humanist educators

*. . . my greatest joy is in victory: to conquer enemies, to pursue them and steal their possessions, to make their women cry, to ride on fast horses and return to my wife and daughters.*
**Chinghis Khan**

# 22 The Mongol Intrusion



| | |
|---|---|
| 1167–1227 | Life of Chinghis Khan |
| 1221–1258 | Mongol conquests of Persia and Iraq |
| 1227–1279 | Conquest of China |
| 1227–1480 | Khanate of the Golden Horde in Russia |
| 1258–1349 | Il Khan Dynasty in the Islamic heartlands |
| 1260 | Mongols defeated at Ain Jalut |
| 1271–1368 | Yuan Dynasty in China |

The Asian world in the period after the decline of the Abbasid caliphate in the West and the fall of the Tang Dynasty in the East was in continuous upheaval. Waves of nomadic, pastoralist peoples emigrated out of the steppes of central Asia seeking new pasturelands for their flocks and wealth to plunder. In the lands of Islam, between the ninth and the early thirteenth centuries, this emigration was experienced as the peaceful arrival of Turkish tribes. China, on the other hand, had already had a long history of attacks by Turco-Mongolian "barbarians" from the North. For the most part, both of these great civilizations had found ways of dealing with such nomadic peoples: in the Islamic East, by converting them and, in China, by building a Great Wall to keep them out. In the thirteenth century, these methods no longer worked. The civilizations of Asia, as well as eastern Europe, were about to experience a barbarian invasion at the hands of a new steppe land force—the Mongols.

## Background

### *The West*

Ethnically speaking, Islam's origins were Arabic and Persian. The Bedouins who had conquered Persia in the 640s were quickly absorbed by the much more sophisticated and numerous Persians. Unlike the Arabs, the Persians had long been accustomed to serving as rulers and models for others, and they reasserted those talents after mass conversion to Islam. For two centuries, the message of the Qur'an came through an Arab-Persian filter. In the 900s, however, a new ethnic group, the Turkish peoples, began to dominate the religion and culture. In the next centuries, the Seljuk Turks (see Chapter 15), who initially took over the Baghdad caliphate, and their Mongol successors gave Islam a Turco-Mongol cast that it retained for centuries. Conversion of these steppe peoples had proved to be an effective way of winning a potential enemy over

Dean Conger/Corbis

**Mongols with Their Ponies.** Mongol soldiers typically traveled with as many as five ponies, because they provided swift, sure transport as well as a food source. The Mongols' ability to carry out lightning attacks and to fire accurately from the backs of these mounts was the key to their military successes.

to being a useful ally. The Seljuks, for example, were successful in resuming the jihads against the Byzantines. However, when a new threat appeared at Islam's doorstep in the early 1200s, the caliphs and sultans of Persia and Iraq were unable to contain it.

## The East

As was seen in Chapter 17, China's Tang Dynasty had begun falling apart early in the tenth century as a result of internal conflicts. However, another contributing factor to China's decline was the continual threats to its northern borders from barbarian tribes. The Tang rulers had tried to deal with this menace by allying themselves with one tribe to defeat others. First, it was a tribe called the Uigurs; after them, it was the Kirghiz. The latter proved to be unmanageable, however, and they eventually overthrew Tang rule in China. The Song emperors who followed the Tang tried dealing with the barbarian problem in much the same fashion as their predecessors had, but their weakness could not stop the Kirghiz from invading northern China. In addition, the Great Wall had fallen into a state of disrepair and was becoming ineffective at keeping the nomads out of the North. By the early 1200s, yet another tribe, the Jurchen, arose out of Manchuria to threaten Song rule. Faced with this new menace, the Song ruler once again turned to the old tactic of playing one tribe off against another. This time, however, the decision was fatal. Their new allies from the Gobi Desert, the Mongols, slaughtered the Jurchen, but with the sweet taste of victory in his mouth, their leader, Chinghis Khan, moved to take control of China as well.

Dean Conger/Corbis

**A Mongol Yurt.** At the time of the Mongol conquests, these tent-like shelters were ideal for a nomadic, war-like people who were constantly on the move. The yurts were made from felt, which provided relatively good insulation against all kinds of temperature extremes.

**Chinghis Khan.** Chinghis united the Mongol clan leaders for the first time in their history and, as the first of the Great Khans, created a world empire that included much of the Eurasian landmass.

## The Mongols

In the beginning, the Mongols were a relatively small group of steppe nomads. Their sources of food were their herds of livestock and what they could obtain by hunting, while their small, but strong Mongol ponies served them as both mode of transportation and food source. Being nomadic, they lived in felt, tentlike structures called **yurts**, and their highest level of leadership was clan elders and tribal warlords.

The prime advantage of the Mongols in war was their ability to cover long distances more rapidly than any of their enemies. Virtually living on their small, hardy ponies, Mongol warriors combined the tactic of surprise with an uncanny accuracy with the bow and arrow and the ability to use massed cavalry against their mainly infantry opponents. The Mongols would bypass walled strongholds against which a cavalry charge would be ineffective and then starve their enemies into submission by controlling the surrounding countryside.

### *Chinghis Khan and the Rise of the Mongols*

If one measures greatness by the territorial extent of a person's conquests, then there can be no doubt at all that Chinghis Khan was the greatest ruler in world history. He was originally named Temujin but was given the title Chinghis Khan ("Great King") in later life. Before his death in 1227, he had come to rule a vast territory from the South Russian steppes to the China Sea. His sons and successors expanded the Mongol empire even farther, until it was easily the largest the world has ever seen.

Temujin was born about 1167 into a violent landscape and had to struggle almost from birth against harsh competitors. At the time of his birth, Mongolian life centered around numerous tribes that warred against one another continuously, when they were not assaulting the richer lands of the Chinese and Koreans. Temujin enjoyed years of successful conquest in these tribal wars. Greatly feared for his ferocity and ruthlessness, by 1196 he had become powerful enough to assert personal control over all of the Mongol tribes. In 1206, at a meeting of the *Khuraltai,* the Grand Council of clan elders at the capital of Karakorum, he accepted the title of Great King (Chinghis Khan) of the Mongols and imposed tight military order on his hundreds of thousands of followers. For the first time in their history, the Mongols were united under one leader.

Chinghis Khan combined traditional Mongol fighting methods with new forms of organization to forge his armies into a remarkably efficient war machine. First, he divided them into light and heavy cavalry. The light units relied purely on the swiftness of their horses and their light weapons of swords, bows, and arrows to make lightning strikes. The heavy cavalry units added Chinese-style armor to the usual light, Mongol weapons. To maintain both political and military unity, Chinghis never allowed his army to remain organized along traditional tribal lines, so he restructured it by mixing all of the tribal warriors into new units consisting of members from many different tribal and clan groups. The largest army unit, the *Tumen,* consisted of 10,000 men and was further divided into smaller tactical units of 1,000, 100, and 10.

### *The Conquests*

The Mongol conquests proceeded in three phases. The first lasted from 1206, when Chinghis and his army attacked China unsuccessfully, to his death in 1227. The initial failure in China forced Chinghis to direct his armies westward against the Turks and Persians. Proud cities such as Bokhara, Samarkand, and Herat, all centers of a rich Muslim civilization, were overwhelmed after desperate resistance, and their populations were massacred or led into slavery. Some cities would never recover their former wealth and importance. Mosques were turned into stables and libraries were burned. Never had such destruction been seen; word of an approaching Mongol army was sometimes enough to inspire wholesale flight. Everywhere, the invaders distinguished themselves by their exceptional bloodthirstiness toward those who resisted (see the two Law and Government boxes), and everywhere they were despised as cultural inferiors. This was particularly true in China, but also in the Christian and Muslim lands they overran. Many of the conquered territories had been under Persian Muslim rule for centuries and had developed a highly civilized lifestyle.

Following these successes, Chinghis headed north. In 1222, he crossed the Caspian Sea and invaded southern Russia. He and the Mongols attacked Novgorod, again striking so much fear into the Russians that they called the Mongols **Tartars**, "people from Hell."

Sated by these victories, Chinghis and his followers returned to Mongolia and gave the peoples to the West a temporary reprieve. His stay in his homelands did not last very long, though, and in 1227 he was again on the road to more battles. Not to be denied a victory and having failed once, he launched a second invasion of northern China. Again, terror was used liberally as his most effective weapon, and he massacred all Chinese in his path, including women, children, and even pets. The warlord finally had conquered the entire world that was known to him, including Mongolia, northern China, Turkistan, Afghanistan, Persia, and Russia. His success in China was short-lived, however, and his death in 1227 ended the first phase of the Mongol eruption.

By then, the Mongols believed that their great spirit-god, Tengri, had commanded them to conquer the entire world, and they came close to doing so in the second and third phases of their conquests. Chinghis's successors returned to Russia to add to the previous conquests and also defeated the Teutonic Knights of Germany along the way, driving their army back almost to the walls of Vienna. The sudden death in 1241of another Great Khan, however, saved the city, as the Mongols hastily retreated to Mongolia to choose a new leader. Afterward, the Mongols under Chinghis's grandson, Hulegu, returned to Persia and Iraq in 1251, and in 1258 the great city of the caliphs, Baghdad, suffered the same fate as so many before it. What had been one of the greatest cities in the world was severely plundered by Mongol troops; scholars have estimated that 80,000 of its citizens were killed. Among these was the last Baghdad caliph of the once proud and mighty Abbasid Dynasty, along with his son and heir. Some of the family managed to escape and flee

LAW AND GOVERNMENT

## The Mongol Army

**SHORTLY AFTER THE DEVASTATING MONGOL ATTACK,** a high-ranking Persian Muslim, Ala-ad-Din-Juvaini, wrote *The History of the World Conqueror.* Clearly impressed by the new overlords, he spoke of the discipline of the Mongol army:

> What army can equal the Mongol army? In time of action when attacking and assaulting, they are like trained wild beasts out after game, and in the days of peace and security they are like sheep, yielding milk, and wool and many other useful things. In misfortune and adversity they are free of dissension and opposition. It is an army after the fashion of a peasantry, being liable to all manner of contributions, and rendering without complaint what is enjoined upon it. . . . It is also a peasantry in the guise of an army, all of them, great and small, noble and base, in time of battle becoming swordsmen, archers and lancers in whatever manner the occasion requires. . . .
>
> Their obedience and submissiveness is such that if there be a commander of a hundred thousand [men] between whom and the Khan there is a distance of sunrise and sunset, and if he but commit some fault, the Khan dispatches a single horseman to punish him after the manner prescribed; if his head has been demanded, he cuts it off, and if gold be required, he takes it from him.

### *Analyze and Interpret*

What reasons can you give to explain these apparent contradictions in the men who formed the Mongol army? Are they, in fact, contradictions? What does the Mongol army have in common with any good army?

Source: Ala-ad-Din Ata-Malik Juvaini, *Ghenghis Khan: The History of the World Conqueror,* trans. J. A. Boyle (Manchester: Manchester University Press, 1997), Vol. 1, p. 23; cited in *The Islamic World,* ed. W. H. McNeill and M. R. Waldman (Oxford: Oxford University Press, 1973).

westward to Egypt, where a much-reduced caliphate was maintained for 250 years in a humbler state under the protection of an Egyptian sultanate.

## THE MONGOL EMPIRE

It would be easy to assume, from their methods of waging war, that the intrusion of the Mongols into the great centers of civilization, like those of Islam and China, brought only destruction. While that surely was the case during the initial conquests, the Mongol hordes also opened some notable possibilities for the traders and merchants among the peoples they had conquered. For about a century, the ***Pax Mongolica*** (Peace of the Mongols) extended for many thousands of miles, all under the supervision of the Great Khan and the relatives and clan leaders he appointed as subordinates from his headquarters in Karakorum. Goods could be safely transported from the coast of China to the towns of the eastern Mediterranean, so long as a tribute or tax was paid to the Khan's agents. It was the first and only time that all of mainland Asia (except southern India) was under the rule of a single power (see Map 22.1), and a few areas and cities prospered to an unprecedented degree as a result. The global effect of this unparalleled degree of control over the major trade routes

LAW AND GOVERNMENT

### A Muslim Describes the Mongol Invasion

**THE MONGOLS PURPOSELY USED TERRORISM** as one way to subdue their enemies, sometimes even without a fight. This description by Ibn al-Athir, a thirteenth-century Muslim, of the Mongol conquest of the Middle East reveals how effective a weapon this fear sometimes was.

> . . . For even Antichrist will spare such as follow him, though he destroy those who oppose him, but these Tatars spared none, slaying women and men and children, ripping open pregnant women and killing unborn babes. Verily to God do we belong, and unto Him do we return, and there is no strength and no power save in God, the High, the Almighty, in face of this catastrophe, whereof the sparks flew far and wide, and the hurt was universal; and which passed over the lands like clouds driven by the wind. For these were a people who emerged from the confines of China. . . .
>
> . . . Now this is a thing the like of which ear has not heard; for Alexander, concerning whom historians agree that he conquered the world, did not do so with such swiftness, but only in the space of about ten years; neither did he slay, but was satisfied that men should be subject to him. But these Tatars conquered most of the habitable globe, and the best, the most flourishing and most populous part thereof, and that whereof the inhabitants were the most advanced in character and conduct, in about a year; nor did any country escape their devastations which did not fearfully expect them and dread their arrival.
>
> . . . It is now time for us to describe how they first burst forth into the lands. Stories have been related to me, which the hearer can scarcely credit, as to the terror of the Tatars, which God Almighty cast into men's hearts; so that it is said that a single one of them would enter a village or a quarter wherein were many people, and would continue to slay them one after another, none daring to stretch forth his hand against this horseman. And I have heard that one of them took a man captive, but had not with him any weapon wherewith to kill him; and he said to his prisoner, "Lay your head on the ground and do not move," and he did so, and the Tatar went and fetched his sword and slew him therewith. Another man related to me as follows: "I was going," said he, "with seventeen others along a road, and there met us a Tatar horseman, and bade us bind one another's arms. My companions began to do as he bade them, but I said to them, 'He is but one man; wherefore, then, should we not kill him and flee?' They replied, 'We are afraid.' I said, 'This man intends to kill you immediately; let us therefore rather kill him, that perhaps God may deliver us.' But I swear by God that not one of them dared to do this, so I took a knife and slew him, and we fled and escaped." And such occurrences were many.

#### *Analyze and Interpret*

Where does the author seem to have gotten this information? How much truth do you think there was in this report? Assuming some of it might be exaggeration, how do you suppose such stories originated? What sort of an impact did they have? Do you know of any other instances where terrorism was purposely employed in history as a weapon?

Source: Edward G. Browne, *A Literary History of Persia* (Cambridge: Cambridge University Press, 1902), Vol. II, pp. 427–431.

Scanned by Jerome S. Arkenberg, Cal. State Fullerton. The text has been modernized by Prof. Arkenberg.

**HistoryNow™**

***To read more of Ibn al-Athir's* On the Tatars, *point your browser to the documents area of* HistoryNow.**

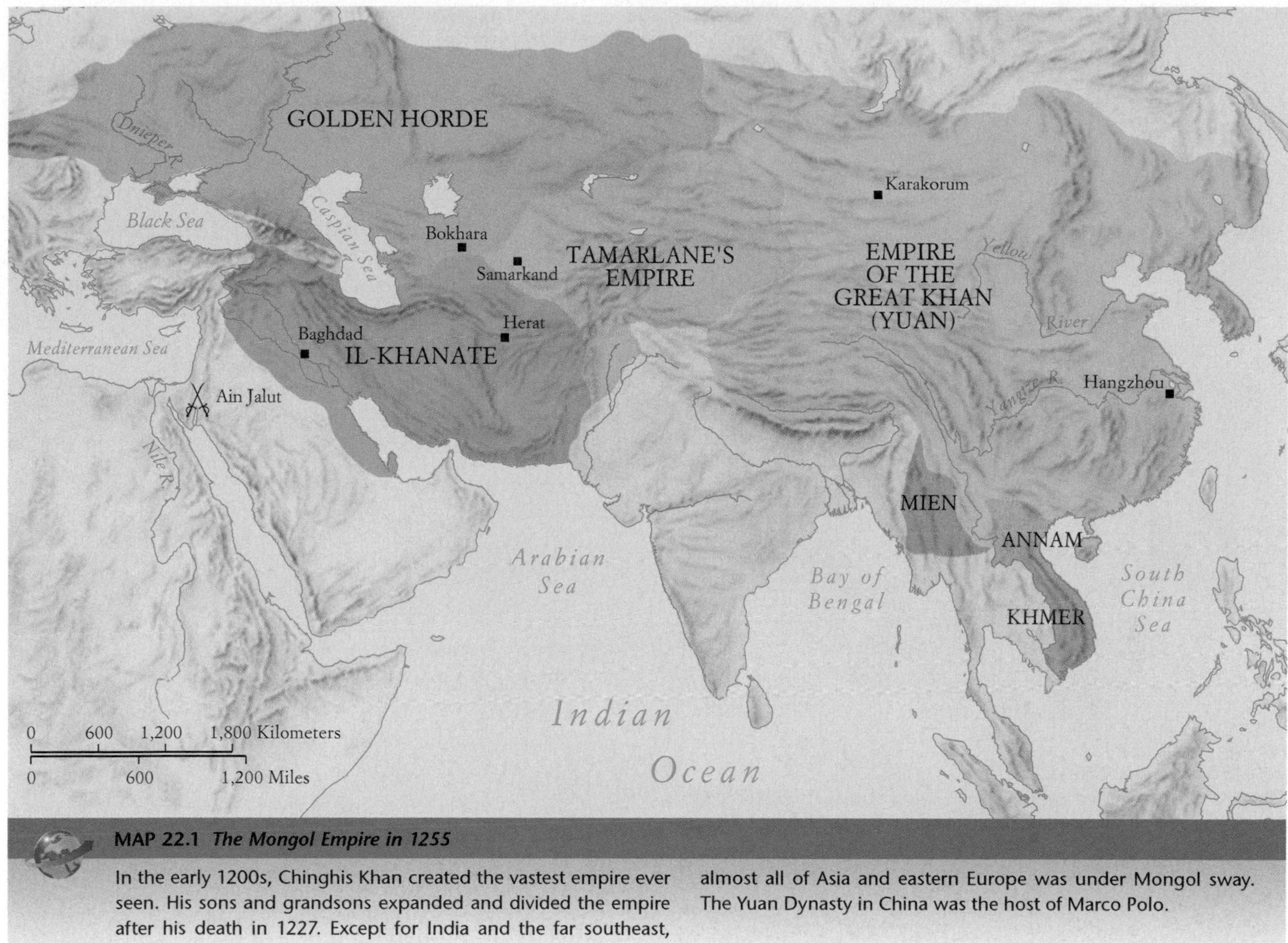


**MAP 22.1** *The Mongol Empire in 1255*

In the early 1200s, Chinghis Khan created the vastest empire ever seen. His sons and grandsons expanded and divided the empire after his death in 1227. Except for India and the far southeast, almost all of Asia and eastern Europe was under Mongol sway. The Yuan Dynasty in China was the host of Marco Polo.

linking East and West clearly contributed to the prosperity that western Europe enjoyed in the later Middle Ages (Chapter 19), and indirectly, at least, was an enabling factor behind the Italian Renaissance (Chapter 21).

## In China

To administer this great expanse of territory, Chinghis Khan installed members of his family in positions of command as he fought his way into western Asia. After his death, his sons and grandsons divided the huge empire among themselves. The richest part, China, went to the **Yuan Dynasty**, whose most illustrious member was Kubilai Khan, the host of Marco Polo. In 1279, Kubilai completed the conquests of China that had begun under Chinghis Khan. For half a century, the Chinese had made successful use of gunpowder to keep the Mongols at bay. They developed an early, primitive type of gun, called the fire lance, which permitted them to discharge several arrows at once against their fearsome attackers. This tactic had given them an edge for a while, but it figuratively backfired when the Mongols learned the secrets of the new weapon and used it themselves.

Kubilai and his followers tried to transform China into their notion of what a land should be: one that resembled the grassy steppe lands from whence they had come. Not fully understanding agriculture, they plowed up productive farmland to graze their horses and camels. One sage advisor to Kubilai, however, finally realized the wastefulness of such measures and convinced the Great Khan to abandon this behavior. After all, farmers who were allowed to cultivate could produce tribute; prevented from following their livelihood, they could produce nothing. Moreover, the Mongols soon learned to rely more on the Chinese and their institutions for help in governing.

China during the years of Yuan rule was divided into a hierarchy, with Mongol officials, called "stamp wielders," at the top. The old Confucian examination system of earlier dynasties was discarded. The Mongols fought against assimilation. To find suitably educated people to staff government positions, they relied on foreigners more than on their Chinese subjects, and they accorded foreigners a

**Marco Polo.** As a foreigner, Marco Polo was trusted more than the native-born Chinese by the great Kubilai Khan.

higher status than they did the Chinese. Many of these foreign recruits were Muslims, so Islam began making significant inroads into the eastern parts of China at this time, in addition to the Far West. The fact that Kubilai preferred foreigners over native Chinese explains why Marco Polo was given an important position when he visited the court of Kubilai Khan from 1275 to 1292.

The Mongols could not long remain entirely resistant to Chinese influences, however. Confucianism, while not encouraged, was at least tolerated. The universalism of Buddhism proved to be more appealing to the Mongols than native Chinese religions and philosophy, and even though the Mongols continued to segregate themselves from the Chinese, that faith found many converts among the barbarians.

The *Pax Mongolica* also meant that Yuan rule was a time of considerable prosperity for China, just as it was throughout the rest of the empire. It marked the end of further invasions from the North, a time of peace for a huge swath of territory, and the peaceful passage of merchants and caravans, which proved to be an enormous boon that helped offset the horrors of the initial invasions.

## *In Russia*

Once the Russians were subdued, the Mongols there proved to be unexpectedly tolerant. Called the **Khanate of the Golden Horde**, the Mongols settled down and converted to marginally more civilized ways. For the most part, they remained content simply to extract tribute from their Russian subjects, otherwise leaving them to their customary ways and Russian Orthodox Christianity. Eventually, too, most Mongols adopted Islam and its highly sophisticated culture. As in other regions over which they ruled, the Mongol Khans' ability to impose universal peace and stability went a long way toward assuring Russians under their rule greater peace and prosperity than they had enjoyed previously. The Khanate of the Golden Horde was also the longest lasting of the four sub-khanates, lasting until 1480 before the Russians under the Muscovite principality finally ended the Mongols' regime.

## *In the Middle East*

Once Hulegu's hordes crushed Abbasid defenses and overran Baghdad, they continued their conquests to the West. Aleppo was sacked when it resisted, but Damascus surrendered and was spared. Neither Christians, Hindus, nor Buddhists had been able to stop them, and only their defeat in 1260 by the Egyptian sultanate's army at **Ain Jalut**, near Nazareth in Palestine, saved the remaining Muslim lands from further destruction. Coming just two years after the Mongol conquest of Baghdad in 1258, this victory revived Muslim resistance and is one of the handful of truly decisive battles of world history.

Hulegu and his successors ruled the Islamic heartlands from Azerbaijan for the next ninety-one years as the dynasty of the Il Khans. They were slow to convert to Islam, but as elsewhere the Mongols remained tolerant of their subjects' faith, and their rule was benign. This peaceful rule was terminated by a series of especially savage wars launched by another Turco-Mongolian warlord by the name of Timur-Lenk, or Tamarlane. Ironically, Tamarlane was a convert to Islam, but that did not prevent him from sweeping away everything in his path in a campaign of devastation upon entering eastern Iran in 1379. He went on to conquer virtually everything between northern India and Moscow, leaving behind him only death and ruin across the entire eastern Islamic world. His conquests seem to have served no purpose beyond conquest for its own sake. He made no real effort to create anything positive. He died in 1405, soon after defeating the Ottoman Sultan Bayezid in a Syrian battle, and left nothing behind. Under his sons, Tamarlane's so-called Timurid Empire dissolved almost as quickly as it had been conquered.

## Fragmentation of the Empire

The Mongols had five Great Khans in the 1200s, beginning with Chinghis and ending with the death of Kubilai Khan in 1294 (see Table 22.1). After that, the ethnic segments of the huge empire went their separate ways. The nomadic culture and the Mongols' approach to government (exploitation through conquest) would have made it difficult to maintain their vast domain under a single center, even if much better communications and a much larger pool of loyal officials had been available. Because these resources were not available, the original unified conquest broke up within a century. First China, then Russia and the Middle Eastern lands separated from one another under sub-khanates with their own conflicting interests. Successive intra-Mongol fights for regional supremacy after 1280 further weakened the power of the dynasty.

The second and third generations of Mongol rulers were more sensitive to their subjects' needs and expectations and included some exceptionally able men. Their adoption of one or another of the competing religions of Asia also enhanced their prestige, for a time at least. In China, Kubilai Khan favored Buddhism. One of the Middle Eastern Il Khan rulers adopted the Muslim faith in the 1290s and simultaneously began the revival of Persian power and prestige. The Russian-based Golden Horde khans also adopted Islam in the late 1200s, but their conversion had no influence on the Russian people, who remained steadfast in their Eastern Orthodox Christianity.

**TABLE 22.1** ***The Great Khans of the Mongols***

| | |
|---|---|
| Chinghis Khan | 1206–1227 |
| Ogodei Khan | 1229–1241 |
| Guyuk Khan | 1246–1248 |
| Mongke Khan | 1251–1259 |
| Kubilai Khan | 1260–1294 |

Gradually, the Mongols' far more numerous Christian (Russia, Near East), Muslim (Middle East, India), and Buddhist (China, Tibet) subjects began to make their presence felt, as they civilized and to some degree absorbed their conquerors. By the mid-1300s, the empire was disintegrating into its preconquest component parts, and rebellions against Mongol rulers were multiplying. In China and Persia first (late 1300s), then the Near East and Russia (1400s), Mongol rule became a bad memory. The former rulers were either absorbed into the subject populations or retired back into their desolate Central Asian homelands.

## Summary

The tribes of the central and eastern Asian steppe lands had long been a thorn in the side of their more settled neighbors to their west and south. The Chinese had been forced to build the Great Wall as a defense against the Mongols' continual depredations, and pressures against the Mongols' western neighbors forced the Germanic tribes and, in the ninth century, the Turks to migrate to the West, eventually contributing to the destruction of the western Roman Empire and the unsettling of the eastern Islamic Empire. The rise of the Mongols under their notorious warlord Chinghis Khan must be understood partly against this deep background. Yet, Chinghis's exceptional abilities as a leader unified the Mongols, and the formidable military talents of the mounted Mongol warriors accounted for their singular success as conquerors.

As always seems to be the case with the most successful conquerors in history, their victims saw them as exceptionally uncivilized. To some degree, the Mongols' reputation as particularly barbarous conquerors can be attributed to this view. However, these accusations also seem to bear some truth, given that the Great Khans tried to spare their own blood and that of their soldiers through deliberate campaigns of terror tactics. Cities fell and, in many cases, peoples surrendered without a fight. Whatever the truth of the stories told about them, the Mongols undoubtedly created history's greatest empire, having conquered an unprecedented swath of territory that included most of the Eurasian landmass by the end of the thirteenth century. Once their invasions were completed, the Mongols settled down to a more peaceful existence and managed to create a zone of peace and prosperity that this enormous region had never before enjoyed.

## Identification Terms

Test your knowledge of this chapter's key concepts by defining the following terms. If you can't recall the meaning of certain terms, refresh your memory by looking up the boldfaced term in the chapter, turning to the Glossary at the end of the book, or working with the flashcards that are available on the *World Civilizations* Companion Website: **http://history.wadsworth.com/adler04.**

Ain Jalut
Khanate of the Golden Horde
*Pax Mongolica*
Tartars
Yuan Dynasty
yurts

## Test Your Knowledge

Test your knowledge of this chapter by answering the following questions. Complete answers appear at the end of the book. You may also take this quiz interactively and find even more quiz questions on the *World Civilizations* Companion Website: **http://history.wadsworth.com/adler04.**

1. Judging by the previous strategies followed by the Tang and Song emperors of China in dealing with northern barbarians, when faced with the Mongol threat, one would have expected the Song to resort to
   a. seeking military assistance from the caliphs of Baghdad.
   b. recruiting a powerful army of mercenaries to defend their realm.
   c. relying on Japanese samurai to ward them off.
   d. playing off another steppe land ally against the Mongols.
   e. retreating farther south into China.
2. Before Chinghis was named as the Great Khan in 1206, it can be said that the Mongols
   a. were led by tribal warlords.
   b. already had seen the rise of previous Great Khans.
   c. were divided into numerous warring tribes.
   d. were attempting to invade China.
   e. were as described in both a and c.
3. The principal military advantage the Mongols enjoyed over their opponents lay in
   a. their ability to shoot bows and arrows accurately from horseback at full gallop.
   b. the genius of their war leaders in matters of strategy.
   c. their skillful use of military intelligence.
   d. their absolute belief in the power of their war god.
   e. b and d.
4. Which of these is the correct sequence of Chinghis Khan's conquests?
   a. China, Mongolia, Afghanistan, Persia, and Russia
   b. Mongolia, Persia, Russia, China, and Afghanistan
   c. Mongolia, Turks, Persians, Russia, and northern China
   d. Mongolia, Persia, Turkistan, China, and Russia
   e. Mongolia, China, Turkistan, Persia, and Russia
5. Through the use of terror, the Mongols
   a. easily overran all enemies.
   b. often were able to cow enemies into surrender without a fight.
   c. sometimes frightened themselves.
   d. were so successful in defeating opponents that they no longer had to use weapons.
   e. frightened all of their enemies into thinking they were from hell.
6. After the Mongol conquests, the Abbasid caliphate
   a. was extinguished.
   b. continued to exist in a reduced state in Egypt.
   c. was relocated to Azerbaijan under the Il Khans.
   d. continued to exist in Baghdad under the domination of the Il Khans.
   e. was protected by the Khanate of the Golden Horde in Russia.
7. It appears that the principal difference between Mongol rule in China and in the Middle East is that the Mongols
   a. were more resistant to assimilation in Persia.
   b. preferred Islamic civilization.
   c. admired Abbasid rule.
   d. were more resistant to assimilation in China.
   e. resorted to the use of terror more frequently in governing China.
8. Russia was left to the Khanate called the
   a. Golden Horde.
   b. Abbasids.
   c. Il Khans.

d. Timurids.
e. Yuan.

9. The Timurids differed from the Il Khans in which respect?
   a. They were Buddhists.
   b. They were Christians.
   c. They were Muslims.
   d. They conquered the Muscovites.
   e. They left no lasting empire.

10. Which of the following can be said of the Mongol conquests as a whole?
    a. They were totally destructive.
    b. The Mongols were generally tolerant of their conquered subjects.
    c. They were good for long-distance trade.
    d. They usually resulted in a cultural decline wherever they happened.
    e. They were as described in both b and c.

## InfoTrac College Edition

Visit the source collections at

**http://infotrac.thomsonlearning.com**

and use the Search function with the following key term:

Mongol

## Wadsworth History Website Resources

Visit the World History Resource Center at **http://history.wadsworth.com/world** for a wealth of general resources, and the *World Civilizations* Companion Website at **http://history.wadsworth.com/adler04** for resources specific to this textbook.

## HistoryNow

Enter *HistoryNow* using the access card that is available for *World Civilizations*. *HistoryNow* will assist you in understanding the content in this chapter with lesson plans generated for your needs. In addition, you can read the following documents, and many more, online:

Marco Polo, *Prologue to Travels*

Ibn al-Athir, *On the Tatars*

# Worldview Three

## Law and Government

## Society and Economy

### Europeans

**Law and Government:** A long-drawn struggle occurs between papacy and monarchs for supremacy within the new kingdoms emerging from the imperial collapse. Law degenerates badly in the early period, but begins a comeback on the Roman model in medieval centuries. Faint beginnings of the modern state and rule by bureaucracy appear at the end of the period in the western European kingdoms.

**Society and Economy:** By the end of this period, the town-dwelling bourgeoisie has become significant in western Europe and is challenging the traditional noble–landlord social order. Feudal serfdom in the West diminishes and becomes almost extinct after the Black Death but is rejuvenated in the eastern countries. Long-distance trade gradually resumes following the establishment of stable monarchic governments in the West. Europeans seek new trade opportunities via ocean routes to the eastern entrepôts as the fifteenth century ends. Also, the new economic form called capitalism is promoted by various developments in credit facilities for business and in the new mobility of wealth and wealth-producing production.

### East Asians

**Law and Government:** A thousand-year-long golden age for China commences, which recovers in the late 500s from a second period of disintegration and prospers during the ensuing Tang and Song periods. Mongol conquest in the thirteenth century interrupts but does not severely damage the Chinese "mandate of heaven" monarchy, which resumes under the vigorous new Ming Dynasty in 1300s. Law and bureaucratic mandarin government operate generally to good effect for peace and stability, particularly in the South, where nomads cannot easily reach. Japan selectively emulates the Chinese system, but the imperial court never exerts control over the nation in a like fashion to China; feudal nobility resists the bureaucratic system and negates it entirely in the later part of this period by erecting the shogunate as the true locus of government powers.

**Society and Economy:** Farming continues in both China and Japan as the means of livelihood for a huge majority, but in China the cities' growth during the Tang and Song eras is impressive. Towns with populations of more than 1 million are known. Domestic trade in every type of good is active, but only limited contacts are made with Western foreigners until the arrival of seafaring Europeans in the 1500s. Travel and commerce over the Silk Road is stimulated by the Mongol hegemony in the thirteenth and fourteenth centuries, and Chinese–Central Asian contacts multiply. The sudden rise and fall of Chinese maritime expeditions in the fifteenth century demonstrate the powers of the government versus the interests of the mercantile class.

### Hindus

**Law and Government:** Written law is still exceptional in this oral civilization. Government is exercised by a tiny minority of high-caste warriors and confirmed by the brahmin priests. Villages govern themselves with little contact with central or regional authorities except taxation. Effective central government is the exception, because of frequent nomadic invasions from the north. Toward the end of the period, these invasions create a ruling Muslim minority within the Hindu mass.

**Society and Economy:** Village fieldwork as free or bonded laborers is the norm throughout Indian history for the majority. Domestic and external trade with Southeast Asia and the Muslims to the west is important in the few cities. Colonial outreach to Southeast Asia and Pacific islanders is strong in South India. Cotton cloth, spices, and precious metals are exported.

# Equilibrium among Polycentric Civilizations, 500–1500 C.E.

## Patterns of Belief

Eastern Europe and Russia are brought into Byzantine Orthodox orbit in the 800s to 1000s. Political-religious divisions between East and West reach a climax with the formal schism between Constantinople and Rome in 1054. Eastern Orthodoxy is closely associated with the state and falls under royal or imperial dominion, especially in Russia. Roman clergy, on the other hand, is often in conflict with Western kings after the reform of the papacy in the tenth and eleventh centuries. Clerical reform comes and goes throughout the late medieval age, as the Christian church accumulates great wealth and the accompanying temptation for misuse.

In China, Buddhism rivals and then blends with Confucian tenets among the educated. Peasantry continues ancestor worship and Daoism. In Japan, Buddhism enters from Korea in the sixth century, subdivides into several noncompetitive sects, and strongly affects national Shinto religion. Neither country produces a clergy or much theology; ethics are derived from nonsupernatural sources in both. Philosophy is Buddhist-based in both and focuses on questions of daily life rather than abstract ideas. Warrior creeds become increasingly dominant in feudal Japan. Zen Buddhism is particularly popular in Japan after 1100s.

Vedic Hinduism is transformed in response to Buddhist challenge and gradually recaptures almost all of Indians' allegiance. Both religions accept the multiple nature of truth, contrasting with both Christians and Muslims. A strong ethical tone dominates, as exemplified in the Upanishads in Hinduism, teachings of Mahavira among the Jains, and the Eightfold Path of Buddha. Near the end of the period, Muslim Turks establish their rule in North India and will come to dominate the northern two-thirds of the region via the Delhi Sultanate. Muslim persecution accelerates Buddhist decline.

## Arts and Culture

After centuries of relative crudity of form, the Gothic architectural style takes root and spreads rapidly in the twelfth and thirteenth centuries, stimulating associated plastic arts for church and civic building decor. In the Italian Renaissance, the Gothic style is supplanted by a neoclassicism based on rediscovered Greek and Roman ideas of beauty. The vernacular also comes to replace Latin after the 1300s in popular literature. Painting, sculpture, architecture, and metalwork profit from novel techniques and ideas. Secularism and individualism permeate Renaissance art and civic culture of the ruling class.

Landscape painting, porcelain, bronzes, inlay work, silk weaving, and several forms of literature (notably, poetry and the first novels) are highly developed in both China and Japan. Japanese take numerous Chinese forms, but alter them to suit Japanese taste. Some art forms, such as Zen gardens and No drama for the Japanese and jade sculpture and porcelain for the Chinese, are peculiar to each nation. Upper-class life allows more artistic freedom to Japanese women than to their counterparts in wholly patriarchal China.

Art forms emphasize interweaving of gods and humans and mutual dependency. Much Indian art is lost as a result of climate and repeated invasions. Buddhist cave shrines and paintings are major repositories of extant art from the early part of the period. Much sculpture created in stone and metal is of high quality. Indian artistic influence is felt throughout Southeast Asian mainland and Indonesia. History and literature are almost nonexistent throughout this period.

## Science and Technology

After universities are founded in the 1200s, advances in humanities occur, but little in science. Technology attracts some interest, especially after the devastation of the Black Death and the reduction of the labor force, but few breakthroughs occur except in agriculture, where the three-field system, horse collar, use of animal manure, and better plows follow one another. New energy sources are developed from the introduction of windmills and watermills in northwestern Europe.

Both science and technology are highly developed in China throughout this period. Many inventions are produced, including gunpowder, printing with movable type, paper made from wood pulp, navigational aids, a water pump, and a ship's rudder. The Japanese are not so active in these areas and depend heavily on Chinese importations but produce exceptional metalwork.

Selective scientific advances are made. Math is particularly strong (e.g., zero concept, decimal system, much algebra). Pharmacy and medicine are also well-developed. Excellent metalwork is created. Technology is dormant because labor is abundant.

# Worldview Three

## Law and Government

## Society and Economy

### Muslims

**Law and Government:** Law is based on the Qur'an as interpreted by ulama and the qadis. Government is also derived directly from the doctrines of the Prophet and *hadith* tradition. The caliph is head of state and head of religion, as well as commander-in-chief, although the sultans supplant the caliphs as the de facto heads of state after the tenth century. No separation of any type exists between religion and state. Only Muslims are full citizens; others are excluded from office holding but are not necessarily oppressed.

**Society and Economy:** A mixed economy is based on both urban and rural institutions. High levels of sophistication are attained in trade and finance. Mercantile activity of all types is strongly developed, built on previous Eastern civilizations and extensive trading contacts. Agriculture is organized along feudal lines. Wealth is open to all, Muslim and infidel, although non-Muslims are required to pay additional taxes. Enormous variations occur in the relative prosperity of Muslim groups, dependent on previous history and regional economy.

### Africans

**Law and Government:** Law is almost always oral and customary until the arrival of Muslim traders/conquerors in the North and East. Government is based on ethnic affiliations, ranging from semidivine monarchs with cadres of officials to practically family-level autonomy from all external authority. Large areas below the Sahara never organize formal governments but remain "stateless societies" in which oral tradition and custom determine social behavior.

**Society and Economy:** Varied lifestyles depend on changing climate and terrain. Nomadism is prevalent among desert Berbers; agriculture is important in the rain forest zone, savanna grasslands, and coastal plains; additional livestock breeding takes place in all regions except the rain forest. Local trade is made in foodstuffs, salt, pottery, and metals. Long-distance trade across the desert supports large-scale governments beginning in Ghana of the late first millennium C.E. Gold, salt, copper, iron, slaves, and animal by-products are major trade items. Active commerce occurs in collaboration with Arabs and Indians across the Indian Ocean to Arabia and points farther east beginning in the late first millennium C.E.

### Americans

**Law and Government:** A general absence of writing means reliance on customary law. Where states exist, government is generally a divine monarchy of limited powers, with a large group of royal kin sharing in prestige and income from tribute. Priesthood is always powerful, sometimes dominant. Conquest of neighbors is the usual means of constructing imperial control over large areas. Causes of decline of these states are seldom known, although warfare, environmental degradation, and climatic change are the most likely explanations.

**Society and Economy:** These are the only major ancient civilizations not located in river plains or valleys and not dependent on irrigated farms. Both Mesoamerican and Peruvian centers depend on agricultural surplus generated by new crops. Most subjects are farmers, but a few large urban areas (Tenochtitlán, Teotihuacán, Cuzco) appear in time. North of the Rio Grande River, smaller-scale but significant civilizations develop in the Southwest (Puebloan) and east of the Mississippi River (Cahokia and Iroquois). Considerable internal trade occurs, but no contact is made with extra-American civilizations.

# Equilibrium among Polycentric Civilizations, 500–1500 c.e.

## Patterns of Belief

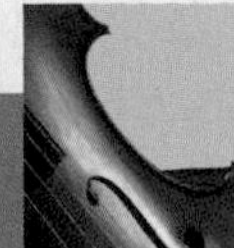

## Arts and Culture

## Science and Technology

Religious affiliation is the basic organizing principle of public life. Islam is strongly exclusivistic and monopolistic in regard to truth. No pressure is exerted on non-Muslims to convert, although many conquered peoples do still. No formal priesthood exists, but the ulama religious scholars advise the caliph and come to be popularly regarded as principal experts on holy law. The Muslim faith clashes head-on with the similar Christianity. Split between Sunni and Shi'a soon destroys original Islamic unity and accentuates power struggles in the Middle East.

Art of all types is strongly influenced by Qur'anic prohibition of human "counterfeits" of God's work. Architecture, interior decor, and landscaping are particular strong points in plastic arts, as are poetry, storytelling, and history in literature. Respect is given for ancient achievements of Greeks in both sciences and philosophy. Society is strongly patriarchal.

Sciences initially and for a long time are promoted by Arab willingness to learn from Greeks and Persians. Major advances are made in math, chemistry, astronomy, and medicine, but by 1300, science is languishing in comparison with the West. Technology is selectively introduced, especially in maritime affairs and, for a time, in war. Muslims are frequently the first alien beneficiaries of earlier Hindu and Chinese breakthroughs.

Widespread belief is held in the power of nature and family spirits. Arrival of Muslims begins after about 700, and sub-Saharan peoples are slowly converted, although veneration of nature and ancestral spirits continues to be common even among Muslims. Christianity is isolated in Nubia and Ethiopia after the seventh century.

Art is entirely devoted to religion or quasi-religious purposes, few of which are understood today. Fine bronzes and carvings are created in parts of the sub-Saharan West and in the Southeast. Nok terra cotta work is the oldest surviving art (seventh century). The wholly oral culture produced no written literature in this era, although extensive oral traditions produced and preserved rich traditions of history and verbal art.

Science is stultified in contrast with other parts of the globe. Lack of written languages hampers retention and exchange of complex information, although farm-based societies have complex systems of astronomy and astrology. Methods of iron-making and metals extraction are relatively advanced. Extensive systems of irrigation are used in some locations.

Religious belief is now unknown in detail. The gods are often fearful, demonic rulers of the afterworld. Faith strongly resembles aspects of Mesopotamia, with human sacrifice on a large scale in at least some of the ruling groups (Aztec, Maya). No apparent connections exist between religion and ethics.

Much pre-Columbian plastic and pictorial artwork survives but little literature has been found. Art serves theology and cosmology. Extraordinary relief sculpture is made in Central America. Architecture highly developed in both Peru and Mexico. The symbolism of much pre-Columbian art is unknown to us.

Technology is highly developed in certain fashions, notably engineering of large stone masses in buildings and fortifications. Mayan mathematics and complex but accurate chronology are other examples. Mastery of hydraulics at Tenochtitlán, massive stone structures in Mayan cities, and Incan road building over very difficult terrain in the Andes demanded extensive science knowledge, but no written records exist.

# PART FOUR

ARCTIC OCEAN
NORTH AMERICA
Mexico
ATLANTIC OCEAN
PACIFIC OCEAN
SOUTH AMERICA
Cuzco
ATLANTIC OCEAN
EUROPE
OTTOMAN EMPIRE
AFRICA
ASIA
RUSSIA
SAFAVID EMPIRE
MUGHAL EMPIRE
Goa
CHINA
JAPAN
Macao
SOUTHEAST ASIA
INDIAN OCEAN
AUSTRALIA
Europeans
West Asians
Americans
South and East Asians

# Disequilibrium: The Western Encounter with the Non-Western World, 1500–1700 c.e.

Within fifty years on either side of 1500 c.e., a host of events or processes contributed to an atmosphere of rising confidence in the power of European governments and their supportive institutions. In the political and military realm, the Mongol yoke in Russia was lifted; the Turks, victorious at Constantinople, failed in an attempt to seize Vienna and central Europe; the Hundred Years' War had ended and the French recovery commenced. The economy finally recovered from the ravages of the Black Death, and maritime trade had increased significantly, as had the sophistication of commercial and financial instruments. The shameful derogation of the papal dignity brought about by the Babylonian Captivity and the Great Schism had ended. The worst of the peasant Jacqueries had been put down, and a peaceable transition from feudal agrarianism seemed possible, at least in the West.

But aside from these general developments, the epoch centered on 1500 is usually heralded as the beginning of the modern era because of two specific complexes of events: the questioning of traditional authority manifested in the Protestant Reformation and the voyages of discovery that revealed the possibilities of the globe to Europeans' imagination—and greed. Both of these complexes contributed, in very different ways, to the expansion of Europe's reach and authority that took place in the next 300 years, until Europeans began to claim a prerogative to decide the fates of others as almost a God-given right. This tendency was particularly striking in the American colonies, where the native Amerindians were either obliterated or virtually enslaved by their overlords, but it was also the case, although in a much more limited way, for eastern and southern Asia, the coast of Africa, and the island or Arctic peripheries of a world that was larger and more varied than anyone had formerly supposed.

The difference between 1500 and 1850 in this regard might well be illustrated by comparing the Aztecs' Tenochtitlán, which amazed the envious Cortés, with the sleepy, dusty villages to which Mexico's Indians were later confined. Similarly, one might compare the army of the Persian Safavid rulers of the early sixteenth century that reduced the mighty Moghuls to supplicants for peace with the raggedy mob that attempted—in vain—to stop a handful of British from installing themselves on the Khyber Pass three centuries later. The West, whether represented by illiterate Spanish freebooters or Oxfordian British bureaucrats, seemed destined to surpass or be invincible against what one unrepentant imperialist called the "lesser breeds." Part Four examines the massive changes that were slowly evincing themselves during these three centuries of heightening interactions between the West and the rest of the world, interactions that by the end of the period had effected a state of disequilibrium in the ecumene that existed since the early stages of the common era.

The voyages of discovery of the fifteenth and sixteenth centuries, the opening of maritime commerce across the Indian and Atlantic Oceans, and the resultant Columbian Exchange and the slave trade are the subject of Chapter 23. Chapter 24 considers in detail the successful Lutheran and Calvinist challenges to the papal church and their permanent effects on Western sensibilities. Chapters 25 and 26 examine the absolutist idea, constitutionalism, and their expression in religious warfare and the desire for stability; the evolving differences in the social and economic structures of western and eastern Europe are also considered.

Chapter 27 shifts the focus to Asia, where the rise and fall of the great Muslim empires of central Asia and India are discussed. China's centuries of glory following the ejection of the Mongols through the early Qing Dynasty are analyzed in Chapter 28. The history of pre–Meiji Restoration Japan and Southeast Asia before 1700 follow in Chapter 29. Finally, the Iberian colonies of America and their struggle for independent existence are outlined in Chapter 30.

*I have come to believe that this is a mighty continent which was hitherto unknown.*
Christopher Columbus

# 23 A Larger World Opens

Maritime Exploration in the 1400s

Overseas Empires and Their Effects
Portuguese Pioneers
The Spanish Empire in the Americas
The African Slave Trade Opens
Dutch and English Merchant-Adventurers

Mercantilism

The Columbian Exchange

European Impacts and Vice Versa
The Fate of the Amerindians
Racism's Beginnings

| | |
|---|---|
| Mid-1400s | Portuguese begin voyages of exploration |
| 1492 | Christopher Columbus reaches Americas |
| 1498 | Vasco da Gama arrives in India |
| Early 1500s | Transatlantic slave trade begins |
| 1519–1540 | Spanish conquer Aztecs and Incans |
| 1522 | First circumnavigation of globe completed |
| 1602 | Dutch East India Company founded |

The unparalleled overseas expansion of Europe in the later fifteenth and early sixteenth centuries opened a new era of intercontinental contacts. What were the motives for the rapid series of adventuresome voyages? They ranged from Christian missionary impulses to the common desire to get rich. Backed to varying degrees by their royal governments, Portuguese, Spanish, Dutch, French, and English seafarers opened the world to European commerce, settlement, and eventual dominion. Through the Columbian Exchange initiated in 1492, the New World entered European consciousness and was radically and permanently changed by European settlers. In most of the world, however, the presence of a relative handful of foreigners in coastal "factories" or as occasional traders meant little change in traditional activities and attitudes. Not until the later eighteenth century was the European presence a threat to the continuation of accustomed African, Asian, and Polynesian lifestyles.

## Maritime Exploration in the 1400s

The Vikings in their graceful longboats had made voyages across the North Atlantic from Scandinavia to Greenland and on to North America as early as 1000 C.E., but the northern voyages were too risky to serve as the channel for European expansion, and Scandinavia's population base was too small. The Vikings' tiny colonies did not last.

Four hundred years later, major advances in technology had transformed maritime commerce. The development of new sail rigging, the magnetic compass, and the astrolabe (an instrument used to determine the altitude of the sun or other celestial bodies); a new hull design; and systematic navigational charts enabled Western seamen, led by the Portuguese, to conquer the stormy Atlantic. Their claims to dominion over their newly discovered territories were backed up by firearms of all sizes. Most of these inventions were originally the products of the Chinese and Muslims. The Europeans had found them in the traditional interchange ports of the eastern Mediterranean and then improved on them.

By the end of the fifteenth century, the map of the Eastern Hemisphere was gradually becoming familiar to Europeans. Knowledge of the high culture of China was current by the early 1400s. Overland traders, mostly Muslims, had established an active trade with China via the famous Silk Road through central Asia and served as intermediaries to Europe. Marco Polo's great adventure was well known even earlier, after the appearance of his book about his many years of service to Kubilai Khan (see Chapter 17).

Most of Europe's luxury imports had long come from China and India, while the Spice Islands (as they were called by Europeans) of Southeast Asia had been the source of the most valuable items in international exchange (see Map 23.1). In the fourteenth century, this trade was disrupted, first by the Ottoman Turkish conquest of the eastern Mediterranean and then by the breakup of the Mongol Empire, which had formed a single unit reaching from China to western Russia.

Security of transit across Asia was threatened, as was the Europeans' long-established and profitable interchange of goods with the Arabs and Persians. In 1453, the great depot of Eastern wares, Constantinople, fell into the

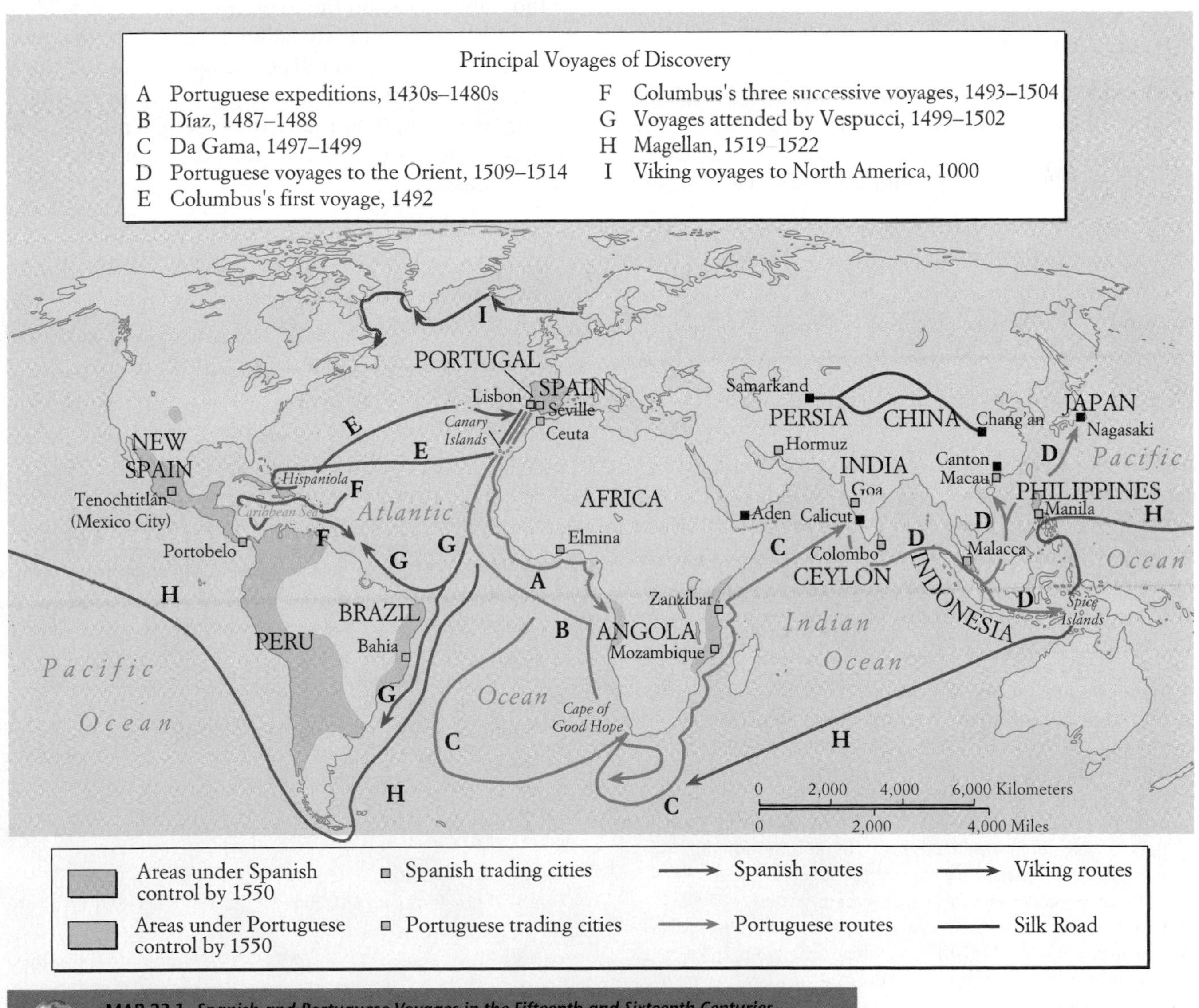


**MAP 23.1** *Spanish and Portuguese Voyages in the Fifteenth and Sixteenth Centuries*

The shaded areas indicate the portions of the newly explored regions that were mapped and settled. Unshaded areas indicate those that remained unexplored and relatively unknown.

hands of the Turks. With direct access to this old gateway to the East now lost, Europeans became more interested than ever in finding a direct sea route to the East by circumnavigating Africa. This route would allow them to bypass the hostile Turks and perhaps even cut out the Arab, Persian, and Indian middlemen—a tempting prospect.

## Overseas Empires and Their Effects

First the Portuguese and the Spanish and then the Dutch, English, and French created overseas empires that had far-reaching effects both at home and abroad.

### *Portuguese Pioneers*

In the middle of the 1400s, insignificant and impoverished Portugal took advantage of its geographical position to begin a rapid phase of European expansion. Under the guidance of the visionary Prince Henry the Navigator (1394–1460), the Portuguese sponsored a series of exploratory voyages down the west coast of Africa and out into the ocean as far as the Azores (about one-third the distance to the Caribbean) in a search for African gold and pepper. In 1488, the Portuguese captain Bartolomeo Diaz made a crucial advance by successfully rounding the Cape of Good Hope. Some years later, Vasco da Gama sailed across the Indian Ocean to the west coast of India. (For a closer look at da Gama's exploits, see Science and Technology.) Trying to follow a new route around the southern tip of Africa that took him far to the west, Pedro Alvarez Cabral got blown all the way across the Atlantic, making landfall in Brazil, which he promptly claimed for Portugal. By 1510, Portuguese flags were flying over Goa in India and Macão on the coast of China (see Map 23.1). In 1511, the extraordinary admiral Afonso da Albuquerque seized the great port-depot of Malacca at the tip of the Malay peninsula. With the capital of their Indian Ocean empire in Goa, the Portuguese became the controllers of the most profitable sea trade in the world (see Chapter 18).

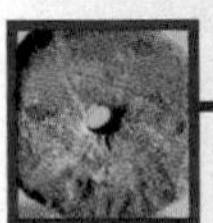

SCIENCE AND TECHNOLOGY

### Vasco da Gama's First Contacts in East Africa

**ONE OF THE MOST DARING** of all the explorers sailing in the name of Portugal or Spain was Vasco da Gama, the first to round the tip of Africa and sail on to India. Da Gama made landfall on the Indian coast in 1498 before returning safely to Lisbon the following year. He kept a detailed diary of his epoch-making voyage, from which the following comments on the non-Muslim peoples of the East African littoral are taken.

> These people are black, and the men are of good physique, they go about naked except that they wear small pieces of cotton cloth with which they cover their genitals, and the Senhores [chiefs] of the land wear larger cloths. The young women in this land look good; they have their lips pierced in three places and they wear some pieces of twisted tin. These people were very much at ease with us, and brought out to us in the vessels what they had, in dugout canoes. . . .
>
> After we had been here two or three days there came out two Senhores of this land to see us, they were so haughty that they did not value anything which was given to them. One of them was wearing a cap on his head with piping worked in silk, and the other a furry cap of green satin. There came in their company a youth who, we gathered from gestures, came from another far country, and said that he had already seen great vessels like those that carried us. With these signs we rejoiced greatly, because it seemed to us that we were going to reach where we wanted to go. . . .
>
> This land, it seemed to us, is densely populated. There are in it many villages and towns. The women seemed to be more numerous than men, because when there came 20 men there came 40 women. . . . The arms of these people are very large bows and arrows, and assagais [spears] of iron. In this land there seemed to be much copper, which they wore on their legs and arms and in their kinky hair. Equally used is tin, which they place on the hilts of daggers, the sheaths are of iron. The people greatly prize linen cloth, and they gave us as much of this copper for as many shirts as we cared to give.

#### *Analyze and Interpret*

What seems to have been the attitude of the East Africans toward these European strangers? To what do you attribute this view? From where do you suppose the previously seen "vessels" had come? To what kinds of material technology does it appear the Africans had access? Where do you think they got it?

Source: Harry Stephan, ed. *The Diary of Vasco da Gama (Travels through African Waters 1497–1499)* (Sydney: Phillips, 1998), pp. 32–33.

The Portuguese empire was really only a string of fortified stations called "factories," from which the Portuguese brought back shiploads of the much sought-after spices, gold, porcelain, and silk obtained from their trading partners in East Africa and the Southeast Asian mainland and islands. The Portuguese paid for these imports initially with metal wares, cloth, and trinkets, and later with firearms and liquor. The Lisbon government was the initiator and main beneficiary of this trade, because Portugal's small upper and middle classes were unable to pay sufficiently to outfit ships for the expeditions.

The era of Portuguese leadership was brief. The country was too poor and its population too small to maintain this lucrative but thinly spread empire. By the late 1500s, the aggressively expanding Dutch merchants had already forced Portugal out of some of its overseas stations. Previously independent Portugal was incorporated into Catholic Spain in 1580, which gave the Dutch and English Protestants an excuse to attack the Portuguese everywhere. Eventually, by the end of the seventeenth century, Portugal was left with only Angola and the Kongo kingdom in West Africa, plus Macão, Goa, Brazil, and a few additional enclaves and trading posts scattered along the coastal regions of the Indian Ocean.

How did a relative handful of European intruders establish themselves as regionally dominant authorities in these distant corners of the globe? In the Indian Ocean and Southeast Asia, the patterns established by the Portuguese were followed by all of their successors. The European outreach was seaborne, and control of the sea was the crucial element. Local populations that tried to resist quickly learned that it was not profitable to confront the European ships with arms, because the Europeans would generally win. Their naval cannon, more advanced methods of rigging, more maneuverable hulls, better battle discipline, and higher levels of training assured them of success in almost all engagements. The intruders avoided land warfare, unless and until mastery of the surrounding seas was assured, and in that case, land warfare was rarely necessary.

After an initial display of martial strength, the newcomers were usually content to deal with and through established local leaders in securing the spices, cotton cloth, silk, and other luxuries that they sought. In the normal course of events, the Europeans made treaties with paramount regional rulers that assured them a dominant position in the export market. This action meant the elimination of the Muslim or Hindu merchants, who until the sixteenth century controlled the Indian Ocean trade and who were the instigators of whatever initial resistance was made. The local ruler's position was not directly threatened unless he should put up armed resistance—a rare occurrence in view of the Europeans' naval advantage and willingness to sell guns to neighboring peoples who might be used as allies against him. The game thus often turned on the principle of divide and conquer.

A kind of partnership thus evolved between the local chieftains and the new arrivals, in which both had sufficient reasons to maintain the status quo against those who might challenge it. The Portuguese frequently made the mistake of alienating the local population by their brutality and their attempts to exclude all competition, but the Dutch and, later, the British were more circumspect. Unlike the Portuguese, they made no attempt until the nineteenth century to bring Africans and Asians to Christianity. As a general rule, after the sixteenth-century Portuguese missionary efforts had subsided, the Europeans interfered little with existing laws, religion, and customs unless they felt compelled to do so to gain their commercial ends. Such interference was rare in both Asia and Africa. There, the European goal was to derive the maximum profit from trade, and they avoided anything that would threaten the smooth execution of that trade. The Spanish and Portuguese empires in the Americas were a different proposition, however.

## *The Spanish Empire in the Americas*

By the dawn of the sixteenth century, a newly unified Spanish kingdom was close behind and in some areas competing with Portugal in the race for world empire. A larger domestic resource base and extraordinary finds of precious metals enabled Spain to achieve more permanent success than its neighbor. The Italian visionary Christopher Columbus was able to persuade King Ferdinand and Queen Isabella to support his dream of a shortcut to the "Indies" by heading *west* over the Atlantic, which he thought was only a few hundred miles wide. The first of Columbus's Spanish-financed voyages resulted in his discovery of the American continents. He made three more voyages before his death and was still convinced that China lay just over the horizon of the Caribbean Sea.

By then, the Spanish crown had engaged a series of other voyagers, including Amerigo Vespucci, who eventually gave his name to the New World that Columbus and others were exploring. In 1519–1521, the formidable Hernán Cortés conquered the Aztec Empire in Mexico. Soon Spanish explorers had penetrated north into what is now California and Arizona. By the 1540s, Spain controlled most of northern South America as well as all of Central America, the larger Caribbean islands, and the South and Southwest of what is now the United States.

Perhaps the greatest of these ventures was the fantastic voyage of Ferdinand Magellan. Starting from Spain in 1519, his ships were the first to circumnavigate the world. A few survivors (not including the unlucky Magellan)

Service Historique de la Marine, Vincennes, France/Lauros/Giraudon/Bridgeman Art Library

**A Portuguese Galleon.** In what kind of vessel did the early explorers set sail? Ships such as these opened the trade routes to the East and to Brazil and the Caribbean for the Lisbon government in the sixteenth and seventeenth centuries. In their later days, two or three rows of cannons gave them heavy firepower as well as cargo space.

limped back into Seville in 1522 and reported that the world was indeed round. Most educated people already thought so, but Magellan's voyage proved that the Earth had no real ends and that it was possible to go around the southern tip of the New World into the more or less familiar waters of East Asia.

Like the Portuguese, the Spaniards' motives for exploration were mixed between a desire to convert the heathen to the Roman Catholic Church and thus gain a strong advantage against the burgeoning Protestants (see Chapter 24) and the desire for wealth and social respectability. Land, too, was increasingly in short supply in Europe, especially for the younger offspring of the nobility and the landed gentry. Gold, God, glory, and acquiring land were the motives most frequently in play. It is often difficult to tell which was uppermost. Sometimes, however—as in the cases of Francisco Pizarro in Peru and Hernán Cortés in Mexico—it is easier. By whatever motivation, the middle of the 1500s saw the Spanish adventurers creating an empire that reached as far as the Philippine Islands. In the terms of the royal charters granted to Columbus and his successors, the Spanish crown claimed the lion's share of treasures found by the explorers. Indian gold and silver (*bullion*) thus poured into the royal treasury in Madrid. Those metals, in turn, allowed Spain to become the most powerful European state in the sixteenth and seventeenth centuries.

Unlike the Portuguese, the Spanish frequently came to stay at their overseas posts. Whereas the Portuguese were primarily interested in quick profits from the trade in luxury items from the East, the Spanish noble explorers were accompanied by priests, who set up missions among the Indians, and by a number of lowborn men (later women, also), who were prepared to get rich more slowly. They did so by taking land and workers from among the native population.

Finding that the much dreamed-of cities of gold and silver, or the *El Dorados,* were mirages, the Spanish immigrants gradually created agricultural colonies in much of Central and South America, using first Amerindian and then black labor. Some of these workers were more or less free to come and go, but an increasing number were slaves, imported from Africa. The Spanish colonies thus saw the growth of a multiracial society—Africans, Amerindians, and Europeans—in which the Europeans held the dominant political and social positions from the outset. The dominance of the whites was to assume increasing importance for the societies and economies of these lands both during their 300 years as colonies and later as independent states.

## The African Slave Trade Opens

The European export of slaves from Africa commenced in the fifteenth century. When the Portuguese ventured down the West African coast, they quickly discovered that selling black house slaves to the European nobility could be a lucrative business, but the slave trade remained small in scale through the 1490s and began to grow only when slaves started to be shipped across the Atlantic. By the mid-1530s, Portugal had shipped moderate numbers of slaves to the Spanish Caribbean and to its own colony of Brazil, and the trans-Atlantic trade remained almost a Portuguese monopoly until into the next century. At that time, Dutch, French, and then English traders moved into the business and dominated it throughout its great expansion in the eighteenth century until its gradual abolition.

Few European women traveled to the Americas in the early years of colonization, so the Spaniards often married Amerindian or black women or kept them as concu-

**The Slave Ship.** This engraving shows the usual arrangements for transport of black slaves in the Atlantic trade. The ship was the *Albanez,* with cargo from the Guinea coast and headed for the Caribbean. It was boarded and taken as a prize by the HMS *Albatross* in 1840, as part of the British effort to outlaw slave trading. Food and water were lowered into the hold through the hatch on a once-daily basis. Some slavers permitted short periods on deck for their cargo, but most did not.

bines. As a result, **mestizos** (the offspring of Amerindians and whites) and **mulattos** (the children of Africans and whites) soon outnumbered Caucasians in many colonies. The same thing happened in Portuguese Brazil, where over time a huge number of African slaves were imported to till the sugarcane fields that provided that colony with its chief export. Here, the populace was commonly the offspring of Portuguese and African unions, rather than the Spanish-Indian mixture found to the north.

## Dutch and English Merchant-Adventurers

***Holland.*** When Portugal's grip on its Indian Ocean trade began to falter, the Dutch Protestant merchants combined a fine eye for profit with religious zeal to fill the vacuum. In the late sixteenth century, the Netherlands gained independence from Spain. Controlling their own affairs after that, the bourgeois ship owners and merchants of the Dutch and Flemish towns quickly moved into the forefront of the race for trade. By the opening of the seventeenth century, Amsterdam and Antwerp were the major destinations of Far Eastern shippers, and Lisbon had fallen into a secondary position.

Dutch interest in the eastern seas was straightforward and hard-edged. They wanted to accumulate wealth by creating a monopoly of demand, buying shiploads of Southeast Asian luxury goods at low prices and selling the goods at high prices in Europe. Many of the Asian suppliers were Muslims, and their relationship with the Catholic Portuguese had been strained or hostile. They preferred to deal with the Dutch Protestants, who were simply businessmen with no desire to be missionaries. If the suppliers were for one or another reason reluctant to sell, the Dutch persuaded them by various means, usually involving Dutch superiority in naval gunnery.

The Dutch focused on the East Indies spice and luxury trade, but they also established settler colonies at Cape Town in South Africa, in New Amsterdam across the Atlantic, and on several islands in the Caribbean. These colonies were less attractive to the Dutch and eventually surrendered to other powers, such as England. New Amsterdam became New York at the close of the first of two naval wars in the seventeenth century that made England the premier colonial power along the East Coast of the future United States.

How did such a small nation (Holland did not possess more than 2.5 million people at this juncture) carry out this vast overseas enterprise while it was struggling to free itself from its Spanish overlords? A chief reason for the Dutch success was the East India Company: a private firm chartered by the government in 1602, the company had a monopoly on Dutch trading in the Pacific. The company eventually took over the Portuguese spice and luxury trade in the East and proved to be an enormous bonanza for its stockholders. The traders were usually temporary partners. A partnership would be set up for one or more voyages, with both cost and profits split among the shareholders, while minimizing risks for all. The traders hired captains and crews who would be most likely to succeed in filling the ship's hold at minimal cost, whatever the means or consequences. Later in the seventeenth century, the focus of attention shifted from importing spices and luxury goods to the alluring profits to be made in the trans-Atlantic trade in African slaves.

***England.*** The English colonial venture was slow in getting started. When the Portuguese and Spaniards were dividing up the newly discovered continent of America and the Far Eastern trade, England was just emerging from a lengthy struggle for dynastic power called the War of the Roses (see Chapter 21). Starting in the 1530s, the country was then preoccupied for a generation with the split from Rome under Henry VIII and its consequences (see Chapter 24). Then came the disappointing failure of Sir Walter Raleigh's "Lost Colony" on the Carolina coast in the 1580s and a war with Spain.

Only in the early 1600s did the English begin to enter the discovery and colonizing business in any systematic way. Like the Dutch, the English efforts were organized by private parties or groups and were not under the direction of the royal government. The London East India Company (often called the British East India Company), founded in 1600, is a good example. Similar to its Dutch counterpart, it was a private enterprise with wide political as well as commercial powers in dealing with foreigners and with its own military resources.

After two victorious wars against the Dutch in the 1650s and 1660s, the English were the world's leading naval power, although the Dutch still maintained their lead in the carrying trade to and from Europe. The East Asian colonial trade was not important to them, however, and they soon gave up their attempts to penetrate the Dutch monopoly on East Indian luxuries, choosing to concentrate on India. (The only important English station in Southeast Asia was the great fortress port of Singapore, which was not acquired until the nineteenth century.)

English colonies in the seventeenth century were concentrated in North America and the Caribbean, and an odd mixture they were. The northern colonies were filled with Protestant dissidents who could not abide the Anglican Church regime: Puritans, Congregationalists, and Quakers. Maryland was a refuge for persecuted Catholics. Virginia and the Carolinas began as real estate speculations. They were essentially get-rich-quick schemes devised by nobles or wealthy commoners who thought they could sell off their American holdings to individual settlers at a fat profit. Georgia began as a noble experiment by a group of philanthropists who sought to give convicts a second chance.

Elsewhere, the English were less inclined to settle new lands than to make their fortunes pirating Spanish galleons or competing with the Dutch in the slave trade. What the Dutch had stolen from the Portuguese, the English stole in part from the Dutch. This was equally true in the New World, where the Dutch challenge to Portuguese and Spanish hegemony in the Caribbean was superseded by the English and French in the eighteenth century.

***France.*** The colonial empire of France parallels that of England. While they were relatively late in entering the race, the French sought overseas possessions and/or trade factories throughout the world to support their prospering domestic economy. From Canada (as early as 1608, one year after Jamestown in Virginia), to the west coast of Africa (as early as 1639) and India (in the early eighteenth century), the servants of the Bourbon kings contested both their Catholic co-religionists (Portugal, Spain) and their Protestant rivals (Holland, Britain) for mercantile advantage and the extension of royal powers. Thus, the French, too, reflected the seventeenth-century trend to allow state policies to be dictated more by secular interests than by religious adherences, a process we will examine in detail in Chapter 25.

## Mercantilism

During this epoch, governments attempted to control their economies through a process later termed ***mercantilism***. Under mercantilism, the chief goal of economic policy was a favorable balance of trade, with the value of a country's exports exceeding the cost of its imports. To achieve this goal, the royal government intervened in the market constantly and attempted to secure advantage to itself and the population at large by carefully supervising every aspect of commerce and investment. The practice reached its highest development in seventeenth- and eighteenth-century France, but it was subscribed to almost everywhere.

As for colonial policy, mercantilism held that only goods and services that originated in the home country could be (legally) exported to the colonies and that the colonies' exports must go to the home country for use there or re-export. Thus, the colonies' most essential functions were to serve as captive markets for home-country producers and to provide raw materials at low cost for home-country importers.

## The Columbian Exchange

The coming of the Europeans to the New World resulted in important changes in the resources, habits, and values of both the Amerindians and the whites. Among the well-known introductions by the Europeans to the Western Hemisphere were horses, pigs, cattle, sheep, and goats; iron; firearms; sailing ships; and, less tangibly, the entire system of economics we call capitalism.

But the Columbian Exchange had another side: a reverse flow of products and influences from the Americas to Europe and through Europe to the other continents.

Educated Europeans after about 1520 became aware of how huge and relatively unknown the Earth was and how varied the peoples inhabiting it were. This knowledge came as a surprise to many Europeans, and they were eager to learn more. The literature of discovery and exploration became extraordinarily popular during the sixteenth and seventeenth centuries.

From this literature, Europeans learned, among other things, that the Christian moral code was but one of several; that the natural sciences were not of overwhelming interest or importance to most of humanity; that an effective education could take myriad forms and have myriad goals; and that viewpoints formed by tradition and habit are not necessarily correct, useful, or the only conceivable ones. Initially just curious about the Earth's other inhabitants, upper-class Europeans gradually began to develop a certain tolerance for other peoples' views and habits. This tolerance slowly deepened in the seventeenth and especially the eighteenth century as Europe emerged from its religious wars. The previously favored view of unknown peoples probably being "anthropophagi" (man eaters) began giving way to the concept of the "noble savage," whose unspoiled morality might put the sophisticated European to shame.

Contacts with the Americas also led to changes in Europe. Some crops such as sugarcane and rice that were already known in Europe but that could not be profitably grown there were found to prosper in the New World. Their cultivation formed the basis for the earliest plantations in the Caribbean basin and the introduction of slavery into the New World. In addition, a series of new crops were introduced to the European, Asian, and African diets. Tobacco, several varieties of beans and peas, potatoes, squashes, rice, maize, bananas, manioc, and others stemmed originally from American or Far Eastern lands. First regarded as novelties—much like the occasional Indian or African visitor—these crops came to be used as food and fodder. The most important for Europe was the white or Irish potato, an Andean native, which was initially considered fit only for cattle and pigs but was gradually adopted by northern Europeans in the eighteenth century. By the end of that century, the potato had become the most important part of the peasants' diet in several countries. The potato was the chief reason European farms were able to feed the spectacular increase in population that started in the later 1700s.

So much additional coinage was put into circulation in Europe from the Mexican and Peruvian silver mines that it generated massive inflation. In the seventeenth century, the Spanish court used the silver to pay army suppliers, shipyards, and soldiers, and from their hands, it went on into the general economy. Spain suffered most in the long run from the inflation its bullion imports caused. Moreover, with its tiny middle class, Spain resisted technological innovation and industrialization, so when the rest of Europe began industrializing, Spanish gold and silver went into the pockets of foreign suppliers, carriers, and artisans rather than into domestic investments or business. This situation would prove fateful in the next century.

In a period of inflation, when money becomes cheap and goods or services become dear, people who can convert their wealth quickly to goods and services are in an enviable position. Those whose wealth is illiquid and cannot be easily converted are at a disadvantage. As a result, the landholders—many of whom were nobles who thought it beneath them to pay attention to money matters—lost economic strength. The middle classes, who could sell their services and expertise at rising rates, did well. Best off were the merchants, who could buy cheap and hold before selling at higher prices. But even the unskilled or skilled workers in the towns were in a relatively better position than the landlords: wages rose about as fast as prices in this century.

In many feudal remnant areas, where serfs paid token rents in return for small parcels of arable land, the landlord was dealt a heavy blow. Prices rose for everything the noble landlords needed and wanted, while their rents, sanctioned by centuries of custom, remained about the same. Many of them had been living beyond their means for generations, borrowing money wherever they could with land as security. Unaware of the reasons for the economic changes and unable to anticipate the results, many landlords faced disaster during the later sixteenth century and could not avoid bankruptcy when their long-established mortgages were called. Much land changed hands at this time, from impoverished nobles to peasants or to the newly rich from the towns. Serfdom in the traditional pattern became impractical or unprofitable. Already weakened by long-term changes in European society, serfdom was abolished in most of Western Europe.

## European Impacts and Vice Versa

How strong was the European impact on the Amerindian cultures of the Western Hemisphere and on the peoples of the Far East, sub-Saharan Africa, and the Pacific Rim? Historians agree that it was enormous in some areas, but much less so in others. The Portuguese and others' trading factories on the African and Asian coasts had minimal impacts on the lives of the peoples of the interior. Only in exceptional circumstances was the presence of the Europeans a prominent factor in native consciousness. Even in the areas most directly affected by slaving such as

**INDIAN LABOR.** The Amerindian population was put to hard labor by the Spanish conquistadors either through arrangements between the Spaniards and local chiefs or by force. This sixteenth-century sketch shows the shipment of arms (including a cannon barrel and balls) across a range of mountains in Mexico. The absence of beasts of burden in Mesoamerica meant that humans had to shoulder every load.

Senegambia, the Nigerian Delta, and Angola, the consensus of recent scholarly opinion holds that few if any massive changes occurred in the course of ordinary affairs, social or economic, as a result of slaving alone. Rather, the foreign slavers' interests were filtered through the existing networks of local authority and custom.

Spain's American settler colonies and Brazil were quite different in these respects. Here the intruders quickly and radically terminated existing Amerindian authority structures, replacing them with Spanish/Portuguese models. In the economy, the *encomienda* estates on which first Amerindians were forced to live and toil replaced the villages with their free labor. Although the encomiendas were soon abolished, Spanish and Portuguese exploitation of helpless Amerindians and Africans continued on rice and sugar plantations, which replaced gold and silver mines.

As with the exchanges in agricultural products, the stream of external influences was not simply one way, from Europe to the rest of the world. In the Americas, a noticeable degree of change was wrought in the Spanish and Portuguese culture by prolonged exposure to Amerindian and African habits and attitudes. An example would be the adoption of maize culture by the mestizo and Spanish populations in Mexico. Another would be the incorporation of Amerindian hydraulic farming technique. In another part of the early imperial world created by the voyages of discovery, the architecture of the Dutch colonial town of Batavia (Jakarta) was soon converted from the trim and tight homes and warehouses of blustery Amsterdam to the different demands of the Javanese climate.

Perhaps it is most accurate to say that in the settler colonies of the Western Hemisphere, the local peoples were extensively and sometimes disastrously affected by the arrival of the whites, but in the rest of the world, including sub-Saharan Africa, the Asian mainland, and the South Pacific islands, the Europeans were less disruptive to the existing state of affairs. Sometimes local peoples even succeeded in manipulating the Europeans to their own advantage, as in West Africa and Mughal India. This would remain true until the nineteenth century. Promoted by industrialization at that time, the European impacts multiplied, became more profound, and changed in nature so as to subordinate the indigenous peoples in every sense.

## The Fate of the Amerindians

By far the worst human consequences of the European expansion were the tragic fates imposed on the native Amerindians of the Caribbean and Central America in the first century of Spanish conquest (see the eyewitness report by Bartolomé de Las Casas in the Evidence of the Past box). Although the Spanish crown imposed several regulatory measures to protect the Indians after 1540, little could be done to inhibit the spread of epidemic disease (measles and influenza, as well as the major killer, smallpox) in the Amerindian villages. As a general rule, because they had not been exposed to childhood diseases

Robert Frerck/Odyssey Productions, Inc.

**THE NATIVE AMERICAN VOICE IN MEXICAN CATHOLICISM.** This detail from the Church of Tonantzintla in Puebla, Mexico, illustrates another aspect of the Columbian Exchange. Indigenous peoples often interpreted European culture and religion through the filter of their own experiences. In this representation of various Roman Catholic saints, Native American artisans depicted their rain god, Tlaloc, in the upper, middle portion of the picture.

like measles and smallpox, the immune systems of the Amerindians were unable to cope with the diseases brought by the newcomers, whereas the Spaniards were much less affected by the Amerindian maladies. (Which ethnic group is responsible for the appearance of syphilis is much argued.)

Smallpox was a particular curse. The population of Mexico, which was perhaps as high as 20 million at the coming of Cortés, was reduced to 2 million only sixty years later, largely as a result of smallpox epidemics. On the Caribbean islands, few Amerindians survived into the seventeenth century in Cuba and the smaller islands. The same story repeated itself in the viceroyalty of Peru, where as many as 80 percent of the native population died in the sixteenth century. Only in modern times have the Amerindians recovered from this unprecedented disaster.

## Racism's Beginnings

Africans came into European society for the first time in appreciable numbers during the fifteenth century. At that time the first faint signs of white racism appeared. The first slaves from Africa were introduced to Europe through Muslim channels. Their rich owners mostly regarded them as novelties, and they were kept as tokens of wealth or artistic taste. Some free black people lived in Mediterranean Europe, where they worked as sailors, musicians, and actors, but they were not numerous enough for the average European to have any firsthand contact.

Many Europeans thought of black people in terms dictated either by the Bible or by Muslim prejudices imbibed unconsciously over time. The biblical references were generally negative: black was the color of the sinful, the opposite of light in the world. "Black-hearted," "a black scoundrel," and "black intentions" are a few examples of the mental connection that was made between the color black and everything evil and contemptible. The Arab slave traders in both West and East Africa who supplied some of the European as well as the Asiatic markets were another source of prejudice. They were contemptuous of non-Muslim Africans of western Sudan or the East African coast in whose flesh they had dealt for centuries before the European trade began. These merchants' point of view was easily transferred to their Italian and Portuguese partners. However, once the European slave trade became big business in the seventeenth century, white racism became the mental cornerstone of a pervasive and viciously exploitative slave-based economy in many parts of the Western Hemisphere.

EVIDENCE OF THE PAST

## Bartolomé de las Casas's Report on the Indies

**Violence toward the conquered** is a commonplace event in history, and nowhere is this more evident than in the history of the state religions. Using inhumane means to propagate Christianity was a cynical cover for some of the Spanish conquistadors in their obsessive search for Indian gold. They were resisted, however, in this bloodthirsty enterprise by one of their own number.

Bartolomé de las Casas (1474–1567), a Dominican priest who had been a conquistador and slaveholder in the Caribbean in his youth, turned his back on his former life and devoted himself to protecting the Amerindians under Spanish rule. In his bold exposé entitled *Brief Relation of the Destruction of the Indies* (1522), he began an uncompromising campaign to show the horrendous treatment meted out by his fellow Spanish to the native populations of the New World. So graphic and terrible were his accounts that foreign powers hostile to Spain (notably, England) were able to use the records for centuries to perpetuate the so-called Black Legend of the viciousness of Spanish colonialism.

The Granger Collection, New York

**The Conquistadors Arrive.** This Aztec painting shows a skirmish between the Spaniards on horse and their Amerindian allies, and Aztec defenders. The Amerindians are armed with obsidian-edged swords capable of cutting off the head of a horse with a single blow.

**Of the Island of Hispaniola**

The Christians, with their horses and swords and lances, began to slaughter and practice strange cruelties among them. They penetrated into the country and spared neither children nor the aged, nor pregnant women, nor those in childbirth, all of whom they ran through the body and lacerated, as though they were assaulting so many lambs herded into the sheepfold.

They made bets as to who could slit a man in two, or cut off his head at one blow . . . they tore babes from their mothers' breasts by the feet, and dashed their heads against the rocks. Others, they seized by the shoulders and threw into the rivers, laughing and joking, and when they fell into the water they exclaimed, "boil the body of So-and-so! . . ."

They made a gallows just high enough for the feet to nearly touch the ground, and by thirteens, in honour and reverence of our Redeemer and the 12 Apostles, they put wood underneath and, with fire, they burned the Indians alive.

They wrapped the bodies of others entirely in dry straw, binding them in it and setting fire to it; and so they burned them. They cut off the hands of all they wished to take alive, made them carry them pinned on to their bodies, and said "Go and carry these letters," that is, take the news to those who have fled to the mountains. . . .

I once saw that they had four or five of the chief lords [Indians] stretched on a gridiron to burn them, and I think there were also two or three pairs of gridirons, where they were burning others. And because they cried aloud and annoyed the Captain or prevented him from sleeping, he commanded that they should be strangled; the officer who was burning them was worse than a hangman and did not wish to suffocate them, but with his own hands he gagged them, so that they should not make themselves heard, and he stirred up the fire until they roasted slowly, according to his pleasure. I know this man's name, and knew his relations in Sevilla. I saw all the above things and numberless others.

And because all the [Indian] people who could flee, hid among the mountains and climbed the crags to escape from men so deprived of humanity . . . the Spaniards taught and trained the fiercest boarhounds to tear an Indian to pieces as soon as they saw him. . . . And because sometimes, though rarely, the Indians killed a few Christians for just cause, they made a law among themselves that for one Christian whom the Indians might kill, the Christians should kill a hundred Indians.

### *Analyze and Interpret*

Besides de las Casas, other Spanish priests tried to protect the Amerindians against cruelty, but usually in vain. What measures might have been taken by the clergy to diminish such cruelty? Was it logical to expect the priests or bishops to intervene effectively? What does the colonial record show?

Source: Bartolomé de las Casas, *A Very Brief Account of the Destruction of the Indies,* trans. F. A. McNutt (Cleveland: Clark, 1909), pp. 312–319.

## Summary

The explosive widening of Europe's horizons in the sixteenth century, in both the geographic sense and the psychological sense, was one side of the Columbian Exchange. A series of colonial empires were created, first by the Portuguese and Spanish and then by the Dutch, English, and French. The original objective of the government-funded explorers was to find new, more secure trade routes to the East, but soon their motives changed to a mixture of enrichment, missionary activity, and prestige: gold, God, and glory.

The import of great quantities of precious metals created severe inflation and promoted the rise of the business/commercial classes. The discovery of customs and values that were different from those of Europeans gradually induced Europeans to adopt new attitudes of tolerance. The overseas expansion also added important new foods to the European diet.

For the non-Western hosts, this colonial and commercial outreach had mainly negative consequences, although circumstances varied from place to place. The most devastating effects were certainly in Spain's American colonies, where the indigenous peoples were almost wiped out by disease and oppression. In West Africa, East Africa, and the Asian mainland, the European trading presence had little overall effect on ordinary life at this time. Racism's beginnings, however, can be traced to its roots in the African slave trade commencing in this era.

## Identification Terms

Test your knowledge of this chapter's key concepts by defining the following terms. If you can't recall the meaning of certain terms, refresh your memory by looking up the boldfaced term in the chapter, turning to the Glossary at the end of the book, or working with the flashcards that are available on the *World Civilizations* Companion Website: **http://history.wadsworth.com/adler04**.

mercantilism
mestizos
mulattos

## Test Your Knowledge

Test your knowledge of this chapter by answering the following questions. Complete answers appear at the end of the book. You may also take this quiz interactively and find even more quiz questions on the *World Civilizations* Companion Website: **http://history.wadsworth.com/adler04**.

1. The fifteenth- and sixteenth-century voyages of exploration were stimulated mainly by
   a. European curiosity about other peoples.
   b. the determination to obtain more farming land for a growing population.
   c. the individual explorers' hopes of enrichment.
   d. the discovery that the Earth was in fact a sphere without "ends."
   e. new technology.
2. Which of the following was *not* proved by Magellan's epic voyage?
   a. The globe was more compact than had been believed.
   b. The globe was indeed spherical.
   c. A sea passage existed south of the tip of South America.
   d. The islands called "Spice Lands" could be reached from the East.
   e. The journey was a long and difficult one.
3. Which of the following nations was most persistently committed to converting the natives of the newly discovered regions to Christianity?
   a. Spain
   b. Holland
   c. England
   d. Portugal
   e. France

4. What is the correct sequence of explorer-traders in the Far East?
   a. Spanish, English, French
   b. Spanish, Portuguese, Dutch
   c. Dutch, English, Spanish
   d. Portuguese, Dutch, English
   e. Spanish, Portuguese, English
5. The first to engage in the slave trade were the
   a. Dutch.
   b. Portuguese.
   c. Danes.
   d. English.
   e. Spanish.
6. Which of the following reasons was least likely to be the motive for a Dutch captain's voyage of discovery?
   a. A desire to deal the Roman church a blow
   b. A search for personal enrichment
   c. A quest to find another lifestyle for himself in a foreign land
   d. The intention of establishing trade relations with a new partner
   e. The desire to serve as a middleman between East Asia and Europe
7. Mercantilism aimed first of all at
   a. securing financial rewards for the entrepreneurs.
   b. allowing the impoverished a chance at rising in society.
   c. bringing maximum income to the royal throne.
   d. securing a favorable balance of foreign trade.
   e. developing a wide range of products for export.
8. Which proved to be the most important of the various new foods introduced into European diets by the voyages of discovery?
   a. Tomatoes
   b. Rice
   c. Potatoes
   d. Coffee
   e. Wheat
9. The sixteenth-century inflation affected which group most negatively?
   a. Landholding nobles
   b. Urban merchants
   c. Wage laborers
   d. Skilled white-collar workers
   e. Church officials
10. The most devastating effects on the native population brought about by European discovery occurred in
   a. India.
   b. Latin America.
   c. West Africa.
   d. Southeast Asia.
   e. North America.

## InfoTrac College Edition

Visit the source collections at

**http://infotrac.thomsonlearning.com**

and use the Search function with the following key terms:

Vasco da Gama Christopher Columbus mercantilism

## Wadsworth History Website Resources

Visit the World History Resource Center at **http://history.wadsworth.com/world** for a wealth of general resources, and the *World Civilizations* Companion Website at **http://history.wadsworth.com/adler04** for resources specific to this textbook.

## HistoryNow

Enter *HistoryNow* using the access card that is available for *World Civilizations*. *HistoryNow* will assist you in understanding the content of this chapter with lesson plans generated for your needs. In addition, you can read the following documents, and many more, online:

Prince Henry the Navigator, *Chronicle of the Discovery and Conquest of Guinea*

Selections from Christopher Columbus's Journal

*I have often been resolved to live uprightly, and to lead a true godly life, and to set everything aside that would hinder this, but it was far from being put in execution. I am not able to effect that good which I intend.*
Martin Luther

# 24 The Protestant Reformation



| | |
|---|---|
| 1517 | Posting of the *Ninety-five Theses* |
| 1521 | Excommunication of Luther |
| 1534 | Act of Supremacy (England) |
| 1540s | Calvinism spreads through much of Europe |
| 1555 | Peace of Augsburg divides Germans |
| 1572 | St. Bartholomew's Day Massacre |
| 1588 | English defeat Spanish Armada |
| 1593 | Henry IV restores peace in France |

The split in Christian belief and church organization that is termed the Protestant Reformation brought enormous consequences in its wake. Its beginning coincided with the high point of the Era of Discovery by Europeans. Taken together, these developments provide the basis for dividing Western civilization's history into the premodern and modern eras around 1500.

What the opening of the transatlantic and trans–Indian Ocean worlds did for the consciousness of physical geography in European minds, the Reformation did for the mental geography of all Christians. New continents of belief and identity emerged from the spiritual voyages of the early Protestants. Luther and Calvin worked not only a re-formation but also a trans-formation of the church and its members.

## Luther and the German National Church

The upheaval called the **Reformation** of the early sixteenth century had its roots in political and social developments as much as in religious disputes. The longstanding arguments within the Christian community over various points of doctrine or practices had already led to rebellions against the Rome-led majority on several occasions. In the major instances in thirteenth-century France, fourteenth-century England, and fifteenth-century Bohemia, religious rebels (the official term is *heretics,* or "wrong thinkers") had battled the papal church. Eventually, all of them had been suppressed or driven underground. But now, in sixteenth-century Germany, Martin Luther

(1483–1546) found an enthusiastic reception for his challenges to Rome among the majority of his fellow Germans.

Why was the church in the German lands particularly susceptible to the call for reform? The disintegration of the German medieval kingdom had been followed by the birth of dozens of separate, little principalities and city-states, such as Hamburg and Frankfurt, that could not well resist the encroachments of the powerful papacy in their internal affairs. Unlike the nations of centrally governed France, England, and Spain, whose monarchs jealously guarded their sources of revenue, the German populations were systematically milked by Rome and forced to pay taxes and involuntary donations. Many of the German rulers were angry at seeing the tax funds they needed going off to a foreign power and sometimes used for goals they did not support. These rulers were eagerly searching for some popular basis to challenge Rome. They found it in the teachings of Luther.

Luther was a monk who had briefly witnessed at first hand the corruption and crass commercialism of the sixteenth-century Roman *curia* (court). When he returned to the University of Wittenberg in Saxony, where he had been appointed chaplain, he used his powerful oratory to arouse the community against the abuses he had seen. He especially opposed the church's practice of selling *indulgences*—forgiveness of the spiritual guilt created by sins—rather than insisting that the faithful earn forgiveness by prayer and good works.

In 1517, a major indulgence sales campaign opened in Germany under even more scandalous pretexts than usual. Much of the money raised was destined to be used to pay off a debt incurred by an ambitious noble churchman, rather than for any ecclesiastical purpose. Observing what was happening, the chaplain at Wittenberg decided to take his stand. On October 31, 1517, Luther announced his discontent by posting the famous ***Ninety-five Theses*** on his church door. In these questions, Luther raised objections not only to many of the papacy's practices, such as indulgence campaigns, but also to the whole doctrine of papal supremacy. He contended that if the papacy had ever been intended by God to be the moral mentor of the Christian community, it had lost that claim through its present corruption.

## Luther's Beliefs

Luther had more profound doubts about the righteousness of the papal church than merely its claims to universal leadership, however. His youth had been a long struggle against the conviction that he was damned to hell. Intensive study of the Bible eventually convinced him that only through the freely given grace of a merciful God might he, or any person, reach immortal salvation.

The Catholic Church, on the other hand, taught that men and women must manifest their Christian faith by doing good works and leading good lives. If they did so, they might be considered to have earned a heavenly future. Martin Luther rejected this notion. He believed that faith alone was the factor through which Christians might reach bliss in the afterlife and that faith was given by God and not in any way earned by naturally sinful man. It is this doctrine of **justification by faith** that most clearly marks off Lutheranism from the papal teachings.

As the meaning of Luther's statements penetrated into the clerical hierarchy, he was implored, then commanded, to cease. Instead, his confidence rose, and in a series of brilliantly forceful pamphlets written in the German vernacular, he explained his views to a rapidly increasing audience. By 1520, he was becoming a household word among educated people and even among the peasantry. He was excommunicated in 1521 by the pope for refusing to recant, and in the same year, he was declared an outlaw by Emperor Charles V.



**MARTIN LUTHER.** This contemporary portrait by Lucas V. Cranach is generally considered to be an accurate rendition of the great German church reformer in midlife. Both the strengths and weaknesses of Luther's peasant character are revealed.

The Catholic emperor was an ally of the pope, but the emperor had his hands full with myriad other problems, notably the assault of the Ottoman Turks. Charles had no desire to add an unnecessary civil war to the long list of tasks he faced. He took action against Luther only belatedly and halfheartedly, hoping that in some way an acceptable compromise might be reached.

Threatened by the imperial and papal officials, Luther sought and quickly found the protection of the ruler of Saxony, as well as much of the German princely class. They saw in his moral objections to Rome the excuse they had been seeking for advancing their political aspirations. They encouraged Luther to organize a national church free from papal overlords.

With this protection and encouragement, Luther's teachings spread rapidly, aided by the newly invented printing press and by the power and conviction of his sermons and writings. By the mid-1520s, Lutheran congregations, rejecting the papal authority and condemning Rome as the fount of all evil, had sprung up throughout most of Germany and were appearing in Scandinavia as well. The unity of Western Christianity had been shattered.

Collection of Albert Rilliet, Geneva, Switzerland/Lauros/Giraudon/Bridgeman Art Library

**JOHN CALVIN.** This Swiss portrait of the "pope of Geneva" in his younger days depicts Calvin in a fur neckpiece. This bit of bourgeois indulgence would probably not have been worn by an older Calvin.

## CALVIN AND INTERNATIONAL PROTESTANTISM

It was not Luther, the German peasant's son, but John Calvin (1509–1564), the French lawyer, who made the Protestant movement an international theological rebellion against Rome. Luther always saw himself as a specifically German patriot, as well as a pious Christian, and his translations of the Scriptures were written in a powerful idiomatic German. (Luther's role in creating the modern German language is roughly the same as the role Shakespeare played in the development of English.) Calvin, on the contrary, detached himself from national feeling and saw himself as the emissary and servant of a God who ruled all nations. Luther wanted the German Christian body to be cleansed of papal corruption; Calvin wanted the entire Christian community to be made over into the image of what he thought God intended. When he was done, a good part of it had been.

Calvin was born into a middle-class family of church officeholders who educated him for a career in the law. When he was twenty-five, he became a Protestant, inspired by some Swiss sympathizers with Luther. For most of the rest of his life, Calvin was "the pope of Geneva," laying down the law to that city's residents and having a major influence on much of the rest of Europe's religious development.

Calvin believed that the papal church was hopelessly distorted. It must be obliterated, and new forms and practices (which were supposedly a return to the practices of early Christianity) must be introduced. In ***The Institutes of the Christian Religion*** (1536), Calvin set out his beliefs and doctrines with the precision and clarity of a lawyer. From this work came much of the intellectual content of Protestantism for the next 200 years.

Calvin's single most dramatic change from both Rome and Luther was his insistence that God predestined souls. That is, a soul was meant either for heaven or hell for all eternity, but at the same time, the individual retained free will to choose good or evil. The soul destined for hell would inevitably choose evil—but did not have to! It was a harsh theology. Calvin believed that humanity had been eternally stained by Adam's sin and that most souls were destined for hellfire.

Despite its doctrinal fierceness, Calvin's message found a response throughout Europe. By the 1540s, Calvinists were appearing in Germany, the Netherlands, Scotland,

England, and France, as well as Switzerland. Geneva had become the Protestant Rome, with Calvin serving as its priestly ruler until his death in 1564.

## Calvinism and Lutheranism Compared

What were some of the similarities and differences between the beliefs of Luther and Calvin (who never met and had little affection for one another)? First, Luther believed that faith alone, which could not be earned, was the only prerequisite for salvation. Good works were encouraged, but they had little or no influence on the Last Judgment. Calvin demanded works as well as faith to indicate that a person was attempting to follow God's order on Earth.

Later, Calvinists saw their performance of good works as a mark that they were among the Elect, the souls predestined for heaven. The emphasis in some places and times shifted subtly from doing good works as a sign of serving God to believing that God would logically favor the members of the Elect. Therefore, those who were "doing well" in the earthly sense were probably among the Elect. From this concept, some later students of religion saw Calvinist beliefs as the basis for the triumph of the capitalist spirit in certain parts of Europe. In effect, a God worthy of man's love and worship could rationally be expected to smile on those who did his bidding in this life as well as the next.

Second, Luther saw the clergy as civic as well as spiritual guides for mankind. He believed in a definite hierarchy of authority within the church, and he retained bishops, who maintained their crucially important power to appoint priests. The bishops themselves had to pass inspection by the civil authorities, a subordination that was to prove fateful for the German Church. In time, the Lutheran pastors and bishops became fully dependent on the state that employed them, rarely defying it on moral grounds. Lutheranism became a state church, not only in Germany but also in Scandinavia, where it had become dominant by the mid-1500s. In contrast, Calvin insisted on the moral independence of the church from the state. He maintained that the clergy as well as laity had a duty to oppose any immoral acts of government, no matter what the cost to themselves. In conflicts between the will of God and the will of kings, the Calvinist must enlist on the side of God.

More than Lutherans, the Calvinists thought of the entire community, lay and clerical alike, as equal members of the church on Earth. Calvinists also insisted on the power of the congregation to select and discharge pastors at will, inspired by God's word. They never established a hierarchy of clerics. There were no Calvinist bishops but only presbyters, or elected elders, who spoke for their fellow parishioners in regional or national assemblies. The government of the church thus included both clerical and lay leaders. The combination gave the church's pronouncements great political as well as moral force.

**THE CALVINIST CHURCH.** This painting is by a Dutch sixteenth-century master, Hendrik van Steenwyck, who portrays the "purified" interior of the Antwerp cathedral after it was taken over by Calvinists. Contrast this church with the Notre Dame de Paris presented in Chapter 19.

By around 1570, Calvin's followers had gained control of the Christian community in several places: the Dutch-speaking Netherlands, Scotland, western France, and parts of northern Germany and Poland. In the rest of France, Austria, Hungary, and England, they were still a minority, but a growing one. Whereas Lutheranism was confined to the German-speaking countries and Scandinavia and did not spread much after 1550 or so, Calvinism was an international faith that appealed to all nations and identified with none. Carried on the ships of the Dutch and English explorers and emigrants of the seventeenth and eighteenth centuries, it continued to spread throughout the modern world.

## Other Early Protestant Faiths

The followers of a radical sect called **Anabaptists** (Rebaptizers) were briefly a threat to both Catholics and Lutherans, but they were put down with extreme cruelty by both. The Anabaptists originated in Switzerland and spread rapidly throughout German Europe. They believed in adult baptism, a priesthood of all believers, and—most disturbingly—a primitive communism and sharing of worldly possessions. Both as radicals in religious affairs and as social revolutionaries, the Anabaptists were oppressed by all of their neighbors. After their efforts to establish a republic in the Rhineland city of Münster were bloodily suppressed, the Anabaptists were driven underground. Their beliefs continued to evolve, and they emerged much later in the New World as Mennonites, Amish, and similar groups.

Yet another Protestant creed emerged early in Switzerland (which was a hotbed of religious protest). Founded by Ulrich Zwingli (1484–1531), it was generally similar to Lutheran belief, although Zwingli claimed he had arrived at his doctrine independently. The inability of Zwingli's adherents and the Lutherans to cooperate left Zwingli's stronghold in Zurich open to attack by the Catholic Swiss. The Protestants were defeated in the battle, and Zwingli was killed. This use of bloody force to settle religious strife was an ominous note. It was to become increasingly common as Protestant beliefs spread and undermined the traditional religious structures.

### *The Church of England*

As was often the case, England went its own way. The English Reformation differed from the Reformation on the Continent yet followed the general trend of European affairs. The English reformers were originally inspired by Lutheran ideas, but they adopted more Calvinist views as time went on. However, the Church of England, or Anglican Confession, came to be neither Lutheran nor Calvinist nor Catholic, but a hybrid of all three.

**A Protestant View of the Pope.** Clothed in hellish splendor and hung about with the horrible symbols of Satan, the Roman pope is revealed for all to see in this sixteenth-century cartoon.

The reform movement in England had its origins in the widespread popular resentment against Rome and the higher clergy, who were viewed as more the tools of the pope than as good English patriots. As we have seen, already in the 1300s a group called the Lollards had rebelled against the clerical claim to sole authority in interpreting the word of God and papal supremacy. The movement had been put down, but its memory persisted in many parts of England.

But it was the peculiar marital problems of King Henry VIII (1490–1547) that finally brought the church in England into conflict with Rome. Henry needed a male successor, but by the late 1520s, his chances of having one with his elderly Spanish wife Catherine were bleak. Therefore, he wanted to have the marriage annulled by the pope (who alone had that power), so he could marry some young Englishwoman who would presumably be able to produce the desired heir.

After trying to evade the issue for years, the pope refused the annulment for reasons that were partly political and partly moral. Between 1532 and 1534, Henry took the matter into his own hands. Still believing himself to be a good Catholic, he intimidated Parliament into declaring him the "only supreme head of the church in England"—the **Act of Supremacy of 1534**. Now, as head of the church, Henry could dictate to the English bishops. He proceeded to put away his unwanted wife and marry the tragic Anne Boleyn, who was already pregnant with his child.

Much other legislation followed that asserted that the monarch, and not the Roman pope, was the determiner of what the church could and could not do in England. Those who resisted, such as the king's chancellor Thomas More, paid with their heads or were imprisoned. Henry went on to marry and divorce several more times before his death in 1547, but he did at least secure a son, the future King Edward VI, from one of these unhappy alliances. Two daughters also survived, the half-sisters Mary and Elizabeth.

***Henry's Successors.*** Henry's actions changed English religious beliefs very little, although the Calvinist reformation was gaining ground in both England and Scotland. But under the sickly boy-king Edward (ruled 1547–1553), Protestant views became dominant among the English governing group, and the Scots were led by the powerful oratory of John Knox into Calvinism (the Presbyterian Church). At Edward's death, it seemed almost certain that some form of Protestant worship would become the official church under the succeeding ruler.

But popular support for Mary (ruled 1553–1558), the Catholic daughter of Henry VIII's first, Spanish Catholic wife, was too strong to be overridden by the Protestant party at court. Just as they had feared, Mary proved to be a single-minded adherent of the papal church, and she restored Catholicism to its official status during her brief reign. Protestant conspirators were put to death without hesitation (hence, she is called "Bloody Mary" in English Protestant mythology).

Finally, the confused state of English official religion was gradually cleared by the political skills of Mary's half-sister and successor, Elizabeth I (ruled 1558–1603). She ruled for half a century with great success while defying all royal traditions by remaining the Virgin Queen and dying childless (see the box). She was able to arrive at a compromise between the Roman and Protestant doctrines, which was accepted by a steadily increasing majority and came to be termed the Church of England. In most respects, it retained the theology and doctrine of the Roman Church, including bishops, rituals, and sacraments, but its head was not the pope but the English monarch, who appointed the bishops and their chief, the archbishop of Canterbury. The strict Calvinists were not happy with this arrangement and wished to "purify" the church by removing all remnants of popery. These **Puritans** presented problems for the English rulers throughout the seventeenth century.

## The Counter-Reformation

Belatedly realizing what a momentous challenge was being mounted, the papacy finally came to grips with the problem of Protestantism in a positive fashion during the 1540s. Pope Paul III (served 1534–1549) moved to counter some of the excesses that had given the Roman authorities a bad name and set up a high-level commission to see what might be done to "clean up" the clergy. Eventually, the church decided to pursue two major lines of counterattack against the Protestants: a thorough examination of doctrines and practices, such as had not been attempted for more than 1,000 years, combined with an entirely novel emphasis on instruction of the young and education of all Christians in the precepts of their religion. These measures together are known as the **Counter-Reformation**.

The Council of Trent (1545–1563) was the first general attempt to examine the church's basic doctrines and goals since the days of the Roman Empire. Meeting for three lengthy sessions divided by years of preparatory work, the bishops and theologians decided that Protestant attacks could best be met by clearly and conclusively defining what Catholics believed. (Protestants were invited to attend, but only as observers; none did.) As a means of strengthening religious practice, this was a positive move, for the legitimacy and accuracy of many church doctrines had come increasingly into doubt since the 1300s. But the council's work had an unintended negative effect on the desired reunification of Christianity: the doctrinal lines separating Catholic and Protestant were now firmly drawn, and they could not be ignored or blurred by the many individuals in both camps who had been trying to arrange a compromise. Now one side or the other would have to give in on specific issues, a prospect neither side was prepared for.

The founding of the **Jesuit Order** was the most striking example of the second aspect of the Counter-Reformation. In 1540, Pope Paul III accorded to the Spanish nobleman Ignatius of Loyola the right to organize an entirely new religious group, which he termed the Society of Jesus, or Jesuits. Their mission was to win, or win back, the minds and hearts of humanity for the Catholic Church through patient, careful instruction that would bring the word of God and of his deputy on Earth, the pope, to everyone. While the Jesuits were working to ensure that all Catholics learned correct doctrine, the *Index* of forbidden books was created and the **Inquisition** revived to ensure that no Catholic deviated from that doctrine. These institutions greatly expanded the church's powers to censor the writings and supervise the beliefs of its adherents.

# Elizabeth I of England (1533–1603)

**In the late sixteenth century,** England became for the first time a power to be reckoned with in world affairs. What had been an island kingdom with little direct influence on any other country except its immediate neighbors across the Channel gradually reached equality with the other major Western military and naval powers: France and Spain. But England's achievement was not just in military affairs. It also experienced a magnificent flowering of the arts and a solid advance in the economy, which finally lifted the nation out of the long depression that had followed the fourteenth-century plague and the long, losing war with France.

The guiding spirit for this comeback was Elizabeth I, queen of England from 1558 until her death in 1603. The daughter of Henry VIII and his second wife, the ill-fated Anne Boleyn, Elizabeth emerged from a heavily shadowed girlhood to become one of the most beloved of British lawgivers. Elizabeth was an intelligent, well-educated woman with gifts in several domains. One of her most remarkable achievements was that she managed to retain her powers without a husband, son, or father in the still very male-oriented world in which she moved.

Born in 1533, she was only three years old when her mother was executed. She was declared illegitimate by order of the disappointed Henry, who had wished for a son. But after her father's death, Parliament established her as third in line to the throne, behind her half-brother Edward and her Catholic half-sister Mary. During Mary's reign (1553–1558), Elizabeth was imprisoned for a time, but she was careful to stay clear of the hectic Protestant-Catholic struggles of the day. By so doing, she managed to stay alive until she could become ruler in her own right.

Her rule began amid many internal dangers. The Catholic party in England opposed her as a suspected Protestant. The Calvinists opposed her as being too much like her father Henry, who never accepted Protestant theology. The Scots were becoming rabid Calvinists who despised the English halfway measures in religious affairs. On top of this, the government was deeply in debt.

Elizabeth showed great insight in selecting her officials and maintained good relations with Parliament. She conducted diplomatic affairs with farsightedness and found she could use her status as an unmarried queen to definite advantage. Philip of Spain, widower of her half-sister Mary, made several proposals of marriage and political unity that Elizabeth cleverly held off without ever quite saying no. She kept England out of the religious wars that were raging in various parts of Europe for most of her reign, but in one of these wars, against her ex-suitor Philip, the Virgin Queen led her people most memorably.

Private Collection/Bridgeman Art Library

**Elizabeth I of England.** The Armada Portrait, perhaps the most famous, was painted by an anonymous artist in the late sixteenth century. Elizabeth was vain, despite being no beauty, and was always receptive to flattery, without in the least being influenced by it in matters of state.

In 1588, after long negotiations failed, Philip sent the Spanish Armada to punish England for aiding the rebellious Dutch Calvinists across the Channel. The queen rallied her sailors in a stirring visit before the battle. The resulting defeat of the Armada not only signaled England's rise to naval equality with Spain but also made Elizabeth the most popular monarch England had ever seen.

A golden age of English literature coincided with Elizabeth's rule, thanks in some part to her active support of all the arts. Her well-known vanity induced her to spend large sums to ensure the splendor of her court despite her equally well-known miserliness. The Elizabethan Age produced Shakespeare, Marlowe, Spenser, and Bacon. By the end of the sixteenth century, English literature for the first time could hold a place of honor in any assembly of national arts.

Elizabeth's version of Protestant belief—the Church of England—proved acceptable to most of her subjects and finally settled the stormy waves of sixteenth-century English church affairs. By the end of her long reign, "Good Queen Bess" had become a stock phrase that most people believed, from barons to peasants.

## *Analyze and Interpret*

Given that an unmarried queen was considered a political risk, what reasons of state could have impelled Elizabeth to remain "the Virgin Queen"? What political capital did she make out of creating the hybrid Church of England that otherwise would have been denied her?

Both became steadily more important in Catholic countries during the next century, as what both sides regarded as a contest between ultimate Truth and abhorrent falsity intensified.

## Religious Wars and Their Outcomes to 1600

The Counter-Reformation stiffened the Catholics' will to resist the Lutheran and Calvinist attacks, which had, at first, almost overwhelmed the unprepared and inflexible Roman authorities. By 1555, the **Peace of Augsburg** had concluded a ten-year civil war by dividing Germany into Catholic and Lutheran parcels, but it made no allowances for the growing number of Calvinists or other Protestants.

In the rest of Europe, the picture was mixed by the late 1500s (see Map 24.1). As we have just seen, England went through several changes of religious leadership, but it eventually emerged with a special sort of Protestant belief as its official religion. Scandinavia became Lutheran in its entirety, almost without violence. Austria, Hungary, and Poland remained mostly Catholic, but with large minorities of Calvinists and Lutherans, who received a degree of tolerance from the authorities. Spain and Italy had successfully repelled the Protestant challenge, and the counter-reform was in full swing. Russia and southeastern Europe were almost unaffected by Protestantism, being either hostile to both varieties of Western Christianity (Russia) or under the political control of Muslims. In two countries, however, the issue of religious affiliation was in hot dispute and caused much bloodshed in the later 1500s.

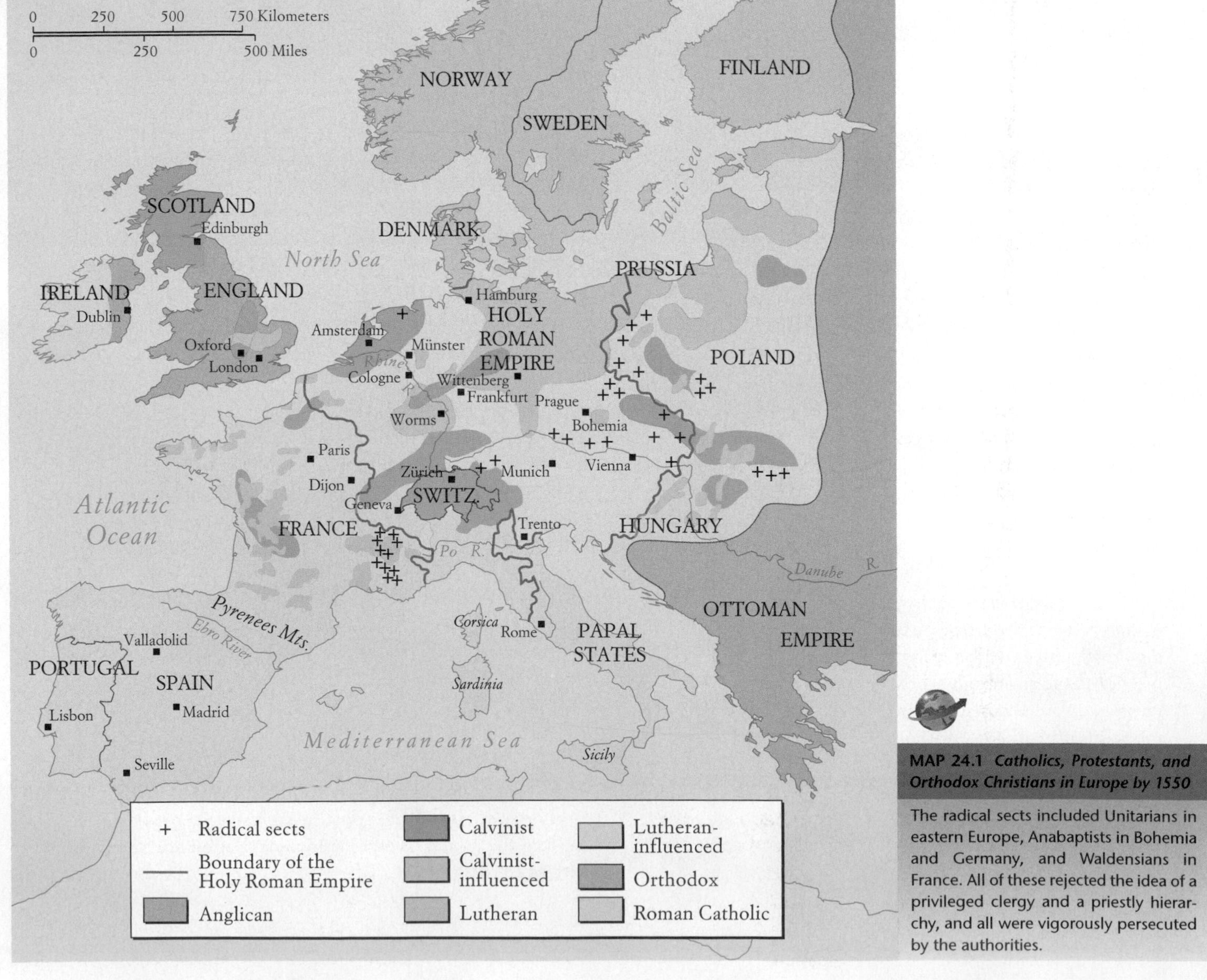


**MAP 24.1** *Catholics, Protestants, and Orthodox Christians in Europe by 1550*

The radical sects included Unitarians in eastern Europe, Anabaptists in Bohemia and Germany, and Waldensians in France. All of these rejected the idea of a privileged clergy and a priestly hierarchy, and all were vigorously persecuted by the authorities.

### France

France remained Catholic at the level of the throne but developed a large, important Calvinist minority, especially among the nobility and the urbanites. For a brief time the Catholic monarchs and the Calvinists attempted to live with one another, but religious wars began in the 1570s that threatened to wreck the country. The Evidence of the Past box on the St. Bartholomew's Day Massacre gives an eyewitness view of the violence.

After some years, the Calvinists found a politician of genius, Henry of Navarre, who profited from the assassination of his Catholic rival to become King Henry IV of France. In 1593, he agreed to accept Catholicism to win the support of most French ("Paris is worth a mass," he is reported to have said). He became the most popular king in French history. His Protestant upbringing inspired the Calvinist minority to trust him, and he did not disappoint them.

In 1598, Henry made the first significant European attempt at religious toleration as state policy by issuing the *Edict of Nantes*. It gave the million or so French Calvinists—the Huguenots—freedom to worship without harassment in certain areas, to hold office, and to fortify their towns. This last provision demonstrates that the edict was more in the nature of a truce than a peace. It held, however, for the better part of a century. During that time, France rose to become the premier power in Europe.

### The Spanish Netherlands

The Spanish Netherlands (modern Holland and Belgium) were ruled from Madrid by King Philip II, the most potent monarch of the second half of the sixteenth century. He had inherited an empire that included Spain, much of Italy, and the Low Countries in Europe, plus the enormous Spanish overseas empire begun by the voyages of Columbus.

But Philip was a man with a mission, or rather two missions: the reestablishment of Catholicism among the Protestant "heretics" and the defeat of the Muslim Turks in the Mediterranean and the Near East. These missions imposed heavy demands on Spanish resources, which even the flow of gold and silver out of the American colonies could not fully cover. Generally successful in his wars against the Turks, Philip could not handle a combined political-religious revolt in Spain's recently acquired province of the Netherlands that broke out in the 1560s. The Netherlands were a hotbed of both Lutheran and Calvinist doctrines, and the self-confident members of the large middle class were much disturbed at the Spanish aliens' attempt to enforce on them the Counter-Reformation and papal supremacy.

Thanks to Spanish overextension, the revolt of the Netherlanders succeeded in holding Philip's feared professional army at bay. The wars were fought with ferocity on both sides. While Philip saw himself as the agent of legitimacy and the Counter-Reformation, the Dutch rebels were aided militarily and financially by the English Protestants across the Channel. The English support was partly based on religious affinity, but even more on the traditional English dislike of a great power's control of England's closest trading partners.

In the mid-1580s, the friction came to a head. Philip (who had earlier tried to convince Elizabeth I to become his wife) became incensed at the execution of the Catholic Mary, Queen of Scots, by order of Elizabeth, who had imprisoned this possible competitor for England's throne. With the reluctant support of the pope, Philip prepared the vast Armada of 1588 to invade England and reconquer that country for the "True Church."

The devastating defeat of the Armada—as much by a storm as by English ships—gave a great boost to the Protestant cause everywhere: It relieved the pressure on the Huguenots to accept Catholic overlordship in France; it saved the Dutch Calvinists until they could gain full independence some decades later; and the defeat of the Armada marks the emergence of England as a major power, both in Europe and overseas.

Spain remained the premier military power long after the Armada disaster, but the country in a sense never recovered from this event. Other fleets were built, bullion from Mexican and Peruvian mines continued to pour into Madrid's treasury, and the Spanish infantry was still the best trained and equipped of all the European armies, but the other powers were able to keep Spain in check from now on, until its inherent economic weaknesses reduced it to a second-line nation by the end of the seventeenth century.

## THE LEGACY OF THE REFORMATION

The Protestant movement made a deep impression on the general course of history in Europe for centuries. It is one of the chief reasons European history is conventionally divided into "modern" versus "medieval" around 1500. The religious unity of all western Europe under the Roman pope was irrevocably shattered, and with the end of such unity inevitably came political and cultural conflicts. For a century and a half after Luther's defiance of the papal command to be silent, much of Europe was engaged in internal acrimony that wracked the continent from the Netherlands to Hungary. In some countries, such as Italy, Spain, Sweden, and Scotland, one or the other faith was dominant and proceeded to harass and exile those who thought differently. In others, such as Austria, Germany, France, and the Netherlands, the question of religious supremacy was bitterly contested. Separation of church and state was not even dreamed of, nor was freedom of conscience. These strictly modern ideas were not seriously taken up even by educated persons until the eighteenth century.

In the Protestant societies, the abolition of the monasteries and convents and the emphasis on vernacular preaching helped integrate the clergy and the laity and thus blurred one of the chief class divisions that had been accepted in Europe since the opening of the Middle Age. Combined with the important roles of the middle-class Protestants in spreading and securing reform, this development provided new opportunities for the ambitious and hardworking to rise up the social ladder.

Some of the other long-term cultural changes that resulted from the Reformation included the following:

1. *Higher literacy and start of mass education.* In much of Protestant Europe in particular, the exhortation to learn and obey Scripture provided an incentive to read that the common folk had never had before. The rapid spread of printing after 1520 was largely a result of Protestant tracts and the impact they were seen to have on their large audiences.
2. *Emphasis on individual moral responsibility.* Rejecting the Catholic assurance that the clergy knew best what was necessary and proper in the conduct of life, the Protestants underlined the responsibility of individual believers to determine through divine guidance and reading Scripture what they must do to attain salvation.
3. *Closer identification of the clergy with the people they served.* Both the Catholic and Protestant churches came to recognize that the church existed as much for the masses of faithful as it did for the clergy—a realization that was often absent previously—and that the belief of the faithful was the essence of the church on Earth.

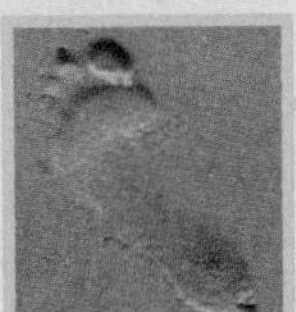

EVIDENCE OF THE PAST

## The St. Bartholomew's Day Massacre

**DURING THE SIXTEENTH-CENTURY** religious wars in Europe, no battlefield was contested more ferociously by both sides than France. Not only did France contain Europe's largest population, but it lay between the Protestant North and the Catholic South. Although the bulk of the peasantry and the royal family remained Catholic, an influential and determined minority of nobles and bourgeoisie became Calvinists, or "Huguenots."

By 1572, because of the political astuteness of their leader, Gaspard de Coligny, the Huguenots were close to a takeover of the French government. However, the queen mother, Catherine de Medici, and the Catholic warlord Henry, duke de Guise, turned the weak-minded King Charles IX against Coligny. The result was a conspiracy that began with Coligny's assassination on August 24, 1572 (St. Bartholomew's Day), and quickly degenerated into a wholesale massacre of the entire Protestant population of Paris: men, women, and children. The death toll is estimated to have approached 10,000, and the streets and alleys reeked of the stench of decaying corpses for weeks afterward.

According to an anonymous Protestant eyewitness who was among the fortunate few to escape the carnage, vicious cruelties were committed without number, setting the scene for what would become twenty years of intermittent civil war in France:

> In an instant, the whole city was filled with dead bodies of every sex and age, and indeed amid such confusion and disorder that everyone was allowed to kill whoever he pleased, whether or not that person belonged to the [Protestant] religion, provided that he had something to be taken, or was an enemy. So it came about that many Papists themselves were slain, even several priests. . . .
>
> No one can count the many cruelties that accompanied these murders. . . . Most of them were run through with daggers or poniards; their bodies were stabbed, their members mutilated, they were mocked and insulted with gibes sharper than pointed swords . . . they knocked several old people senseless, banging their heads against the stones of the quay and then throwing them half dead into the water [the Seine River]. A little child in swaddling clothes was dragged through the streets with a belt round his neck by boys nine or ten years old. Another small child, carried by one of the butchers, played with the man's beard and smiled up at him, but instead of being moved to compassion, the barbarous fiend ran him through with his dagger, then threw him into the water so red with blood that it did not return to its original color for a long time.

### *Analyze and Interpret*

What event in your memory seems most similar to the St. Bartholomew's Day Massacre? What are the dissimiliarities?

Source: Excerpted from Julian Coudy, *The Huguenot Wars,* trans. Julie Kernon (Radnor, PA: Chilton, 1969).

History Now™

***To read another eyewitness account of the St. Bartholomew's Day Massacre, point your browser to the documents area of* HistoryNow.**

4. *Increase in conflicts and intolerance.* Much of Europe fell into civil wars that were initially set off by religious disputes. These wars were often bloody and produced much needless destruction by both sides in the name of theological truth. Religious affiliation greatly exacerbated dynastic and the emergent national conflicts.

The Catholic-Protestant clashes led to intellectual arrogance and self-righteousness not only in religion but in general among those who wielded power. Open debate and discussion of contested matters became almost impossible between the two parts of Western Christianity for a century or more.

## SUMMARY

As much as the discovery of the New World, the Protestant movement gave birth to the modern era in the West. The protests of Luther, Calvin, and many others against what they saw as the unrighteous and distorted teachings of the Roman papacy had immense long-term reverberations in Western culture. The reformers combined a new emphasis on individual morality with assertions of the ability and duty of Christians to read the Gospels and take into their own hands the search for salvation.

Among Calvinists, the material welfare of the Elect on Earth was linked to their quality of being saved, a link that would gradually produce what later generations called the "Protestant ethic." The Catholic response was the Counter-Reformation, which, spearheaded by the Jesuits, eventually reclaimed much of the Protestant territories for the Roman Church at the cost of an alarming rise in religiously inspired conflict. Warfare of an unprecedentedly bloody nature broke out in the Netherlands and in France and Germany between groups asserting their possession of the only correct theology. Europe entered the Modern Age in a flurry of fierce antagonisms among Christians, some of which were to continue for generations and permanently split apart previous communities.

## IDENTIFICATION TERMS

Test your knowledge of this chapter's key concepts by defining the following terms. If you can't recall the meaning of certain terms, refresh your memory by looking up the boldfaced term in the chapter, turning to the Glossary at the end of the book, or working with the flashcards that are available on the *World Civilizations* Companion Website **http://history.wadsworth.com/adler04**.

Act of Supremacy of 1534
Anabaptists
Counter-Reformation
Inquisition
Jesuit Order
justification by faith
*Ninety-five Theses*
Peace of Augsburg
Puritans
Reformation
*The Institutes of the Christian Religion*

## TEST YOUR KNOWLEDGE

Test your knowledge of this chapter by answering the following questions. Complete answers appear at the end of the book. You may also take this quiz interactively and find even more quiz questions on the *World Civilizations* Companion Website **http://history.wadsworth.com/adler04**.

1. The posting of the *Ninety-five Theses* was immediately caused by
   a. Luther's outrage over the ignorance of the clergy.
   b. Luther's conviction that he must challenge papal domination.
   c. Luther's anger over the sale of indulgences.
   d. the tyranny of the local Roman Catholic bishop.
   e. Luther's anger that church tithes were being siphoned out of Germany to Rome.
2. Which of the following practices/beliefs is associated with Calvinism?
   a. The basic goodness of humans
   b. Predestination of souls
   c. Religious freedom for all
   d. Indulgences
   e. The rejection of good works as necessary for eternal salvation

3. Which of these men died fighting for his beliefs?
   a. John Calvin
   b. Martin Luther
   c. Ulrich Zwingli
   d. Henry VIII
   e. Henry IV
4. Henry VIII's reform of English religious organization occurred
   a. after study in the Holy Land.
   b. for primarily religious-doctrinal reasons.
   c. for primarily political-dynastic reasons.
   d. at the urging of the pope.
   e. after he experienced a vision from the Archangel Gabriel.
5. The term *Counter-Reformation* applies to
   a. a movement in Germany aimed at extinguishing the Lutherans.
   b. the strong resistance of the Roman clergy to real reforms.
   c. a Europe-wide campaign to win back the Protestants to Rome.
   d. the political and military efforts of the German emperor to crush the Protestants.
   e. the attempt by German princes to suppress Luther's ideas.
6. The Jesuit Order was founded specifically
   a. to train Catholic soldiers for battle.
   b. to oversee the activities of the Inquisition.
   c. to act as the pope's first-line troop in religious wars.
   d. to open a new type of monastery.
   e. to recover through education fallen-away Catholics.
7. The St. Bartholomew's Day bloodshed was
   a. the result of the Catholic fanatics' hatred of Protestants in France.
   b. the revenge of the English Calvinists on the English Catholics.
   c. the upshot of a failed attempt to overturn the Catholic dynasty in Spain.
   d. the slaughter of rebel peasantry in Flanders.
   e. the massacre of French Catholics by Huguenots.
8. The *Edict of Nantes*
   a. expelled all Protestants from Catholic France.
   b. gave Protestants in France a degree of official toleration.
   c. brought civic and legal equality to Protestants in France.
   d. ended the war between Catholic France and Protestant England.
   e. established religious tolerance between Spain and France.
9. Which of the provinces of King Philip of Spain caused him the most problems over religion?
   a. the American colonies
   b. the Netherlands
   c. the Italian provinces
   d. Spain
   e. the Caribbean
10. One of the chief negative effects of the Reformation on Europe was
   a. the lessening of educational opportunity.
   b. the loss of national identities.
   c. the diminished tolerance for variations from official doctrine.
   d. the decreased opportunities for social climbing.
   e. a loss of power for the clergy.

## InfoTrac College Edition

Visit the source collections at

**http://infotrac.thomsonlearning.com**

and use the Search function with the following key terms:

Reformation Counter-Reformation
Martin and Luther not King

## Wadsworth History Website Resources

Visit the World History Resource Center at **http://history.wadsworth.com/world** for a wealth of general resources, and the *World Civilizations* Companion Website at **http://history.wadsworth.com/adler04** for resources specific to this textbook.

## HistoryNow

Enter *HistoryNow* using the access card that is available for *World Civilizations*. *HistoryNow* will assist you in understanding the content of this chapter with lesson plans generated for your needs. In addition, you can read the following documents, and many more, online:

Martin Luther, *Ninety-five Theses*

John Calvin, selections from *The Institutes of the Christian Religion*

King Henry IV, *Edict of Nantes*

*The great and chief end of men's uniting into commonwealths, and putting themselves under governments, is the preservation of their property.*
John Locke

# 25 Foundations of the European States

The Thirty Years' War
The Treaty of Westphalia, 1648
Spain's Decline

Theory and Practice of Royal Absolutism
French Government under Louis XIV

Revolt against Royal Absolutism: Seventeenth-Century England
Civil War: Cromwell's Commonwealth
Restoration and Glorious Revolution of 1688

Political Theory: Hobbes and Locke

| | |
|---|---|
| 1603–1625 | James I (England) |
| 1610–1643 | Louis XIII (France) |
| 1618–1648 | Thirty Years' War/Treaty of Westphalia |
| 1649–1651 | Civil War in England |
| 1653–1658 | England under Oliver Cromwell's Commonwealth |
| 1660 | Restoration of Charles II (England) |
| 1661–1715 | Louis XIV (France) |
| 1688–1689 | Glorious Revolution/William and Mary |

In Europe, the seventeenth century saw the birth of the modern state as distinct from the domain of a ruling monarch. During this century, the powers attached to a governing office began to be separated from the person of the occupant of the office. This separation allowed the creation over time of a group of professional servants of the state, or bureaucrats, people who exercised authority not because of who they were, but because of the offices they held. Religious conflict between Protestant and Catholic continued but gave way to political-economic issues in state-to-state relations. The maritime countries of northwestern Europe became steadily more important thanks to overseas commerce, while the central and eastern European states suffered heavy reverses from wars, the Turkish menace, and commercial and technological stagnation.

Royal courts constantly sought ways to enhance their growing powers over all their subjects. These varied from west to east in both type and effectiveness. But by the early eighteenth century, some form of monarchic absolutism was in force in every major country except Britain. In this chapter, we focus on the Germanies, France, and England.

## The Thirty Years' War

The Thirty Years' War, which wrecked the German states and was the most destructive conflict Europe had seen for centuries, arose from religious intolerance, but it quickly became a struggle for territory and worldly power on the part of the multiple contestants. The war began in 1618, when the Habsburg Holy Roman Emperor attempted to check the spread of Protestant sentiments in part of his empire, the present-day Czech Republic or Bohemia, as it was then called. This led to a rebellion, which the Habsburg forces put down forcefully at the Battle of White Mountain near Prague in 1621. A forced re-Catholicization began.

The defeated Protestants did not submit but found allies among their co-religionists in southern and eastern Germany. From this point, the war became an all-German civil war between the imperial armies of the Catholic emperor,

**The Thirty Years' War.** In this panorama by Jan Brueghel, the horror of war in the seventeenth century is brought home. Turned loose on the hapless peasants and townspeople, the mercenaries who made up the professional armies of the day killed and stole as they pleased.

**Henry IV and His Queen.** The great Flemish painter Peter Paul Rubens created this imaginary scene of the French king taking leave of his wife, Marie de Médici, to take command of the army fighting the Habsburg emperor. Between the royal figures is their little son who would grow up to be King Louis XIII and father of Louis XIV.

on the one side, and Lutherans and Calvinists on the other. By 1635, the war had become an international struggle beyond consideration of religion. The Protestant kings of Scandinavia and the Catholic French monarchy supported the Protestants, whereas the Spanish cousins of the Habsburgs assaulted the French.

## *The Treaty of Westphalia, 1648*

For thirteen more years, France, Holland, Sweden, and the German Protestant states fought on against the Holy Roman Emperor and Spain. Most of the fighting was in Germany. The country was thoroughly ravaged by both sides, which sent forces into the field with instructions to "forage"—that is, to rob the natives of food and fodder, while killing any who resisted.

Finally, a peace, the **Treaty of Westphalia**, was worked out in 1648 after five years of haggling. The big winners were France and Sweden, with the latter suddenly emerging as a major power in northern Europe (see Map 25.1). The losers were Spain and, to a lesser degree, the Austrian-based Habsburgs, who saw any chance of reuniting Germany under Catholic control fade. From 1648 on, Germany ceased to exist as a political concept and broke up into dozens, then hundreds of small kingdoms and principalities, some Catholic and some Protestant (see Map 25.2).

The Peace of Westphalia was the first modern state treaty. From start to finish, its clauses underlined the decisive importance of the sovereign state, rather than the dynasty that ruled it or the religion its population professed. Theological uniformity was replaced by secular control of territory and population as the supreme goal of the rival powers.

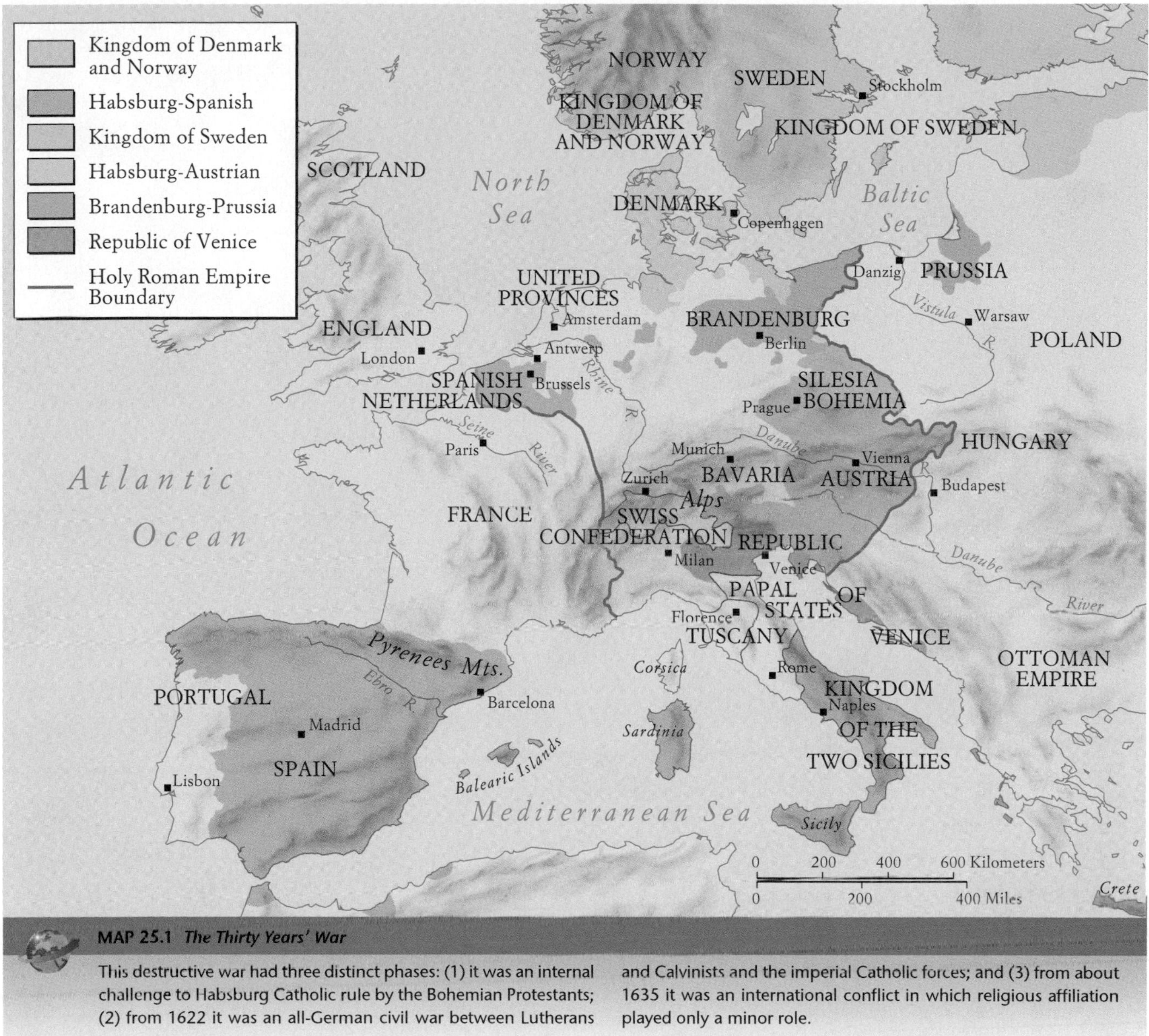


**MAP 25.1** ***The Thirty Years' War***

This destructive war had three distinct phases: (1) it was an internal challenge to Habsburg Catholic rule by the Bohemian Protestants; (2) from 1622 it was an all-German civil war between Lutherans and Calvinists and the imperial Catholic forces; and (3) from about 1635 it was an international conflict in which religious affiliation played only a minor role.

What did the treaty bring? In religious affiliations, despite all the bloodshed, things were left much as they had been in 1618. The principle that had first been enunciated in the Peace of Augsburg 100 years earlier—*cuius regio, eius religio* ("the ruler determines religious affiliation")—was now extended to the Calvinists, as well as Lutherans and Catholics. Northern and eastern Germany were heavily Protestant, while the South and most of the Rhine valley remained Catholic. This division negated any chance of German political unity for the next two centuries.

The Thirty Years' War was an economic disaster for the Germans. Plague, smallpox, famine, and the casualties of war may have carried off as many as one-third of the population. The division of Germany into small states made it all the more difficult to recover as a nation. For a long while to come, a political power vacuum would exist in the center of Europe, and the Germans would be thought of as a nation of poets and musicians rather than a political force.

## Spain's Decline

For Spain, the ultimate results were almost as painful, although the war was not fought on Spanish territory. The Dutch Protestants gained full independence from Madrid, and Portugal, which had been under Spanish rule for sixty years, rebelled successfully in 1640. The war with France was foolishly resumed until Spain was forced to make peace in 1659. By that date, the tremendous military and naval advantages that Spain's government had once possessed had all been used up. Spain's government was

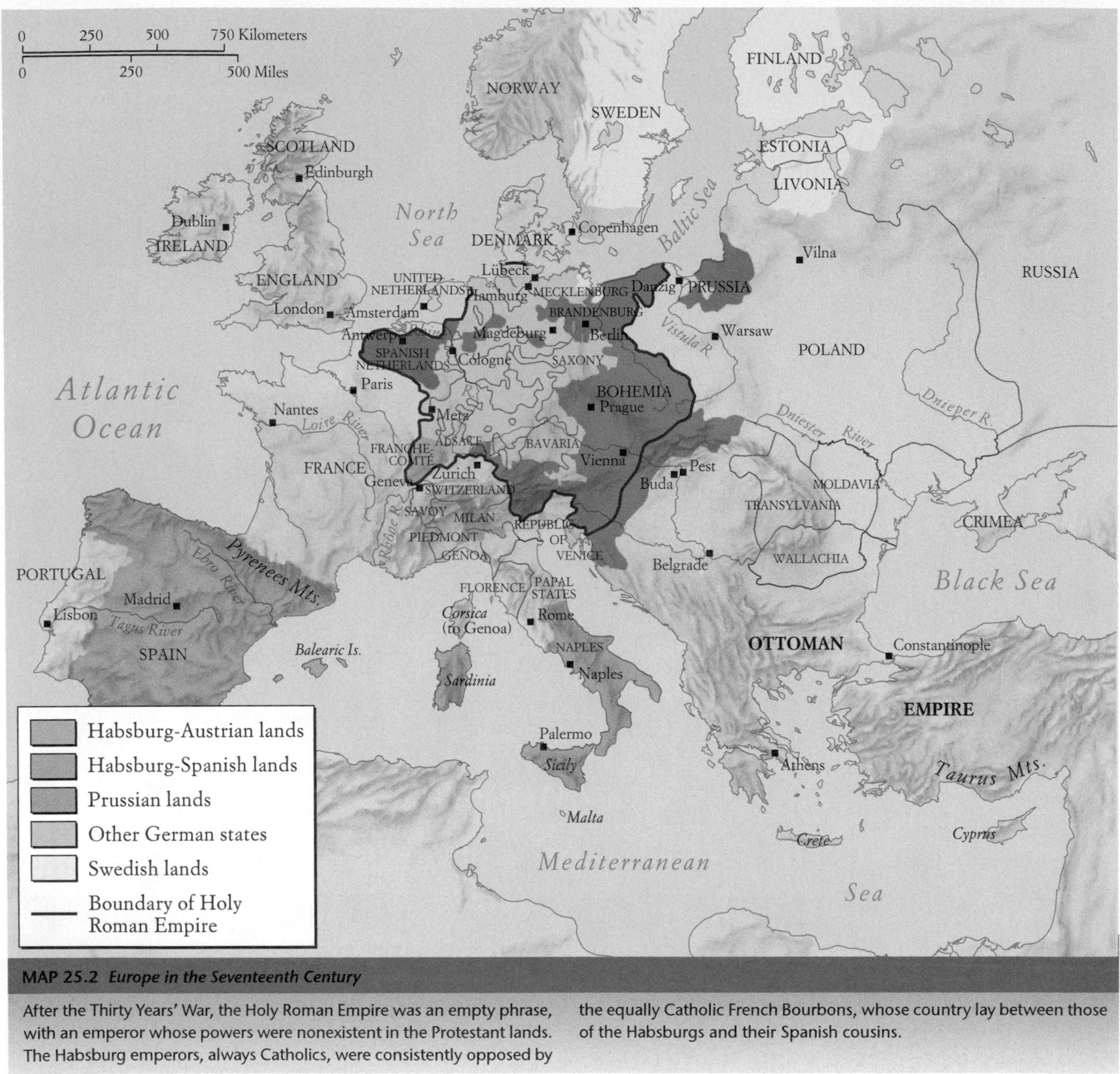


**MAP 25.2** *Europe in the Seventeenth Century*

After the Thirty Years' War, the Holy Roman Empire was an empty phrase, with an emperor whose powers were nonexistent in the Protestant lands. The Habsburg emperors, always Catholics, were consistently opposed by the equally Catholic French Bourbons, whose country lay between those of the Habsburgs and their Spanish cousins.

bankrupt, and its incoming shipments of overseas bullion were now much reduced. Worse, the domestic economy had seen little or no development for a century and a half.

How did this happen to what had been clearly the strongest state in Europe? The influx of Mexican and Peruvian silver had made much of Europe rich in one way or another (see Chapter 23), but ordinary Spaniards—still overwhelmingly rural and agrarian—were as poor as ever and perhaps even poorer, because the Spanish crown, the nobility, and the church were notoriously unproductive users of the vast wealth that went through their hands in the sixteenth and seventeenth centuries. The costs of taking on the role of defender of the papal religion throughout Europe had been steep, and to these were added the defense of the Mediterranean basin from the Turkish advance. The epitome of the noble Spaniard had been fixed in the long struggle to expel the Moors: the warrior, weapon in hand, intent on preserving honor and destroying his enemy. There was no room here for the vision of the merchant or the entrepreneur. Money exerted no attractions in itself, only as a means to an "honorable" end, such as that striven for by the immortal Don Quixote. In this Spain, a capitalist, investing, accumulating middle class could not develop, and remnants of feudalism were everywhere apparent in the economy as well as the social arrangements. Despite much effort in the eighteenth century to regain its former status, Spain was now condemned to a second rank in European and world affairs.

## Theory and Practice of Royal Absolutism

The theory of royal absolutism existed in the Middle Age, but the upheavals caused by the Hundred Years' War in France and England, the Black Death in the fourteenth century (see Chapter 20), and the wars of religion following Luther's revolt had distracted the rulers' attention and weakened their powers. Now, in the seventeenth century, they got back to the business of asserting their sacred rights (see the Patterns of Belief box).

The outstanding theorist of absolutism was a French lawyer, Jean Bodin, who stated in a widely read book that "sovereignty consists in giving laws to the people without their consent." Sovereignty cannot be divided; it must remain in the hands of a single individual or one institution. For France, Bodin insisted that this person should be the French monarch, who had "absolute power" to give his people law. Another Frenchman, Bishop Bossuet, gave a theological gloss to Bodin's ideas by claiming that kings received their august powers from God and that to defy them as a rebel was to commit a mortal sin.

Does this mean the monarch had to answer to no one or could safely ignore what his people said and felt? No, the king had to answer to his Christian conscience and eventually to his Creator, as did everyone, and any king who attempted to rule against public opinion or the well-meant advice of his councilors was a fool. But the king was and should be the final source of legitimate authority in politics and law. Bodin arrived at this theory in part because of the times in which he lived. His book was published at the height of the French religious struggles in the 1570s, when it appeared that without a strong, respected monarch, France might collapse as a state.

Bodin found his most potent and effective adherent in Cardinal Richelieu (1585–1642), the prime minister for the young Louis XIII in the 1620s and 1630s. Richelieu was the real founder of absolute monarchy in France—and most of Europe soon imitated Paris. Following the murder of the peacemaking Henry IV in 1610, Protestant-Catholic antipathy in France had increased. Henry's Italian widow Marie de Médici was the regent for her young son, but much of the Huguenot nobility held her in contempt, despising her frivolity and her partisan Catholicism in equal measure. Unable to control the constant intrigues around her, she turned to the strong-minded and talented Richelieu. Despite being a prince of the church, Richelieu believed wholeheartedly in the primacy of the state over any other earthly institution. *Raison d'état* (reason of state) was sufficient to justify almost any action by government, he thought. The state represented order, the rule of law, and security for the citizenry. If it weakened or collapsed, general suffering would result. The government had a moral obligation to avoid that eventuality at all costs.

The cardinal set up a cadre of officials (***intendants***) who kept a sharp eye on what was happening in the provinces and reported to the king's ministers. Thus, the faint outlines of a centralized and centralizing bureaucracy began to appear: these men were picked for their posts at least partially on merit, depended on the central authority for pay and prestige, and subordinated local loyalties and personal preferences to the demands and policies of the center. The cardinal-minister used them to check the independence of the provincial nobles, particularly the Huguenots. He used armed force on several occasions and summarily executed rebels.

Richelieu was the real ruler of France until he died in 1642, followed a bit later by his king. The cardinal had handpicked as his successor as chief minister another Catholic churchman, Cardinal Mazarin, who had the same values as his master. The new king, Louis XIV (ruled 1643–1715), was but five years old, so the government remained in Mazarin's hands for many years. The young Louis was brought up to believe that kingship was the highest calling on Earth and that its powers were complete and unlimited except by God—and perhaps not by him, either!

### French Government under Louis XIV

Louis XIV had the longest reign of any monarch in European history. In the last fifty-four of those years, he was his own chief minister, totally dominating French government. He was the incarnation of absolute monarchy, believing in *divine right,* which said that the monarchy's powers flowed from God and that the king's subjects should regard him as God's representative in civil affairs.

The late seventeenth and eighteenth centuries were the Age of France or, more precisely, the Age of Louis XIV. Not only in government, but also in the arts, the lifestyle of the wealthy and the highborn, military affairs, and language and literature, France set the pace. What Florence had been to the Renaissance, Paris was to the European cultural and political world of the eighteenth century. King Louis allegedly once said, "I am the state," a statement he truly believed. He saw himself as not just a human being with immense powers and prestige but as the very flesh and blood of France. It is to his credit that he took kingship very seriously, working twelve hours a day at the tedious, complex task of trying to govern a country that was still subdivided in many conflicting ways and notoriously difficult to govern. In this task he was greatly aided by a series of first-rate ministerial helpers—the marquis of Louvois, Jean-Baptiste Colbert, Sebastien de Vauban, and others—each of whom made major contributions to the theory and practice of his chosen field.

Below these top levels, the intendants continued to serve the monarch as his eyes and ears in the provinces.

## Queen Christina of Sweden (1626–1689)

"**Far from beautiful,** short in stature, pockmarked in face and with a slight humpback": such was the less than prepossessing description of a woman who would make her mark on her nation and her contemporaries in ways still not forgotten—or forgiven. Her political foibles might be overlooked, but it was impossible for her fellow Lutherans to accept her conversion to Rome in an era when religious affiliation was frequently the trigger for civil war.

Christina of Sweden was the sole surviving child of King Gustavus Adolphus, the warrior-king who died at the head of his Lutheran troops in the Thirty Years' War in Germany. When he died, Christina was only six years old, and a regency was established for the next twelve years. Prodigal and imperious by nature, the young girl did not take kindly to advice in matters public or private. She was brilliant in intellect and passionate in temperament and found it irritating to listen to those she regarded as her social or intellectual inferiors.

In 1644, she was crowned queen of Sweden, which at that time included most of Scandinavia and had the best army in Europe. Wanting to rid herself of the chief regent Oxenstierna and knowing that she could not do so as long as the war in Germany raged, she pressured her advisers to end the war as soon as possible. Still Sweden emerged from the conflict as a major power, and its twenty-two-year-old queen now became a major player in the intricate game of high diplomacy. But like the English with Elizabeth a generation earlier, many Swedes thought it unnatural—and perhaps foolhardy—to allow the nation's fate to hang on the actions of a mere unmarried woman.

Musee des Beaux-Arts, Beziers, France/Lauros/Giraudon/Bridgeman Art Library

**Queen Christina of Sweden.**

The Swedish estates (clerics, nobles, and commoners) strongly pressured the queen to marry as soon as possible, but she resisted just as strongly. Raised to believe herself the linchpin of her country's fate, she found it difficult to think of herself as only the channel by which a male could steer the ship of state. Disgusted with her countrymen, she was only barely persuaded to withdraw her abdication in 1651. In the same year, Christina also rejected the Lutheranism of almost all her compatriots and began to neglect the business of state in favor of her personal affairs, including her various lovers.

Her relations with the nobility worsened when she created more than 400 new nobles in an attempt to gain popularity and thus angered the proud old Swedish families. Friction mounted steadily, and in June 1654 her second offer to abdicate was gladly accepted. Dressed in the male attire she often wore that gave rise to many speculations regarding her sexuality, Christina left Stockholm at once and proceeded to Rome. En route, she insulted her fellow Swedes and her upbringing by accepting the Catholic faith and proclaiming herself the ally of the pope. To her surprise and dismay, practically none of her former subjects chose to follow. Instead, she became a "nonperson" in Stockholm's seats of power. She spent most of the rest of her sixty-three years in Rome, where she involved herself with papal politics and with lovers from both clergy and laity.

Christina's authentic fame rests on her extraordinary artistic taste and her lavish generosity in acting on it. The queen-in-exile, as she liked to think of herself, was the Roman patroness of the great musicians Alessandro Scarlatti and Arcangelo Corelli, who wrote some of their finest work in her honor; the protector of the gifted architect and sculptor Giovanni Bernini, who crowned his lifework with the plans for St. Peter's Square; and the sponsor of the first opera company in Rome. Her house was a treasure trove of seventeenth-century Italian and Flemish artworks, and at her death her library became an important addition to the Vatican's library, the greatest in all of Europe.

Left alone and living off the charity of the pope, Christina, the heiress of the great Gustavus Adolphus, had her last wish fulfilled by being buried in the cathedral of St. Peter's. Her Swedish Lutheran subjects erected no monuments to her memory.

### *Analyze and Interpret*

Why was it particularly difficult for Sweden's nobility to accept a woman as ruler in the seventeenth century? How significant do you believe it to be that a woman chooses to dress like a man, as Christina often did, when she occupies high public positions?

Louvre, Paris, France/Giraudon/Bridgeman Art Library

**LOUIS XIV.** This masterful portrait by the court painter Rigaud shows Louis as he would have liked to appear to his subjects. The "well-turned leg" was considered to be an absolute essential for royal figures. Louis's wig and ermine cape were also necessities for a king.

Louis's bureaucrats were the best-trained and most reliable servants their king could obtain. He selected their middle and lower ranks from the middle classes as much as from the nobility. Many latter-day French nobles were the heirs of commoners who were rewarded for outstanding service to King Louis XIV or were given the much-sought-after opportunity of purchasing an office that carried noble status with it.

Louis was steeped in Richelieu's concepts from childhood and was determined to establish the royal throne as the sole seat of sovereignty. To do so, he had to nullify the independent powers of the aristocrats in the provinces. He did this by forcing them to come to Versailles, his magnificent palace outside Paris, where they vied for his favor and he could keep them under a watchful eye. He was generally successful at this effort. By his death, the previously potent nobles had been reduced to a decorative, parasitic fringe group, with few real powers and few responsibilities save those granted by the king.

Louis's revocation of the *Edict of Nantes* in 1685 was a mistake, which led to the loss of a valuable asset: the Huguenots, who emigrated en masse in the following decade. By allowing them to do so, the king hoped to emphasize the unity of Catholic France. He mistakenly thought that most of the Calvinists had been reconverted anyway and that the edict was no longer needed. Welcomed to Protestant Europe, some 200,000 Huguenots served as bastions of anti-French activity and propaganda against the monarch in the series of wars on which he now embarked.

***Wars of Louis XIV*** Although Louis kept the peace for the first thirty-five years of his reign, his overpowering thirst for glory led him to provoke four conflicts with England, Holland, and most of the German states, led by the Austrian Habsburgs in the last twenty years. The most important was the final one, the War of the Spanish Succession (1700–1713), in which France tried to seize control of much-weakened Spain and its empire and was checked by a coalition led by England. The war bankrupted France and was extremely unpopular among the French people by its end. France succeeded only in placing a member of the

Giraudon/Bridgeman Art Library

**VERSAILLES.** The view is from the garden side, with the grand fountain in the foreground. The palace lies a few miles outside Paris and is now one of the most visited tourist centers in Europe. Built by increments from the seventeenth through the eighteenth century, Versailles set the architectural and landscaping pace for the rest of the Western world's royalty.

Bourbon family (the French dynasty) on the Spanish throne, but under the condition that Spain and France would never be joined together. England, the chief winner, gained control of part of French Canada, the Spanish Caribbean islands, and the key to the Mediterranean, Gibraltar. The war began the worldwide struggle between England and France for mastery of a colonial empire.

### *Strengths and Weaknesses of French Absolutism*

Louis XIV gave all of Europe a model of what could be accomplished by a strong king and a wealthy country. His well-paid officials were the most disciplined and most effective that any Western country had seen. Through them, the king kept a constant watch on the country as a whole. Anything that happened in the provinces was soon known at Versailles and received a royal response whenever necessary. The palace was awe-inspiring, serving to reinforce Louis's prestige and power in visible fashion. Versailles, originally a mere hunting lodge for Louis XIII, was made into the largest and most impressive secular structure in Europe. It was surrounded by hundreds of acres of manicured gardens and parks and was large enough to house the immense court and its servants. Its halls were the museums of the Bourbon Dynasty and remained so until the Revolution.

But problems also persisted. Finance was always the sore point for aspiring kings, and Louis spent huge amounts of cash in his quest for military and civil glory. A helter-skelter system of tax "farms," concessions for tax collection in the provinces, did not work well. Begun in the early seventeenth century, the system suffered from a growing disparity between what was collected and what was eventually forwarded to the court. Pushed by his ministers, the king considered the possibility of introducing taxes on the lands of the church and the nobles but was dissuaded from this radical step. Instead, taxes on the peasant majority were increased, especially after the wars began.

The financial problem of the monarchy was in fact never solved. Of all European countries, France was the most favored by nature, and its agricultural economy was the most diverse. But the French peasants were slowly becoming aware of the contrasts between the taxes they had to bear and the exemptions of various sorts enjoyed by the privileged orders of the clergy and nobility. When that discontent would be later joined by the resentment of the much-enlarged group of middle-class townspeople during the course of the eighteenth century, the potential for revolution would exist.

## Revolt against Royal Absolutism: Seventeenth-Century England

At the death of Queen Elizabeth in 1603, the English crown passed by prearrangement to Elizabeth's nearest male Protestant relative, the Stuart king James VI of Scotland, who became James I (ruled 1603–1625) of England. James was a great believer in absolutism and the divine right of kings and quickly alienated the English Parliament with his insistence that the Crown should have sole control over taxes and the budget. James's lack of respect for English customs, his blatant homosexuality, and his arrogance combined to make him highly unpopular by the end of his reign. His greatest achievement was his selection of a committee of distinguished churchmen, who produced in short order the most influential English book ever written: the King James Version of the Bible.

The England that James ruled was fast developing into a society in which the commercial and professional classes had a great deal of political savvy and were becoming used to the exercise of local and regional power. Although the highest level of the government in London was still, as everywhere, dominated by the nobility, the well-off merchants and municipal officials who were represented by Parliament's House of Commons now insisted on their rights to have final input on taxation and much else in national policy. They were armed with a tradition of parliamentary government that was already four centuries old. They could not be intimidated easily.

Another topic of acrid debate between the king and his subjects was the proper course in religious affairs. James had been brought up as a Scot Calvinist but had agreed to adopt Anglicanism (the Church of England) as king of England. In truth, many people believed he sympathized with Rome, which made the Anglicans nervous and appalled the growing number of Puritans.

It is impossible to say how numerous the Puritans were because Puritanism was more a state of mind than a formal affiliation. Puritans were inclined to accept the Calvinist social values: hard work, thrift, and a sober lifestyle that aimed at finding its true rewards in eternity. The Puritans liked to think of poverty as the deserved accompaniment of sin and of wealth and social status as the just rewards of a good Christian, a member of the Elect. The capitalist ethic was well-rooted in them, and they, in turn, were well-represented in the business classes of England. In the House of Commons, they were now a majority.

Absolutist king and Puritan Parliament clashed repeatedly in the 1620s over taxation and religion. By the time James died in 1625, Parliament was on the point of revolt. James was succeeded by his son Charles I (ruled 1625–1649), who soon turned out to be as difficult as his father. When the Commons attempted to impose limits on his taxing powers, he refused to honor the ancient custom of calling a Parliament at least every third year. He attempted to bring England into the Thirty Years' War against strong public opinion that held that England had no interest in that conflict. He appointed an archbishop of Canterbury who many people believed was a sympathizer with popery, and he was at least as provocatively stubborn as his father had been. Finding that Parliament would not cooperate with him, he sent it home in 1629 and ruled without its advice and consent.

Charles's marriage to a French Catholic princess had stirred up much resentment, and his high-handed attitude toward the Calvinist clergy finally offended his Scot subjects so badly that in 1640 they rose in revolt. Charles needed money—lots of it—to raise an army against them. That meant he had to impose new taxes, which in turn meant he had to summon Parliament.

By this time, Parliament had not met for eleven years, and when the representatives came together, they were in no mood to support an arrogant and unpopular king's demands. Instead, Parliament passed a series of restrictive laws on the royal powers, but the king maneuvered to bypass them in clear violation of English traditions. When the increasingly radical Puritans in Parliament insisted on direct control of military affairs, Charles raised an army of royalist supporters, and this action led directly to the beginning of civil war in 1642.

### *Civil War: Cromwell's Commonwealth*

Britain divided about evenly between supporters of the king (the Anglican clergy, most of the nobility, and most peasants) and supporters of Parliament (most townspeople, the merchant and commercial classes, the Puritans, and the Scots). Regional and local economic interests often dictated political allegiance. After several years of intermittent struggle, the war ended with Charles's defeat. Parliament then tried the king for treason. After a rump trial, he was found guilty and executed in 1649. (See Evidence of the Past for more on Charles's death.)

This was the first and only time that the British had executed their king and the first time since the beginnings of the modern state system that *any* European people had turned so decisively on their legitimate sovereign. The experience was agonizing even for the king's sworn enemies among the Puritans, and it led to a great deal of debate over where sovereignty resided and how legal process in government should be defined and protected. Over time, the modern Anglo-American ideals of constitutional government evolved from this debate.

After the king's execution, Parliament declared that England was a *commonwealth*—that is, a republic with no monarch. Its executive was the chief organizer of the triumphant Puritan army, Oliver Cromwell, who had gained a deserved reputation as a man of iron will and fierce rectitude. During his turbulent tenure as Lord Protector (1653–1658), a comprehensive attempt was made to eliminate such vices as dancing, drinking, making merry on the Sabbath, and theatrical performances. Such efforts to limit human enjoyment had the predictable result: when Cromwell died, few people wanted to hear more about Puritan government.

Cromwell's rule had also become unpopular because of the high taxes he levied (with the cooperation of an

EVIDENCE OF THE PAST

## The Death of Charles I

**MOST SHOCKING TO TRADITION** and the pieties of medieval beliefs about royalty, the English Revolution actually put to death a legitimate king, Charles I. After losing the civil war to the troops of the Roundheads' leader, Cromwell, the king was captured and brought to trial on the count of treason. The Roundhead Parliament convicted him, and by one vote they condemned him to death. An eyewitness who was a royalist sympathizer describes the king's last moments:

> To the executioner, he said: "I shall say but very short prayers, and when I thrust out my hands—"
>
> Then he called to the bishop for his cap, and having put it on, asked the executioner:
>
> "Does my hair trouble you?"
>
> [The executioner] desired him to put it all under his cap; which, as he was doing by the help of the bishop and executioner, he turned to the bishop and said:
>
> "I have a good cause and a gracious God on my side . . . ."
>
> After a very short pause, his Majesty stretching forth his hands the executioner at one blow [of his axe] severed his head from his body; which, being held up and shown to the people, was with his body put into a coffin covered with black velvet and carried into his lodging [in the Tower of London].
>
> His blood was taken up by diverse persons for different ends: by some as trophies of their villainy; by others as relics of a martyr; and in some hath had the same effect, by blessing of God which was often found in his sacred touch when living.

### *Analyze and Interpret*

What might be the reasons for making the execution of a king a public spectacle?

Source: Louis L. Snyder and Richard B. Morris, eds., *They Saw It Happen* (Harrisburg, PA: Stackpole, 1951). Reprinted with permission.

**History Now™**

***To read the death warrant of Charles I, point your browser to the documents area of* HistoryNow.**

intimidated Parliament) to pay for frequent military expeditions. He put down rebellions against English rule in Catholic Ireland and Calvinist Scotland with bloody force, thereby laying the groundwork for a Great Britain that would include these formerly quite separate countries as well as England and Wales. A maritime war with Holland in the 1650s brought England far along the road to control of the seven seas and in North America the rich prize of the former Dutch colony of New Amsterdam.

Three years before his death, the Lord Protector tired of parliamentary quibbling and instituted a forthright military dictatorship. When Cromwell's weak son attempted in vain to fill his father's shoes, parliamentary negotiations with the exiled son of Charles I were begun. After eighteen months, the **Restoration** was completed with the return of King Charles II (ruled 1660–1685) to his native land.

## *Restoration and Glorious Revolution of 1688*

King Charles had learned the lessons that had cost his father his head. Charles also wished to exercise absolute powers but knew when he had to compromise. As he once said, he had "no wish to go on my travels again."

The pendulum of power in British government had swung decisively toward the House of Commons during the revolutionary era, and Charles made his peace with the Commons by establishing the beginnings of the ministerial system. The king appointed several of his trusted friends to carry out policy, but these men had to answer to parliamentary questioning. Gradually, this informal arrangement became a fundamental part of government and was formalized when the party system got under way in the eighteenth century. From it came the modern British cabinet, with its collective responsibility for policy and its reliance on parliamentary votes of confidence to continue its authority as a government.

Charles cared little about religion (his private life was a continual sexual scandal, and real or alleged royal bastards abounded), but many members of Parliament did. They proceeded to make it legally impossible for anyone but an Anglican to hold office, vote, or attend the universities. The measure was a reaction against the Puritans, Quakers, and Catholics who had caused such turmoil for England over the past quarter century. But this law—the **Test Act**—was too restrictive to be supported by the majority in the long run. It was gradually eased, first for other Protestants, then for Catholics and Jews, until it was finally abandoned in the nineteenth century.

One aspect of Charles's religious policy helped create problems for his successor, however. Under a secret arrangement with King Louis XIV of France, Charles was to receive a large annual monetary payment in exchange for returning England to Catholicism. Although nothing ever came of the rather absurd pact, the news inevitably leaked out in Britain and created a wave of anti-Catholicism that led to a virtual panic. Thus, when it became clear that the aging and (legitimately) childless Charles would be succeeded by his younger brother, James, who had become a practicing Catholic while in exile in France, the English viewed their new king with a great deal of suspicion from the outset.

James II (ruled 1685–1688) made things worse by flinging insult after insult at the Protestants in and out of Parliament and by deliberately ignoring the provisions of the Test Act in his official appointments. So long as the king had no Catholic children to succeed him, the English could grit their teeth and wait for the elderly man's death. But in 1688 his young second wife unexpectedly produced a healthy baby son who would be raised a Catholic and would presumably rule Britain for many years. To many, this prospect was too much to bear.

Practically all of England rebelled against King James in the **Glorious Revolution of 1688** that ended the Stuart male line on the English throne. James again went into French exile accompanied by his family, while parliamentary committees stepped into the vacuum in London. After brief negotiations to establish the boundaries of governing power, William of Orange, the Dutch Calvinist husband of James's daughter Mary, was invited to rule England jointly with his Protestant wife. So, as the guests of a self-confident Parliament, began the reign of William and Mary (1689–1702).

***Significance of the Glorious Revolution*** The revolution against James Stuart had been swift and almost bloodless; its significance was political and constitutional, not military or economic. Sovereignty shifted from the monarch to his or her subjects, as represented by their elected Parliament. From now on England was a constitutional state. The king or queen was the partner of Parliament in matters of high policy, both domestic and foreign. William and Mary had accepted the offer of the throne from a parliamentary delegation. What parliamentary committees had given, they could also legitimately take away. Although relations were generally cordial, the royal pair was never allowed to forget that.

The most concrete result of the Glorious Revolution was the **Bill of Rights**, which was adopted by Parliament in 1689. Its most important provisions spelled out the rights and powers of Parliament versus the Crown:

- Law was to be made only by Parliament and could not be suspended by the king.
- Members of Parliament were immune from prosecution when acting in their official capacities.
- The king could not impose taxes or raise an army without prior approval by Parliament.

In addition, the Bill of Rights ensured the independence of the judiciary from royal pressures, prohibited standing armies in peacetime, extended freedom of worship to non-Anglican Protestants, and stipulated that the throne should always be held by a Protestant.

The Glorious Revolution was the world's first significant move toward full parliamentary government, but it was definitely *not* a democratic revolution. The great majority of the English and other Britons did not have the vote at any level beyond the village council. That right would have to wait until near the end of the nineteenth century. And women of any class would not have political equality in Britain until the twentieth century (see the Society and Economy box for a view of their status in guilds).

In accordance with the 1701 Act of Succession worked out by Parliament and the king, Mary's younger sister Anne succeeded William and Mary on the English throne. Like them, she died without surviving children. Now Parliament exercised its new powers under the act to invite the duke of Hanover, a distant German relative of King James I and the nearest male Protestant relation to the deceased queen, to become King George I (ruled 1714–1727). George thus introduced the **Hanoverian Dynasty** to Great Britain.

The first two Georges lived mostly in Hanover, could barely speak English, and showed little interest in the intricacies of English political life. Both were content to leave policy making to trusted confidants among the aristocrats and landed gentry who still dominated both houses of Parliament. Robert Walpole, the prime minister for more than twenty years (1721–1742), was the central figure in British government and the key developer of the ministerial government that had begun under King Charles II. Under Walpole, the frequently absent monarchs were manipulated by the parliamentary leadership more and more, so that Parliament became the more important force in most aspects of internal policy. While foreign affairs and the military still belonged primarily in the Crown's domain, Parliament was supreme in legislation and finance.

## Political Theory: Hobbes and Locke

Two British political philosophers formed the basis of public debate on the nature of government during the tumultuous seventeenth century. Thomas Hobbes (1588–1679) thought that the pregovernmental "state of nature" had been a riotous anarchy, a "war of all against all." A strong government was essential to restrain humans'

SOCIETY AND ECONOMY

### Women and the Guilds

**The change in females' economic status** from the Middle Age to the early modern epoch was clearly downward. The near-equality that working women had enjoyed with males in the fifteenth century had deteriorated sharply by the late seventeenth, when this statement was made by a young German tradesman:

> Women are shut out from our guild and cannot be trained by a master. The reason is, they are given the leadership of the family, under the supervision of their husbands. Because it is impossible to know who will be their husband when girls are still children, it is better and more suitable to their sex to teach them the domestic arts, which any husband will appreciate. It is also better for everyone that each sex does what is proper for it, and doesn't attempt to butt into the other's affairs while ignoring or neglecting their own.
>
> I might add, that a woman who moves in male circles [namely, journeymen, who were almost always bachelors] puts herself in danger to her good reputation. . . . It is certainly better that men, and not women, learn a trade, as not everything can be learned at home or during the apprenticeship, but must be picked up through experience and "wandering." From this comes the old saying of the journeymen: "what I haven't learned, I got from my wandering." But wandering doesn't suit women's place in the world, as they would return from their Wanderjahre with their reputation in tatters, and therefore there is another axiom: "journeymen who haven't done their Wanderjahre, and maidens who have, are equally dubious." To lead, protect and command is the duty of a master, and is rightly given over to the male sex.

#### *Analyze and Interpret*

What do you think of the defense of exclusion of women from the guilds? Given that females are often physically able to perform the same tasks as males, do you think that should be the primary consideration in job assignments?

Source: Dora Schuster, *Die Stellung der Frau in der Zunftverfassung* (Berlin: 1927).

natural impulses to improve their own lot by harming their neighbors. Recognizing this need to restrain violence, early societies soon gave birth to the idea of the state and to the state's living embodiment, the monarch. The state, which Hobbes termed *Leviathan* in his famous book of 1651, was both the creature and the master of man. The state commanded absolute obedience from all. Those who rebelled should be crushed without mercy for the protection of the rest (see the Law and Government box).

LAW AND GOVERNMENT

## Hobbes's *Leviathan*

**THOMAS HOBBES PUBLISHED *LEVIATHAN*** in 1651 to provide a philosophical basis for absolutist monarchy that went beyond the conventional idea of "divine right." Much influenced by the events of the day in England—the civil war was raging—Hobbes wished to demonstrate that strong control of the body politic by a monarch was a political necessity. Note how he bases all effective lawmaking on people's fear of punishment by a superior force, and not at all by the action of reason or compassion. He is interested in establishment of an effective governing authority, and not in the moral and/or reasonable basis for it. He had no illusions about the benign nature of mankind. The following excerpts come from the opening section of the second part of *Leviathan,* where the author summarizes his case:

> The final cause, end, or design of men (who naturally love liberty, and dominion over others) in the introduction of that restraint upon themselves . . . is the foresight of their own preservation, and of a more contented life thereby; that is to say, of getting themselves out of that miserable condition of war, when there is no visible power to keep them in awe, and tie them by fear of punishment to the performance of their covenants.
>
> For the laws of nature . . . without the terror of some power to cause them to be observed, are contrary to our natural passions. . . . And covenants without the sword are but words, and of no strength to secure a man at all. . . . And in all places where men have lived in small families, to rob and spoil one another has been a trade, and so far from being reputed against the law of nature, the greater spoils they gained, the greater was their honor. . . . And as small families did then; so now do cities and kingdoms, which are but greater families. . . .
>
> It is true that certain living creatures, as bees and ants, live sociably with one another . . . and therefore some man may perhaps desire to know, why mankind cannot do the same. To which I answer
>
> First, that men are continually in competition for honor and dignity, which these creatures are not. . . .
>
> Secondly, that amongst these creatures, the common good differs not from the private; and being by nature inclined to their private, they procure thereby the common benefit.
>
> Thirdly, that these creatures, having not [as man] the use of reason, do not see, nor think they see any fault, in the administration of their private business: whereas among men, there are very many that think themselves wiser, and abler to govern the public, better than the rest; and these strive to reform and innovate, one this way, another that way; and thereby bring it into distraction and civil war.
>
> Lastly, the agreement of these creatures is natural; that of men, is by covenant only, which is artificial; and therefore it is no wonder if there be somewhat else required to make their agreement constant and lasting; which is a common power, to keep them in awe, and to direct their action to the common benefit.
>
> The only way to erect such a common power . . . [is] to confer all their power and strength upon one man, or upon one assembly of men, that may reduce all their wills, by plurality of voices, unto one will . . . as if every man should say to every man, *I authorize and give up my right of governing myself to this man, or to this assembly of men, on this condition, that thou give up thy right to him, and authorize all his actions in like manner.*
>
> And he that carries this power is called *sovereign,* and said to have *sovereign power,* and everyone besides him is his *subject.*
>
> The attaining of this sovereign power is by two ways. One, by natural force . . . the other, is when men agree amongst themselves to submit to some man or assembly of men, voluntarily, in confidence to be protected by him against all others. This latter may be called a political Commonwealth.

### *Analyze and Interpret*

Do you believe Hobbes is wrong in his assumption that only fear of superior force keeps people in a more or less peaceable community? What might a devout Calvinist have to say about that assumption? How do *Leviathan* and *The Prince* by Machiavelli resemble or contradict one another?

Source: From *The English Works of Thomas Hobbes,* ed. Thomas Molesworth, vol. 3, chap. 17.

**HistoryNow™**

***To read further selections from* Leviathan, *point your browser to the documents area of* HistoryNow.**

Hobbes's uncompromising pessimism about human nature was countered at the end of the seventeenth century by the writings of John Locke (1632–1704). In his most famous work, the *Two Treatises of Civil Government,* Locke said that all men possess certain natural rights, derived from the fact that they were reasonable creatures. Some of those rights were voluntarily given up to form a government that would protect and enhance the remaining ones: the rights to life, liberty, and property. No prince might interfere with such rights or claim to have one-sided powers to define the citizenry's welfare. Insofar as the government fulfilled its duties, it should enjoy the citizens' support and loyal service. When it did not, it had no claim to their support, and they could righteously push it aside and form a new government.

Whereas Hobbes's words were harsh and shocking to most English people of his time, Locke's message fell on much more welcoming ground. His readers, like the author, were members of the middle and upper classes, who possessed properties and freedoms they were determined to protect from the claims of absolutist monarchs. The English Revolution of the 1640s and the events of the 1680s had given them confidence that their views were both correct and workable. Locke's arguments made good sense to them, and he was also to become the most important political philosopher for the English colonials in North America.

## Summary

The Thirty Years' War wrecked Germany while providing a forcible resolution to the question of religious conflict in post-Reformation Europe. The Treaty of Westphalia, which ended the war, was founded on state interests, rather than religious doctrine or dynastic claims. From the early seventeenth century on, doctrines of faith took an ever-decreasing role in forming state policy. The Catholic but anti-Habsburg French emerged as the chief beneficiaries of the conflict in Germany. France replaced Habsburg Spain as the prime force in military and political affairs and, under the guidance of Richelieu and the long-lived Louis XIV, became the role model for the rest of the aspiring absolutist monarchies on the Continent.

The English Revolution, sparked by the attempts of the Stuart kings to emulate Louis XIV, ended in clear victory for the antiabsolutist side. Led by the Puritan rebels against Charles I, the wealthier, educated segment of the English people successfully asserted their claims to be equal to the Crown in defining national policies and the rights of citizens. The Glorious Revolution of 1688 cemented these gains. The seeds thus planted would sprout continuously in the Western world for the next two centuries, especially in the British colonies in North America. Given a theoretical underpinning by philosophers such as John Locke and practical form by the 1689 Bill of Rights, the idea of a society that was contractual rather than authoritarian in its political basis began to emerge. Along with this came the ideal of a state that guaranteed liberty and legal equality for all its subjects.

## Identification Terms

Test your knowledge of this chapter's key concepts by defining the following terms. If you can't recall the meaning of certain terms, refresh your memory by looking up the boldfaced term in the chapter, turning to the Glossary at the end of the book, or working with the flashcards that are available on the *World Civilizations* Companion Website **http://history.wadsworth.com/adler04**.

Bill of Rights
Glorious Revolution of 1688
Hanoverian Dynasty
*intendants*
Restoration (English)
Test Act
Treaty of Westphalia

## Test Your Knowledge

Test your knowledge of this chapter by answering the following questions. Complete answers appear at the end of the book. You may also take this quiz interactively and find even more quiz questions on the *World Civilizations* Companion Website **http://history.wadsworth.com/adler04**.

1. The Thirty Years' War began
   a. as a struggle for religious freedom for Protestant reformers in Bohemia.
   b. as a contest between Calvinists and Lutherans in Germany.
   c. as a political contest between Germans and French in the Rhineland.
   d. as an attempt by the French to re-Catholicize their nation.
   e. as none of these.
2. In its final stage, the Thirty Years' War became
   a. the first religious war in Europe.
   b. a political struggle for European hegemony.
   c. a struggle between the Roman pope and various Protestant groups.
   d. a struggle between the Habsburgs and Bourbons.
   e. a religious struggle between Lutherans and Calvinists.
3. Under the terms of the Treaty of Westphalia, the principle of *crius regio, eius religio* was extended to
   a. Catholics.
   b. Protestants.
   c. Lutherans.
   d. Anglicans.
   e. Calvinists.
4. The founder of absolute monarchy in France was
   a. Jean Bodin.
   b. Louis XIV.
   c. Cardinal Richelieu.
   d. Cardinal Mazarin.
   e. Henry IV.
5. *Raison d'état* is most accurately translated as
   a. the power of a duly constituted government to do virtually anything to maintain internal order.
   b. a false reason given by a spokesperson to justify what the government desires.
   c. a pretext used by a government to justify illegal acts.
   d. the state's legal power to make war.
   e. the power of the state to choose its people's religion.
6. Which of the following characteristics was *not* true of the government of Louis XIV?
   a. It was based on parliamentary policy making.
   b. It was Catholic in religion.
   c. It was staffed by many members of the middle classes.
   d. It was highly concentrated in the person of the king.
   e. It succeeded in nullifying the actual powers of the aristocrats.
7. Which of the following seventeenth-century English monarchs was most successful in retaining the support of Parliament?
   a. James II
   b. Charles I
   c. James I
   d. Charles II
   e. William of Orange
8. William and Mary came to rule England
   a. at the invitation of Parliament.
   b. as the successors to Cromwell after his death.
   c. as the conquerors of Cromwell's Commonwealth.
   d. as the brother and sister of the last Stuart king. after the death of Mary's father, Charles II.
9. England's 1701 Act of Succession eventually brought which dynasty to rule the country?
   a. Tudors
   b. Hanovers
   c. Windsors
   d. Stuarts
   e. None of these
10. The message conveyed by Hobbes's *Leviathan* was in brief that
    a. man would find his way to a better future.
    b. man could make more progress once religion was abolished.
    c. man was irredeemably stained by original sin.
    d. man needed a powerful government to avoid anarchy.
    e. man by nature would do good if taught to do so.

## InfoTrac College Edition

Visit the source collections at

**http://infotrac.thomsonlearning.com**

and use the Search function with the following key terms:

Thirty Years' War    Louis XIV    Oliver Cromwell

## Wadsworth History Website Resources

Visit the World History Resource Center at **http://history.wadsworth.com/world** for a wealth of general resources, and the *World Civilizations* Companion Website at **http://history.wadsworth.com/adler04** for resources specific to this textbook.

## HistoryNow

Enter *HistoryNow* using the access card that is available for *World Civilizations*. *HistoryNow* will assist you in understanding the content in this chapter with lesson plans generated for your needs. In addition, you can read the following documents, and many more, online:

The Treaty of Westphalia

Thomas Hobbes, selections from *Leviathan*

John Locke, "An Essay Concerning Human Understanding"

*After I had seen [Peter I] often and had conversed with him, I could not but adore the depth of the providence of God that raised up so furious a man to so absolute an authority over so great a part of the world.*

**Bishop Burnet**

# 26 EASTERN EUROPEAN EMPIRES



| | |
|---|---|
| 1533–1584 | IVAN IV, THE TERRIBLE (RUSSIA) |
| EARLY 1600S–1613 | TIME OF TROUBLES (RUSSIA) ENDED BY FIRST ROMANOV CZAR |
| 1640–1688 | FREDERICK WILLIAM, THE GREAT ELECTOR (PRUSSIA) |
| 1682–1724 | PETER I, THE GREAT (RUSSIA) |
| LATE 1600S–1700S | OTTOMAN DECLINE |
| 1713–1740 | FREDERICK WILLIAM I (PRUSSIA) |
| 1740–1786 | FREDERICK II, THE GREAT (PRUSSIA) |
| 1740–1748 | WAR OF THE AUSTRIAN SUCCESSION |
| 1740–1780 | MARIA THERESA (AUSTRIA) |
| 1756–1763 | SEVEN YEARS' WAR |
| 1762–1796 | CATHERINE II, THE GREAT (RUSSIA) |
| 1772–1795 | POLISH PARTITIONS |

ROYAL ABSOLUTISM BEGAN TO DEVELOP in eastern Europe at about the same time as in western Europe—that is, in the sixteenth century—but it proceeded further and was not challenged or checked until much later. The gap between East and West in this regard is one of the outstanding determinants of modern European history. Eastern Europe, lagging in the evolution toward personal freedoms and the abolition of class privilege, became a fundamentally different society from western Europe. In the seventeenth and eighteenth centuries, three states—Russia, Austria, and Prussia—came to dominate this "other Europe" in which absolutist government and feudal society still prevailed.

The borders of the eastern European states were extremely unstable, partly because of war, political backwardness, and centuries of forced and voluntary migrations. This instability both contributed to the rise of absolutist monarchic government and acted against its effectiveness. By the end of the eighteenth century, eastern Europe had westernized its ruling aristocracy, but deep differences remained between Europe east of the Elbe River and west of that traditional dividing line.

## ABSOLUTISM EAST OF THE ELBE

The reasons for these differences varied, some being economic, others social and political in character. What were the most important of these factors? Absolute monarchy was able to develop more completely in eastern Europe largely because of the nature of its agrarian economy. Feudal monoculture estates lasted much longer in Russia, Poland, and Hungary than in France, England, and Sweden. The social cleavage between noble lord and peasant serf was enabled and perpetuated by the rising profits the landlords were able to wring from their large estates. The grain necessary for the expanding populations of the cities of western and central Europe was produced on these holdings—a business that became increasingly profitable for landlords who could produce the crop cheaply with nonfree labor.

The struggle between noble landowners and the royal government was resolved in eastern Europe by a silent compromise: the monarchs surrendered full control over the peasants to the landlords in return for the landlords' loyalty and service to the Crown. As time passed, the once-weak monarchs steadily gained power through control of the sole permitted armed forces, and the nobles became their servants, just as the peasants were servants to the nobles. The ranks between noble and peasant, which had been crucially important in the West as allies of the Crown, here played no role. No effective middle-class voice was ever heard in constitutional affairs east of the Elbe. Why? The towns were too few and too impoverished, and the small urban populations never gained self-government and economic freedom as in the West. In part through actual use of armed force against the rebel nobles as in Russia, and in part through its threat, as in Prussia and Austria, the royal dynasts were gradually able to subordinate all classes and interests to themselves, and the continuity of legitimate royal power had become the pivot on which all society revolved by the eighteenth century.

The three states' political evolution was not identical, however. Russia became the most autocratic by far. The Romanov czar was not beholden to any earthly power in Russian legal theory; his will was law. On the contrary, the power of the Austrian emperor—always a member of the Habsburg Dynasty—was sharply limited by the high nobility until the later eighteenth century. The Prussian king—a Hohenzollern—originally had fewer supreme powers than the Romanovs but more than the Habsburgs. Eventually, the Prussian king was to become in fact the most powerful and successful of the three, and from Prussia came modern Germany. We will look at Prussia first and then at the other two states.

## Prussia's Rise

As we have seen, after the Thirty Years' War (1618–1648), much of Germany was in a state of economic decay and political confusion. The 300-odd German states and statelets were divided along religious lines: about half were Catholic and half Protestant. Neither accepted the other, and distrust and animosities were always present. The famines and epidemics that accompanied the war had led one-third of the population to an early death, and whole regions almost reverted to wasteland. From this unpromising situation, however, arose one of the major powers of modern Europe, Prussia-Germany (see Map 26.1).

The rise of the small and economically insignificant Prussia during the later seventeenth and eighteenth centuries was largely attributable to the Hohenzollern princes who occupied the Prussian throne from 1640 to 1786. Frederick William, the **Great Elector** (ruled 1640–1688), was a man of iron will and great talent. He united his previously separate family holdings of Prussia, Brandenburg, and some small areas in western Germany into a single government that was known thereafter simply as Prussia. During his reign, Berlin began its rise from a simple market town to a capital city. A sign of his strength was his victory over the powerful feudal lords in a constitutional struggle over who would have the final word regarding taxes.

Through such measures, the Great Elector tripled the government's revenues and then spent much of the increase on his prize: a new professional army. Every fourteenth male citizen was a member of the army on active service. No other European country even came close to this ratio. Frederick William only once had to use this force directly against a foreign enemy. Its existence was enough to intimidate his many opponents both inside and outside of Prussia's borders.

Frederick William also began the understanding between king and nobles that gradually came to characterize Prussian politics until

Brandenburg, 1415
Prussian acquisitions to 1740
Conquest of Silesia by 1748
From Poland as result of First Partition, 1772
0 125 250 500 Kilometers
0 125 250 Miles
Baltic Sea
EAST PRUSSIA
Danzig
POMERANIA
WEST PRUSSIA
UNITED NETHERLANDS
BRANDENBURG
Elbe R.
Potsdam
Berlin
Poznan
Vistula R.
Warsaw
Magdeburg
Cologne
Rhine R.
Leipzig
SAXONY
Oder R.
POLAND
Dresden
SILESIA
Frankfurt
BOHEMIA
Prague

**MAP 26.1** *The Expansion of Prussia, 1640–1795*

Prussia was originally the home of Slavic tribes that were conquered and absorbed by Germanic neighbors in Brandenburg. The acquision of prosperous Rhine Valley principalities and of rich Silesia were key factors in bringing formerly insignificant Prussia to the forefront of European power politics.

the twentieth century. The Crown handed over the peasants to the noble landlords, who acted as their judge and jury and reduced most of them to a condition of misery as serfs. In return, the Crown was allowed almost total control over national policy, while the noble landlords' sons were expected to serve in the growing military and civil bureaucracy that Frederick William was creating.

During the reign of the Great Elector and for a long time thereafter, many of the Prussian ***Junkers*** (landowning nobles) were not yet resigned to their inferior position as adjuncts to the monarch, but they could not bring themselves to look for help from the most likely quarter. In the struggle over constitutional rights, the nobles ignored the third party that might have been able to tip the balance against the king: the townspeople. As in the rest of eastern Europe, the Prussian urban middle classes did not play the crucial role they had in western Europe. They could not strike a "deal" with either king or nobles to guarantee their own rights. They had to pay the taxes from which the nobles' lands were exempt, and their social and political status remained much lower than that of the Junkers.

After Frederick William's death, his son Frederick I and grandson Frederick William I ruled Prussia until 1740. By clever diplomacy in the War of the Spanish Succession, Frederick I was able to raise his rank from prince to the much loftier king of Prussia, while Frederick William I (ruled 1713–1740) was even more intent than his grandfather on building the finest army in Europe. He was the real founder of Prussia-Germany's military tradition and its deserved reputation as the most efficiently governed state on the Continent.

During the reign of Frederick William I, Prussia was aptly called "an army with a country." Military priorities and military discipline were enforced everywhere in government, and the most talented young men by now automatically entered state service, rather than going into business or the arts and sciences. The aristocratic bureaucrats were known far and wide as dedicated, hardworking servants of their king, whether in uniform (which they generally preferred) or in civilian clothing. The officer corps became the highest social group in the nation, enjoying even its own legal code separate from the civil society.

The series of notable Hohenzollern monarchs culminated in the eighteenth century with Frederick II, the Great (ruled 1740–1786), who is generally seen as one of the most talented kings in modern history. A shrewd judge of people and situations, Frederick was cultivated and cynical, daring, and calculating. A fine musician, his literary and artistic inclinations as a youth were so strong as to have him defy his overbearing father and toy with the idea of abdicating his rights in order to become a private citizen. But a sense of duty combined with unlimited ambition to abort this romantic notion.

As king, Frederick proved to be one of the most effective in an age of outstanding monarchs. His victories against Austria in Silesia (and later in the Seven Years' War) enabled Prussia to rise into the first rank of European powers. Under Frederick's rule, the Prussian economy prospered. The universal adoption of the potato as a staple enabled the rising population to subsist on that formerly condemned product of the marginal agricultural land of Northeast Germany. The Prussian territorial gains in western Germany were brought together under the efficient bureaucracy that Frederick continued to develop. Frederick II cleverly associated the Prussian monarchy with a reviving German sense of national unity. With him began the "German dualism," the century-long contest between Austria and Prussia, Vienna and Berlin, for leadership of the German-speaking people, the most numerous in Europe.

## THE HABSBURG DOMAINS

Prussia's rival for eventual political supremacy over the fragmented Germans was Habsburg Austria. Based in Vienna, the **Habsburg Dynasty** ruled over three quite different areas: Austria proper, Bohemia (the present-day Czech Republic), and Hungary (see Map 26.2). In addition, the Habsburgs found allies among the southern German Catholics, who sympathized with their Austrian cousins and had strong antipathies toward the Prussian Protestants.

The dynasty had acquired Hungary and Bohemia through lucky marriages in the sixteenth century. At that time, much of Hungary was still occupied by the Ottoman Turks (see the next section). It was liberated by Habsburg armies at the end of the seventeenth century. Although a potentially rich agricultural country, Hungary had been laid to waste by the Turks during their long occupation. By the end of the eighteenth century, it had been revivified and repopulated by Catholic Germans and others under the close control of the Vienna government.

Bohemia was even more valuable. It had been severely hurt by the Thirty Years' War but had scored a quick comeback. Commerce and manufacturing were more developed here than in any other Habsburg dominion. As a center of the arts and commerce, Prague at this juncture was almost as important as Vienna. It was inhabited almost entirely by Germans and Jews, however. The Czechs themselves were still peasants, ruled over by foreign nobles imported by the Catholic emperor as a result of the native nobles' support of the Protestants in the Thirty Years' War.

### *The Struggle against Turkey*

Toward the end of the seventeenth century, Austria was being threatened on several sides. Against its southern and eastern flanks, the Ottoman Turks were still a menacing

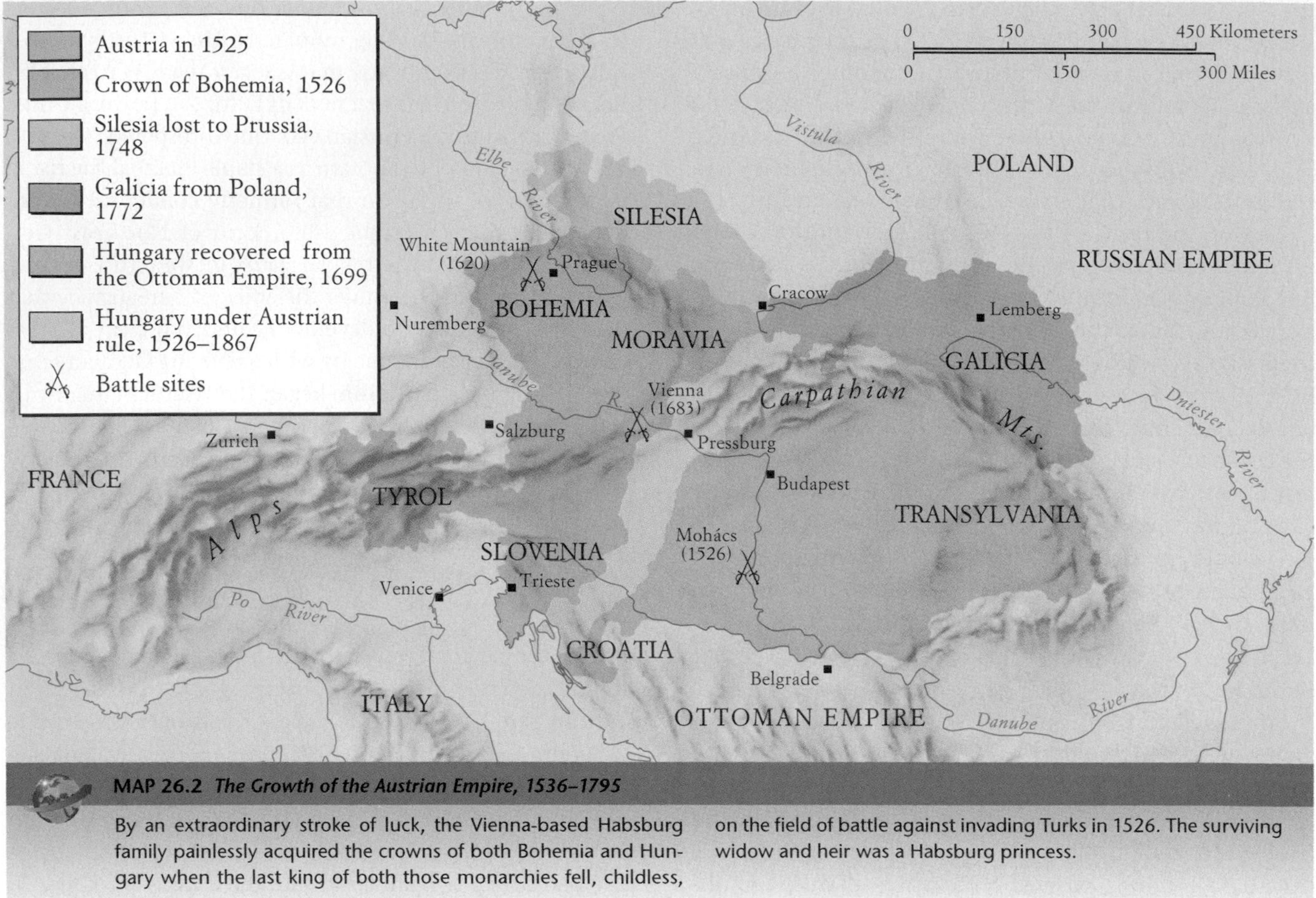


**MAP 26.2** ***The Growth of the Austrian Empire, 1536–1795***

By an extraordinary stroke of luck, the Vienna-based Habsburg family painlessly acquired the crowns of both Bohemia and Hungary when the last king of both those monarchies fell, childless, on the field of battle against invading Turks in 1526. The surviving widow and heir was a Habsburg princess.

foe, and they mounted an invasion that reached the outskirts of Vienna in 1683. In the west, the French monarch Louis XIV was readying the War of the Spanish Succession (1700–1715). Louis's object was to make Spain, including its overseas possessions, an integral part of France and thereby make France the decisive power in continental affairs. The Ottomans' attack was beaten off, and the counterattack against Turkey went well at first, but then Austria's preparations for the imminent war with France allowed the Turks to recoup their strength. The Treaty of Karlowitz in 1699 regained Hungary for the Habsburgs but did not definitively end the Ottoman menace to Austria. In this conflict, the chief architect of Austrian greatness in the eighteenth century, Prince Eugen of Savoy, first won renown. He then successfully led the imperial forces against the army of Louis XIV along the Rhine before returning to the Ottoman front, where he won a decisive victory at Belgrade in 1716. From this point on, the Ottomans were almost always on the defensive against the Christian powers opposing them. The threat of a Turkish invasion of central Europe was eliminated, and Austria became a leading power for the first time.

This new power, however, had a flaw that became apparent with time. Ethnically, the empire of Austria was the least integrated of all European countries. It included no fewer than ten different nationalities: Germans, Hungarians, Italians, Croats, Serbs, Slovenes, Poles, Czechs, Slovaks, and Ukrainians. In this historical epoch, few if any Europeans were conscious of their national affiliations in the modern, political sense and were thus not disturbed at being ruled by nonnatives or being unable to use their native tongues in court proceedings or schools. Nevertheless, as late as the mid-eighteenth century, the Habsburg lands resembled a "salad" of nations and regions that had little in common except rule by the dynasty in Vienna.

Maria Theresa, the only surviving child of the previous emperor, became the first and only female to rule Austria (1740–1780). Accepted only reluctantly by the still-semifeudal nobility, she became one of the most successful of the Habsburg rulers. She and her son Joseph II (ruled 1780–1790) did much to modernize the Austrian armed forces and civil bureaucracy. (See the Law and Government box for more on the prickly relationship of these two.) She was also the first to introduce some coherence

LAW AND GOVERNMENT

## Mother and Son in the Habsburg Family

**WE GET AN EXTRAORDINARY INSIGHT** into royal family relations among the Austrian Habsburg Dynasty of the eighteenth century via a letter composed by Leopold, younger son of Maria Theresa and younger brother of her co-ruler, Kaiser Joseph. Although the two brothers supported each other in many ways, Leopold had an unsparing eye for Joseph's weak points. It should be noted that Leopold succeeded his brother on the Habsburg throne after Joseph's early death, and in the opinion of many contemporaries, he was the most talented ruler in that family's lengthy history. However, his reign lasted only two years (1790–1792) before he, too, died of sudden illness.

Schloss Schonbrunn, Vienna, Austria/Bridgeman Art Library

**MARIA THERESA AND HER SONS.** Empress Maria Theresa of Austria with four of her sons: (left to right) Joseph (1741–1790), her co-ruler; Ferdinand (1754–1806); Leopold (1747–1792), who succeeded Joseph; and Maximilian (1756–1801).

> When they [that is, the empress and her co-ruler Joseph] are together there is uninterrupted strife and contradictions, and if the Kaiser takes a step or gave an order without telling her, she is always put out of sorts. . . . She sees how many want to curry the Kaiser's favor by complaining about her and telling him how much better things will go when he is in command. She claims she will abdicate, as people can't seem to wait for the passing of the crown to Joseph. . . . She has the greatest jealousy of all who speak or even write to the Kaiser, suspecting them of making common cause against her. With Joseph she is always arguing, even over trifles, and they are never of one voice and mind.
>
> The worst is, all these arguments and conflicts of opinion are publicly known, because both of them speak openly about such things, and that means that among the officials and in fact among all the public there are people who claim that they are either of the Kaiser's faction or that of the empress, and are therefor being persecuted. This makes a very bad impression upon the diplomats at court, as well as harming the affairs of government and discouraging everybody. . . .
>
> The Kaiser has many talents and capabilities; he quickly comprehends, and has the gift of both good memory and articulate speech. He understands well how to get his ideas across, verbally and on paper. In recent days he has been of a bad temper, it seems because of frustration that he is not yet able to exercise sole power, but must still depend on the empress' acquiescence. He complains a lot about that. He is a hard, powerful man, full of ambition, who will do most anything to be talked about and be praised. . . . He can stand for no contradiction, and is a believer in wilful, even brutal principles of action, and is an adherent of the most uncompromising, strongest despotism. He loves no one, makes a friendly face towards only those whom he thinks he needs because of their special talents, but makes mockery even of them when it pleases him. He contemns everything that did not originate with himself.

Source: Adapted from Karl Guthas, *Kaiser Joseph II* (Munich: Zsolnay, 1989).

### *Analyze and Interpret*

This letter was written to an official of the Habsburg government. Does it surprise you to read such candid remarks coming from a royal person about his own family's performance on the throne he hoped to inherit? Why or why not?

---

and uniformity to the Habsburg government. Despite losing Silesia to the Prussians in the **War of the Austrian Succession** (1740–1748) at the outset of her reign, she slowly welded the various provinces and kingdoms into a single entity under a centralized government headquartered in the impressive royal city. Thanks to Russian initiatives (see the next section), Austria even gained some territory from neighboring Poland.

Much later, in the mid-nineteenth century, when it gradually became clear that Austria was losing the battle over the future allegiance of the German-speaking people, the Austrians turned east and south to realize their version of colonial expansion. By so doing, they encountered the Turks, who had sunk into second-level status and would not have been a serious obstacle if they had been forced to stand alone. But in the nineteenth century,

**The Belvedere in Vienna.** This palace was built by and for Prince Eugen of Savoy, greatest of the Habsburg generals in the wars of the late seventeenth and early eighteenth centuries. It is a perfect example of Austrian baroque architecture.

British Library, London, UK/Bridgeman Art Library

Europe's diplomats agreed to let the Turks continue to control southeastern Europe (the Balkans), so as to avoid the inevitable conflicts that would ensue if the Turks were pushed aside and replaced by others. Foremost among those contenders were the newly powerful Russians.

## Russia under the Czars

Russia's government rose from centuries of retardation and near-disintegration to attain great power status in the eighteenth century (see Map 26.3). Until the 1200s, Russia had been an independent Christian principality based on the impressive city of Kiev, with extensive trading and cultural contacts with both western and Mediterranean Europe through the Baltic and Black Seas. The Russians had been converted to Orthodox Christianity by Greek missionaries in the late 900s and had remained closely attached to Constantinople in secular, cultural, and religious doctrine for the next three centuries.

But in 1241, the fierce, pagan Mongols under the successors of Chinghis Khan had conquered the principality of Kiev and settled down to rule the Russians for the next 240 years (see Chapter 22). During that period, Russia's formerly numerous contacts with both eastern and western Europe were almost completely severed or neglected, and the Russians retrogressed in many differing fashions, ranging from literacy rates to peasant superstitions. Even their crafts and skills declined. For example, in the sixteenth century, after the Mongols were overthrown, the seat of Russian government, the Kremlin in Moscow, was rebuilt in stone rather than wood, but Italian masons had to be brought in because the Russians could no longer handle large-scale projects as they had in the eleventh and twelfth centuries when they built their great stone churches in Kiev.

Their governmental institutions also deteriorated. The Russian princes connived and maneuvered to serve as agents and intermediaries of the Mongol khan, who played them off against each other for almost two centuries. Moscow, one of the dozen or so principalities into which Russia was divided after the conquest, came through cunning, perseverance, and good luck to overshadow its rivals even during the Mongol era.

Shifting alliances between Russians, Mongols, and the briefly potent Lithuanian state on the western borders marked the entire fourteenth century. Taking advantage of a temporary split in the upper rank of the occupying *orda* (horde), one Muscovite prince actually defeated the Mongol cavalry in 1380, but he could not follow up his victory. But in the fifteenth century, the princes of Moscow gained steadily on their several rivals. Using every available means, from marriages to bribery, the Muscovites brought neighboring Slavic principalities under their control as the Mongol grip slowly loosened.

The **Mongol Yoke**, as the Russians call it, was finally thrown off in a bloodless rebellion led by Moscow in 1480. The once-fearsome Golden Horde's remnant retired eastward into the Siberian steppe, and the Russians slowly reemerged into European view. The English traders, the German diplomats, and the Greek clerics who now arrived looked on the Russians as residents of a "rude and barbarous kingdom."

In fact, as late as the 1600s, few western Europeans gave any thought to Russia or the Russians. Trade relations were eventually established with Britain through the Arctic seas and later with the Scandinavians and Germans through the Baltic. (Hostile Poles and Turks interdicted overland access.) But beyond some raw materials

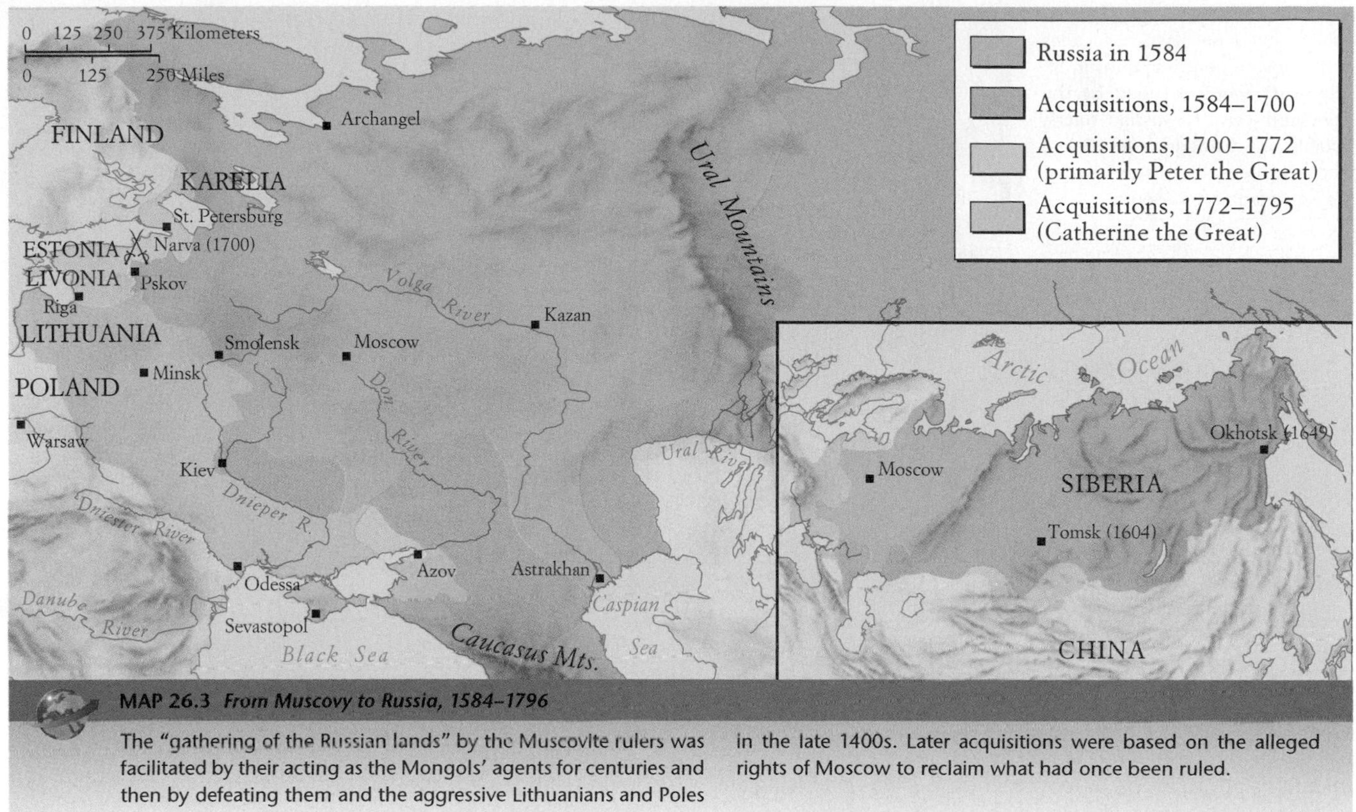


**MAP 26.3** *From Muscovy to Russia, 1584–1796*

The "gathering of the Russian lands" by the Muscovite rulers was facilitated by their acting as the Mongols' agents for centuries and then by defeating them and the aggressive Lithuanians and Poles in the late 1400s. Later acquisitions were based on the alleged rights of Moscow to reclaim what had once been ruled.

available elsewhere and some exotic items such as ermine skins, there seemed little reason to confront the extraordinary challenges involved in trading with this alien society. Militarily and politically, it had nothing to offer the West, and whatever technical and cultural progress was made in Russia during these centuries almost always stemmed from Western—particularly German and Swedish—sources.

## Russia's Antipathies to the West

The Russians were in any case not inclined to welcome Western ideas and visitors except on a highly selective basis. The Orthodox church had been crucially important in keeping alive national identity during the Yoke, and most Russians responded with an uncompromising attachment to its doctrines and clergy. Their distrust of Western Christians was strong. The sporadic attempts of both papal and Protestant missionaries to convert the Russian "heretics" contributed, of course, to this distrust and dislike on the Russians' side. The ill-concealed disdain of the Europeans for their backward hosts in Moscow, Novgorod, and other trade markets sharpened native *xenophobia* (antipathy to foreigners).

Culturally, Russia experienced almost nothing of the consequences of the Protestant revolt against Rome or

**PETER THE GREAT.** The great reformer/modernizer of backward Russia, painted in the early years of his reign.

**A Prospect of St. Petersburg.** The beautiful neoclassical facades of the government buildings in St. Petersburg were ordained by the eighteenth-century Russian rulers, notably by Catherine the Great, whose winter palace later became the Hermitage art museum.

Giraudon/Art Resource, NY

the Renaissance, a situation that greatly heightened the differences between it and the rest of Europe. The Renaissance glorification of individuality, of examination of the human potential, of daring to oppose was to make no impact east of Poland. In religious affairs, the Russians either were ignorant of or rejected the changes Western Christianity had undergone, such as the enhanced role of the laity in the church, the emphasis on individual piety and Bible reading, and the restrictions on the clergy's power. Protestant doctrines were regarded either as negligible tamperings with a basically erroneous Roman faith or—worse—Western surrender to the lures of a false rationalism that could only lead to eternal perdition.

Above all, from their Byzantine-inspired beginnings, the Russian clergy had accepted the role of partner of the civil government in maintaining good order on Earth. Unlike the papal or Protestant West, the Russian Christian establishment accorded the government full authority over the earthly concerns of the faithful. This tradition had been much strengthened by the church's close support of the Muscovite princes' struggle to free Russia from the Mongols. The high Orthodox clerics saw their role as helper and moral partner of the government in the mutual and interdependent tasks of saving Russian souls and preserving the Russian state.

## Absolutism in Russia: Peter I

The expansion of the Muscovite principality into a major state picked up its pace during the sixteenth century. The czar Ivan IV, the Terrible (ruled 1533–1584), encouraged exploration and settlement of the vast and almost unpopulated Siberia. He brushed aside the Mongol remnants in a program of conquest that reached the Pacific shores as early as 1639—6,000 miles from Muscovy proper. Soon after, Russia was brought into formal contacts with China for the first time—a fateful meeting and the onset of a difficult relationship along the longest land border in the world.

Like the countries of western Europe, Russia adopted a form of divine right monarchy in the seventeenth century. Already in the previous century, Ivan the Terrible had established a brutal model by persecuting all who dared question his rights. So fearful had been his harassment of his nobles (*boyars*) that many of them abandoned their lands and positions and fled. Those who chose to remain often paid with their lives for nonexistent "treason" or "betrayal." Whether Ivan became clinically paranoid is open to question. Mad or not, he bullied and terrified the Russian upper classes in a fashion that would have certainly led to revolt in other countries of the age, but in Russia, no such rebellion occurred in his day.

A Time of Troubles in the early seventeenth century threatened the state's existence. The ancient dynasty of Kievan princes died out, and various nobles vied with armed force for the vacant throne. A serf rebellion added to the turmoil, and the Poles and Swedes on the western borders took advantage of the confusion to annex huge slices of Russian territory. Nevertheless, recovery under the new **Romanov Dynasty** (1613–1917) was fairly rapid. By the middle 1600s, Moscow was pressing the Poles and Swedes back to the Baltic shores and reclaiming some of the territories lost to these invaders and to the Ottoman Turks in the Far South during the previous fifty years.

Peter I, the Great (ruled 1682–1724), is the outstanding example of Russian royal absolutism. Brutal he may have been, but there is no question of Peter's sanity. In fact, his foreign policy was one of the shrewdest of his age. Like Ivan IV, however, he was in no way inclined to share power with any group or institution and believed the fate of the country was solely his to decide. There were attempts to rebel against Peter, but they were put down with great cruelty. Nobles and peasants suffered equally if they resisted.

The impact of the human whirlwind called Peter on stolid, isolated, and conservative Russia is impossible to categorize. He was the first Russian ruler to set foot outside the country and to recognize how primitive Russia was in comparison with the leading countries of Europe. He brought thousands of foreign specialists, craftsmen, artists, and engineers to Russia on contract to practice their specialties while teaching the Russians. These individuals—many of whom eventually settled in Russia—acted as yeast in the Russian dough and had inordinate influence on the country's progress in the next century.

Peter was the driving force for an enormously ambitious, partly successful attempt to make Russia into a fully European-style society. He did westernize many Russian public institutions and even the private lives of the upper 2 to 3 percent of the society. This tiny minority of gentry or noble landowners/officials assisted the czar in governing his vast country; they were swept up into lifelong service to the state, much against their will. In Peter's scheme, the peasants (five-sixths of the population) were to serve the nobility on their estates and feed the townspeople; the nobles were to serve the government as both military and civil bureaucrats at the beck and call of the czar; and the czar, in turn, saw himself as the chief servant of the state.

The Granger Collection, NY

**A Royal Barber.** Peter's many domestic opponents saw him as an atheistic upstart and vandalizer of all that the conservative Russians held sacred. Here Peter personally clips the beard of a dignified noble who refused to pay the tax on beards that the czar imposed in his modernization drive.

Defeating the Swedes and Poles, Peter established a new capital at St. Petersburg to be Russia's long-sought "window on the West," through which all sorts of Western ideas and values might flow. He began the slow, state-guided modernization of what had been a backward economy; he built a navy and made Russia a maritime power for the first time; he also encouraged such cultural breakthroughs as the first newspaper, the first learned journal, the Academy of Sciences, and the first technical schools.

But Peter also made Russian serfdom even more rigid and more comprehensive. He used his modernized, professional army not only against foreign enemies in his constant wars but also against his own peasant rebels. He discouraged any independent political activity and made the Orthodox clergy into mere agents of the civil government under a secular head. His cruelty bordered on sadism, and his personal life was filled with excess. Perhaps, as he himself said, it was impossible to avoid every evil in a country as difficult to govern as Russia. In any event, he remains the watershed figure of Russia's long history.

## Two Eastern Powers in Eclipse

In the East, two former great powers—Poland and Turkey—were gradually eclipsed by the rising stars of their competitors. By the end of the eighteenth century they had been reduced to a negligible quantity or removed from the map.

### *Poland*

The Polish kingdom had come into existence in the 900s under native Slavic princes who converted to Western Christianity. Under pressure from the Germans pushing eastward, the Poles expanded into ethnic Lithuanian and Russian/Ukrainian territory between the twelfth and sixteenth centuries. In the 1500s, Poland reached from the Baltic to the Black Sea, making it easily the largest European state west of Russia. It shared in the European Roman Christian culture in every way, while rejecting and condemning the Orthodox culture of the Russians. The Polish nobles were numerous and powerful, and they had instituted a system of serfdom over their Polish and non-Polish subjects that was as oppressive as any in the world.

The native dynasty died out in the 1500s, and the Polish nobles successfully pressed for an elective monarchy that would give them decisive powers. From then on, the succession to the Polish throne was a type of international auction: whoever promised the most freedom to the noble voters was the winner and next king. As a result, centralized and effective government ceased to exist. Poland became a series of petty feudal fiefdoms headed by the great magnates—that is, large landholding families.

Under the famous ***liberum* veto**—perhaps the most absurd technique for governance ever devised—a single individual could veto any proposed legislation of the *sejm* (national parliament of nobles). Poland was truly what its proud motto asserted: a republic of aristocrats. No one else counted. The small urban middle classes lost all influence on national policy, and the peasantry had never had any. The king, often a foreigner who had no roots whatever among the Poles, had to be content with being a figurehead, or he could not attain the post in the first place. The clergy was a noble domain. In the 1700s, Poland resembled a feudal monarchy of western Europe five centuries earlier. Even the royal army ceased to exist, and the nation's defense was put into the unstable hands of the "confederations"—the magnates and their clients.

Chateau de Versailles, France/Bridgeman Art Library

**STANISLAS LESCZINSKI, KING OF POLAND.** One of several Polish monarchs in the seventeenth and eighteenth centuries who were installed in power through foreign intervention or bribery of the noble electors. Lesczinski was supposed to be a Russian puppet, but he discovered Polish patriotism once he sat on the throne. Note the artist's balancing of military armor with a decidedly unmilitary face.

***The Polish Partitions*** This situation was too tempting to Poland's neighbors to be allowed to continue. In the seventeenth century, the kingdom was seriously weakened by rebellions among the Ukrainian peasants and invasions by the Swedes. A long war against the Muscovites for control of the lower stretches of the important Dnieper waterway to the Black Sea had resulted in a decisive defeat, and the Turks had seized and kept the area along the Black Sea coast that had formerly been under Polish sovereignty.

In 1772, the Russian empress Catherine II decided that a favorable moment had arrived to solve the problem of a weakening Poland on Russia's western borders. Coordinating her plans with Frederick II of Prussia and Maria Theresa of Austria, she found a transparent pretext to demand Polish subordination. When the nobles attempted resistance, the upshot was the First Partition, whereby about one-third of Poland was annexed to the three conspirators' lands (see Map 26.3).

The tremendous shock at last awakened a reform party among the aristocrats in Warsaw. Further impetus to reform was provided by the example of the American Revolution and its constitutional aftermath in the 1780s. In 1791, the noble Diet produced a remarkably liberal, forward-looking document for future Polish government. Serfdom was abolished, and many other significant reforms were enacted.

Catherine used this "unauthorized" constitution as a pretext for renewed armed intervention in the form of the Second Partition, which took another large slice for Russia and Prussia in 1793. The Poles in desperation then rebelled in an uprising led by the same Thaddeus Kosciusko who had assisted General George Washington in America a few years earlier. After a brave fight, the rebels were crushed, and Poland disappeared from the map in the ensuing Third Partition of 1795 (Russia, Prussia, and Austria).

Throughout the nineteenth century, Polish patriots in and outside the country constantly reminded the world that a previously unthinkable event had happened: an established state had been swallowed up by its greedy neighbors. They attempted two major uprisings (1831 and 1863–1864) against foreign rule. Much later, in the waning days of World War I, the revolution in Russia and the defeat of the Germans and Austrians allowed the Polish state to be re-created by the peace treaty.

## Turkey

The other unsuccessful empire in eastern Europe was Ottoman Turkey. The Turks had invaded the Balkans in the later 1300s and gradually expanded their territory north, west, and east through the later 1500s. After a period of equilibrium of power, they then began to lose ground. The most visible turning point came in 1683, at the second siege of Vienna when the Ottoman attackers were beaten off with heavy loss.

At this point, a newly modernizing and powerful Russia joined with Austria to counter the Turks throughout the eighteenth century, and the fortunes of the Ottomans came to depend on how well the two Christian empires were able to coordinate their policies and armies. When they were in harmony, the Turks were consistently pushed back. But when, as often, the two powers were pursuing different aims, the Turks were able to hold their own.

From 1790 on, the Austrians came to fear Russian territorial ambitions in eastern Europe more than Turkish assault and ceased to make war on the Ottomans. By this time, however, the Turks had weakened sufficiently that they were repeatedly defeated by the Russians acting alone. Finally, all of the other great powers stepped in to restrain Russia and support the sultan's government in its feeble attempts to modernize and survive.

Why was the Ottoman government unable to adapt effectively to the demands of a modern state and civil society? Certainly, a basic problem was the inability to devise an effective substitute for military conquest as the reason for government to exist. Thus, when military conquest was no longer easily possible against the Europeans (roughly about 1600), the government no longer commanded the respect and moral authority it had enjoyed earlier.

Furthermore, the entire tradition of the Ottoman state emphasized the crucial importance of religion as the foundation stone of public life and institutions. Islam was never intended to be merely a matter of conscience. This attitude, which grew stronger rather than weaker as time passed, meant that a large part of the population was always excluded from consideration as a creative or constructive force. In southeastern Europe, 80 to 90 percent of the native populace remained Christian everywhere except Bosnia. For the Turkish overlords,these were the *raja,* the barely human who were destined to serve and enrich the Islamic ruling minority. A modern civic society could not be created on such a basis.

In addition, the bureaucracy and military, which had originally served the sultan faithfully and effectively in the conquered lands, became corrupt and self-seeking as time passed. Foremost in this were the **Janissaries**, the professional soldiers who gradually became a kind of parallel officialdom in eastern Europe, rivaling and often ignoring the Istanbul appointees. The Janissaries also blocked every effort to modernize the armed forces of the sultan after 1700 because the changes would have threatened their privileges. For example, they resisted the introduction of modern field artillery drawn by horses because their tradition was to employ heavy siege guns, which could only be moved very slowly and were meant to be used only against immobile targets. The Turks were therefore consistently outgunned in battles in the open field after about 1700 and suffered heavy casualties before they could engage the enemy.

The Janissaries' corruption and greed in dealing with their Christian subjects and serfs triggered several rebellions in the Balkans in the eighteenth and nineteenth centuries. Too entrenched to be disciplined by the central government, the Janissaries were ultimately eliminated by government-inspired massacre in Istanbul in the 1830s.

Finally, the Ottomans as an economic entity were weakened by corrupt local governors who withheld collected taxes from the central government and so oppressed their non-Muslim subjects that they rebelled and/or failed to produce taxable objects. The local officials could then justify their failure to forward tax money to Istanbul by claiming that it was needed to combat rebellion or to supervise an increasingly restive subject population. In many parts of the Balkans, the Christian peasants habitually went "into the hills" to evade the Muslim landlords, which, of course, further reduced the tax funds collected. Banditry was widespread. In some of the more backward areas, such as Montenegro and Albania, it became a profession. So long as most of the victims were Muslims, no social stigma attached to it.

For all of these reasons, the Ottomans were destined to fall behind their European enemies and were unable to catch up despite sporadic reform attempts by the sultans and grand viziers. The government's problem was not that it was ignorant of what was happening in its domains but that it was physically and morally unable to correct the situation. In the end, this inability condemned the government in Istanbul to a slow death.

## Summary

The eastern European dynasties were able to grow and foil the occasional efforts to restrict their royal powers because neither of the two potential secular counterforces—the limited urban classes and the nobility—could find ways to substitute themselves for the throne. The clergy in all three eastern Christian empires were mainly a part of the machinery of government rather than an autonomous moral force that could challenge the government. These factors, while true everywhere to some extent, were particularly noteworthy in the Orthodox lands.

The rise of the Prussian Hohenzollern Kingdom began in earnest in the mid-1600s when the Great Elector cleverly made his petty state into a factor in the Thirty Years' War, while subordinating the nobility to a centralized government. Continued by his successors, the elector's policies culminated in the reign of his great-grandson Freder- ick II, one of the most effective monarchs of European history.

The Habsburgs of Austria took a different path. Through fortunate marriage alliances, they gradually came to rule a large empire based on Bohemia and Hungary as well as Austria proper. The weaknesses of this state were partially addressed by the efforts of Empress Maria Theresa, who brought a degree of centralization and uniformity to the government. But Austria's great problem—its potentially competing nationalities—remained.

After an obstacle-filled climb from obscurity under the Mongols, the Muscovite principality "gathered the Russian lands" in the 1500s and began to expand eastward. Its Polish, Turkish, and Swedish rivals in the West were gradually overcome by lengthy wars. The Russian nobility, once all-powerful, were reduced by the various devices of the czars to more or less willing servants of the imperial throne. As in Prussia, this collaboration of throne and noble had been secured by giving the estate-owning nobility full powers over the unfortunate serfs and the sparse and insignificant urban residents.

Two other former great powers in the East had been either swallowed up by their neighbors or reduced to impotence by the late eighteenth century. The partitions of the later eighteenth century caused Poland to disappear as a sovereign state, and the Ottomans were so checked and weakened by both internal and external factors as to become a negligible factor in European affairs.

## Identification Terms

Test your knowledge of this chapter's key concepts by defining the following terms. If you can't recall the meaning of certain terms, refresh your memory by looking up the boldfaced term in the chapter, turning to the Glossary at the end of the book, or working with the flashcards that are available on the *World Civilizations* Companion Website **http://history.wadsworth.com/adler04**.

Great Elector (Frederick William)
Habsburg Dynasty
Janissaries
*Junkers*
*liberum* veto
Mongol Yoke
Romanov Dynasty
War of the Austrian Succession

## Test Your Knowledge

Test your knowledge of this chapter by answering the following questions. Complete answers appear at the end of the book. You may also take this quiz interactively and find even more quiz questions on the *World Civilizations* Companion Website **http://history.wadsworth.com/adler04**.

1. East of the Elbe, the feudal landlords of the fifteenth through seventeenth centuries
   a. maintained or increased their local powers and prestige.
   b. regularly overthrew the royal governments.
   c. suffered a general decline economically.
   d. practically became extinct with the rise of urban life.
   e. had little to do with the peasants under their control.
2. Which of the following did the Great Elector of Prussia *not* do?
   a. He made a tacit alliance with the landlord-nobles.
   b. He ensured the political and social prestige of the peasants.
   c. He greatly increased the financial resources of the government.
   d. He began the tradition of noble military and civil service to the government.
   e. He built up a new professional army.
3. The foundation of Frederick William's success in establishing strong royal government in Prussia was his
   a. ability to intimidate the rebellious nobles into submission.
   b. success at waging war against the rebel peasants.
   c. ability to bribe his enemies.
   d. strong alliance with Peter the Great of Russia.
   e. tacit bargain with his nobles.

4. The eastern European leader who is viewed as one of the most talented kings in modern history is
   a. Peter the Great.
   b. Ivan the Terrible.
   c. Maria Theresa.
   d. Frederick William I.
   e. Frederick II, the Great.
5. Maria Theresa's major achievement for Austria was
   a. to conquer more territories from the Turks.
   b. to bring order into the workings of government.
   c. to defeat the claims of the Prussians to Austrian lands.
   d. to clean up the corruption in society.
   e. to leave a strong son behind who would rule for thirty years after her death.
6. A great difference between Ivan IV, the Terrible, and Peter I, the Great, is
   a. the savagery of the first and the subtlety of the second.
   b. the minimal successes of Ivan and the tremendous ones of Peter.
   c. the tender consideration shown to the nobles by Peter.
   d. the degree to which they incorporated Western ideas into their country.
   e. their views about the concept of absolute rule.
7. The most striking difference between the absolutist governments in East and West was
   a. the almost complete lack of a middle class in the East.
   b. the ability of the peasants to express their political opinions to the central government.
   c. the coordination of the policies of the official church and the government.
   d. the degree to which constitutions restrained them in their policies.
   e. the development of professional armies in the East but not in the West.
8. The two nations that had the least success in the competition for power in eastern Europe were
   a. Austria and Russia.
   b. Turkey and Poland.
   c. Poland and Russia.
   d. Turkey and Prussia.
   e. Austria and Turkey.
9. The *liberum* veto was a device by which
   a. one individual could prohibit the passage of a proposed law.
   b. a family member had the right to secure liberty for a political prisoner.
   c. the king could veto any measure passed by the Polish parliament.
   d. only a noble had the right to full liberty.
   e. the parliament could overturn decisions of the king.
10. All but one of the following factors contributed to the decline of Turkish prestige after 1600:
   a. The inability of the government to justify its existence other than for conquest of territory
   b. The decrease in the flow of taxes to the capital because of corruption
   c. The high percentage of Christians in the empire, who were disdained by their rulers
   d. The decline of the effectiveness of Turkish weaponry and tactics in war
   e. The tacit understanding among other nations that allowed Russia to completely envelop the Ottoman Empire

## InfoTrac College Edition

Visit the source collections at

**http://infotrac.thomsonlearning.com**

and use the Search function with the following key terms:

Habsburg or Hapsburg    Ottoman Empire
Peter the Great

## Wadsworth History Website Resources

Visit the World History Resource Center at **http://history.wadsworth.com/world** for a wealth of general resources, and the *World Civilizations* Companion Website at **http://history.wadsworth.com/adler04** for resources specific to this textbook.

## HistoryNow

Enter *HistoryNow* using the access card that is available for *World Civilizations*. *HistoryNow* will assist you in understanding the content in this chapter with lesson plans generated for your needs. In addition, you can read the following documents, and many more, online:

"The Secret History of the Reign of Jan Sobieski," 1683

*He who cannot love another human being is ignorant of life's joy.*
Sa'adi

# 27 The Rise and Fall of the Muslim Empires



| | |
|---|---|
| *c.* 1250 | Osman founds the *ghazi* Ottoman state |
| 1300s–1500s | Ottoman Empire expands and flourishes |
| 1453 | Mehmed the Conqueror seizes Constantinople/Istanbul |
| 1520–1566 | Reign of Suleiman the Magnificent |
| 1500s–1722 | Safavid Empire in Persia |
| 1556–1605 | Reign of Akbar the Great of India |
| 1587–1629 | Reign of Shah Abbas the Great of Persia |
| 1500s–mid-1800s | Mughal Empire in India |

At the time when Europe slowly began finding its way out of centuries of feudal disintegration to early statehood, and East Asian governments experienced challenges from both external and internal rivals, Islamic empires in Asia and Africa experienced seemingly endless upheavals. The Islamic world did not have a middle age of governmental evolution and consolidation. Instead, destructive wars that set Muslims against Muslims wracked the world of Islam and contributed much to its slow decline after 1600.

In Chapters 14, 15, and in parts of Chapter 16, we looked at how Islam expanded rapidly in the tropical zone between Spain and India. Within remarkably few decades, Arab Bedouin armies carried the message of Muhammad the Prophet from Mecca in all directions on the blades of their conquering swords. The civilization that sprang from this message and conquest was a mixture of Arab, Greek, Persian, Egyptian, Spanish, African, and Southeast Asian—the most cosmopolitan civilization in world history.

In the thirteenth century, the capital city of the Abbasid caliphs remained at Baghdad, but by then the Islamic world had become severely fractured into dozens of competing, quarreling states and sects. More devastating still, in that century the Mongols swept into the Islamic heartland in central and western Asia, destroying every sign of settled life in their path and establishing brief rule over half the world (see Chapter 22). After their disappearance, the Ottoman Turks gave Islam a new forward thrust. By the 1500s, the Ottomans had succeeded in capturing Constantinople and reigned over enormous territories reaching from Gibraltar to Iraq. Farther east and somewhat later, the Safavids in Persia and the Mughals in India established Muslim dynasties that endured into the early modern age.

## The Ottoman Empire

The Mongols had smashed the Persian center of Islam in the 1250s, conquered Baghdad in 1258, and left the caliph as one of the corpses of those who had dared oppose them. At this time, the all-conquering intruders intended to wipe out the rest of the Islamic states that reached as far as Spain. One of these was the Ottoman principality in what is now Turkey, which took full advantage of the Mongols' defeat at Ain Jalut to maintain its independence.

The arrival of the Ottoman Dynasty in Asia Minor and their subsequent rise to the status of most powerful state in the Islamic world was the partial consequence of two developments that had preceded them. The first of these was the Turkification of the caliphate that had begun as early as the ninth century C.E. The nomadic Turkish tribes began migrating from their homelands in the steppes of Central Asia early in that century, and soon large numbers of them were inhabiting the eastern lands of the Abbasid caliphate. Faced with increasing challenges to their authority from Kharijites and Shi'ites, the Abbasid caliphs were forced to rely on the skills of these fearsome fighters to help quell revolts. Soon, Turkish troops under Turkish commanders were largely staffing the armies of the caliphate, but the real power resided in Baghdad under the Seljuk sultans (see Chapter 15). Once in power in Baghdad, the Seljuks resumed the Muslim offensive against the rejuvenated Byzantine Empire in the eleventh century. In 1071, a crucial Seljuk victory over the Byzantines at the **Battle of Manzikert** gave the Turks direct access to Asia Minor for the first time. They established the Rum Sultanate in eastern Asia Minor and continued their *jihad* against the Christian enemies to the west.

The second important development was the growing importance of the ***dervish***, or Sufi, orders in Islam. As explained in Chapter 15, many Muslims embraced mystical forms of Islam after the death of al-Ghazzali in 1111 C.E. Many dervishes/sufis formed religious associations or brotherhoods (*tariqas*). In most cases, these were organized around a central religious figure, or shaykh, whom the dervishes believed possessed extraordinary spiritual authority and who was responsible for the spiritual and intellectual direction of his followers. Typically, too, the dervish order was organized into grades, much like a secret society (like the Masons in western Europe), and initiates graduated into higher levels of the order as they were allowed access to secret knowledge known only to members of these higher levels.

The Ottoman Empire began around 1250, when a Turkish chieftain named Osman (after whom the dynasty was named) and his group of followers entered into the service of the Rum sultans of eastern Asia Minor. Osman was given a small fiefdom in western Asia Minor to wage *jihad* against the Byzantines. Thus, the empire began as a *ghazi* state; that is, one made up of ***ghazis***, or frontier warriors, whose express purpose was waging holy war against the Christians. Osman's tiny state was initially organized around two dervish orders, and besides being a warlord, the authority of Osman and his early successors appears to have come from their positions as shaykhs of one or both of these dervish orders.

Osman succeeded in becoming independent when the Mongols destroyed the Rum Sultanate soon after they overran Baghdad. By the time he died, Osman had established a core Ottoman state that included most of western Asia Minor through continual warfare against both his Muslim and non-Muslim neighbors. His son and successor, Orhan (ruled 1326–1359), continued this policy of expansion, and he began the conquest of what remained of the Byzantine Empire on the Balkan peninsula.

More important, as the Ottoman *ghazi* state continued to grow, Orhan reorganized it along feudal lines. Feudal estates were parceled out among the commanders of the mounted army. Orhan was also noted for creating the system by which the growing numbers of various nationalities and religious groups were absorbed into the burgeoning Ottoman Empire. Each group was organized as a *vilayet;* that is, as a separate minority under the leadership of an appointed shaykh, who answered directly to the sultan and his officials. Each vilayet was allowed a degree of self-regulation under its shaykh, and its rights were protected.

By the 1450s, the empire had grown to include all of Asia Minor and most of the Balkans south of modern-day Hungary. Of the Byzantine Empire, only the great capital of Constantinople remained. After several failed attempts to capture the great fortress city of the Christians on the western side of the narrow waterway separating Europe

**MEHMED THE CONQUEROR.** The conqueror of Constantinople is portrayed in this Turkish miniature smelling a rose, symbolizing his cultural interests, as well as gripping a handkerchief, a symbol of his power.

Topkapi Palace Museum, Istanbul, Turkey/Giraudon/Bridgeman Art Library from Asia, Sultan Mehmed the Conqueror (ruled 1451–1481) succeeded in taking this prize. A long siege weakened the Christians' resistance, and the sultan's new bronze cannon destroyed the walls. In 1453, the city finally surrendered. Under the new name of Istanbul, it became the capital of the Ottoman Empire from that time forward. By the reign of **Suleiman the Magnificent** (r. 1520–1566), Hungary, Romania, southern Poland, and southern Russia had been added to the sultan's domain, while in North Africa and the Middle East all of the Islamic states from Morocco to Persia had accepted his overlordship (see Map 27.1). At this stage, Ottoman military power was unmatched in the world.

## Ottoman Government

Ottoman glory reached its apex during the reign of Suleiman the Magnificent, a sultan whose resources and abilities certainly matched any of his fellow rulers in an age of formidable women and men (Elizabeth I of England, Akbar the Great in India, and Ivan the Terrible in Russia). The government he presided over was composed of the "ruling institution" and the "religious institution." At the head of both stood the sultan. The ruling institution was what we would call the civil government, composed of various levels of officials from the **grand vizier** (prime minister) down. Most members of the ruling institution were originally non-Muslims who had converted to the Muslim faith.

The religious institution was parallel to the ruling institution. Its members were collectively the *ulama,* or learned men of the law, the *Sharia,* which was derived from the holy book of Islam, the Qur'an. The sultan appointed a high official as the head of this vast bureaucracy called the ***Shaykh al-Islam***. The religious institution lent its great moral authority to the ruling institution. It was in effect a junior partner of the government. In the ordinary course of events, conflict between the two was unthinkable.

The army was part of the ruling institution. The Ottoman army was far superior to European militaries by virtue of its professionalization and discipline. At its heart

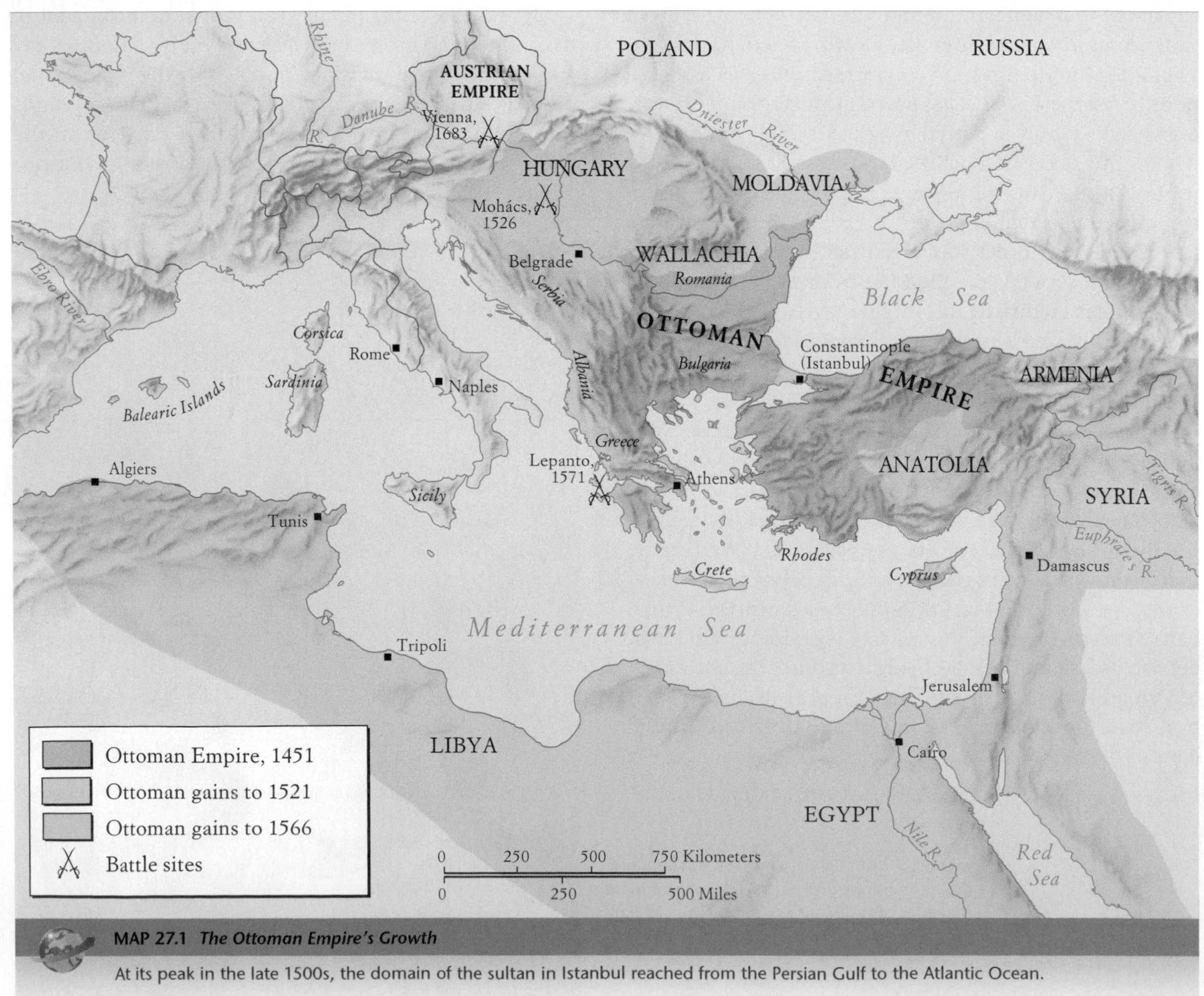


**MAP 27.1** *The Ottoman Empire's Growth*

At its peak in the late 1500s, the domain of the sultan in Istanbul reached from the Persian Gulf to the Atlantic Ocean.

were the well-trained and well-armed **janissaries**, an elite infantry corps. The Ottomans used a system called the ***devshirme*** to staff the janissary units of the army and other high positions within the sultan's administration. Essentially this system was based on seizing Balkan Christian boys at a tender age, converting them to Islam, and giving them unlimited chances to advance themselves in both army and government. The system was designed to create new units of the army and the ruling institution, staffed by servants whose only loyalty was to the sultan. Some of the most brilliant leaders of the Ottoman state in the sixteenth through eighteenth centuries were these willing slaves of the sultan (as they proudly termed themselves), recruited from the infidel.

Through the devshirme, the Ottoman state for many years successfully avoided the weakening of the central authority that was inevitable with the kind of feudal system Orhan had created in the fourteenth century. Instead, by the time of Mehmed and Suleiman, the bulk of the standing army was a mobile, permanent corps that could be shifted about throughout the huge empire controlled by Istanbul. Therefore, aside from the cavalry corps, most soldiers came to depend on salaries paid directly to them by the central government. The Janissaries and other new infantry corpsmen remained loyal to the central government alone because of their lack of local connections and the fact that they rarely remained in one place very long.

As long as the Janissaries conformed to this ideal, the Ottoman governmental system operated smoothly and effectively. The provincial authorities obeyed the central government or were soon replaced and punished. But after about 1650, when the professional army was able to obtain land and develop the connections to purely local affairs that landholding entailed, a lengthy period of decline commenced.

## Non-Muslims under Ottoman Rule

The treatment of non-Muslims varied over time. In the early centuries of Ottoman rule (1300–1600), official treatment of Christians and Jews was generally fair. These "People of the Book" were distinctly limited in what we would call civil rights, could not hold office, could not proselytize for converts or bear arms, and suffered many other disadvantages, but they were not forced to convert to Islam and could run their own civil and cultural affairs on the local and even provincial level. They were taxed, but not excessively. Until the seventeenth century, the public lives of minorities within the *vilayet* system seem to have assured them more security than most Jews or Muslims living under Christian rule could expect. On the other hand, the brutality with which the Ottomans treated defeated opponents and the forceful application of the *devshirme* proved the limits of Ottoman tolerance for the rights of subject populations.

The majority of the Balkan population was Orthodox Christian. Under Turkish rule, those peasants were almost always decently treated until the seventeenth century. They were allowed to elect their own headmen in their villages; go to Christian services; and otherwise baptize, marry, and bury their dead according to their traditions. Like other non-Muslims, they were more heavily taxed than Muslims, but they were allowed to own land and businesses and to move about freely.

In the course of the seventeenth century, however, the condition of the Balkan Christians deteriorated badly for several reasons, including the central government's increasing need for tax funds, the increasing hostility toward all infidels at Istanbul, and a moral breakdown in provincial and local government. "The fish stinks from the head," says an old Turkish proverb, and the bad example of the harem government in the capital was having effects in the villages.

During the eighteenth century, the condition of the Balkan Christians had become sufficiently oppressive that they began looking for liberation by their independent neighbors, Austria and Russia. From now on, the Ottomans had to treat their Christian subjects as potential or actual traitors, which made the tensions between ruler and ruled still worse. By the nineteenth and twentieth centuries, the treatment of Christian minorities, such as the Greeks, Armenians, and others, at times was about as bad in the Islamic Near East as any people have ever had to endure. Unfortunately for the Balkan states today, these old hatreds that Ottoman rule brought to the region remain the primary source of the ethnic and religious conflicts that continue to plague it.

## The Zenith of the Ottoman Empire: Suleiman and After

The Ottoman Empire reached its peak during the reign of *Suleiman the Magnificent* in the sixteenth century. Many consider Suleiman to have been the empire's greatest ruler. Even in a dynasty that had many long-reigning sultans, the length of Suleiman's rule was remarkably long, from 1520 to1566. His was an outstandingly stable rule in which it seemed that everything the sultan attempted to accomplish succeeded.

Immediately, when Suleiman came to the throne at 26 years of age, he was successful in extending control over all of North Africa. For many years, the Spanish and the Portuguese had attacked and occupied the port cities of Morocco and Algeria. To deal with them, Suleiman formed an alliance with a corsair by the name of Khair ad-Din Barbarossa. The attacks that followed by the combined fleets of Khair ad-Din and the well-armed Ottomans were effective in pushing the Iberians out of Tunis and Algiers. Suleiman also seized the island of Rhodes, which the Christian Knights of St. John hitherto had defended successfully against the Ottomans for centuries. With these victories, Suleiman came close to rivaling ancient Rome by winning complete control over the entire Mediterranean Sea. In southeastern Europe, the sultan's huge army seized the cities of Belgrade and Budapest. Suleiman's next and boldest move was against the capital of the Austrian Empire, Vienna. After a siege that lasted through the summer in 1529, autumn and colder weather finally obliged Suleiman to make an orderly withdrawal. Although the attack failed, it marked the crest of a long wave of Ottoman expansion in Europe.

As they had stacked conquest on top of conquest, the Ottoman sultans increasingly had come to be regarded by Muslims all over as the new caliphs of the Muslim *Umma* (see Chapter 14). With the golden age of the Abbasids long past, Muslims needed a powerful ruler who could assume the responsibilities of religious leadership that were essential to Islam. Ottomans such as Mehmed and Suleiman filled that need admirably. Besides his attacks on Christian Europe, for example, Suleiman defeated a powerful Safavid Shi'ite state in Iran (see following section) and managed to occupy Iraq. He also took charge of making the crucial arrangements for the annual pilgrimages to Mecca. In addition, he remodeled the Tomb of the Prophet Muhammad in Medina and the famous Dome of the Rock mosque in Jerusalem.

Despite the continued conquests and the unprecedented levels of prestige and influence achieved by the sultanate under this monarch, already harbingers of future problems surfaced during Suleiman's reign. He introduced new practices that were followed by the sultans who came after him, all of which ultimately proved disadvantageous to the empire. For example, after the demoralizing losses of his favorite grand vizier and his son, Mustafa, to harem intrigues (see Evidence of the Past), Suleiman showed less and less interest in the day-to-day details of governing than had been the case beforehand. He withdrew from daily meetings of his ***divan,*** or royal council, allowing his new grand viziers to assume power, if not actual responsibility. The annual *jihads* and conquests continued, but Suleiman and his successors again deferred to their viziers and other military officials (who were given the title of *pasha*) for their execution.

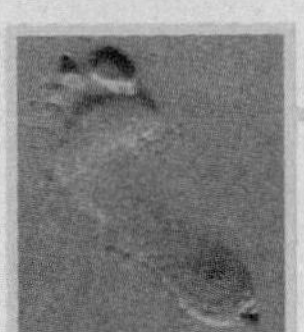

EVIDENCE OF THE PAST

## Harem Intrigue in the Death of Suleiman's Favorite Son

**The following is an eyewitness account** of a visit with Suleiman by Ogier Ghislain de Busbecq, who had been sent as the Austrian ambassador to the court of the Sultan near the end of his reign. As can be seen, Busbecq was impressed by the Sultan. However, take particular note of the hint of intrigue in the Sultan's harem with the account of the scheming of Roxilana, his favorite wife, to have Suleiman's favorite son, Mustapha, put to death.

> The Sultan was seated on a rather low sofa, no more than a foot from the ground and spread with many costly coverlets and cushions embroidered with exquisite work. Near him were his bows and arrows. His expression, as I have said, is anything but smiling, and has a sternness which, though sad is full of majesty . . .
>
> . . . He is beginning to feel the weight of years, but his dignity of demeanor and his general physical appearance are worthy of the ruler of so vast an empire. . . . Even in his earlier years he did not indulge in wine or in those unnatural vices to which the Turks are often addicted. Even his bitterest critics can find nothing more serious to allege against him than his undue submission to his wife [Roxilana] and its result in his somewhat [hasty] action in putting Mustapha . . . to death, which is generally [blamed on Roxilana's] employment of love potions and incantations. It is generally agreed that, ever since he promoted her to the rank of his lawful wife, he has possessed no [slave wives], although there is no law to prevent his doing so. He is a strict guardian of his religion and its ceremonies. . . . For his age—he has almost reached his sixtieth year—he enjoys quite good health, though his bad complexion may be due to some hidden malady; and indeed it is generally believed that he has an incurable ulcer or gangrene on his leg. The defect of complexion he remedies by painting his face with a coating of red powder.

### *Analyze and Interpret*

What effect did the death of Mustapha seem to have on the great sultan?

Source: From Edward Foster, trans. *The Turkish Letters of Ogier Ghiselin de Busbecq, Imperial Ambassador at Constantinople, 1554-1562* (Oxford: Clarendon Press, 1927), pp. 58–59, 65–66.

History Now™

***To read about a visit to another of Suleiman's wives, point your browser to the documents area of* HistoryNow.**

The remainder of the sixteenth century and most of the seventeenth amounted to a stalemate between the Islamic East and the Christian West. This period saw growing difficulties for the Ottomans and the other great Muslim empires, especially in their dealings with the West. Yet, there was little or no actual loss of territory. In 1683, the Ottomans even managed again to muster sufficient resources for a second assault on Vienna. This assault failed, but unlike the failure of the first one in 1529, this one was followed by a disastrous defeat at the hands of a Habsburg army led by Eugen of Savoy. Finally, in 1699, the Ottomans were forced to sign the **Treaty of Karlowitz**, a momentous document that, after centuries of continuous expansion, forced the Ottoman sultan for the first time to cede territory to his European opponents.

## The Muslim Empires in Persia and India

In the sixteenth and seventeenth centuries, the Sufi and Shi'ite divisions, which had existed within the theology of Islam for many centuries, became noticeably stronger. The Sufi mystics sought a different path to God than orthodox Muslims (see Chapter 14). Some of the Sufi of Central Asia adopted the historical views of the Shi'ites, who reject all of Muhammad's successors who were not related directly to him by blood or marriage. In the eighth century, as we saw in Chapter 15, this belief resulted in a major split between the Shi'ite minority and the Sunni majority, who believed that the caliph, or successor to the Prophet, could be anyone qualified by nobility of purpose and abilities. From that original dispute over succession gradually emerged a series of doctrinal differences. Much of Islamic history can be best conceived of within the framework of the rivalry between the Shi'ite and Sunni factions.

### *The Safavid Realm*

Within the Islamic world, the greatest rival of the Ottoman Empire after the sixteenth century was the **Safavid Empire** of Persia. Therefore, it is ironic that they shared similar origins. The embryonic Safavid state began in the region of Tabriz, west of the Caspian Sea, and like the Ottoman ghazi state it was organized around a Turkish Sufi association. This brotherhood took its name from its founder, Safi ad-Din (shortened as "Safavid"), who claimed to be a descendant of Muhammad. By the fifteenth century, the Safavid state came to differ from the Ottoman orders in one important aspect, however: it converted to Shi'ite Islam. The Safavids became a major threat to the Ottomans when they evolved a militant theology that advocated the supremacy of Shi'ism through the force of arms. Spreading their views through propaganda, they converted many Turkish tribes in Iran, Syria, and eastern Asia Minor. These Shi'ites took over much of the Persian Muslim state, and from that base they waged frequent wars on their Sunni competitors to the west. In the early 1500s, a leader named Ismail, claiming to be a representative of the hidden Shi'a Imam, succeeded in capturing much of Persia and Iraq, including Baghdad, and made himself *shah* (king). With these successes, Ismail proclaimed Shi'ism to be the official cult of the Safavid state. Thus was founded the Safavid Empire, which lasted for two centuries and was a strong competitor to the Ottomans, who were Sunni Muslims (see Map 27.2). This doctrinal opposition to Sunni Islam and political rivalry with the Ottoman Empire became especially sharp by the early seventeenth century, and it reached its height during the reign of Shah Abbas I (ruled 1587–1629), the greatest of the Safavid rulers.

The European opponents of the Turks, who were then still established deep in central Europe, aided Shah Abbas in his conflicts with Istanbul. Several foreigners occupied high positions in his government, as Abbas strove to avoid favoring any one group within his multiethnic realm. His beautifully planned new capital at Isfahan was a center of exquisite art and artisanry, notably in textiles, rugs, ceramics, and paintings. The Safavid period is considered the cultural high point of the long history of Persia and the Iranian people. Just as in the case of Suleiman the Magnificent, the reign of Abbas represented the high point of Safavid rule in Persia. Following his reign, a gradual decline resulted from encroachments by highly independent Turco-Iranian tribesman. Making things even more complicated were the gradual and caustic influences of European imperialists The empire slowly lost vigor and collapsed altogether in the 1720s under Turkish and Afghani attacks. It is worth noting that, like the European Christians, the various subdivisions within Islam fought as much against each other as against the infidel. A common religion is rarely able to counter the claims of territorial, economic, or military advantage in the choice between war and peace.

### *The Mughal Empire*

When we last looked at the Indian subcontinent in Chapter 16, we commented on the gradual revival of Hindu culture under the Gupta Dynasty in the fourth and fifth centuries C.E. and the Golden Age that ensued. Very early in Islam's history, during the late 600s, Arabs and Persians had moved into the Indus valley and seized the province of Sind at its lower extremity. This was the beginning of a long, ongoing struggle between Hindu and Muslim in the northwest borderlands. Out of this struggle, 800 years after the province of Sind was captured, one of the most

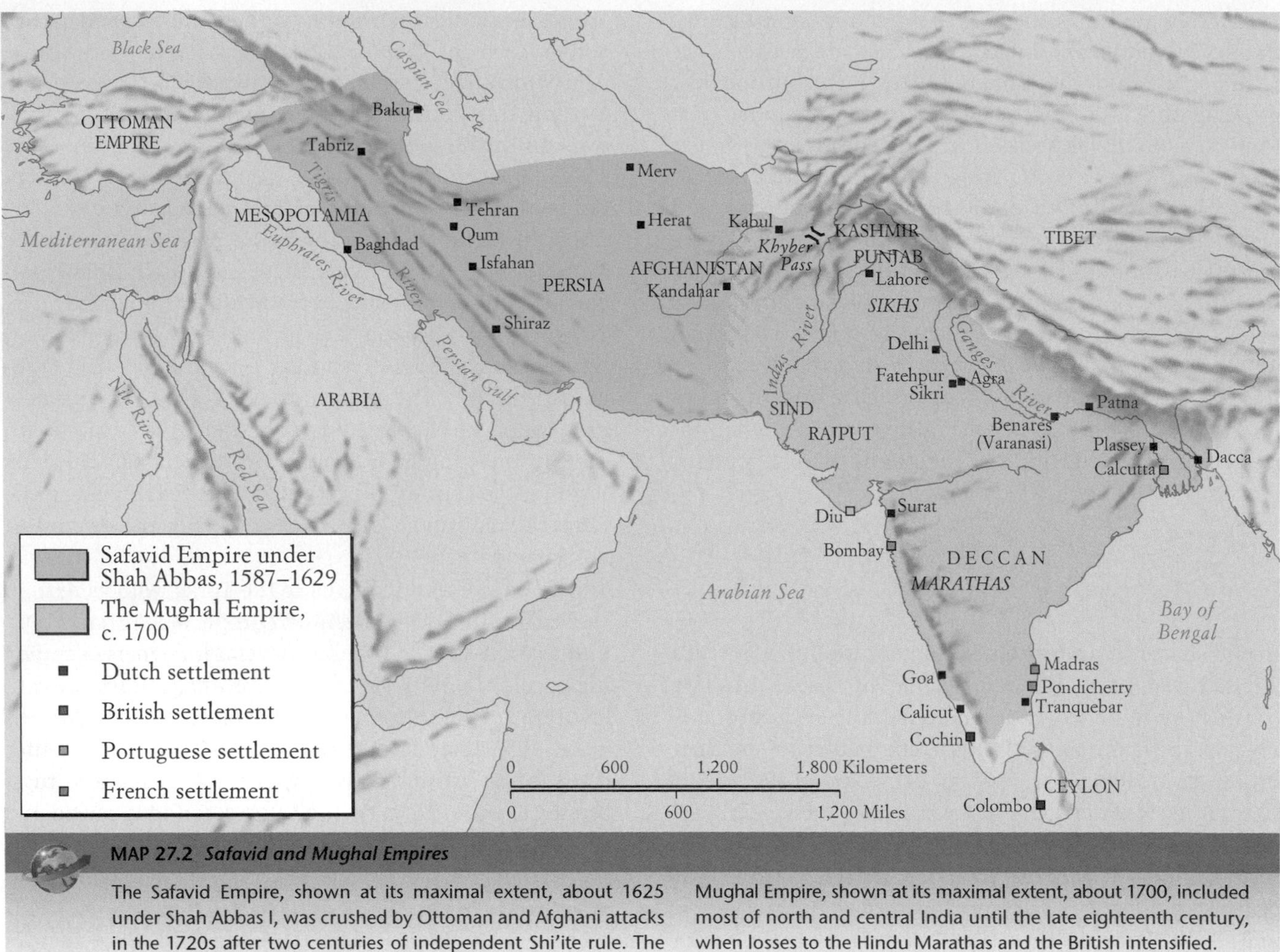


**MAP 27.2** *Safavid and Mughal Empires*

The Safavid Empire, shown at its maximal extent, about 1625 under Shah Abbas I, was crushed by Ottoman and Afghani attacks in the 1720s after two centuries of independent Shi'ite rule. The Mughal Empire, shown at its maximal extent, about 1700, included most of north and central India until the late eighteenth century, when losses to the Hindu Marathas and the British intensified.

impressive Muslim empires in world history was created in northern India by a branch of the Turks known as the **Mughals**.

The word *Mughal* is a corruption of the name *Mongol,* to whom the Turks were distantly related. Muslims from Central Asia had raided and attempted to invade northern India since the 900s but had been repulsed by the dominant Hindus. As was seen in Chapter 16, in the early 1200s, the Delhi Sultanate was established by a Turkish slave army operating from their base at Ghazni in Afghanistan. Within a century, the sultanate controlled much of the Indian subcontinent, reaching down into the Deccan. Divorced from their Hindu subjects by every aspect of culture, language, and religion, the sultans and their courts attempted at first to convert the Hindus and then, failing that, to humiliate and exploit them.

The original dynasty was soon overthrown, but it was succeeded by other Central Asian Muslims who fought among themselves for mastery even as they extended their rule southward. Aided by continuing disunity among their Hindu opponents, Mongols, Turks, Persians, and Afghanis fought for control of the entire width of the Indian subcontinent from the Indus to the Ganges. At last, a leader, Babur, who was able to persuade his fellow princes to follow him, arose again from the Afghan base. Brilliantly successful battle tactics allowed him to conquer much of the territory once ruled by the Delhi sultans. By the time of his death in 1530, he had established the Mughal Muslim Indian dynasty. This man's grandson and successor was Akbar the Great (ruled 1556–1605). Akbar was the most distinguished Indian ruler since Ashoka in the third century B.C.E. He was perhaps the greatest statesman Asia has ever produced.

Akbar earned his title "the Great" in several different ways. He splendidly fulfilled the usual demands made on a warrior-king to crush his enemies and enlarge his kingdom. Under his guidance and generalship, the Mughal Empire came to control most of the subcontinent—the first time a central government had accomplished this feat since the day of the Mauryan kings. Second, despite his own youthful illiteracy, he completely reorganized the central government, developed an efficient multinational bureaucracy to run it, and introduced many innovative reforms in society. Third and most strikingly,

Akbar practiced a policy of religious and social toleration that was most unusual in the sixteenth century. He was at least formally a Muslim, ruling a Muslim-dominated empire, but he allowed all faiths including Christianity to flourish and to compete for converts in his lands.

Because most of his subjects were Hindus, Akbar thought it particularly important to heal the breach between them and the Muslim minority. His initiatives toward creating an ethnically equal society were remarkable. He married a Hindu princess, and Aurangzeb, one of his sons by a Hindu woman, eventually succeeded him. Hindus were given equal opportunities to obtain all but the highest government posts, and the Hindu warrior caste called Rajputs became his willing allies in governance. By repealing the odious poll tax (*jizya*) on non-Muslims, Akbar earned the lasting gratitude of most of his subjects. The sorrow that existed among both Muslims and non-Muslims at Akbar's death was the most sincere tribute to his character.

Midway in his long reign, around 1580, Akbar decided to build an entirely new capital at Fatehpur Sikri, some distance from the traditional royal cities of Delhi and Agra. This palace-city was soon abandoned and is now a ruin, but its beauty and magnificence were famous throughout the Muslim world. The court library reputedly possessed more than 24,000 volumes, making it easily the largest collection of books in the world at this time. Akbar's love of learning encouraged sages of all religions and all parts of the Asian world to come to his court at his expense as teachers and students. (See the Science and Technology box about his interest in science.) His cultivation of the official Persian language brought new dimensions to Indian literature. The ties with Persian culture enabled by the language contributed substantially to the revival of a sense of national unity among Hindus, which they had lacked since the Gupta era.

***Society and Culture*** India under the Mughals remained a hodgepodge of different peoples, as well as different religions and languages. Besides the civilized Indians, there were still many tribal groups, especially in the rain forest regions of the eastern coast, whom neither Hindu nor Muslims considered fully human and often enslaved.

The caste system continued to be refined in constant subdivisions among Hindus. Although the Muslims never acknowledged the caste system, it did serve as a useful wall to minimize frictions between subject and ruler. Despite extensive business and administrative dealings between the two religious communities, social intercourse was unusual at any level. Even among the majority Hindus, culturally based barriers existed that had nothing to do with caste.

A new religion, derived from the doctrines of both Hindu and Muslim, arose in the Far North during the seventeenth century. At first dedicated to finding a middle ground between the two dominant faiths, it eventually became a separate creed, called the religion of the **Sikhs**. Generally closer to Hindu belief (but rejecting caste), the Sikhs fought the last Mughal rulers and dominated the northwestern Punjab province. (They currently represent perhaps 5 percent of the total population of India and strive still for full autonomy on either side of the India–Pakistan border.)

After Emperor Aurangzeb (r. 1668–1707), the governing class was almost entirely Muslim again, and aspiring Hindus sometimes imitated their habits of dress and manners. A notable example was *purdah,* the seclusion of women, which was adopted by the upper castes of Hindus. Many foreigners, especially from the Middle East, came into the country to make their fortunes, often at the luxurious and free-spending courts of not only the emperor but also subsidiary officials. Prevented by imperial decrees from accumulating heritable land and office, the Muslim upper class took much pride in funding institutions of learning and supporting artists of all types.

Wolfgang Kaehler

**Akbar's Palace at Fatehpur Sikri.** The palace-city erected by Akbar the Great outside Agra is now mostly ruins. It was abandoned soon after Akbar's death by his successor as Great Mughal. However, the blending of traditional Indian materials and architectural features with Islamic motifs fit with Akbar's policies that encouraged the creation of a unified, Indo-Islamic society.

SCIENCE AND TECHNOLOGY

## Practical Science in Akbar's India

**Akbar the Great lived a century** earlier than Russia's Peter the Great, but both rulers had certain similar traits that are striking. They shared a strong interest in practical application of scientific knowledge and the desire to learn by doing. We know of Akbar's interests both from the reporting of several Jesuit priests who resided at the Delhi court while attempting to convert the emperor to Christianity and from the memoirs of the Muslim courtier-scientist, Abul Fazl, one of Akbar's favorites.

In 1580, Jesuit father Henriques noted that "Akbar knows a little of all trades, and sometimes loves to practise them before his people, either as a carpenter, or as a blacksmith, or as an armorer." Another said that he "is so devoted to building that he sometimes quarries stone himself along with the other workmen." These inclinations, so reminiscent of Peter during his grand tour of western Europe, were also employed in learning the goldsmith's and lacemaker's trades and the manufacture of guns. Like the Russian, Akbar believed that to truly value a product by another's hand, you must first learn how to make it yourself.

Akbar prided himself also in his inventions—or what he claimed were his inventions. Abul Fazl tells us that the prince originated the use of a *khas*-frame, a method of using hollow bamboo stalks stuffed with a fragrant root called *khas,* then pouring water over the bamboo, with the effect of cooling the area within the frame, "so that winter seems to arrive in the midst of summer."

Not only that, but His Majesty was a pioneer of refrigeration technique. He apparently was familiar with basic chemical reactions, so that he could enjoy a cooling drink.

> [Akbar] made saltpeter, which creates such tumult in the form of gunpowder, the means of cooling water, so that both the poor and the rich were made happy. . . . A ser of water is poured into a bottle made of pewter or silver and its mouth is closed. In a pan two and one half sers of saltpeter are mixed with five sers of water, and the closed bottle is moved round and round within that mixture for the space of half a *ghari* [about twelve minutes]. The water within the bottle gets very cold.

### *Analyze and Interpret*

If Akbar and Peter were alike in their fascination with technology, can you point out some ways in which their personalities were different? Refer to Chapter 26.

Source: Irfan Habib, *Akbar and His India* (Calcutta: Oxford University Press, 1997), p. 128 ff.

In the fine arts, the Mughal rulers made a conscious and successful effort to introduce the great traditions of Persian culture into India, where they blended with the native forms in literature, drama, and architecture. The quatrains of Omar Khayyam's ***Rubaiyat***, which have long been famous throughout the world, held a special appeal for Mughal poets, who attempted to imitate them (see the Patterns of Belief box for an excerpt from the *Rubaiyat*).

The **Taj Mahal**, tomb of the much-loved wife of the seventeenth-century emperor Shah Jahan, is the most famous example of a Persian-Indian architectural style, but it is only one of many, as exemplified by the ruins of Fatehpur Sikri, the equally imposing Red Fort at Agra, as well as a whole series of mosques. Much painting of every type and format from book miniatures to frescos also survives from this era and shows traces of Arab and Chinese, as well as Persian, influence. By this time, Muslim artists ignored the ancient religious prohibition against reproducing the human form. The wonderful variety of portraits, court scenes, gardens, and townscapes is exceeded only by the precision and color sense of the artists.

The Muslims had an extensive system of religious schools (*madresh*), while the local Brahmins took care of the minimal needs for literacy in the Hindu villages by acting as open-air schoolmasters. Increasingly, the Muslims used the newly created Urdu language (now the official language in Pakistan) rather than the Sanskrit of the Hindus.

Like the Safavid Persians to their west, the Mughals were an exceptionally cosmopolitan dynasty, well aware of cultural affairs in and outside of their own country and anxious to make a good impression in foreign eyes. They welcomed European travelers. Like Marco Polo's reports about Kubilai Khan's China, the sixteenth- and seventeenth-century tales of visitors to the Great Mughal were only belatedly and grudgingly believed. Such cultivation and display of luxury were still beyond Europeans' experience.

***The Mughal Economy*** The existing agrarian system was but slightly disturbed by the substitution of Muslim for Hindu authority. Beginning with the Delhi sultans, courtiers and officials were awarded a parcel of land

# The *Rubaiyat* of Omar Khayyam

**PERHAPS THE MOST-QUOTED POEM** in the English language is a nineteenth-century translation of a twelfth-century Persian philosopher, who may or may not have written the original. The *Rubaiyat* of Omar Khayyam is a collection of four-line verses that became associated with his name long after his death in 1122. Edward Fitzgerald, who had taught himself Persian while passing his days as a Victorian country gentleman, published them in 1859 in a very free translation. Instantly finding a public, the *Rubaiyat* was reprinted several times during Fitzgerald's life and many more since then.

The poem speaks in unforgettably lovely words of our common fate. Morality is all too often a negation of joy. Death comes all too soon: in wine is the only solace. The verse story, of which only a fragment is given here, opens with the poet watching the break of dawn after a night of revelry:

1
Awake! for Morning in the Bowl of Night
Has flung the Stone that puts the Stars to Flight
And lo! the Hunter of the East has caught
The Sultan's Turret in a Noose of Light.

2
Dreaming when Dawn's Left Hand was in the Sky
I heard a Voice within the Tavern cry,
"Awake, my Little ones, and fill the Cup
"Before Life's Liquor in its Cup be dry."

7
Come, fill the Cup, and in the Fire of Spring
The winter Garment of Repentance fling
The Bird of Time has but a little way
To fly—and Lo! the Bird is on the Wing.

14
The Worldly Hope men set their Hearts upon
Turns Ashes—or it prospers; and anon,
Like Snow upon the Desert's dusty Face
Lighting a little Hour or two—is gone.

15
And those who husbanded the Golden Grain
And those who flung it to the Winds like Rain
Alike to no such aureate Earth are turn'd*
As, buried once, Men want dug up again.

16
I think that never blows† so red
The Rose as where some buried Caesar bled;
That every Hyacinth the Garden wears
Dropt in its Lap from some once lovely Head.

19
Ah, my Beloved, fill the Cup that clears
Today of past Regrets and future Fears—
*Tomorrow?*—Why, Tomorrow I may be
Myself with Yesterday's Sev'n Thousand Years.

20
Lo! some we loved, the loveliest and best
That Time and Fate of all their Vintage prest
Have drunk their Cup a Round or two before,
And one by one crept silently to Rest.

21
And we, that now make merry in the Room
They left, and Summer dresses in new Bloom,
Ourselves must we beneath the Couch of Earth
Descend, ourselves to make a Couch—for whom?

22
Ah, make the most of what we yet may spend,
Before we too into the Dust descend;
Dust into Dust, and under Dust, to lie,
Sans Wine, sans Song, sans Singer, and—sans End!

23
Alike for those who for TODAY prepare,
And those that after a TOMORROW stare,
A Muezzin from the Tower of Darkness cries
"Fools! your Reward is neither here nor there!"

24
Why, all the Saints and Sages who discuss'd
Of the Two Worlds so learnedly, are thrust
Like foolish Prophets forth; their Words to Scorn
Are scatter'd, and their Mouths are stop'd with Dust.

25
Oh, come with old Khayyam, and leave the Wise
To talk; one thing is certain, that Life flies;
One thing is certain, and the Rest is Lies;
The Flower that once has blown for ever dies.

*"Aureate earth . . ." means once buried, the body is no golden treasure.

†The verb "to blow" here means "to bloom."

## *Analyze and Interpret*

Do you sympathize with the poetic point of view? Why or why not? Would a Sufi mystic or a Christian monk have agreed with it? Given the religious origins and foundation of Islamic societies, how do you suppose such a point of view would have been accommodated?

Source: *The Rubaiyat of Omar Khayyam,* trans. and ed. Edward Fitzgerald (New York: Dover, 1991).

**History Now™**

***To read more of the* Rubaiyat, *point your browser to the documents area of* HistoryNow.**

Bridgeman Art Library

**The Taj Mahal.** This seventeenth-century tomb was designed in Indo-Persian style as the resting place of the beloved wife of Mughal emperor Shah Jahan. Building commenced in 1632 and was completed eleven years later. Four identical facades surround a central dome 240 feet high. The whole complex is supplemented by gardens and the river that flows beside it.

consonant with their dignity and sufficient taxes to allow them to maintain a specified number of fighting men and their equipment. This system of rewarding individuals who rendered either civil or military duties to the state was called the *mansabdari*. Some mansabdars maintained small armies of 5,000 or even 10,000 men. When the sultanate weakened, they established themselves as petty kings, joining the universal fray in northern India for territory and prestige. This system was carried over into the Mughal period. Perhaps half of the mansabdars under Akbar were Hindus, creating a loyalty to the imperial government that continued even under Aurangzeb's determined Islamic regime.

The peasants on the mansabdar's domain were somewhat better off than their contemporary counterparts in Europe or China. Most of them were tenants rather than outright proprietors, but they were not yet haunted by the shortage of agrarian land that would arrive, as it did in China, during the later eighteenth century. Their lives were bounded by the village, caste, and tax collectors. The latter were generally no worse than in other places, and their demand for one-third to one-half of the crop was bearable if the harvest was productive.

## Summary

The three principal Muslim empires that occupied most of the Asian continent between 1250 and 1800 were able to hold their own militarily and culturally with their Chinese, Hindu, and Christian competitors. Often warring among themselves, they were still able to maintain their borders and prestige for 200 to 600 years. After the terrible destruction rendered by the Mongols, the Muslims of the Middle East absorbed their invaders and rebuilt their cities. Chief and most enduring among their states were those of the Ottoman Turks and the Indian Mughals. The Ottomans profited from the Mongol destruction of Baghdad and the Rum Sultanate by erecting their own powerful *ghazi* state and even eventually took Constantinople (Istanbul) for their capital. Under a series of warrior-sultans, the Ottoman leaders extended their power to the gates of Vienna before internal weakness drove them back in the 1700s. By the nineteenth century, the Ottomans had become so weak that they were sustained only by the rivalry of the major European powers. Thus, the dreaded sixteenth-century empire of Suleiman had been degraded to the sick man of Europe so-called by a British statesman.

For two centuries, the Shi'ite dynasty of the Safavids reclaimed grandeur for Persia and Iraq, where they ruled until they were brought down by the superior power of their Sunni rivals in Istanbul. The Mughals descended on Hindu India in the early sixteenth century and set up one of the few regimes in Indian history that managed to rule most of this intensely varied subcontinent successfully. Under the extraordinary Akbar the Great, this regime reached its apex, only to decline slowly during the following century.

## Identification Terms

Test your knowledge of this chapter's key concepts by defining the following terms. If you can't recall the meaning of certain terms, refresh your memory by looking up the boldfaced term in the chapter, turning to the Glossary at the end of the book, or working with the flashcards that are available on the *World Civilizations* Companion Website **http://history.wadsworth.com/adler04**.

*dervish*
*devshirme*
*divan*
*ghazis*
grand vizier
janissaries
Karlowitz, Treaty of
Manzikert, Battle of
Mughals
*Rubaiyat*
Safavid Empire
*Shaykh al-Islam*
Sikhs
Suleiman the Magnificent
Taj Mahal

## Test Your Knowledge

Test your knowledge of this chapter by answering the following questions. Complete answers appear at the end of the book. You may also take this quiz interactively and find even more quiz questions on the *World Civilizations* Companion Website **http://history.wadsworth.com/adler04**.

1. Taken together at their height, the Ottoman, Mughal, and Safavid empires
   a. extended from the Atlantic Ocean to Australia.
   b. included all of Asia except the Japanese islands.
   c. could be termed a united political territory.
   d. extended from the Atlantic to the Ganges River valley.
   e. included such diverse areas as Iraq, India, and Italy.
2. The Ottoman Empire began
   a. as a Shia *dervish* order.
   b. as a *ghazi* frontier state.
   c. as a Byzantine state.
   d. subordinate to the Abbasid caliphs.
   e. as a combination of three formerly competing dynasties.
3. Which of the following was *not* accepted by Ottoman statecraft?
   a. The precepts and prescriptions of the Qur'an
   b. The function of the sultan as leader of the faithful
   c. The favored situation of the Muslims over the non-Muslim subjects
   d. The necessity to have at least one major Christian ally
   e. A grand vizier who served as the highest civil official
4. The treatment of non-Muslims in the Balkans under Ottoman rule
   a. deteriorated sharply in the seventeenth and eighteenth centuries.
   b. improved as the powers of the sultan diminished.
   c. tended to become better the farther away they were from the capital.
   d. depended entirely on the whims of the ruling sultan.
   e. deteriorated for a short time in the seventeenth century, but by 1900 was much improved.
5. Suleiman the Magnificent accomplished all of these *except*
   a. driving the Europeans out of North Africa.
   b. conquering Vienna.
   c. remodeling several monumental buildings.
   d. assuming leadership of the Islamic Empire.
   e. taking charge of the arrangements for the pilgrimage to Mecca.
6. Shi'ite Muslims
   a. believe the Qur'an is only partly correct.
   b. make up the largest single group of Islamic people.
   c. reject the prophetic vocation of Muhammad.
   d. believe the leader of Islam must be descended from the prophet Muhammad.
   e. refuse to admit Sufis into their sect.
7. The Ottoman and Safavid empires were similar in one respect: they both were
   a. governed by a sultan and a grand vizier.
   b. organized in their beginnings around a Sufi order.
   c. organized to fight as holy warriors against Christian infidels.
   d. weakened by the demoralizing effects of harem intrigues.
   e. based on the Sunni sect of Islam.

8. The Muslim rulers of the Safavid Dynasty were
   a. the conquerors of Constantinople.
   b. the allies of the Mughals in India.
   c. a Persian family that converted to Shi'ite Islam.
   d. the first conquerors of Persia for Islam.
   e. militant warriors who cared little for the arts.
9. The attitudes and policies of Akbar the Great regarding Hindus were that of
   a. tolerance.
   b. religious fanaticism.
   c. a desire to secularize them if he could not convert them.
   d. indifference.
   e. disdain.
10. The most universally revered of the Indian Mughal rulers was
   a. Aurangzeb.
   b. Akbar.
   c. Ashoka.
   d. Abbas.
   e. Babur.

## InfoTrac College Edition

Visit the source collections at

**http://infotrac.thomsonlearning.com**

and use the Search function with the following key terms:

Ottoman Empire Sufi Sufism

## Wadsworth History Website Resources

Visit the World History Resource Center at **http://history.wadsworth.com/world** for a wealth of general resources, and the *World Civilizations* Companion Website at **http://history.wadsworth.com/adler04** for resources specific to this textbook.

## HistoryNow

Enter *HistoryNow* using the access card that is available for *World Civilizations*. *HistoryNow* will assist you in understanding the content in this chapter with lesson plans generated for your needs. In addition, you can read the following documents, and many more, online:

Sidi Ali Reis, *Mirat ul Memalik* (*The Mirror of Countries*)

Omar Khayyam, the *Rubaiyat*

*Great wealth is from heaven; modest wealth is from diligence.*
Chinese Folk Saying

# 28 China from the Ming through the Early Qing Dynasty

Ming China, 1368–1644

Economic Progress
Urbanization and Technology

The Ming Political System
The Bureaucracy

Dealing with Foreigners

The Manzhou Invaders: Qing Dynasty
Manzhou Government

Qing Culture and Economy
Progress and Problems

| | |
|---|---|
| 1368–1644 | Ming Dynasty |
| 1400s | Maritime expeditions |
| 1500s | First contacts with Europeans |
| 1644–1911 | Qing (Manzhou) Dynasty |
| 1700s | Economic growth; population rises, trade increases |

The ages of China do not coincide with those of Europe. China had no Middle Age or Renaissance of the fourteenth century. The outstanding facts in China's development between 1000 C.E. and 1500 C.E. were the humiliating conquest by the Mongols and their overthrow by the rebellion that began the Ming Dynasty. For more than 200 years, the Ming rulers remained vigorous, providing the Chinese with a degree of stability and prosperity that contemporary Europeans would have envied. But the sustained creative advance in the sciences and basic technologies that had allowed China to overshadow all rivals during the thousand years between the beginning of the Song and the end of the Ming dynasties (600–1600) was slowly drawing to a close. China was being overtaken in these areas by the West, but as late as the eighteenth century, this was hardly evident to anyone. Possessed of an ancient and marvelous high culture, China was still convinced of its own superiority and was as yet far from being forced to admit its weaknesses.

## Ming China, 1368–1644

The Ming was the last pure Chinese dynasty. It began with the overthrow of the hated Mongols, who had ruled China for 100 years. Founded by the peasant Zhu, who had displayed masterful military talents in leading a motley band of rebel armies, the Ming would last 300 years. Zhu, who took the imperial title Hongwu (meaning The Generous Warrior), was an individual of great talents and great cruelty. In many ways, his fierce ruthlessness was reminiscent of the First Emperor. He built the city of Nanjing (Nanking) as his capital near the coast on the Yangtze River. His son and successor, Yongle, was even more talented as a general and an administrator. During Yongle's twenty-two-year reign (1402–1424), China gained more or less its present heartlands, reaching from Korea to Vietnam and inward to Mongolia (see Map 28.1). The eastern half of the Great Wall was rebuilt, and the armies of China were everywhere triumphant against their Mongol and Turkish nomad opponents.

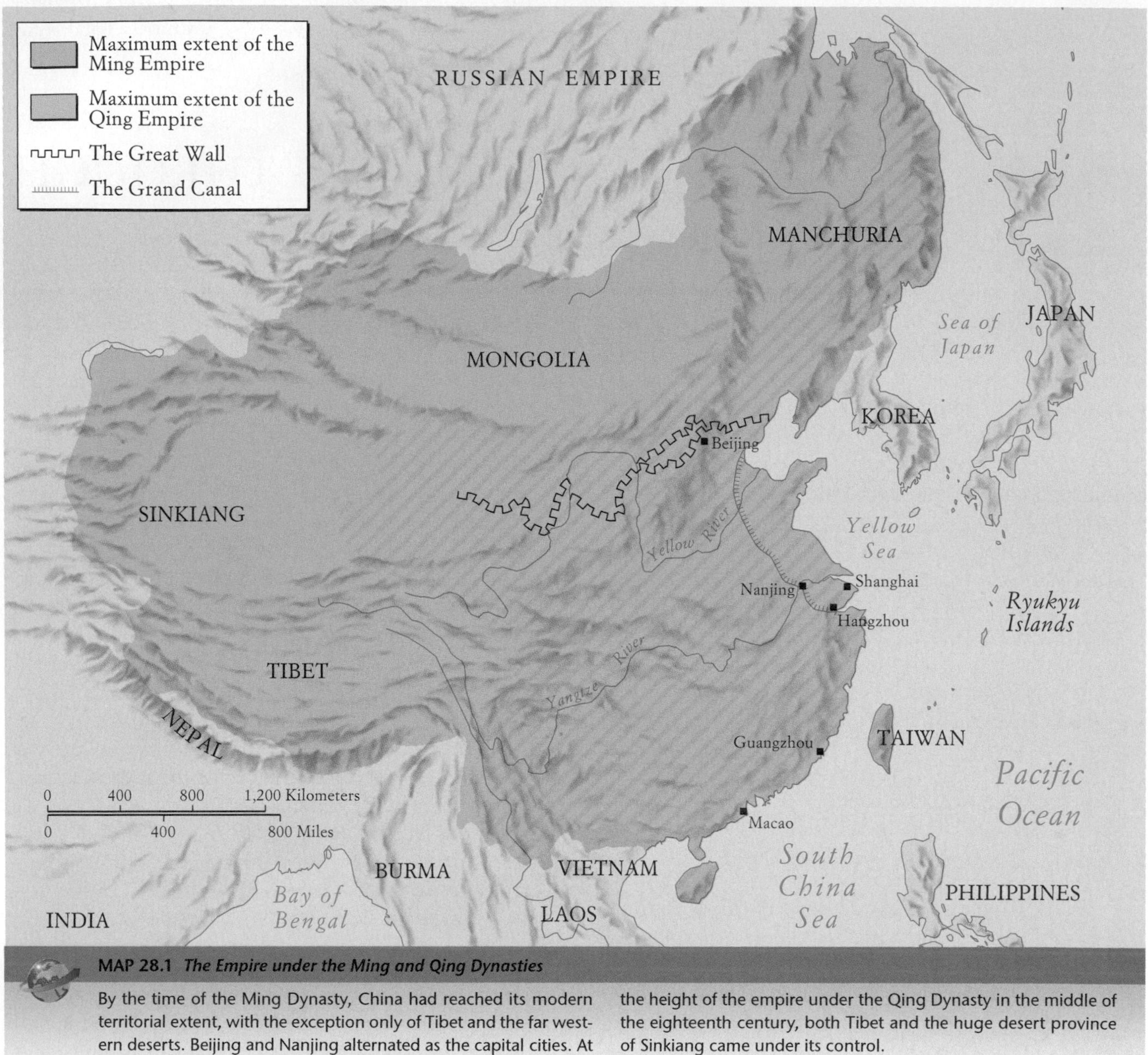


**MAP 28.1** ***The Empire under the Ming and Qing Dynasties***

By the time of the Ming Dynasty, China had reached its modern territorial extent, with the exception only of Tibet and the far western deserts. Beijing and Nanjing alternated as the capital cities. At the height of the empire under the Qing Dynasty in the middle of the eighteenth century, both Tibet and the huge desert province of Sinkiang came under its control.

In the Ming era, China generally had an effective government. One sign of this was the sharp rise in population throughout the dynastic period. When the Ming took power, bubonic plague (the same epidemic that was simultaneously raging in Europe; see Chapter 20) and Mongol savagery had reduced the population to about 60 million, the same size it had been in the Tang period, 500 years earlier. The population rose to perhaps 150 million by 1600, the most dramatic rise yet experienced by any society.

This new population necessitated an equally dramatic rise in food supply. The old center of Chinese food production, the Yangtze basin in south-central China, was not able to meet the demand. A new area for rice cultivation in the extreme south near Vietnam was developed during the Ming, and some new crops from the Americas such as corn, squash, peanuts, and beans made their way into Chinese fields via the trans-Pacific trade with the Portuguese and Spanish. Interestingly, the Irish or white potato, which would become the staple food crop of northern European peasants in the eighteenth century, was introduced into China but did not catch on. Because rice has greater nutritional value than the potato, this turned out to be a boon for China.

## Economic Progress

Commercial activity steadily increased until it was probably more commonplace in China than in any other country of the world by the 1600s. A larger percentage of the labor force was directly engaged in buying, selling, and transporting goods than in any other land. The merchants remained quite low on the social ladder but were acquiring sufficient money to provide them with a comfortable and cultivated lifestyle.

Commercial contact with the Europeans started in the early 1500s with the coming of the Portuguese into the Indian and, soon, the Pacific oceans. Originally welcomed, the Portuguese behaved so badly that the Chinese quickly limited them to a single port, Macao. Here, in return for silver from the Americas, the Portuguese obtained luxurious and exotic goods that brought exorbitant prices from European nobles, who coveted them for the prestige they conveyed. A merchant who could take a few crates of first-class Chinese porcelain tableware back to Europe could make enough profit to start his own firm.

### *Urbanization and Technology*

The Ming period also saw an enormous increase in the number of urban dwellers. Some Chinese cities, serving as marketplaces for the rural majority and as administrative and cultural centers, grew to have several hundred thousand inhabitants; one or two possibly had more than a million at a time when no European town had a population of even 100,000. In these Chinese metropolises, almost anything was available for money, and the kind of abject poverty that would arise later was probably still unknown. In general, the villagers and city dwellers of Ming China seem to have been decently housed and fed.

Historians have often asked why China with its large, financially sophisticated commercial class and a leadership role in so many ideas and techniques did not make the breakthrough into a mechanical mode of industry. Why, in other words, did the Chinese fail to make the leap from the "commercial revolution" of the later Ming period to an "industrial revolution" of the kind that began in the West a century later? Various answers have been proposed, but no single one is satisfactory. The Chinese esteem for artists and scholars and the tendency of such people to place little emphasis on accumulation of material goods must be part of the explanation. Engineers and inventors were never prominent in China's culture, even though Chinese science and technology led the world until at least the 1200s. Also, the Confucian ethos did not admire the capitalist entrepreneur or his activities. It was the retention of the old, not the invention of the new, that inspired properly educated Chinese. In the end, we can only attest that China did not experience an industrial-technical breakthrough. If it had, China and not western Europe would have been the dominant power of the world in the past three centuries.

## The Ming Political System

As always since Han times, the Chinese government culminated in the person of an all-powerful but not divine emperor, who ruled by the mandate of Heaven through a highly trained bureaucracy derived substantially from talented men of all classes and backgrounds. Hongwu, the peasant rebel commander, brought militaristic and authoritarian ways to the government he headed. The first Ming ruler divided China into fifteen provinces, subdivided into numerous counties, an arrangement that has survived almost intact into the present day. He made occupations hereditary and classified the population into three chief groups: peasants, soldiers, and workers. Supposedly, the class into which people were born would determine the course of their lives, but this was much truer on paper than in reality. China was far too vast and the bureaucracy far too small to allow this restrictive and antitraditional theory to be successfully put into practice.

**Festival at the River.** This is part of a thirty-three-foot-long scroll painted in the Ming Dynasty era portraying one of the several civic festivals that marked the Chinese calendar. The emperor's participation in these festivals was an important part of his functions as head of government and holder of the mandate of heaven.

But the emperor's powers during the early Ming were probably greater than ever before. Hongwu created a corps of palace eunuchs, men without families who had been raised since boyhood to be totally dedicated servants of the ruler. They served as his eyes and ears, and during periods of weak leadership, the eunuchs often exercised almost dictatorial powers over the regular officials, because they alone had direct access to the emperor. This practice, of course, led to much abuse, and the eunuchs were hated and feared by most Chinese. Curiously, the eunuchs never seem to have attempted to overthrow a legitimate ruler, although some Ming emperors practically turned the government over to them. The imperial corps of eunuchs lasted into the twentieth century, though their powers were much diminished by then.

**EXAMINATIONS FOR GOVERNMENT POSTS.** This seventeenth-century painting shows the examinations for government posts in progress. Despite years of preparation, very few candidates were successful at the higher levels.

After a brief sojourn in Nanjing during the rule of the first Ming emperor, the government was returned to the northern city of Beijing (Peking), which was originally built by the Mongols. In its center was the **Forbidden City**, a quarter-mile-square area of great palaces, offices, and living quarters for the higher officials. No ordinary person was ever permitted within its massive walls. The Forbidden City was expanded several times during the Ming, until it came to house more than 20,000 men and women, who served the emperor or his enormous official family. Its upkeep and the lavish entertainments and feasts that were regularly put on for thousands were a heavy burden on the whole country.

## The Bureaucracy

The basis for entry and success in the bureaucracy remained the same as it had been for the last 1,500 years: mastery of the Confucian philosophy and ethics. Confucianism grew stronger than ever. Many schools were founded solely to prepare boys for the government service exams. These exams, which had been suspended by the Mongols, were immediately reinstated by the first Ming emperor. Their essentials would not change until the twentieth century. The exams were administered every other year at the lowest (county) level and every third year at the provincial capitals. Each candidate was assigned a tiny cubicle in which he slept and ate under constant surveillance when not writing his essays during the three to five days of the examination.

Only a tiny minority was successful in obtaining an official post even at the province level. The most distinguished of these would then compete for the central government posts every third year, and the successful ones were considered the most prestigious of all of the "men of Han."

Unchanged for centuries, the exams influenced all Chinese education and kept what we now call the curriculum to a very narrow range. After basic reading, writing, and arithmetic, most Chinese schooling was aimed only at preparing students for the civil service examinations. It consisted of a good deal of rote memorization and required extensive knowledge of the various interpretations of Confucian thought. Imagination, creativity, and individuality were definitely not desired. Over the long term, this limited education put China's officials at a distinct disadvantage when confronted with situations that required flexibility and vision. On the other hand, the uniform preparation of all Chinese officials gave the country an especially cohesive governing class, the mandarins (see Chapter 17), and conflicts generated by differing philosophies of government were rare or nonexistent. Until recently, civil upheaval and antagonism never occurred *within* the governing class, only *between* it and some outer group (usually foreigners, eunuchs, or provincial usurpers). This unity of view and the loyalty it engendered were valuable in preserving China from threatened disintegration on repeated occasions.

In the early Ming period, both the government and most of the educated population agreed on the vital prin-

**MING VASE.** This superb example of Chinese porcelain was made in the seventeenth century, possibly for the developing export trade with Europe.

ciples of a good civic life and how to construct it. All officials, from the emperor down to the minor collector of customs in some obscure port, were accepted by the masses as their proper authorities. The ever-recurring question of how to meet the modest demands of the peasantry for survival without alienating the often rapacious landlord-officials was handled effectively. Unfortunately, this harmony declined in later years, as weak emperors ignored the examples set by the dynasty's founders.

## DEALING WITH FOREIGNERS

The Mongols and other nomadic peoples on the northern and northwestern frontiers were still a constant menace after they had been expelled from China proper. Much of the large military budget of Ming China was spent on maintaining the 2,000 miles of the Great Wall, large sections of which had to be rebuilt to defend against potential invaders. To do this job, a huge army—well over a million strong—was kept in constant readiness. The main reason for moving the capital back to Beijing from Nanjing was to better direct the defense effort.

The rulers at Beijing followed the ancient stratagem of "use the barbarian against the barbarian" whenever they could, but twice they miscalculated, and the tribes were able to put aside their squabbles and unite in campaigns against the Chinese. The first time, the Mongols actually defeated and captured the emperor, liberating him only after payment of a tremendous ransom. The second time, they smashed a major Chinese army and overran Beijing itself in 1550. Eventually, both incursions were forced back, and the dynasty was reestablished.

With the Japanese, relations proceeded on two planes: that of hostility toward pirates and smugglers and that of legitimate and beneficial exchange. From the fourteenth century, pirate-traders (there was little distinction) from Japan had appeared in Korean and north Chinese waters. Gradually, they became bolder and often joined Chinese pirates to raid coastal ports well into the south. Because the Japanese could always flee out of reach in their islands, the Chinese could only try to improve their defenses, rather than exterminate the enemy fleets. During the sixteenth century, the Beijing government actually abandoned many coastal areas to the pirates, hoping this tactic would enable them to protect the rest.

Otherwise, the Ming period was a high point in cultural and commercial interchange between China and Japan. Direct Chinese-Japanese relations concentrated on trading between a few Japanese *daimyo* and Chinese merchants, a private business supervised by the respective governments. Several of the shoguns of Japan (see Chapter 29) were great admirers of Chinese culture and saw to it that Japan's doors were thrown widely open to Chinese ideas as well as artifacts.

The trading activity with the Japanese was exceptional, however. Generally speaking, China's rulers believed that the Empire of the Middle needed little from the outside world. A brief but significant excursion onto the Indian Ocean trade routes seemed to underline this conviction. The **Maritime Expeditions** of the early 1400s are a notable departure from the general course of Chinese expansionist policy, in that they were naval rather than land ventures. Between 1405 and 1433, huge fleets carrying as many as 30,000 sailors and soldiers traveled south to the East Indies, and as far west as the coast of Africa. The expeditions were sponsored by the government, and at the emperor's order, they stopped as suddenly as they had begun. Their purpose remains unclear, but it does not seem to have been commercial. The fleets made no attempt to plant colonies or to set up a network of trading posts. Nor did the expeditions leave a long-term mark on Chinese consciousness or awareness of the achievements and interests of the world outside.

The Maritime Expeditions were a striking demonstration of how advanced Chinese seamanship, ship design, and equipment were and how confident the Chinese were in their dealings with foreigners of all types. Although China certainly possessed the necessary technology (shipbuilding, compass, rudder, sails) to make a success of overseas exploration and commerce, the government decided not to use it. The government's refusal was the end of the matter. The large mercantile class had no alternative but to accept it because the merchants had neither the influence at court nor the high status in society that could have enabled the voyages to continue. In this sense, the failure to pursue the avenues opened by the expeditions reflects the differences between the Chinese and European governments and the relative importance of merchants and entrepreneurial vision in the two cultures.

Contacts with Westerners during the Ming era were limited to a few trading enterprises, mainly Portuguese or Dutch, and occasional missionaries, mainly Jesuits from Spain or Rome. The Portuguese, who arrived in 1514 before any other Europeans, made themselves so offensive to Chinese standards of behavior that they were expelled, then confined to the tiny Macao port, near Guangzhou. The missionaries got off to a considerably more favorable start. They made enormous efforts to empathize with the Confucian mentalities of the upper-class Chinese officials and to adapt Christian doctrines to Chinese psyches. Several of the missionaries were well-trained natural scientists and were able to interest their hosts in their religious message via their demonstrations of Western mechanical and technical innovations.

Outstanding in this regard was Matteo Ricci (1551–1610), a Jesuit who obtained access to the emperor thanks to his scientific expertise, adoption of Chinese ways of thought, and mastery of the difficult language. Ricci and his successors established a Christian bridgehead in the intellectual focal point of China that for a century or more looked as though it might be able to broaden its appeal and convert the masses. But this was not to be. (See the Science and Technology box for some of Ricci's remarks on Chinese technology and his insights into Chinese culture.)

## The Manzhou Invaders: Qing Dynasty

The end of the Ming Dynasty came after a slow, painful decline in the mid-seventeenth century. A series of ineffective emperors had allowed government power to slip into the hands of corrupt and hated eunuchs, who made decisions on the basis of bribes, without responsibility for their consequences. Court cliques contended for supreme power. The costs of the multitude of imperial court officials and hangers-on were enormous and could be met only by squeezing taxes out of an already hard-pressed peasantry. Peasant rebellions began to multiply as the government's ability to restrain rapacious landlords declined. The administrative apparatus, undermined by the eunuch cliques at court, ceased to function. Adding to the troubles was the popularity among the mandarins of an extreme version of scholarly Confucianism that rejected innovation.

The Manzhou tribesmen living north of the Great Wall in **Manchuria** had paid tribute to the Beijing emperor but had never accepted his overlordship. When the rebellions led to anarchy in several northern provinces, the Manzhou saw their chance. The Manzhou governing group admired Chinese culture and made it clear that if and when they were victorious, conservative Chinese would have nothing to fear from them. Presenting themselves as the alternative to banditry and even revolution, the Manzhou invaders gradually won the support of much of the mandarin class. One province after another went over to them rather than face continuous rebellion. The last Ming ruler, faced with certain defeat, committed suicide. Thus was founded the last dynasty of imperial China, the Manzhou or Qing (Pure) (1664–1911). In its opening generations, it was to be one of the most successful as well.

### *Manzhou Government*

When the **Qing Dynasty** was at the apex of its power and wealth, China had by far the largest population under one government and the largest territory of any country in the world (see Map 28.1). China reached its largest territorial extent at this time. The Manzhou had been close to Chinese civilization for many years and had become partially sinicized (adopted Chinese culture), so the transition from Ming to Qing rule was nothing like the upheaval that had followed the Mongol conquest in the 1200s. Many Ming officials and generals joined with the conquerors voluntarily from the start. Many others joined under pressure or as it became apparent that the Manzhou were not savages and were adopting Chinese traditions in government. High positions in the central and even the provincial governments were in fact occupied by two individuals: one Manzhou, one Chinese. Chinese provincial governors were overseen by Manzhou, and the army was sharply divided between the two ethnic groups, with the Manzhou having superior status as the so-called Bannermen, who occupied key garrisons.

Like most new dynasties, the Manzhou were strong reformers in their early years, bringing order and respect for authority, snapping the whip over insubordinate officials in the provinces, and attempting to ensure justice in the village. The two greatest Manzhou leaders were the emperors Kangxi (Kang-hsi; ruled 1662–1722) and his grandson Qienlong (Chien Lung; ruled 1736–1795). Their unusually long reigns allowed them to put their stamps on the bureaucracy and develop long-range policies. Both were strong personalities, intelligent and well-educated men who approached their duties with the greatest seriousness. Both attempted to keep Manzhou and Chinese separate to some degree, although the Manzhou were always a tiny minority (perhaps 2 percent) of the popula-

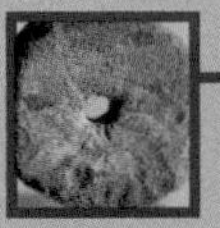

SCIENCE AND TECHNOLOGY

## Chinese Inventions

**In the sixteenth century,** an Italian priest named Matteo Ricci was invited by the emperor to reside at the court in Beijing in the capacity of court astronomer. Ricci had learned Chinese and drew on his learned background in the sciences to both instruct and entertain his hosts. His journals were published shortly after his death in 1610 and gave Europeans their first eyewitness glimpse of the Ming Dynasty civilization and the first knowledgeable insight into Chinese affairs since Marco Polo's report three centuries earlier.

All of the known metals without exception are to be found in China. . . . From molten iron they fashion many more things than we do, for example, cauldrons, pots, bells, gongs, mortars . . . martial weapons, instruments of torture, and a great number of other things equal in workmanship to our own metalcraft. . . . The ordinary tableware of the Chinese is clay pottery. There is nothing like it in European pottery either from the standpoint of the material itself or its thin and fragile construction. The finest specimens of porcelain are made from clay found in the province of Kiam and these are shipped not only to every part of China but even to the remotest corners of Europe where they are highly prized. . . . This porcelain too will bear the heat of hot foods without cracking, and if it is broken and sewed with a brass wire it will hold liquids without any leakage. . . .

Finally we should say something about the saltpeter, which is quite plentiful but which is not used extensively in the preparation of gunpowder, because the Chinese are not expert in the use of guns and artillery and make but little use of these in warfare. Saltpeter, however, is used in lavish quantities in making fireworks for display at public games and on festival days. The Chinese take great pleasure in such exhibitions and make them the chief attraction of all their festivities. Their skill in the manufacture of fireworks is really extraordinary and there is scarcely anything which they cannot cleverly imitate with them. They are especially adept at reproducing battles and in making rotating spheres of fire, fiery trees, fruit, and the like, and they seem to have no regard for expense where fireworks are concerned. . . .

The art of printing was practiced in China at a date somewhat earlier than that assigned to the beginning of printing in Europe. . . . It is quite certain that the Chinese knew the art of printing at least five centuries ago, and some of them assert that printing was known to their people before the beginning of the Christian era. . . .

Their method of making printed books is quite ingenious. The text is written in ink, with a brush made of very fine hair, on a sheet of paper which is inverted and pasted on a wooden tablet. When the paper has become thoroughly dry, its surface is scraped off quickly and with great skill, until nothing but a fine tissue bearing the characters remains on the wooden tablet. Then with a steel graver, the workman cuts away the surface following the outlines of the characters, until these alone stand out in low relief. From such a block a skilled printer can make copies with incredible speed, turning out as many as fifteen hundred copies in a single day. Chinese printers are so skilled at turning out these blocks that no more time is consumed in making one of them than would be required by one of our printers in setting up a form of [moveable metallic] type and making the necessary corrections. . . .

The simplicity of Chinese printing is what accounts for the exceedingly large number of books in circulation here and the ridiculously low prices at which they are sold. Such facts as these would scarcely be believed by one who had not witnessed them.

### *Analyze and Interpret*

Why do you think the Chinese did not use gunpowder technology in war as in entertainments? In light of what Ricci reports, is contemporary European preference for metallic type justified?

Source: P. Stearns et al., eds. *Documents in World History: Vol. 2. The Modern Centuries* (New York: Harper & Row, 1988).

**History Now™**

***To read futher selections from Ricci's "The Art of Printing," point your browser to the documents area of* HistoryNow.**

tion and were steadily sinicized after the early 1700s by intermarriage and free choice. (See the Law and Government box for more on Kangxi.)

Kangxi was the almost exact contemporary of Louis XIV of France and, like him, was the longest-lived ruler of his country's history. From all accounts, Kangxi was a remarkable man with a quick intellect and a fine gift for administration. He retained the traditional Chinese system of six ministries advising and implementing the decrees of the Son of Heaven in Beijing. He did much to improve the waterways, which were always of great importance for transportation in China. Rivers were dredged, and canals and dams built. He was particularly active in economic policy making, both domestically and toward the Western

LAW AND GOVERNMENT

## Kangxi's Sacred Edict

**EMPEROR KANGXI, THE SEVENTEENTH-CENTURY** Qing dynast, was perhaps the greatest of all the Chinese rulers, in part because of the extraordinary duration of his hold on the throne. In 1670, he issued a Sacred Edict to popularize Confucian values among the people.

1. Esteem most highly filial piety and brotherly submission, in order to give due importance to the social relations.
2. Behave with generosity toward your kindred, in order to illustrate harmony and benignity.
3. Cultivate peace and concord in your neighborhoods, in order to prevent quarrels and litigations.
4. Recognize the importance of husbandry and the culture of the mulberry tree, in order to ensure a sufficiency of clothing and food.
5. Show that you prize moderation and economy, in order to prevent the lavish waste of your means.
6. Give weight to colleges and schools, in order to make correct the practice of the scholar.
7. Extirpate strange principles, in order to exalt the correct doctrine.
8. Lecture on the laws, in order to warn the ignorant and obstinate.
9. Elucidate propriety and yielding courtesy, in order to make manners and customs good.
10. Labor diligently at your proper callings, in order to stabilize the will of the people.
11. Instruct sons and younger brothers, in order to prevent them from doing what is wrong.
12. Put a stop to false accusations, in order to preserve the honest and good.
13. Warn against sheltering deserters, in order to avoid being involved in their punishment.
14. Fully remit your taxes, in order to avoid being pressed for payment.
15. Unite in hundreds and tithing, in order to put an end to thefts and robbery.
16. Remove enmity and anger, in order to show the importance due to the person and life.

### *Analyze and Interpret*

What might Kangxi's motives have been in promoting such values to the common people?

Source: From *Popular Culture in Late Imperial China* by David Johnson et al. 

merchants whose vessels were now starting to appear regularly in Chinese ports. After decades of negotiations, Kangxi opened four ports to European traders and allowed them to set up small permanent enclaves there. This decision was to have fateful consequences in the mid-nineteenth century, when the Beijing government was in much weaker hands.

Kangxi's grandson Qienlong was a great warrior and perceptive administrator. He eradicated the persistent Mongol raiders on the western borders and brought Tibet under Chinese control for the first time (see Map 28.1). The peculiar fashion of dealing with neighboring independent kingdoms such as Korea as though they were voluntary satellites of China (tributaries) was extended to much of Southeast Asia at this time. Qienlong ruled through the last two-thirds of the eighteenth century, and we know a good deal about both him and his grandfather because Jesuit missionaries still resided in Beijing during this era. Their perceptive reports to Rome contributed to the interest in everything Chinese that was so manifest in late eighteenth-century Europe.

The early Manzhou emperors were unusually vigorous leaders, and the Chinese economy and society responded positively to their lengthy rule until the mid-nineteenth century, when the dynasty's power and prestige suffered under a combination of Western military intrusions and a growing population crisis. (This period is covered in Chapter 43.)

## QING CULTURE AND ECONOMY

Although the Manzhou were looked on as foreign barbarians originally, and they exerted themselves to remain separate from the Chinese masses, no break in fundamental cultural styles occurred between the Ming and Qing dynasties. As in earlier China, the most respected cultural activities were philosophy, history, calligraphy, poetry, and painting. In literature, a new form matured in the 1500s: the novel. Perhaps inspired by the Japanese example, a series of written stories about both gentry life and ordinary people appeared during the late Ming and Qing eras. Best known are the *Book of the Golden Lotus* and ***The Dream of the Red Chamber***, the latter a product of the eighteenth century. Most of the authors are unknown, and the books that have survived are probably a small portion of those actually produced. Some of the stories are pornographic, a variety of literature that the Chinese evidently enjoyed despite official disapproval.

Porcelain reached such artistry in the eighteenth century that it became a major form of Chinese aesthetic creation. Throughout the Western world, the wealthy sought fine "china" as tableware and objets d'art and were willing to pay nearly any price for the beautiful blue-and-white Ming wares brought back by the Dutch and English ships from the South China ports. Chinese painting on scrolls and screens was also imported in large amounts, as were silks and other luxury items for the households of the nobility and wealthy urbanites. The popular decorative style termed *chinoiserie* reflected late-eighteenth-century Europe's admiration for Chinese artifacts and good taste. The "Clipper ships" of New England made the long voyage around Cape Horn and across the Pacific in the first half of the nineteenth century to reap enormous profits carrying luxury goods in both directions: sea otter furs from Alaska and the Pacific Northwest and porcelain, tea, and jade from China.

During the Ming and Qing periods, far more people were participating in the creation and enjoyment of formal culture than ever before. By the 1700s, China had a large number of educated people who were able to purchase the tangible goods produced by a host of skilled artists. Schools and academies of higher learning educated the children of anyone who could afford the fees, generally members of the scholar-official class who had been governing China since the Han Dynasty.

In this era (from the 1500s on), however, China definitely lost its lead in science and technology to the West, which it had maintained for the previous thousand years. Developing a sensitivity to beauty, such as the art of calligraphy, was considered as essential to proper education in China as mastering literacy and basic math. Painting, poetry, and meditation were considered far more important than physics or accounting or chemistry. This ongoing downgrading of the quantitative sciences and the technical advances they spawned in the West was to be a massively negative turning point in international power relations for China. Aesthetic sensitivities and artistic excellence proved to be little aid when confronted by cannons and steam engines.

## Progress and Problems

Among the outstanding achievements of the early Qing emperors were improvements in agriculture and engineering that benefited uncounted numbers of ordinary Chinese. Kangxi, for example, did much to ensure that the South China "rice bowl" was made even more productive and that the Grand Canal linking the Yellow River with the central coast ports and the Yangtze basin was kept in good order. New hybrid rice allowed rice culture to be extended and increased yields, which in turn supported an expansion in population.

Internal trade in the large cities and many market towns continued the upsurge that had begun during the Ming Dynasty and became ever more important in this era. Although most Chinese—perhaps 80 percent—remained villagers working the land, there were now large numbers of shopkeepers, market porters, carters, artisans, moneylenders, and all the other occupations of commercial life. Money circulated freely as both coin and paper, the coins being minted of Spanish silver brought from the South American colonies to Manila and Guangzhou to trade for silk and porcelain.

All in all, the Chinese in the early Qing period were probably living as well as any other people in the world and better than most Europeans. But this high standard of living worsened in later days, when for the first time the population's growth exceeded the ability of the agrarian economy to allow suitable productive work for it. By the nineteenth century, almost all of the land that had adequate precipitation or was easily irrigable for crops had already been brought under the plow. The major improvements possible in rice farming had already been made, and yields did not continue to rise as they had previously. Machine industry had not yet arrived in China (and would not for many years), and trade with the outside world was narrowly focused and on a relatively small scale that government policy refused to expand. (China wanted very few material things from the non-Chinese, in any case.) In the nineteenth century, rural China began to experience massive famines and endemic poverty that were the result of too-rapid growth in population in a technically backward society without the desire or means to shift to new production modes.

# Summary

The overthrow of the Mongols introduced another of the great Chinese dynasties: the Ming. Blessed by exceptionally able emperors in the early decades, the Ming imitated their Tang Dynasty model and made notable improvements in agriculture and commerce. Urban life expanded, and the urban bourgeoisie of merchants became economically (but not politically) important. The borders were extended well to the west and north, and the barbarian nomads thrust once again behind the Great Wall for a couple of centuries.

In the classic pattern, however, the Ming's grip on government and people weakened, and the costs of a huge court and army pressed heavily on the overtaxed population. When rebellions began in the northern provinces, the people were encouraged by the promises of change offered by the invading Manzhou in the northeast. Triumphant, the Manzhou leader began the final dynastic period in China's 3,000-year history, that of the Qing.

The two first Qing emperors were extraordinarily able men, who in the eighteenth century led China to one of the summits of its national existence. The economy prospered, and overpopulation was not yet a problem. In the arts there was extraordinary refinement and development of new literary forms. But in science and technology, China now lagged far behind the West, and the coming century was destined to be filled with political and cultural humiliations. China entered the modern age unprepared to handle the type of problems that it faced on the eve of the European intrusion: growing impoverishment, military backwardness, and technical retardation. First the Europeans and then the Japanese would find ways to take advantage of these handicaps.

## Identification Terms

Test your knowledge of this chapter's key concepts by defining the following terms. If you can't recall the meaning of certain terms, refresh your memory by looking up the boldfaced term in the chapter, turning to the Glossary at the end of the book, or working with the flashcards that are available on the *World Civilizations* Companion Website **http://history.wadsworth.com/adler04**.

*The Dream of the Red Chamber*
Forbidden City
Manchuria
Maritime Expeditions
Qing Dynasty

## Test Your Knowledge

Test your knowledge of this chapter by answering the following questions. Complete answers appear at the end of the book. You may also take this quiz interactively and find even more quiz questions on the *World Civilizations* Companion Website **http://history.wadsworth.com/adler04**.

1. The most serious menace to China's stability during the 1300s and 1400s was
   a. the Japanese coastal pirates.
   b. the Mongol conquerors from the north.
   c. the conspiracies of the palace eunuchs.
   d. the invasions of the Vietnamese in the south.
   e. the isolation that caused the Chinese to fall behind the rest of the world.
2. The last dynasty to be of pure Chinese origin was the
   a. Manzhou.
   b. Song.
   c. Tang.
   d. Ming.
   e. Qin.
3. China's first commercial contact with Europeans was with the
   a. British.
   b. Dutch.
   c. Spanish.
   d. Greeks.
   e. Portuguese.
4. The emperor Hongwu initiated a period during which only the __________ had direct access to the emperor.
   a. royal family.
   b. leading merchants.
   c. government officials.
   d. palace eunuchs.
   e. military leaders.

5. During the Ming/Manzhou era, China was ruled by a bureaucracy that was
   a. selected on the basis of aristocratic birth.
   b. controlled by a professional military establishment.
   c. dominated by the Buddhist priesthood.
   d. selected on the basis of written examinations.
   e. unconcerned about the Chinese peasantry.
6. During the Ming period, Chinese-Japanese contacts were
   a. restricted to occasional commerce and raids by Japanese pirates.
   b. thriving on a number of fronts, both commercial and cultural.
   c. hostile and infrequent.
   d. marked by the Japanese willingness to accept China's dominance.
   e. exceptional, in that the Chinese adopted Japanese technology.
7. The Maritime Expeditions of the fifteenth century were
   a. the product of contacts with Arab traders.
   b. the result of Mongol invaders who had occupied China.
   c. the government-sponsored explorations of the Indian Ocean.
   d. begun at the initiative of private traders.
   e. an opportunity for the Chinese to show the rest of the world their superiority.
8. The replacement of the Ming by the Manzhou Qing Dynasty was
   a. caused by a Japanese invasion of China and collapse of the Ming.
   b. a gradual armed takeover from a demoralized government.
   c. carried out by Westerners, who were anxious to install a "tame" government in Beijing.
   d. caused by Western Christian missionaries hostile to the Ming.
   e. the natural result of cultural interaction between the two groups.
9. The outstanding Qing emperors of the eighteenth century
   a. learned much of political value to them from the West.
   b. were cruel tyrants in their treatment of the common Chinese.
   c. split governmental responsibility between Manzhou and Chinese.
   d. tried hard to expand commerce between China and Europe.
   e. rejected the traditional Chinese bureaucracy in favor of absolute rule.
10. Which of the following did *not* figure prominently in Manzhou cultural achievement?
    a. Poetry
    b. Landscape painting
    c. Theology
    d. Fictional narratives
    e. Calligraphy

## InfoTrac College Edition

Visit the source collections at

**http://infotrac.thomsonlearning.com**

and use the Search function with the following key terms:

Ming China    China history

## Wadsworth History Website Resources

Visit the World History Resource Center at **http://history.wadsworth.com/world** for a wealth of general resources, and the *World Civilizations* Companion Website at **http://history.wadsworth.com/adler04** for resources specific to this textbook.

## HistoryNow

Enter *HistoryNow* using the access card that is available for *World Civilizations*. *HistoryNow* will assist you in understanding the content in this chapter with lesson plans generated for your needs. In addition, you can read the following documents, and many more, online:

Matteo Ricci, "The Art of Printing"

Pere du Halde, "The Chinese Educational System"

The Dream of the Red Chamber

*The white chrysanthemum*
*Even when lifted to the eye*
*Remains immaculate.*
**Basho**

# 29 Japan and Colonial Southeast Asia



| | |
|---|---|
| 1543 | First European contacts with Japan |
| c. 1600 | Tokugawa shogunate established |
| c. 1630s | Christianity suppressed; foreigners expelled/*sakoku* begins |
| 1600s–1700s | Money economy and commercial society develop |
| 1853–1854 | Perry opens Japan to trade; *sakoku* ends |

Before the 1500s, the Japanese islands' contacts with the outer world were only with Korea and China. The arrival of Portuguese trader-explorers brought change to a substantial segment of society, which adopted Christian belief. But this trend was later reversed by government action, and in a remarkable turnabout, the Japanese entered a long period of self-imposed seclusion.

Southeast Asia also experienced the European outreach, but in a highly localized and restricted manner, linked to the exclusive interest of the newcomers in the spice trade. Only much later, in the nineteenth century, did Europeans begin to develop Southeast Asian colonies.

## Japan

Although akin to China in some ways, Japan was very different in many others. The political power of the emperor in Kyoto was weak throughout early modern times, and Japan became a collection of feudal provinces controlled by clans. In the century between the 1460s and the 1570s, the warrior-nobles (***daimyo***) had engaged in a frenzy of the "strong eating the weak." Finally, a series of military strongmen managed to restore order, culminating in the establishment of a type of centralized feudalism, the **shogunate**.

The first European contacts occurred in the mid-1500s, when traders and missionaries were allowed to establish themselves on Japanese soil. One of the most important trade items brought by the Portuguese was firearms. Another was the Christian Bible. Contacts with Europe were complicated by Japanese distrust of the Christian faith and its hints of submission to an alien culture. The shogun eventually decided that this danger was intolerable. Within a generation's time, Japan withdrew behind a wall of enforced isolation from the world, from which it would not emerge until the nineteenth century.

## First European Contacts: Christianity

The Portuguese arrived in Japanese ports for the first time in 1543, looking for additional opportunities to make money from their active trading with all the Eastern countries. They took Chinese silk to Japan and Japanese silver to China and used the profits from both to buy spices in the South Pacific islands to bring back to Portugal.

One of the first influences from the West to reach the thus-far isolated Japanese was Christianity, which arrived via the numerous Catholic missionaries sponsored by the Society of Jesus (Jesuits). The Jesuit order had been founded to fight Protestantism only a few years earlier, and its missionaries were well educated and highly motivated. For various reasons, a fair number of the daimyo were sympathetic to the Jesuit efforts and converted to Christianity during the 1550s and 1560s. By the year 1600, it is estimated that 300,000 Japanese had converted. That number would have constituted a far higher percentage of the population than do Christians in modern times.

At this time, most Japanese were adherents of either Shinto or one of the many varieties of Buddhism. Why did the ruling group allow the missionaries free access to the people? And why did the Japanese initially prove more receptive to Christianity than, for example, the Chinese or the Indians? It is impossible to say with certainty. One reason was the personal example of the Jesuits, led by St. Francis Xavier, who greatly impressed their hosts with their piety and learning.

Other changes were under way. In the later 1500s, a movement for Japanese national unity led by Oda Nobunaga (1523–1582), a feudal lord who had fought his way to regional power, was getting under way. In the 1570s, the brutal Nobunaga succeeded in capturing Kyoto and most of the central island of Honshu, but he was killed by one of his cohorts. Following Nobunaga's death, his lieutenant Toyotomi Hideyoshi took over. Aided by the first large-scale use of firearms in Japan, Hideyoshi had visions of Asian, if not worldwide, supremacy. He invaded Korea with a well-equipped army of 150,000 as a first step toward the conquest of Ming China. Repulsed in 1592, he was in the midst of a second attempt when he died in 1598. After a couple of years of struggle among Hideyoshi's would-be successors, the formidable warrior and statesman Tokugawa Ieyasu (ruled 1603–1616) seized the baton. (See the Law and Government box.)

Tokugawa ceased the abortive invasion of the mainland and by 1600 had beaten down his several internal rivals. Thus began the 250 years of the Tokugawa shogunate, a military regency exercised in the name of an emperor who had become largely a figurehead. Tokugawa "ate the pie that Nobunaga made and Hideyoshi baked" goes the schoolchildren's axiom in modern Japan. He was the decisive figure in premodern Japanese history, using a selective violence against the daimyo to permit a special form of centralized governance.

## The Tokugawa Shogunate

Once in power, Tokugawa continued and expanded the changes that Hideyoshi had begun. By disarming the peasants, Tokugawa removed much of the source of the rebellions that had haunted Japan during the preceding century. From this time on, only the professional warrior class, the ***samurai***, and their daimyo employers had the right to own weapons. The daimyo, who were roughly equivalent to the barons of Europe some centuries earlier, were expected to spend half their time at the court of the shogun, where they would be under the watchful eyes of the shogun and his network of informers.

Museo Nacional de Soares dos Reis, Porto, Portugal/Giraudon/Bridgeman Art Library

**Arrival of the Portuguese.** Note the black slave unloading the goods, showing that the Portuguese were already using black labor in their trans–Indian Ocean trade in the first half of the seventeenth century. The Japanese observer is possibly the merchant for whom the goods were consigned, and the monkey is the ship's mascot.

LAW AND GOVERNMENT

# Tokugawa Ieyasu (1542–1616)

**On March 8, 1616, the shogun** Tokugawa Ieyasu died. According to his wish, he was buried in Nikko, a beautiful wood ninety miles north of Tokyo. His tomb stands at the end of a long avenue of great gardens. Posthumously, Tokugawa was given the title "Noble of the First Rank, Great Light of the East, Great Incarnation of the Buddha." He was already acknowledged as the individual who brought law to a lawless society.

Tokugawa Ieyasu (that is, Ieyasu of the Tokugawa clan) was born in 1542. During the last decades of the sixteenth century, he became an ally of Toyotomi Hideyoshi, the most powerful of all the feudal aristocrats who divided the country among themselves.

When Hideyoshi died unexpectedly in 1598, Ieyasu and another man were the prime candidates to succeed him. Tokugawa assembled a force of 80,000 feudal warriors, while his opponent led a coalition of 130,000. In the decisive battle of Sekigahara in 1600, the outnumbered Tokugawa forces claimed the field. In the next few years, Ieyasu destroyed the coalition's resistance and secured the shogun's office for himself and his second son. Ieyasu's victory was a turning point of great importance. For the next 250 years, the Japanese were forced to live in peace with one another. This "Era of Great Peace" was marked by the Tokugawa clan's uninterrupted control of the shogunate in Edo (Tokyo), while the semi-divine emperor resided in Kyoto and remained the symbolic center of Japanese patriotism.

Ieyasu was an extraordinarily gifted man. Coming out of the samurai tradition of military training, he was nevertheless able to appreciate the blessings of a permanent peace. He carefully redivided the feudal lords' domains throughout the islands to ensure his control over all of them. He established the daimyo as the officials of his kingdom. They were given considerable freedom to do as they pleased in their own backyards, so long as their loyalty to the shogun was not in doubt. Ieyasu and his successors in the 1600s did much to improve and nationalize Japan's economy, particularly among the peasant majority. The heimin or plain folk were divided into three basic groups: farmers, artisans, and traders, in that rank order. Farmers were generally regarded as honorable people, while traders were originally looked down upon, as in China. At the bottom of the social scale were the despised *hinin,* who were equivalent to the Indian untouchables. Unlike the untouchables, however, the hinin were able to rise in status.

**Tokugawa Ieyasu.** This portrait was done after the powerful warrior had assured his position as shogun in 1603.

Private Collection/ Bridgeman Art Library

In many ways, Tokugawa Ieyasu was the father of traditional Japan. The political institutions of the country did not change in any significant way after him until the late nineteenth century. He lives on in the pantheon of Japan's heroes as a model of military virtue, who reluctantly employed harsh and even brutal measures in order to bring about the rule of law in a lawless society.

## *Analyze and Interpret*

Would there have been many alternatives to Tokugawa's method of imposing order in sixteenth-century Japan? What problems may arise from having absolute powers supposedly in one man's (the emperor's) hands, while another actually exercises them? How might this arrangement be compared to similar situations throughout history (for example, the later Abbasid caliphate, as in Chapter 15)?

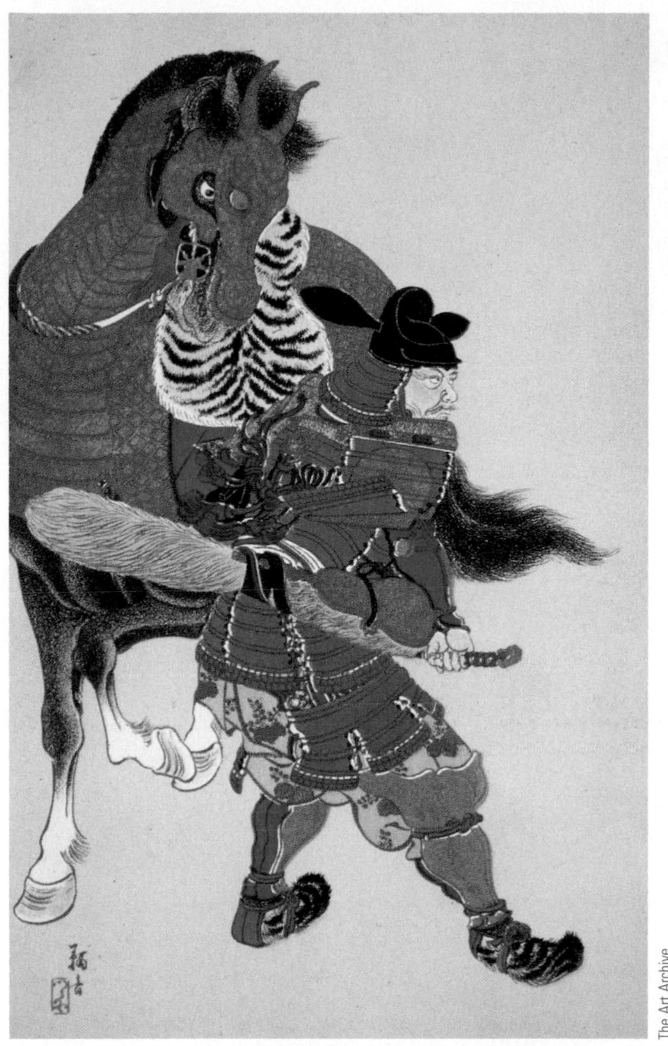


**Hideyoshi as Samurai.** This later illustration of General Hideyoshi allows close inspection of the traditional samurai costume and weapons.

In the early 1600s, the Tokugawa shoguns began to withdraw Japan into seclusion from outside influences. Earlier, Hideyoshi had had misgivings about the activities of the Jesuits within his domains, and in 1587 he had issued an order, which was later revoked, that they should leave. After newly arrived members of the Franciscan Order attempted to meddle in the shogunate's internal affairs, Tokugawa acted. He evicted the Christian missionaries who had been in the country for half a century and put heavy pressure on the Christian Japanese to reconvert to Buddhism. After Christian peasants supported a revolt in 1637, pressure turned into outright persecution. Death became the standard penalty for Christian affiliation. In a few places, the Christians maintained their faith through "underground" churches and priests, but the majority gradually gave up their religion in the face of heavy state penalties and their neighbors' antagonism.

At the same time, Japan's extensive mercantile contacts with the Europeans and Chinese were almost entirely severed. Only a handful of Dutch and Portuguese traders/residents were allowed to remain in two ports (notably, Nagasaki, where two Dutch ships coming from the East Indies were allowed to land each year). (See Map 29.1.) The building of oceangoing ships by Japanese was forbidden. No foreigners could come to Japan, and no Japanese were allowed to reside abroad (with a few exceptions). Japanese who were living abroad were forbidden to return. The previously lively trade with China was sharply curtailed.

This isolation (called ***sakoku*** in Japanese history) lasted until the mid-nineteenth century. It was a remarkable experiment with highly successful results so far as the ruling group was concerned. Japan went its own way and was ignored by the rest of the world.

## Shogun, Emperor, and Daimyo

The Tokugawa shoguns continued the dual nature of Japanese government, whereby the shogunate was established at **Edo** (later Tokyo) while the emperor resided in the imperial palace at **Kyoto** and occupied himself with ritual and ceremony as the current holder of the lineage of the Sun Goddess who had created Japan eons earlier (see Chapter 18). True power in both a military and a political sense remained with the shogun, who now headed a council of state composed of daimyo aristocrats. An individual who was always a member of the Tokugawa clan acted in the name of the emperor while closely overseeing some twenty large and perhaps two hundred small land-holding daimyo, who acted both as his agents and as autonomous regents in their own domains. The shogun controlled about one-fourth of Japan as his own fiefdom. This system continued without important change until 1867.

The daimyo were the key players in governance and posed a constant potential threat to Tokugawa's arrangements. As the source of military power on the local level, they could tear down any shogun if they united against him. Therefore, to secure the center, the shogun had to play the daimyo against each other in the countryside. He did this by constant intervention and manipulation, setting one clan against another in the competition for imperial favor. The shogun controlled the domains near Edo or put them in the hands of dependable allies. Domains on the outlying islands went to rival daimyo clans, which would counterbalance one another. Meanwhile, the wives and children of the more important daimyo families were required to live permanently at Edo, where they served as hostages for loyal behavior. The whole system of supervision and surveillance much resembled Louis XIV's arrangements at Versailles in seventeenth-century France.

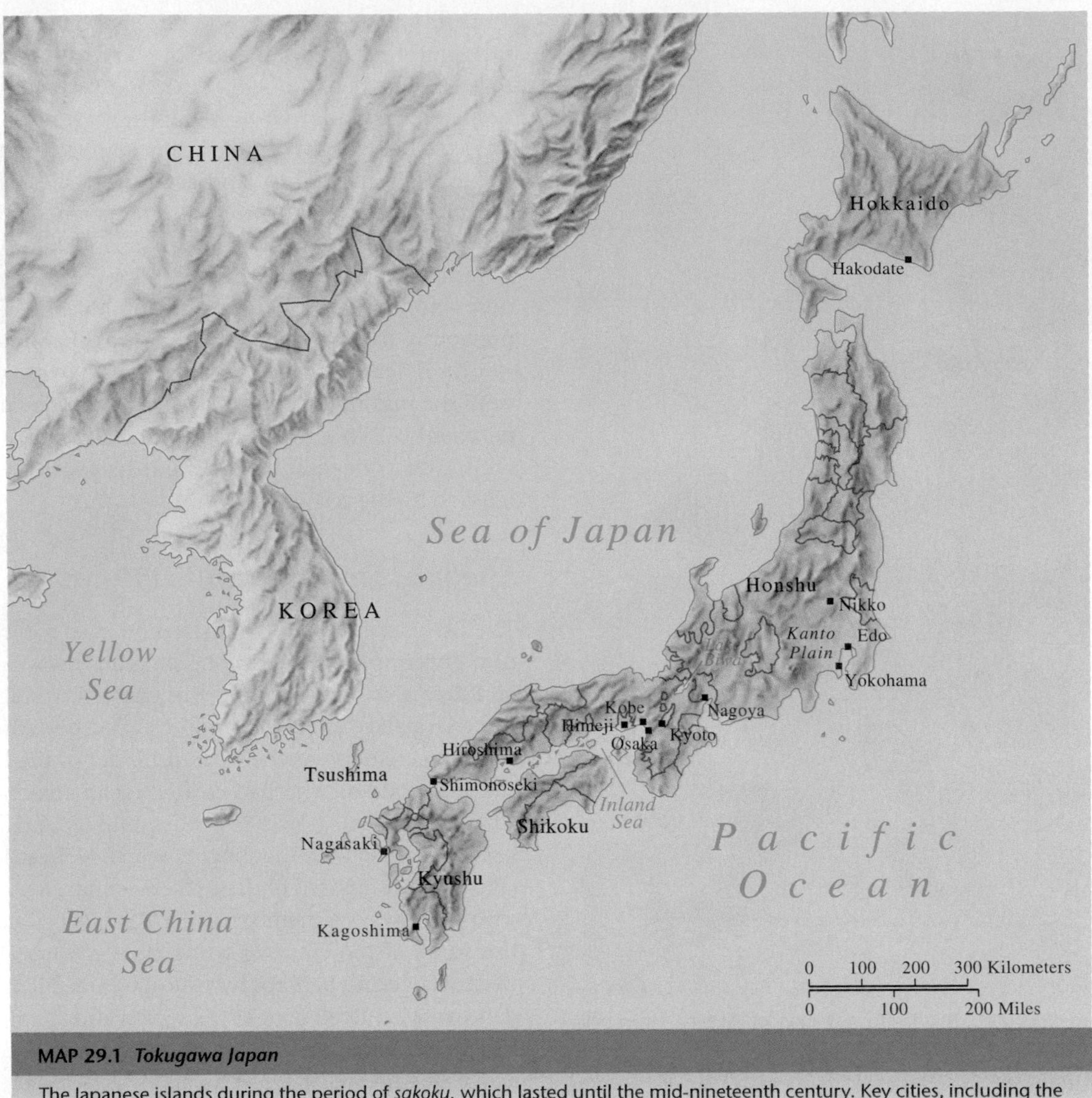


**MAP 29.1 *Tokugawa Japan***

The Japanese islands during the period of *sakoku*, which lasted until the mid-nineteenth century. Key cities, including the shogunate's capital, Edo, are shown.

## *Economic Advances*

Japan's society and economy changed markedly during these centuries of isolation. One of the most remarkable results of sakoku was the great growth of population and domestic trade. The population doubled in the seventeenth century and continued to increase gradually throughout the remainder of the Tokugawa period. Closing off trade with foreigners apparently stimulated internal production, rather than discouraged it, and domestic trade rose accordingly. The internal peace imposed by the powerful and respected government of the shogunate certainly helped. The daimyo aristocracy had an ever-increasing appetite for fine wares such as silk and ceramics. Their fortress-palaces in Edo and on their domains reflected both their more refined taste and their increasing ability to satisfy it.

The merchants, who previously had occupied a rather low niche in Japanese society (as in China) and had never been important in government, now gradually gained a much more prominent place. Formerly, the mercantile and craft guilds had restricted access to the market, but the early shoguns forced them to dissolve, thereby allowing many new and creative actors to come onto the entrepreneurial stage. Even so, the merchants as a class were still not as respected as were government officials, scholars, and especially the daimyo and their samurai. Nevertheless, the merchants' growing wealth, which they often lent—at high interest—to impoverished samurai, began to enhance their prestige. A money economy gradually replaced the universal reliance on barter in the villages.

Commercialization and distribution networks for artisans invaded the previously self-sufficient lifestyle of the country folk. Banks and the use of credit became more common during the later Tokugawa period. Some historians see the growth of a specifically Japanese form of capitalism long before Japan's entry into the world economic system in the later nineteenth century.

### *Peasants and Urbanites*

The condition of the peasants, who still made up the vast majority of the population, improved somewhat under the early Tokugawa regime. Since the beginnings of the shogunate under the Fujiwara clan, the peasantry had been sacrificed to keep the daimyo and their samurai retainers satisfied. In most of the Japanese lands, the peasant was no better than a serf and lived in misery. In the early Tokugawa era, the peasants received some protection from exploitation, and the shogun's government claimed that agriculture was the most honorable of ordinary occupations. But the government's taxes were heavy, taking up to 60 percent of the rice crop, which was by far the most important harvest. In later years, the increasing misery of some peasants led to many provincial rebellions, not against the shogun but against the local daimyo who were the peasants' landlords. These revolts, although numerous, were on a much smaller scale than those that would trouble Manzhou (or Manchu) China in the same nineteenth-century epoch.

Cities grew rapidly during the first half of the Tokugawa period but more slowly later. Both Osaka and Kyoto were estimated to have more than 400,000 inhabitants in the eighteenth century, and Edo perhaps as many as 1 million. All three cities were bigger than any town in Europe at that date. The urban population ranged from wealthy daimyo and merchants at the top, through tens of thousands of less fortunate traders, shopkeepers, and officials of all types in the middle, and many hundreds of thousands of skilled and unskilled workers, casual laborers, beggars, prostitutes, artists, and the unlucky samurai at the bottom. Most Japanese, however, still lived as before in small towns and villages. They depended on local farming, timbering, or fishing for their livelihood and had only occasional and superficial contact with the urban culture. Until the twentieth century, the rhythms of country life and rice culture were the dominant influence on the self-image and the lifestyle of the Japanese people.

## Taming the Samurai

In the seventeenth and eighteenth centuries, the samurai caste, which had been the military servants of the wealthy daimyo and their "enforcers" with the peasants, lost most of its prestige in Japanese society. Estimated to make up as much as 7 percent of the population at the time of establishment of the Tokugawa regime, the samurai had now become superfluous.

With the creation of the lasting domestic peace, there was literally nothing for them to do in their traditional profession. They were not allowed to become merchants or to adopt another lifestyle, nor could they easily bring themselves to do so after centuries of proud segregation from the common herd. The Edo government encouraged the samurai to do what they naturally wished to do: enjoy themselves beyond their means. Borrowing from the merchants, the samurai tried to outdo one another in every sort of showy display. After a generation or two, the result was mass bankruptcies and social disgrace.

The fallen samurai were replaced in social status by newcomers, who were finding they could advance through commerce or through the civil bureaucracy. As in the West, this bureaucracy was slowly assuming the place of the feudal barons and becoming the day-to-day authority in governance. The samurai lost out to a new class of people: men who did not know how to wield a sword but were good with a pen. Trained only to make war and raised in the bushido code of the warrior, most of the samurai were ill-equipped to transition from warrior to desk-sitting official of the shogun or a daimyo lord. Most samurai seem to have gradually sunk into poverty and

**"Sunrise."** This woodcut by the famed engraver Hiroshige (1797–1858) shows a typical procession of laborers going to work in a seaside town, while the fishermen raise sail and the rice sellers ready their booths for the morning trade along the quay. The long net is presumably for capturing birds that will be put into the cages and sold.

loss of status as they reverted to the peasant life of their long-ago ancestors.

## Tokugawa Arts and Learning

The almost 250 years of peace of the Tokugawa period produced a rich tapestry of new cultural ideas and practices in Japan. Some of the older ideas, originally imported from China, were now adapted to become almost entirely Japanese in form and content. The upper classes continued to prefer Buddhism in one form or another, with a strong admixture of Confucian secular ethics. Among the people, Shinto and the less intellectual forms of Buddhism formed the matrix of belief about this world and the next. Japanese religious style tended to accept human nature as it is without the overtones of penitence and reform so prominent in Western thought. As before, a strong current of eclecticism blended Buddhism with other systems of belief and practice.

### *Literature and Its Audiences*

Literacy rates were quite high in Japan and continued to increase in the later years of the Tokugawa period, when perhaps as many as 50 percent of the males could read and write the cheap product of wood-block printing presses. This percentage was at least equal to the literacy rate in central Europe of the day and was facilitated by the relative ease of learning the phonetic written language (in distinct contrast to Chinese, the original source of Japanese writing).

Literature aimed at popular entertainment began to appear in new forms that were a far cry from the elegant and restrained traditions of the past. Poetry, novels, social satires, and Kabuki plays were the foremost types of literature. By this era, all of these forms had been liberated from imitation of classical Chinese models, and several were entirely original to the Japanese.

**Haiku** poems, especially in the hands of the revered seventeenth-century poet Basho, were extraordinarily compact revelations of profound thought. In three lines and seventeen syllables (always), the poet reflected the Zen Buddhist conviction that the greatest of mysteries can only be stated—never analyzed. Saikaku's contributions in fiction matched those of Basho in poetry, also during the late seventeenth century. His novels and stories about ordinary people are noteworthy for their passion and the underlying sense of comedy with which the characters are observed. Saikaku's stories, like Basho's verse, are read today in Japan with the same admiration afforded to them for centuries. (See Arts and Culture box.)

**Kabuki** is a peculiarly Japanese form of drama. It is highly realistic, often humorous and satirical, and sometimes violent in both action and emotions. For its settings, it often used the "floating world," the unstable but attractive world of brothels, shady teahouses, and gambling dens. Kabuki was wildly popular among the upper classes in seventeenth- and eighteenth-century Japan. It was not unusual for a particularly successful actor (males played all parts) to become a pampered "star." Actors were often also male prostitutes, just as actresses in the West were often female prostitutes at this time. Homosexuality was strongly frowned on by the shogunate authorities, but it had already had a long tradition among the samurai and some branches of Buddhism.

### *Adaptation and Originality*

In the fine arts, Japan may have drawn its initial inspiration from Chinese models, but it always turned those models into something different, something specifically Japanese. This pattern can be found in landscape painting, poetry, adventure and romance stories, gardens, and ceramics—in any art medium that both peoples have pursued. The Japanese versions were often filled with a playful humor that was missing in the Chinese original and were almost always consciously close to nature, the soil, and the peasantry. The refined intellectualism common to Chinese arts appeared less frequently in Japan. As a random example, the rough-and-tumble of Kabuki and the pornographic jokes that the actors constantly employed were specifically Japanese and had no close equivalent in China.

The merchants who had prospered during the Tokugawa era were especially important as patrons of the arts. Again, a parallel can be drawn to the European experience, but with differences. The European bourgeoisie became important commissioners of art two centuries earlier than the Japanese merchants and did so in self-confident rivalry with the nobles and church. Japan had no established church, and the bourgeoisie never dared challenge the daimyo nobility for taste-setting primacy. Nevertheless, high-quality painting and wood-block prints displaying a tremendous variety of subjects and techniques came to adorn the homes and collections of the rich merchants. In fact, much of what the modern world knows of seventeenth- and eighteenth-century Japanese society is attributable to the knowing eye and talented hands of the artists rather than to historians. Unlike the Chinese, the Japanese never revered compilers of records. There are no Japanese equivalents of the great Chinese histories.

## Response to the Western Challenge

In the later Tokugawa, the main emphasis of Japanese thought shifted from Buddhist to Confucian ideals, which is another way of saying that it changed from an otherworldly emphasis to an empirical concern with this world.

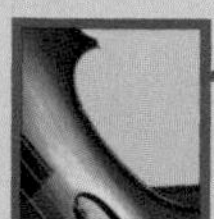

ARTS AND CULTURE

## The Origins and Evolution of Haiku

**Haiku is undoubtedly the most** distinctive and well-known form of traditional Japanese poetry. Haiku has changed somewhat over the centuries since the time of Basho, and today it is typically a three-line, 17-syllable verse form consisting of three metrical units of 5, 7, and 5 syllables. Three related terms, *haiku, hokku,* and *haika,* have often caused considerable confusion. What we know today as haiku had its beginnings as hokku, a "starting verse" of a much longer chain of verses known as haika. The hokku was the most important part of a haika poem; therefore, it was an especially prestigious form of poetry from its inception. Before long, therefore, poets began composing hokkus by themselves. One nineteenth-century master in particular, Masaoka Shiki, formally established the haiku in the 1890s in the form in which it is now known. Here are a few samples of the poetry of Basho:

An old pond!
A frog jumps in—
The sound of water.

The first soft snow!
Enough to bend the leaves
Of the jonquil low.

In the cicada's cry
No sign can foretell
How soon it must die.

No one travels
Along this way but I,
This autumn evening.

In all the rains of May
there is one thing not hidden—
the bridge at Seta Bay.

The year's first day
thoughts and loneliness;
the autumn dusk is here.

Clouds appear
and bring to men a chance to rest
from looking at the moon.

Harvest moon:
around the pond I wander
and the night is gone.

Poverty's child—
he starts to grind the rice,
and gazes at the moon.

No blossoms and no moon,
and he is drinking sake
all alone!

Won't you come and see
loneliness? Just one leaf
from the *kiri* tree.

Temple bells die out.
The fragrant blossoms remain.
A perfect evening!

### *Analyze and Interpret*

To what do you attribute the appeal of this simple poetic form? What seems to be the poems' purpose, if any?

Source: From Haiku for People, http://www.toyomasu.com/haiku/#Basho.

The Japanese version of Confucianism was, as always, different from the Chinese. The secular, politically pragmatic nature of Confucius's doctrines comes through more emphatically in Japan. The Chinese mandarins of the nineteenth century had little tolerance for deviation from the prescribed version of the Master. But in Japan, several schools of thought contended and were unimpeded by an official prescription of right and wrong. Another difference was that whereas China had no room for a shogun, Japan had no room for the mandate of Heaven. Chinese tradition held that only China could be the Confucian "Empire of the Middle." The Japanese, on the other hand, although confident they were in that desirable position of centrality and balance, believed they need not ignore the achievements of other, less fortunate but not entirely misguided folk.

What was the significance of this pragmatic secularism for Japan? It helped prepare the ruling daimyo group for the invasion of Western ideas that came in the mid-nineteenth century. The Japanese elite were able to abandon their seclusion and investigate whatever Western technology could offer them with an open mind. In sharp contrast to China, when the Western avalanche could no longer be evaded, the Japanese governing class accepted it with little inherent resistance or cultural confusion.

At the outset of the Tokugawa shogunate, the Japanese educated classes were perhaps as familiar with science and technology as were the Westerners. Sakoku necessarily inhibited further progress. The Scientific Revolution and its accompanying technological advances were unknown in Japan, and the Enlightenment of the eighteenth century was equally foreign to the cultural landscape of even the most refined citizens (see Chapter 30). From the early 1800s, a few Japanese scholars and officials were aware that the West (including nearby Russia) was well ahead of them in certain areas, especially the natural sciences and medicine, and that much could be learned from the Westerners. These Japanese were in contact with the handful of Dutch merchants who had been allowed to stay in Japan, and they occasionally read Western science texts. "Dutch medicine," as Western anatomy, pharmacy, and surgery were called, was fairly well-known in upper-class Japan in the early nineteenth century, although it did not yet have much prestige.

Michael S. Yamashita/Corbis

**HIMEJI CASTLE.** This relatively late construction, known as the White Egret to the Japanese, stands today as a major tourist attraction. The massive stone walls successfully resisted all attackers.

When the American naval commander Matthew Perry arrived with his "black ships" to forcibly open the country to foreign traders in 1853 and 1854, the Japanese were not as ill-prepared as one might assume after two centuries of isolation. Aided by the practical and secular Confucian philosophy they had imbibed, the sparse but important Western scientific books they had studied, and the carefully balanced government they had evolved by trial and error, the Edo government, the daimyo, and their subofficials were able to absorb Western ideas and techniques by choice rather than by force. Rather than looking down their cultured noses at what the "hairy barbarians" might be bringing, the Japanese were able to say, "If it works to our benefit (or can be made to), use it." Unlike China, the West decidedly did not overwhelm the Japanese. On the contrary, they were true to their nation's tradition by showing themselves to be confident and pragmatic adapters of what they thought could be useful to themselves, rejecting the rest.

## SOUTHEAST ASIA

The territories in Southeast Asia that had succeeded in achieving political organization before the appearance of European traders and missionaries had little reason to fear or even take much notice of them until a much later era. Contacts were limited to coastal towns and were mainly commercial. In the 1600s, the Dutch had driven the Portuguese entirely out of the islands' spice trade, and they had established a loose partnership with the local Muslim sultans in Java and Sumatra in assuring the continuance of that trade with Europe. After a brief contest with the Dutch, the British, in the form of the East India Company, had withdrawn from the Spice Islands to concentrate on Indian cotton goods. Only in the Spanish Philippines was a European presence pervasive and politically dominant over a sizable area.

Most of the insular Asians were by now converted to Islam, a process that began in the 1400s through contact with Arab and Indian Muslim traders. Except for the island of Bali, the original syncretistic blend of Hindu with animist beliefs that had been India's legacy had faded away. Only in the Philippines was there a Christian element.

If the islands were relatively untouched by the early European traders, the mainland populations were even less so. In the 1700s, the three states of Thailand, Burma, and Vietnam dominated the area. The first two were by then part of the *Hinayana* Buddhist world, while Vietnam under Chinese influence had remained with the *Mahayana* version of the faith. The once-potent Khmer state of Cambodia had been divided between the Thais and the Viets by stages during the fifteenth through seventeenth centuries. Nowhere was there a visible European influence so late as the end of the eighteenth century, but this was to change radically in the next century.

### *The Colonial Experience*

In the early nineteenth century, a generation of European administrator-scholars entered into colonial careers following the Napoleonic wars (see Chapter 32). These men were products of the Enlightenment and were often sincerely dedicated to humane treatment of their Southeast Asian charges while still being convinced adherents of Western cultural superiority. Foremost among them was Sir Thomas Raffles, the founder of Singapore and the first European to take serious interest in the history and archaeology of the precolonial societies. Although Raffles was entrusted with oversight of affairs for only a few brief years in Java, his reforming policies aimed at promoting peasant prosperity and local government autonomy persisted as a model, which was unfortunately not often followed in the century to come.

Indonesia was returned to Dutch rule in 1824 by a treaty that finally settled the ancient Anglo-Dutch rivalry. In the century that followed, Dutch administrators gradually expanded their controls, both political and economic, over the hundreds of inhabited islands that make up the "East Indies" (see Map 29.2). The bloody five-year Java War (1825–1830) was the decisive step, establishing Dutch sovereignty once and for all over this most important of the Indonesian lands. Other battles had to be fought in Sumatra and in the Celebes at the end of the nineteenth century. Only then was a true Dutch colony, rather than a trade partnership, created.

In the economic sphere, the Dutch directed a change from a limited, spice export trade with the homeland to an expansive, commodity-oriented trade during the mid-nineteenth century. This change was accomplished via the "**culture system**," a refined form of peonage through which the peasants were obliged to deliver a major part of their crops to Dutch buyers at minimal prices. This system brought poverty to the Indonesians and great profits for the Dutch and Chinese middlemen, especially from the export of coffee, which replaced spices as the most important crop in the colony. The blatant abuses of the peasant laborers finally led to humanitarian reforms in the latter part of the century, but by this time, Java and Bali had been thrust into a cycle of declining availability of land and a rising population of rural tenants working absentee landlord estates. The resentments thus bred would inspire a tide of nationalist sentiment in the early twentieth century.

In mainland Asia, the assertion of Western colonial power extended first to the Burmese kingdom. As the British East India Company gradually transformed from a private commercial venture into a colonial government in India (see Chapter 32), its agents came into conflict with the claims of the Burmese rulers to certain frontier districts. A brief war ensued, with the customary results in favor of the Europeans. The process was renewed twice more in the mid-nineteenth century, and the Burmese eventually submitted to imperial oversight as a province of British India.

The sultans of Malaya (in the lower reach of the long Malay peninsula) followed a somewhat different route into the imperial camp. Here, the British at Singapore were joined by an influx of Chinese who quickly came to dominate the increasing trade going through the Straits of Malacca. By the 1870s (following the opening of the Suez Canal linking the Mediterranean and the Red Sea), this was the world's busiest waterway. Steamships and sailing vessels of many nations carried trade between Asian countries and took part in the long-distance transport between Asia and Europe. The remarkable growth of world markets for tin and rubber, both of which were found in abundance in the peninsula, also spurred alien business interests there. One after the other, the undeveloped sultanates were peaceably melded into the British "Straits Settlements," with a large population of immigrant Chinese in the mines and plantations. By the opening of the twentieth century, this jerry-built aggregation had become the colony of Malaya.

Vietnam fell under French dominion in this same epoch, largely because of the imperial ambitions of a handful of French leaders, who felt that Paris was falling behind London in the race for colonial riches. A secondary reason was the determination of the Catholic leadership in France to use Vietnam as the portal to the conversion of China to the Roman faith. French missionaries had been engaged among the Viets since the seventeenth century and had made considerable progress by

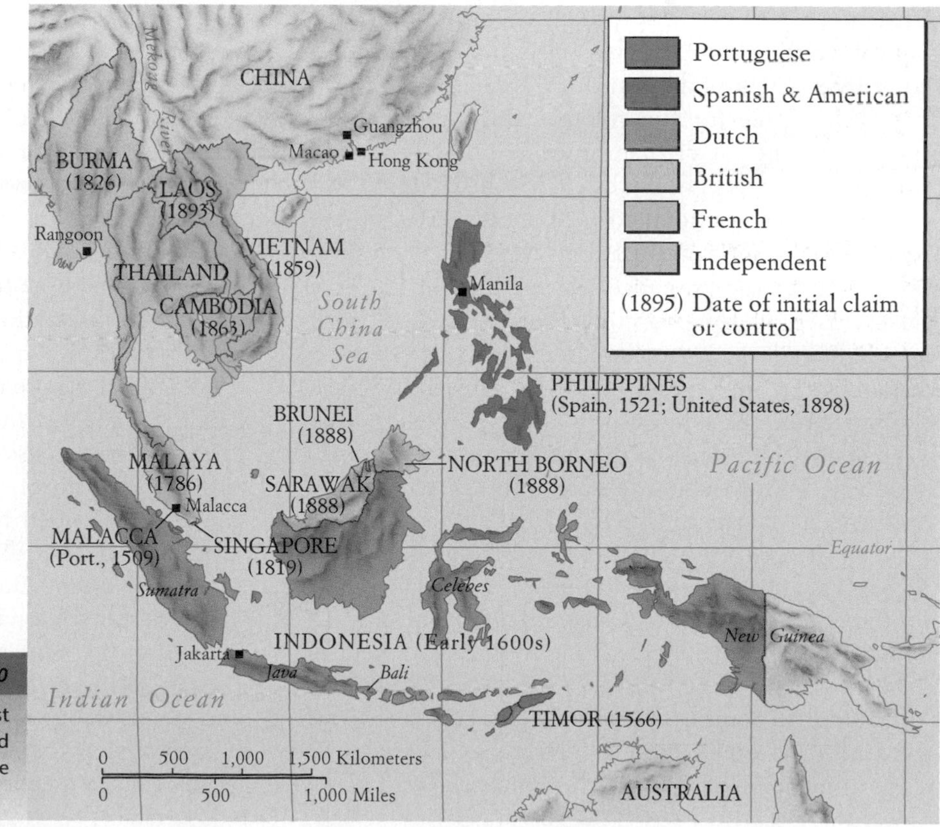

**MAP 29.2 *Colonial Southeast Asia, c. 1850***

At this point, European imperialism was just getting under way on the mainland but had a long history in the islands of Java and the Philippines.

**SINGAPORE'S INNER HARBOR.** The hundreds of sampans crowding the waterways of modern Singapore have not changed in design or use for several hundred years, since the Europeans first arrived in the Straits area.

Charles E. Rotkin/Corbis

the early years of the nineteenth century. At that time, they and their converts were subjected to an intense anti-Catholic campaign by a successful contestant in the recurrent civil wars that marked Vietnamese history in the nineteenth century. This was the justification for French military intervention that began in the 1850s and continued at intervals until all of the **Union of Indochina**—the official name for the colony, which included the present-day states of Vietnam, Laos, and Cambodia—fell under Parisian oversight by the end of the century.

As in Malaya, economic development picked up rapidly after the coming of the Europeans. Capital and steam power brought the great rice-growing area of the lower Mekong River valley into production for the first time, and Vietnam became the premier exporter of rice to the world markets. Rubber plantations followed. Unfortunately, the rice fields and plantations were owned either by aliens or by a small clique of aristocrats who were friendly to the French. The economic lot of the Vietnamese villagers deteriorated as a result of the new developments. Just as in Dutch-ruled Indonesia, the visible and growing cleft between the mass of the inhabitants and the European/bourgeois governmental class inspired the rise of strong nationalism among some of the newly educated.

Among the Southeast Asian nations, only Thailand (still known as Siam) escaped the colonial net and remained independent. How did this happen? It was partly a result of the 1893 agreement between the British in India and the French in Indochina that it would be convenient to maintain a buffer between their respective colonies, and that could only be Thailand. Thai independence was also partly the result of the remarkable vision and diplomatic skills of two nineteenth-century Thai kings, Mongkut (ruled 1851–1868) and his son and successor, Chulalongkorn (ruled 1868–1910). The two kings together brought their country into the modern age, introducing a wide variety of Western-style governmental and technical ideas into the still traditional Thai culture. These reforms ranged from overhauls of the judicial system to setting up a telegraph line, from abolition of the traditional prostration in the royal presence to the first printing press.

Although the premier foreign influence remained Britain, the Thai kings made it a point to invite advisers from many nations to assist them in their campaign of modernization. Not only were foreigners made to feel secure and well rewarded for their efforts, but the numerous members of the ruling clan were also encouraged to undergo Western education in several different countries before returning to take up their governmental duties. As a result of these policies of openness and technical progress, Thailand entered the twentieth century not only independent but also poised to meet Western cultural imperialism with an awakening sense of Thai national pride and a conviction of equality with the aliens.

## Summary

After a century of unchecked feudal warfare in Japan, three strongmen arose in the late sixteenth century to re-create effective centralized government. Last and most important was Tokugawa Ieyasu, who crushed or neutralized all opposition, including that of the Christian converts who were the product of the first European contacts with Japan in the mid-1500s.

By the 1630s, Japan was rapidly isolating itself from the world under the Tokugawa shogunate. The chief goal of the Tokugawa shoguns was a class-based political stability, which they successfully pursued for centuries. The shogun controlled all contacts with foreigners and gradually ended all interaction to isolate the island empire for more than 200 years. The daimyo nobility were carefully controlled by the shogun in Edo, who ruled from behind the imperial throne. Massive social changes took place at the same time the feudal political structure remained immobile. While urban merchants rose in the socioeconomic balance and peasants became wage laborers, the samurai slowly declined into obsolescence.

Population surged and the general economy prospered. The arts, particularly literature and painting, flourished. When Japan's solitude was finally broken, the governing elite were ready to deal with the challenge of Western science and technology constructively.

In Southeast Asia, the colonial period commenced with Dutch and Spanish presence in the Indonesian and Philippine Islands, respectively. But as late as the end of the eighteenth century, the Western traders and missionaries had had relatively little impact on the mass of the native inhabitants of the islands and even less on the mainland. This situation changed gradually but with increasing rapidity. The nineteenth century saw both a transformation of the former subsistence economy of the peasantry and the introduction of direct European control of government both in the islands and on the mainland. By 1900, the entire region, except for Thailand, had become a European colony.

## Identification Terms

Test your knowledge of this chapter's key concepts by defining the following terms. If you can't recall the meaning of certain terms, refresh your memory by looking up the boldfaced term in the chapter, turning to the Glossary at the end of the book, or working with the flashcards that are available on the *World Civilizations* Companion Website **http://history.wadsworth.com/adler04**.

culture system
*daimyo*
Edo
haiku
Kabuki
Kyoto
*sakoku*
*samurai*
shogunate
Union of Indochina

## Test Your Knowledge

Test your knowledge of this chapter by answering the following questions. Complete answers appear at the end of the book. You may also take this quiz interactively and find even more quiz questions on the *World Civilizations* Companion Website **http://history.wadsworth.com/adler04**.

1. The early Christian missionaries to Japan
   a. found a hostile reception.
   b. were mainly Protestants.
   c. made the mistake of trying to conquer the Buddhist natives.
   d. were welcomed and given a hearing.
   e. were evicted from the country within five years of their arrival.
2. The Shinto faith is best described as
   a. the native Japanese religion.
   b. the Japanese Holy Scripture.
   c. a mixture of Christianity and Japanese pagan belief.
   d. a variety of Buddhism imported from Korea.
   e. a reaction to the proselytizing of the Jesuits.

3. The Tokugawa shogun is best described as a
   a. military dictator.
   b. military adviser to the emperor.
   c. chief of government under the supposed supervision of the emperor.
   d. symbolic and religious leader under the emperor's supervision.
   e. feudal lord who first implemented shogunate rule.
4. The government system created by the shoguns in the 1600s
   a. allowed the local chieftains called *daimyo* to rule unchecked.
   b. was an imitation of the Chinese system of mandarin officials.
   c. made the daimyo dependent on the shogun's favor.
   d. used the emperor as military chief while the shoguns ruled all else.
   e. provided imperial protection for the families of the daimyo.
5. Which of the following did *not* occur during the Tokugawa period?
   a. Japanese elite thought shifted from Buddhist to Confucian patterns.
   b. Japanese formal culture stagnated in its continued isolation from the world.
   c. Trade and economic activity generally increased.
   d. Internal peace and order were effectively maintained.
   e. The elite samurai faded into obsolescence.
6. The reduction of the samurai's influence in public affairs was
   a. carried out through government-ordered purges.
   b. attempted but not achieved during the shogunate period.
   c. achieved by eliminating internal warfare through a strong government.
   d. achieved by encouraging them to become merchants and landlords.
   e. opposed by the shoguns but supported by the emperor.
7. The Kabuki drama
   a. specialized in dreamy romantic comedies.
   b. was limited in appeal to the samurai and daimyo.
   c. depicted drama in daily life in a realistic, humorous way.
   d. was an import from China.
   e. portrayed in realistic fashion the military exploits of the samurai.
8. Which of the following art forms was an original Japanese invention?
   a. Wood-block printing
   b. Haiku
   c. Nature poetry
   d. Weaving of silk tapestry
   e. The epic poem
9. The "culture system" was introduced in
   a. French Vietnam to ensure a supply of rice to the peasantry.
   b. Dutch Indonesia to ensure export profits.
   c. British Malaya to get the rubber plantations started.
   d. the Spanish Philippines to support the Catholic Church clergy.
   e. Japan to facilitate the opening of port cities to Western trade.
10. Thailand's continuing independence is largely attributable to
   a. the conflict between Vietnam and Burma.
   b. the determination of the Thai people.
   c. the protection afforded by the Manchu emperors in China.
   d. the desire for a buffer between India and Indochina.
   e. the desire of the Thai people to modernize their country.

## InfoTrac College Edition

Visit the source collections at

**http://infotrac.thomsonlearning.com**

and use the Search function with the following key terms:

Japan history     Tokugawa

## Wadsworth History Website Resources

Visit the World History Resource Center at **http://history.wadsworth.com/world** for a wealth of general resources, and the *World Civilizations* Companion Website at **http://history.wadsworth.com/adler04** for resources specific to this textbook.

## HistoryNow

Enter *HistoryNow* using the access card that is available for *World Civilizations*. *HistoryNow* will assist you in understanding the content in this chapter with lesson plans generated for your needs. In addition, you can read the following documents, and many more, online:

Honda Toshiaki, "A Secret Plan for Government"

Kaibara Ekken or Kaibara Token, "Greater Learning for Women"

*[The conquest] was neither a victory nor a defeat. It was the dolorous birth of the mestizo people.*
Anonymous Inscription at the Site of Final Aztec Defeat

# 30 From Conquest to Colonies in Hispanic America



| | |
|---|---|
| 1520s–1810s | Latin America under Spanish/Portuguese rule |
| 1650s–1750 | Stagnation under a weakened Spain |
| 1760–1790 | Revival of economy under Carlos III |
| 1793–1804 | Haitian slave rebellion and independence |

The arrival of the Europeans in the New World started an enormous exchange of crops and commodities, modalities, and techniques. The beginning and most important phase of this exchange was conducted under the auspices of the Spanish and Portuguese conquistadores, who so rapidly conquered the Indian populations in the sixteenth century. For the next 300 years, most of the newly discovered lands were administered by a colonial system that superimposed Iberian Christian economic institutions, habits, and values on existing indigenous ones. The form of colonial lifestyle that gradually evolved in Latin America was the product of the native Indians and the imported black slaves, as much as of the whites.

## The Fall of the Aztec and Inca Empires

We have seen (Chapter 23) that the initial phase of Spanish exploration in the Caribbean was dominated by the search for treasure. The "Indies" of Columbus were reputed to be lands of gold and spices, waiting to be exploited by the first individual who might happen upon them. Within a few years, however, this image was obliterated by the realities of the Caribbean islands, where gold was nonexistent. The search then shifted to the mainland, and the immediate result was the conquest of the Aztecs in Mexico and the Incas in Peru.

The Aztec capital fell in 1521 to conquistador Hernán Cortés, who began construction of Mexico City with stones from the leveled pyramids. Within a decade, Francisco Pizarro used the tactics of Cortés to conquer the Inca empire in South America. Pizarro, based in Panama, followed rumors of gold to the south, and by 1532 he had taken the Inca capital, Cuzco. Just as in Aztec Mexico, when the Spanish arrived in Peru, they found many allies to help them overthrow the Cuzco government, which was engaged in civil war. Also as in Mexico, the Spanish were immeasurably helped by the coincidence of their arrival with Indian expectations of the return of a white-skinned deity, who had departed in a distant past and, according to legend, would return in triumph to punish his enemies. Like the Aztec emperor Moctezuma, the Inca somewhat naively trusted the newcomers. The viral pandemics (smallpox, measles, and influenza) carried by the Spaniards to Mexico and Peru decimated the Indians' ranks while hardly affecting the Spaniards. The Native Americans perceived that their deities and leaders were powerless against the scourges of the conquistadores, while the apparently superior Catholic religion was able to protect its faithful. The generous social assistance programs of the Incas (see Chapter 12) were no longer enough to win the active loyalty of the Inca's subjects. Pizarro and his band, which was even smaller than that of Cortés in Mexico, were able to take the Inca king hostage and demolish the regime in a short time in the Peruvian lowlands and valleys. Some of the imperial family and their officials escaped to the high mountains and attempted to rule from there for another thirty years before being crushed. Spain showed little interest in the sparsely populated areas of northern Mexico and in southern South America, whose recalcitrant Amerindian groups raided frontier settlements throughout and even after the colonial period.

## The Colonial Experience

Spain's colonization of the New World focused on the conquered areas of the Aztec and Maya dominions (the colonial viceroyalty of New Spain) and the Inca empire (the viceroyalty of Peru). These areas had treasure in gratifying abundance, both in gold and, in even greater amounts, silver. Here Indian resistance was broken, and the small groups of Spaniards made themselves into regional chieftains, each with his Spanish entourage. One-fifth (*quinto*) of what was discovered or stolen belonged to the royal government; the remainder could be divided up as the conquistadores saw fit. Agricultural production was greatly enriched by the introduction of draft animals and new crops (cotton, wheat, rice, sugar cane, citrus fruits). The survivors of the pre-Columbian empires furnished a ready-made free labor pool, which was accustomed to organized labor for tribute to a central authority.

In this earliest period, until about 1560, the Spanish crown, which in theory was the ultimate proprietor of all the new lands, allowed the conquerors of the Indians the ***encomienda***, or the right to demand uncompensated labor from the natives as a reward for the risks and hardships of exploration. This soon led to such abuses that the priests who were charged with converting the Indians to Christianity (especially the determined and brave Dominican Bartolomé de las Casas) protested vigorously to Madrid, and the encomienda was abolished midway through the sixteenth century on paper, although somewhat later in fact.

It should be noted that the Spanish in America have long had an unjustified reputation for cruelty and indifference to Indian welfare (the "Black Legend"). It is true that most of the motley group of fortune seekers who constituted the conquistadores had no consideration whatever for the Indians; the Carib Taino tribe, for example, literally disappeared within a generation under their onslaught. But again and again during the sixteenth century, both the Spanish home government and its agents, the viceroyal councils in the Americas, intervened as best they could to ameliorate and protect the welfare of the natives. The colonial histories of other nations have no equivalent to the flat prohibition of Indian slavery or the precise outline of the rights of the Indians and the duties of the Spanish overlords that were features of the Spanish American administration as early as the 1560s. That the colonial elites recognized these prohibitions in theory but did not necessarily enforce them in practice is also, unfortunately, true. But the general thrust of law, legislation, and instructions to the bureaucracy in New Spain (Mexico) and Peru was definitely more solicitous of humane treatment of the natives than the colonial administrations of Holland or Britain in a later and supposedly more enlightened epoch.

This consideration, however, could not prevent a demographic disaster without parallel in history. Owing in part to a kind of soul sickness induced by their enslavement and subservience but much more to epidemic diseases brought by the whites and unfamiliar to the Indians, the populations of these civilized, agricultural folk crashed horrifically (see Chapter 23). By the mid-seventeenth century, the Indian populations had begun to recover but never did so fully. Latin American populations only reached their pre-Columbian levels in the nineteenth century, when the influx of blacks and whites had created a wholly different ethnic mix.

### Colonial Administration

The Spanish administration in most of the Americas and the Portuguese system in Brazil were essentially similar. Under the auspices of the home government, an explorer/conqueror was originally allowed nearly unlimited proprietary powers in the new land. Soon, however, he was displaced by a royal council set up with exclusive powers over commerce, crafts, mining, and every type of foreign trade. Stringent controls were imposed through a viceroy or governor appointed by the Spanish government in Madrid and responsible solely to it. Judicial and military matters were also handled through the councils or the colonial *audiencia* (court) in each province. The only hints of elective government were in the bottom ranks of the bureaucracy: the early Spanish town councils (*cabildos*) and the traditional communes of the Indian villages.

The colonial administration was dominated by Iberian-born nobles (*peninsulares*). It was highly bureaucratized and mirrored the home government in its composition and aims. A great deal of paper dealing with legal cases, regulations, appointment procedures, tax rolls, and censuses flowed back and forth across the Atlantic. From the mid-sixteenth century, the government's basic aim was to maximize fiscal and commercial revenues for the home country.

Secondarily, the government wished to provide an avenue of upward mobility for ambitious young men in the administration of the colonies. The viceroys of New Spain and of Peru were established in the mid-sixteenth century, and the holders of these posts were always peninsulares. A few of them were able administrators; most were court favorites being rewarded with a sinecure with opportunities for wealth. Despite all attempts to ensure Madrid's controls over colonial policies, the sheer distance involved and the insecurity of ocean travel meant that the local officials—normally ***criollos*** (native-born people of Iberian race in Latin America)—had considerable autonomy. Their care of their Indian and mestizo charges varied from blatant exploitation to admirable solicitude.

### The Church in the Colonies

Another Iberian institution was as strong as the civil government in the colonies: the Catholic Church. Filled with the combative spirit and sense of high mission that were a legacy of the long *reconquista* struggle against the Moors, the missionaries were anxious to add the Central and South American Indians to the church's ranks. In this endeavor the Madrid authorities supported them. A church stood at the center of every town in the new lands; all other buildings were oriented around it. The bishops, nominated by the Crown, were as important in the administration of a given area as the civil governors; cultural and educational matters pertaining to both Europeans and Indians were in their hands. In its baroque buildings and artworks, the church left a long-lasting physical imprint throughout the Spanish and Portuguese colonies. The spiritual imprint was even more profound, continuing to the present day.

## The Early Economic Structure

The major element in the economy of the early Spanish colonies was the mining of precious metals. Everything else served that end. (Brazil, the Portuguese colony, was originally a sugarcane plantation, but later it also emphasized mining.) The agricultural estates, which were first encomiendas and then ***haciendas***—rural plantation-villages with at least technically free wage labor—existed primarily to supply food for the mining communities. Handicraft industries made gloves and textiles, prepared foods, and provided blacksmithing services for the same market. There were few exports beyond the produce of the mines and a handful of cash crops such as sugar and indigo.

Rights to export goods to the Spanish colonies were limited to Spaniards; the goods could be carried only in Spanish ships, which left from one port, Seville (later also Cádiz), twice a year. From Latin America, another flotilla

**A Baroque Church.** The intricate façade of this church in Guanajuato, Mexico, is a good example of the Spanish baroque style that the colonial governors and artists of the seventeenth century brought to Latin America. The work was performed by native craftsmen, who frequently used Indian motifs in combination with the Spanish designs.

Danny Lehman/Corbis

laden with the bullion mined the previous year left annually from the Mexican port of Vera Cruz. The restrictions on these flotillas were intended to protect the returning treasure from the Americas from pirates and to restrict what was sent to and taken from the colonies.

The great bonanza of the early years was the "mountain of silver" at Potosí in what is now Bolivia. Next to it came the Mexican mines north of Mexico City. The silver that flowed from the New World to Seville (and from Acapulco to Manila) from the 1540s to the 1640s far overshadowed the gold taken from Moctezuma and the Inca in the conquest period. When the volume declined drastically in the 1640s, the Madrid government experienced a crisis. Production stayed relatively low for a century, but thanks to new technology and increased incentives, it reached great heights in the later eighteenth century before declining again, this time for good.

The input of bullion did not produce lasting constructive results in Spain. Some of it flowed on through royal or private hands to enrich the western European shippers, financiers, merchants, and manufacturers who supplied Iberia with every type of good and service in the sixteenth and seventeenth centuries. Perhaps a third wound up in Chinese hands to pay for the Spanish version of the triangular trade across the Pacific: Spanish galleons left Acapulco, Mexico, loaded with silver and bound for Manila, where they met Chinese ships loaded with silk and porcelain, which, after transshipment across Mexico or Panama, wound up in Seville and might be reshipped back to the Caribbean. Less than half of the Spanish silver remained in Spanish hands, but this was enough to start an inflationary spiral there that seized all of Europe by the end of the sixteenth century and brought ruin to many landholding nobles (see Chapter 23).

## Stagnation and Revival in the Eighteenth Century

The later seventeenth century and the first decades of the eighteenth were a period of stagnation and decline in New Spain. The last Spanish Habsburg kings were so weak that local strongmen in Latin America were able to overshadow the audiencia and *corregidores* (municipal authorities) of the viceroyal governments. The once-annual treasure fleets were sailing only sporadically, and the total supply of American bullion was down sharply from its high point. Several of the larger Caribbean islands were captured by the British, French, or Dutch or were taken over by buccaneers. The import/export controls imposed by the Madrid government were falling apart, because non-Spaniards were able to ignore the prohibitions against trading with the colonies, were granted exemptions, or collaborated with the criollos in smuggling in systematic fashion. By now the colonies could produce the bulk of their necessities and no longer had to import them.

At this juncture, the Spanish government experienced a revival as a new dynasty, an offshoot of the French Bourbons, took over in Madrid in 1701 as a result of the war of Spanish Succession (see Chapter 25). Especially under King Carlos III (ruled 1759–1788), who figured among the most enlightened monarchs of the eighteenth century, thoroughgoing reform was applied to the Indies. A form of free trade was introduced, the navy and military were strengthened, and a new system of *intendants,* responsible to the center on the French Bourbon model, was able to make Spanish colonial government much more effective. Taxes were collected as they had not been for years, and smuggling and corruption were reduced. The two Spanish American viceroyalties were subdivided into four: New Spain, Peru, New Granada (northern South America), and Rio de la Plata (Argentina and central South America). The officials for these new divisions continued to be drawn almost exclusively from the peninsula, an affront that the people in the colonies did not easily swallow. Another point of contention was that many criollo clergymen were among the Jesuit missionaries banished by the anticlerical Bourbons from the Iberian empire. Colonists throughout the Western Hemisphere rose up in protest against the expulsion of the Jesuits, who had won the hearts and minds of all, and who from their exile encouraged the emerging sense of Hispano-American identity among criollos and mestizos alike.

The reforms did not benefit the mass of Indian and mestizo inhabitants at all. Indian population increased (perhaps doubling) in the eighteenth century, creating an irresistible temptation to hacienda owners to press this defenseless and unskilled group into forced labor in the expanding plantation agriculture. The market for these products was not only the seemingly insatiable demand for sugar in Europe and North America but also the rapidly growing population in the colonies. The foreseeable result was an expansion of brutal serfdom, generating a series of Indian uprisings. The most notable was led by Tupac Amaru, a descendant of the Inca, in the 1780s. The viceroyal government of Peru was nearly toppled before the revolt was put down. A few years later in the Caribbean island of Haiti (then Saint Domingue), a black ex-slave named Toussaint L'Ouverture led an uprising of slaves that ended French dominion on that island. The Toussaint rebellion eventually succeeded in attaining complete independence for Haiti, and it made an indelible impression on both the friends and enemies of the daring idea of a general abolition of slavery.

The oppressed Indians and enslaved blacks were by no means the only Latin Americans who were discontented in the last years of the eighteenth century. Economic policy reforms, however needed, were also sometimes painful to the native-born criollos. With free trade, imports from Europe became considerably cheaper, hurting domestic producers. And the remarkable increase in silver production as a result of new mining techniques and new discoveries did not flow to the benefit of the locals but rather to what was more often now viewed as an alien government in Madrid. The untying of the former restrictions on trade and manufactures had a distinctly stimulative effect on the intellectual atmosphere of the criollo urbanites. After decades of somnolence, there arose within a small but crucially important minority a spirit of criticism and inquiry, which reflected the stirring of European liberalism we shall examine in Chapter 32.

**A Hacendado and His Family.** This nineteenth-century scene shows a Mexican hacendado, owner of a large plantation, with his wife and one of his overseers. The elaborate costumes were impractical but necessary in maintaining social distance from the peons.

In the 1770s, the criollo elite witnessed the successful (North) American revolt against Britain, and a few years later, the radical French revolution doctrines seized their attention. In both of these foreign upheavals, they believed they saw many similarities with their own grievances against their government, similarities that were to be ultimately persuasive for their own rebellion.

## Colonial Society and Culture

The class system was based on the degree of "purity" of Spanish bloodlines. In a legal sense, both peninsulares and criollos were considered Spanish. However, the peninsulares considered themselves superior to their criollo cousins, whom they supposed were even physically inferior by virtue of their birth in the Americas. The peninsulares occupied the uppermost ranks of society, church, and government, and they excluded the criollos from positions of power to prevent the formation of a strong native-born elite that might threaten the dominance of the peninsulares. Yet the criollos (especially the descendants of the conquistadores), being owners of haciendas and mines, were often wealthier than the peninsulares. Both groups did their utmost to re-create Spanish life in the New World.

Social life was centered in the cities and towns, because the Spaniards preferred urban life. The elite lifestyle was slow-paced and leisurely, consisting of carriage rides and other outings to display their finery, religious ceremonies and festivals, and diversions such as gambling, bullfights, and the popular baroque poetry contests. It was said that the (mostly bad) colonial poets were a "flock of noisy magpies." For the men, there were cockfights, liaisons with the beautiful mixed-blood women, and other indulgences. The criollos, relegated to secondary status, cultivated intellectual and literary pursuits to enrich the limited cultural environment. Although the Inquisition prohibited reading novels and other heretical material, and the printing presses in Mexico and Lima produced mostly religious material, secular books were nonetheless widely available, and the criollo intellectuals kept abreast of Enlightenment thought and the latest European literary currents. Women were mainly limited to religious literature. The monastery or convent were also options for the criollos. In the more lenient religious orders, the "cells" were more like suites of rooms.

In this strongly patriarchal society, women lacked independent legal status and were expected to obey their fathers, brothers, or husbands unconditionally. Spanish women were carefully protected, because their family's honor depended on their irreproachable behavior. The daughters of criollos were married, if possible, to newly arrived peninsulares to ensure the family's prestige. Young men were sent to Spain or France for higher education. Young women were given a rudimentary education by tutors at home, and a few learned domestic and social arts at mission schools, but they were denied any higher education. In the final analysis, elite women had three alternatives: marriage, spinsterhood, or the convent. Widows of comfortable financial status were the

Museo de America, Madrid, Spain/Giraudon/Bridgeman Art Library

**Sister Juana Inés de la Cruz.** Sister Juana was the finest poet of her day in the Spanish empire, an extraordinary achievement given the constraints on colonial women. Sister Juana, although beautiful and accomplished, was a poor, illegitimate criolla. She became a nun in order to pursue her studies and writing, but she came under criticism from her superiors for such wordly pursuits and eventually renounced books in order to save her soul.

most independent women in colonial times; they were free to make their own decisions, and they often ran the family businesses with great success.

The *mestizos,* or "mixed-blood," sons of Spanish men and Indian women, became adept at creating roles for themselves in a society that had originally despised them as mongrels. They served as intermediaries and interpreters among the elites, the Indians, and other categories of mixed-blood peoples. Mestizos were excluded from the universities and from positions in the church and the government. They could be soldiers but not officers, artisans' apprentices but not master craftsmen. Mestizos might be tenant farmers or hacienda managers. The mestizo horsemen of the Argentine grasslands (the *pampas*) found their niche as providers of contraband cowhides and tallow.

The fifteen other categories of mixed-blood peoples were more severely restricted than the mestizos and were not permitted to bear arms. African-Americans were at the bottom of the social pyramid. Along with the surviving Indians, they slaved from dawn to dusk in the mines, on haciendas and plantations, in sweatshops and mills, for little or no pay. Their only opportunities for rest were the Sunday mass and markets and the occasional festival. Non-Spanish women were less restricted because the Amerindian and African cultures were less patriarchal in origin.

The subdued Amerindians lived in a variety of other settings besides haciendas and plantations. After the decimation of the Native Americans in the Caribbean, the Spanish policy was to protect the Indians and facilitate their Christianization by keeping them separate from abusive Spaniards. Indians were exempt from some taxes, and because they were viewed as children in the eyes of the Church, they were beyond the reach of the Inquisition.

The Granger Collection, New York

**The Indian Virgin of Guadalupe.** Hispanic Catholicism took on new forms in the American colonies, as Indians and Africans blended Catholic saints with their precontact deities. The miraculous appearance of the Indian Virgin Mary occurred not long after the conquest, at a site sacred to the Aztec Earth goddess, where a cathedral was built.

# Forced Labor and Debt Peonage in the Colonies

**The luxurious lifestyle of the colonial** elites was supported by the labors of their inferiors in the social pyramid: Native Americans, Africans, and mestizos. They toiled in the textile mills and on the haciendas, where conditions (although wretched) were still preferable to working in the mines, as detailed in the following description:

In the 1620s, a Spanish monk traveled through the Spanish colonies in the Americas, making careful observation of what he witnessed, among which was the workings of early textile mills and how they got their labor.

"There are in this city [Puebla, in central Mexico] large woolen mills in which they weave quantities of fine cloth. . . . To keep their mills supplied with labor, they maintain individuals who are engaged and hired to snare poor innocents; seeing some Indian who is a stranger to the town, with some trickery or pretense, such as hiring him to carry something, like a porter, and paying him cash, they get him into the mill; once inside, they drop the deception, and the poor fellow never again gets outside that prison until he dies and they carry him out for burial.

In this way they have gathered in and duped many married Indians with families, who have passed into oblivion here for 20 years, or longer, or their whole lives, without their wives and children knowing anything about them; for even if they want to get out, they cannot, thanks to the great watchfulness with which the doormen guard the exits. These Indians are occupied in carding, spinning, weaving, and the other operations of making cloth; and thus the owners make their profits by these unjust and unlawful means.

And although the Royal Council of the Indies, with the holy zeal which animates it in the service of God our Lord, of his Majesty, and of the Indians' welfare, has tried to remedy this evil . . . and the Viceroy of New Spain appoints mill inspectors to visit them and remedy such matters, nevertheless, since most of those who set out on such commissions aim rather at their own enrichment, however much it may weigh upon their consciences, than at the relief of the Indians, and since the mill owners pay them well, they leave the wretched Indians in the same slavery; and even if some of them are fired with holy zeal to remedy such abuses when they visit the mills, the mill owners keep places provided in the mills in which they hide the wretched Indians against their will, so that they do not see or find them, and the poor fellows cannot complain against their wrongs."

Source: A. Vásquez de Espinosa, *Compendium and Description of the West Indies,* trans. C. Clark (Washington, DC: Smithsonian, 1942).

Spanish royal officials described the plight of the Indians in Peru, who not only paid the tribute tax, but also were condemned to the serfdom of debt **peonage;** that is, perpetually working off debts forced on them by their masters.

On farming haciendas, an Indian subject . . . earns from fourteen to eighteen pesos a year. . . . In addition, the hacendado assigns him a piece of land, about twenty to thirty yards square in size, to grow his food. In return the Indian must work three hundred days in the year, leaving him sixty-five days of rest for Sundays, other church holidays, illness, or some accident that may prevent him from working. The *mayordomo* (foreman) of the hacienda keeps careful record of the days worked by the Indian in order to settle accounts with him at the end of the year.

From his wage the master deducts the eight pesos of royal tribute that the Indian must pay; assuming that the Indian earns eighteen pesos, the most he can earn, he is left with ten pesos. From this amount the master deducts 2.25 pesos to pay for three yards of coarse cloth . . . [for] a cloak to cover his nakedness. He now has 7.75 pesos with which to feed and dress his wife and children, if he has a family, and to pay the church fees demanded by the parish priest. But . . . since he cannot raise on his little plot all the food he needs for his family, he must get from the hacendado each month two bushels of maize, [at] more than double the price if he could buy elsewhere, [an annual total of] nine pesos, which is 1.75 pesos more than the Indian has left. Thus the unhappy Indian, after working three hundred days of the year for his master and cultivating his little plot in his free time, and receiving only a coarse cloak and twelve bushels of maize, is in debt 1.75 pesos, and must continue to work for his master the following year [borrowing more money for church rites and emergencies]. . . . Since it is impossible for the poor Indian to [pay the debt], he remains a slave all his life and, contrary to natural law and the law of nations, after his death his sons must continue to work to pay the debt of their father.

Source: Jorge Juan and Antonio de Ulloa, *Noticias secretas de América* (Madrid, 1918), 2 vols., I, pp. 290–292, as quoted in Benjamin Keen, ed., *Latin American Civilization,* 4th ed. (Boulder and London: Westview Press, 1986), pp. 75–76.

## *Analyze and Interpret*

Contrast the actual treatment of the colonial Amerindians to the treatment intended by royal decrees for their protection. What factors might account for the difference between the ideal and the actual treatment?

## Festivals in Cuzco, Peru

**THE CORPUS CHRISTI FESTIVAL,** with its fascinating blend of traditional Hispanic Catholicism and ancient Inca motifs, was witnessed by a travelling criollo postal inspector in the eighteenth century. The enthusiasm of the Indians for the Corpus Christi procession of the image of the crucified Christ may hark back to a pre-Columbian ceremony in which the mummies of past Incas were carried in processions both reverent and festive.

> Religious festivals: The great Catholic festival of God (Corpus Christi) begins in June and ends in August. These days are celebrated with devotion and amusement in the poorest towns in Spain and the Indies. The serious devotions are observed in the church ceremonies . . . and continue in the processions of the high clergy and the inquisitors, followed by the cabildo (town council) and all the nobility with their best finery, [all to accompany the holy image of Christ, while He is revered by the spectators, and the Host is administered.]
>
> The second part of the procession is truly diverting [to the observer]. . . . [T]he ancient dances of the Indios that converge on Cuzco . . . are very solemn in content because the Indians are of naturally serious temperament. Their main adornments are made of heavy silver, which they rent from various mestizos who engage in this trade. . . . The [traditional Spanish floats and oversized figures], although they have no connection with Catholic rites [because the Indians have substituted precolumbian motifs], are approved by the authorities as a festival gift, because they make the people happy."

This second description by the same traveler shows Carnival celebrations by various segments of Cuzco's population. It is apparent that, no matter their social class, the colonists celebrated to the utmost every possible occasion.

> A secular festival [Carnival]: The festivities consist chiefly of bullfights, lasting from the first of the year till Lent. . . . As soon as one [bull] tires, he is released in one of the side streets for the amusement of the populace. . . . The employees of the farms, riding fast horses, are usually the ones who take part, as well as young men on foot, generally Indians, who correspond to the lower class in Spain. . . .
>
> The nobility of Cuzco appear in the plaza on fine horses beautifully adorned with velvet . . . gold and silver. The clothing of the horsemen is often made of the choicest fabrics of Lyon, France. . . . These horsemen are attendants to the mayor and his cabinet, who . . . watch the bullfighting, or greet the ladies and receive their gifts of fine candies or perfumed water, tossed from the balconies. . . . [T]he ladies have bags of cheap candy to throw to the crowd that throws them back, and those of the lower class pick them up and sell them to the men on horseback.
>
> At the end of the festivities, fireworks are set off, . . . then everyone retires to prepare for the dawn of Ash Wednesday.

Robert Frerck/Odyssey Productions, Inc.

**CORPUS CHRISTI IN CUZCO TODAY.** The Corpus Christi festival continues to attract visitors today.

### *Analyze and Interpret*

What do these passages reveal about the relationship between colonial social life and the Catholic religion?

Source: Alonso Carrió de la Vandera, *El Lazarillo de ciegos caminantes* (The Guide of Blind Travelers), Chapter XXII (Lima, 1775–1776), trans. Willis Knapp Jones in *Spanish American Literature in Translation,* Vol. 1 (New York: Ungar, 1966), pp. 93–95.

Communally run Indian towns, vestiges of the pre-Columbian empires, were remote from the Hispanic towns and were left intact. The only outsiders they saw were priests and tribute collectors (the infamously corrupt *corregidores*). In areas where the Indians had dispersed and a demand arose for their labor in the mines, the Spanish rounded them up and settled them in newly established Spanish-run towns, where clergy saw to their instruction in the Catholic faith, and where they were readily accessible for tribute labor. Finally, the religious orders collected the Indians in missions, where they received the rudiments of religious indoctrination and were taught useful crafts. Treatment of the Indians in the missions ranged from exploitative to benevolent, but even in the best of cases, they were legally classified as minors and treated as children.

The Indians throughout the colonies adopted Christianity, identifying particularly with the consoling figure of the Virgin Mary (similar to their earth goddesses) and with the crucified Christ (whose suffering paralleled their own traumatic conquest). To varying degrees, the Catholic saints were blended with pre-Columbian deities. A group of Indians devoutly praying at a saint's altar in a baroque cathedral might well be paying homage to the Inca or Aztec deity hidden under the statue's skirts. In the Caribbean areas, the Africans equated Catholic saints to Orusha deities, resulting in syncretic belief systems such as *santería,* which is still practiced by most Cubans.

## Summary

The Iberian conquest of Latin America was a clash of cultures that devastated the pre-Columbian civilizations but set the stage for the creation of a new society that blended contributions from Native Americans, Iberians, and later, Africans. As the conquerors and explorers became colonists, they replaced the Aztec and Inca masters at the top of the socioeconomic ladder. The conquerors' thirst for gold and elite status could be quenched only with the labor of the Indians. The Iberian monarchs, aided by progressive missionaries, tried in vain to protect their spiritually innocent Indian charges in order to convert them humanely to Christianity.

The colonial experience in Latin America was quite different from that in Asia, North America, or Africa. Many Europeans eventually settled there but remained far outnumbered by the native Indians and the imported blacks. The church and government worked together to create a society that imitated that of the mother countries, while remaining different in many essentials. The unique melding of Iberian with Indian and African cultures proceeded at differing tempos in different places.

After the flow of American bullion to the Old World tapered off in the mid-seventeenth century, a long period of stagnation and neglect ensued. A century later, the Spanish Bourbons supervised an economic and political revival in Latin America with mixed results. While the economies of the colonies were stimulated, so was resentment against continued foreign rule. By the early 1800s, armed rebellion against the mother country was imminent, inspired in part by the North American and French models.

## Identification Terms

Test your knowledge of this chapter's key concepts by defining the following terms. If you can't recall the meaning of certain terms, refresh your memory by looking up the boldfaced term in the chapter, turning to the Glossary at the end of the book, or working with the flashcards that are available on the *World Civilizations* Companion Website **http://history.wadsworth.com/adler04.**

*criollos*
*encomienda*
*haciendas*
peonage

## Test Your Knowledge

Test your knowledge of this chapter by answering the following questions. Complete answers appear at the end of the book. You may also take this quiz interactively and find even more quiz questions on the *World Civilizations* Companion Website **http://history.wadsworth.com/adler04.**

1. Which of following Spanish terms does not apply to Latin American social or ethnic divisions?
   a. Criollo
   b. Menudo
   c. Mestizo
   d. Zambo
   e. Mulatto
2. Which of the following factors helped bring about the rapid fall of both the Aztec and Inca empires?
   a. The Indians thought Cortés and Pizarro were devils.
   b. The conquistadores lost their Indian allies against the emperors.
   c. The conquistadores bribed Moctezuma and Atahualpa to betray their people.
   d. The Indians had steel weapons capable of killing an armored horseman.
   e. Masses of Indians died or were weakened by foreign diseases.
3. The following were introduced to the Americas by the Iberians:
   a. Turkeys and tobacco
   b. Chocolate and maize
   c. Cattle, sugar cane, and wheat
   d. Pyramids and potatoes
   e. Tomatoes and tortillas
4. Which of these were main features of the colonial system?
   a. Viceroyalties and cabildos
   b. Democratic elections
   c. Free trade among the viceroyalties
   d. The predominance of small farms owned by mulattos
   e. Separation of church and civil government
5. Of the following elements, which were important goals of the Spanish in the New World?
   a. Gold and silver
   b. Religious conversion of the Amerindians
   c. Establishment of new industries
   d. The Black Legend
   e. Both a and b
6. One result of the Bourbon reforms was
   a. decentralization of power and more autonomy for the colonies.
   b. vast improvements in the Indians' quality of life.
   c. mercantilism and trade monopolies.
   d. more efficient government and less corruption.
   e. mine closures and the breakup of huge haciendas.
7. The only successful rebellion by slaves in the Western Hemisphere occurred in
   a. Haiti.
   b. Cuba.
   c. Colombia.
   d. Brazil.
   e. Mexico.
8. Which factor led to the discontent of the criollos with colonial rule?
   a. The consolidation of two viceroyalties into one
   b. The peninsulares' exclusion of criollos from the upper echelons of government and society
   c. The expulsion of the Muslim Moors
   d. The Monroe Doctrine
   e. The Black Legend
9. Colonial Amerindians usually worked
   a. in the colonial government.
   b. in mines, mills, and religious missions.
   c. as foremen on the haciendas.
   d. for inflated wages and comfortable retirements.
   e. part time as horsebreakers.
10. The colonial mestizos
    a. were not exempt from taxation and the Inquisition.
    b. were never nomadic horsemen.
    c. served as links between the Indian and Spanish populations.
    d. were encouraged to attend university.
    e. could be military officers.

## InfoTrac College Edition

Visit the source collections at

**http://infotrac.thomsonlearning.com**

and use the Search function with the following key terms:

Latin America history

## Wadsworth History Website Resources

Visit the World History Resource Center at **http://history.wadsworth.com/world** for a wealth of general resources, and the *World Civilizations* Companion Website at **http://history.wadsworth.com/adler04** for resources specific to this textbook.

## HistoryNow

Enter *HistoryNow* using the access card that is available for *World Civilizations*. *HistoryNow* will assist you in understanding the content in this chapter with lesson plans generated for your needs. In addition, you can read the following documents, and many more, online:

Aztec Accounts of the Conquest of Mexico

Hernán Cortés, "Second Letter to Charles V"

# Worldview Four

| |  Law and Government |  Society and Economy |
|---|---|---|
| **Europeans** | Law and government are based on class, but the effect of religious wars is to make them increasingly secular. Absolutist monarchy is the rule, with few exceptions (England, Holland). Nobles and landlords rule free peasants in West, serfs in East. State and church are still intertwined; religious tolerance is considered dangerous to public order by most governments. | The economy continues to diversify, with strong capitalist character, especially in Protestant nations. The urban middle class becomes prominent in business and commerce. Class divisions and the number of impoverished people increase, with abject serfdom common east of the Elbe River. Machine industry begins in the later eighteenth century in western Europe. |
| **West Asians** | Government among the Muslims continues along traditional Qur'anic lines, and law follows the *Sharia.* Ottomans bring the Muslim international empire to its apex in the sixteenth century, but they cannot sustain the momentum after 1700. The Safavid Dynasty in Persia has 200 years of glory but exhausts itself between Ottoman and Mughal rivals in Turkey and India. | Highly commercialized, complex trade further evolves among Muslim countries as well as between them and the non-Muslims. Slavery remains common, mainly from African sources. Wealth is generated from gold mines in West Africa, spices from East Asia, and carrying trade between India/China and the West via the Mediterranean. |
| **South and East Asians** | The Western presence is not yet decisive but is becoming steadily more apparent. Many South Pacific island territories have been under Western colonial administration since the 1500s. Japan originally welcomes Westerners but then shuts itself off in *sakoku.* China continues as an imperial dynasty ruling through mandarin bureaucracy after the Manzhou replace the Ming in 1600s. India's north and center are unified under the Mughal dynasts in Delhi with European colonies beginning to occupy the coasts after 1700. | Japan prospers and advances while maintaining *sakoku* isolation; China has its last great age under the early Qing before suffering humiliation from European hands: North and South are brought firmly together by extensive trade. Mughul India is still a well-organized, prosperous country, with much commerce with Southeast Asia and islands. Merchants and craftsmen multiply, but everywhere the agrarian village is the mainstay of the economy. |
| **Americans** | By the mid-1500s, Spain and Portugal have established Iberian law and viceroyalties from Mexico to Argentina. Natives are subordinated to a small minority of whites. Highly centralized colonial governments are committed to the mercantilist system and discouragement of autonomy. Reversal of these policies occurs in the later 1700s and proves the cradle of independency movement. | Mercantilism is enforced until the later 1700s, with colonial artisans and manufacturers obstructed by Madrid and London. Mining and plantation agriculture are the dominant large-scale economic activities in the Latin colonies. Most of the population in both the North and the South lives in agrarian subsistence economy. |

# DISEQUILIBRIUM: THE WESTERN ENCOUNTER WITH THE NON-WESTERN WORLD, 1500–1700 C.E.

|  PATTERNS OF BELIEF |  ARTS AND CULTURE |  SCIENCE AND TECHNOLOGY |
| --- | --- | --- |
| Christian unity is broken by Protestant Reform. The papal church is severely challenged, but it regains some lost ground in the seventeenth century. Churches become nationalistic, and theology is more narrowly defined. Skepticism and secularism increase after 1700, leading to increased religious tolerance by the end of the eighteenth century. Enlightenment dominates intellectual affairs after c. 1750. | The Renaissance continues in plastic arts; the great age of baroque architecture, sculpture, and painting thrives in Catholic Europe. Neoclassicism of the eighteenth century is led by France. Vernacular literature flourishes in all countries. Western orchestral music begins. Authors become professionals, and the arts begin to be democratized. | Physical, math-based sciences flourish in the "scientific revolution" of the seventeenth century. Science replaces scripture and tradition as the source of truth for many educated persons. Technology becomes much more important. Weaponry enables the West to dominate all of its opponents. Improved agriculture enables the population explosion of the eighteenth century. The beginnings of the Industrial Revolution are manifested in England. |
| *Ulema* and Islamic tradition resist the accumulating evidence of Western superiority and attempt to ignore or refute it on doctrinal grounds. Religious orthodoxy is severely challenged in various parts of the empire (e.g., Sufi, Shi'a) and becomes increasingly defensive. Islamic expansion makes its last major surge into the Asian heartland (Mughal India). | This is the high point of Islamic art forms under Ottoman, Safavid, and Mughal aegis. Architecture, ceramics, miniature painting, and calligraphy are some particular strengths. | Sciences are neglected; the original mental capital derived from Greek and Persian sources is now exhausted, and no new impulses are discovered. Technology also lags, with almost all new ideas coming from the West rejected as inferior or blasphemous. By the end of this period, Westerners are moving into the preferred posts in commerce of the Ottoman and Mughal empires (capitulations, East India Company). |
| Religious beliefs undergo no basic changes from the prevalent Buddhism (China, Japan, Southeast Asia); Hinduism (most of India, parts of Southeast Asia); Islam (North India, Afghanistan, East Indies); and Shinto (Japan). Christianity briefly flourishes in Japan until it is suppressed by Tokugawa shoguns in the 1600s, but it makes little headway in China and India. | Superb paintings and drawings on porcelain, bamboo, and silk are created in China and Japan. Calligraphy is a major art form. *Kabuki* and *No* plays are invented in Japan, and novels appear in China. Poetry of nature is admired. In India, the Taj Mahal, frescoes, enamel work, and Mughal architecture are high points. | Sciences throughout Asia fall rapidly behind Europe by the end of this period. The exceptions are in medicine and pharmacy. China adopts defensive seclusion from new ideas under mandarin officials. Technology also lags, as overpopulation begins to be a problem at the end of this period, further reducing the need for labor-saving devices or methods. |
| Catholicism makes a somewhat deeper impression on Latin American Indians, but religion remains a mixed cult of pre-Christian and Christian beliefs, supervised by *criollo* priesthood and Spanish hierarchs. | The church in Latin America remains the major sponsor of the formal arts, but folk arts derived from pre-Columbian imagery remain universal. Baroque churches are the center of social life. Little domestic literature is written, but secular Enlightenment makes inroads into a small educated class by the mid-eighteenth century. | Science and technology in Latin colonies are totally dependent on the stagnant mother country and have no importance to illiterate masses. Enlightened monarchs of the later 1700s make some improvements, but these are temporary and partial. In North America, the Enlightenment finds ready acceptance and lively intellectual exchanges. |

# PART FIVE

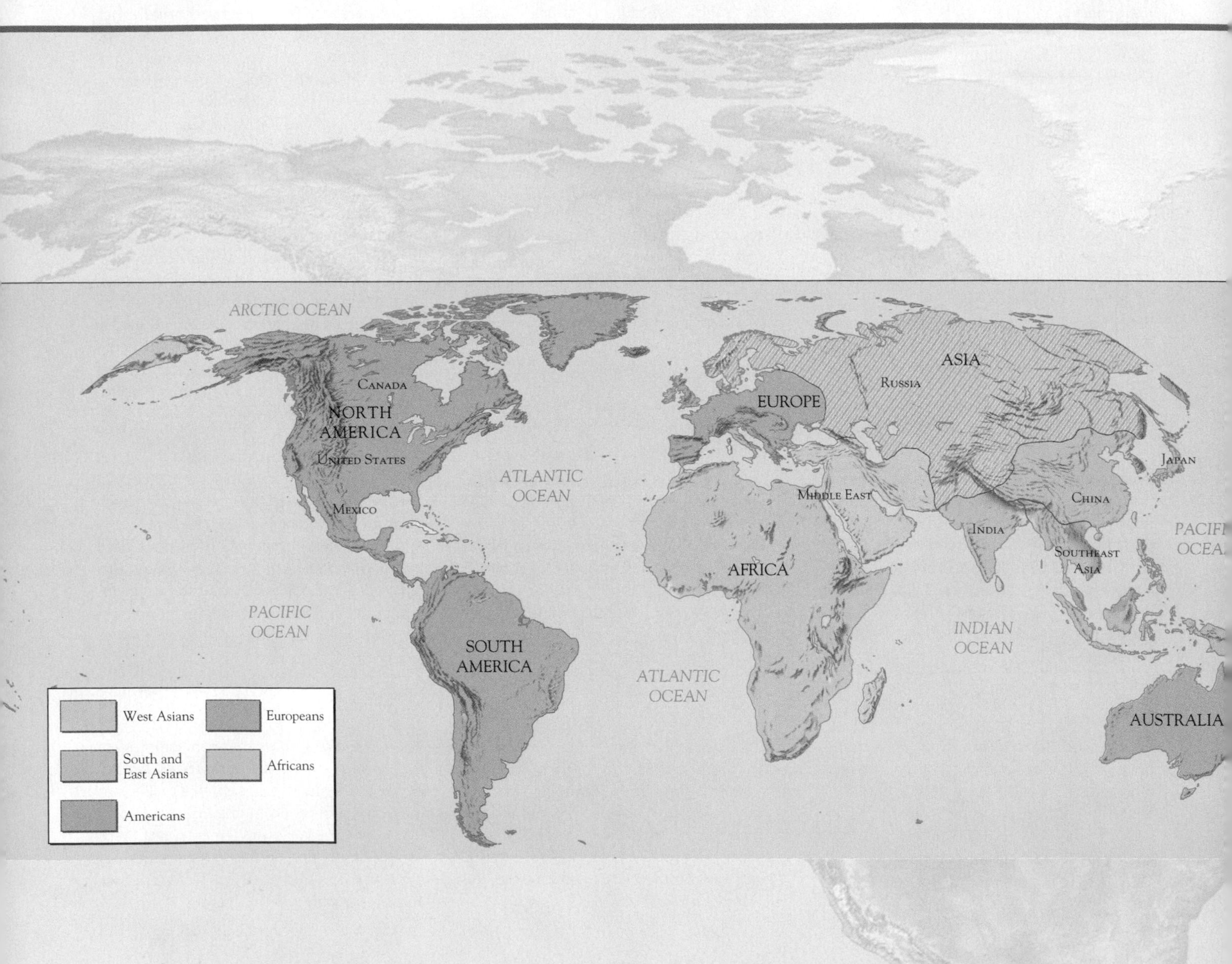
ARCTIC OCEAN
Canada
NORTH AMERICA
United States
Mexico
ATLANTIC OCEAN
PACIFIC OCEAN
SOUTH AMERICA
ATLANTIC OCEAN
EUROPE
AFRICA
Middle East
Russia
ASIA
India
China
Japan
Southeast Asia
INDIAN OCEAN
AUSTRALIA
West Asians
Europeans
South and East Asians
Africans
Americans

# Revolutions, Ideology, and the New Imperialism, 1700–1920

After rising secularism had gradually dampened the Europe-wide crisis generated by the Protestant challenge to the papal church, the seventeenth century witnessed the first wave of "scientific revolutions" that would mark modern times. For the first time since the Greeks, the West took the forefront in advances in knowledge about this world and its natural phenomena (Chapter 31).

The same curiosity and willingness to challenge ancient authority that impelled the breakthroughs in natural science were a bit later applied to the "Science of Man," as the eighteenth-century Enlightenment called it. The Enlightenment was the project of an urban upper class determined to bring Reason and its child Wisdom to take their rightful places in the halls of government as well as the school and home. Filled with a sense of sacred mission, the philosophes fought the intolerance and ignorance of the past, most especially the darkness surrounding the established church and absolutist throne (Chapter 32).

What they desired in political and constitutional affairs seemingly came to pass in the first flush of the popular revolution in France, but the original reforms were soon overshadowed by a radical democracy and soon a dictatorship employing terror against all who opposed it. The Napoleonic empire's aggressions confirmed the negative impression gained by most observers outside France and also strengthened the eventual victors' resolve to limit and control both political and social change (Chapter 33).

Following the pattern established in late-eighteenth-century Britain, the rest of western Europe entered the industrial epoch in the ensuing century by stages. The initial Industrial Revolution was powered by steam and concentrated on a few basic commodity production processes. Its immediate social repercussions were bitter for the masses of poor laborers in the new towns but were gradually ameliorated (Chapter 34). In the meantime, the postrevolutionary peace was disturbed by clashes between reactionary monarchies and the rising forces of economic and political liberalism, culminating in the rebellions of 1848–1849 in much of Europe (Chapter 35).

The short-term failure of most of the 1848 rebellions was caused largely by the new ethnically based nationalism that had arisen in many lands as an indirect result of the French Revolution. The situation was exacerbated by the cleft between the bourgeois political liberals and the socially radical working classes, which came to light during the revolts. By the 1870s, this cleft was being bridged in the western, democratizing states, although it was still quite wide in the eastern and southern parts of Europe (Chapter 36).

Meanwhile, with the shift in the military balance of power between the West and the East, Europe became increasingly aggressive overseas. Islamic powers such as those of the Ottomans, the Safavids, and the Mughals were at a disadvantage for the first time in dealing with the European powers. Chapter 37 examines the responses of the Islamic peoples of the Near and Middle East to this changed situation. Chapter 38 provides an overview of precolonial Africa in this period of transition as well. Finally, the Iberian colonies of America and their struggle for independent existence are outlined in Chapter 39.

Advancing industrial development, now powered by the new energy sources of petroleum and electricity, helped bring about further democratization as well as a rising wave of Marxian socialism as the nineteenth century entered its final quarter (Chapter 40).

The physical sciences and some of the social sciences also took imposing strides in the second half of the nineteenth century and had various effects on the European popular consciousness (Chapter 41). The nineteenth century's naïve faith in progress had a horrid demise in the catastrophic World War I, with fateful impacts on both the West and the non-Western world (Chapter 42).

*If I have seen farther than others, it is because I have stood on the shoulders of giants.*
Isaac Newton

# 31 The Scientific Revolution and Its Enlightened Aftermath



| | |
|---|---|
| 1543 | Nicholas Copernicus, *Revolution of the Heavenly Bodies* |
| c. 1575–c. 1650 | Francis Bacon, Galileo Galilei, René Descartes |
| 1687 | Isaac Newton, *Principia Mathematica:* law of gravitation |
| 1690 | John Locke, *Essay Concerning Human Understanding* |
| 1730s–1789 | Enlightenment flourishes |
| 1776 | Adam Smith, *Wealth of Nations* |
| 1776 | Thomas Jefferson, Declaration of Independence |

Perhaps the most far-reaching of all the "revolutions" since the introduction of agricultural life in the Neolithic Age was the early modern era's change in educated persons' thinking about natural phenomena, their laws, and their relation to a presumed Creator. This Scientific Revolution became fully evident in the work of the eighteenth-century *philosophes,* but its major outlines were drawn earlier, when the focus of European intellectual work gradually shifted away from theology to the mathematical and empirical sciences. By the end of the eighteenth century, it had proceeded so far among the educated classes that a new worldview was taken for granted, one that seriously challenged the medieval conviction that an omniscient God ordained and guided the natural processes, including the life and eternal fate of mankind. While the consolidation of royal absolutism seemed to be rigorously proceeding in most of Europe during the seventeenth and eighteenth centuries, the sciences successfully undermined traditional theology's claims and by so doing countered the royal throne's aspirations to be taken as God's chosen representative on earth.

## The Scientific Revolution of the Seventeenth Century

So great were the achievements during this epoch that one of the outstanding modern philosophers has said that "the two centuries [that followed] have been living upon the accumulated capital of ideas provided for them by the genius of the seventeenth century." The natural sciences—that is, those based primarily on observed phenomena of nature—experienced a huge upswing in importance and accuracy. A new style of examining phenomena, the **scientific method**, came into common usage. It was composed of two elements: careful observation and systematic experimentation based on that observation. Interpretation of the results of the experiments, largely relying on mathematical measurement, was then employed to achieve new and verified knowledge.

The most significant advances in the sciences came from posing new types of questions rather than from collecting new facts. Different questions led directly to novel avenues of investigation, and those led to new data being observed and experimented with. For example, René Descartes (1596–1650), one of the founders of the mathematical style of investigation, wished to take humanity to a higher plane of perfection than ever yet achieved. To do so, he separated the material from the nonmaterial universe completely, insisting that the material world could be comprehended by mathematical formulas that existed entirely apart from the human mind. If that was so, knowledge of these broad laws of number and quantity could provide explanations—hitherto lacking—of observed phenomena. The proper way to understand the material world, then, was to formulate broad generalizations of a quantitative nature and employ them to explain specific events or processes. This approach, in which one went from a general law to a particular example of that law observed by the human mind, was called **deductive reasoning**.

Another method of accumulating knowledge about the natural world was exemplified in the writings of the Englishman Francis Bacon (1561–1626). Bacon insisted that contrary to traditional belief, most ideas and principles that explain nature had not yet been discovered or developed but lay buried, like so many gems under the earth, awaiting uncovering. Like Descartes, he looked forward to a better, more completely understood world, but this world was to be created by the persistent and careful observation of phenomena without any preconceived laws or general explanations of them, a process that became known as **inductive reasoning**.

Bacon was not methodical in his science or his reasoning. His close association with the concept of inductive reasoning is perhaps not really deserved, but his writings did encourage later scientists to practice the **empirical method** of gathering data and then forming generalizations. *Empirical* means the evidence obtained by observation through the five senses, which is then worked up into varying hypotheses (assumptions) that may be subjected to experiment. This style of assembling and verifying knowledge blossomed in the seventeenth century and later became the normal fashion of proceeding in all of the sciences.

## *Background of the Scientific Revolution*

Why did the spectacular advances in natural science occur in the seventeenth century rather than earlier or later? There is no single answer to this question. As with most important changes in the status quo of human knowledge, several factors both material and immaterial came together at that time to encourage more rapid progress than before, but this is not to say that no progress had been under way previously. It is now accepted that the old view of medieval science as a laughable collection of superstitions and crackpot experiments is quite wrong. The medieval universities harbored many people who seriously undertook to widen the horizons of knowledge and had some success in doing so. The long search for magical elements to convert base metal into gold, as an important instance, did much to found the science of chemistry.

The real problem of medieval and Renaissance science seems to have been not its superstitions but its exaggerated reliance on authority, rather than evidence. The great Greek philosophers of science—Aristotle, Ptolemy, Galen, Eratosthenes, and Archimedes—were held in excessive reverence as the givers of final truth. The weakening of this reverence, or perhaps intimidation by the ancients, made possible the breakthroughs of the sixteenth and seventeenth centuries.

Stimulated and aided by the reports of the explorers and voyagers in the New World, scholars accumulated a mass of evidence about nature and geography that both amplified and contradicted some of what the traditional authorities had taught. Such evidence could be ignored only at the risk of retarding the power and wealth of the whole exploring society. Still more important, perhaps, was the rapid advance in the mathematical capabilities of Europeans. At the beginning of the sixteenth century, European math was still at the same level as in the seventh century. Only with the recovery of the Greek and Hellenistic mathematical works could it advance into new areas: logarithms, calculus, and decimals. By the mid-seventeenth century, math had become as much a device for theoretical exploration as for counting.

Another mass of data that partly contradicted what the Greeks had believed was the product of new instruments. The new math made possible analyses of the physical world that had never before been attempted. Instruments of all sorts (sensitive scales, pressure gauges, microscopes, telescopes, thermometers, chronometers) came along one after the other to assist in this analysis. It was now possible to measure, weigh, divide, and synthesize the world in ways that explained the previously inexplicable.

## The Progress of Scientific Knowledge: Copernicus to Newton

The rediscovery of the Greco-Roman scientific treatises by the Renaissance scholars (often working from Arabic translations of the Greek and Latin originals) stimulated curiosity while providing a series of new insights into the makeup of the natural world—insights that contradicted the conventional wisdom of the day. This progress was sharply interrupted by the wars of religion in the sixteenth century, when the focus shifted away from science to clashing theologies. Only with the exhaustion of those religious antipathies after the Thirty Years' War did scientific endeavors once again take a primordial position in educated men's affairs.

Our emphasis on seventeenth-century events does not mean that modern science commenced then. The acknowledged breakthrough advance in empirical knowledge of the natural world came a century earlier with the *Revolution of the Heavenly Bodies,* the pioneering treatise on astronomy by the Polish scholar Nicholas Copernicus (1473–1543). Copernicus cast severe doubt on the traditional and generally accepted theory of an Earth-centered (**geocentric**) universe, which he criticized as unnaturally complex and difficult to understand. Copernicus's observations led him to conclude that the Earth revolved around a fixed sun, a belief first advanced by Hellenistic Greek astronomers. A cautious and devout Catholic, Copernicus published his conclusions only in the year of his death. The church ignored his theory at first, although it was ridiculed by both Luther and Calvin, but when **heliocentrism** began to win adherents in large numbers, both Rome and the Protestants officially condemned it as contrary to both Scripture and common sense.

Two astronomer-mathematicians who emerged a generation after Copernicus also deserve our attention. The first was an eccentric Dane, Tycho Brahe (1546–1601), who spent much of his life taking endless, precise measurements of the cosmic rotation of the visible planets. Using these data, Tycho's student, the German Johannes Kepler (1571–1630), went on to formulate the *three laws of celestial mechanics,* which showed that the heavenly bodies moved in great ellipses (ovals) around the sun, rather than in the perfect circles that had been believed necessary as the handiwork of a perfect Creator. This insight explained what had been previously inexplicable and made Copernicus's proposals still more persuasive.

In the early 1600s, an Italian professor at Pisa named Galileo Galilei (1564–1642) used his improvement of the telescope to rewrite the rules of cosmology as handed down from the ancients. His discoveries strongly supported Copernicus's suppositions that the universe was sun centered and that the Earth was a relatively small,

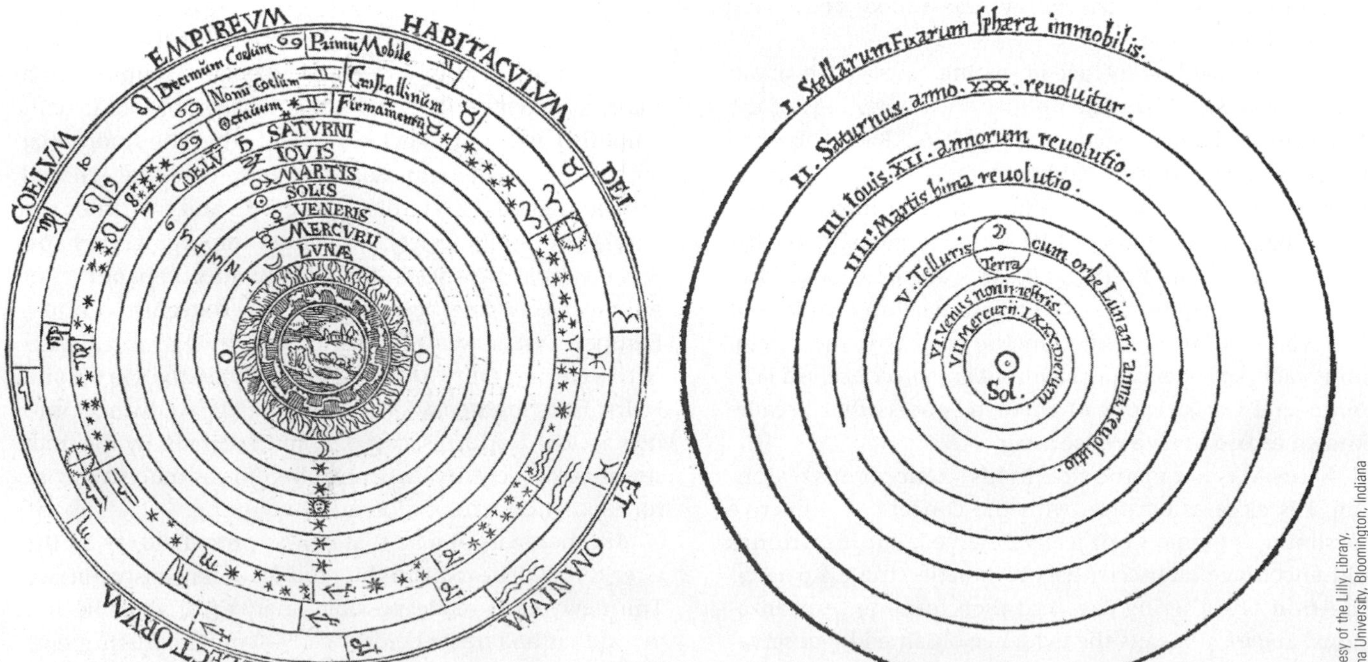


**The Two Cosmoses.** Contrasted here are the two visions of the cosmos. The first dates from the sixteenth century before Copernicus's death and shows the geocentric universe and the sun (Solis) between Venus and Mars. The second is from the first edition of Copernicus's great work and shows the heliocentric universe.

Courtesy of the Lilly Library, Indiana University, Bloomington, Indiana insignificant planet in a huge solar system. Not only did Galileo's astronomy force clerical authorities to a reconsideration of the condemned theory of Copernicus, but his physics contributed to the final overthrow of Aristotle's long reign as master physicist. Through his work with falling bodies and the laws of motion, Galileo came close to discovering the fundamental law of all nature: the law of gravity.

When Galileo died in 1642, the whole traditional view of the physical universe as an impenetrable mystery—created by God for his own reasons and not responsive to human inquiries—was beginning to come apart. The limiting horizons that had been in place for many centuries were steadily receding as the seventeenth century progressed. What was still needed was some overarching explanation of the physical world order, which was now being revealed as though through a semitransparent curtain.

The genius of Isaac Newton (1642–1727) put the capstone of the new science in place. While still a student at Cambridge University, he theorized that there must be a "master key" to the edifice of the universe. In the century and a quarter since Copernicus, a great deal had been discovered or strongly indicated about the laws of nature. Still lacking, however, was a universally applicable explanation of the most basic property of matter: movement.

In the 1660s, Newton occupied himself with the study of physics. At that time he evolved his deceptively simple-looking theorem, the most famous in the history of the world: $E = M^2/D^2$. This was the formula of the law of gravitation, although it yet lacked mathematical proof. After many more years of research, Newton published his conclusions and their proofs in the *Principia Mathematica* in 1687. The *Principia* was the most influential book on science in the seventeenth century and was soon known from one end of educated Europe to the other. (See the Science and Technology box for more on Newton.)

Newton proposed a new universe. The physical cosmos was a sort of gigantic clockwork in which every part played a particular role and every movement and change was explained by the operation of law. It was humans' proud duty and privilege to identify those laws and in so doing to penetrate to the heart of the God-created universe.

## Religion and Science in the Seventeenth Century

How did the official churches react to this challenge to tradition? Both Catholic and Protestant preachers felt that relegating the Earth to a secondary, dependent position in the universe was at least an implied rejection of Holy Scripture (the Old Testament story about the sun standing still at the battle of Jericho, for example). It also downgraded the jewel of God's creation, human beings, who lived on this inferior Earth and were presumably limited to it. The Catholic Galileo was threatened with imprisonment if he did not retract parts of what he had published in one of his books on science. He spent his final years under house arrest by order of the pope.

Were these condemnations justified? Most of the seventeenth-century scientists considered themselves good Christians and made no attempt to rule a divine being out of the universe. A devout Anglican, Newton spent most of his later life embarked on religious speculations and obscure theological inquiries. Descartes, like Copernicus before him, was a Catholic who saw no conflict between what he taught about the nature of the material world and what he believed about the spiritual one. Quite to the contrary, Descartes believed that his speculations only pointed more clearly to the existence of a divine intelligence in the universe.

Most ordinary people were unmoved by the revelations of science. The peasants never heard of them, and even urban dwellers were ignorant of them except for the privileged few whose education went beyond the three Rs. The fourth R, religion, generally retained the strong grip on the daily lives and beliefs of common folk that it had always had.

But the church's truth, resting as it did on revelation rather than empirical data, was being challenged—at first only tangentially, but later more confrontationally—by the truth of science. And science's truth had potent appeal for men and women who were weary of the strife of theologians and the claims of priests and pastors. Science's truth had no axes to grind for one party or another. It was not linked to politics or to a social group's advantage or disadvantage. It was self-evident and could sometimes be used to benefit the ordinary person; for example, through its conversion to new technology (although the connections between science and technology were as yet almost entirely undeveloped).

Increasingly, educated people were beginning to wonder whether it was more useful to know whether the Holy Eucharist should be given in two forms than to know how digestion takes place in the stomach or some similar aspect of the new physical science. Science came to be seen as an alternative to theology in finding useful knowledge and applying it to society's multiple problems.

In this regard, two of the most important thinkers of the seventeenth century were the agnostic Dutch Jew Baruch Spinoza and the pious Catholic Frenchman Blaise Pascal. Spinoza was a great questioner, who after leaving Judaism finally found some measure of peace by perceiving his God in all creation—*pantheism.* His rejection of a personal deity earned him a great deal of trouble, but his thought influenced generations. Pascal wrote his *Pensées* (*Thoughts*) to calm a troubled mind and produced a work that has been considered one of the greatest of Christian

# Isaac Newton (1642–1727)

**THE MAN MANY CONSIDER TO BE THE MOST** distinguished scientist of all history, Sir Isaac Newton, was born on Christmas Day, 1642, in Lancashire, England. Best recognized as the discoverer of the law of gravity, Newton was equally famed for his work in optics, higher mathematics, and physics in his own day. He was a distinct exception to the rule that pioneers are not appreciated; his career as both a Cambridge professor and government official under William and Mary was brilliant and adequately rewarded.

Although his father was a farmer with little property, Newton received an exceptional education. He completed studies at the local grammar school near his home village, with the aid and encouragement of the Anglican vicar, who was a graduate of Cambridge. With this gentleman's recommendation, Isaac won a scholarship to the university in 1661, graduating in 1665 with what would now be called a major in natural science. He wished to go on for the M.A. degree at once, but an outbreak of plague forced the university to close in both 1666 and 1667, and Newton returned home.

During these years, his great, groundbreaking work on gravity was basically outlined. The notion that all physical being was, so to speak, tied together by a single principle—that of gravity—took shape in the twenty-five-year-old's long studies at his family home in Woolsthorpe. Newton gradually refined and expanded his theory when he returned to Cambridge, first as an M.A. candidate, then as a professor in 1669. He held this post until his honor-filled retirement in 1701.

Although Newton apparently regarded gravitation as a fact as early as the 1660s, he hesitated in publishing his work until 1687. In that year, his *Principia Mathematica,* or *Mathematical Principles of Natural Philosophy,* was finally published in London and soon afterward in most of the capitals of Europe. Rarely has a scientific book been hailed so universally as a work of genius. At the same time, Newton was bringing out fundamentally important work on the spectrum, proving that light was composed of colored particles. Newton is also generally credited with being the co-discoverer of calculus, along with his rival Gottfried Leibniz. The two men were working independently, and their quarrel over who was first became one of the Scientific Revolution's less appetizing anecdotes.

In his later years, Newton's dedication to Old Testament studies and theology surpassed his scientific interests. Newton was a master of Greek and Hebrew and spent much energy on his researches into the Old Testament prophecies.

Highly placed friends secured his appointment as warden of the royal mint in 1696, a lucrative post that Newton was grateful to have. In 1703, he was elected president of the Royal Society, the premier scientific post in England, and was reelected every year thereafter until his death. The queen knighted Sir Isaac in 1705 for services to his country as well as to the realm of science. Newton died at eighty-five years of age, heaped with honors and substantial wealth. On his deathbed he is supposed to have said, "If I have seen farther than others, it is because I have stood on the shoulders of giants." After a state funeral, he was buried in the walls of Westminster Abbey.

The famous story of the falling apple just may be true; no one will ever know.

ISAAC NEWTON

## Analyze and Interpret

Contrast the fashion in which Newton gave his formula on gravitation to the world and the way such an announcement might be made today by modern scientists. Why do you think he chose to use Latin as his vehicle, so late in the 1680s?

**History Now™**

*To read some of Isaac Newton's* **Principia**, *point your browser to the documents area of* **HistoryNow.**

consolations ever since. The fact that Pascal was highly suspect to the French clerical establishment only added to his later fame.

## The Science Of Man

Until modern times, the natural sciences were regarded as a branch of philosophy rather than a separate intellectual discipline, but as a branch of philosophy they had obtained some respectability. Already in the Renaissance, math and physics began to establish a place in the university curriculum. Their prestige was still relatively low, and they could not rival medicine, law, or theology in attracting students, but they did begin to form their own rules of evidence and analysis.

As the mathematics-based sciences came to be accepted as the sources of much previously unknown truth, the previous relation between natural science and philosophy underwent a gradual but decisive reversal. Philosophy, which had been the more inclusive term, encompassing science, now became for many persons a branch of science, and a somewhat dubious one at that. Insomuch as an object of thought could not be measured and weighed, it ceased to be worthy of close attention. Such individuals held that *only* what could be determined in its existence by the tools of science was reachable by the power of reason and useful to humans. They did not deny that other phenomena that were not measurable and not reachable by reason existed, but they insisted that these phenomena should have only a secondary place in the hierarchy of human values.

Among those phenomena, of course, were religious belief, artistic creativity, wonder, imagination, ethics, and political theory, to mention only a few. None of these could be measured, and none could be brought under uniform and predictable laws. Or could they? A body of thought gradually arose that said these phenomena, too, might be subject to law, analyzable through mathematical computations, and comprehensible in the same way as physics. The *Science of Man,* not man as an anatomical construct or an example of biological systems but as a thinker, political actor, and artist, began to form. By the early eighteenth century, this science—which we now call social science—was competing with physical science for the attention of the educated classes.

## The Enlightenment

Eighteenth-century intellectual leaders saw no reason why what had been done in the natural sciences could not be attempted in the social sciences. They wanted to put history, politics, jurisprudence, and economics under the same logical lenses that had been applied to math and physics. Spurred on by such hopes, the **Enlightenment** was born.

Above all, the eighteenth century in western Europe was distinguished from what had come before by the attitudes that educated persons exhibited in the affairs of everyday life: the atmosphere of their mental life. Two key characteristics assert themselves again and again: optimism and rationality. Here *optimism* refers to the belief that change is possible and controllable in society at large, while *rationality* refers to the idea that the universe and all creatures within it, especially humans, are comprehensible, predictable, and lawful. The commitment to a rational view of the universe usually embraced a similar commitment to *secularism*—that is, a downgrading or outright rejection of the importance of supernatural religion. The Enlightenment preferred to see humanity as capable of creating its own moral code for its own benefit and in accord with the precepts of a rational mind.

How did this translate to concrete activity? The ways of viewing the physical world that math and physics had introduced were now applied—or an attempt was made to apply them—to the world's social, political, and moral aspects. If physicists could measure the weight of the Earth's atmosphere (and they now could), then why couldn't historians isolate the exact causes of cultural retardation and determine how to avoid them in the future? Why couldn't criminologists build a model prison and establish a regime there that would turn out completely rehabilitated prisoners? Why couldn't political scientists calibrate various methods of selecting public officials to ensure that only the best were elected?

### Formative Figures and Basic Ideas

Although the movement was a truly international one, the two outstanding progenitors of the Enlightenment's ideals were the Englishmen Isaac Newton and John Locke. As we have already seen, Newton was the greatest scientific mind of his age, and Locke was the leading mapper of the political path that England embarked on with the Glorious Revolution of 1688 (see Chapter 28).

Newton's greatest contribution to science—related to but even more important than the law of gravity—was his insistence on rational, lawful principles in all operations of physical nature. He rejected supernatural causes as an explanation of the natural world. Because nature is rational, human society as part of nature should be rational in its organization and function.

Locke was as much a psychologist as a political scientist; he set forth his view of the mind in the immensely influential ***Essay Concerning Human Understanding***

(1690). Here he said that the mind is a blank page until experience and environment write on it and mold it. Thus, human nature is dynamic and unfixed; it has been in the past and will be in the future formed by external experience, and this experience is capable of being controlled. Thus, humans are not condemned to repeat endlessly the sin of Adam and the mistakes of the past. They can and must take charge of their destiny; they can perfect themselves.

More than anything else, this faith in *perfectibility* is the distinguishing innovation of the Enlightenment. For the previous seventeen centuries, the Christian idea of guilt from the sin of Adam as an insuperable barrier to human perfection had been the foundation stone of Western moral philosophy. Now, the eighteenth century proposed to move the house off this foundation and erect it anew. Progress, both moral and physical, was reachable and real. The study of history showed how far humans had come and how far they still had to go. The past was filled with error and blindness, but it could be—*must* be—learned from, so that it could light the way to a better future.

The reformers believed that mass religious belief was generally controlled by those who profited from ignorance and prejudice, and was everywhere used as a tool to obscure the truth. They took an especially harsh view of the Roman Catholic clergy. Where the church had obtained a monopolistic position in the state and was the official church, the reformers believed that inevitable corruption had made it a parasite that should be cast off as soon as possible and replaced with freedom of conscience and worship.

In the reformers' view, education was the salvation of humankind. It should be promoted at every opportunity everywhere. Insofar as people were educated, they were good. The fully educated would be unerring seekers of the best that life held, defenders of the helpless, teachers of the misguided, and the liberators of the oppressed.

## The Philosophes and Their Ideals

The Enlightenment was a view of life, a philosophy, and that meant it must have its philosophers. Generically known by the French term ***philosophes***, they included men and women of both thought and action, scientists and philosophers, who were committed to the cause of reform. Despite their often intense personal differences, they were united in their desire for progress, by which they meant controlled changes.

Several of the outstanding philosophes were French. Paris, and secondarily London, was the center of the Enlightenment's activities (it was a decidedly urban phenomenon), but the philosophes kept in frequent touch with one another through a network of clubs and correspondents that covered the map of Europe (see Map 31.1). They included the Frenchmen Voltaire (François-Marie Arouet), Baron Montesquieu, Denis Diderot, and Jean-Jacques Rousseau; the English and Scots David Hume, Adam Smith, and Samuel Johnson; the Germans Josef von Sonnenfels, Gotthold Lessing, and August Ludwig von Schlozer; and the Italians Lodovico Muratori and Cesare Beccaria; but the list could be made as long as one wants. The Americans Thomas Jefferson, Benjamin Franklin, and John Adams belong as well. The Enlightenment had no

**The Establishment of the French Academy of Sciences and the Observatory.** Louis XIV sits in the center as the scientists who depend on his support for their work scramble around him to display their achievements.

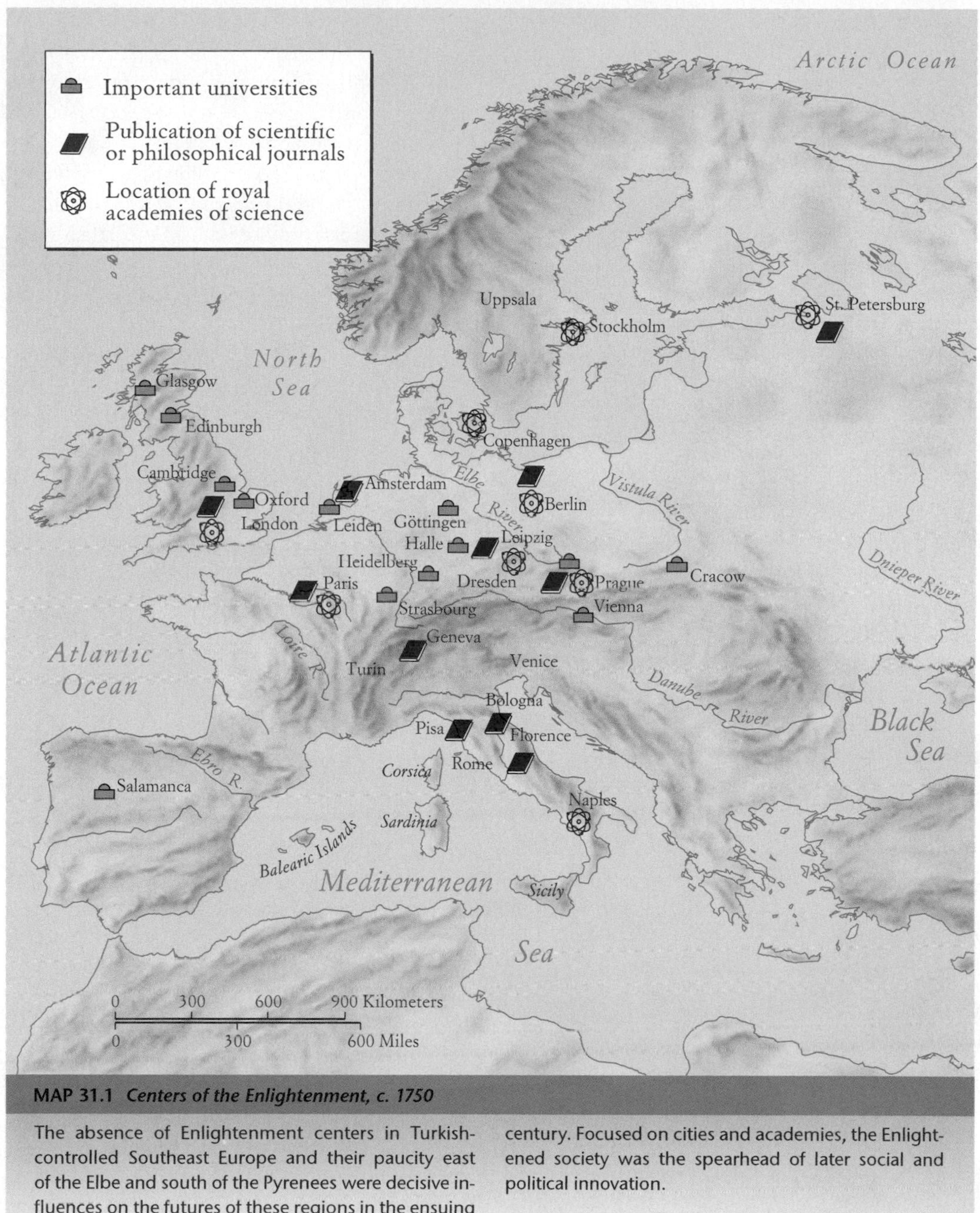


**MAP 31.1** ***Centers of the Enlightenment, c. 1750***

The absence of Enlightenment centers in Turkish-controlled Southeast Europe and their paucity east of the Elbe and south of the Pyrenees were decisive influences on the futures of these regions in the ensuing century. Focused on cities and academies, the Enlightened society was the spearhead of later social and political innovation.

territorial boundaries, although it was much narrower and shallower in eastern Europe than in the West and had much less impact on the public conduct of government. (See the Science and Technology box for more on Franklin.)

Chronologically, the earliest evidence of enlightened activity in organized fashion dates from the 1730s. The period of most active endeavor ended with the French Revolution's political crises. The high point was in the 1770s and 1780s, when various governments from North America to Russia experimented with, gave lip service to, or fully adopted one after another of the favored ideas of the philosophes.

Beyond the commitment to reform, it is difficult to find a common denominator in these ideas because the philosophes themselves are difficult to categorize. Some of them were the first public atheists, but most were at least outward Christians, and some were pious clergymen. Muratori, for example, was a priest. Most believed constitutional monarchy was the best form of government, whereas others were uncompromising republicans.

In the physical sciences, some believed unreservedly in the Baconian procedure of going to the sense-perceptible data (empirical science), others doubted all knowledge that was not reducible to mathematics, and still others

SCIENCE AND TECHNOLOGY

## Franklin as Scientist

**Ben Franklin is better known** to Americans as a political activist and philosopher, but he is equally entitled to be in the front rank of those who created the Enlightenment's views of science. His work in isolating and controlling electricity was fundamental, and his interest in the subject was, as almost always with him, closely tied to the practical applications it might contain. But to ascertain those applications, certain experiments were necessary:

Franklin spoke of electricity as fire, but this fire, he thought, was the result of a disturbance between the equilibrium of the "positive" and the "negative" fiery fluids that he conceived electricity to be. All bodies, in his view, contained such electrical fluid: a "plus" body, containing more than its normal amount, is positively electrified and tends to discharge its surplus into a body containing a normal amount or less; a "minus" body, containing less than a normal amount, is negatively electrified and will draw electricity from a body containing a normal amount or more.

**Franklin at his Laboratory.** This nineteenth-century French engraving shows the American diplomat-scientist investigating the attraction and repulsion of electrical ions. Franklin was convinced that someday electricity could be rendered useful to humankind.

The Granger Collection, New York

His work with lightning rods to protect buildings from such electrical discharges was at first rejected as "visionary" by the Royal Society in London but was soon validated: Two French scientists, de Lor and d'Alibard, tested Franklin's theory by erecting a pointed iron rod fifty feet high; they instructed a guard to touch the rod with an insulated brass wire if, in their absence, thunder clouds should pass overhead. The clouds came, the guard touched the rod not only with wire but also with his hands, sparks flew and crackled, and the guard was severely shocked. De Lor and d'Alibard confirmed the guard's report by further tests and informed the Académie des Sciences that: "Franklin's idea is no longer a conjecture, but reality."

Franklin, however, was not satisfied; he wished to make the identity of lightning and electricity evident by "extracting" lightning with something sent up into the storm cloud. In June 1752, as a thunderstorm began, he sent up on strong twine a kite made of silk; a sharply pointed wire projected some twelve inches from the top of the kite to act as a lightning attractor; and at the observer's end of the twine, a key was fastened with a silk ribbon. In sending to England directions for repeating the experiment, Franklin indicated the results:

> When the rain has wet the kite twine so that it can conduct the electric fire freely, you will find it stream out plentifully from the key at the approach of your knuckle, and with this key a phial [Leiden jar] may be charged, and from electric fire thus obtained spirits may be kindled, and all other electric experiments performed . . . and therefore the sameness of the electrical matter with that of lightning completely demonstrated.

### Analyze and Interpret

Why do you think it generally took a century or more to convert knowledge of science into technology that was useful to humans, before our own days?

Source: W. and A. Durant, *The Story of Civilization* (New York: Simon & Schuster, 1965), vol. 9, p. 520.

classified quantifiable knowledge as inherently inferior. Some were hopeful of gradual improvement in human affairs (ameliorationism); others were convinced that nothing important could be accomplished without radical, even revolutionary changes in society.

The philosophes did not hesitate to argue with one another as well as with their conservative opponents. Much of the literature of the later eighteenth century consists of pamphlets and newspapers arguing one or another favorite idea. In a society where literacy levels made wide distribution of printed matter a paying proposition for the first time, the philosophes fully used the available channels to get their various messages into the public domain.

***Common Goals.*** Although they differed on specifics, most of the philosophes agreed on many general points. In political theory, they universally acclaimed the idea of a *balance of governmental powers* between executive and legislature, as presented in Baron Montesquieu's famous ***Spirit of the Laws*** (1748), perhaps the most influential of a century of influential books on government. In it, the French aristocrat argued for the careful division of powers to prevent any one branch from becoming too strong and dictatorial. He thought that of current governments, the British example came closest to perfection in that line (he did not really understand the British system, however), and his ideas strongly influenced the makers of both the U.S. and the French revolutions and their ensuing constitutions.

The *constitutional limitation of monarchic power* was considered an absolute essential of decent government. The brilliant Voltaire (1694–1778), in particular, led the charge here, because he had a good deal of personal experience with royal persecution in his native France before becoming such a celebrity that kings desired his witty company. He, too, admired the British system of ensuring civil rights and condemned the French lack of such safeguards.

The philosophes also agreed that *freedom of conscience* must be ensured at least for all varieties of Christians, if not Jews and atheists as well. "Established" or tax-supported churches should be abolished, and no one faith or sect should be equipped with governmental powers (as was the case in all European countries at this time).

All persons should enjoy a fundamental *equality before the law.* The philosophes saw this as a basic right that no government could take away or diminish. In line with this principle, punishments were to be blind to class distinctions among criminals; the baron would be whipped just like the peasant. Meanwhile, those who had talent should have increased possibilities for upward mobility. This did not mean that the philosophes were democrats; almost all of them agreed that humans, being differently gifted, should definitely *not* have equal social and political rights.

The philosophes were convinced that the cause of most misery was ignorance, not evil intentions or sin. They were thus picking up a thread that had been running through the fabric of Western intellectual discussion since the Renaissance: that the main causes of man's inhumanity to man were to be found in ignorance and that in a good society, such ignorance would not be tolerated. This view led the philosophes to call for *state-supervised, mandatory education* through the elementary grades as perhaps the most important practical reform for the general benefit.

Most philosophes viewed the *abolition of most forms of censorship* as a positive step toward the free society they wished to see realized. Just where the lines should be drawn was a topic of debate, however; some of them would permit direct attacks on Christianity or any religion, for instance, whereas others would not.

In addition to censorship, the philosophes did not agree on several other broad areas of public affairs. Some would have abolished the barriers to social equality, so that, for example, all government posts would be open to commoners; others feared that this would guarantee the rule of the mob. A few, such as the Marquis de Lafayette and the North Americans, became republicans; most thought that monarchy was a natural and necessary arrangement for the good of all.

## Economic Thought: Adam Smith

The outstanding figure in eighteenth-century economic thought was undoubtedly the Scotsman Adam Smith (1723–1790). In his ***Wealth of Nations***, which was published in 1776 and soon became a European best-seller in several languages, Smith put forth the gospel of free trade and free markets. Smith is often described as saying that the smaller the government's role in the national economy, the better, and that a free market could solve all economic problems to the benefit of all. *Laissez-faire* (Let them do what they will) was supposedly his trademark, but this is oversimplification of Smith's ideas. In reality, he acknowledged that government intervention in one form or another was necessary for society's well-being in many instances.

Smith is, however, rightly credited with being the father of free enterprise as that term is used in the modern West. In *The Wealth of Nations,* he laid out in persuasive detail his conviction that an "unseen hand" operated through a free market in goods and services to bring the ultimate consumers what they needed and wanted at prices they were willing to pay. Smith criticized mercantilism, the ruling economic wisdom of his time, for operating to the disadvantage of most consumers. As in so many other instances, his doctrines followed the Enlightenment's underlying conviction that the sum of abundant individual liberties must be collective well-being. Whether this is true, seen from the perspective of the twenty-first century, is debatable; to the eighteenth-century reformers, it was a matter of faith.

## Educational Theory and the Popularization of Knowledge

One of the least orthodox of the philosophes, Jean-Jacques Rousseau (1712–1778), was the most influential of all in the vitally important field of pedagogy and educational philosophy. Rousseau was a maverick in believing that children can and *must* follow their inherent interests in a proper education and that the teacher should

The Granger Collection, New York

**The Wheelwrights' Trade.** One of the lasting values of the Encyclopédie was the exact illustration by copper engravings of the various trades and handicrafts of the eighteenth century. Pictured here are five steps in the making of carriage wheels.

use those interests to steer the child in the wished-for directions. Rousseau had little following in his own lifetime, but his ideas strongly influenced some of the revolutionary leaders a few years later and gained more adherents in the nineteenth century. He is now regarded as the founder of modern pedagogical theory and, along with Smith, is probably the most important of the philosophes to the present age.

In the mid-eighteenth century, Europeans were able to profit for the first time from the popularization of science and intellectual discourse that had come about through the Scientific Revolution. The upper classes developed a passion for collecting, ordering, and indexing knowledge about the natural world and humans' relations with it and with each other. The century also saw the initial attempts to make science comprehensible and accessible to the masses.

The most noted of these was the immensely successful French ***Encyclopédie***, which contained thirty-five volumes and thousands of individual articles on literally every-

**Dual Portraits: Voltaire and Rousseau.** Two faces of the Enlightenment are shown here, when they were young men. Voltaire's confident smile suited the man who wrote the savagely satirical *Candide*, while Rousseau's moral seriousness comes across in this portrait of the author as a young man.

(a) Musee Antoine Lecuyer, Saint-Quentin, France/Giraudon/Bridgeman Art Library
(b) National Gallery of Scotland, Edinburgh, Scotland/Bridgeman Art Library

thing under the sun. Its general editor was Denis Diderot (1713–1784), assisted by Jean d'Alembert, who saw the work through in fifteen years (1751–1765) against enormous odds. Contributors to the *Encyclopédie* (the first of its kind) included the outstanding intellectuals of Europe. The philosophical articles were often controversial, and their "slant" was always in the direction favored by the more liberal philosophes. (Not the least valuable part of the enterprise were the numerous volumes of illustrations, which are the greatest single source of information on early technology.) The expensive *Encyclopédie* sold more than 15,000 copies, a huge number for the day, and was found on personal library shelves from one end of Europe to the other, as well as in the Americas and Russia.

## Ideals of the Enlightenment: Reason, Liberty, Happiness

*Reason* was the key word in every philosophical treatise and every political tract of the Enlightenment. What was reasonable was good; what was good was reasonable. The philosophes took for granted that the reasoning faculty was humans' highest gift and that its exercise would, sooner or later, guarantee a decent and just society on Earth.

Liberty was the birthright of all, but it was often stolen away by kings and their agents. Liberty meant the personal freedom to do and say anything that did not harm the rights of another person or institution or threaten the welfare of society.

Happiness was another birthright of all humans. They should not have to defer happiness until a problematic eternity; it should be accessible here and now. In a reasonable, natural world, ordinary men and women would be able to engage in what one of the outstanding philosophes called "the pursuit of happiness" (Thomas Jefferson in the Declaration of Independence).

All of the ideals of the philosophes flowed together in the concept of *progress*. For the first time in European history, the belief that humans were engaged in an ultimately successful search for a new state of being here on Earth crystallized among a large group. The confidence and energy that were once directed to the attainment of heaven were now transferred to the improvement of earthly life. Progress was inevitable, and it was the individual's proud task to assist in its coming.

## The Audience of the Philosophes

How thoroughly did the Enlightenment penetrate European society? It was not by any means a mass movement. Its advocates, both male and female, were most at home amid the high culture of the urban elite. (See the Society and Economy box on the enlightened female.) There were probably more fans of the acid satire of Voltaire in Paris than in all the rest of France and more readers of Hume in London than in all the remainder of the British Isles. It was an age of brilliant conversationalists, and the hostesses who could bring the celebrated minds of the day together were indispensable to the whole movement. In the "salons" of Madame X or Madame Y were heard the exchanges of ideas and opinions that were the heartbeat of the Enlightenment.

The movement hardly ever attempted direct communication with the masses. In any case, most were still illiterate and could not absorb this highly language-dependent message. Others, especially among the peasants, rejected it as atheist or antitraditional. Only the upper strata—the educated professional and merchant, the occasional aristocrat and liberal-minded clergyman—made up the audience of the philosophes, bought the *Encyclopédie,* and were converted to the ideals of progress, tolerance, and liberty. Most of these adherents would

**COOK AND BANKS IN HAWAII.** Captain Cook, discoverer of the Hawaiian Islands and much of the southern Pacific, is shown examining some of the exotic birds and wildlife of Hawaii. Beside him is the official naturalist of Cook's carefully planned expeditions, William Banks.

SOCIETY AND ECONOMY

## The Enlightened Female

**A RECENT AUTHOR GIVES US** a quick introduction to the Enlightenment's differing opinions on the capablities of the female mind:

> The eighteenth century saw the triumph of the idea that women have a specifically female nature. The triumph was essentially the work of physicians and the philosophes. More than ever before they speculated on what makes a woman and what differentiates and separates her from man. . . . All agreed that women are half of humankind, but once that statement was made their positions diverged.
>
> One current of thought . . . introduced the notion of equality into the *querelle*. Asserting that "the mind has no sex" [this current] insisted that reason, which defines membership in the human species was proper to men and women alike. . . .
>
> The opposing and clearly predominant attitude had two illustrious spokesmen, one a physician and the other a philosophe: Jean-Jacques Rousseau and Pierre Roussel. . . . Reducing current opinion to a system, they sparked a dynamic movement that produced a harvest of writings, medical and/or philosophical, on the specificity of the female. For all these authors the woman represented admittedly half of the human species, but a half that was fundamentally different. From difference they passed on rapidly to inequality, and from inequality to inferiority. . . .
>
> The woman could not have the same type of reason as the man. Like the rest of her person, her reason was subject to her genital organs. This explained much of her weakness, hence her inferiority. She was an eternal invalid, regularly subject to ills proper to her—a true handicap that meant she could not possibly lead an active life in society. . . . "Women's status," Rousseau and the physicians asserted, is to be a mother, and they added that her anatomy predestined her to that role. What followed from that maternal function and her physiological weakness was a less active life, a "passive state" (Roussel) dictated by nature. . . . Each sex had its own functions, willed by nature: men's functions were public, women's were private; and it would be subversive to confuse the two.
>
> The century of triumphant reason was thus not free of paradoxes. In a society where the sexes mixed (at least in France) on nearly all occasions, where women were at the heart of social life, both in the street and in the literary circles, a reigning ideology incontrovertibly divided the qualities, the space, and the social roles of the sexes. . . . Whereas the Enlightenment fought prejudice as the enemy of reason, the philosophers had no intention of abandoning their own prejudices where women were concerned.

### *Analyze and Interpret*

What side of this perennial argument over the nature and capacities of women do you take? Do you believe that there is a real difference in the quality of female from male reason, or is this a "male myth"? If true, is it necessarily a mark of inferiority?

Source: Dominique Godineau, *"The Enlightened Woman," in Enlightenment Portraits,* ed. M. Vovell (Chicago: University of Chicago Press, 1997), pp. 395–399, 409–411.

undoubtedly have been appalled by the prospect of revolution, and they had no sympathy for the occasional voice that considered violence against an evil government acceptable.

The Enlightenment was, then, an intellectual training ground for the coming explosion at the end of the eighteenth century. In its insistence on human perfectibility, the necessity of intellectual and religious freedoms, and the need to demolish the barriers to talent that everywhere kept the privileged apart from the nonprivileged, the Enlightenment spirit served as an unintentional forerunner for something far more radical than itself: the revolution.

## SUMMARY

In the sixteenth century, the Renaissance scholars' rediscovery of classical learning and its methods produced an acceptance of empirical observation as a method of deducing truth about the physical world. This new attitude was responsible for the Scientific Revolution, which was at first confined to the physical sciences but inevitably spread to other things. Inductive reasoning based on observation and tested by experiment became commonplace in the educated classes. Mathematics was especially crucial to this process.

A century later, the confidence that the method of science was adequate to unlock previously incomprehensible mysteries had spread to the social sciences: the Science of Man. The same overreaching law that governed the rotation of the planets operated—or should operate—in politics and government. When that law was finally understood, all would fall into place, and the Earth would cease to be out of joint.

The conviction that progress was inevitable and that humans were good and wanted good for others was the product of a relatively small but very influential group of philosophes in France and other countries. They were the leaders of a significant transformation of Western thought that was gradually embraced by most members of the educated classes during the course of the eighteenth century. This transformation is termed the Enlightenment. The philosophes were obsessed by reason and the reasonable and saw nature as the ultimate referent in these respects. A phenomenon of the urban, educated classes, the Enlightenment made little impact on the masses but prepared the way for middle-class leadership of the coming revolutions.

## IDENTIFICATION TERMS

Test your knowledge of this chapter's key concepts by defining the following terms. If you can't recall the meaning of certain terms, refresh your memory by looking up the boldfaced term in the chapter, turning to the Glossary at the end of the book, or working with the flashcards that are available on the *World Civilizations* Companion Website **http://history.wadsworth.com/adler04.**

deductive reasoning
empirical method
*Encyclopédie*
Enlightenment
*Essay Concerning Human Understanding*
geocentric
heliocentrism
inductive reasoning
*philosophes*
scientific method
*Spirit of the Laws*
*Wealth of Nations*

## TEST YOUR KNOWLEDGE

Test your knowledge of this chapter by answering the following questions. Complete answers appear at the end of the book. You may also take this quiz interactively and find even more quiz questions on the *World Civilizations* Companion Website **http://history.wadsworth.com/adler04.**

1. The source of the major elements of medieval European thought in the physical sciences was
   a. Augustus Caesar.
   b. Aristotle.
   c. Virgil.
   d. St. Augustine.
   e. Archimedes.
2. Developments in which two sciences were at the heart of the advances of the sixteenth and seventeenth centuries?
   a. Physics and astronomy
   b. Math and chemistry
   c. Math and medicine
   d. Biology and chemistry
   e. Biology and astronomy

3. Kepler's great contribution to science was
   a. his theory of the creation of the universe.
   b. the three laws of celestial mechanics.
   c. the discovery of the planet Jupiter.
   d. his theory of the geocentric nature of the universe.
   e. his development of the empirical method of reasoning.
4. Which of the following did *not* make his fame as a natural scientist?
   a. Galileo
   b. Spinoza
   c. Copernicus
   d. Brahe
   e. Kepler
5. Newton's conception of the universe is often described as
   a. an apparent order that cannot be comprehended by humans.
   b. an incoherent agglomeration of unrelated phenomena.
   c. a mirage of order that exists only in the human mind.
   d. a machine of perfect order and laws.
   e. complete chaos.
6. By the end of the seventeenth century, educated Europeans were generally
   a. ready to abandon the search for a more intelligible natural science.
   b. considering applying the scientific method to the study of humans.
   c. impelled toward atheism by the conflicts between religion and science.
   d. abandoning Bacon's empiricism for Descartes' inductive reasoning.
   e. returning to religion as the center of their existence.
7. The key concepts of the Enlightenment were
   a. science and religion.
   b. faith and prayer.
   c. optimism and rationality.
   d. democracy and freedom.
   e. community and religion.
8. Which of the following was *not* a common goal held by the philosophes?
   a. Fundamental equality before the law
   b. A more rigid class system
   c. State-supervised education
   d. Constitutional limitations on rulers
   e. The separation of church and state
9. Which of the following was particularly interested in reforming education?
   a. Rousseau
   b. Diderot
   c. Hume
   d. Voltaire
   e. Montesquieu
10. The Enlightenment is best described as a phenomenon that
    a. was generally limited to an urban, educated group.
    b. was found more or less equally throughout Christendom.
    c. reached quickly into the consciousness of most people.
    d. was generally favorable to the idea of an official religion.
    e. was contained to the country of France.

## InfoTrac College Edition

Visit the source collections at

**http://infotrac.thomsonlearning.com**

and use the Search function with the following key terms:

Isaac Newton or Copernicus    Enlightenment

Rousseau

## Wadsworth History Website Resources

Visit the World History Resource Center at **http://history.wadsworth.com/world** for a wealth of general resources, and the *World Civilizations* Companion Website at **http://history.wadsworth.com/adler04** for resources specific to this textbook.

## History Now

Enter *HistoryNow* using the access card that is available for *World Civilizations*. *HistoryNow* will assist you in understanding the content in this chapter with lesson plans generated for your needs. In addition, you can read the following documents, and many more, online:

René Descartes, *Discourse on Method*

Isaac Newton, *Principia*

Voltaire, entries from *Philosophical Dictionary*

*The American Revolution broke out, and the doctrine of the sovereignty of the people came out of the townships and took possession of the State.*
Alexis de Tocqueville

# 32 Liberalism and the Challenge to Absolute Monarchy



1756–1763 Seven Years' War (French and Indian War)

1765 Stamp Act

1773 Boston Tea Party

1775 Fighting begins at Lexington and Concord

1776 *Common Sense;* Declaration of Independence

1781 Articles of Confederation

1783 Treaty of Paris

1789 U.S. Constitution adopted

Among the most important long-term consequences of the Scientific Revolution and the subsequent Enlightenment was the set of beliefs called *liberalism.* It took especially strong root in the Anglo-Saxon countries, where it was also fostered by the events of 1688 and the writings of John Locke (see Chapter 21).

The political revolutions in America and France were different in course and outcome, but they were linked by a common origin in the belief in the inherent freedom and moral equality of men. This belief was at the heart of liberal politics and economics and could not be reconciled with the existing state of affairs in either the American colonies or France in the late eighteenth century. In this chapter, we will look at the linkage of liberal thought with the particular problems of the American colonies; in the following one, at the troubles in France.

In America, the more radical colonists' discontent with their status grew to the point of rebellion in the 1770s. The term *rebellion* is usually associated with starving workers or exploited peasants. On the contrary, the American Revolution was led by a prosperous middle class, who had nothing against their government except that final authority was located in London and not directly responsible to them.

## The Liberal Creed

Where did the liberal creed begin, and what were its essentials? Liberalism was born in the form identified by the modern world in the late eighteenth century. Its roots go back much further, to the Protestant Reformation and the seventeenth-century political philosophers in England. The basic principles of liberalism are a commitment to (1) the liberty of the individual in religion and person and (2) the equality of individuals in the eyes of God and the laws.

Eighteenth-century liberals were children of the Enlightenment and thus especially noticeable in France and England, much less so in central, southern, and eastern Europe, where that movement had taken only superficial root. They believed in the necessity of equality before the law and freedom of movement, conscience, assembly, and the press. They considered censorship both ineffective and repressive, and they despised the inborn privileges accorded to the aristocracy. They thought that a state religion was almost inevitably corrupt and that individuals should have the power to choose in which fashion they would serve and obey their God.

Liberals originally did not believe in equality for all in political or social matters but only in restricted legal and economic senses. They subscribed to what we would now call "the level playing field" theory—that is, that all people should have the opportunity to prove themselves in the competition for wealth and the prestige that comes with it. Those who were weaker or less talented should be allowed to fail, as this was nature's way of allowing the best to show what they had to offer and keeping the best on top.

The liberals of the eighteenth century reflected the general optimism of the Enlightenment about human nature. Like most of the philosophes, the liberals believed that the good would inevitably triumph and that humans would recognize evil in whatever disguises it might assume for the short term. They believed that rational progress was possible and—in the long run—certain. They believed that education was the best cure for most of society's problems. (The enthusiasm for education carried over to a fascination with new technology that could demonstrate the innate mastery of men over nature. See the Science and Technology box for one of the more exotic examples.)

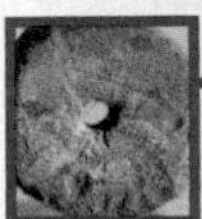

SCIENCE AND TECHNOLOGY

## The First Manned Flight in England, 1784

VICENTE LUNARDI, A NEAPOLITAN DIPLOMAT IN LONDON, was a pioneer of the new science of aeronautics, born of the Enlightenment. In the 1780s, a rage for balloon flights swept Europe, with the first successful attempts being made in France at the very moment the American Revolution had been completed and the French upheaval was gathering momentum. In this passage, Lunardi recollects his first flight in London, as an impatient crowd surrounds the anchored balloon and one accident after another delays the ascent:

> I now determined on my immediate ascension, being assured by the dread of any accident which might consign me and my Balloon to the fury of the populace, whose impatience had wrought them up to a degree of ferment. An affecting, because unpremeditated testimony of approbation and interest in my fate, was here given.
>
> The Prince of Wales, and the whole surrounding assembly almost at one instant, took off their hats, hailed my resolution, and expressed the kindest and most cordial wishes for my safety and success. At five minutes past two, the last gun was fired, the cords [holding the Balloon] were divided, and the Balloon rose, the company returning my signals of adieu with the most unfeigned acclamations and applause. The effect was that of a miracle on the multitudes which surrounded the place; and they passed from incredulity and menace into the most extravagant expressions of approbation and joy.
>
> At the height of twenty yards, the Balloon was a little depressed by the wind, which had a fine effect; it held me over the ground for a few seconds, and seemed to pause majestically before its departure. On discharging a part of the ballast, it ascended to the height of two hundred yards. As a multitude lay before me of a hundred and fifty thousand people who had not seen my ascent from the ground, I had recourse to every stratagem to let them know I was in the gallery [basket] and they literally rent the air with their acclamations and applause. In these stratagems I devoted my flag and worked my oars, one of which was immediately broken and fell from me, a pigeon too escaped, which with a dog and a cat were the only companions of my excursion.
>
> When the thermometer had fallen from 68 to 61 degrees I perceived a great difference in the temperature of the air. I became very cold and found it necessary to take a few glasses of wine. I likewise ate the leg of a chicken, but my bread and other provisions had been rendered useless by being mixed with sand, which I carried as ballast.
>
> When the thermometer was at fifty, the effect of the atmosphere and the combination of circumstances around produced a calm delight, which is inexpressible, and which no situation on earth could give. The stillness, extent, and magnificence of the scene rendered it highly awful. . . . I saw streets as lines, all animated with beings, whom I knew to be men and women, but which I should otherwise have had difficulty in describing. . . . All the moving mass had no object but myself, and the transition from the suspicion, and perhaps contempt of the preceding hour, to the affectionate transport, admiration, and glory of the present moment, was not without its effect on my mind.

Lunardi went on to land safely a few miles outside London in a farmer's yard, and the first balloon flight in England was the topic of every journal and café conversation for a week. Note that the cheerful custom of taking a glass of wine or two while making a balloon flight dates back to the origins, not always because of the cold!

### *Analyze and Interpret*

Only a few days previously, a French balloonist had been threatened and his vehicle destroyed by an angry crowd awaiting the delayed ascent. Why might the common folk be suspicious and/or violent when confronted by new technology? What does the often-expressed fear of the common people indicate about social relations in the late eighteenth century in Europe?

Source: V. Lunardi, *An Account of the First Aerial Voyage in England* (London, 1784).

In matters of government, they sympathized with John Locke and Baron Montesquieu. These men thought that the powers of government must be both spread among various organs and restricted by a checks and balances system in which the legislative, judicial, and executive powers were held by separate hands. Liberals believed that representative government operating through a property-based franchise was the most workable and most just system. They rejected aristocracy (even though there were many liberal nobles) as being outmoded, a government by the few for the few. But they mistrusted total democracy, which they thought would lead to rule by the "mob" of uneducated, propertyless, and easily misled. They were willing to have a monarchy, so long as the monarch's powers were checked by a constitution of laws, by a free parliament, and by free and secure judges.

**THE TEA PARTY IN BOSTON, 1773.** This contemporary engraving shows the colonists emptying cases of tea into Boston harbor to express their contempt for the new excise-tax laws imposed by Parliament. Their disguise as Indians neither fooled nor was intended to fool anyone.



In the liberal view, the legislature should be the most powerful branch of government. It should be elected by and from the "solid citizens"—that is, from among the liberal sympathizers: educated and well-off landowners, professionals, merchants, and the lower ranks of the nobles. They all believed that in structure, if not in practice, the government of eighteenth-century England should be the model for the world. They admired its segregation of parliamentary and royal powers, with Parliament holding the whip hand in matters of domestic policies. They thought England after the Glorious Revolution had achieved a happy blend of individual freedoms within proper limits, allowing the responsible and forward-looking elements to retain political and social dominance.

## THE AMERICAN REVOLUTIONARY WAR

In this context, it was natural that the British American colonies were strongholds of liberal thought and sympathy. Men like George Washington, Thomas Jefferson, James Madison, Benjamin Franklin, and many others were ardent supporters of the liberal view. They had pored over Locke and Montesquieu and digested their ideas. They had much less fear of popular democracy than the home country, because the masses of desperate poor who might threaten the continued leadership of the middle- and upper-class liberals in Europe were not present in America. In fact, the 3 million or so free colonists were probably the materially best-off large group of individuals in the world.

The American Revolutionary War began with a routine dispute between the British government and its subjects over taxation. Fighting the war of the Austrian Succession (Queen Anne's War) and the **Seven Years' War** (French and Indian War), which lasted from 1754 to 1763 in North America, had cost the British government a considerable sum, while the American colonists had contributed little to meet those expenses. The necessity of maintaining a much larger standing army to garrison Canada and the new American frontiers meant that London would be faced with a budgetary drain for the foreseeable future. Therefore, Parliament imposed a series of new taxes on the colonists, most notably the **Stamp Act of 1765**, which created such a furor that it was quickly repealed. The **Navigation Acts**, demanding the use of British ships in commerce between the colonies and other areas, which had been loosely enforced until now, were tightened and applied more rigidly.

These British demands fell on colonists who in the Hanoverian Dynasty era had become thoroughly accustomed to running their own households. The American colonies had the highest per capita income in the Western world in 1775, and they paid among the lowest taxes. They were the great success story of European settlement colonies, and they had achieved this condition without much guidance or interference from the London government. The Americans were used to a high degree of democratic government in local and provincial affairs. Many now felt they were being unduly pushed about by the ministers of King George III, and they resolved to let their feelings be known. The focal point of discontent was in the Massachusetts Bay colony, where maritime commerce was most developed.

The Boston Tea Party of 1773 was a dramatic rejection of the right of the Crown to change the terms of colonial trade in favor of British merchants. When the London government replied to the defiant and illegal acts of the Bostonians by sending troops and closing the crucially important Boston harbor, the clash came much closer. One act led to another as the stakes were raised on both sides. Finally, in April 1775, the "shots heard 'round the world" were fired by the Minutemen in Lexington, and the War for Independence—the first full-blown revolt by a European colony against its home country—was on.

What did the rebellious colonists want? At the outset, the moderate faction in the Continental Congress, which the rebels summoned to provide political leadership, was in control. They demanded "no taxation without representation" and other, relatively mild slogans upholding the alleged rights of Englishmen after the Glorious Revolution of 1688. But by 1776, after blood had flowed, a more uncompromising group, led by Patrick Henry and Jefferson, assumed the leadership role. This group wanted nothing less than independence from Britain, and in the Declaration of Independence, Jefferson wrote their program and battle cry (see the Law and Government box for excerpts from this work as well as a comparable French declaration). The great popularity of the radical pamphlet ***Common Sense*** by the newly arrived Thomas Paine showed how inflamed some tempers had become (see the Law and Government box on page 429 for more on Paine).

LAW AND GOVERNMENT

## The Declaration of Independence of 1776 and the Declaration of the Rights of Man and Citizen of 1789

**The American 1776 Declaration of Independence** and the French 1789 Declaration of the Rights of Man and Citizen were products of individuals who had studied the same authors and were committed to the same visions of government's proper role.

### THE DECLARATION OF INDEPENDENCE OF 1776

We hold these truths to be self-evident, that all men are created equal, that they are endowed by their Creator with certain inalienable rights, that among these are life, liberty, and the pursuit of happiness. That to secure these rights, governments are instituted among men, deriving their just powers from the consent of the governed. That whenever any form of government becomes destructive of these ends, it is the right of the people to alter or to abolish it, and to institute new government, laying its foundation on such principles and organizing its powers in such form, as to them shall seem most likely to effect their safety and happiness.

### THE DECLARATION OF THE RIGHTS OF MAN AND CITIZEN OF 1789

The representatives of the French people, organized in National Assembly . . . recognize and proclaim, in the presence and under the auspices of the Supreme Being, the following rights of man and citizen:

1. Men are born equal and remain free and equal in rights. . . .
2. The aim of every political association is the preservation of the natural and inalienable rights of man; these rights are liberty, property, security, and resistance to oppression; . . .
4. Liberty consists of the power to do whatever is not injurious to others; thus the enjoyment of the natural rights of every man has for its limits only those that assure other members of society the enjoyment of those same rights;
5. The law has the right to forbid only actions which are injurious to society. Whatever is not forbidden by law may not be prevented, and no one may be constrained to do what it does not prescribe.
6. Law is the expression of the general will. . . . All citizens, being equal before it, are equally admissible to all public offices, positions, and employments.
7. No man may be accused, arrested, or detained except in the cases determined by law, and according to the forms prescribed thereby. . . .
10. No one is to be disquieted because of his opinions, even religious, provided their manifestation does not disturb the public order established by law.
11. Free communication of ideas and opinions is one of the most precious of the rights of man. . . .
17. Since property is a sacred and inviolate right, no one may be deprived thereof unless a legally established public necessity obviously requires it.

### *Analyze and Interpret*

Point out if and where you see that the American declaration was intent on dissolving political ties with what the colonists considered an unjust and alien government, and that the French document was aimed at generic reform of a monarchy that had neglected its duties to its people.

**HistoryNow™**

***To read all of the Declaration of Independence, point your browser to the documents area of HistoryNow.***

LAW AND GOVERNMENT

## Thomas Paine (1737–1809)

**Of all those who might be called** the liberal instigators of the American Revolution, Tom Paine must take pride of place. When he came to the colonies in 1774, he was an unknown English acquaintance of Benjamin Franklin. Two years later, he was one of the foremost figures in America, but at that point his extraordinary public career was just beginning.

Paine was born into rural poverty in 1737 and had to leave school at age thirteen to go to work to supplement the family's meager income. For the next quarter century, he failed at everything he tried, from seaman to schoolteacher. His appointment as excise collector (a hated post among the people) in 1762 was revoked because of an improper entry in his records. Although he managed to be reinstated in 1766, he remained under a cloud of suspicion and was dismissed again in 1774 for reasons that are unclear. At this juncture, friends introduced him to Franklin, who had come to London to represent the North American colonies before Parliament.

At his invitation, Paine arrived in Philadelphia in late 1774 and began writing for Franklin's *Pennsylvania Magazine*. A few months later, he became editor of the magazine. His contributions were marked by a gift for rhetoric and a radical turn of mind on public issues.

In early 1776, his pamphlet *Common Sense* appeared. The work immediately became a best-seller in the colonies and was reprinted in several European countries as well. Paine had a way with memorable phrases. *Common Sense* made a powerful argument not only against colonial government but also against the person of George III as a "hardened, sullen Pharaoh." In a mere seventy-nine pages, the pamphlet gave discontented Americans both abstract arguments and concrete objections against being ruled by a distant, uncaring, and allegedly tyrannical monarch.

General Washington and other leaders at once recognized Paine's merits and his potential to assist in the revolutionary cause. Between 1776 and 1783, in support of the rebels, he produced the papers known collectively as *The Crisis:* "These are the times that try men's souls . . ." with references to "the summer soldier and the sunshine patriot."

In 1787 Paine returned to England for a short visit. Delays kept him until 1789, and while there, he was swept up in the initial liberal euphoria about the French Revolution. He wrote *The Rights of Man* (1791) to defend the Revolution against the increasing number of English critics. Having to flee England, Paine went to France and was elected to the Convention of 1793 despite being a foreigner. But here his independent attitude also made him an uncomfortable ally, and he was imprisoned for almost a year during the Reign of Terror. Released by the intercession of the American minister James Monroe, Paine wrote *The Age of Reason* (1794), a pamphlet denouncing revealed religions, especially Christianity, and challenging people to exercise their capacity to find a morality independent of faith.

When Paine finally returned to America in 1802, he was astonished and depressed to find that the outrage over his attack on religion had overwhelmed all gratitude for his services in the Revolution. Former friends such as John Adams and his family avoided him, and the children in his adopted town of New Rochelle, New York, taunted him. After several years of living as a social pariah on his farm, he died in 1809 and was denied the burial in a Quaker cemetery he had requested. A final bizarre note was added when a project to take his remains back to England failed because of the bankruptcy of one of the principals, and the coffin, which was seized as an "asset," disappeared forever.

### *Analyze and Interpret*

Tom Paine once wrote, "It is absurd that a continent be ruled by an island." Do you agree in the sense that Paine meant? Do you think Paine's treatment after returning to America was justified given that almost all of his fellow citizens were God-fearing Christians?

**History Now™**

***To read selections from* Common Sense*, point your browser to the documents area of* HistoryNow.**

Not all colonists agreed by any means. Besides the very hesitant moderates, many persons in all of the colonies remained true to the Crown, and these Loyalists later either were maltreated by their fellow Americans or chose to emigrate at war's end. The conflict was as much a civil war as a rebellion. Even families were split. Washington's troops froze during the savage winter at Valley Forge, while in nearby Philadelphia most of the populace enjoyed their comforts under British occupation and protection.

The military outcome was eventually dictated by three factors favoring the rebels: (1) the logistic effort needed to transport and supply a large army overseas; (2) the aid provided to the rebels by the French fleet and French money; and (3) the only halfhearted support given to

Capitol Collection, Washington, DC/Bridgeman Art Library

**JULY 4, 1776.** This well-known painting by the American John Trumbull shows Jefferson as he presented his final draft of the Declaration of Independence to the Continental Congress in Philadelphia.

the Crown's efforts by the sharply split Parliament in London.

Under the **Alliance of 1778**, the French supplied the Americans with much material aid, contributed some manpower, and, above all, prevented the British navy from controlling the coasts. By 1779, after the critical defeat at Saratoga, it was clear that the second-rate British commanders had no plans worth mentioning and could not put aside their mutual jealousies to join forces against Washington. Even if they had, the many London sympathizers with the Americans, both in and out of Parliament, would negate any full-fledged war effort. The defeat of General Lord Cornwallis at Yorktown in 1781 spelled the end of armed hostilities, and the Peace of Paris officially ended the war in 1783.

## Results of the American Revolution in European Opinion

What exactly was the American Revolution? We are accustomed to thinking of a revolution as necessarily involving an abrupt change in the economic and social structures, but this was not the case in the new United States. The existing political, economic, and social circumstances of the citizenry, whether white or black, were scarcely changed by independence. The War for Independence had been won, but this was not at all the same as a revolution.

The real American Revolution was slower to manifest itself and did so only by degrees after 1783. By the Paris treaty, the thirteen former colonies were recognized as a sovereign nation, equal to any other. All of the territory west of the Appalachians to the Mississippi was open to the new nation (see Map 32.1). For the first time, a major state (Switzerland preceded the United States but did not qualify as a major state) would have a republican form of government—that is, one that had no monarch and in which sovereignty rested ultimately in the people at large. Lawmaking power would be exercised by a representative body that was responsible to the citizenry through the electoral process. Most of the (white male) citizens would be entitled to vote and to hold office. They would enjoy freedom of religion, be fully equal before the law, and have no economic restrictions imposed on them by birth, residence, or circumstance. The establishment of *that* form of government and *those* freedoms was the American Revolution, not the forcible severance of ties with London, however remarkable that had been.

A few years after independence, the ex-colonists acknowledged the severe shortcomings of the 1781 Articles of Confederation, which had been their first try at bonding the states together. They set about creating a workable, permanent system of government. The outcome of the effort, the U.S. Constitution of 1789, is now one of the oldest constitutions in the world. This document was drafted by men raised in the liberal traditions of the eighteenth century. The framers of the Constitution under which Americans still live were conservatives in their approach to social institutions but liberals in their approach to individual freedom.

They wished to create a system that would allow free play to individual talent and ambition and protect individual rights, while still asserting the primacy of the state. They believed in freedom of opportunity, while rejecting political and social equality. They believed in equality before the law and in conscience, but like Locke, they believed in the sacred rights of property and hence left slavery untouched.

More than the successful war, the Constitution strongly influenced educated European opinion. Against many expectations, it demonstrated that a large number of men could create a moderate system of self-government with elected representatives and without an aristocracy or a monarch at its head. Many European liberals had in-

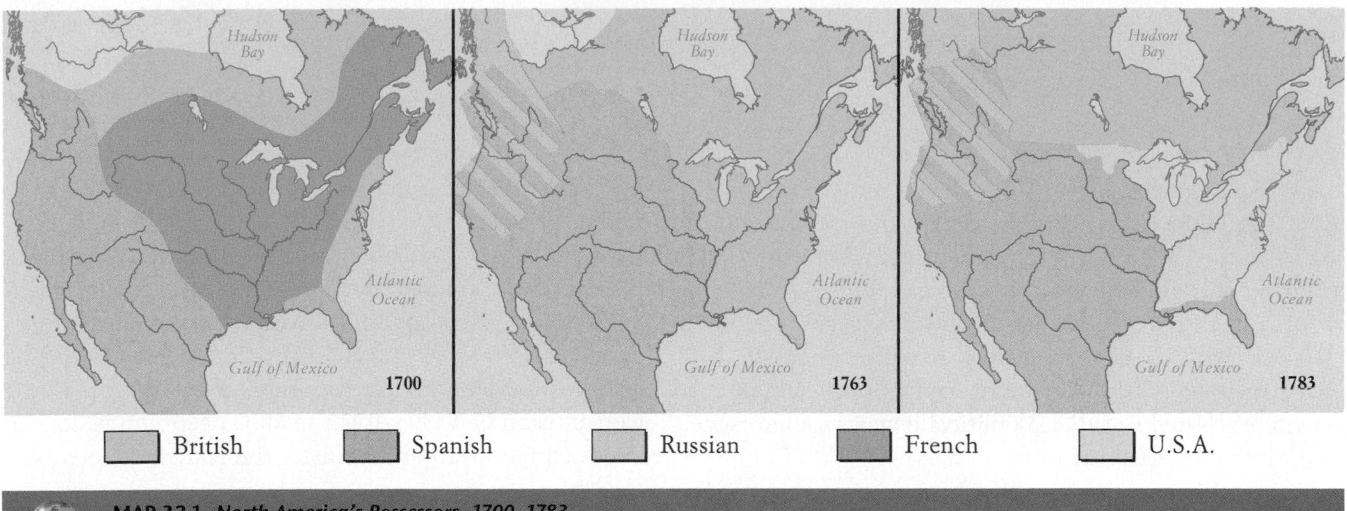


**MAP 32.1** ***North America's Possessors, 1700–1783***

The changing balance of power in Europe's affairs was closely reflected in North America in the eighteenth century.

formed themselves in detail about the United States. Some of them even came to fight in the rebellion (the French Marquis de Lafayette, the Poles Kazimierz Pulaski and Tadeusz Kosciuszko, and the German Baron von Steuben among many others). They were an effective propaganda apparatus, and they were seconded by the equally effective work of Americans such as Franklin, Jefferson, and the Adamses, who resided for a time in Europe as officials of the new country.

On the continent, the American innovations received the most attention in France. The rebellion had many friends in enlightened society, including some in the royal government who welcomed this weakening of the British winner of the Seven Years' War. Many French officers had been in America and had contact with the leading American figures. The drawing rooms of the Parisian elite were filled with talk about America. Some of it was negative: the crude Americans would soon see that government must be either by the king and his responsible officials or by the mob—no third way was possible, given human nature. But much of the talk was enthusiastically favorable. More and more persons of high social standing were convinced that the present French monarchic system was in terrible need of reform, and they looked to some aspects of the American experiment for models of what they wished to introduce at home.

Like the Enlightenment, the liberal frame of reference in politics was to contribute mightily in a few more years to a movement for reform that would go much further than originally intended.

Musee de la Ville de Paris, Musee Carnavalet, Paris, France/Giraudon/Bridgeman Art Library

**LAFAYETTE, MARQUIS DE FRANCE.** This engraving shows Lafayette as the adherent of the earliest stage of the revolution in France, when he was commander of the Garde Nationale, 1790. He was soon disillusioned by the increasing terror.

## Summary

Liberal politics was the product of beliefs dating to the Protestant Reformation and the seventeenth-century English revolution against absolutism. Its fundamental principles asserted the equality and liberty of individuals in both the moral and the legal sense. Liberals believed that all were entitled to the opportunity to prove their merits in economic competition, but they generally rejected social and political equality as impractical for the foreseeable future.

The British colonies in America were strongholds of liberalism, and those convictions led directly to the rebellion against British rule in 1775. Thanks in part to French military and financial aid and the lukewarm support of the war effort by Parliament, the rebellion was successful: the American republic was born, the first large-scale experiment in liberal politics. Although the War for Independence was won, the true American Revolution took longer to develop. Its paramount expression came in the Constitution of 1789, which made a deep impression on educated Europeans, particularly the French adherents of reform.

## Identification Terms

Test your knowledge of this chapter's key concepts by defining the following terms. If you can't recall the meaning of certain terms, refresh your memory by looking up the boldfaced term in the chapter, turning to the Glossary at the end of the book, or working with the flashcards that are available on the *World Civilizations* Companion Website **http://history.wadsworth.com/adler04**.

Alliance of 1778
*Common Sense*
Navigation Acts
Seven Years' War
Stamp Act of 1765

## Test Your Knowledge

Test your knowledge of this chapter by answering the following questions. Complete answers appear at the end of the book. You may also take this quiz interactively and find even more quiz questions on the *World Civilizations* Companion Website **http://history.wadsworth.com/adler04**.

1. Eighteenth-century liberals thought that
   a. all individuals should have equal opportunities to amass wealth.
   b. all individuals should have basic necessities guaranteed to them.
   c. men and women were essentially equal in talents and abilities.
   d. social and cultural position should be about the same for all.
   e. a total democracy was the only government that could succeed in the long run.
2. In matters of religion, eighteenth-century liberals normally believed that
   a. there should be an officially designated and supported faith.
   b. all individuals should have freedom to believe as they saw fit.
   c. the government must have authority over religion because of its connection with politics.
   d. all humans were naturally inclined to evil and sinfulness.
   e. the best religion was one that recognized the worth of humanity.
3. The essence of Baron Montesquieu's theses on government is that
   a. power should clearly be concentrated in the executive.
   b. lawmaking powers should be shared between the federal and state levels of government.
   c. elections should be guaranteed to be held within short time periods.
   d. powers should be divided among three branches of government.

e. the aristocracy, having more to gain, would work harder to make a representative government successful.

4. An important reason for the democratic spirit among the North American colonists in the era before 1776 was the
   a. natural inclinations of colonials toward equality for all.
   b. total absence of the social divisions commonly found in Europe.
   c. habit of religious tolerance in the American traditions.
   d. absence of masses of poor people who might have threatened social revolution.
   e. need for all colonists to work together against the perceived abuses of Parliament.
5. The main reason that the American colonists resented the Navigation Acts and other such laws was that they
   a. believed the taxes were too high.
   b. resented Britain's renewed restrictions after years of ruling their own affairs.
   c. preferred to trade with countries other than Britain.
   d. did not recognize the sovereignty of George III.
   e. new restrictions placed a tremendous strain on the colonies' meager resources.
6. Thomas Paine's first radical writing in the American colonies was
   a. the popular pamphlet, *Common Sense.*
   b. a small pamphlet used as a model by Thomas Jefferson for the Declaration of Independence.
   c. *The Rights of Man.*
   d. a series of papers known as *The Crisis.*
   e. editorials in the *Pennsylvania Magazine.*
7. Which of the following was *not* a reason for American victory in the Revolutionary War?
   a. The division in Parliament about the conduct of the war
   b. The military mediocrity of the British commanding officers
   c. The better equipment of the American forces
   d. French aid to the rebels
   e. The petty jealousies among the British officers
8. The impact in Europe of the American Revolution can best be summarized as
   a. important and influential among the educated classes everywhere.
   b. important in Great Britain but not acknowledged widely elsewhere.
   c. minimal except among a handful of liberals.
   d. important in a military but not a political sense.
   e. sufficient to anger conservative Europeans who still believed in the divine right of kings.
9. To liberal-minded Europeans, the success of the American Revolution meant above all that
   a. force is most important in political affairs.
   b. democracy should be introduced to their own governments.
   c. the teachings of the Enlightenment were feasible.
   d. Americans were more aggressive than other Westerners.
   e. all monarchies had become obsolete.
10. The American Revolution had the most direct impact on the citizens of
   a. England.
   b. Scotland.
   c. Germany.
   d. Spain.
   e. France.

## InfoTrac College Edition

Visit the source collections at

**http://infotrac.thomsonlearning.com**

and use the Search function with the following key terms:

John Locke American Revolution

Thomas Paine or Tom Paine

## Wadsworth History Website Resources

Visit the World History Resource Center at **http://history.wadsworth.com/world** for a wealth of general resources, and the *World Civilizations* Companion Website at **http://history.wadsworth.com/adler04** for resources specific to this textbook.

## HistoryNow

Enter *HistoryNow* using the access card that is available for *World Civilizations. HistoryNow* will assist you in understanding the content in this chapter with lesson plans generated for your needs. In addition, you can read the following documents, and many more, online:

Thomas Jefferson, "The Declaration of Independence"

Thomas Paine, selections from *Common Sense*

*The effect of liberty upon individuals is that they may do as they please; we ought to see what it will please them to do before we risk congratulations.*
**Edmund Burke**

# 33 The French Revolution and the Empire of Napoleon



| | |
|---|---|
| 1715–1774 | Reign of Louis XV |
| 1774–1792 | Reign of Louis XVI |
| 1789–1791 | First phase of the Revolution: Constitutional monarchy |
| 1792–1794 | Second phase of the Revolution: Jacobin Terror |
| 1795–1799 | Third phase of the Revolution: Thermidorean Reaction |
| 1800–1814 | The Revolution terminated: Napoleonic empire |
| 1815 | The Vienna Settlement |

The watershed of modern political history is the upheaval called the French Revolution that struck France and then all of Europe in the last years of the eighteenth century. More than what had happened in the American colonies a few years earlier, the unrest in France challenged every tradition and shook every pillar of the establishment. During its unpredictable and violent course evolved the ideas of popular democracy, social equality, and personal liberty, which the Revolution originally stood for but later betrayed. What started as a French aristocratic rebellion against royal taxes became the milepost from which all modern political and social developments in the Western world are measured.

## The Background of the Crisis

The Revolution of 1789 in France was triggered by a dispute over finances and taxation between monarch and subjects, just as the American Revolution was. But the tax question could have been remedied, if the deeper problems of the royal government in Paris had not been so intense and so complex.

Since the death of the "Sun King," Louis XIV, in 1715, the quality and the morale of French officialdom had declined. Louis's immediate successor was his great-grandson (he had outlived both his son and grandsons), Louis XV, a young boy. For many years during his youth, actual power had been exercised by a group of nobles who used the opportunity to loosen the controls put on them by the Sun King's monopoly of power. Intent mainly on personal luxuries, they abused their powers and their newly regained freedom. Corruption and bribery began to appear in the courts and in administrative offices where it was previously not tolerated. The middle-class professional officials who had been the heart and soul of Louis XIV's bureaucracy were passed over or ignored in favor of the aristocrats who monopolized the highest offices, by right of birth.

How did this deterioration come about? By nature, Louis XV was not suited to the demands of absolutist government. He was intelligent but cynical and preferred play to work. When he did take action, he delegated power to sycophants and careerists and refused to involve himself if he could avoid it.

But the tax revenue problems could not be put off indefinitely. During the mid-eighteenth century, France engaged in a series of costly and losing wars against Britain overseas and against Austria and then Prussia on the Continent (War of the Austrian Succession, 1740–1747; Seven Years' War, 1756–1763). Taxes had to be increased, but from whose pockets? The urban middle classes and the peasantry were already paying a disproportionate amount, while the state church (the greatest single property owner in France) and the nobles were paying next to nothing, claiming ancient exemptions granted by medieval kings. By the time of Louis XV's death in 1774, the government was already on the verge of bankruptcy, unable to pay its military forces on time and forced to go to several moneylenders (notably, the Rothschild family) to meet current accounts.

Louis XV was succeeded by his weak-minded and indecisive grandson Louis XVI (ruled 1774–1792). A sympathetic and decent person, Louis was in no way qualified to lead an unstable country that was rapidly approaching a financial crisis. Specifically, he could not be expected to limit the vast expenditures that were wasted on the maintenance and frivolities (such as the amusements of Queen Marie Antoinette) of the royal court at Versailles. Nor would he take an effective stand against the rising political pretensions of the nobility. This latter group, acting through their regional assemblies—the *parlements*—claimed to be the true defenders of French liberties. In practice, this claim translated into an adamant refusal to pay their share of taxes.

This was the situation in 1778 when the royal government decided to enter the American rebellion on the side of the colonials, to weaken Britain and perhaps to reclaim what it had lost in the Seven Years' War earlier (that is, Canada and the Mississippi valley). The expenses of this effort were very high for France. And by now, much of the entire budget had to be funded by borrowed money at rates of interest that rose higher and higher because of the justified fear that the government would declare bankruptcy and refuse to honor its outstanding debts. (This had happened before in France.) Half of the revenues had to be paid out just to meet the interest due on current accounts. No one knew when or whether the principal could be repaid.

Faced with the refusal—once more—of the nobles and the clergy to pay even a token sum, the king reluctantly agreed to the election of an assemblage that had been forgotten for 175 years: the **Estates General**, or parliament representing all segments of the society of all France. No Estates had been convoked since 1614, because after that time first Richelieu and then Louis XIV had embarked on absolutist royal government.

## Constitutional Monarchy

According to tradition, the members of the Estates General would be elected from and by their own colleagues. There were three "estates," or orders of society: the First Estate was made up of the clergy, the Second consisted of the nobility, and the Third included everyone else. Rich or poor, rural or urban, educated or illiterate, all people who were neither in the church nor of the nobility were in the **Third Estate**. Tradition further held that each estate voted as a bloc, so that only three votes would be cast on any issue. Because the two "privileged" estates could always form a majority against the commoners, they were assured of retaining their privileges if they stayed together.

### *Calling of the Estates*

The first two estates made up only about 3 percent of the total population of France, but the nobles and clergy dominated every aspect of public life except commerce and manufacturing. They were the exclusive holders of political power above the local level. They were the king's powerful servants and concession holders, and they had every social privilege imaginable. They lived a life apart from the great majority, with their own customs and their own entertainments. They looked on the commoners with contempt and, sometimes, fear. They held a very large share of the property in France—about 40 percent of the real estate and an even higher share of income-producing enterprises and offices of all sorts.

Some of the representatives of the First and Second Estates were liberal-minded individuals who sympathized with the demands for reform. Their leadership and assistance were crucially important to the success of the Revolution's first phase.

The Third Estate, the commoners, was represented mainly by lawyers and minor officials. A very few delegates were peasants, but there were virtually no representatives from the vast mass of artisans, employees, and illiterate laborers. The Third Estate's major complaints were the legal and social inequalities in the kingdom and their own lack of political representation. The Estate's guiding principles and its political philosophy were taken straight from the liberal Enlightenment. (See the Society and Economy box for more on the Third Estate.)

In the spring of 1789, the elected Estates General convened at Versailles, the site of the royal palace and

SOCIETY AND ECONOMY

## What Is the Third Estate?

**The original ideals of the French Revolution** were moderate and primarily concerned with eliminating the special privileges of the church and the nobles. By the 1780s, most of the French populace understood more or less clearly that they were severely disadvantaged by the various exemptions and concessions that the 3 percent of the population belonging to the privileged classes held.

No one better expressed the sentiments of the middle classes (the bourgeoisie) at this time than the priest Emmanuel Sieyes (1748–1836) in a pamphlet entitled *What Is the Third Estate?*

> We must ask ourselves three questions:
>
> 1. What is the Third Estate? Everything.
> 2. What has it been till now in the political order? Nothing.
> 3. What does it want to be? Something. . . .
>
> Who is bold enough to maintain that the Third Estate does not contain within itself all that is needful to constitute a complete nation? It is like a strong and robust man with one arm still in chains. If the privileged order were removed, the nation would not be something less, but something more!
>
> What then is the Third Estate? All; but an "all" which is fettered and oppressed.
>
> What would it be without the privileged order? It would be all; but free and flourishing. Nothing will go well without the Third Estate; everything would go considerably better without the two others.

### Analyze and Interpret

How would you have answered the same questions?

Source: Emmanuel Sieyes, *What Is the Third Estate?* trans. M. Blondel. Reprinted with permission of Greenwood Publishing Group, Inc., Westport, CT.

government just outside Paris. Immediately, a dispute arose over voting. The Third Estate demanded "one man, one vote," which would have given it the majority when joined with known sympathizers from the others. The other two orders refused, and the king was called on to decide. After attempting a vain show of force, Louis XVI caved in to the demands of the commoners. Some renegades from the privileged then joined with the Third Estate to declare themselves the National Constituent Assembly. On June 20, 1789, they resolved not to disperse until they had given the country a constitution. In effect, this *was* the French Revolution, for if this self-appointed assembly were allowed to stand, the old order of absolutist monarchy would end.

## The National Assembly and Its Constitution

What the Assembly wanted was a moderate, constitutional monarchy like England's, but the king's hope to reestablish control and the refusal of most of the nobility and clergy to go along with the Assembly's project made a confrontation unavoidable. The confrontation came in the summer of 1789, beginning with the storming of the Bastille (the royal prison in Paris). For the next several months, the Parisian mob, whipped up by radicals from all over the country, played a major role in the course of political events, the first time in modern history that the urban "underclass" asserted such direct influence. The moderates and conservatives who dominated the Assembly were forced to listen to and heed the demands of the poor, who staged a series of bread riots and wild demonstrations around the Assembly's meeting place.

On August 4, 1789, the nobles who had joined the Assembly made a voluntary renunciation of their feudal rights, effectively ending serfdom and the nobility's legal privileges in France forever. A little later, the Assembly adopted the **Declaration of the Rights of Man and Citizen**, which went much farther than the almost simultaneous first ten amendments—the Bill of Rights—of the American Constitution. (For a sampling of historic documents from both France and the United States, see the box in Chapter 32.)

This democratic manifesto was followed by the **Civil Constitution of the Clergy**, meaning the Catholic clergy in France. This measure allowed the state to confiscate the church's property and made the priests into (unwilling) agents of the emerging new government—paid by it and therefore controlled by it. This radical act was a misreading of the country's temper, because most French were still obedient Catholics and rallied to the support of the church's continued independence. The pope in Rome condemned the Civil Constitution, and with the resistance against it began the counterrevolution.

By the end of 1791, the new constitution had been completed. It provided for powers to be shared between king and parliament along the English lines, but with even stronger powers for the parliament. A national election for this new Legislative Assembly was ordained and carried through.

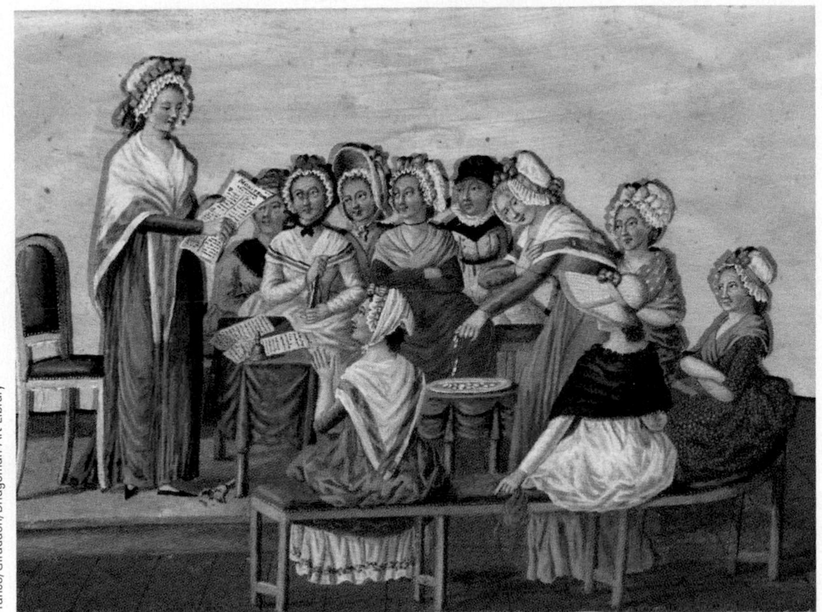

Musee de la Ville de Paris, Musee Carnavalet, Paris, France/Giraudon/Bridgeman Art Library

**Female Patriots, 1790.** A club of women discusses the latest decrees of the revolutionary government, while a collection plate is set up for the relief of those families who have suffered in the cause.

## Jacobin Terror

The conservative monarchic governments of Europe led by Austria and Prussia were closely watching what was happening, and they were determined to restore Louis XVI to his rightful powers with armed force. The counterrevolutionary war began in the summer of 1792. Combined with the misguided attempt of Queen Marie Antoinette and Louis to flee the country, the war changed the internal atmosphere at a blow. Until 1792, the moderates, who wished to retain the monarchy and to avoid any challenge to the rule of property, had been in control. Now the radical element called the **Jacobins** (their original headquarters was in the Parisian convent of the Jacobin order of nuns) took over the Legislative Assembly. The moderates were soon driven into silence or exiled.

What did the new masters of France want? The Jacobins were determined to extend the Revolution, to guarantee the eradication of aristocratic privileges and royal absolutism, and to put the common man in the driver's seat. They dissolved the Legislative Assembly and called a National Convention, elected by universal male suffrage, into being. In Paris, a self-appointed Jacobin Commune established itself as the legal authority. By early 1793, the war emergency encouraged the Jacobins to institute a *Reign of Terror* against all enemies within the country. This was history's first mass purge of people on account of their social origins or suspected beliefs. Over the next year or so, between 25,000 and 40,000 victims were guillotined, and many tens of thousands more were imprisoned or exiled by the extraordinary Courts of the People, which were everywhere.

Among the early victims of the Terror was the king. Held as a prisoner since his foiled attempt to escape France, he was given a mock trial for treason and beheaded in January 1793. Marie Antoinette followed him to the guillotine in October. The killing of the king and queen was an enormous shock to the many Europeans who believed in liberal ideals and had seen the first stage of the Revolution as their implementation. From 1793 on, the educated classes of Europe were sharply divided between friends and enemies of the Revolution, with more and more tending toward the latter camp as the atrocities of the Terror were recognized. What had started in 1789 as a high-principled campaign for justice, liberty, and progress had degenerated into a bloodbath.

Musee de la Ville de Paris, Musee Carnavalet, Paris, France/Giraudon/Bridgeman Art Library

**A French Cartoon from 1792.** In this engraving, the enraged peasant finds himself unchained and reaches for his weapons while the shocked priest and noble recoil in horror.

After September 1792, France was no longer a monarchy but a republic. The executive power was exercised by the National Convention's **Committee of Public Safety** with dictatorial authority. Maximilien Robespierre was its leading member and the theoretician of the Revolution. (For more about Robespierre, see the Law and Government box.)

The years 1793–1794 were the height of the Revolution. The Jacobins produced many novel ideas and techniques of power that would be imitated in revolutions to

LAW AND GOVERNMENT

## Maximilien Robespierre (1758–1794)

**The most dreaded name in all of France** during the Reign of Terror of 1793–1794 was that of the leader of the Committee of Public Safety, Maximilien Robespierre. A small figure with a high-pitched voice, he had come to the forefront during the National Assembly in 1790–1791 as an advocate of a republican democracy. His power base was the Society of Jacobins in Paris.

Robespierre was the driving force behind the steady radicalization of the Legislative Assembly in 1792 and its successor, the Convention. He engineered the declaration of the republic in August 1792 and justified the horrific massacre of imprisoned nobles and clerics in September as a necessary step in preparing France to defend its Revolution. Attacked by his enemies in the Convention as a would-be dictator, he defied them to find any stain on his patriotism and his selflessness in the revolutionary cause.

Musee de la Ville de Paris, Musee Carnavalet, Paris, France/Giraudon/Bridgeman Art Library

**Robespierre.** An anonymous eighteenth-century portrait of the man whom some considered the pure and selfless servant of the little people and others viewed as the personification of evil.

His election to the Committee of Public Safety in July 1793 meant a sharp turn toward even more shocking measures. In the fall, he led the Convention into pronouncing the Republic of Virtue, an attempt to supplant Christianity and all religion in France. Patriotism would henceforth be measured by devotion to reason and the people rather than to God and king. The names of the days and the months were changed to rid them of all overtones of gods and saints, and the counting of the years began anew, with the declaration of the republic in 1792 being Year One. Churches were renamed Temples of Reason, and the Catholic clergy was subjected to both ridicule and bloody persecution. Much of this change went far beyond what Robespierre had intended, but he was powerless to stop the frenzy that he had helped set loose among the *sans-culottes* (urban working class) and the provincial Jacobins.

Robespierre found it necessary to eliminate even his coworkers in the committee and the Convention for being lukewarm supporters of the Revolution. He believed he was destined to cleanse the ranks of all who would falter on the road to perfection. In June 1794, he pushed the notorious Law of 22 Prairial through an intimidated Convention (Prairial was the name of the month in the revolutionary calendar). This allowed kangaroo courts all over France to issue the supreme penalty with or without substantive evidence of hostility to the government. In that summer, thousands of innocents were guillotined, either because they were anonymously denounced or simply because they were members of a "hostile" class such as the nobles. Robespierre justified these actions in a speech saying that because the Terror was but an inflexible application of justice, it was a virtue and must be applauded.

In July 1794, the increasingly isolated Robespierre rose in the Convention to denounce the backsliders and the hesitant. In the past, such speeches had foretold another series of arrests by the People's Courts. This time, by prearrangement, the Convention shouted him down and arrested him. On the following day, July 28, he was guillotined amid sighs of relief and curses.

### *Analyze and Interpret*

Can you think of the counterpart of Robespierre in a more recent revolution? What case can be made for the application of terror against the internal enemies of a radical political movement? What case against it?

History Now™

***To read Robespierre's "Address to the National Convention," point your browser to the documents area of HistoryNow.***

**The Levée en Masse.** In 1792, the National Convention created a new, massive army composed of volunteers from all classes and, later, conscripts. Here, citizens enthusiastically sign up while receiving money payments for their enrollment.

Giraudon/Art Resource, NY

come over the next two centuries. They insisted on the following three points:

- That all men were legally, socially, and politically equal—*Egalité*
- That they were free in mind and body—*Liberté*
- That they were, or should be, brothers—*Fraternité*

They elevated reason and patriotism to entirely new heights, making these faculties into virtues that were supposed to supplant the old ones of religion and subservience. They recognized no neutrality, nor would they tolerate neutrals. Those who did not support the People's Revolution were necessarily its enemies and would be treated accordingly. These were novel and shocking thoughts to the conservative forces inside and outside France. It seemed to them that the Jacobins' systematic rejection of traditional authority must lead to chaos rather than freedom.

Believing the royal professional military to be a dubious ally, the Jacobins also started the ***levée en masse*** (conscript army) to defend the Revolution. With the aid of many recruits from the former royal forces (such as Napoleon Bonaparte), they developed and used that army so effectively that the French were on the offensive from 1794 onward against the conservative coalition. And they completed the wholesale confiscation and distribution of royal, noble, and clerical land to the peasants, thereby eliminating one of the major causes of complaint in pre-1789 France. The nobility and the church had lost their economic bases. They would never get them back.

## Reaction and Consolidation

The machinery of terror was quickly dismantled after the execution of Robespierre, as the pervasive fear had become too great for most French, even radicals, to live with. The period 1794–1795 is termed the *Thermidorean Reaction* against the excesses of the Reign of Terror. The name comes from Thermidor, the new name for August, the month after which Robespierre fell. In place of the Jacobin-led poor who had greatly influenced government policy until now, the middle classes and the wealthy came again to the fore. They chose several of their own to form a new executive, called the **Directory**, and by sharp restriction of the franchise created a much more conservative-minded assembly, derived largely from the propertied classes.

The five directors were soon maneuvering for power and squabbling among themselves. Meanwhile, the economic condition of the urban poor grew desperate, and the ongoing war created a severe inflation and a new class of wealthy profiteers. The peasantry sought in vain for legal recognition of its newly seized lands, while neither the clergy nor its secularist detractors were satisfied with the relationship between state and church. These various discontents could be contained only so long as the revolution was winning on the battlefield and the prospect for final victory looked good.

### *The Bonapartist Era Opens*

From 1794 to 1798, French armies seemed irresistible (see Map 33.1). A young and well-connected general named Napoleon Bonaparte distinguished himself in the campaigns that forced the Austrians and Prussians to make a losing peace with France. In 1798, however, Russia joined the anti-French coalition, and Britain remained an enemy that would not give in. Napoleon persuaded the Directors to send him with a large army to Egypt to cut off the British commercial route to the East and thus induce this "nation of shopkeepers" to make peace. The ill-thought-out Egyptian campaign of 1798–1799 turned into a disaster, but Napoleon saved his reputation by returning home in time and letting his subordinates take the eventual blame. His ambitious wife, Josephine, and

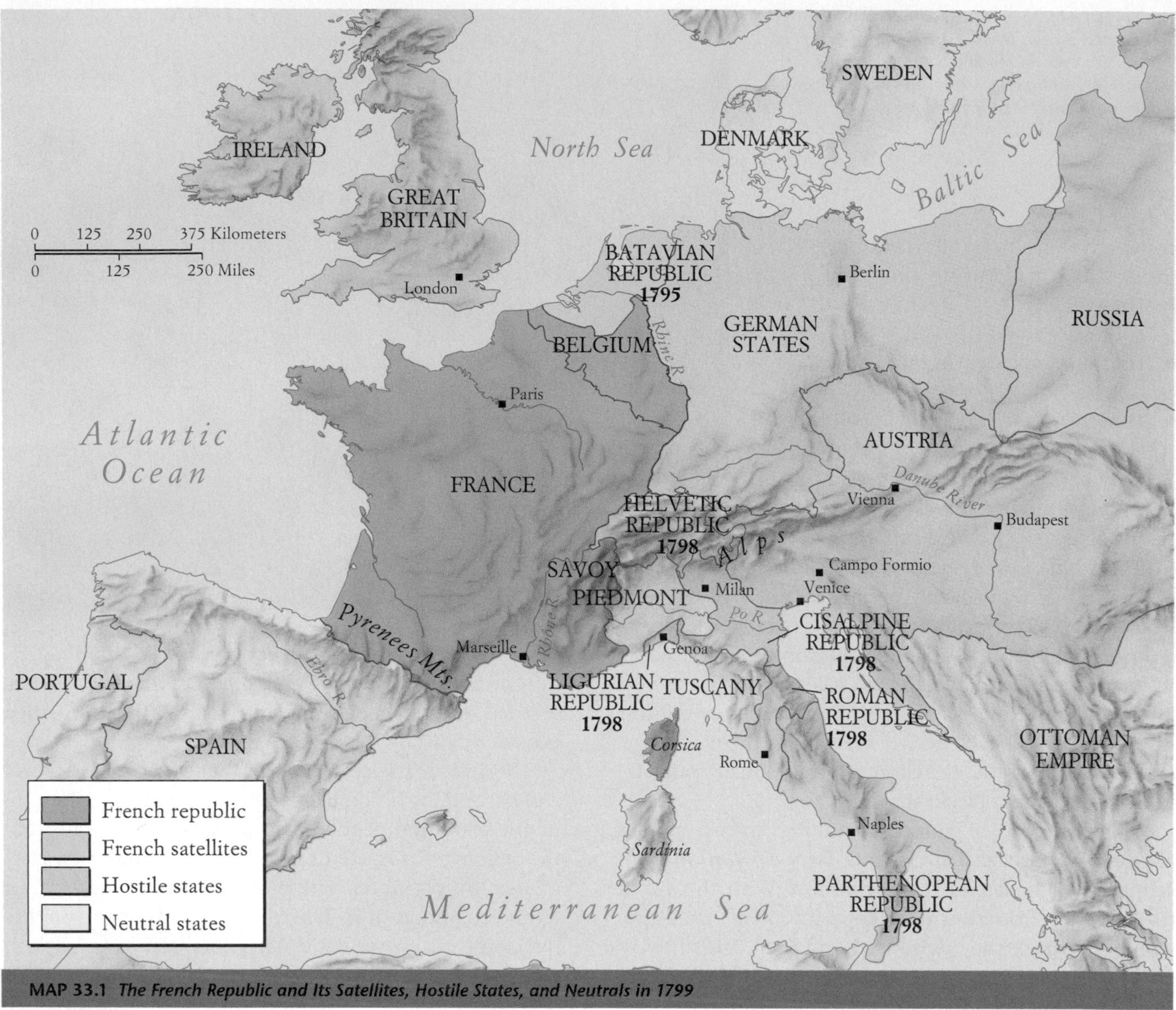

**MAP 33.1** *The French Republic and Its Satellites, Hostile States, and Neutrals in 1799*

his friends had told him that the time was ripe to brush aside the unpopular government and take command in France. In November 1799, he acted on their advice.

Finding little resistance in defense of the by-now vastly unpopular Directors, Bonaparte and his army accomplices pulled off the coup d'état of 18 Brumaire. It made Napoleon **First Consul** of France, holding supreme civil and military power in his ambitious hands. A new era was about to begin, led by a thirty-year-old Corsican who had risen dramatically since entering the revolutionary army six years previously as a young lieutenant.

Confident of his talent and his vast energies, Napoleon as First Consul (1799–1804) pretended to obey a new constitution that was concocted by his agents in the tame legislature he allowed to stand. He suppressed all political opposition and solidified his already-high standing with the public by carrying out a series of acts, called collectively the **Napoleonic Settlement**. It embraced the following:

- Establishing the *concordat* with the papacy in 1801. This agreement pacified the French clergy and the peasants by declaring that Catholicism was the semi-official religion, but it also pleased the strong anticlerical party by making the Catholic Church and clergy a part of the state apparatus and putting them under strict controls.
- Creating administrative and judicial systems that have lasted in France until the present day. Napoleon created a highly centralized network that went far to integrate and standardize the formerly diverse provincial governments and connect the regions more tightly with the capital.
- Granting legal title to the peasants for the lands they had seized earlier in the revolution

- Giving the country new uniform civil and criminal codes of law (the **Civil Code of 1804**; see the Law and Government box for more on this code.)
- Putting the new single national currency and the government's finances in good order
- Establishing social peace by allowing the exiles to return if they agreed to support the new France
- Crushing royalist plots to return the Bourbons, and also crushing the radical Jacobin remnants

## French Dominion over Europe

In 1804, Napoleon felt the time was ripe to do what everyone had long expected: He crowned himself monarch of France. His intention was to found a Bonaparte dynasty that would replace the Bourbons. He took the formal title of emperor, because by then France controlled several non-French peoples. As long as his wars went well, he was so popular at home that he could raise vast conscript armies and levy heavy taxes to support their expense, employing a legislature and bureaucracy that were completely his creatures. And the wars went well for France for several years.

Napoleon was perhaps the greatest military strategist of the modern era. He devised and led one victorious campaign after another, often against superior numbers, between 1796 and 1809. His implacable enemy was Britain, which actively supported the various coalitions against him by contributions of troops, ships, and money. War reigned between France and Britain uninterruptedly (save a few months in 1802) for twenty-two years, 1793–1814. French armies conquered Spain, Portugal, the Italian peninsula, Austria (three times), Prussia, and Holland, all of which were incorporated into France directly, made into satellites, or neutralized. He also defeated a Russian army sent against France and was on the verge of invading England when his defeat in a major sea battle at Trafalgar off the Spanish coast in 1805 put that plan to rest forever.

Napoleon's relations with Russia were always edgy, even after its decisive defeat at French hands in 1807. By 1810, Napoleon was convinced that the czar, Alexander I, was preparing hostilities again and would form an alliance with the English. He decided on a preemptive strike. In the summer of 1812, the invasion began from its Polish base with a huge army of 600,000, including Frenchmen, their coerced allies, and some volunteers.

Napoleon's campaign in Russia is one of the epic stories of modern war. After initial successes against the retreating

LAW AND GOVERNMENT

### The Civil Code of 1804

**The systematic reworking of French law** called the Civil Code of 1804 proved to be one of the most lasting and most important bequests of the French Revolution. Whereas the radical democratic spirit and the atheism of the Jacobins was soon submerged and the French military dominion over much of the Continent was ended by Waterloo, the Napoleonic code had a supranational influence not only on the continent of Europe but also on Latin America and the European colonies.

One of the code's important aspects was its conservative and patriarchal definition of the rights of females, a definition that would not be substantially altered in France until the twentieth century. Those definitions and distinctions between male and female included the following:

- The legal residence of a married woman was that designated by her husband.
- Women could not serve as witnesses or institute lawsuits in court.
- Female adultery was punishable by imprisonment or fines; male adultery was legally blameless unless the illicit partner was brought into the wife's home.
- Generally, a married or single woman had no control over property.
- Married women's wages were legally the property of their husbands, and a married woman could not engage in business or sign contracts without the permission of her husband.

These restrictions on females remained essentially unchanged until the entry of large numbers of women into the labor force in Europe and the resultant necessity of allowing them greater management of their independent incomes. The crises generated in society by World Wars I and II also contributed greatly to this movement.

#### *Analyze and Interpret*

How do the code's restrictions on women's rights compare with those in earlier laws affecting women, such as the Code of Hammurabi, the Laws of Manu, and the Qur'an?

**The Plum Pudding in Danger.** This satirical cartoon by noted British illustrator James Gillray was done in 1805, when it briefly appeared that Napoleon was more interested in carving off Europe for his empire than in striking a deal with Britain and ending the lengthy war. The Englishman is William Pitt, prime minister throughout the war years.

Russian army, the French belatedly realized that they had fallen into a lethal trap: exposure and starvation claimed most of those who survived the guerrilla warfare of the long winter retreat from Moscow. Perhaps one-third of the original force found their way to friendly Polish soil.

*La Grande Armée,* Napoleon's magnificent weapon with which he had ruled Europe for the preceding decade, was irretrievably broken despite his frantic efforts to rebuild it. The culminating **Battle of the Nations** at Leipzig in 1813 ended in French defeat at the hands of combined Russian, Prussian, and Austrian forces. Occupied Europe was then gradually freed of French troops and governors. In March 1814, Paris was surrendered and occupied, and Bonaparte was forced to abdicate.

**Retreat from Moscow.** This rendering of the retreat of Napoleon's Grande Armée through the snowy wastes of Russia in the winter of 1812 captures well the atmosphere of desperation that engulfed the once proud ranks of the French invaders.

**Napoleon Leading His Troops.** This magnificent if imaginary scene of Napoleon crossing the Alps was created by the great French painter J. L. David (1748–1825) to give the French a vision of their emperor they could not forget.

## Napoleon: Pro or Con

The debate over Napoleon's greatness as a leader and statesman has occupied the French and others for almost two centuries. Opinions divide nearly as sharply now as during his lifetime. Although some see him as a man of genius and the founder of a progressive, stable social order, others see him as a dictator whose visions for society were always subordinate to his concern for his own welfare and glory.

There can be little doubt that he was an able administrator and selector of talent. In those crucial capacities, he came closer to the ideal "enlightened despot" than any other ruler of his day or earlier. In contrast to the recent Bourbon regime, his government was for years efficient, able, popular, and relatively honest. Men of ability could move upward regardless of their social background. Although by no means a revolutionary himself, Napoleon kept the promises that the French Revolution had made to the peasants and to the middle classes. He confirmed, though he may not have originated, many of the liberals' favorite measures, such as the disestablishment of the Catholic Church, equality before the law, and the abolition of privilege by birth. His codes provided a modern, uniform basis for all French law, both civil and criminal (though the subordination of women was kept very much intact). His administrative reforms replaced the huge mishmash that had been the French regional and provincial bureaucracy with a thoroughly rational centralized system. Now power was concentrated in the government in Paris, which appointed and oversaw the provincial and local officials.

But the imperial regime developed more than a few blemishes as well. After about 1808, the French government was a dictatorship in which individual liberties depended on Napoleon's wishes. No political parties were allowed, and the Napoleonic legislature was at all times a sham. The press was so heavily controlled that it became meaningless. Political life was forced underground and degenerated into a series of conspiracies. An internal spy system had informants everywhere.

In the occupied or satellite territories that made up the Napoleonic empire (see Map 33.2), governmental policies were often harsh even when enlightened, and patriots who opposed French orders were executed without mercy. The non-French populations were steadily exploited. They were expected to pay new and onerous taxes, to furnish conscripts for the French armies, and to trade on terms that were advantageous to the French. Napoleon also strongly promoted the nationalist spirit that had been so

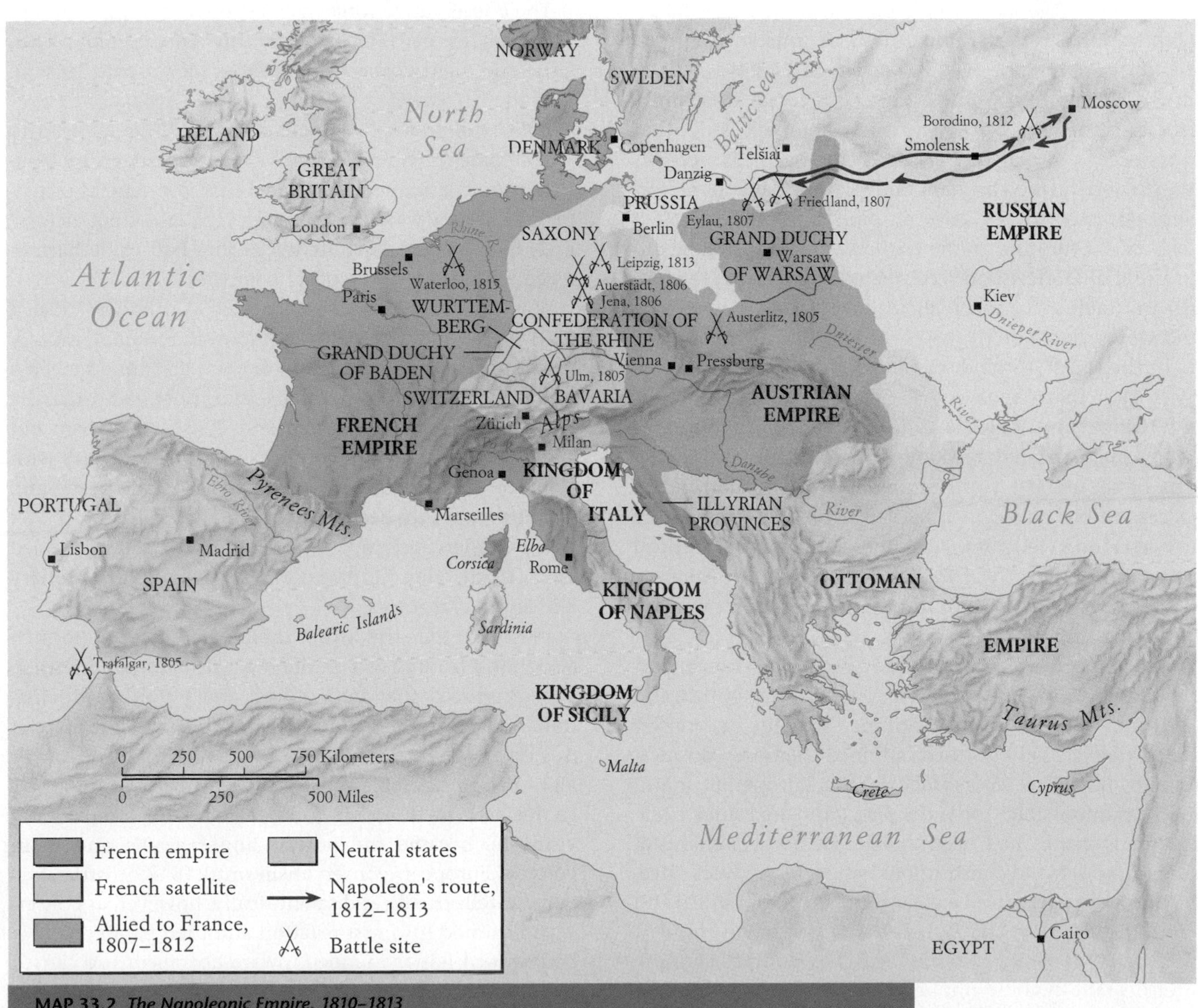


**MAP 33.2** *The Napoleonic Empire, 1810–1813*

Except for Britain and Russia, Napoleon controlled almost all of Europe by 1810, either directly through incorporation into his empire or by coerced alliances.

important to the early years of the Revolution, but only as long as the subject peoples accepted the leadership of Paris. When they did not, they were regarded as traitors and dealt with accordingly. The Prussian liberals, especially, learned this to their dismay when, in true national spirit, they attempted to reject French overlords after royal Prussia's defeat in 1806.

There is also no doubt that as time went on, Bonaparte became increasingly cynical and indifferent to the welfare of the masses he once claimed to champion against their aristocratic oppressors. His willingness to create a new class of nobles, based on alleged merit but actually too often mere opportunists and sycophants of the Bonapartist regime, was not unnoticed by the idealists.

## The Vienna Settlement

With Napoleon exiled (in luxurious circumstances) to the island of Elba in the Mediterranean, the allies who had united against him went to Vienna to try to work out a general settlement of the extremely complex issues that two decades of war had created. Originally, France was not invited, but the brilliant and slippery Talleyrand, foreign minister to the now-restored Bourbon monarch Louis XVIII (brother to the last king), used his talents to ensure that France soon received an equal seat at the bargaining table. (For more about Talleyrand, see the Law and Government box.)

In the midst of the discussions came the news in February 1815 that Napoleon had fled Elba, landed in southern France, and issued a call to all of his followers to renew the war. They responded with enthusiasm in the tens of thousands. The Hundred Days campaign nearly succeeded but ended in total defeat for the Bonapartists at **Waterloo** in Belgium. This time, Napoleon was shipped off as a prisoner of war to a rock in the South Atlantic, St. Helena, where he lived out the remaining six years of his life writing his memoirs.

In Vienna, the "Big Four" victors—Austria, Prussia, Russia, and England—were busy working out the political and territorial outlines of a new Europe. Actually, the conservative powers, led by Austria's Prince Clemens von Metternich, hoped to reconstruct the old Europe but found that was impossible. Too much had happened since 1789: too many hopes had been awakened, borders changed, kings removed, and constitutions issued. In the years since, Europe had experienced a great watershed in political and social history. The "Old System" of European government and society (***l'ancien régime***) was like Humpty Dumpty after his fall—it could not be reconstructed.

After nearly coming to blows on the thorny question of what should happen to Poland—a state that had been partially re-created by Napoleon—the four victors hammered out a series of agreements that collectively gave Europe its political borders for the next hundred years. They were guided in their work by several underlying principles:

1. *Legitimacy in government.* Kings were restored to their thrones, and radical constitutions written by pro-French revolutionaries were thrown out or rewritten to reflect more conservative themes. Revolutions would henceforth be suppressed by international collaboration and intervention.
2. *International cooperation to maintain peace.* The victors (and soon also France) formed an alliance with regular meetings of foreign ministers. The Quadruple Alliance lasted for only a decade, but its principles of international responsibility for peace guided diplomatic meetings throughout the century from 1815 to 1914.
3. *Discouragement of nationalism and liberalism in politics.* The conservative forces saw both nationalism and liberalism as evils brought by the French radicals to Europe. Neither was recognized as a legitimate demand of the citizenry.
4. *Balance of power.* No single state would be allowed to dominate the Continent as had France under Napoleon.

Within the framework created by these general principles, what now were the agendas of the four chief victors? Each had, in fact, separate needs that had to be harmonized with those of the other countries.

Russia, under the visionary Czar Alexander I (ruled 1801–1825), had been the main force in the final military defeat of the French and now for the first time played a leading role in European affairs. Alexander had originally sympathized with liberalism and constitutionalism but came to mistrust those concepts after the struggles with Napoleon began. Led by mystical hopes for peace and harmony, the czar became a conservative autocrat in later years. Under Alexander's successor, Nicholas I (ruled 1825–1855), the country became a bastion of reactionary and antiliberal forces.

Austria under the astute diplomat Prince Metternich also took a leading role in the reconstruction. Metternich was convinced that nationalism and popular participation in government would ruin the multinational state of Austria and then all of Europe. He fought these ideas with all of his considerable skill and energy. Because he stayed at the helm of Vienna's foreign policy for almost forty years, he became the outstanding example and main voice of European conservatism until 1848. Austria stagnated intellectually and scientifically, however, as conservatism turned into first reaction and then paralysis.

Prussia originally tended toward liberalism and carried out internal reforms under a group of statesmen who admired the constitutional phase of the French Revolution. But, after the defeat of the French, the Prussian king Frederick William III made clear his distaste for constitu-

LAW AND GOVERNMENT

## Talleyrand (1754–1836)

**Maurice de Talleyrand-Perigord,** prince of Benevento, diplomat extraordinaire, and foreign minister of France under five different regimes, was born in 1754 as the second son of a high noble family. As was customary for that time and that class, his upbringing was turned over to a nurse and a governess, while his mother and father were in constant attendance at the royal court. When Talleyrand was five, a fall injured his foot and lamed him for life. It also deprived him of the army career that would normally have been his lot. When he was thirteen, his parents sent him to a seminary against his will, and he never forgave them or the church he was supposed to serve.

Through family influence, Talleyrand was consecrated bishop of Autun in 1789, and he at once joined with the moderate members of the Third Estate in the deliberations of the Estates General at Versailles. In general, he endorsed the state's confiscation of the church's property, the Civil Constitution of the Clergy, and the subordination of the religious establishment to the government. For these opinions, he was excommunicated by the pope and spent the rest of his long life as a layman.

Talleyrand's demonstrated administrative and diplomatic abilities caused the National Assembly to name him as a special emissary to Great Britain in 1792. But the Revolution's radical turn later in 1792, especially the execution of the king and queen, frightened Talleyrand, who remained an adherent of constitutionalism and tolerance all of his life. Expelled from Britain after the war broke out, he went to the United States (whose society he did not care for) for two years and then returned to France under the Directory in 1796. He served as foreign minister both for the Directory and for Napoleon, whose triumphant takeover in 1799 Talleyrand had a hand in preparing. For the next eight years, Talleyrand was the most important man in France except for the emperor. He constantly tried to tame Napoleon's ambitions and to work out a permanent peace between France and the rest of Europe. He was convinced that Bonaparte's cynical disregard of the interests of other powers would not succeed in the long run, although it was sustained at the moment by superior force. But he could not get his master to see things in this light, and after the peace of Tilsit in 1807, Talleyrand resigned his ministry.

When Napoleon abdicated and the defeated French began negotiations with the allies, Talleyrand's career resumed with a flourish, as he was able to induce Czar Alexander I of Russia to support the return of the Bourbon family to the throne of France in the name of the sacred principle of "legitimacy." He was also crucial to the decision to allow France to come to the Congress of Vienna as an almost equal member rather than as a defeated enemy. Talleyrand's skill at protecting French national interest at Vienna became legendary. He was rewarded by being appointed France's foreign minister once again in 1815, this time by the restored Bourbon Louis XVIII. Shortly afterward, he resigned the post, however, preferring to retire to a life of ease and social activity at his country mansion.

He was by now immensely rich, having taken full advantage of many opportunities to increase his wealth during the Napoleonic era. His many enemies in Paris claimed that he had acquired his money illegally, and the accusations were at least partly true: he had taken part in schemes to manipulate the nation's finances for his own advantage more than once.

In 1830, the old man emerged briefly into the political limelight once again as a supporter of the "Citizen King" Louis Philippe, who took the throne after the July revolution in that year. Louis wished to make him foreign minister once more, but Talleyrand preferred to be ambassador to London, where he negotiated the treaty that made England and France formal allies for the first time in centuries. In 1834, he resigned his post and returned to France to die. In his final weeks, he reconciled himself to the Catholic Church and died with honors showered on him as one of the greatest statesmen of the age. He had terminated a loveless marriage in 1815 and left no legitimate heirs.

### *Analyze and Interpret*

Was Talleyrand a flexible diplomat, who attempted in his own way to serve the cause of peace, or a "titled scoundrel" as he was called by many? Does serving many different masters well necessarily imply moral weakness in an official?

---

tional government and succeeded in turning back the political clock for a generation. As a nation, Prussia came out of the wars with France strengthened and expanded, with improved technology and an aggressive entrepreneurial class. By the 1830s, it had the best educational system in Europe and was in a position to contest Austria for the lead in pan-German affairs.

Great Britain was clearly the leading naval power and one of the strongest military forces in Europe by 1815, but the British governing class primarily wanted to concentrate on its business interests to take advantage of the big lead it had established since 1780 in the race to industrialize (see the next chapter). The British liberals always felt uncomfortable on the same side of the table as Czar Alexander and Metternich, and by 1825, they had abandoned the Quadruple Alliance system. Having helped establish the balance of power on the Continent, they retreated into "splendid isolation" for the rest of the nineteenth century. They involved themselves in Europe's affairs only when they deemed that their commercial and business interests were endangered.

These four powers plus France would mold Europe's destinies for the rest of the nineteenth century. The others had little to say beyond their own borders. Italy was not yet formed into a single state and would in any case remain in the second tier in international affairs. Spain subsided into a third-rank state, especially after losing its empire in the Western Hemisphere early in the nineteenth century (see Chapter 39). Turkey was "the sick man of Europe," increasingly powerless to protect its southeast European possessions. Already during the Napoleonic era, the Scandinavian countries had adopted the neutral course that they would henceforth maintain in world political affairs.

## Overall Estimate of the Vienna Settlement

During the later nineteenth century, the treaty making at Vienna was criticized on many grounds. The aristocratic negotiators meeting in their secluded drawing rooms ignored the growing forces of popular democracy, national feeling, liberalism, and social reform. They drew up territorial boundaries in ignorance of and disregard for popular emotions and restored kings to their thrones without the citizenry's support. The treaty makers were a small handful of upper-class men, contemptuous of the ordinary people and their right to participate in politics and government.

All of these criticisms are more or less true. Yet, if success is measured by the practical test of enduring peace, it would be hard to find another great international settlement as successful as the treaty of Vienna of 1815. The borders it established endured without serious challenge for fifty years until the German and Italian petty states were unified into two great powers. With the single exception of the Franco-Prussian conflict of 1870, Europe did not experience an important, costly war until the outbreak of World War I in 1914. The great multilateral conflicts that had marked the late seventeenth and all of the eighteenth centuries were avoided, and Europe had three generations of peaceable economic expansion both at home and overseas.

The Vienna Treaties were followed by a century of cultural and material progress for the middle classes and toward the end, at least, for the common people as well. That this was not the specific intent of the peacemakers is beside the point. Any judgment of the treaties must consider that the massive social and economic changes witnessed by the nineteenth century were successfully accommodated within the international relationships established in 1815.

## Summary

The problems of the French monarchy in the late eighteenth century were cumulative and profound. Inspired by the Enlightenment and the example of the U.S. Revolutionary War, many French were convinced that the weak and directionless regime of King Louis XVI must change. In 1789, they were able to overcome the stubborn resistance of both king and nobility to bring about a moderate constitutional monarchy. Within two years, however, this situation was turned into a radical social upheaval by the Jacobins and their supporters among the nation's poor. The *ancien régime* of rule by an absolutist monarch and a privileged church and nobility could not survive this challenge despite the attempt by France's conservative neighbors to save it through armed intervention.

The exigencies of invasion and war combined to create the Reign of Terror led by the Jacobin Committee of Public Safety. This egalitarian dictatorship was overthrown after two years, and a consolidation begun under the Directory in 1795. Corruption and incompetence weakened the Directory to a point that allowed a military coup by the young general Napoleon Bonaparte in 1799.

Napoleon's authoritarian settlement of the Revolution's conflicts within France was successful, and his wars in the name of defense of the Revolution went well for several years. For a long and important decade, most of western and central Europe were under French sway. The 1812 Russia campaign was disastrous, however, and the retreat soon led to defeat in 1814 and its Waterloo sequel. At the Vienna congress of victors, a framework of compromise between reaction against and grudging acceptance of the Revolution's principles was worked out; despite its attempt to ignore popular nationalism and other defects, it allowed Europe a century of peace and progress.

## Identification Terms

Test your knowledge of this chapter's key concepts by defining the following terms. If you can't recall the meaning of certain terms, refresh your memory by looking up the boldfaced term in the chapter, turning to the Glossary at the end of the book, or working with the flashcards that are available on the *World Civilizations* Companion Website: **http://history.wadsworth.com/adler04.**

Battle of the Nations
Civil Code of 1804
Civil Constitution of the Clergy
Committee of Public Safety
Declaration of the Rights of Man and Citizen
Directory
Estates General
First Consul
Jacobins
*l'ancien régime*
*levée en masse*
Napoleonic Settlement
Third Estate
Waterloo

## Test Your Knowledge

Test your knowledge of this chapter by answering the following questions. Complete answers appear at the end of the book. You may also take this quiz interactively and find even more quiz questions on the *World Civilizations* Companion Website: **http://history.wadsworth.com/adler04.**

1. The trigger for the outbreak of revolution in France was
   a. the refusal of the nobles and the clergy to pay their share of taxes.
   b. peasant unrest caused by landlord abuses.
   c. an armed rebellion by outraged middle-class taxpayers.
   d. the assassination of the king.
   e. the frivolous excesses of Queen Marie Antoinette.
2. The Third Estate in France consisted of
   a. the peasants.
   b. the urban dwellers of all types.
   c. everyone outside the ranks of the nobility and the clergy.
   d. the children of the nobles who had no right of succession.
   e. those outside the Catholic faith.
3. The opening phase of the French Revolution saw the demand for
   a. a republic.
   b. a military dictatorship.
   c. a representative democracy.
   d. a constitutional monarchy.
   e. an end to civil government that was tied to the Catholic Church.
4. Abbé Emmanuel Sieyes wrote a much-read pamphlet in 1789 that
   a. attacked the whole idea of the monarchy in France.
   b. defended the rights of the Third Estate.
   c. demanded the separation of church and state.
   d. urged the immediate introduction of a proletarian dictatorship.
   e. mirrored the American Declaration of Independence.
5. Napoleon came to power in 1799 because of the
   a. public reaction against the Terror of the Jacobins.
   b. complete anarchy in France after Robespierre's fall.
   c. threat of the counterrevolutionaries.
   d. unpopularity of the Directory.
   e. success he had attained in the war against Britain in Egypt.
6. The battle at Trafalgar
   a. ensured French domination of most of the Continent.
   b. frustrated a potential French invasion of England.
   c. knocked the Russians out of the anti-French coalition.
   d. made it necessary for France to sell the Louisiana Territory to the United States.
   e. was Napoleon's last victory over England.
7. Which of the following did Napoleon *not* preside over in France?
   a. The signing of a *concordat* with the Vatican
   b. The creation of a new administrative system
   c. The enactment of uniform legal codes for the whole country
   d. The elimination of the Catholic clergy's influence on French opinion
   e. The establishment of a uniform currency
8. The chief conservative powers at the Vienna peace conference were
   a. Prussia, Russia, and Austria.
   b. Prussia, Russia, and Britain.
   c. Austria, Russia, and France.
   d. Russia, Prussia, and France.
   e. France, Prussia, and Austria.

9. Which of the following was least considered in the negotiations at Vienna?
   a. The right of forcibly deposed monarchs to regain their thrones
   b. The right of working people to determine their form of government
   c. The right of states to retain adequate territory and resources for defense
   d. The responsibility of nations to work together to promote peace
   e. The need to suppress rebellions in the future

10. Which country of post-1815 Europe does the phrase "splendid isolation" apply to most directly?
   a. Great Britain
   b. France
   c. Russia
   d. Turkey
   e. Austria

## InfoTrac College Edition

Visit the source collections at

**http://infotrac.thomsonlearning.com**

and use the Search function with the following key terms:

French Revolution    Napoleon    Napoleonic Wars

## Wadsworth History Website Resources

Visit the World History Resource Center at **http://history.wadsworth.com/world** for a wealth of general resources, and the *World Civilizations* Companion Website at **http://history.wadsworth.com/adler04** for resources specific to this textbook.

## HistoryNow

Enter *HistoryNow* using the access card that is available for *World Civilizations*. *HistoryNow* will assist you in understanding the content in this chapter with lesson plans generated for your needs. In addition, you can read the following documents, and many more, online:

*Cahiers de Doléances* (*Lists of Grievances* in response to Louis XVI's call for delegates to the Estates General)

Maximilien Robespierre, "Address to the National Convention"

Napoleon Bonaparte, "The Coup d'État of 18 Brumaire"

*Steam is an Englishman.*
Anonymous

# 34 Europe's Industrialization and Its Social Consequences



| | |
|---|---|
| 1700s | Increase in trade, population, and agricultural production |
| 1750–1850 | Change in premarital relationships and family structure |
| 1760s–1820s | First Industrial Revolution in Britain/steam power |
| c. 1815–c. 1860s | Industrialization of northwestern Europe |
| 1830 | First railroad completed in Britain |
| Late 1800s | Second Industrial Revolution/petroleum and electricity |

The rapid industrial development that gripped Europe in the nineteenth century was a direct outgrowth of the Scientific Revolution and, like that earlier event, was not really so much a revolution as a steady accretion of new knowledge and techniques. It was made possible by another "revolution": the transformation of agriculture that took place at the same time. England led in both of these transformations, and the rest of Europe only slowly and unevenly fell into line.

And to what extent were the lifestyles of ordinary people altered during the transition from a preindustrial to an industrial society? We shall see that the change was substantial, but it was gradual in most cases and only really remarkable over a generation or more. Taken all in all, however, the lives of many Europeans changed more in the century between 1750 and 1850 than they had in all preceding centuries together.

## Prerequisites for Industrial Production

Historians have identified several factors that are necessary for an economy to engage in large-scale industrial production. All of these were present in England by the late eighteenth century:

1. *Upsurge in world trade.* The expanding market for European goods and services created by the new colonies was matched by the large volume of exports from those colonies destined for European consumption. In the eighteenth century, French overseas trading grew more than tenfold, and the English were not far behind. Intra-European trade also grew spectacularly, as the colonial goods were often reexported to third parties.
2. *Rising population.* The increased demand for imports was largely a result of the rapidly rising population of most of the Continent and England. Although the precise reasons for this rise are still in dispute, it is clear that the death rate steadily fell and the birth rate steadily rose in Europe after 1750. The English population, for instance, quadrupled in a century—a phenomenon never before recorded in history from natural increase alone.
3. *Increased flow of money.* Commercial expansion required additional capital. Money was needed to finance the purchase of goods until they could be resold. Many individuals tried to profit from the rising consumption by building new factories, port facilities, and warehouses—all of which required money or credit. Capital was raised by the expanding stock markets, partnerships and speculations, and the issue of paper money backed by the bullion coming from America.
4. *Experienced managers and entrepreneurs.* By the later eighteenth century, several pockets of entrepreneurial expertise could be found, primarily in London, Antwerp, Amsterdam, and other cities of northwestern Europe. All of these places had already had two centuries of experience in colonial trade. Now they were the home of numerous individuals who had had experience in organizing and managing fairly large enterprises. These people knew how to calculate risks, how to spread them, and how to use the corporate form of organization and insurance to minimize them. They knew how to raise capital, secure credit, and share profit. They were relatively open to new ideas and new technology that promised good returns on investment.

## Agrarian Improvements

If industrial society was to be possible, Europe's farmers would have to produce sufficient food to feed the growing urban labor force. To ensure this production, the crop yields had to be increased. Everywhere in seventeenth-century Europe, croplands were tended in much the same way and with much the same results as in the Middle Age. The ratio of grain harvested to seed sown, for an important example, was still only about 3 or 4 to 1, which was far too low.

The most important single step toward modernizing farming was the change from open fields to enclosures, which enabled progressive proprietors to cultivate their lands as they saw fit. These newly enclosed fields were capable of producing two crops yearly, while only one-third, rather than the traditional one-half, lay fallow. The enclosed field system originated in Holland, which had the densest population in all of Europe and consequently the most precious agrarian land. The Dutch also pioneered many other new techniques that improved crop yields, including the intensive use of manure fertilizer, rotation between root crops such as potatoes and seed crops such as wheat, the use of hybrid seeds, and land drainage.

From Holland the new agrarian practices spread quickly to Britain, and as it became apparent that landowners using the new methods and crops could make profits equal to those of the industrial manufacturer but at much less risk, many larger landlords took up the new idea of market farming (that is, producing for an urban market rather than for village subsistence). This was the advent of agrarian capitalism, in which reducing unit costs and raising the volume of product were just as important as in industrial production.

Without these improvements in agriculture, the huge numbers of ex-farm laborers required by industry and commerce in the nineteenth century might not have become available. They certainly could not have been adequately fed. Not only were they fed, but many of them were fed considerably better than ever before.

## The Method of Machine Industry

Industrial production is aimed above all at *lessening the unit cost of production through improved technology.* The changes that occurred in late eighteenth- and early nineteenth-century consumption took place not so much because new products were produced but because industrialized technology allowed the production of familiar products in greater quantity and at lesser cost.

For example, one of the chief early products of industry was underclothing for men and women. There was nothing new about its design, raw material, or general method of production. What was new and revolutionary was the much lower price for a shirt or underpants when those items were woven on a machine—a power loom—

from textiles that had been spun by machine from flax or cotton that had been cleaned and deseeded by machine. The factory owner could sell to wholesale outlets at much lower unit prices because perhaps five machine-made shirts could be produced for the cost of one previously handwoven shirt. The wholesaler could then place those five shirts with a single retailer because the price was so low that the retailer could be sure of disposing of all five quickly. Men and women who had previously not worn underclothing because of its high cost were now able and willing to buy several sets.

Most early industrial products were simply variations of previously handworked items that had been adapted to a mode of production that used machines for all or part of the process. These products included clothing and shoes, lumber, rough furniture, bricks, coal, and pig iron. Sophisticated or new products came only gradually, when inventors and entrepreneurs had developed a clearer vision of what could be accomplished with the new machinery and had developed a trained labor force.

### The Factory

Before the eighteenth century, it was unusual for a single employer to have more than a handful of workers on the payroll directly. Very often, people often took in some type of raw material, such as rough bolts of cloth, and worked it up into a finished consumer product in their own homes, working on their own schedules, and being paid when they had completed the task assigned. This was commonly called the **"putting-out" system** because the same entrepreneur secured the raw material, found the parties who would work it, and collected the finished product for sale elsewhere. He bore the risks and made all of the profits, while the workers received a piecework wage. Most clothing, draperies, shoes, kitchenware, harness, and table utensils, as examples, were made this way in early modern days. The wages earned were an important part of the income of many rural and urban families.

The shift to factory production was as important in changing lifestyles in the Western world as the industrial products themselves were. In the new **factory system**, an entrepreneur or a company gathered together perhaps hundreds of individual workers under one roof and one managerial eye. They were paid on a prefixed pay scale and worked under tight discipline on a single, repetitive part of the production process. See the Society and Economy boxes for more about labor practices during this era.

No longer did the individual workers function as partners of the employer and have a good deal to say about the conditions and pay they received. No longer would workers have much to say about how their skills would be employed, the nature of what they were making, or where it would be sold or to whom. All of those decisions and many others were now exclusively made by the employer, the capitalist entrepreneur who controlled the factory (or mine, or foundry, or railroad).

## England: The Initial Leader in Industrialism

Why did England take the early lead in the industrial production of goods and services? There were several reasons:

1. *Entrepreneurial experience.* Already in the early eighteenth century, the English were the Western world's most experienced traders and entrepreneurs. The English colonies were spread around the world, and the North American colonies were the biggest markets for goods outside Europe. The English national bank had existed as a credit and finance institution since 1603, rates of interest were lower than anywhere else, and the English stock markets were the world's largest and most flexible for raising capital.
2. *Population increase.* As mentioned earlier, the English population rose about 15 percent per decade throughout the eighteenth century, generating a huge increase in demand and an equally huge increase in the potential or actual labor supply.
3. *Energy, or "Steam is an Englishman."* The key to industrialization as a mechanical process was a new source of energy: steam. The English pioneered the inventions that made steam engines the standard form of mechanical energy during the nineteenth century. All over the world, English steam engines opened the path to industrialized production of goods.
4. *Agricultural improvements.* The improvements in agricultural production made it possible for the farmers to not only feed the rapidly growing urban sector but to do so with fewer workers in the fields. The excess rural population then migrated from the countryside, contributing to the growth of the urban sector's demand for foodstuffs.
5. *Key raw materials.* England controlled much of the two basic raw materials of early industry: coal and cotton. The English coalfields were large and easy to access. They provided the fuel for the new steam engines and used those engines extensively to produce coal more cheaply than anywhere in Europe. Cotton came from India, which was by now an English colony, and from the North American colonies. It was carried across the ocean almost entirely in English ships, woven in English factories, and the finished cloth was exported to the rest of Europe without effective competition for a century.
6. *Transportation.* England had the most favorable internal transport system. The geography and topography

SOCIETY AND ECONOMY

## Textile Mills' Labor

**FOLLOWING THE VICTORY OVER NAPOLEON,** a wave of industrial unrest broke over England, as the working conditions of early industrial society became intolerable both to the workers themselves and to the awakening conscience of part of the liberal middle classes. In the 1830s and 1840s, a series of parliamentary commissions were charged with investigating the conditions of working and living among the factory and mine laborers. Their reports shocked the British public and were followed by some of the earliest attempts to control the "free market" endorsed by the more extreme followers of Adam Smith.

The following is an excerpt from a commission report on child labor, interviewing a witness named Abraham Whitehead. His and other, similar testimony led directly to the first child labor law in British history, passed in 1833:

> What is your business?—A clothier
>
> Where do you reside?—At Scholes, near Holmfirth.
>
> Is that not in the centre of very considerable woollen mills?— Yes, I live nearly in the centre of thirty to forty woollen mills. . . .
>
> Are the children and young persons of both sexes employed in these mills?—Yes
>
> At how early an age are children employed?—The youngest age at which children are employed is never under five, but some are employed between five and six. . . .
>
> How early have you observed these young children going to their work?—In the summertime I have frequently seen them going to work between five and six in the morning, and I know the general practice is for them to go as early to all the mills. . . .
>
> How late in the evening have you seen them at work, or remarked them returning to their homes?—I have seen them at work in the summer season between nine and ten in the evening: they continue to work as long as they can see, and they can see to work in these mills as long as you could see to read. . . .
>
> Your business as a clothier has often led you into these mills?—Frequently.
>
> What has been the treatment that these children received in the mills, to keep them attentive for so many hours at such early ages?—They are generally cruelly treated, so cruelly treated that they dare not hardly for their lives be late to work in the morning. . . . I have seen them so fatigued, they appear in such a state of apathy and insensibility as really not to know whether they are doing their work or not. . . .

### *Analyze and Interpret*

The committee's report was unpopular with many parents of working children, because it recommended limiting the hours and types of work they might do. What would you think of this attitude? Is it still true of some parents? Can it be justified?

Source: *"The Report of the Committee on the Bill to Regulate the Labour of Children,"* British Seasonal Papers 15 (London: n.p., 1832), p. 195.

**History Now™**

***To read another account, by J. L. Hammond, of labor during the Industrial Revolution, including child labor, point your browser to the documents area of* HistoryNow.**

of England made the country ideal for moving goods to market. Not only were there few natural obstacles to travel and transport, but the river system, connected by canals in the eighteenth century, made transportation cheaper and safer than elsewhere.

As a result of these advantages, it was natural for England to take the lead in industry (see Map 34.1). In the generation between 1740 and 1780, England produced a variety of mechanical inventions, including Richard Arkwright's spinning machine, called the *spinning jenny,* and Samuel Crompton's *mule,* which made yarn or thread. By 1800, these machines had been joined by others, including the cotton gin, invented by an American, Eli Whitney, and Edmund Cartwright's power loom. Together, these inventions revolutionized the production of cotton cloth. Machines that still used water or animal power were now quickly replaced by the perfected steam engines designed by James Watt and Matthew Boulton. Cheap and reliable steam power became the standard energy source of the Western world's machines for the next hundred years.

Engineers of all sorts, bridge builders, railroad and tramway developers, and mining superintendents—in short, all types of the nineteenth century's burgeoning technical aristocracy—were first and foremost England's contribution to the industrial world.

## SPREAD OF THE INDUSTRIAL REVOLUTION

From England the new processes spread slowly during the eighteenth and early nineteenth centuries. No other country had England's peculiar combination of advantages, but there were other reasons for this tardiness. A major factor was England's attempt to treat industrial

SOCIETY AND ECONOMY

## Adam Smith on Specialization

**One of the outstanding innovative results** of early industrialization was the specialization of labor. Tasks that previously had been performed by two or three individual craftspeople working at their own pace and in their own sequence were broken up by the early factory operators into distinct phases, each with its own machine-supported applications by individual workers.

Adam Smith (1723–1790) anticipated these results in his epoch-making book *The Wealth of Nations,* written in 1776 when the Industrial Revolution's effects were just barely discernible in Great Britain. Smith provided the economic and philosophical bases of liberalism, as that word was used in the eighteenth and nineteenth centuries. In the following excerpt, he considers the division of labor, which the introduction of factories was greatly stimulating.

**Chapter I: Of the Division of Labor**

To take an example, therefore, from a very trifling manufacture; but one in which the division of labor has been very often taken notice of, the trade of the pin-maker; a workman not educated to this business (which the division of labor has rendered a distinct trade), nor acquainted with the use of the machinery employed in it (to the invention of which the same division of labor has probably given occasion), could scarce with his utmost industry, make one pin in a day, and certainly could not make twenty. But in the way in which this business is now carried on, not only the whole work is a peculiar trade, but it is divided into a number of branches, of which the greater part are likewise peculiar trades. One man draws the wire, another straightens it, a third cuts it, a fourth points it, a fifth grinds it at the top to receive the pin-head; to make the head requires two or three distinct operations; to put it on is a peculiar business, to whiten the pins is another; it is even a trade by itself to put them into the paper; and the important business of making a pin is, in this manner, divided into about eighteen distinct operations, which in some manufactories, are performed by distinct hands, though in others the same man will perform perhaps two or three of them.

I have seen a small manufactory of this kind where ten men only were employed . . . they could when they exerted themselves make among them about twelve pounds of pins per day. There are in a pound upwards of four thousand pins of a middling size. Those ten persons, therefore, could make among them upwards of forty-eight thousand pins in a day. Each person, therefore, making a tenth part of forty-eight thousand pins, might be considered as making four thousand, eight hundred pins in a day. But if they had all [worked] separately and independently, and without any of them having been educated to this peculiar business, they certainly could not each of them have made twenty, perhaps not one pin in a day; that is, certainly, not the two hundred and fortieth, perhaps not the four thousand eight hundredth part of what they are at present capable of performing, in consequence of proper division and combination of their different operations.

Source: Adam Smith, *An Inquiry into the Nature and Causes of the Wealth of Nations,* ed. Edwin Canaan (New York: Modern Library, 1994).

### *Analyze and Interpret*

Does Smith show any appreciation of the psychic results of the new method? What might some of the subsidiary results of this type of specialization be?

**History Now™**

***To read further selections from* The Wealth of Nations, *point your browser to the documents area of* HistoryNow.**

techniques as state secrets. These restrictions could not be effectively enforced, and the theoretical knowledge of machine design and technology spread into northern Europe and the United States after about 1820.

Another factor retarding industrialization was the long Napoleonic wars, which disrupted the normal communications and commerce between the Continent and England for the quarter-century between 1793 and 1815. It would take another generation before even the more advanced areas of western Europe could rival Britain in industrial techniques.

By about 1830, the areas on the Continent closest to England had begun to industrialize part of their productive capacity. Belgium and northern France began to use steam power first in coal and textile production, the same industries that had initiated the use of steam in England. By the 1860s, industrial techniques had spread to the Rhine valley, especially the Ruhr coal and iron fields, as well as to parts of northern Italy and the northern United States (see Map 34.2).

Nevertheless, even as late as the 1860s, eastern Europe, Russia, and Iberia (Spain and Portugal), as well as most of Italy, were almost untouched by the industrial lifestyle and industrial production. These regions all lacked one or more of the important factors that had to come together for industrialization to proceed. They became the permanent, involuntary clients of the industrialized regions. Some areas, such as eastern Europe and the Balkans, were

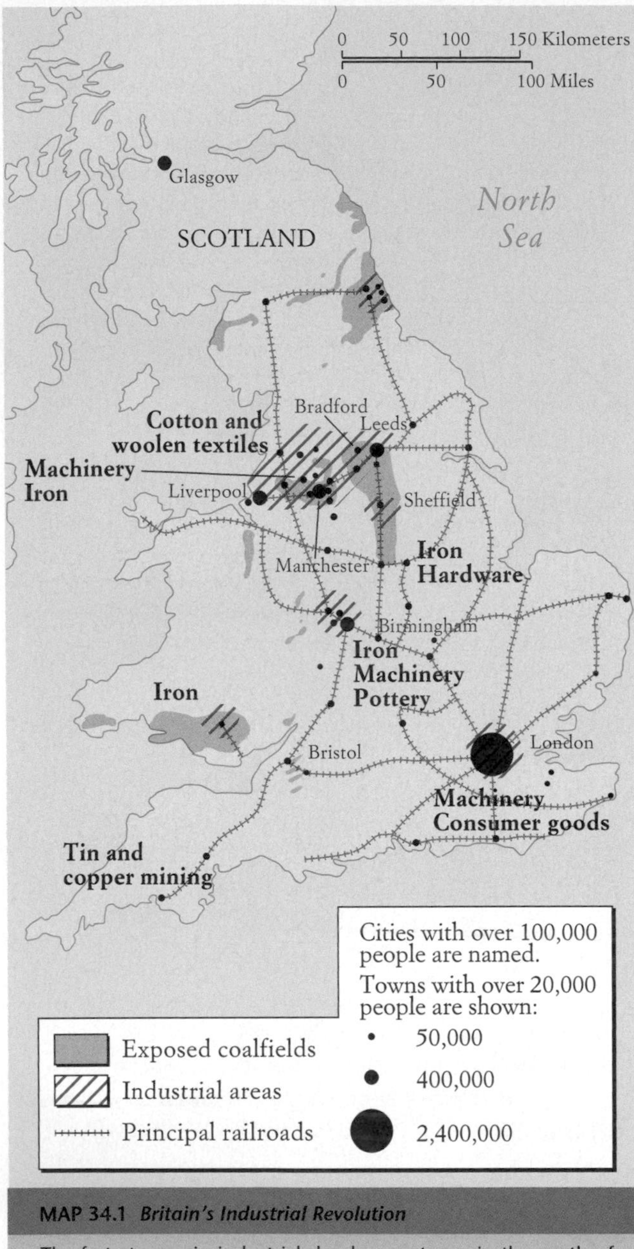


**MAP 34.1** ***Britain's Industrial Revolution***

The fastest pace in industrial development was in the north of England, where coal and textile production combined to create strong attraction for laboring immigrants.

still untouched well into the middle of the twentieth century. Industrialization was not automatic or inevitable, and large parts of the non-Western world are still only superficially and partially industrialized in their essential production techniques.

## Railroads

One of the most spectacular results of steam power was the railroad. Again, Britain led the way, but in this instance, the new invention spread rapidly. The first commercial use of steam railroading was in 1830, when a line connected Liverpool and Manchester, two of the newly important British industrial towns. By the 1840s, lines were under way in most countries of the old and new worlds, including Russia and the United States.

Most early rail lines were built by private companies, but railroads were costly, and the large debts the owners incurred were often more than the lines could sustain during the frequent downturns in the economic cycle. As a result, many railroads went bankrupt and were taken over by the government. By the 1860s, most railroad lines were in government hands everywhere but in the United States.

The steam locomotive was the heart of a railroad. Yet the locomotive's mechanics were so simple that only a few years after the first one was mounted on its track, it had reached a state of perfection that hardly changed over the next century. Bigger and slightly more efficient locomotives were built, but they were essentially the same machine as the famous *Rocket* of the 1830 Liverpool–Manchester line.

The railroad dramatically reduced the costs of shipping and personal travel. It also greatly increased the security of moving goods and people over long distances. By as early as 1850, trains were steaming along in excess of fifty miles per hour—a speed that seemed almost diabolical to many onlookers. By that year it was possible to travel from London to Edinburgh overnight in safety and comfort. Twenty years earlier, the same journey had taken four or five jolting, banging days in a stagecoach, and the train cost less as well. The railroad had an impact on the first half of the nineteenth century similar to the impact of the automobile on the first half of the twentieth—another "revolution"!

Ironbridge Gorge Museum, Telford, Shropshire, UK/Bridgeman Art Library

**OPENING OF ROYAL ALBERT BRIDGE.** Named in honor of Queen Victoria's husband, this span was a design by I. K. Brunel and one of the triumphs of the transport revolution spawned by industrialization.

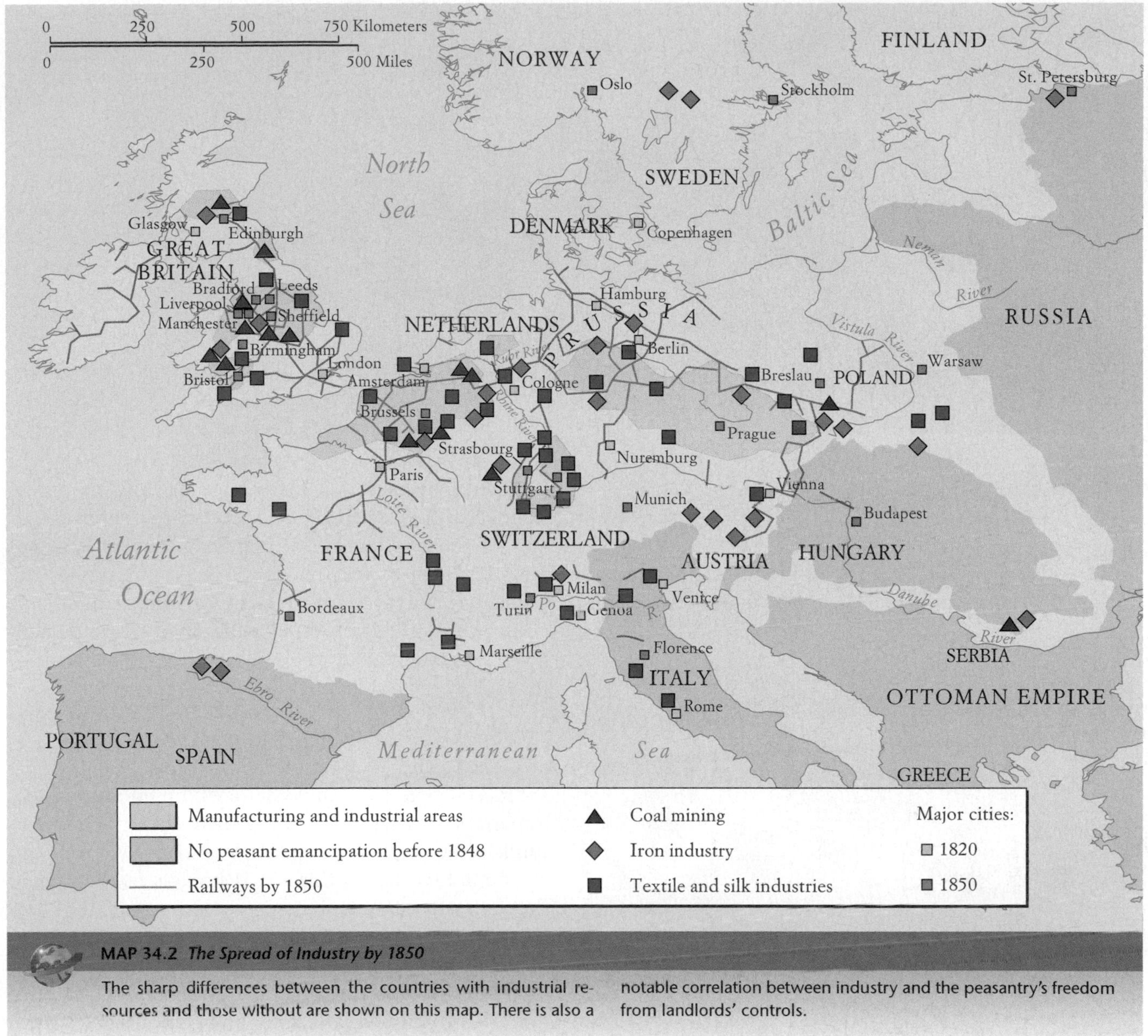


**MAP 34.2** ***The Spread of Industry by 1850***

The sharp differences between the countries with industrial resources and those without are shown on this map. There is also a notable correlation between industry and the peasantry's freedom from landlords' controls.

## Phases of the Industrial Revolution

Industrial work and lifestyles did not develop rapidly as a onetime occurrence at the end of the eighteenth century. The changes that began then have continued to the present day, but they can be divided into certain discernible stages.

The **First Industrial Revolution**, which lasted in Europe from about 1760 to 1820, was marked by the predominance of Britain, the central importance of a new supply of energy from steam, and the production of textiles and iron in the factory setting.

The **Second Industrial Revolution** began in the later part of the nineteenth century in various parts of western Europe and produced modern applied science or technology. The chemical and petroleum industries especially came to the fore in this phase, and a new source of energy was developed—electricity. National leadership shifted gradually from Great Britain to Germany (after its formation in 1871) and the post–Civil War United States.

In our own time, industrial production has spread rapidly into many countries that were previously untouched, or almost so, by these revolutions. At the same time, the older industrial countries in the West have moved on to a postindustrial society, in which the production of goods

**RAIL STATION.** This magnificent 1862 illustration by the British painter W. Powell Frith captures the bustling activity of a Victorian-era station and the crowds who were glad to board the "iron horse."

Royal Holloway and Bedford New College, Surrey, UK/Bridgeman Art Library

Bibliotheque des Arts Decoratifs, Paris, France/Archives Charmet/Bridgeman Art Library

**THE *ROCKET*, 1829.** This engraving shows George Stephenson's locomotive as it traveled across the English countryside in 1829. Essentially a steam boiler laid on its side with pistons and wheels, the *Rocket* quickly outdistanced its stagecoach competitors between Liverpool and Manchester.

in factories and their transport by railroad has given way in importance to the provision of services and information relying on electronic transmissions. We are, in fact, living through a Third Industrial Revolution symbolized and powered by the computer.

## Traditional Social Structures and Impacts of Early Industry

During the later eighteenth century in Britain and France (where the records are best preserved), a massive, widespread change in social habits and relationships became apparent. The causes of this change are not well understood, but they seem to be linked with the arrival of Enlightenment science as a competing primary source of ethical guidance with religion. The beginnings of the Industrial Age accelerated changes that had already begun. One striking example is the structure of the family and the household.

### *The Structure of the Family and Household*

For most people, the family they are born into is the most important social institution in their lives. We tend to think of the family as unchanging: a man, a woman, and their children. But is this so? Historians once assumed that for many centuries before industrialization, the European family had a standard structure, which varied little. This family, so it was thought, was characterized by an extended kin group living under one roof, high rates of illegitimate children, and early universal marriage. Now, however, researchers have established that this stereotype of the preindustrial family is false. The characteristics that were assumed to be commonplace were in fact uncommon during the preindustrial centuries.

Instead, it is now clear that major changes in the family structure took place beginning in the middle of the eighteenth century *before* industry became common. Three changes were particularly noticeable:

1. A lowering of the average age of marriage from the previous 27 for both men and women to about 22 for women and 23.5 for men by 1850
2. A sharp increase in the bastardy rate, beginning in the towns but soon also becoming common in the rural areas, where the majority of the population lived
3. A steady increase in the previously low number of aged persons (over sixty) who had to be cared for by younger generations

## The Place of Children

Until the eighteenth century, only the wealthy or the nobility could afford to give much loving attention to infants or very young children. The reason was simple: The mortality rate for infants and children was so high that it discouraged people from putting much financial or emotional investment into them. In many places, three of five children of ordinary people normally would die before age ten, and another would die before age twenty.

Diseases of every type hit children (and the aged) harder than others. In times of famine, young children were often the first victims. Household and farm accidents of a lethal nature were an everyday affair among children (we frequently hear of children drowning in the farm pond or the well, being kicked by a horse, cut by sharp tools, or burned to death). In those days, when medical care for rural people was nonexistent and hospitals were feared, even minor burns or slight infections would become aggravated and often result in death, weeks or months later.

Therefore, the usual attitude toward the infant was a mix of indifference with a good deal of realistic caution about his or her prospects. Most peasants and workers viewed children below age seven or so as debit factors: they demanded time-consuming care and feeding without being able to contribute anything to the family resources. Only after they had become strong and rational enough to do adult work were they looked on as assets.

The urban classes and the wealthy could afford to take a more relaxed attitude toward children's work, but their emotional relations with the young child were about as distant as the peasant's. Urban children died as readily and as unpredictably as rural children. It only made "biological sense" to restrict maternal love and paternal pride to those children who were old enough to have a good chance of a long life. And for most people, the point of having children was to provide a primitive form of social security. Children were expected to see to it that their parents did not suffer the ultimate indignity of a beggarly old age or have to throw themselves on the charity of others when ill or disabled.

At some point between 1750 and 1850, a change became evident, as parents began to show what we now consider normal parental love and tenderness toward newborn and young children. This change occurred first in the better-off segment of society and then seeped downward into the lives of the majority. Why did it happen?

Several factors can be identified: the declining child mortality rate, which gradually increased the chances that a child would survive; the rising numbers of middle-class people who did not need children's labor but valued them for their own sake; and the influence of educational reformers such as Jean-Jacques Rousseau, Johann Heinrich Pestalozzi, and Friedrich Herbert. These reformers insisted that children should be given more humane education and treated as unformed, responsive individuals rather than as contrary creatures whose naturally mischievous ways must be corrected by constant strict discipline.

Another influence on the attitudes of adults toward young children was the introduction of general public instruction in state-supervised and funded schools, which began in Prussia and Austria, among other places, in the mid-1700s. Clearly, children worthy of being educated at parental tax expense were valuable for more than just serving as attendants in their parents' old age (for which the children needed no education).

## Relations between Men and Women

Marriage among the rural folk and most urbanites was still a contract between two families rather than the result of individual erotic attraction. But this, too, changed during the eighteenth century in Europe. Not only did people marry at an earlier age as the century progressed, but social relations among the young also became considerably freer.

Mary Evans Picture Library

**The Flower Girl.** "That girl seems to know you, George!" says the suspicious wife as the flower girl recognizes a customer of her other wares. Prostitution was widespread in the early Industrial Age.

In the later eighteenth century, premarital sex without marriage plans seems to have occurred with increasing frequency. Both sexes, in countryside and town, were able to "get away" with behavior that previously the full weight of social opinion would have prevented. Why this happened is a subject of some debate among historians. Some say that a psychological sea change occurred after 1750 that allowed new freedoms in the sexual sphere. Others, the majority, say that the young people simply seized the increasing opportunities that a more mobile society gave them to get together outside the watchful oversight of pastors, parents, and elders.

For most women, marriage was still the main career option, but demographic changes made it impossible for some women to marry. Although the number of males and females is about equal at birth, unmarried females begin to outnumber males after about age twenty-five. This discrepancy was larger in the past than now because males were affected disproportionately by accidents and violence. Consequently, there were fewer eligible males than females in the age cohort most likely to marry. Many women were never able to marry. These "spinsters" were common in all social strata except the very highest. Their married relatives often took shameless advantage of them, forcing them to work as child watchers, laborers, maids, and seamstresses in return for minimal room and board.

## Occupations and Mobility

Although most people continued to work directly with and on the land (farming, tending orchards, fishing, timbering, shepherding), the number engaged in urban occupations and nonmanual work was gradually increasing by the 1750s. As methods of agriculture improved, large estates could reduce the number of farm laborers they employed. These displaced persons could normally escape poverty only by moving away to a new life as wage earners in the towns.

Some small minority of these ex-farmers had the intelligence, drive, and luck to take up a skilled trade or nonmanual work, perhaps as bookkeepers, sales clerks, or schoolteachers (for which the only real qualification was semiliteracy). Any who could make their way into these occupations would move upward in the social scale and find the opportunity to better themselves by imitating the manners and ideas of the socially superior classes.

The rapidly increasing overseas commerce of the eighteenth and early nineteenth centuries extended the horizons of ambitious youths, a good many of whom had left their ancestral villages because they saw only too clearly what a miserable future awaited them there. Some of them ended up in one or another of the colonies, but the majority stayed at home, unable to bring themselves to take the leap into the dark that emigration entailed.

Because there were absolutely no government provisions to aid the needy, the threat of unemployment and of literal starvation was often very real. Many young men spent years teetering on the edge of the abyss, before they had sufficiently mastered a trade, established themselves in business, or inherited some land to farm, so that they could set themselves up as the head of a family household. (See the Society and Economy box for one youth's adventures.)

### *Female Occupations*

For young women, the choices were considerably narrower. There were essentially only two options: they could stay at home, hoping for a successful marriage to a local youth of their own class, or they could go into service—that is, join the millions of teenaged daughters of peasants and laborers who left home to become live-in servants. The prevalence of servants is difficult for twenty-first-century Americans to imagine. Practically every household, even relatively poor ones, had one or more. It was not at all unusual for a poor farmer's house to harbor one or two servant girls as well as a male laborer or two. No middle- or upper-class house in the nineteenth century was without its servant staff, mainly females from rural families who came to town to seek work. Sometimes the servants were related by blood or marriage to the household; sometimes not.

Many of these young women left their employers after shorter or longer periods of service, having found a suitable marriage partner with whom to "set up," but many others stayed for life. They remained unmarried, contributing part of their meager wage to support the old folks in the village. Some of these women practically became members of the family and were cared for in their old age, but many were turned out like so many used-up horses when they became too old to work.

By the early nineteenth century, when factory work had become fairly common in Britain, young women also had the option of taking a job tending a machine. The earliest factories were often staffed by entire families, but increasingly, young women and children replaced the male adults and family units in the unskilled jobs such as cotton spinning and mechanical weaving. The owners of the textile and shoe mills found that young women would work for lower wages than young men commanded and were more reliable. Many country girls preferred factory jobs, where they could be with their peers and have some freedom in their off hours, to going into domestic service with its many restrictions.

SOCIETY AND ECONOMY

## A Navvy's Life on the Tramp

**THE ANONYMOUS AUTHOR OF THIS PIECE** was born about 1820 in England. When he left home at about twenty years of age, he was already well acquainted with hard work. Like tens of thousands of other young men, he could find no place in the traditional village economy and went "on the tramp," taking pickup laboring jobs with farmers or railroad gangs. He would do any other unskilled work he could find. Many men (and a few women) who could not find a suitable place for themselves in the home village pursued this life for years, sometimes even into old age.

**Family and Earliest Work**

My father was a labouring man, earning nine shillings a week in the best of times [about the equivalent of $135 currently]. . . . There was a wonderful large family of us—eleven was born, but we died down to six. I remember one winter, we was very bad off, for we boys could get no employment, and no one in the family was working but father. He only got fourteen pence a day to keep eight of us in firing and everything. It was a hard matter to get enough to eat.

The first work I ever did was to mind two little lads for a farmer, I drawed them about in a little cart, for which I got my breakfast and a penny a day. When I got older, I went to tending sheep. I was about seven years old then.

**On the Tramp**

After I left home I started on the road "tramping" about the country, looking for work. Sometimes I'd stop a few weeks with one master, then go on again, travelling about; never long at a time in the one place. I soon got into bad company and bad ways. . . . This is the way we'd carry on. Perhaps I'd light on [meet] an old mate somewhere about the country, and we'd go rambling together from one place to another. If we earned any money, we'd go to a public house [tavern], and stop there two or three days, till we'd spent it all, or till the publican turned us out drunk and helpless to the world. Having no money to pay for a lodging, we had to lie under a hedge, and in the morning we'd get up thinking, "What shall we do?" "Where shall we go?" And perhaps it would come over us, "Well, I'll never do the like again."

We'd wander on till we could find a gang of men at work at some railroad or large building; sometimes they would help us and sometimes they would not. Once I travelled about for three days without having anything to eat.

. . . [W]hile I was in Yorkshire I met with a young gentleman who had a fine house of his own, but would spend all his time in the beershop. One day he saw me there and called out, "Well, old navvy," he says, "can you drink a quart of ale?"

"Thank you, sir," says I.

"Well, if you will stop along of me, I'll keep you in drink, as long as you like to sing me songs," says he.

"Master," says I, "I'll have you! I do like my beer."

. . . I stopped with him a fortnight drinking Yorkshire ale at 6 pence a quart, while he drank rum and brandy, and soda water between whiles. But at the fortnight's end I had to run away. I could not stand it any longer. He'd have killed me with it if I'd gone on.

It was not long after this that I got sent to prison. I was working at Hastings, when we struck [went out on strike] there. The ganger [foreman], he came up and then he upped with his fist and knocked me down; and as fast as I got up he hit me down again. . . . They come and ta'en us the next day, and had us locked up in Lewes Gaol; two of us got two months, and the other one month. We was all very happy and comfortable there, though we were kept rather short of victuals. There they learnt me to spin mops, and it was there that I got hold of most of my scholarship.

### *Analyze and Interpret*

Does our author think his life exceptional in its hardships? What does the comment on the "eleven . . . who died down to six" tell you of family life and intrafamilial relations at the time?

Source: "Life of a Navvy," in *Useful Toil,* ed., J. Burnet (New York: Penguin, 1984), p. 55. 

## THE MIGRATION TO THE CITIES: URBANIZED SOCIETY

Throughout the Western world, a massive flight to the cities began in the eighteenth century and continued almost unchecked through the twentieth century. Most of the migrants from the countryside were young people in the prime of life. The precise reasons for this **urban migration** varied considerably from place to place and era to era, but three motives underlay it everywhere:

1. *Human curiosity and the desire for change.* The young in every culture are more open to change and more eager to embrace it than their elders. When it became relatively easy to move about and experience new things, new places, and new people, young people took advantage of the changed conditions.

**TEXTILE MILL WORKERS.** This early photo shows the noisy and dangerous conditions of work in a mid-nineteenth-century mill. The many exposed machinery parts were constantly jamming, often at the expense of a worker's daily wages.

The Art Archive

2. *The desire to improve economic and social status.* The variety of occupations that the towns offered, the opportunity to gain at least a minimal education, and the belief that talent and ambition had a freer field in the town than in the ancestral village inspired many persons to move.
3. *The desire to find better marital partners.* Young women in particular, whose prospects of finding a desirable husband in their village were tightly restricted by their families' demands and social standing and who could not easily rebel, took the opportunity to search elsewhere.

Beyond these subjective motivations, we should note the objective economic fact that by the nineteenth century, the shift of an entire society from a rural to an urban majority was, for the first time in history, viable and sustainable. The gradual spread of commerce and long-distance communications and financial credit arrangements allowed towns to grow regardless of the local food-producing capacity. Bristol in England, Lyon in France, Brussels in Belgium, and Oslo in Norway, to cite some examples at random, no longer depended on the ability of the agricultural region close by to supply their daily bread and meat. They could, and did, get their supplies from Canada, Denmark, or wherever it was most convenient.

## Urban Growth

In the eighteenth century, this urbanization of society was advancing rapidly: among the metropolises, London's population rose from 700,000 in 1700 to about 1 million in 1800. Berlin tripled in size to about 175,000. Paris rose from about 300,000 to 500,000 in the same period. In every Western country, the number of towns with populations between 10,000 and 25,000 grew considerably. These towns served as important administrative, cultural, and economic centers for the provinces.

The bulk of the new industry and manufacturing was concentrated in these smaller towns as the Industrial Revolution gradually got under way. Land was cheaper there than in the great metropolises, and the smaller towns were usually closer to the raw material sources. Manchester, the English textile center, for example, had a population of about 7,000 in the 1740s. By 1790, the population had risen to about 25,000, and it gained at least 50 percent every decade for the next half-century.

The census of 1851 showed that for the first time, a majority of the people in England lived in an urban setting (that is, in places with more than 5,000 inhabitants). About 25 percent of the population of France and Germany lived in urban areas. But the percentage was lower in southern and eastern Europe, where industry was not yet established.

## Urban Classes and Lifestyles

In the eighteenth-century towns, social classes were quite distinct. At the top, dominating politics and setting the cultural tone, was the nobility. In some places, particu-

The Art Archive

**MANCHESTER, ENGLAND, AT MIDCENTURY.** This moody portrait of the outstanding industrial town in Britain conveys the uncompromising ugliness of the environment created by the early factories.

larly in western Europe and Scandinavia, the aristocrats increasingly intermarried with wealthy commoners—bankers, merchants, officials of the self-governing cities—and together they formed the governing group.

Beneath them was an urban upper-middle class, or classes, who included less wealthy merchants, landlords, tradesmen, and professionals. These well-educated, upwardly mobile men and their families constituted what the French called the ***bourgeoisie***. Many of them opposed the pretensions of the nobles and their wealthy allies and were on a collision course with the aristocratic governors—a collision that finally exploded in the French Revolution at the end of the century.

Below the bourgeoisie were the lower-middle classes, also primarily urban, composed of clerks, artisans, skilled workers, and independent shopkeepers. They were desperately afraid of falling back into the class from which they had emerged: the workers who labored in semiskilled or unskilled jobs for an employer. The lower-middle classes mimicked their social betters among the bourgeoisie, a class to which they might ascend with luck, time, and good marriages.

This lower-middle class, more than the still relatively small and fragmented working classes, generated most of the social discontents that marked the late eighteenth and early nineteenth centuries. Only in the later nineteenth century, when the industrial working classes had become much larger and more important in the social structure, did they successfully assert themselves.

## Diet and Nutrition

At the same time that industrialization was beginning, the diet and health of ordinary citizens were gradually transformed. For many centuries, European common people had been accustomed to depending on an uneven mix of grains, cheese, sporadic meats and fowl, and a few seasonal fruits to maintain life. Much depended on local weather and harvests. The season determined what provisions would be available for human consumption. In late winter and spring, the supplies put away at harvest would begin to run short, and hunger became a constant companion to much of the population.

Local famine was commonplace throughout the early eighteenth century everywhere. In such times, it was not unusual for grain to be rotting in barns fifty miles or so from where people were starving for lack of it. Transport networks for bulk goods were primitive or nonexistent in the more backward regions. Only the towns commanded a more or less sophisticated supply system, with stored reserves and emergency powers over the population in times of crisis. In the countryside, every decade or so in one part of Europe or another, people starved in large numbers.

By the end of that same century, famines had become a rarity, and Europeans were in fact eating considerably better than ever. What happened to change the situation? First, water transportation was much improved, as were the roads, which had formerly been in an abysmal condition. Second, new and more productive agricultural methods, seeds, and crop rotations had increased food production in western Europe, while in eastern Europe the spread of serfdom on latifundia estates allowed an increasing amount of grain to be exported to the West. Third, the diet of Europeans had greatly expanded and improved. The potato had become a dependable staple for the poor, and its nutritional value was exceptional. Milk and dairy products were considerably more common, although they were still viewed with suspicion by many. Meat and fish, always desired but too expensive to be enjoyed by the poor, were coming to be a standard part of the diet of all but the very poor by the end of the century.

Changing diets had a basic impact on health. The diet of the rich was excessively dependent on protein (meat)

Private Collection/The Stapleton Collection/Bridgeman Art Library

**Slum Life in Late-Nineteenth-Century Britain.** This photograph was made in London's East End, where dead-end alleyways like this were the rule and children rarely saw anything green and growing from one month to the next.

and carbohydrates (sweets, fats), with a shortage of vitamins. With the coming of new foods from the colonies such as potatoes, maize, beans, and squash, this protein-loaded diet became more balanced. For the poor, the potato in particular meant the difference between life and death for many hundreds of thousands of northern Europeans, who came to depend on it as much as they did on bread. In the latter part of the century, citrus fruits and exotic vegetables began to show up on the tables of the middle and upper classes, adding another dimension to the diet. These were the products of the semitropical colonies, as was sugar from cane, which now replaced honey.

## Public Health

Although the lives of ordinary people were improving in several respects, in many areas conditions were hardly better at all. For example, although diet was generally improving, medical and surgical conditions showed little change over the century. Being admitted to a hospital was still almost a death warrant, and the poor would absolutely refuse to go, preferring to die at home. Doctoring was a hit-or-miss proposition, with primitive diagnosis backed up by even more primitive treatment. Surgery was a horror, with no pain deadener but whiskey until well into the nineteenth century. Amputations were the last resort in many cases, and the resultant wounds frequently became infected and killed the patient if shock had not already done so.

Doctors and pharmacists still did not receive formal training in schools of medicine. The trainees completed a haphazard apprenticeship with a doctor, who may or may not have known more than his apprentice. All sorts of quacks were active, bilking the public with their "Electrical Magnetic Beds" and "Elixirs of Paradise." Both the educated and the uneducated had a low opinion of doctors.

Medical facts now taken for granted were unknown then. The functions of many of the internal organs, germ theory, the dangers of infection, and fever treatment were still guesswork or not known at all. The mentally ill were just beginning to be given some treatment besides the traditional approach, under which violent patients were locked up under awful conditions and others were kept at the family home. All in all, the treatment of the human mind and body when they fell ill was hardly improved over what the Romans had done 2,000 years earlier. Some would say it was worse.

### *Housing and Sanitation*

The most urgent problem facing the industrial towns in the early part of the nineteenth century was sanitation. In the dreary rows of cheap rental housing (hastily built largely by the mill and factory owners as an additional source of income), overcrowding to an incredible degree was commonplace. Even the most basic sanitary facilities were largely missing. Ventilation of interior rooms was nonexistent, and all types of infectious disease ran rampant. Tuberculosis (TB, or consumption) rapidly became the number one cause of death in nineteenth-century Britain. It bred in the damp, unventilated back rooms and spread easily through the workers' slums, where several people—often unrelated—crowded into every miserable abode.

Privacy was impossible for the working class to obtain. Illegitimacy and incest were constant menaces to family cohesion and security. In report after report to the British Parliament in the 1830s and 1840s, shocked middle-class investigators noted that sleeping five and six to a bed was common, that boys and girls in their teens were frequently forced to sleep together for lack of space, and that greedy landlords regularly extracted the maximal rent by allowing several poverty-stricken families to share the same tiny apartments.

**Seven Dials.** This 1872 engraving by Gustave Doré captures the irrepressible vitality of the worst slum in London. Seven Dials was known far and wide as a thieves' haven and a pickpocket's bazaar. Some of the stolen wares were brazenly put on display immediately for sale, perhaps to the former owners.

Similar conditions were soon found on the Continent as industry spread. For many years, civic authorities were either unable or unwilling to tackle the huge tasks of ensuring decent living conditions for the poorer classes. (Recall that the poor did not yet have the vote anywhere.) Despite the relative youth of the new urban populations, towns and cities normally had a higher death rate than birthrate. Only the huge influx of new blood from the villages kept the towns expanding.

## Living Standards

As the Industrial Age began, the gap between the living conditions of the European rich and poor became wider than ever before in history. The aristocracy and the handful of wealthy commoners lived a luxurious and self-indulgent life. The higher nobility and court officials were expected to have squadrons of servants, meals with fourteen courses and ten wines, palaces in the towns and manors in the countryside, and personal jewelry whose value was equal to the yearly cash incomes of a whole province of peasants. Great wealth, although almost always hereditary, was thought to be a reward for merit and should be displayed as an intrinsic duty as well as honor.

The lifestyle of the urban middle classes was much more modest, although some of the richest, such as bankers, might have six times the income of the poorer aristocrats. Secure in their solid townhouses, surrounded by domestic servants, the members of the middle classes entertained modestly if at all and concentrated on their counting-houses, investments, shops, businesses, and legal firms. They devoted much attention to their extensive families. The wife was expected to be a thrifty, farsighted manager of the household, and the husband was the source of authority for the children and the bearer of the most precious possession of all, the family honor.

For most people in urban areas, material life was gradually improving, but the lower fringes of the working classes and the many beggars, casual laborers, and wandering peddlers and craftspeople were hard put to keep bread on the table and their children in clothes. Poverty was perhaps never so grim in European cities as in the early nineteenth century, when it became more visible because of the much increased numbers of abjectly poor, and it had not yet called forth the social welfare measures that would become common by the twentieth century. As industrial work began to become common in the towns, the uprooted ex-peasants who supplied most of the labor often experienced a decline in living standards for a while, until they or their families found ways to cope with the demands of the factory and the town lifestyle. This decline could last for an entire first generation of migrants, and only their children benefited from the often painful transition.

## Reforms and Improvements

To the credit of the British aristocrats who still controlled Parliament, as early as the 1820s, after the war emergency had passed, several reform proposals to aid the working classes were introduced. By the 1830s, some of the worst abuses in the workplace were attacked. The **Factory Acts** of 1819 and 1833 limited the employment of young children and provided that they should be given at least a little education at their place of work. (Still, it remained entirely legal for a nine-year-old to do heavy labor for eight-hour workdays and for a thirteen-year-old to work twelve hours a day, six days a week!)

Women and boys under the age of ten were not permitted to work in the mines after 1842. Until then, much of the deep underground work, which was highly dangerous and exhausting to anyone, was done by women and young children. In most textile manufacturing, physical strength was not as important as quickness and endurance. Women and children were paid much less than men demanded, and their smaller size allowed them to move about in the crowded machine halls with more agility than men. Boys as young as seven years of age were regularly employed in twelve- or thirteen-hour shifts until the passage of the 1833 act. The families of young working children often opposed and circumvented the reforms, which threatened to diminish the potential family income. No more substantial reform legislation was passed until the early twentieth century.

Little was done to improve basic sanitation in worker housing until the 1860s. In 1842, a pioneering report by Edwin Chadwick on the horrible conditions in the slums and how they might be corrected through modern sewage and water purification systems began to draw attention. But not until the great cholera scare of 1858, when London was threatened by a major outbreak of this lethal waterborne disease, was action taken. (Read more about this epidemic in the Science and Technology box.) Then the upper and middle classes realized that although epidemic diseases such as cholera might originate in the slums, they could and would soon spread to other residential areas. At about the same time, the restructuring of its primitive sewer system allowed Paris for the first time to manage its waste disposal problem. Led by the two capitals, the provincial city authorities soon began to plan and install equivalent systems. By the end of the nineteenth century, European city life was again reasonably healthy for all but the poorest slum dwellers.

SCIENCE AND TECHNOLOGY

## Cholera Arrives in Manchester, 1832

**The most dreaded disease** of the nineteenth century was cholera. Borne by polluted water, it was particularly lethal in the crowded industrial slums springing up in the first half of the century throughout western Europe. The worst epidemic occurred in 1832, moving briskly from Russia through central Europe into Britain. In this excerpt, one of the leading medical researchers of the age tells us of the first case in Manchester, where it was going to kill several thousand people in a period of weeks. It would take another British cholera outbreak, in the 1850s, to finally prove the disease's spread through germ-laden water and lead to its eventual control:

> I had requested the younger members of the staff, charged with the visitation of outpatients of the infirmary, to give me the earliest information of the occurrence of any cases of cholera. I had a scientific wish to trace the mode of its propagation and to ascertain if possible by what means it would be introduced into the town. My purpose was to ascertain whether there was any, and if so, what, link or connection between the physical and social evils, to which my attention had been so long directed. . . .
>
> [A sick Irish laborer living in the dank, polluted slum called Irishtown is reported to the doctor, who goes to visit him.]
>
> I sat by the man's bed for an hour during which the pulse became gradually weaker. In a second hour it became almost extinct, and it was apparent that the patient would die. His wife and three children were in the room . . . as the evening approached I sent the young surgeon to have in readiness the cholera van not far away. We were surrounded by an excitable Irish population, and it was obviously desirable to remove the body as soon as possible, and then the family, and to lock up the house before any alarm was given. . . .
>
> No case of Asiatic cholera had occurred in Manchester, yet notwithstanding the total absence of characteristic symptoms in this case, I was convinced that the contagion had arrived, and the patient had been its first victim. The Knott Hill Hospital was a cotton factory stripped of its machinery; on my arrival here I found the widow and her three children with a nurse grouped round a fire at one end of a gloomy ward. . . . None of them showed any sign of disease, and I left the ward to take some refreshment. On my return, the infant had been sick in its mother's lap, had made a faint cry, and had died. The mother was naturally full of terror and distress, for the child had had no medicine, had been fed only from its mother's breast, and consequently, she could have no doubt that it perished from the same causes as its father. I sat with her and the nurse by the fire very late into the night. While I was there the children did not wake, nor seem in any way disturbed, and at length I thought I might myself seek some repose. When I returned about six o'clock in the morning, another child had severe cramps and some sickness, and while I stood by the bedside, it died. Then later, the third and eldest child had all the characteristic symptoms and perished in one or two hours. In the course of the day the mother likewise suffered from a severe and rapid succession of the characteristic symptoms and died, so that within twenty-four hours the whole family was extinct.

Source: Frank Smith, *The Life and Work of Sir James Kay-Shuttleworth* (London: n.p., 1923).

### *Analyze and Interpret*

What does the doctor mean by "any link or connection between the physical and social evils"? Why was it logical that the early cases of cholera would be found among the inhabitants of a place called "Irishtown" at this time and place? And why would the doctor want to conceal evidence of cholera infection among the inhabitants?

# Summary

Industrial methods of producing goods via machinery entered European life gradually in the mid-eighteenth century, with England as the leader. The English had several natural advantages and social characteristics that enabled them to expand their lead over the rest of the world until well into the nineteenth century. This First Industrial Revolution was largely dependent on two related changes: the increase in agrarian production and the rapid rise in population and attendant demand for consumer goods. Without these, the factory system of concentrated labor under single management and discipline would not have been feasible.

The industrial system spread slowly at first, because of the wars and the difficulty of replicating the English advantages. By the mid-nineteenth century, however, industrialization had spread into much of northern and western Europe and the United States. Coal mining and textiles were two of the initial industries to be affected, and the steam engine became the major energy source for all types of industry. The railroad, introduced in the 1830s, soon effected massive change in the transport of goods and people and contributed to the success of the industrial system in substantial ways. A Second Industrial Revolution commenced in the late nineteenth century, fueled by petroleum and electricity, and a third is currently under way in the provision of services rather than goods.

The social change introduced by mechanized industry took many forms, affecting family relations, occupational mobility, urbanization, and diet. The family was changed by a decreasing age of marriage and a sharp rise in illegitimacy. Children came to be valued as creatures worthy of love in their own right. Several new occupations were opened to both men and women in factories and mills as industry spread, while the traditional servant jobs multiplied in the expanding cities and towns.

Living standards varied from an unprecedented opulence among the rich to an actual decline in the conditions of recent urban migrants. Slums appeared in the new industrial quarters, which were horribly lacking in basic sanitation and privacy. Nevertheless, to the working classes, the attractions of the towns were manifold and irresistible, particularly for those who sought a better life than the traditional social and economic restrictions that the villages allowed. A richer and more varied diet even for the poor gradually made itself felt in better health. By the end of the nineteenth century, sanitation and workers' living and labor conditions had visibly improved.

## Identification Terms

Test your knowledge of this chapter's key concepts by defining the following terms. If you can't recall the meaning of certain terms, refresh your memory by looking up the boldfaced term in the chapter, turning to the Glossary at the end of the book, or working with the flashcards that are available on the *World Civilizations* Companion Website **http://history.wadsworth.com/adler04**.

*bourgeoisie*
Factory Acts
factory system
First Industrial Revolution
"putting-out" system
Second Industrial Revolution
urban migration

## Test Your Knowledge

Test your knowledge of this chapter by answering the following questions. Complete answers appear at the end of the book. You may also take this quiz interactively and find even more quiz questions on the *World Civilizations* Companion Website: **http://history.wadsworth.com/adler04**.

1. The basic aim of industrial production technique is to
   a. provide more employment opportunities for the labor force.
   b. allow a greater variety of jobs.
   c. lower the unit cost of production.
   d. discipline and organize the labor force more efficiently.
   e. move farm workers into cities to work in factories.
2. James Watt was the inventor of
   a. an entirely new form of mechanical energy.
   b. the power loom for weaving.
   c. a new machine called the "spinning jenny."
   d. an improved and more flexible form of steam-driven machine.
   e. a device for raising water from flooded mines.
3. The chief driving force for the Industrial Revolution in eighteenth-century England was
   a. the threat of being overshadowed by France in the world economy.
   b. the invention of an improved source of energy.
   c. the creation of the British overseas colonial empire.
   d. the encouragement of the British government.
   e. the development of the business corporation.
4. The first major industry to feel the effect of industrial production was
   a. lumbering.
   b. railroads.
   c. grain farming.
   d. paper making.
   e. textiles.

5. Development of competitive industry on the Continent was delayed by
   a. the Napoleonic wars and their attendant disruption of trade.
   b. lack of interest.
   c. the upper classes' contempt for profit making.
   d. lack of suitable and basic natural resources.
   e. the need for strong agrarian societies.
6. Around the mid-eighteenth century, the European population
   a. began to rise as a result of declining mortality and rising birthrates.
   b. started to stabilize after a century of steady increase.
   c. tapered off from the sharp decline that had marked the sixteenth and seventeenth centuries.
   d. began to rise as a result of medical breakthroughs against epidemics.
   e. suffered a severe drop because of emigration.
7. Marriage in preindustrial European society could be best described as
   a. a relationship based on love between two people.
   b. a contractual relation formed mostly by economic and social aspirations.
   c. a contractual relation that conformed closely to biological drives.
   d. an economic relationship between two individuals.
   e. a strategy to "cover" the sexual activities engaged in by the young anyway.
8. An important function of children in preindustrial society was
   a. to serve in the landlord's military forces.
   b. to elevate themselves socially and thus to honor their parents.
   c. to bring grandsons into the world and so carry on the family name.
   d. to pray for the departed souls of their deceased parents.
   e. to serve as security for their parents in their old age.
9. In the early industrial period, the most common employment for a female
   a. involved prostitution at least part-time.
   b. was as a domestic household servant.
   c. was in one or another white-collar jobs.
   d. was to substitute for a man temporarily as needed.
   e. was as a field worker.
10. The governing class in the cities in the eighteenth century was composed of
   a. the aristocracy and the wealthiest commoners, who had intermarried.
   b. the military commanders responsible to the royal government.
   c. the masses of urban commoners who had obtained the vote.
   d. the hereditary aristocracy.
   e. the few young people who were financially able to attend universities.

## InfoTrac College Edition

Visit the source collections at

**http://infotrac.thomsonlearning.com**

and use the Search function with the following key terms:

industrial revolution    industrial development

family nineteenth century    Chartism

Romanticism

## Wadsworth History Website Resources

Visit the World History Resource Center at **http://history.wadsworth.com/world** for a wealth of general resources, and the *World Civilizations* Companion Website at **http://history.wadsworth.com/adler04** for resources specific to this textbook.

## HistoryNow

Enter *HistoryNow* using the access card that is available for *World Civilizations*. *HistoryNow* will assist you in understanding the content in this chapter with lesson plans generated for your needs. In addition, you can read the following documents, and many more, online:

Selections from Adam Smith, *The Wealth of Nations*

Excerpts from Charles Dickens, *Hard Times*

*The folk learn more from a defeat than the kings do from a victory.*
**Alessandro Manzoni**

# 35 Europe in Ideological Conflict



| | |
|---|---|
| 1815–1850 | Economic liberalism, conservatism, nationalism, and socialism emerge |
| 1830 | July Revolution (France): Louis Philippe (1830–1848) |
| 1832 | Reform Act in Great Britain |
| 1848 | Popular revolts in France, Austria, Prussia, Italy |
| 1849–1850 | Failure of revolts/conservatives regain control |

The ancien regime of pre-1789 Europe could not be brought back despite the efforts of the conservative leaders at the Vienna congress. But in countries other than France, many of the political, legal, and social reforms that the French Revolution had brought or attempted to bring were delayed or even temporarily reversed. In France, however, the changes since 1789 were too popular to be ignored in the post-1815 settlement, and the forces unleashed by the economic changes that had been taking place in England—the First Industrial Revolution, as it has come to be called—were going to remake the society of western Europe by the mid-nineteenth century. The throne-shaking revolts of 1848 were the direct, though delayed, result of the changes set in motion by industrialization and by the ideas of 1789.

## Liberalism in Politics and Economics

Much of the history of the past two centuries, especially in Europe, has been a reflection of a sustained *dual revolution* in politics and economics. What exactly is meant or implied by that term? The political revolution was highlighted by events in the United States between 1775 and 1789 and in France between 1789 and 1800, which we looked at in earlier chapters. In the first example, a republic of federated states was born, committed to political democracy and the legal equality of all citizens: government of the people, by the people, and for the people. In the second, the ancient class privileges given to the highborn were declared extinct, and the way upward into social and political distinction was opened to all who had the talent and ambition to tread it.

The economic revolution was slower and less spectacular, but it was at least as important over the long run. It was generated by the changes in industrial production that took place beginning in the second half of the eighteenth century, particularly in Britain; by the conquest of space through the railroads; and by the immense growth of population in Europe and the United States, which provided formerly undreamed-of markets for consumer products.

The two revolutions fused together, reinforcing one another in all kinds of ways. Two examples will suffice:

1. In the 1790s, during the period of the Directory in France, a tiny group of conspirators tried to popularize the first "socialist" ideas, although they did not use that term. Their vague hopes of eliminating property-based distinctions and sharing equally the products of human labor got nowhere. The leaders were soon arrested and put to death as pernicious agitators of the poor. A generation later, when the horrible working conditions produced by early industrialization were being recognized simultaneously with the political beliefs of liberal democracy, another group of theorists arose in Britain and France. They were determined to replace the abuses and exploitation of early capitalism with the humane ideals of equality and mutual care. This was the origin of an organized, multinational effort to introduce governmental responsibility for the welfare of the citizenry, which eventually triumphed to a greater or lesser degree in several countries.
2. The eighteenth-century political revolution was guided by the middle classes—the lawyers, teachers, and merchants—on their own behalf. They had little sympathy with democracy as we now understand that term. Later, in the post-1815 period of reaction, the more perceptive among them recognized that without the active assistance of much of the laboring classes, they could not gain and hold power against the aristocracy. The industrial laboring classes were growing rapidly but lacked leadership from within their own ranks. Instead, "renegades" from the middle classes became more or less radical democrats and led the struggle to help the industrial laborers find their rightful voice in the political arena. During the later nineteenth century, a partnership grew up in western Europe between the middle-class reformers and newly enfranchised working-class voters, which brought about substantial improvement in the condition of ordinary people.

We have already explored the fundamental principles of liberal thought (see Chapter 32). Inspired by the philosophical concepts of Locke, Montesquieu, and others, middle- and upper-class reformers believed that so long as law and custom prevented most people from enjoying certain fundamental liberties and rights, the human race would fail to fulfill its high destiny.

These liberal sons and daughters of the Enlightenment everywhere formed a "party of reform," dedicated to changing the traditional, class-based system of political representation. By 1815, much had been achieved in those respects in America and France, but the conservative reaction nullified some of those gains everywhere in Europe. Only in France and England was much of the liberal political agenda retained. Here, men of property had the vote, all men were equal in the eyes of the law, and royal powers were sharply curtailed by written laws that could not be easily manipulated. Parliaments in both countries, similar to Congress in the United States, were responsible to the voters, rather than to the king, and freedom of conscience was guaranteed.

**The Wanderer in the Sea of Clouds.** Caspar Friedrich was the best known and possibly the most technically accomplished of the early generation of Romantic painters. He painted this brooding introspective in 1818.

### The Gospel of Free Enterprise

Another side of the liberal philosophy focused on freedoms in the marketplace and the rebellion against the traditional restrictions imposed by mercantilism. In contrast to political liberalism's gradual evolution from diverse sources, economic liberalism grew directly from the path-breaking work of Adam Smith, whose ideas were mentioned briefly in Chapter 32. What did Smith's adherents want?

- *Laissez-faire.* If government would only let them alone to do what they saw best fit (laissez-faire), the merchants and manufacturers of every nation would produce goods and services to meet the demands of the market most efficiently and economically.
- *Free trade.* The existing mercantile system of quotas, licenses, and subsidies should be eliminated as quickly as possible, and the most efficient producers should be allowed to trade with any place and anyone who desired their goods at prices that the free market would set.
- *The less government, the better.* As the first two conditions suggest, the economic liberals despised governmental controls of any sort in the economy (even though Smith made certain important exceptions to laissez-faire). They believed that the free market alone would provide proper guidance for policy decisions and that it was government's task simply to follow these guidelines as they revealed themselves over time. Any interference in the economy they condemned as an obstruction to the prosperity of the nation. The famous "unseen hand" of the free market should be allowed to do its beneficial work for all.

In early-nineteenth-century England, extreme economic liberalism, often called **Manchester liberalism** because of its popularity with the cotton mill owners in Manchester, provided the employers of industrial labor with an excuse for the systematic exploitation of the weak. They drew on theorists such as Thomas Malthus (*An Essay on Population,* published in 1798) and David Ricardo (*The Iron Law of Wages,* published in 1817). Using these sources, the Manchester liberals were able to demonstrate that the poor would always be poor because of their excessive birthrate and other moral faults, and that it was the well-off people's duty to protect their material advantages by any means they could. Since sympathizers with this line of thought—the Whigs—came into control of the British House of Commons after the electoral **Reform Act of 1832**, the government was largely unsympathetic toward the idea of social protection of the lower classes. Only in the 1870s and later did a sufficient number of reformers emerge who rejected this heartless attitude and busied themselves with the improvement of the lot of the poor majority.

## CONSERVATISM

The liberals, though gaining strength, were by no means the sole players in the European political field after 1815. Supported by the wave of anti-Napoleonic nationalism, conservative forces in Britain and France were powerful for at least a generation longer. In central and eastern Europe, the conservative wave became sheer reaction and lasted much longer. Conservatism in the first half of the nineteenth century meant one of two things. One was *moderate conservatism,* an attempt to take the milder liberal ideas of the day and adapt them to the service of the traditional institutions such as monarchy, established religion, and class-based legal and social distinctions. The other was *reaction,* a total rejection of the ideas of the American and French revolutions and a determination to turn the clock back.

### Moderate Conservatism

Conservatives of all stripes believed that an official religion was a necessity for instilling proper respect for law and tradition. They could not imagine a state in which church and government were separated by law. They supported a constitution but rejected political democracy as being the rule of the mob. They believed that only those who had a stake in society, evidenced by property, could and would take on the burdens of self-government with the requisite seriousness and respect for legal procedure. They thought that just as differences in talent would always exist, so also should differences in privilege. Some conservatives rejected the idea of privilege by birth. Others embraced it as the best way to ensure that a responsible group would remain in continuous command of the ship of state.

Moderate conservatism was supported by a large percentage of ordinary Europeans, probably a majority, who had been appalled by Jacobin radicalism and then angered by Napoleon's arrogance and his economic exploitation of non-French subjects. The clergy, both Catholic and Protestant, were the leaders of moderate conservatism in much of the Continent. The more enlightened aristocrats, who could see what would happen if turning the clock back were to be adopted as state policy, also contributed to moderate conservatism. They wished to avoid revolutions in the future by making some necessary concessions now.

In economics, the moderates generally favored the continuation of government controls in trade (especially foreign trade) and industry. They thought that Smith was well meaning but wrong and that without such supervision by the authorities, the national welfare would only be harmed by selfish and greedy entrepreneurs.

Because many of the nonclerical conservatives depended on land rents, any drastic change in the existing restrictive economic system would almost certainly harm their interests. Much of their wealth was tied up in inherited land, which could not be mortgaged or sold by the terms of inheritance. They were not happy watching financial speculation, commerce, and manufacturing replace land rent as the primary source of prestige and large income.

### *Reaction*

Reactive conservatism was the rule in Prussia, Austria, and Russia, where few if any political concessions were made to the new social structures being created by the changing modes of production. This led to explosive pressures, which eventually burst forth in the revolts of 1848 and the upheaval of World War I and its revolutionary aftermath. In Prussia and Austria, the reactionary conservatives ruled for a generation after 1815. They denied a constitution; retained the established church, whether Catholic or Protestant; and maintained strict class distinctions in justice, taxation, and voting rights. Both countries also maintained a form of serfdom until 1848.

In Russia (which meant not only the Russian ethnic groups but also much of what is now independent eastern Europe), the reactionaries were also in command. Czar Alexander I had died in 1825 without ever giving his nation the constitutional government that he had toyed with since his accession to the throne twenty-five years earlier. He was followed on the throne by his younger brother, Nicholas I (ruled 1825–1855), a sincere believer in God's designation of autocracy for Russia and a dyed-in-the-wool reactionary. Nicholas's inclinations were reinforced by the botched attempt of a handful of idealistic rebels (the "Decembrists") to organize a revolution and impose a constitution on liberal lines in December 1825. During Nicholas's reign, Russia was called the **Gendarme of Europe**, eager and ready to send troops to put down liberal agitation or revolutionary change wherever it might rear its ugly head. All of Europe was split during the entire post-Napoleonic generation between these reactionary forces and their liberal opponents. Some version of this struggle could be found in every quarter of the European realm.

## NATIONALISM

Besides the struggle between liberal and conservative, another source of conflict was evidencing itself in post-1815 Europe: popular nationalist feeling. Modern political nationalism has its origins in France between 1792 and 1795, when the Jacobins insisted on the duties imposed on all citizens by patriotism. Later, when the French occupied half of Europe, their subjects' patriotic reaction against the occupier contributed mightily to the growth of nationalism.

Nationalism and liberalism marched well together in several nations, especially Britain and France. Conservatives, on the other hand, were usually split on the question of nationalism. Many conservatives denounced it as a trick exercised by demagogues to fool the common people into supporting ill-advised and revolutionary actions. They could not forget its origins.

Early **nationalism** was generally a culturally benign phenomenon. It was positive in its goals and tolerant in its outlook. Thus, to be aware of being French did not mean to reject the Germans or English as inferiors. One could simultaneously strive for the freedom of the individual and the free nation. Sometime in the 1840s and later, however, nationalism in much of Europe lost its constructive, tolerant character. This later phase was marked by the rise of negative qualities that we in modern times are thoroughly familiar with: "we" versus "they" and right against wrong; nationalism as a zero-sum game in which one nation's gain is another's loss and vice versa. This nationalism was characterized by a conviction of cultural superiority over other nations and by a sense of mission—the belief that one's nation was bringing the light to other, less fortunate neighbors. It degenerated to its worst in the Balkans and eastern Europe, where many distinct peoples lived in mixed communities and regions without clear territorial lines. Here, nationalism soon became an excuse for one war after another in the later nineteenth and early twentieth centuries.

## SOCIALISM IN THE PRE-MARX ERA

Usually, the word *socialism* is associated with the political and economic creed first systematically proposed by Karl Marx, but that connection did not always exist. As we have seen, the earliest socialists were a handful of conspirators in France in the 1790s. Once they were eliminated by governmental repression, no others arose to take their place until a generation later. All of these preceded Marx.

What did the early socialist thinkers wish to achieve? What constituted this phenomenon of socialism? Its goals were both social and economic. Three chief economic goals were involved:

1. *A planned economy.* The unregulated free market was an entirely wasteful, haphazard way of supplying the needs and wants of most people.
2. *Greater equality.* There was too much for the rich, too little for the rest, and too few ways in which that situation could be changed peaceably and fairly.
3. *Ownership of income-producing property by the state rather than private parties.* Only the state was powerful enough

to resist the wealthy and ensure that the means of producing wealth were not controlled by a few for their own exclusive benefit.

The pre-Marxian nineteenth-century socialists were often later termed *utopian,* because what they wanted allegedly could never be secured so long as acquisitive human nature remained as it was. But that label (originated by Karl Marx) is inherently unfair to them. What they wanted has been, in large part, achieved by modern societies all over the globe.

The most influential of the early socialists worked in France. The reform-minded nobleman Henri de Saint-Simon (1760–1825) was perhaps the most important of all. He believed that industrialized society had the potential to be the fairest, as well as the most productive, society the world had ever seen. He believed further that the state (that is, the government) had the positive duty to look out for those who were unable to look out for themselves—the misfits, the incompetent, and the disabled. Because industrialized production would be so much more lavish than anything previously seen, the economy of scarcity would be abolished soon, and it would be no hardship for the productive majority to care for these "welfare cases." Saint-Simon thought that private industry and government must combine in planning this economy of abundance that was surely coming.

Charles Fourier and Pierre Proudhon were active later than Saint-Simon and had differing views. Fourier was an obsessive theorist of technology and organization. His vision of special, self-contained units of precisely 1,620 persons living and working together was one of the oddities of early social thought (see the Society and Economy box). Fourier was particularly important as a forerunner of feminist equality in work and politics and as the upholder of the demands of the emotional, passionate side of human nature in industrialized society.

Proudhon was the first modern anarchist. He believed the power of the state must be destroyed if men and women were ever to be truly free and capable of living humane lives. Unlike most socialists, Proudhon was convinced that government was at best a barely tolerable evil. He thought it was always controlled by the wealthy and was almost always the oppressor of the poor. In 1840, he posed his famous question, *What Is Property?* and gave a resounding answer: Property is nothing but organized theft! It has been stolen from the sole creator of value, the worker, by the owning class. And it should be taken back—by force, if necessary.

In England, utopian socialism in the early nineteenth century took a different direction; its leading figure was a businessman, Robert Owen. Owen was a remarkable man whose hard work and ambition made him a wealthy mill owner at the age of twenty-seven. Inspired by a rugged Christianity, he then decided to give much of his wealth and power to his workforce. At his famous cooperative textile mill in New Lanark, Scotland, Owen put his theories into practice and created a profitable enterprise that also provided well for every need of its workers and their families. Although not all of his visions worked out so well (the American experimental community he founded in the 1820s was a quick disaster), Owen remained convinced that industrial production and a decent life for workers were compatible and within reach.

In the 1840s, socialism was still very much an idea or theory of outsiders. It was not taken seriously by most people and was condemned as being against the laws of God and man by most of those who *did* take notice of it. Economic liberals thundered against it as unnatural. Middle-class political liberals were appalled at the prospect of hordes of uneducated industrial workers being admitted into equality in government. All types of conservatives thought socialism terribly misunderstood human nature and hence was foredoomed to fail.

## POLITICAL EVENTS TO 1848

In the period just after the Vienna settlement of 1815, European international affairs were relatively calm (see Map 35.1). The Quadruple Alliance of the victors formed at Vienna was easily strong enough to suppress any attempts to overthrow the peace, as long as its members agreed. Revolts by liberals in Spain (1820) and Italy (1822) were quickly squelched, but a nationalist guerrilla war by the Greeks against their Turkish overlords (1827–1830) was allowed to commence and eventually succeed because it was a special circumstance of Christian versus Muslim. (The Greek rebellion had a special connection to nineteenth-century English literature; see the Arts and Culture box on Lord Byron.)

During this decade, the Spanish-American colonies were also allowed to break away from backward Spain, which was too weak to suppress their revolts by itself. First Mexico, then most of South America rebelled against Madrid and became independent states by 1825. Brazil, Portugal's one colony in the New World, also broke away during this same period (see Chapter 30).

### *The Liberal States: France and Britain*

In an almost bloodless revolution in July 1830, the French middle classes threw out their unpopular Bourbon ruler, who had foolishly attempted to install an absolutist government. In his place came the "Citizen King," Louis Philippe (ruled 1830–1848). Louis gladly accepted from Parliament a moderately liberal constitution, which called him "king of the French," rather than the traditional king of France, and stated that sovereignty lay in the people, not in the throne. This was a novelty in monarchic government that would be widely accepted later.

SOCIETY AND ECONOMY

## Charles Fourier (1772–1837)

**The most interesting of all the early** socialist theorizers was the Frenchman Charles Fourier. Although perhaps not entirely sane, he nevertheless pinpointed many of the unpleasant truths about modern industrial society seventy-five or a hundred years before those truths were accepted by most.

Fourier was born into a well-off family in a provincial city and received an excellent education, but he lost his property during the French Revolution. He fought for the Napoleonic regime for two years, but ill health forced him to resign his army post. He then began a life of scholarship and propagandizing his ideas.

In 1808, he anonymously published his basic work, *The Theory of the Four Movements,* in which he explains that human society has been corrupted by the unnatural restraints that we impose on ourselves. Only when those restraints have been lifted will humans achieve their potential. Fourier's focus on the importance of emotions, or passions, and on the necessity of women finding satisfaction in their emotional life make him an important forerunner of the feminist movement. However, Fourier's demand that passions be given free expression quickly stamped him as an eccentric and a dangerous challenger to accepted values.

In the economic aspect of this doctrine, Fourier worked out an answer to the blight of early industrialization: the socioeconomic unit he called the *phalanx* (Greek for a military unit). He insisted that individualism and the competition it fostered were the prime cause of social evils. The new society would consist of voluntary associations, where cooperation would be the rule in every aspect of life.

The phalanx envisioned by Fourier consisted of exactly 1,620 persons, equally divided by sex, with sufficient farmland around the common dwelling and workplace—the *phalanstery*—to supply the members with food. Work would be assigned as much as possible by preference, but the dirty tasks would be rotated, and there would be no "high" or "low" occupations. The work would be suited to the natural temperaments of different age and gender groups. For example, young children with their natural affinity for dirt would be assigned to act as public scavengers and garbage collectors! Those who desired could marry, but all could rightfully engage in free sexual expression, which was considered a basic human need. Needless to add, such reasoning did not convince many people in a Europe that was still largely controlled by church and censor.

Although he led a reclusive life, Fourier continued to publicize his theories to his dying day, but he never had the satisfaction of seeing them translated into fact. Despite the best efforts of his friends and converts, there was but one French experiment with Fourierism, as the theory was termed by the 1830s. It ended quickly in total failure. Instead, Fourier's most important impact was in the New World. Several American experiments in communal living in the first half of the nineteenth century drew their inspiration and some of their structure from Fourier. Brook Farm, the famous New England venture in an intellectual and communal society, was one of these.

In his later life, Fourier devoted his energies to finding a rich backer, who would supply the necessary capital to establish a phalanstery, or a series of them, under his own supervision. Reportedly, having published an appeal for the equivalent of a million dollars or so in his tiny newspaper, Fourier would go to his office at noon on the appointed day to wait for the unknown benefactor to drop the money in his lap. No matter how many times the benefactor failed to appear, the next time the notice ran, Fourier would go in all confidence to wait for the gift.

This sort of unworldliness pervaded Fourierism, as well as its founder, and kept the authorities from becoming too concerned about his challenge to the status quo. Fourier was contemptuous of the competing theories of Saint-Simon and Owen, believing that their failure to appreciate the importance of human passions rendered their whole approach to socioeconomic questions invalid. Although it is beyond dispute that much of his own theory would, if applied, do more damage than good to people, it is still impressive to note how well Fourier understood some of the damage that modern individualistic and competitive societies inflict on their members. While the phalanxes and phalansteries may be condemned without hesitation as unworkable daydreams, the emotional repression, social isolation, and alienation from one's fellow beings that they were meant to counter are also indisputably bad for the human body and soul.

### Analyze and Interpret

What would happen among your college classmates if a Fourier phalanx were to be erected along his principles? What do you think of Fourier's insistence that human emotions must be considered in providing a work environment?

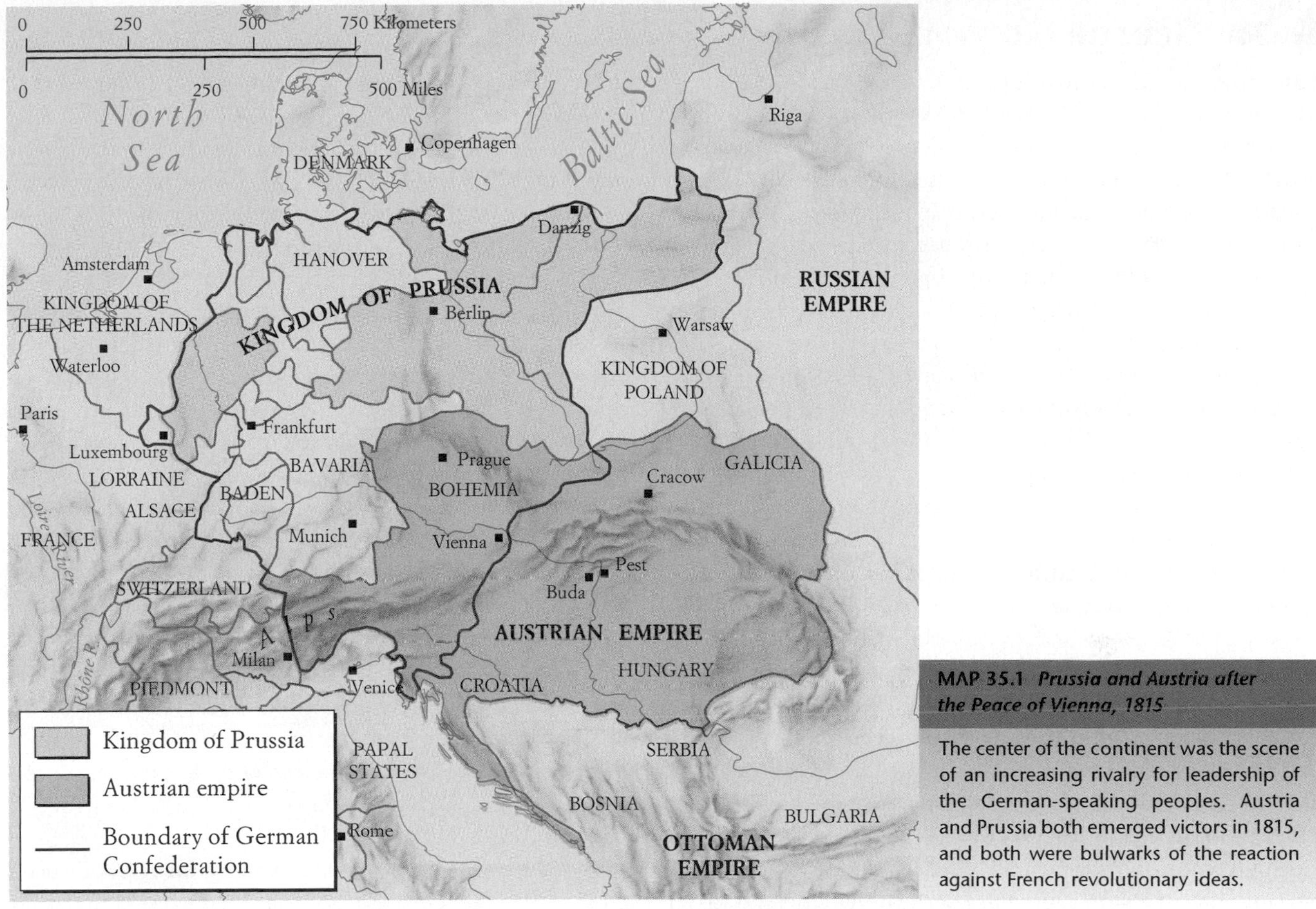


**MAP 35.1** ***Prussia and Austria after the Peace of Vienna, 1815***

The center of the continent was the scene of an increasing rivalry for leadership of the German-speaking peoples. Austria and Prussia both emerged victors in 1815, and both were bulwarks of the reaction against French revolutionary ideas.

The **July Monarchy**, as the eighteen years of Louis Philippe's reign are generally called, was a major step forward for both economic and political liberalism. The middle class and especially the new upper class of wealth (not birth) did well under this government. The rising number of urban poor and industrial workers found little sympathy from it, however. Troops were repeatedly used to break strikes and to control the populace. Citizen rights were granted and usually observed by the government, but those rights were much more extensive for the well-off than for the majority. Social tensions were steadily building and could not be held in check forever. Victor Hugo's great novel *Les Misérables* is the best mirror of this epoch.

In Great Britain—the other country favoring the liberal views—the major fact of political life during the 1820s to 1840s was the rising influence of the mercantile and manufacturing classes. In 1832, the most important reform of voting rights since the Glorious Revolution was finally passed over the protests of the Conservative Party (**Tories**) by their opponents in Parliament, the Liberals (**Whigs**). This Reform Act of 1832 stripped away many of the traditional political advantages of the landholding aristocrats and strengthened the previously weak urban middle classes. Overnight, the House of Commons seats controlled by *rotten boroughs* (very few voters) and *pocket boroughs* (controlled by a single family) were eliminated, and the seats thus made free were distributed to urban and industrial districts. Because these latter were controlled by the Liberals, the composition of the Commons changed drastically. The Whigs would remain in charge for the next thirty-five years.

By making Parliament into a more representative national body and giving the vote to a large number of property holders who previously had been denied it, British government diminished the danger of revolution. The British middle classes were assured of a forum—Parliament—in which their voice would be heard and through which they could attain peaceable, orderly change. In the later nineteenth century, these concessions would be extended downward from the propertied classes to the unpropertied, working classes. Revolution and radical socialism never gained much following among the common folk in Britain for that reason.

## The Reactionary States: Austria, Russia, and Prussia

In the reactionary countries, the story was different. In Austria, Russia, and the Germanies, the rulers spent the generation after Napoleon attempting to hold back all

ARTS AND CULTURE

## George Gordon, Lord Byron (1788–1824)

**The triumph of the Industrial Age** also saw a vigorous reaction against it in the **Romantic movement,** which seized on much of Europe during the mid-nineteenth century. Beginning in Britain, this movement first attacked the excessive faith in rationalism that characterized the later-eighteenth-century Enlightenment. By the 1820s, it had become a rejection of the narrow moneygrubbing that many believed had come into British urban life with the Industrial Revolution. A recognition of the power of the emotions came to be seen as an essential element of all the arts, but particularly the art most given to expression of feeling—poetry. Among the British Romantic poets, George Gordon (Lord Byron) took the first place through not only the magnificence of his verse but also the enormous publicity his unconventional life generated. Several of the finest Romantic poems are from his pen, but Lord Byron's place in history has also benefited from what would now be called successful media exposure.

Born to a dissipated and irresponsible father and a loving but unbalanced mother, Byron's early years were unstable. He was lamed by a clubfoot that grew worse under the attentions of a quack doctor who tried to heal the boy with painful braces. His erratic schooling was successful at least in arousing a love of literature and encouraging his inclination to write. At age sixteen, he fell in love with Mary Chatworth, a slightly older girl whose tantalizing cold-blooded attitude toward her teenage admirer, Byron later said, was the turning point of his emotional life. From this time on, this handsome and passionate man became involved in a steady procession of short- and long-term affairs with women of all descriptions. There is much evidence of sexual ambivalence as well in his relations with men both in Britain and abroad.

Byron's poetic efforts began to see the light of day in 1807, when he was a student at Cambridge. His gifts were equally apparent in his lyrics and in his satires of his detractors, which could be savage. In 1809, he entered the House of Lords (his father had been a minor noble) and soon took off for a two-year visit to the Continent. Most of his time was spent in Greece, a place and a people for whom he developed a lasting affection.

The major literary product of his trip was the magnificent *Childe Harold's Pilgrimage,* which became the rage of all London and made Byron's reputation overnight. The long poem beautifully caught the moods of the growing reaction against conventional manners and values, personified in the autobiographical Childe Harold. The magnetic Byron now took advantage of his notoriety to enter into one sexual affair after another—an "abyss of sensuality," as he put it, enhanced by both wine and drugs.

National Portrait Library, London, UK/Bridgeman Art Library

**Byron as the Giaour.** This portrait was painted in 1813, shortly after Lord Byron returned from his tour of the Near East, which produced several of his best poems and established his fame.

Seeking perhaps some stable influence, in early 1815, he suddenly married a rich young woman, but the marriage went awry almost as soon as it commenced. Only a scant year later, his wife was hurrying back to her parents and requesting legal separation despite her just-born daughter. After some unpretty squeezing of his in-laws for money, Byron agreed to sign the separation papers; in those days, this was tantamount to an admission of guilt. His social reputation was now destroyed, not only by the scandalous separation but also by dark hints, never denied and much later confirmed, that he had committed incest with his half-sister, Augusta Leigh. In 1816, he left to visit his friend, the poet Percy Bysshe Shelley, in Switzerland. He never set foot in Britain again.

For the final seven years of his life, Byron was mainly in Italy, where he wrote much of his finest work, including the *Don Juan* epic as well as several of his poetic dramas. The Italian years were made happy by his permanent attachment to the young Teresa Guiccioli, the love of his life, who finally released him from the aimless philandering he had engaged in for fifteen years.

In 1823, the Greeks' rebellion against their Turkish overlords attracted Byron's attention, and he hastened to Greece to put his money and energies into the cause. He contracted a lethal fever and died in his adoptive country in 1824. Throughout the rest of the century, his reputation grew, not only as a poet but as the literary symbol of the brave but doomed individual who challenges the destiny of ordinary souls and must eventually pay for his temerity by defeat and death. Denied the honor of burial in Westminster Abbey because of his shocking escapades, Byron finally received a memorial stone in the abbey floor in 1969. His beloved Greeks had acted much earlier to memorialize him in their own country.

### *Analyze and Interpret*

Should the character or private life of a great artist influence one's judgment of him or her as an artist? Do you think Byron's political banning from England was a legitimate expression of society's condemnation of his private life?

thought of political liberalism. Through censorship, police and military force, diplomacy, and eventually war, they threw a dam across the tide of reform, which held more or less tightly until 1848. The Austrian emperor, the Russian czar, and the Prussian king rejected the kind of concessions the French and British governments had made to their citizens. As a result, revolt seemed to many thinking people the only hope of bringing these countries into modern political and economic life.

Austria had a special problem in that it was a multinational society in a time of increasing national conflict. It was for this reason that foreign minister Prince Metternich was determined to wall off Austrian politics from liberal ideas. He saw that whereas liberalism fostered nationalism, the conservative point of view generally disregarded national divisions as irrelevant and looked at people solely in terms of social class. Until 1848, in Austria, one's social background was far more important than one's ethnic group. The governing class was composed of a multiethnic aristocracy, where it mattered not at all whether a person was a Pole, a Hungarian, a Croat, or a German by blood. What counted was birth in the aristocracy.

## The Revolts of 1848

The revolt that broke out in the streets of working-class Paris in late February 1848 was destined to sweep through Europe from one end to the other during the next year. These revolts of the lower classes against their stepchild position in society combined with an explosion of nationalist conflicts and assertions of popular sovereignty against kings and emperors to set all of Europe aflame (see Map 35.2). Of the major countries, only Britain and Russia were spared, the first because there was no intense dissatisfaction with the government, and the second because the government seemed too strong to be challenged.

The revolts did not have a single cause, and it is impossible to bring them down to a lowest common denominator. Nor did they have the same outcome. In some cases, the revolutionaries were partly successful (Italian states, France, Scandinavia), but in others (German states, Austria), they were defeated in the short term.

Nevertheless, at least three underlying similarities can be established: (1) the revolts were led initially by middle-class liberals, not by the workers and/or the peasants; (2) the workers soon grew disappointed with the liberals' hesitancy and created their own more violent revolutions against both aristocrats and the middle classes; and (3) national divisions contributed significantly to the failure of the revolts throughout central and eastern Europe.

### *Two Phases*

In the initial stages, the revolts appeared to be on the verge of success. In France, the exhausted and impotent July Monarchy fell within days, and France was turned into a republic for a few years. In the German states, several kings and princes were brushed aside by popular assemblies that claimed supreme powers and enacted liberal constitutions. Within the Austrian Empire, the Hungarians and the Italians declared themselves independent, while the German-Austrians attempted to set up a liberal and constitutional monarchy. In the "Springtime

Louvre, Paris, France/Bridgeman Art Library

**Liberty Leading the People.** This often-reproduced painting by Eugène Delacroix shows the female Liberty (the national French symbol of Marianne) leading the way in the revolution of 1830. Delacroix, the foremost Romantic painter of his day, was probably the illegitimate son of the much-traveled bishop, Talleyrand.

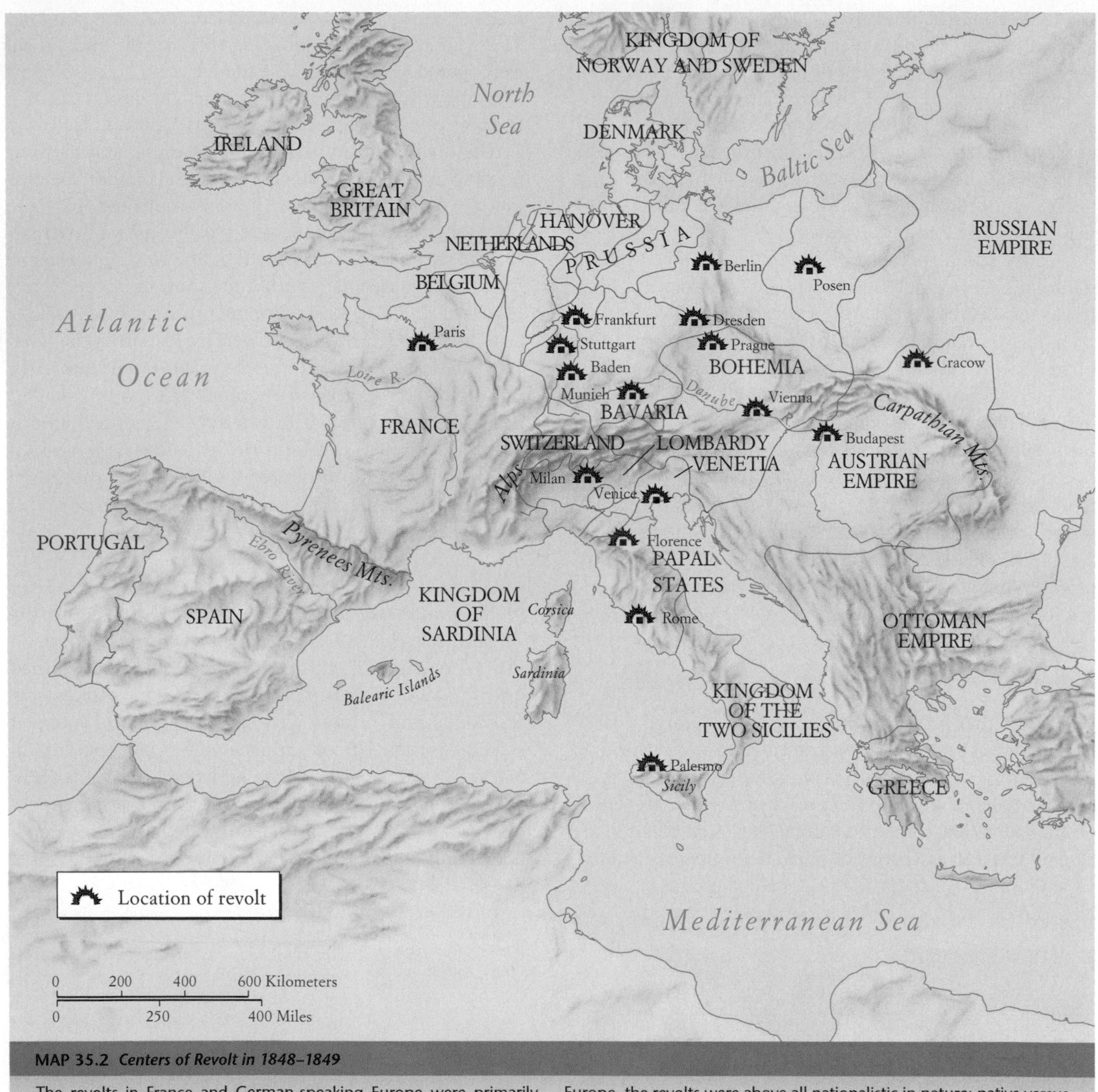


**MAP 35.2** ***Centers of Revolt in 1848–1849***

The revolts in France and German-speaking Europe were primarily political in nature: liberal versus conservative. In southern and eastern Europe, the revolts were above all nationalistic in nature: native versus alien overlord.

of Nations," it looked for a while as though the reactionaries had been routed, but appearances were deceptive. The military generally remained loyal to the monarchies, and the churches rallied round the throne. The peasants, who were still a majority of the population outside Britain, remained on the sidelines everywhere, because they could see no common ground with the urban liberals or workers after the abolition of serfdom was accomplished.

The second phase of the revolts opened them to defeat. When the workers in Paris, Vienna, and Berlin went into the streets to demand not only constitutional government but also decent working conditions and better pay and housing, the liberals got "cold feet." If they had to choose between the continued rule of the aristocracy and Crown and radical social change in favor of the masses, the middle classes would take the first alternative. They figured, more or less correctly, that time was on their side in their efforts to obtain political power peaceably. If they encouraged thoroughgoing reform of the socioeconomic system, on the other hand, they had no way of knowing what would happen in the long run. The

Historisches Museum der Stadt, Vienna, Austria/Bridgeman Art Library

**BARRICADES IN VIENNA.** Edouard Ritter painted this canvas shortly after the events it depicts in revolutionary Vienna. Bourgeois revolutionaries atop the hill make common cause for a brief interval with the laborers gathered below.

liberals, composed overwhelmingly of urban middle-class property holders, were more afraid of some form of socialism than they were of continued aristocratic privilege and royal absolutism.

## Consequences

In instance after instance, during 1848 and 1849, this open or barely concealed split between the middle class and the lower class enabled the conservative forces to defeat the goals of both in the short term. The liberals got only a conditioned increase in political representation. The workers got nothing but bayonets.

1. *France.* The Second Republic established by the revolt lasted but three years before Louis Napoleon (Napoleon III), nephew of the great Bonaparte, used the power of the republican presidency to which he had been elected in 1848 to declare himself emperor. So began the Second Empire in France, which was to last twenty years. It saw the realization of most of the liberals' economic and political goals, but little for the workers.
2. *Prussia.* After a year of wrangling about the exact form and provisions of a liberal constitution for a united Germany, the middle-class **Frankfurt Assembly** dissolved in complete failure. Led by Prussia, the bulk of the German states reverted to the conservative regimes that had been briefly pushed aside by the revolts. German liberals had suffered a permanent defeat—one they would not recover from for a century.
3. *Austria.* The new Austrian emperor, eighteen-year-old Franz Joseph (ruled 1848–1916), relied on his aristocratic advisers to gradually regain control of the revolutionary situation, which had forced Metternich out and briefly turned Austria into a constitutional and liberal regime. Playing off one nationality against the other, the Vienna government crushed the independence movements of the Czechs, Hungarians, and Italians within the empire and then intimidated the German liberals in Austria proper. By the summer of 1849, reaction was unchecked, and Austria was embarked on a decade of old-fashioned royal absolutism.
4. *Italy.* It is important to remember that as yet there was no unified Italy. It was rather a collection of small kingdoms and the Papal States. The north was controlled by Austria, the middle was divided between the kingdom of **Sardinia-Piedmont** and the papacy, and the south and Sicily were controlled by the reactionary kingdom of Naples. Liberal Italians had long wanted to unite Italy under a constitutional monarchy. They favored the Sardinian kingdom as the basis of this monarchy because it was the only state that had a native Italian, secular ruler. Many middle-class Italians, especially those in the northern cities, were anticlerical and antipapal. They viewed the popes as political reactionaries and upholders of class privilege. For several of the nineteenth-century popes, this was a fair judgment.

In 1848, anti-Austrian and antipapal riots broke out in various parts of Italy. Sardinia declared war on Austria, believing that Vienna was too occupied with other crises to defend its Italian possessions. This proved to be a mistake. The Austrians were decisive victors. Pope Pius IX (in power 1846–1875) was so frightened by the Roman mobs that he opposed any type of liberalism from then on. In 1849, it appeared that a united Italy was as far away as it had ever been.

Thus, the revolts and attempted revolutions had accomplished very little by 1850. Both middle-class liberals and working-class radicals had been defeated by military force or its threat. Yet, within a generation's time, almost all that the middle classes had fought for and even some of the demands of the radicals had come into being in many European capitals. Reaction proved unable to meet the needs of the day, and the necessity to introduce a more or less industrialized economy overrode the objections of the Old Guard. Many of the thousands who were imprisoned for treason or violating public order from 1849 to 1850 would live to see the day when their governments freely gave the rights they had fought for and been punished for seeking.

## Summary

The dual revolutions in politics and economics started in the later eighteenth century but matured in the nineteenth. In the era after the Napoleonic wars, Europe divided politically into liberal, conservative, and reactionary segments, all of which were attempting to meet the new challenges thrown up by the Americans' successful revolt against their colonial overlord and the French Revolution.

In politics, the conservatives reluctantly discovered that the French upheaval and its spread by Napoleon's armies had changed traditional relationships so that they could not be successfully reconstructed. Despite the defeat of the French radicals by their own countrymen and the defeat of Napoleon by the rest of Europe, some of the seeds planted by each would sprout in a generation's time.

The liberal spirit that was forcing its way into prominence in France and Britain took a less benign form in economics than in politics. The ideas of Adam Smith and others were selectively adopted by the Manchester liberals and used to justify harsh exploitation of the workers. They triggered experiments with socialism that attracted little attention because of their utopian nature and, in most cases, quick failure. In the reactionary empires of eastern Europe, the liberals failed to gain ground throughout the generation after the Vienna settlement.

The Europe-wide revolts of 1848 mostly failed in the short run, but the forces in society that had touched them off proved too strong to resist, and they triumphed to at least a limited extent in the following generations. One reason for the initial failure was the rising sense of conflicting nationalism in multiethnic states. Another was the divergence between the mainly political goals of the liberal middle classes and the mainly economic and social goals of the workers.

## Identification Terms

Test your knowledge of this chapter's key concepts by defining the following terms. If you can't recall the meaning of certain terms, refresh your memory by looking up the boldfaced term in the chapter, turning to the Glossary at the end of the book, or working with the flashcards that are available on the *World Civilizations* Companion Website **http://history.wadsworth.com/adler04**.

Frankfurt Assembly (1848)
Gendarme of Europe
July Monarchy
Manchester liberalism
nationalism
Reform Act of 1832
Romantic movement
Sardinia-Piedmont
Tories
Whigs

## Test Your Knowledge

Test your knowledge of this chapter by answering the following questions. Complete answers appear at the end of the book. You may also take this quiz interactively and find even more quiz questions on the *World Civilizations* Companion Website: **http://history.wadsworth.com/adler04.**

1. Which of following would a moderate conservative be most likely to support?
   a. An officially established church with preeminent rights in education
   b. An absolutist monarch ruling with no constitutional restraints
   c. A proposal to sever any connections between church and schools
   d. A proposal to give poor and rich alike an equal vote
   e. A removal of governmental controls on commerce and manufacturing
2. Which of the following had its modern birth in the 1789–1814 era?
   a. Constitutional monarchy
   b. Nationalism
   c. Autocracy
   d. Meritocracy
   e. Liberalism
3. The Gendarme of Europe was
   a. France.
   b. Great Britain.
   c. Russia.

d. Germany.
e. Turkey.

4. The most uncompromisingly radical of Europe's early socialists was
   a. Henri Saint-Simon.
   b. Pierre Proudhon.
   c. Robert Owen.
   d. Charles Fourier.
   e. Karl Marx.
5. Charles Fourier propagandized for a society structured
   a. in large states with dictatorial leadership by the working classes.
   b. in a military fashion.
   c. in small communities of self-directing workers.
   d. in communities of fellow believers housed in monasteries.
   e. in small states governed by the wealthy.
6. The most notable success in early socialist experiments was
   a. the New Lanark mill of Robert Owen.
   b. the phalanstery of Charles Fourier.
   c. the anarchy promoted by Pierre Proudhon.
   d. the communal society proposed by the French revolutionaries.
   e. the implementation of feminist ideas in France by Charles Fourier.
7. The most important parliamentary act in nineteenth-century British history was the
   a. passage of the United Kingdom Act.
   b. passage of the Reform Act of 1832.
   c. decision to exile Napoleon to St. Helena.
   d. passage of the Factory Act of 1819.
   e. ousting of the Tories from Parliament.
8. The revolts of 1848 began in
   a. Belgium with an outbreak against Dutch rule.
   b. Paris with demonstrations against the July Monarchy.
   c. London with hunger marches in the slums.
   d. St. Petersburg with protests against the Crimean War.
   e. the Austrian Empire with a declaration of independence by the Hungarians and Italians.
9. Which country was least affected by the revolts of 1848?
   a. France
   b. Great Britain
   c. Italy
   d. Austria
   e. Prussia
10. In response to the Italian riots of 1848,
    a. Pope Pius IX spoke out on behalf of the oppressed.
    b. Austria allowed the riots to continue for several months unchecked, being preoccupied with problems elsewhere.
    c. Italy gained its independence from Austria.
    d. liberals from Vienna came to help the Italian protesters.
    e. Pope Pius IX turned away from all liberal causes from that point on.

## InfoTrac College Edition

Visit the source collections at

**http://infotrac.thomsonlearning.com**

and use the Search function with the following key terms:

Adam Smith nationalism

## Wadsworth History Website Resources

Visit the World History Resource Center at **http://history.wadsworth.com/world** for a wealth of general resources, and the *World Civilizations* Companion Website at **http://history.wadsworth.com/adler04** for resources specific to this textbook.

## HistoryNow

Enter *HistoryNow* using the access card that is available for *World Civilizations. HistoryNow* will assist you in understanding the content in this chapter with lesson plans generated for your needs. In addition, you can read the following documents, and many more, online:

Adam Smith, selected chapters from *The Wealth of Nations*

Thomas Malthus, *An Essay on the Principle of Population*

*The war of the peoples will be more terrible than those of kings.*
Winston Churchill

# 36 Consolidation of National States



| | |
|---|---|
| 1851–1871 | Louis Napoleon (Napoleon III): Second Empire (France) |
| 1853–1856 | Crimean War |
| 1859–1870 | Unification of Italy |
| 1861 | Freeing of serfs in Russia/ Civil War in the United States |
| 1862–1871 | Unification of Germany |
| 1867 | *Ausgleich:* Dual monarchy established in Austria-Hungary |
| 1870 | Franco-Prussian War |

After the defeats of 1848, European liberals and nationalists were in retreat during the next decade, and conservative statesmen were everywhere in control. But only twenty to thirty years later, many of the goals of the liberals had been reached, and nationalism was already one of the givens of policy making. The elements of modern political democracy were visible in several nations, notably Britain and the post–Civil War United States. The universal male franchise was introduced in several countries. Governments in many places legalized labor unions, and Russia freed its serfs. The Western world was entering the next phase of the dual revolution—that is, the Second Industrial Revolution and the massive social changes that accompanied it.

## Russia

Since victory over Napoleon in 1814, the armed might of Russia had lain like a menacing bear on Europe's eastern perimeters. The revolts of 1848–1849 had brought Russia's army into Hungary to assist the Habsburg Dynasty in its hour of crisis, and the reactionary czar Nicholas I had rejoiced in his role of Gendarme of Europe. Now the Romanov Dynasty's own hour of crisis approached, this time generated by foreign challenges.

### Defeat in the Crimea

The first severe failure of the international alliances set up by the Vienna treaties was the **Crimean War** (1853–1856) between Russia on one side and England, France, and Turkey on the other. An awkward war that no one wanted, it represented an accidental breakdown of the system established a generation earlier. Expansionary ambitions led Czar Nicholas I to demand Turkish concessions in southeastern Europe. Once assured of British and French help, the Turks unexpectedly resisted. The conflict was mostly fought on the Crimean peninsula in the Black Sea (see Map 36.1).

Militarily, the war was a general debacle for all concerned. The Russian commanders and logistics were even less competent than those of the allies, so in time Russia had to sue for peace. The Peace of Paris of 1856 was a drastic diplomatic defeat for St. Petersburg, and for the next twenty years, Russia was essentially bottled up in the south, unable to gain the much-desired naval access to the Mediterranean. The Russian Colossus, which had intimidated Europe since crushing Napoleon, was seen to have feet of clay. Its pressing internal problems would have to be addressed if it were to play any sizable role in future world affairs. Its self-appointed role as reactionary watchman would have to be abandoned for a time.

What were these internal concerns, and how were they eventually addressed by a hesitant imperial government in St. Petersburg?

## The Great Reforms

The military embarrassment in the Crimea hardened the determination of the new ruler, **Czar Alexander II** (ruled 1855–1881), to tackle Russia's primary social and economic

**MAP 36.1** *Europe after 1871*

The unification of the Germanies and of the Italian peninsula had been completed by 1871, but southeastern Europe was still in political flux. A disintegrating Turkey meant that Bosnia would soon fall under Austrian occupation, and a lost war against Russia would force the Ottomans to recognize the independence of Serbia, Montenegro, Romania, and Bulgaria in 1878. In 1912, a new war allowed the kingdom of Albania to emerge from the Ottoman Empire, while Greece and Serbia were enlarged.

**The Crimean War.** The war in the Crimea was the first to be photographed. Here, the English journalist Roger Fenton shows us an officer and men of the Fourth Dragoons in their encampment in 1855. At their side is one of the first military nurses, a colleague of Florence Nightingale.

Corbis

problem: the question of the serfs. For the previous half century, educated Russians had been debating what could and should be done to bring the almost 50 percent of the population who lived in legal bondage into freedom and productivity. Various czars since Catherine the Great had proposed various steps to better the serfs' condition, but in the end, little had been done. The overwhelmingly rural serfs still lived in almost total illiteracy, ignorance, and superstition. Not only were they growing increasingly resentful of their noble landlords and masters, but they were an immense drag on the Russian economy. Living in stagnant poverty as they had for centuries, they had no money to consume anything except what they made or grew themselves. Nor could they contribute to the nation's capital for desperately needed financial and industrial investments.

In 1859, a determined Alexander commanded a quick resolution of the serf problem, based on these principles:

- Freeing the serfs from the judicial and administrative control of their landlords and making them legally equal to other citizens with full personal liberty
- Giving the serfs a substantial part of the estate land that they had previously worked for their master, and compensating the landlord with government bonds, redeemable by annual payments from the peasants
- Anchoring the ex-serfs to the land by making them collectively responsible for the two most basic duties of the citizenry: paying the fixed tax of the village community (*mir*) and supplying a quota of conscripts for the army

Over the next two years, a special Court Commission worked out the complex details, and on February 19, 1861, the most massive emancipation order ever issued by any government abolished serfdom in Russia. About 55 million individuals—serfs and their dependents—were directly affected.

What was the result of the long-sought emancipation? It was only a very limited success. Many serfs were disappointed with their allotted portions of land, which were either small or of poor quality. And instead of outright possession of the land, they received only a tentative title subject to several restrictions imposed by the government. The serfs could not mortgage the land or sell it without permission from the village council, which was difficult to obtain. So, instead of creating a class of prosperous, politically and socially engaged farmers as the authorities in St. Petersburg had hoped, the emancipation of the serfs actually made a good many worse off than before—much like the condition of many of the freed slaves in the U.S. South after the Civil War. Rural misery and ignorance were only gradually and partially abated in the generation following 1861.

Besides emancipation, Alexander II presided over several other major reforms in Russian public life. These **Great Reforms**, as they are called, included the following:

- *Local government.* The central government reorganized local and provincial authority, changing its previously purely appointive nature. It allowed the election of a county commission, called the *zemstvo board.* Originally, the zemstvo boards had few real powers, but they acted as a catalyst of civic spirit and helped the local peasants become aware of what they could do to better their lives. From the zemstvo boards came many of the middle-class reformers and liberals who attempted to avert revolution before World War I by persuading the imperial government to make timely concessions to democracy.
- *Judicial system.* The Russian court system was so antiquated and corrupt (bribing the judge was common) that it barely functioned. In 1864, Czar Alexander decreed a complete overhaul, and soon the courts were on the level of the western European countries. The class of lawyers and judges who emerged played a leading role in politics from then on, often to the dismay of the authorities who resented their liberal leanings.

- *Army reform.* In 1873, the conscription, training, length of service, and many other aspects of the Russian army were completely revamped. The army became less a penal institution and more an educational and engineering facility, used by the government to do something about the very low level of rural education. The maximum service time was set at two years for most youth and less for the educated.

Seen in the longer perspective, however, what Alexander did not do was more important than what he did. Like several of his predecessors, he did not think the time ripe for Russia to have a constitution, an elected national legislature, or strong local government bodies. Russia's central authority remained what it had always been, an autocracy (government by a single person having unlimited power). The czar alone ultimately decided law and policy, and the people were viewed as simply passive recipients of the government's demands. This failure to change the basic governmental institutions would prove to be a crucial mistake. The continuing autocratic nature of Russian government blocked the way to peaceable political evolution and forced serious reformers all too often to become revolutionaries.

Ironically, it was during the reign of the reforming Alexander II that the Russian revolutionary movement became for the first time a serious threat. In the 1870s, both socialism and anarchism found their first adherents in the urban **intelligentsia**, the intellectuals and activists drawn mostly from the thin ranks of the professional class. Every variety of revolutionary doctrine was to be found in the Russian underground by the 1890s, ranging from orthodox Marxism through peasant communes to nihilistic terrorism. As late as 1905, however, the government of the czar still seemed to be in undisputed control of the illiterate peasants and a small and doctrinally divided group of socialist workers in the towns.

## FRANCE

The nephew of the great Napoleon won the presidential election in France that was held in the wake of the 1848 revolt. Riding on his uncle's name and claiming to be a sincere republican, Louis Napoleon—or "Napoleon the Little," as he was at once nicknamed by his enemies—was the first modern ruler who understood how to manipulate the democratic franchise to create a quasi-dictatorship. What he did in France during the 1850s showed the power of modern propaganda when controlled by an individual who knew how and when to appeal to his people.

Within a few months of his election, Napoleon sensed that there would be no effective opposition if he imitated his uncle and made himself emperor of the French, as Napoleon III. This Second Empire lasted twenty years, which divide into two distinct segments. Until the 1860s, it was an authoritarian regime led by one man's vision. After that, Napoleon gradually liberalized his rule and allowed political opposition. The main reason for the change was his increasingly unpopular and misconceived foreign policy: a frivolous colonial adventure in Mexico in 1863–1864, failure to stop an aggressively expanding Prussia, and inability, in the eyes of Catholic France, to protect the pope from the Italian secularists. These problems made trouble for Napoleon at home. To ameliorate them, he then had to encourage a previously tame legislature to share leadership responsibilities.

Napoleon was more successful in changing the primarily agrarian France of 1851 into a mixed economy with the firm beginnings of industrial development in place by 1870. Paris was the only large industrial city and was regarded as a foreign place by much of the French public, in much the same way as midwesterners in the United States looked on New York City. But by 1870, capitalist industry was also taking root in many smaller cities, such as Lyon,

Hulton-Deutsch Collection/Corbis

**ESCAPE BY BALLOON, PARIS, 1870.** In this dramatic photo, the head of the French government, Prime Minister Leon Gambetta, eludes the Prussian blockade of Paris by balloon. Despite Gambetta's efforts to continue resistance, the war was lost through the early mistakes of Emperor Louis Napoleon.

Marseilles, Nancy, Brest, and Rouen. Britain and Germany were still far ahead of France in industrial development, but at least the French were beginning to make up the difference.

Napoleon and his Second Empire came to a disgraceful finish in the **Franco-Prussian War** of 1870, which was the emperor's last foreign policy miscalculation. Foolishly taking the field, he was captured by the enemy, forced to abdicate, and died in quiet exile in England. At the end of the war, the first attempt at socialist revolution had taken place in Paris—the capital city whose residents strongly resented the terms of the peace settlement—but the army crushed the group with great bloodshed. This **Paris Commune of 1871** was extremely unwelcome to the majority of the French. From this time onward, the split between the conservative villages of the French provinces and the radical workers and intellectuals of "red" Paris that had originated in the French Revolution of 1789 was wide open. It would remain that way for much of the following century.

Following the lost war, the monarchists (who certainly at this juncture represented the majority of the French) failed to agree on a single candidate. This quarrel enabled those who favored a republic to gradually establish themselves in power. By 1875, the **Third Republic** was more or less in place: it was a liberal state with a strong legislature (the National Assembly) and a weak presidential executive. A confused mass of political parties ranged across the whole spectrum from extreme reactionaries to Marxists and anarchists. About the only political topic that most French agreed on during the later nineteenth century was the necessity of someday gaining revenge on Bismarck's Germany and reclaiming the "Lost Provinces" of Alsace and Lorraine (shown on Map 36.2).

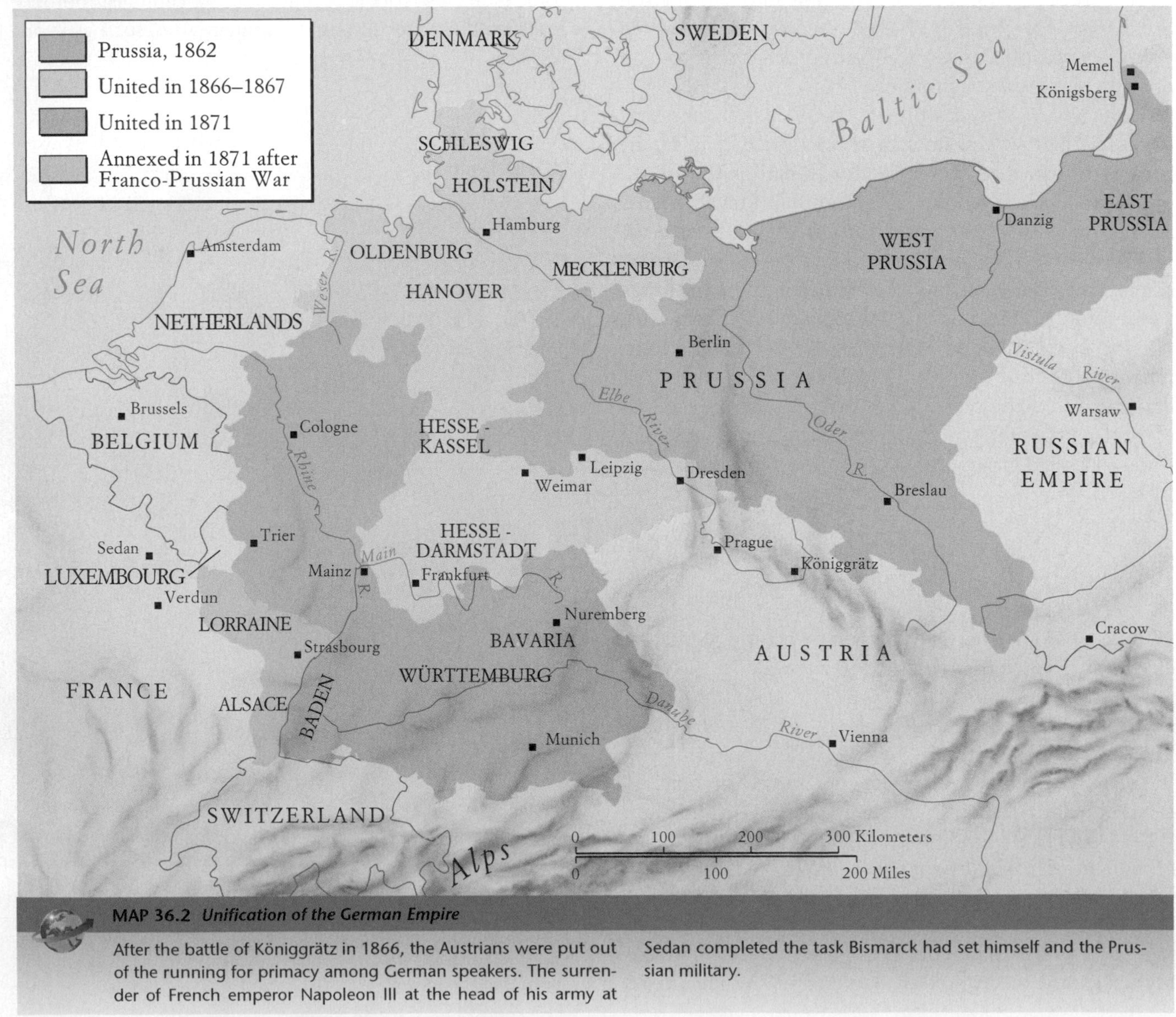


MAP 36.2 *Unification of the German Empire*

After the battle of Königgrätz in 1866, the Austrians were put out of the running for primacy among German speakers. The surrender of French emperor Napoleon III at the head of his army at Sedan completed the task Bismarck had set himself and the Prussian military.

## The Unification of Italy

One of the major changes in the political map of nineteenth-century Europe was the completion of the unification of Italy (see Map 36.3). This had been the goal of two generations of Italian statesmen and revolutionaries, going back to the Napoleonic wars. In the 1860s, unification was thrust through over the opposition of both Austria, which controlled much of northern Italy, and Pope Pius IX, whose experiences and inclinations led him to despise and dread a secular, liberal Italy. Austria's opposition could only be ended through warfare. The pope's opposition was never actually ended, but it was made harmless.

The father of Italian unification was the liberal-minded aristocrat Count Camillo Cavour (1810–1861), who became the prime minister of the kingdom of Sardinia in 1852. Cavour was a moderate who believed in constitutional monarchy and firmly rejected radical social change. Sardinia had long been the best hope of those who wanted a united Italy. It was better known as **Piedmont**, because the center of political gravity in the kingdom had long since moved from backward Sardinia to progressive and modern Turin at "the foot of the mountains." Cavour strongly supported economic progress, and during the 1850s, he built Piedmont into the leading economic force in all of Italy, as well as the major political power.

Cavour fully realized that Austria would never willingly let go of its Italian provinces and that Piedmont alone was too weak to force it to do so (as had been demonstrated in 1848). Therefore, a foreign ally was needed, and that ally could only be France. Carefully, he drew the all-too-willing Napoleon III into a so-called defensive alliance and then provoked a war with Vienna in 1859. Faced with the French-Piedmont alliance, the Austrians were outmatched and forfeited the large Lombard province to Cavour.

As Cavour had reckoned, after the defeat of Austria, much of the rest of Italy threw in its lot with Piedmont. The newly christened kingdom of Italy, based in Turin, now embraced about half of the peninsula. The rest was divided among the pope, the reactionary Bourbon king of Naples and Sicily, who wished to remain independent, and the remaining Austrian possessions.

The romantic and popular revolutionary Giuseppe Garibaldi now entered the scene, leading a volunteer army ("The Thousand Red Shirts") through southern Italy, routing the royal government of Naples and joining Sicily and southern Italy to the Italian kingdom in 1861 (see the Law and Government box). A few months later, Cavour died, with the job of unification-by-conquest almost complete.

Two pieces of the picture still remained to be fitted in: the Austrian province of Venetia and the Papal States

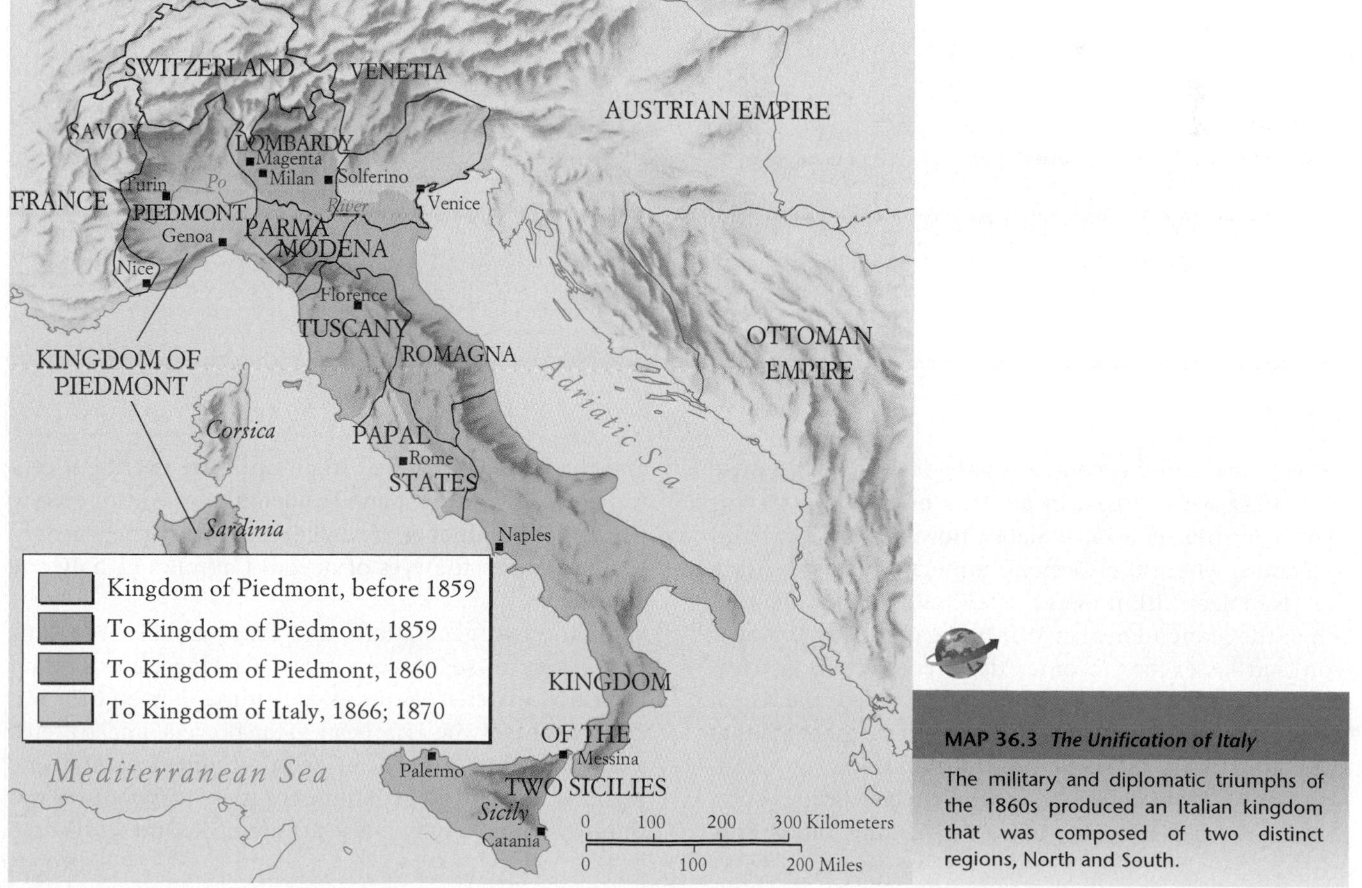


**MAP 36.3** *The Unification of Italy*

The military and diplomatic triumphs of the 1860s produced an Italian kingdom that was composed of two distinct regions, North and South.

L A W   A N D   G O V E R N M E N T

## Giuseppe Garibaldi (1807–1882)

**The creation of new national states** inevitably involved bloodshed as well as negotiation. Every bit of territory within the European continent had long since been occupied by ethnic groups, who by the nineteenth century had made their claims to national existence legitimate, although they still might lack sovereign statehood. The Italian and the German peoples entered unified political existence at almost simultaneous dates, in part because of the extraordinary abilities of individuals. These men found varying ways to create and exercise personal authority. In Italy, Giuseppe Garibaldi's romantic charisma fascinated a generation of his countrymen.

Born in Nice in 1807, Garibaldi grew up in the full flush of the national feeling unleashed by the French Revolution and its extension through Napoleon's troops. He was a subject of the small kingdom of Sardinia-Piedmont, but as a dedicated republican, he took part in an abortive plot against the king and had to flee for his life to South America in 1835. There he participated in several attempts to install a republic in Brazil and to secure independence for Uruguay. He also became an enthusiast for the ideas of his fellow Italian Giuseppe Mazzini, perhaps the most admirable of the nineteenth-century revolutionaries in his steadfast conviction that the brotherhood of man could only rise from the smoking ruins of monarchic government.

In 1848, Garibaldi hastened back to his native land to join the fight against Austria. After its defeat, he reluctantly put aside his republican convictions and became an ally of Count Cavour's diplomacy aimed at making the king of Sardinia, Victor Emmanuel II, the eventual king of united Italy. In 1859, Garibaldi again joined with Cavour in Sardinia (or Piedmont, as the kingdom was increasingly known) against the Austrians by embarking on the crowning adventure of an adventurous life: the conquest of Sicily and southern Italy for the forces of unity. At this time, Sicily and the southern third of the peninsula were poorly governed by one of the most unpopular monarchs of Europe, Francis II of the house of Bourbon. With his One Thousand volunteers (who had been outfitted and trained in the north), Garibaldi succeeded in routing the royalists first in Sicily (at the battle of Calatafimi in June 1860) and then on the mainland (at the Volturno River). All of Italy except the Papal States around Rome and the city itself were now under the control of either Piedmont or Garibaldi. Finally, the Franco-Prussian War of 1870 allowed Victor Emmanuel to ignore the pope's condemnation and move his forces into Rome and make it the capital of the united Italy.

Garibaldi became a delegate to the new Italian parliament, but his true place in history was accorded to him by the Italian people, who regarded him as the chief hero of their long campaign to throw out foreign rulers and native oppressors. By the time of his death, he had become almost an object of worship among the common people of his country.

Archives Larousse, Paris, France/Bridgeman Art Library

**Garibaldi**

### *Analyze and Interpret*

Whom do you think was more important for success in leading a radical change in politics, the Cavours or the Garibaldis? Is there always room for both?

centered on Rome. Venetia was gained in 1866, as a prize for joining with Prussia in another brief victorious war against Austria. The Papal States, however, were guarded by France, where the Catholic population was insisting that Napoleon III preserve traditional papal liberties. When the Franco-Prussian War broke out in 1870, Napoleon had an excuse to order the French garrison withdrawn. The Piedmontese quickly annexed the Papal States and made Rome the capital of the new Italian kingdom. The pope was reduced to the status of quasi-prisoner within Vatican City, a tiny enclave in the center of Rome. The relationship between the kingdom of Italy and the papacy remained frigid until the twentieth century. Papal resentment and condemnation contributed to the early difficulties of the Italian state and discredited it to some extent in the eyes of devout Catholics in Italy and elsewhere.

In the two generations that followed, the new Italy was a very mixed success story. Lacking all important industrial material resources except manpower, Italy was the weakest of the European great powers, and suffered from a large gap between self-proclaimed stature and political, social, and economic realities. This country was in most ways really two distinct countries: the industrializing, urban, liberal North and the agrarian, rural, feudal South.

The South (from Rome down) and Sicily were controlled by reactionary aristocrats, mainly absentee landowners whose impoverished peasants still lived in serfdom in everything but name. The Catholic Church was all-powerful and an ally of the aristocracy. The population outside the towns resembled its Russian equivalent; it was almost entirely illiterate, superstitious, and unaware of anything outside its native region. The South had no modern industry or transport, and no prospects of any.

The North (from Florence up) was controlled by educated wealthy landowners and a large commercial middle class, who lived and worked in good-sized cities such as Turin, Milan, and Venice. These towns, which had ties to transalpine Europe, were rapidly industrializing, producing a proletariat who would soon be one of Europe's most fertile fields for socialist ideas. The average income in Milan was three or four times what it was in Palermo, Catania, or Naples. The northerners viewed the Sicilians and the South in general with contempt and despair, refusing to regard them as equal fellow citizens of the new state. The "national culture," as well as government money, was tilted heavily in favor of the North and would remain that way into the mid-twentieth century. Almost all of the millions of Italian emigrants to North and South America came from the overpopulated, backward South.

## The Unification of the Germans

During the same years that the Italians were attempting to construct one state came the unification of Germany (see Map 36.2). As the new Italy was an extension of the kingdom of Sardinia, so the new Germany was an extension of the kingdom of Prussia. Like Italy, Germany was the product of both diplomacy and war. But here the similarities mostly ended.

The creation of the German Empire (*Deutsches Reich*), as it was called, was the most important politico-economic development of the later nineteenth century in Europe. Far more than Italy, Germany was an economic and military powerhouse, and it became the most important military force in the world by the 1880s. Germany would surpass Britain as the foremost industrial power as early as 1890 and would be rivaled only by the United States in the early twentieth century.

The fashion by which Germany was united would have a dominant influence on the later history of the country. It followed the conservative, even reactionary realization of the vision of two men: the Prussian king William I (ruled 1861–1888) and, more important, his chancellor and trusted friend Otto von Bismarck (1815–1898). Bismarck was the outstanding European statesman of the entire nineteenth century, and his shadow hung over the German nation until 1945. For good or evil, modern Germany was largely the product of Bismarck's mind and hand.

A Junker aristocrat, Bismarck deeply distrusted liberalism, while remaining a nationalist to the core. Like almost all nineteenth-century patriots, he wished to see the German people united rather than remain fragmented among the sixteen kingdoms and city-states left by the 1815 Treaty of Vienna. Above all, he wanted to complete what many years of Prussian policies had attempted with only modest success: to unify all Germans under the political leadership of Berlin. A chief reason for the failure thus far was the determined opposition of the other major Germanic state: Austria. Austria insisted on a seat in any pan-German political arrangement, and its size and prestige in the early nineteenth century assured it a leading seat if such an arrangement ever came about.

**Bismarck and the Young Kaiser, 1888.** The tension between the ambitious young William II and his chancellor Bismarck comes through even in this formal photo. William found it impossible to continue his predecessor's warm relations with the old man who had piloted Prussia and Germany since 1862.

Bildarchiv Preussischer Kulturbesitz, Berlin

The Prussians resisted Austria's pretensions, in part because they considered the Austrian empire not really a German territory at all. Within Austria's borders were more non-Germans than Germans, as we have seen. In 1848, this tension between ***kleindeutsch*** ("little German," Germans only) and ***grossdeutsch*** ("big German," or Germans predominantly) did much to wreck the hopes of the constitutionalists at Frankfurt and allow the reestablishment of absolutist monarchy in most of the Germanic lands.

Bismarck was a decided kleindeutsch adherent, and his policy aimed at removing the Austrians from German affairs as soon as possible. To this end, he cleverly manipulated the Vienna government into a situation where, no matter what Austria did, it came out looking opposed to German unity. Bismarck then provoked Austria into declaring war on Prussia, so that Austria appeared to be the aggressor in the eyes of the other Germans, who tried to remain neutral. The **Austro-Prussian War** of 1866 was over in one bloody battle, won unexpectedly by the Prussians using their new railway system and repeating rifles. Instead of seeking territory or money damages, Bismarck insisted only that Austria withdraw from German political affairs, leaving the field to Prussia.

The capstone of Bismarck's policy for unity was to provoke a third war, this one against the traditional enemy west of the Rhine. The Franco-Prussian War of 1870–1871 was the result of clever deception by the Prussian chancellor to maneuver the French into becoming the formal aggressor. As Bismarck had reckoned, the other German states could no longer remain neutral in this situation. Fevered nationalist opinion forced the governments to join the Prussians, as fellow Germans, against the ancient enemy.

Soon the captured Napoleon III had to abdicate, and France sued for peace. Bismarck now put forward the Prussian king as emperor of Germany as a wave of national triumph swept the country. The Germans, after all, were the most numerous nation in Europe and had been artificially divided for many centuries. Only the Austro-Germans and the neutral Swiss stayed outside the new homeland, which counted 70 million inhabitants and extended from Alsace (annexed from France) almost to Warsaw and from the North Sea to the Alps.

The new empire was a decidedly conservative state. Bismarck drew up a constitution that replicated that of Prussia. In the *Reichstag,* the national legislature, it was the Prussian delegation that counted, and votes in Prussia were based on property: one-third of the legislators were elected by the top 5 percent of property holders. The government ministers were responsible not to the Reichstag but to the king. Behind everything was the looming, stern figure of Bismarck, whose power in the imperial government would be almost unchallenged for the next nineteen years. Only the coming of a new monarch, William II in 1888, would loosen the old Junker's grip.

## AUSTRIA-HUNGARY

In the center of the European map stood the Austrian empire. The fourth largest state in population, and third largest in territory, Austria under the guidance of its longtime foreign minister Metternich had played a major role in international affairs for a full generation after 1815. After the national-liberal revolts of 1848 had been crushed, a decade of absolutist rule had ensued under the young kaiser Franz Joseph.

During this decade, considerable internal progress had been made, both economic and cultural, but these successes were outweighed by setbacks in foreign policy and by the refusal of the defeated Hungarian nationalists to participate in central government. Since the Hungarians were the second largest group in the empire and had a long tradition of self-government, their boycott crippled internal politics.

After the defeats in Italy in 1859 and by Prussia in 1866, the kaiser had to come to terms with them. He did so in the **Ausgleich of 1867**, a compromise that divided Austria into roughly equal halves, Austria and Hungary. Each was independent of the other in everything except foreign policy, defense, and some financial matters. Each had its own constitution on generally liberal principles. The *Dual Monarchy,* as it came to be called, was a unique political arrangement held together by the person of the ruler, the army, the Catholic Church, and a supranational bureaucracy and nobility. The Hungarians, given wide-ranging domestic power, were temporarily placated.

The minority peoples within the empire—Czechs, Slovaks, Croats, Serbs, Italians, and others—were less satisfied (see Map 36.4). Those living in Hungary were now under the uncompromising domination of the highly nationalistic Hungarians (Magyars), which they strongly resented. Those in Austria were subordinate to the Austro-Germans, and for a time, the internal affairs of this half of the Dual Monarchy were more harmonious. But by the 1890s, the "national" question was heating up here as well. The fairly liberal, constitutional government was paralyzed by the obstructionist minorities in Parliament. To get anything done, the emperor had to violate his own constitution and rule by decree. Austria-Hungary became the prime European example of the negative aspects of nationalism.

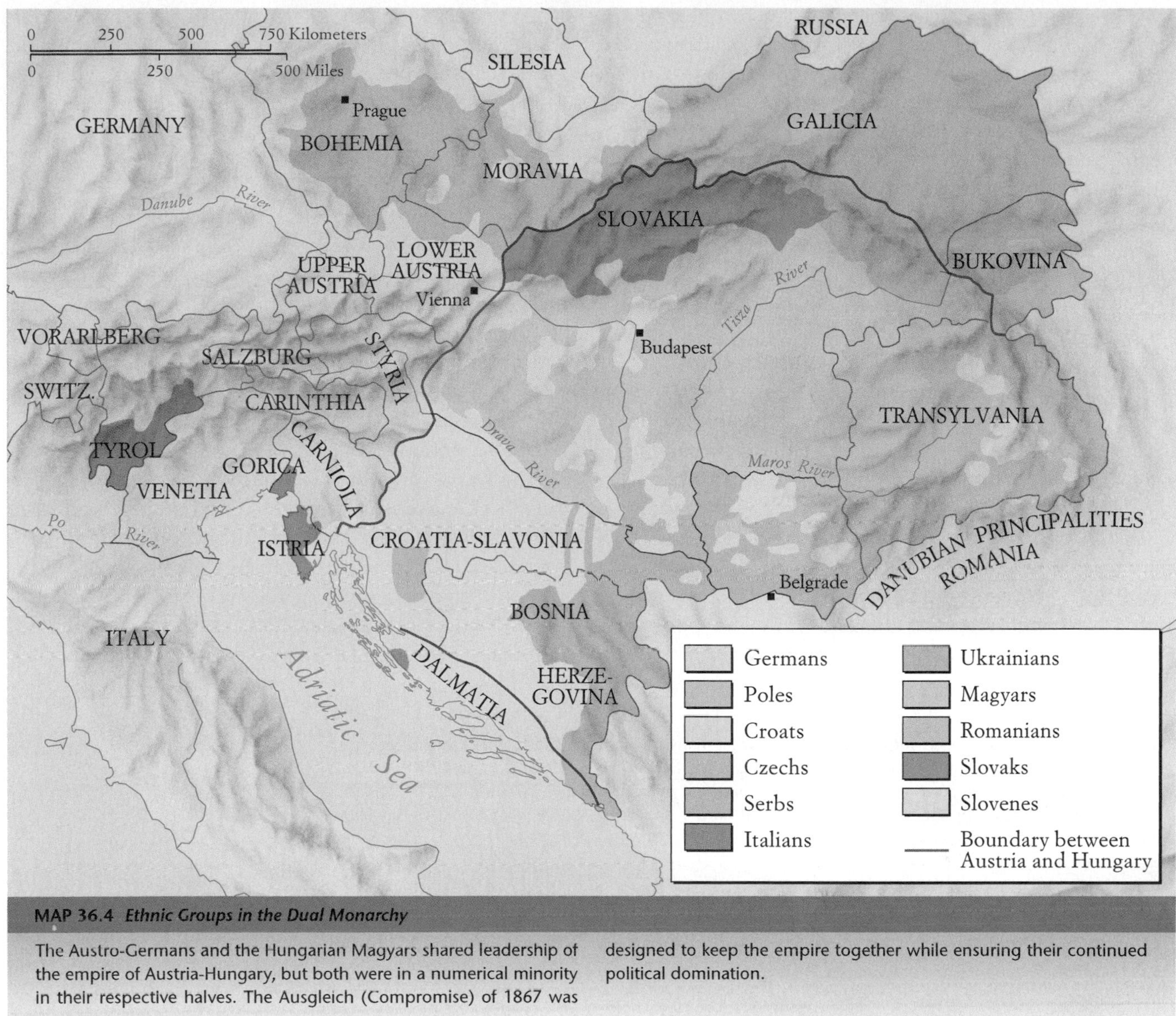


**MAP 36.4** *Ethnic Groups in the Dual Monarchy*

The Austro-Germans and the Hungarian Magyars shared leadership of the empire of Austria-Hungary, but both were in a numerical minority in their respective halves. The Ausgleich (Compromise) of 1867 was designed to keep the empire together while ensuring their continued political domination.

## The United States

At its independence from Britain, the United States was still an agrarian society, with its 4 million inhabitants concentrated along the eastern coast. Skilled tradesmen and master craftsmen were in short supply, and 85 percent of the labor force were farmers and their auxiliary helpers and servants. Even in the urbanized areas of New England and the mid-Atlantic region, as late as 1800 there was practically no large-scale commercial production.

### *Industrial Progress*

By the Civil War, seventy years later, this situation had changed markedly. Thanks to steady waves of immigrants from Europe and slaves from Africa, the United States had more inhabitants than Great Britain—about 30 million. Half a dozen cities had populations of more than 100,000, and farm labor now made up less than half of the total. The dependence on British engineering and machinery that had characterized the first generation after independence (and made the United States the best customer outside of Europe for British exporters) was now entirely gone. American manufacturers and industrial techniques were rapidly proving they could compete throughout the world.

New England was the original center of American industry. Factories producing consumer goods such as textiles and shoes, harnesses and wagons, and metal tools and kitchenware located there. They took advantage of both the abundant waterpower provided by the many rivers and the large pool of labor from the overcrowded and poverty-stricken rural areas. New England's expanding population had long since exceeded the supply of reasonably arable farmland. The new immigrants who came by the tens of thousands in the 1830s and 1840s often found they had only two choices: they could try the unsettled frontier life in the West or go to work in a factory, railroad, mine, or construction site, becoming employees of others in one capacity or another. Most chose the latter mode of living, believing its rewards were safer and more predictable.

Mill towns such as Lowell, Massachusetts, and Bridgeport, Connecticut, became common. They were similar in many ways to those in England but less dreary and unsanitary because of cheaper land and a different building style. Compared to the early industrial towns in Europe, where workers for the most part faced exploitation and limited horizons, American towns offered a degree of democracy and social mobility. Although the stories of Horatio Alger ascents from rags to riches were mostly myths, Americans generally did have far more opportunities to improve their condition than were available to the working class in Europe. The belief that a relatively high degree of economic equality and opportunity was and must remain open to Americans permanently shaped American political and social ideals.

## The Nature of U.S. Industrialization

Three characteristics of U.S. industrialization are especially notable. The first was the enormous advantage that an imposing array of natural resources gave the American industrialist and entrepreneur. No other country in the world approached the riches to be found on and under the American earth of the mid-nineteenth century. Added to these was the steady stream of immigrant labor, much of it in the prime of life and composed of the most flexible and ambitious elements.

The second was the advantage of not being the pioneer, a characteristic the United States shared with all other industrializing nations outside of Great Britain. Americans were able to use British know-how and capital, and they avoided some of the technical and financial blind alleys that the English had experienced in their initial stages. By midcentury, the U.S. entrepreneurs in such

**Protest and Repression.** This engraving illustrates what many middle-class British and European people feared would be the inevitable result of labor organization. In 1887, a contingent of socialist workers attempted to hold a protest parade against current government policies, and at St. Martin's Lane in London were violently broken up by the "bobbies." Britain was among the last of the Western countries to allow unions and the right of strikers to demonstrate.

Mary Evans Picture Library

vital areas as land and sea transport, iron making, and mining were catching up to or surpassing their teachers. The U.S. gross industrial product was already as large as that of the rest of Europe outside Britain.

The third characteristic was the rugged individualist, risk-taking nature of capitalism in nineteenth-century America. Men such as the railroad barons Cornelius Vanderbilt and Edward H. Harriman, banking wizard John Pierpont Morgan, and steel makers Andrew Carnegie and Henry Clay Frick came into their own only after the Civil War, when American industry and finance exploded forward. But the practice of enjoying total freedom from governmental and public opinion in one's method of business and use of money was already deeply ingrained and would not be modified until the twentieth century. This tradition stands in contrast to the experiences of both England and the Continent, where government, tradition, or a degree of social conscience exercised some controls over the way the early industrialists made and spent their money.

## The Modern Nation-State

We have seen that in the quarter-century between 1850 and 1875, great political changes occurred in several major European states: Russia, France, Italy, Germany, and Austria-Hungary (review Map 36.1). These changes were accompanied by sweeping changes in the economy and the structure of society. Toward the period's end, the Second Industrial Revolution—powered by petroleum and electricity—was in full swing, bringing technological advances that had a direct impact on the everyday lives of everyday people.

What emerged in Europe and the United States during these years was in fact the modern nation-state, in which an ethnic group (the nation) exercises control over a territory (the state) through domination and mass participation in government. Its political-governmental outlines had been initiated in the French Revolution but were not perfected until the industrial-technical breakthroughs of the late nineteenth century.

A host of familiar concepts first came into daily life during this period, including the following:

- Mass political parties electing legislatures and executives who were more or less responsible to their voters
- Mass school systems turning out disciplined, trained minds to take over the technical tasks of a much more complex society and economy
- Labor unions representing the rapidly increasing numbers of workers negotiating with the representatives of impersonal corporations

All of these developments were characterized by a large group, a mass or class, coming into a predominant position, while the individual and his or her idiosyncracies, desires, inclinations, and so forth receded into the background.

## The New Imperialism

The last half of the nineteenth century also witnessed an extraordinary surge in Western activity in the non-Western world. While the "scramble for Africa" was the most spectacular example (see Chapter 38), much of Asia and the Pacific islands were also the objects of a huge landgrab by the United States and Japan as well as the European powers.

What was behind this sudden burst of imperial expansion? One factor was the conviction in the European capitals that a state must either expand its power and territory or watch them shrink. There could be no standing still in the race for international respect. Another factor was the coming of the oceangoing steamship in the 1860s. With its ability to carry much larger cargoes over much longer distances on a cost-efficient basis, the steamship changed the rules of international maritime trade. Now it became imperative for trading nations to obtain secure refueling harbors, which meant assured military control over a far-flung network of colonial ports.

The third factor behind imperialism was that many statesmen assumed that new colonies would soak up the excess production of industrial consumer goods that was already looming in Europe and the United States. This economic consideration was generally accepted as a rationale for the industrialized nations to secure new markets in what we now term the *developing countries*.

Finally, and by no means least, many well-intentioned folk at all levels of American and European society felt that it was, in Rudyard Kipling's phrase, the "**white man's burden**" to "civilize" the Asians and Africans, whether they desired that happy state or not. In other words, what was happening to the non-Western world was not a power play by rapacious foreign exploiters but an act of duty toward fellow humans who—perhaps without acknowledging it—needed the West's magnanimous aid. The combination of all these factors in varying degrees justified to both government and citizens the surge of Western military and economic power into the Asiatic and African lands that we examined in Part Four.

## Summary

The 1860s and 1870s produced major changes in almost all of the political and territorial maps of continental Europe. The modern nation-state with its mass-participatory institutions was coming into existence, although its pace varied from place to place. In Russia, attempts at basic reform fell short because of the Court's and nobility's fearfulness and reluctance to allow the people—particularly the newly liberated serfs—a full share in governing themselves. Instead, the aborted political reforms resulted in the growth of a revolutionary movement that would blossom in the early twentieth century. In France, the empire of Napoleon III brought progress internally but failed in foreign policy and was destroyed by the lost war with Prussia. Italy was finally unified in the 1860s, in part voluntarily and in part through conquest by the kingdom of Sardinia-Piedmont. What emerged, however, was two Italies, south and north, that had little in common and would remain isolated from each other for generations.

The German chancellor Bismarck was the most successful of the statesmen who attempted to realize national destiny. Unified by war and nationalist fervor, Germans entered into a Prussia-dominated empire after 1871 and immediately became the most potent military force on the Continent. One of the countries the new empire surpassed was Austria-Hungary, a former rival that was now defeated militarily and split by conflicting nationalisms.

In the United States, steady industrial growth on a regional level in New England was greatly expanded on a national scale after the Civil War. By the end of the century, the American economy rivaled Germany's for leadership of the industrial world. In the last half of the century, the West engaged in a new imperialism that was driven by disparate motives and particularly focused on Asia and Africa.

## Identification Terms

Test your knowledge of this chapter's key concepts by defining the following terms. If you can't recall the meaning of certain terms, refresh your memory by looking up the boldfaced term in the chapter, turning to the Glossary at the end of the book, or working with the flashcards that are available on the *World Civilizations* Companion Website **http://history.wadsworth.com/adler04**.

Ausgleich of 1867
Austro-Prussian War
Crimean War
Czar Alexander II
Franco-Prussian War
Great Reforms
*grossdeutsch*
intelligentsia
*kleindeutsch*
Paris Commune of 1871
Piedmont
Third Republic of France
white man's burden

## Test Your Knowledge

Test your knowledge of this chapter by answering the following questions. Complete answers appear at the end of the book. You may also take this quiz interactively and find even more quiz questions on the *World Civilizations* Companion Website: **http://history.wadsworth.com/adler04**.

1. The biggest single governmental problem in mid-nineteenth-century Russia was how to
   a. defend the enormous borders against simultaneous attacks.
   b. make the czar's government more efficient.
   c. bring the serfs into the national economy.
   d. bring the military into the modern technical age.
   e. industrialize the country enough for it to compete with other countries.

2. The Paris Commune was
   a. an attempt to impose a socialist regime under Karl Marx on France.
   b. an imaginative attempt to introduce democracy through popular vote.
   c. an uprising against the imperial government that had lost a war.

d. a kind of new religion prompted by anti-Christian radicals.
e. a group of Parisian artists who gathered to support each other in perfecting their craft.

3. Cavour's role in unifying Italy was that of
a. the diplomat-statesman.
b. the rabble-rousing tribune of the people.
c. the military commander.
d. the right-hand man of the pope.
e. the author of the Italian constitution.

4. Garibaldi's contribution to Italy's unity is best described as that of
a. the militant romantic.
b. the calculating politician.
c. the religious prophet.
d. the financial wizard.
e. the judicial father-figure.

5. The crucial question for Bismarck as Prussia's chancellor in the 1860s was how to
a. strengthen the army.
b. crush the socialists' opposition.
c. unite the German people politically.
d. strengthen the constitutional rights of the citizens.
e. use his military to best effect.

6. The Franco-Prussian War represented first and foremost
a. a major shift in the European balance of power.
b. a victory of a land power over a naval one.
c. a lesson to would-be autocrats such as Napoleon III that the citizens' will could not be ignored in modern politics.
d. the rising powers of the socialists in dictating policy to government.
e. a victory of a naval power over a land one.

7. The most serious problem facing late-nineteenth-century Austria was
a. the constant rebellions of the peasantry.
b. the friction among the various nationalities.
c. the pressure against its borders from the rising power of Germany.
d. the lack of policy continuity at the top—that is, on the throne.
e. the lack of a strong military.

8. The United States became one of the top industrial powers
a. after the Civil War.
b. through profiting from the free labor of black slaves.
c. as soon as New England had been colonized.
d. by the expansion across the Mississippi River.
e. by stealing ideas from the British.

9. One significant aspect of the modern nation-state is
a. the development of independent thought and action among individuals.
b. the need for close ties between church and state.
c. the subordination of the individual to the community.
d. an increase in social welfare spending.
e. a greater tolerance for members of opposing groups.

10. The "new imperialism" differed from the older variety by being more
a. oriented toward the Pacific Rim lands.
b. closely supervised by government officials.
c. concerned with the state than with the rights of individuals.
d. individualistic in its leadership.
e. driven by industrial market considerations.

## InfoTrac College Edition

Visit the source collections at

**http://infotrac.thomsonlearning.com**

and use the Search function with the following key terms:

Crimean War    Habsburg or Hapsburg

## Wadsworth History Website Resources

Visit the World History Resource Center at **http://history.wadsworth.com/world** for a wealth of general resources, and the *World Civilizations* Companion Website at **http://history.wadsworth.com/adler04** for resources specific to this textbook.

## HistoryNow

Enter *HistoryNow* using the access card that is available for *World Civilizations*. *HistoryNow* will assist you in understanding the content in this chapter with lesson plans generated for your needs. In addition, you can read the following documents, and many more, online:

Otto von Bismarck, *Memoirs*

Otto von Bismarck, "Letter on the Capture of Napoleon III"

*The Islamic religion is a religion of unity throughout. It is not a religion of conflicting principles but is built squarely on reason, while Divine revelation is its surest pillar.*
Shaykh Muhammad Abduh

# 37 The Islamic World and India, 1600–1917

The Decline of the Muslim Empires
The Strengths and Weaknesses of Ottoman Civilization
The Decline of the Ottoman Empire
Safavid and Mughal Decline

The Muslim Countries until World War I

Reforms of the Muslim Ruling Elites
The Tanzimat
Egypt and Sudan under Muhammad Ali and Khedive Ismail
Reforms under the Iranian Shahs

Social and Intellectual Responses
Wahhabi Fundamentalism and Jihad
The Salafiyya Movement
Arab Nationalism

| | |
|---|---|
| 1500s–1722 | Safavid Empire in Persia |
| 1526–1857 | Mughal Empire in India |
| early 1600s | Ottoman decline begins |
| c. 1700–1830 | External attacks on Ottoman Empire |
| late 1700s | Wahhabist movement begins |
| 1880–1898 | Mahdi rebellion in Sudan |
| 1890s | Beginnings of Salafiyya and Arab nationalist movements |

For the great Islamic empires, the seventeenth and eighteenth centuries were a time of steady social and political decline and loss of power against the West. The European counteroffensive against Islam had begun already in the Middle Ages, as Iberian Crusaders fought for the reconquest of Spain and Portugal, and French, German, and English armies tried to retake Palestine, albeit unsuccessfully. Until the sixteenth century, the civilization and armies of Islam enjoyed the advantage and there remained a standoff between Europe and the great Muslim empires, but by the mid-eighteenth century the European Renaissance and the Scientific Revolution, which was perhaps its most important byproduct, altered the balance of power in Europe's favor. European fleets invaded the Indian Ocean, defeating the navies of the Ottoman sultans and their Indian allies, and occupied the most important commercial centers from Mozambique to Macao. Slowly, too, the battle for control of the Mediterranean shifted in favor of Venice and the Habsburgs and their Spanish allies after a key naval victory that was fought off the coast of Italy, at Lepanto, in 1571. On land, a "Holy League," organized by the pope in the late 1600s and led by the Ottomans' old rivals the Habsburgs of Austria, gained the military advantage in the Balkans. By the time of Catherine the Great, Russian armies began driving the Ottomans and Safavids out of their possessions around the Caspian and Black seas.

Since the eighteenth century, Islamic peoples and states have remained on the defensive as Western imperialism and ideas have created steady inroads into their midst. The eighteenth- and nineteenth-century responses of Islam to these incursions are the same paradigms that are still with the world today. The initial responses took the form of state-directed reforms that tried to control and limit the impact of Western ideas, particularly those concerning religion and culture, but the more enduring responses were those broader ones that arose out of Islamic leadership and societies as a whole.

## The Decline of the Muslim Empires

### *The Strengths and Weaknesses of Ottoman Civilization*

The strengths of the Ottomans were most evident during the earlier centuries of their rule, as one would expect, and the weaknesses later. But some of each are clear throughout the long reign of the Ottoman dynasty that lasted from about 1300 to 1922. Aside from their military merits, their strengths included extraordinary artistic sensitivity in literature, architecture, and symbolic imagery; a commitment to justice for all, no matter how weak; a tolerance for nonbelievers that was unusual for its time; and a literary language (Turkish with an Arabic-Persian overlay) that was truly an international bond as well as the channel for a rich literature. In economic and administrative affairs, the Ottomans had a far more efficient tax system and better control of their provincial authorities than any European government of the fourteenth through sixteenth centuries. Unfortunately, these institutions were to weaken later on.

Although the sultans were assisted by a vast bureaucracy, among the Ottomans' weaknesses were a government that depended for the most part on the qualities and energy of one or two individuals, the sultan and the grand vizier. It was no accident that the name of the empire was that of its founding figure, Osman (in Turkish, it was called the Osmanli Empire), and of its ruling dynasty. The sultans were not just the principal administrators: the sultanate provided the institutional machinery and energy that drove it. It was the central fact of the empire. Other weaknesses included a theory of government that was essentially military in nature and needed constant new conquests to justify and maintain itself; an almost complete inability to convert the Qur'an-based Sharia code of law to changing necessities in legal administration; a collective blind eye to the importance of secular education and to all types of technology; and an excessive reverence for tradition, which produced the kind of stagnation that follows from excessive conservatism.

From the middle of the 1700s on, the weaknesses of the Ottoman state in Europe rendered it prey to an increasingly aggressive West. First the Habsburg Dynasty in Vienna, then the Russian Romanovs went on the counterattack against Turkey in Europe, driving back its frontiers step by step (see Map 37.1). In the early 1800s, rising national consciousness among the native peoples of the Balkans made them rebel against an Ottoman control that had become increasingly intolerant and oppressive as it

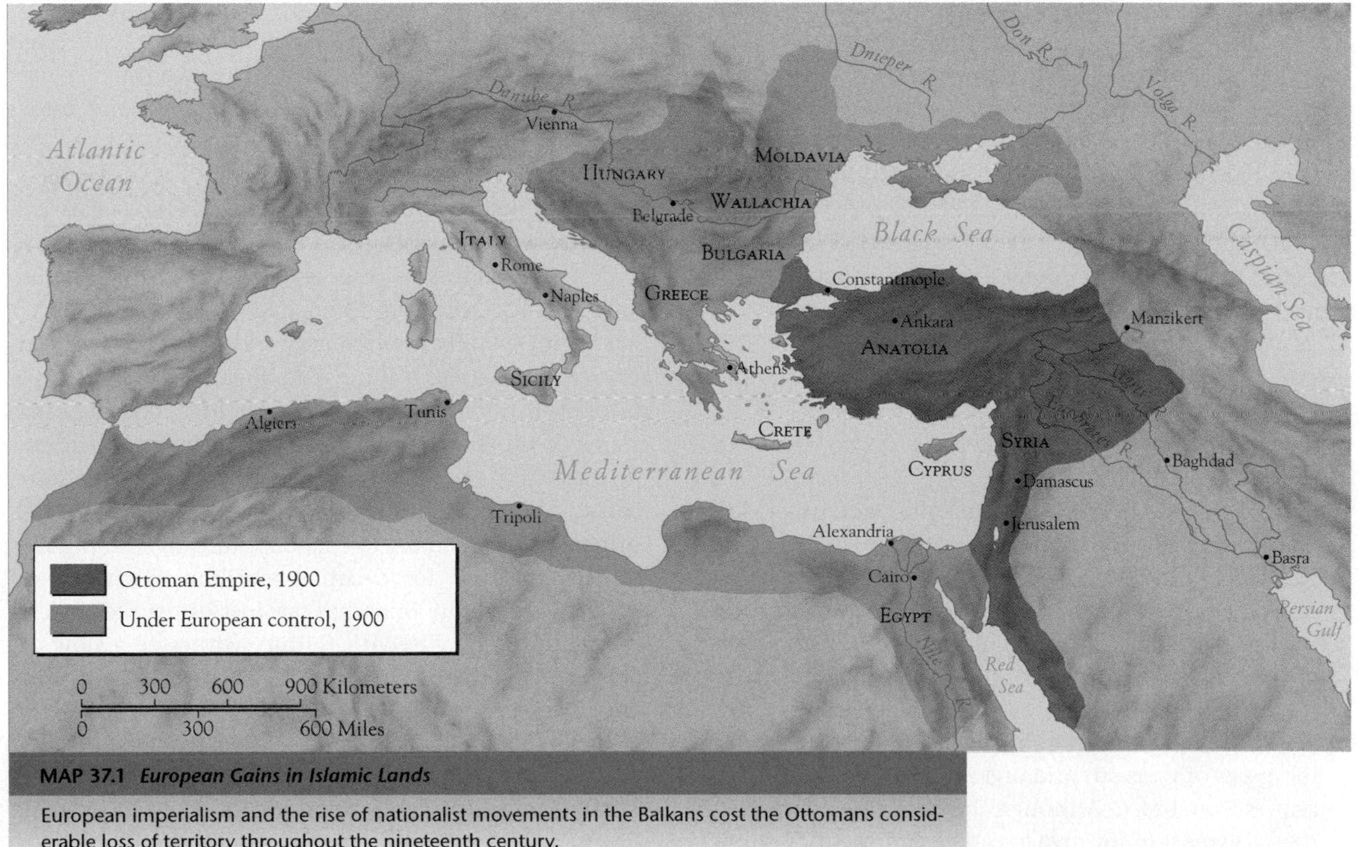


**MAP 37.1** ***European Gains in Islamic Lands***

European imperialism and the rise of nationalist movements in the Balkans cost the Ottomans considerable loss of territory throughout the nineteenth century.

declined. The European powers provided them with encouragement and assistance until the Turks' domain was reduced to Bulgaria, Albania, and northern Greece. At that point, about 1830, the external attacks ceased when the aggressors became wary of one another. The "sick man of Europe" was allowed to linger on his deathbed until 1918 only because his heirs could not agree on the division of the estate.

## The Decline of the Ottoman Empire

Suleiman's reign (1520–1566) was the high point of the sultan's authority and also of the efficiency and prestige of the central government. Beginning with Suleiman's son and successor Selim the Sot (!), many of the sultans became captives of their own viziers and of the intrigues constantly spun within the harem. After 1603, rather than exposing young princes to the rigors of military service, as had been past practice, the sultans began to restrict their sons to being reared entirely within the harem. There, as the sultanate began to decline, the power of the harem and the court bureaucracy grew. More and more, young princes were subject to manipulation by court eunuchs and the sultans' many wives and concubines, who vied for power or to see their sons succeed to the throne. Whichever prince succeeded to the throne, this practice gravely weakened his fitness to rule.

Nevertheless, the empire did not run straight downhill after 1600. Once every few decades, a dedicated grand vizier or a strong-willed sultan attempted to reverse the decay. He would enforce reforms, sweep out the corrupt or rebellious officials in one province or another, and make sure the army was obedient, but then the rot would set in again. By the end of the 1700s, effective reversal was becoming impossible.

Besides the personal qualities of the sultan, several other factors contributed to the long decline:

1. *Economic.* Starting around 1550, the shift of European trade routes from the Muslim-controlled Near and Middle East to the Atlantic Ocean (and later the Pacific Ocean) dealt a heavy, long-term blow to Ottoman prosperity.
2. *Military.* After the 1570s, the Janissaries and other elite units were allowed to marry and settle down in a given garrison, which gradually eroded their loyalties to the central government and allowed them to become local strongmen with local sympathies, often allying with local craft guilds and in conflict with government interests. Moreover, by the seventeenth century the Ottomans reached the limits of expansion possible with the types of weapons and organization on which their armies were based. Although the Ottoman armies had been the most innovative in earlier centuries (for example, in the use of artillery and firearms), a conservative resistance to further change and nepotism set in, particularly among the Janissary corps. The repeated failures of Ottoman armies to win decisively when far from their winter quarters in Istanbul meant that the military initiative passed to the Europeans by the late 1600s.
3. *Technological.* From the seventeenth century on, the Ottomans failed to comprehend how Western technology and science were changing. Increasingly, they found themselves unready when confronted in tests of power. They almost always responded by attempting to ignore the unpleasant realities. They failed to acknowledge or give up old ways when the situation demanded change. This characteristic was spectacularly apparent in military sciences, where the once-pioneering Turks fell far behind the West in all spheres, including training, organization, weapons, and tactics.

## Safavid and Mughal Decline

None of the Safavid rulers who followed Akbar the Great matched his statesmanship. Consequently, by the 1700s, the Safavids had disappeared as a dynasty. In contrast to the Ottomans and Mughals, they had been unable to advance from an empire relying on its original tribal alliance to a centralized bureaucratic empire. Though they had tried, with the help of Georgian Janissary-type infantries, in the end they fell victim to invading Afghan tribesmen and a renewal of tribal competition in Iran through most of the 1700s. At the end of the century, a new dynasty, the Qajars, established themselves, and under them Iran continued to remain under tribal rule. The Qajars, however, tried with mixed results to bureaucratize Iran in the course of the nineteenth century.

In India, Aurangzeb (ruled 1656–1707), though a triumphant warrior, was responsible for reversing the climate of toleration that Akbar had introduced and that had been generally maintained for the ensuing half century. Aurangzeb was a confirmed Muslim, and he reintroduced a distinctly Islamic character to public life. This change heightened the latent frictions between the ruling class and their Hindu, Zoroastrian, Jain, and (few) Christian subjects. Although his large, efficient, and tax-eating army was too big to challenge directly, Aurangzeb's rule set the stage for eventual rebellion by the Hindu majority, led by the Marathas, against his weaker successors. The entire eighteenth century witnessed a slow decline of the emperor's powers and prestige and a gradual whittling off of the territory he controlled. The latter condition was the result of both internal (Maratha) and external (European) challengers.

In the expanding empires of the Safavids in Persia and the Mughals in India, the appearance of European explorers and traders during the 1500s did not create much of a stir. At that time, the European presence in India was limited to a relative handful of traders in a few ports such as Goa and Calicut.

The Portuguese were the first Europeans to arrive in India, followed by the Dutch, English, and French. By the end of the 1600s, the Portuguese "factories" except Goa had been absorbed first by the Dutch, then by the English. After some tentative skirmishing on the seas (demonstrating that no non-Western force could hold its own against the European navies), the Mughals had settled into a mutually comfortable relationship with the British centered on trade goods in both directions, with luxury goods flowing to the West and firearms going in the opposite direction. The privately owned British East India Company, founded in 1603, was given monopolistic concessions to trade Indian goods, notably tea and cotton cloth, to the West and bring in a few European items in return.

For a long time, the arrangement worked out harmoniously. At times, the East India Company made large profits, though as a whole profits rose and fell wildly, while the members of the Mughal upper class were pleased with their access to European firearms, metal, and fabrics. Within the company's handful of port enclaves, all power over both Englishmen and Indians was vested in the English superintendent, who had strict reminders not to involve himself in local politics.

The arrival of the French in the 1670s put some strain on English–Mughal relations, as Paris was already in competition with London for a colonial empire. Under the brilliant administrator Joseph François Dupleix (Governor-General of French possessions in India, 1742–1754) the French made an effort to enlist the Indians as allies, not just trading partners. The British then responded similarly. By the 1740s, the frequent European wars between Britain and France involved their Indian outposts as well. On the French side, Dupleix commanded tens of thousands of Indian troops. On the British side, Robert Clive was just as active. They fought one another even while the home countries were at peace.

In India as in North America, the Seven Years' War (1756–1763) was the decisive round in the contest. British control of the sea proved more important than French victories on land. By the Treaty of Paris in 1763, control of much of India fell into British hands through the intermediation of the East India Company, but Parliament was by now unwilling to trust such a costly asset entirely to private hands, and a statute in 1773 divided political oversight between London and the company. In the 1780s, Lord Cornwallis (lately, commander-in-chief of the British forces in Virginia) was put in charge of the Indian possessions, and others who followed him crushed the occasional Muslim or Hindu attempts to defy British power. Increasingly, those rajahs who did not obey London's wishes were forcibly replaced by British civil governors. One after another, the many subdivisions of the subcontinent were incorporated into the British-ruled empire.

## The Muslim Countries until World War I

The three Muslim empires of earlier times in Asia were either overthrown or much weakened by the nineteenth century. The Mughals in India, the Safavid Persians, and the Ottoman Turks had been overwhelmed by Western military and financial powers where they came into conflict with them. By the mid-1800s, the British had made most of India an outright colony, and Persia was effectively divided into Russian and British spheres. The Ottomans had been repeatedly defeated by Russia in Europe and had been forced to watch as even the façade of their political overlordship in North Africa faded away and was lost to invading French armies after 1830 (see Chapter 38). Napoleon invaded Egypt in 1798, and while he and his army were expelled by an Anglo-Ottoman alliance in 1804, for all practical purposes Egypt became independent under its new military governor, Muhammad Ali Pasha. Finally, in 1882, Britain invaded and occupied Egypt, adding that country to its worldwide empire. Only in the Middle East did some substance of Turkish control remain.

But these political and military weaknesses were not the only indicators of decline. The Islamic world would have to overcome a series of psychological and technical barriers if it were to regain its equality with the West. The fundamental tradition of Islam, wherever it attained power, was to understand itself as a community of righteous believers who were actively spreading the sole authentic word of God and establishing his rule on Earth. For a thousand years, since the time of the prophet Muhammad, this viewpoint had been the driving force behind the expansion of the religion around the globe.

From about the mid-eighteenth century, however, this view could no longer be sustained, as the unbelievers took over former Muslim territories from the Balkans to the islands of Southeast Asia. The learned and powerful men of Islam reacted in several ways. Some assumed that these reverses were temporary and would soon be regained. Others looked—for the first time—to the West for inspiration in technology and, above all, military science, to help them to counter and overcome Western superiority.

Unfortunately for Muslim ambitions, the first trend prevailed over the second. The ulama and the imams of the Ottoman domains could not accept the secularism of post–French Revolution Europe, but a few grudgingly recognized that Muslim practice would have to incorporate some Western elements if it was not to be utterly overwhelmed.

Yet they still believed in the inherent superiority of the community of God (*Dar al-Islam*) over the unbelievers (*Dar al-Harb*). As a result, they only sporadically and inconsistently attempted to adopt some European science and technology without changing the conservative cast of Islamic education and government, which frowned on innovation.

A vast body of traditions and prejudices opposed those few who attempted to bring large-scale Western ideas into Islam. Even some of the Ottoman sultans who recognized that resisting the West without the assistance of Western science and education would be hopeless were unable to carry through their plans of reform against the twin obstacles of tradition and fatalistic apathy. By the mid-nineteenth century, Islam, as a religious community and as a political association, was in a nearly moribund state. Unwilling to adapt beyond a few superficial phenomena, the Muslim nations were seemingly destined to a future in which they were the permanent pawns of the European powers.

## Reforms of the Muslim Ruling Elites

By the 1890s, this inability to resist external pressure had produced four different responses in the Muslim world. The first of these was simply *ignoring* or *rejecting* the changes that were occurring around them. This was the easiest response, and many of the ulama and the general population continued to take for granted the superiority of all things Islamic over other ways and ideas. The second amounted to attempts at *accommodation,* which began when the ruling elites in the Ottoman Empire, Egypt, and Iran tried to impose limited, largely military reforms. The third was the beginnings of what is now called *Islamic fundamentalism.* The fourth was *pan-Arabism* or *Arab nationalism,* which are related but not identical attempts to create a sense of unity among the Arab peoples of the Middle East and North Africa.

### The Tanzimat

The Ottoman Empire was the first Islamic state to try modernizing along European lines, and in many respects it was the one that experimented the longest and whose attempts ultimately went the deepest in changing Ottoman society as a whole. Egypt and Iran also tried to implement similar reforms in the 1800s. However, in each of these cases the reforms were state-directed—that is, they did not begin as a popular response to the Western challenge—and the ruling elite intended to limit them only to the military sphere.

With the further defeats and losses of territory that came after the Treaty of Karlowitz in 1699, the Ottoman sultans and grand viziers of the eighteenth century finally realized that they had lost the military advantage to the Europeans. To save the sultanate and what remained of the Empire, they had to modernize the Ottoman military machinery. As early as 1719, the grand vizier tried introducing reforms that were essentially conservative: the objective was not a wholesale reform of Ottoman society or Islamic institutions, but rather was limited to improving military instruction. Alas, in 1730, a popular uprising against these "Frankish (European) manners" ended Damad's experiment, and the grand vizier paid for his perceived mistakes by being executed. Other similarly brief and unsuccessful experiments were tried in the following decades. Sultan Selim III was the first to initiate the far-reaching and successful reforms, later called the **Tanzimat** ("New Order") **Reforms**. Beginning in 1793, he tightened government control over the crumbling and corrupt provinces, and created new schools for the training of officers who were to become the backbone of a new, European-style Ottoman army and navy. European instructors were brought in, books were imported—many

Michael Nicholson/Corbis

**Ottoman Sultan Selim III.** Selim was the first to institute the permanent and thoroughgoing reforms of the Ottoman military and administration known as the Tanzimat.

from France and reflecting the new thought of the European Enlightenment—and a new library was made available to the students. Again, though, in 1807, another uprising of the ulama and the Janissaries deposed Selim and temporarily set back the reforms.

The next sultan, Mahmud II, permanently reignited the reorganization in 1826 when he ended the opposition of the Janissaries and the ulama once and for all after luring them into an ambush. Immediately afterward, he dismantled the Janissary corps, banned the religious (Sufi) brotherhoods, and seized all sources of funding previously controlled by the ulama (waqfs, for example). New reforms promptly followed, as the sultan and his viziers created schools for training students in European languages and sciences, and set new controls over education, administration, and communications. When Abdul Mejid succeeded to the sultanate in 1839, he added even more far-reaching reforms, called the Tanzimat. The **Rose Chamber Rescript of 1839** revolutionized Islamic society by declaring the legal equality of all Ottoman subjects, regardless of religion or ethnicity. In the succeeding decades (1839–1861), Mejid reinforced the terms of the Rose Chamber Rescript by replacing the moribund feudal estate system with individual land ownership and by creating a new law code modeled on European paradigms and new courts to administer it equally to all their subjects.

Up to this point, the reforms remained state-directed, but in 1861, the Tanzimat entered a new phase. A new sultan, Abdul Aziz, proved to be a reactionary who was opposed to further liberalizations of Islamic law and society. By then the direction and extent of reform had begun to slip from state control. Decades of training Ottoman subjects in European sciences and ideas (including those of Enlightenment liberalism) had created a broader base and momentum for change. A group of young intellectuals and journalists, called the **Young Ottomans**, had started to exert pressure for the political liberalization of Ottoman society. Using European nations as their model, they clamored to replace the sultanate with a constitutional monarchy and parliamentary system. In 1876, when Abdul Aziz died, they and other reformers within the government supported Abdul Hamid II for the succession, on the promise that he would liberalize the government. The reformers got their constitution, and an election was held for the first time in Ottoman history for the creation of a parliament. Once in power, however, Abdul Hamid proved to be just another autocrat: he ended the Tanzimat by dismissing the parliament and suspending the constitution. Throughout his long reign (1876–1909), he used a vast system of spies to put down all resistance and impose strict control over all Ottoman subjects. He also gradually began to ally the empire with Germany. A nationalist reform party of army officers deposed him in 1909 and set up a military *junta* in place of the sultanate. Called the Committee for Union and Progress (CUP), it continued to govern using the policies and methods Abdul Hamid had established. More important, perhaps, the CUP led the Ottoman Empire into World War I as an ally of Germany.

Historical Picture Archive/Corbis

**A Janissary.** This portrait shows one of the Sultan's Janissary corps as they appeared about the time of Sultan Selim III. At one time the elite of the Ottoman army, the Janissaries had become largely reactionary by the eighteenth century. It was a revolt of the Janissaries that ended Selim's reforms in 1806–07.

Bettmann/Corbis

**SULTAN ABDUL HAMID II.** The last sultan of the Ottoman Empire and the last Islamic caliph, Abdul Hamid ended the Tanzimat. Throughout his long reign from 1876 to 1909, he suppressed liberal reforms and the growing Arab nationalist movement.

## *Egypt and Sudan under Muhammad Ali and Khedive Ismail*

Appointed as the Ottoman viceroy to Egypt in 1805, **Muhammad Ali Pasha** filled the political vacuum that had been left in Egypt after the forced withdrawal of French forces in 1805. His reign in Egypt was highly unusual for two reasons: (1) its longevity, lasting until 1848, and (2) his success in modernizing the armed forces. He accomplished the first of these goals through bribery and intimidation: regular gifts of large sums of cash were sent to the sultan and influential members of the Ottoman Court to ensure that he would not be removed from his position. By such methods, he succeeded not only in ensuring that he would remain as Egypt's governor, but also that the position would remain in his family. (The last of his line, King Farouk, was deposed in 1952.)

Far more important for Egypt, though, were Muhammad Ali's reforms. An Albanian by birth, he had served in the Ottoman forces against the French. In those years, he had become utterly convinced of the military superiority of European armies, so to strengthen his position he implemented a far-reaching program of military reforms similar to what was occurring in Istanbul at that time. Above all, he turned to the French for his models. Missions were dispatched to France to pursue studies in military science, engineering, and medicine. He brought scores of French technicians and officers to Egypt to advise him. He forcefully conscripted thousands of Egyptian peasants, whom he outfitted with the latest weapons, and placed them under the command of Turkish and European officers. To help support these measures, he established munitions industries and created a modern system of schools and public health. He encouraged private landownership, and sugar and cotton were added as important new cash crops. State monopolies of vital industries such as sugar refining, plus textile, iron, and weapons manufacturing, were established. Emboldened by his successes, the viceroy also expanded his holdings outside of Egypt. Much like the ancient pharaohs, he sent his armies up the Nile to occupy the Sudan. The Egyptians founded the city of Khartoum as their primary command center. In 1838, he sent his son to invade Syria, challenging Ottoman authority there. Unfortunately, this aggressiveness against the Ottoman sultanate invited Anglo-French intervention, and the viceroy's navy was destroyed in a battle fought off the coast of Greece in 1839. This disappointment set back the Egyptian reform movement for several decades.

Under Muhammad Ali, foreign investment played a key part in Egypt's modernization. This continued under his successors, particularly in the building of Egypt's railroads and the construction of the Suez Canal, which British and French investors largely capitalized. This created a difficult problem for Egypt's rulers, who were forced to wrestle with the enormous debts they incurred to foreign banks and other investors. The third of Muhammad Ali's sons to rule, Ismail, greatly added to the problem because he loved everything European. It was his fondest desire to make Egypt into a European nation, and he hoped to be accepted by European leaders as one of them. Therefore, when the Suez Canal was opened for the first time in 1869, he spent lavishly on a huge fête, to which he invited all of the European heads of state and royal families. To impress them, he commissioned the Italian composer, Verdi, to compose an opera, *Aida,* and he rebuilt large parts of Cairo and Alexandria to resemble Paris. Ultimately, he bankrupted his country and was forced to sell Egypt's shares in the Suez Canal Company to Britain. Worse, he was forced by the European powers to turn over the management of Egypt's treasury to a committee made up largely of his principal investors. An uprising of army officers who opposed this European intervention finally forced Britain to occupy Egypt in 1882 in order to protect its interests in the canal. Britain installed Ismail's son as the new khedive, and they remained as a colonial occupier in Egypt until 1922.

**Muhammad Ali Pasha of Egypt.** Many consider Muhammad Ali to have been the founder of modern Egypt. His reforms of the army reached into many other aspects of Egyptian life, including its economy.

Bettmann/Corbis

**The Harem of a Cairo Shaykh, ca. 1870.** The harem actually was the private quarters of a Muslim home, the place where women and children were protected from strangers.

Victoria & Albert Museum, London, UK/Bridgeman Art Library

The Egyptian occupation of the Sudan led to some unexpected resistance, which also entangled the British. Between 1881 and 1885, Muhammad Ahmad, called **the Mahdi** ("the Expected One"), led a successful revolt against Egyptian (and British) presence there. Khedive Ismail sent a British officer, General Charles Gordon, as his governor of the Sudan, but Gordon was killed in an assault by the Mahdi's followers on Khartoum. The Mahdist rebellion combined elements of national resistance to foreign rule and Islamic, fundamentalist reaction against innovations. Following his victory, Muhammad Ahmad formed a government in which he imposed traditional laws and established courts of Islamic judges to enforce Islamic law. Believing he was sent as a savior of Islam, a Mahdi, he believed he communicated directly with God, so he also modified Islam's Five Pillars to support the principle that loyalty to him was part of true belief. Muhammad Ahmad died of typhus six months after the capture of Khartoum, but the Mahdiyya lasted until British forces finally defeated the rebels in 1898 and set up a protectorate over the Sudan.

## *Reforms under the Iranian Shahs*

Under the Safavid shahs and the Qajar Dynasty that replaced them in the eighteenth century, Iran did not experience the full impact of growing European cultural superiority and military might that the Ottoman Empire did in the 1700s. Consequently, it did not start down the path of reform until well into the nineteenth century. Shah Nasir ad-Din was the first Qajar ruler to introduce significant restructuring. Like Selim III and Muhammad Ali Pasha, he tried to reform the shah's army to counter steady Russian encroachment in the Caspian Sea region and British expansion in India. The result was an intensification of military and commercial ties with the West, and gradually Iran was drawn into the world market. As Iranians developed a taste for imports, more turned to growing cash crops such as tobacco, cotton, and opium to pay for imports.

Under pressure from Britain to lower tariffs, Iran imported a flood of cheap European-manufactured goods, putting indigenous producers out of business. Moreover, for help in building modern transport and communications systems, Nasir ad-Din made overly generous concessions to European firms. In 1890, the granting of a tobacco monopoly to a British firm created a serious crisis when, led by a Muslim cleric by the name of Jamal ad-Din al-Afghani, national resistance to foreign interference in Iran broke out. Afghani, fearing Big Power political intervention in Muslim countries such as Iran, convinced local merchants that the concessions would bring harm to local people and compromise Iran's religious and political autonomy. The shah expelled Afghani from the country in 1891, but he was forced in the end to withdraw the monopoly when another cleric declared a national prohibition on the smoking of tobacco. However, the Western control over Iran's mineral and oil rights was established by another concession to the Anglo-Iranian Oil Company, and between 1908 and 1912, Iran began its first exports of oil to the industrial West.

Meanwhile, as happened in Turkey under Young Ottoman leadership in the 1870s, demands for a constitutional and representative government to broaden the government and make it more democratic began circulating among Iran's young, increasingly Western-educated intelligentsia. The catalyst for this movement was Shah Muzaffar ad-Din's attempts at punishing Tehran's merchants for price-fixing. The ulama and young intellectuals united in defending the merchants and demanding reforms to curb the shah's actions. Popular support grew so fast that Shah Muzaffar was obliged to capitulate to the protesters' demands for a constitution and a *Majlis* (National Assembly). In 1907, the Majlis convened for the first time, but the shah's willingness to use military force against the Majlis for many years effectively weakened it. Although the movement for popular reform ended in a partial failure, nationalist feelings had been born in Iran, and the constitution and the popular movement that supported it remained vivid memories among Iranian reformers that had their echoes in the 1950s and in 1979 (Chapter 54).

## Social and Intellectual Responses

### *Wahhabi Fundamentalism and Jihad*

Throughout its long history, Islam has witnessed periodic episodes of revivalism. Sometimes, especially during times when Islam was in crisis, these developments took a decidedly fundamentalist and violent form. At other times, as was the case in the late 1800s, they assumed the character of movements of reform and accommodation. A modern example of the former, violent reaction, was **Wahhabism**, a militant reform begun in the late 1700s when a desert shaykh, Muhammad ibn Abd al-Wahhab (1703–1792), joined forces with a tribal leader, Muhammad ibn Saud (from whom the Saudi royal family is descended). Together, they fought a jihad to purge Islam of sufis, Shi'ites, and all others whom they accused of introducing innovations, which they believed were responsible for the decline of Islam. Largely inspired by the ultraconservative writing of a late-thirteenth-century theologian, Ibn Taymiyya (see Patterns of Belief), the Wahhabis believed that Islam would survive attacks against it by its enemies only by returning to the fundamental sources of the faith, namely the Qur'an and collections of oral traditions (called *hadith*) concerning the prophet Muhammad. Only the example of the primitive Islamic community as it was assumed to have existed at Medina in the time of Muhammad served as an acceptable model to the Wahhabis for Muslim life. Therefore, all Muslims had to be forced to follow that example. Ibn Abd al-Wahhab labeled all who disagreed with this view as heretics deserving of death.

These zealots declared holy war on all neighboring tribes to force them to accept their more purified version of Islam. "Enforcers of obedience" maintained moral order, and they still do so in modern Saudi Arabia. "Objectionable innovations" targeted for destruction even included mosque minarets and grave markers; therefore, they even planned attacks on the tomb of the prophet Muhammad in Medina. In 1802 they destroyed the tomb of the Shi'ite Imam Husayn at Karbala, Iraq. In 1803 they succeeded in capturing Mecca, the holiest city of Islam, and Medina, where they destroyed the markers of Muhammad's grave. The Ottoman sultan, Mahmud II, sent Muhammad Ali Pasha in 1811 to drive them out. As the original fundamentalist sect of Islam, Wahhabism has inspired many similar violent reactions to change, especially to any innovations originating in the West. In the nineteenth century, to a varying extent, it helped inspire resistance to European ideas and imperialism in Africa and the Middle East.

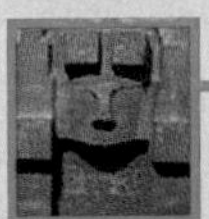

PATTERNS OF BELIEF

## The Founding Figure of Islamic Fundamentalism and Reform

**MANY MUSLIMS TODAY CONSIDER** Taqi al-Din ibn Taymiyya (1263–1328) to have been the leading intellectual of the ultraconservative Hanbali school of Islamic thought in the Middle Ages. His writings inspired the eighteenth-century Wahhabi movement, an Islamic fundamentalist movement founded by Muhammad ibn 'Abd al-Wahhab, and also influenced the reform thought (Salafiyya) of Shaykh Muhammad Abduh and others.

The son of a Hanbali scholar, Ibn Taymiyya received his education in Damascus, where afterward he lived for about fifteen years as a schoolmaster. Living at a time when the Muslim world was divided internally by sectarian differences and under repeated assaults by Christian Crusaders and the Mongol armies (Chapter 17), he sought to overcome the problems of Islam by reviving a strictly literal interpretation of the Qur'an and Islamic law of the prophet Muhammad and by opposing customs and innovations he considered to be illegal innovations, such as sufism and the worshipping of saints. Because of the zeal with which he expressed his opinions, he offended many secular and religious officials. He spent much of his life in various prisons in Cairo, Alexandria, and Damascus, and finally died in prison.

Ibn Taymiyya was convinced of the utter perfection of Islam. Furthermore, as did most ulama, he thought Muhammad had been both the Messenger of God and the perfect Muslim. Reasoning thus, to him later additions to Islam, such as theological speculation, sufism, and saint worship, detracted from the perfection of Islam as it was in Muhammad's days. To solve current problems, he struggled to revive an understanding of Islam as Muhammad and his close companions (*Salaf*, hence the adjective *Salafiyya* sometimes is applied to his Revivalism) had originally defined the faith. Although the ulama of all four schools of Islamic law (*Sharia*) accepted this last point, where Ibn Taymiyya and most Hanbali scholars differed was in their rejection of every other form of Islam, or sources of Islam other than the Qur'an and the traditions of the prophet. He stated that the goal of a true Muslim was not to think or speculate about God, nor to "know" Him, nor love Him, nor to seek Him in any way. Rather, he thought the only legitimate goals for a Muslim were to *carry out* God's will through worshipping Him and obeying Him. Any other form of religious belief and practice for Muslims was mere "innovation" (*bida*), hence unbelief (*kufr*). Therefore, in his words, it was the duty of every Muslim to wage jihad against anyone who failed to subscribe to these beliefs:

> The command to participate in jihad and the mention of its merits occur innumerable times in the Koran and the Sunna. Therefore it is the best voluntary [religious] act that man can perform. . . . Jihad implies all kinds of worship, both in its inner and outer forms. More than any other act it implies love and devotion for God, Who is exalted, trust in Him, the surrender of one's life and property to Him, patience, asceticism, remembrance of God and all kinds of other acts [of worship]. . . . Since lawful warfare is essentially jihad and since its aim is that the religion is God's entirely and God's word is uppermost, therefore according to all Muslims, those who stand in the way of this aim must be fought.

### Analyze and Interpret

In your experience, how do the views of Ibn Taymiyya compare to the views of religious fundamentalists or revivalists of other religions, such as Christian, Jewish, and Hindu fundamentalists?

Source: Rudolph Peters, *Jihad in Classical and Modern Islam* (Princeton, NJ: Markus Wiener Publishers, 1996), pp. 47–49.

Today, Wahhabist-inspired fundamentalism is notorious for fueling Islamic terrorism against America and other Western nations. Fundamentalism was and is marked by a thoroughgoing rejection of Western influences and Western ideas, including such notions as political democracy, religious toleration, the equality of citizens, and various other offshoots of the Age of Enlightenment and the American and French revolutions. To a fundamentalist (the word is a recent appellation), the task of government is to bring about the reign of Allah and his faithful on Earth—nothing less and nothing more. Any obstacles that stand in the way of this process should be swept aside, by persuasion if possible, but by force (jihad) if necessary. There can be no compromise with the enemies of God or with their varied tools and facilitators, such as secular schools, mixed-religion marriages, and nonconfessional parliaments. In the rise of Wahhabism in Arabia and the bitter resistance by Abd al-Qadir's followers to the French in Algeria (see Chapter 38), modern Islamic fundamentalism found its first heroes. Many others would come forth in the twentieth century.

## The Salafiyya Movement

Not all who advocated a return to the early community of Islam did so by demanding the wholesale rejection of all things Western. As we saw previously, Muslims who lived under autocratic regimes (such as the Ottomans and the

Qajars) agitated for Western-style liberal democracies and constitutional governments to replace the systems they had lived under for centuries, but others wanted even more, namely the reform of Islam to permit modern ideas and ways of life to penetrate Islamic societies. Chafing under European occupation of parts of Africa and the Middle East, some Muslim leaders in Egypt and India in the 1890s were distressed that Islamic civilization had fallen hopelessly behind the West, especially in technology and the sciences. One of these concerned leaders was Jamal ad-Din al-Afghani, who urged Muslims to reform themselves in order to find the strength to meet the challenges of the West. Afghani believed that the key to the future of Islam was to reject blind obedience to religious tradition, and he called for Islam to modernize itself.

It was left to the Egyptian shaykh Muhammad Abduh to develop a program of reform. Between 1889 and 1905, Abduh served as the grand mufti and as the rector of Egypt's most prestigious mosque university, the Azhar. In these positions, he was able to influence many students and intellectuals to accept limited modifications of Islamic law and thus admit the teaching of new subjects, such as science and geography. Above all, he realized this change required discarding adherence to tradition that had been the rule since the tenth century. Calling for modernization based on Islamic principles, Abduh and his followers began what came to be known as the **Salafiyya movement**. Rather than simply accepting the ways of the past, even the ways of the early community, as Ibn Taymiyya and the Wahhabists had advocated, Abduh called for returning to the days of the "pious ancestors" (*Salaf,* from which Salafiyya comes) before the tenth century, to the time when Islamic civilization led the world in intellectual experimentation. Firmly adhering to the belief that God favored Muslims, Abduh believed Allah could not desire to see Muslims in their present state of inferiority and subjection to "Christian" Westerners. Rather, he reasoned, God wished the Muslims to return to the days of free intellectual enquiry when they studied all of the sciences. That focus, he believed, would enable them to catch up with the West.

Many of Abduh's ideas spread rapidly in some intellectual circles throughout the Islamic world. Seyyid Ahmad Khan and Muhammad Iqbal advocated similar reforms for the modernization of India, as did Shaykh al-Amin bin Ali Mazrui and Shaykh Abdallah Saleh Farsy in East Africa, for example. Unfortunately, though, most ulama continued to ignore all innovations.

## Arab Nationalism

Pan-Arabism is an outgrowth of Arab national consciousness that began to be articulated in the late nineteenth century, especially among Lebanese and Egyptian Christians. (Note that the word *Arab* or *Arabic* refers to an ethnic group, not a religious one. There are many Arab Christians in Egypt, Lebanon, and Syria, and they were among the leaders of Arab nationalism.) Ottoman recognition of the equality of all Ottoman subjects in the nineteenth century, regardless of religion, meant that they could no longer refuse admission to missionaries to work among the Christian communities of the empire. The establishment of mission schools in Lebanon and Egypt gradually introduced Christian Arabs to the Enlightenment ideas of political liberalism and nationalism for the first time. In Beirut, editors of a few small Christian newspapers called for increased political self-identity among all Arabs, regardless of religion. These ideas spread rapidly into Syria, Egypt, and Iraq, where they appealed especially to anti-Turkish dissidents, who wished to see an end to Ottoman rule. By the 1890s, various vocal Arabic societies had appeared, which advocated political independence from the Ottoman Empire for the Arab provinces.

The reaction of the autocratic Sultan Abdul Hamid to these ideas was predictable: he was able to use his secret police to suppress such talk and hound the leaders of the Pan-Arab movement into hiding. Agents were sent disguised as ulama to exacerbate tensions and traditional rivalries between tribes, clans, and families, as well as between Christians and Muslims. These actions were temporarily alleviated when the officers to the CUP deposed the Sultan in 1909, but soon conservatives within the junta clamped down on Arab aspirations by ordering that all ethnically based organizations be disbanded. None of this action seriously discouraged the Arab nationalist movement, though. In 1905, many were openly promoting the creation of an independent, Arabic-speaking nation, stretching from Iraq to the Suez Canal. By 1913, as the Ottoman Empire was on the brink of entering a world war as an ally of Germany, an Arab Congress met in Paris to hammer out a consensus scheme for an autonomous Arab state. Although the Congress failed to gain the support of the major Western powers that they had hoped for, events during the war soon changed the whole history of the Pan-Arab movement, as well as of the entire Middle East (see Chapter 54).

## Summary

Their worldwide expansion in the Age of Discovery brought Europeans into more frequent and, inevitably, more violent contact with other world civilizations. For many centuries beforehand, Muslims and European Christians had fought across religious frontiers in periodic "holy wars," and in these encounters, both intellectually and militarily, the Muslims generally had enjoyed the upper hand. In the centuries following the Renaissance, the balance of power between Europe and the lands of Islam began shifting slowly in favor of the West, so bewildered Muslims responded in several ways that set the pattern for interactions between Western nations and Muslim peoples that have continued to this day. Although these responses differed considerably, they all shared two features: (1) their continued religious base, and because they were religious, (2) the continued assumption of the superiority of all things Islamic, even to a Western civilization that clearly had become wealthier and more powerful.

Because of this assumption, for example, the first responses of the eighteenth and nineteenth centuries were state-directed and limited to relatively insignificant borrowings from Western technology, particularly military technology. Muslim leaders were willing to learn from the West, provided that what they learned did not affect what they believed were rules for living and truths that Allah had mandated. Inevitably, though, such attempts at maintaining a barrier between science and religion had to fail, especially because what the Muslims coveted, science—hence, the scientific method—derived from a Western revolution in thought that was so highly secular. In the modern era, Westerners learned not to discard their beliefs, but to suspend them in trying to understand and master their world while leaving what happened after death to their faiths. So, in the end, Muslim religious extremists have found that their greatest "enemy" was not Western Christianity, but Western secularism. Islamic civilization, like the medieval civilization that modern Westerners finally discarded, has struggled to separate religion from everyday life.

## Identification Terms

Test your knowledge of this chapter's key concepts by defining the following terms. If you can't recall the meaning of certain terms, refresh your memory by looking up the boldfaced term in the chapter, turning to the Glossary at the end of the book, or working with the flashcards that are available on the *World Civilizations* Companion Website **http://history.wadsworth.com/adler04**.

The Mahdi
Muhammad Ali Pasha
Rose Chamber Rescript of 1839
Salafiyya movement
Tanzimat Reforms
Wahhabism
Young Ottomans

## Test Your Knowledge

Test your knowledge of this chapter by answering the following questions. Complete answers appear at the end of the book. You may also take this quiz interactively and find even more quiz questions on the *World Civilizations* Companion Website: **http://history.wadsworth.com/adler04**.

1. A major source of internal trouble for the Ottoman rulers of the eighteenth and nineteenth centuries was
   a. the spreading atheism of most of the Turkish upper class.
   b. the professional military units called Janissaries.
   c. the missionaries from Europe in the Ottoman cities.
   d. the attacks from the Mughal Empire of India.
   e. their inability to control their police forces.
2. The original objective of the British East India Company in India was to
   a. study native customs.
   b. use India as a base for further Asian conquests
   c. conquer and convert the Hindus to Christianity.
   d. colonize southern India for the British Crown.
   e. control the tea and cotton trade with Europe.

3. Which of these was not cited as a reason why the Ottoman Empire weakened after the seventeenth century?
   a. The empire became militarily overextended.
   b. New trade routes bypassed Ottoman territories, weakening the economy.
   c. Later sultans were less well prepared to rule, passing much of their youth in the harem.
   d. The sultans failed to perceive the growing threats posed by the Western powers.
   e. Islamic attitudes and institutions helped to block needed changes.
4. Which of the following is/are true about the Tanzimat Reforms?
   a. They were initiated and directed by the sultans' government.
   b. They were popularly supported from their inception.
   c. They failed in their objectives.
   d. They were forced on the Ottomans by the European powers.
   e. Both a and d are true.
5. The Rose Chamber Rescript was significant because it
   a. ended the Ottoman monarchy.
   b. advocated the creation of a new, modern army.
   c. established the legal equality of all Ottoman subjects.
   d. banned Islamic law.
   e. ended the feudal system of military estates.
6. An Islamic leader who influenced movements for reform in both Iran and Egypt and who advocated Islamic modernization was
   a. Nasir ad-Din.
   b. Muhammad Abduh.
   c. Mahmud II.
   d. Abdul Hamid II.
   e. Al-Afghani.
7. In Iran, national resistance to a reform-minded government finally gelled around the issue of
   a. government attempts to stop merchants from fixing prices.
   b. efforts by the Shahs to modernize their armies.
   c. attempts by the government to regulate education.
   d. government concessions of monopolies to foreigners.
   e. Both a and b
8. Many people today trace the roots of Islamic fundamentalist violence to
   a. the Salafiyya movement.
   b. the Sudanese Mahdiyya.
   c. the writings of Ibn Taymiyya.
   d. eighteenth-century Wahhabism.
   e. the establishment of the kingdom of Saudi Arabia.
9. In many respects, the founder of modern Egypt was
   a. Nasir ad-Din.
   b. Mahmud II.
   c. Selim III.
   d. Muhammad Ali.
   e. Khedive Ismail.
10. The Mahdist uprising in the Sudan was a result of
   a. efforts by the Egyptian Khedive to modernize Sudanese society.
   b. the Egyptian occupation.
   c. the British occupation.
   d. Sultan Abdul Hamid's efforts to suppress Arab nationalism.
   e. the expansion of the slave trade under Egyptian rule.

## InfoTrac College Edition

Visit the source collections at

**http://infotrac.thomsonlearning.com**

and use the Search function with the following key terms:

Ottoman Empire     Sufi     Islam

## Wadsworth History Website Resources

Visit the World History Resource Center at **http://history.wadsworth.com/world** for a wealth of general resources, and the *World Civilizations* Companion Website at **http://history.wadsworth.com/adler04** for resources specific to this textbook.

## HistoryNow

Enter *HistoryNow* using the access card that is available for *World Civilizations*. *HistoryNow* will assist you in understanding the content in this chapter with lesson plans generated for your needs. In addition, you can read the following documents, and many more, online:

Young Turks, "Proclamation for the Ottoman Empire"

Biography of Sultan Abdul Hamid II

*We are people because of other people.*
Sotho Proverb

# 38 Africa in the Era of Informal Empire

| | |
|---|---|
| 1650–1870 | Height of Atlantic slave trade |
| 1652 | Dutch East India Company founds Cape Colony, South Africa |
| c. 1770–1840 | Warfare and migrations throughout southern and eastern Africa |
| 1832 | Sayyid Sa'id founds Sultanate of Zanzibar |
| 1830s | French begin to assert control over North Africa |
| 1840s | Christian missionaries and explorers begin to move into interior |
| 1850s–1860s | French begin extending their control up the Senegal River |



The centuries that followed the first appearance of Europeans in Africa were ones of both decline and growth for Africans. These centuries until about 1880 in African history are often characterized as the era of **Informal Empire**—that is to say, the era when Europeans remained content with limited involvement in Africa. Until then, Europeans remained confined to the coastal regions. Conquest and the creation of formal colonies, especially of the continent's vast interior, was something in which European governments were not prepared to invest blood and treasure. Interest remained limited to commerce, and permanent settlement was out of the question for most Europeans. Therefore, Europeans had by far their greatest, and perhaps most destructive, impact on the coastal regions. Africans living there or in the near interior experienced the greatest changes, especially where the effects of the slave trade were felt. However, describing the history of the entire African continent entirely in terms of the European presence would be an oversimplification. Many other things were happening in Africa that had little or nothing to do with Europeans. While the European presence in Africa was an important and growing factor in African history during the centuries before 1880, Africans found their own ways of dealing with it.

## The Era of Informal Empire

Long after the first Europeans had arrived on the coasts of West Africa in the second half of the fifteenth century, they had penetrated very little into the enormous depths of the continent or into the interior life of the people. Aside from the Dutch at the Cape of Good Hope and the Portuguese colony of Angola, Europeans in the three centuries after 1480 established no permanent settlements. Instead, trade was often conducted by sailors right on coastal beaches, or fortified trading posts like the famous Elmina Castle on the Gold Coast (present-day Ghana) were founded at wide intervals. Staffed by a literal handful of European traders and their African employees, these trading stations, or **factories**, as they were called, naturally had a strong impact on African life in areas near the coasts. However, the farther one went inland from these European enclaves, the less effect they had. African leaders usually dealt with the white traders on an equal or even advantageous basis, because the whites depended entirely on the African leaders to gather slaves, gold, pepper, and animal byproducts that the interior produced for export.

In contrast to the Americas and Asia, most of Africa's interior remained free from outside interventions. The chief reason seems to have been the ability of the early traders to get what they wanted without having to establish permanent settlements or long-term relationships. Of course, what they originally came for was gold and a list of exotic products for which Africa was the only source. In this sense, the early African experience with the Europeans was similar to that of the Southeast Asian peoples: minimal and highly selective contact. Soon, however, slaves took the place of gold as the most profitable and most pursued item of trade. Coastal peoples in mutually profitable fashion delivered both slaves and goods to the Europeans, who saw no persuasive reason to risk the dangers of a long journey into unknown territory to get what African middlemen would deliver—for a price. There was certainly profit enough for all, and the coastal peoples and their rulers possessed sufficient authority and knowledge of trading practices to know how to deal with the newcomers.

The model established in the 1400s by the exploring Portuguese was followed closely by their several successors along the western African coast. The European traders could not and did not simply overwhelm the Africans and seize what they wanted. Europeans did not possess any real military advantage over Africans until the late nineteenth century. Moreover, any such attempt at the use of force would have resulted at the very least in stopping all future trade. And for the entire four centuries of European precolonial contact with West Africa, the Portuguese, Dutch, British, French, and others were engaged in commercial competition, which African leaders at times could manipulate to their own advantage.

Also discouraging permanent settlement were the devastating diseases that were endemic. With its tropical climate, Africa was afflicted more than Europe by fevers such as malaria, cholera, sleeping sickness, typhus, and typhoid fever. The western coast in particular had long had the reputation of being a "white man's graveyard." A recent authority on the question estimates that the mortality rate among white traders and seamen on the West African coast might have surpassed even that of the African slaves shipped across the Atlantic: 25 to 50 percent *per year*! Adding to such formidable obstacles were the oppressively hot climate and the unknown and difficult terrain. To protect their middleman positions in trading with Europeans, who seemed always to have been willing to think the worst of Africans and their "strange" ways, coastal peoples often gave false accounts of savage peoples inhabiting the interior, who supposedly lay in wait to murder any innocent traveler or explorer who turned up in their midst. Such, then, were the unfortunate origins of the image of Africa as the "Dark Continent," an image that was difficult to dispel and that persists to some degree even today among the ignorant.

As noted in Chapter 13, Africa's geography and climate make traveling inward from the coast especially difficult. Thanks to the tsetse fly, the primary carrier of "sleeping sickness," horses and mules are unable to survive throughout most of the central and southern two-thirds of the continent, and the wheel was unknown in equatorial Africa before Europeans introduced it. All goods of whatever nature depended on human muscle for transport. The interior plateaus drop off sharply to the coastal plains, creating rapids and waterfalls that make long-distance river transport impossible in much of the continent. Only the Nile, the Niger in the west, and the Congo in the center are sporadically navigable far into the interior. All three of these rivers were controlled by substantial states when the Europeans arrived, and the Nile valley was in Muslim hands.

## The Slave Trade and Its Results

Slavery was an old institution that was found at some time or another among virtually all peoples, even Africans, and it long predated the transatlantic trade. In ancient and medieval times, unfortunates of all ethnic backgrounds, including Greeks, Turks, Mongols, Africans, and various Slavic peoples, filled the demand for slaves. War and poverty provided the primary reasons for enslaving human beings, whereas ethnic and racial prejudices had contributed to it only indirectly. Ancient and medieval slavery also took many forms. It was formally recognized in the Qur'an, for example, yet Muslims were encouraged to treat their slaves with compassion and to free those who converted to Islam. Among Africans, slavery was usually closely akin to indentured labor or even a sort of remote kinship.

In Africa, the slave trade existed long before the arrival of Europeans south of the Sahara. Berber and Arab Muslims transported thousands from that broad region called the Sudan, moving them across the Saharan desert and the Red Sea, and to a lesser extent from East Africa and across the Indian Ocean. Despite this prior trade, no topic in African history has been as sensitive and controversial as the extent and results of the transatlantic slave trade (see Map 38.1). The European settlement of the Western Hemisphere and their establishment of plantation systems there created the demand for cheap labor. Their first

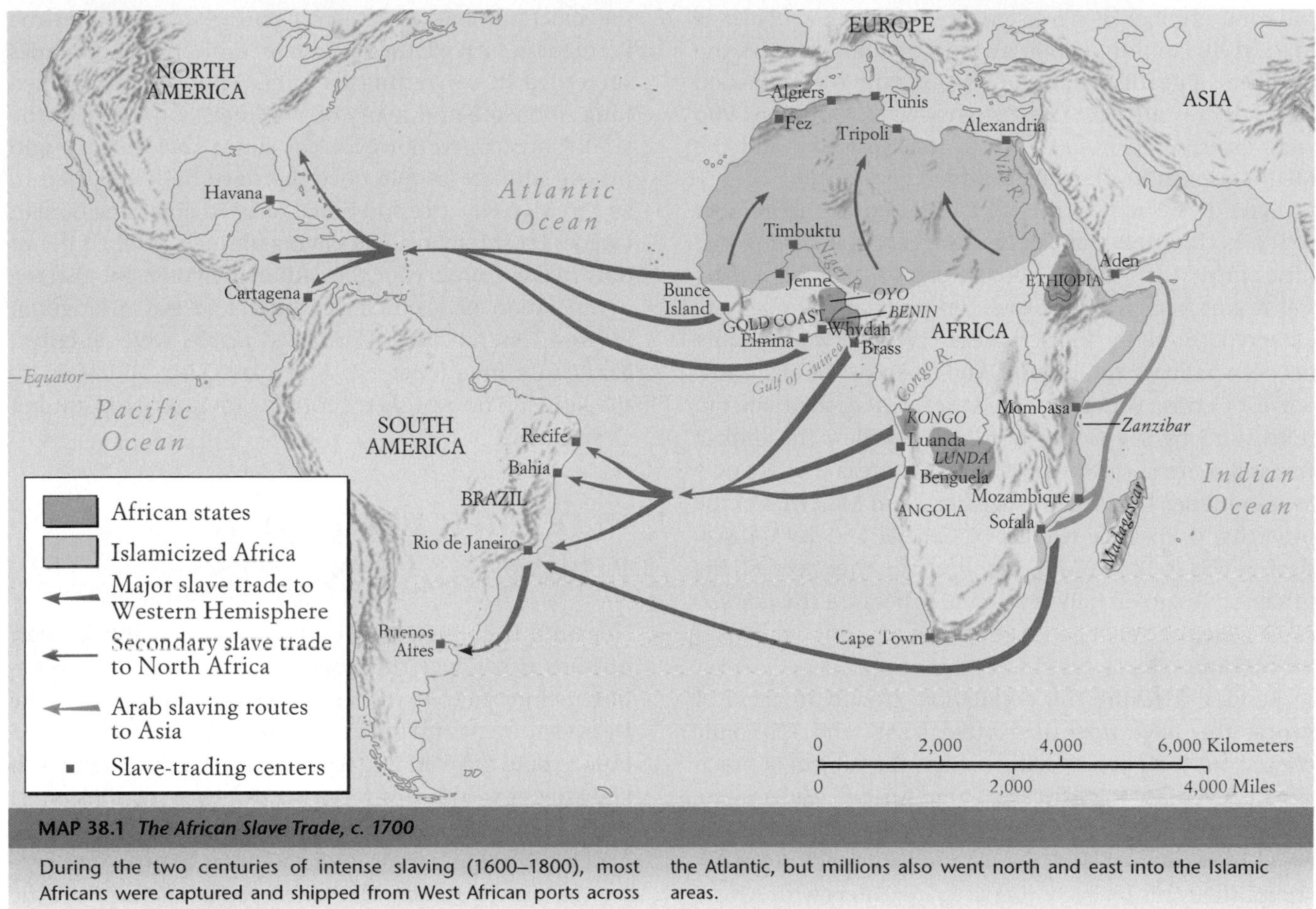


**MAP 38.1** *The African Slave Trade, c. 1700*

During the two centuries of intense slaving (1600–1800), most Africans were captured and shipped from West African ports across the Atlantic, but millions also went north and east into the Islamic areas.

choice to meet that need was Native Americans, but diseases destroyed up to 90 percent of the Native American population and forced the Europeans to look elsewhere. Given the prior existence of slavery, it cannot be said that racism, per se, motivated their initial choice of Africans to replace Native Americans; more obvious contributing factors in the beginning were the Africans' ability to survive the harsh transatlantic crossing and to resist disease. However, the brutality of the system of trade and transport and the form of slavery in which slaves were reduced to chattel helped engender racism, and racist assumptions about Africans provided the excuses on which the "system" was based.

The Portuguese were the first to engage in the business of slavery. They purchased the first slaves from the region of the Senegal River around 1448, and the slave trade continued until the early 1500s more or less haphazardly, probably numbering no more than a few hundred per year. By 1520, however, Portuguese immigrants established sugar plantations on the offshore islands of Principe and São Tomé, to which slaves soon were being exported. Until about 1640, relatively few slaves were exported to the New World, but the demand quickly increased thereafter, and the Dutch replaced the Portuguese for a few decades of the seventeenth century as the principal dealers and transporters of slaves. (A Dutch ship sold the first slaves to the colony of Jamestown, Virginia, when tobacco first was being tried there as a cash crop.) By the end of the seventeenth century, the English, French, Danes, and others began challenging the Dutch near-monopoly. The following century saw the trade at its zenith, and after the founding of the Royal African Company in 1672, the English quickly came to dominate it until 1807, when Parliament finally banned it.

The greatest debates have centered on the statistics of slavery. One problem is the lack of sufficient and uniformly reliable data, and another concerns issues of interpretation. How many slaves were sold and bought? And where? And how did these numbers change over time? Furthermore, what crucial information might one *not* expect to find in the data, such as census figures and birth and mortality rates? Given these difficulties, refinement is impossible, and one is driven to make only the crudest approximations of the numbers involved and the impact they had. The lowest estimates that have been made are that 8 million human beings were exported from Africa to the New World in the 220 years between 1650 and 1870, the high point of the trade. Others calculate that the total number of slaves exported might have been as high as 40 million, if one includes in those figures the numbers of deaths that occurred along the way. Added to these figures are estimates of another 3.5 million who were transported from Africa to the Near East and the Mediterranean in the same period.

Even if one accepts the lowest figures for the number of slaves exported, this does not suggest that slaving had little impact on African populations or that the impact was uniform in all areas. Slaves for the Atlantic trade were gathered primarily in two areas: West Africa (roughly between Senegal and Nigeria) and the coast of what now is West Central Africa. In East Africa, where the trade ran northward by sea to the Muslim countries, the impact was still more narrowly focused on the areas that are now Mozambique, Tanzania, Madagascar, and Malawi. On the other hand, in large regions of Central and East Africa, slaving was of little or no importance, either because the inhabitants successfully resisted it or because the populations were too small and scattered to offer an easy target for capture.

Besides checking the population growth in parts of Africa, the slave trade had other social and economic effects, but their precise nature is also the subject of much debate, even among Africans. Some African leaders were indisputably able to reap an advantage for themselves and for at least some of their people from the trade. They accomplished this by becoming active partners with whites in securing new human supplies and by using the proceeds of the trade in ways that increased their material prestige and powers. Leaders especially prized firearms, which they then used to enhance their power to gather more slaves. This trade specifically helped create or at least enhance the power of several kingdoms of varying size, particularly those of the so-called Slave Coast, which included the littorals of what now are the African nations of Togo, Benin, and Nigeria. African states that benefited particularly from the slave trade in this region included the kingdoms of Dahomey and Oyo as well as the Niger Delta city-states of Bonny, Brass, Calabar, Nembe, and Warri.

Slaving and the raids or local wars that it generated were also indisputably a major cause of the chaotic bloodshed observed and condemned by nineteenth-century Europeans. Above all, firearms were responsible for this situation. Guns were needed not only to hunt for slaves, but also to defend oneself from would-be slave hunters. Africans often found themselves at a considerable disadvantage when confronted by Europeans wanting slaves: either they had to provide the slaves in return for the firearms, or the firearms were sold to others who were willing to provide the slaves. If people refused to become a part of the system, they could expect to become its victims. The results could be catastrophic, as had occurred, for example, in the great kingdom of the Kongo during the sixteenth and seventeenth centuries. Soon after the Portuguese arrived there, Roman Catholic missionaries succeeded in converting its king, whom they renamed King Affonso I, and many of the chiefs and elders of the land. Christianity, however, could not save the king and his unfortunate people once the slave traders moved in and were given a free and brutal hand in obtaining human cargoes for shipment. The slaving business resulted in not only massive misery for the captured victims but also the degeneration of a previously large and stable kingdom in West Central Africa. These sad results were described eloquently in a letter the Kongolese king addressed to the king of Portugal, his "brother," in 1526 (see Law and Government).

## Intensification of European Contacts

Not until the nineteenth century did most sub-Saharan Africans experience the heavy hand of foreign domination. Before then, Europeans remained indifferent to the Dark Continent and believed its people and its lands had little to offer the world, in terms of either knowledge worth knowing or wealth worth having. For these reasons, most white men who came to Africa restricted their interest in Africa to trade and their interest in Africans to those peoples of the coastlands who could provide them with the few goods they desired. Except for the French in North Africa, the Portuguese in Angola, and the Boers of Dutch descent in South Africa, the Europeans saw no reason to take any interest in, much less disturb, the patchwork of kingdoms that existed mostly in the interior of the continent. The result was that, in 1800, Europeans knew hardly more about the interior than their ancestors had known in the fifth century. Not even the basic geography of the river systems was understood, and the quest for the sources of the Nile, which lasted until the 1860s, was one of the great adventure stories of the Victorian era.

From 1800 onward, this indifference and ignorance changed gradually. Several reasons account for this change. The first of these was humanitarian. After centuries of being steeped in the inhumanity of the slave trade, Europeans—first and especially those who were most involved in it, the English—simply rediscovered their conscience in the 1790s. A movement to end the slave trade and slavery arose out of late-eighteenth-century Christian evangelism. This was particularly true with the appearance of the Wesleyan (Methodist) movement among the new urban poor of Britain's early Industrial Revolution. Men like John Wesley and Thomas Fowell Buxton led a vigorous **Anti-Slavery Movement**, which soon acquired many supporters in high places. In 1807, they persuaded the British Parliament, the United States (1808), and other

## The Letter of King Affonso of Kongo, 1526

**The kingdom of Kongo** was the best organized and most extensive of all the African states encountered by the Europeans in their early explorations. Extending many hundreds of miles on either side of the river, Kongo encompassed most of today's Angola and much of the territory of the Democratic Republic of the Congo. The Portuguese, who sent missionaries to the court of Kongo's powerful and wealthy king at the same time as Columbus's voyages to the Caribbean, were delighted at being able to report the conversion to Catholic Christianity of the ruler they dubbed Affonso I (ruled 1506–1543). Affonso collaborated closely with his Portuguese protectors and business partners in a rapidly expanding slave and luxury goods trade. He also founded the only African dynasty of Christian rulers, which lasted until the final collapse of the Kongo kingdom in the later seventeenth century under the combined weight of the slave trade and rebellion by provincial chiefs, who used firearms and the profits obtained from the slave trade against the king's authority. This letter, dated October 18, 1526, by King Affonso to the King of Portugal explains the predicament into which his kingdom had been reduced by the slave trade.

> Moreover, Sir, in our Kingdoms there is another great inconvenience which is of little service to God, and this is that many of our people [*naturaes*], keenly desirous as they are of the wares and things of your Kingdoms, which are brought here by your people, and in order to satisfy their voracious appetite, seize many of our people . . . and very often it happens that they kidnap even noblemen and sons of noblemen, and our relatives, and take them to be sold to the white men who are in our kingdoms. . . .
>
> And as soon as they are taken by the white men they are immediately ironed and branded with fire, and when they are carried to be embarked, if they are caught by our guards' men the whites allege that they have bought them but they cannot say from whom, so that it is our duty to do justice and to restore to the freemen their freedom, but it cannot be done if your subjects feel offended, as they claim to be.
>
> And to avoid such a great evil we passed a law so that any white man living in our Kingdoms and wanting to purchase goods in any way should first inform three of our noblemen and officials of our court whom we rely upon in this matter, and these are Dom Pedro Manipanza and Dom Manuel Manisaba, our chief usher, and Goncala Pires our chief freighter, who should investigate if the mentioned goods are captives or free men, and if cleared by them there will be no further doubt nor embargo for them to be taken and embarked. But if the white men do not comply with it they will lose the aforementioned goods. And if we do them this favour and concession it is for the part Your Highness has in it, since we know that it is in your service too that these goods are taken from our Kingdom, otherwise we should not consent to this. . . .

### *Analyze and Interpret*

What are the trade "goods" referred to in the document? What does the use of this term suggest about the sixteenth-century attitude toward slaves? What seems to be the nature of the relationship between Affonso and the king of Portugal? Did Affonso and his ministers seem to have control over the situation he describes? What seem to be the reasons why or why not? Why do these Africans all have Portuguese names?

Source: Excerpted from Visconde de Paiva-Manso, *História do Congo (Documentos)* (Lisbon, 1877). Reprinted in Basil Davidson, *African Civilization Revisited* (Trenton, NJ: Africa World Press, 1991), pp. 224-225.

European nations after the Napoleonic Wars, to officially end the slave trade. To enforce these laws, Britain used its powerful Royal Navy to patrol the coastal areas of West and East Africa, where the trade was most active. Colonies were established at Freetown in Sierra Leone (by Britain) and Libreville in what is now Gabon (by France) for slaves who had been freed through these measures. Right behind these reformers came missionaries who were anxious to convert these freed slaves and other Africans for God and Christ. Missionary societies were begun in Europe and America to train men and women to go into the "field" as evangelists to minister to the souls of Africans and as medical missionaries to minister to their bodies.

Another reason for the changed attitudes was simple curiosity: the desire to explore the world's last great unexplored regions. The most noted of the nineteenth-century journeyers into the interior of the Dark Continent were either missionaries such as David Livingstone or explorer-adventurers such as the Frenchman René Caillé, the German Heinrich Barth, the Englishman Richard Francis Burton, and the Anglo-American Henry Morton Stanley. The sharply competitive search for the source of the Nile River was largely responsible for opening knowledge of the vast interior of East Africa in the 1860s and 1870s to the outside world, while the exploration of the Niger and Congo basins did the same for West and

Central Africa. Livingstone was the first European to be acknowledged as having crossed the entire African continent east to west, although there is evidence that he was preceded by half a century by a Portuguese explorer. The British journalist Stanley, made famous by his well-publicized search for an allegedly lost Livingstone, went on to become a major African explorer in the 1870s and "opened up" the Congo to colonial status as an agent of the king of the Belgians, Leopold II.

Finally, there was the profit motive. Commercial interest in Africa was not new in the nineteenth century, but previously most had believed that Africa possessed little more to offer the world than slaves, gold, and animal by-products such as ivory and skins. That perception changed when the gold and slave trade began winding down, and the Industrial Revolution in nineteenth-century Europe and America created new needs for industrial raw materials and markets for its finished, manufactured goods (Chapter 34). After having witnessed firsthand the effects of the slave trade in East and Central Africa, David Livingstone, perhaps unwittingly, contributed to this new interest in Africa when he observed that, if "Christianity and commerce" might be offered, Africans would be weaned away from the slave trade. Trading companies like Britain's Royal Niger Company and various firms operating out of northern Germany and Marseilles, France, began marking off their respective "spheres of influence" all over Africa, wherein they exercised monopolistic control of trade in highly sought-after local products such as palm oil, the principal lubricant of the First Industrial Revolution.

**Photograph of the famous English missionary and explorer, David Livingstone.** Livingstone represented the nineteenth-century evangelical movement. Like many Europeans, he believed that Africans needed saving from slavery and "primitivism." His desire was to introduce "civilization" and Christianity to Africans.

Bettmann/Corbis

Gradually then, as the nineteenth century passed and new forms of interest in Africa developed, the conditions for the sudden, late-nineteenth-century competition among the major European powers, called the "Scramble for Africa" (see Chapter 52), fell into place.

## North Africa

Another factor that motivated Europeans to seek colonies in Africa and other parts of the world was nationalism. As a ploy to shore up a weak and unpopular monarchy, the French government hoped to stir up nationalistic feelings by embarking on a new course of conquest unseen since the days of Napoleon. Beginning in 1830, using the threat of piracy as an excuse, France launched invasions of Morocco and Algeria. Morocco remained theoretically independent under its sultan, who was supervised by a "resident-general" appointed by the French government in Paris. Less heavily populated and less stable, Algeria was easily seized from a decaying Turkish administration and made into a formal French colony as early as 1847. Eventually, more than a million French immigrants settled on the richly soiled region between the Atlas Mountains and Algeria's Mediterranean coast. Algeria became the sole African region in which this type of intensive, agriculturally oriented European settlement occurred, until diamonds and gold were discovered in late-nineteenth-century South Africa. The Arabs and indigenous Berbers in Algeria were treated by Europeans as unwelcome foreigners in their own country, and many were required to work the lands of absentee landlords for meager pay. Nearly the same process occurred later in neighboring Tunisia. Thus, by the later nineteenth century, the whole western half of Africa north of the Sahara was within the French orbit.

The eastern Mediterranean coast of Africa had still been part of the dying Ottoman Empire, but the Turkish regents had been able to exercise little real control over these lands for centuries and could not defend them successfully from European ambitions for long. In 1798, Napoleon invaded Egypt, and once he was expelled by combined Turkish and British arms, the Ottoman sultan appointed the Albanian Muhammad Ali as the viceroy of Egypt. In the years afterward, Muhammad Ali succeeded in establishing himself and his successors as a quasi-independent regime. In 1821, he extended Egyptian control into the Sudan. In 1869, during the reign of his son and successor, the Khedive Ismail, the French completed the construction of the Suez Canal. In 1882, fearing Egyptian seizure of this strategically vital asset, the British invaded and added Egypt to their worldwide empire. For their part, the Italians took over the (then) wastelands of Libya in 1911.

In all of these lands, Islam was the religion of the great majority. As both the local leadership and the Turks in Istanbul proved themselves unable to act effectively in the face of aggressive Europeans, Islam underwent a revival in many parts of the Islamic world (see Chapter 37), including Africa. Sometimes this revival took the form of *jihads,* holy wars to expel Christian "infidels." In the thousand years since Islam had first been introduced to Africa, it had become fused with local forms of economic and cultural life. Therefore, when Europeans invaded Africa, threatening to impose an alien religion and culture, religion provided a natural foundation for organizing resistance. Without question, the hardest fought and longest lasting of these struggles was the jihad of Abd al-Qadir in Algeria. Like others who led similarly inspired wars in Africa (see following West Africa section), Abd al-Qadir was a local leader of a Sufi brotherhood; more specifically, he was a ***marabout***, a charismatic leader of holy men who inhabited a complex of monastery-like lodges among the desert and mountain Berbers. Abd al-Qadir was able to base his struggle against the French on his personal religious charisma and on effective use of the preexisting network of lodges. The jihad began in 1841, and by 1847, Abd al-Qadir was captured and exiled; however, the jihad continued until 1879 before the French finally prevailed against this "proto-nationalist" struggle, which in many respects presaged the Algerian war of independence in the 1950s (Chapter 52).

Hulton-Deutsch/Corbis

**PORTRAIT OF ABD AL-QADIR.** The Algerian Abd al-Qadir led the Islamic resistance to French invasion for many years.

## West Africa

By the early nineteenth century, the French and the British were the leading European powers operating in West Africa, each having created respective "spheres of influence" in which their merchants carried out business under the protection of their governments. In these areas, the slave trade had been the major occupation of Europeans and their African collaborators for centuries. After slaves were banned by acts of Parliament from British ships in 1807 and from British imperial territory in 1834, the principal slaving centers moved southward into the Portuguese colony of Angola. Here the trade continued flourishing until the American Civil War removed a major destination and the abolition of slavery in Brazil in 1888 eliminated the most important one. (The U.S. Congress prohibited the importation of slaves in 1808, but they continued to be smuggled into the southern United States even during the Civil War.)

As the new "legitimate trade" replaced the slave trade, agricultural exports from Africa and imports of European metal, cloth, and manufactured goods became its foundation all over Africa. In their few locations in West Africa, the French and British, as well as the Portuguese, had staked out monopolistic control of local markets along the coast and the banks of the major rivers of the region. The French were largely concentrated along the Senegal River and the British in the lower Niger River basin (Nigeria), the Gold Coast (Ghana), Sierra Leone, and the Gambia. The vast interior remained unaffected for the most part, although events there ultimately became a major influence on the decision of the French to conquer the West African interior.

Beyond the coastal regions, Islam was the dominant religion in West Africa long before the nineteenth century (Chapter 13). The great medieval commercial empires of Mali and Songhay and others had played important roles in this process in West Africa: mosques were built, Arabic literacy spread, and Muslim traders carried Islam ever farther into the coastal hinterlands. Despite conversions, however, many African Muslims clung to ancestor veneration, spirit possession, sacrifice, and divination rites that were rooted in their pre- or non-Islamic past. Even rulers of Muslim states allowed practices to persist that were forbidden by Islamic law, such as allowing their own subjects (who were Muslims) to be sold as slaves to Europeans and the collection of illegal taxes.

Beginning in the seventeenth century, the first of a series of holy wars began in the region of Senegal and Guinea in response to these shortcomings. Others followed across the western and central Sudan over the next two centuries, but the most important of these were the jihads of Usman dan Fodio and al-Hajj Umar Tal in the nineteenth century.

The origins of the jihad of Usman dan Fodio began in the 1790s and arose from a dispute between a Muslim holy man and the king of a Hausa city-state called Gobir. The Hausa are a people found in the northern part of modern Nigeria. Like the Swahili of East Africa, they lived in city-states. (See Map 38.2.) He began preaching against the local Habe ruler of Gobir, whom he accused of infidelity. A crisis finally led to declaration of a holy war, and between 1804 and the time of Usman's death in 1817, a series of jihads vanquished not just Gobir, but all of the city-states of Hausaland and even the neighboring countries of Nupe and Ilorin in northern Yoruba country to the South. With the capital of his new "caliphate" at Sokoto, the Islamic empire Usman created consisted of several satellite emirates, each of which centered on the major Hausa states and all of which were governed by Islamic law. Although dan Fodio died soon after the completion of his jihad, his son, Muhammad Bello, succeeded him. His competence and long life put his father's accomplishment on a stable foundation, and the Sokoto caliphate endured through the colonial era.

The success of the jihad of Usman dan Fodio inspired similar Islamic revolutions to the west, particularly among the Tukolor people in the area between the Niger and Senegal rivers. Whereas the earlier holy wars fought by dan Fodio and others were directed against the non-Islamic practices of local rulers, the jihad of al-Hajj Umar Tal followed a more deliberate plan of conquest and Islamic state building. Umar left his native Futa Toro in 1826 to set off on the pilgrimage, and after spending several years at the court of Muhammad Bello, he returned to Futa Jallon on the headwaters of the Senegal River. There he set up a school and began building a circle of followers, until in the 1840s he launched his jihad against neighboring Islamic states to the east. By the 1860s, he had managed to extend his conquests as far as the upper Niger, where he forced many to convert to Islam and established the Islamic Sharia as the backbone of his government. These wars got him into difficulties with the French, who had established themselves on the lower reaches of the Senegal River to the west of Umar's growing empire. Louis Faidherbe, the governor of Senegal, feared Umar's designs on French holdings and used Umar's ambitions as a reason to extend control farther up the river. As we shall see in Chapter 52, with imperial

**A Miniature Hausa Quran of the Sixteenth to Seventeenth Century and the Period before the Jihad of Usman dan Fodio.** This design was used for "magical" purposes, such as a form of fortune telling, and indicates the "unorthodox" forms of Islam that developed as Islam penetrated south of the Sahara and against which Usman dan Fodio and al-Hajj Umar fought.

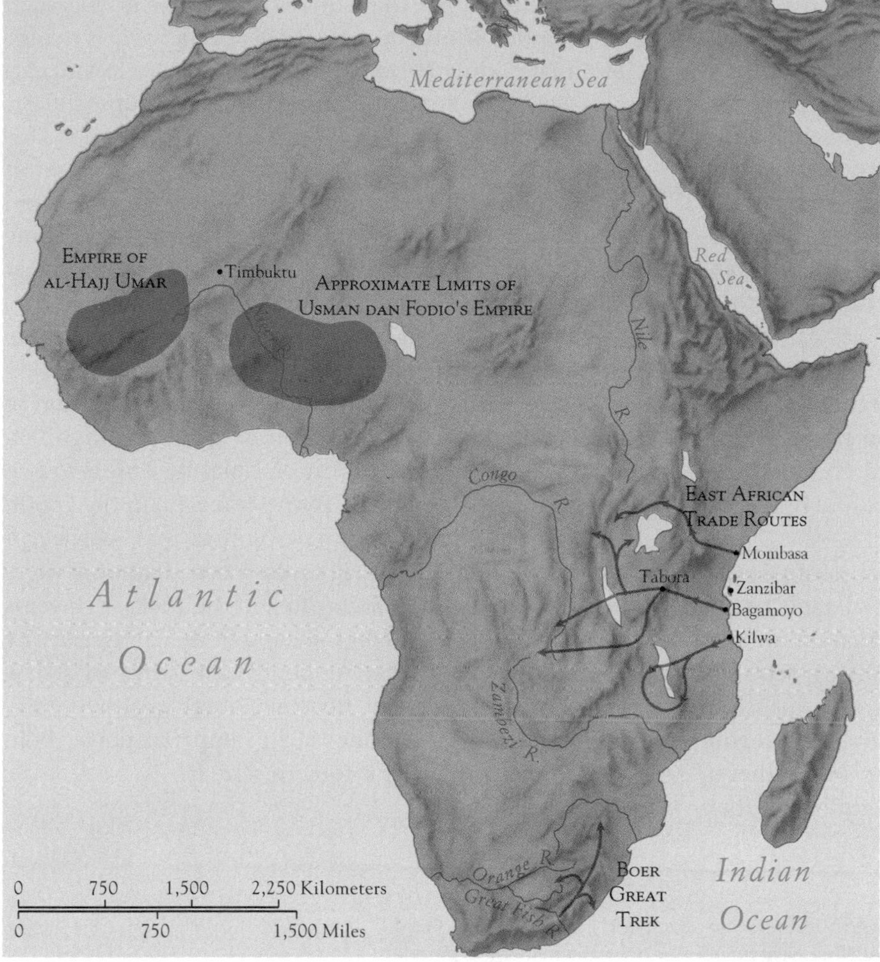


MAP 38.2 *Africa in the Nineteenth Century*

ambitions of their own in this region of West Africa, the French were able to exploit divisions among Umar's sons and resentments against his forced conversions to their considerable advantage in the 1880s and 1890s, and to extend their own colonial empire to include most of West Africa.

## South Africa

The Cape Colony in extreme southern Africa was the other large area, along with Algeria, where whites settled in some numbers before the late nineteenth century. Capetown was founded in 1652 when the Dutch East India Company decided to establish a colony in South Africa as a place where company ships making the long voyage to and from the East Indies could take on supplies of fresh meat and vegetables and where their sick could receive attention. Although the Dutch colonists sent by the company originally were required to provide these services, soon many demanded—and got—the company's permission to settle new farmlands to the east of the Cape. These so-called **Boers** (Dutch for farmers) founded new western Cape settlements at Stellenbosch and Graf Reinet and steadily displaced the indigenous, cattle-herding Khoikhoi ("Hottentot") peoples they encountered. From the beginning, relations with African peoples were almost never conducted on a basis of racial equality. As Boer migrants, or **Trekboers**, moved ever-farther inland, they swept aside the indigenous peoples and dispossessed them of their lands and livestock. Labor was a perpetual problem in the colony, so slaves were imported from other parts of Africa, Indonesia, India, and Madagascar. Some racial mixing inevitably occurred, producing a new social element in Cape society, the so-called **Coloureds**. Slaves, Africans, and Coloureds either had to accept a permanently subservient role in Boer society or flee, as many did, living on the northern and eastern fringes of Cape Colony and occasionally raiding for cattle among Boer farmsteads on the eastern frontier.

Until the recent past, when majority rule was introduced into South Africa, the Boers maintained an old myth that their ancestors had preceded Bantu-speaking Africans in settling South Africa. In fact, archaeological and linguistic evidence indicates that Khoisan peoples had inhabited southern Africa for tens of thousands of years, and Bantu-speaking peoples had been present in South Africa since as early as the fourth century (Chapter 13). Essentially village dwellers, the Bantu-speaking peoples were economically more diversified than the Khoisan and Khoikhoi. They had an iron-based technology and lived as mixed farmers, supplemented by livestock breeding. Gradually, they occupied the eastern Cape and the inland high plateau, where rainfall levels could support their way of life. As for their political organization, available evidence suggests that until the eighteenth century, these Bantu-speaking peoples had lived in loosely organized paramount chieftaincies. The Zulu and closely related peoples, such as the Xhosa, steadily pushed southward along the broad coastal plain, until they finally encountered the Boers around the Fish River in the eighteenth century. What followed was a military stalemate. Neither Africans nor Boers could push the other aside.

In 1815, as part of the Vienna settlement of the Napoleonic wars, Britain occupied the Cape, and the colony became subject to English law and slightly more liberal ideas about racial relations. Having enjoyed substantial self-government, the Boers of the eastern frontier resented British efforts to bring order and more humane treatment of Africans. In particular, they resented British efforts to restrict slavery and cut off much of the supply of free labor on which the Boers depended. Beginning in 1836, in an effort to escape the English, the Boers started a northward migration away from the Cape in what was called the **Great Trek**. Once in the interior, they drove out the local Sotho peoples, fought and defeated the mighty Zulu, and set up independent Boer republics to the north of the Orange and Vaal rivers, where they could continue the old ways undisturbed: the Orange Free State and its neighboring Transvaal.

Meanwhile, the northern and eastern areas into which the Boers thrust themselves had seen considerable transformations among the Bantu-speaking Africans in the century before. For reasons that are still being debated, about the time the Trekboers had begun their expansion out of the western Cape, levels of conflict had begun rising among the Bantu-speaking peoples of Southeast Africa. This caused the formation of powerful states that were organized for warfare under formidable leaders such as the famous **Shaka** of the Zulu people, as well as others. Continual raiding by Africans for land, women, and cattle, as well as by Boers and even Coloured groups (the latter two for slaves), caused considerable migration of African populations, many of whom sought the protection of these powerful warlords, whereas other areas became depopulated. To escape the pressures of warfare, some migrated out of South Africa altogether and fled into other regions of southern and East Africa (Map 38.2).

As for Boer–British relations, all went well for a time, because the Boer republics and the British Cape Colony were situated far apart. In 1879, fearing the reputation of the Zulu, the British army succeeded in eliminating them as a threat to the occupation of Natal by Europeans in what is known as the **Zulu War**. Moreover, in the 1860s, the long-standing European perception that Africa had little value changed permanently when diamonds were discovered at Kimberly. Soon after, in the 1880s, rich veins of gold were also found on the Rand in the Transvaal. The diamond and gold fever suddenly cast Africa in a new light: it was a continent rich in natural wealth waiting to be exploited by anyone or any imperial power bold enough to do whatever it took to seize it.

**DIAMOND MINING.** The richest diamond-mining district in the world was found in the 1860s by British prospectors in South Africa. Massive amounts of hard labor were required to bring the mines into production, leading directly to much harsher working and living conditions for the Africans who supplied this labor.

## East Africa

East Africa felt the most direct impact of Arab and Swahili traders, who had long preceded the Europeans in slaving and other commerce in African goods. Swahili towns such as Paté, Mombasa, Zanzibar, and Kilwa were busy entrepôts in the Indian Ocean trade for centuries. In these coastal regions, the Swahili-speaking people had developed a highly cosmopolitan lifestyle, with trading networks that extended along a broad stretch of the coast from Mogadishu to Mozambique as well as into the interior (Chapter 13). The urban Swahili were Muslims, whereas most of the hinterland peoples continued to follow local religious beliefs and practices. These city-states were commercial in nature, trading across the Indian Ocean as partners of their fellow Muslims in southern and eastern Arabia, Iraq, Iran, and India.

Although slaving had formed a small part of this coastal trade for many centuries, it is unlikely that the volume of the East African trade had ever approached that of the West African business, whether Arab or European. The demand for slaves changed suddenly, however, in the eighteenth century. In 1698, the Omani Arabs (from Oman, in southeastern Arabia) expelled the Portuguese and occupied all points of the coast north of Mozambique, and almost a century later the French settled the Indian Ocean islands of Mauritius and Réunion. Plantation economies in the Persian Gulf and on Mauritius and Réunion created an unprecedented demand for slaves, most of which were obtained from the Central African interior and exported through Kilwa Kivinje and Zanzibar.

Further encouragement to the East African trade was given in 1832 when the Sultan of Oman, Sayyid Sa'id bin Sultan al-Busaidi, moved the headquarters of his sultanate to Zanzibar. After developing what came to be known as the **Zanzibar Sultanate**, Sayyid Sa'id and his successors extended their control over the entire Swahili coast of East Africa. However, theirs was a commercial empire above all else. All coastal trade was directed through Zanzibar, where the Sultans collected a standard 3 percent duty. Sayyid Sa'id encouraged the creation of a plantation economy in East Africa, so Arabs and Indian immigrants displaced the local Swahili in Zanzibar, and large numbers of slaves were employed in cultivating cloves. Inland from many coastal towns, too, Arabs and local Swahili alike turned to plantation farming, where grains were cultivated for export. Under such a growing demand, trade in slaves and ivory soon reached inland beyond the East African lakes region as far as Uganda and the eastern Congo River basin. In 1873, the trade finally was ended when the British convinced Sa'id's son to agree to abolish the export of slaves permanently. However, the practice of slavery continued in East Africa until finally it, too, was ended during the colonial period.

**SULTAN BARGHASH.** A proud Arab, Sultan Barghash tried resisting European interference in the slave trade of Zanzibar. In the end, he was forced to submit to ending the slave trade and became dependent on the British for his political survival.

## SUMMARY

In many ways, Africa from the seventeenth through the late nineteenth centuries was in transition. Most parts of the interior of the continent remained relatively unaffected by any European efforts to control or alter the lands and lives of its peoples. For one thing, before the last quarter of the nineteenth century, Europe simply did not possess the power to conquer such a vast continent; for another, it lacked any will to do so. European interest in Africa remained entirely commercial, and as long as there were plenty of Africans who were willing, or whom Europeans could persuade, to supply the slaves and exotic tropical products they demanded, there was no reason for Europeans ever to think of wasting money and manpower on conquest. In the one place where

Europeans did settle before the nineteenth century, South Africa, the relatively few hunting and pastoralist peoples the Europeans met in the western Cape were easily defeated. However, in the late eighteenth century, once these white settlers encountered the much more numerous and advanced Bantu-speaking peoples in the northern and eastern parts, their advance was halted. Therefore, European governments showed no official interest in colonizing Africa during the first great age of imperialism, when attention was directed primarily to Asia and America. The only exception was the French, who began the conquest of North Africa. There they found that Islam could be a major obstacle to conquest, a fact of which they were to be reminded repeatedly later when they launched the conquest of the Sudan.

All of the reasons Europeans had for official disinterest in Africa changed after about 1880, in what is called the age of the New Imperialism. As will be seen in Chapter 52, all of the major European powers experienced dramatically changed attitudes toward Africa and the potential difficulties and responsibilities that empire building there would entail. All of the major powers, and a couple of minor ones as well, would engage in carving up what one empire builder, King Leopold II of Belgium, called "this magnificent African cake."

## Identification Terms

Test your knowledge of this chapter's key concepts by defining the following terms. If you can't recall the meaning of certain terms, refresh your memory by looking up the boldfaced term in the chapter, turning to the Glossary at the end of the book, or working with the flashcards that are available on the *World Civilizations* Companion Website **http://history.wadsworth.com/adler04**.

Anti-Slavery Movement
Boers
Coloureds
factories
Great Trek
Informal Empire
*marabout*
Shaka
Trekboers
Zanzibar Sultanate
Zulu War

## Test Your Knowledge

Test your knowledge of this chapter by answering the following questions. Complete answers appear at the end of the book. You may also take this quiz interactively and find even more quiz questions on the *World Civilizations* Companion Website: **http://history.wadsworth.com/adler04**.

1. The most extensive contacts between Europeans and Africans in the period of Informal Empire were those initiated by
   a. Christian missionaries.
   b. traveling merchants.
   c. European sportsmen/hunters.
   d. medical practitioners on both sides.
   e. European explorers and adventurers.
2. In his letter to the King of Portugal, King Affonso I of the Kongo blamed the rising instability in his kingdom on
   a. slave traders.
   b. the Boers.
   c. the Portuguese-sponsored war against him.
   d. an Islamic jihad.
   e. the actions of Christian missionaries.
3. In the nineteenth century, most of the northwestern part of Africa fell under the control of
   a. Spain.
   b. Germany
   c. Italy.
   d. England.
   e. France
4. What can be said about the slave trade?
   a. It had positive effects on some African societies.
   b. It had negative effects on some Africans.
   c. The exact numbers who were sold into slavery are uncertain.
   d. The firearms that were sold to cooperative Africans reduced the amount of violence the slave trade brought.
   e. Answers a, b, and c

5. Before the 1880s, the most widespread, externally introduced religion in Africa was
   a. Buddhism.
   b. Protestantism.
   c. Hinduism.
   d. Islam.
   e. Roman Catholicism.
6. One major cause of the West African jihads was
   a. the practice followed by Muslim rulers of allowing non-Muslims to settle among Muslims.
   b. the practice followed by Muslim rulers of allowing non-Muslims to marry Muslim women.
   c. continued observance of non-Islamic practices among West African Muslims and their rulers.
   d. continued involvement of West Africans in the slave trade despite Islamic injunctions against it.
   e. slave raiding conducted among Muslims by non-Muslim coastal peoples.
7. The jihadist activities in West Africa were partly
   a. a reaction to the increased levels of violence caused by the slave trade.
   b. inspired by an expected return of Muhammad.
   c. inspired by Islamic revivalism in Arabia and the Islamic heartlands.
   d. inspired by the resistance of Abd al-Qadir to the French invasion of Algeria.
   e. a reaction to growing activities by Christian missionaries in Africa.
8. The Dutch who founded the Cape Colony in South Africa in 1652 came there for what purpose?
   a. To spread Christianity among the Africans
   b. To create a station where Dutch East India Company ships could take on supplies
   c. To conquer the local African population and seize their livestock
   d. To seek freedom of religion
   e. To trade and seek other new economic opportunities among the African population
9. Who was responsible for the increase in slavery and the slave trade in East Africa after the eighteenth century?
   a. The French
   b. Indian merchants
   c. French and Indian merchants
   d. The Omani Arabs and the French
   e. The Omani Arabs
10. The coastal cities of East Africa in the nineteenth century
   a. already had centuries of trading history by the time they were put under Omani rule.
   b. were already part of Christian culture.
   c. had never before experienced foreign contacts.
   d. were enclaves of Arab colonists.
   e. exported no slaves.

## InfoTrac College Edition

Visit the source collections at

**http://infotrac.thomsonlearning.com**

and use the Search function with the following key terms:

Africa slave trade

## Wadsworth History Website Resources

Visit the World History Resource Center at **http://history.wadsworth.com/world** for a wealth of general resources, and the *World Civilizations* Companion Website at **http://history.wadsworth.com/adler04** for resources specific to this textbook.

## HistoryNow

Enter *HistoryNow* using the access card that is available for *World Civilizations*. *HistoryNow* will assist you in understanding the content in this chapter with lesson plans generated for your needs. In addition, you can read the following documents, and many more, online:

Henry Morton Stanley, excerpts from *How I Found Livingstone*

Charles Dudley Warner, *Up the Cataracts of the Nile*

*America is ungovernable. Those who served the revolution have been ploughing the sea.*
**Simón Bolívar**

# 39 Latin America from Independence to Dependent States

The Independence Movements

The Age of Chaos and Caudillos

National Consolidation under Oligarchies

Social Distinctions

Land and Labor

Latin American and Caribbean Cultures

| | |
|---|---|
| 1810s–1820s | Wars of independence throughout Latin America |
| 1822–1889 | Brazil independent under constitutional monarchy |
| 1830s–1850s | Chaos, military coups, and caudillos |
| 1850s–1900s | National consolidation under oligarchies |
| 1898 | Cuba and Puerto Rico break with Spain |

The nineteenth century in Latin America is full of paradoxes and contradictions. The *criollos* of the late colonial period were eager to take power from the peninsulares, but their position of dominance over the lower classes depended on the legitimacy of the Crown's authority. In the Spanish colonies, the criollos were forced to declare independence in order to *avoid* liberal reforms from Madrid. The protracted wars of independence lasted from 1810 to 1825, but the following thirty years were anything but peaceful. With the monarchy gone (except in Brazil's independent monarchy), the center could not hold, and the criollo factions in most countries, lacking any political experience, could not unite to find a middle ground between the extremes of absolutism and republicanism. A new period of violence and civil wars, punctuated by despotic military regimes proclaiming themselves as saviors of society, lasted until the second half of the century, when a new generation of elites dressed their oligarchies (government by a few) in republican clothing. The booming **monoculture** economies (that is, economies reliant on just one or two crops) were based on exporting raw materials, which brought high prices due to growing demand in the industrialized world. As a result, the Latin American economies were dependent on foreign imports and investment, a type of economic colonialism that, in the following century, would lead to debilitating economic and political dependence on more developed countries. Meanwhile, the masses benefited little from independence; the new elites, following the colonial tradition, ignored the needs of the poor on whose labor they depended. Century's end saw the creation of new, politically aware middle and working classes, who would challenge the oligarchies in the twentieth century.

## The Independence Movements

By 1800 in Spanish America, the peninsulares and criollos, although legally equal in status, actually had become two distinct castes with conflicting interests. The criollos had become dissatisfied with rule by Madrid and Lisbon for reasons both commercial and political. Criollo resentment of the Spanish colonial regime was high because, although the Bourbon free-trade reforms had made the colonies more prosperous, they were forced to pay higher taxes, and the Crown still treated the colonies merely as sources of wealth for Spain. Educated criollos who had been exposed to the Enlightenment ideals of individual liberty and equality, and who had been inspired by the French and American revolutions, began to contemplate independence from Spain. Most of all, they aspired to a political revolution so that they might replace the peninsulares in the highest positions, something that had been denied to them for centuries. The criollos were not interested in revolutionary social change or with improving the lot of the lower classes. In fact, in many areas, they were outnumbered by the *castas,* Africans, and Indians, and felt threatened by them. The successful slave revolt in Haiti, as well as rebellions by groups of *castas* in Mexico and Peru, served as a warning to the criollos to avoid social reforms in order to protect their own interests.

In the decade between 1810 and 1822, one after another of the Iberian colonies in the Americas declared their independence and escaped from the grip of the mother countries. The revolts against Spain, Portugal, and France were *not* uprisings of the common people against their masters and landlords. On the contrary, with the single exception of the black slaves in French Haiti, all of the revolutions were led by the native-born whites who formed the elite class. After the persecution of rebels like the Venezuelan criollo Francisco de Miranda, who in 1806 led a handful of U.S. volunteers in an ill-fated attack against the viceroyalty of Nueva Granada, most criollos limited themselves to discussing their ideas of liberation under cover of the scientific and economic clubs that had been fashionable under the Bourbon kings.

The Napoleonic invasion of Spain and Portugal in 1808 (see Chapter 33) set in motion independence movements throughout the colonies. The Spanish monarchs were taken to France, and Napoleon's brother occupied the throne of Spain. The criollos' first concern was that Napoleon's victory over the Spanish and Portuguese monarchies would result in some type of radical, antielite reforms in the colonies. To *prevent* such reforms, various criollo groups in the Spanish colonies proclaimed that they were severing their colonial ties and taking over political leadership. They summoned the town councils (the one place where criollos had power) to decide their response to the sudden absence of the Spanish king. Would they transfer their obedience to the viceroys until the Spaniards defeated the French and the king was back on his throne? Or would they form their own local governments, to rule in the monarch's name, as occurred in Spain? From Mexico to Argentina, the councils declared new governments and banished the viceroys on the authentic grounds that the colonies legally belonged to the Spanish Crown, not to the Spanish nation. The new criollo governments would ostensibly be stewards of the American colonies until they could be returned to the king. It was not long before the king's representatives, the viceroys, were driven out and independence was declared. After a long struggle, the peninsulares followed the viceroys as well. Altogether, the wars of independence of the Spanish colonies lasted more than fifteen years, from 1810 to 1825, when the last Spanish soldiers left Peru.

Three of the Latin American warriors for independence were particularly important:

1. *Miguel Hidalgo,* the Mexican priest who started the revolt against Spain in 1810;
2. *José de San Martín,* who liberated Argentina and Chile with his volunteer army;
3. *Simón Bolívar,* who liberated northern South America and is the best known and most revered of the three.

In each colony, other men also contributed to the success of the rebellions: Agustín Morelos in Mexico, Bernardo O'Higgins in Chile and Peru, and the Portuguese Prince Pedro in Brazil, among many more. But it should be repeated that, outside of Haiti, the revolts were led and carried through by conservative or wealthy men, who had no interest at all in social reforms or political equality.

The restored monarchs of Spain and Portugal were far too weak and too preoccupied with their internal affairs after Napoleon's eventual defeat to interfere. The faint hope of the Madrid government that it could find European support for an overseas expedition to "restore order" was put to rest in 1823 when the U.S. president James Monroe issued the **Monroe Doctrine**, protecting Latin America from European interference. Latin America was thus acknowledged to be independent, at least in terms of international law. Within a few years, no fewer than nine sovereign states had appeared from the wreckage of the former Spanish dominions, and a generation later, this number had reached eighteen. All hope of a large, integrated entity reaching from Texas to Cape Horn had to be soon abandoned, as regional and personal quarrels came to the fore.

The most farsighted and most tragic of the heroes of the early independence era was Simón Bolívar (1793–1847), who struggled throughout the 1820s to bring the various regions together under a federal constitution modeled on the U.S. Constitution. He failed at this task, and at the end of his life he declared, "America is ungovernable . . . elections are battles, freedom anarchy, and life a torment." This black depression was the result of seeing one reasonable plan for Latin American union and progress after another fail because of the indifference of the people or sabotage by selfish personal interests.

The great question in the early years of the revolutions in Latin America was whether the new governments should be monarchies or republics. The example of the newly independent United States was well known in Latin America, and many criollos thought that a republic

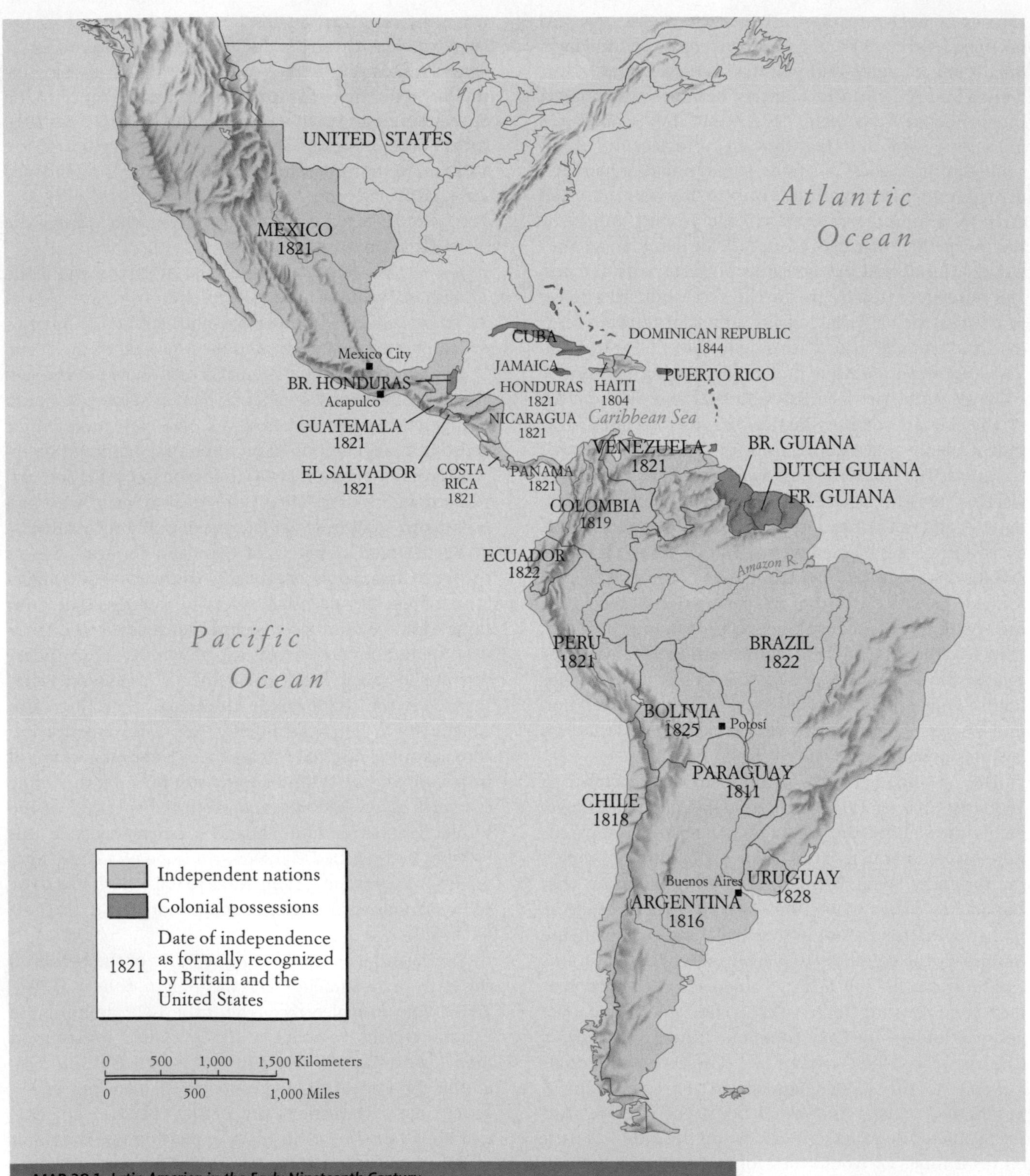


**MAP 39.1** *Latin America in the Early Nineteenth Century*

This map shows the changes in status after 1804, when Haiti was effectively made independent by a slave rebellion.

Bettmann/Corbis

**General Simón Bolívar Leading His Troops.** Images and statues of the revered "Liberator" are seen all over South America.

was the only form of government suitable for the new nations (see Map 39.1). But many were fearful of the power of the mob, and especially of the mestizos and blacks. They rejected the sharp break with tradition that a republican form of government necessarily represented; instead, they wanted a monarchy. The struggle between the two schools of thought went on throughout the revolutionary decades of the 1810s and 1820s. Except in Brazil, the battle was eventually won by the republicans, who protected the rights of property and the existing social structure by placing supreme powers in a legislature elected through a narrowly drawn franchise. The efforts of some to introduce democratic forms were generally repulsed until the twentieth century.

The Portuguese colony of Brazil took a more peaceful route to independence. When Napoleon's army reached Portugal, the royal family sought refuge in Brazil, ruling what remained of their empire from their court in Rio de Janeiro. Eventually, when the king and queen returned to Portugal, the Brazilian elites, preferring a monarchy, pressured Prince Dom Pedro to remain in Brazil. After he submitted to their entreaties, Pedro declared independence and led a constitutional monarchy, which ensured the unity of the new nation. By now too weak to do otherwise, the once-great imperial power, Portugal, chose not to make any effort to retain her colony. Thus, the transition to independence was far smoother for Brazil than it was for Spanish Latin America. Although Brazil faced the same obstacles of regional separatism, conflicts between conservatives and liberals, and questions about the role

Archivo Iconografico, S.A./Corbis

**Brazilians Cheer Their New King.** Dom Pedro I liberated Brazil; he and his son, Dom Pedro II, were benign constitutional monarchs.

of the Church, Brazil's constitutional monarch worked with the various factions to resolve the problems of the newborn nation. In 1889, after the progressive king Dom Pedro II supported the emancipation of the African slaves, the same elites who had supported him turned against him because their wealth depended on slave labor. Dom Pedro was ousted by an unlikely coalition of these disgruntled elites and liberal factions that for decades had pushed for a democratic republic and the end of the monarchy.

The main outlines of nineteenth-century politics were delineated by the struggle between liberals and conservatives. On the liberal side were those inspired by the French Revolution's original goals: the liberty and fraternity of humankind and the abolition of artificial class distinctions. Mostly from the embryonic middle stratum of society, they regarded Bolívar as their leader and thought the proper form of political organization was a federation, exemplified by the United States. Most of the liberals came from a commercial or professional background and were strong promoters of economic development.

The conservatives generally were either landed gentry or had connections with the powerful Catholic clergy. Like all conservatives, they emphasized stability and protection of property rights first and foremost. They looked on the Indians and mestizos as wards who could be trained only gradually toward full citizenship, but who in the meantime had to be excluded from political and social rights. The conservatives would support a republic only if their traditional preferences were guaranteed; if not, they could be counted on to finance and direct the next "revolution."

## The Age of Chaos and Caudillos

Bolívar once said, prophetically, "I fear peace more than war." The thirty years of instability and violence that followed the wars of independence proved that his fears were well founded. Latin America lacked three elements present in the newly independent United States: a middle class with a strong work ethic, experience in self-government, and a fairly homogeneous population. Everywhere in Latin America, the civil government operated in the shadow of the military, and the frequent dictators almost always came from the army ranks. Government policy was tightly controlled by a small group of wealthy individuals, who were closely linked with the military officer corps. The prestige of the military man was an unfortunate consequence of the battles for independence—unfortunate, that is, for constitutional process and the rule of law.

Few of the Spanish American nations escaped the anarchy and chaos of the 1820s to the 1850s that gave rise to the military strongmen. The frequent "revolutions" and "manifestos" were shadow plays, disguising the raw greed that impelled almost all of the actors. The vacuum of authority, left by the deposed monarchy and a weakened Church, resulted in the reassertion of regionalism and the power of the local political bosses, which the colonial regime had just barely been able to contain.

The ***caudillo,*** the epitome of the military strongman, would rise and assert populist dictatorial rule for a time. He maneuvered for supreme power, using a combination of personal charisma, force of arms, political skills, and patronage. The caudillos who achieved national prominence were the only leaders who had proven capable of quelling the endemic squabbling among the numerous petty regional chieftains. Almost always, these individuals soon made peace with the large landlords and other criollos who had traditionally governed. Social reforms were forgotten for another generation, while the caudillo became corrupt and wealthy. When internal affairs seemed to become too dangerous for their continued survival, many caudillos would find one excuse or another to divert attention by starting a war with their neighbors. For this reason, much of Latin America was at war over pointless territorial disputes throughout most of the nineteenth century.

One of the most infamous examples of such a caudillo is Juan Manuel Rosas, who ruled Buenos Aires, then all of Argentina, from 1828 to 1852. Born a criollo, as a young man he rejected all things Spanish and became a hacendado (owner of a large plantation) with a successful beef-salting business. He trained himself to be expert at the skills of the gauchos, gaining the respect of his gaucho ranch hands, and eventually subduing the gaucho chieftains who were ravaging Argentina with their warfare. As governor of the province of Buenos Aires, Rosas aspired to the presidency; however, he did not stage a national coup. Instead, he astutely waited until the civil wars had become so destructive of social order that the Buenos Aires elites begged him to reimpose stability as president with unlimited powers.

Rosas adopted the label of "federalist" while governing as an authoritarian centralist. He called himself "Restorer of the Law," but his opponents called him "Tyrant of the Argentine." His crimes against the people far outweighed the economic improvements he managed to achieve. Rosas's personal police force mercilessly persecuted anyone who opposed him, from peons to intellectuals. Meanwhile, the elites, who were anxious for peace at any price, looked the other way when the heads of innocent victims appeared on pikes in Buenos Aires and when Rosas refused to grant a stay of execution to a young criolla named Camila O'Gorman who had been impregnated by her priest-lover. Rosas was finally deposed by a coalition of the gauchos who realized they had been duped and by the exiled intellectuals (such as the future president, Domingo Faustino Sarmiento) whose writings marshaled international opinion against the tyrant. Rosas's most constructive legacy was that the movement to oust him unified Argentinians of all factions against despotism as the easy road to peace and order.

During the second half of the nineteenth century, liberal leaders such as Sarmiento in Argentina and Benito Juárez in Mexico established the foundations of oligarchic civil republics. (See Law and Government box.) Brazil, Chile, Uruguay, and Costa Rica also achieved constitutional stability based on civil governments. Unfortunately, the lower classes in these republics were excluded once again; in fact, they were considered an obstacle to progress. What is more, in most Hispanoamerican countries, the authoritarian tradition of the caudillo predominated during the nineteenth and well into the twentieth century.

## National Consolidation under Oligarchies

During the second half of the century, a new generation of elites in Argentina, Mexico, Chile, and a few other countries recognized the need for reconstruction after decades of civil war. The political and economic reorganization of the new states took place according to the principles of liberalism: secular government, the protection of individual property rights, free trade, and modernization

LAW AND GOVERNMENT

### Plans for the Political Organization of Argentina

**The leading Argentinian jurist Juan Alberdi** wrote a book that had a great influence on the drafting of the Constitution of 1853, a year after the despot Rosas had been toppled, when the country was still struggling over whether to have a federal or centralized government. This selection defines "civilization" in the optimistic tone of nineteenth-century liberalism and could apply equally to all of Latin America, although Argentina benefited most from his ideas.

> We are incapable of either perfect federation or of a perfect [centralized] government, because we are poor, we are insufficiently educated, we are few. . . . Democracy itself fits in badly with our conditions, yet we live in it and are incapable of living without it. The same thing will happen with our . . . general system of government; it will be incomplete, but at the same time it will be inevitable. . . . Unity, after all, is not the starting point but the goal of all governments; history proclaims this and reason proves that it is so.
>
> [The] constitutions [of the 1820s] fulfilled their mission. The men who drew them up understood their epoch and knew how to serve it. . . . But the nations of Latin America now [of the 1850s] have other needs. The same approach can no longer apply. . . . What we must now do is to emancipate our countries from their miserable economic backwardness. . . . Today we must strive for free immigration, liberty of commerce, railroads, the navigation of our rivers, the tilling of our soil, free enterprise, not instead of our initial principles of independence and democracy, but as essential means of assuring ourselves that these will cease being mere words and will become realities. . . . We must begin by building up our young national bodies.
>
> The only sensible constitution for a country in this condition is one which will make its [unpopulated] wilderness disappear. . . . In America to govern is to populate [with immigrants, preferably from nothern Europe] . . . in the sense that to populate is to educate, to improve, to civilize, to enrich, and make great, spontaneously and rapidly, as has happened in the United States. . . . The end [objective] of constitutional policy and government in America, then, is essentially economic.

#### *Analyze and Interpret*

What tenets of nineteenth-century liberalism does Alberdi mention? Which of these did Argentina carry out during its national consolidation in the second half of the century? Do you agree with the author that the leaders of the 1820s "knew their epoch and . . . how to serve it?" In 1900, it was predicted that, of the two great American immigrant countries, Argentina and the United States, Argentina would become the greatest world power. Why do you think that did not happen?

Source: Juan Bautista Alberdi, *Bases y puntos de partida para la organización política de la República Argentina,* 1852, as cited in English translation in John Crow, *The Epic of Latin America* (New York: Doubleday, 1971).

following European models. The liberal reforms were initially more successful in Argentina than in Mexico.

After the fall of Rosas, Argentina's civil governments took crucial steps toward modernization and political organization under a new constitution. The southern Indian territories of Patagonia were conquered, and hostile Indians were either subdued or exterminated. After decades of disputes between Buenos Aires and the hinterland, Buenos Aires became a federal district and capital of the country. The infrastructure was developed with the help of the British: roads and railroads were built, barbed wire sectioned off the Pampas into ranches, and a large-scale livestock industry was developed. Under Sarmiento, the "Schoolmaster President," public schools were created, and primary education was declared free and obligatory. Henceforth, Argentina would have one of the highest literacy rates in the Western Hemisphere. Immigration was encouraged to help populate the empty territories and to improve the racial mix. The liberal leaders denigrated Hispanic traditions and the mestizo culture of the gauchos and emulated what they saw as the superior civilizations of the United States and Britain.

Mexico during the second half of the century, after the overthrow of the caudillo Santa Anna, faced more obstacles to national organization than did Argentina. The Catholic Church and its conservative supporters were more entrenched, and the mestizos and Indians more numerous. Benito Juárez, a full-blooded Zapotec Indian who, like his contemporary, Abraham Lincoln, rose from humble origins to become president, is revered as the spirit and soul of his country and protector of its independence. Juárez was a liberal reformer who also planted the seed for a whole series of changes in the national consciousness of his country toward the relative importance of criollo and mestizo values. In a society long known for its aristocratic views, he awakened Mexican nationalism and steered his people on the lengthy and rocky path toward political democracy. As minister of justice in the new government that succeeded Santa Anna, Juárez was primarily responsible for the creation of the strongly liberal and reformist constitution of 1857. All of these activities brought him the solid opposition of the conservative elements, notably the entrenched hacendados and the higher churchmen. This opposition led to the War of Reform (1858–1861), in which the liberals were able to beat back the challenge of the reactionary groups and preserve the constitution under Juárez's leadership as acting president.

After the War of the French Intervention (1862–1867), when Napoleon III tried in vain to make Mexico a French colony, and a final, ill-fated attempt by the Mexican conservatives to install a monarchy, Juárez was reelected president. However, the struggle between liberals and conservatives was as fierce as ever and showed no signs of abating after the victory over the French. Like other Latin American reformers, Juárez ended his life painfully aware of the difficulties in getting his fellow Mexicans to agree on even the most basic elements of political and social progress.

Mexico was not yet ready for the ideals put forth in Juárez's Constitution of 1857. The reaction to the Reform came in the form of a forty-year dictatorship under the caudillo Porfirio Diaz. The vision of Juárez and the liberal reformers would be realized only after the Revolution of 1910–1920, when the Constitution of 1917 reintroduced the principles first put forth in 1857, such as separation of church and state and secular education.

By the last quarter of the nineteenth century, the once-idle criollo elite class in Argentina, Mexico, and elsewhere had become entrepreneurs in their booming, export-based economies. Their prosperity was linked with the Gilded Age in Europe and the United States; in fact, because the Spanish American countries exported raw materials and imported the products they did not yet produce, their wealth came from a kind of economic colonialism.

**Portrait of Benito Juárez, Father of Modern Mexico.** The president of Mexico, Vicente Fox (2000–2006), admires a portrait of former President Benito Juárez.

Reuters/Corbis

The criollos were interested in pursuing political power in order to protect their agriculture, livestock, and mining interests. Accordingly, they imposed political control either indirectly, through mestizo dictators (like Díaz in Mexico, and his peers in Venezuela and Peru), or directly, through nominally republican oligarchies where elections were fraudulent (in Chile and Peru). The railroads built to carry products to the ports were also used to transport federal troops to quell local uprisings. By ensuring stability, the elites were able to attract foreign investment and, in turn, promote growth of the import-export economy. By the early twentieth century, Latin America had developed some textile and food processing factories, and the service industries were robust (transportation, government bureaucracy, and commerce, among others). Two results of the growing native enterprises were to have repercussions far into the following century. First, there was the creation of an urban, educated middle sector (professionals, merchants, and small businessmen) that would demand to be included in the power structure. Second, the streams of immigrants who were invited to join working classes (except in Mexico and Cuba, which had large indigenous or African work forces) organized into mutual societies, and eventually labor unions, creating demands for better pay and working conditions.

## Social Distinctions

In the constitutions that were worked out after independence, all legal distinctions among the citizens of the new states were declared void. Slavery was abolished in most (but not all) of them, but that did not mean that no social class distinctions existed. The Latin society of the colonial period had already evolved a clear scale of prestige: the "pure-blooded" criollos were at the top, various levels of Europeanized mestizos were in the middle, and the non-European ***castas*** (free people of color), Indians, and black ex-slaves were at the bottom. This order was reinforced by the prevailing nineteenth-century "scientific" theory that the white masters were inherently superior to their workers of color. Because people were born into their places on the scale, Latin American society is frequently called a "classist society." Status was largely visible at a glance, because skin color was an important factor in determining who was who. Although Latin society was relatively free of the legal and political prejudice against the dark-skinned population that the people of the United States only partly overcame in the Civil War, the society had a distinct social gradient by complexion that was (and is) taken for granted.

States with numerous pure-blooded Indians (most of South and all of Central America) refused to allow this group to participate as equals in either political or cultural life and made no effort to introduce them into national public affairs for several generations. These restrictions were not necessarily a bad thing: most of the Indians had neither experience nor interest in government beyond the village or tribal levels.

In free Latin America as under Spain, the towns were the center of everything that was important: politics, administration, cultural events, commerce, and industry. The criollos were disproportionately prominent in the towns. The countryside was inhabited by the bulk of the population: mestizo or Indian small farmers, farm and pastoral laborers, and many hundreds of thousands of people who had no visible means of support. The absentee landlords lived in town, looked toward Europe, and left daily control of the rural plantations to agents and managers.

For the mestizo and Indian masses, life was a losing struggle against poverty; the people lacked good land, industrial jobs, and enterprise in the ruling group that were needed to induce change for the better. Although slavery was forbidden, *peonage* became commonplace on the haciendas. Peonage was a form of coerced labor that served to repay real or alleged debt owed to the employer; it was not much different from slavery for the victim and perhaps even more lucrative for the master.

The universal backwardness of the rural majority was a chief reason for the stagnation of national politics throughout most of the nineteenth century. Illiteracy and desperate poverty were normal; the hierarchy of social classes from colonial days did not change. The Indians, blacks, and their mixed-blood offspring remained mostly outside of public life, although they technically became free and equal citizens when slavery was abolished (Brazil did not abolish slavery until 1888, when it became the last of the Western Hemisphere countries to do so). Blacks and Indians had more opportunity for mobility in Latin America than in North America, however. Latin American society was willing to consider light-skinned mulattos and mestizos as equivalent to Europeans rather than holding that miscegenation (mixed blood) was an insuperable obstacle to social status. Relative wealth, skills, and education counted for more than blood alone. For example, if an Indian left his village and traditional lifestyle and became Hispanicized, in terms of lifestyle and social status, he was no long considered an Indian. The Mexican president Benito Juárez (see previous discussion), who was Indian by birth but criollo by lifestyle, epitomized the social mobility of the fortunate gifted individual of humble origins.

## Land and Labor

Land (the source of livelihood for most people) was held in huge blocks by a few families, who often claimed descent from the conquistadores. Sometimes they had land grants from the king to prove it; more often, their ancestors had simply taken over vast tracts from the helpless Indians.

Because land was useless without labor, first the Indians and then (in Brazil and the Caribbean) imported blacks were forced to work it as slaves.

Slave agriculture is normally profitable only where monoculture plantations can produce for a large market. For this reason, Latin American agriculture came to be based on one or two export crops in each region—an economically precarious system. Originally, the cash crops were sugar and rice destined for the European or North American markets. Later, bananas, coffee, and citrus in the more tropical lands and cattle and wheat in the more temperate climates became the main exports. Almost all the labor of clearing land, raising and harvesting the crop, and transporting it to market was done by hand. Machinery was practically nonexistent well into the twentieth century, because with labor so cheap, the landholders had no need for machines.

The size of the *latifundios* (big rural plantations) actually grew after independence. Their owners were practically little kings within the republics. Although these great landowners did not carry formal titles of nobility after independence, they might as well have done so, because they comprised an aristocracy in the truest sense. Mostly of European blood, they intermarried with one another exclusively; their sons went into high government office or the army officers' cadres by right of birth. In the nineteenth century, this aristocracy lived very well, in both the material and the intellectual senses, but they inherited the lack of social responsibility that also marked their ancestors. They either could not see or would not recognize that the miserable conditions of the majority of their fellow citizens eventually posed a danger to themselves (see Society and Economy box).

SOCIETY AND ECONOMY

## The Monstrous Division of Land in Mexico

**One of Mexico's most committed** nineteenth-century liberals, Ponciano Arriaga, spoke eloquently about land reform at the convention that hammered out Benito Juárez's Reform Constitution of 1857. Arriaga and his small group were among the few liberals of the time who cared about the hacienda system that kept millions of peons in misery. His speech is visionary, in that it spells out the main triggers of the Mexican Revolution of 1910–1920, waged by the peasants for "land, bread, and liberty." Ironically, the Constitution of 1857 emphasized private over corporate ownership of land. The same "reform" statutes that divested the Church of its vast landholdings, and hacendados of unused lands, also shrunk the communal Indian lands that had been protected since the colonial New Laws of the Indies. In other words, between 1857 and 1910, untold numbers of Indians wound up working as serfs on land that had been theirs for centuries.

> With some honorable exceptions, the rich landowners of Mexico . . . resemble the feudal lords of the Middle Ages. On his seignorial land, . . . the landowner makes and executes laws, administers justice and exercises civil power, imposes taxes and fines, has his own jails and irons, metes out punishments and tortures, monopolizes commerce, and forbids the conduct without his permission of any business but that of the estate. The judges or officials who exercise on the hacienda the powers attached to public authority are usually the master's servants or tenants, his retainers, incapable of enforcing any law but the will of the master.
>
> An astounding variety of devices are employed to exploit the peons or tenants, to turn a profit from their sweat and labor. They are compelled to work without pay even on days traditionally set aside for rest. They must accept rotten seeds or sick animals whose cost is charged to their miserable wages. They must pay enormous parish fees [much more than] the fees that the owner has arranged beforehand with the parish priest. They must make all their purchases on the hacienda, using tokens or paper money that do not circulate elsewhere. At certain seasons of the year they are assigned articles of poor quality, whose price is set by the owner, constituting a debt which they can never repay. They are forbidden to use pastures and woods, firewood and water, or even the wild fruit of the fields, save with the express permission of the master. In fine, they are subject to a completely unlimited and irresponsible power.

### *Analyze and Interpret*

Do you think the problems outlined in Arriaga's speech were unique to Mexico (refer back to Chapter 30, Society and Economy)? Why were most nineteenth-century liberals unwilling to address the problems of peonage? Why do you think Benito Juárez, as the leader of the Reform and as an Indian, did not include in the Constitution of 1857 a statute protecting the Indians' communal lands?

Source: Francisco Zarco, *Historia del congreso estraordinario constituyente de 1856 y 1857* (Mexico, 1857), 2 vols., Vol. I, pp. 546–555, as translated by Benjamin Keen, ed., in *Latin American Civilization*, 6th ed. (Boulder, CO: Westview Press, 1996), pp. 273–274.

**HistoryNow™**

***To read another view of haciendas, written by George M. McBride in 1923, point your browser to the documents area of* HistoryNow.**

Private Collection/Bridgeman Art Library

**SUGAR-CANE WORKERS IN CENTRAL AMERICA.** In many places in Latin America, people, not machines, do the heavy labor.

## LATIN AMERICAN AND CARIBBEAN CULTURES

The prevalent culture of Latin America owes as much to the European background of its original colonists as does the culture of North America. The two differ, of course. The ideas and values introduced into Latin America were predominantly Spanish or Portuguese, Roman Catholic, and patriarchal rather than British, Protestant, and (relatively) genderless as in the United States and Canada.

Whereas Iberian culture is supreme on the mainland, the Caribbean islands reflect the African origins of their black populations. The native Amerindian populations of the islands were exterminated or fled early and have been entirely supplanted by African ex-slaves and mulattos. Thus, the Caribbean culture is very different from the Iberian and is not properly considered a part of Latin America.

From these different roots have developed very different societies. As an example, until recently, public life in Latin countries was as much dominated by males as were ancient Greece and the Islamic civilizations. The adoption of the Napoleonic codes of law in these countries contributed to the persistence of the idea that the male is legally and socially responsible for the female. On the contrary, the black ex-slave societies of the Caribbean islands followed the African example of giving females a quasi-equal position in private and—to some degree—public affairs.

The Catholic Church in Latin America was guaranteed a supervisory role in most aspects of public life and private morals. It was from the start and remained an official church, supported by donations and taxes. It had little competition. Catholicism was the religion of the vast majority of the general population and of the entire ruling group. (As in the European homelands, Latin America has simultaneously had a strong tradition of anticlericalism.) The high clergy were automatically men of influence and did not hesitate to intervene in political affairs when they sensed that the church or their own family interests were threatened.

In the nineteenth century, the church was responsible for most educational institutions and practically all social welfare organs. At times, in some places, the church made a sincere effort at lifting the Amerindians and poor mestizos toward justice and dignity, even when doing so meant breaking with the ruling group from which much of the higher clergy came, but these episodes were the exception. Class ties generally seemed stronger than a sense of obligation to the common people, and the clergy were content to conform to the current ideas of their lay peers.

Peter Turnley/Corbis

**WOMAN IN HAITI CARRYING GOODS ON HER HEAD.** A scene from Caribbean work life. Haiti, a former French colony, is not properly considered part of Latin America.

Cultural stratification is particularly strong in Latin America and has long been an obstacle to national unity. Until the early twentieth century, the landowner–official group who controlled public life regarded themselves as Europeans residing in another continent, rather than as Latin Americans, much the same as the British colonists regarded themselves as Britons living in Australia or the French settlers regarded themselves as French living in Africa. The elite read European literature, taught their children European languages in European-directed schools, and dressed in current European fashions. When they grew tired of their surroundings, they often spent a year or two in a European capital. Many sent their older children to European schools and universities as a matter of course. When asked about family origins, young men and women would say they came from some Spanish town, which their ancestors had left (often as poverty-stricken emigrants) 300 years earlier! They did not recognize a Latin American culture that was separate and distinct from Iberia. They spent much of their lives attempting to keep up with contemporary European culture and trying to replicate it in their alien environment.

A powerful reason for the great difference between Latin and North American social habits and history in this regard was that the whites in Central and South America perceived Amerindian culture as a much greater threat than did the European settlers of North America. The Amerindians of Latin America were far more numerous than their North American cousins. The Spanish and Portuguese conquerors wanted to maintain a sharp distinction between themselves and the natives. This distinction gradually gave way, as a result of the large number of ordinary people who intermarried with the Indians and created the mestizo culture that predominates in many present-day Latin countries. But the ruling class rigorously maintained the distinction, remaining at heart Europeans who lived in Peru, Brazil, or Colombia, *not* Peruvians, Brazilians, or Colombians. For them, intermarriage was unthinkable.

## Summary

We have seen how difficult it was for Latin America to make relatively rapid transitions from colonial states to independent statehood. One should remember this period in the history of the Latin American nations not only for the violence, turmoil, and imperfect results, but also for the extraordinary feat of accomplishing in less than a century a process that took three or four hundred years in other parts of the world.

Criollo resentment against continued foreign rule increased under the late colonial reforms. Armed rebellion against Spain followed on the North American and French models, and by 1825, the colonials had established independent republics that Spain and Portugal could not recapture. Independence proved easier to establish than to govern, however. Military men and local caudillos became the ultimate arbiters of politics, despite grand-sounding manifestos and constitutions. An urban elite of absentee landlords maintained power despite numerous "revolutions."

The agrarian economy became dependent on the exports to western European and North American states. The rural majority lived in agrarian villages or haciendas in conditions that differed little from serfdom. Little manufacturing could develop, because of both the widespread poverty of the internal market and the openness of that market to imports from abroad. By the end of the nineteenth century, Latin America was perhaps tied more closely to foreign economic interests than it had ever been in the colonial era. The newly formed nations could not become truly politically independent because their economic dependence on countries such as the United States and Britain led to interference in their internal political affairs.

The disparities between the governing criollo cliques and the mestizo, black, and Amerindian masses were underlined by cultural orientations. The members of the upper class considered themselves Iberians and Europeans displaced in a Latin American atmosphere.

## Identification Terms

Test your knowledge of this chapter's key concepts by defining the following terms. If you can't recall the meaning of certain terms, refresh your memory by looking up the boldfaced term in the chapter, turning to the Glossary at the end of the book, or working with the flashcards that are available on the *World Civilizations* Companion Website **http://history.wadsworth.com/adler04.**

*castas*
*caudillo*
monoculture
Monroe Doctrine

## Test Your Knowledge

Test your knowledge of this chapter by answering the following questions. Complete answers appear at the end of the book. You may also take this quiz interactively and find even more quiz questions on the *World Civilizations* Companion Website: **http://history.wadsworth.com/adler04.**

1. The only successful rebellion by slaves in the Western Hemisphere occurred in
   a. Haiti.
   b. Cuba.
   c. Colombia.
   d. Brazil.
   e. Ecuador
2. Which of the following does *not* describe the conditions under which the Latin Americans gained independence?
   a. In the wake of the Napoleonic invasion of Spain
   b. As a result of the Spanish king's intolerable tyranny
   c. As a counter to a feared movement toward radical democracy
   d. Inspired by the successful North American and French revolutions
   e. The criollos' resentment of being subordinate to the peninsulares
3. Brazil avoided a violent transition from colony to nation because
   a. the plantation slaves, although numerous, were prevented from fighting.
   b. the colonial Brazilians had plenty of experience with self-governance.
   c. Brazil, by choice, operated as a constitutional monarchy for much of the nineteenth century.
   d. the Brazilian criollos were more interested in fiestas than in politics.
   e. the British intervened and stopped the budding revolution.
4. Caudillo is the Latin American term for
   a. a retired general who has been honored in civil life.
   b. an appointed governor of a province.
   c. a usurping strongman.
   d. a priest who has entered politics.
   e. a person of mixed blood who rises to prominence.
5. The tyrant Juan Manuel de Rosas was not
   a. criollo by birth.
   b. raised as a gaucho.
   c. merciless with his opponents.
   d. defeated partly by the writings of his opponents.
   e. president of Argentina.
6. Which of the following does not describe Benito Juárez?
   a. A pure-blooded Indian
   b. A committed defender of Mexican nationalism
   c. A devout ally of the Catholic clergy
   d. The father of Mexico's constitution
   e. The leader of the Reform movement
7. The Latin criollos of the independence movement were interested mainly in
   a. obtaining more land for themselves.
   b. keeping U.S. influences out of their homelands.
   c. achieving the installation of popular democratic government.
   d. ousting Europeans from their countries.
   e. maintaining political control against the Indian or mestizo masses to protect their livelihoods.
8. Which of the following is most correct? Racism in the Latin countries has traditionally been
   a. wholly contingent on the economic position of the affected person.
   b. expressed as prejudice but not persecution against the dark skinned.
   c. less overt but more harmful overall to good relations than in North America.

d. divorced from skin color but reflective of religious prejudices.
e. harshly practiced and based completely on a person's color.

9. Which was the last country in the Americas to outlaw slavery?
a. Honduras
b. Brazil
c. United States
d. Mexico
e. Argentina

10. *Monoculture* and *latifundio* are terms usually associated with
a. pastoral societies.
b. self-sufficient farmers.
c. growing of garden produce for local consumption.
d. large-scale, forced labor production for export.
e. nomadic gauchos.

## InfoTrac College Edition

Visit the source collections at

**http://infotrac.thomsonlearning.com**

and use the Search function with the following key terms:

Latin America history
Monroe Doctrine
Law and Government
Economy

## Wadsworth History Website Resources

Visit the World History Resource Center at **http://history.wadsworth.com/world** for a wealth of general resources, and the *World Civilizations* Companion Website at **http://history.wadsworth.com/adler04** for resources specific to this textbook.

## HistoryNow

Enter *HistoryNow* using the access card that is available for *World Civilizations*. *HistoryNow* will assist you in understanding the content in this chapter with lesson plans generated for your needs. In addition, you can read the following documents, and many more, online:

Simón Bolívar, "Message to the Congress of Angostura"

George M. McBride, "Haciendas," from *The Land Systems of Mexico*, 1923

*Hence all society would appear to arrange itself into four different classes: (1) those that will work, (2) those that cannot work, (3) those that will not work, and (4) those that need not work.*
Henry Mayhew

# 40 Advanced Industrial Society



| | |
|---|---|
| 1848 | *Communist Manifesto* |
| c. 1850–c. 1910 | Massive emigration from Europe |
| c. 1870s | Second Industrial Revolution begins |
| 1870s–1914 | Urbanization increases/Labor unions and mass democratic politics emerge/Marxist socialism strengthens |

Throughout the nineteenth century, the West (that is, western Europe and the United States) was clearly the dominant factor in world political and military developments. And this colonial subordination of much of the rest of the globe to Europe was a reflection above all of the West's large and increasing lead in technology and economic organization.

In the half-century between 1860 and World War I, Europe and the United States themselves went through a peaceful change of massive dimensions. As in the eighteenth century, a dual revolution was propelled by a shift in the sources of energy, which then was reflected in social organization and national politics. As the First Industrial Revolution was driven by steam, the Second Industrial Revolution was driven by petroleum and electricity. These two energy sources transformed urban life and made the city clearly the dominant social organism. Urban areas produced new businesses, new organizations of workers, new professions, and new lifestyles.

In these decades, socialism became for the first time a major force in several countries. As enunciated by Marx, it posed a severe threat from below to the combined aristocratic/bourgeois rule that had become the norm in European politics and economies. Also, while the non-Western world was being incorporated into the new financial and commercial system, Europeans were emigrating in massive numbers to selected areas of the globe, primarily for economic reasons. The Americas and particularly the United States were the favored destinations.

## The Second Industrial Revolution

As in the late eighteenth century, population growth and rising demand for consumer goods necessitated new energy sources. Europe's overall population exclusive of Russia rose from 265 million to 401 million in the second

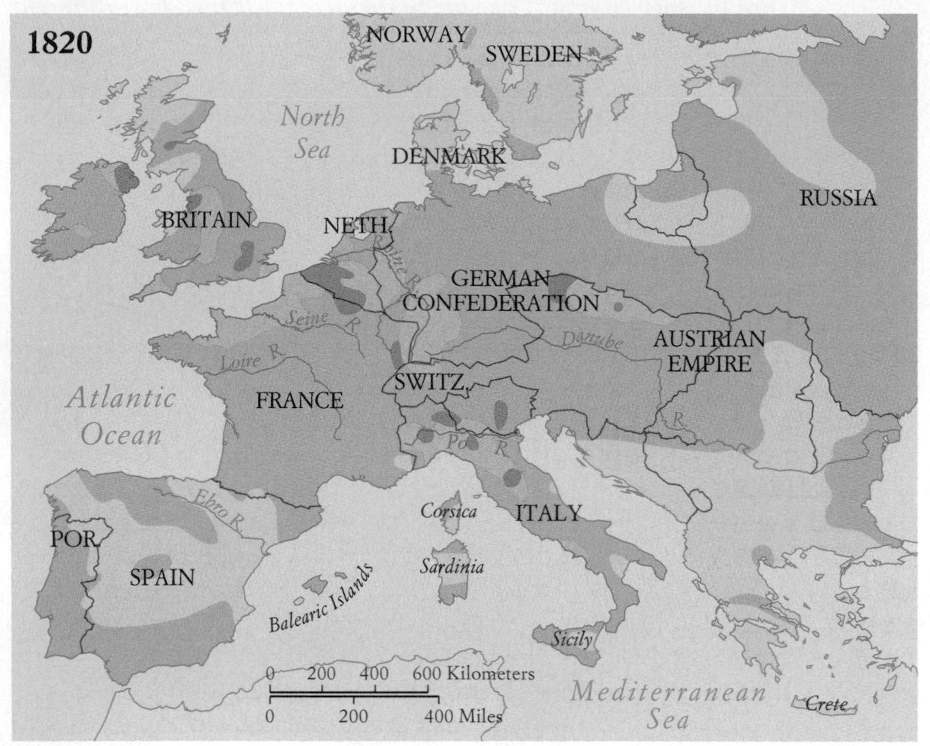


Inhabitants per square mile

<20 | 20–50 | 50–100 | 100+

**MAP 40.1** ***European Population Growth in the Nineteenth Century***

The Italian peninsula and parts of central and eastern Europe saw the most dramatic increases in population density during the eighty-year period from 1820 to 1900. In some rural areas in these lands, the lack of industry and the poor soil productivity had created an overpopulation crisis that was only ameliorated by emigration. Government was caught up in conflict with itself; emigration was discouraged and made difficult by national policy (particularly in Russia), while local authorities promoted it. In the latter third of the century, most of the younger male residents of whole villages and counties emigrated to the New World. Some intended to return—and did so—but the majority stayed in their new homelands.

half of the nineteenth century (see Map 40.1). Despite the stabilization of the average western European family at 2.5 children at the end of the century—the eastern Europeans were substantially more fertile—the previous huge increase, combined with a sharp rise in real income, created a large market for consumer goods and services of all types.

A definite rise in material standards of living was visible throughout Europe west of Russia. With fewer children's hands now necessary for labor, those who were

**A Paris Street Scene.** This view of the Montparnasse tram station was taken in 1900. The regularity of the building façades was one of the results of the massive rebuilding of this former slum undertaken by the government of Louis Napoleon in the 1860s.



born profited from better public health and nutrition to live longer, healthier lives. They could and did consume more. Goods that were almost unknown in European workers' houses in the early 1800s now became common: machine-produced footwear and clothes, nursing bottles for babies, gas or electric lighting, and books and newspapers.

Adding to this internal market was the rapidly expanding overseas market, both in the European colonies and in some of the independent nations of America and Asia. The surge of imperial ventures that began in the 1850s brought major increases in the availability of raw materials as well as the number of potential consumers in the Asian and African marketplaces. The volume of world trade shot upward in the later nineteenth century, and the West controlled that trade entirely. Britain, Germany, and the United States were the main beneficiaries.

## New Energy Sources

The big lead in industrial production that Great Britain had established in the early nineteenth century gradually narrowed after 1850. Belgium and northern France were the centers of the Continent's initial industries, followed by parts of Germany and Italy. After the unification of those two countries, their industrial growth accelerated sharply. As an important example, Germany's steel and iron production exceeded Britain's by 1893 and was almost double British production by 1914.

Whole new industries sprang up, seemingly overnight. Chemicals, oil refining, steamship building, turbines and electrical machinery, and, toward the end of the 1890s, the automobile industry are outstanding examples. But perhaps the most important of all the new developments was the taming and application of electricity to both industrial and domestic uses.

Electricity had been recognized as a potentially useful natural phenomenon since the eighteenth century (the days of Ben Franklin), but no practical use could be made of it then. In the 1870s, this situation changed dramatically as a result of the work of German, American, and French researchers. The development of generators and transformers allowed direct current to be sent wherever desired cheaply and efficiently, and then transformed into easily used, safe, alternating current. The first big urban power plant was constructed in 1881, and electric power was soon being used to light streets, power trams, and bring artificial light into hundreds of thousands of city homes and factories. Soon after, electrical machinery was being used in thousands of industrial applications. Electric railways and subway systems were introduced in every major European city by the 1890s. Probably no other series of inventions contributed so much to easing the physical labor and improving the material life of ordinary people.

Petroleum was the second new energy source. The internal combustion engine, which drew its power from the controlled explosion of gasoline injected into cylinders, was invented in 1876. Although it was clearly an impressive means of producing energy, its full potential was not apparent until the German engineers Daimler and Benz put the engine on a carriage and connected the cylinder pistons with the wheels. Benz's work in the late 1880s is generally credited with the emergence of the gasoline-powered automobile as a practical, reliable mode of transport, although literally dozens of other German, French, American, and British experimenters also contributed in major fashion to its development.

Petroleum and its by-product, natural gas, were to have many other uses, including lighting, heating, and driving stationary engines and pumps. From petroleum also came a whole range of important new chemicals. Then as now, Europe west of Russia had very little oil and depended on imports from other places. American capital (Rockefeller's Standard Oil) and American exploration and drilling techniques soon led the world in the race for oil production.

The Second Industrial Revolution depended largely on scientific research. The Germans with their well-equipped university and industrial laboratories quickly took over the lead in this area and held it without serious competition for many years. Their carefully organized and well-funded research enabled the Germans to dominate new European industry after 1870. The British, the former leaders, were slow to realize that the rules of industrial competition had changed. They put little money into research, from either government or private hands. By 1890, Britain's technological expertise and innovation were falling steadily behind Germany's, and this growing gap had much to do with the rising competition between the two countries in political and diplomatic affairs.

### *New Forms of Business Organization*

New forms of business organization accompanied the new energy applications. In the first century of the industrial age (1760–1860), the standard form of industry had been the private partnership or proprietorship. It was limited deliberately to a small handful of owner-managers, some of whom might work alongside their employees in the office or even on the shop floor. When more capital was needed for expansion, it was borrowed on a short-term basis for specific needs. The public was *not* invited in, and the banks and investment companies were not partners but only facilitators in arranging funds.

In the second industrial age (c. 1860–1920), the **corporation** rather than the partnership became the standard, and the corporation was often permanently financed by banks, which thus became part owners of the company. *Joint stock companies,* whose shares were traded on public stock exchanges in every European capital, were formed to raise huge amounts of capital from the investing public. The shareholders were technically the owners of the company, but, in fact, they had little or nothing to say about management policy, which was the purview of a board of directors with whom the investor normally had no contacts. This separation of ownership and management was one of the most striking changes in business and commerce of all sorts in the later nineteenth century, and it continues to the present.

## Social Accompaniments of the Second Industrial Revolution

The Second Industrial Revolution accelerated several trends that had begun during the first. Four were particularly important:

1. *Urbanization.* The outstanding feature in Western demography throughout the nineteenth century was the rapid growth of urban areas. Britain was the first European country to urbanize. In 1851, the census revealed that more than half of the English people lived in towns and cities. (At this time, by comparison, only 22 percent of Americans were urban dwellers.) By 1900, Britain alone had more cities with populations of more than 100,000 than there had been on all of the Continent in 1800. Industrial jobs were a major reason for migration to the cities, but they were by no means the only reason, as we saw in Chapter 39. Better education, leisure activities, and marital prospects were also strong incentives.
2. *Organization of labor.* After the failure of the 1848 revolutions, the workers on the Continent rarely attempted to gain better conditions by street riots or mass demonstrations. Instead, they took to organizing labor unions, which would fight for improvements in a legal way and attempt to gain government support against abusive employers. In so doing, the Continental workers were following the lead of the British, who had attempted to win reforms in their conditions of life and labor through the **Chartist movement** of the 1840s. Although their short-term goals were frustrated by conservative resistance and police repression, the Chartists initiated a long-term change both in and outside Parliament toward greater democracy and fairer distribution of the country's wealth.

   In the 1870s, Great Britain became the first major country to fully legalize labor unions, giving them the right to strike, picket, and boycott. In the 1880s, France took the same course, and in 1890 Germany did also. By the turn of the twentieth century, all western European nations except Spain and Portugal had conceded the rights of labor to use all nonviolent means available in the struggle for a better life.

3. *Social reforms*. The unions did give the laboring classes a new and fairly effective way to express their grievances and sometimes win redress for them. By 1914, few workers had to endure the sort of systematically inhumane working conditions that were common during the first industrial age. Child labor laws and industrial safety regulations were now common and enforced by both national and local authorities. A few countries had some provisions for worker employment security and pensions (Bismarck's Germany led in these respects). Even worker health and accident insurance was frequently provided by the government, if not the employer.

   The early unions were sometimes socialist in orientation, sometimes not. By the 1890s, however, the Marxist revolutionary socialists were close to taking over the labor movement in several key countries. (The United States was a notable exception; Marxism was never popular there.) This action frightened many employers and their partners in government, and they attempted to suppress or intimidate the socialist leaders. The last decade before World War I saw many bitter disputes between management and labor all over Europe and in the United States. Labor violence was common.
4. *Mass democratic politics*. An important effect of industrial life was the coming of mass politics and parties. In the last third of the century, almost all European governments as well as the United States allowed all of their male citizens to vote, regardless of property qualifications: Germany in 1871, France in 1875, Britain in 1884, and Spain in 1890. Only Russia, Hungary, and Italy stood firm against universal male suffrage as late as 1905. By the outbreak of World War I in 1914, all of Europe had male universal suffrage. This advance strongly stimulated the formation of large, tightly organized political parties. Before that time, the people who had the vote were property holders, relatively well educated, and generally aware of the issues of national politics. They did not need an organization to get out the vote, because they knew very well what was at stake in elections and made voting a major part of their public lives.

   Now, the much-enlarged number of voters had to be informed about the issues and organized into groups that would identify their interests, and act on them. The vehicle for doing this was a mass political party, equipped with newspapers, local organs and offices, speakers, and propaganda material. Most of the new voters were men of the working classes, and the new parties concentrated their efforts on them.

## Socialism after 1848: Marxism

The failure of the 1848 revolts inspired much analysis. National antagonisms and the passivity of the countryfolk were important, but the chief reason, all contemporary observers agreed, was the split between the liberal leaders—professionals and intellectuals—and the urban working classes. This split allowed the conservatives to gain a breathing space after their initial panic and then to mount a political and military counterattack that was successful almost everywhere (see Chapter 35).

Why did the split between the middle-class liberals and the workers occur? The liberals generally did not want social reforms. They only wanted to substitute themselves for the conservatives in the seats of political power. The workers, on the other hand, were economically desperate and wished to gain for themselves the type of thoroughgoing change in the alignments of power that the French peasants had won in the wake of the 1789 revolution. When it became clear to the liberals that the workers wanted to go much further down the revolutionary road, they withdrew to the sidelines or

**Suffragettes.** One of the many late-nineteenth-century demonstrations for women's voting rights, this one was in the United States. In most cases, the Western countries did not grant female suffrage until after World War I.

Bettmann/Corbis

actually joined with the conservatives, as happened in Vienna, Paris, and Berlin. In the end, the protection of property meant more than political or social ideals.

## Marxist Theory

One close observer of this development was Karl Marx (1818–1883). A German Jew whose family had been assimilated into Prussian Protestantism, Marx grew up in the Rhineland town of Trier. Soon after his graduation from the University of Berlin in 1842, he became deeply involved in radical politics. Pursued by the Prussian police, he had to leave his native city and flee to France as a political refugee. There, he came to know his lifelong colleague, Friedrich Engels, the wealthy, radical son of a German industrialist. The two men formed a close working relationship that was ideal for Marx, who devoted his entire adult life to research and writing, and organizing revolutionary socialist parties. (See Patterns of Belief.)

In 1848, coincidentally, just before the revolt in France, Marx and Engels published perhaps the most famous pamphlet in all of European history: the ***Communist Manifesto***. Marx predicted the coming of a new social order, which he called *communism,* as an inevitable reaction against the abuses of bourgeois capitalism. When this order would come, he did not predict, but he clearly expected to see communist society arise within his lifetime. It was equally clear that Marx and Engels expected communism would be born in a violent revolution by the industrial workers, the proletariat who had been reduced to abject misery and had little or no hope of escaping it as long as capital ruled. (See the Law and Government box.)

PATTERNS OF BELIEF

### Karl Marx (1818–1883)

> The critical thing is not to understand the world, but to change it!

**WITH THIS MAXIM AS HIS POLESTAR,** the philosopher Karl Marx became the most notorious, most quoted, and most influential social reformer of the nineteenth and twentieth centuries. The recent demise of that distortion of his ideas called Soviet communism has put his name and reputation under a heavy cloud from which they may never recover. But for 150 years, Marx and Marxism provided much of the world's dissatisfied citizenry with what they perceived to be their best hope of better times.

Marx was born into a well-to-do Jewish family in Trier, Germany, which at that time was part of the kingdom of Prussia. He studied at the universities of Bonn and Berlin, where his major interest was philosophy, but his interests soon expanded to include economics and sociology, two sciences that were still in their infancies. By the mid-1840s, he was slowly shaping his radical critique of contemporary European society by drawing on all three disciplines: German philosophy, English economics, and French social thought.

Prevented by his Jewish background from realizing his original plan of teaching in a university, Marx returned to Trier after graduating from the University of Berlin. In 1842, he opened a small newspaper, the *Rhenish Gazette,* which was dedicated to promoting social and political reform. He soon got into trouble with the conservative authorities and had to flee to escape arrest. He lived briefly in Paris, where he came to know his lifelong supporter Friedrich Engels, son of a wealthy German manufacturer. Engels and Marx collaborated on the *Communist Manifesto,* which was published just weeks before the 1848 revolutions.

Soon Marx aroused the suspicions of the French authorities and had to move on. An attempt to enter German politics as a revolutionary leader failed, and again Marx had to flee his native country, this time to London, where Engels was ready to help. Marx spent the rest of his life in English exile, living in genteel poverty with his German wife and several children.

The world around Marx was in the throes of the first wave of industrialism, and it was not an attractive place for most working people. Air and water pollution were common in the factory towns and in the working-class sections of the cities. Public health was neglected, medical help was restricted to the well-to-do, and welfare facilities of any type were almost nonexistent.

Women and children worked at exhausting jobs for very low pay, and workers were frequently fired without warning to make room for someone else who agreed to work for less. Neither law nor custom protected the workers' rights against their employers, and among the employers, cut-throat competition was the rule. Government intervention to ensure a "level playing field" in the marketplace was unknown. When governmental power was occasionally employed, it was always in favor of the status quo, which meant against the workers.

Marx observed this scene closely and was convinced that the situation must soon erupt in proletarian revolution. The explosion would come first in the most advanced industrial countries, which meant at this time Britain, parts of Germany

The proletarian revolution was inevitable, according to Marx, and the only questions were the precise timing and how it might be helped along by those who wished to be on the side of progress and justice. Marx issued an invitation to all righteous persons to join with the ignorant and miserable proletariat in hastening the day of triumph. Once the revolution of the downtrodden was successful in gaining political power, a "dictatorship of the proletariat" (not further defined) was to be created, which would preside over the gradual transformation to a just society.

What was the ultimate goal of Marxist revolution? According to Marx, it was a communist society, in which private control/ownership of the means of production would be abolished and men and women would be essentially equal and free to develop their full human potential. For the first time in history, said Marx, the old boast of the Greeks that "Man is the measure of all things" would be fulfilled. A society would be created in which "the free development of each is the condition for the free development of all."

At the time, no government took notice of the *Communist Manifesto.* None of the important 1848 revolutionary groups had heard of it or its authors, but in time this changed. During the 1850s and 1860s, Marx and Engels gradually emerged as two of the leading socialist thinkers and speakers. From his London base (England had the most liberal political association and censorship laws in Europe), Marx worked on his great analysis of mid-nineteenth-century industrial society, *Capital* (1867–1873). This work was the basis of Marx's boast that his socialism was scientific, unlike the utopian (that is, impractical) socialism of earlier days.

and France, and possibly the United States. While Engels provided financial assistance, Marx dedicated many years to working out a theory of history and social development that would make sense of the chaos and allow a rational hope of a better world in the future. Eventually, he produced *Das Kapital,* or *Capital,* the bible of scientific socialism, which was published in the original German in 1867 and translated into most European languages by the later nineteenth century. Almost all of the work was done in the Reading Room of the British Museum, which Marx visited with clocklike regularity for decades.

In 1864, Marx organized the International Workingmen's Association. This so-called First International lasted only a few years before it collapsed in internal arguments about how the revolution of the proletariat should best be accomplished. Marx was always a headstrong character and was most unwilling to allow others to have their say. Like many prophets, he came to think that any who disagreed with him were ignorant or malicious. Engels was one of the few intimates who remained faithful to the master to the end.

In 1883, Marx died in the same poverty in which he had lived in the London suburb of Hampstead for most of his life. At his death, the proletarian revolution seemed further away than ever, but the movement was slowly growing. It would make giant strides in several countries in the 1890s, and in far-off Russia, a country that Marx held in contempt for its backwardness, a certain Vladimir Ilich Ulyanov, better known as Lenin, was studying *Capital* with an eye toward the Russian future.

**Karl and Jenny Marx.** Marx spent most of his life in English exile with his long-suffering German wife, Jenny.

## *Analyze and Interpret*

What theory or philosophy do you think has taken the place of Marxist socialism as a hope for the world's exploited and oppressed workers? Or do you think that Marxism has not been defeated, but only temporarily rejected as a social philosophy?

LAW AND GOVERNMENT

## Communist Manifesto

**THE MOST WELL-KNOWN OF THE NINETEENTH** century's various revolutionary challenges was the manifesto produced by Karl Marx and Friedrich Engels in 1848 as a platform for the tiny Communist League they had recently founded in London. Most later Marxist doctrine appeared in this essay in capsule form. The following excerpts concern mainly the theory of the formation of classes and the struggle between them in history:

> The history of all hitherto existing society is the history of class struggle. Freeman and slave, patrician and plebian, lord and serf, guildmaster and journeyman, in a word, oppressor and oppressed, stood in constant opposition to one another, carried on an uninterrupted, now hidden, now open fight, that each time ended either in a revolutionary reconstitution of society at large, or in the common ruin of the contending classes. . . .
>
> The modern bourgeois society . . . has not done away with class antagonisms. It has but established new forms of struggle in place of the old ones.
>
> Our epoch, the epoch of the bourgeoisie, possesses, however, this distinctive feature: it has simplified the class antagonisms. Society as a whole is more and more splitting up into two hostile camps, into two great classes directly facing one another: Bourgeoisie and Proletariat. . . .
>
> [T]he bourgeoisie has at last, since the establishment of modern industry and of the world market, conquered for itself, in the modern representative State, exclusive political sway. The executive of the modern State is but a committee for managing the common affairs of the whole bourgeoisie. . . .
>
> In proportion as the bourgeoisie, i.e., capital developed, in the same proportion as the proletariat, the modern working class, developed; a class of laborers, who live only so long as they find work, and who find work only so long as their labor increases capital. . . .
>
> Owing to the extensive use of machinery and to division of labor, the work of the proletarians has lost all individual character, and consequently, all charm for the workman. He becomes an appendage of the machine. . . . In proportion, therefore, as the repulsiveness of the work increases, the wage decreases.
>
> All previous historical movements were movements of minorities. The proletarian movement is the self-conscious, independent movement of the immense majority, in the interest of the immense majority. The proletariat, the lowest stratum of our present society, cannot stir, cannot raise itself without the whole super-incumbent strata of official society being sprung into the air.
>
> What the bourgeoisie produces above all, are its own gravediggers. Its fall and the victory of the proletariat are equally inevitable.
>
> The Communists disdain to conceal their views and aims. They openly declare that their ends can be attained only by the forcible overthrow of all existing social conditions. Let the ruling classes tremble at a communistic revolution. The proletarians have nothing to lose but their chains. They have a world to win.
>
> Working men of all countries, Unite!

### *Analyze and Interpret*

Do you agree that class struggles have largely defined history, especially in modern times? Do you think that a just society can be reached through violent revolution? Can it only be reached through violent revolution?

Source: Excerpted from Karl Marx and Friedrich Engels, *The Communist Manifesto* (New York: Signet Classic, 1998).

**History Now™**

*To read more of* **The Communist Manifesto,** *point your browser to the documents area of* **HistoryNow.**

Marx was a child of his times. The 1840s were the "dismal decade," years of the crudest exploitation of the workers by greedy or frightened employers. They were frightened because many were being driven to the wall by the relentless competition of the free market. As these small business owners desperately looked for ways to lower production costs, they usually resorted to reducing wages. Because what Marx called a "reserve army" of starving unemployed workers were always ready to work at almost any wage, the most elementary job security was totally absent. The result was often an extremely low pay scale for the semiskilled and unskilled workers who made up most of the early industrial labor force. Marx was not alone in believing that this condition would persist until it was changed by militant force from below.

## *Marxist Organizations*

When the Paris Commune arose in the wake of the lost war with Prussia in 1871, Marx mistakenly thought that the dawn of social revolution had come and enthusiastically greeted the radical oratory of the *Communards*. The Commune was speedily crushed, but socialist parties came into being everywhere after 1871 and grew steadily over the next decades. By the end of the century, the socialists were the primary voice of the industrial working class in most countries. Their common denominator was a demand for radical rearrangement of the existing socioeconomic order. Some of these parties were anti-Marxist in doctrine, either preferring some form of anarchism (see the next section) or wishing to operate mainly through labor unions (a tendency that Marx anathematized as mere reformism), but most were Marxist and subscribed to the principles laid out in *Capital* by the master.

The most important socialist parties were in Germany, Austria, Belgium, and France. In southern Europe, they were outnumbered by anarchists and syndicalists (see the next section). In Britain and the United States, no socialist party had a wide following, and in Russia, the Marxists were still a tiny exile group at the end of the century.

## Rivals of Marxism

In Mediterranean Europe and Russia, the theory of politics called **anarchism** captured many minds. Anarchism is the rejection of the state and the powers that the modern state exercises over its citizenry. Its followers believe that all government is necessarily prone to corruption. Only such authority as is necessary to avoid conflict over property or civil rights of the citizens should be surrendered by the citizens to their government. Even then, the least possible authority should be granted, and only on a small-scale, localized basis. Anarchists simply do not trust any government. They believe that sooner or later every government will succumb to the temptation to restrict its citizens' freedoms without just cause.

As a theory, anarchism goes back to the ancient Greeks, but the modern founders of anarchism are the Frenchman Pierre Proudhon, whom we have already encountered (see Chapter 35) and the Russian Michael Bakunin (1827–1876). Bakunin developed the *propaganda of the deed,* the idea that a dramatic, violent act was the most effective way to gather converts for anarchism. The deeds his followers performed were acts of political terror: they carried out bombings and assassinations in the hopes of shaking the structures of government from the top down. In the two decades between 1885 and 1905, the high point of anarchism, about 300 notable lives were sacrificed to this belief, including several reigning kings and queens, prime ministers, presidents (including the U.S. president William McKinley in 1901), and assorted generals.

Was the propaganda of the deed successful? It succeeded nowhere. Both governments and popular opinion reacted strongly against the terrorists. Eventually, the theory of anarchism itself became discredited because of its association with political murders. After World War I, little was heard of it until the 1960s.

**Syndicalism** is a form of political action by the working classes. It is founded on the belief that only the laboring classes and peasants should govern, because only they contribute a substantial asset to society through their work. Instead of the false verbal sparring and make-believe of the political parties, the laborers must create a large-scale association of persons employed in the same type of work. This association, called a *syndicate,* would represent the economic and social interests of the members and confer with other syndicates to find common political means for progress in economics and justice in society. Like anarchism, and unlike communism, syndicalism did not wish to abolish private property but to limit its political power and distribute it more evenly.

Syndicalism was stronger than socialism in Spain and Portugal and was a strong rival to it among the peasantry in Italy and France. Syndicalist government offered the poorly paid and insecure working classes and small peasants a theoretical way upward without going to the socialist extreme of class warfare and the abolition of private property. It never succeeded in establishing control of a national government.

### *Reform and Revisionism*

In Great Britain, the labor force was never much attracted to either socialism or its rivals as a solution to the dual problems of concentrated wealth and concentrated poverty. Instead, British workers in the later nineteenth century focused on gaining higher pay and better working conditions through a moderate reformism that centered on the right to strike and organize unions. In 1906, the reformist, non-Marxist **Labour Party** was formed on a platform of more equitable distribution of wealth. The new party gradually attracted the vote of most union members and much of the lower middle class. It was able to replace the Liberal Party as the main opponent of the Conservatives after World War I.

In the 1880s, Chancellor Bismarck attempted to crush the appeal of socialism in Germany by an attack on two fronts. First, he outlawed the Marxist socialist party, which had been organized in 1875, claiming that it was a revolutionary group that intended to ultimately destroy the state. Then he tried to show that socialism was unnecessary because the powerful and progressive German state would look out adequately for the workers' welfare. During the 1880s, a series of new laws instituting unemployment insurance, accident and health protection, and worker pensions made Bismarck's Germany the most progressive state in the world in terms of social policy.

The blunt attack on the Marxists did not succeed. After a few years, there were more German socialists than ever, and in 1890, the antisocialist law was repealed as an unadmitted failure. The German Social Democratic Party (SD) steadily gained votes, attracting not only workers but also the lower middle classes and civil servants. With several newspapers, a tight network of local offices, and an extensive member/financial base in the German labor unions, the German party set the pace for socialists throughout Europe.

In 1899, a leading SD theorist, Eduard Bernstein, published a book in which he claimed that the SDs would soon become strong enough to take over the state in peaceful, constitutional fashion. Socialism would then be introduced through the workings of a parliament and government controlled by the Marxists. Thus, the idea of violent revolution in the streets was outmoded. According to Bernstein, Marx (who had died sixteen years earlier) could not foresee that capitalism would be so altered by democracy that the workers would be able to counter it through the ballot rather than on the barricades. The triumph of social justice could and should be obtained without bloodshed.

This idea was heatedly denounced by many in the **Second International**, the Europe-wide association of socialists founded in 1889, but the theory attracted the party leadership in the more industrially advanced countries, especially in Germany and France. By the coming of World War I, **revisionism** (the adaptation of Marxist socialism that aimed to introduce basic reform through parliamentary acts rather than through revolution) was a strong rival to orthodox Marxism as the true path to the workers' paradise. (See Society and Economy for a view of one worker's reality.)

## Emigration Overseas

The largest human migration in world history took place from Europe to overseas destinations during the second half of the nineteenth century. What caused this world-reshaping move? In general, the triggers were economic, but the emigrations began with the political upheaval of 1848, when tens of thousands of Germans and Austrians looked to America for the freedoms they feared they would never have in their homelands.

From about 2.5 million in the 1850s, total net emigration from Europe rose each decade until it peaked in the years just before World War I. By then, about 12 million people had left Europe in a ten-year period, a number about equal to the entire population of Scandinavia at that time. The war shut this stream down almost com-

SOCIETY AND ECONOMY

### Home Work: Berlin 1898

**One of the plagues of working life** in the big European cities was the spread of home work into the tenements of the poor. Particularly the so-called needle trades depended on massive numbers of male and female production workers laboring in their own apartments for up to sixteen hours per day. Paid by the piece, the cutting and sewing was done in miserably overcrowded and unsanitary conditions. The family's one or two rooms usually had to serve as nursery, kitchen, sitting room, and bedroom as well as workplace. Children as young as nine were typically part of the "labor force." For the employers, the use of the workers' apartments meant saving the costs of not only the factory building and machinery but also worker pensions, sick pay, holidays, and so on, which they might otherwise have to bear. The following is excerpted from an 1898 exposé of conditions in Berlin:

> [T]he mother of a multitudinous family said, compared to her one-windowed room where her children slept, cried, played, and worked, she would far rather be in the factory where she had worked for awhile. As against the disorder and noise of her own household, the quiet and regularized factory environment was like a vacation, and she often could scarcely bring herself to return to her home after the work-day. But the infant child was constantly sick, and she had to give up her factory job. Now she sewed blouses all day long, and for longer worktime she earned actually less. Besides this, at home the needs of the children were constantly thrust into her eyes, while the necessity of steady work to support them demanded her full attention, and so she was always neglecting one task in order to do another. Her life had become an exhausting chase, so that "I think each morning that I simply can't get up and start another day."
>
> Another Berliner widow and mother of three told the census-taker in a few words her painful situation: "Because work and illness made it impossible to raise my children properly at home, I took them to an orphanage. But my mother's feelings couldn't be overcome, and after three months I brought them all home again. I hope that they can somehow raise and supervise themselves: I cannot."

#### *Analyze and Interpret*

What has happened to orphanages in our time? Why? Are there fewer children who require public assistance?

Source: Annette Kuhn and Jorn Rusen, eds., *Frauen in der Geschichte* (Dusseldorf: Pädigogischer Verlag Schwann, 1982), vol. 2, pp. 229ff., citing two German authors of inquests in 1898 and 1904.

pletely, and it never again reached those dimensions. In all, some 60 million Europeans emigrated during the nineteenth century and did not return. (Return to the homeland was common: about one of three emigrants to the United States eventually returned to the home country for reasons ranging from homesickness to deportation.)

## Destinations

Where were all of these people headed? The river of migrants flowed mainly to the New World, but Australia, New Zealand, and (for Russians exclusively) Siberia were also important destinations. The French colony of Algeria and the British colony of South Africa also attracted large groups of emigrants. (See Figure 40.1.)

In terms of proportionate impact on a given nation, Argentina was the most dramatic example of immigration in the world. About 3 percent of the total Argentine population arrived from Europe (mostly Spain and Italy) every year in the early twentieth century—three times the rate that the United States gained from the same source. But in absolute terms, the United States was easily the most popular single destination. It received about 45 percent of the grand total of immigrants worldwide during the nineteenth century.

Why did these emigrants leave? First and foremost, they were seeking better economic conditions. The rise and fall of emigration rates corresponded closely to European business cycles. In hard times, more left for the "land of golden opportunities," but a large proportion left because they were dissatisfied with domestic political and social conditions and had little faith that the future held any more promise than the present.

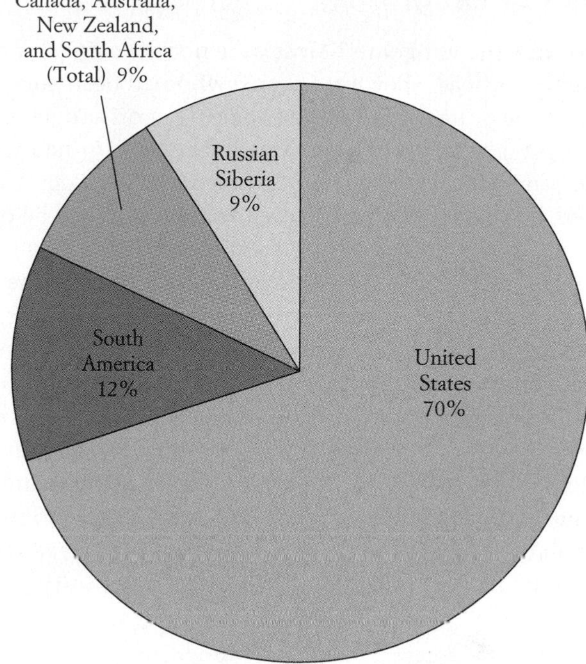


FIGURE 40.1 *European Emigrants' Destinations, 1800–1960*
The United States was easily the most preferred destination, with South America (mainly Argentina and Brazil) a distant second. What countries did the emigrants leave? Great Britain and Ireland supplied about 33 percent of the total; Italy, about 30 percent; and the rest of Europe, the remainder. The ethnic balance shifted steadily from northern and western Europe to southern and eastern as the nineteenth century matured. At the peak of European emigration in the decade just before World War I, an average of about 1.2 million emigrated annually.

**THE DINING HALL AT ELLIS ISLAND.** This 1906 photo captures the human faces who poured through the huge New York immigrant facility, which has recently been made into a museum. By this time, the dominant nationalities were Italian and eastern European. New York City's population was more than one-third foreign-born during this era.

## Types of Emigrants

Who were the emigrants? Most were not the very poor or ignorant. Instead, they were people who had been able to save a little or had relatives who were better off and helped them get a start. Many were small farmers who had too little land to ever get much farther up the ladder and feared for their sons' future when that little would be divided again by inheritance. Some were skilled craftsmen, who believed guild-type restrictions would prevent them from becoming independent entrepreneurs. Some were educated people who saw no chance of fully using their education in a class-bound society. In the later phases of the movement, the poor and ignorant also began to leave, assisted by relatives who had emigrated earlier and had managed to establish themselves in their new lands. Unmarried young men were the largest single contingent of emigrants, followed by young girls, usually the sisters and/or fiancées of males already in the new country.

The ethnic origins of the emigrants varied by chronology of departure. Most of those who left for the New World in the mid-nineteenth century were from Britain, Ireland, and Germany. In the later decades, they tended to be from eastern and southern European countries. By World War I, the Austro-Hungarians, Russians, Poles, and, above all, the Italians supplied the great bulk of the emigrants. A disproportionate number were Jews from the Russian empire (including Poland) who were fleeing racial persecution.

By the later nineteenth century, in the industrial economies of northern and western Europe, the working classes could find reasonably secure factory and white-collar jobs. Hence, they were less likely to emigrate than the unemployed and underemployed peasants and laborers of eastern and southern Europe. As a rule, the more literate and better prepared went to North America, Australia, or South Africa. South America received mainly those with lesser prospects.

Corbis

**Lower East Side of New York.** This magnificent "slice of life" shows Mulberry Street, one of the chief street markets in slum New York, in about 1900. Much of the population of such neighborhoods spent little of the day inside their cramped apartments, if they could help it.

## Summary

A Second Industrial Revolution was fueled by the electrical and petroleum industries and the myriad uses to which these new sources of energy were applied in the last third of the nineteenth century. The newly developed corporation replaced the partnership, and banks and joint stock companies became the usual means of raising capital in this same period.

In this second phase of industrialization, mass political parties became commonplace throughout western Europe. They sometimes represented newly organized labor and were almost always based on the rapidly expanding urban centers. By 1900, most industrial countries had introduced the universal male franchise. These developments contributed to the steady gains of socialism, particularly the Marxist variety after about 1880. Karl Marx's theories posited inevitable class warfare and a revolution of the proletariat against its capitalist oppressors. At the end of the century, this view was increasingly challenged by revisionism and/or other rivals in the search for a more just distribution of national wealth.

The later nineteenth century also saw the most extensive emigration in recorded history, as up to 60 million Europeans opted to leave their homelands permanently and travel to the New World or other areas for better economic or political prospects.

## Identification Terms

Test your knowledge of this chapter's key concepts by defining the following terms. If you can't recall the meaning of certain terms, refresh your memory by looking up the boldfaced term in the chapter, turning to the Glossary at the end of the book, or working with the flashcards that are available on the *World Civilizations* Companion Website **http://history.wadsworth.com/adler04**.

anarchism
Chartist movement
*Communist Manifesto*
corporation
Labour Party
revisionism
Second International
Syndicalism

## Test Your Knowledge

Test your knowledge of this chapter by answering the following questions. Complete answers appear at the end of the book. You may also take this quiz interactively and find even more quiz questions on the *World Civilizations* Companion Website: **http://history.wadsworth.com/adler04**.

1. The Second Industrial Revolution was generated by
   a. the worker revolts of 1848.
   b. capitalist exploitation of the workers to the maximum extent possible.
   c. industrial research and electrical energy.
   d. mining and iron making.
   e. scientific experimentation.
2. The countries that were in the forefront of the Second Industrial Revolution were
   a. Britain and the United States.
   b. the United States and Germany.
   c. Japan and the United States.
   d. Germany and Britain.
   e. Japan and Britain.
3. The most important of the new forms of business emerging in the late nineteenth century was the
   a. partnership.
   b. proprietorship.
   c. nonprofit company.
   d. corporation.
   e. savings and loan industry.
4. Labor unions first gained the legal right to organize and to strike in
   a. Germany.
   b. the United States.
   c. Britain.
   d. Holland.
   e. France.

5. The first European country to pass laws providing for universal male suffrage was
   a. Italy.
   b. Britain.
   c. France.
   d. Spain.
   e. Germany.
6. Which of the following pairs is logically incorrect?
   a. Karl Marx and scientific socialism
   b. Eduard Bernstein and revisionist socialism
   c. Michael Bakunin and anarchism
   d. Pierre Proudhon and anarchism
   e. All of these are paired correctly.
7. Which of these systems of government would operate only under the auspices of the laboring classes and the peasants?
   a. Communism
   b. Socialism
   c. Anarchism
   d. Legalism
   e. Syndicalism
8. The bulk of the European emigrants of the nineteenth century were
   a. landless laborers seeking a new start in North and South America.
   b. dissatisfied small farmers, businessmen, artisans, and skilled laborers.
   c. Jews and others fleeing political persecution.
   d. relatively successful shop owners, artisans, and white-collar workers.
   e. wealthy families who wanted the benefits of living in the world's most modern nation.
9. In the early twentieth century, the country supplying the largest number of emigrants to the United States was
   a. Germany.
   b. Ireland.
   c. Russia.
   d. Italy.
   e. France.
10. Which of the following was *not* a new phenomenon in the late nineteenth century?
   a. The corporation as the dominant form of business organization
   b. The spread of anarchist philosophy
   c. A dramatic rise in emigration to the United States from Europe
   d. Revision of the Marxist plan of violent revolution
   e. The growth of political parties

## InfoTrac College Edition

Visit the source collections at

**http://infotrac.thomsonlearning.com**

and use the Search function with the following key terms:

Marxism socialism history anarchism

## Wadsworth History Website Resources

Visit the World History Resource Center at **http://history.wadsworth.com/world** for a wealth of general resources, and the *World Civilizations* Companion Website at **http://history.wadsworth.com/adler04** for resources specific to this textbook.

## HistoryNow

Enter *HistoryNow* using the access card that is available for *World Civilizations*. *HistoryNow* will assist you in understanding the content in this chapter with lesson plans generated for your needs. In addition, you can read the following documents, and many more, online:

Karl Marx and Friedrich Engels, *The Communist Manifesto*

*Discovery consists of seeing what everyone has seen and thinking what no one has thought.*
Albert Szent-Gyorgi

# 41 Modern Science and Its Implications



| | |
|---|---|
| 1859 | Charles Darwin, *The Origin of Species* |
| 1871 | *The Descent of Man* |
| 1880s–1920 | Curie, Planck, Einstein, Freud, Jung, Pavlov |
| 1891 | *Rerum novarum* |
| 1895–1920 | Durkheim and Weber |
| 1920s–1930s | Christian revival |

In the West, the eighty years between 1860 and 1940 proved to be one of the most dazzling periods of innovation and change in intellectual history. In the last years of the nineteenth century, it was still possible for sophisticated persons to hold to a Newtonian view of the universe: the physical world or cosmos was a composition of law-abiding matter, finite in its dimensions and predictable in its actions. Fifty years later, most of the "hard" or natural sciences and especially physics, biology, and astronomy had been radically changed by some new factual data and many new interpretations of old data. The social, or "soft," sciences such as psychology, sociology, and economics had undergone a somewhat lesser transformation, although here the novel ideas encountered more resistance because they could not be easily demonstrated as factually correct.

Religion, too, experienced striking changes. Long in retreat before an aggressive secularism, some Western Christians had come to believe that their religion was evolving like other human thought and that the Bible was properly subject to interpretations that would differ sharply in various ages and circumstances. But some fundamentalist denominations moved instead toward an uncompromising insistence on literal interpretation of the Bible as the sole source of God's unchanging truth.

## The Physical Sciences

In the second half of the nineteenth century, the mental frame of reference implied or dictated by rationalism and science became much more commonplace than ever before. By century's end, educated individuals throughout most of the Western world accepted the proposition that empirical science was the main source of accurate and valuable information. Religious revelation, authority, and/or tradition were not seen as legitimate rivals.

In the first half of the twentieth century, the preponderance of science over competing worldviews became stronger still. Theology and philosophy, which previously had some persuasive claim to presenting a comprehensive explanation of the processes and purpose of human life, became the narrowly defined and exotic preserves of a handful of clerics and academics. In the universities of the West, which became for the first time the recognized intellectual centers of the world, the physical sciences became increasingly specialized while attracting more students. Meanwhile, armies of scientific researchers garnered the lion's share of academic budgets and prestige. Although ever fewer people were able to understand the intricacies of the new research, the educated public still maintained its belief in the method of science and its handmaiden technology as the most efficacious way of solving human problems. This viewpoint was weakened but survived even the cataclysms of the two world wars.

Corbis

**THE GORILLA'S REPROACH.** Thomas Nast was a well-known political cartoonist of the day, and this cartoon was one of his favorites.

## Biology

The shift from theology to science and hence from spiritual to material causation had begun with the Scientific Revolution of earlier days (see Chapter 31), but certain nineteenth-century ideas hastened its pace greatly. Darwinian biology was perhaps the most important.

In 1859, the Englishman Charles Darwin published ***The Origin of Species***, a book that did for biology what Adam Smith's *Wealth of Nations* had done for economics. The controversy the book set off roiled European and American society for more than a generation and generated acrid public and private debate. In the end, the Darwinian view generally won out over its detractors.

What did Darwin say? Basically, he argued that through a process of **natural selection**, the individual species of plants and animals (inferentially including humans) evolved slowly from unknown ancestors. The organisms that possessed some marginal advantage in the constant struggle for survival would live long enough to create descendants that also bore those assets in their genes. For example, a flower seed with sufficient "feathers" to float a long distance through the air would more likely find suitable ground to germinate than those with few or none. Slowly over time, that seed type would come to replace others in a given area and survive where others died off.

This is a mechanical explanation of nature's variety and of the evolution of species. It is similar to stating that an automobile moves along a highway because its wheels are propelled by a drive shaft and axles, which are themselves driven by a motor. That is all true, of course, but it leaves out any mention of a person sitting in the driver's seat and turning the ignition key. Darwin carried Newton's mechanistic explanation of the cosmos into the domain of living things. In so doing, he eliminated the role of an intelligent Creator, or God, who had ordered nature toward a definite purpose and goal: glorifying himself and instructing humans. God was superfluous in Darwinian science and, being superfluous, should be ignored.

Darwin carried this theme forward with his 1871 ***The Descent of Man***, which specifically included humans in the evolutionary process. It treated the morals and ethics they developed as the product of mechanical, naturalistic processes, not of an all-knowing and directing God. If the ability of our thumbs to close upon our fingers chiefly distinguishes humans from apes, as some biologists believe, then what some call the human conscience may also be just a product of evolutionary experience, aimed at physical survival rather than justice and obedience to the will of a Creator-Judge.

Contrary to general impressions, Darwin did not explain why natural selection occurs or the factors that caused some variance from the norm (a mutation) that resulted in the survival of one species and the expiration of others. That task was left to an Austrian monk named Gregor Mendel, who worked out the principles of modern genetics in many years of unrecognized labor with the common pea in his monastery garden. And it should be added that Darwin's work was matched, simultaneously, by the independent research of Alfred Russell Wallace, another English amateur, who never sought or received public notice until after Darwin's work had taken over the stage. (For a sample of Darwin's writings, see the Science and Technology box).

SCIENCE AND TECHNOLOGY

## Charles Darwin Reflects on *The Origin of Species*

**TOWARD THE END OF HIS LIFE,** Charles Darwin wrote an autobiographical sketch for his children in which he outlined his feelings about his epoch-making work. The following excerpts are taken from his reflections on the modification of animal and bird species he had observed during his 1836 voyage on the *Beagle* to the Galápagos Islands. The reference to success in adapting plants and animals to man's uses is to the ongoing breeding of improved livestock and crops. The reference to "Malthus on Population" is to the pamphlet that this author had given the world in 1798, claiming that the food supply would always lag behind the number of mouths to feed adequately.

> It was evident that such facts as these [that is, certain species' changes] as well as many others could be explained on the supposition that species gradually become modified; and the subject haunted me. But it was equally evident that neither the action of the surrounding conditions, nor the will of the organisms (especially in the case of plants), could account for the innumerable cases in which organisms of every kind are beautifully adapted to their habits of life—for instance a woodpecker or tree-frog to climb trees, or a seed for dispersal by hooks or plumes. I had always been much struck by such adaptations, and until these could be explained it seemed to me almost useless to endeavour to prove by indirect evidence that species have been modified.
>
> I soon perceived that Selection was the key-stone of man's success in making useful races of animals and plants. But how selection could be applied to organisms living in a state of nature remained for some time a mystery to me. In October 1838, that is fifteen months after I had begun my systematic inquiry, I happened to read for amusement "Malthus on Population," and being well prepared to appreciate the struggle for existence which everywhere goes on from long continued observation of the habits of animals and plants, it at once struck me that under these circumstances favourable variations would tend to be preserved and unfavourable ones to be destroyed. The result of this would be formation of new species.

After many hesitations and delays, Darwin finally decided to publish the book he had been incubating since 1837:

> In September 1858 I set to work by the strong advice of Lyell and Hooker* to prepare a volume on the transmutation of species, but was often interrupted by ill health. . . . It was published under the title of the "Origin of Species" in November 1859. Though considerably added to and corrected in the later editions it has remained substantially the same book.
>
> It has sometimes been said that the success of the *Origin* proved "that the subject was in the air," or "that men's minds were prepared for it." I do not think that this is strictly true, for I occasionally sounded not a few naturalists, and never happened across a single one who seemed to doubt about the permanence of species. Even Lyell and Hooker, though they would listen with interest to me, never seemed to agree. I tried once or twice to explain to able men what I meant by natural selection, but signally failed. What I believe strictly true is that innumerable well-observed facts were stored in the minds of naturalists ready to take their proper places, as soon as any theory which would receive them was sufficiently explained.

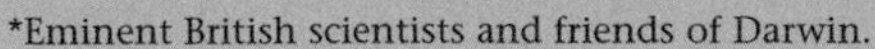

*Eminent British scientists and friends of Darwin.

Bettmann/Corbis

**CHARLES DARWIN.** Darwin's gravity assisted him to overcome the many critics and doubters who found his application of the theory of evolution to man offensive.

### *Analyze and Interpret*

Do you agree that scientific discoveries are awaiting a theory that will sufficiently explain facts already "well observed"? What comes first, the theory that explains or the facts that back up the theory?

Source: *Autobiographies: Charles Darwin; Thomas H. Huxley,* ed. Gavin de Beer (Oxford: Oxford University Press, 1974), pp. 70–74, 84.

**HistoryNow™**

***To read more selections from* The Origin of Species, *point your browser to the documents area of* HistoryNow.**

## Physics

In physics the pathbreakers were Ernst Mach (1838–1916), Wilhelm Roentgen (1845–1923), Max Planck (1858–1947), and Albert Einstein (1879–1955). The fact that all four were educated in German universities is an indication of the emphasis on scientific research in the German educational system (see Chapter 36). This model was gradually extended throughout the Western world.

Mach's several publications in the 1880s and 1890s contributed importantly to the underlying concept of all twentieth-century physics: the impossibility of applying philosophical logic to physical matter. Mach believed that scientists could only determine what their intellect and equipment told them about matter, not what matter actually was or did. What a later German physicist would call the "Uncertainty Principle" had replaced the Newtonian world machine and substituted mere probability for law.

Roentgen discovered X-rays, by which solid objects could be penetrated by a form of energy that made their interiors visible. His work, published at the end of the nineteenth century, immediately gave rise to experimentation with subatomic particles, especially in the laboratory of the Englishmen J. J. Thompson and Ernest Rutherford (1871–1937). Rutherford, who was a pioneer in the discovery of radioactivity and splitting the atom, is one of the great names of modern science. His work, in turn, was materially helped by the simultaneous research conducted by the French radiologist Marie Curie (1867–1934), whose laboratory work with radium proved that mass and energy were not separate but could be converted into one another under certain conditions.

Planck headed a major research lab for many years and revolutionized the study of energy with his *quantum theory,* by which energy is discharged in a not fully predictable series of emissions from its sources, rather than as a smooth and uniform stream. Quantum theory explained otherwise contradictory data about the motion of objects and subatomic matter such as electrons and protons.

Then, in 1905, the young Swiss German Einstein published the most famous paper on physics since Newton, the first of his theories on relativity. Einstein insisted that space and time formed a continuous whole and that measurement of both space and time depended as much on the observer as on the subjects of the measurement themselves. He saw time as a "fourth dimension" of space rather than as an independent concept. Eleven years later, Einstein published his ***General Theory of Relativity***, which announced the birth of twentieth-century physics (and the death of the Newtonian model).

Mary Evans Picture Library

**X-Ray Examination.** The drawing shows the discoverer of the X-ray, Wilhelm Roentgen, giving a young patient an examination with one of the earliest machines. Roentgen was awarded the Nobel Prize in 1901 for his hugely beneficial invention, which allowed surgeons to work with unprecedented success on the body's interior bones and organs.

Topham Picture Library/Image Works

**The Young Einstein.** This photo was taken about 1902, when Einstein was twenty-three and yet an unknown dabbler in theoretical physics.

How does twentieth-century physics differ from the Newtonian conception? Several fundamental ideas are prominent:

- *Uncertainty.* In dealing with some forms of energy and with subatomic particles, modern science does not assume that cause-and-effect relations are reliable. Strong probability replaces certainty as the best obtainable result. No Newtonian laws apply except in the most crude fashions.
- *Relativity.* The observer's status affects the supposedly independent object observed. Some would say that the very fact of observation changes the nature of the object or process observed, so that no neutral observation is possible.
- *Interchangeability of matter and energy.* Under specified conditions, the Newtonian distinction between matter and energy falls away, and one becomes the other.

These mind-bending novelties have been recognized and acted on by only a small handful of specialists, mainly in the universities. They have removed modern physics from the comprehension of most ordinary people, even well-educated ones. The assumption, so common in the nineteenth century, that physical science would be the key to a fully comprehensible universe, in which matter and energy would be the reliable servants of intellect, was dashed by the physical scientists themselves. Their ever-more exotic research and its unsettling results widened the previously narrow gap between professional scientists and educated laypeople.

This intellectual divorce between the mass of people and the holders of specialized scientific knowledge has become a subject of concern that continues to the present day. The nonspecialists in positions of responsibility are often placed in an intolerable situation when dealing with economic policy, for example. Statesmen and politicians rarely comprehend the scientific background of the internal development policies they are implementing or their possible dangers. For another example, the naïveté of the early proponents of nuclear power plants, who had no understanding of the menace posed by a nuclear meltdown, became a major embarrassment, or worse. The lawmaking and political authorities were forced to rely on scientific advisers who had every professional interest in seeing the plants built. This dilemma of contemporary government is not going to be easily solved.

### Astronomy

In astronomy the major changes in the scientific paradigm are more recent. The last fifty years have seen fantastic advances and an ongoing debate. The advances were mainly technological: huge new telescopes and radio devices, space vehicles that venture far into the cosmos to report on distant planets, and spectroscopes that analyze light emitted eons ago from the stars. As a result of this new technology, we know much more about the nature of the universe than before. Space probes have revealed that planets such as Mars and Saturn are physically quite different than previously thought, whereas the moon has become almost familiar territory. The universe is now thought to be much larger than once believed—perhaps infinite—and to contain millions or billions of stars.

Strictly speaking, the debate is not astronomical in character but rather metaphysical ("beyond physics"). It revolves around how this huge universe was created and how it will develop. The widely supported **"big bang" theory** holds that the universe originated several billion years ago with a cosmic explosion of a great fireball, which is still flinging fragments of matter—stars—farther out into space. Some think that the expansion will end with a general cooling and dying off of all life-supporting planets. Others believe that gravity will gradually slow the expansion and bring all of the scattered fragments together again, only to have another big bang and repeat the process.

A third group—creationists—rejects both of these naturalistic explanations and holds to the Christian tradition that an Intelligent Being created the cosmos and all within it in accord with a preconceived plan. In the same way, some respected scientists accept the overwhelming evidence for the slow physical evolution of humans but insist that the separate, instantaneous creation of an immortal soul within *Homo sapiens* by a God is a perfectly possible hypothesis.

## The Social Sciences

The social sciences have human beings, collectively or individually, as their subject matter. They include psychology, sociology, anthropology, economics, and political science. These disciplines were strongly affected by the waves of new ideas and data produced by the physical sciences in the later nineteenth century. Just as the sciences of the seventeenth-century innovators slowly percolated into the consciousness of historians and political philosophers to produce the Enlightenment, so did the innovations and technological breakthroughs of the nineteenth-century physicists and biologists affect the worldviews of the sociologists and psychologists who followed. The effect was probably most spectacular and controversial in psychology.

### Psychology

Psychology has been radically altered by the widely held modern conviction that its major purpose should be to heal sick minds, rather than to merely understand how

AP/Wide World Photos

**The Consultation Room in Freud's Apartment.** This is the famous couch on which Freud's patients reclined while the psychiatrist listened to their "free associations" and took notes.

the mind works. In the twentieth century, psychiatry—the healing process—has come to be an important branch of medicine. No one individual has been more crucial to this transformation than Sigmund Freud (1856–1939), a doctor from Vienna, Austria, who developed a theory of psychiatric treatment called psychoanalysis.

Freud believed that not the conscious but the unconscious mind is the controlling factor of the deepest mental life. In effect, he was rejecting the principle of rationality—that is, that men and women are capable and desirous of reasoned acts—on which all previous psychological theory had been built. Psychoanalysis attempts to help the patient first recognize, and then do something about, the distorted impressions of reality that produce social or individual disabilities. Based on Freud's convictions, the sexual drive is the chief motor of the unconscious, childhood events are almost always the source of mental and emotional problems in adult life, and the eternal struggle between the libido, or pleasure principle, and the superego, which might be translated as conscience, will never be entirely resolved within the human mind.

Freud has had several major competitors in explaining the mind's workings and how the sick might be cured. The Swiss Carl Jung (1875–1961) was one of Freud's early collaborators, but he broke with the master (as did many others) and founded his own psychological school that emphasized religious symbolism and archetypal ideas shared by all humans in their unconscious as the bedrock of mental activity.

Ivan Pavlov (1849–1936) is considered the founder of behaviorism, a widely supported theory that insists that the rewards and punishments given to various types of behavior are the controlling factors of individual psychology. Pavlov's work with dogs in his native Russia before World War I made him famous. His work was importantly expanded and supplemented by the Americans William James (1842–1910) and B. F. Skinner (1904–1990) in the early and middle decades of the past century.

In recent years, the former sharp division of psychologists into pro- and anti-Freud camps has softened. Although much of Freud's theoretical work is now rejected or discredited from universal application, a good deal more has been accepted as conventional wisdom. When we use terms such as *inferiority complex, Freudian slip,* and *Oedipus complex* in everyday speech, we are paying verbal tribute to the Austrian explorer of the mystery of inner space. (For more about Freud, see the Arts and Culture box.)

## *Anthropology and Sociology*

Both anthropology and sociology treat humans as a species rather than as individuals. These two new sciences flourished greatly in the twentieth century. Anthropology as a scientific discipline is an indirect product of Darwinian biology, although some work was done earlier. It is divided into two basic varieties: (1) physical, dealing with humans as an animal species, and (2) cultural, dealing with humans as the constructors of systems of values. Especially since World War II, great advances have been achieved in extending our knowledge of the human species far back into prehistoric time. Combining with archaeology and the new subscience of sociobiology, these paleoanthropologists have learned much about the physical and cultural aspects of earlier human life. They have posited

ARTS AND CULTURE

## Sigmund Freud (1856–1939)

**THE FOUNDER OF MODERN PSYCHOTHERAPY,** Sigmund Freud is one of the three Germans of Jewish descent who radically changed the physical and social sciences of the Western world in a relatively brief epoch. (The others were Albert Einstein and Karl Marx.) In some ways, Freud's contribution was perhaps even more penetrating than the others, because the popularized versions of his theories have long since become part of the everyday mental equipment of even minimally educated persons. His innovative work has proved extraordinarily controversial, even more than a century later.

Freud was born in Bohemia (now the Czech Republic), a province of the Habsburg empire. He entered medical studies at the University of Vienna in 1885 and lived in that city for almost his entire life. He became increasingly interested in the interlinking of the mind and the body, especially as this was evidenced by hysteria, or the breakdown of certain bodily functions under extreme stress. His attempt to show that the underlying cause of hysteria (almost always found in females) was some type of sexual fear or trauma offended the prevalent ethical sensitivities and made him *persona non grata* among his medical cohorts. A few years later, his insistence on the sexuality of small children as well as the sexual meanings of dreams cemented this rejection by the Viennese public.

But Freud was not put off by the disdain of his colleaques. Between 1900 and 1910, he published several major studies in psychology and psychotherapeutic practice that won him international recognition. In this period, he developed his ideas on the possibility of reaching and healing unconscious sources of mental anguish by means of free association: encouraging the patient to "talk out" the mental link between outwardly unrelated topics or feelings. This approach came to be called *psychoanalysis*. The doctor's role was to listen encouragingly rather than to intervene actively. In essence, the patient would in time come to recognize the source of his or her ills and heal him or herself.

Bettmann/Corbis

**SIGMUND FREUD.** The Austrian psychiatrist photographed in his middle years.

By the mid-1920s, most of the original work in Freud's psychotherapeutic theories had been completed. He remained at the head of the International Psychoanalytical Association and continued his private practice in Vienna, where he had married and raised a family. Most of his later writings are concerned with cultural topics rather than medical ones, including his influential books *Civilization and Its Discontents* and *Moses and Monotheism*.

The antagonism Freud aroused through his insistence on the sexual nature of much human activity was only increased by his equal insistence on the primacy of the unconscious in directing human action. Freud's assertions that humans are only sporadically rational and intermittently aware of why they thought or did certain things fell at the time on stony ground, particularly in his native country. Many thought it no great loss when the "degenerate Jewish manipulator" Freud had to leave Vienna for London in the wake of the Nazi takeover in 1938. Already suffering from a painful cancer of the jaw, he died shortly after arriving there.

Sigmund Freud was a pioneer of the huge, dark spaces of the human psyche. Much of what he insisted on has now been revised or even rejected by the majority of psychiatrists, but it is perhaps no exaggeration to give him the title "Columbus of the Soul."

### *Analyze and Interpret*

How much of Freud's insistence on sexuality as the prime motivator of unconscious activity do you agree with? What other motivators strike you as important inputs into the unconscious?

**HistoryNow™**

***To read more excerpts from* The Interpretation of Dreams, *point your browser to the documents area of* HistoryNow.**

several theories and ideas about the nature of humans that sharply contradict the previous, traditional concepts and that have strongly influenced current anthropological research.

Sociology also came of age in the late nineteenth century. Unlike most fields of science that are the product of many disparate contributors, sociology can trace its basic theory to a small handful of brilliant individuals. First was Auguste Comte (1798–1857), a Frenchman whose philosophical treatise, *The Positive Philosophy,* insisted that laws of social behavior existed and were just as readily knowable as the laws of physical behavior. In this view, humans advance through three stages of ability to perceive knowledge, culminating in the scientific stage just now being entered. Truth could and must be obtained by the application of positivism, by which Comte meant that only empirical, measurable data were reliable and that a philosophy that attempts to identify spiritual, nonmaterialistic forces or values was falsely conceived and impossible.

Comte's view of sociology as the culmination of all the sciences inspired many imitators. In the last years of the nineteenth century, the French sociologist Emile Durkheim (1858–1917) and the German Max Weber (1864–1920) were equally important as formative influences. In his special way, Karl Marx was perhaps the greatest of the nineteenth-century figures who studied the "science of society."

Several Americans were also at the forefront of sociology's development, especially in the early twentieth century when American universities took up the discipline with enthusiasm. The underlying premise of sociology seemed to be particularly appealing to American habits of mind: if one knew enough of the laws of social behavior, then one could alter that behavior in positive and planned ways. This mode of thought fit well with the preeminently American view of society as an instrument that might be tuned by conscious human interventions. But in many minds, this optimism was eventually countered by profound misgivings about the course of human society.

One offshoot of the Darwinian discoveries in biology was a reexamination of human ethics. More especially, can a code of ethics originate through a particular set of environmental influences? If so, can one type of behavior be promoted over another in some rational manner? Do ethics themselves evolve, or are they permanently instilled by a Superior Being, as fundamentalist Christians believe?

Herbert Spencer (1820–1903) was the most noted of the upholders of social Darwinism, a philosophy that held that ethics are evolutionary in nature and that free competition is the main engine of social progress. As among the plants and animals, the fittest will survive, as a ruthless nature demands. Although Spencer did not intend such a result, his philosophy of unbridled social competition made it all too easy for the powerful to justify their own position as the proper, even the inevitable, reward for their superiority. As for the poor or the unfortunate, their misery was the equally inevitable result of their natural inferiority. Social Darwinism was a temporarily fashionable pseudophilosophy at the end of the nineteenth century, and its adherents by no means entirely disappeared in the twentieth.

## The Malaise in Twentieth-Century Society

With all of the triumphs scored in understanding the physical universe, and the growing acceptance of science as the most certain path to useful knowledge, many people at the nineteenth century's end still felt uneasy about the road ahead. This malaise (apprehensive feeling) became much more tangible and widespread after World War I. What had happened?

In unintended ways, psychology has contributed as much to the insecurity and uncertainty that cloud modern lives in the West as the revolution in physics has. Both sciences often leave the observer with the feeling that things are not as they outwardly seem. In psychology, the Freudians insist that the brute instinct is as important as the reason. In physics, matter can suddenly turn into its opposite, nonmatter, and the course and nature of such transformations cannot be predicted accurately nor fully understood. Traditional knowledge is no longer applicable or insufficient, and traditional authority has shown itself incompetent to give clear answers to new questions. Freud himself claimed, with a note of ambivalent pride, that his work had finished the destruction of the medieval view of humans begun by the cosmology of Copernicus and continued by the biology of Darwin. While Copernicus had reduced humankind to being residents of a minor planet in a cosmos of many similar planets, Darwin had torn down the precious wall distinguishing beasts and man. Now Freud had shown that these human beings did not and could not fully control their own acts or perceptions.

These new perceptions had widespread consequences. One of the prominent features of the social sciences in the twentieth century was the spread of **cultural relativism**. The nineteenth century's assurance that whatever was the standard in Europe should become the standard of the world's behavior was largely demolished. The recent generations raised in Western culture are much less convinced that there is but one proper way to raise small children, inculcate respect for the aged, assign suitable gender roles, and so forth, than was the case a century ago. An appreciation of the variety of ways to solve a generic task, such as instructing the young in what they will need to prosper, has become more common among Western people. It is interesting that this is happening at exactly the time when the rest of the world is voluntarily imitating the West in many respects. This cultural relativism is another face of the general abandonment of traditional ethnocentrism that is an earmark of late twentieth-century thought, in the West, especially, but also throughout "the global village" the world has become.

## Religious Thought and Practice

During the nineteenth century, the Christian Church came under siege throughout Europe. Both Catholic and Protestant believers found themselves portrayed by numerous opponents as inappropriate, even hateful relics from a forgotten medieval age who were against progress, rationalism, and anything modern.

### *Churches under Attack*

Attacks came from several quarters. Intellectuals, in particular, rejected the traditional arguments of religion and the clergy's claim to represent a higher order of authority than mere human beings. Liberals rejected the stubborn conservatism of the clergy and the peasants who were the church's most faithful followers. Marxists laughed at the gullibility of the pious believer ("pie in the sky when you die"), while agitating against the churches, which they regarded as slavish tools of the bourgeois class, like other institutions of the modern state.

These varied attacks had substantial effect. By the 1890s, much of the middle classes refused to tithe and had little respect for the parish curate, while the European working class had almost entirely ceased to attend church. In France only a minority of the Catholic peasantry went to hear the priest on occasions other than their wedding day. Like the English and the Germans, the French urban workers were practically strangers to organized religion. In Italy and Spain, where the papal religion was still an established church, anticlericalism was common in all classes, even though most peasants still supported the church as an essential part of their life.

Positivist science was a strong weapon in the attackers' arsenal. The intellectual battle over Darwin's biology was won by the Darwinians by century's end, although the topic was still acrimoniously debated in some sectors. The long struggle over lay versus religious control of public education was settled everywhere in the West by the coming of state-supported and directed schools in which the religious denominations were excluded or restricted. Religious belief was removed from the qualifications of officeholders, civil servants, and voters. Everywhere but Russia, by the 1870s, Jews and atheists were made fully equal with Christians in law, if not always in practice. Among the larger part of the educated and influential classes, secularism was taken for granted as the wave of the future in European (and American) civic culture.

### *The Christian Revival*

Meanwhile, the churches everywhere were struggling to renew themselves and regain at least some of the lost ground. In parts of the United States, the fundamentalist Protestant creeds became strong rivals of the Lutherans, Anglicans, and other, less aggressively evangelical churches. The somewhat similar British Nonconformists (those Protestants who did not "conform" to the Anglican credo, such as Methodists, Presbyterians, Quakers, and Unitarians) showed formidable tenacity in their missionary work and the foundation of hundreds of schools.

In Germany, Chancellor Bismarck made a major error in attempting to consolidate support for his government by attacking the Catholic Church. This "Kulturkampf" ended in the 1880s with a rout of the Bismarck forces. The church emerged stronger than ever and founded a political party, which was the second largest in the German parliament by 1910. The necessity of meeting the Darwinian challenge and the positivist critics of the Bible made it obligatory for both Catholics and Protestants to reexamine their basis of literal belief. Soon, a school of Christian Bible exegesis on scientific foundations contributed to a revival of intellectually credible research.

In 1891, the unfortunate tradition of papal rejection of all that was new was broken by Leo XIII's major encyclical (papal letter): ***Rerum novarum*** ("About new things"). In this, the pope strongly supported the ideals of social justice for the working classes and the poor, while continuing to denounce atheistic socialism. For the next fifty years, *Rerum novarum* provided a guideline for loyal Catholics who wished to create a more liberal, less exploitative economic order. They frequently found themselves opposed by the clergy and their coreligionists in positions of power throughout the Western world.

World War I dealt a heavy blow to all organized religions. Many members of the clergy in all denominations were caught up in the patriotic hysteria of the early weeks of the war and outdid themselves in blessing the troops and the battleships, declaring, "Gott mit uns!" (God's on our side). The ghastly reality of the trenches quickly put an end to such claims. Radical discontent at the endless bloodletting sharpened the critiques. The clergy were denounced as willing pawns of the various governments that controlled their incomes and status. After the 1917 Russian Revolution, Marxist propaganda skillfully intensified these negative feelings both inside and outside of Russia.

A small minority reacted differently. They saw the war and the following period of upheaval as the inevitable results of a godless, mechanistic progressivism that had little of value to offer humans' spiritual nature. In the 1920s and 1930s, both Protestant and Catholic communities in the Western world experienced a perceptible, though limited, revival of Christian belief.

A few intellectuals, too, were ready to risk the contempt of their fellows by taking an overtly religious point of view in the interwar era. Among them were Paul Claudel and Etienne Gilson in France, Karl Jaspers and Reinhold Niebuhr in Germany, T. S. Eliot in Britain, and Dorothy Day in the United States. They were a tiny minority, but that did not deter them from hoping and working for a Christian renaissance out of the blood and terror of the war.

## Summary

Advances in the physical sciences multiplied and fed off one another in the second half of the nineteenth century, leading to an explosive ferment in the opening half of the twentieth. Darwinian biology led the parade of theory and data that together profoundly altered the existing concepts of the physical universe and its creatures, including human beings. The Newtonian cosmology was overthrown by a New Physics pioneered by German researchers. Somewhat later, theoretical astronomy also entered a revolutionary era, which had its own impact on age-old habits of belief.

In the social sciences, the disputed revelations of Freud were equally disturbing to traditionalists. For those who followed the master, human consciousness was overshadowed by irrational forces beyond its awareness, and the soul was reduced to a biochemical entity, if it existed at all. What was left of traditional morality was ascribed to a psyche entangled in its own irrational fears and follies. Less controversially, sociology and anthropology emerged as accepted academic disciplines and provided new ways of contemplating humans as a community.

Throughout the nineteenth century, the Christian religion had been assaulted by self-doubt and persuasive scientific adversaries. Much of the population no longer attended or honored the traditional ceremonies. Tardily, both Protestant and Catholic organs took up the challenge. Reaction against positivist science and liberal changes in official church attitudes had assisted a slight recovery by the turn of the century. This limited revival was strengthened in the 1920s and 1930s by the revulsion against World War I.

## Identification Terms

Test your knowledge of this chapter's key concepts by defining the following terms. If you can't recall the meaning of certain terms, refresh your memory by looking up the boldfaced term in the chapter, turning to the Glossary at the end of the book, or working with the flashcards that are available on the *World Civilizations* Companion Website **http://history.wadsworth.com/adler04**.

"big bang" theory
cultural relativism
*The Descent of Man*
*General Theory of Relativity*
natural selection
*The Origin of Species*
*Rerum novarum*

## Test Your Knowledge

Test your knowledge of this chapter by answering the following questions. Complete answers appear at the end of the book. You may also take this quiz interactively and find even more quiz questions on the *World Civilizations* Companion Website: **http://history.wadsworth.com/adler04.**

1. Darwinian biology was ultimately based on
   a. Christian theology.
   b. a mechanical view of the cosmos.
   c. a belief in random change in species.
   d. a belief in a kind of deism much like Newton's.
   e. observation of people.

2. The Uncertainty Principle refers to modern
   a. psychology.
   b. physics.
   c. history.
   d. economics.
   e. sociology.

3. The most clear-cut similarity among later nineteenth-century physicists is their
   a. belief in Christianity.
   b. involvement in an antiwar movement.
   c. reliance on individual research.
   d. unhappy domestic lives.
   e. training in German methodology.
4. Which of the following was *not* embraced by Freudian psychology?
   a. The superego is engaged in a struggle against the libido.
   b. The sex drive lies at the bottom of much unconscious activity.
   c. Humans are basically seeking rational answers to their difficulties.
   d. Conscious actions are often reflections of unconscious motives.
   e. Unconscious sources of mental anguish could be healed.
5. Freud's theories of psychology
   a. encouraged the belief in rational planning as an answer to misery.
   b. were supported most ardently in his home city of Vienna.
   c. were thought to be insulting by many of his colleagues.
   d. were based on the study of behavior of animals.
   e. built on Darwin's theories of evolution.
6. Which of the following pairs is *least* logically paired?
   a. Mach and Einstein
   b. Freud and Jung
   c. Marie Curie and Ernest Rutherford
   d. Auguste Comte and Wilhelm Roentgen
   e. Charles Darwin and Alfred Russell Wallace
7. Which pair fits *most* logically together in terms of their interests?
   a. Durkheim and Weber
   b. Niebuhr and Mach
   c. Jung and Einstein
   d. Darwin and Rutherford
   e. Curie and Spencer
8. As a general rule, twentieth-century Christian belief in the Western world
   a. became nearly extinct after World War II.
   b. developed an entirely new view of Christ.
   c. became much stronger as a result of World War I.
   d. recovered some support among intellectuals.
   e. has never recovered from the loss of prestige it suffered because of World War I.
9. Auguste Comte believed that
   a. sociology was less important than psychology.
   b. sociology was the social science that would bring the greatest concrete changes to society.
   c. Karl Marx was the greatest nineteenth-century figure.
   d. truth could not be obtained without using the senses.
   e. sociology was the culmination of all the sciences.
10. In the *Rerum novarum,* Catholics found papal support for being
    a. more liberal.
    b. more conservative.
    c. more militant.
    d. stronger proselytizers.
    e. more socialistic.

## InfoTrac College Edition

Visit the source collections at

**http://infotrac.thomsonlearning.com**

and use the Search function with the following key terms:

Charles Darwin    Sigmund Freud    Social Darwinism

## Wadsworth History Website Resources

Visit the World History Resource Center at **http://history.wadsworth.com/world** for a wealth of general resources, and the *World Civilizations* Companion Website at **http://history.wadsworth.com/adler04** for resources specific to this textbook.

## HistoryNow

Enter *HistoryNow* using the access card that is available for *World Civilizations. HistoryNow* will assist you in understanding the content in this chapter with lesson plans generated for your needs. In addition, you can read the following documents, and many more, online:

Charles Darwin, selected chapters from *The Origin of Species*

Sigmund Freud, excerpts from *The Interpretation of Dreams*

*The lights are going out all over Europe. We shall not see them lit again in our lifetime.*
Lord Grey, British Foreign Minister

# 42 World War I and Its Disputed Settlement



| | |
|---|---|
| 1882 | Triple Alliance: Germany, Austria-Hungary, Italy |
| 1894 | Franco-Russian Treaty |
| 1904 | Anglo-French Entente |
| 1907 | Anglo-Russian Agreement |
| 1914–1918 | World War I |
| 1917 | United States enters war; Russia withdraws |
| 1919–1920 | Paris peace treaties |

In several senses, the nineteenth century and its convictions of inevitable, benevolent Progress lasted until 1914, when "the lights went out all over Europe," as one British statesman put it. And the twentieth century thus began not in 1900 but in 1918, when by far the bloodiest and most bitter war fought until then finally ended.

World War I was a savage European fratricide and the deathblow to the belief that progress and prosperity were almost automatic. By war's end, much of the youth and the political ideals of the Western world lay in ruins on the battlefields and at home. Disillusionment was rampant, and the stage was set for revolution in several countries. From a war that had no true victors in Europe, the United States and Japan emerged as major powers, while the Western imperial image suffered damage in Asia and Africa that was never repaired.

## Prewar Diplomacy

After defeating France in the short Franco-Prussian War of 1870–1871, the German chancellor Bismarck knew that the French would be yearning for revenge. Weakening France to the maximum accordingly made good strategic sense. Thus, Germany seized the two border provinces of Alsace and Lorraine, a move that deprived an industrializing France of its main sources of iron and coal.

### *The Triple Alliance*

Bismarck also wished to keep France isolated, knowing that France alone could not hope to defeat the newly united and powerful Germany. Toward that end, he promoted alliances with Austria-Hungary and Russia. These states were engaged in a strong rivalry over the fate of the weakened Ottoman Empire, and Bismarck intended to bind them together with Germany as the "swing" partner, so that neither would join France.

For more than twenty years, Bismarck's system worked well. A "satiated" Germany had what it wanted, and peace was preserved because France was indeed too weak to move alone and could not find allies. (Britain in this epoch was practicing "splendid isolation" from continental affairs and in any case had no quarrel with Germany and no friendship toward France.)

When newly unified Italy began to want to play a role in international affairs, Bismarck was able to persuade the Italians that their desires for colonial expansion would have a better hearing in Berlin than in Paris. Italy eventually joined Germany and Austria in the **Triple Alliance** of 1882, which said, in essence, that if any one of the three were attacked, the other two would hasten to its aid.

In 1890, however, the linchpin of the system was removed when the old chancellor was dismissed by the young Kaiser William II (ruled 1888–1918). William was not a man to remain willingly in the shadow of another. He was determined to conduct his own foreign policy, and he did so immediately by going out of his way to alienate Russia, allowing a previous treaty of friendship to lapse. As a result, the Russians suddenly showed some interest in negotiating with the French, who had been patiently waiting for just such an opportunity. In 1893–1894, France and Russia signed a defensive military alliance. The pact did not mention a specific antagonist, but it was clearly aimed at Germany.

### *The Anglo-French Entente and the Anglo-Russian Agreement*

The cordial relations between Britain and Prussia-Germany, which had prevailed throughout the nineteenth century, gave way to an unprecedented hostility in the early 1900s for several reasons:

- Germany's newly confident industrial and commercial imperialists were demanding that Kaiser William carve out a big slice of the few remaining potential colonial regions before the French and British swallowed them all.
- The Boer War in South Africa (1899–1902) aroused considerable anti-British feeling among the Germans. These sentiments, fed by the sensationalist penny press in London, were quickly reciprocated by the British public.
- Germany's announcement in 1907 that it intended to build a world-class navy was taken as a deliberate provocation that must be answered by British countermeasures.
- The belligerent "sword rattling" in which the impetuous and insecure kaiser indulged during the decade before 1914 contributed significantly to the developing tensions. Under William II, the German government often gave the impression that it was more interested in throwing its considerable weight about than in solving diplomatic crises peaceably.

By 1904, the British had decided that post-Bismarck Germany was a greater menace to their interests than France, the traditional continental enemy. In that year, Britain and France signed the **Anglo-French *Entente*** (understanding). Without being explicit, it was understood that Britain would come to the aid of France in a defensive war. Again, no other power was named in the pact, but its meaning was quite clear.

The final step in the division of Europe into conflicting blocs was the creation of a link between Britain and Russia, which had been on opposite sides of everything since the Napoleonic wars had ended. Here, the French served as middlemen, replicating the earlier German role between Russia and Austria-Hungary. In 1907, Britain and Russia signed the **Anglo-Russian Agreement**, which was much like the Anglo-French Entente. Now Germany, Austria, and Italy on the one side faced Britain, France, and Russia on the other. The stage had been set. The action was sure to follow.

## CAUSES OF THE WAR

What caused World War I? This question has occupied three generations of historians. Like most wars, World War I had two types of causes: (1) the proximate cause, or the event that actually triggered hostilities, and (2) the more decisive remote causes, or the trail of gunpowder that led to the explosion.

The proximate cause was the assassination of Archduke Franz Ferdinand, the heir to the Austrian throne, on June 28, 1914, in the town of Sarajevo in Bosnia, which was at that time an Austrian possession. Bosnia had been transferred from Turkish to Austrian rule by international agreement in 1878, following one of several uprisings. The transfer from one alien overlord to another had not placated the Bosnian Serbs, who wished to join with the independent Serbian kingdom adjoining Bosnia (see Map 42.1). The archduke was murdered by a conspiracy of Serbian nationalist youths who were convinced that the assassination would somehow induce Austria to abandon its Serb-populated possessions. They were, of course, wrong.

The war also had several remote causes:

- *Nationalism.* Extreme nationalist sentiment had been rising steadily, particularly among the various small

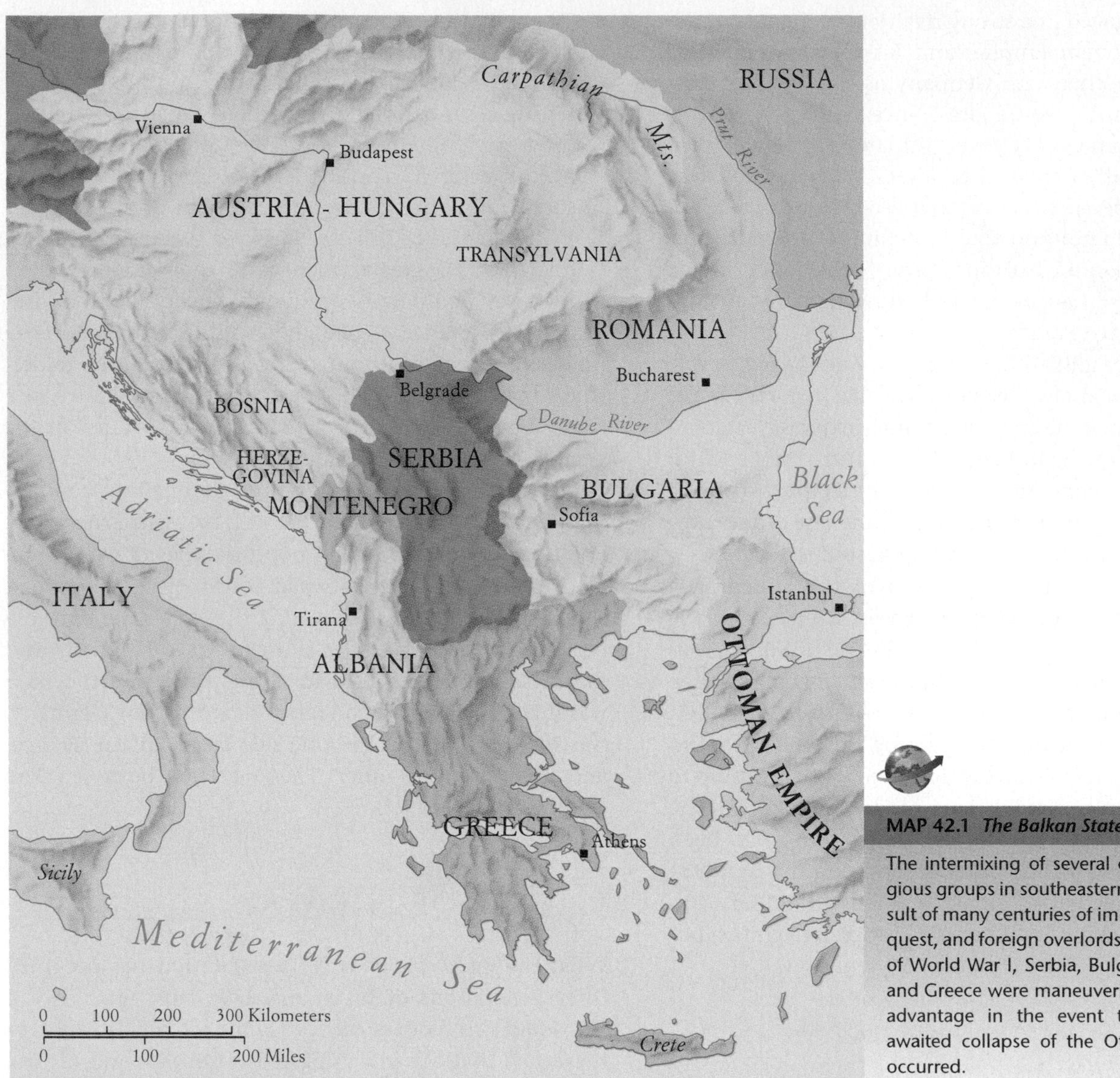


**MAP 42.1** *The Balkan States, 1914*

The intermixing of several ethnic and religious groups in southeastern Europe is a result of many centuries of immigration, conquest, and foreign overlordship. On the eve of World War I, Serbia, Bulgaria, Romania, and Greece were maneuvering for national advantage in the event that the long-awaited collapse of the Ottoman Empire occurred.

peoples who inhabited the areas of southeastern Europe that had been held for centuries by the Turks. Some of these peoples were the clients of the Austrians, some were the clients of the Russians, and some had no patron. All were determined to seize as much territory as possible for their own nations when the capsizing Ottoman Empire finally sank.

- *International imperialism.* Austria, Russia, Britain, France, Germany, and Italy all shared in the frenzy of the new imperialism of the late nineteenth century. At the time, many believed that those nations that were not expanding their territories and populations would be the certain losers in the sharpening industrial competition among the developed nations. This doctrine of expansion and conflict among the capitalists was a cornerstone of Marxist propaganda.
- *Weariness of peace.* A long generation of peace (1871–1914) had allowed Europeans to forget how quickly war can fan the embers of discontent into revolution and anarchy. In addition, some influential persons in public life were convinced that war ennobled the human spirit and that Europe had "suffered" through too many years of peace since 1815. They actually longed for the challenges of war as the ultimate test that would separate the wheat from the chaff among the nations.

After a month's ominous silence, the Austrian government presented the government of independent Serbia (from which the assassins had obtained their weapons and possibly their inspiration) with a forty-eight-hour ultimatum. Acceptance of the conditions would mean in effect the surrender of Serbian independence, while refusal meant war. The Serbs chose war.

## Military Action, 1914–1918

Within a week in early August, all but one of the members of the two blocs formed over the past two decades were also at war. The exception was Italy, which bargained with both sides for the next several months. Austria-Hungary was joined at once by Germany, Turkey, and Bulgaria (in 1915). Joining Serbia were Russia, France, Britain, Italy (in 1915), and Romania (in 1916). The United States and Greece entered the fray in 1917 on the Entente or Allied side, as it was generally called.

In its military aspect, World War I was almost entirely a European phenomenon, although members of the Allies came from all continents by the time it was over. The battlefronts were (1) the *Western front* in France and Belgium, which was the decisive one (see Map 42.2); (2) the *Eastern or Russian front,* which reached from the Baltic Sea to the Aegean but was always secondary (see Map 42.3); and (3) the *Alpine front,* which involved only Italy and Austria-Hungary and had no major influence on the course of the conflict.

Bettmann/Corbis

**Apprehension of Gavrilo Princip in Sarajevo.** What happened to the archduke's assassin? He was seized immediately by the Sarajevo police and rushed into prison before he could be lynched. He died in an Austrian prison from tuberculosis in 1918.

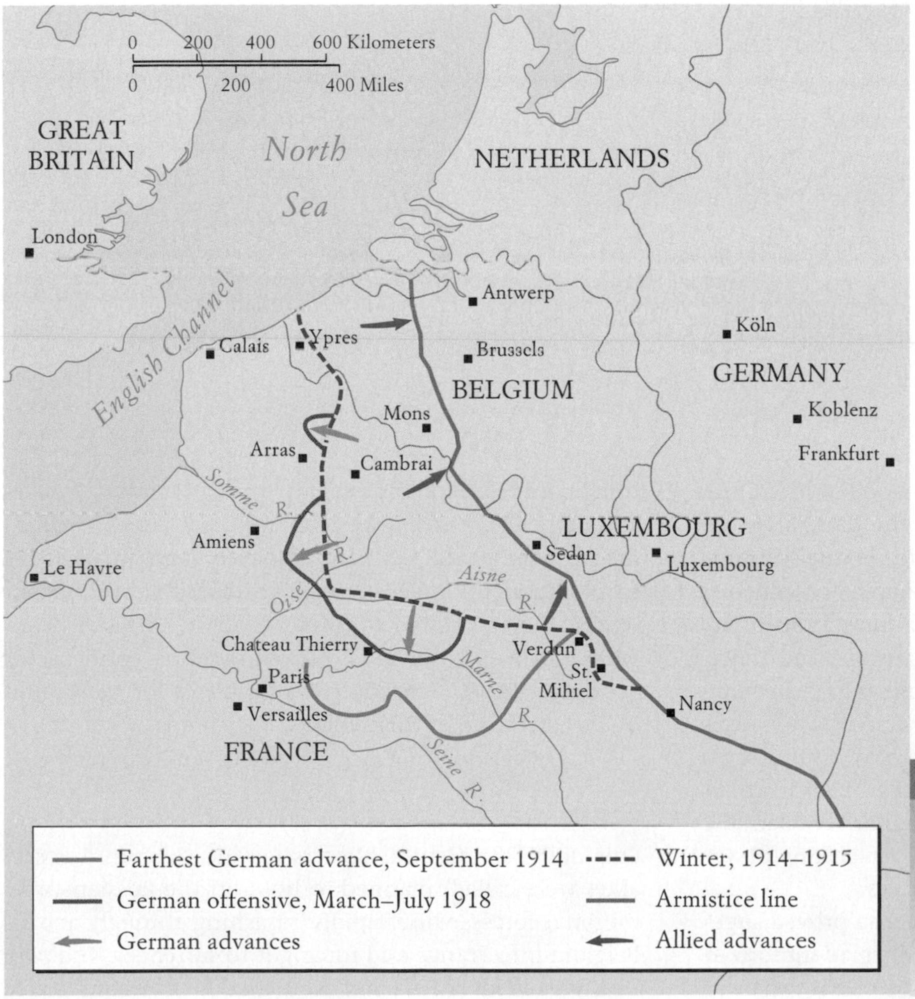

— Farthest German advance, September 1914
— German offensive, March–July 1918
← German advances
---- Winter, 1914–1915
— Armistice line
← Allied advances

**MAP 42.2** ***The Western Front in World War I***

Neither the Germans nor the Allies were able to move more than a few miles forward after the initial German attack was contained in the fall of 1914. Artillery, minefields, and machine guns stopped any assault on the opposing trenches with massive losses.

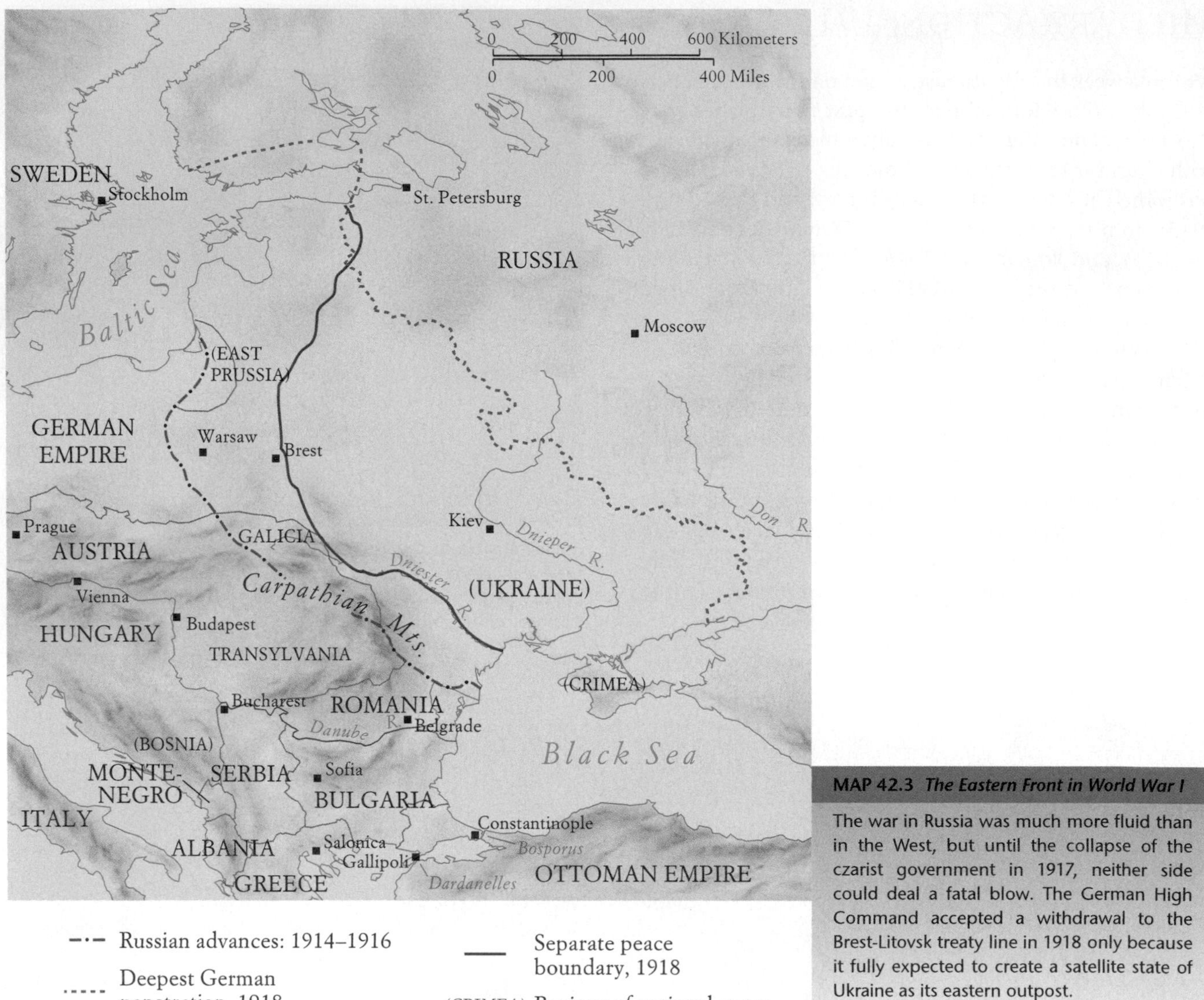


**MAP 42.3** ***The Eastern Front in World War I***

The war in Russia was much more fluid than in the West, but until the collapse of the czarist government in 1917, neither side could deal a fatal blow. The German High Command accepted a withdrawal to the Brest-Litovsk treaty line in 1918 only because it fully expected to create a satellite state of Ukraine as its eastern outpost.

The course of the war was unforeseen. As so often, the military experts were mistaken, and the generals were unprepared. This was particularly true on the Western front. The experts had thought that thanks to railroads, motor vehicles, telephones, and radio communications, as well as the use of much heavier cannons and much larger armies than had been seen before, whichever side got the upper hand in the early days would have a decisive advantage. The offense would also have a big advantage over the defense, thought the experts. The war would be won within a few weeks by the superior attacker, just as in a chess game between experts in which one player gains the advantage in the opening moves.

Just the opposite happened: the defense proved superior to the offense. Instead of large numbers of motorized troops scoring breakthroughs against the enemy, the war turned out to be endless slogging through muddy trenches and hopeless, cruelly wasteful infantry attacks against machine guns while artillery knocked every living thing to perdition for miles around. Instead of lasting a few weeks, the war lasted four and a quarter ghastly years, with a loss of life far in excess of any other conflict ever yet experienced. (See Evidence of the Past for an account of a soldier's life in the trenches.)

## The Bloody Stalemate

Originally, the Central Powers (as the German-Austrian allies were called) planned to hold off the Russians with minimal forces while rapidly smashing through neutral Belgium into France and forcing it to surrender. The plan nearly worked. In late August 1914, the Germans got to within a few miles of Paris, only to be permanently stalled along the river Marne by heroic French resistance. Aided now by a British army that grew rapidly, the French were able to contain one tremendous German attack after another for four years. From the English Channel to Switzerland, the battle lines did not move more than a few miles, as millions of men on both sides met their death.

## U.S. Entry and Russian Exit

The entry of the United States into the war in April 1917 was vitally important to the Allies. The American decision was triggered by the resumption of unrestricted submarine war by the German High Command. Strong protests after U.S. ships and American lives had been lost to torpedoes had brought a lull in attacks for almost two years, during which time the United States maintained its formal neutral stance. In fact, President Woodrow Wilson and most of his advisers had been sympathetic to the Allied cause from the beginning, yet the public's opinion was sharply divided.

Many Americans were recent immigrants from the lands of the Central Powers and had emotional ties to them. Wilson found it politically inadvisable to intervene in the war until after winning the 1916 presidential election, although some persuasive reason could be found for doing so. In early 1917, several Allied ships carrying American passengers were sunk, giving the pro-Allied party in Washington a dramatic and plausible excuse for intervention.

The American entry into the conflict counterbalanced the collapse of the Russian war effort following the revolutions of 1917 (see Chapter 44) and the terrible losses suffered by the Allies in the Somme River offensive in the

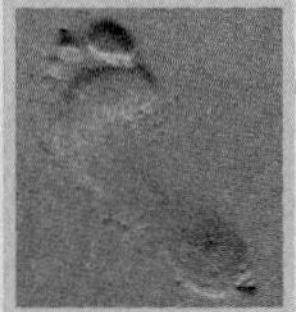

EVIDENCE OF THE PAST

## Erich Maria Remarque, *All Quiet on the Western Front*

**IN EVEN THE MOST HORRIFYING NIGHTMARE,** no one who enthusiastically marched or cheered on those who were marching into World War I could have foreseen the dehumanizing brutality that the four years 1914–1918 would bring. The German writer Erich Maria Remarque was conscripted into the imperial army soon after the outbreak of the war. In his 1927 novel, *All Quiet on the Western Front,* which became an international best-seller, he recounted what he had observed through the ghastly, violent experiences of young German soldiers such as himself:

> We wake in the middle of the night. The earth booms. Heavy fire is falling on us. We crouch into corners. . . . Slowly the grey light trickles into the outpost, and pales the flashes of the shells. Morning has come. The explosion of mines mingles with the gunfire; that is the most dementing convulsion of all. The whole area where they go off becomes one grave. . . .
>
> The dull thud of gas shells mingles with the crashes of the high explosives. A bell sounds between the explosions, gongs and metal clappers warning everyone: Gas! . . . These first few minutes with the [gas] masks decide between life and death: is it tightly woven? I remember the awful sights in the hospitals: the gas patients who in day-long suffocation cough their burnt lungs up in clots.
>
> We lie under the network of arching shells and live in a suspense. Over us Chance hovers. If a shot comes, we can duck, that is all; we neither know nor can determine where it will fall.
>
> It is this Chance which makes us indifferent. A few months ago I was sitting in a dugout playing *skat;* after a while, I stood up and went to visit some friends in another dugout. On my return nothing more was to be seen of the first one: it had been blown to pieces with a direct hit. I went back to the second and arrived just in time to lend a hand digging it out. In the interval it had been buried.
>
> The brown earth, the torn, blasted earth, with a greasy shine under the sun's rays; the earth is the background of this restless gloomy world of automatons . . . into our pierced and shattered souls bores the torturing image of the brown earth with the greasy sun and the convulsed and dead soldiers, who lie there . . . who cry and clutch at our legs as we spring away over them. We have lost all feeling for one another. We can hardly control ourselves when our hunted glance lights on the form of some other man. We are insensible, dead men who through some trick, some dreadful magic, are still able to run and to kill.

### Analyze and Interpret

This novel of World War I was written by a German but earned great worldwide praise. Why do you think this happened?

History Now™

***To read another first-person account of the war, point your browser to the documents area of HistoryNow.***

**Battle of Verdun.** The fortress city of Verdun, near the German frontier, was utterly destroyed in a sixteen-month-long attack costing both sides more than a half-million casualties.

Bettmann/Corbis

summer of 1916. The American war industry and military met the demands placed on them by the exhausted British and French surprisingly rapidly. Men and war supplies sent from U.S. ports during the winter and spring of 1918 allowed the desperate French to hold on against the final German offensive.

## Collapse of the Central Powers

In the fall of 1918, the Central Powers suddenly collapsed. The Austrians asked for peace without conditions in mid-October, by which time the Bulgarians and Turks had already withdrawn. The High Command now advised the kaiser to accept the armistice conditions that President Wilson had presented some weeks earlier, which had been based on the **Fourteen Points** he had enunciated in a speech in January 1918. In summary, the Fourteen Points looked for a "peace without victors," self-determination for the repressed nationalities, disarmament, freedom of the seas for all, and an international body to keep the peace permanently.

On November 9, 1918, the kaiser handed power to a just-created provisional government. Mainly members of the Social Democratic Party, this government immediately asked for an end to hostilities. On November 11, the long bloodbath came to an end. Everywhere, German troops were still standing on foreign soil, and Germany itself had experienced none of the destruction wrought by war on Allied lands. Those facts were to be very important in

Bettmann/Corbis

**Aerial Dogfight on the Western Front.** Both sides quickly recognized the potential of the airplane for reconnaissance and artillery spotting. Spectacular dogfights between opposing planes were a daily occurrence.

future days. They allowed the impression that Germany had been defeated not by foreign troops or war exhaustion but by the betrayal of some scheming politicians.

## The Home Front during the War

After the outburst of manic enthusiasm that overtook all of the belligerent populations in the first weeks of war (and the total failure of the Marxist socialists' hopes for an international general strike), both governments and people came to realize that a long, hard struggle lay ahead. Several steps had to be taken if the demands of this first "total war" were to be met. By 1916, all combatants had acted to ensure that civilians would fully support the battlefronts. Among the most important measures they took were the following:

- *Full mobilization of the civilian population.* Unlike all previous wars, World War I did not allow the unarmed masses to remain neutral. Led by Germany but soon imitated by France and the others, the authorities insisted that everyone had a role to play in attaining victory. The governments made wholesale use of every type of propaganda available: print media, exhibitions, parades, veterans' speaking tours, and so on. Starting in 1915, they indulged in hate propaganda. Much of it was deliberate lies. All of it was meant to transform the civil population into a productive machine to fight the enemy.

  Food was rationed, and so were fuel and clothing. All active males aged seventeen to sixty were considered "soldiers in the war for production" and could be ordered about almost like the troops in battle. Even women were pressed into various kinds of unprecedented service, as described later.
- *Government control of the economy.* Much more than in any previous war, the governments took command of the entire production system. Labor was allocated by bureaucratic command, and so were raw materials, currency, and imports of all types. New taxes were levied to prevent any excess profit from war contracts. Wage rates, rents, and consumer prices were also controlled by government order. All or almost all of these measures were novelties being tried for the first time.
- *Female labor.* Because millions of men were no longer available to the civil economy after 1914, women were induced to fill their places by various means, including high pay, patriotic appeals, and even coercion. Dozens of occupations that were previously off-limits to women were now opened to them, including jobs involving heavy physical labor or considerable authority. Women worked as police officers, tram drivers, truck drivers, bank tellers, carters, and munitions factory laborers and held a host of civil service jobs that had been previously reserved for men.

In this way, a new world of work opportunity opened for women. After some initial resistance by the labor unions, women were generally accepted as replacements for men and given more or less equal pay. In particular, their ability to do repetitive industrial jobs exceeded male expectations and earned them new respect as productive employees. In every belligerent country, women made up at least 30 percent of the total civilian labor force by war's end—a far higher percentage than in peacetime.

### Social Behavior

As in most wars, the insecurity of life and the desire to accommodate the young men going off to fight resulted in a slackening of traditional standards for both sexes, but especially for women. Public demonstrations of affection between the sexes became acceptable even among the

**Female Workers, World War I.** The draining off of males to battlefields after 1914 opened the way for millions of women to enter jobs that were previously unknown to them. In this 1917 photo, female paper mill workers show they can handle heavy labor.

UPI/Bettmann/Corbis

respectable classes. Women insisted on access to some form of mechanical birth control as extramarital and premarital sex became more common. Standards of conduct and dress for girls and women became more relaxed. Factory work inspired shorter and less voluminous dresses—it was even possible to show a bit of leg without automatically being considered "fast" by one's peers. Alcohol consumption by both sexes rose sharply despite attempts to discourage it by all governments (which were concerned about worker absenteeism in the war plants).

Unlike previous wars, so many men were involved and the casualty rates suffered by most belligerents were so high that the slackening of moral restraint during the war had a profound and permanent effect on postwar society. Marriageable men were in short supply for years afterward, and the imbalance between men and women aged twenty to thirty-five influenced what was considered acceptable sexual conduct. After the war, it proved impossible to put young men and women back into the tight customary constraints of prewar society.

In addition, the many millions of conscripts in the armies had been torn out of their accustomed and expected slots in life. For better or worse, many, especially rural youth, never returned to their prewar lifestyles. "How're you gonna keep them down on the farm after they've seen Paree?" went the popular song in the United States. That was a relevant question, and not just for Americans.

### Psychic Consequences

Perhaps the most significant of all the consequences of World War I was its effect on the collective European psyche. Three effects in particular stand out in retrospect:

1. *Political disillusionment.* Even while the war was being fought, many were disillusioned of its purpose, its justification, and the prospects for meaningful victory, and their mood spread despite intensive propaganda campaigns by all the belligerent nations. After 1916, the war became one of brutal attrition. Basically, both sides were trying to hold on until the other gave up. As the casualty lists lengthened without any decisive victories for either side, the survivors in the trenches and their loved ones back home came to doubt as never before the wisdom of their political and military leaders. Men were dying by the millions, but what was being fought for remained unclear. When the war ended, disillusionment with the peace was widespread even among the victorious Allies. Some thought it too mild, and others too harsh. Despite Wilson's promises, the losers universally regarded the peace as one of vengeance.
2. *Skepticism toward authority.* The feelings of betrayal and disappointment were especially common among the veterans who came back from the battlefields. They regarded most military and political leaders as heartless blunderers who had no concern for ordinary people. All authority figures were now suspect: the clergy who had blessed each side's cannons, the diplomats who had not been able to prevent the war, and the teachers and professors who had led the foolish cheering at its outbreak. None of the old guides for right and wrong could be trusted; all of them had acted out of ignorance, cowardice, or self-interest.
3. *An end to the religion of science and progress.* Before 1914, most educated Europeans assumed that the next generation would be able to solve most of the problems that still haunted their own. They believed that material and spiritual progress were inevitable. The war ended that naïve optimism for soldiers and civilians alike. They had seen the mutual slaughter end with no clear achievement for the victors and with chaos for the losers. As the spiritual and economic costs to all sides became apparent, many people began to doubt whether there had even been any victors. The faith of the European bourgeoisie in liberalism, parliamentary government, and the triumph of science looked absurd in 1919, as the smoke of battle cleared and the cemeteries filled. Not progress, but revolution and a kind of vicious nihilism (belief in nothing) were on the day's menu.

The dismay was not universal, however. For some a triumphant new day had dawned after the carnage. In the fine arts, a whole series of new ideas, new perspectives, and challenging new theories emerged during or soon after the war. (We will look at them in Chapter 48.) On the political side, many eastern and central European nationalists were initially gratified at the outcome of the war, because the peace negotiations fulfilled many of their dreams of regional dominance and sovereignty. The feminists were pleased because women gained the vote in almost every country, largely as a result of the promises made by desperate politicians during the war emergency. And the Marxist socialists or communists were filled with surging hopes of a Europe-wide proletarian revolution, brought on by the sufferings of the common people during the conflict and the general rejection of the prewar political order. These hopes were ignited by the success of the revolution in November 1917 and the installation of a Marxist socialist regime in Moscow (see Chapter 44, as well as Law and Government on pages 568–569).

## The Peace Treaties, 1919–1920

The German surrender was based on acceptance of an armistice offered by the Allies in November 1918. A permanent peace arrangement was worked out in Paris during the first months of 1919. The last of five separate treaties with the losing nations (Austria, Hungary, Bulgaria, and Turkey, as well as Germany) was signed in August 1920.

The popular leader of the victorious Allies was clearly the American president Woodrow Wilson. Much of the European public saw him as a knight in shining armor because of his earlier proclamation of "a peace without victors" and his support of "open diplomacy." But Wilson's popularity did not carry into the closed-door negotiations in Paris. He was soon blocked by the other Allied leaders, who were convinced that the president's slogans and plans were naïve. Georges Clemenceau, the French premier, and Vittorio Orlando, the Italian premier, were opposed to a peace without victors, which to them meant political suicide or worse. David Lloyd George, the British prime minister, was originally a bit more sympathetic to the American, but he, too, turned against Wilson when the president attempted to make his Fourteen Points the basis of the peace. Each of the European leaders had good reasons for rejecting one or more of the Points as being inapplicable or foolish, and they united against the American on their mutual behalf. The points, supposedly the basis of the peace, were eventually applied in a highly selective manner or ignored altogether.

The negotiations were conducted in secret (despite Wilson's earlier promises) and involved only the victors. Germany, Austria, Hungary, Bulgaria, and Turkey were each given a piece of paper to sign without further parlays. They were told that if they did not, the war would be resumed. Unwillingly, each signed during 1919–1920. Especially for the Germans, this peace was a bitter pill that would not be forgotten.

## *Conflicting Principles and Their Compromise*

What came out of the Paris negotiations?

***Territorially*** Germany lost 10 percent of its land and its population to the new states of Poland and Czechoslovakia. Alsace-Lorraine, the "Lost Provinces" of 1870, went back to France (see Map 42.4).

Austria's empire was completely dismantled, a process that had become inevitable during the closing days of the war when each of the major components had declared its independence from Vienna and the last Habsburg ruler had abdicated. The new **Successor states**, as they were called, were Austria, Hungary, Czechoslovakia, Poland, and Yugoslavia. In addition, Romania was greatly enlarged. Bulgaria lost some land to Romania, Yugoslavia, and Greece.

Turkey's empire was also completely dissolved, and its Middle Eastern lands were partitioned among the Allies: Jordan, Palestine, Iraq, Syria, Arabia, and Lebanon became French or British protectorates. The Turkish core area of Anatolia came under a military dictatorship led by the ex-officer Mustapha Kemal.

***Ethnically*** Some of Wilson's plans for self-determination became a reality, but others were ignored. The old multinational empires had collapsed and were replaced by states in which one ethnic group had at least a majority. But each of the eastern European Successor states included a large number of minority groups. Some were as much as 30 percent of the total population. Czechoslovakia and Yugoslavia were the most vulnerable in this respect. The Germans living within Czechoslovakia made up close to one-third of the population, and the Magyars, Germans, Albanians, and others in Yugoslavia were a strong counterweight to the dominant Slavs.

Everywhere, the attempts of the peacemakers to draw up ethnically correct borders were frustrated by strategic, economic, geographic, or political considerations. The resulting ethnic map between Germany and the new Soviet Russia and between the Baltic and the Aegean seas looked like a crazy quilt. Protections were formally extended to the minorities by the special treaties that all Successor states were required to sign upon entry into the League of Nations, a new international organization established to maintain peace and promote amity among nations (discussed later in this chapter). Chauvinist governments soon were ignoring these protections almost without reprimand, because there was no mechanism to enforce them. National and religious minorities were often made the objects of systematic prejudice throughout the interwar era.

***Politically*** Germany was tagged with full responsibility for starting the war (**Paragraph 231 of the Versailles Treaty**), which no German could accept as true. This allowed the European Allies (Wilson would not) to claim reparations for wartime damages from the losers. The amount of damages was to be calculated (solely by the victors) at some future date. It eventually was announced as $33 billion (perhaps eight times that in year 2004 value). The **reparations question** was to be one of the chief bones of contention in international affairs for the next fifteen years. (See Law and Government on page 571 for excerpts from the Versailles Treaty.)

The defeated states and some of the Successors became republics, having lost their various royal/imperial rulers during the final days of the conflict. The last Habsburg emperor, Charles I, lived out his days in exile. The Hohenzollern kaiser was gone from Berlin (he died in Dutch exile), and the last Romanov czar died as a hostage of the Bolsheviks in 1918. The Turkish sultan was also gone, deposed by the Kemal government.

The new states of Czechoslovakia, Poland, and the three tiny Baltic states were parliamentary republics.

LAW AND GOVERNMENT

## Nicky and Sunny

**OVER THE CENTURIES, THE EUROPEAN** royal families have had considerably more than their share of unusual characters, but neither Czar Nicholas II of the Romanovs nor his czarina, Alexandra, could be considered eccentric. Both were exceptionally handsome specimens, the czar standing over six feet tall and his wife, the former Princess Alix of Hesse, even more regal in appearance than her husband. With the exception of the hemophilia in Alix's family, neither had a physical or mental handicap of any substance that would present obstacles to a successful reign.

Alix was twenty-two when she was wed in 1894 to the twenty-six-year-old czar, who had just succeeded his dead father on the throne. In accord with the usual terms of a Russian noble wedding, she gave up her Lutheran faith and became a member of the Orthodox Church, taking the name Alexandra Feodorovna Romanov.

Nicholas II admired his father greatly and was determined to rule in a similar, ultraconservative fashion. Unfortunately for him, he did not possess his father's personality. Where Alexander III had been blindly self-righteous, Nicholas was hesitant. Where Alexander had ignored criticism, Nicholas was confused by it. Nicholas regretted the necessity of using his efficient secret police (*Okhrana*) against the revolutionaries; Alexander never regretted anything.

Alexandra soon convinced herself that she was the divinely ordained counterbalance to Nicholas's indecision and softness. For several years after coming to Russia, she remained in the background, content to supervise the rearing of the five handsome children (four girls and a boy) she bore the czar in the years around 1900. But in 1908, a fateful meeting between Alexandra and the corrupt "holy beggar" Rasputin led to changes that eventually rocked the Russian government's foundations. In a crisis, Rasputin was able, probably through hypnotism, to arrest the hemophilia threatening the life of the young heir-apparent Alexander. From that moment on, the czarina came increasingly under Rasputin's influence; by 1912, "our friend," as Alexandra called him, came to have real power in the appointment of officials and even in domestic policies.

Rasputin's wholly selfish motives reinforced Alexandra's natural inclinations in government. In many letters to her traveling husband, the czarina encouraged Nicholas to resist all concessions to constitutional government, liberal ideals, and anything smacking of democracy. She despised parliaments and all their works. She is said to have believed that the last truly great Russian leader was Ivan the Terrible; since his time, the rulers of Russia had made entirely too many concessions to the mob and to the rotten intellectuals.

When World War I broke out, Nicholas's government was in serious disarray, caught between the mock constitutionalism adopted after the aborted revolution of 1905 and the basic inclinations of the royal couple and their friends. In 1915, Nicholas left St. Petersburg and assumed direct command of the poorly trained and equipped armies. Alexandra, who had come to rely increasingly on Rasputin's advice, was left in charge at the palace. The many letters exchanged between the couple (the Nicky/Sunny correspondence) show their deep

Constitutional monarchies (Yugoslavia, Romania, Bulgaria, Albania) were continued in the Balkans. In all of these entities, democracy was given lip service and often little more.

***Diplomatically*** The Paris treaties created an organ that was new in world history, a **League of Nations** with universal membership that was to act as a permanent board of mediation when international conflicts arose. The league was Wilson's brainchild, and to obtain it, he had been willing to accept all of the injuries that had been inflicted on his other ideas by the European statesmen.

As it happened, despite his best efforts, Wilson was not able to sell his fellow Americans on the idea of the league. Partly because of concern about involving the United States indefinitely in Europe's tangled affairs, and partly because of Wilson's intractability, the U.S. Senate rejected the Paris treaties in 1919. The United States eventually made separate treaties with each of the defeated states, duplicating the Paris treaties with the exception of the League of Nations paragraph.

## Evaluation of the Treaties

Criticism of the peace signed in Paris began as soon as the ink dried, and it came not only from the losing nations but from a good portion of the victors as well. Some of the victors' complaints came from fear that the losers had been left too well off. Many people in France feared that Germany could and would rise once more despite its partial dismemberment and the extraordinary costs of reparations. But some of these concerns arose from the conviction that the peace had been guided by vengeance and mutual affection but also demonstrate how weak Nicholas was in contrast to his forceful—and hopelessly wrongheaded—wife. Even the murder of Rasputin by some patriots in December 1916 did not help matters; the rift between the palace and the hastily reconvoked parliament was by now too deep, and the Romanovs' unpopularity too widespread among the people. The March Revolution of 1917 was inevitable (see Chapter 44).

Under the Provisional Government, the royal family was placed under a loose form of house arrest in one of their homes. When the Bolsheviks took command in November 1917, they were moved to what appeared to be a safe haven in a provincial town. But the entire family was massacred by Lenin's personal order in July 1918, when it seemed that anti-Bolsheviks might free them and use them as a unifying force against the Leninists. Nicky and Sunny went bravely to their graves, according to eyewitness reports that have become available only in the last few years. All five of the dead children have now been definitively identified through DNA comparisons, although false reports of a surviving daughter (Anastasia) circulated for more than half a century.

Bettmann/Corbis

**The Romanov Family in 1916.** Portrait of Czar Nicholas II and his family: Empress Alexandra, with Crown Prince Alexis at her feet, and Anastasia to her father's left.

## *Analyze and Interpret*

Do you think, under the traditional Russian system of absolute power in the hands of the czar, that Alexandra's guidance/interference in government was illegitimate? Or was she filling a vacuum left by Nicholas's dislike for the task and therefore justified?

**HistoryNow™**

***To read Nicholas's Abdication, point your browser to the documents area of* HistoryNow.**

that all of the high-flown principles of the Allied governments had been ignored in the dealings in Paris. After all, the peace negotiated in Paris was *not* a peace without victors, nor did it guarantee self-determination, nor did it end imperialism or carry through many of the other ideals that the wartime Allies had proclaimed.

The most scathing Allied critique came from the young British economist John Maynard Keynes, who believed that the Allies had attempted to impose a "Carthaginian peace" (total destruction) on Germany that could not succeed. Keynes had enormous contempt for Wilson, and his opinions soon became fashionable among influential people in both Britain and the United States. Both groups regarded the French and Italians as greedy and stupid in their shortsighted fixation on temporary advantage.

The failure of the Versailles Treaty in the Senate was a major turning point in postwar diplomacy. With no commitment to the League of Nations, America could and did turn its attention to Europe only when and how it chose for twenty years. And without the assurance of U.S. support through the league, France was left to face a resurgent Germany by itself in the early postwar era. As a result, the French position became more hard-line than ever and drove France and Britain farther apart at the time when close coordination was most necessary.

Perhaps the worst aspect of the peace was that it tried to ignore certain political realities. Russia, now under Bolshevik rule, was not even invited to send a representative to Paris. Confirmed as a pariah nation, it was allowed no access to negotiations that would surely affect its status and future in world affairs. The losing nations, above all Germany, were presented with a fait accompli that was intensely disagreeable to them and that they believed was totally unjust. Neither Germany nor Russia, two of the

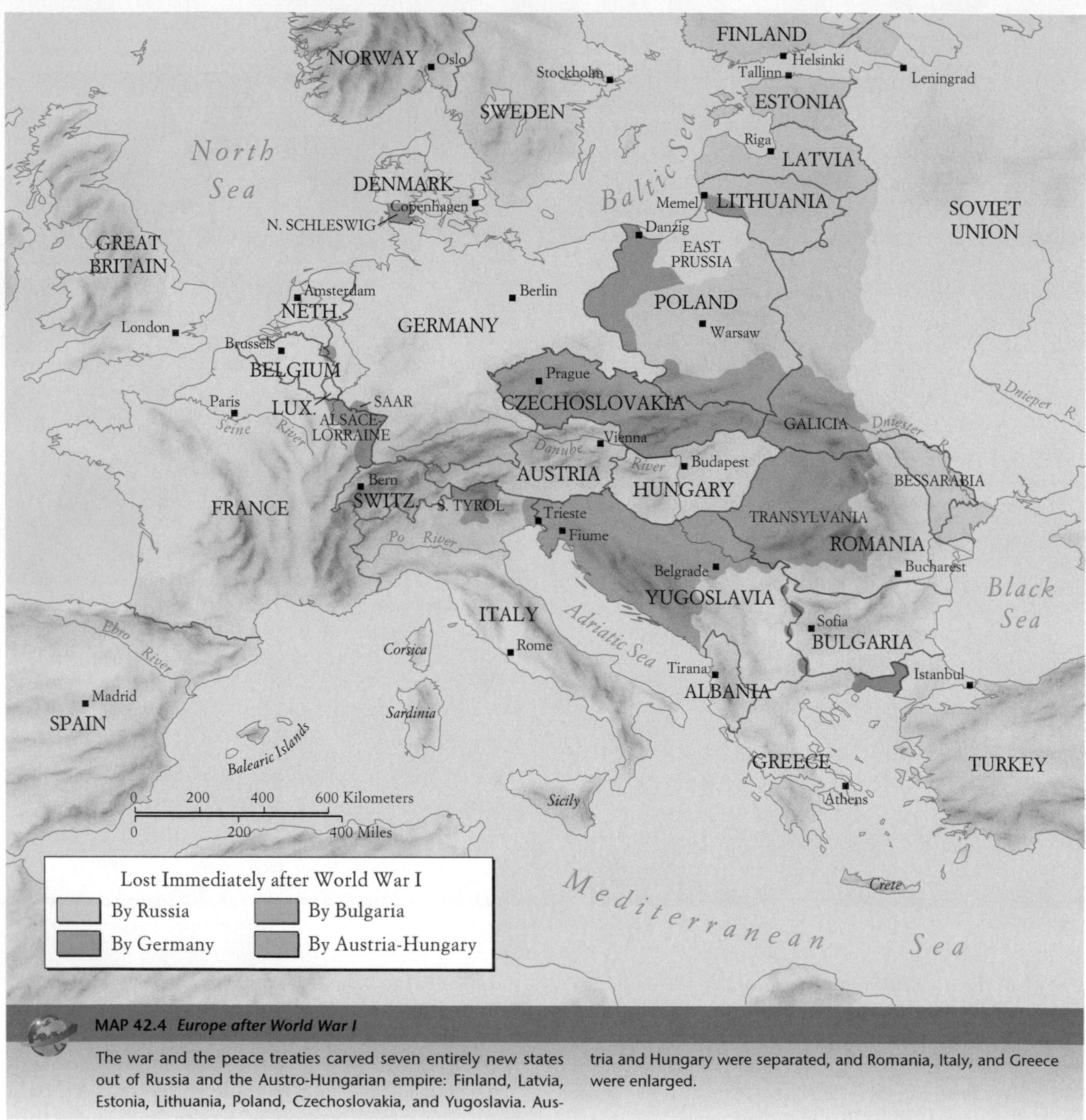


**MAP 42.4** ***Europe after World War I***

The war and the peace treaties carved seven entirely new states out of Russia and the Austro-Hungarian empire: Finland, Latvia, Estonia, Lithuania, Poland, Czechoslovakia, and Yugoslavia. Austria and Hungary were separated, and Romania, Italy, and Greece were enlarged.

strongest states in the world, was allowed to join the League of Nations for several years. Germany was commanded to disarm almost entirely, yet no machinery was in place to enforce that unrealistic demand, and none was ever created.

The league was supposed to be not only the enforcer of the Paris treaties but also the keeper of the peace for the indefinite future. Yet the weak Secretariat had no armed force at its disposal, and the league members never had any intention of creating one. The league's effectiveness was going to depend on the goodwill of the member governments, and some of those governments were filled with anything but goodwill toward their neighbors.

The 1919 treaties were not as harsh as they have sometimes been painted, but they were a long way from the hopes of the Wilsonians and much of the world's population, who were trying to recover from the "war to end wars." As it turned out, the treaties lasted less than twenty years. What Europe had found in 1919 was not peace, but a short armistice between two terribly destructive wars.

LAW AND GOVERNMENT

## The Versailles Treaty, 1919

**THE VERSAILLES TREATY HAS BEEN ARGUED** over since it was signed, portrayed by supporters as a strict but just limitation on the powers of an aggressive Germany to make war, and by its critics as a vindictive act of revenge. Beyond clipping off 10 percent of German prewar territory and population, the treaty's numerous articles went into great detail on topics as widely separate as German citizens' rights in the former African colonies and the supplying of the Allied forces of occupation that were to be stationed temporarily in western Germany.

Some of the more pertinent articles for the status of postwar Germany are cited here:

> Article 119. Germany renounces in favor of the Principal Allied and Associated Powers all her rights and titles over her overseas possessions. [These possessions were mainly in Africa, on the China coast and in the southern Pacific islands.]
>
> Article 160. By a date which must not be later than March 31, 1920 the German Army must not comprise more than seven divisions of infantry and three divisions of cavalry.
>
> After that date, the total number of effectives . . . must not exceed one hundred thousand men. . . .*
>
> The Army shall be devoted exclusively to the maintenance of order within the territory and to the control of the frontiers.
>
> The total effective strength of officers, including staffs, must not exceed four thousand. . . .
>
> The German General Staff and all similar organizations shall be dissolved and shall not be reconstituted in any form. . . .
>
> Article 180. All fortified works, fortresses and field works situated in German territory to the west of a line drawn fifty miles to the east of the Rhine shall be disarmed and disassembled. . . .
>
> Article 198. The armed forces of Germany must not include any military or naval air forces. . . .
>
> Article 231. The Allied and Associated Governments affirm and Germany accepts the responsibility of Germany and her allies for causing all the loss and damage to which the Allied and Associated Governments and their nationals have been subjected as a consequence of the war imposed upon them by the aggression of Germany and her allies.
>
> Article 233. The amount of the above damage for which compensation is to be made by Germany shall be determined by an Inter-Allied Commission, to be called the Reparation Commission.†

*The 100,000-man limit was quickly gotten around, as part of the more or less open defiance of the Versailles armed force restrictions that took place after 1921 (see Chapter 45).

†The total reparations figure due from Germany was $33 billion in gold, as presented by the Commission in 1921. Of this, about one-third was eventually paid, mainly in goods (see Chapter 45).

### *Analyze and Interpret*

Do you think these peace conditions were reasonable? What were the provisions of the treaty to enforce them?

Source: Treaty of Peace with Germany.

**History Now™**

***To read the entire Treaty of Versailles, point your browser to the documents area of* HistoryNow.**

## SUMMARY

The system erected by Bismarck to keep France isolated and helpless broke down after the impetuous William II took over the direction of foreign policy in Berlin. Within a decade, the blocs that would contest World War I had been formed. When a Serbian nationalist youth assassinated the heir to the Austrian throne in 1914, a general war broke out that, contrary to expectations, lasted for more than four years.

The battlefields where huge slaughters took place were matched in importance by the home fronts, where governments intervened in unprecedented ways to spur the civilian war effort. Women in particular were affected, as the desperate need for labor impelled politicians in all countries to forget prewar restrictions on female activity.

The war aims of all the combatants were poorly understood and never honestly expressed. As the casualty lists soared, a sense of disillusionment and anger toward established authority spread. Even the so-called victors experienced feelings of revulsion at the disparity between the huge sacrifices demanded and the minimal results gained. This disgust was strengthened as it became apparent that the "peace without victors" was not to be. The social and psychic consequences of the war were enormous and permanent.

The Paris treaties were despised by the losers and satisfied few of the victors with their compromises between the optimistic visions of President Wilson and the hard realities of international and national politics. The former empires of eastern Europe were dismantled, and a group of Successor states established in accord with political and strategic advantage rather than ethnic justice.

## Identification Terms

Test your knowledge of this chapter's key concepts by defining the following terms. If you can't recall the meaning of certain terms, refresh your memory by looking up the boldfaced term in the chapter, turning to the Glossary at the end of the book, or working with the flashcards that are available on the *World Civilizations* Companion Website **http://history.wadsworth.com/adler04**.

Anglo-French *Entente*
Anglo-Russian Agreement
Fourteen Points
League of Nations
Paragraph 231 of the Versailles Treaty
reparations question
Successor states
Triple Alliance

## Test Your Knowledge

Test your knowledge of this chapter by answering the following questions. Complete answers appear at the end of the book. You may also take this quiz interactively and find even more quiz questions on the *World Civilizations* Companion Website: **http://history.wadsworth.com/adler04**.

1. The Bismarckian system of alliances for Germany was meant to
   a. restrain Russia and Austria and to isolate France.
   b. allow Austria to expand to the south and east.
   c. encourage peace with France indefinitely.
   d. force Russia to submit to German eastern expansion.
   e. keep Russia from intervening if Germany invaded Belgium.
2. The Triple Alliance of 1882, which was renewed through 1914, was composed of
   a. Italy, France, and Britain.
   b. Austria, Russia, and Germany.
   c. Germany, Austria, and Italy.
   d. France, Britain, and Russia.
   e. Germany, Britain, and Italy.
3. Which of the following was *not* a remote cause of World War I?
   a. Aggressive imperialism practiced by several nations
   b. An inclination toward the "supreme test" of war among some leaders
   c. The belligerent nationalism of the Balkan states
   d. Racial antipathies between colonies and their home countries
   e. The belief among many nations that a war was inevitable
4. Which of the following was *true* of World War I?
   a. Participants were shocked at the speed with which the Germans seized territory.
   b. Most soldiers spent most of their time waiting to be called to the front.
   c. Infantry attacks were surprisingly successful, given the strength of enemy fortifications.
   d. Machine guns were not as useful as had been hoped, because few recruits received adequate training in their use.
   e. Contrary to what most people had expected, defensive positions were more effective than were offensive maneuvers.
5. In the spring of 1917, two unrelated events changed the course of the war; they were
   a. the failure of the submarine campaign and the entry of Italy into the war.
   b. the success of the socialist revolution in Russia and the first use of conscripts by France.
   c. the toppling of the czarist government in Russia and the entry of the United States into the war.
   d. the collapse of the French government and the entry of Britain into the war.
   e. the use of submarine warfare and the entry of France into the war.

6. Which of the following did *not* accompany the wartime use of females in the economy?
   a. A widening of the gap between the wages paid to males and females for their labor
   b. A demonstration of the women's ability to do many physical tasks
   c. Less male restrictiveness toward female public activities
   d. Less distinction between traditionally male and female jobs
   A desire among many women to retain their wartime jobs after the war ended
7. A chief novelty brought by World War I was
   a. the use of naval blockades.
   b. the desire of the belligerents to gain postwar economic advantages.
   c. the use of conscripts rather than all-volunteer armies.
   d. the massive intervention of government into the war economy in all nations.
   e. the use of the machine gun.
8. Czarina Alexandra was all but one of the following:
   a. A firm-willed and energetic woman
   b. An opponent of parliamentary government
   c. A politically reactionary character
   d. A regal princess who fulfilled the role of czarina admirably
   e. A reluctant and timid player in Russian governmental affairs
9. In the aftermath of the Versailles Treaty, which of these countries functioned as parliamentary republics?
   a. Yugoslavia and Romania
   b. Albania and Czechoslovakia
   c. Austria and Bulgaria
   d. Bulgaria and Albania
   e. Czechoslovakia and Poland
10. The most serious complaint against the Paris treaties was that they
   a. failed to punish the losers severely enough to keep them down.
   b. failed to recognize basic international political realities.
   c. did not give enough national self-determination.
   d. ignored ethnic boundaries entirely when redrawing the map.
   e. allowed France to punish Germany too severely.

## InfoTrac College Edition

Visit the source collections at

**http://infotrac.thomsonlearning.com**

and use the Search function with the following key terms:

World War, 1914–1918 Versailles Treaty Nicholas II

## Wadsworth History Website Resources

Visit the World History Resource Center at **http://history.wadsworth.com/world** for a wealth of general resources, and the *World Civilizations* Companion Website at **http://history.wadsworth.com/adler04** for resources specific to this textbook.

## HistoryNow

Enter *HistoryNow* using the access card that is available for *World Civilizations*. *HistoryNow* will assist you in understanding the content in this chapter with lesson plans generated for your needs. In addition, you can read the following documents, and many more, online:

Woodrow Wilson, "Proposal for Declaration of War"

Woodrow Wilson, "Fourteen Points"

Treaty of Versailles

# Worldview Five

| |  Law and Government |  Society and Economy |
|---|---|---|
| **Europeans** | After the French Revolution, civil law is based on a secular viewpoint rather than religious authority. Government becomes steadily more sophisticated, and bureaucracy is universal in advanced societies. Colonial imperialism revives under new auspices in mid-century and is extended to Asia and Africa by armed force and economic activity. | Industrialization develops throughout this period, with deep regional variations of pace and impacts. By 1920, northern and western Europe are far more industrial than the east and south. Capitalist structures and processes are challenged by newly organized Marxist groups in most countries. Mechanized, factory-based modes of production replace handwork after the Second Industrial Revolution commences in the later part of the nineteenth century. |
| **West Asians** | Muslim regions are subordinated increasingly to Western imperialism. Islamic states in the Middle East are reduced to satellites or taken over entirely by Europeans. The Ottomans are helpless to defend their interests, and their empire crumbles. | The economy of West Asia is heavily damaged by the rise of Atlantic maritime trade and by the continuing decline of Muslim empires. Machine industry is still unknown at the end of this period, and a huge technological gap has opened between the West and Muslim worlds. |
| **Africans** | The long-unknown African interior is penetrated after 1840 by various Western imperialist missions and by private individuals; the "scramble" for previously independent Africa is completed by the 1890s. | Slaving disrupts some established trade patterns in the West, making some of the coastal states (Dahomey) more powerful, while undermining others (Hausa, Songhay). Agriculture spreads, aided by the introduction of new crops from the Americas and South Asia. Bantu areas in the east and south develop extensive trade with Arab and Portuguese coastal towns. |
| **South and East Asians** | The Tokugawa shogunate and Manzhou Dynasty continue in Japan and China throughout most of the period. Both encounter Western penetration and aggression after 1840 but respond in sharply different fashions; the Meiji Restoration in Japan is successful, but Manzhou China collapses into anarchy. The Muslim Mughals in India also fail to deal with the West successfully and are eliminated as governors by both Hindus and Europeans. Southeastern Asia and the Pacific islands are mainly appropriated by British and French colonists in the second half of the century. | China begins to feel an overpopulation problem in the early part of the period, whereas Japan continues to prosper and urbanize. The urban population, and particularly the merchants in both countries, gain prestige and some power in government, whereas the peasantry sinks into further poverty. After the Meiji Restoration (1867), Japan rapidly industrializes and soon is the leading economic power in Asia. China belatedly attempts economic reforms, but tiny progressive forces cannot overcome mandarin traditionalism. India enters an urban age and selective industrial development as a British colony. |
| **Americans** | After 1825, both North and South Americans are independent peoples pursuing different goals in government and law. North Americans continue their heritage of constitutional and representative government within a democratic republican form; South Americans also adopt a republican form but are unable to translate it into effective constitutional democracy. Throughout Latin America, criollos continue to rule as before over the mestizo majority. The industrializing United States pioneers universal enfranchisement of whites, while the slavery question has to be decided finally by a bloody civil war. | After unspectacular but steady growth up to 1860, North America's industrial economy, propelled by large-scale immigration, explodes after the Civil War. By 1920, the United States is the most potent industrial nation in the world. Latin America receives relatively little immigration and little capital investment until the early twentieth century; industry is minimal, and the overwhelmingly agrarian society is still controlled by a relative handful of wealthy families that depend on monocultural exports. |

# Revolutions, Ideology, and the New Imperialism, 1700–1920

|  Patterns of Belief | 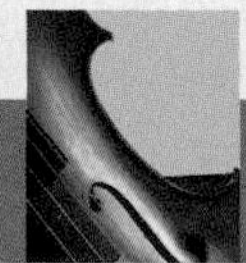 Arts and Culture |  Science and Technology |
|---|---|---|
| The Enlightenment and French and American revolutions attack official churches and the link between the state and church. Secularist philosophies become widely accepted, and after Darwin, traditional Christianity is seen as antiscientific by many educated persons. A philosophy of inevitable progress based on the advance of science becomes popular. | Major achievements are attained in all plastic and pictorial arts. Neoclassicism is followed by Romanticism and Realism as the leading schools of art and literature. The late nineteenth and early twentieth centuries are especially significant for innovations. The beginnings of mass culture are facilitated by rapidly advancing technologies such as radio, telephony, and cinema. | The spectacular advances of the physical and biological sciences are rivaled toward the end of this period by innovations in the social sciences. Technological breakthroughs multiply, utilizing new energy sources. Positivism is the ruling philosophy, but it is challenged at the end of the nineteenth century by a discrediting of Newtonian physics and antirationalist trends in the arts. |
| This is the nadir of Muslim religious and cultural vitality. Secularism is rejected by traditionalists, who dominate society. Toward the end of the period, some signs of revival are seen via Arab nationalism. | Art forms in both Muslim and animist regions stultify or become imitative of previous work. Still, some fine artisanry is produced in Persia, the Ottoman Empire, and the few parts of Africa where the machine products of the West have not yet penetrated. | This period is the nadir of Asian science and technology as compared with the West and with North America. Occasional attempts to remedy this lag through modern education are blocked by religious fundamentalism and by the rising anti-Western feelings of Muslim populace. |
| Both North and sub-Saharan Africa are dominated by Western cultural influences, and Christian missionaries exert significant influence on the non-Muslim areas. African native animism continues unchanged by European "factories," which have no interest in missionary work, but Muslims make steady progress in sub-Saharan conversions, reaching into the Congo basin by period's end. | Reduced wealth and a sense of impotence in confronting the colonial masters contribute to the decline of creativity. | Africans as yet lack a basis of scientific knowledge in the modern sense. |
| Muslims and Hindus peaceably contest for allegiance of northern Indians under Mughal rule, while both religions see the rise of strong minority sects. In China and Japan, Buddhism in several forms blends with Confucian and Dao beliefs (China) and Shintoism (Japan). Neo-Confucian philosophy in China also influences the Japanese. Christian missionary efforts in all three countries bring relatively minor returns. | In China and Japan, the later eighteenth century is a high point in both pictorial and literary arts. Luxury items of bronze, porcelain, silk, and jade enjoy enormous prestige in the West. Mughal arts are extraordinarily cosmopolitan and reach a high degree of excellence as independent political powers wane. | Until 1867, Japan continues to lag behind the West but then rapidly closes the gap in science and technology. Official China resists Western ways and does not develop the scientific outlook or sufficient Western contacts to make much difference. The traditional Muslim and Hindu views of life hinder India's progress in this respect, although a few upper-caste individuals respond to British examples and encouragement toward a modern Western viewpoint. |
| Secularism triumphs in the founding legal codes of both Americas, although Catholicism is the practical religion of state in most of Latin America. In the United States, separation of church and state is taken farther and becomes generally accepted. The United States and Canada share in the general debate over the place of religion versus science that Darwinian biology has begun. In Latin America, anticlericalism of most of the criollo intellectuals is carried to an extreme, confronting a clerical establishment that remains feudal. | Both Americas are still essentially dependents of European art forms and fashions throughout most of the period. Only in folk art or in the figure of an occasional eccentric can a native genius be discerned. Signs of rebellion against this traditional conformism are multiplying at the end of the nineteenth century, and the early twentieth century sees a definite change toward cultural autonomy, especially in the United States. | In North America in the later part of the period, the physical sciences and their accompanying technology make major advances, although they are still lagging the most developed parts of Europe. By 1920, the gaps have been closed in almost all fields. In Latin America, the gaps widen except for the tiny minority of educated and well-off people. A key difference in the two continents can be found in access to the educational systems and the place of the sciences within them. |

# PART SIX

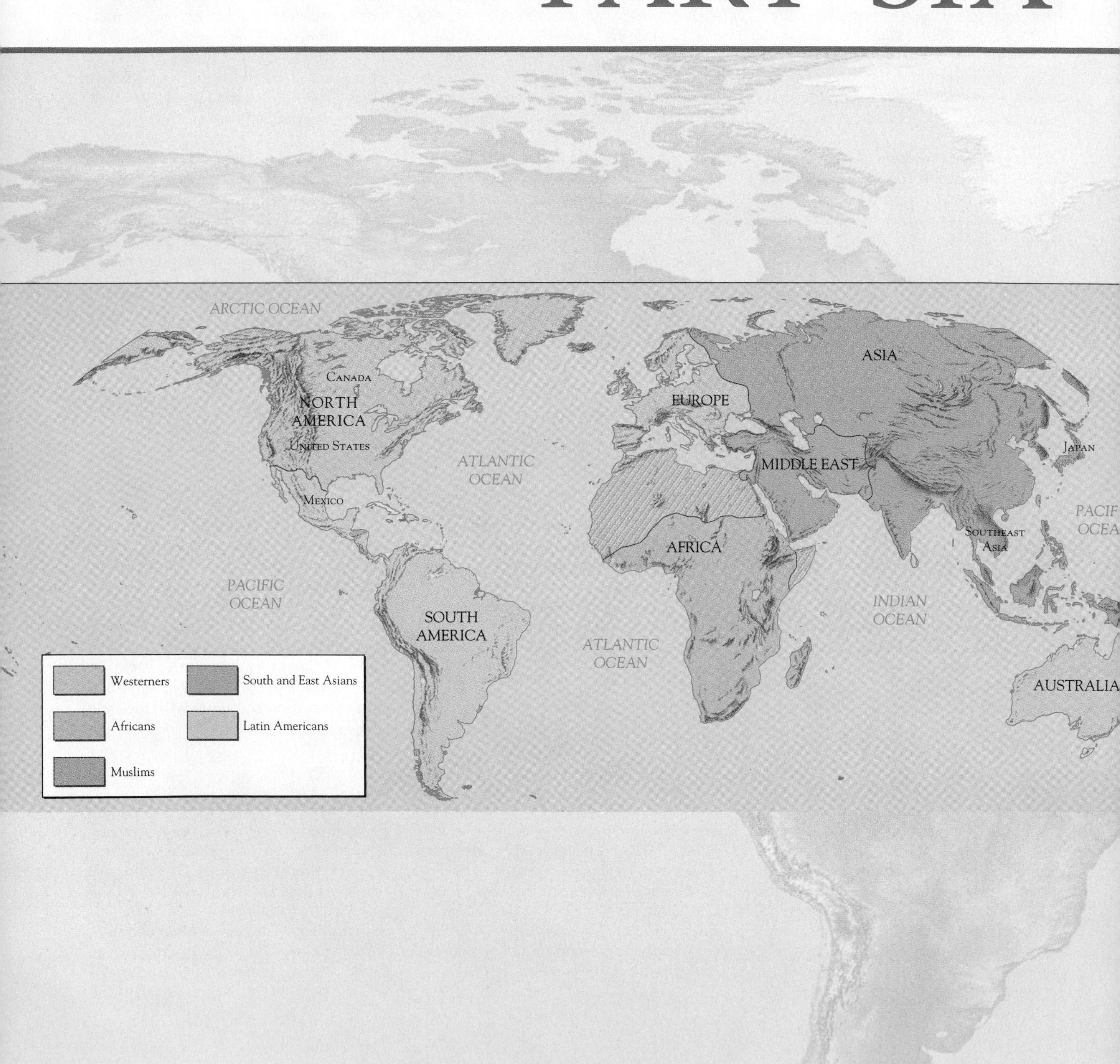
ARCTIC OCEAN
CANADA
NORTH AMERICA
UNITED STATES
MEXICO
ATLANTIC OCEAN
PACIFIC OCEAN
SOUTH AMERICA
ATLANTIC OCEAN
EUROPE
ASIA
MIDDLE EAST
JAPAN
SOUTHEAST ASIA
AFRICA
INDIAN OCEAN
AUSTRALIA
Westerners
Africans
Muslims
South and East Asians
Latin Americans

# Equilibrium Reestablished: The Twentieth-Century World and Beyond, 1920–Present

Part Six examines the last nine decades of intensifying interaction between the East and West. These years have seen the unilateral military and political authority of the West modified and weakened throughout the non-Western world, while Western cultural forms have expanded into heretofore-untouched regions. New constellations of power, both military and economic, have arisen, sometimes to fall again, as in the case of communist Russia. East Asia has become a major nexus of development, and South and Southeast Asia have emerged from the shadow of colonial status with vigor and confidence. For Africa and Latin America, the story has not been so positive; both remain on the periphery of power and in an essentially dependent relationship with the West.

In the wake of the disastrous World War I, the central and eastern European nations generally gravitated into various forms of authoritarian government and bade sour farewell to the classical liberal ideals and presumptions about human nature. Fascism in superficially varied forms won popular support and governmental power in several countries.

Britain, France, Scandinavia, and the United States resisted this trend during the interwar period, but after 1930, it was not the liberal democracies, which seemed helpless and exhausted, that seized the imagination and captured the sympathies of many of the world's less fortunate peoples. They turned instead to the novel socioeconomic experiment mounted by the Bolsheviks after seizing power in a war-prostrate Russia. Under Josef Stalin's brutal aegis, traditional Russia was transformed by the Five-Year Plans and the Stalinist aberration of Marxism.

Catalyzed by the lust for revenge and the expansionary dreams of Adolf Hitler and his fellow Nazi visionaries, World War II broke out in 1939. The unnatural anti-Nazi partnership of Britain, the United States, and Stalinist Russia fell apart, however, immediately after the common enemy was overwhelmed. The Cold War began and lasted for a long and often terrifying generation of crises. For a time, the world seemed on the verge of becoming divided into the permanent fiefs of the two atomic superpowers: the United States and the Soviet Union. But western Europe, which had seemed finished in the ruins of 1945, got back on its economic feet with American aid and by the mid 1950s was showing an astonishing vitality.

In eastern Europe, the allegedly revolutionary message of communism was revealed to be no more than the ideologically enlarged shadow thrown by a crude Great Power, rather than a new dispensation for humankind. This impression was then demonstrated by the abject collapse of the spiritually bankrupt communist regimes at the beginning of the 1990s.

In the non-Western world, the reestablishment of national autonomy went through several stages. In the interwar era, the formation of a critically important native intelligentsia was completed. The two world wars revealed the weaknesses of Western governments and generated much support for national self-determination throughout the world. Either by armed force or by moral suasion, the once-subject colonies became newly sovereign nations and took their place proudly in a United Nations organization that had originally been planned as a great power club. A kind of cultural and political equilibrium among the members of an increasingly polycentric world was in the process of being painfully and tentatively reasserted. Using the intellectual and moral resources opened to them by Western ideas and ideals, the other three-quarters of humanity were determined to make themselves heard and listened to as this violent century came to its end.

Chapter 43 opens this part by reviewing the attempt to make World War I comprehensible to its survivors. Chapter 44 is the story of the first generation of Soviet Russian government, from Lenin's coup to the enthronement of Stalin. Chapter 45 puts the totalitarian idea—and particularly the Nazi dictatorship—under the spotlight.

Chapter 46 examines the momentous events that occurred in East Asia during the century between 1840 and 1949.

World War II is the subject of Chapter 47, which also looks at the strains that quickly broke down the victorious alliance against the Axis. Chapter 48 departs from our usual political-chronological standpoint to review some outstanding aspects of modern culture. The Cold War between the United States and the Soviet Union is the focus of Chapter 49. This is followed in Chapter 50 by an examination of the decolonizing phenomenon after the war and the staggering problems of the developing countries since the 1950s.

Chapter 51 reviews the history of the countries on the Pacific's western shores and of South Asia since the end of World War II. Africa is the subject of Chapter 52, which looks at the immense difficulties confronting the sub-Saharan states as they crossed the bridge of independence. In Chapter 53, the same problem-oriented survey is made, this time of the Latin American countries throughout the twentieth century. In Chapter 54, the focal point is the Islamic community, particularly the Middle East. The collapse of the Marxist regimes in Europe is analyzed in Chapter 55. Our final chapter, 56, looks at some aspects of contemporary society, both East and West, and summarizes the immediate challenges awaiting in the new millennium.

*I do not worship the masses, that new divinity created by democracy and socialism. . . . History proves that it is always minorities . . . that produce profound changes in human society.*
Benito Mussolini

# 43 A Fragile Balance: Europe in the Twenties



| | |
|---|---|
| 1919 | Weimar Republic established in Germany |
| 1922 | Mussolini in power in Italy |
| 1923 | France occupies Ruhr/Inflation in Germany |
| 1925 | Locarno Pact/Facist dictatorship begins in Italy |
| 1926 | General strike in Britain |
| 1927–1930 | Economic and political stability |

World War I had profound and disturbing effects in every corner of Europe. The 1919 peace treaties were resented intensely by the losers and did not satisfy the winners. Most of the eastern half of the continent was in continuous upheaval for several years. Russia had given birth to the world's first socialist society in 1917 and then attempted to export its Bolshevik revolution by legal and illegal channels. In the immediate postwar era, defeated Germany underwent the world's worst devaluation of money, ruining millions. In supposedly victorious Italy, a brutal new totalitarian style of governing called fascism had its violent birth. It was soon after emulated and refined in the irrational philosophy of the German Nazis. For several years, international resentments and rivalries, aggressive Bolshevism, and rampant nationalism made another conflict appear inevitable, but by the late 1920s, Europe seemed more stable, and the threat of renewed war was more distant. For a few years, it seemed that European society might weather the crisis that 1914 had set off.

## Political and Economic Backdrop

### Political Diversity

The United States and, to a lesser degree, Europe saw the rapid democratization of politics, in part because of the extension of the franchise to women and the poorer classes. Political parties had ceased to be defined strictly by class. Some parties broadened sufficiently to include workers *and* members of the middle class, aristocrats *and* intellectuals. (This process really accelerated in Europe only after World War II.) Property alone no longer dictated political affiliation, as it often had in the past. The nineteenth-century division into liberal and conservative made less and less sense as cultural experience, secularization, social philosophy, and other intangibles helped shape the political inclinations of a given individual. Any parties that continued to represent a single interest group at either end of the social scale were destined to give way to those that attracted a diverse mix. The only important exception were the Marxists, who claimed a proprietary interest in both progress and the proletariat, and a few ethnic parties in the Successor states of eastern Europe.

### Keynesian Economics

In national economics, the two major innovations of the first half of the twentieth century were (1) the recognition that governments could and probably should intervene to smooth out the roller coaster of the traditional business cycle and (2) the spread and Russianization of Marxist communism.

John Maynard Keynes (1883–1946), the British economist whom we encountered in connection with his harsh critique of the Treaty of Versailles (see Chapter 42), proved to be the most influential economic theorist of the century. He insisted that government had the power and the duty to lessen the violent ups and downs of the business cycle by pumping new money into the credit system in hard times (such as the 1930s). By doing so, the millions of private investors, business owners, and speculators whose collective decisions determined the course of the economy would get the credit they needed to engage in new enterprise. Eventually, the increased tax revenues generated by this stimulus would recompense the government for its expenditures and enable it to prevent inflation from accelerating too rapidly. A growth economy with some inflation was both attainable and more desirable than the nineteenth-century "boom-and-bust" cycles that had caused much misery.

Keynes's thought did not find many adherents among government leaders before World War II. President Franklin D. Roosevelt instituted some halfhearted measures along Keynesian lines during the Great Depression of the 1930s, but they had relatively little effect. Only after 1945 were Keynes's ideas tried in earnest. Since that time, it has become standard procedure for Western governments to counter the economic cycle by "pump priming" in times of unemployment and deflation. Essentially, this means pouring new government expenditures into the economy at a time when the government's income (taxes) is declining. Because increasing taxes during a recession is politically difficult, a government that follows Keynes's ideas must either borrow from its own citizens (by issuing bonds or Treasury notes) or use its powers to inflate by running the money printing presses a bit faster.

The debate as to whether Keynes's ideas actually work continues. Certainly, governments have often abused Keynesian pump priming for the sake of political advantage, and it probably has contributed to long-term inflation, which hits the lower classes hardest. Since the 1970s, free-market theory and practice have experienced a significant revival—not the untrammeled market that the nineteenth-century liberals expounded, but rather a kind of partnership of business and government in the global markets that technology has opened. Examples include the economic policies of President Ronald Reagan in the United States and Prime Minister Margaret Thatcher in Britain. Most recently, several Southeast Asian nations and the postcommunist governments of eastern Europe have embraced this modified free-market idea. Such theory rejects the Keynesian view in part and accepts the inevitability of some ups and downs in the national economy, while encouraging the "survival of the fittest" in the global markets.

### Marxist Successes and the Soviet Chimera

The other major phenomenon of international economics after World War I was the flourishing of the Marxist gospel among both workers and intellectuals in much of the world. That the inexperienced and supposedly incompetent "Reds" of revolutionary Russia (see Chapter 44) could turn the new Union of Soviet Socialist Republics (USSR) into an industrial great power by the 1930s seemed to demonstrate the correctness of Karl Marx's analysis of the world's ailments. What had been done in backward, isolated Russia, many reasoned, must and would be done in the rest of the world.

In the early 1920s, new communist parties, inspired and guided by the Russian pioneers, sprang up in every industrial country and many colonies. From the sitting rooms where intellectuals worried that they might be left behind "on the ashheap of history" to the docks and mines where painfully idealistic communist workers labored, the Marxist belief spread into all social groups and classes. Even some of the "bourgeois exploiters" saw the light and abandoned their own narrow class interests to join the forces of progress and equity.

During the Great Depression of the 1930s (discussed in Chapter 44), the Marxists made substantial progress among not only the miserable unemployed but also the many intellectuals and artists who concluded that capitalism had definitively failed, that its day was done, and that the page had to be turned. The Marxist sympathizers delighted in contrasting the millions of out-of-work, embittered men and women in the Western democracies with the picture (often entirely false) painted by Soviet propaganda of happy workers going off to their tasks of "building Socialism in one country" (the Soviet Union) with confidence and dignity.

## Totalitarian Government

In eastern Europe outside the new communist Soviet Union, totalitarian forces were at work. The word *totalitarian* means an attempt—more or less successful—to impose *total* control over the public life and serious intervention into the private lives of a society, and by so doing to create a state in which loyalty to the Leader is the supreme virtue and all dissent is treason. **Totalitarianism** is a twentieth-century phenomenon. Before then, such an attempt had not been made, in part because it was not technically possible, but largely because other institutions such as the churches and the universities strongly resisted the idea.

The atmosphere of unquestioning obedience to governmental authority that was a necessary prelude to totalitarianism was a product of World War I. The full mobilization of the civilian population behind the war effort was new in history. No one could escape. The wartime governments took full control of the economy, instituting rationing, allocations of labor and materials to industry, wage ceilings, and price controls. Citizens were expected to sacrifice their accustomed personal freedoms for victory. The majority readily accepted the government's crude censorship and propaganda. Those who refused were vulnerable to both legal and social retributions.

### Five Characteristics

What would a totalitarian state and society mean in practice?

1. The traditional boundaries between public and private affairs of citizens would be redefined or obliterated. Much that had been considered private would now be declared public and thus a matter for governmental concern and control. Even family relationships and aesthetic values would fall into this category.
2. The state would become an extension of the Leader's will. Government policy would be the implementation of what "the people" truly wanted, as interpreted by the Leader.
3. The bond between people and Leader would be made concrete and visible by the single allowed party, a mass organization created to form a link between the two. The "people" would be understood to include only those belonging to the majority ethnic group (Italians, Germans, or whoever). The others, "aliens," would to one degree or another be considered intruders and have no inherent rights at all.
4. Because the Leader and the people would be joined by a mystic bond allowing the Leader to be the sole authentic interpreter of the collective will, there would be no need for political competition or discussion. Parliaments and traditional parties could all be eliminated. They were merely selfish interests seeking to confuse the people and negate their true welfare, which lay in the Leader's hands.
5. The collective would be all; the individual, nothing. Individual conscience, affections, and interests would be rigorously subordinated to the needs and demands of the people and the Leader, as expressed at various levels through the party.

### Antirationalism

Totalitarian governments often deliberately turned away from reason and cultivated a kind of *antirationalism* as a philosophy. Instincts were raised above logic—"thinking with the blood," as the Nazis would put it. Such antirationalism was an outgrowth of the late nineteenth century, when a cult of violence appeared among some intellectual fringe groups in Europe. World War I then showed how far civilized humans could descend toward their animal origins. Instead of being revolted by the futile bloodletting of the war, totalitarian theorists often seized on the experiences in the trenches as representing authentic human nature: violent, instinctual, collective.

*Struggle* was the key concept for totalitarian states. The struggle of the people and their Leader was never completed. Victory was always conditional and partial, because another enemy was always lurking somewhere. The enemies were both domestic and foreign ("international Bolshevism," "Jewish conspiracies," "encircling capitalists"), and it was necessary to be constantly on guard against their tricks and destructive ploys.

*Action* was also essential, although it often lacked any clear goal. As Benito Mussolini once said, "Act forcefully . . . the reason for doing so will appear." In other words, don't worry about why something is done; the act of doing it will produce its own rationale in time. Inevitably, this approach often led to contradictory and illogical policies, but reasonable action was not high on the list of totalitarian priorities.

## Italian Fascism

The first example of an attempt at totalitarian government was **fascism** in Italy. (See the Evidence of the Past box for more.) Mussolini was the first political figure to see what might be accomplished by blending the techniques of wartime government with an appeal to national sentiment and the resentments of the masses. In his *fascisti,* he brought together traditional underdogs of society and gave them a chance to feel like top dogs. The fascists claimed to be the vanguard of an epoch of national glory, made possible by a radical change in the very nature of social organization and led by a man of destiny: ***Il Duce*** ("the Leader").

After the war had ended, Italian workers and peasants became extremely discontented with their liberal parliamentary government. At the Paris peace talks, Italy gained much less than it had hoped for and been promised by France and Britain. The economy was in critical condition because of the sudden end of wartime industrial contracts and the failure to plan for peace. Emigration to the United States, the traditional haven for unemployed Italians, ended when the United States enacted restrictive laws in the early 1920s. The Bolshevik success in Russia was well publicized by the socialists, who soon split into moderates and communists (as did every other European socialist party).

EVIDENCE OF THE PAST

### Theory of Fascism

**Benito Mussolini tried for years** to avoid spelling out exactly what the aims of his fascist movement were and what the good Fascist Party member should believe. He did this in part because he rejected the restrictions such a definition would place on his freedom of intellectual movement and in part because explaining what fascism stood for was difficult (though saying what it was *against* was relatively easy).

In 1932, however, after seven years of dictatorial powers, Mussolini decided that the time had come. An article entitled "The Political and Social Doctrine of Fascism," signed by Il Duce, appeared that year in the Italian national encyclopedia. The following are excerpts from this article, which is as close as Mussolini ever came to attempting a rationale of his movement:

> Fascism was not the nursling of a doctrine worked out beforehand with detailed elaboration; it was born of the need for action and it was itself from the beginning practical rather than theoretical; it was not merely another political party but, even in the first two years, in opposition to all political parties . . . a living movement.
>
> Fascism, the more it considers and observes the future and the development of humanity quite apart from political considerations of the moment, believes neither in the possibility nor the utility of perpetual peace. It thus repudiates the doctrine of Pacifism—born of a renunciation of the struggle and an act of cowardice in the face of sacrifice. War alone brings up to its highest tension all human energy and puts the stamp of nobility upon the peoples who have the courage to meet it. All other trials are substitutes which never really put men into the position where they have to make the great decision—the alternative of life or death. . . .
>
> Such a conception of life makes Fascism the complete opposite of that doctrine, the base of so-called scientific or Marxian Socialism, the materialist conception of history. . . . Fascism now and always believes in holiness and in heroism, that is to say, in actions influenced by no economic motives, direct or indirect. . . .
>
> After Socialism, Fascism combats as well the whole complex system of democratic ideology, and repudiates it, whether in its theoretical premises or in its practical applications. Fascism denies that the majority, by the simple fact that it is a majority, can direct human society; it denies that numbers alone can govern by means of periodic consultations [that is, elections], and it affirms the immutable, beneficial, and fruitful inequality of mankind.

#### *Analyze and Interpret*

Show in three or four instances the ways in which this statement contradicts the beliefs expressed or implied by the American Declaration of Independence and the U.S. Constitution.

Source: *Mussolini and Italian Fascism,* ed. S. W. Halperin (Princeton, NJ: Van Nostrand, 1964), citing the *Encyclopedia Italiano* (1931), vol. 14.

History Now™

***To read Mussolini's entire piece on fascism, point your browser to the documents area of* HistoryNow.**

An ex-socialist named Benito Mussolini now came forward as a mercenary strikebreaker and bullyboy in the employ of frightened industrialists and landowners. His party took its name from the ancient Roman symbol of law and order, the *fasces* (a bundle of rods with an ax in the center) carried by the bodyguard of the consul. At first very small, the Fascist Party grew by leaps and bounds in 1921–1922 with the secret support of the antisocialist government itself. Fear of communism, frustrated nationalism, and the accumulated resentments of the underdogs made a potent combination, and Mussolini harnessed and rode that combination into power.

In October 1922, Mussolini pulled off a bloodless coup by inducing the weak King Victor Emmanuel III to appoint him as premier. This was grandiosely termed Mussolini's **March on Rome**. For two years, he ruled by more or less legal and constitutional methods. The fascists were only a small minority in parliament, but their opponents were badly divided. Then, in 1924, Mussolini rigged elections that returned fascists to a large majority of parliamentary seats. He proceeded to form a one-party state; by the end of 1926, he had forced the other parties to "voluntarily" disband or had driven them underground (like the communists). Those who protested or attempted resistance were harassed and imprisoned by a brutal secret police. (See the Law and Government box for more on Mussolini.)

### Fascist Economic and Social Policies

*Fascist economics* was a mixture of socialism-without-Marx and laissez-faire. Private property was never disturbed, but the state played a much larger role than heretofore in directing both industry and commerce. Fascist party councils operated at all levels to enforce the government's wishes and distribute government contracts. Organized labor was pressed into becoming an arm of the government. For a few years, this system worked reasonably well and avoided or dampened the class struggles that were plaguing much of democratically governed Europe during the 1920s and 1930s.

Until the mid-1930s, Mussolini was genuinely popular. Despite his comic-opera strutting and bombast, so long as he did not involve Italy in war, most Italians were fascinated by his undeniable charisma. They believed in his efforts to make Italy a major power for the first time. Drawing freely on his original socialism, he promised action on behalf of the common people, and to some extent he delivered—*autostrade* (highways), pregnancy leaves, vacation pay, agricultural credit for the peasants, and the like—but his price was always total control of the nation's politics, enforced by his Black Shirt thugs.

Throughout the later 1920s and 1930s, Mussolini was attempting to erect a totalitarian state, but he was to be only partly successful. The master builders were across the Alps to the north and across the wide eastern European plains.

## Germany in the Postwar Era

The new republican government in Berlin came under fire from its first day. It was mainly supported by the Social Democratic Party, which had adopted revisionism in the prewar years and was therefore prepared to accept a parliamentary role. It had the thankless task of attempting to fill the vacuum left by the military and civil collapse at the end of the war. Very soon the government was forced to accept the hated Versailles Treaty, an act that damned it in the eyes of the nationalists and conservatives forever.

Simultaneously, the new government was threatened by Russian-inspired attempts to spread the Bolshevik revolution among the German working classes. In early 1919, the German communists attempted to replicate what their Russian colleagues had done in November 1917. This coup d'état was put down by the German army, which despite defeat had remained a powerful force under its conservative generals. The generals now chose to go along with the despised Social Democrats rather than risk a communist takeover. This tacit partnership lasted throughout the 1920s.

In July 1919, the government adopted a new fundamental law, called the Weimar Constitution after the town where it was framed. The constitution was a high-minded, liberal, democratic document, but the government it established was already so tarnished in the eyes of many that neither the constitution nor the state it created was considered truly German and legitimate. As long as economic conditions were tolerable and the menace of a communist coup remained, the **Weimar Republic** was not in too much danger from the conservatives, but once these conditions no longer prevailed, the danger was imminent.

### Reparations

The most painful part of the Paris peace to Germany was the insistence of the French (less so the Italians and British) that Germany bore the full financial responsibility for war damages and therefore must pay reparations. After much delay, the Allies finally presented the full bill in 1921: $33 billion (in 1920 dollars)—approximately the value of Germany's total gross national product for five years! This was supposed to be paid in either gold or goods in annual installments over the next several years.

Paying such sums would have utterly bankrupted the banking system of a wounded Germany, and the government attempted to reason with the French, but the Paris

# Benito Mussolini (1883–1945)

**THE TOTALITARIAN STATE WAS FIRST** attempted in Italy. Its aura of single-minded unity and violence was carefully promoted by ceaseless sloganeering and use of every type of modern propaganda. Coercion of all who resisted was portrayed as the citizen's duty.

The Fascist Party of Italy was the creation of an ex-socialist named Benito Mussolini, the son of a blacksmith, who had obtained an education and become a journalist for socialist newspapers. In 1912, he had become the editor of the major Socialist Party newspaper; from that platform, he called for revolution and regularly denounced all wars in standard Marxist terms as an invention of the capitalists to keep the international proletariat divided and helpless. When World War I broke out, however, Mussolini renounced his pacifism and campaigned for intervention on the side of the Allies; for that, he was kicked out of the Socialists and proceeded to found a nationalist paper. When Italy entered the war in May 1915, he at once volunteered for front-line duty and in 1917 was wounded in action. He returned to his newspaper, *Il Popolo d'Italia,* and spent the rest of the war demanding that Italy find its overdue respect and national glory in combat.

Bettmann/Corbis

**BENITO MUSSOLINI.** Il Duce greets the crowd from his office balcony on the occasion of the fifteenth anniversary of the Fascist Party, 1935.

The end of the war found an exhausted but supposedly victorious Italy deprived of much of what it had been promised, by President Woodrow Wilson's insistence on a peace based on national self-determination. Mussolini rode the ensuing wave of chauvinist reaction and fear of Bolshevism to proclaim himself the patriot who would lead the Italian nation to its just rewards. Appealing cleverly to the whole political spectrum, from the peasants and workers in desperate economic straits, to the ultraconservative landlords of the south, the fascist leader appeared to many Italians as the Man of Destiny.

By mid-1922, the fascist black-shirted "squads" were found in every Italian town, composed of disillusioned veterans, unemployed workers, and the flotsam and jetsam of unstable men seeking to find their place in a radically disrupted postwar era. Strengthened by a stream of undercover subsidies from the right-wing parties, the fascists moved into the vacuum in Italian politics left by the bankruptcy of the wartime government's policies.

The 1920s saw the first application of systematic violence, organized and directed from above, against political opponents in a European state. This violence, aimed at obtaining complete conformity of the populace to the wishes of a semimythic Leader (Il Duce), was promoted by innumerable slogans and distortions of the truth:

> "Mussolini is always right."
> "Believe! Obey! Fight!"
> "Better to live one day as a lion than a hundred years like a sheep!"
> "A minute on the battlefield is worth a lifetime of peace!"
> "Nothing has ever been won in history without bloodshed."

## *Analyze and Interpret*

Do appeals such as those described here still find resonance in contemporary politics? Can you give some examples?

government would not negotiate. In 1921 and 1922, the Germans actually made most of the required payments, but in 1923, they asked for a two-year moratorium (suspension of payment). The French responded by sending troops to occupy Germany's industrial heartland, the Ruhr area along the lower Rhine. The occupying force was instructed to seize everything that was produced, mainly iron and coal. Berlin then encouraged the Ruhr workers to engage in massive nonviolent resistance through strikes that effectively shut down all production.

### Inflation and Middle-Class Ruin

The Ruhr occupation and shutdown set off the final spiral of the inflation that had afflicted the German Reichsmark since 1919. The inflation ruined many people in Germany's large middle class, which had been the backbone of its productive society for many years. At the height of the inflation, money was literally not worth the paper it was printed on—one U.S. dollar purchased 800 *million* Reichsmarks in late 1923. A few speculators and persons with access to foreign currencies made fortunes overnight, but most people suffered. People who lived on fixed incomes, as did much of the middle class, were wiped out. Many were reduced to begging, stealing, and selling family heirlooms to avoid starving. They would not forget.

Bettmann/Corbis

**THE EFFECTS OF INFLATION.** Money to burn? This German housewife uses worthless currency to light a fire in her cooking stove. In the early 1920s, the value of the German mark had fallen incredibly.

The inflation was ended by a government loan in U.S. dollars to the German national bank, which reassured people that the paper currency had something of value behind it once more. At the same time, in 1924, the U.S.-sponsored **Dawes Plan** induced the French to leave the Ruhr, forgo some of the reparations payments, and spread the remaining installments over a considerably longer time period, if the Germans would resume payments. This agreement held up for a few years (1924–1929), but the psychic and financial damage to the strongest elements of German society could not be made good. They had seen the thrifty turned into beggars while clever thieves became wealthy. They hated the society and government that had permitted such things. From now on, many of them were looking for someone who could impose order on a world that had betrayed their legitimate expectations.

## EASTERN EUROPE

In the Successor states, parliamentary democracy and constitutional government were facing rocky roads after the war. By the mid-1930s, almost all of the eastern European states had devolved into authoritarian dictatorships. Czechoslovakia was the only one that retained its democratic and constitutional nature throughout the interwar period. Not coincidentally, it was also by far the most industrially developed, with a vibrant, well-organized working class.

Poland, which had been newly re-created from slices of Germany and Russia, had no democratic tradition and huge economic problems. Its difficulties were compounded by the fact that one-third of its population were not Poles and did not want to be within Polish borders. By 1926, Marshal Jozef Pilsudski, a World War I military hero, had brushed aside the quarreling and ineffectual parliament and established a conservative dictatorship.

Hungary had lost more than half of its prewar territory and population, making economic progress impossible even during the relatively prosperous years of the later 1920s. Embittered Magyar nationalism was the sole shared rallying point for the socialist left and the chauvinist right. No major figure or party was willing to accept the dictates of the peace treaty. Manipulating the parties and acting as a sort of conservative father figure throughout the interwar era was Miklos Horthy, a former Austro-Hungarian officer who called himself "regent" (for the former Habsburg emperor).

In Romania, an alleged Allied victor in World War I, the prewar monarchy carried over and provided a façade behind which the two chief parties maneuvered for control. Both were corrupt, and neither represented the interests of the vast majority: the impoverished and illiterate Romanian peasantry. Parliamentary government was a series of cynical deals between the parties or between them and the king.

In the new country of Yugoslavia and the defeated Bulgaria, similar constitutional monarchies were in place. Here parties representing all segments of the population were present, but the small urban bourgeoisie exercised parliamentary control in its own interest and against the peasant majority. This manipulation was facilitated by the several divisions of the populace along ethnic and religious lines and by the maneuvers of a clique of "patriots" at the royal palace.

In all of the eastern European states, fear of Bolshevism was intense among the governing classes even though the industrial workers were so few and the peasants so conservative as to make the Bolshevik appeal very limited. In most of these countries, the native Communist Party was soon outlawed. Its small, mostly urban memberships were driven underground.

The most pressing problem of the eastern European states was alike from Poland to Albania: their economies were still based on an underdeveloped, subsistence agriculture. Between 60 and 85 percent of the people either were outside the cash economy or derived an erratic and unreliable livelihood from low-paying grain or pastoral agriculture. So long as the world commercial picture was bright and they could export their primary products (grain, hides, lumber), the eastern Europeans could get along, but when the Great Depression of the 1930s began, this picture quickly changed.

Chauvinist nationalism was the universal blight of the eastern Europeans. Every state east of Germany had a large number of minority citizens, most of whom were living unwillingly under alien rule. Many of them (such as the Magyars in Czechoslovakia and Romania, the Germans in the same states and in Poland, and the Austrians in northern Italy) were vulnerable to **irredentism**, the movement to split away from one's present country in order to unite with a neighboring, ethnically similar state. The fact that Wilson's promise of self-determination was only partially fulfilled at Paris aggravated the condition of those who found themselves left outside of their ethnic state borders. This situation would cause intense political problems throughout the interwar era in eastern Europe.

## THE WESTERN DEMOCRACIES

The two major European political and social democracies, Britain and France, had several advantages in the 1920s. At least formally, they had been the victors in a war that no European state had really won. Their economies and male labor forces had been hard hit by the war, but not so badly as Germany's, and they had not suffered the destructive inflation of the losing powers. They had much deeper democratic roots than the other states, and their governments were committed to constitutional processes.

### Britain

This does not mean, however, that Britain and France did not have serious problems. For Great Britain, the two most serious issues were economic: (1) unemployment and (2) reduced availability of capital. The British labor force suffered severe and chronic unemployment throughout the entire interwar period for many reasons. During the war, the United States had replaced Britain as the financial center of the world. The British Empire could no longer be relied on to absorb the products of English mines and factories. Wartime losses had dramatically reduced the earnings of the world's largest merchant marine, and British goods and services were now rivaled or overshadowed by several competitors (notably the United States and Japan) in world markets.

**UNEMPLOYMENT IN BRITAIN.** Why were the British unable to solve their continuing unemployment problem, which became evident in the early 1920s as the economy contracted after the war? The wartime transfer of overseas markets and financial power to the United States was a major factor, as was the obsolescence of much English industry.

The Granger Collection, New York

**General Strike in Britain.** The May 1926 general strike in Great Britain was called by the trade unions to underline their protest at the continued high unemployment rate. One reason it failed to produce results was the flexibility displayed by the many nonstrikers in meeting the challenge, such as that of these office workers shown riding to work in a truck.

Reduced profits and trade opportunities were reflected in the long decline of capital invested by the British in Britain and around the world. Where once the English led all nations by a large margin in profitable investments, such as tramway lines in Argentina, railroads in India, and fishing canneries in Japan, they now often lacked the capital to invest. Furthermore, Britain, which had once been the world leader in technology, had slipped behind the United States and Germany in the late nineteenth century and was falling even farther behind now.

These conditions explain the long depression that gripped Britain early and permanently during the interwar period, when millions were "on the dole" (welfare). One result was the sudden rise of the **Labour Party**, a non-Marxist socialist group, to second place in British selections. The new party displaced the Liberals and was even able to elect a Labour government in 1924 over its Conservative opponent. Labour carried great hopes, but it had no more success than the Conservatives and Liberals in curing the nation's ills. A union-organized general strike in 1926—the first in a democratically governed country—was also a failure. Despite all efforts, the unemployment rate stayed around 10 percent. No one had a quick answer to what was ailing Britain.

## France

In France, on the contrary, economic problems were not apparent in the 1920s. France had a well-balanced national economy, and German reparations and the return of the rich provinces of Alsace and Lorraine after 1918 helped it. But like the other belligerents, France had been seriously weakened by the loss of 1.5 million of its most productive citizens in the war, and German reparations could only slowly make up for the $23 billion in estimated material damage to French property. France's most serious dilemma was more of a psychic and/or social nature: the fear of a powerful, vengeance-minded Germany on its eastern border, and the deeply felt conviction that no cause, not even national survival, was sufficient to justify another such bloodletting.

## The United States

In the United States, after the passion aroused by the fight over the League of Nations had subsided, a series of conservative Republican administrations (those of Warren Harding, Calvin Coolidge, and Herbert Hoover) had been content to preside over a laissez-faire and prospering domestic economy. Foreign policy questions were overshadowed by the general embitterment over the Europeans' "ingratitude" for U.S. contributions to the victory and the Allies' irritating laxity in repaying their war loans. The extensive social reform crusades of the early-twentieth-century Progressives were put aside, and, in Coolidge's words, the business of America once again became business.

Fundamental domestic changes were taking place in this decade, although most were unnoticed at the time. (See the Society and Economy box for more on the Roaring Twenties.) The Second Industrial Revolution was now complete. Corporations and the hugely expanded stock market they generated completely dominated both commerce and industry. The consumer economy became much larger thanks to new techniques, such as assembly-line production, retail chain stores, and enormously increased advertising. Suburban living became popular, and

SOCIETY AND ECONOMY

## The Roaring Twenties

**A LARGE PART OF THE REASON** for looking at World War I as a significant break between epochs of modern history is to be found in changes in popular culture. In literature, entertainment, apparel, communication media, social customs—in short, in almost all facets of interpersonal and intergroup relations—the world of the late 1920s was considerably changed from that of 1914. A few examples follow (and others will be dealt with in Chapter 48).

In transport and communication, the airline industry was transformed in a space of fifteen years from the manufacture of a few dozen fragile "kites" for daredevil backyard pilots to the production of hundreds of craft large enough to carry first mail, then passengers over thousands of miles on a regular schedule. Telephony was limited to the large businesses and commercial users in a handful of Western countries before the war; residential service was unusual outside of the larger cities. By 1925 in the United States (which led the world in this area, as in many other technical advances), the business without a phone was a rarity, and the telephone lines were rapidly taking the place of the telegraph everywhere.

The changes announced themselves more in the tone and content of literature than in its forms. The more profound analysis of motivation, the much franker treatment of gender relations, the use of novel technique, and many other breaks with tradition marked both the European and the American books of the twenties. Disillusionment was a frequent note, except in the numerous ranks of the communists and their fellow travelers, who affected to see a new world coming.

Entertainment media became both more varied and more commercialized. The advent of the radio was in part responsible, as was the great popularity of the cheap phonograph record for musical reproduction. Professional sports experienced a steady upsurge in their spectator figures. The reduction of the work week to 45 and then 40 hours allowed an increase in time for hobbies and vacation trips, although this trend, too, was markedly more apparent in the United States than in Europe. Most important was the coming of the movie theater, a topic looked at in detail in Chapter 48.

The loosening of the restrictions on female attendance in public places and events during the wartime years has been noted. This relaxation continued in the 1920s, showing itself not only in allowances for women to enter almost any establishment without the previously mandatory escorting male, but also in permissible language, forms of address, dress, and many types of social manners. In concrete terms, the young lady of, say, 1928 in Berlin, London, or Paris might appear unescorted in a hotel bar, greet and be greeted by some of the male patrons affectionately, order and drink a martini cocktail while smoking a cigarette, and then proceed on her way in her stylish outfit of knee-length silk and high heels, without anyone imploring the manager to cease allowing his premises to be abused by "loose women."

### *Analyze and Interpret*

Women are supposedly the guardians of public and private morality. Is this true in your experience? Or is it another example of male delusion about the other sex?

the blurring of traditional class divisions, which had always been an American characteristic, picked up speed. The well-dressed clerk could not be distinguished from the store manager in appearances and tastes; the blue-collar factory hand and the company's stockholders ate the same cornflakes for breakfast and sat in the same grandstand at the baseball game; and the automobile, led by Henry Ford's low-priced and mass-produced creations, swept the country.

The nation as an economic enterprise profited greatly from U.S. involvement in World War I, and the population had suffered little damage compared to the European nations. By the early 1920s, the United States had replaced Britain as the Western Hemisphere's source of technology, trade, and finance and had become the prime creditor nation in world trade. Only a few pessimists were worried about the indiscriminate speculative activity on the New York Stock Exchange.

## International Relations on the Eve of the Depression

The late 1920s saw considerable hope that the lessons of world war had been learned and that war would soon become obsolete. After the failure of the Ruhr occupation and the ensuing economic chaos, the French spirit of vengeance against Germany gave way to a more cooperative stance. In 1925, the two countries signed the **Locarno Pact**, which was to be the high-water mark of interwar diplomacy for peace. Locarno allowed Germany to join the League of Nations in return for its promise to accept its frontier with France and Belgium as permanent. Soon afterward, the Soviet Union was also allowed to join the league. In the same spirit, a series of conferences and agreements were held toward the goal of limiting armaments worldwide.

**LINDBERGH PREPARES FOR TAKEOFF.** Colonel Lindbergh became an instant—if reluctant—hero with the first solo flight across the Atlantic in 1927. He is shown here just before takeoff in his all-metal monoplane, the *Spirit of St. Louis*.

By this time, the U.S. president was the internationally sophisticated Herbert Hoover, a different individual from his immediate predecessors Harding and Coolidge, neither of whom had ever set foot in Europe. With Washington's tacit blessings, the flow of investment money from the United States to Europe, particularly Germany, was ever increasing as the profits (on paper) from speculating on the bubbling stock market made many Americans feel rich.

By 1928, Europe appeared to be en route to full recovery from the economic effects of the war. Dollar loans and private investment had helped reestablish German prosperity, and the Germans could thus manage their reduced reparations payments to France and Britain. These countries could then begin to repay the large loans they had received from the United States during the war. For four years, this circular flow of money worked well for all concerned. The eastern European agricultural products were bought in large quantities by the western European industrial nations. Except in Britain, unemployment was under control.

Even the West's hostility and fear toward Bolshevism cooled, as the Russians ceased to trumpet their confident calls for world revolution and started to behave like reasonable, if somewhat unorthodox, business partners in world trade. It was indicative that by the later 1920s, Soviet diplomats had given up the workers' caps and boots they had donned ten years earlier and returned to formal dress of top hat and tails.

The fear that European workers would gravitate en masse toward Bolshevik Russia had proved to be exaggerated. Much communist energy was wasted in fighting the socialists who had refused to join the Communist (Third) International, founded and headquartered in Moscow. Even conservative politicians began to look on the communists, whether in Russia or at home, as a less urgent danger than they had originally appeared to be. In 1929, European international relations seemed to be in a healing mode. The wounds of war were closing, and good economic times allowed old enemies to think of one another as potential partners. Hope was in the air.

## SUMMARY

In the immediate postwar years, the political situation was extremely unstable in central and eastern Europe, with Russian Bolshevism seeking to expand westward and a series of new states without constitutional stability groping for survival.

The twentieth-century phenomenon of totalitarian government found several homes in Europe after World War I. One experiment occurred in Italy with the fascism of Benito Mussolini, but the German Nazi state under Adolf Hitler would be the most notable and aggressive example. The Weimar Republic of Germany began its history encumbered with the guilt of signing the Versailles Treaty and presiding over a spectacular inflation, two handicaps that it could never overcome in the eyes of many citizens. In Italy, a demagogue named Mussolini bluffed his way to governmental power in 1922 and then proceeded to turn his country into a quasi-totalitarian state.

In the Western democracies, the search for economic

recovery seemed to be successful in France, but less so in a subtly weakened Britain. The United States immediately withdrew from its European wartime activity and devoted itself to domestic affairs under conservative Republican administrations. It enjoyed general prosperity partly as a result of taking the role Britain had vacated in world financial and commercial affairs.

By the end of the decade, international conferences had secured partial successes in disarmament, border guarantees, and pledges of peace. The spread of Bolshevism seemed to have been checked, and the Russians became less threatening. As the decade entered its last year, most signs were hopeful for amity and continued economic progress.

## Identification Terms

Test your knowledge of this chapter's key concepts by defining the following terms. If you can't recall the meaning of certain terms, refresh your memory by looking up the boldfaced term in the chapter, turning to the Glossary at the end of the book, or working with the flashcards that are available on the *World Civilizations* Companion Website **http://history.wadsworth.com/adler04**.

Dawes Plan
fascism
*Il Duce*
irredentism
Labour Party
Locarno Pact
March on Rome
totalitarianism
Weimar Republic

## Test Your Knowledge

Test your knowledge of this chapter by answering the following questions. Complete answers appear at the end of the book. You may also take this quiz interactively and find even more quiz questions on the *World Civilizations* Companion Website: **http://history.wadsworth.com/adler04**.

1. The necessary prelude to the development of the totalitarian state was
   a. World War I.
   b. the French Revolution.
   c. the precepts of *Mein Kampf*.
   d. the Bolshevik Party charter.
   e. Nazism.
2. Which of the following is *not* associated with modern totalitarian government?
   a. Continuous striving toward changing goals
   b. Distinctions between private behavior and affairs of public policy
   c. Subordination of the individual to the state
   d. Leadership exercised by a single semisacred individual
   e. A single allowed party
3. Mussolini made his political debut as
   a. a communist organizer in postwar Italy.
   b. a strikebreaker.
   c. a military officer.
   d. a liberal parliamentary delegate.
   e. a writer of scathing editorials against the government.
4. The March on Rome
   a. was a papal visit.
   b. left almost 2,000 people dead.
   c. took place when Hitler visited Mussolini.
   d. was Mussolini's first review of the troops under his command.
   e. brought Mussolini to power.
5. The postwar German state was the product of
   a. a communist coup following Germany's military defeat in the war.
   b. the Allied Powers' intervention and postwar occupation.
   c. a liberal constitution written by the Social Democrats and their allies.
   d. a generals' dictatorship imposed to prevent an attempted communist takeover.
   e. a new republic that worked to enforce the will of the people.
6. The nation that suffered most dramatically from inflation after World War I was
   a. France.
   b. Russia.
   c. Germany.
   d. Britain.
   e. Poland.
7. The Dawes Plan was a
   a. proposal by U.S. financiers to ensure Germany's recovery and payment of reparations.
   b. U.S. government plan to carry out the punishment of Germany.

c. British-French scheme to ensure German payment of reparations.
d. U.S. government plan to try to get the country out of the Great Depression.
e. proposal by the victors of World War I to outlaw war.

8. The most serious problem for the countries of eastern Europe during the 1930s was that
a. ethnic minorities inside artificially constructed borders could not get along.
b. the communist government of the Soviet Union continued to try to annex them.
c. President Wilson was out of office, and no one in the United States seemed to care about them.
d. Britain and France were so far ahead of them technologically.
e. their agriculture-based economies suffered terribly during the Great Depression.

9. The nation that had the most deep-rooted unemployment problem in postwar Europe was
a. Great Britain.
b. Germany.
c. France.
d. Italy.
e. Belgium.

10. The high point for hopes of a lasting European peace was
a. the signing of the Locarno Pact in 1925.
b. the removal of the French from the Ruhr in 1923.
c. the entry of Germany into the League of Nations.
d. the diplomatic recognition of the Soviet Union by France and Britain in 1921.
e. the lifting of economic sanctions against Germany in 1924.

## InfoTrac College Edition

Visit the source collections at

**http://infotrac.thomsonlearning.com**

and use the Search function with the following key terms:

Weimar Republic Mussolini fascism

## Wadsworth History Website Resources

Visit the World History Resource Center at **http://history.wadsworth.com/world** for a wealth of general resources, and the *World Civilizations* Companion Website at **http://history.wadsworth.com/adler04** for resources specific to this textbook.

## HistoryNow

Enter *HistoryNow* using the access card that is available for *World Civilizations*. *HistoryNow* will assist you in understanding the content in this chapter with lesson plans generated for your needs. In addition, you can read the following documents, and many more, online:

"The 25 Points 1920: An Early Nazi Program"

Benito Mussolini, "What Is Fascism?"

*It is true that liberty is precious—so precious that it must be rationed.*
**Vladimir Lenin**

# 44 THE SOVIET EXPERIMENT TO WORLD WAR II



| | |
|---|---|
| 1917 | MARCH/OCTOBER REVOLUTIONS |
| 1918 | TREATY OF BREST-LITOVSK/ CIVIL WAR BEGINS |
| 1921 | NEW ECONOMIC POLICY |
| 1927 | STALIN EMERGES AS LEADER |
| 1929 | FIRST FIVE-YEAR PLAN BEGINS |
| 1936–1938 | GREAT PURGE |

ONE OF THE CHIEF BY-PRODUCTS of World War I was a radical experiment in social organization that seized Russia and was destined to last for seventy-five years. In 1917, the Russian Marxists took advantage of the disruptions, resentments, and weaknesses caused by the war to carry out revolution. The first socialist state, the Union of Soviet Socialist Republics (USSR), was born under the watchful eye of a handful of ambitious, visionary men around Vladimir Lenin. Their communist government, which proudly called itself the realization of Marx's "dictatorship of the proletariat," was a frightening phenomenon to most of the rest of the world. But everywhere some men and women were inspired by its example and wished to imitate it in their own countries during the interwar period.

## THE MARCH REVOLUTION, 1917

What had set the stage for this radical upheaval? By 1917, the imperial government of Russia had been brought to the point of collapse by the demands of total war. Twelve years earlier, an aborted revolution had finally brought a constitution and the elements of modern parliamentary government to the Russian people. But the broadly democratic aims of the Revolution of 1905 had been frustrated by a combination of force and guile, and the czar maintained an autocratic grip on the policy-making machinery as the World War began.

In the opening years of World War I, the Russians suffered huge casualties and lost extensive territory to the Germans and Austrians. Their generals were the least competent of all the belligerents. The czar's officials were unable or unwilling to enlist popular support for the conflict.

As the wartime defeats and mistakes piled up, the maintenance of obedience became impossible. By spring 1917, the food supply for the cities was becoming tenuous, and bread riots were breaking out. Finally, the demoralized garrison troops refused to obey orders from their superiors. With no prior planning, no bloodshed, and no organization, the **March Revolution** came about simply when the unpopular and confused Czar Nicholas II suddenly abdicated his throne. A committee of the *Duma* (the parliament), which had been ignored and almost powerless until now, moved into the vacuum thus created and took over the government of Russia. The Duma committee, which called itself the **Provisional Government,** intended to create a new, democratic constitution and hold free elections as soon as possible.

The new government was a weak foundation on which to attempt to build a democratic society, however. It had no mandate from the people but had simply appointed itself. Leadership soon passed into the hands of Alexander Kerensky, a moderate, non-Marxist socialist who had little understanding of the depths of the people's antiwar mood. The peasants—about 80 percent of the population—were desperately tired of this war, whose aims they had never understood and which they hated because it was devouring their sons. If peace were not soon achieved, they would refuse to grow and ship food to the cities, and Russian government of any kind must collapse. But Kerensky thought that Russia dare not make a separate, losing peace despite the ominous tide of discontent. He believed that only a victorious peace would allow the newborn Russian democracy to survive, and he was therefore determined to keep Russia in the war.

## The Bolsheviks

The people's war weariness opened the way for the uncompromising Marxists, or **Bolsheviks,** led by the brilliant tactician Vladimir Lenin (1870–1924). Before the spring of 1917, Lenin had been a refugee from his native land, living in Swiss and German exile for twenty years, plotting and propaganizing incessantly for the triumph of the socialist revolution. He was the leader of a movement that had perhaps 100,000 members and sympathizers in the entire Russian imperial population of about 160 million.

Under Lenin's aegis, the Bolsheviks had changed Marx a great deal to make his ideas fit with the Russian realities.

**Lenin in His Tomb.** Embalmed at his death in 1924, the founder of the USSR rests in an elaborate mausoleum on Red Square in the heart of Moscow. Given an annual "touch-up," the body can remain in good condition for centuries, but it may soon be relocated to the Ulyanov family plot in a St. Petersburg cemetery.

AKG London

Lenin insisted on a full-time, professional leadership supervising a conspiratorial, clandestine party. Unlike Marx, he believed that such a party could hasten the coming of the revolution and that the peasantry could be led into revolutionary action. Lenin thought that in a country such as Russia, where the urban workers' class was at most about 5 percent of the population in 1910, only a movement that galvanized peasant discontent stood a chance of success. Lenin was clear that the vague dictatorship of the proletariat that Marx had talked about would quickly become a dictatorship of the Bolsheviks. Within that party, the small group around Lenin, called the Central Committee, would rule in fact.

The Bolshevik leader returned to Russia immediately after the March Revolution, when the new government, anxious to display its democratic credentials, allowed total freedom to all political groups. Through the summer of 1917, Lenin and the Provisional Government under Kerensky dueled for power. The chosen arena was the *soviets* (councils) of workers and soldiers, which had formed all over Russia. Chairing the supremely important St. Petersburg soviet was Leon Trotsky (1879–1940), Lenin's dynamic second-in-command, who was able to lead the body into the Bolshevik camp.

In the short term, the fate of the country necessarily would be determined by which group could secure the allegiance of the armed forces. The imperial army had been disintegrating since the spring, with mass desertions commonplace. The peasant soldiers hated the war, and a wide cleft had opened between them and their middle- and upper-class officers. Into this rift, Bolshevik pacifist and revolutionary propaganda was pouring and finding a ready audience.

Kerensky decided to accede to the demands of his hard-pressed allies in the West and gamble everything on an ill-prepared summer offensive, which was soon turned into a rout by the Germans' counterattack. By September, the enemy was at the gates of St. Petersburg, and the army was visibly collapsing. The cities were on the point of mass starvation, and the peasants were taking the law into their own hands and dividing up the estates of their helpless landlords, much as their French counterparts had done a century and a quarter earlier.

## The October Revolution

By mid-October, Lenin had convinced a hesitant Central Committee that the time for armed revolutionary action was at hand. He insisted that the brilliantly simple Bolshevik slogans of "All power to the Soviets" and "Land, bread, peace" would carry the day despite the tiny number of Bolsheviks.

On the evening of October 26, Old Style (November 6 by the modern calendar), the Bolsheviks used their sympathizers among the workers and soldiers in St. Petersburg to seize government headquarters and take control of the city. The **Great October Revolution** of Soviet folklore was in fact a coup d'état that cost only a few hundred lives to topple a government that, as Lenin had insisted, had practically no support left among the people. In the next few weeks, Moscow and other major industrial towns followed St. Petersburg by installing Bolshevik authorities after engaging in varying amounts of armed struggle in the streets. (See the Law and Government box for Lenin's speech to the Soviet after the revolution.)

What about the 80 percent of the population outside of the cities? For several months, the countryside remained almost untouched by these urban events, with one exception: in the villages, the peasants took advantage of the breakdown of government to seize the land they had long craved from the hands of the nobles and the church. For the peasants, the redistribution of land from absentee landlords to themselves was the beginning and the end of revolution. Of Marxist theory about collectivization of agriculture, they knew and wanted to know nothing at all.

Lenin moved swiftly to establish the Bolshevik dictatorship, using both armed force and the massive confusion that had overtaken all levels of Russian government after October. By December, large economic enterprises of all types were being confiscated and put under government supervision. The first version of the dreaded political police, the ***Cheka,*** had been formed and was being employed against various enemies. The remnants of the imperial army were being bolshevized and turned into a weapon for use against internal opponents.

## Civil War

Against heavy opposition from his own associates, Lenin insisted that Russia must make immediate peace with the Germans and Austrians. His rationale proved to be correct: a civil war against the many enemies of Bolshevism was bound to come soon, and the party could not afford to still be fighting a foreign foe when it did. In March 1918, the harsh **Treaty of Brest-Litovsk** was signed with the Central Powers. The collapse of the Central Powers eight months later made this treaty a dead letter. By that time, the Bolshevik "Reds" were engaged in a massive and very bloody civil war, which was to last two and a half years and cause about as many Russian deaths as had occurred in World War I.

The Reds won this conflict for several reasons. They were far better organized and coordinated by a unitary

LAW AND GOVERNMENT

## Lenin's Speech to the Soviet

**IMMEDIATELY AFTER THE BOLSHEVIK** revolution of 1917 in Russia, Vladimir Lenin outlined his party's priorities and longer-range goals in a speech to the Petrograd (St. Petersburg) Soviet, which was now under the control of the Bolsheviks and their sympathizers. The uncompromising directness is typical of Lenin's speaking style. He was at this time entirely confident that the workers in the rest of the combatant nations would join Russia in revolt against their capitalist governments and that peace would come because the workers would refuse to fight their proletarian brothers any longer.

> Comrades! The workmen's and peasants' revolution, the need of which the Bolsheviks have emphasized many times, has come to pass.
>
> What is the significance of this revolution? Its significance is, in the first place, that we shall have a soviet government, without the participation of bourgeoisie of any type. The oppressed masses will of themselves form a government. The old state machinery will be smashed into bits, and in its place will rise a new machinery of government created by the soviet's organizations. From now on there is a new page in the history of Russia, and the present, third Russian revolution [that is, counting the abortive 1905 uprising] shall in its final result lead to the victory of socialism.
>
> One of our immediate tasks is to put an end to the war at once. But in order to end the war, which is closely bound up with the present capitalistic system, it is necessary to overthrow capitalism itself. In this work we shall have the aid of the world labor movement, which has already begun to develop in Italy, England, and Germany.
>
> A just and immediate offer of peace by us to the international democracy will find a warm response everywhere among the international proletariat masses. In the interior of Russia a large part of the peasantry has said: Enough playing with the capitalists! We will go with the workers!
>
> We shall secure the confidence of the peasants by one decree, which will wipe out the private property of the landowners. The peasants will understand that their only salvation is in union with the workers.
>
> We will establish a real control by labor in production. We have now learned to work together in a friendly manner, as is evident from this revolution. We have the force of mass organization which has conquered all, and which will lead the proletariat to world revolution.
>
> We should now occupy ourselves in Russia in building up a proletarian socialist state.
>
> Long live the world-wide socialist revolution!

### *Analyze and Interpret*

Why could Lenin think at this juncture that other nations' proletariats would join with the Russians in revolution against their capitalist governments? Why would the "peasants understand that their only salvation is in union with the workers"?

**History Now™**

***To read excerpts from Lenin's* State and Revolution, *point your browser to the documents area of HistoryNow.***

leadership than were their opponent "Whites." Despite his total lack of military experience, Lenin's colleague Trotsky proved to be an inspiring and effective commander-in-chief of the Red Army, which he created in record time. The Reds had a big advantage in that they controlled most of the interior of European Russia, including the major cities of St. Petersburg and Moscow and the rail networks that served them (see Map 44.1). The opposition armies, separated by vast distances from one another, were often at cross-purposes, did not trust one another, and had little coordination in either military or political goals. Moreover, the Whites were decisively defeated in the propaganda battles, in which the Reds played up the White generals' multiple links with both the old regime and the landlords. Personal rivalries also damaged the White leadership.

The intervention of several foreign powers in the civil war also became a Red asset, although it was intended to assist the Whites. In early 1918, fearing that the Bolsheviks would take Russia out of the war and that matériel meant for the old imperial army would fall into enemy hands, the French and British sent small forces into Russia. Inevitably, these forces clashed with the Reds, and the foreigners (including a small U.S. detachment in the far north) began actively assisting the Whites. Overall, the foreign intervention provided little practical help for the Whites but gave the Leninists an effective propaganda weapon for rallying support among the Russian people.

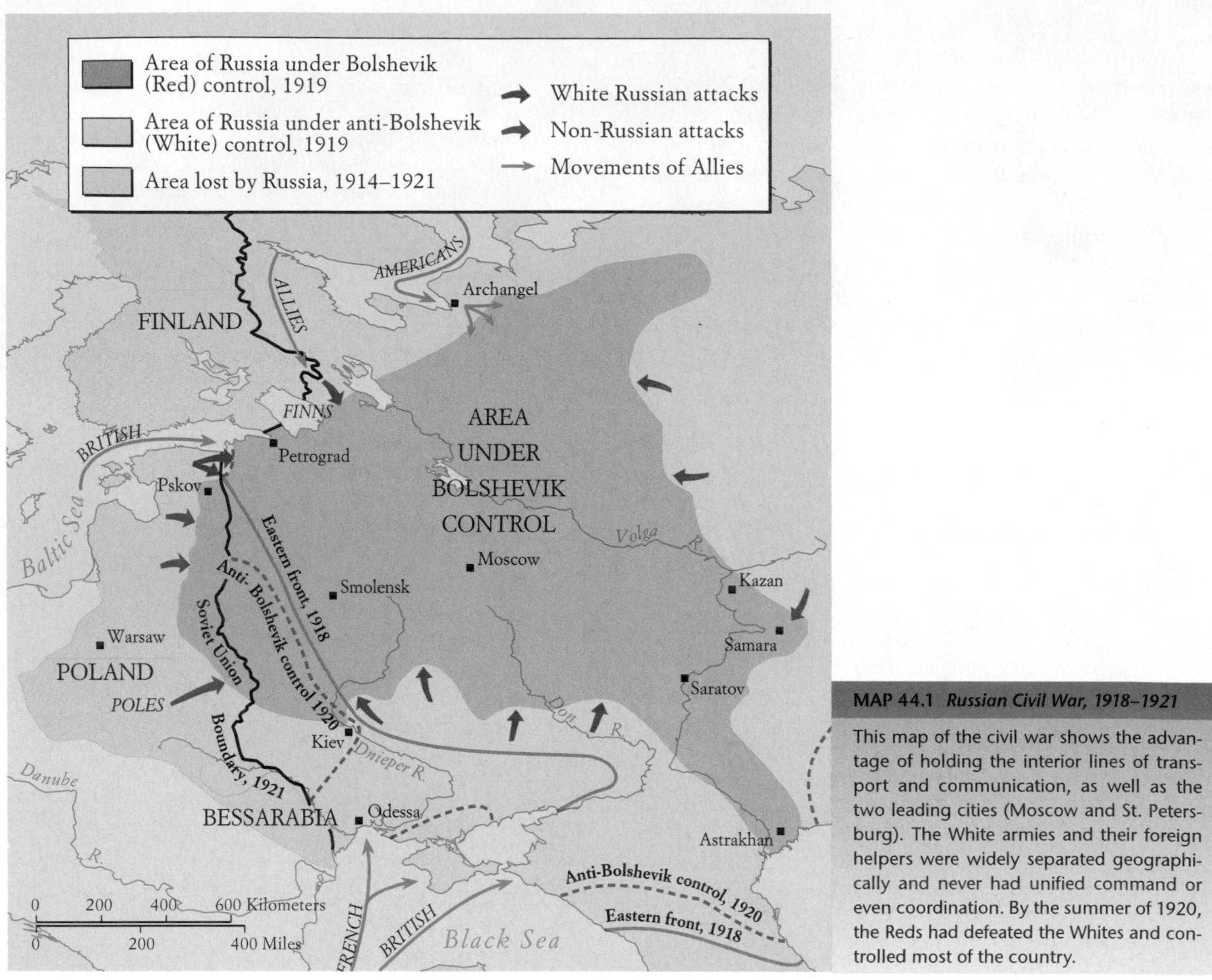


**MAP 44.1** ***Russian Civil War, 1918–1921***

This map of the civil war shows the advantage of holding the interior lines of transport and communication, as well as the two leading cities (Moscow and St. Petersburg). The White armies and their foreign helpers were widely separated geographically and never had unified command or even coordination. By the summer of 1920, the Reds had defeated the Whites and controlled most of the country.

# Economic Revival and Internal Struggles

By the summer of 1921, the Bolsheviks were close enough to victory that they abolished their coercive "War Communism"—the label they used for rule at the point of a gun. Lenin had employed this method since 1918 through the Red Army and the Cheka, and it had sustained the Bolshevik rule, but only at great costs. Along with terrible famine and the disruptions of civil war, War Communism had reduced the Russian gross national product to an estimated 20 percent of what it had been in 1913!

In place of War Communism, Lenin now prescribed the **New Economic Policy (NEP),** which encouraged small-scale capitalist business and profit seekers, while retaining "the commanding heights" of the national economy firmly in state hands. By this time, state hands meant Bolshevik hands. The Communist Party of the Soviet Union (CPSU), headed by Lenin and his colleagues, was in sole control of both economic and political affairs. By 1922, all other parties had been banned, and Russia was fast becoming a totalitarian state.

After being wounded in an attempted assassination, Lenin suffered a series of strokes starting in 1922. Power in everyday affairs was transferred to an inside group of the Central Committee, called the *Politburo* (Political Bureau). This group included Lenin's closest colleagues. Trotsky was the best known and seemed to hold the dominant position within the party's innermost circle, but when Lenin died in January 1924 without naming anyone to succeed him, a power struggle was already under way.

One of Trotsky's rivals was Josef Stalin (1879–1953), a tested party worker since early youth. He was esteemed by Lenin for his administrative abilities and hard work. At the end of his life, however, Lenin had turned against Stalin because of his "rudeness" and his contempt for others' opinions.

Lenin was too late in reaching this conclusion: Stalin, as the party general secretary (administrator), had already cemented his position. Brilliantly manipulating others,

**Stalin as a Young Bolshevik.** These police file photos were taken in 1912 or 1913 and show the thirty-four-year-old Stalin after one of his several arrests as a suspected revolutionary.



Stalin was able to defeat first Trotsky and then other contestants for Lenin's position in the mid- and late 1920s. By 1927, he was the leader of the majority faction in the Politburo and thus of the Communist Party. By 1932, Stalin was becoming dictator of the Soviet Union's entire public life. By 1937, he was the undisputed master of 180 million people. (See the Law and Government box for more on Trotsky.)

Under the NEP, both the agrarian and the industrial economy had made a stunning recovery by late 1928 from the lows of the early postwar era. The peasants were apparently content and producing well on their newly acquired private farms. Industrial production exceeded that of 1913. To foreign businessmen interested in Russian contracts, it appeared that Bolshevism's revolutionary bark was much worse than its bite. One could, after all, do good capitalist business with the Soviets, but only a few months later, the entire picture changed.

## The Five-Year Plans

At Stalin's command, the **First Five-Year Plan** of 1929–1933 was adopted. It would transform the Soviet Union in several ways. The "Second Revolution" had started.

Russia was still an overwhelmingly rural, agrarian society, backward in every way compared with western Europe or the United States. Throughout the 1920s, some party members had been discontented with the "two steps forward, one step back" concessions of the NEP. In their view, the good proletarian workers in the cities were still at the mercy of the "reactionary" peasants who fed them. Very little additional investment had been made in industry, which was seen as the key to a socialist society.

In the fall of 1928, many of the more prosperous peasants decided to hold back their grain until they could get better prices in the state-controlled markets. Stalin used this perceived "betrayal" as a reason to start the drive for agricultural collectivization and rapid industrialization, which would go on at a breathtaking pace until World War II brought it to a temporary halt.

Stalin's Five-Year Plan was intended to kill three major birds with one enormous stone: (1) the age-old resistance of private landholders to any kind of government supervision would be broken by massive pressure to collectivize; (2) a huge increase in investment would be allocated to heavy industry and infrastructure (such as transportation and communication systems) to modernize the backward society; and (3) the organization and efforts required to achieve the first two goals would enable the total

# Leon Trotsky (1879–1940)

**Lev Davidovitch Bronstein**, better known by far as Leon Trotsky, was born to a prosperous Jewish farmer in southern Ukraine in 1879. Like many other Russian revolutionary figures, Trotsky's career as a radical challenger of the status quo began early, while he was in high school in Odessa. In 1898, he underwent the traditional coming-of-age ceremony for eastern European reformers: arrest by the political police.

Exiled to Siberia in 1900, Trotsky escaped two years later and fled abroad, where he met Vladimir Lenin and other leaders of the budding Russian Marxist movement. Even in that highly intellectual and aggressive company, young Trotsky stood out by force of character and self-assurance. Opposed to Lenin's version of Marxism, Trotsky later adopted an independent standpoint of his own, refusing to submit to the discipline Lenin demanded of all his followers but not condemning Bolshevism outright. During the short-lived Revolution of 1905, Trotsky had momentary power as chairman of the Petersburg Soviet of Workers. He again was exiled and again escaped to Europe in 1907.

Corbis

**Leon Trotsky**

Still opposed in principle to Bolshevism during the early years of the war, Trotsky changed his mind after the March 1917 revolution. He now fell under Lenin's powerful personality and joined him as his right-hand man. Trotsky was second only to Lenin in preparing the October Revolution that brought them to power. After a brief stint as commissar for foreign affairs, Trotsky then took over as commissar for war in 1918. His brilliance as a strategist and his ruthlessness were major reasons for the Reds' victory in the civil war that wrecked Russia between 1918 and 1921.

In the struggle for succession to Lenin, which began as early as 1922, Trotsky seemed to most to be the inevitable choice, but Stalin and others were determined this would not happen and proved to be both less scrupulous and more in tune with party members' thinking than Trotsky. One step after another forced the civil war hero out of the Central Committee, then out of the commissariat for war, then out of the party, and finally, in 1929, into foreign exile. In 1940, after several moves, Trotsky was murdered on Stalin's orders in his final refuge in Mexico.

A tiny, unprepossessing figure with thick glasses, Trotsky was possessed of almost incredible energy and single-mindedness. He was totally uncompromising and totally convinced of his own correctness in things political. Like his hero Lenin, he never allowed what the Bolsheviks called "bourgeois sentiment" to interfere with his dedication to a communist triumph. Again like Lenin, his force of personality attracted a clique of followers who were entirely devoted to him, but he lacked the organizational skills of his master and was never interested in the day-to-day administrative detail.

Trotsky became a hero to some because of his unremitting and devastating criticism of Stalin's dictatorship, at a time—the 1930s—when few other reformers were willing to see just how repressive Stalin's regime had become. Trotsky believed, as Mao Zedong would later, that bureaucracy was the great danger to revolutions, and he condemned it among communists as well as capitalists. He was a steadfast adherent of "permanent revolution" and the opponent of Stalin's "socialism in one country." He believed that if the communist revolution did not spread, it would inevitably degenerate under a dictator such as Stalin. Trotsky's attempt to found an anti-Stalin Fourth International did not get far, but his charisma and his vivid writings about the Russian Revolution of 1917 have guaranteed him a place in the pantheon of twentieth-century revolutionaries.

## *Analyze and Interpret*

Why are succession problems frequently violent, even lethal, in revolutionary governments?

integration of the citizenry into the CPSU-controlled political process.

## Agrarian Collectivization

In 1929, Stalin began his collectivization campaign as a way to "win the class war in the villages"—that is, the alleged struggle between the poor peasants and those who were better off. The richer peasants (*kulaks*) were to be dispossessed by force. The poorer peasants were to be forced onto newly founded collective farms under party supervision.

As many as 10 million peasants are estimated to have died in the collectivization drive between 1929 and 1933, most of them in an artificially caused famine. Determined to break the peasants' persistent resistance, Stalin authorized the use of the Red Army as well as armed party militants against the villages. Millions were driven off their land and out of their houses and condemned to wander as starving beggars. Their former land, machinery, and animals were turned over to the new *collectives*. These enormous farms, which were run like factories with wage labor by party bosses, proved to be inefficient, largely because the peasants heartily disliked their new situation and felt little responsibility and even less incentive to produce. Throughout the Soviet Union's history, agriculture remained a major weakness of the economy.

The collectivization struggle left deep scars, and its costs were still being paid a generation later. Stalin rammed it through because he believed it was essential if the Soviet Union were to survive. The ignorant, conservative peasants must be brought under direct government control, and their numbers reduced by forcing them into a new industrial labor force. Both of these goals were eventually reached, but at a price that no rational economist could justify.

## Industrial Progress

Stalin's second goal was rapid industrialization. Here again, the costs were very high, but their justification was easier. Soviet gains in industry between 1929 and 1940 were truly impressive. In percentage terms, the growth achieved in several branches of heavy industry and infrastructure was greater than any country in history has ever achieved in an equivalent period—about 400 percent even by conservative estimates. Whole industrial cities rose up from the Siberian or Central Asian plains, built partly by forced labor and partly by idealists who believed in Stalin and in communism's vision of a new life. Throughout the economy, "fulfilling the Plan" became all-important. Untouched by free-market realities and constraints, the Soviet managers plunged ahead in a wild race to raise total production.

The new industry turned out capital goods, not consumer items. Consumer goods such as clothes and baby carriages became more difficult to obtain, and their prices rose ever higher throughout the 1930s. When a suit of clothes could be found, it cost the equivalent of four months' wages for a skilled worker. Items such as refrigerators, automobiles, and washing machines were out of the question. Even basic food had to be rationed for a while because of the drop in production caused by collectivization. It is testimony to the extraordinary capacity of the Russian people to suffer in silence that so much was accomplished at such high costs with so little reward for those doing it.

The uprootings and hardships caused by the industrialization drive in the 1930s were nearly as severe as those caused by collectivization in the countryside. And much of the work on the new mines, canals, logging operations, and other projects was performed by Stalin's slave laborers. By conservative estimates, fully 10 percent of the 1930s Soviet gross national product was produced by prisoners of the NKVD (one of the several successive names for the Soviet political police).

Hulton-Deutsch Collection/Corbis

**Lenin and Stalin: A Faked Photograph.** This photo of the two leaders, purportedly taken shortly before Lenin's death and used extensively by the Stalinist propaganda machine to show the closeness of their relationship, is known to have been "doctored." Stalin's figure was placed into the photo later. Lenin came to distrust Stalin in his last days but took only ineffective measures to warn the party against him.

## The Stalinist Dictatorship

The third goal of the Five-Year Plans was, in effect, a revolution by Stalin and a changed Communist Party against the Soviet peoples. In 1928, Stalin was chief of a CPSU that was still an elite organization. It was relatively small (about 6 percent of the adult population) and difficult to join. The party was tightly disciplined and composed of intellectuals, white-collar personnel, and some workers. It included very few peasants and few women above the lowest ranks. Many members still knew little of Stalin and were totally unaware of the secret high-level struggles for control in the Politburo.

Stalin emerged as the Boss (*vozhd*) on his fiftieth birthday in 1929, when a tremendous fuss was made over his role as Lenin's successor. From this time on, no one else in the Soviet hierarchy was allowed to rival Stalin in press coverage or authority. From the early 1930s, every party member lived in Stalin's shadow. He proved to be a master of Mafia-style politics, never forgetting who had helped and who had hurt him in his climb. Absolutely vindictive toward political rivals and enemies (they were the same to him), his character has long fascinated many Russian and foreign analysts. (See the Society and Economy box.)

Stalin cultivated an image of mystery. Unlike his fellow dictators, he had no gift for speech making, and he never indulged in the dramatics that other dictators constantly employed in their public appearances. After 1935, he was rarely seen in public—and then only under totally controlled circumstances.

Although he was a Georgian by birth, Stalin became a strong Russian nationalist and soon transformed what had been a truly supranational movement under Lenin into a Russian one. He took the international communist organization, called the Comintern (Communist International) and based in Moscow, and turned it into an organ of Russian foreign policy. No foreign communists dared to challenge the policies dictated by Stalin's stooges on the governing board of the Comintern, even when, as sometimes happened, those policies were directly opposed to the interests of the Communist Party in the foreigners' own country. In the communist world, Moscow alone called the tune.

### The Purges: A Terrorized Society

Although Stalin had crushed his high-level opponents by 1933, he still had some opposition in the party. In 1935, he apparently decided that he must crush those opponents, too. He proceeded to do so over the next few years in a fashion that shocked and mystified the world.

Between 1936 and late 1938, Moscow was the scene of a series of **show trials,** where leading party members were accused of absurd charges of treason and sabotage. Virtually all of Lenin's surviving comrades had disappeared from public sight by 1939, and Stalin was alone as master. Hundreds of thousands of ordinary citizens were arrested at the same time for alleged crimes against the state and sentenced to prison or to the Siberian labor camps, where most of them eventually died.

Corbis

**Victory in the Five-Year Plan.** Soviet propaganda for the "Workers Paradise" created by Stalin's dictatorship particularly liked to show the alleged enthusiasm of the peasantry for their new tasks. This view was often the opposite of the truth.

## Josef Stalin, Husband and Father

**ONE OF THE STRANGER OCCURRENCES** of twentieth-century history was the appearance of a Soviet Russian citizen at the New Delhi, India, embassy of the United States in 1966, asking for political asylum. The Russian's name was Svetlana Alliluyeva Stalin; she was the only surviving child of the Soviet dictator, Josef Stalin. At age forty, she had decided she had had enough of life in the country her father had formed.

Svetlana Stalin was born in 1926 to the second wife of Stalin, Nadezhda Alliluyeva, as her second child. Nadezhda (Nadja) had been only seventeen when she married, while Stalin was a thirty-nine-year-old widower. He had married a fellow worker in the underground revolutionary movement in 1905, with whom he had one son, Jakov, before his wife's untimely death in 1907. As a harried and secretive Bolshevik revolutionary and political exile in Siberia, Stalin had had little time or opportunity to found a second family. But in the aftermath of the successful coup d'état of November 1917, he had courted and married the young Nadezhda, starting a new family in the Kremlin apartments.

Svetlana had been raised in the citadel of the Marxist revolution. As she wrote in her first memoir of her Soviet life, her father's ability to control the fate of millions was nothing to her compared to the fact of whether he did or did not take her on his lap for a brief moment between his endless conferences. Stalin may have been a distant and harsh-mannered father to her and her two brothers, but she makes it clear that for her early childhood years, he fulfilled her modest demands.

The marriage of Josef and Nadezhda was too heavily burdened to survive, however. The increasing paranoia of the Soviet dictator intruded ever more into his family life. In 1932, Nadezhda committed suicide; the motives and the details remain a secret, even in post-Soviet Russia. The impact on Svetlana, now age six, was overwhelming; she had been closer to her warm-hearted and ever-present mother than to her father, and she never recovered from her loss. Gradually alienated from her father, she married and divorced twice before she was thirty and led a tormented internal life—by her own words—even as a member of the Soviet elite.

During World War II, both Svetlana's half-brother Jakov and her brother Vasili were active in the Soviet forces. Jakov died in a German POW camp after his father had refused a proferred exchange of prisoners that would have freed him in return for some high-ranking German officers. Vasili survived the war as a combat aviator but met an early death from alcoholism, in part induced by Stalin's icy rejection of him as an incompetent.

In the United States, Svetlana published her memoir of her early life to worldwide success: *Twenty Letters to a Friend* (1967) was an instant best-seller. Becoming an American citizen, she married a Virginia architect in 1970 and added a new daughter to the two grown children from her Russian marriages. (Both of those had opted to remain in the USSR when their mother defected.)

The American marriage also failed, however, and in 1984 Svetlana temporarily returned to the Soviet Union, longing to see her older children and trying to find a foothold in that rapidly changing political environment. In 1986, she opted to return to the United States and then went to live her remaining years in Great Britain. Her erratic and painful course shows that after more than sixty years, she still lived in "Stalin's Shadow," as she has titled a second book of family recollections published not long ago. Like millions of other Soviet citizens who felt the dictator's iron fist, although never within his family orbit, she could only strive to put a permanently scarred life back together.

### Analyze and Interpret

Does the revelation of a personal, "human" side of a dictator induce you to make allowances for his public evils and brutalities? Should it? Do you sympathize with Svetlana Stalin, or do you believe her to be only the spoiled weakling that some critics see in her ?

**History Now™**

*To read more of Stalin's* **Trotskyism or Leninism?** *and* **Industrialization of the Country,** *point your browser to the documents area of* **HistoryNow.**

To this day, historians do not agree on an explanation of why the purge happened. What is known is that between 1935 and the end of Stalin's life in 1953, perhaps *10 million* Soviet citizens were at one time or another banished to prison camps without trial and almost always without proof of violation of current Soviet law. Everyone had a close relative or friend who had been spirited away, usually in the night, by the dreaded secret police. These "administrative measures," based on anonymous denunciations, were conducted completely outside of the usual court system, and often the prisoners were never told their crimes, even after serving many years. Some survived their sentences, but very many did not. It was commonplace for the camp overseers to extend the original sentences, adding five more years for such "offenses" as trading a bit of bread for a pair of socks.

Stalin never offered an explanation for his actions, then or later. One thing is certain: if Stalin instituted the **Great Purge** to terrorize the party and Soviet society into complete obedience, he succeeded. Until his death, no one in the party, military, or general society dared oppose him openly.

How did Stalin's dictatorship compare with Adolf Hitler's—that other terrifying Western dictatorship of the twentieth century? One major difference should be noted: Stalin posed as the champion of the underdog everywhere, whereas Hitler was the champion only of the Germans. We will see in Chapter 47 that Hitler's narrowly racist ideology had no vision of the beneficial transformation of human society, whereas Stalin's international communism did. Stalin and his assistants were able to fashion that vision so that a significant portion of the world, from China to Cuba, came to believe it—for a time.

## Life under the Dictatorship

Stalin and his associates believed that a "new Soviet man" would emerge after a few years of Soviet rule. In this ideal, they were sadly mistaken. The Soviet people continued to be old-style human beings with all their faults, but a new type of society did emerge in the Soviet Union, and it had both good and bad points.

### *Possibilities Expanded*

On the good side, the forced-draft industrialization and modernization under the Five-Year Plans allowed a very large number of human beings to improve their professional prospects dramatically. Mass education of even a rather primitive sort enabled many people to hold jobs and assume responsibilities that they could not have handled or would never have been offered in the old society. Many illiterate peasants saw their sons and daughters obtain degrees in advanced technology, while the new Soviet schools turned out engineers by the millions. For example, Nikita Khrushchev, Stalin's successor as head of the Communist Party, worked as a coal miner in his early years before becoming a full-time communist organizer.

Millions of Russian and Soviet women were emancipated from a life that offered them no real opportunities to use their minds or develop their talents. Despite much propaganda to the contrary, the Soviet leaders did not really believe in equality for women, and the highest positions remained overwhelmingly male until the Soviet Union's collapse, but the leaders *did* believe in additional skilled labor, male or female. By the end of the 1930s, most Soviet women worked outside of the home. Living standards were very low, and the woman's additional income was crucial for many Soviet families. Still, the door to a more varied, more challenging life had been opened and would not be closed again.

Then, a basic "safety net" was established for all citizens. Outside of the camps, no one starved, and no one was allowed to die like an animal because of lack of human care. According to the Soviet constitution, every citizen had a right (and a duty!) to a job. Medical care was free, all workers received pensions, and education was open and free to all politically reliable persons. There were truly no ceilings to talent, provided that one either was a sincere communist or paid the necessary lip service to the system. Few found either of these attitudes intolerable.

Sovfoto/Eastphoto

**The Soviet Drive for Literacy.** An undeniable benefit of the Soviet Union to its people was the effective campaign for adult literacy introduced in the 1920s. By the end of the Second Five-Year Plan in 1937, most men and women had some ability to read and write.

### *Liberties Suppressed*

On the bad side were all of the drawbacks we have already mentioned as inherent in the Stalinist dictatorship: lack of any political freedom, terror and lawlessness, and low standards of living. There were other disadvantages, too: religious persecution, cultural censorship, constant indoctrination with a simplistic and distorted version of Marxism, and constant interference with private lives. For a certain time, during the 1920s and early 1930s, many well-meaning people in and outside the Soviet Union were able to rationalize the bad aspects of Soviet life by balancing them against the good. They accepted the Stalinist statement "You can't make an omelet without breaking eggs." They believed that within a few years, Soviet society would be the envy of the capitalists in the West. Then, the glories of developed socialism would be wonderful to behold, and the evils of the transition period would be soon forgotten.

The terror of the purges of the mid-1930s disillusioned many, however, and the continued iron dictatorship after World War II discouraged many more. Even the youths, who had been the most enthusiastic members of the party and the hardest workers, were disappointed that the enormous sacrifices made during World War II seemed to go unappreciated by the Leader. The CPSU lost its spirit and its moral authority as the voice of revolutionary ideals. In the postwar years, it came to resemble just another huge bureaucracy, providing a ladder upward for opportunists and manipulators. The only real talent necessary for a successful party career became to pretend to worship Stalin.

## Material and Social Welfare in the Interwar Soviet Union

Material life under Stalin was very hard. Starting from a low level, Russians' living standards became far worse than those of any other European people. The new industrial cities were plagued by a continuing, unsolvable housing crisis. On average, people were living worse in 1950 than they had in 1930. The typical Moscow apartment housed four adults *per room,* and often they were members of unrelated families sharing a kitchen and a one-floor-down toilet. There was a total lack of privacy in urban apartments, with devastating effects on family living conditions. Until the mid-1950s, certain basic foods were still rationed—long after the defeated Germans had overcome such shortages.

Social problems were sometimes met head-on by government action, and sometimes ignored. The divorce and abortion rates shot up in the 1920s in line with the communist-supported emancipation of Russian women. In the mid-1930s, Stalin reintroduced tight restrictions on abortion and divorce and rewarded women who bore many children with cash and medals ("Heroine of Socialist Labor"). The underlying reason for this change in policy was the shortage of labor in Soviet industry and agriculture, both of which were extraordinarily inefficient in their use of labor and which suffered from endemic low productivity.

Soviet medical care was supposedly free to all but was spotty in quality, and party membership was a definite advantage. Clinics were established for the first time throughout the countryside, but the problems of poor nutrition, superstition about prenatal and postnatal care, and the large Muslim population's distrust of all Western-style medicine were great handicaps to overcome in lowering the epidemic death rate or infant mortality.

Alcoholism remained what it had always been in Russia: a serious obstacle to labor efficiency and a drain on resources. Repeated government campaigns for sobriety had only limited effects on the peasants and urban workers. Home brew was common despite heavy penalties on its production.

Some common crimes were effectively reduced, at least for a time. (The Soviet government was always reluctant to provide accurate statistics on social problems, especially crime.) Prostitution became rare for a while, partly because the original Bolshevik attitude toward sex was quite liberal: men and women were equals and should be able to arrange their sexual activities as they saw fit without interference. This changed over time to a much stricter Puritanism. Financial offenses, such as embezzlement and fraud, were almost eliminated because opportunities to commit them were originally almost nonexistent. This, too, was to change radically in later days. Theft, on the other hand, became common, as all classes of people frequently had to resort to it in order to survive during the civil war; later, the attitude became that stealing from a government-owned shop or enterprise was not really a crime, as all property belonged to "the people," hence to no one. Violence against persons increased in the early Soviet period, when civil war, starving wanderers, and class struggle were commonplace and provided some cover for personal criminal acts. So far as could be seen from statistics, violent crimes then reverted to their original, prerevolutionary patterns.

## Summary

The Bolshevik revolution of 1917 was one of the milestones of modern history. For a long time, millions of idealists considered it the definitive dawn of a new age. No other modern social or economic movement has convinced so many different people that it was the solution to society's various ills.

Lenin's installation of a dictatorship by the Communist Party immediately after the revolution broke the ground for the Stalinist rule of later date. After a hidden power struggle, Leon Trotsky, the presumed successor to Lenin, was overcome by Josef Stalin, who had mastered the art of closed-group infighting better than any of his competitors. In a few more years, he had made himself the master of his country in unprecedented fashion.

In 1928, the introduction of the First Five-Year Plan was a Second Revolution. Agrarian life was transformed by collectivization of the peasants, and the USSR became a major industrial power. Midway through the 1930s, the Great Purge of both party and people began, claiming millions of innocent victims. Stalinist policies helped the material welfare of some large segments of the Soviet populace. These measures improved education, professional opportunities, and medical care and generally allowed the population to live a more modern lifestyle, but the Soviet people paid high prices for these advantages. They gave up all political and economic liberties and suffered through a generation of great hardships under the dictatorial rule of the party and its omnipotent head.

## Identification Terms

Test your knowledge of this chapter's key concepts by defining the following terms. If you can't recall the meaning of certain terms, refresh your memory by looking up the boldfaced term in the chapter, turning to the Glossary at the end of the book, or working with the flashcards that are available on the *World Civilizations* Companion Website **http://history.wadsworth.com/adler04**.

Bolsheviks
*Cheka*
First Five-Year Plan
Great Purge
Great October Revolution
March Revolution
New Economic Policy (NEP)
Provisional Government
show trials
Treaty of Brest-Litovsk

## Test Your Knowledge

Test your knowledge of this chapter by answering the following questions. Complete answers appear at the end of the book. You may also take this quiz interactively and find even more quiz questions on the *World Civilizations* Companion Website: **http://history.wadsworth.com/adler04.**

1. The March Revolution in Russia took place without real opposition after
   a. Alexander Kerensky spoke in Moscow and called for the people to rebel.
   b. Czar Nicholas II abdicated the throne.
   c. Vladimir Lenin returned to Russia.
   d. Leon Trotsky took control of the military.
   e. Russia and Germany signed the Treaty of Brest-Litovsk.
2. In the early 1920s, Lenin's closest associate and apparent successor as leader of the Soviet Party and state was
   a. Stalin.
   b. Trotsky.
   c. Khrushchev.
   d. Romanov.
   e. Kerensky.
3. The October Revolution began in the city of
   a. Leningrad.
   b. Moscow.
   c. St. Petersburg.
   d. Kiev.
   e. Stalingrad.
4. By 1921 in Russia,
   a. a large part of the population was taking up arms against communism.
   b. the majority of Russians had become communists.

c. a civil war had greatly worsened the damage sustained during World War I.
d. the economy had almost recovered from wartime damages.
e. the White Russians were on the verge of winning the civil war.

5. During the Five-Year Plans, the peasants were
a. finally liberated from dependence on the government.
b. ignored by the authorities, who were concentrating on industry.
c. deprived of most of their private property.
d. given a major boost in productivity by government action.
e. relegated to the fringes of society, but left in charge of their own lands.

6. The Five-Year Plans called for
a. subordination of the Communist Party to the government.
b. rapid, forced industrialization.
c. distribution of the farmlands to the peasants.
d. war on the Western democracies.
e. the reinstitution of religion in the Soviet Union.

7. Which of the following were *not* members of the new communist elite in the Soviet Union?
a. Artists and writers
b. Party officials
c. Intellectuals
d. Technical managers
e. Medical specialists

8. The Great Purges started
a. after an assassination attempt on Stalin.
b. after evidence of a foreign spy ring within the Communist party was uncovered.
c. because of a rebellion of party leaders against the Five-Year Plans.
d. because of Stalin's suspicions about his associates' loyalty.
e. after Stalin became concerned about the growing strength of Leon Trotsky.

9. One of the chief rewards for the workers in the new Soviet Union of the 1930s was
a. improved and expanded housing.
b. mass educational facilities.
c. a decisive voice in public affairs.
d. security of life and property against the state.
e. improvements in their working conditions.

10. Which of the following is most descriptive of the Stalinist era in the Soviet Union?
a. Most people had seen their lives improve somewhat between 1930 and 1950.
b. Divorce rates rose throughout the period, but government sanctions led to lower abortion rates.
c. Free medical care was equally available to all citizens.
d. Rates of fraud and embezzlement dropped significantly, but thievery became much more common.
e. Government efforts almost eliminated the problem of alcoholism.

## InfoTrac College Edition

Visit the source collections at

**http://infotrac.thomsonlearning.com**

and use the Search function with the following key terms:

Russia Revolution Bolshevik Joseph Stalin

## Wadsworth History Website Resources

Visit the World History Resource Center at **http://history.wadsworth.com/world** for a wealth of general resources, and the *World Civilizations* Companion Website at **http://history.wadsworth.com/adler04** for resources specific to this textbook.

## HistoryNow

Enter *HistoryNow* using the access card that is available for *World Civilizations*. *HistoryNow* will assist you in understanding the content in this chapter with lesson plans generated for your needs. In addition, you can read the following documents, and many more, online:

Vladimir Lenin, excerpts from *State and Revolution*

Josef Stalin, *Trotskyism or Leninism?*

Josef Stalin, *Industrialization of the Country*

*One does not establish a dictatorship in order to make a revolution; one makes a revolution in order to establish a dictatorship.*
George Orwell, 1984

# 45 Totalitarianism Refined: The Nazi State



| | |
|---|---|
| 1920 | Hitler takes charge of NSDAP |
| 1923 | Munich putsch fails |
| 1924 | *Mein Kampf* |
| 1930–1932 | Great Depression in Germany |
| 1933 | Hitler becomes chancellor/ Enabling Law |
| 1935 | Nuremberg Laws on race |
| 1936–1939 | Nazi preparation for war |
| 1938 | "Kristallnacht"/Harassment of Jews intensifies |

In the twentieth century, a new form of state organization came into the world—the savage form called totalitarianism (see Chapter 43). It was an unprecedented denial of the traditional freedom of the individual citizen, in order to glorify and strengthen the powers of the state. Was totalitarianism the result of some peculiar, temporary combination of circumstances in the political-economic spectrum of the 1920s and 1930s? Or was what occurred in those years in several European countries the result of the inevitable stresses generated by the modern nation-state, and therefore the possible harbinger of worse things still to come? The experts still argue about these questions.

Totalitarian states were necessarily always ruled by a dictator, but not all dictatorships were necessarily totalitarian. The interwar years (1919–1939) saw the rise of several dictatorships in various parts of the world. Most of these regimes were not totalitarian in character. In this chapter, we concentrate on the most aggressive and militant of totalitarian states: that erected by Adolf Hitler, the leader of Nazi Germany from 1933 until his death at the end of World War II. Hitler had taken some of his strategies and tactics from the Italian Fascist pioneers, but he soon refined and systematized them to an extent not approached by the followers of Mussolini.

## Hitler and the Thousand-Year Reich

The "honor" of creating the most ruthless totalitarian system was divided between the communist dictatorship of Josef Stalin in Russia (see Chapter 44) and the Nazi dictatorship of Adolf Hitler in Germany. We have seen that Stalin attained tremendous power by cynically manipulating an idealistic movement aimed at bringing first Russia and then the world into a new era of equality and freedom. The German dictator had no such visions, however.

### *Hitler's Early Career*

Adolf Hitler was born an Austrian citizen in 1889. He was the only child of a strict father and a loving mother who spoiled him in every way her limited resources allowed. When he was seventeen, he went off to Vienna in hopes of an art career. Rejected as having no talent, he survived for the next few years on the fringes of urban society, living hand to mouth on money from home. He fully absorbed the anti-Semitism prevalent in Vienna at this time, and his constant reading convinced him of the falsity of typical "bourgeois" values and politics, but he despised

Marxism, which was the most common hope and refuge of social outsiders like himself. When World War I broke out, Hitler was a young malcontent of twenty-five, still searching for some philosophy that would make sense of a world that had rejected him.

Enlisting immediately, Hitler distinguished himself for bravery under fire, receiving the Iron Cross. The wartime experience gave him his first idea of his life's purpose. With millions of other demobilized men, he spent the first months of the postwar era in a state of shock and despair, seeing the socialist government that had replaced the kaiser and accepted the Versailles Treaty as the betrayers of the nation. As time passed, he became determined to join those who were aiming to overturn the government.

In 1920, Hitler took over a tiny group of would-be reformers and renamed them the National Socialist German Workers Party (NSDAP), or "Nazis" for short. Devoting his fanatical energy to the party, he rapidly attracted new members in the Munich area, where he had been living since before the war. In 1923, Hitler, supported by a few discontented army officers, attempted a ***putsch*** (coup d'état) in Munich, but it failed miserably. Arrested for treason, he used the trial to gain national notoriety. He was sentenced to five years in prison by a sympathetic judge and used the year he actually served to write his autobiography and call to arms: ***Mein Kampf*** (*My Struggle*).

## The Nazi Program

In wild and ranting prose, *Mein Kampf* laid out what Hitler saw as Germany's present problems and their solutions. It insisted on all of the following:

- *Anti-Semitism*. Jews were declared born enemies of all proper German values and traitors to the nation.
- *Rejection of the Versailles Treaty and German war guilt.* Hitler called the treaty the most unfair in world history, dictated by a (temporarily) strong France against a helpless, tricked Germany.
- *Confiscation of illicit war profits*. This measure was aimed mainly at Jews but also at non-Jewish German industrialists. This point reflected the Nazis' claim to be socialists (though anti-Marxist).
- *Protection of the middle classes from ruinous competition.* The Nazis made a special show of paying attention to the growing concerns of the shopkeepers and white-collar workers who feared that they were being forced downward on the economic ladder by big business.
- *Land redistribution for the peasants*. With this pseudo-socialist measure, Hitler claimed to be protecting the peasants who were being squeezed out by large landholders.

The basic tenor of *Mein Kampf* and of Nazi speeches and literature in the 1920s was consistent: hatred for the existing situation in Germany and the determination to change it radically. The "Marxist-Zionist" government that had accepted the Versailles Treaty had given a "stab in the back" to the brave German army in 1918. Germany must be reborn and once again gain its rightful place! Whatever means were necessary to do this were justified, as only the strong would survive in a jungle world of competing nations.

After the failure of the Munich putsch, Hitler swore that he would come to power by constitutional, legal means. No one could later say that he had acted against the will of his people. From the moment that he was released from jail, he devoted himself tirelessly to organizing, speech making, and electioneering from one end of the country to the other.

Hitler was an extremely gifted rabble-rouser who quickly learned how to appeal to various groups in language they could not forget. His targets were always the same: Jews, the signers of the Versailles Treaty, the communists, and the clique of businessmen and bureaucrats who supposedly pulled the strings behind the scenes. (For more about Hitler's life and his appeal, see the Law and Government box.)

Between 1925 and 1929, which were prosperous years for Weimar Germany, the Nazis made little headway among the masses of industrial workers, who remained loyal to either the Social Democrats or the large, legal German Communist Party. But the Nazis did pick up voters among the members of the middle classes who had been ruined in the great inflation and among the numerous white-collar workers who saw their relative status slipping in postwar Germany. As late as the elections of 1928, the Nazis received only 2.6 percent of the vote and 12 seats in the Reichstag. In comparison, the Communists had 77 seats, and the Social Democrats had 156. The rest of the Reichstag's 500 seats were held by moderate or conservative parties that regarded Hitler as a loose cannon who might possibly be useful against the socialists but could not be taken seriously as a politician.

## The Great Depression's Effects

The collapse of the German (and world) economy in 1930–1931 set the stage for Nazi political success. In late 1929, the New York Stock Exchange went into a tailspin that soon had effects on every aspect of finance in the Western world. Germany was particularly affected because for years German industrialists and municipalities had been relying on American investment and loans. Suddenly, this credit was cut off as loans were called in on short notice. Instead of new investment, international finance and trade shrank steadily as each nation attempted to protect itself from external competition by raising tariffs and limiting imports.

## Adolf Hitler (1889–1945)

**Despite many tries,** no one has been able to explain satisfactorily why Adolf Hitler's political and social doctrines were so attractive to most German people. During the 1930s, few Germans were disturbed by his anti-Semitic and antiforeigner slogans, his manic nationalism, or his crude and violent ideas for renovating the German nation.

True, the plight of the Germans after World War I and the struggle for survival during the first years of the Great Depression contributed to their acceptance of Hitler's views. The orderly and progressive world of Kaiser William II had crumbled before their eyes. Germany was forced to yield to a partial Allied occupation and to give up most of its much-honored army and its equipment. Most irritating of all, Germany was forced to accept a peace treaty that branded it as the sole culprit for causing the ruinous war and was required to pay many billions of dollars as compensation to the victors.

The punishment was far greater than most had anticipated, and the common people suffered the consequences. Inflation, unemployment, and political turmoil spread. The fear of communism was acute among the middle classes, while the laborers and intellectuals struggled to make their voices heard. The old system was thoroughly discredited, and Germans looked for a new architect of morals. In 1923, a candidate appeared who had not yet found his proper voice. His name was Adolf Hitler.

Hitler had served during the war and—like millions of other front-line soldiers—emerged from that experience with contempt for the politicians and the traditional leaders of his people. He was looking for revenge against the "dark forces," which he sensed had thus far prevented him and those like him from assuming their rightful place in society and prevented Germany as a nation from reaching its rightful, dominant place in the world.

In 1920 Hitler found his chance at the head of a tiny party of malcontents. Rapidly expanding its membership through his mesmerizing ability to capture a crowd, Hitler entered into a half-baked scheme to take over the government in 1923, when the terrible postwar inflation and popular turmoil were at their height. The attempted coup failed with fourteen deaths. Hitler was tried for treason, turned the courtroom into a rostrum for his passionate attacks on the Jews and socialists, and was jailed for a year.

From 1924 on, the Nazi movement slowly gained strength. Hitler became an ever-more skilled manipulator of political propaganda and gathered around him a mixed band of dreamers, brutes, ambitious climbers, and opportunists. Some of them firmly believed in the Führer and his self-proclaimed mission to save Germany and bring a New Order to Europe. Others hitched their wagons to his star without necessarily believing the wild rantings in *Mein Kampf.* Few took his promises to exterminate Jews and communists as anything more than a rabble-rouser's empty words.

Hitler's personality was a collection of contradictions. He despised organized religion and proclaimed himself untrammeled by common morality, yet he lived a life of ascetic restraint. A strict vegetarian and teetotaler, he frowned on the more boisterous and indulgent lifestyle of some of his followers (such as the fat hedonist Göring). He was fascinated by the power of the intellect and will, yet held intellectuals in contempt. He would work thirty-six hours at a stretch, yet went into nervous collapse and secluded himself from his officials in several political crises. He was a notorious charmer of susceptible women, yet abstained from all sexual relations and was probably impotent.

He was perhaps the most murderous power holder of the twentieth century, committing endless atrocities against Germans and other human beings, yet he had a deep reverence for the arts and considerable artistic talent. Perhaps a hint of the truth lies in his artistic personality: when his paintings were exhibited after the war, critics were impressed by his talent for rendering structural accuracy but noted his inability to sketch the human form.

### *Analyze and Interpret*

Why do you think Hitler seized on the Jews as the German people's most dangerous enemy? Is it unusual for a political leader to hold sharply contradictory views of moral standards for himself versus for the mass of people?

**History Now™**

***To read some of Hitler's speeches, point your browser to the documents area of* HistoryNow.**

The results for Germany were horrendous: the number of unemployed rose from 2.25 million in early 1930 to more than 6 million two years later (about 25 percent of the total labor force), and this figure does not count involuntary part-time workers or the many women who withdrew from the labor market permanently. In no other country, not even the United States, was the industrial economy so hard hit.

The governing coalition of Social Democrats and moderate conservatives fell apart under this strain. In the frequent elections necessitated by the collapse of the coalition, the middle-of-the-road parties steadily lost seats to the extremes on right and left: the Nazis and the Communists. In an election for the Reichstag in mid-1930, the Nazis won a total of 107 seats, second only to the weakening SDs.

As the economy continued downhill, Hitler promised immediate, decisive action to aid the unemployed and the farmers. In another national election in early 1932, the Nazis won 14.5 million votes of a total of about 35 million. The Nazis were now the largest single party but still lacked a majority. Their attacks on the government and the other parties intensified both verbally and, increasingly, in the streets.

## *The* Machtergreifung

Finally, in a move aimed at moderating Hitler by putting him into a position where he had to take responsibility rather than just criticize, the conservative advisers of the old president, Paul von Hindenburg, appointed Hitler chancellor on January 30, 1933. Within eight weeks, Hitler had transformed the government into a Nazi dictatorship, and technically, he had accomplished this ***Machtergreifung,*** or seizure of power, by constitutional procedures, as he had promised.

The Granger Collection, New York

**Our Last Hope, Hitler.** This poster depicting economic depression on a mass scale was part of Hitler's unsuccessful 1932 presidential campaign as the National Socialist Party candidate.

The Granger Collection, New York

**Nazis or Bolsheviks?** This effective appeal to the German populace to choose between the Nazis or bolshevism was part of the campaign to discredit any moderate solutions to the Depression and its attendant misery.

How did this transformation occur? It involved two complementary processes: the capture of legal authority for the Nazis and the elimination of competing political groups. First, the Nazis whipped up hysteria over an alleged communist revolutionary plot. Under the constitution's emergency provision, Hitler as chancellor introduced the equivalent of martial law and used it to round up tens of thousands of his opponents in the next weeks. After the election that Hitler called for in March (in which the Nazis still failed to gain a simple majority), all communist and some Social Democratic delegates to the Reichstag were arrested as traitors. Finally, in late March, the Nazi-dominated rump parliament enacted the so-called *Enabling Act,* giving Hitler's government the power to rule by decree until the emergency had passed. It did not pass for the next twelve years, until Hitler was dead in the ruins of Berlin.

UPI/Bettmann/Corbis

**An All-German Party Parade.** A major reason for the Nazi success was the masterly touch of drama accompanying the party's functions. The impression of overwhelming force was fostered by slogans and banners that proclaimed the party's strength in every part of the homeland.

The German Communist Party was immediately outlawed, and the Social Democrats were banned a few weeks later. One by one, the centrist and moderate parties disappeared, either by dissolving themselves or by being abolished by Nazi decree. In mid-1933, the Nazis were the only legal political organization left in Germany. In its various subgroups for women, youths, professional associations, farmers, and others, all patriotic Germans could find their place.

Hitler completed the process of consolidating power with a purge within the party itself. This was the infamous *Night of the Long Knives* in June 1934, when the paramilitary ***Sturmabteilung*** (Storm Troopers, or SA), who had been very important to the Nazi movement as bullyboys, were cut down to size. Using another of his suborganizations, the new ***Schutzstaffel***, or SS, Hitler murdered several hundred of the Storm Troop leaders. By doing so, he both rid himself of potentially serious rivals and placated the German army generals, who rightly saw in the brown-shirted Storm Troop a menace to their own position as the nation's military leaders.

## The Nazi Domestic Regime

When the Nazis took power, the NSDAP had an active membership of about 1 million and probably twice that many supporters who could be counted on to show up for major party affairs or contribute some money. By 1934, about 15 percent of the total population had joined the Nazi Party. The numbers rose steadily thereafter. By the middle of the war, about one-fifth of adult Germans belonged, although many joined under severe pressure and contributed nothing except mandatory dues.

Rank-and-file party members were drawn from all elements of the population, but the leaders were normally young men from the working and lower-middle classes. Like the Russian communists, the Nazis were a party of young men who were in a hurry and had no patience with negotiation or gradual reform. Unlike the communists, they saw themselves not so much as implementing a revolution but as restoring proud Germanic traditions that had been allowed to decay.

The party was represented in all parts of Germany, which were now reorganized into *Gaue,* or districts under the command of a *Gauleiter* (a district party boss). Special organizations tended to the explanation and practice of party doctrine for different parts of the population. But there was remarkably little "philosophy" in Nazism; the emotional rantings of *Mein Kampf* and the even more confused babbling of Julius Rosenberg's brochures, which no one could render intelligible, were the official credos of the movement. In the end, the Nazi phenomenon depended on a primitive German nationalism and resentments of the peace treaty and the Jews.

As under the Bismarckian and Weimar governments, Prussia was the most important region in Germany. The brilliant and unscrupulous propagandist Joseph Goebbels

(1897–1945) was Hitler's deputy here. Another member of Hitler's small circle of intimates was Hermann Göring (1893–1946), the rotund, wisecracking, and entirely cynical pilot-hero of World War I who was generally seen as the number-two man in the hierarchy.

From his release from the Munich jail, Hitler's policies were designed to make Germany into a totalitarian state, and they did so considerably more thoroughly and more rapidly than Mussolini was able to accomplish in Italy. His right arm in this process was Heinrich Himmler (1900–1945), the head of the SS and of the *Gestapo,* or political police. Himmler was Hitler's most loyal colleague, and he was charged with overseeing the internal security of the Nazi regime. Himmler's SS operated the concentration camps that had opened as early as 1934 within Germany, and later in the conquered territories, a branch of the SS conducted the Holocaust of the Jews, setting up the slave labor camps and installing a reign of terror against all possible resistance. (See the Law and Government box for more on Himmler's ideas.)

LAW AND GOVERNMENT

## Heinrich Himmler's Speech to the SS

**Heinrich Himmler was perhaps** the most detested—and feared—man in the world, until he died at his own hand in the Nazi collapse in 1945. A totally insignificant-looking individual with rimless eyeglasses through which he peered nearsightedly, Himmler was the willing slave of the Führer. In return for his doglike devotion, he was entrusted with the leadership of the SS, the *Schutzstaffel,* or bodyguard of Hitler, which he built up into an elite branch of the German military.

Himmler was given the responsibility of implementing the Final Solution of the Jewish Question. The following selection is a partial transcript of a speech that Himmler gave to an SS conclave in Poland on October 4, 1943. Note the peculiar combination of secrecy and an attempt to excite pride in what the concentration camp guards were being asked to do.

> I also want to make reference before you here, in complete frankness, to a really grave matter. Among ourselves, this once, it shall be uttered quite frankly; but in public we will never speak of it. Just as we did not hesitate on June 30, 1934,* to do our duty as ordered, to stand up against the wall comrades who had violated their duty, and shoot them, so we have never talked about this, and never will. . . . Each of us shuddered, and yet each one knew that he would do it again if it were ordered and if it were necessary.
>
> I am referring to the evacuation of the Jews, the annihilation of the Jewish people. This is one of the things that can be easily said: "The Jewish people is going to be annihilated" says every Party member. "Sure, it's in our program, elimination of the Jews, annihilation—we'll take care of it." And then they all come trudging in, 80 million worthy Germans, and each one of them has his one "decent Jew." Sure, the others are swine, but *this* one is an A-1 Jew.
>
> Of all those who talk this way, not one has seen it happen, not one has been through it. Most of you know what it means to see a hundred corpses side by side, or five hundred, or a thousand. To have stuck this out and—excepting cases of human weakness—to have kept our integrity, that is what has made us hard. In our history, this is an unwritten and never-to-be-written page of glory, for we know how difficult we would have made it for ourselves if today—amid the bombing raids, the hardships and deprivations of war—we still had the Jews in every city as secret saboteurs, agitators, and demagogues. If the Jews were still situated in the body of the German people, we probably would have reached the 1916–1917 stage by now.
>
> The wealth they had we have taken from them. We have taken none of it for ourselves . . . whoever takes so much as a Mark of it for himself is a dead man. A number of SS men—not very many—have transgressed, and they will die without mercy. We had the moral right, we had the duty toward our people, to kill this people who wished to kill us. But we do not have the right to enrich ourselves with so much as a fur coat, a watch, a Mark, or even a cigarette or anything else. Having exterminated a germ, we do not want in the end to be infected by the germ, and die of it. I will not stand by and let even a small rotten spot develop, or take hold.
>
> Wherever it may form, we together will cauterize it. All in all, however, we can say that we have carried out this heaviest of all our tasks in a spirit of love for our people. Our inward being, our soul, has not suffered injury from it.

### *Analyze and Interpret*

Why does Himmler insist on the absolute honesty of the SS in dealing with Jews' property? What do you think he refers to when in the last sentence he talks of "our inward being, our soul"?

*The Night of the Long Knives, when the SA was eliminated.

Source: "The Holocaust Reader," in *Readings in World Civilizations,* ed. Lucy Dawidowicz (Metuchen, NJ: Behrman House, 1976). Copyright 1976, Behrman House, Inc.

**History Now™**

***To read "The Final Solution," point your browser to the documents area of* HistoryNow.**

Corbis

**Nuremberg Nazi Rally, 1938.** The massive display of strength and unity so dear to the Nazis was nowhere better on view than at the regular rallies held in the Bavarian town of Nuremberg. In this photo, Hitler exchanges salutes with party officials.

## The "Jewish Question"

The most horrible of the Nazi policies was the genocide against the Jews. For the first time in modern history, a systematic, cold-blooded war of extermination was practiced against a noncombatant people, solely on the basis of race. The war against the Jews went through four distinct phases in the twelve years of Nazi rule between 1933 and 1945:

1. From March 1933 to 1935, German Jews were publicly humiliated and excluded from government jobs.
2. In September 1935, the **Nuremberg Laws** prohibiting social contacts between Jews and "Aryans" (defined as persons with no Jewish blood for two generations on both sides of their family) made Jews into noncitizens. The government began to harass Jews constantly and push them either to emigrate or enter urban ghettos for easier surveillance.
3. In November 1938, new policies made it almost impossible for Jews to engage in public life and business and forbade emigration unless they surrendered all their property in Germany and went as paupers. By this time, many thousands of "antistate" Jews (communists, SD members, anti-Nazis) had been consigned to the camps.
4. At the **Wannsee conference** in Berlin in 1942, the **Final Solution** for the "Jewish problem" was approved by Hitler. The Jews were rounded up from the ghettos throughout Germany and occupied Europe and sent to the death camps in Poland. The Holocaust had begun and would not end until Germany's defeat in 1945. By then, some 6 million Jews from all over central and eastern Europe had been murdered, starved to death, or otherwise fallen victim to Himmler's henchmen. Of the more than 2 million Jews living in Germany in 1933, only a few tens of thousands had survived at the close of the war, overlooked or hidden by sympathetic neighbors.

Keystone Press/Image Works

**Dehumanizing of the Jews.** The Nazis viewed Jewish–Christian sexual relations as pollution of German blood. The woman's sign reads, "I am the biggest pig in the place and get involved only with Jews." The Jewish man's placard says, "As a Jewish fellow, I take only German girls to my room." The public humiliation of such couples began immediately after the Nazis came to power in 1933.

## Nazi Economic Policy

Economic policy in the Nazi state was a peculiar mixture of a fake "socialism" and an accommodation of the big businesses and cartels that had dominated Germany for a generation. As in Mussolini's Italy, the government's economic policies generated some measure of social reform. Workers and farmers were idealized in propaganda as the true Aryan Germans, but private property remained untouched, and the capitalist process was subjected to only sporadic and selective interference by the government. The labor unions, like every other type of public association, were fully subordinated to the party and became arms of the Nazi octopus. Strikes were illegal, and the Marxist idea of class conflict was officially declared nonexistent among Germans.

Hultan-Deutsch Collection/Corbis

**HITLER YOUTH.** At the annual mass rally of Nazi organizations in Nuremberg, the uniformed Hitler Youth were always given a prominent place to salute the Führer's carefully staged arrival. Membership was all but mandatory; those who didn't join were singled out for social ostracism.

Dictatorial governments
Parliamentary governments

**MAP 45.1** ***Europe in 1939 at Eve of World War II***

Most of Europe was under dictatorial rule of various types by the end of the 1930s. The impact of the Great Depression pushed some of the former parliamentary democracies into the dictatorship column during the middle of the 1930s. Only Britain, France, and the Scandinavians kept alive the reality of democratic politics.

Hitler had come to power partly on the strength of his promises to end the unemployment problem. From 1933 to 1936, he instituted measures that were effective at providing jobs. The huge road construction and public works programs he began in 1934 absorbed a large portion of the pool of unemployed. With rearmament, the military was greatly enlarged, and munitions factories and their suppliers received government orders. Raw materials were rapidly stockpiled. Synthetics for the vital raw materials that Germany lacked (petroleum, rubber, tin, and many other exotic minerals) were invented in government-supported laboratories and produced in new factories.

Already by 1936, Hitler was putting Germany on a war footing. Labor was allocated according to government priorities. Government ministries decided what would be imported and exported. In the western border region, a huge "West Wall" was being erected. This system of fortifications would mirror the fortified French Maginot Line across the frontier. The *autobahns* (expressways) were crisscrossing the country, creating a system that could move men and material quickly in case of war.

By 1937, the number of unemployed was down to 400,000 (from 6 million), and a labor shortage was developing. Unmarried women and youths were put into more or less compulsory organizations to relieve the shortfall. In every German village and town, Nazi Youth organizations gave boys and girls ages seven to twenty-one a place to get together with their peers for both work and fun while imbibing the Nazi viewpoints. The nation was prosperous, the Great Depression became a dim memory, and many millions of Germans were proud of their government and their ***Führer.***

# Summary

The defeat in 1918, the runaway inflation of the early 1920s, and the weak and unpopular socialist government combined to exert a devastating effect on German national morale. Millions of voters lost faith in liberal democracy and the parliamentary process. So long as the economic situation remained favorable, this political weakness was manageable, but the onset of the world depression brought on a crisis from which the gifted demagogue Adolf Hitler and his Nazi Party emerged triumphant in 1933. The Nazis could soon boast that the Führer made good on his promises to his people. He had obtained government power legally, and an intimidated legislature gave him dictatorial authority soon after.

By the mid-1930s, rearmament and a vigorous social investment policy had restored German prosperity. Most Germans were content with Hitler's guidance. His ranting anti-Semitism and brutal harassment of all opposition elements did not overly disturb the majority, who had found prosperity, security, and a sense of national purpose that had been sorely lacking.

## Identification Terms

Test your knowledge of this chapter's key concepts by defining the following terms. If you can't recall the meaning of certain terms, refresh your memory by looking up the boldfaced term in the chapter, turning to the Glossary at the end of the book, or working with the flashcards that are available on the *World Civilizations* Companion Website **http://history.wadsworth.com/adler04**.

*Führer*
Final Solution
*Machtergreifung*
*Mein Kampf*
Nuremberg Laws
*putsch*
*Schutzstaffel/SS*
*Sturmabteilung/SA*
Wannsee conference

## Test Your Knowledge

Test your knowledge of this chapter by answering the following questions. Complete answers appear at the end of the book. You may also take this quiz interactively and find even more quiz questions on the *World Civilizations* Companion Website: **http://history.wadsworth.com/adler04**.

1. Hitler's major political ideas were formed
   a. during his early manhood in Vienna.
   b. as a reaction to the Great Depression.
   c. during his boyhood in rural Austria.
   d. after he formed the Nazi Party in the postwar era.
   e. during his incarceration after the 1923 putsch.
2. Which of the following was *not* a part of Hitler's call to arms in *Mein Kampf*?
   a. Protection of the middle classes
   b. Rejection of the Versailles Treaty
   c. Land redistribution
   d. Confiscation of money and goods gained as a result of World War I
   e. Government ownership of all property
3. Which of the following did *not* help Hitler in his bid for political power?
   a. His sympathy for Marxist theory and practice
   b. His gift for influencing the masses
   c. The ineptitude of the democratic leaders in meeting the economic crisis
   d. Massive economic hardship
   e. His personal charisma
4. The political party that held the most seats in the Reichstag at the beginning of the Great Depression was the
   a. Communist party.
   b. Fascist party.
   c. Social Democrat party.
   d. Nazi party.
   e. Liberal party.
5. The German chancellorship came to Hitler in 1933 through
   a. legal appointment.
   b. a conspiracy.
   c. an overwhelming electoral victory.
   d. armed force.
   e. a military takeover.
6. The Enabling Act
   a. made Hitler Chancellor of Germany.
   b. gave Nazis in the Reichstag absolute power.
   c. outlawed the Communist party.
   d. gave Hitler's government the right to rule by decree.
   e. banned the Social Democratic party.
7. The internal purge of the Nazi movement was called
   a. the Day of Judgment.
   b. the Night of the Long Knives.
   c. the Second Coming.
   d. the Führer's Triumph.
   e. Bloody Sunday.
8. Hitler's head of the SS and the Gestapo was
   a. Goebbels.
   b. Himmler.
   c. Göring.
   d. Gauleiter.
   e. Bismarck
9. The Nuremberg Laws
   a. outlawed the German Communist Party.
   b. laid out the details of the Nazi dictatorship in Germany.
   c. detailed who was Jewish and what that meant.
   d. were the formal rejection of the reparations bill from World War I.
   e. expelled all Jews from Germany.
10. Which was *not* true of Hitler's government during the 1930s?
   a. Its policy was increasingly anti-Semitic.
   b. It was successful in eliminating mass unemployment.
   c. It allowed only one party to represent the German people.
   d. Its economic policy abolished private ownership.
   e. It built up a strong military in defiance of the Treaty of Versailles.

## InfoTrac College Edition

Visit the source collections at

**http://infotrac.thomsonlearning.com**

and use the Search function with the following key terms:

Hitler    Nazi or Nazism    Totalitarianism

## Wadsworth History Website Resources

Visit the World History Resource Center at **http://history.wadsworth.com/world** for a wealth of general resources, and the *World Civilizations* Companion Website at **http://history.wadsworth.com/adler04** for resources specific to this textbook.

## History Now

Enter *HistoryNow* using the access card that is available for *World Civilizations*. *HistoryNow* will assist you in understanding the content in this chapter with lesson plans generated for your needs. In addition, you can read the following documents, and many more, online:

Adolf Hitler, "Proclamation to the German Nation"

Adolf Hitler, "Speech to the Reichstag"

Wannsee conference, "The Final Solution"

*The art of government is the organization of idolatry.*
George Bernard Shaw

# 46 East Asia in a Century of Change



| | |
|---|---|
| 1840–1911 | Decline of the Qing (Manzhou) Dynasty in China |
| 1868 | Meiji Restoration and beginning of reforms in Japan |
| 1895 | First Sino-Japanese War |
| 1904–1905 | Russo-Japanese War |
| 1910 | Japan annexes Korea |
| 1912 | Founding of Chinese Republic |
| 1937 | Beginning of Second Sino-Japanese War |
| 1941–1945 | Pacific Allies' War against Japan |
| 1947–1949 | Civil War in China |

The explosive development of Western technology and military prowess in the nineteenth century had an impact on East Asia somewhat earlier than elsewhere in the nonindustrial world. By the 1850s, China, Japan, and Southeast Asia had all felt the iron hand of the West in their commercial and political relations with the rest of the world.

How did these widely variant nations meet this unexpected challenge to their identities, generated by a Western culture to which neither of them had paid much attention previously? China and Japan could hardly have chosen more different ways of dealing with the new situation. Nor could the outcomes have been more different. By the opening of the twentieth century, China suffered a collapsing government attempting to preside over a society torn by unbridgeable gaps. In contrast, Japan had undergone one of the most remarkable self-willed transformations known to history. An aggressive imperialism brought Japan into conflict with a struggling China in the 1930s and later with the West. Meanwhile, Southeast Asia had gradually become a group of white-ruled colonies where European values and education were loosely and superficially imposed on the traditional cultures.

## China

The Qing (Manzhou) Dynasty had originated outside China in Manchuria and had come to China as conquerors, ruling from 1644 onward. This last dynasty of imperial China was notably successful in its early generations (see Chapter 30), but by the mid-nineteenth century it had weakened considerably. Problems such as overpopulation and resultant famine developed in parts of China, while the almost entirely agrarian/handicraft domestic economy stagnated.

### *The Manzhou Decline*

China's modern history begins with the **Opium Wars** (1840–1842). In the eighteenth century, the British East India Company had developed a lucrative trade in Indian opium with south China. The drug had at long last given Westerners an exchange commodity for the luxury goods they imported from China and had to pay for with precious gold and silver. Previously little known in China, cheap opium became a major public health problem in the coastal cities, and its illegal trade disrupted the empire's finances. After some ineffective protests to the East India officials and the British government, in the 1830s the Chinese finally decided to take strong measures to prevent the drug's importation. This led to a naval war, which was predictably one-sided, given the huge differences between British and Chinese weaponry and naval tactics.

In 1842, the Beijing government signed the first of the "**unequal treaties**" between a weakening China and the Western powers. China, in effect, lost control of some of its territory and its trade patterns to a foreign power. The treaties opened up the previously closed Chinese coastal towns to British merchants and consuls. (This was the beginning of the British colony of Hong Kong.) The resident British were subject to British law, not Chinese law. Although not specifically mentioned in the treaty, the opium trade would continue.

The treaty with Britain was followed by others with France and, later, with Russia and Germany. All of the treaties were similar. All were extorted from a Chinese government that was still attempting to deal with the West as its ancestors in the sixteenth and seventeenth centuries had dealt with foreigners—as a superior dealing with inferiors. This was by now so far from reality that it became a bad joke among the Europeans. With the exception of some missionaries who were intent on bringing Christ to the Buddhist or Daoist masses, most Europeans in China in the nineteenth and twentieth centuries were there as imperialist fortune seekers. The Chinese resented these Westerners intensely, humiliated by their new inability to protect themselves from the "foreign devils." (See one official's scheme to meet an aspect of China's crisis in the Society and Economy box.)

SOCIETY AND ECONOMY

## A Novel Cure for the Opium Plague

**By no means were all Chinese officials** blind to what was happening to their country in the nineteenth century or without ideas about how to meet the crisis ensuing from the lost Opium Wars and the Taiping Rebellion. Yi Tsan sent this memorandum to the imperial throne in the 1860s:

> The situation China faces today is unprecedented, and what has worked in the past, to our sorrow, no longer works today. In today's world all the nations have been suddenly thrown together, and the normal approach to making China wealthy and strong has become woefully inadequate. . . .
>
> The Westerners' most effective weapon in butchering our financial well-being has been and still is opium, the poison of which permeates into every corner of the nation. We exchange precious silver for harmful drugs, and the total amount of silver that has flowed out of the country during the past fifty years is so large that we have cease to count. The more we ban the opium traffic, the more the people violate the ban. Meanwhile, the Westerners, sitting there comfortably and radiating a self-satisfied smile, collect their profit. They will not be satisfied until every Chinese looks like a skeleton and every Chinese penny goes into their pockets. . . .
>
> However, as long as we cannot prevent people from taking opium, we might as well let people manufacture opium of their own, so at least we can reduce the amount of silver that flows from the country. Yet the government strictly enforces the law that bans the cultivation of native poppies. . . . The official policy seems to be that anyone who wishes to smoke opium must buy it from foreigners. In the name of eradicating the opium poison, our government and its officials, although unwittingly, have brought the greatest harm to our own country on behalf of opium traders from abroad. . . . It is true that under the treaties we cannot prevent foreigners from shipping opium to China; it is also true, nevertheless, that the treaties do not prohibit us from growing our own. As native opium will completely displace foreign opium in the domestic market in thirty or forty years, we can then do whatever we please about the opium problem without involving either the treaties or the foreigners. Then we can either impose heavy taxation on opium consumption or introduce strict rules governing opium traffic. In either case, opium will gradually disappear from the market and the number of opium smokers will slowly decrease until, eventually, there are neither opium nor opium smokers. All this, of course, requires patience.

### *Analyze and Interpret*

How effective do you believe Yi's cure for the opium epidemic would be? Do you think that the suggested "heavy taxation" and "strict rules" would work to ensure the gradual disappearance of the drug once it was legalized?

Source: *Modern China*, ed. and trans. Dun J. Li (New York: Scribner's, 1978), pp. 68–69.

***The Taiping Rebellion*** The losses to the European powers, bad as they were, were overshadowed in the 1850s through early 1870s by the Taiping and Nien rebellions. Of the two, the **Taiping** episode was the more widespread and more disastrous. For more than twenty years, during which the Chinese suffered perhaps 20 million deaths, rebel generals led a motley band of poverty-stricken peasants and urban workers against the Qing emperors. The Taipings' success in the early years of the revolt brought them wide support from many educated Chinese, who were sickened by the government's inability to resist the foreigners. The upheaval was encouraged by several factors:

- Discontent with the corruption and incompetence of the government officials
- The rapidly worsening problems of overpopulation in much of south China
- The strong appeal of the Taipings' economic reform proposals
- The total ineffectiveness of the Qing armed forces

For a few years, the Taipings set up a countergovernment in central China that controlled about half the total area of the country. Their leader, the visionary Hung Hsiu-chuan, had been exposed to Christian missions and believed himself to be Jesus's younger brother. Hung originally enjoyed sympathy from the West, in part because he seemed to want to imitate Western ways. Some thought he was the would-be founder of a Christian China. But the Taipings also opposed opium smoking and further giveaways of Chinese rights to foreigners. The Western powers thus opted to support the Qing, because they knew the government would give them little trouble in the future. At that point, the rebels began to quarrel among themselves; by 1864, they were breaking up. The government soon defeated them and executed Hung.

For a time, the Nien presented almost as fierce a threat to the Beijing emperor. They controlled large areas of the southwest and northwest of the empire and threatened to link up with the Taipings. Total collapse seemed imminent.

***Failure of the Late Manzhou Restoration*** The government was unexpectedly saved by a group of provincial officials and landlords. They organized regional armies to take the place of the failed central forces. Their effort is known as the "late Manzhou restoration" of the 1870s.

The new governors were reformers, and their policy of **Self-Strengthening** aimed at giving China the means to hold its own against the foreign barbarians once more. They addressed the peasants' myriad problems by instituting land reform measures and encouraging them to grow new crops with more nutritive value. Long-neglected public works programs, such as flood control projects on the Yellow (Huang) and Yangtze rivers, were taken in hand with good effect.

Self-Strengthening attempted to introduce Western methods and technologies, while retaining traditional Confucian values in the Chinese educated class. The examination system was tightened to eliminate favoritism, but candidates were still tested on the Confucian classics. Business affairs received much more attention than heretofore but continued to play a supporting role, rather than being allowed to take center stage in Chinese life.

This attempt to blend West and East had only partial success. New leaders who could both quote the classics and design a steam-driven factory did not appear as hoped, and traditionalist, ultraconservative attitudes remained too strong to be overcome among the scholar-officials. The **Empress Dowager Cixi** (1835–1908), who managed to hold on to power for almost fifty years (1861–1907), was not opposed to reform in principle, but she was also not in favor of it. The only thing that mattered to her was retaining her own position. An expert in political infighting, she was a kind of evil genius of China's government, pulling the strings for many years in the name of her son and her nephew, both powerless child-emperors. (For more about this wily ruler, see the Law and Government box.)

Mainly because of her foot dragging, the Chinese military forces were in poor shape in the first Sino-Japanese war, fought with Japan in 1894–1895 over Korea. Japan was rapidly pulling this traditional buffer between Japan and China into its orbit in the 1890s. The Chinese were decisively defeated in the war. Japan later annexed Korea and thus announced that it was replacing China as the most powerful Asian nation (a shift that remained in effect until Japan's defeat in World War II).

## Chinese Disintegration after 1895

The defeat in 1895 was an even ruder shock to the Chinese leaders than the string of humiliations by the Westerners had been. For many centuries the mandarins had looked on Japan and the Japanese as pitiable imitators of infinitely superior China. Now modern weapons and armies had been shown to be superior to refined culture and Confucian integrity, even in non-Western hands.

In the wake of the defeat, China again had to submit to a wave of foreign imperialist pressure. Russian, German, and British, as well as Japanese, trade extortions were forced on the Beijing officials, backed by governmental threats. Christian missionaries were granted unprecedented freedoms to attempt the conversion of the mostly unreceptive natives. Coastal enclaves became special spheres of interest for one power or another. The Chinese government conceded that its ancient tributary of Vietnam was now the property of the French colonialists. Control of Korea had been surrendered to Japan (over the heads of the Koreans). Manchuria was all but given to the Russians in the north.

## Empress Cixi (1835–1908)

**The last effective ruler of the empire of China,** the empress Cixi was an extraordinary woman who defied every cliché about Asian women. Born in 1835 to a provincial gentry family, she was married to the weak Qing emperor Hsien Feng as a child and bore him his only surviving child. When Hsien died in 1861, Cixi took full advantage of her position to have her young son named emperor while she exercised ruling powers in his name. This period, which lasted for twelve years, was the first time Cixi ruled a nation that traditionally despised women who attempted a public role. Two other periods were to follow.

All accounts agree that the empress was a person of more than usual intelligence, but her real strength was her ability to anticipate what others wanted and make sure that they were dependent on her goodwill to get it. She was a master of everyday psychology. She supervised a court and a government that had become so filled with intrigue that every action—indeed, almost every word—could carry multiple meanings.

**Empress Cixi.** Dressed in formal court costume, the manipulative empress is shown at the height of her powers around the turn of the twentieth century.

The Qing Dynasty had come to China as conquerors and insisted for a time on maintaining the signs that they, and not the "men of Han," as the Chinese called themselves, were in charge. But since the Opium Wars (1840–1842), the central government was under severe attack and had shown little imagination in trying to meet the challenge. Foreigners ranging from Christian missionaries to soldiers of fortune had overrun the port cities, turning the Chinese into second-class citizens in their own country. Native rebels, above all the Taipings, had almost overturned Chinese imperial government in the 1860s and 1870s. Much of the blame in the officials' eyes rested squarely on the woman at the head of the imperial court, but blaming her was one thing; removing her was another.

When her young son died in 1875, Cixi managed to have her infant nephew placed on the throne with herself as regent for the ensuing fifteen years. She outmaneuvered the boy's father, Prince Kung, and eliminated him from the court completely. Even after the nephew came of age and assumed power for himself, most decisions remained in the hands of the empress. When he attempted to put through some badly needed governmental reforms, she removed him and reassumed power herself in 1898. It was she who manipulated the Boxers into becoming her tool for defying the foreign powers that were carving up China.

A determined and intelligent ruler such as Cixi might have been able to bring the tottering Qing Dynasty through its crisis, if she had not been so intent on simply preserving her own position. To do so, she was not above arranging the murder of those who opposed her at court, offering massive bribes, or using government monies for her private ends. The most sensational case was her use of the navy budget to rebuild the Beijing Summer Palace. China's most famous and most awe-inspiring ship was actually a life-size replica made of white marble and resting permanently in a reflecting pool at the palace!

Although not opposed to all reform, Cixi resisted many measures that were needed to modernize the decrepit bureaucracy and military. She played one group of provincial lords off another with great expertise, so that no single faction could challenge her directly. Even as an old woman of seventy-four, she was not ready to step aside and appointed a distant relative, the infant Pu Yi, as last emperor of China in 1908. A few weeks later, she was dead, and the empire itself was on its deathbed.

### *Analyze and Interpret*

Do you think the traditional Chinese distaste for female rule accentuated or restrained Cixi's ambitions? What, if any, restraints did the Chinese system offer to prevent a ruler such as Cixi from injuring the country?

The **Boxer Rebellion** (1900) was an attempted answer to this wave of foreign exploitation. The Boxers were a fanatical, quasi-religious society who believed that they had nothing to fear from bullets. Rebelling at first against Beijing, they changed their course when the sly old empress joined with them in starting a crusade to cleanse China of the foreign devils, but the Boxers had no effective leadership or weaponry. After a few months, an international military force shipped off to China from various European capitals crushed the rebellion and further humiliated the tottering dynasty by demanding cash indemnities. The failure of the Boxers convinced even the most conservative leaders that the old, Confucian-based government could no longer be maintained. China had to change or disappear as a state, and a series of radical reform proposals now came forth from various quarters.

***The New China Movement*** By the end of the nineteenth century, a small but growing handful of young Chinese had been given a Western-style education, generally through the influence of missionaries who had adopted them. The most important of these was the intellectual Kang Yu-wei (1858–1927), who argued against the common notion that Confucian philosophy represented an unchanging and unchangeable model of government and society. Kang taught that Confucius was a reformer and that reform was a basic ingredient of his philosophy. Kang believed that history was evolutionary, not static, and that history was moving forward in China, as in the rest of the world, toward democratic government.

Collectively, Kang's ideas were called the **New China Movement**, and they spread widely among educated people in the 1890s. By 1898, the stage was set for an attempt at revolution from above, similar to that carried out by Peter the Great in eighteenth-century Russia. But this attempt was not successful, and its supporters in Beijing were forced to flee for their lives. For a few more years, under the manipulations of the empress, the status quo prevailed. It was clear that if China were to be changed, it would have to be done from below by the exasperated and desperate people.

***The Chinese Republic*** An important step toward a new China was the abolition of the Confucian examinations for government office in 1905. This move opened the way for aspiring officials with modern ideas, many of whom had been educated in the West or in rapidly westernizing Japan. The Western-educated liberal Sun Yat-sen (1866–1925) was the intellectual leader of an antigovernment reform movement that quickly swept the whole country. Sun was trained as a medical doctor in Honolulu and Hong Kong, and on returning to his country, he gradually became convinced that a revolution from below was the only answer to China's many ills. He took up the cause of reform ("Three Principles") among the overtaxed and impoverished peasantry, believing that China could regain political harmony only after a measure of social justice had been established.

The long-awaited revolution against the feeble and incompetent government came in 1911. After Cixi's death three years earlier, the dynasty was so weak that few would defend it when it was challenged. Originally, Sun was called to head the new parliamentary government, but to avoid civil war, the head of the Army, General Yuan Shikai, soon replaced him. The Republic of China was formally declared in 1912. The last child emperor was forced to abdicate and lived long enough to see the installation of Mao's communist government many years later.

For a few years, General Yuan was master of China and intended to become the next emperor, but his failure to stop the Japanese incursions on the coast during World War I made him unpopular, and he died in disgrace in 1916. For the next decade, China was in anarchy, ruled by warlords (local strongmen, often ex-bandits) with private armies. More important was the fast growth of fanatical nationalism among the urban classes, particularly the educated youth. Sun was the theoretical leader of this movement, but he was a poor organizer, and the national party he founded, the **Kuomintang**, or KMT, split into many factions during the 1920s.

The whole nationalist-reformist phase of China's development in the early twentieth century is called the **May Fourth Movement**, because of an incident in 1919 when

**Boxer Rebel Awaits Beheading, 1901.** Surrounded by European troops, Chinese hangmen prepare to behead a captured Boxer.

thousands of Beijing students and youth protested the Versailles Treaty's gift of a part of China to Japan. The movement had no single leader, and its various subgroups went off in many directions. Eventually, the reform ideas it propagated would provide some of the momentum for the communist takeover after World War II. Mao Zedong himself was one of the outraged students who swore that China would no longer be the pawn of foreigners and capitalists who exploited Chinese backwardness.

## *Chiang Kai-shek's Regime*

Sun Yat-sen's most able and aggressive lieutenant was Chiang Kai-shek, who headed the KMT's military branch. After the founder's death in 1925, Chiang moved quickly to take over leadership, while maintaining the liaison with the tiny Chinese Communist Party (CCP) that Sun had established in the early 1920s to assist in modernizing the state. In 1926, Chiang felt strong enough to go after the warlords who had made themselves into petty kings in the north and northeast and bring them under effective central control. This Northern Expedition was a success, and several provinces were recovered. Strengthened by this and by the increasing support of Chinese financial circles, Chiang decided to finish off the communists who had displayed disturbing support in Shanghai and a few other coastal cities. In 1927, he conducted a sweeping blood purge of all suspected communists, killing tens of thousands before it was over. The CCP appeared to have suffered an irremediable defeat. Chiang was clearly in control and established himself as the president of a national KMT government in Beijing a few months later.

**CHIANG KAI-SHEK AND MADAME CHIANG.** The newsweekly *Time* selected Chiang and his spouse as "Man and Wife of the Year, 1937." Madame Chiang handled much of the diplomacy of China with the Western powers in this epoch.

The Kuomintang government under Chiang (1928–1975) was a barely disguised dictatorship, led by a man who believed in force as the ultimate political argument. He had married a westernized Chinese plutocrat, who successfully acted as his intermediary when dealing with Western governments throughout his long career. Chiang believed the obstacles to making China into a sovereign, respected state were first the Japanese and then the communists. As time passed, however, that order began to reverse. Under new leaders, the CCP had staged a quick recovery from the events of 1927 and, within a few years, had established a strong base among the peasants in south China.

Knowing that he did not as yet have the strength to challenge the superior weaponry and training of the Japanese, Chiang threw his 700,000-man army against the communists. He drove them from their rural strongholds into the famous **Long March of 1934**, an epic of guerrilla war. Under their rising star Mao Zedong, an original force of perhaps 100,000 poorly armed peasants wandered more than 6,000 miles through western China. A year later, the 10,000 or so survivors of starvation and combat barricaded themselves in Shensi in the far northwest near the Mongolian border. Here, during the remainder of the 1930s, they preached the Marxist gospel to the desperately poor peasants around them.

In this belief, they were following Mao's new precept: the Chinese peasants are a true revolutionary force, and no revolution will succeed without them. Mao pursued peasant support in clever and concrete ways. He never spoke of collectivization but only of justice, lower interest rates, and fair distribution of land. The members of the CCP became village teachers—the first ever in this province—and made sure that the communist army did not behave like earlier Chinese armies and "liberate" what they needed and wanted from the helpless farmers. Soon the locals were sufficiently impressed with Mao's forces that they began to join them.

## *The Sino-Japanese War and the Maoist Challenge*

Americans sometimes forget that for four years before Pearl Harbor, the Japanese and Chinese were engaged in a bloody war. This conflict had actually begun with the Japanese aggression in Manchuria in 1931, but it had been sporadic until a minor incident in the summer of 1937 gave the Japanese commanders the pretext they had long

**Mao in Yunan, 1930s.** This undoubtedly staged photo wishes to show Mao's convivial side. During the desperate struggle against the forces of Chiang Kai-shek, there was usually little time for peasant interviews with the communist leadership.

Eastfoto

sought to begin war. After a few months of unequal fighting, the two major cities of Beijing and Nanjing had fallen, and much of coastal China was under Japanese control.

Instead of submitting and becoming a Japanese puppet as expected, Chiang elected to move his government many hundreds of miles west and attempt to hold out until he could find allies. The move inland meant, however, that Chiang was isolated from his main areas of support. Furthermore, the KMT army and officials appeared to the local people around the new command city of Chongqing (Chunking) as a swarm of devouring locusts. Famine was endemic in this poverty-stricken region, and official corruption in the army and civil government was widespread.

Morale deteriorated steadily under these conditions, especially since Chiang refused to actively fight the Japanese invader. After the attack on Pearl Harbor, he had decided that Tokyo would eventually be defeated by the Americans and that the communists under Mao were China's real enemy. Protected in his mountainous refuge, he wanted to husband his forces. When the war ended in 1945, Chiang was the commander of a large but poorly equipped and demoralized garrison army that had no combat experience and was living parasitically on its own people.

The Maoists, on the other hand, made steady progress in winning over the anti-Japanese elements among the people, especially the peasants. They claimed to be nationalists and patriots as well as reformers, and they fought the invader at every opportunity from their bases in the northwest. Mao set up a local government system that was far more just and more respectful of the peasants than the KMT had been. He introduced democratic practices that won the communists the support of many of the intellectuals and the workers. Mao's armed force grew by large numbers during the war years to a total of almost 1 million men in organized units, plus many thousands of guerrilla fighters behind the Japanese lines. The CCP set up mass organizations with branches in every village for women, youth, educators, and others.

***Communist Victory*** At the Pacific war's end, Chiang's army was about three times the size of Mao's, and now that the Americans had disposed of the Japanese, he was confident of victory over the internal rivals. The civil war broke out soon after the Japanese surrendered. The United States at first backed Chiang with supplies and money but could not counter the effects of years of corrupt KMT rule, inaction, and failure on Chiang's part to appreciate what China's peasant masses wanted. While the KMT armies deserted, the communist forces enjoyed wide and growing support. The superior fighting spirit and military tactics of the Maoists turned the tide decisively in 1948, when Beijing and the big port cities fell into their hands.

By October 1949, all of China was under Mao's control, and Chiang with several hundred thousand KMT men were refugees on the Chinese offshore island of Taiwan. Here, they set up a regime that called itself the Republic of China and was recognized as the legitimate government of China by the anticommunist world for some time to come. But "Red" China (properly the People's Republic of China, or PRC), with the world's largest population, was now presumably a devoted Cold War ally of the Soviet Union under the ruthless communist Mao and was aiming at world revolution side by side with the Soviets.

## JAPAN

In the mid-nineteenth century, Japan's two centuries of seclusion under the Tokugawa shoguns ended, and the country began to be transformed.

### The Emergence of Modern Japan

The trigger for Japan's modernization was the forceful "opening of Japan" by the American commodore Matthew Perry in 1853 and 1854 (see Chapter 31). In the name of international commerce, Perry extorted a treaty from the shogun that allowed U.S. ships to dock and do business in Japanese ports. This treaty was soon followed by similar agreements with the European trading nations. With the country divided over whether to allow the "pale-faced barbarians" into the ports, a brief conflict broke out among the daimyo lords for the shogun's power, and a few resident foreigners were molested. In 1863, a retaliatory attack by Western naval forces revealed how far Japan had fallen behind in the arts of war.

Japan seemed on the brink of being reduced to the same helplessness as China, but at this point, a decisive difference emerged. Some of the daimyo and samurai faced the causes and consequences of Japanese impotence squarely: they decided to imitate the West as rapidly as possible. These men engineered the revolt against the shogunate in 1867 that is termed the **Meiji Restoration** because, in a formal sense, the emperor was restored to the center of political- governmental life and the shogunate was abolished. In control, however, was not the emperor but the powerful daimyo, who had seen that the semifeudal shogunate was obsolete and now replaced it with a new style of government.

Starting in 1871, one major reform after another came out of the imperial capital in Tokyo (formerly Edo). All were modeled on the West. Unlike their neighbors across the China Sea, the Japanese leaders were willing and able to add up the pluses and minuses of accepting Western ideas and come to definite, consensual decisions about them. Then they systematically carried out reforms, even at the expense of cherished tradition.

***Meiji Reforms*** The major reforms of the Meiji Restoration included the following:

- *Military.* The daimyo-samurai feudal forces were removed in favor of a conscript army with a modern organization, modern weaponry, and professional discipline.
- *Financial.* A new national tax system and a new national bank and currency were established; credit facilities and corporations on the Western model were introduced.
- *Agrarian.* Land was redistributed, quasi-feudal dues were abolished, and ownership was established clearly and securely by survey.
- *Constitutional.* In 1889, a group of notables framed an entirely new constitution. It gave the parliamentary vote to a small electorate and allowed the emperor considerable but not supreme power over the government elected by the parliament.

By no means did all Japanese support these reforms. The samurai majority were so discontented by their total loss of status (even their precious swords were taken from them in 1876) that they attempted to rebel several times, only to be crushed by the new army. The new tax system, which required money payments to the government rather than service to the daimyo, reduced many peasants from landowners to tenants and was unpopular, but after twenty years, the reform element in Tokyo was unshakably entrenched.

Students were sent abroad by the hundreds annually to study Western science and Western government. For a time, everything Western was highly fashionable in Japan, from pocket watches to Darwinian biology. As elsewhere, the most potent of all the Western influences was the modern sense of nationalism, which struck Japanese youth just as strongly as it had Chinese. New political parties sprang up and vigorously contested the seats in the lower house of the Diet (parliament), even though only about 5 percent of the male population had the franchise. The constitution of 1889 was modeled after the German constitution authored by Bismarck and reserved decisive powers to the wealthy voters and the imperial ministers. The emperor was sovereign, not the people. He was also commander-in-chief of the armed forces, and the ministers answered solely to him, not to the parliament.

At the same time, the Meiji leaders made sure that the ancient regime and the traditional values of the people were held in high esteem. The reformers strongly supported the Shinto faith, which revered the emperor as the quasi-divine leader of his country. The constitution (which remained in force until 1945) explicitly stated that "the empire of Japan shall be governed by a line of emperors unbroken forever." The Meiji reformers made no attempt to throw out what they thought of as truly Japanese. Rather, the reform consciously—and successfully—aimed at making Japanese of all classes into good patriot-citizens.

Industrial development received much attention from the outset. Government funds were directed to railroad construction, shipyards, mines, and munitions under the supervision of foreign technicians. Later, in the 1890s, many of these costly enterprises were sold at bargain rates to combinations of individual investors. Thus began the peculiar Japanese form of government-assisted large corporations called *zaibatsu,* which came to dominate the nation's economy.

New banks were founded to provide credit for entrepreneurs, and the internal transport of people and goods was greatly eased by the construction of a dense network of railways. Mountainous terrain and the island geography had physically isolated much of Japan's population until the early twentieth century, but the railroads changed that.

Agriculture became more productive as taxes were paid in fixed amounts of money rather than produce, and peasants were able for the first time to buy, mortgage, and sell land freely. Silk—in demand everywhere in the industrial world—was the big money crop, rising from 2.3 million pounds in 1870 to 93 million in 1929. Japan's mechanization of silk production practically blew the Chinese out of the world market they had previously dominated. Rice production—the key Japanese commodity—also rose sharply, more than doubling in tonnage produced in one generation's time.

Asian Art and Archaeology, Inc./Corbis

**Japan's First Railway.** In 1872 the Tokyo-Yokohama rail line was opened, only a few years after the Meiji reform era began. Built under the direction of Western engineers, the line fascinated the Japanese, who portrayed it in traditional woodcut style.

***Foreign Successes*** The foreign policy of Meiji Japan was aggressive and grew more so as time went on. The challenge to "big brother" China in 1895 was a great success. Another success was the gradual elimination of the unequal treaties signed with the Western powers in the 1850s and 1860s. Like China, the Japanese authorities had at first agreed to a series of treaties that allowed Westerners to enjoy extraterritoriality. Persistent negotiations reversed this situation by the end of the nineteenth century, and Japan became the first Asian power in modern times to trade with Europeans as equals.

But the big breakthrough for Japanese prestige in foreign eyes was the Russo-Japanese War of 1904–1905. This war, the first between an Asian and a European nation that ended in victory for the Asians, announced to the world that Japan had arrived as a major power. The formal annexation of occupied Korea was a major result of the war, and the Japanese nationalists felt cheated that they had not obtained still more reparation from the beaten Russians. They would have their chance a few years later, when the Bolshevik revolution and civil war made Russia temporarily helpless. After nominally participating on the Allied side in World War I, Japan attempted to seize eastern Siberia as its reward from the Soviets. Pressured mainly by the United States, the Japanese reluctantly agreed to evacuate in 1922 but kept their eyes firmly on the huge border province of Manchuria as a possible field for imperial expansion.

## Between the World Wars

The foundation of civil government in Japan was aided substantially by the fact that economic prosperity for the upper and middle classes continued without setback for the entire reign of the first Meiji emperor (1868–1912). World War I armament production then gave the entire economy a boost but also created severe inflation, which caused serious rioting in 1918. The 1920s and 1930s saw a strengthening of the army in politics, a factor that Japan had not previously experienced. The career officers often resented their diminished position in Japanese life compared to what the samurai had once had. Considering themselves to be the samurai descendants and the most devoted and reliable exponents of all that was good in Japanese culture, the officers came to hold the parliamentary politicians in contempt.

In the early and most difficult years of the Great Depression, the officers' ambitions were particularly attracted to resource-rich Manchuria. In 1931, they in effect rebelled against the Tokyo civil government and seized the prov-

**Tanks Patrolling Nanjing, 1937.** The "rape of Nanjing" was the opening of the second Sino-Japanese war, 1937–1945. Here, Japanese armor patrols among the ruins of China's second city.



ince from the weak hands of China. From this point onward, Japan's army was engaged in an undeclared war against China and also against its own government in Tokyo. The Chinese war became an open struggle only after 1937, but the war against the civil government was already won in 1932. From that year, the military was in effective command of Japan's domestic and foreign policies. Any civilians who opposed the aggressive and self-confident generals and admirals were soon silenced.

In 1936, Japan, whose military shared the usual contempt for Marxism among army men, joined the Hitler-sponsored Anti-Comintern Pact. By 1937, Japan was formally at war with Chiang Kai-shek's government and had close to 1 million men in China. The alliance with Hitler (and Mussolini) was supposedly strengthened by the signing of the 1940 Tripartite (three-sided) Pact, but the Japanese resented not being informed of Hitler's decision to go to war against the West in 1939. When Germany decided to attack Russia in 1941, the Japanese were again not informed, and they decided to remain neutral despite the provisions of the pact and inciting German anger. The Japanese had, in fact, little to do with their supposed ally throughout World War II. The war in the Pacific was almost entirely distinct from the European conflict in timing, motivation, and contestants.

The Japanese attacked Pearl Harbor, Hawaii, in December 1941 because the Tokyo military command was convinced that war was inevitable if the United States would not go along with Japan's plans for imperialist expansion in Asia. Because the U.S. government showed no signs of changing its expressed resistance after long negotiations, the Tokyo general staff wished to strike first and hoped that greater willpower would overcome greater resources (see Chapter 49).

For about eight months, it seemed that the Japanese might be correct. Then, with the great naval battles of the mid-Pacific in the summer of 1942, the tides of war changed. From that point on, it was apparent to most observers (including many of Japan's leaders) that the best Japan could hope for was a negotiated peace that would leave it the dominant power in the western Pacific. Those hopes steadily diminished and were finally dashed with the explosions over Hiroshima and Nagasaki in August 1945.

## Southeast Asia

Although China and Japan managed to maintain their formal independence from the Europeans, the Asians in the southeast of the continent and in the Pacific Islands were not so fortunate. In the nineteenth century, all those who had not already become part of a European empire fell under one or another of the great powers, except Thailand, which played off various rivals and thereby retained independence (see Map 46.1 and Chapter 31).

In the middle of the twentieth century, the kingdom of Burma, which had been independent for many centuries, fell under British rule through imperialist war and was united to British India. At the same time, the British colonial fiefs in Malaya and especially Singapore, the port at its tip, began to experience a great economic upsurge. The tin mines and rubber plantations that sprang forth in interior Malaya attracted much British capital and Chinese labor. By the end of the century, Singapore was a large city serving shipping from around the industrial world as well as East Asia. The political leadership was entirely British, but the Chinese dominated trade and commerce, and their business acumen enabled them to maintain equality with the resident Europeans in all except political matters.

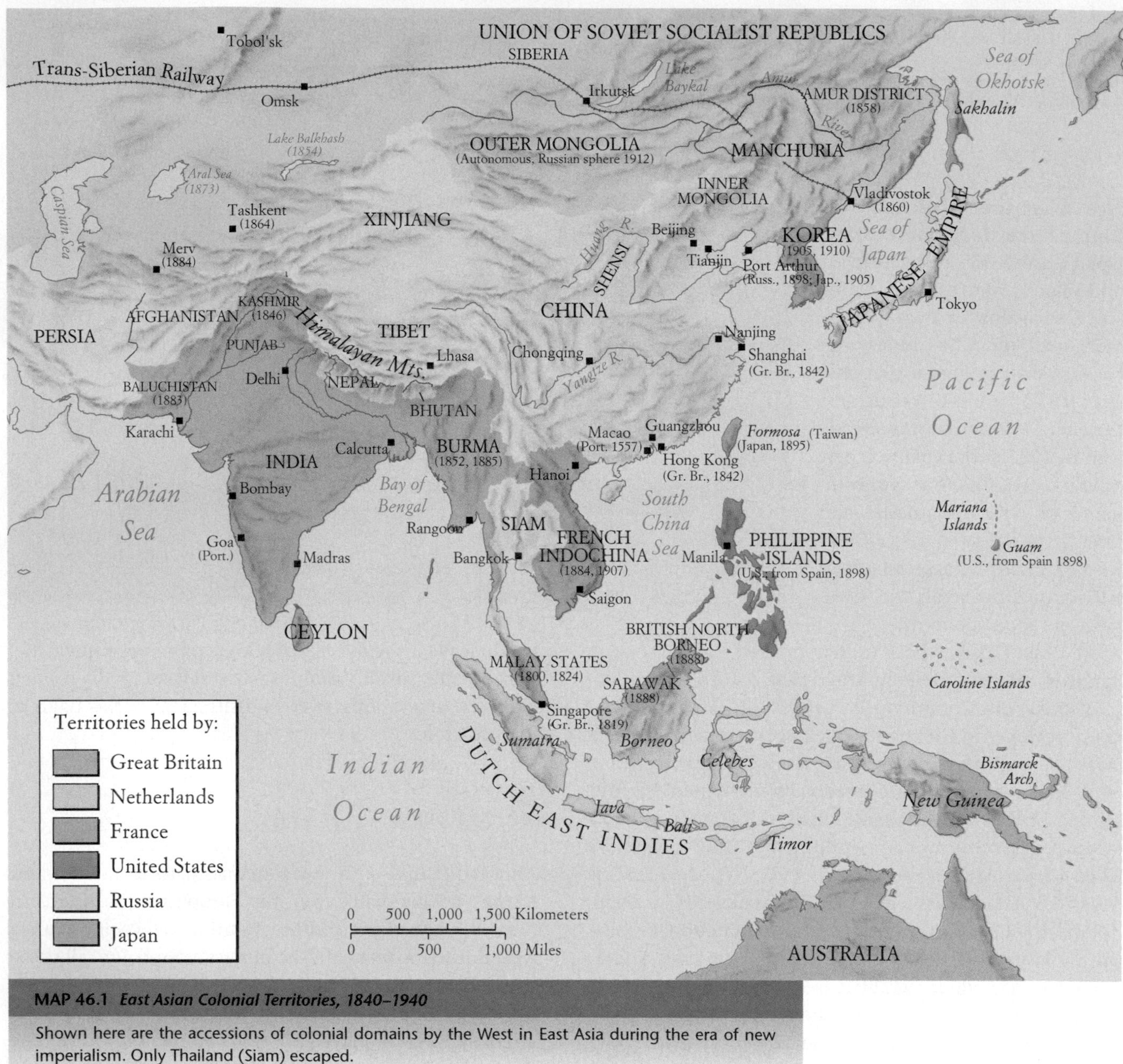


**MAP 46.1** *East Asian Colonial Territories, 1840–1940*

Shown here are the accessions of colonial domains by the West in East Asia during the era of new imperialism. Only Thailand (Siam) escaped.

The French presence centered on Indochina, or Vietnam, Laos, and Cambodia, as they are now called. The French had seized Indochina by stages, starting in the 1850s. They were aided by the same invulnerable naïveté that impeded an effective Chinese response to European aggression: the mandarins simply could not believe that their superior culture was endangered. In 1859, France used a pretext to seize Saigon and, a few years later, Cambodia. Following a brief war with China in 1885, the French then took over all of Vietnam and Laos.

In time, tens of thousands of French came to Indochina to make their careers and/or fortunes as officials, teachers, rubber plantation owners, and adventurers of all sorts. Like the British in Malaya, the French introduced some beneficial changes into the economy and society, making southern Vietnam, for example, into an enormously fertile rice bowl that exported its product throughout East Asia. They opened village schools, ended the practical slavery of women, forbade the marriages of children, and introduced new cash crops (rubber and coffee). But as happened everywhere else in colonial Asia, these improvements in social and economic possibilities benefited mainly the small minority of alien middlemen (mainly immigrant Chinese) and native landlords, and they were outweighed in nationalist eyes by the humiliations suffered at the hands of the European conquerors and overlords.

In the major maritime colonies of Dutch Indonesia and the Spanish Philippine Islands, the Europeans had a much longer presence, dating to the seventeenth century.

The Indonesian islands had been placed under a limited (in the geographic sense) Dutch rule in the 1600s, when bold Hollanders had driven out their Portuguese rivals for the rich spice export trade. Since then little had changed until the mid-nineteenth century. At that juncture, the nature of colonial controls had tightened, and their impact expanded with the introduction of the "culture system" of coerced cropping of specific commodities. Dutch overlords gradually conquered and replaced native leaders, and a small group controlled large estates that produced coffee and sugar at high profits. Despite efforts to assist them after 1870, the Indonesian peasants suffered, as massive population growth turned many of them into landless semiserfs for Dutch and Chinese landlords.

Alone among the Asian lands taken over by European rule, the Philippines became a nation in which the majority was Christian. This fact heightened the Filipinos' resentment when Spain continued to deny them political and social rights. The southern half of the Philippine archipelago was never brought under European rule, and here the Muslim faith was paramount among an aggregation of sultanates. A rebellion against the stagnant and faltering Spanish rule broke out in the northern islands in the late 1890s. It was still going on when the Americans became embroiled in war with Spain and captured the islands (1899–1900).

Because the United States was originally no more inclined to give the Filipinos their independence than the Spaniards had been, the rebellion turned against the Americans and persisted for two more years before it was finally extinguished. What had been promoted as a "liberation" became an occupation. Even though American policy became steadily more benevolent and advantageous to the Filipinos and independence was promised in the 1930s, the Philippines had to wait another decade before attaining sovereignty immediately after World War II.

## SUMMARY

China and Japan met the overwhelming challenge of Western intervention in vastly different ways. The Chinese mandarins, unwilling to leave the false security that Confucian philosophy and many centuries of assured superiority gave them, went down a blind alley of hopeless resistance and denial until they were pushed aside by rebellion and revolution at the beginning of the twentieth century. In contrast, the Japanese upper classes soon recognized the advantages to be gained by selectively adopting Western ways and used them to their own, highly nationalistic ends during the Meiji Restoration of the late nineteenth century.

China's halfhearted and confused experiment with a democratic republic came to an end in World War II, when the corrupt Chiang Kai-shek regime was unable to rally nationalist support against either the Japanese or Mao's communists. After two years of civil war, Mao took Chinese fate in his confident hands. Japan's civil government was much more stable and successful than China's until the 1930s, when a restive and ambitious military establishment pushed it aside and put the country on a wartime footing with an invasion of China. Then, in 1941, they entered World War II with the attack on Pearl Harbor.

Elsewhere, almost all of Southeast Asia was a European colony, and by the early twentieth century, this region was experiencing a buildup of frustrated nationalism among both intellectuals and ordinary folk. This became even truer after the Asians witnessed the humiliation of Russia by Japan in 1905 and the mutual slaughter of Europeans in World War I. In retrospect, the late nineteenth and early twentieth centuries were the high point of European domination of Asia. After World War II, the tide would turn toward a closer balance in East–West relations.

## IDENTIFICATION TERMS

Test your knowledge of this chapter's key concepts by defining the following terms. If you can't recall the meaning of certain terms, refresh your memory by looking up the boldfaced term in the chapter, turning to the Glossary at the end of the book, or working with the flashcards that are available on the *World Civilizations* Companion Website **http://history.wadsworth.com/adler04.**

Boxer Rebellion
Empress Dowager Cixi
Kuomintang
Long March of 1934
May Fourth Movement
Meiji Restoration
New China Movement
Opium Wars
Self-strengthening
Taiping
unequal treaties

## Test Your Knowledge

Test your knowledge of this chapter by answering the following questions. Complete answers appear at the end of the book. You may also take this quiz interactively and find even more quiz questions on the *World Civilizations* Companion Website: **http://history.wadsworth.com/adler04**.

1. The beginning of China's clear inability to withstand foreign pressure is found in
   a. the outcome of the Opium Wars.
   b. the repression of the Boxer Rebellion.
   c. the defeat at the hands of the Japanese in 1895.
   d. the concessions in Manchuria to the Russians in 1901.
   e. the concessions made to the British in the 1820s.
2. The most devastating rebellion in China's history was
   a. the Boxer Rebellion.
   b. the Nakamura Rising.
   c. the Taiping Rebellion.
   d. the Long March.
   e. the Manzhou Rebellion.
3. The "late Manzhou restoration" was
   a. a successful attempt by the bureaucracy to renew itself.
   b. a cultural movement in the late nineteenth century that replaced Western forms with Chinese models of literature and art.
   c. the short-lived regeneration of the government by local gentry leaders after the Taiping and Nien rebellions were put down.
   d. the substitution of a new young emperor for the old empress by the army.
   e. a brief period of Japanese rule in China during the last years of the nineteenth century.
4. The New China Movement was founded on the premise that
   a. Confucius had been wrong in his philosophy of self-regulation.
   b. reform had been a significant part of Confucius's life and teaching.
   c. the best example of forward momentum for a modern country was that of Russia under Peter the Great.
   d. history was static, and any changes would necessarily involve revolution.
   e. if China were to survive, it must chart its own course in defiance of Western oversight.
5. Mao Zedong formulated his ideas within the context of
   a. thc Boxer Rebellion.
   b. World War II.
   c. the New China Movement.
   d. the Opium Wars.
   e. the May Fourth Movement.
6. One of the main reasons for the success of Mao Zedong's communist forces in China's civil war was
   a. the fact that his army was about three times the size of the Nationalist forces.
   b. his strength among the country's intellectuals.
   c. the lack of a will to fight among Nationalist forces.
   d. the resentment among many Chinese toward American support for the Nationalists.
   e. the peasants' resentment of Chiang Kai-shek's corruption and inaction.
7. The Meiji Restoration in Japan saw
   a. the return of the emperor to supreme governing power.
   b. a turning away from the West to a renewed isolation.
   c. the reinstallation of the samurai and daimyo to power.
   d. the adoption of Western techniques and ideas by Japan's rulers.
   e. the construction of a new capital city for the shogun at Tokyo.
8. The single most important foreign policy success of post-1853 Japan was
   a. winning the war against China in 1895.
   b. forcing the Boxer rebels to surrender in China in 1901.
   c. winning the war against Russia in 1904–1905.
   d. signing the Anglo-Japanese Treaty of 1902.
   e. the successful construction of a long-range naval fleet.
9. Which of the following places was *not* made into a European colony?
   a. Thailand
   b. Indonesia
   c. Malaya
   d. Burma
   e. Vietnam
10. In the 1800s, the only southeast Asian nation whose dominant faith was Christianity was
    a. Thailand.
    b. the Philippines.
    c. Indonesia.
    d. Cambodia.
    e. Malaya.

## InfoTrac College Edition

Visit the source collections at

**http://infotrac.thomsonlearning.com**

and use the Search function with the following key terms:

China history    Mao Zedong    Japan history

## Wadsworth History Website Resources

Visit the World History Resource Center at **http://history.wadsworth.com/world** for a wealth of general resources, and the *World Civilizations* Companion Website at **http://history.wadsworth.com/adler04** for resources specific to this textbook.

## HistoryNow

Enter *HistoryNow* using the access card that is available for *World Civilizations*. *HistoryNow* will assist you in understanding the content in this chapter with lesson plans generated for your needs. In addition, you can read the following documents, and many more, online:

"The Taiping Rebellion"

Fei Ch'i-hao, "The Boxer Rebellion"

Yao Chen-Yuan, "My Adventures During the Boxer War"

Sun Yat-sen, "Fundamentals of National Reconstruction"

*I have been actuated by love and loyalty to my people in all my thoughts, acts, and life. They gave me the strength to make the most difficult decisions which have ever confronted mortal man.*

**Adolf Hitler**

# 47 World War II

THE RISE AND FALL OF COLLECTIVE SECURITY
The Spanish Civil War

HITLER'S MARCH TO WAR, 1935–1939
The Reoccupation of the Rhineland
*Anschluss* in Austria
Munich, 1938
The Nazi-Soviet Nonaggression Pact

WORLD WAR II
The European Theater
The Pacific Theater

THE ONSET OF THE COLD WAR
Wartime Alliance and Continuing Mistrust
The Original Issues

| | |
|---|---|
| 1931 | Japanese seizure of Manchuria |
| 1935 | Ethiopian War |
| 1936–1939 | Spanish Civil War |
| 1938 | *Anschluss* of Austria/Munich conference |
| 1939–1945 | War in Europe |
| 1941–1945 | War in Pacific |
| 1945 | Yalta and Potsdam conferences among Allies |
| 1945–1948 | Eastern Europe comes under Soviet control/Cold War begins |

For the first fifteen years after the end of World War I, the peace held together. Despite the bitter complaints of the losers, especially the Germans, the Paris treaties were backed up by French diplomacy and the potential application of military force by France and Britain. For a brief period in the late 1920s, the Germans voluntarily adopted a policy of "fulfillment," adhering to the provisions of the treaties. But with the worldwide economic collapse and the coming of Adolf Hitler to power in the early 1930s, the treaties were unilaterally rejected and an atmosphere of international hostility resumed. The impotence of the League of Nations was quickly evident, and Hitler successfully bluffed his way forward until he felt himself in an invulnerable position to undertake a war of vengeance and conquest.

## The Rise and Fall of Collective Security

When the French saw the U.S. Senate reject Woodrow Wilson's League of Nations and realized that the British were having second thoughts about continuing their wartime alliance, they hurriedly took independent steps to protect France from potential German revenge. To this end, France signed a military alliance with Poland, Czechoslovakia, and Romania, three of Germany's eastern neighbors. This *Little Entente* stated that if Germany attacked any of the signatories, the others would give assistance. Also, France stayed on good terms with fascist Italy throughout the 1920s, and the French consistently argued that the league must take unified action against any potential aggressor nation; an attack on one was an attack against all.

Even before Hitler's seizure of power, however, the Paris-inspired policy of "collective security" against a resurgent Germany was under severe strain. For one thing, the aggressive stirring of international revolutionary hopes by the Bolsheviks meant that Soviet Russia was an outcast (see Chapter 44). For years, it was not invited to join the League of Nations, and even after a reluctant invitation was extended, it was not considered a suitable ally by the capitalist democracies. For another, Japan, a member of the league, totally disregarded the league's disapproval of its invasion of Manchuria in 1931 and got away without penalty. The league could only express its moral condemnation.

The league's powerlessness was revealed even more clearly in 1935 in a case that was much closer to European affairs. Hoping to revive his sagging popularity with the Italian people, Benito Mussolini started a blatantly imperialistic war with Ethiopia. The Ethiopians appealed to the league and obtained a vote that clearly branded Italy as an aggressor nation. But neither Paris nor London would take decisive measures, such as banning oil shipments to Italy, which had no oil of its own. In the end, the triumphant invaders were not even threatened in their occupation of Ethiopia. The League of Nations had been shown to have no teeth. Collective security had been struck a hard but not yet lethal blow.

### *The Spanish Civil War*

All hope for collective security was finished off by the Spanish Civil War, which broke out in the summer of 1936. Spain in the 1930s was a sharply divided nation. Its liberals had recently forced out an ineffectual monarch and declared a republic, but the public remained divided among every variety of leftist group, moderate democrats, and fascists. Like most of the Spanish upper classes, many army commanders were afraid that Spain might soon come under a communist government if current trends were not checked. To prevent such a takeover, they entered into a military revolt, supported by the Catholic Church, much of the peasantry, and most of the middle classes.

Despite open support for the rebel forces from both Mussolini and Hitler, the Western democracies refused to take sides and declared an embargo on shipments of arms and matériel to both contestants. In the circumstances, this was the same as assisting the rebels led by General Francisco Franco against the legitimate Spanish government.

Josef Stalin decided early on that the Spanish conflict was a golden opportunity. It might allow the Soviet Union to gain popularity among the many Western antifascists who as yet could not sympathize with communism. The Comintern orchestrated an international campaign to assist the outnumbered and outgunned Spanish Loyalists in the name of a **Popular Front** against fascism. For two years, the Soviets abandoned their previous vicious propaganda against the democratic socialists in all countries. In some instances, Popular Front tactics were quite successful. Much Soviet military aid was sent to Spain, and some tens of thousands of volunteers from all over the world (including the United States) came to fight with the Loyalists.

Hitler's and Mussolini's arms and advisers were more numerous and more effective in the long run, however. In the spring of 1939, the Loyalists surrendered, and Franco established himself as the military dictator of his country for the next generation. Although friendly to the fascist dictators, he stubbornly defended his freedom of action and never allowed himself to be their tool. Like Sweden, Switzerland, and Portugal, Spain sat out World War II as a neutral party.

## HITLER'S MARCH TO WAR, 1935–1939

Since 1922, the fascist Mussolini had made no effort to conceal his contempt for the Western democracies, but Germany, much more than Italy, represented the real danger to the Paris treaties. Even before gaining power, Hitler had sworn to overturn the Versailles Treaty, and he proceeded to take Germany out of the League of Nations almost immediately—in 1933.

Did Hitler intend a major war from the outset of his dictatorship? This question is still much debated. Historians generally agree that he realized that the program of German hegemony described in *Mein Kampf* could only be made reality through war, because it entailed a major expansion of German territory eastward into Slavic lands (Poland and Russia). But he seems to have had no concrete plans for war until about 1936, when he instructed the General Staff to prepare them.

In 1935, Hitler had formally renounced the provisions of the Versailles Treaty that limited German armaments. This move had symbolic rather than practical importance, because the treaty limitations had been ignored even during the Weimar era. A few months later, he started conscription for a much larger army and the creation of a large *Luftwaffe* (air force). Neither France nor Britain reacted beyond a few words of diplomatic dismay and disapproval.

### *The Reoccupation of the Rhineland*

In 1936, Hitler sent a small force into the Rhineland, the area of Germany west of the Rhine on the French borders. Under both the Versailles and Locarno agreements, the Rhineland was supposed to be permanently demilitarized. To the French, stationing German troops there was a direct threat to France's security, but in the moment of decision, France said that it did not want to act alone, and Britain said it would not support France in an offensive action. What the British and French did not know was that the German army was more frightened of the consequences of the Rhineland adventure than they were. The General Staff strongly opposed the action, advising Hitler not to try this ploy, because the army as yet was in no condition to resist Allied attacks. Hitler insisted on proceeding with his bluff and scored a great psychic and diplomatic triumph over his own generals as well as the French. From this point, the quite erroneous legend of Hitler the master strategist was born.

From 1936 on, Germany was rapidly rearming, while France and Britain were paralyzed by defeatism or pacifism among both the general public and the government officials. In Britain, where the English Channel still gave a false feeling of security, many members of the Conservative government leaned toward appeasement of der Führer and were ready to abandon France. Much of the party leadership was more fearful of a Bolshevik revolution than of a fascist or Nazi society. Some hoped that a Hitler-like figure would rise in Britain and put "order" back into the Depression-wracked country. The French, for their part, put all of their hopes into the huge defensive network—the Maginot Line—built during the 1920s along their eastern borders—and into their allies in eastern Europe.

Also in 1936, Hitler and Mussolini reached a close understanding, the Rome–Berlin **Axis Pact**, which made them allies in case of war. This agreement eliminated any hopes the French might have had that Mussolini would side with France and against Germany.

## Anschluss *in Austria*

In 1938, the pace of events picked up. Hitler, an Austrian by birth, had always intended to bring about the "natural union" of his birthplace with Germany. The ***Anschluss*** (joining) was explicitly forbidden by the Versailles Treaty, but by this time that was a dead letter. In Austria, the Nazis had strong support. Most Austrians were German by blood, and they regarded the enforced separation from the Reich as an act of vengeance by the Allies. An earlier attempt at a Nazi coup in 1934 had failed because of Mussolini's resistance. Now, in 1938, Mussolini was Hitler's ally, and the Anschluss could go forward. It was completed in March by a bloodless occupation of the small country on Germany's southern borders, and Nazi rule was thus extended to another 7 million people.

Next to fall was the Successor State of Czechoslovakia, a country created by the Versailles Treaty that Hitler had always hated. Linked militarily with France, it contained within its borders 3.5 million Germans, the Sudetenlander minority who were strongly pro-Hitler. Under the direction of Berlin, the Sudeten Germans agitated against the democratic, pro-Western government in Prague. Concessions were made, but the Germans always demanded more. After the Anschluss in Austria, it appeared to be only a matter of time before the Germans acted. The attitude of the British government was the key. If Britain supported Czech armed resistance, the French promised to honor their Little Entente treaty obligation and move against Germany.

## *Munich, 1938*

In September 1938, Hitler brought the British prime minister Neville Chamberlain and the French premier Edouard Daladier to a conference at Munich, where they were joined by Mussolini. After several days of threats and negotiations, Hitler succeeded in extracting the **Munich Agreements** from the democratic leaders. The Czechs were sacrificed entirely, although Hitler had to wait a few months before taking the final slice. Chamberlain returned to Britain waving a piece of paper that he claimed guaranteed "peace in our time." One year later, Britain and Germany were at war.

Almost before the ink was dry on the Munich Agreements, Hitler started pressuring Poland about its treatment of its German minority. These Germans lived in solid blocs on the borders with Germany and in the so-called Free City of Danzig (Gdansk) in the Polish Corridor to the sea between Germany and its province of East Prussia (see Map 47.1).

Prodded by British public opinion and the speeches of Winston Churchill in Parliament, Chamberlain now at last moved firmly. In March 1939, he signed a pact with Poland, guaranteeing British (and French) aid if Germany attacked. Hitler did not take this threat seriously, because he knew that the Allies could aid Poland only by attacking Germany in the West, but the French, having put their military in an entirely defensive orientation behind the Maginot Line, were not prepared to go on the offensive. Of more concern to Hitler was the attitude of the other nearby great power, the Soviet Union.

## *The Nazi-Soviet Nonaggression Pact*

At this point, the only convincing threat to Hitler's war plans was the possibility of having to face the Soviet Union in the east and the Allies in the west simultaneously—the two-front war that had proved disastrous in 1914–1918. But even at this stage, neither Chamberlain nor Daladier nor their conservative advisers could bring themselves to ask the communist Stalin to enter an alliance. In fact, the Russians were equally as suspicious of the West's motives as Paris and London were of Moscow. Stalin had not forgotten that the Soviet Union had been excluded from the postwar arrangements and treaties. Nor had he overlooked the fact that when the chips were down, Britain and France had sacrificed their ally Czechoslovakia rather than coordinate action with the Soviet Union, as Stalin had offered to do through Czech intermediaries.

Even so, it was a terrific shock to communists and to all antifascists everywhere to hear, on August 23, 1939, that Stalin and Hitler had signed a **Nonaggression Pact**. By its terms, the Soviet Union agreed to remain neutral in a war involving Germany. In return, Hitler agreed that the Russians could occupy the three small Baltic states (Estonia, Latvia, and Lithuania), eastern Poland, and a slice of Romania. These areas had once belonged to imperial Russia and were still claimed by the Soviets. Both sides affirmed their "friendship." Hitler no longer had to worry

**MAP 47.1** ***World War II in Europe***

In contrast to World War I (1914–1918), World War II was decided militarily as much or more on the Eastern fronts as in the West. Until the war's end, the largest part of Nazi forces was deployed in Russia and occupied eastern Europe. Civilian and military casualties far outstripped those of World War I, again mainly in the East, where slave labor was extensively recruited and the extermination camps were located.

about what Russia might do if he attacked Poland and the Allies came to the Poles' aid as they had promised. The Nonaggression Pact made war certain.

For communists all over the world, the pact represented a 180-degree turn in the party line, and they were entirely unprepared. Hitler was now the head of a friendly government. The Popular Front against fascism died overnight. Many members of the Communist Party outside the Soviet Union dropped out, unable to swallow this latest subordination of truth and others' national interests to the momentary advantage of the Soviets. But Stalin had gained some time. The Soviet Union did not enter World War II for almost two more years. Whether he used the time well to prepare for war is a topic of debate to the present day.

## World War II

World War II can be divided into three major chronological periods and two geographic areas, or theaters. Chronologically, the first phase of the conflict saw the German and later the Japanese victories and expansion from 1939 to late 1942. The second phase was the Allied counterattack from late 1942 through 1943, which checked and contained both enemies. The third phase was the steady Allied advance in 1944 and 1945, bringing final victory in August 1945.

## The European Theater

Geographically, the European theater (including North Africa) was the focus of Allied efforts until the German surrender in May 1945. Then, the emphasis shifted to the Pacific, but the anti-Japanese campaign was unexpectedly shortened by the atomic bombs and Japan's ensuing surrender. The United States, alone among the belligerents, played an important role on both fronts. The Pacific theater was fundamentally a conflict between Japan and the United States. The Soviet Union was drawn into the European war in mid-1941 but maintained neutrality with Germany's ally Japan until the final three weeks. (We will consider the Pacific war as an adjunct of the European theater, as indeed it was for all combatants except Japan and China.)

***Phase 1: Axis Blitzkrieg*** German *blitzkrieg* ("lightning war") machine smashed into Poland on September 1, 1939 (see Map 47.1). Britain and France retaliated by declaring war on Germany two days later. Italy remained neutral for the time being (the Axis Pact did not demand immediate assistance to the other partner), and so did

LAW AND GOVERNMENT

## Winston Churchill (1874–1965)

**Each year the American newsmagazine** *Time* selects a "Man of the Year" to appear on the cover of the last issue of the year, but a few years ago, *Time* decided that one individual should qualify as "Man of the Century." That person was the British statesman, author, artist, and warrior Winston Churchill. Yet some might ask which century Churchill best represents: the nineteenth, in whose traditions he immersed himself and fought for, or the twentieth, in which he found himself a natural hero, but somewhat out of step with the majority of his country's political and social viewpoints. The novelties introduced into British political life by mass democracy and the coming of the welfare state, as well as the worldwide backlash against colonialism following World War II, were difficult for Churchill to understand and accept.

Churchill was born to an American mother and a British aristocratic father in 1874. Born to privilege, Winston was a lonely child, unwanted and generally ignored by his parents. He was sent to the military academy at Sandhurst and served in India and the Sudan as an army officer. Resigning his commission to have more personal freedom, Churchill covered the Boer War as a correspondent for a London paper. He quickly made a name for himself through his journalistic exploits, especially his escape from Boer captivity.

In 1900, he was elected to the House of Commons as a Tory (Conservative). Four years later, he made the first of several political jumps by joining the rival Liberals and was rewarded by being appointed undersecretary for the colonies in the Liberal government of 1905–1908. Other high posts in succeeding Liberal governments followed, while Churchill developed a solid reputation as an incisive speaker and wily parliamentarian. But in World War I, as First Sea Lord (that is, secretary of the navy), Churchill suffered a severe blow when the Gallipoli campaign, which he had strongly supported, was an abysmal failure. He was forced out of government for a time.

In 1924, he switched back to the Tory side as chancellor of the exchequer (minister of finance), a post he held until the Tories were defeated in the elections of 1929. During this period, he defended the idea of the continuing British Empire and condemned Mohandas Gandhi's campaign for Indian self-government. He also led the opposition to organized labor and the general strike of 1926. These positions alienated large groups of voters for differing reasons, and after 1929, Churchill was out of government (but still in Parliament) for the entire decade preceding World War II.

During his "exile" in the 1930s, Churchill continued the writing career that had begun with journalism, but his passion for active politicking could not be satisfied with literary achievement, and he longed to get back into action. Churchill was appalled at the inability of the British upper classes to recognize the menace of Hitler and the fascist movements on the Continent. Again and again, he called on the government to strengthen the country's defenses and to take action against the Nazi aggression. In the fall of 1939, with a major war under way, the discredited government of Neville Chamberlain was forced out, and the country turned to the man whose warning had proved so correct. Winston Churchill now stepped like some fierce, confident bulldog into the seat of power that he had been preparing for since boyhood. For millions of Britons,

Germany's other ally, Japan, and the United States, Spain, the Scandinavian countries, and the Balkan countries. The Soviet Union remained neutral as well, but it moved quickly to occupy the promised segments of eastern Europe in accord with the Nonaggression Pact.

Poland fell almost at once to the well-trained, well-armed Germans despite brave resistance. Soviet forces occupied the eastern half of the country. For several months, all was quiet. Then, in the spring of 1940, Hitler struck. France fell to the German tanks (now assisted by the Italians) within a few weeks. Denmark, the Netherlands, Belgium, and Norway were overwhelmed before France. By July, Britain stood alone against a Nazi regime that controlled Europe from the Russian border to the Pyrenees.

For the next several months, the Luftwaffe attempted to bomb England into submission, as many experts feared would be possible with the huge new planes and their large bomb loads. But the Battle of Britain, fought entirely in the air, ended with a clear victory for the defenders. The Channel was still under British control, and Hitler's plans for an invasion, like those of Napoleon a century and a half earlier, had to be abandoned. Just before the fall of France, Churchill had replaced Chamberlain as head of the British government, and he personified the "British bulldog" who would never give up. His magnificent speeches and leadership rallied the British people, cemented the growing Anglo-American sympathies, and played a key role in the Allies' eventual victory. (See the Law and Government box for more on this leader.)

Churchill *was* the government, incarnating in his jowly face and stubborn chin the determination not to yield to the enemy's bombs or threats.

But almost immediately after final victory, his stubborn conservatism and unwillingness to cater to an electorate that had made enormous wartime sacrifices and now wanted the Labour Party's promised "welfare state" made him unpopular, and he was voted out of office. Six years later, with the public dissatisfied by Labour's inability to get the economy into high gear, another election returned the Tories and Churchill to power. He governed until his retirement in 1955. The final ten years of Churchill's life were dedicated to writing his impressive *History of the English-Speaking Peoples,* to go on the shelf next to his magisterial *History of the Second World War* completed earlier. In 1953, he was awarded the Nobel Prize for literature.

Besides his political leadership, Churchill was known for his biting wit and mental quickness. Once the playwright and Labour supporter George Bernard Shaw sent him two tickets to a Shaw premiere. "Bring a friend, if you have one," wrote Shaw on the accompanying note. Churchill returned the tickets with regrets, saying that he could, however, use some for the second performance, "if there is one."

Bettmann/Corbis

**WINSTON CHURCHILL.** Statesman, soldier, historian, journalist, and artist, Churchill was an extraordinary man in extraordinary times.

### *Analyze and Interpret*

Do you think that Churchill deserves his honors as Man of the Century? Whom might you put up for that title instead?

**HistoryNow™**

***To read some of Churchill's speeches, point your browser to the documents area of* HistoryNow.**

The high point of the war for the Nazis came in 1941, when attacks on Yugoslavia (April), Greece (May), and the Soviet Union (June) were all successful. The Germans gained huge new territories and turned all of eastern Europe into either a Nazi satellite (Romania, Bulgaria, Hungary) or an occupied land (the Ukraine, Poland, and western Russia).

**Operation Barbarossa**, the code name for the attack on Russia, got off to a tremendous start, because Stalin's government was caught entirely by surprise despite repeated warnings from spies and Allied sources. In the first two days alone, some 2,000 Russian planes were destroyed on the ground, and a half million men were taken prisoner by the end of the first month. The Red Army, which was still recovering from the purge of its officers in 1937–1938, looked as though it had been all but knocked out of the war. At this critical point, Hitler overruled his generals and insisted on diverting many of his forces southward, toward the grain and oil of Ukraine and the Black Sea area, rather than heading straight for Moscow. As a consequence, the Germans were struck by the numbing cold of an early winter before they could take the capital, and Stalin was given precious time to rally and reinforce. For all practical purposes, the Germans had lost their chance for a quick, decisive victory on the Eastern front already in the fall of 1941.

***Phase 2: Allied Counterattack*** In December 1941, the attack on Pearl Harbor brought the United States into the war against Japan and its allies, Germany and Italy. In many ways, the U.S. entry into World War II and its later decisive role in it was similar to what had occurred in World War I. As the oppressive nature of the German occupation regime in Europe became known to the American public, opinion began running strongly in support of London and against Berlin. Thus, the attack on Pearl Harbor only accelerated a process that was already under way toward the entry of the United States into the conflict.

Although the American peacetime military was very small and poorly equipped, U.S. industrial resources were immense and played the same important role that they had in 1917–1918. Neither Japan nor Germany had the wherewithal to hold out indefinitely against this power. In an economic sense, the outcome of the war was decided as early as December 1941, but the Allies' eventual victory was far from clear at the time. The Germans had been checked in Russia but not defeated. Their Italian ally was not much help but did contribute to the takeover of North Africa and the Balkans and the blockade of the British forces in Egypt. German submarines threatened Britain's supply lines from the United States for the next two years and were defeated (by the convoy system) only after heavy losses.

In the summer of 1942, the Russians were again pushed back hundreds of miles by superior German armor and aircraft. Stalin then ordered a "not one step backward" defense of the strategic city of **Stalingrad** on the Volga. Historians agree that the ensuing battle in the fall and winter of 1942 was the turning point of the war in Europe. The Nazis lost an entire army, which was surrounded and captured, and from this point on, they were defending more than attacking. At the same time, the Western Allies were at last counterattacking. By the summer of 1943, the Germans and Italians had been driven from Africa, and the Allies landed in southern Italy. After a few months, the discredited Nazi puppet Mussolini fell, and Italy capitulated in September.

***Phase 3: Allied Victory*** In Europe, the tide had turned decisively in 1943. An Allied army landed in the south of France and started pushing northward. In the Balkans, the German occupiers were under heavy attack by partisans

**Ruins of Hamburg, 1945.** The terrible destruction visited on the German cities by Allied bombing is vividly displayed here. The port of Hamburg was destroyed in two days and nights in 1944 by a huge firestorm set off by incendiary bombs.

Yad Vashem Film and Photo Archive

**THE HOLOCAUST: THE EXTERMINATION CAMP AT AUSCHWITZ.** After his initial success in the east, Hitler set in motion the machinery for the physical annihilation of Europe's Jews. Shown here is a group of Hungarian Jewish women and children who have just arrived at Auschwitz, a major extermination camp. The picture was taken shortly before their deaths.

(guerrillas) supplied by the Allies. By late 1944, Greece, Yugoslavia, Bulgaria, and Albania had been cleared of Axis forces, but the main theater of the war in Europe was on the Russian front, where the Germans had the bulk of their forces. Here, too, the Nazis were forced steadily back, and by the fall of 1944, they were again on German soil. Poland, Hungary, and Romania had all been freed of the occupiers. The Red Army became entrenched in those countries, while it pursued the retreating Germans.

The human losses on the Eastern front were immense. The Nazis had treated the occupied areas with great brutality, taking millions for slave labor in German factories and mines. Millions more starved to death. The large Jewish populations of Poland, Hungary, and Romania as well as the western Soviet Union were systematically exterminated in the gas chambers of Auschwitz, Belsen, Maidenek, and the other death camps set up by the SS.

Stalin's repeated calls for a **Second Front** in the West were finally answered by the June 1944 invasion across the English Channel by British, American, and Canadian forces (the invasion began on June 6, or **D-day**). For the next several months, fighting raged in northern France and Belgium without a decision, but by the winter of 1944–1945, Allied troops were on Germany's western border. The next spring the fighting was carried deep into Germany from both east and west.

On May 1, 1945, a half-mad Hitler committed suicide in the smoking ruins of his Berlin bunker, as the Russians entered the city. Several of his closest associates chose the same death, but others fled and were hunted down for trial at Nuremberg as war criminals. Germany's formal surrender—unconditionally this time—took place on May 8. In accordance with previous agreements, the Russians occupied eastern Germany, including East Berlin. The British and Americans controlled the western part of the country.

## The Pacific Theater

In the Pacific theater, naval battles in 1942 checked what had been a rapid Japanese advance (see Map 47.2). All of Southeast Asia and many Pacific islands had fallen to the flag of the Rising Sun, and the Japanese were threatening Australia and India by the middle of that year, but by the end of 1942, it was clear that the United States was recovering from Pearl Harbor. The **Battle of the Coral Sea** had nullified the Japanese threat to Australia, and British India proved ready to defend itself rather than passively submit, as Tokyo had hoped.

Even with the bulk of the U.S. war effort going toward Europe and the Russians remaining neutral, the Japanese did not have the raw materials or the manpower to keep up with the demands of prolonged conflict over so wide an area. (The Japanese high command knew this. They had counted heavily on the attack on Pearl Harbor to "knock out" American power in the Pacific or at least to make the United States amenable to a negotiated peace that would leave Japan in control of the western Pacific.)

In 1943–1944, the United States rolled the Japanese back, taking one Pacific island chain after another in bloody fighting. The Philippines were liberated from Tokyo's forces in late 1944 in a campaign led by the American commander Douglas MacArthur, the chief architect of the victory in the Pacific. The Japanese homelands

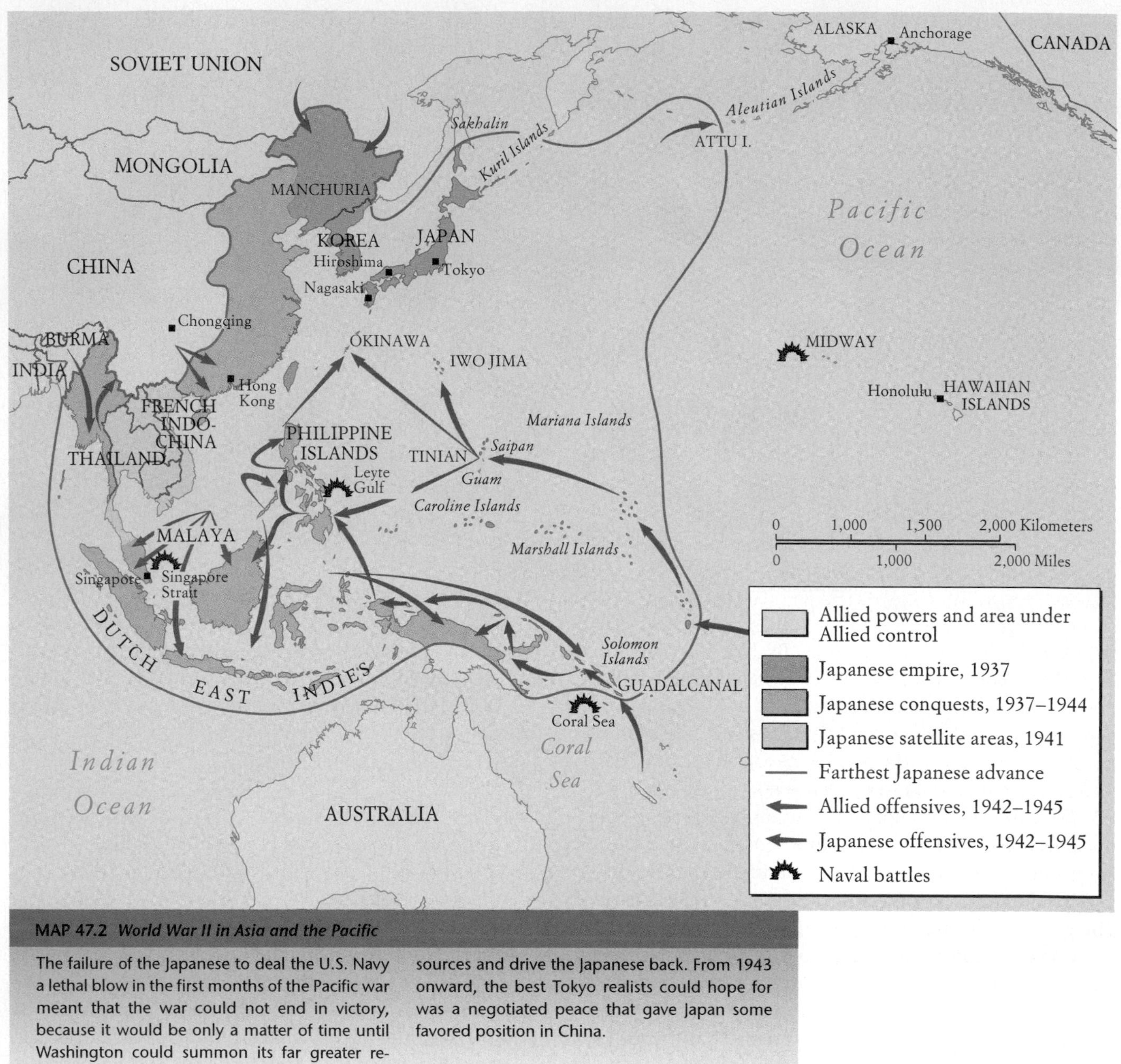


**MAP 47.2** ***World War II in Asia and the Pacific***

The failure of the Japanese to deal the U.S. Navy a lethal blow in the first months of the Pacific war meant that the war could not end in victory, because it would be only a matter of time until Washington could summon its far greater resources and drive the Japanese back. From 1943 onward, the best Tokyo realists could hope for was a negotiated peace that gave Japan some favored position in China.

were pummeled by constant bombing from these newly captured island bases.

***Japanese Defeat and Surrender*** The end of the Pacific war came quickly after the Nazi capitulation. During 1944–1945, the Japanese occupation forces had been gradually forced from maritime Southeast Asia. Burma and Indochina had been cleared when the Japanese withdrew to return to their homeland. The long war between Japan and China was also now swinging in favor of the communist army under Mao Zedong (see Chapter 46).

The Americans were preparing for massive casualties in a planned invasion of the Japanese islands when they dropped atomic bombs on Hiroshima and Nagasaki in August 1945. Within a few days, the Japanese government indicated its readiness to surrender, and the formal act was completed on August 15, 1945. The sole condition was that Emperor Hirohito be allowed to remain on his throne.

Should the atomic bombs have been used? This issue has remained profoundly acrimonious. Critics say that the bombing of the two Japanese cities was admittedly aimed against civilians rather than military targets and cite the huge loss of civilian life (more than 70,000 of a population of about 200,000) in Hiroshima. This was entirely unnecessary, they say, because Japan would soon have surrendered to overwhelming Allied forces in any case. Another school of criticism thinks that the real reason for the bombing was that the U.S. government was looking ahead to the postwar era and wished to intimidate the Soviets.

On the other side, the defenders of President Harry S. Truman and the U.S. high command point out that the Japanese had shown fanatical determination to resist and would have stalwartly defended their home islands. Some estimates at the time allegedly thought more than a million U.S. casualties and countless more Japanese might have been expected before the fighting was over. To avoid such massive casualties, the atomic attack was entirely justified in their view. In any case, the sight of the enormous mushroom cloud of an atomic explosion would hover like some ghastly phantom over the entire postwar era. The knowledge that humans now had the power to entirely destroy themselves was the most fearsome insight to come out of World War II.

The other balance sheets of the war were almost as terrible. More people died in World War II than in any other disaster in recorded history. The final count will never be known for certain, but it is thought that about 30 million people died as a direct result of hostilities around the world. The most devastating casualties were suffered by the Jews of Europe, followed by the Russians and the Germans. In material categories, much of central and eastern Europe was reduced to shambles by ground or air war, and many parts of Italy and France also suffered severe damage. Many Japanese and Chinese districts were in bad shape from bombings and (in China) years of ground war. Everywhere, the survivors stood on the edge of an abyss. Starvation, cold, epidemic disease, family disintegration, and psychic disorientation posed distinct threats to humane life in much of the world.

## The Onset of the Cold War

During the conflict, the Allies had not been able to agree on their postwar aims. Between the Western Allies and the Soviets stood a wall of mistrust that had been veiled temporarily but had by no means been dismantled. As soon as the victory over the Axis powers was secured, the dimensions of this wall were again visible for all to see.

### *Wartime Alliance and Continuing Mistrust*

The so-called Cold War between the Soviet Union and the West began as early as 1945. During the war against the Axis, three Allied summit conferences (Tehran in 1943, Yalta and Potsdam in 1945) had been held. The main concrete results of these meetings were to assure the Soviets of political-military dominion over eastern Europe after the war, to assign parts of conquered Germany to Allied armies of occupation, and to move Germany's eastern border a hundred miles to the west. Moving Germany's border would allow the Soviet border with Poland to be moved west a similar distance, fulfilling an old demand of the Soviets dating back to 1919.

The immediate trigger for inter-Allied suspicion was the Soviets' clear disregard for their commitments in eastern Europe and Germany. At the **Yalta conference** in February 1945, the participants had agreed that free elections would be held as soon as wartime conditions might permit, even though all of these nations fell under what was conceded to be a Soviet "sphere of interest." Already at the Potsdam Conference in July 1945, it was apparent that major problems were arising. From Stalin's point of view (the only one of the Big Three still in power), the assurance of freedom in any real sense for these nations was unjustified presumption on the West's part. Since 1918, the nations of eastern Europe had consistently been hostile to the Soviet Union and would undoubtedly continue to be so, given the chance. Therefore, the only freedom for them that the Soviets would agree to was the freedom to choose between various types of Soviet overlordship. The eastern Europeans could install their own native Communist Party dictatorship, or they could accept the Soviet one—in either case, backed up by the Red Army already on the scene.

From the Western point of view (which increasingly meant the U.S. perspective), Stalin's government was violating the plain meaning of the promises it had made about eastern Europe and eastern Germany. Also, the tiny Communist Parties were being falsely portrayed as the voices of the majority of Poles, Hungarians, and the like by Soviet media, and governments composed of their members were being imposed on anticommunist majorities through rigged elections and political terror.

Both sides were correct in these accusations. The almost inevitable rivalry between the United States and the Soviet Union in the contest for postwar leadership was the basic reason for the Cold War. Which side was indeed the more culpable for the fifteen years of extreme tension that followed is not easily answered except by those who have a doctrinal commitment to Marxism or its capitalist opponents. The following assertions seem in order now.

Until Stalin's death in 1953, the Soviets were certainly trying to expand their direct and indirect controls over Europe. The large Communist Parties of France and Italy (which consistently obtained more than 25 percent of the vote in postwar elections) were regarded as Trojan horses by all other democratic leaders, and rightly so. These parties had shown themselves to be the slavish followers of Moscow's commands, and if they had obtained power, they would have attempted to turn those democracies

Bettmann/Corbis

**The Big Three at Yalta, February 1945.** This final summit meeting among the three Allied leaders—Churchill, Roosevelt, and Stalin—came a few months before the German surrender. It was devoted to arranging the Soviet Union's entry into the Pacific war against Japan and the fate of postwar eastern Europe.

into imitations of the Soviet Union. World revolution was still seen as a desirable and attainable goal by some communists, possibly including Stalin. The progress of the Maoist rebellion against the Chinese government in the late 1940s certainly buoyed these hopes, while greatly alarming American opinion.

On the other hand, the U.S. military and some U.S. political leaders were almost paranoid in their fears of communism. They were prone to see Muscovite plots everywhere and to think all communists shared a monolithic commitment to Moscow's version of Marx, employing the same goals and methods. Like the most fanatical communists, they could not imagine a world where communists and capitalists might coexist. They viewed the exclusively U.S.-controlled atomic bomb as the ultimate "persuader" for a proper world order.

## The Original Issues

During the immediate postwar years, several specific issues concerning Germany and eastern Europe brought the two superpowers—the United States and the Soviet Union—into a permanently hostile stance:

- *Reparations in Germany.* The Soviet Union claimed, more or less accurately, that the Allies soon reneged on their promises to give the Russians a certain amount of West German goods and materials, as reparations for war damage.
- *"Denazification" of German government and industry.* Again, the Russians were correct in accusing the West of not pursuing the Nazi element vigorously, as soon as the Cold War frictions began. By 1949, the Western powers had dropped denazification altogether, as an unwelcome diversion from the main issue of strengthening Germany as a barrier to the spread of communism.
- *The creation of a new currency for the Allied sectors of Germany in 1948.* Without consulting its increasingly difficult Russian occupation "partner," the West put through a new currency (the deutsche mark, which is still in use), which split the supposed unity of the occupation zones in economic and financial affairs.
- *The Berlin government and the Berlin blockade in 1948–1949.* The Russians showed no interest in maintaining the agreed-on Allied Control Council (where they could be always outvoted) and made East Berlin and East Germany practically a separate administration as early as 1946. In 1948, Stalin attempted to bluff the Western allies out of Berlin altogether by imposing a blockade on all ground access. The Allies defeated the **Berlin blockade** by airlifting food and vital supplies for six months, and Stalin eventually lifted it (see Chapter 49).
- *The country-by-country Soviet takeover of eastern Europe between 1945 and 1948.* From the moment the Red Army arrived, terror of every kind was freely applied against anticommunists. For a brief time after the war's end, the Communist Parties attempted service to democratic ideals by forming political coalitions with noncommunists who had not been compromised during the Nazi occupation. Under Moscow's guidance, these coalitions were turned into "fronts" in which the noncommunists were either powerless or stooges. Protests by Western observers were ignored or denounced. The communists then took the leading positions in all of the provisional governments and used their powers to prepare for "free" elections. The elections were held at some point between 1945 and 1947 and returned a predictable overwhelming majority for the Communist Parties and their docile fellow travelers. Stalinist constitutions were adopted, the protecting Red Army was invited to remain for an indefinite period, and the satellite regime was complete.

Many other factors could be mentioned, but the general picture should already be clear: the wartime alliance was only a weak marriage of convenience against Hitler and was bound to collapse as soon as the mutual enemy was gone. After 1946 at the latest, neither side had any real interest in cooperating to establish world peace except on terms it could dictate. For an entire generation, the world and especially Europe would lie in the shadow thrown by the atomic mushroom, with the paralyzing knowledge that a struggle between the two superpowers meant the third, and final, world war.

## Summary

World War II came about through a series of aggressive steps taken by the fascist and Nazi dictatorships in the later 1930s against the defeatist and indecisive democratic states of western Europe. Hitler quickly recognized the weakness of his opponents and rode his support by most Germans to a position of seeming invincibility in foreign affairs. The remilitarization of the Rhineland was followed by the annexation of Austria and Czechoslovakia, and finally the assault against Poland in September 1939 that began the general war.

In the first three years of war, the battles were mainly decided in favor of the Axis powers led by Germany, but the Battle of Stalingrad and the defeat of the Axis in North Africa marked a definite military turning point in the fall of 1942. In a long-range sense, the entry of the United States into the war following the Japanese attack on Hawaii was the turning point, even though it took a full year for the Americans to make much difference on the fighting fronts.

By late 1944, the writing was clearly on the wall for both the Germans and the Japanese, and attention turned to the postwar settlement with the Soviet ally. Despite some attempts, this settlement had not been spelled out in detail during the war because of the continuing mistrust between East and West. As soon as the fighting had stopped (May 1945 in Europe, August 1945 in the Pacific), the papered-over cracks in the wartime alliance became plain and soon produced a Cold War atmosphere. The political fate of eastern Europe and the administration of defeated Germany were the two focal points of what proved to be a generation of conflict between the West, led by the United States, and the communist world, headed by Soviet Russia.

## Identification Terms

Test your knowledge of this chapter's key concepts by defining the following terms. If you can't recall the meaning of certain terms, refresh your memory by looking up the boldfaced term in the chapter, turning to the Glossary at the end of the book, or working with the flashcards that are available on the *World Civilizations* Companion Website **http://history.wadsworth.com/adler04**.

*Anschluss*
Axis Pact
Berlin blockade
Coral Sea, Battle of the
D-day
Munich Agreements
Nonaggression Pact
Operation Barbarossa
Popular Front
Second Front
Stalingrad
Yalta conference

## Test Your Knowledge

Test your knowledge of this chapter by answering the following questions. Complete answers appear at the end of the book. You may also take this quiz interactively and find even more quiz questions on the *World Civilizations* Companion Website: **http://history.wadsworth.com/adler04**.

1. One ostensible reason for the Spanish Civil War was the military's fear of
   a. the country's new republic.
   b. a fascist takeover.
   c. communism.
   d. Mussolini.
   e. a return to monarchy.
2. Which of the following was *not* a German-instigated step toward World War II?
   a. The occupation of the Rhineland
   b. The invasion of Ethiopia
   c. The seizure of the Sudetenland
   d. The Nonaggression Pact of 1939
   e. The buildup of a military force
3. A chief reason for Britain's prolonged appeasement of Hitler was that
   a. the British government wanted a counterweight to France on the Continent.
   b. he was seen by some leaders as an anticommunist bulwark.
   c. the British government of the late 1930s was strongly pro-German.

d. he was seen as a way to tame the eastern European troublemakers.
e. the United States urged Britain to stay out of any dangerous situations.

4. At the Munich conference in 1938,
   a. Austria was sacrificed to a Nazi invasion.
   b. Czechoslovakia was abandoned by its Western allies.
   c. Soviet Russia was invited to join the League of Nations.
   d. Hitler and Mussolini decided on war.
   e. Neville Chamberlain first began to understand the true evil of Adolf Hitler.
5. World War II was started by the Nazi invasion of
   a. France.
   b. Austria.
   c. Poland.
   d. Czechoslovakia.
   e. Belgium.
6. Which of these did *not* occur during the first phase of World War II?
   a. The German blitzkrieg against Denmark and Norway
   b. The D-day invasion of France
   c. The occupation and neutralization of France by Germany
   d. The invasion of Russia
   e. The conquest by Germany of the Balkans
7. Winston Churchill first became a public figure when he
   a. became the leader of the British government.
   b. was elected to Parliament.
   c. was a journalist in Africa.
   d. was a navy minister in World War I.
   e. spoke out against Chamberlain's support of Hitler.
8. The turning point in favor of the Allies in World War II from a military point of view was
   a. the fall and winter of 1942.
   b. the fall of 1944.
   c. the spring and summer of 1940.
   d. the summer of 1941.
   e. the summer of 1944.
9. The battle that halted Japanese aims to take Australia was the Battle of
   a. Yalta.
   b. Midway.
   c. the Philippines.
   d. the Coral Sea.
   e. Hiroshima.
10. The focal point of the Yalta conference among the Allied leaders in 1945 was
   a. the future of Japan.
   b. the postwar political arrangements in eastern Europe.
   c. the details of a peace treaty with Germany.
   d. the signing of a peace treaty with Italy.
   e. a plan to liberate the Jews in occupied Poland.

## InfoTrac College Edition

Visit the source collections at

**http://infotrac.thomsonlearning.com**

and use the Search function with the following key terms:

World War, 1939–1945 Holocaust Winston Churchill

## Wadsworth History Website Resources

Visit the World History Resource Center at **http://history.wadsworth.com/world** for a wealth of general resources, and the *World Civilizations* Companion Website at **http://history.wadsworth.com/adler04** for resources specific to this textbook.

## HistoryNow

Enter *HistoryNow* using the access card that is available for *World Civilizations*. *HistoryNow* will assist you in understanding the content in this chapter with lesson plans generated for your needs. In addition, you can read the following documents, and many more, online:

Adolf Hitler, Proclamation to the German Nation

Adolf Hitler, Speech to the Reichstag

Winston Churchill, Speech to the French, 1940

Winston Churchill, Speech to the Italians, 1940

Franklin Delano Roosevelt, "Four Freedoms"

*I respect the idea of God too much to hold it responsible for a world as absurd as this one.*
**Georges Duhamel**

# 48 High and Low Cultures in the West



| | |
|---|---|
| 1880s–1890s | Post-Impressionist painting begins/ Modernism in the arts |
| Early 1900s | Modernism in literature, music |
| 1920s | Radio commercialized/Movies become major entertainment medium/ Recorded music |
| 1930s | Television invented/Cheap paperback books |
| 1960s | FM radio/audiotape recordings/ Business and research computing |
| 1970s | First VCRs and video cameras |
| 1980s | CD recordings/Large-screen TVs |
| 1990s | The home computer age/The Internet |

In the just-completed century, the arts and their audiences have undergone one more of those radical reorientations that we have termed revolutions when placed in a political or economic context. The twentieth century was unprecedentedly receptive to new cultural trends and new ways of communicating both ideas and feelings. Frenetic experimentation has been the hallmark of Western culture since World War I. Many forms have been borrowed from non-Western sources, and artists in several media have not hesitated to reject the historical traditions of their art. Popular media, with no traditions to restrict them, have sprung up like weeds, feeding on technological innovation.

In painting and literature, especially, an almost complete break with the modalities of earlier times was attempted and occasionally was successful. Such attempts often led to dead ends, however, and the older models were able to hold the allegiance of the audience majority. The century ended with a distinct gap between the "high" and the "low" cultures, which differ not only in the media employed but also in their content, their aims, and their audiences.

## Fragmentation and Alienation

If we were to select a single keyword to describe twentieth-century Western culture, it might well be *fragmentation.* All authorities agree that never before have so many conflicting approaches to the common problems of human life and art been pursued. Value systems and aesthetic judgments collide head-on with depressing regularity. There often seems to be so little common ground that no lasting consensus can be achieved.

The sense of what is necessary and proper for the fulfillment of a satisfying human life, which the educated saw as a self-evident proposition in the eighteenth and nineteenth centuries, no longer seems to exist. Artists and writers insist that individual viewpoints, shaped by specific experience, are the only valid points of reference for creative work. The result is frequently an art from which unity of message, form, and technique has been eliminated. What remains often looks like chaos to the observer. What has happened? Why and how has this fragmentation, or incoherence, occurred? Is it profoundly harmful to our society or merely another mode of cultural expression, as legitimate and creative as any that preceded it?

The creative arts in the past century have been dominated by alienated individuals who are in conflict with their human environment. *Alienation* means to become a stranger and find oneself at odds with the values of your fellows or unable to communicate with them. This is hardly a new phenomenon among artists. Since the beginning of modern times, artists have often felt like outsiders in society, as many were, but in the past century this feeling has deepened and become more aggressively expressed. The early twentieth-century Dada movement repudiated all obligations to communicate intelligibly to the public. As its manifesto proudly stated, "Art is a private matter; the artist does it for himself; any work of art that can be understood is the product of a journalist."

The Dadaists were too extreme to be taken seriously by most people, but many serious artists also believed that the artist's first duty was always to be true to him- or herself. In practice, this has meant that in painting, fiction, poetry, and to a lesser extent music and sculpture, innovative artists frequently abandoned the forms and even the contents of the classical past. Meterless verse, abstract figures in painting and sculpture, music composed of equal parts silence and dissonance, and stream-of-consciousness narrative were the essence of their art to many of the most noted recent practitioners.

How did the previous high-culture audience react? Many found it all too confusing. Artists in all fields discovered that they had to choose between disproportionate sectors of the public when preparing their work. A dual-level audience had arisen: the elite who favored innovators although their art was perceived to be "difficult," and the much larger group that included those who visited museums to admire the portraits of a Rembrandt, went to concert halls to hear the works of Bach and Beethoven, and read poetry that they felt they could understand at first sight. Between the two groups and the artists that each supports, there was and is little communication or shared ground.

Much modern art makes a great many people uncomfortable. The temptation to dismiss the creators as baffling egocentrics or outright frauds is strong. Sometimes, no doubt, this suspicion is justified. The fine arts in our times have become in some instances a commodity like any other, exhibiting the usual marketing techniques of clever agents and sellers, but this is certainly not always the case. In the twentieth century, almost all of the arts in the West experienced a tremendous burst of creativity, such as has not been seen since the Renaissance. Let's look at a few common characteristics of this explosion and then at a few of the individual art forms exemplifying them.

## Modernism

Certain common features of recent Western art and culture can be summed up conveniently in the word **modernism**. It carries several implications, the foremost of which are as follows:

- *Form is emphasized at the expense of content.* Because many modern artists were convinced that even a sympathetic and knowledgeable audience could not uniformly comprehend what they were saying, they mini- mized the message (content) and gave full attention to the medium (form). This obsession with form led to novels that shifted narrators and time frame without warning; poetry that seemed much more concerned with the printed format than with the sense of the words; and sculpture that was entirely "abstract"—that is, unrecognizable in life—and given such a title as *Figure 19.*
- *A systematic and determined rejection of the classical models.* At no epoch of the past did artists so generally attempt to find new—perhaps shockingly new—ways to express themselves. Not only new techniques but also wholly new conceptions and philosophies of art were trotted out, following one another in rapid succession from the 1870s (painting), the 1890s (poetry), and the 1900s (music and dance) to the 1910s (literature and sculpture).
- *A conscious search for non-Western inspiration.* This was particularly true in the figurative arts—painting, sculpture, weaving, ceramics—in which East Asian and African and Polynesian forms had a great vogue.

### Modern Painting

Painting has frequently been the pathbreaker in times of change in the high culture. What the eye can see is universal, making painted pictures capable of reaching the largest audiences in the most straightforward fashion. In the 1870s, the **Impressionists** began the long march away from realism and toward abstraction. The Impressionists (working mainly in Paris, which remained the painting capital until the 1950s) were concerned not with realism, which they wanted to leave to the newly invented camera, but with the nature of light and color. In the 1880s and 1890s, center stage went to the **post-Impressionists**, who focused on mass and line and were daring innovators in their use of color. Several of them (Paul Cézanne, Claude Monet) were the pioneers of twentieth-century forms and are revered as the creators of modern classics in painting.

At the end of the nineteenth century and the first decade of the twentieth, cubism and abstract art appeared, again first in Paris. The key descriptor of this new school is "nonrepresentational": the painter makes little or no attempt to represent external reality as the eye sees it. Piet

Mondrian was perhaps the leading exponent of **abstractionism**, but the most influential figurative artist of the entire century was Pablo Picasso, a Spaniard who chose to live and work in France for most of his long and highly innovative life. (For more about Picasso and his work, see the Arts and Culture box.)

During the first decades of the twentieth century, expressionism and other, smaller schools emphasized the primacy of the emotions through line, color, and composition. After World War II, the Americans led by Jackson Pollock, Hans Koenigsberger, and others took the lead by combining pure abstraction and new ways of putting the paint on the canvas (sometimes by apparently random splattering). This **abstract expressionism** remained the chief form of avant-garde painting in the second half of the century, although it has a half-dozen competitors, including its diametrical opposite, a photographic neorealism. Many attempts to discover profundity in the commonplace and vulgar (pop art, op art) have also been made in the past fifty years—with limited success in the public.

Hans Namuth/Photo Researchers

**JACKSON POLLOCK, 1951.** The American painter, who was the founder and most noted exponent of abstract expressionism, charged his enormous canvases with raw energy. Splattering apparently random flecks from his brush onto the canvas, Pollock's work convinced most critics that it contained both form and content of genius.

## Modern Literature

In literature the departure from tradition is as sharply defined and uncompromising as it has been in painting. Novelists, playwrights, and especially poets have turned their backs on the models of narrative and description enshrined by the past. They have experimented with every conceivable aspect of their craft: grammar and meter, characterization, narrative flow, point of view, and even the very language. Some poets and novelists employ what seems almost a private vocabulary, which, like the Red Queen's in *Alice in Wonderland,* means "what I want it to mean."

The inevitable upshot of this fevered experimentation has again been the loss of much of the traditional audience. Modernist poetry, for example, demands so much effort to follow the poet's vision that it is exhausting to most casual readers. Although a poem by Delmore Schwartz may be in every "serious" anthology of twentieth-century verse, it is seldom quoted by lovers of poetry. Instead, their lists of favorites are likely to include any of several poems by Robert Frost. With their familiar English and adherence to traditional rules of poetic construction, Frost's verse seems easily understood by a mass audience.

The same is true of novels and novelists. In both style and content, some modern writing is so intent on giving voice to the writer's subjective viewpoints that the essential communication of ideas and events gets lost or is never attempted. This *fascination with the self,* at the expense of the reader, "turns off" a large part of the public from modernist fiction.

Two examples among hundreds may be found in the novels of the American Donald Barthelme (b. 1931) and the film scripts of the Frenchman Alain Resnais (b. 1922). Although praised highly by critics, their work is appreciated by only a select few who are willing to attempt the hard work of analysis they demand and who are not deterred by their deliberate obscurity. Time may reveal that Barthelme and Resnais are great artists, but most of the contemporary reading and filmgoing public seems content to remain happily ignorant of them and their work.

In some instances, the modernists have been rewarded by widespread recognition from the public as well as the critics. The artistry and originality of these authors are undeniable. James Joyce (1882–1941), Samuel Beckett (1906–1980), Marcel Proust (1871–1922), and Virginia Woolf (1882–1941) had the creative power to overcome old forms and break new ground. Joyce was the author of two novels that were immediately recognized as marvelously original works. *Ulysses* (1917) and *Finnegan's Wake* (1934) employed the "stream of consciousness" technique to a degree and with an effect never seen before. Joyce succeeded in portraying the ordinary life of an individual as

ARTS AND CULTURE

## Pablo Picasso (1881–1973)

Underwood and Underwood/Corbis

**Picasso.** The twentieth century's most influential artist.

**Rare indeed are the artists who can claim** to be the originators of an entirely new technical conception of their art. Rarer still are those who can make that claim and also be the creators of the two most important paintings of an entire century. Pablo Picasso, a Spaniard who lived most of his life in France, is that exception. In his technical innovation, his tremendously original imagination, and his versatility, he had no peers in the twentieth century.

Picasso studied in Paris in the early 1900s after a brief training in Barcelona. At that time innovators from every European country and the Americas were eagerly flocking there to join the many established painters, sculptors, and authors. From the earliest days of his boyhood, Picasso had known what he wished to do with his life. His pursuit of artistic excellence was single-minded and uncompromising from that period on.

Picasso's painting career went through several more or less distinct phases. In his first years, his so-called Blue Period, he focused on the melancholy lives of the urban poor, using predominantly blue tones. Later, during his Rose Period, which began in 1905, he used a lighter palette of colors to convey more carefree scenes, many taken from life in the circus. In 1907, Picasso's *Les Demoiselles d'Avignon* became a sensation, first among his fellow artists and then among the artistic public at large. *Les Demoiselles* was the first major work of cubism and the signal for an entirely new conception of how the artist might present external reality on canvas. In showing the distorted figures of three young girls, the painting reflected in vivid colors the impressions of African sculptures that Picasso and the rest of artistic Europe had recently experienced. The rigid mathematical basis of cubism led directly to the abstractionist style, which Picasso himself never joined but which inspired a generation of painter-innovators after World War I.

In the 1930s as the war clouds gathered, Picasso refused for years to involve himself directly with political affairs, but in 1937 he surprised the world with a second landmark work, the passionate mural *Guernica,* in memory of the agony of that small and previously unnoticed city that had been heavily bombed by Franco's planes in the current Spanish Civil War. A condemnation of fascist brutality and war, the huge painting was the twentieth century's most remarkable work of artistic propaganda. It is now located in the Museum of Modern Art in New York City.

Picasso settled after World War II in southern France with his third wife and devoted himself mainly to sculpture and ceramics. Among his best-known work in this period was the long series on the life of the character from Spanish literature, Don Quixote, and his faithful Sancho Panza. Picasso was through and through a Spanish artist but refused to return to his beloved Catalonia (the area around Barcelona) until the tyrant Franco was dead. That meant never, for Franco outlived the artist.

Picasso's genius lay in his ability to see through the conventional forms and beyond them. So strong was his influence that much of what the world calls modern painting is identified by the signature "Picasso." He was a master of line, and much of his postwar work was in graphics rather than paint. With a few strokes of the crayon or pen, he could bring a scene to the viewer complete in every essential. In the ten years after World War II, he lent his name and reputation to the communists. Like many others, his commitment to truth as he saw it led him to an almost childlike faith in the good intentions of those who pretended to agree with him.

### *Analyze and Interpret*

Do you think artists have an obligation to voice their protest or support of political activity, as leaders or molders of opinion? Or should they segregate their artistic lives entirely from their activities as citizens, if any?

experienced by his unconscious mind, as though relating a dream. *Finnegan's Wake* was too abstruse for the public (much of its effect came from a huge series of obscure puns), but *Ulysses* has become a modern classic.

Beckett's series of plays, written after World War II, were technically so inventive that they found an international audience despite their profound pessimism about humans and their fate. *Waiting for Godot* is his most famous work. Others include *Endgame* and *Krapp's Last Tape.* Beckett sees humans as unfortunate worms who sporadically delude themselves into believing that this life holds something besides disappointment and despair. It is a horrifyingly grim picture that this reclusive Irishman paints of humans and all their hopes.

Gianni Giansanti/Corbis Sygma

**SARTRE AND SIMONE DE BEAUVOIR.** These two intellectuals established an extraordinary partnership in both their professional and personal lives in the postwar era.

Proust's portraits of upper-class Parisians in the beginning of the twentieth century were important not for what he said but for the way he said it. Proust was a neurotic who lived almost entirely in a cork-lined retreat in his wealthy home, exercising his memory and his imagination to attempt a total recall of the details of life. It is a testament to his success that his multivolume novel *Remembrance of Things Past* is universally accorded a place among the three or four most influential fictional works of the first part of that century.

Woolf's fiction, also written in the early decades of the twentieth century, has been highly influential in both matters of style and content. *To the Lighthouse* and *Mrs. Dalloway,* both published in the 1920s, are her most significant works of fiction. She also wrote a pathbreaking feminist tract, *A Room of One's Own,* which has found much resonance in the last twenty-five years.

## Modern Philosophy

Philosophy has not been exempt from the profound changes in traditional thought that mark recent times in the West. Twentieth-century philosophical systems have been divided between those that seek a new basis for human freedom and those that deny freedom as a myth and insist on the essential meaninglessness of life. Much recent philosophy focuses on the role of language: how it is created and how it relates to material reality. Behind this interest is the conviction that the so-called spirit or soul has no existence other than a linguistic one; that is, because we talk about it, it exists.

The question of existence itself is the primary concern of **existentialism**, which has been perhaps the leading school of philosophy in this century. Existentialism, which originated in Europe, rejects the various higher meanings that religion or philosophers have attempted to find in human life. It demands that one accept the inherent pointlessness of life. At the same time, most existentialists, led by Jean-Paul Sartre (1905–1980), insist that humans are free to supply their own meaning, and in fact they *must* do so. Existentialism blossomed after World War II, when the anguish created by this second bloody conflict within a single generation seemed to spell the end of European and, perhaps, Western culture. Seen in historical perspective, existentialism may be understood as a reaction against the rather naïve optimism and faith in science as the great "fixer" of human problems that marked the late nineteenth century.

Like the arts and literature, twentieth-century philosophy was strongly affected by the uncertainty and cultural relativism that may be traced to Darwinian and Freudian theory, on the one side, and post-Newtonian physics, on the other (see Chapter 43). In the present day, most adherents of one philosophical school would not dare accuse their opponents in another school of heresy or attempt to silence them. No one, it seems, has that type of self-assurance any longer in this culture of probabilities and relative ethics. This relativism is the other side of the coin of tolerance and sensitivity to others' values that the twentieth century so espoused—or at least paid lip service to.

# POPULAR ARTS AND CULTURE

Popular, or low, culture has undergone an explosion in both variety and accessibility. The mass media (television, movies, paperbacks, radio, popular magazines, newspapers, tape and disc recordings) has never had such a large audience as in the late twentieth century. This audience transcends the political boundaries that previously fragmented and restricted it. New technology has been largely responsible for this explosion. Easily the most important at the moment are the vast reach of the Internet and the personal computer, but there have been important predecessors. At the outset of the twentieth century, two inventions were quickly converted to commercial entertainment: the motion picture and the radio. Both were products of the two decades just before World War I and were developed by Europeans and Americans working independently (Thomas Edison, Guglielmo Marconi, the Lumiere brothers, Lee De Forest). After the war, both came into their own as channels of mass communication.

## Movies

The movies (the more elegant term *cinema* was never accepted in the United States) were first shown in arcades and outdoors. The first narrative film was *The Great Train Robbery* (1903). New York City was the initial home of the motion-picture makers, and the American industry was to be the pacesetter of the world cinema for most of the century. By 1920, stars such as Charlie Chaplin, Buster Keaton, and Mary Pickford were well established. The studio system, whereby the film creators were financed and thus controlled by distant investors, was already in operation. This uneasy marriage of artistic creativity and hardheaded money making was to be the keynote of the international cinema and particularly of Hollywood, which replaced New York as the center of moviemaking in the United States during World War I. By 1927, the first talking movie was produced (Al Jolson in *The Jazz Singer*), and films were on the way to becoming the number-one entertainment medium of the world—a position they retained until the advent of television after World War II.

## Radio

Like the movies, radio emerged rapidly from the laboratory to become a commercial enterprise of major importance. The brilliant Italian experimenter Guglielmo Marconi was successful in transmitting signals through the air ("wireless") over long distances in 1901. Two years later, the invention of the vacuum tube enabled voice and music to be carried. The demands of military communications during World War I sped up radio transmission technology and improved receivers. The first commercial radio broadcasts began in the early 1920s. Within a few years, networks of broadcasting stations had been formed by the same combination of creative scientists and entrepreneurs as in the film industry.

In Europe and other parts of the world, the government normally controlled radio broadcasting. These governments saw in radio the same possibilities for influencing the citizenry that were inherent in the postal service and the telephone network. In the United States, however, radio was from the start a commercial venture, and the ever-present advertisements were a standard part of the radio-listening experience.

Radio and movies provided not only entrepreneurs but also politicians and cultural leaders with undreamed-of means of reaching a national audience. Many people in positions of power quickly recognized this potential. The use of both media for propaganda as well as commercial and educational purposes was one of the key breakthroughs in the manipulation of democratic societies. The Soviet and Nazi leaders both adeptly used film and radio in the 1930s and 1940s.

But it was probably in the extension of knowledge of what was happening in the world—the "news"—that the radio set and the movie screen made their greatest contributions to twentieth-century culture. The radio told and the movie newsreel showed your grandparents' generation what was going on outside their own cultural circles in a way that neither books nor newspapers could rival. Not only politics but also manners, fashion, humor, language, and education were intensely affected. In the interwar period, about two of every five adults went to a movie at least once a week in Britain and the United States. Never before had such a large percentage of the population participated in a single form of recreational activity except eating, drinking, and possibly sex.

## Music

Music for the masses came into its own in the twentieth century. The technology of Edison's phonograph and its lineal descendants the tape player, compact disc player, and laser were joined to forms of popular music that expressed a great deal more than the simple urge to sing and dance. Since the 1950s, various forms of rock-and-roll have captured the allegiance of much of the world's youth. The West's "youth revolt" of the late 1960s was a thoroughly international phenomenon, and its anthems were drawn equally from folk music and rock.

But rock was just the latest addition to a parade of musical types that drew from both European and African-American sources in the early twentieth century. The European sources included the artificial folk songs of the Broadway stage and the vaudeville halls. More important was the black contribution—jazz—the name given to that mix of gospel song, African rhythms, and erotic blues shouting that was popularized by black musicians in New Orleans and later in Memphis and Chicago. Once introduced into the mainstream white culture via traveling nightclub bands and early radio, jazz was cleaned up and tamed for middle-class consumption via phonographs.

The processing of folk songs and jazz into commercial products began with the "crooners" of the 1920s. It continued through the swing bands of the 1930s and 1940s, the beboppers and rock-and-roll of the 1950s, and the folk revival of the 1960s. Keeping close pace with the rise of stars such as Elvis Presley, The Beatles, The Rolling Stones, and The Supremes was the stream of mechanical innovations that made popular music an ever-present accompaniment to most of the rituals of life for Western people under age thirty. The high-fidelity stereo system, Walkman portable tape player, FM broadcasting technology, and automobile sound system are all part of this stream. Nowhere is the close and formative relation between technology and mass culture so clear as in the production, distribution, and consumption of popular music.

### Television

The powerful impressions left by radio and movies on the popular mind were equalled or even overshadowed, however, by those delivered by a post–World War II development—television. Invented by Americans and Britons in the early 1930s, TV came into commercial use only after the war. Already by 1950, television had replaced radio as the prime entertainer in the American home, and a few years later, it was threatening to drive the neighborhood movie theaters out of business. Left behind by the Americans at first, Europeans closed the television gap in the 1960s. As with other forms of mass media, the European governments monopolized the broadcasting studios until private commercial stations were permitted in the 1970s and 1980s.

More even than films, television shows have the immediacy and emotional power of a picture, especially when that picture is edited (that is, manipulated to give a particular effect) by a knowing hand. Television's takeover of news reporting on all levels—local, national, and international—is striking evidence of how deeply the flickering images of the small screen have penetrated into the world's life and thought. Most recently, even war in Iraq and Afghanistan has been captured by TV's cameras and fitted into its schedules. Newspapers, which were the chief news medium in the nineteenth century and the first half of the twentieth, are rapidly being converted into bulletin boards for local retail advertisers and human-interest storybooks. A newspaper cannot compete with television for quick, colorful reporting of what is happening around us or around the globe.

## Mass Culture and Its Critics

Between the high culture of the patrons of art museums, contributors to the Metropolitan Opera, and subscribers to the *New York Review of Books* and the low culture of the Elvis Presley cultists, readers of comic books, and fans of the National Football League exists a transition ground whose importance and nature are the subject of much debate. In a famous essay dating from the early 1960s, the critic Dwight MacDonald dubbed this large group of in-betweeners **Masscult**. MacDonald believed that Masscult was a disastrous phenomenon, representing the surrender of the higher to the lower echelon. He thought that the Masscult participants were rapidly losing the ability to tell the real from the phony and could not distinguish the art and music that came from an authentic artist from that generated by some advertising agency's robots. Better to have honest ignorance, he said, than the tasteless banality of a half-educated flock of pretenders. Authentic culture—the culture that historically has created the models and set the standards of the world civilizations—has always been an elitist phenomenon and always will be. Insofar as it becomes amassed, it declines in value.

Others are not so sure. They argue that Masscult has come about because of the unparalleled access to education that the Western nations, at least, have enjoyed since World War II; the cultural variety that the communications explosion of the late twentieth century produced; and the openness to experiment and toleration of artistic novelty. In their view, Masscult is a praiseworthy reflection of the lower classes' efforts to rise up the ladder of cultural taste. These observers do not deny that Masscult's

**Andy Warhol.** One of the iconic figures of popular art forms in the 1960s and 1970s was the painter, photographer, and filmmaker Andy Warhol. Photographed here with rock icon Mick Jagger in 1977, Warhol was the best-known leader of a peculiar band of "subterranean" artists who considered themselves rebels against mainstream culture but who were adept at profiting from it.

Lynn Goldsmith/Corbis

judgments and preferences are frequently misguided or manipulated. They merely ask when the masses of people ever before had a chance, such as they now enjoy, to educate themselves and refine their taste. In short, they ask MacDonald to give the Masscult time to mature and develop better taste and surer judgments. Then, the process will be reversed with the low culture being uplifted, rather than the high culture being made banal.

Whichever side of this argument one takes, it is beyond dispute that twentieth-century technology has provided most of the Western world's populations with access to cultural opportunities in an unprecedented fashion. Radio broadcasts, films, television, and cheap paperbacks have been followed by videocassettes and recorders, computer imagery, portable telephones, and a seemingly unending parade of home entertainment devices that quickly filter down in the market's hierarchy from luxury items to common expectations. In the latest epoch, access to the cybernetic reality of the Internet and the instantaneous communication possibilities of e-mail and wireless telephony have further foreshortened the distance that once separated all of us from one another. We are all now children of the electronic age, and the "technological imperative" that was once conceived of as operating only in the science labs has now transformed the consumer market: If it can be done, it will be done! And sold!

## Summary

The first half of the twentieth century saw an expansion of cultural opportunities for the masses that has no parallel. New means of communication across distance have joined with new leisure and widespread prosperity in the Western world to allow tremendously widened access to ideas, arts, and news. Commercial entertainment has become one of the chief industries of the modern age and reaches into every level of society with its wares of film, music, sports, and television shows.

Whether this trend is truly uplifting the formerly ignorant masses into the lofty realm of high culture is a topic of debate. Some think that the worthwhile has given way to the despicable. The high-culture purists have seen their position eroded by the modernist movement in the early part of the century, which permitted artists to forget their former obligation to communicate in easily comprehended ways. By doing so, much literature and pictorial art of a high-culture type were removed from the experience of ordinary people. They turned instead to the models of culture being supplied increasingly through commercially driven entertainment media. Such low-culture channels have always existed but could be ignored by the tastemakers until the twentieth century, when they have penetrated into so many levels of society as to become what some critics call Masscult, the legitimation of banality.

## Identification Terms

Test your knowledge of this chapter's key concepts by defining the following terms. If you can't recall the meaning of certain terms, refresh your memory by looking up the boldfaced term in the chapter, turning to the Glossary at the end of the book, or working with the flashcards that are available on the *World Civilizations* Companion Website **http://history.wadsworth.com/adler04**.

abstract expressionism
abstractionism
existentialism
Impressionists
Masscult
modernism
post-Impressionists

## Test Your Knowledge

Test your knowledge of this chapter by answering the following questions. Complete answers appear at the end of the book. You may also take this quiz interactively and find even more quiz questions on the *World Civilizations* Companion Website: **http://history.wadsworth.com/adler04**.

1. The art movement of the early twentieth century that attacked all accepted standards and forms was
   a. abstractionism.
   b. cubism.
   c. Dadaism.
   d. expressionism.
   e. conceptualism.
2. Modernism in twentieth-century arts implies, among other things, that
   a. the message of the artwork to its audience should be uniformly understood.
   b. content is more important than form.
   c. the artist cannot be held responsible for differing perceptions of his or her work.
   d. the artist has the duty to attempt something novel in his or her art.
   e. the artist has a responsibility to his or her viewer to make the meaning of the work clear.
3. A characteristic of twentieth-century Western art forms was
   a. a reverence for the great classical masters.
   b. a timidity in attempting to devise new forms.
   c. an interest in non-Western ideas and forms.
   d. an obsession with propagandizing the audience.
   e. a desire to bring art to the masses.
4. Abstract painting seeks to project
   a. a photographic vision of external objects.
   b. a blueprint for understanding reality.
   c. an internal mood or feeling divorced from external imagery.
   d. a self-portrait of the artist.
   e. a realistic image of the artist's vision about a particular event.
5. "Stream of consciousness" in prose was most memorably employed by
   a. James Joyce.
   b. Samuel Beckett.
   c. Jean-Paul Sartre.
   d. Sigmund Freud.
   e. Leo Tolstoy.
6. The convinced existentialist believes that
   a. life is hardly worth living, as it is devoid of all values.
   b. values are created for others by a handful of strong individuals.
   c. each age creates its own moral values.
   d. each individual must create his or her own values.
   e. there is no such thing as values.
7. Virginia Woolf's *A Room of One's Own* has been praised as a ________ work.
   a. historiographic
   b. psychoanalytic
   c. philosophical
   d. feminist
   e. sociological
8. The greatest contribution of the radio and motion picture industries in their early years was
   a. introducing audiences to new products.
   b. providing a forum for political campaigns.
   c. providing escapist entertainment.
   d. allowing governments to explain their programs to the general public.
   e. informing the general public about news events taking place throughout the world.
9. Popular music in the mid- and late twentieth century
   a. has been dominated by non-Westerners.
   b. has been much affected by technology.
   c. is less important to general culture than it has been in the past.
   d. is more limited to certain ethnic groups than before.
   e. has polarized the world rather than bringing people together.
10. Which of the following would *not* be considered a good example of Masscult?
   a. A radio comedy broadcast
   b. A monument to Beethoven
   c. A *People* magazine feature on a new art gallery
   d. A television program on interior decorating
   e. An Internet discussion board whose topic is the Impressionist artists

## InfoTrac College Edition

Visit the source collections at

**http://infotrac.thomsonlearning.com**

and use the Search function with the following key terms:

modernism existentialism

## Wadsworth History Website Resources

Visit the World History Resource Center at **http://history.wadsworth.com/world** for a wealth of general resources, and the *World Civilizations* Companion Website at **http://history.wadsworth.com/adler04** for resources specific to this textbook.

## HistoryNow

Enter *HistoryNow* using the access card that is available for *World Civilizations*. *HistoryNow* will assist you in understanding the content in this chapter with lesson plans generated for your needs.

*We are eyeball to eyeball . . . and I think the other fellow just blinked.*
U.S. Secretary of State Dean Rusk, October 1962

# 49 Superpower Rivalry and the European Recovery

| | |
|---|---|
| 1947 | Marshall Plan and Truman Doctrine |
| 1948–1949 | Blockade of Berlin/NATO and Warsaw Pact |
| 1950s | Western European economic recovery/ Stalinization of eastern Europe |
| 1950–1953 | Korean War |
| 1957 | Treaty of Rome establishes European Economic Community (EEC) |
| 1961 | Berlin Wall |
| 1962 | Cuban Missile Crisis |
| 1970s | Détente in Cold War |
| 1979 | Soviet invasion of Afghanistan |



As World War II ended, the two great victorious powers were becoming increasingly suspicious of each other's intentions. Leadership in the Western world was passing to the United States from Britain and France for the indefinite future. In the East, Stalin's Union of Soviet Socialist Republics (USSR) was the engine of a drive to make the world over according to Marx. The two superpowers would have to find a way to settle their differences peaceably or plunge the world into atomic conflict that would leave both in smoking ruins. For the two decades after 1945, the question of atomic war overshadowed everything else in world affairs and dictated the terms of all international settlements.

The Cold War became the stage on which the other vast drama of postwar diplomacy was played: the ending, forcible or peaceable, of the colonial system in the non-Western world. The links between the two struggles were many. In those same decades (1945–1965), Europe staged a remarkable recovery from both the material and the spiritual damages of war. Although many had almost written off Europe as a loss, the nations in the noncommunist two-thirds of Europe were exceeding prewar levels of production as early as 1950. In the next thirty years, they succeeded in progressing far down the road to economic unity, and the ancient hopes of political unification looked increasingly attainable.

## Conflict in the Postwar Generation

The hostility between the United States and the Soviet Union had both proximate and remote causes. We briefly reviewed the immediate causes in Chapter 47: the Soviets' insistence on "friendly" regimes along the western borders of their country and the arguments over the treatment of postwar Germany and the defeated Nazis. But these disputes were only specific reflections of the broader, more remote causes: the friction between two militarily powerful states, each of which had a tradition of strong nationalism and was convinced its politics and social organization were based on an exclusive truth. The Russian communists (who were at all times the directing force within the Soviet Union) believed that in Stalin's version of Marxism they had found the ultimate answers to the problem of making humans happy on Earth. The Americans thought their forebears had produced, and they had maintained, a political and economic system that reflected the justified aspirations of all right-thinking people everywhere. The war against fascism had briefly brought these two nations into the same political bed. Now that the war was won, their latent ideological antagonism must inevitably make itself apparent. (See the Law and Government box on "The Iron Curtain.")

## The Division of Europe

Both superpowers realized that control of Germany meant control of most of Europe. The focus of conflict soon shifted from the elections and governments of the eastern European countries (which were clearly within the Russian zone of dominion) to defeated Germany. Germany was divided into originally three and then four occupation zones: Russian, American, British, and French. Already in 1946, arguments over industrial reparations from Germany had broken out. The Russians confiscated everything movable in their zone, shipping it back to the badly wounded USSR, while the Americans, British, and French soon decided that stripping Germany of its industrial capacity would only bring on political and social chaos and possibly a communist revolution.

To counter the menace of Soviet expansion and to speed up the still slow recovery, in the summer of 1947, U.S. secretary of state General George Marshall put forth the **Marshall Plan** for reconstruction of the European economy. It proved to be one of the most successful foreign policy initiatives ever undertaken and was largely responsible for the beginning of the European recovery.

The **Truman Doctrine** was also announced in 1947. Named for the then-president, it committed the United States to defend governments throughout the world when they were threatened by communist inspired subversion. This policy was a historic departure from the traditional U.S. position of refusing the "entangling alliances" warned against long ago by George Washington.

LAW AND GOVERNMENT

### The Iron Curtain

IN THE SPRING OF 1946, Winston Churchill, just retired by the voters from his job as British wartime prime minister, visited the United States as a guest of President Harry Truman. In Westminster, Missouri, he gave a speech that caught the attention of the whole world and gave the phrase "Iron Curtain" to the language. His purposes were to alert the U.S. government and public to what was happening in Soviet-controlled eastern Europe and to assure a united stand against it.

> A shadow has fallen upon the scenes so lately lighted by the Allied victory. Nobody knows what Soviet Russia and its Communist international organization intends to do in the immediate future, or what are the limits, if any, to their expansionist and proselytizing tendencies. . . . From Stettin in the Baltic to Trieste in the Adriatic,* an iron curtain has descended across the Continent. Behind that line lie all the capitals of the ancient states of Central and eastern Europe. Warsaw, Berlin, Prague, Vienna, Budapest, Belgrade, Bucharest and Sofia, all these famous cities and the populations around them lie in what I must call the Soviet sphere, and all are subject in one form or another, not only to Soviet influence but to a very high and, in many cases, increasing measure of control from Moscow. . . . The Communist parties, which were very small in all these Eastern States of Europe, have been raised to pre-eminence and power far beyond their numbers and are seeking everywhere to obtain totalitarian control.
>
> I do not believe that Soviet Russia desires war. What they desire are the fruits of war and the indefinite expansion of their power and doctrines. . . . Our difficulties and dangers will not be removed by closing our eyes to them. They will not be removed by mere waiting to see what happens; nor will they be removed by a policy of appeasement. What is needed is a settlement, and the longer this is delayed, the more difficult it will be and the greater our dangers will become.

*A line drawn between these two cities would enclose to its east the areas of Europe recently taken by the Red Army and made into Soviet satellites.

#### Analyze and Interpret

How might the situation described by Churchill have been expected? To what extent might the United States and Britain have been complicit in the division of Europe?

**HistoryNow™**

***To read the entire text of Churchill's speech, "The Sinews of Peace," as well as Joseph Stalin's reply, point your browser to the documents area of HistoryNow.***

**The Nuremberg Trial, 1946.** Shortly after the German surrender, the Allies put several leading Nazis on trial for "crimes against humanity." The months-long trial was presided over by judges from Russia, the United States, Britain, and France. It resulted in the convictions of all but three of the defendants, who were sentenced to varying terms in prison or to death. Hermann Göring, the number-two Nazi (far left, first row), cheated the hangman by taking cyanide.

Corbis

The acceptance of the policy by the U.S. Congress and the public indicated that a decisive change in attitude had taken place since Woodrow Wilson's League of Nations was rejected in 1919. The United States was now prepared, however reluctantly, to shoulder the burdens of what was soon termed "free world" leadership.

The Soviet blockade of Berlin in 1948 (see Chapter 47) was decisive in showing there was no hope of reviving the wartime alliance and that Stalin was committed to expanding communism into the European heartland. The key to containment of this threat was a West-oriented Germany. Conjured from the three Western zones in September 1949, West Germany (*Bundesrepublik Deutschland*) was larger and more powerful than its Russian-created counterpart, the Deutsche Demokratische Republik, or East Germany, which came into existence a few weeks later.

The North Atlantic Treaty Organization (**NATO**) was similarly an outgrowth of the East–West struggle. Created in April 1949, it was Washington's solution to the need for an international military organ dedicated to stopping the spread of communism. It originally counted twelve western European and North American members—later increased to fifteen—who pledged to come to the aid of one another if attacked. The Soviet answer quickly came with the **Warsaw Pact**, which made the communist governments of eastern Europe military allies. The pact merely formalized what had been true since the series of Marxist takeovers in 1945–1948.

Not only Germany but now all of Europe was thus divided into two enemy blocs, along with a handful of militarily insignificant neutrals (Austria, Finland, Spain, Sweden, and Switzerland). (See Map 49.1.) The situation

**The Berlin Airlift.** After Stalin blocked all surface routes into West Berlin, the Allies responded by starting an airlift of supplies from their occupation zones in western Germany into the isolated city. Beginning in June 1948, the airlift continued for eleven months until the Soviets allowed overland access again, tacitly admitting defeat.

Bettmann/Corbis

whereby the Continent was more or less at the military mercy of two non-European powers, Russia and the United States, was a definite novelty in history. In the late 1940s and through the 1950s, it appeared that whatever the Europeans might be able to do about their own prosperity, they would remain the junior partners of outside powers in military affairs and diplomacy.

## Grudging Coexistence

In 1950, the **Korean War** broke out when South Korea, a U.S. satellite, was invaded by North Korea, a Soviet satellite. Within a year, the conflict had become an international war, with the United States providing the leadership in the South and the Chinese (*not* the Soviets) coming to the aid of their hard-pressed North Korean allies. The fighting ended in deadlock, and a truce was finally signed in 1953 (which still exists).

Josef Stalin also died in that year, and with him died the most aggressive phase of the Cold War. His successors, however fanatical their communist belief, were never so given to paranoia as Stalin had been in his later years. After a behind-the-scenes power struggle, Nikita Khrushchev (1894–1971) emerged as Stalin's successor, chief of the Communist Party and the government. Khrushchev, the son of peasants, was very different from the secretive, mysterious Stalin. Although just as convinced that Marxism must inevitably triumph in the whole world, he was

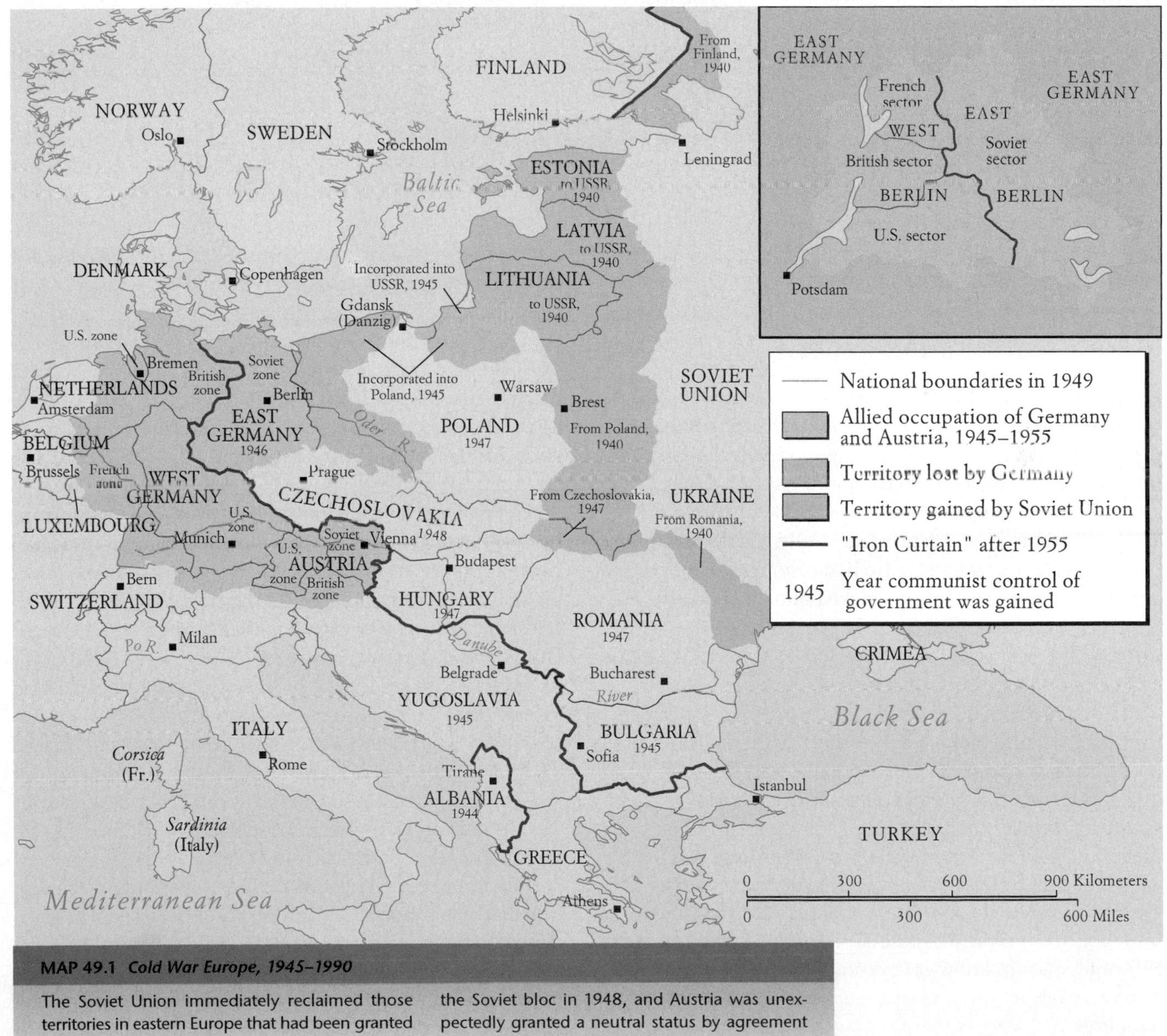


**MAP 49.1** *Cold War Europe, 1945–1990*

The Soviet Union immediately reclaimed those territories in eastern Europe that had been granted to it by the Nonaggression Pact of 1939 and added half of East Prussia. Yugoslavia was thrust from the Soviet bloc in 1948, and Austria was unexpectedly granted a neutral status by agreement among the occupying nations in 1955. Germany remained divided until the autumn of 1990.

generally more open in his dealings with the West and less menacing. He said he believed in peaceful coexistence with the West, and he challenged the West to engage in economic rather than military competition—a challenge that would turn into a bad joke for the Russians later.

Khrushchev was not about to give up what World War II had brought to the Soviet Union or to release the eastern Europeans from their bonds to communism, however. In 1956, when the Hungarians rose up in revolt against their highly unpopular satellite government, he sent Soviet tanks to restore order and keep Hungary firmly within the Soviet orbit. The failure of the NATO powers to take any action made it clear that the West had accepted the Soviet-style regimes in eastern Europe, however much it might denounce their illegality and repression. Since 1949, the Russians possessed their own atomic weaponry, and in the shadow of the mushroom cloud, the *pax Sovietica* (Soviet peace) was deemed acceptable.

**BUDAPEST, 1956.** The fierceness of the resistance to the Russian invasion is shown in the face of this female resistance fighter. Many of the Hungarian "freedom fighters" fled to sanctuary in western Europe or the United States.



## *From Cuban Missiles to NATO's Decline*

The Cold War was sharpened with the sudden erection of the **Berlin Wall** in 1961 by the East Germans to prevent the steady outflow of political refugees. The success of this unparalleled division of a city and a nation perhaps inspired Khrushchev to make an unexpected gamble in an attempt to help his Cuban Marxist ally, Fidel Castro, in 1962. Three years earlier, Castro had conquered Cuba with a motley army of insurgents, kicked out the corrupt government, and then declared his allegiance to Marxism. An abortive U.S.-sponsored invasion at the Bay of Pigs had been a total failure. Fearing another attempt, Castro asked the Russians for military help. Khrushchev decided to install intermediate-range rockets with nuclear warheads, and the project was well under way when it was discovered by U.S. aerial surveillance over Cuba.

After a few days of extreme tension, the Soviets backed down and removed their weapons when presented with an ultimatum by President John F. Kennedy. Kennedy allowed Khrushchev some room for maneuver by making some concessions on U.S. bases in Asia, along with a promise not to attempt another invasion. Both sides could thus claim to have achieved their goals when the missiles were withdrawn.

The world fright over the **Cuban Missile Crisis** stimulated the nuclear powers to make more serious efforts to reduce the level of hostility (see the Law and Government box on this topic). In 1963, they signed the **Nuclear Test Ban**, limiting the testing of atomic weapons in the atmosphere. Under the new leadership of Willy Brandt, the West German government after years of resistance moved to recognize the postwar borders to its east and thus to establish better relations with its communist neighbors and with the Soviet Union. This German ***Ostpolitik*** (Eastern policy) was a key point in reducing tensions in Europe.

By the mid-1960s, then, the Cold War was less confrontational. The ideology of communist revolution had become a minor part of the Soviets' baggage in international affairs; it had been replaced by the predictable, selfish interest of a great power with imperialist motives. The Soviet Union was becoming a conservative state—a stable factor in world politics—despite its revolutionary slogans. The best evidence of this shift was the failure of the Soviets to provide military support for the communist side in the Vietnam conflict during the later 1960s (see Chapter 51).

The progress of **détente** (relaxation) between the Soviet Union and the West was marred but not derailed by the Soviet invasion of Czechoslovakia in 1968, when that nation attempted to oust its Stalinist overlords through a peaceful revolution. The United States was again not inclined to involve NATO in this "internal matter," and communist rule was reimposed without bloodshed. Coming in a year when many Western nations experienced explosive internal frictions between government and citizens, the Czechs' misfortunes were soon forgotten in the West.

## Cuban Missiles in 1962

**IN THE FALL OF 1962,** the stunning discovery that the Soviets had secretly deployed nuclear-tipped intermediate-range missiles in Castro's Cuba ignited the most dangerous incident in the generation-long Cold War. Aerial photography of the island during September and October gradually confirmed that Russian engineers were building missile launch sites and bringing in a large number of missiles by ship. If fired, the missiles already transported could destroy much of the eastern United States.

Faced with the cruelest dilemma of any postwar presidency, John F. Kennedy had to frame a response that was absolutely firm yet restrained and not provocative. A nuclear war might well have been the price of miscalculation. After the Soviets were quietly put on notice that Washington was aware of what was going on, and they had not responded, Kennedy decided it was necessary to "go public" with the news. For some days, the White House continued the agonizing search for the most unambiguous wording, designed to put maximum pressure on the Soviet leader Nikita Khrushchev while giving him an opportunity to retreat without losing face. On October 22, Kennedy made a televised address to a nervous nation and world:

> Good evening, my fellow citizens.
>
> This government, as promised, has maintained the closest surveillance of the Soviet military build-up on the island of Cuba. Within the past week, unmistakable evidence has established the fact that a series of offensive missile sites are now in preparation on that imprisoned island. . . .
>
> This secret, swift, and extraordinary build-up of communist missiles—in an area well known to have a special and historical relationship with the United States and the nations of the Western hemisphere—in violation of Soviet assurances, and in defiance of American and hemispheric policy—this sudden, clandestine decision to station strategic weapons for the first time outside Soviet soil is a deliberately provocative and unjustified change in the status quo which cannot be accepted by this country if our courage and our commitments are ever to be trusted again by either friend or foe.
>
> . . . All ships of any kind bound for Cuba from whatever nation or port will, if found to contain cargoes of offensive weapons, be turned back.
>
> . . . It shall be the policy of this nation to regard any nuclear missile launched from Cuba against any nation in the Western hemisphere as an attack by the Soviet Union on the United States, requiring a full retaliatory response upon the Soviet Union.
>
> . . . I call upon Chairman Khrushchev to halt and eliminate this clandestine, reckless, and provocative threat to world peace, and to stable relations between the two nations. . . .

After a few horribly tense days, the Russians agreed to dismantle and withdraw their missiles in return for a face-saving pledge on Kennedy's part that the United States would not attempt another invasion of Castro's island. The crisis was over.

### *Analyze and Interpret*

What factors might have prompted Soviet Premier Nikita Khrushchev to arm Cuba this way? Do you think it was a deliberate provocation? How might Khrushchev have viewed the situation?

Source: Elie Abel, *The Cuban Missile Crisis* (Philadelphia: Lippincott, 1966).

**History Now™**

***To read the entire text of Kennedy's speech, point your browser to the documents area of HistoryNow.***

The NATO alliance was not so close-knit by this time. Under war hero General Charles de Gaulle, France had no sympathy for what it considered the American obsession about the Soviets. The bombastic Khrushchev had been replaced in 1964 by a tight group of *apparatchiks* headed by Leonid Brezhnev (1906–1982), who showed little commitment to any type of revolution or foreign policy gambles. De Gaulle and many others thought western Europe was no longer seriously threatened by violent communist intervention, and France withdrew its military from NATO command in 1962.

The decline of NATO reflected the shift from foreign to domestic policy issues that preoccupied European leaders in the 1960s. Generated originally by student discontent with the outmoded educational and cultural institutions carried over from the prewar era, protests of every type (the "youth revolt") soon erupted against the policies and politics of governments and other forms of traditional authority. These protests—often violent—reached a peak in 1968, when European disaffection with NATO support of the U.S. war in Vietnam and with the continuing arms race between the East and West reached tidal wave proportions. Not only was the defense against a fading Marxism becoming superfluous, but to European minds, there were far more urgent and profitable areas for their governments to pursue.

## Europe's Economic Recovery

Cast into the shadows by the disasters of the first half of the century, Europe had reemerged by the last quarter of the twentieth century as the most important locale of technical, financial, and commercial power in the world. The word *renaissance* is not too strong to use in describing the developments in western Europe since 1945. In that year, the Continent was an economic ruin for the most part, and two external powers were contesting for supremacy over what was left intact. By 1965, the western European countries had surpassed every measure of prewar prosperity and were rapidly regaining independence of action in politics.

### Factors Promoting Prosperity

What had happened to encourage this rebirth? Five factors in particular can be identified:

1. *Marshall Plan aid* was remarkably successful in restarting the stalled economies of both the former enemies and the allies. For five years (1947–1951), Austria, West Germany, France, Britain, Italy, and others benefited from this fund of U.S. dollars available for loan. The conditions imposed by supervisory agencies ensured a new spirit of collaboration not only between governments but also between government and employers for the benefit of the general public.
2. *Social reforms* were enacted immediately after the war to provide benefits for ordinary citizens that they had long sought. Pensions for all, universal medical insurance, family allowances, paid vacations, paid schooling, and other changes all gave the working classes a new sense of being part of the process. Now they felt they had a stake in the success of their country.
3. *Effective national planning* provided intelligent direction for the economy without eliminating individual enterprise and its profit reward. The "mixed economy"—with some industries and financial institutions directly controlled by the government, some totally private, and many in between—came to be the rule from Scandinavia to Portugal.
4. *A large, willing labor pool* in most countries allowed employers and entrepreneurs to expand at will when they saw opportunities. The unions, which had generally opposed employers as a matter of principle in the prewar era, now cooperated because socially conscious politicians protected and expanded their rights to a point where they now had an important voice in management.
5. *Free trade was made general.* The tariff, quota, and license barriers of the 1930s were gradually junked among the NATO countries; the various national currencies were made easily convertible and transferable; and international investment—much from the United States—was simplified and directly encouraged.

For these reasons, the growth of the western European economies was little short of sensational after the immediate postwar years. West Germany led the way in these "economic miracles" of the 1950s, but France, Italy, and the Benelux nations (Belgium, Luxembourg, and the Netherlands) were close behind. Only Britain did not do well because of an overly tradition-bound mentality and the breakup of the Commonwealth trading bloc that had long given British industry a false sense of security from competition. The *average* rate of growth in western European gross national product during 1948–1972 was approximately 4.5 percent per annum—an unbelievable achievement over a full quarter-century. Some nations did much better, and no recessions or business crises occurred.

The United States promoted much of this economic development by pouring in new capital first through the Marshall Plan and then much more through private investment by U.S. companies. By the 1960s, many Euro-

Hulton-Deutsch Collection/Corbis

**Volkswagen Assembly Line.** This plant, a frequent target of Allied bombers, led the way into mass production of cheap automotive transport for millions of European consumers.

peans were becoming concerned that their economies were being tied too closely to the United States or that Europe had become a kind of voluntary satellite to the Colossus across the Atlantic.

In retrospect, it is clear that the early 1960s represented the apex of American economic influence and political power in Europe. Subsequently, the intervention in Vietnam combined with the erosion of the dollar's value to weaken U.S. moral and financial prestige. President Richard M. Nixon's reluctant decision to allow the dollar to find its own level in the international gold market (1971) immediately demonstrated that the U.S. currency had become overvalued, and the Swiss franc and the German mark began to rise steadily against it. The financial event dramatized the more general economic changes that had been taking place under the surface, bringing Europe collectively back into a status of balance with the United States (and far overshadowing the Soviet Union).

### European Unity

As the economies of the various western European states recovered and then boomed in the 1950s, the old dream of supranational union quickly took on new life. For a couple of generations, some Europeans had looked to the day when the nations would give way to some kind of federation (with or without a powerful central organ). Now at the end of a gruesome war that had been caused, at least in part, by German and French enmity, these visionaries saw their best opportunity ever. With the strong backing of the United States—a successful federation—they would turn Europe into a new and peaceable political organism.

The main actors in this movement were the leaders of the Christian Democratic parties in Italy, France, Belgium, and West Germany. These middle-of-the-road Catholic parties had become the leading political forces in their countries immediately after the war. Their leaders in the early 1950s were gifted men, such as Alcide de Gasperi in Italy, Konrad Adenauer in West Germany, and Robert Schuman in France. They shared a consensus on future politics for the Continent. They believed that inter-European wars were an absolute disaster and must be avoided through political controls over each nation by some type of international group. Being realists, they thought that the best way to form this political association was to create economic ties among the potential members, which would grow so strong and all-embracing that an individual government could not logically consider waging war against its partners. First would come the economic bonds, then the social, and eventually the political ones.

In chronological order, the most important steps in this process of unifying western Europe (communist Europe was for obvious reasons a hostile bystander until the 1990s) were the following:

- 1947: The founding of the *Organization for European Economic Cooperation (OEEC)*. The OEEC was the supervisory arm of the Marshall Plan aid to Europe.
- 1951: The founding of the *European Coal and Steel Community.* France, West Germany, the Benelux nations, and Italy agreed to subordinate their individual needs in coal and steel to a supranational council. The system worked splendidly, and the six countries formed the nucleus of the Common Market of Europe.
- 1957: The **Treaty of Rome**, the founding charter of the **European Economic Community (EEC)**. The EEC was the fundamental organ for European unity in the past forty years, and the current European Union evolved from it. The EEC is responsible for the *Common Market,* which now embraces most of Europe's countries in a single, nondiscriminatory trading system.

  The EEC was meant to become the vehicle by which Europe would be drawn into social as well as economic integration. It has largely achieved these aims for its original twelve members, which have now expanded to twenty-five.
- 1992: The **Maastricht Treaty**. This treaty gave extensive powers to the European Parliament (created in 1957 by the Treaty of Rome) and facilitated economic and financial intercourse among the member states.

The name of the organization (headquartered in Brussels) that supervises these affairs is now simply the *European Union (EU)*. By 1998, labor, money, credit, raw materials and manufactures, communications, and personal travel flowed across the national boundaries of fifteen European states with few, if any, restrictions. In 2002, a single, unified currency, the *euro,* went into effect. All European states, except traditionally neutral Switzerland, have joined or are candidates to join the EU. Several of the former communist states have applied for membership. Ten joined on May 1, 2004: Cyprus, Czech Republic, Estonia, Hungary, Latvia, Lithuania, Malta, Poland, Slovakia, and Slovenia. Even without those states and the former Soviet Union, the EU now contains the largest, richest single market in the world—more than 400 million consumers.

## THE COMMUNIST BLOC, 1947–1980

Eastern Europe (that is, Poland, Hungary, the Czech and Slovak Republics, Romania, former Yugoslavia, Bulgaria, and Albania), where the communists took over after World War II, developed very differently. Here, the orthodox Marxist program was put into effect, following the lead of the Soviet Union. For several years, the development of heavy industry and transportation was the number-one priority. Labor and capital were placed into heavy industry at the expense of agriculture and all consumer goods.

This Stalinist phase lasted from the late 1940s to the mid-1950s. As in the Soviet Union, it resulted in a huge increase in industrial capacities and the partial industrialization of these previously backward, peasant economies. Urban areas in particular grew by leaps and bounds as the abundant excess labor of the rural areas was siphoned off by the demand for workers in the new industry. As in Soviet Central Asia a generation earlier, whole new towns sprouted out of the fields, built around the new steel plant or the new chemical complex. Agriculture was collectivized and then relegated to permanent stepchild status in the budget.

After Stalin's death in 1953, somewhat more attention was paid to the consumer's needs, although the standard of living in communist Europe lagged far behind that in western Europe at all times. Khrushchev, Stalin's successor, summed up the period between 1955 and 1970 when he called it "goulash communism," communism that would put some meat in the pot. By the early 1960s, it was possible for people with professions or skills—and perhaps with good Communist Party connections—to live fairly comfortably and to hope for a better future still for their children.

Salaries and wages were very low by Western standards, but medical care and education at all levels were free, and rents and food prices were low. In this way, the communist governments more or less satisfied a large proportion of their subjects economically, especially those who had been on the lower end of the social ladder in precommunist days.

In the 1970s, however, in one communist-ruled country after another, the economic advance halted and went into reverse as far as most consumers were concerned. The Marxist "command economy," which was always struggling with major defects, now showed increasing signs of breaking down altogether. Workers' discontents radically increased, and the governments' attempts to placate them with concessions backfired. As periodicals and television reception from the West were legalized and Western tourism increased, eastern Europeans had a better opportunity to see how miserably they fared in contrast to their Western counterparts.

The "technology gap" was growing more rapidly than ever before to the huge disadvantage of the communists, not only in international economics but also at home. The average man in Warsaw, Budapest, or Moscow recognized how far behind his society was and how hopeless its chances of catching up were. And the average working woman was rapidly tiring of the dubious benefits that communism had given her: a double task inside and outside the home, lower pay than males and "glass ceilings" in her work, declining health care, and other handicaps in both public and private life. In the face of this rising wave of discontent, the rigid old men who were in charge of the Communist Party and government in all of the eastern European communist lands were paralyzed. They simply did not know what to do, short of abandoning the system to which they had devoted their lives and that had treated *them,* at least, quite well. As the 1970s became the 1980s, all of the European communist countries drifted and stagnated at the top, while the steam was building up below. And, of course, the safety valve of protest—democratic politics and free elections—did not exist. We take up subsequent developments in Chapter 55.

## Summary

The field of ruins that was Europe in 1945 gave birth to new economic and political life in a surprisingly short time. With U.S. aid, but mainly by their own determination and energy, the western Europeans came back strongly and created a stable, prosperous economy by the 1960s. Progress in economic unity gave strong encouragement to hopes of eventual sociopolitical integration of the European heartland.

During the same two postwar decades, the Cold War waxed and waned in accord with U.S. and Soviet initiatives and gambles such as the Berlin blockade. So long as Josef Stalin lived, it seemed impossible to find an accommodation that would take the world out from under the atomic mushroom cloud. His successor, Nikita Khrushchev, proved more flexible despite erecting the Berlin Wall in 1961 and the missile adventure in Cuba in 1962. Peaceful coexistence became the slogan of the day, leading to a considerable relaxation in East–West relations by the mid-1960s.

Internally, the eastern European communist states went through a Stalinist phase of heavy industrial development that transformed these peasant economies into modern, urban-based ones. But the industrial development was not matched by an increase in living standards, and the previous gap between East and West in this respect grew steadily larger in the 1970s. By the early 1980s, the slowdown in the chase for prosperity was noticeable everywhere in the Soviet bloc, and discontent was rising.

## Identification Terms

Test your knowledge of this chapter's key concepts by defining the following terms. If you can't recall the meaning of certain terms, refresh your memory by looking up the boldfaced term in the chapter, turning to the Glossary at the end of the book, or working with the flashcards that are available on the *World Civilizations* Companion Website **http://history.wadsworth.com/adler04**.

Berlin Wall
Cuban Missile Crisis
détente
European Economic Community (EEC)
Korean War
Maastricht Treaty
Marshall Plan
NATO
Nuclear Test Ban
*Ostpolitik*
Treaty of Rome
Truman Doctrine
Warsaw Pact

## Test Your Knowledge

Test your knowledge of this chapter by answering the following questions. Complete answers appear at the end of the book. You may also take this quiz interactively and find even more quiz questions on the *World Civilizations* Companion Website: **http://history.wadsworth.com/adler04**.

1. The most dangerous phase of the Cold War's early period (1946–1950) was
   a. the Soviet attempt to blockade access to West Berlin.
   b. the Soviet decision to assist North Korea's invasion of South Korea.
   c. the arguments over proper operation of the military government in Berlin.
   d. the Western Allies' attempt to get a democratic government in Poland.
   e. the Soviet construction of the Berlin Wall.
2. Khrushchev emerged as successor to Stalin in the Soviet Union
   a. from the public election held in 1954.
   b. after much backstage maneuvering.
   c. on a platform of anti-Stalinism and more democracy in the Communist Party of the Soviet Union.
   d. because of his wide popular appeal to Russians.
   e. because there was no one who could provide a viable alternative to him.
3. Khrushchev may have been inspired to place nuclear missiles in Cuba by
   a. Fidel Castro's imposition of a communist government there.
   b. the success of the Berlin blockade.
   c. the failed Bay of Pigs invasion.
   d. his admiration for Castro.
   e. the success of the Berlin Wall.
4. What is the correct chronology of these events?
   a. Berlin Wall erection, Berlin blockade, Cuban Missile Crisis, Korean War
   b. Berlin blockade, Korean War, Berlin Wall erection, Cuban Missile Crisis
   c. Korean War, Berlin blockade, Berlin Wall erection, Cuban Missile Crisis
   d. Korean War, Cuban Missile Crisis, Berlin blockade, Berlin Wall erection
   e. Berlin blockade, Cuban Missile Crisis, Berlin Wall erection, Korean War
5. General Charles de Gaulle was
   a. the United States' most dedicated ally in NATO.
   b. the founder of the Free French movement in World War II.
   c. the leader of a coup against the civil government in the 1960s.
   d. the supreme commander of French forces during the early months of World War II.
   e. the president of France for three decades.
6. The economic "miracle" of West Germany during the 1950s was founded on
   a. a mixed state and private economy.
   b. free-market capitalism with few restrictions.
   c. the decision to create a model welfare state.
   d. extensive imports from Britain and the United States.
   e. a tremendous amount of financial donations from the United States and neighboring western European countries.
7. Early postwar leadership in western Europe was generally held by
   a. socialist parties that severed ties with the communists.
   b. coalitions of communists and socialists.
   c. moderate conservatives in the Christian Democratic parties.
   d. strong conservatives rejecting all aspects of socialism.
   e. strong coalitions between conservatives and labor groups.

8. The Common Market in Europe was originated by
   a. the Treaty of Versailles in 1919.
   b. the wartime Alliance of the United States, Britain, and the Soviet Union.
   c. the NATO treaty in 1949.
   d. the Treaty of Rome in 1957.
   e. the union of Europe's steel and coal companies.
9. During the early years of communism in Eastern Europe, the economic emphasis was on
   a. consumer goods.
   b. a military buildup.
   c. the development of transportation networks and heavy industry.
   d. teaching the citizenry about the virtues of communism.
   e. the development of countermeasures to the Marshall Plan.
10. Which description of communist Europe's economic progress is most correct?
   a. Much industrial progress from 1945 to 1955, then tapering off to stagnation in the 1970s
   b. Poor results until Stalin's death, then rapid improvement until the 1970s
   c. Gradual change from agrarian to industrial economy during the 1950s and 1960s with a switch to consumer products successfully undertaken in the 1970s and 1980s
   d. A continuous disaster of poor planning and lack of expertise
   e. Moderate economic success in countries such as Yugoslavia and East Germany

## InfoTrac College Edition

Visit the source collections at

**http://infotrac.thomsonlearning.com**

and use the Search function with the following key terms:

Cold War

Soviet Union relations with the United States

Single European Market

## Wadsworth History Website Resources

Visit the World History Resource Center at **http://history.wadsworth.com/world** for a wealth of general resources, and the *World Civilizations* Companion Website at **http://history.wadsworth.com/adler04** for resources specific to this textbook.

## HistoryNow

Enter *HistoryNow* using the access card that is available for *World Civilizations*. *HistoryNow* will assist you in understanding the content in this chapter with lesson plans generated for your needs. In addition, you can read the following documents, and many more, online:

The Truman Doctrine

The Marshall Plan

Winston Churchill, "The Sinews of Peace"

John F. Kennedy, "Address on the Cuban Crisis"

*The moment the slave resolves that he will no longer be a slave, his fetters fall. Freedom and slavery are mental states.*
Mohandas Gandhi

# 50 Decolonization and the Third World



| | |
|---|---|
| 1945–1975 | End of Western colonies |
| 1946–1947 | Philippines, India, Pakistan become independent |
| 1919 | Indonesia attains independence |
| 1954 | French rule ends in Indochina |
| 1957 | Ghana becomes first sub-Saharan colony to attain independence |
| 1960s | Most British, French, Belgian colonies become independent |
| 1970s | Portuguese driven from African colonies |
| 1989–1991 | Soviet empire collapses |
| 1994 | Majority, democratic rule in South Africa |

The fifty years after World War II saw the end of the colonial empires that had been built up since 1500 by the European powers. In the Western colonies, the end came soon after the war. In 1945, many hundreds of millions of Asians, Africans, Polynesians, and others were governed by Europeans from distant capitals. By the end of the 1970s, practically none were. These unexpected developments gave birth to the so-called Third World as a counterforce to the superpower blocs of the Cold War years.

In the late 1980s, the last of the colonial powers, the Soviet Union, confessed its inability to coerce continued obedience from its eastern European and Asian satellites and released them from imposed communist rule. A short time later, the collapse of the Soviet Union allowed the emergence of several new independent states from its ruins (see Chapter 55).

**Decolonization**, or the "retreat from empire," as it has been frequently called, was a major turning point in world history. Europe (and North America and Japan) continues to exercise great power over the non-Europeans, but today this influence is subtler. It is basically economic rather than political and military in nature. Until America's military intervention in Iraq in 2003, it was inconceivable that a Western country would attempt to install an openly colonial regime in any non-Western land, if only for fear of the penalties it would suffer from its own neighbors. Since the collapse of the Soviet system in the early 1990s, the same can be said of the Russians. For most of the world, colonialism as an overt political relationship is "history."

## Decolonization's Causes

What brought about this unexpectedly rapid end to a story that dated back to the sixteenth-century Western expansion? The movement toward decolonization had several major causes. In certain instances, such as India, Vietnam, and the Philippines, the rise to independent, sovereign status was the culmination of a generation or more of struggle—sometimes with gun in hand. In other cases, such as French-speaking West and Central Africa, Libya, and Iraq, independence came as a more or less sudden "gift" from the home country, sometimes to populations that were only partly ready for the event. Whatever the individual circumstances, all of the independence-seeking colonies profited from some general developments that had occurred during the immediate postwar years:

- *Rising nationalism in Asia and Africa.* National pride and a burning resentment of Western dominion were in all cases the driving forces of decolonization. European rule had sown the seed of its own dissolution in the colonies by creating a small but vitally important intelligentsia among subject peoples. The products of European-founded schools, these individuals had sometimes obtained higher education in the mother country. There they had learned not only academic subjects but also to reject the inferior status they suffered at home. They also absorbed Western nationalism and Western techniques of political organization (both legal and illegal). (The value of imitating Western models was quickly learned; see the Law and Government box on "Vietnam's Declaration of Independence.") In a few cases, such as the Vietnamese Ho Chi Minh (1890–1969) in France, the intelligentsia encountered and adopted Marxism as a path to successful revolution. The Asian militants' efforts to build a popular following were aided by the repeated humiliations Japan inflicted on European/American armies and navies early in World War II, which revealed that the colonial powers were not invincible.
- *Loss of European moral authority.* In the nineteenth and early twentieth centuries, most Europeans looked on their colonies with the sense that in ruling them they were doing the right thing—that is, meeting their duties as carriers of the "white man's burden." By the 1950s, the conviction that they were destined to rule others had been much weakened by the experiences of the two world wars and by the postwar spirit of egalitarian democracy. The façade of moral and cultural superiority that lay behind the largely mythical "white man's burden" was stripped away by the contradictions and even hypocrisies of colonial rule. Moreover, having suffered from two highly destructive "civil" wars (World Wars I and II), Europeans' self-assurance about their own fitness to govern foreign peoples had evaporated.
- *Temporary prostration of Europe.* After the war until about 1960, Europe's six overseas colonial powers (Belgium, Britain, France, Italy, the Netherlands, and Portugal) were absorbed with repairing the damage caused by the war and/or reforming the low-tech economies, social antagonisms, and obsolete educational systems they had carried over from the 1930s. The public had no interest in supervising "difficult" colonials or pouring badly needed capital and labor into colonial projects that, like many previous ones, might never work out. The postwar elections of socialist-leaning governments in Europe, such as Britain's Labour Party, also introduced a new spirit that was more critical of imperial responsibilities, especially in light of the difficulties being faced by their populations in recovering from the effects of the wars.
- *Opposition to the continuation of colonies in both Allied war aims and U.S. policy.* The stated aims of the United Nations, founded at the end of World War II by the Western powers, were clearly anticolonial, and the United States, which played such a major role in postwar Europe, had always felt uneasy about holding colonies, even its own. (It acknowledged Philippine independence as early as 1946.) In light of these facts, the Western countries' release of their colonies between 1946 and 1974 becomes more understandable, especially when one considers the tremendous costs visited on the colonial powers when and where they tried to stop the march toward independence in Southeast Asia and parts of Africa. By the 1970s, only the Soviet Union was still an important colonial country, holding eastern Europeans as unwilling satellites and suppliers.

## Dismantling of Western Colonies

How did decolonization proceed? Britain led the way by making good on the Labour Party's wartime promise to release India from the British Commonwealth. For many years, British Conservative governments had steadfastly opposed the peaceable but unrelenting movement for independence led by the Hindu Congress Party and its founder, Mohandas Gandhi (1869–1948). Gandhi's magnificent ability to reveal the moral inconsistencies in the British position made him an unbeatable opponent, however, and the Labour Party had been gradually won over to his point of view.

In 1945, Labour won the first postwar election, and negotiations with Gandhi and his associate Jawaharlal Nehru were begun. It soon became clear that the Hindu leaders could not speak for the large Muslim minority, which demanded separate statehood. The British government, immersed in the severe postwar problems at home, tried in vain to resolve this dilemma. In 1947, independence was granted to India on a ready-or-not basis.

# Vietnam's Declaration of Independence, 1946

**Ho Chi Minh remained in Vietnam** throughout World War II, organizing and leading the Viet Minh guerrillas against the Japanese occupiers. Ho and his people expected to be treated as allies by the French after the war, but instead they were told they must return to colonial status. In September 1945, the Viet Minh leadership made this reply, which draws cleverly on the history of both France and the United States to justify itself. Note that Ho by no means had the "entire Vietnamese people" behind him at this juncture and was hoping to bluff the French and embarrass the Americans with this Vietnamese Declaration of Independence. That independence was in fact achieved only after thirty years of near-continuous fighting.

"All men are created equal. They are endowed by their Creator with certain inalienable rights; among these are Life, Liberty, and the pursuit of Happiness." This immortal statement was made in the Declaration of Independence of the United States of America in 1776. In a broader sense, this means: all the peoples of the earth are equal from birth, all the peoples have a right to live, to be happy, and to be free.

The Declaration of the French Revolution made in 1791 on the Rights of Man and Citizen also states: "All men are born free and with equal rights, and must always remain free and have equal rights."

Those are undeniable truths.

Nevertheless, for more than eighty years, the French imperialists, abusing the standard of Liberty, Equality, and Fraternity, have violated our Fatherland and oppressed our fellow citizens. They have acted contrary to the ideals of humanity and justice. . . .

They have built more prisons than schools. They have mercilessly slain our patriots; they have drowned our uprisings in rivers of blood. . . .

In the field of economics, they have fleeced us to the backbone, impoverished our people, and devastated our land. . . .

In the Autumn of 1940 when the Japanese Fascists violated Indochina's territory to establish new bases in their fight against the Allies, the French imperialists went down on bended knee and handed over our country to them. Thus, from that date our people were subjected to the double yoke of the French and the Japanese. Their sufferings and miseries increased. . . .

After the Japanese had surrendered to the Allies, our whole people rose to regain our national sovereignty and to found the Democratic Republic of Vietnam.

The truth is that we have wrested our independence from the Japanese, and not from the French. The French had fled, the Japanese have capitulated. Our people have broken the chains which for nearly a century have fettered them and have won independence for the Fatherland.

Black Star/Stockphoto

**Ho Chi Minh with His Generals.** The Vietnamese leader of the long war against France and then the United States plots his next moves. "Uncle" Ho was an outstanding representative of the large group of Third World nationalists determined to lead their peoples into independence by any means possible after World War II.

For these reasons, we, members of the Provisional Government, representing the entire Vietnamese people, declare that from now on we break off all relations of a colonial character with France; we repeal all the international obligations that France has so far subscribed to on behalf of Vietnam, and we abolish all the special rights that the French have unlawfully acquired in our Fatherland.

## *Analyze and Interpret*

To what extent do you think Ho's use of the French and American ideals was sincere? Do you think he was justified in his criticisms of France? Why?

Source: *Selected Works of Ho Chi Minh,* vol. 3 (Hanoi: 1960–1962).

History Now™

***To read the entire Declaration, point your browser to the documents area of* HistoryNow.**

The immediate result was a bloody civil war, fought by Hindus and Muslims over the corpse, so to speak, of Gandhi, who had been assassinated by a fanatic. From this war came two new states, India and Pakistan (and eventually Bangladesh, the former East Pakistan), which remain hostile to this day and engage in mutual misunderstandings. Frequent border disputes also erupt, such as the current antagonisms over Kashmir that brought both nations to the brink of possible nuclear war in 2003. It was a shaky beginning to the decolonization movement.

Elsewhere, however, the British generally managed things more adroitly. Burma and Sri Lanka (Ceylon) gained their independence peaceably by mutual agreement in the late 1940s. **Ghana** (Gold Coast) became the first colony in sub-Saharan Africa to be granted self-government. It was then recognized as a sovereign member of the voluntary association called the *British Commonwealth* in 1957. Almost the entire list of British colonies, from Malaysia to Belize (British Honduras) in Central America, quickly followed. By the mid-1960s, even such minor holdings as the islands of the south Pacific (Fiji, the Solomon Islands) and the Bahamas were granted either self-government under the Crown or full independence.

In France, the attitude of the public and government toward retaining the colonial empire underwent a sharp shift around 1960. This reversal was generated by the unhappy results (for France) of its colonial wars in Vietnam (1945–1954) and Algeria (1958–1961). Both of these proved lost causes that led to many thousands of French casualties and much discontent at home. In 1958, the war hero General Charles de Gaulle became president of France and almost immediately began to change course on the colonial question. Within four years, most of the former possessions had been granted independence and membership in a French version of the British Commonwealth. The members of this community remain closely linked with France in economics and culture but go their individual ways in international affairs. With some bitter exceptions, the French were successful, as were the British, in retaining a position of privilege and influence in their former colonies. Despite strong nationalism among the former subjects, the ties generated by common languages and education often survived the political scission.

The Belgians, Dutch, and Portuguese, on the other hand, were all forced from their Asian and African possessions by a combination of uprisings and international pressure exerted in the United Nations. These small European countries had relatively more prestige and wealth invested in their colonies and gave them up only reluctantly. The Belgians were compelled to grant self-rule in the huge African Congo by threatened rebellion in 1961. The Dutch let go of their Indonesian empire only after prolonged and vain fighting against the nationalists in the late 1940s. The Portuguese gave up their outposts in Africa also under severe pressure from a guerrilla war beginning in the early 1970s.

## Problems of the Third World

What have the former colonies achieved in the generation or more since attaining their independence? Have they been able to fulfill the hopes of the nationalist intellectuals and the dedicated dreamers who were so instrumental in their creation?

Until the mid-twentieth century, the writing of history in the United States or any other Western country was largely concerned with the acts of a relatively small minority of the world's peoples: namely, the inhabitants of Europe and North America. But the largest part of the world's population has always been located primarily in Asia and Africa. The majority live in what formerly was called the "Third World" (that is, of neither the American nor the Soviet side of the Cold War) of less developed and scarcely developed countries such as Togo, Afghanistan, and Bolivia. In these countries, the per capita cash income is perhaps one-twentieth of the West's, and this material poverty is reflected by a basically different set of cultural values and fewer opportunities in a world that is still dominated by Western capitalism.

In fact, three-fourths of the more than 6 billion people inhabiting the world in 2004 lived in the poorer countries. This predominance in numbers has not yet been translated into cultural and economic predominance—and perhaps never will be—but with the global village beckoning in the twenty-first century, we in the West had better prepare to encounter and assist these people if we intend to live in peace. Many observers believe the gap that currently exists between the developed and less developed countries cannot be sustained much longer without severe repercussions.

What is a Third World society? The rapid economic and social development of some non-Western nations in recent years makes it imperative to distinguish among countries that used to be lumped together under that term. Thus, the following description applies to only the least developed nations of the world, some of which are in the Americas, but most of which are located in Asia and Africa. Economically speaking, it is a society in which poverty is the rule, and some form of agriculture still makes up a high proportion (more than 50 percent) of the gross national product. Unskilled labor is predominant in both town and country; for most there remain few opportunities for higher education and economic advancement; and the industrial and larger commercial

**Flight from Terror.** Millions of Muslim refugees piled onto trains to flee the outbreaks of ethnic violence that marked the 1947 division of British India into two sovereign states. Hindus living in the new Pakistan suffered a similar fate.

enterprises are commonly controlled by foreign capital and dependent on world markets. Industry is most often engaged in unsophisticated processing of raw materials, primarily for export to the "first world" nations for manufacture into finished products. Policies imposed on these subject peoples during the colonial era encouraged the production of commodities and raw materials (and labor during the era of the slave trade, see Chapter 38) for Europe's and America's factories, but also discouraged the development of local forms of manufacturing. Many Third World nations, although now free of colonial rule, remain underdeveloped as a result of high tariffs that First World nations continue to impose on finished products from poor, Third World nations. Such disadvantageous and discriminatory economic practices usually are called **neocolonialism**.

Politically speaking, a Third World society is one in which a small elite, often derived from the bureaucracy of the colonial era, controls access to power and wealth. Again, their roots go back to the privileged few of the colonial era who were favored by their former colonial masters with Western-style educations. (Perhaps the most egregious hypocrisy of colonialism was the claim to a "civilizing" role in Africa, even though no effort was made to extend education to the overwhelming majority of subject peoples.) One political party or the army controls public life, often with dictatorial power. Large landholders are dominant in the countryside, overshadowing or intimidating the far more numerous and disadvantaged small farmers and landless laborers.

Socially speaking, it is a society in which the overpopulation problem is severe and is worsening each year. Males still exercise control over females within the family and have far more rights and prestige outside of it. Education is highly desired and prestigious but often is still beyond the means of too many people and ill designed for the present tasks. The clan or the extended family is far more important than in developed countries. Upward mobility is still possible but is becoming more difficult to achieve as the gap between the rich and the poor widens and as opportunities for the many become ever more meager. An unhealthy imbalance between burgeoning town and stagnant country life is steadily more apparent.

Internationally speaking, a Third World country is one that in most ways is still dependent on the more developed countries—sometimes as much so as when it was formally a colony. Once it achieved independence in the days of the Cold War, both the West and the former Soviet bloc treated it basically as a pawn in their foreign policy designs. Since the Cold War ended, its weak bargaining powers have almost always been reduced even further.

Since the collapse of the Soviet bloc and the discrediting of Marxist economics (see Chapter 55), the tension between the rival ideologies of communism and capitalism can no longer be turned to third-party advantage in the competition for political and economic power. Additionally, the leaders of the Western world have given the highest priority to international aid programs for the Russians and eastern Europeans, to avoid chaos as those peoples attempt to make the transition to a free market. Moreover, attitudes of cultural superiority and even racism continue to bedevil thoughts and behaviors of some Westerners toward non-Europeans. In the post–Cold War world, the needs of even some of the poorest and most helpless African and Asian peoples are given lower priority. Consequently, less aid has been made available for these countries.

For some nations, the standard of living has actually declined since they attained independence. Africa is a particularly tragic case. The famine and banditry afflicting much of the **Sahel** (Sudan, Somalia, Ethiopia) in recent years are manifestations of this decline. So are the dictatorships that are the rule in African governments. Where dictators are absent, it is often only because social antagonisms (Somalia, Rwanda), religious warfare (Sudan), or a combination of these (Democratic Republic of Congo) have prevented a single individual or party from seizing power. Almost everywhere, the root causes of these evils are a population that is too large for the available resources, continuing first world policies, misapplied technology, and an unequal distribution of power and wealth.

## The Population of the Earth

A book appeared in the 1970s with the arresting title *The Population Bomb*. Written by a respected biologist, Paul Ehrlich, at an American university, it warned that a time was rapidly approaching when the Earth would face massive, prolonged famine. The rate of population growth in the less developed countries threatened to overwhelm the Earth's capacity to grow food.

Professor Ehrlich's prognosis of early famine proved erroneous. The Green Revolution, plus a series of good crop years around the globe, actually increased the ratio of available food to mouths, but many believe Ehrlich's basic argument is still valid: inevitably, starvation will come. They point to the examples of the African Sahel, Bangladesh since independence, and many of the Andean populations in South America, to assert that the number of consumers is exceeding the available resources. It is just a matter of time, they argue, until the well-fed will be using lethal weapons to hold off the starving hordes.

Other observers, however, argue that Ehrlich and similar doomsayers are not taking the so-called **demographic transition** into account. This transition occurs when parents stop viewing many children as a familial and economic necessity and instead produce a smaller number of better-cared-for children. Historically, this has occurred when a society becomes industrialized and urbanized. Children then become less economically necessary to the family, and a lower mortality rate means that most will live to maturity. Hence, parents no longer need to have many children to ensure that some will survive to care for them in their old age. Because the three continents (Africa, Asia, and South America) where the large majority of the nonindustrial peoples live are rapidly developing urban and industrialized societies, it was hoped that the birthrates would drop substantially within a generation, but this has not happened.

In Latin America, parts of Asia, and much of Africa, birthrates have remained at levels that are double or triple Western rates. The "gap" between the present-day medical and technological capacities to preserve and prolong life and the cultural demands to have children early and frequently so that some will survive into adulthood has not closed as swiftly as was hoped. Efforts to lower the birthrate by artificial means (condoms, the Pill) have worked in some places but failed in others. The most impressive results have been obtained in China through massive government intervention in private life as well as constant propaganda for one-child families. Neither of these measures would be acceptable in most countries.

Yet, some means of controlling the hugely increasing demands of the world's population on every type of natural resource (including privacy, quietude, or undisturbed contemplation) must be found soon, presumably. The human inhabitants of Spaceship Earth are increasing in geometric fashion. The Earth's first half-billion inhabitants took perhaps 50,000 years to appear, and the second half-billion appeared over 500 years (1300–1800), but the last half-billion of the 1990 total of 5.5 billion people came aboard in a period of ten to twelve years! Most of this last half-billion live in the less developed countries, where the rate of natural increase—births over deaths without counting migration—is two to four times that of the industrial world.

## Misapplied Technology

The developed countries' postwar attempts to assist the former colonies and the Latin American states sometimes compounded the difficulties those nations were already experiencing. In nations with a superabundance of labor, where the economy could not supply more than a few months' paid labor for many citizens, the World Bank and other international agencies frequently promoted industrial projects that actually *lessened* job opportunities. Instead of encouraging the continued use of shovels and baskets or similarly technologically primitive but economically productive means of moving earth, for example, the agencies shipped in bulldozers and large dump trucks to construct a new dam or mine. In agriculture, a local government's request for modern heavy equipment for plowing or the newest mechanical milking machines for its dairies would be granted, even when the predictable net result for the local labor market would be devastating. The cowherd and other laborers thus thrust out of work only contributed to the problems of the poverty-stricken villages or the overcrowded city slums. This preference for short-term "show" rather than long-term improvement characterized many of the Third World's domestic and internationally funded postwar projects.

Ill-conceived technology also frequently had unfortunate ecological consequences. The Aswan Dam project in Egypt is a good example. Built with Soviet aid in the 1950s, the huge dam and the lake it created radically altered the ecology of the lower Nile River. Although the lake (despite tremendous loss from evaporation) supplied tens of thousands of acres with water for irrigation, downstream from the dam the changes were entirely for the worse. A variety of snail that previously had not lived in the lower Nile waters began to flourish there, causing a massive outbreak of epidemic disease. The schools of Mediterranean fish that had previously been fed from the flooding Nile delta disappeared; with them went the food supply of many Egyptians and the livelihood of many more who had netted the fish and sold them. The new upstream lands now under irrigation from Lake Nasser could not make up the deficit for the hungry Egyptian peasants, because almost all of these lands were devoted to cotton or other industrial crops for export.

All told, the efforts of the Third World nations to achieve industrial and/or agrarian development in the thirty years following World War II were unsuccessful in raising living standards for the masses of people. Some groups did prosper, and some regions did much better than others, notably the western rim of the Pacific Ocean, but in much of Africa and Latin America, the few rich got richer, the many poor stayed poor, and those in between did not multiply as hoped. The uneven distribution of wealth is best displayed by some comparative figures. In the industrialized Western nations, the personal income of the uppermost 10 percent of society is about five times the income of the bottom 10 percent. In the comparatively well-off Mexico, the disparity in income has grown over the past decades, until by the 1990s the upper 10 percent were receiving *twenty-seven times* as much as the bottom 10 percent.

## Summary

Decolonization came in the first quarter-century after World War II, as the colonial powers realized that economic exhaustion and anticolonial sentiment made it impossible to retain their former possessions in Asia and Africa. Beginning with the difficult and bloody severance of India and Pakistan from the British Empire, the colonial structures were dismantled or toppled by armed revolts between 1947 and 1974. While the British gave their remaining subjects uncontested self-government and then sovereignty in the 1960s, the French were at first less pliant. First in Vietnam and then in North Africa, they engaged in extended warfare that eventually resulted in defeat and withdrawal. Only then under de Gaulle did they achieve a workable postcolonial relationship. The French mistakes were imitated by the Dutch, Belgians, and Portuguese, all of whom had to be driven out of their colonies by nationalist rebellions during the 1940s through the 1970s. In the Soviet instance, the attempt to retain satellites persisted into the 1980s.

The Third World that emerged from the postcolonial settlements was a hodgepodge of different states and societies, but to some degree all suffered from generic handicaps in dealing with the "First World" West and the "Second World" communist states. Maldistribution of national wealth, misapplication of technological assets, and the overwhelming growth of population were three of the worst problems.

## Identification Terms

Test your knowledge of this chapter's key concepts by defining the following terms. If you can't recall the meaning of certain terms, refresh your memory by looking up the boldfaced term in the chapter, turning to the Glossary at the end of the book, or working with the flashcards that are available on the *World Civilizations* Companion Website **http://history.wadsworth.com/adler04**.

decolonization
demographic transition
Ghana
neocolonialism
Sahel

## Test Your Knowledge

Test your knowledge of this chapter by answering the following questions. Complete answers appear at the end of the book. You may also take this quiz interactively and find even more quiz questions on the *World Civilizations* Companion Website: **http://history.wadsworth.com/adler04**.

1. Which was *not* a strong motivation for the rapid decolonization after World War II?
   a. U.S. opposition to continued colonial holdings
   b. The war-caused weakness of most colonial powers' economies
   c. The weakening of Europeans' confidence in their ability to rule others well
   d. The communists' accusations of Western imperialism
   e. Newly elected Socialist governments in Europe that favored their own development over colonial responsibilities
2. Which of the following African countries fought a long war against a colonial power and eventually won its independence?
   a. Nigeria
   b. Egypt
   c. Algeria
   d. South Africa
   e. The former Belgian Congo
3. The decolonization process generally went ahead with the least violence in
   a. Southeast Asia.
   b. French North Africa.
   c. The Middle East.
   d. Portuguese Africa.
   e. British Africa.
4. The last surviving major colonial power was
   a. Portugal.
   b. the Soviet Union.
   c. the United States.
   d. France.
   e. Belgium.
5. What proportion of the world's population currently lives in the less developed countries?
   a. One-half
   b. Two-thirds
   c. Three-fourths
   d. Four-fifths
   e. One-eighth
6. One of the prominent identifying factors for a Third World society is
   a. a prospering rural and agrarian economy.
   b. the problem of overpopulation.
   c. a reluctance to accept foreign aid.
   d. equal status for young males and females.
   e. a steady drain of population into the cities.
7. Which of the following was *not* a factor in lessening the West's attention to the problems of the Third World in recent years?
   a. The collapse of the communist hopes of revolution
   b. The diversion of foreign aid to the former communist lands of Europe
   c. The inability of Third World nations to collaborate effectively in international negotiations
   d. The slowing rate of population growth in most ex-colonial countries
   e. The effects of continuing attitudes of racial and cultural superiority among some Western leaders
8. The "demographic transition" means
   a. a change from a youthful to an elderly population.
   b. a change from an excess of males to an excess of females in a given population.
   c. the evolution of a bigger, stronger average size in human bodies.
   d. the change from high birthrates to lower ones as a population modernizes.
   e. a change from rule by one tribe to another.
9. Political and economic inequality in many Third World nations has its roots in
   a. colonial policies.
   b. racial discrimination.
   c. religious strife.
   d. ethnic rivalries.
   e. constitutions that favor military or dictatorial rule.
10. Third World nations suffer from underdevelopment due to
   a. First world nations' high tariffs on Third World goods.
   b. Colonial policies that discouraged industrialization.
   c. Low priority given to aid to Third World nations.
   d. a, b, and c.
   e. a and b only.

## InfoTrac College Edition

Visit the source collections at

**http://infotrac.thomsonlearning.com**

and use the Search function with the following key terms:

decolonization Gandhi developing countries

## Wadsworth History Website Resources

Visit the World History Resource Center at **http://history.wadsworth.com/world** for a wealth of general resources and the *World Civilizations* Companion Website at **http://history.wadsworth.com/adler04** for resources specific to this textbook.

## HistoryNow

Enter *HistoryNow* using the access card that is available for *World Civilizations*. *HistoryNow* will assist you in understanding the content in this chapter with lesson plans generated for your needs. In addition, you can read the following documents, and many more, online:

Mohandas Gandhi, "Indian Home Rule"

Jawaharlal Nehru, Speech on the Granting of Indian Independence

Vietnamese Declaration of Independence

*A revolution is not a dinner party.*
Mao Zedong

# 51 The New Asia



| | |
|---|---|
| 1945–1952 | U.S. occupation of Japan |
| 1949–1976 | Mao Zedong leads China |
| 1950–1953 | Korean War |
| 1950–1990 | Japanese economic success |
| 1955–1973 | U.S. involvement in Vietnam War |
| 1958–1959 | Great Leap Forward in China |
| 1966–1976 | Great Proletarian Cultural Revolution in China |
| 1975 | Vietnam reunified under communist government |
| 1976–1997 | China under Deng Xiaoping |
| 1984 | Assassination of Indira Gandhi |
| 1989 | Tiananmen Square massacre |
| 1990–present | Japanese economic recession |
| 2002 | China admitted to the World Trade Organization |

The two leading Asian powers had both suffered greatly during the war and were temporarily restricted in their international roles while recovering. China and Japan continued to take sharply differing paths to establishing modern societies. China chose the path of revolution and became the world's largest Marxist state. Japan adapted Western ideas and technology to fit its own culture and became for a time the world's exemplary economic success.

Whereas World War I had brought relatively minor change to these areas, World War II proved to be the wellspring of major transformations. Many areas in eastern and southern Asia had been in colonial status and were intent on gaining full independence as soon as the war was concluded. The U.S.-held Philippines were the first to do so, followed by India and the European possessions in Southeast Asia and the Pacific islands. By the end of the twentieth century, several newly independent states had attained international significance by taking full advantage of a rapidly changing global economy.

## Mao's China, 1949–1976

A triumphant Mao Zedong proclaimed the People's Republic of China (PRC) in the fall of 1949. It entered into a formal alliance with the Soviet Union a few months later. Government and all social institutions were reorganized on Soviet communist lines, and for the first ten years, the Soviets were both its helpers and its mentors.

The conquest of the world's largest population had essentially been the work of one man—Chairman (of the

Chinese Communist Party's Central Committee) Mao, with the help of some brilliant assistants, especially Zhou Enlai. Although Mao had profited from some Soviet arms and economic support and guidance since the 1930s, in its fundamentals Chinese communism was his creation. No one else, not even Stalin, had played much of a role besides him in Chinese eyes. This was to be a critical factor in the years to come.

Mao was convinced that in an agrarian society such as China's (about 90 percent of the population were peasants), the correct path to socialism could only lie through a revolutionary peasantry. Thus, at all times during his rule, keeping the peasants with him was his chief concern. What the urbanites thought and did was of secondary importance. Mao's long and fruitful contacts with the rural folk also seem to have made him increasingly distrustful of intellectuals—an untraditional attitude for a Chinese leader and one that would have horrendous effects in the 1960s Cultural Revolution.

In its first three years (1949–1952), the regime instituted the basic policies it would employ to ensure political and social control indefinitely. In the countryside, land was expropriated from the landlords, and many—perhaps millions—of them were killed or imprisoned. The land was first redistributed to the peasants and then in 1955–1957 collectivized as the Soviets had done in their Five-Year Plan. Although millions more were killed or allowed to starve in the great famines of 1960–1962, the peasants did not resist as fiercely as in the Soviet Union. Why not? In part, because of the ancient Chinese tradition of regarding the central government as the legitimate source of authority and in part because so many desperately poor peasants supported the new arrangements ardently.

The new social organ called the *commune* was made the basis of rural production and of government, with disastrous effects for both the agricultural and the industrial economies. The communes were so large (about 25,000 persons) and their responsibilities so unclear that they could not function. As a result of poor planning and low incentives, food production barely matched the rapidly increasing population, even in good years. When bad harvests came after 1960, mass famine was inevitable. To keep the industrial plant functioning at all, grain was confiscated from the communes mercilessly, and the peasants starved just as they had in Russia earlier, under war communism and during the Five-Year Plans. Eventually, the communes were abolished, and smaller units were created that resembled the traditional villages except that land and work were collectivized.

The Chinese pursued industrial expansion in the same fashion as the Soviets had earlier, emphasizing heavy industry at the expense of consumer goods. A Stalinist Five-Year Plan instituted in 1953 produced substantial results in metals, coal, and other basic goods for industry, but Mao had become impatient with Soviet models and plans. In 1958, he personally introduced the **Great Leap Forward**. This attempt at overnight mass industrialization was an enormously costly failure (the infamous "backyard steelmaking," for example). It accelerated the growing gap between the Chinese and their Russian mentors, especially between Mao and Nikita Khrushchev.

The Russians criticized Mao for foolishly attempting the impossible and also for allowing himself to be made into the sort of Great Father in China that Stalin had been in Russia. In 1956, Khrushchev had just finished revealing Stalin's true nature to a shocked communist world, and he had no intention of allowing Mao to step up onto the vacant pedestal. On his side, a confident Mao made it clear that while he was no great admirer of Stalin or any other foreigner, he believed that true revolutions demanded a nearly supernatural Leader, with whom the ignorant masses might identify—something that Khrushchev never pretended to be or was capable of being.

Furthermore, Mao told the Russians that they had been diverted from the authentic revolutionary path by their fears of losing what they had in a war with capitalism and, moreover, that he intended to take their place as spokesman of the oppressed masses. By 1960, the barely concealed **Sino-Soviet conflict** was splitting the communist ranks. The rift became fully public at the time of the Cuban Missile Crisis, when the Maoists derided the Soviets' fear of U.S. "paper tigers," while Moscow denounced Beijing's readiness to plunge the world into atomic war.

Mao had long been convinced that the Soviet revolution had been suffocated by bureaucratization, and he was determined that China would not share this fate. In 1965, he suddenly called for the **Great Proletarian Cultural Revolution**. This extraordinary upheaval was meant to—and did—turn Chinese society on its head for many years. Like Stalin's "second revolution" of 1929, Mao's plan went far beyond political rearrangement. He wished to create a truly new relationship among party, people, and the exercise of revolutionary power. The attack was aimed primarily at the intellectuals, particularly those in the CCP's cadres of officials.

To achieve his main end, Mao was prepared to undertake what seemed an impossible task: to rid the Chinese people of their reverence for tradition. He called on the youthful **Red Guards**—mainly students—to make war on the older generation and its "empty formalisms." Mao was a profoundly skeptical spirit who distrusted all systems, even those he had created. He wished to introduce the permanent, self-perpetuating revolution, which he thought the Russians had given up in return for peace and a pseudo-Marxist society.

For the next three or four years, China experienced barely controlled, officially inspired anarchy. Professors were publicly humiliated, learned doctors were made to scrub the floors in their hospitals, scholars were abused for having foreign language books in their libraries, and Communist Party secretaries were accused of sabotage. Factional fighting in the party was allowed and encouraged, sometimes in the streets. The economy, only now recovering from the Great Leap Forward's mistakes, again suffered severe damage. Managers and skilled personnel were sent as outcasts to the villages to "learn the revolution's lessons" as barnyard sweepers or potato diggers. For a time, the only qualification for getting a responsible post was to have memorized the *Thought of Chairman Mao,* immortalized in the "**little red book**" that tens of millions of Chinese waved daily like an amulet against unknown evils. In 1969, the anarchy had become so bad that Mao had to call off the Red Guards and put the army in charge of everyday affairs. (For a sampling of the *Thought of Chairman Mao,* see the box.)

The tensions between China and the Soviet Union had erupted in the **Amur River War** as troops stationed on both sides of the frontier sporadically fired on each other. The military chiefs told Mao they could not guarantee what might happen if Russia attacked while the unrest continued. Still, until Mao's death in 1976, the spirit of the Cultural Revolution lived on, especially among the millions of radical, barely literate youth who thought the demolition of the Communist Party's apparatus and the government's disarray presented a once-in-a-lifetime chance for them to get ahead.

Within weeks of Mao's death, the inevitable reaction set in. The Cultural Revolution was first partially and then entirely condemned as a mistake. A collective leadership of party officials moved cautiously but steadily to put Mao's contributions into perspective. In 1980, his portraits, formerly everywhere, were silently removed from all public places. The era of the godlike chairman and his omnipresent little red book was definitely over.

## Recent China

Under Deng Xiaoping (1904–1997), an elderly but vigorous pragmatist, the Chinese Communist Party groped its way forward into the vacuum left by Mao's demise. A prisoner of the Cultural Revolution, Deng was determined to return China to "normal" socialism. He got rid of his enemies, put his supporters in key positions, and allowed greater freedom of expression. His most important achievement was to allow free-market incentives to gradually replace China's old economy, which had been tightly controlled under a system of state ownership. In Deng's words, China would remain *socialist in spirit,* re-

LAW AND GOVERNMENT

### Chairman Mao's Thought

**THE FOUNDER AND MASTER** of the Chinese Communist Party, Mao Zedong, had a peculiarly un-Chinese contempt for the traditional scholar-official (mandarin) class. His feelings were frequently expressed in his many speeches and writings during his long tenure of the party chairmanship:

**Intellectuals and Workers (1942)**

I began life as a student and at school acquired the ways of a student. . . . At that time I felt that the intellectuals were the only clean people in the world, while in comparison workers and peasants were dirty. . . . But after I became a revolutionary and lived with the workers and the peasants and with soldiers of the revolutionary army, I gradually came to know them well, and they came gradually to know me well, too. . . . I came to feel that, compared with the workers and the peasants, the unremolded intellectuals were not clean, and that, in the last analysis, the workers and peasants were the cleanest people, and even though their hands were soiled and their feet smeared with cowdung, they were really cleaner than the bourgeois and petty-bourgeois intellectuals.

#### *Analyze and Interpret*

To what do you attribute Mao's attitudes towards intellectuals? What did this "thought" by the man who became the unchallenged leader of China for many years portend about the place of intellectuals in Mao's China?

Source: *A Revolution Is Not a Dinner Party,* ed. R. Soloman and D. Huey (New York: Anchor, 1975), p. 149f.

**HistoryNow™**

***To read more quotations from Chairman Mao, point your browser to the documents area of HistoryNow.***

Jeff Widener/AP Photos

**The Goddess of Democracy.** Chinese university students modeled this plaster creation after the Statue of Liberty and used it as their rallying point in Tienanmen Square before the massacre of May 1989. Mao's huge portrait looks on disapprovingly.

gardless of the semi-capitalist economic system it seemed to be adopting. During the 1980s and 1990s, prosperity gradually spread into China's hinterlands from the thriving coastal cities of Hong Kong and Shanghai. Deng, who had long been associated with the moderate wing of the party, was particularly interested in establishing better relations with foreign capitalists who might help China recover from Mao's mistakes.

Spurred by President Richard M. Nixon's surprise visit to Beijing in 1972, the China–U.S. relationship had grown somewhat warmer since the ending of the U.S. presence in Vietnam. The Soviet invasion of Afghanistan (1979) increased Chinese interest in coming to a better understanding with the other superpower. Hence, in the 1980s, with U.S. encouragement, considerable progress was made in opening the country to foreigners and democratizing the secretive Communist Party and its iron controls over the political life of the populace. But in 1989, the rapid spread of freedom of thought and expression among university students again frightened the leaders, and when students demonstrators erected a "Goddess of Democracy" statue in Beijing, the leaders reasserted Party control in the infamous **massacre in Tienanmen Square**. Hundreds, perhaps thousands, of young people died fleeing the guns of their own army.

Since that time, China's government has been walking a fine line between diplomatic isolation and a partial acceptance of Western demands for relaxation of its repressive political measures. Relations with the United States especially have remained ambivalent. Simmering resentment over American military alliances with Japan, South Korea, and the nations of Southeast Asia in what they considered their own "sphere of influence" has sometimes made China hypersensitive to any perceived slights. A particular sore spot has been Taiwan, an island about one hundred miles from the mainland to which China has laid claim since 1947. American trade, military assistance, and support for democratic elections in 1996 have further complicated relations between the two nations. Tensions were worsened in April 2001, when a U.S. Navy EP-3 Aries II reconnaissance plane collided with a Chinese F-8 fighter plane, forcing the Navy plane to land at a Chinese base on Hainan Island. Despite this incident, both sides realized the importance of maintaining cooperative relations. The United States supported China's application to become a member of the World Trade Organization, and in 2002 it became a full-fledged

Jeff Widener/AP Photos

**Chinese Youth Defies Tanks.** The never-identified youth stood alone to stop the tanks heading to Tienanmen Square in May 1989. After a brief hesitation, the vehicles rolled around him and continued to another destination.

member, further opening its 1.25 billion people to the regulations and advantages of the world marketplace. Following the al-Qaida attacks on New York's World Trade Center and the Pentagon in Washington, D.C., in September 2001, both nations also found common ground in fighting worldwide terrorist attacks by extremist Muslims, as well as in negotiating an end to tensions caused by North Korea's pursuit of nuclear armaments.

## Postwar Japan to 1952

The defeat and occupation of the Japanese islands by a foreign force (for the first time in history) was a tremendous shock, but it soon proved to be a constructive shock, unleashing a great deal of new energy and innovative thinking. Despite heavy war damage and loss of life, both military and civilian, Japan's economy rebounded with unexpected speed and then proceeded to shoot far ahead of anything it had achieved before.

The government of occupied Japan was an American-supervised affair under General Douglas MacArthur. Unlike the situation in occupied Germany after its defeat, a native civilian government was allowed to function, but it was limited to carrying out the directives of MacArthur's staff. The Japanese accepted all of MacArthur's many reform decrees in politics and social matters almost without criticism. Spiritually and materially exhausted by war and defeat, they were in a mood of self-questioning, which was unusual for this proudly nationalist and confident nation. They seemed ready to accept a new basis for their social and political organization, and their willingness to change made the American occupation a great success.

In the first two years of his regime, MacArthur's office initiated radical changes in the traditional Japanese system, culminating in an entirely new constitution that established a government similar to the British government. The parliament (Diet) was declared the most important branch of government, with sovereignty residing in the Japanese people. The emperor remains in place, but only as a symbol. Japan "forever renounces war as a sovereign right of the nation," maintaining only a small Self-Defense Force.

The war in Korea (1950–1953) was key in elevating the United States from conqueror to protector. The active support given to the North Korean communist army by Mao's China after 1951 made the U.S. armed forces in South Korea and elsewhere in the western Pacific an indispensable guardian for disarmed Japan. Japanese of all persuasions generally recognized the need for U.S. military protection, even though some were disturbed by the U.S.-instigated transformations in their social relations and political culture.

## Independent Japan

In 1952, the occupation ended and Japan again became a sovereign state. It signed a treaty of alliance with the United States that extended the U.S. nuclear umbrella over Japan in any future war. In return, the United States was guaranteed the right to have naval and military bases on Japanese soil for the indefinite future. Although minimally opposed at the time, this treaty caused tensions later, when the socialist and communist parties denounced the treaty as a tool of U.S. imperialism. By then, however, it was clear that Japanese politics tended toward the conservative and that an anti-U.S. position had little appeal. A homogeneous people who value tradition and group approval, the Japanese have never shown much interest in social experimentation or political radicalism.

For the first few years, the Liberal Party was the leading force in independent postwar politics. The Liberals merged with their closest rivals in 1955 and became the Liberal Democratic Party (LDP). For almost forty years, the LDP formed every Japanese government. Despite the name, it was a conservative party, dominated by the big business interests that have always worked closely with government in Japan. The LDP finally went down to defeat in 1993, when it was the culprit in a series of political corruption scandals that rocked the country and the business establishment. Always more an aggregation of financial and economic interests than a political unit, the LDP split into factions and lost out to a coalition of opponents. In most recent days, the LDP's factions have become almost separate parties, fighting one another in the Diet and allowing Socialists and other groups to contest the national leadership effectively. Japan has become a fully democratic state, with governments that reflect both the strengths and weaknesses of that condition.

### *Economic Progress*

The economic success of postwar Japan was admired throughout the world and was even considered as a possible model by the older industrialized states of the West. What explains this success? A combination of external and internal factors contributed to Japan's prosperity from the 1950s through the 1980s.

Externally, Japan benefited from several developments. When the United States assumed the burden of Japan's defense, the budgetary expenditures that would have gone into nonproductive weaponry, housing, and pensions for the military were saved and could be invested in the civilian economy. The Korean War stimulated Japanese industry in many different ways. Also, Japan is entirely dependent on imported oil, and oil was cheap during the initial postwar decades. International credit institutions such as the World Bank and the International Monetary Fund were eager to lend money for investment and the acquisition of technology. Japan soon showed itself to be a willing student and a highly reliable credit risk.

Internally, Japan had the world's highest personal savings rate, and the banks reinvested the savings in new industry. The Japanese labor force was disciplined and skilled and had been well educated in one of the world's most effective primary and secondary school systems. The Japanese population rose throughout the postwar era, providing a large labor pool as well as a growing internal market. Under strong government urging, labor continued to work with employers rather than take an adversarial position. Unions were rewarded with extensive powers in the workplace.

Most of all, in the opinion of many, Japan's postwar surge was the result of the consistent support of business by the government, which made large sums available for ongoing research and development and aggressively promoted business interests in its diplomacy. Business and manufacturing combines (called *zaibatsu*), which originally had been broken up by the Americans, were allowed to reconstitute themselves in a slightly different fashion and with even more political and financial clout. New industrial giants such as Sony and Honda were the product of bold entrepreneurs. Industry and government directed a major effort toward expanding foreign trade, and Japanese trade with almost every noncommunist country rose without interruption during the postwar decades. Japanese goods, including electronic products, automobiles, watches, and cameras, conquered the consumer markets of the globe. The "Made in Japan" label, which had been synonymous with cheap imitations in the prewar era, became a symbol of advanced design and the world's best quality.

All of these factors combined to give Japan the highest rate of growth in gross national product (about 10 percent per annum) in the world during the quarter-century between 1950 and 1975. Since then, the rate of growth has slowed because of several factors: other Asian countries began to compete effectively in the global markets; unsound credit extension saddled banks with enormous loan defaults; and widespread corruption in government–business relations weakened Japan's capacities and self-confidence. In the 1990s, the country slipped into a recession that is not yet overcome.

## *Japanese Society*

Both rural and urban populations benefited from the postwar surge in material progress. After many generations of Buddhist simplicity and restraint, the Japanese have recently become a nation of consumers in the Western sense. Automobiles, television sets, cameras, and all of the other manifestations of personal luxury we have become accustomed to are at least equally evident in Japan's cities. The standard of living is about as high as that in the United States, but many flaws in the picture of prosperity have recently come to light. Much of the surge in the postwar economy, especially in the 1980s, was generated by wild speculation in real estate, enabled by easy bank credit. This "bubble" broke with the first tremor in Japan's export balances, leaving huge numbers of aborted projects and paper losses in its wake. The government has shown itself unable to solve the tangles involved. Housing, for example, remains an acute problem because of the massive influx from the countryside and the shortage of available land where people wish to live. A well-paid manager working in Tokyo may have a two-hour, nerve-grinding commute because finding an affordable apartment any closer is impossible. It has only been since 2003 that the nation has seen the beginnings of a recovery from the stagnation of the previous decade.

More disturbing than the economic stagnation to many is the visible erosion of respect for elements of the nation's Buddhist heritage that has taken place during the last two decades. Some blame this change on the Americanization begun in the occupation years and promoted since then by American entertainment media. Others see the lost war as the fundamental reason why less respect is shown for the older generation and for all authority. In any case, urban youths in particular are increasingly unwilling to continue the age-old deference to the elderly. Embracing the consumer mentality, they resent having to provide support for a generation of older people who can no longer work and take care of themselves. Increasingly, these tasks are pushed off onto governmental agencies, as in the West. This unprecedented "war of the generations," as some alarmists have termed it, is exacerbated by the housing shortage and outlandish rents in the cities, which force young people to remain in their parental homes much longer than they desire.

How have Japanese women fared in this era? They find themselves in a multifaceted struggle to gain economic equality with their husbands and brothers. The constitution gave them legal and political equity but deliberately failed to alter a system that firmly separated male and female. In recent years, Japanese working women have gained some access to jobs that were formerly male preserves, but they still lag behind women in other industrial societies. The "glass ceiling" in Japan may be the most prevalent and impenetrable in the world.

The formerly predominant agricultural sector has been much diminished in the last half-century: now less than 10 percent of the population lives on farms, and many of Japan's villages have become the more or less unwilling locales for second-home colonies of the city dwellers rather than their former self-contained societies. Even more telling of the reduced prestige of the farmer is the recent government decision to allow importation of foreign rice and the implied abandonment of the centuries-old "rice economy" and its commitment to the peasant as the mainstay of Japan's prosperity.

As for leisure and play, the ancient habit of allowing men to go places and engage in activities that were quite out of bounds to women has not been seriously challenged. Company-sponsored visits to geisha bars and nightclubs are still a routine part of white-collar professional life, as is ritualized drunkenness. The wife, on the other hand, usually has undisputed control over the household budget and the handling of the younger children and is at least the equal of her husband in family decision making. Most Japanese women are content with this state of affairs, and divorce rates are relatively low, although climbing. (See the Society and Economy box below for further information.)

SOCIETY AND ECONOMY

## Unsold Goods and Giant Garbage

**TRADITIONAL JAPANESE POLITENESS** has never excluded blunt expressions, especially for those who for one reason or another are vulnerable to social reproof. A Western resident of Tokyo in the 1980s gives us a more current view of femininity, followed by a few examples of contemporary insults by either sex.

> One way to chart the meaning of femininity in Japan is to listen to how the landscape itself is described. A "male hill" is the steeper side of the hill, while the more gently sloping grade is termed the "female hill." . . . Another way of using nature to summarize the character of the sexes is the proverb "Men are pine trees, women are wisteria vines," which means men are the strong base to which women cling.
>
> The positive traits associated with women are bundled up and tied together in the word *onna-rashisa*. Dictionaries define it in terms of being kind, gentle, polite, submissive, and graceful. Sometimes "weak" is included, spurring feminist scholars to protest.
>
> On the other hand the Japanese have several insults based on the linking of women with certain character faults. "Rotten as a woman" is an insult hurled at Japanese men by accusers of both sexes. . . . Both men and women are offended when someone denounces them as "womanish." . . . Women are also the standard for inferiority; one way to show contempt for a man is to call him "less than a woman." Females being inferior to males has been considered so unremarkable that no parallel expression exists.
>
> Although few Japanese stay single for life, there is a large and devilishly clever arsenal of Japanese words for ridiculing people—specifically women—who remain unwed past the so-called marriageable age. The older unmarried woman is "unsold goods." She has become a "widow without going," a play on the popular term for marrying, "to go as a daughter-in-law." . . . One anxiety shared by many women who stay single for life is the fate of their remains after death. According to Japanese custom, women are laid to rest in the family grave of their husband. A woman deemed "unsold merchandise" may have trouble entering the family grave beside her parents if, for example, her older brother's wife opposes. . . .
>
> People in Japan always sort their garbage into three categories for easier disposal: combustible trash like eggshells, fire-resistant rubbish like beer cans, and last but not least, "giant garbage," *sodai gomi,* the big, coarse, hard-to-handle junk like broken refrigerators. Or like retired husbands, in the cruel slang of the 1980s.
>
> Women call their own husbands "giant garbage" to complain that they mope aimlessly about the house, good for nothing, always getting in the way. Until they retired from demanding salaried jobs, these *sodai gomi* spent so little time at home that they never developed their own household niche. While wives devote all their energy to the home, husbands define themselves in terms of their job, as is revealed by another wifely insult for retirees who have been stripped of the company name that provided their identity. They are "unlabeled canned goods."

### *Analyze and Interpret*

Do these two examples conform to your understanding of Japanese women's domestic arrangements with their men?

Source: Kittredge Cherry, *Womansword* (New York: Kodansha International, 1987).

## South and Southeast Asia since Independence

The Indian subcontinent emerged from the colonial era divided between antagonistic Hindu and Muslim segments. It eventually yielded the major separate states of India, which is predominantly Hindu, and Pakistan and Bangladesh, which are mostly Muslim.

### *India*

Today India's social and economic problems are severe, but its adherence to constitutional and political means to devise solutions is an inspiration to democrats throughout the world. Shortly after India gained its independence, Mahatma Gandhi's assassination left the Hindu masses in confusion and sorrow but did not interfere with the erection of the new India. As leader of the majority Congress Party, Gandhi's close associate and designated heir Jawaharlal Nehru (1889–1964) sprang into the breach. Unlike Gandhi, Nehru believed that Western-style industrialization was absolutely necessary to avoid social chaos in India, and he set the country firmly on that path during his fifteen years at the government's head. He also believed that India could best live with neighboring Muslim Pakistan by showing it a strong hand. In practice, this policy meant that India and Pakistan were on a quasi-war footing for the next three decades, largely over the ownership of the rich border province of **Kashmir**, where Muslims predominated but India ruled.

Nehru led India toward a moderate democratic socialism that owed little to Marx and much to the British Labour Party. A mix of state ownership and free enterprise was worked out that has been relatively successful. For many tens of millions of Indians, living standards have risen in the past half-century, but for perhaps 60 percent of the total of 750 million, there has been discouragingly little change from the poverty of preindependence days. The most acute challenge to Indian prosperity, as in so many other developing nations, remains the high rate of population growth. Various governmental campaigns for fewer births have not been successful in the traditionalist villages where most Indians live.

After Nehru's death, in 1966 his daughter Indira Gandhi (no relation to the Mahatma) became the first female prime minister of an Asian state and continued her father's vision of a modern, industrial India. Her increasingly dictatorial style created conflicts with many Congress Party leaders, however, and she was turned out of office in the 1975 general election, only to return in 1980. These peaceable electoral transitions were evidence of the maturity that India—the world's largest democracy—had achieved in its government only a generation after colonial subordination. It was an impressive and heartening performance.

The picture of stability and political consensus has been rudely marred in recent years by increased ethnic and religious friction. Above all, this has been fueled by the rise of religious intolerance among Hindus and Muslims. Hindu nationalists have attacked and destroyed mosques, on one hand, while on the other, the Kashmir problem has become the focus of Muslim terrorist attacks and exchanges of gunfire between soldiers of the Indian and Pakistani armies. During an especially tense period in 2002, both nations threatened nuclear war. Fortunately, the situation has cooled down, and in 2003 and 2004 these two nations have been content to satisfy their rivalries on the soccer field. In the northwest, the Sikh minority is demanding autonomy for their Punjabi province. Its denial by the government of Indira Gandhi was the trigger for her assassination by Sikh extremists in 1984. In the far south, Tamils and Sinhalese are fighting one another in a long-drawn-out, nasty, but little-publicized guerrilla

Bettmann/Corbis

**Indira Gandhi.** The first Asian female prime minister proved herself an adept politician. However, the intense maneuvering required to unite the many factions of the Congress Party became too much for her patience, and her increasingly authoritarian stance defeated her party in national elections in 1975. She returned to power a few years later and was assassinated in 1984 by Sikh fanatics.

war. Outraged by what he thought was the government's favoritism, a Tamil fanatic killed Indira Gandhi's son and successor, Rajiv Gandhi, in 1991, and in the last several years, recurrent riots between militant Hindus and the Muslim minority have sharpened interfaith mistrust.

Given these deep-seated animosities, it is all the more remarkable that Indian democratic government has held together almost without lapse. The Congress Party, which formerly held the allegiance of a large majority, has found itself in increasing electoral difficulty as nationalist parties and regional groups have become prominent. These challengers have won elections in very recent years throughout India and have thus checked whatever opportunities may have once existed for the Congress to make itself into a monolithic grouping on the African model. The large, well-equipped army has not meddled in politics, nor have any civilian adventurers attempted to gain power by using the military.

## *Pakistan and Bangladesh*

When the British withdrew from the subcontinent in 1947, the large Muslim minority demanded separate and sovereign status in a state of their own. The widespread distribution of the Muslim population made it impossible to create this state as a single unit, so West and East Pakistan came into existence. All Muslims not already within their borders were encouraged to migrate to those areas. Together the two Pakistans included about one-fourth of the former British colony's population but considerably less than one-fourth of its human and material resources. These new states suffered from severe handicaps: their economies were undeveloped, and they had no infrastructure and few potential leaders. Under the leadership of the devout Mohammed Ali Jinnah, the two Pakistans were committed from the outset to the supremacy of Islam in public life. This religious emphasis contributed to Pakistan's alienation from, and suspicions of, Nehru's determinedly secular India.

The geographically widely separated states soon discovered that they had nothing in common except Islam, and that was simply not enough to hold them together. With India's assistance, East Pakistan became the independent nation of Bangladesh in 1971. As measured by gross national product per capita, the overpopulated and flood-prone Bangladesh is among the poorest countries in the world. Pakistan is not much farther up the ladder despite a generation of rival Chinese and American foreign-aid programs. Even before the 2001 Afghani conflict, the burden of caring for 3 to 4 million Afghani refugees from the lengthy civil war in that country has added to Pakistan's difficulties. The difficulties the ruling military government under General Musharraf has faced in trying to exert control over the mountainous northern parts that border on Afghanistan have complicated Pakistan's long-standing alliance with the United States since the invasion of Afghanistan in 2002. Almost impossible to control, with its warlike and fiercely independent tribespeople, this part of the country has been a hotbed of Islamic extremism. Under the control of fundamentalist shaykhs, its religious training institutes (*madrasas*) have been breeding grounds that spawned the notorious **Taliban** (literally, "students"), whom the Americans expelled from Afghanistan in 2002. Many believe that Osama bin Laden has continued to escape capture by American and Pakistani forces largely because these tribesmen support his cause and provide shelter to him and his followers.

## *Southeast Asia since World War II*

Stark contrasts are found in the postwar history of mainland and offshore Southeast Asia. During the middle decades of this century, some areas of the region may have experienced more violence than any other place on Earth, while others developed peaceably. Since the expulsion of the Japanese invaders in World War II, insurgents of one stripe or another have challenged the governments of Southeast Asia in several guerrilla campaigns (see Map 51.1). In former French Indochina (that is, Cambodia, Laos, and Vietnam), these insurgencies produced communist governments after long struggles. In Malaya (Malaysia) and the Philippines, leftist guerrillas challenged unsuccessfully in the later 1940s, while in the Dutch East Indies (Indonesia), the campaign for national independence was triumphant. Both Thailand and Burma (Myanmar) withstood significant minority rebellions, but these uprisings were more tribal than revolutionary in nature.

***The War in Vietnam*** The lengthy war in Vietnam began as a nationalist rebellion against the French colonial overlord in the immediate postwar years. Under the Marxist-nationalist Ho Chi Minh, the Viet Minh guerrillas were at last able to drive the French army from the field and install a communist regime in the northern half of the country in 1954. At this point, the U.S. government under President Dwight D. Eisenhower took over the French role in the south, installed an American-funded puppet, and agreed to hold free elections for a national Vietnamese government. But the Americans became convinced that Ho would successfully manipulate any elections, and, as a result, none were ever held. In the ensuing Kennedy administration in the early 1960s, the decision was made to "save" the client government in Saigon from a communist takeover by countering increasing guerrilla activity in the south with U.S. ground and air power. Then President Lyndon B. Johnson, who found that he had inherited a small-scale war, determined to bring it to a successful conclusion. He believed that he could do so without crippling the simultaneous War on Poverty in the United States or his effective support for civil rights for the U.S. black population.

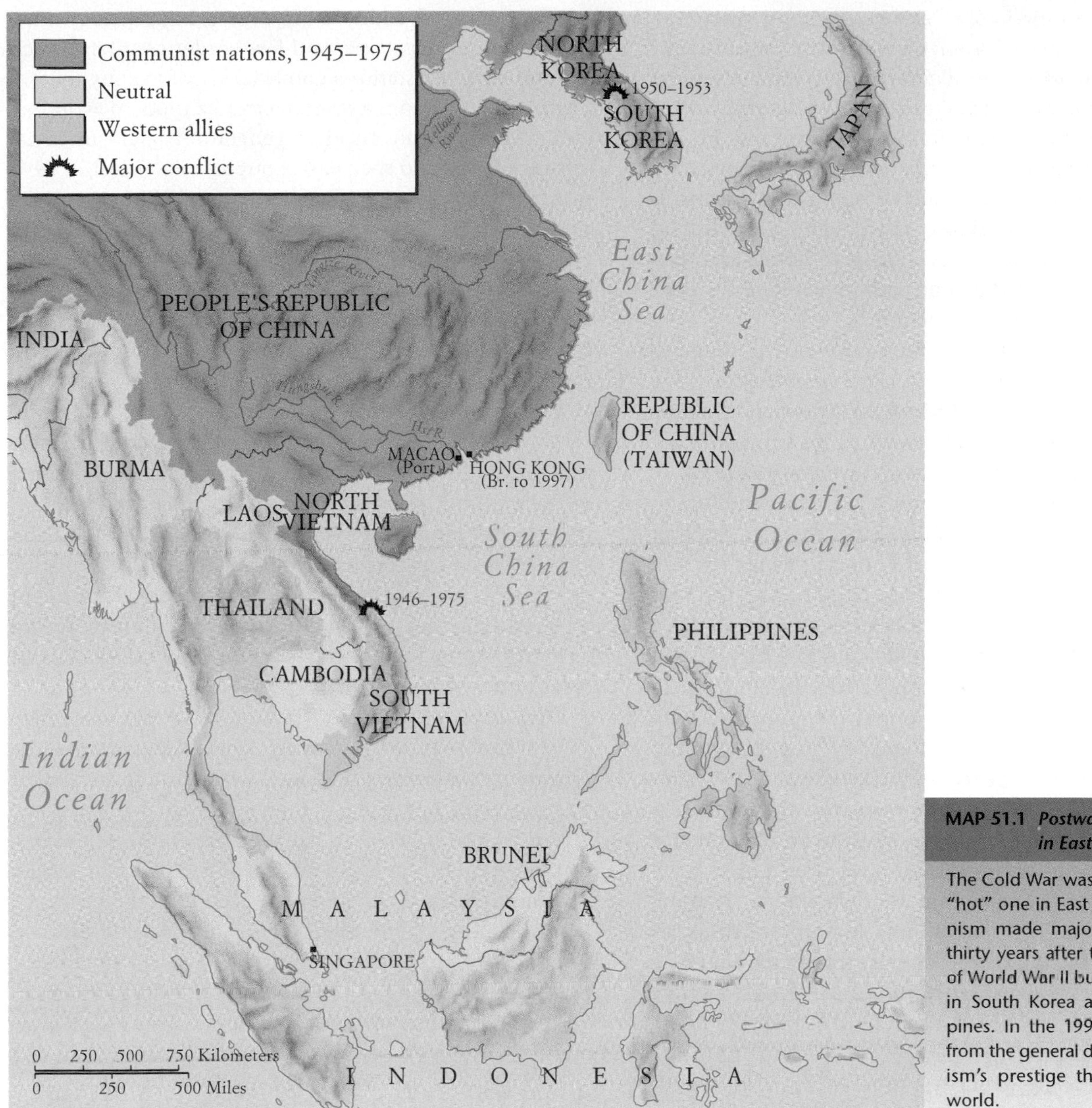


**MAP 51.1** ***Postwar Conflicts in East Asia***

The Cold War was sporadically a "hot" one in East Asia. Communism made major gains in the thirty years after the conclusion of World War II but was checked in South Korea and the Philippines. In the 1990s, it suffered from the general decline in Marxism's prestige throughout the world.

He was wrong on both counts. By 1968, half a million U.S. troops were on the ground in Vietnam. The entire nation was debating the wisdom and the morality of engaging in this faraway, bloody, and apparently unending conflict that appeared on television screens nightly. The War on Poverty had been curtailed by both budgetary and political constraints. The campaign for civil rights had run into African-American resentments, and there was a sharp decline of white liberal support for a president who continued to slog through the morass of Vietnam.

Johnson in effect resigned the presidency by deciding not to seek reelection in 1968, and his Republican successor Richard M. Nixon eventually opted to withdraw U.S. forces in the early 1970s under cover of a supposed "Vietnamization" of the conflict. A patched-together peace was signed with North Vietnam's government in 1973 after a year of negotiations, and the South Vietnamese took over their own defense. By 1975, the corrupt and demoralized Saigon authorities had fallen to their communist opponents, and North and South Vietnam were reunited on standard communist political and economic principles.

Until recently, both West and East relegated the country to a diplomatic limbo. The failure of the Soviets to assist their fellow communists in Vietnam fully brought to light the change in the Cold War and the conclusive nature of the break between the Soviet Union and China. In contrast to 1962, when Khrushchev was willing to gamble in Cuba, the Soviet government under Leonid Brezhnev preferred to forgo a foothold in South Asia and a propaganda advantage in the Third World rather than risk a war where Soviet security was not at stake. For its part, China was an active supplier of the guerrillas but carefully avoided placing its full resources behind the Vietnamese. After the communist reunification, frictions between the supposed allies reached the point where the Chinese briefly invaded Vietnam and withdrew only after giving a lesson to the recalcitrants in Hanoi. Relations between the two countries continue to be strained as Vietnam's commitment to Marxism weakens and the fear of a recurring Chinese dominance is reawakened (see Chapters 18 and 28). In most recent times, the still-communist regime in Hanoi has sought ties with all sources of potential aid for its lagging economy, and thus seems to be following the same path in its economic policies as its large neighbor to the north.

Important though the Vietnam conflict was in international affairs, its most striking consequences were probably within the United States. Many Americans now over age forty formed their views of government, the duty of citizens, and public affairs in general as a result of some type of personal involvement with the issues of the Vietnam War. The 1960s upheavals generated by war protest movements and resistance to what many saw as a wrong-headed and arrogant Washington were second only to the black civil rights movement as a milestone in the domestic affairs of the United States in the twentieth century. With the U.S. invasion of Iraq in 2003, these issues continue to resonate among those Americans who experienced the 1960s. To many of this generation, events appear to have repeated themselves.

### *Progress and the Promise of Future Prosperity*

Other nations of Southeast Asia have been much more successful than the unfortunate Vietnam in escaping from poverty and technological backwardness. Although handicapped by rapid population growth and a still-heavy dependence on agriculture and exports of raw materials in a high-tech world, they are overcoming these obstacles to prosperity.

The "**four little tigers**" of the Pacific Rim—South Korea, Taiwan, Singapore, and Hong Kong—have followed the course plotted by the Japanese. Until recently, they maintained superior growth rates in the drive to establish an electronically driven, information-based economy. They are being joined by Malaysia, and just behind these five are Thailand and Indonesia. Throughout the western Pacific, to foment rapid economic growth based on a modified free market has become the first priority for government, whether Marxist or capitalist in formal ideology. From a backwater status in the early part of this century, industrialized East Asia and Southeast Asia have become a vital part of a mutually dependent global interchange.

With relatively abundant resources, high literacy rates, stable village agriculture, and few border conflicts, much of Southeast Asia stands a good chance of making the difficult transition from a premodern to a modern economy and society within another generation. (The financial misalignments and speculative bubbles that burst in 1998 in several nations put a severe but probably short-lived ripple in this picture of progress.) The major long-term danger is still excessive population growth and the pressures it puts on the social fabric, but this threat is not as acute as elsewhere and is partly countered by steady growth in industrial development, which has drained off the rural excess in constructive fashion.

The most successful exemplars are Hong Kong and Singapore, two city-states with entrepreneurial business as their driving force. Both have found profitable niches in the evolving global interchange of goods and services. (How well Hong Kong can retain this special position after its reannexation to mainland China in 1997 is an open question. Recent efforts by the Chinese government to blunt demands by pro-democracy demonstrators for universal suffrage have created a political stand-off that remains unresolved as of 2004.)

Next come South Korea, Taiwan, and Malaysia, where skilled and politically ruthless leaders encouraged the growth of modern economies. The authoritarian rule that was the norm between 1950 and 1980 is now being replaced by more open and truly democratic arrangements, as the prosperity created for the rich under the earlier generation filters down and widens choices and horizons. Indonesia, the Philippines, and Thailand come next on the ladder of prosperity, while the war-wounded and isolated Burma (Myanmar), Cambodia, and Vietnam remain on the bottom rungs.

Ken Straiton/Corbis

**GINZA SHOPPING DISTRICT.** Postwar Japan has undergone another of its rapid adaptations to Western influences, this time to the global marketplace introduced to the country by the American occupation regime. Here, the Ginza shopping district in downtown Tokyo reflects the new consumer economy of the 1970s.

## Summary

In the second half of the twentieth century, East Asia saw two world powers arise: communist China and capitalist Japan. Taking sharply divergent paths since they contested one another for predominance in World War II, both nations have come to play important roles in world affairs. In China, this role has been primarily military and political. In the case of Japan, it has been entirely economic and commercial up to the present.

As founder of the Chinese Communist Party, Mao Zedong had tremendous influence after his victory in the civil war in the 1940s. His break with his Soviet mentors ten years later divided communism into hostile camps. It also allowed Mao to follow his own path into a communism that focused on the peasants and the necessity of continual revolution. After his death in 1976, his successors soon rejected this path, and the present leaders are experimenting with an unstable mix of socialism in politics and capitalism in the economy. The radical change in generations of leaders that lies just ahead puts a large question mark over the entire situation.

In Japan, the economy and society were modernized and westernized under the American occupation. The American-sponsored constitution allowed a new political culture to take shape that found a wide and positive response in a nation ready to accept change. A sustained partnership between government and business encouraged an unprecedented surge in productivity that was undisturbed by social or political discontents until very recently. Now one of the world's great economic powerhouses, Japan stands on the verge of having to make a decision about its role in international politics and diplomacy.

The Indian subcontinent emerged from the colonial era divided between antagonistic Hindu and Muslim segments. India has shown admirable maturity in retaining democratic politics despite the heavy pressures exerted by ethnic and religious frictions among its several peoples and inadequate, though substantial, economic development. Pakistan faces intimidating problems generated by retarded civic development and by the commitment to hostility with neighboring India.

In Southeast Asia, the picture has brightened in recent years after more than thirty years of violence and wars. Worst of these was the Vietnam conflict, which also had serious repercussions on the United States internally. Several of the former colonies of Southeast Asia are making a successful transition to the high-tech global economy and have excellent prospects for the future.

## Identification Terms

Test your knowledge of this chapter's key concepts by defining the following terms. If you can't recall the meaning of certain terms, refresh your memory by looking up the boldfaced term in the chapter, turning to the Glossary at the end of the book, or working with the flashcards that are available on the *World Civilizations* Companion Website **http://history.wadsworth.com/adler04**.

Amur River War
"four little tigers"
Great Leap Forward
Great Proletarian Cultural Revolution
Kashmir
little red book
massacre in Tienanmen Square
Red Guards
Sino-Soviet conflict
Taliban

## Test Your Knowledge

Test your knowledge of this chapter by answering the following questions. Complete answers appear at the end of the book. You may also take this quiz interactively and find even more quiz questions on the *World Civilizations* Companion Website: **http://history.wadsworth.com/adler04**.

1. China's attempt to make itself industrially independent of outside aid during the 1950s is called the
   a. Self-Strengthening movement.
   b. Red Guard challenge.
   c. China First movement.
   d. Great Five-Year Plan.
   e. Great Leap Forward.
2. What major change in international affairs became fully apparent in the early 1960s?
   a. China and the United States joined forces against the Soviet Union.
   b. China and Japan became allies.
   c. China and the Soviet Union became allies for the first time.

d. China and the Soviet Union became hostile toward each other.
e. China and Japan renewed their hostilities toward each other.

3. Mao started the Great Proletarian Cultural Revolution because he
a. believed that China was in danger of imminent attack.
b. thought that it was the proper time to introduce political democracy.
c. believed that all revolutions should be constantly renewed.
d. wanted to forestall the Soviets' move toward coexistence.
e. thought he could thereby control the peasants.

4. Which of the following statements is *not* true of postwar Japan?
a. It developed the world's highest rate of personal savings.
b. It developed the world's highest sustained growth in gross national product.
c. It came to enjoy the world's most favorable balance of trade.
d. It had the world's highest rate of personal consumption.
e. It became able to fully support the dietary needs of its people.

5. Japan's postwar political scene has been mainly controlled by the
a. Socialist Party.
b. Liberal Democratic Party.
c. emperor through his political allies.
d. labor unions.
e. democratically elected Diet.

6. In recent years, Japanese working women have
a. returned to their prewar habits of withdrawing into the home.
b. been the world's leaders in asserting their political presence.
c. been discriminated against as never before.
d. finally broken through the "glass ceiling."
e. made some gains in attaining equal pay and opportunity.

7. Since attaining independence, India has
a. been a military dictatorship.
b. maintained a large degree of democracy.
c. been steadily at war with one or another of its neighbors.
d. become a single-party, quasi-fascist society.
e. established itself as one of the most autocratic nations in the world.

8. During the Vietnam War, the Soviet Union
a. tried to aid the insurgents in every way possible.
b. consistently tried to bring peace by acting as middleman.
c. took a bystander's role rather than assisting the insurgents.
d. healed the conflict with China to assist Ho Chi Minh.
e. chose to support Cambodia but not Vietnam.

9. Since the 1990s, China's relationship with the United States can best be described as
a. wary.
b. open-handed and warm.
c. frequently hostile.
d. largely conditioned by internal politics.
e. resentful.

10. Pakistan's and India's relations with each other have been colored primarily by
a. fundamental differences in their ruling philosophy.
b. religious differences.
c. rival imperialist ambitions in the region.
d. rivalries and personality conflicts between their leaders.
e. their growing strength in nuclear weapons.

## InfoTrac College Edition

Visit the source collections at

**http://infotrac.thomsonlearning.com**

and use the Search function with the following key terms:

Mao Zedong    China history    Vietnamese conflict

## Wadsworth History Website Resources

Visit the World History Resource Center at **http://history.wadsworth.com/world** for a wealth of general resources and the *World Civilizations* Companion Website at **http://history.wadsworth.com/adler04** for resources specific to this textbook.

## HistoryNow

Enter *HistoryNow* using the access card that is available for *World Civilizations. HistoryNow* will assist you in understanding the content in this chapter with lesson plans generated for your needs. In addition, you can read the following documents, and many more, online:

Mao Tse-tung, selected quotations

*The African woman does not need to be liberated. She has been liberated for many thousands of years.*
Leopold S. Senghor, ex-president of Senegal

# 52 Africa in the Colonial and Independent Eras



| | |
|---|---|
| 1880s–1914 | Almost all of Africa brought under European control |
| 1899–1902 | Boer War in South Africa |
| 1955–1965 | Decolonization of most of Africa |
| 1963 | Organization of African Unity founded |
| 1960s–1970s | Trend toward dictatorship and one-party states/Cold War interventions by United States, USSR, China |
| 1970s–1980s | Overpopulation problem/ Drought, civil wars, AIDS, runaway urbanization wrack the continent |
| 1990–2004 | More stable, open governments appear in several states/Apartheid dies in South Africa/Muslim fundamentalism gains in northern tier |

## Background: The Scramble for Africa, 1880–1914

By the 1880s, sufficient geographic information was known about the interior of the continent to allow the European nations to begin to stake definite claims. Belgium and Germany vied with the British in Central and East Africa. The Portuguese took Angola and Mozambique under firm control at this time. The French cemented their hold on West Africa and parts of the center. Italy took the area around the Horn of Africa and was repulsed when it attempted to add independent Ethiopia to the list. In 1884, all of the major European states met at a conference in Berlin to lay down rules for establishing claims and to avoid overlapping jurisdictions.

By 1900, all of Africa had been allocated to European rule, with the exception of Ethiopia and Liberia (see Map 52.1). No attention whatever was given to local custom or economic relations when the borders of the various colonies were drawn. Whole peoples were split, and teams, sent out from Paris, London, or Berlin to partition the continent, shattered ancient ethnic and social affiliations. That this disregard for African geographic and ecological traditions was an egregious mistake became clear when the colonial system was dismantled after World War II and border disputes occurred all across the continent.

What contributed to the establishment of European sovereignty over Africa? First, after centuries of marginal interest in Africa, Europeans' attitudes changed. The rise of the antislavery movement and humanitarian interest in Africa (see Chapter 38) helped induce a European feeling

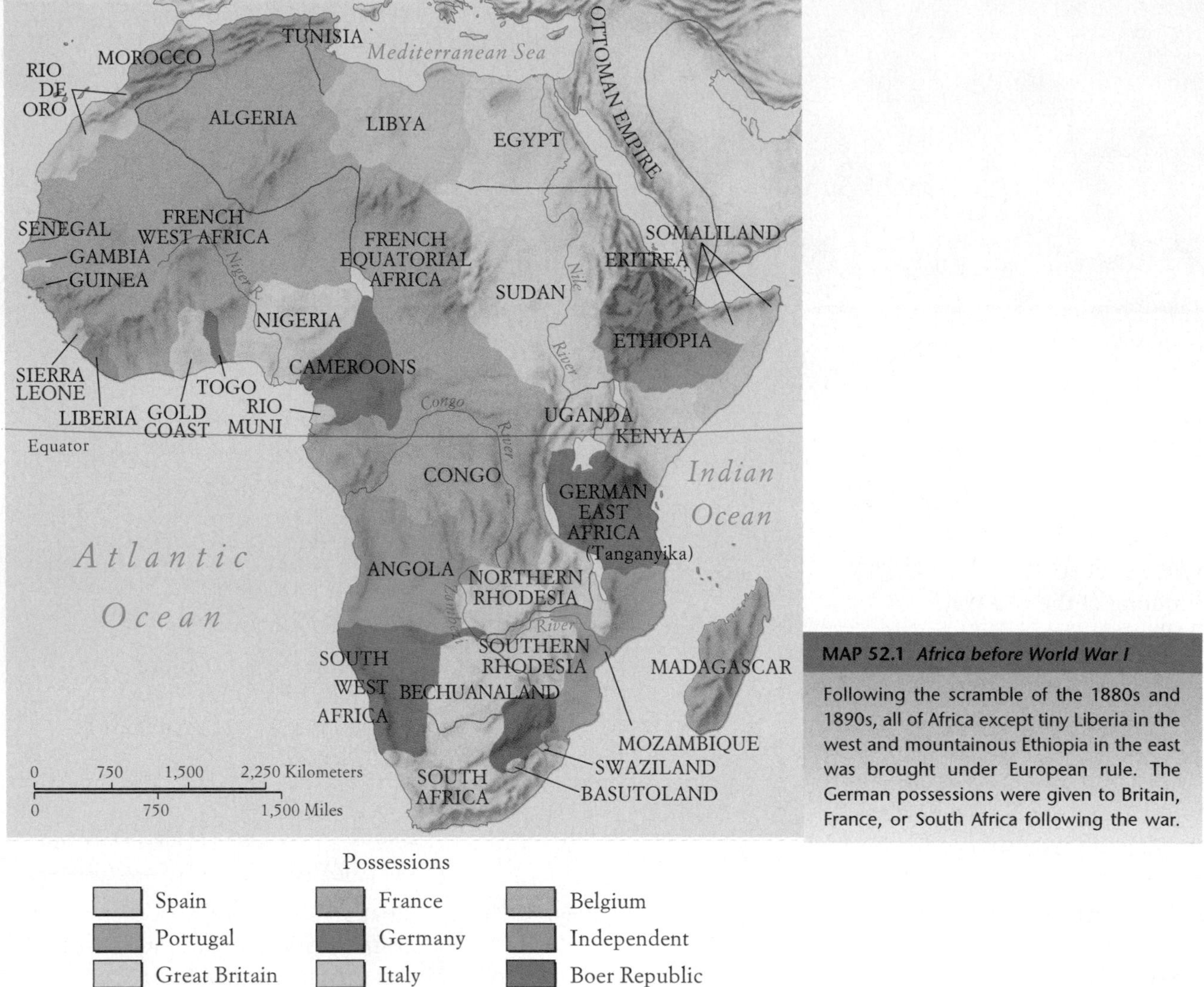


**MAP 52.1** ***Africa before World War I***

Following the scramble of the 1880s and 1890s, all of Africa except tiny Liberia in the west and mountainous Ethiopia in the east was brought under European rule. The German possessions were given to Britain, France, or South Africa following the war.

of paternalism toward Africans. Europeans came to believe they had a "civilizing mission"—often called the **white man's burden**—in Africa. The phrase was first coined in a Rudyard Kipling poem. Second, European capitalism began to play a new role in Africa. With industrialization, European nations needed new sources of raw materials and markets for their manufactured goods. Some, like the missionary David Livingstone, advocated "legitimate trade" as a substitute for the slave trade. Consequently, Western businessmen and women now came to see Africans and their lands in a wholly new light: they could "save" Africans from themselves, while bringing them the mixed blessings of the Bible and Western civilization. Third, the diseases that had made much of Africa "the white man's graveyard" for centuries finally were understood and countered by tropical medicines (quinine for malaria, above all). Mortality per year for whites dropped to about 5 percent in 1900. Finally, in the nineteenth century, Europeans developed mobile artillery, the Gatling and the Maxim machine guns, and the rapid-firing rifle that tipped the balance sharply in favor of those who possessed them versus those who did not.

One of the first tasks of the new overlords was to train an African constabulary under white officers to break up slaving raids and put down resistance to colonial rule. Another was the establishment of district offices, staffed often by young civil servants fresh from the mother country who were given extraordinary responsibilities in maintaining the peace and establishing European administration. In the British colonies, it was not unusual to see a twenty-seven-year-old, three years out of Cambridge and backed only by his constables, given life-and-death authority over a district population of perhaps 30,000 individuals. Direct challenges to the new dispensation were rare. Officers could move about freely without fear in the villages, although the nearest European might be a couple of hundred miles away. Attacks on the Europeans, when they occurred, were almost always motivated by the whites' breaking of religious taboos, taxation, or repeated cruelties.

The three European governments had somewhat different goals for their colonies and administered them in different ways, which were arrived at by necessity and experiment rather than by plan. French possessions were

**THE WHITE MAN'S BURDEN.** This engraving from 1895 shows the European concept of "civilized" administration being brought to the Africans. A district official listens judiciously to the complaint before issuing his decision, backed up if necessary by African soldiery in the background.

Hulton-Deutsch Collection/Woodfin Camp & Associates, Inc.

administered from a central office in Dakar and were linked directly with the Paris government. The Africans were given little margin to govern themselves. Through a system called **assimilation**, the French exerted strong pressure on the upper-caste Africans to learn French and acquire French manners and values. If they did so, they were paternalistically considered as "black Frenchmen and women." They could then enter the colonial bureaucracy and even become French citizens, although very few ever did.

The French made considerable effort to convert Africans to Catholicism, but they met with little success until the twentieth century. Very little economic development occurred in these colonies, which were for the most part desert regions deficient in natural resources or rain forest that discouraged exploration. Only in the twentieth century have modern irrigation works made it possible to develop some agriculture in former French colonies such as Mali, Chad, and Mauritania.

The British possessions to the south were more favored by nature and attracted more attention from those seeking profits. A few colonies (Gold Coast and Nigeria) began as the private possessions of monopoly firms, similar to the British East India Company in India. Sierra Leone began as a refuge for free Africans from intercepted slave ships after the maritime slave trade was banned. The British rulers, whether private or governmental, relied heavily on local assistants, whom they appointed to exercise actual day-to-day government under loose supervision. This system of **indirect rule**, which was similar to what the British did in India, was implemented partly to reduce administrative costs for the home country and to ease the transition from traditional methods of rule.

As a result of the (sometimes coerced) introduction of commercial crops such as peanuts, palm oil, cotton, cocoa, sisal, tea, and coffee in the late nineteenth century, Europeans' African dominions were integrated gradually into the world market. This proved to be yet another mixed blessing. Before the Great Depression, while prices for commodities remained high, the African colonies prospered. As in the rest of colonial Africa, however, the replacement of food crops by cash crops proved to be a disaster for Africans in the long run. Colonial authorities discouraged industrial development. The manufacturing of finished goods was left to the mother countries, and Africans were permitted only to provide raw materials. So when the prices of their cash crops and other raw materials (including mineral exports) fell, Africans' dependence on the world market proved to be "the mother of poverty." Unable to sell their cash crops at reasonable prices, many went hungry or starved when they could not earn enough to purchase food.

## REACTIONS TO EUROPEAN DOMINATION

Although terribly outgunned (literally as well as figuratively), Africans did not passively submit to European overlords. Many African leaders sought to check or defeat the Europeans' encroachments throughout the second half of the nineteenth century. Among the notable struggles was the Zulu War in South Africa. When rich diamond and gold deposits were discovered in the Johannesburg area in the 1880s, Cecil Rhodes, the British capitalists, and developers pushed into Boer territory to open mines and build railroads to serve them. The result was the **Boer War** (1899–1902), won by the British after a bitter struggle. But the Boers still constituted the backbone of white settlements and commerce in South Africa, and the British had to make concessions to them to maintain a manageable colony. The chief concession was to leave the Boers in control of the *apartheid* system of racial segregation. The African population was left with the choice of becoming ill-paid and exploited laborers in the white-owned industries, mines, and farms or remaining on barren reservations, or "Bantustans." Politically, the British maintained oversight of the colony from London and Cape Town, but the Boers dominated in the *veldt* (rural) villages and towns and elected a majority of the colony's legislature.

Other examples of resistance included the fight against the Germans in Tanganyika and the Ashanti resistance against the British in the Gold Coast. But, like the resistance of the Berber rebels against the French in Algeria and Morocco and the Mahdists in Sudan, these attempts failed in the end. With the single exception of the Italians' campaign in Ethiopia, the Europeans' superiority in weaponry and tactics won out, albeit after overcoming resistance that sometimes lasted for years. Against the Maxim guns and exploding artillery, bravery alone was not enough.

Once conquered, the African elites faced two choices: submit and attempt to assume the manners and values of their new masters, or withdraw as far as possible from contact with an alien overlord. In the French and British colonies, African leaders generally chose the first way, encouraged by colonial administrators. In the Belgian, Italian, Portuguese, and German colonies, the Africans often chose the second way, because they were given little opportunity to do anything else until after World War I. In some cases, those who withdrew and remained committed to African tradition retained more prestige in the eyes of their people than those who associated with the conquerors and mimicked their manners. Having seen the power of the Europeans, however, many believed that the whites' ways were superior and sought to associate themselves with those who provided access to them.

Of the three types of Europeans with whom Africans now were in contact—merchants, administrators, and missionaries—the latter perhaps were the most important for the evolution of African culture. Missionary efforts at basic education in the local languages were responsible for the creation of a small group of educated Africans who were determined to become like their white mentors. The education offered rarely went beyond the ABCs. By the 1930s, however, those select few who did advance became conscious of the gap between what the European liberals and intellectuals preached and what the governments practiced in their treatment of the colonial peoples. From their ranks in the mid-twentieth century were to come the nationalist leaders of Africa. They saw that the most telling critique of Western colonial practice was to be found in the classic ideals of the West. Like their Asian counterparts, the African intellectuals used the weapons that their Western education delivered to them to free themselves from colonial authorities to lead their peoples to independence.

## Changes in African Society

By the early twentieth century, the Europeans had completely demolished the traditional division of lands and severely affected the commercial and cultural relations among the Africans. The old boundaries based on topography and clan and ethnic associations had given way to European diplomatic agreements and horse-trading. In the same fashion, traditional African power relations had been either destroyed or severely altered by the imposition of European-style officials, police forces, and courts, manned either by whites or by their African pawns.

Personal relations between masters and underlings varied, sometimes even within the same empire. French officials and African subordinates generally got along well in West Africa but poorly in Central Africa, because of local variations in the French administration. In some instances, the whites and the African Muslim upper class got on well, but most Africans, who saw them both as exploiters, resented them. In colonies with large numbers of settlers, as in British Kenya and South Africa, the whites generally exploited their African labor and established an impenetrable social "color line," regardless of central government policies.

### Undermining of the Old Ways

At the beginning of the twentieth century, although Christianity had already made a slight dent in African traditional religions, the Islamic faith had far more prestige and adherents throughout the northern half of the continent. The burgeoning colonial cities like Dakar, Lagos, and Nairobi increasingly attracted Africans, but the majority continued living in their rural villages. Their standards of living were simple, and illiteracy was nearly universal outside of the cities and the few villages with mission schools, but where they were permitted to continue growing their traditional food crops and breeding their livestock, they were not impoverished in any material sense. However, where forced to turn to cash-cropping or to wage labor, poverty and social disruption tore asunder the cultural fabric of African societies.

Everywhere in the villages, the old ways of the Africans' culture and institutions lingered on, but subtle changes were under way beneath the surface. The "native rulers" appointed by colonial authorities frequently abused the powers given them by the Europeans. Because these powers usually exceeded traditional authority, their villagers only resented them. People found that the guiding spirits of the ancestors no longer seemed to be effective, so more and more youths sought their futures in the white man's religions, schools, cities, and jobs. The white man's medicine likewise provided an ancillary, and often more effective, source of healing. In these and other fashions, mostly unintended, the Europeans' coming as permanent overlords had a cumulatively erosive effect on the old ways. Many Africans found themselves adrift between the colonialists' preferred models of belief and conduct and the age-old traditions of African life.

## Economic Changes

What benefits to the home countries came from the establishment of African colonies? In 1880, the European colonial governments had few if any long-range plans to develop their new territories economically. The chief concern shared among them was to avoid expense or to find ways in which the Africans could be brought to pay for the military and civil expenditures incurred. They had to walk a fine line between excessive expense to the home country taxpayer and excessive coercion or taxation in the colony. A rebellion would be not only distasteful but also expensive to the home government. Ideally, cash-cropping and development of African mineral resources would allow a cost-free colony. For most colonial governments, however, this goal proved to be a mirage. Only a few of the colonies (Gold Coast, Nigeria, Senegal, Kenya, and South Africa) with cash crops such as palm oil, peanuts, coffee, tea, and cotton were better than a break-even proposition for the home nations. The hoped-for large domestic markets for excess European industrial capacity never developed—the Africans' cash incomes were far too small to absorb large quantities of consumer goods, and it proved impossible to attract private investments into Africa on any scale comparable to what was going into the Americas or even Asia. Only in one or two situations, notably the copper mines and rubber plantations of the Congo and the diamond and gold mines of the Cape Colony, did the African bonanza materialize. Cecil Rhodes, the British capitalist and greatest of the private empire builders of the nineteenth century, had envisioned a thorough Europeanization of Africa, driven by railroads and mineral wealth. By 1914, it was already clear that this would not happen.

The individual colonies varied sharply in economic aspects. In the center of the continent, the Congo was a royal plantation, held by a private firm in which the Belgian king held a majority share. Originally explored by Henry Stanley (of Stanley and Livingstone fame), the Belgian Congo was a vast area along Africa's second largest and longest river. It was an important source of several industrial raw materials, especially copper and rubber.

Relatively few Europeans settled permanently here. The main reason for claiming and keeping this kingdom of the West-Central rain forest was to exploit its abundant material resources. A great scandal ensued in the early twentieth century when it was gradually revealed how brutal the royal enterprise had been toward its workers and how little had been done to improve the lives of its African peoples. Despite many assertions that European rule was justified by its potential to benefit Africans, the final judgment is spoken by a simple figure: the population declined by half in twenty years (1885–1905) of Belgian royal oversight.

In a few colonies, the economic impact of colonial rule was visible and direct. In British South and East Africa and in Algeria, whole agricultural districts were taken from the Africans to be used exclusively by the whites. Everywhere, new requirements that taxes had to be paid in money forced Africans into providing cheap labor for white businesses and farms. Closely aligned with business interests, for example, colonial governments pressured the "kaffirs" (Boer term for Africans) of South Africa's gold and diamond mines into their dangerous and exhausting work.

Such methods forced Africans steadily into Western-dominated, capitalist economies of trade and cash. These economic changes undermined centuries-old lifestyles and beliefs that had been rooted in values that traditionally favored family and community ties. In the villages,

**"How the white man trades in the Congo State: bringing in rubber and hostages."** As an example of how white businesses exploited Africans, women and children were kidnapped and held as hostages to force their families to harvest rubber.

Private Collection/Michael Graham-Stewart/Bridgeman Art Library prestige shifted from those who came from respected lineages or who had religious authority to those who accumulated wealth. The way was being prepared for Africans' belated entry into the world marketplaces, albeit often to their considerable disadvantage.

### Independent Africa

Since independence, Africa has become one of the most problematic areas of the world in the most basic terms of political stability, prosperity, and perhaps even survival of some of its peoples. Decolonization has failed to bring the happy solutions that leaders and much of the general population had counted on almost half a century ago. Most of the continent's fifty-odd independent nations have undergone major economic and social transitions, and the results so far have been mixed, at best. Millions have died needlessly from famine, civil wars, and political terror. Millions of others have been reduced to misery as refugees.

What is particularly disturbing to both African and non-African observers is that the cycle of economic deterioration and political repression shows no sign of having run its course. With the exception of South Africa, most indicators are still pointing downward for the continent. The hopes of a generation ago have been severely disappointed.

## The Immediate Post-Independence Years

The decolonization of Africa proceeded rapidly (and unexpectedly peacefully, for the most part) between 1955 and 1965 (see Map 52.2). About thirty-five states derived from the former European colonies emerged in that decade. Since then, independence has been obtained through armed action in the Portuguese colonies in 1975, in the British settler colony of Rhodesia in 1980, and in Eritrea in 1993.

Aside from resurrecting some African names from the precolonial era (Mali, Ghana, and Zaire, among others), the new states showed remarkably little inclination to try to wipe out the two generations of European presence. The various kingdoms and empires that had been established as recently as the mid-nineteenth century by black and Muslim rulers were not reestablished, nor was a serious effort made to do so. Instead, the colonial borders were continued without change. Where they were challenged by secession, as in the Congo, Nigeria, and Ethiopia, they were defended—not always successfully—by armed force. It soon became clear that, despite the severe obstacles to a truly national unity that the colonial-era borders imposed, the new leaderships were determined to keep them. If they acceded to a neighboring state's dismantling, they saw that they were inviting the same misfortune in their own.

It often is said that African independence movements were fueled by nationalism, but this term means something different in Africa than elsewhere. African nationalists were not attempting to bind together a culturally distinct people under a single government within a common territory, as the nineteenth-century European nationalists had tried to do. Instead, the African nationalists wanted modernization and equality with the whites. African nationalism is therefore at base not an ethnic phenomenon but a social and economic one.

The first years of independence saw a wave of optimism about Africa's prospects and specifically about the intentions and abilities of African leaders to install democratic parliamentary republics. In several sub-Saharan states (Tanzania, Kenya, Ghana, and Senegal are examples), men of cosmopolitan culture and political subtlety were placed at the helm. These men were thoroughly familiar with Western forms of government and values. Most had been residents of Europe and the United States. In other states (Zaire, Guinea, Angola, Sierra Leone), less known and less subtle leaders asserted themselves, sometimes through coups against the original elected governments.

The pro-democracy bent disappeared almost immediately, however. The presidents and prime ministers became dictators within five to ten years of independence. Original multiparty systems were replaced by an all-embracing (and completely artificial) "people's union" or "national assembly" single party a year or two later. Ghana, the first colony to gain independence, is a good example. The Western-educated Kwame Nkrumah (1909–1972) was a popularly elected president in 1957. In 1960, he pushed through a new constitution that made him effectively the sole authority, and he banned the opposing politicians and made Ghana a one-party state in 1964. He reigned over it as self-glorifying dictator until he was deposed by an army rebellion.

This sequence of events occurred so regularly as to form a pattern in every part of Africa—Muslim and sub-Saharan, West and East. Why? The answers must be tentative. First, like Eastern Europe, preindependence Africa had no tradition of Western-style political institutions and customs associated with parliamentary give and take. In the colonial era, only the British and French had attempted to prepare their colonies for self-government along such lines, and the process had barely begun before World War II.

When the war ended, the combination of circumstances mentioned in Chapter 47 brought the colonies into a semblance of parliamentary politics with a rush. In most, the "Westminster model" based on British precedents was adopted under European inspiration, but this

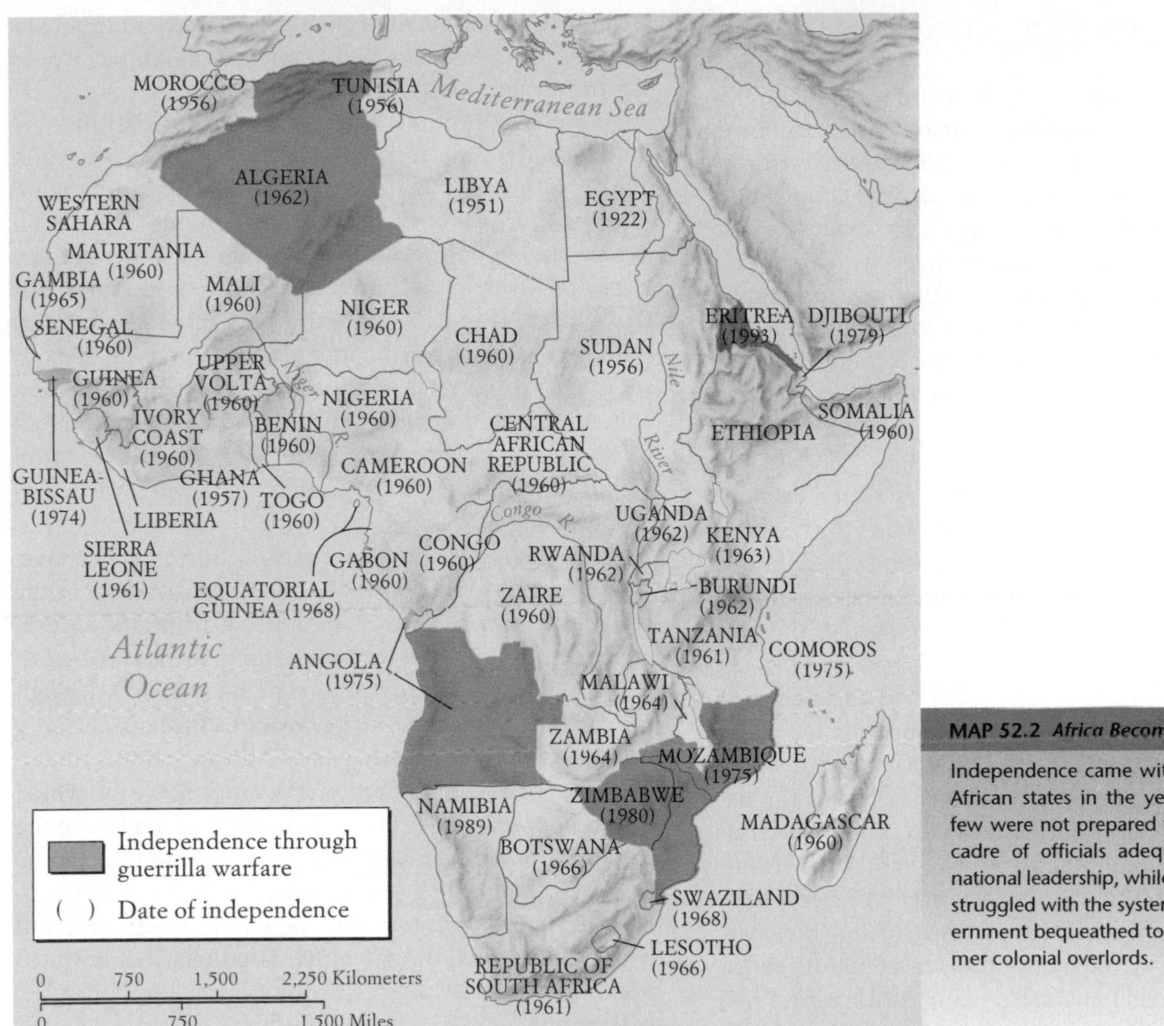


**MAP 52.2** *Africa Becomes Independent*

Independence came with a rush for most African states in the years 1955–1965. A few were not prepared for it and lacked a cadre of officials adequately trained for national leadership, while many others have struggled with the systems of law and government bequeathed to them by their former colonial overlords.

type of government, based on the interplay of a majority party and a loyal opposition whose voice must be permitted to be heard, was alien to Africa. On the contrary, Africa did have a strongly rooted tradition of personal leadership and loyalty to a lineage or kin group, which allowed no place for compromise if victory was in its grasp. Political party divisions in post-independence Africa were normally along such kin group lines, or what the West would call *tribalism*.

In addition, foreign interests sometimes promoted the removal of a democratically elected regime and its replacement by a group, civil or military, which favored the foreigners. This pattern was most visible in nations that were caught up in the Cold War struggles among Russia, China, and the West for control of various parts of the continent. Ethiopia, Somalia, Angola, and Mozambique are examples.

The breakdown of democratic parliamentary government often resulted in the establishment of a military dictatorship. The first in sub-Saharan Africa appeared in Ghana in 1966, but such dictatorships were soon endemic from Nigeria to Somalia and from Algeria to Angola. Some of the generals have come into power with a vision of what they wished to accomplish, but too many have simply wanted power and its accompanying opportunities to get rich. Worst of all have been those who combine the worst features of African regionalism and European terror: the repulsive Jean-Bedel Bokassa in the Central African Republic, Idi Amin in Uganda, and Joseph (Ssese Seko) Mobutu in Zaire (now the Democratic Republic of Congo).

Yet some signs indicate that a better day is dawning. Some of the vicious repressors have been forced out. Popular protests against several of the one-party dictatorships have been increasing, and some of them (the Democratic Republic of Congo, Benin, Ivory Coast) have succeeded in winning the right to establish legal opposition. Only the passage of time will reveal whether this is a trend throughout the continent or only a brief remission in the pattern of authoritarian government.

## The African Economy

Post-independence economies in Africa were naturally the outgrowths of colonial-era policies. In the interwar years, all of the European powers had encouraged the rise of monoculture plantations, producing single crops such as cacao, rubber, coffee, and palm oil for export to the developed world. These plantations were owned and developed by Westerners, but laborers who were sometimes forced to work on the plantations if they could not pay taxes in cash did the actual work. In the colonies with sizable mineral resources, such as Congo, Rhodesia, Angola, and a few others, Westerners similarly owned mines employing African labor.

Domestic manufactures were relatively scarce, because the home countries, which exported goods to the colonies, discouraged them. African enterprises tended to turn out substitutes for imports. For example, a factory might make soap that would otherwise be imported, but not asphalt for paving roads.

The final epoch of the colonial era had changed African economics in several ways. Migratory labor, for example, became more prominent all over the continent. Some went to a new area because of money wages or the demands of coerced labor in lieu of taxes. The cash economy introduced along the new railways and river steamships made it necessary for people who had never seen cash before to earn it, if they wished to buy the new goods introduced by the Europeans. The emphasis on export crops meant that gradually, many Africans who had previously produced all of their own food from their gardens and gathering now had to purchase it, as they would any other commodity.

M. & E. Bernheim/Woodfin Camp & Associates, Inc.

**Boys and Mercedes-Benz.** The delight on the boys' faces as they admire the car is only a partial counterbalance to the reminder of the vast differences in lifestyles between the "Wabenzi" (the Mercedes-Benz people) and the other Africans.

As a producer of raw materials, Africa was hit hard by the Great Depression of the 1930s. Prices on the world market dropped much faster for raw materials than for finished manufactures or consumer goods, so African farmers and miners received less for their exports but had to pay relatively more for their imports. With World War II, the market for raw materials of all kinds revived, and the postwar period until independence was prosperous for African producers. This prosperity was a major reason why Africans and non-Africans alike were optimistic about prospects for the new states. Africa (especially tropical Africa) was thought to be hovering on the verge of an economic "takeoff."

Their optimism was disappointed, however. The takeoff turned out to be a slow crash for most of Africa in the years since independence. For quite some time, the mounting crisis was disguised by international loans and credits. The 1960s saw an influx of foreign aid—mainly through the United Nations and the **World Bank**, but partly from individual countries. Many African nations undertook huge development projects, only some of which made economic sense. "Bigger is better" seemed to be the password. Broad four-lane highways were built in capital cities that had only a few thousand cars, big new terminals in airports that had five flights on a busy day, and twenty-story government office buildings that towered over the cardboard shacks of the poor while remaining half-empty.

Huge amounts of aid money were wasted or stolen by both locals and foreign contractors, who scented easy pickings and paid the necessary bribes. To a large extent, the bribery and waste were products of the Cold War, as the United States and the Soviet Union (and China in some instances) jockeyed for position in a dozen African countries. The United States kept the money flowing to the corrupt and murderous Mobutu regime in power in Zaire because he favored the West. The Soviets were only too pleased to support the Mengistu government in Ethiopia because this tyrannous and blood-stained clique called itself "Marxist-Leninist." Neither side protested or lifted a finger against the insane Idi Amin in Uganda because they had vain hopes of inducing him to join them.

After the OPEC-generated oil shock of the 1970s, the African states found themselves slipping rapidly backward. Except for Nigeria and Angola, very few oil wells existed south of the Sahara, and the quadrupling of oil prices in 1973 hit the developing industries and the general citizenry hard. Inflation quickly got out of hand. The governments attempted to meet the crisis by redoubling their exports, thus encouraging still more monoculture of cash crops such as cotton and rubber. This in turn discouraged growing of domestic food crops, such as rice and sweet potatoes. By the end of the decade, several formerly self-sufficient countries were importing part of their food. Nigeria, for example, chose to use a good chunk of its increased oil revenues to pay a subsidy to importers of food, thus keeping food prices low for consumers but putting local farmers out of business. When the oil bubble burst in the 1980s, Nigeria faced sharply reduced revenues from petroleum and far fewer farms to feed its increased population.

The true dimensions of the problem became visible only in the 1980s. Several events coincided to bring this about: the diminishing domestic food stocks; the prolonged drought in Ethiopia, Somalia, and the Sudan; civil wars in the Sudan, Chad, Angola, Mozambique, and Ethiopia; and the sharp reduction in foreign aid flowing into Africa from international bodies and Cold War opponents. The injurious effects of all of these problems were magnified by the continuing rapid increase in population, which was only partly offset by the equally rapid spread of AIDS in several countries.

In the twenty years from 1960 to 1980, in only about 20 percent of African nations did gross national product (GNP) grow at an annual rate of 2 percent or better, which is considered to be a moderate standard of progress. Nine countries actually had negative growth in this period. In the 1980s, however, the record was still worse. The small farmers and herdsmen who make up a majority in every country in tropical Africa have suffered most from the overpowering changes since independence. Farm output since independence has increased by 2 percent per year at best in most countries, while population growth has averaged more than 3 percent everywhere. One-quarter of sub-Saharan Africans live in what the World Bank calls "chronic food insecurity"—that is, they are hungry.

The abandonment of traditional diet and work patterns in the villages has driven many men to seek work in the exploding cities. Increasingly, labor is flowing from the countryside to the towns, which almost never have adequate employment opportunities for it. Unable to find regularized employment, people are driven into the streets, as in India or Latin America, where they live by hawking bric-a-brac, cooked food, Coca-Cola, or plastic toys to passersby who are as poor as themselves. Previously, theft was almost unknown in African society, but it has now become common, as has street violence in the cities. Hunger and deprivation are the reasons.

## The Population Bomb

The economic and social problems enumerated here are largely the result of one overwhelmingly important fact: Africa is producing too many people for the means available to satisfy their rising expectations. Africa has the world's highest birthrates, averaging 3.3 percent per annum in 1990. In some countries, the rate of national population increase has been more than 4 percent. (Most recent figures show some decline in African birthrates.) As yet, no African country has made a serious effort to control its surplus population. Several governments still maintain that there *is* no overpopulation problem, only a resource availability problem, but this position cannot be sustained in the face of any serious investigation of the facts of African ecology.

Only about 10 percent of African surface soil is suitable for any type of crop cultivation. Much of the farming is carried out on marginal land that is subject to repeated droughts, which come in long cycles. Africa has only 8 million hectares (each hectare equals 2.47 acres) of irrigated land, versus Asia's 135 million. In exactly the same way as in the Amazon basin, one of Africa's most valuable products is being rapidly diminished: the tropical rain forest. Once the big trees (mahogany, above all) are cut down, the nutrient-poor land they have shaded is next to useless for agriculture and is poor even for pasturage. But the lumber has immediate export value, and that has been a sufficient inducement for governments that are desperate for revenues and private owners who are greedy for cash.

The concentration on export crops and timber has seriously disrupted the African ecological balance, and the explosive growth of population has increased the pressures. Nomadic herders in the Sahel, for example, have had to increase their flocks of camels, goats, and cattle, because in a drought cycle, such as was experienced in the 1970s and early 1980s, the animals could not prosper and grow sufficient meat for human consumption. But these increased numbers put even more stress on the vegetation they browse on, magnifying the effects of the drought. As a result, in this area the Sahara is rapidly expanding southward, as the natural vegetation is eliminated.

The popular image of Africa as a vast expanse of jungles and plains filled with lions and elephants is wildly distorted and always has been, but a great deal of big game is left in Africa in certain regions, and the tourist money that it attracts is a major contributor to some African nations (Kenya, Zimbabwe, and Tanzania lead the list). As the population has grown in those countries, however, large regions where lions previously roamed have had to be opened to human habitation. The upshot, predictably, is a conflict between human and animal uses of the land, which, again predictably, the animals always lose. That, in turn, harms the tourist trade, reducing the money available to the governments to assist the excess population in the struggle to stay alive.

The current surge in African population numbers has produced several vicious circles of this sort. The "population bomb" that the ecologists in the 1970s feared would threaten the livability of the entire planet proved to be exaggerated—*except* in tropical Africa where, in some senses, it has exploded. (Recall the dire predictions of Paul Ehrlich and his associates. A prime reason that they have not come true thus far, at least, was the **Green Revolution** in agriculture. Through a combination of fertilizers and new hybrids, yields of corn, rice, and wheat were greatly increased in much of Asia and Latin America, but this outcome did not occur in Africa, where yields have remained low throughout the post-independence period and probably cannot be raised much.)

## Two African States

Two African nations—Kenya and Zimbabwe—illustrate the troubled internal politics of African states since independence.

### *Kenya*

The Texas-sized East African country of Kenya was a British colony until 1963, when the London-trained anthropologist Jomo Kenyatta (c. 1890–1978) became the first president (see Society and Economy). Kenyatta had been accused of collaborating with the Mau Mau guerrillas, who had begun attacking the British settlers as early as 1952 in an attempt to drive them out. The accusation was groundless, but Kenyatta spent years in jail nevertheless, which made his name known to every Kenyan and made him a folk hero to his Kikuyu people, the most numerous of several Kenyan ethnic groups. Kenyatta began auspiciously by assuring the 100,000 British that they were still welcome under African rule. Africanization of land and commerce was pursued and gave many Kikuyu, in particular, a rapid entry into modern and urban living.

By the early 1970s, however, Kenyatta had become the effective dictator of a one-party state. He had silenced the major opposition party by jailing its leaders, and within his own party, the Kenya African National Union (KANU), he had even resorted to assassinations. Regional and ethnic politics soon displaced the concept of national welfare, and the Kikuyu did not hesitate to oppress their fellow citizens for their own advantage.

Kenyatta's successor, Daniel arap Moi, was in command of the country until 2002, and his rule became steadily more repressive. Barely a shred of democratic government was left, while corruption at the top was rampant and the country's urgent problems were ignored. Possessing one of the most industrialized economies in Africa and some of the best agricultural land, Kenya went backward rather than forward in the twenty-six years under Moi's dictatorship. An exploding rate of population growth in the past (as high as 4 percent per annum, the highest in Africa) has contributed to the country's downward spiral. (See the Society and Economy box for more about Kenya.)

### *Zimbabwe*

Zimbabwe, which is about the size of Montana, emerged into independent existence in 1980, the fruit of a lengthy and sometimes-bloody guerrilla war against the British settlers. The conflict began in 1966, when the settlers defied London's commands and set up their own independent government, calling their creation Rhodesia. The whites, who constituted only 5 percent of the population, were eventually worn down and entered into negotiations with the guerrillas. In 1980, the state was

Jason Laure/Woodfin Camp & Associates, Inc.

**Jomo Kenyatta.** Born into Kenya's Kikuyu tribe, Kenyatta traveled to Britain in the 1930s and became an outspoken advocate of African rights in Britain's colonies. Following World War II, he returned to Kenya and was arrested for his alleged participation in the "Mau Mau" rebellion. From Kenya's independence in 1963 until his death in 1978, Kenyatta served as Kenya's first President.

SOCIETY AND ECONOMY

## Changing Times in Kenya

**The following spontaneous comment** on what should be done to make a better life possible comes from a Kenyan village woman, speaking with an interviewer in the late 1970s. The married women of Africa, and particularly those areas like Kenya that had seen most of the good land already taken up, often were left alone by their men folk for months or even years at a time. The men saw the city as the only possible locale for entering the new money economy that had gradually supplanted the traditional barter/labor system of the villages. Sometimes they returned, sometimes not. In the meantime, the women were willy-nilly entering a new life:

> What we need in this village is teachers to teach women handicrafts and sewing and agricultural skills. We have organized a women's group. I am one of the leaders. . . .
>
> It is better to educate a girl than a boy, although one should educate both. Girls are better. They help a lot. See this house? My daughters built it for me. If you don't have any daughters, who will build for you? The boys will marry and take care of their wives—that's all. They don't care about mothers. . . .
>
> My mother has eleven children; she is my father's only wife. She works in the fields and grows the food we eat. She works very hard, but with so many children it is difficult to get enough food or money. All my sisters and brothers go to school. One is already a teacher, and that is why I am trying to learn a profession. If I can get enough schooling I can serve the country and my own family. . . . My life is very different from my mother's. She just stayed in the family until she married. Life is much more difficult now because everybody is dependent on money. Long ago, money was unheard of. No one needed money. But now you can't even get food without cash. Times are very difficult. . . .
>
> If I were in a position of authority, I would really try to educate women. Right now, girls are left behind in education. It costs money, and parents think it is more important to educate boys. But I think that if people are intelligent, there is no difference. Girls and boys should be educated the same. I would make rules and teach women who are not educated and who have never been to school. They, too, must understand what today's problems are. If I have any spare time, I want to learn new things. I would like to learn how to manage my life, my future life, and have enough say in things so that my husband and I could understand one another and share life with our family. And I would change the laws so that men would understand women and their needs and not beat them as they do. . . .
>
> Women feel very hurt because they think their men don't recognize them as human beings. They are unhappy because of this inequality. I am lucky . . . my husband is good. He never took another wife. We are still together. . . . My wish would be that men and women could live as two equal people.

### *Analyze and Interpret*

What similarities and contrasts do you see between this and the Japanese woman's changing role described in Chapter 50? Do you think that a traditional society like Kenya's can modernize and still retain the subordination of women to men? Why or why not?

Source: P. Huston, *Third World Women Speak Out* (New York: Praeger, 1979). 

renamed Zimbabwe, symbolizing the coming of African rule by evoking the ancient city-state. Robert Mugabe, head of the Zimbabwe African National Union (ZANU) and a leader of the guerrilla war, was elected prime minister in the first national election in which Africans participated as equals. Until recently, he had taken a relatively moderate approach to the Africanization of white-owned businesses, land, and cultural institutions despite his party's formal commitment to what it terms African socialism.

Economic progress in this quite rich country has been solidly impressive in the years since independence. The farmers, who make up by far the largest single occupational group, have increased production per acre significantly, aided by government credits and advice. Africans and the very small, but economically important, white minority have established some industry. Social progress has also been substantial in health and education.

Unfortunately, Mugabe has followed the same path as innumerable other African politicians in seeking to establish an overarching unity among disparate ethnic groups by monopolizing politics. From the beginning, he has actively persecuted his chief internal opponents. ZANU swallowed the major opposition party by coerced merger (1987) and has frequently harassed and threatened to ban the others. Adding to the tensions is the fact that the political map is based on ethnic lines dividing the dominant Shona people of Mugabe and the minorities. Resistance to Mugabe has been gradually increasing. He has been hurt internally by the evolution of South Africa away from *apartheid* (the term for segregation of the races in South Africa) and into African rule, because he had long been a leader of the antiapartheid forces internationally and has used that role to justify his increasingly repressive domestic policies. In the last three years, Mugabe has tried to cement his position by encouraging and directing the illegal takeover of white-owned land by his followers. In the general election of 2002, both his domestic rivals and international observers have challenged Mugabe's win. As of this writing, Mugabe remains in control.

## Prospects at the Start of the Twenty-First Century

What will the twenty-first century hold in store for Africa? If one were to listen to the daily news bulletins as the sole source of information, it would be easy to predict a future of chaos, famine, and brutality. These have been a depressingly large part of Africa's fate in the recent past and are presumably what will happen for the indefinite future. This view can be supported by nearly infinite social data. The continent has most of the world's poorest people. In recent studies, it was found that the per capita GNP for Mali was \$190. It was \$155 for Madagascar, \$235 for Tanzania, and \$200 for Niger. In the same year, U.S. per capita GNP was \$16,444. Life expectancies for males and females were forty-five and forty-eight, respectively, in Senegal, forty-two and forty-seven in Angola, forty-five and forty-nine in Mozambique, and thirty-eight and forty in Chad (perhaps the world's lowest). For the United States, they were seventy-four and seventy-eight.

Chad had one physician for every 53,000 residents in 1990. The infant mortality rate in sub-Saharan Africa averages about 125 per 1,000. In the United States, it is about 10 per 1,000. The adult literacy rate in many countries of Africa is below 50 percent overall and far lower among village dwellers. Higher education (postsecondary) is still a rarity, and most higher degrees are issued for the traditional specialties such as law, the humanities, foreign literature, and education. Relatively few students are interested in the applied sciences, engineering, or health specialties, which are precisely the disciplines most needed in their countries. These curricula lack prestige unless they can be studied at a foreign university, a dream that is open to few Africans.

One of the more gloomy and recalcitrant situations is the huge menace of the Acquired Immune Deficiency Syndrome (AIDS) epidemic, which started in Africa and has hit that continent much harder than any other part of the world. According to reliable estimates, in parts of tropical Africa about 30 percent of the population is infected with the Human Immunodeficiency Virus (HIV), and already far more people have died from the disease in Africa than in the rest of the world combined. Until recently, official countermeasures to fight the disease have been weak and ineffective. Strapped by scarce funding and an absence of basic public health facilities, the African governments are relying on the international health authorities to find a solution and bring it to Africa.

In a different arena, the internal and international conflicts afflicting Africa are frightening. Besides the strengthening challenges of the Islamic fundamentalists in the north, almost every country south of the Sahara has some ethnic group that is acutely unhappy with the state of affairs in the national capital. As of 2002, major rebellions were engaged in at least seven countries. Riots and street demonstrations against the current regimes were taking place in another half-dozen. Only in the Republic of South Africa, which is now completing the transition from generations of white-dominated apartheid to majority African rule, is there solid evidence of a new harmony. (See Nelson Mandela's words in the Law and Government box.) The **Organization of African Unity (OAU)**, founded in the wake of the independence surge in the 1960s as both a sounding board and a peacekeeper for the continent, has proved ineffectual in the latter role. It has long since become a club of autocrats who never wish to reprimand one of their neighbors for fear that the example might then be applied to themselves.

In the economy, all of the African states are more or less deeply indebted to the World Bank and a series of private international banks from which they have borrowed

**Elementary School in West Africa.** Often overcrowded, elementary schools are now found in most African villages, and universal education is an acknowledged responsibility of the government. The sexes are usually segregated, as in this math class for seven- and eight-year-olds.

Jerry Cooke/Corbis

## Inaugural Address by Nelson Mandela

**THE RISE OF NELSON MANDELA** to the presidency of the Republic of South Africa must be one of the more amazing events of recent African history. Imprisoned for twenty-five years as a subversive by the white South African government, Mandela remained the rallying point for all those who believed that the day of apartheid must finally pass.

Raised the son and heir of a thoroughly traditional African tribal chief, Mandela broke with his family and culture to gain a legal education in the city. As a thirty-six-year-old black lawyer, he entered the still subterranean world of African nativist politics and rapidly rose to prominence before his career was cut off by prison.

For his mainly black followers in the African National Congress, Mandela's convincing majority in the first universal balloting ever permitted in South Africa was a day of great elation and a satisfying end to an "extraordinary human disaster." But the white and Colored minorities were naturally nervous about what the future might hold. Would Mandela allow his more passionate black adherents to take revenge for their long exclusion from power and from human dignity? Would he remember the humiliations he had suffered both before and during his long imprisonment at the hands of the dominant Afrikaner whites? Or would he attempt to calm the waters stirred by a sometimes bloody electoral campaign and look into the future rather than at the past? His inaugural address of May 10, 1994, was eagerly awaited.

> Today, all of us by our presence here . . . confer glory and hope to newborn liberty. Out of the experience of an extraordinary human disaster which lasted too long must be born a society of which all humanity will be proud.
>
> Our daily deeds as South Africans must produce an actual South African reality that will reinforce humanity's belief in justice, strengthen its confidence in nobility of the human soul, and sustain all our hopes for a glorious life for all.
>
> The time for the healing of the wounds has come. The moment to bridge the chasms that divide us has come. The time to build is upon us. . . .
>
> We have triumphed in the effort to implant hope in the breasts of the millions of our people. We enter into a covenant that we shall build the society in which all South Africans, both black and white, will be able to walk tall, without any fear in their hearts, assured of their inalienable right to human dignity—a rainbow nation at peace with itself and the world. . . .
>
> We dedicate this day to all the heroes and heroines in this country and the rest of the world who sacrificed in so many ways and surrendered their lives so that we could be free. Their dreams have become reality. Freedom is their reward. We understand . . . that there is no easy road to freedom. We know it well that none of us acting alone can achieve success. We must therefore act together as a united people, for national reconciliation, for nation building, for the birth of a new world.
>
> Let there be justice for all. Let there be peace for all. Let there be work, bread, water, and salt for all. Let each know that for each the body, the mind, and the soul have been freed to fulfill themselves. . . .
>
> Let freedom reign! God bless Africa!

### *Analyze and Interpret*

Accused of revolutionary activity, Mandela chose to appeal to a "higher law" in his own defense before a South African court. Do you think such a defense was justified?

**History Now™**

***To read the entire inaugural address, point your browser to the documents area of* HistoryNow.**

large sums in the 1960s and 1970s. Because the prospect that these monies will ever be returned has disappeared, the lenders now insist on internal economic reform in the guise of so-called **Structural Adjustment Programs (SAPs)**. The SAPs supposedly will restart stalled African economies and allow increased export earnings, but the SAP goals are contingent on painful governmental measures to reduce chronic inflation, reduce subsidies to exporters and importers, or other measures that are equally unpopular with the voting public and/or the influential wealthy. As a result, the governments have little incentive to implement the SAPs, once the loan is obtained. With all of these economic and political negatives, is it still possible to look at the first generation of independent Africa as a learning experience that may produce much of value for the continent's peoples? In several instances, a ray of light has entered the political and economic darkness that has engulfed Africa during the past twenty years. Here are a few examples:

- Several of the one-party autocracies established in the 1970s have been forced to surrender power or loosen their grip on it during the past few years. Malawi, Benin, the Ivory Coast, and Mozambique, among others, have to some extent democratized their politics, thanks to popular protest or armed rebellion.
- The end of the Cold War competition for allies has allowed a measure of sanity to creep back into relations between the First and Second Worlds and the

African Third World. Fantasts, tyrants, and kleptocracies (rules of thieves) are no longer supported on the ground that if "we" don't, "they" will.

- International lenders are no longer willing to put up money for construction of personal or national shrines in the form of steel plants with no markets, international airports with no traffic, and hydropower plants with no customers. New projects now must be rationally justified and be suited to the real needs of the country.
- After many unhappy experiences, African governments have toned down or stopped their previous emphasis on cash export crops and focused instead on family farming to meet the constantly growing domestic food demand.
- A change in attitude has been displayed by several African governments and political parties toward women and their roles in society. Women are receiving active support and being encouraged to make their voices heard not only in politics but also in the working economy and in public affairs generally. (See the previous box on Kenyan villagers.)

Africa's future as a part of human society is impossible to predict. This rich continent, with its immense variety in both natural phenomena and human activities, may continue to suffer from a welter of civil wars, tyrannical politics, and economic hardship internally and peripheral status internationally. But it could be that the first generation or two of freedom was a period of growing pains and that the twenty-first century will see a recovery from past internal mistakes, followed by a steady rise from neocolonialism to equality in the world community. "Out of Africa, always something new," said the Roman sage Pliny in 65 C.E., and his words remain true today.

## Summary

The second largest continent has seen some evil days since attaining freedom from colonial status in the 1960s and 1970s. The fond hopes of participatory democracy were largely gone to dust within a few years, as single-party or outright dictatorial regimes took power. Where guerrilla wars had been necessary to attain independence, the warriors imposed themselves in the guise of united fronts or similar vehicles of personal power. In other cases, free elections produced the rule of an ethnic or "tribal" group, whose leadership soon reacted to opposition by creating a dictatorship. In still others, the military reacted to civilian squabbles by brushing them aside. In all instances, the attempt to introduce the Westminster model of parliamentary government has had a rocky path. Corruption has been endemic and has been stimulated by foreign aid and trade arrangements.

In the economy, the new states continued the colonial era's emphasis on cultivating export crops and mining but added a new dependency on international credits for some ill-conceived "prestige" projects. When combined, these factors made Africa vulnerable to conditions no government could control: famine in the wake of droughts, low raw material prices on the world market, and rising food imports to feed an exploding population. In most African countries, the economy has at best been stalled and has often shown actual losses in GNP during the past decade. In recent years, an encouraging shift has occurred toward economic realism and political toleration. Attacking the overpopulation problem is the continent's most pressing task. What the future holds in both politics and living conditions is impossible to know, but Africa will need both luck and assistance from the developed world to overcome its present handicaps.

## Identification Terms

Test your knowledge of this chapter's key concepts by defining the following terms. If you can't recall the meaning of certain terms, refresh your memory by looking up the boldfaced term in the chapter, turning to the Glossary at the end of the book, or working with the flashcards that are available on the *World Civilizations* Companion Website **http://history.wadsworth.com/adler04**.

assimilation
Boer War
Green Revolution
indirect rule
Organization of African Unity (OAU)
Structural Adjustment Programs (SAPs)
white man's burden
World Bank

## Test Your Knowledge

Test your knowledge of this chapter by answering the following questions. Complete answers appear at the end of the book. You may also take this quiz interactively and find even more quiz questions on the *World Civilizations* Companion Website: **http://history.wadsworth.com/adler04**.

1. By 1900, all of the African continent had been colonized by Europeans except
   a. Liberia and Zanzibar.
   b. South Africa and Ethiopia.
   c. Kenya and Tanganyika.
   d. Ethiopia and Liberia.
   e. Ethiopia and Egypt.
2. Which of the following statements about African nations is *false*?
   a. They have fewer educational facilities now than before independence.
   b. They all have primarily rural populations.
   c. They are all aware of their impoverished status in contrast to the West.
   d. They have almost all experienced a colonial past.
   e. Most of them in the twenty-first century are experiencing problems related to epidemics.
3. Which of the following statements most accurately describes the actions of European countries in Africa?
   a. The British imported their own governors, having no confidence in local Africans to rule adequately.
   b. The French tried very hard to convert their colonial subjects to Catholicism.
   c. French subjects were given great latitude in governing themselves.
   d. Most colonial administrators were so fearful of revolt that they almost never left their compounds without being heavily guarded.
   e. Most British officers in Africa were seasoned veterans in their forties.
4. The main reason Europeans were interested in the Belgian Congo was a desire to
   a. explore the Congo River.
   b. maintain a trading center there.
   c. extract slaves for the American trade.
   d. extract gold.
   e. take advantage of its natural resources.
5. From 1965 until recently, the general trend of government in Africa has been toward
   a. one-party dictatorships.
   b. monarchies.
   c. socialist states.
   d. parliamentary democracies.
   e. democratically elected presidencies.
6. In Africa, since independence, the most common population movement has been from
   a. the cities to the rural areas.
   b. the inland cities to the coastal areas.
   c. the nomadic life to the farm villages.
   d. the farm villages to the cities.
   e. the nomadic life to the cities.
7. In terms of the Green Revolution, Africa
   a. benefited more than other places in increasing its food supply.
   b. benefited less than elsewhere.
   c. grew no crops that could have benefited from the revolution.
   d. experienced practically no effect because of the nomadic lifestyle of many inhabitants.
   e. chose not to participate in experiments with new food crops.
8. The career of Jomo Kenyatta can best be summarized as evolving
   a. from terrorist to democratic statesman.
   b. from patriot to terrorist.
   c. from European student to African patriot.
   d. from ignorant African to sophisticated Westerner.
   e. from terrorist to dictator.
9. The Shona people are the majority ethnic group in the country of
   a. Kenya.
   b. Ethiopia.
   c. South Africa.
   d. Zimbabwe.
   e. Tanzania.
10. Which of the following has *not* contributed to African economic missteps since independence?
    a. Misguided notions of establishing national prestige
    b. Desire for personal enrichment
    c. Desire to spread the benefits to maximal numbers of citizens
    d. Frequent use of bribery
    e. The misuse and/or theft of much foreign aid money

## InfoTrac College Edition

Visit the source collections at

**http://infotrac.thomsonlearning.com**

and use the Search function with the following key terms:

Africa Kenya history Nelson Mandela

## Wadsworth History Website Resources

Visit the World History Resource Center at **http://history.wadsworth.com/world** for a wealth of general resources and the *World Civilizations* Companion Website at **http://history.wadsworth.com/adler04** for resources specific to this textbook.

## HistoryNow

Enter *HistoryNow* using the access card that is available for *World Civilizations*. *HistoryNow* will assist you in understanding the content in this chapter with lesson plans generated for your needs. In addition, you can read the following documents, and many more, online:

Jomo Kenyatta, *The Kenya Africa Union Is Not the Mau Mau*

Desmond Tutu, "The Question of South Africa"

Nelson Mandela, Speech on Release from Prison

Nelson Mandela, Inaugural Address

*Those who make peaceful revolution impossible will make violent revolution inevitable.*

John F. Kennedy

# 53 Latin America in the Twentieth Century

| | |
|---|---|
| 1900–1933 | Repeated forceful intervention in Caribbean affairs by the United States |
| 1910–1920 | Mexican Revolution |
| 1930s | Cárdenas presidency in Mexico |
| 1933 | President Franklin Roosevelt begins Good Neighbor Policy |
| 1940s–1955 | Perón in Argentina |
| 1948 | Organization of American States founded |
| 1959 | Castro takes command in Cuba |
| 1961 | Bay of Pigs invasion of Cuba |
| 1970s | Military governments in most of Latin America established |
| 1980s–Early 1990s | U.S. intervention in Grenada, Nicaragua, Panama, Haiti |
| 1990s | Reestablishment of constitutional governments in most of continent |



In the twentieth century, the histories of the twenty countries making up Latin America varied sharply in detail but were generally similar overall. In all cases, the politics and international relationships of the Latin countries were fundamentally influenced by the economic and social problems they faced—problems that were roughly alike from Mexico to Argentina. All of the countries also had to come to terms with the United States, the dominant power in the Americas with the ability—repeatedly demonstrated—to intervene in hemispheric affairs at will.

The worldwide depression of the 1930s was a turning point for the Latin Americans in an economic sense, as some of the larger countries attempted to recover from their loss of export markets by developing the neglected domestic markets and adoption of economic nationalism. Although not completely successful, they did manage a partial escape from the neocolonialism to which they had formerly acquiesced. Since the end of World War II, other attempts have been made to introduce more or less radical changes in both the political and economic structures, but with the exception of a faltering and controversial Marxism in Cuba, these efforts have not been sustained for more than a few years. Deep class divisions have continued, and social problems, especially those generated by population pressure and abject poverty, still look to their amelioration.

## Persistent Dependency

Because of its economic backwardness, Latin America remained dependent on the United States and Europe throughout the nineteenth and early twentieth centuries (many would say until the present). This did not mean merely that Latin America was dependent on outside areas for imports of goods and services it did not produce. In addition, Latin America became increasingly dependent on foreign capital and therefore foreign political approval for domestic investment of all types.

Latin America did not lack export markets. On the contrary, throughout the nineteenth century, demand in the Western world was rising for its raw materials: Bolivian tin, Brazilian coffee and rubber, Chilean copper and fertilizer, Mexican silver and oil, and Argentinian meat and grain. But instead of providing a general stimulus to the Latin economies, the benefits derived from these exports were limited to a mere handful of wealthy families or to foreigners. The native families either sent the profits abroad, used them for their own extraordinarily wasteful lifestyles, or squandered them on poorly considered schemes. Little was invested in rational, farsighted ways by either government or the rich. No attempt was made to strengthen the social fabric by encouraging the poor and the unskilled to become educated and thus qualify themselves to participate in the political process. For that matter, there was rarely an attempt at securing social justice of the most basic sort.

In many cases, the real beneficiaries of the exploitation of Latin America's raw materials were the foreign investors who supplied the necessary capital to get production under way: American mining corporations, European coffee plantation owners, and British shipping firms. None of their profits went into the pockets of *any* of the natives, let alone the workers, and to ensure the continuance of this arrangement, corruption in government was endemic.

The rising disparities between the rich handful and the poor majority created an atmosphere of social unrest in much of the continent. At times in the nineteenth century, the disenchanted and the desperate were able to find a popular leader (*caudillo*) who frightened the wealthy with his threats to install democratic reform. In every case, either the ruling group was able to bribe and co-opt the caudillo or another army-led "revolution" forcibly removed him. In some cases, when the traditional ruling group did not remove the disturber swiftly enough, the United States acted instead. Beginning with the Mexican War of the 1840s, examples of U.S. intervention became more numerous after the Spanish-American War of 1898 brought the North Americans more directly into the Latin world.

The obstacles facing the Latin American countries are similar in many respects, even though their political systems and societies are different, in some cases dramatically so. National economic policy throughout modern Latin America has aimed at escaping from the basic pattern of impoverishment: exporting cheap raw materials and importing expensive manufactured goods and technical expertise. A few countries made significant progress in the middle years of the century, usually in combination with a radicalization of internal politics. For example, in Argentina in the 1940s, the lower classes enthusiastically supported the dictator Juan Perón when he attacked both domestic class privileges and Argentina's import dependency on the United States. In the 1930s under President Lázaro Cárdenas, the Mexicans went further; they actually expropriated U.S. oil firms (with compensation) and withstood the wrath of the Giant to the North until a negotiated agreement was reached.

But in general, the economy of the southern continent (and of its Caribbean outliers) remained nearly as much under the control of external forces as it had been since colonial days. Until well into the twentieth century, the majority of the South American and all of the Central American states remained agrarian societies. They exported raw materials such as coffee, grain, beef, timber, petroleum, and copper ore. They imported the vital elements of industry and personal consumption such as machinery, steel, automobiles, transformers, and telephone wire. In such an equation, the raw material exporters are always at a disadvantage in the marketplace, because their products can almost always be found elsewhere or be replaced by new technologies.

## New and Old Social Problems

By the mid-twentieth century, the Latin American countries were divided into two major groups: the more industrialized and urban societies, which included Argentina, Brazil, and Chile (the ABC countries) and, with reservations, Mexico; and the majority, which remained agrarian and rural. In the first group, the migration of much of the population into the handful of major towns accompanied industrialization, accentuating the accustomed isolation of the countryside from the highly centralized government. The peasants in their adobe villages or the laborers in the mine and ranch country saw the capital city as a distant seat of invisible (and parasitic) powers, rather than as the source of leadership in addressing national problems.

In the cities, the industrial working class was growing rapidly and began to play a new role in national affairs in the 1930s and 1940s under the guidance of populist politicians. Primary education allowed a few of them to rise in the social scale and even join the thin ranks of a native middle class, but in the nonindustrial majority of countries, the people at large remained isolated from the government as they had always been and continued their traditional political passivity. The illiterate mestizo, mulatto, and Indio peasants remained in a backward condition, dominated in every sense by the (often absentee) landowners and with no hope of the social and economic mobility that the cities to some degree offered.

The social and political complexion of a given Latin American country depended largely on the number of its immigrants between about 1890 and 1930. In a select group consisting of the ABC countries plus Uruguay and Costa Rica, immigration from Spain and Italy in particular was large enough to establish and maintain a European culture in the cities and extinguish whatever Amerindian culture the countryside may have once possessed. At first glance, these countries seemed to have favorable prospects for extensive and intensive development. With the exception of Brazil, they had little or no history of slavery and its accompanying social distinctions. Race was not a factor. Basic natural resources were generally adequate to abundant, and good farmland was in sufficient supply. In short, these countries seemed to have enough actual and potential wealth to meet their growing population's needs for a long time to come *if* no human-made obstructions to the exploitation and distribution of that wealth were imposed.

It was precisely such obstructions that led to much of the social tension in Latin America in the twentieth century. In the ABC countries (less so in Uruguay and Costa Rica), the Creole latifundists and their caudillo partners in government prevented the land from being subdivided for the immigrant latecomers in the nineteenth and twentieth centuries. Social discontent in the cities thus could not be relieved by settling the vast and underdeveloped countryside. Mineral wealth such as Chile's copper or Venezuela's oil remained in a few, mainly foreign, hands. Industry and commerce were almost as tightly controlled as the fertile lands were by the nonavailability of credit. In the absence of a vibrant economy that would act as the rising tide that lifts all ships, these nations attempted to find answers to their problems in political doctrine. After 1920 or so, the proffered solutions ranged from a demagogic nationalist populism to total dependency on foreign (meaning mostly U.S.) interests and investment.

Until recently, Latin America's most intractable social problems were in countries such as Colombia, Peru, and Bolivia, where a large Amerindian or mestizo population continued to rival the Iberian culture of the dominant criollos. As late as the 1940s, the criollos normally responded to the perceived menace by attempting to exclude the natives completely from national affairs. Only in recent years has the uppermost class accepted the impossibility of continued political segregation between themselves and the masses.

Now, the ancient chasms between the landowning class and their peon laborers and between criollos and mestizos have been further complicated by the widening gap between urbanites and rural dwellers. In the last thirty years or so, everywhere in Latin America the demographic picture has changed markedly. Propelled by high birthrates as well as migration, the cities are growing at an incredible rate. The *barrios* and *favelas,* the shantytowns that surround every city and often contain more people than the city proper, are the future of Latin society if current trends are not reversed. Overcrowding, unsanitary makeshift accommodations, and the absence of even elementary public services (schools, police, pure water, and the like) are taken for granted in these slums, where some shacks have harbored three generations already. In the meantime, the villages and small towns have become even less important in the affairs of the nation than before. Always a disproportionately urban-based economy, Latin America is becoming a series of huge heads (Mexico City now has an estimated population of about 16 million), weakly supported by anemic bodies.

Unemployment, both urban and rural, is endemic and constant. No reliable figures are kept because it is impossible to do so, but perhaps one-third of the adults in the cities have nothing that U.S. citizens would recognize as a steady job. Income distribution is as bad as or worse now than it ever has been. Even by the standards of the developing world, Latin America has the most skewed distribution of cash income imaginable. A very small group of industrialists, latifundists, and import–export business owners are rewarded handsomely, while a very large number of unskilled urban and agricultural workers have next to nothing. In the middle, the number of professionals, white-collar employees, managers, and small business owners is increasing, but usually they are still too few, too unorganized, and insufficiently independent to play an important role in civic affairs.

## Economic Nationalism

One result of acute social stratification and continuing economic dependency on foreigners has been the wavelike rise of radical reform movements with strongly nationalist overtones. Interestingly, the leaders of such protests have often been military men. The widespread foreign perception of Latin American military leaders as reactionaries who automatically uphold the status quo

Keith Dannemiller/Corbis Saba

**Mexican Rebels Challenge the Government.** In the extreme south of Mexico, where small cliques have controlled the state government of Chiapas for many years, an armed rebellion speaking for the rights of the peasantry broke out in 1995. After some hundreds of casualties, the federal government agreed to negotiations that are still continuing.

has become increasingly erroneous. Depending on the circumstances, they have frequently been at the forefront of economic nationalism.

Seeking to avoid a socialism that ran contrary to Latin individualism and would invite the active disapproval of the United States, the reform leaders of the past century were often strongly influenced by the idea of a Mussolini-type corporate state, in which all sectors of the population would supposedly find adequate representation. The most popular of these broad-based movements appeared in Mexico under Cárdenas in the 1930s and in Argentina a decade later under the Peróns.

## Mexico under Cárdenas

The spasmodic and multisourced revolution that took place in Mexico between 1910 and 1920 was, as has been mentioned, the only genuine social and political change in the first half of the twentieth century. Out of it finally came a single-party government committed to social equalization and redistribution of both wealth and power. In this mestizo country, where a small number of *hacendados* had held all power for generations, such goals were unprecedented—and unfulfillable. In the 1920s, the governing party (later termed the Partido Revolucionario Institucional, or PRI), despite much talk, did little to advance social causes. But under the impact of the depression and the Marxist experiment in Russia, President Cárdenas (governed 1934–1940) tried to give substance to some of the revolution's slogans. He confiscated and redistributed much land to Amerindians and peasants in the poverty-stricken north, expropriated foreign mineral firms, and insisted on Mexican sovereignty in every sense. In so doing, he set the pattern of Mexico for the Mexicans, which most of his successors in office have followed.

His efforts to achieve security and a political voice for the lower classes, however, have generally not been followed, and the gap between the haves and the have-nots in Mexico remains vast. The much-heralded economic boost supposedly offered Mexico by the 1993 erection of the NAFTA free-trade zone with the United States and Canada has not materialized, and the national economy is still far from realizing its productive potential.

In the political arena, the PRI long since became an intricate web of established social powers ranging from labor leaders to intellectuals, all of whom expected—and got—a calculated payoff for their support. Despite undoubted abuses, particularly corruption at the top, the Mexican system has recently allowed an increasing pluralism in politics. The old allocation of political powers to solely a few recognized groups broke down, and scandal plus incompetence has ended the PRI's former death grip on high-level affairs. National elections in 2000 brought the leading opposition party to power, and President Vicente Fox promised, but so far has not delivered, major structural reform. Despite the difficult economic times Mexico has undergone in the last several years, there are some hopeful indications that the country is emerging from neocolonial status and headed into a more stable as well as more democratic epoch.

## Argentina under Perón

In Argentina, Juan Perón and his military and industrialist backers in the 1940s were ardent nationalists, who dreamed of making Argentina the dominant power in Latin America—a status for which it seemed destined by its size, natural resources, and entirely European immigrant population. Perón was one of a group of officers who threw out the elected government in 1943 and soon made himself into its leader. Perón's pro-German sympathies guaranteed that the United States would condemn him, which all but ensured his election in 1946 on a vehemently nationalist platform. His wife Eva (the "Evita" of song and story) was a product of the slums who knew her people intimately. She was always at his side in public, and her personal charisma and undoubtedly sincere concern for the Argentine working classes made her an idol whose popularity among the populace exceeded the colonel's. In terms of political impact, she was the most important woman in twentieth-century American politics, North or South. Her early death in 1952 was in a sense the beginning of the decline of the movement her husband headed.

Bettmann/Corbis

**JUAN AND EVITA PERÓN.** This 1951 photo shows the couple acceding to the "demand" of the Argentine people that they run for reelection.

Perón (or Evita) understood something that eluded most Latin American reformers: to overcome the apathy of the rural dwellers and the tradition of leaving government in the hands of a few, it was necessary to appeal to people in a way that they could respond to, directly and with passion. Such an appeal must concentrate on their many economic and social discontents, not on their political ideals. Perón played on this theme effectively, organizing huge rallies of the lower classes and making inflammatory speeches against the foreign and domestic "exploiters" while simultaneously, though quietly, assuring the entrepreneurs and big business of government contracts and concessions of unprecedented size. It was a fine balancing act between encouraging the egalitarian desires of the ***descamisados*** ("shirtless ones") and reassuring the rich that nothing unbearable was in store and that anyone else in Perón's place would probably be worse. Perón was helped by the fact that the early years of his rule (1946–1955) were a time of large profits for raw material producers, of whom Argentina took a place in the first rank. Like Africa in the immediate post-independence era, the Argentine economy prospered mightily, and the bigger pie allowed a bigger slice for all.

By 1954, however, Perón was confronted by a gradually strengthening democratic opposition. Attempting to keep his popularity among the workers, he allowed the radical socialist wing of the Perónistas more prominence, which alienated his industrial and business support. In that year, he also made the mistake of taking on the Catholic Church—which had originally been mildly favorable toward Perónismo—by attacking its conservative higher clergy. In 1955, the military drove Perón into exile.

During the ensuing decades, the military or its puppets again ruled Argentina, giving way to civil rule only in 1982 after the self-incurred disaster of the brief Falkland Islands War with Britain. Only in the early 1990s did this potentially rich country stabilize politically and find its way—briefly—out of the social conflicts and mismanagement of the economy that mark its history. Like all of Latin America, its economic well-being and social harmony still largely depend on events and processes in

Stephanie Maze/Corbis

**MINING IN BRAZIL.** The wholesale degradation of the natural environment practiced in almost all of the Latin American states since World War II is dramatically shown in this photo of an open-pit gold mine in the Amazon. Such sites rarely or never recover their pristine appearance; government regulation is minimal and often ignored by foreign investors.

which it is essentially a bystander, as the recent national bankruptcy has again demonstrated.

The appeal of nationalism remains strong and will become stronger as the Latins gradually are brought into contact with the world beyond their barrios by the international trade arrangements such as the **North American Free Trade Agreement (NAFTA)** that now links the United States with Canada and Mexico. The so-called Southern Tier free-trading area currently being hammered out among Argentina, Brazil, and Chile seems to be next, and it will presumably be followed by a full-scale globalization of the Latin economies. Whether this setup will bring tangible benefit to the masses of the poor or be just a modern variant on the neocolonialism of the earlier days remains to be seen. In any case, those who clamor for political power in the name of "the people" will always find a ready audience in this sadly unbalanced society. What Mexican peons saw in Cárdenas and Argentinian descamisados in Perón was a leader who, whatever his faults, claimed to stand on *their* side of the social and economic barricades, and that was a rarity they appreciated.

## The Shark and the Sardines

What about the powerful neighbor to the north? During the first two-thirds of the twentieth century, the *Yanquis* repeatedly played a heavy-handed and frankly conservative role in Latin American international affairs. One leader who had experienced firsthand what American influence could do in a small country (Guatemala) called it the relationship of the "shark with the sardines." That may be overstating the case slightly, but there is no doubt that in ways both open and covert, Washington was the court of final appeal in Latin foreign relations and, in some cases, not just foreign relations.

The United States first began to pay close attention to Latin America during the Spanish-American War (1898–1900), which was fought, in part, over the rights of the Cuban people to independence. In the ensuing thirty years, Washington intervened at will in Latin and Caribbean affairs. Incidents ranged from Theodore Roosevelt's creation of Panama as a suitable place to build his desired canal to the sending of armed forces against Mexico and Haiti and the use of the Marines to squelch the rebels of General Sandino—the original Sandinistas—in Nicaragua.

After World War I, U.S. capital and finance took the vacated place of the Europeans with a rush. The dependence of some of the Central American "**banana republics**" on the plantations of the United Fruit Company was merely the most notorious example of the economic imperialism that was practiced throughout Latin America. Cuba's huge sugarcane farms and mills were 80 percent owned by U.S. investors. The big oil strikes in Venezuela were brought in by U.S. firms using U.S. engineers. Mexico's original petroleum fields were dependencies of U.S. firms until nationalization, and 20 percent of the land surface of Mexico's border states was owned or leased by foreign investors in the 1920s, to name only a few examples.

But the story of Latin dependency on the United States has another side. Had it not been for Yankee investment and commerce, the countries to the south would have been even less developed economically and would have sunk deeper into their grossly obsolete system of production and consumption. Until World War II, it's largely true that the Caribbean and northern Latin America (with the exception of Cárdenas's Mexico) were U.S. colonies in everything but name. The bigger question remains: What would have been the Latins' fate in this period in the absence of the United States? Through their own efforts and expertise, they would never have achieved reasonable living standards for even a small segment of their peoples during the first half of the past century (and perhaps not in the second, either). If the U.S. capitalists had not been involved, would the Latin Americans have found more benevolent and selfless sources of help outside the Americas? It seems very doubtful.

In Franklin D. Roosevelt's presidency (1933–1945), the United States embarked on a **Good Neighbor Policy**, treating the Latins more as sovereign nations than as colonies. For many years, no troops were landed to ensure a "stability" acceptable to the United States, but still no one had any doubt where true sovereignty lay in the Western Hemisphere. With World War II and the coming of the Cold War, Washington became more concerned about the political allegiance of the Latin states. In treaties signed immediately after the war, the United States pledged political and economic assistance to the other signatories. In 1948, the **Organization of American States (OAS)** was founded under American auspices and served several useful commercial, cultural, and legal purposes besides its primary one of assuring democratic and pro-Western governments in the hemisphere.

But the real catalyst for U.S. activity was the coming of Fidel Castro to revolutionary power in Cuba (with a program described in the Law and Government box). Originally the organizer of a hopelessly outnumbered band of idealists, Castro surprisingly overturned the corrupt and unpopular Batista government at the beginning of 1959. After a year of increasing tension, he declared himself a Marxist and began systematically persecuting those who openly disagreed with that philosophy, while denouncing the United States as the oppressor of freedom-loving Latin Americans. After he nationalized the extensive U.S. businesses in Cuba, a state of near-war existed between the two countries, culminating in the abortive Bay of Pigs invasion by U.S.-financed anti-Castroites in 1961. A year

# Fidel Castro's Manifesto

**Fidel Castro attempted to begin** a revolutionary movement in Cuba in 1956, three years before a second attempt was successful. The attack on the Moncada Barracks was a failure, and Castro was captured, but he was given an opportunity to broadcast his appeal to the Cuban people by the trial judges. His summation in his own defense is entitled *History Will Absolve Me*. The Cuban revolutionaries regard it as the fundamental statement of Castro's beliefs:

> When we speak of the people we do not mean the comfortable ones, the conservative elements of the nation, who welcome any regime of oppression, any dictatorship, any despotism, prostrating themselves before the master of the moment. . . . When we speak of struggle, the people means the vast unredeemed masses to whom all make promises and whom all deceive; we mean the people who yearn for a better, more dignified and more just nation. . . .
>
> Seven hundred thousand Cubans without work. . . .
>
> Five hundred thousand farm laborers, inhabiting miserable shacks, who work four months of the year and starve the rest. . . .
>
> Four hundred thousand industrial laborers and stevedores whose retirement funds have been embezzled, whose benefits are being taken away . . . whose salaries pass from the hands of the boss to the moneylender. . . .
>
> One hundred thousand small farmers who live and die working on land that is not theirs, looking at it in sadness as Moses looked at the Promised Land, to die without ever owning it. . . .
>
> Thirty thousand teachers and professors who are so devoted, dedicated and necessary to the better destiny of future generations and who are so badly treated and paid. . . .
>
> Twenty thousand small businessmen, weighted down by debt . . . and harangued by a plague of grafting and venal officials.
>
> Ten thousand young professionals . . . who come forth from school with their degrees, anxious to work and full of hope only to find themselves at a dead end with all doors closed. . . .
>
> These are the people, the ones who know misfortune and, therefore, are capable of fighting with limitless courage!
>
> To the people whose desperate roads through life have been paved with the bricks of betrayal and false promises, we were not going to say: "We will eventually give you what you need," but rather—"Here you have it, fight for it with all your might, so that liberty and happiness can be yours!"

Bettmann/Corbis

**Fidel Castro in Havana.** The Cuban revolutionary leader enjoys his triumph in Havana after chasing out the corrupt Batista regime in 1959. The display of guns, as well as the characteristic Castro cigar, were frequent notes in Castro appearances during his early years in power.

## *Analyze and Interpret*

How closely did Castro's actions follow his words when he did manage to secure power in Cuba? Should it have been such an unpleasant surprise to the U.S. government of Dwight Eisenhower when Castro proceeded to nationalize all U.S. industrial properties? Do Castro's statements affect your own understanding of how he has been able to retain power in Cuba for over forty years?

Source: Fidel Castro, *History Will Absolve Me* (London: Cape, 1968).

**HistoryNow™**

***To read some of Fidel Castro's writings, point your browser to the documents area of HistoryNow.***

later, the placement of long-range missiles on the island by the Soviets brought the world to the brink of nuclear war (see Chapter 49).

Since then, relations between the Castro government and Washington have remained frigid. The Cuban revolution, despite some real achievements for the people of the island (literacy, public health, technical education, housing), has proved unable to guarantee a decent material life, especially since Castro's original Soviet and Chinese supporters have collapsed or withdrawn their aid. The revolution has also proved unsuitable for export to the rest of the continent, as Castro had once intended.

No other Latin state ever "went communist," although a few Marxist-leaning governments have been elected (notably, those of Salvador Allende in Chile in 1971 and of the Sandinistas in Nicaragua in the 1980s). All of these have been overtly and covertly undermined by the United States, as have also the attempts by Marxist-led guerrillas or terrorists to seize power. The fiasco of Marxist theory and practice in eastern Europe (see Chapter 55) and the manifest disinterest of the Chinese have all but eliminated this threat to capitalist and democratic governments in the continent.

### *The U.S. Role in Recent Latin Affairs*

In the early days of the Kennedy administration (1961–1963), under the emblem of anti-Castro action, the United States entered into an **Alliance for Progress** with the Latin American states. More than $10 billion was set aside for economic development loans and credits, more than twice the money allocated to postwar Europe under the Marshall Plan. But as so often happens with government programs that are intended to make a quick impression on the electorate, much of the money went to make the rich richer or wound up in the wrong pockets. The single most effective, externally funded program for Latin American development was the quiet work on improving crop yields, done mainly in Mexico during the 1950s and 1960s. This botanical laboratory project gave a tremendous boost to world food grain production, resulting in some places in the Green Revolution that we have mentioned earlier. Its success in greatly stimulating rice, wheat, and other food grain production is a main reason why the threatened world famine has thus far been confined to regions of Africa and has not menaced Latin America and the entire developing world.

In recent years, U.S. involvement with the Caribbean nations has again become openly interventionary and reactionary, but generally within dimensions that the OAS as a whole has been willing to approve. Since 1983, Presidents Ronald Reagan (Grenada, Nicaragua), George Bush (Panama), and Bill Clinton (Haiti) have acted forcefully to protect what they perceived to be U.S. strategic, political, or economic interests in the area. Ongoing efforts funded and guided by the North Americans to control narcotic drug smuggling from several Latin states into the United States have drawn further U.S. intervention, but a return to the pre-1930 system of "gunboat diplomacy" by the United States is hardly possible, even if it were desirable. A major voluntary change in the levers of control occurred in 2000 when the U.S.-built and -managed Panama Canal became part of the sovereign territory of Panama. Pending political questions in the Caribbean basin include possible independence for Puerto Rico (a U.S. territory for the past century) and the fate of Cuba after the inevitable demise of the seventy-seven-year-old Castro.

## Current Issues and Problems

In Latin America as elsewhere, economic and social issues are linked together and have numerous direct political repercussions. In Latin America as a whole, just as in Africa, probably the highest-priority long-term social problem is controlling a rate (2.9 percent) of population growth that is too high for the resources available. Also as in Africa, several governments would contest this assessment, saying that faulty or nonexistent access to resources, both domestic and foreign, generates most social frictions in their countries. There is, in fact, something to be said for this argument. In the eyes of many Latin Americans, the developed world, and especially the United States, has taken unfair and shortsighted advantage of the underdeveloped world during the past century and continues to do so in the following ways:

1. The terms of foreign trade—that is, the rate at which raw materials are exchanged for manufactures, consumer goods, and necessary services—are loaded in favor of the developed countries.
2. Financial credits have been extended to the underdeveloped American nations on an unrealistically "businesslike" basis (high interest and short terms), which nearly guarantees that the loans cannot and will not be repaid on time, if at all. This condition then becomes the basis of demanding still harsher terms for the next loan.
3. Currently, the underdeveloped nations are being pressed to avoid using the main resources they possess—what nature has given them—to ensure a more secure future for the developed minority. Environmental concerns are being used to justify interference in internal affairs such as how many trees are cut down, or where beef cattle should graze, or how many fish should be caught.

What are we to make of these complaints? First, there can be little doubt that Latin America, like the rest of the developing world, has been forced to accept consistently disadvantageous trade conditions, while getting only an occasional and undependable sop in the form of World Bank or bilateral loans and grants. Since World War II, a ton of wheat, a bag of coffee, or a container of bananas purchases less and less of the electrical machinery, office equipment, or insurance policies that the developed countries sell to the underdeveloped nations.

Whether the second accusation is true is debatable. Much of the waste, corruption, or misuse of international credits was indisputably the work of recipients in the developing countries, who had little fear of ever being held personally responsible. At the same time, the international lending community has rarely if ever "pulled" loans that were clearly being diverted to the illicit benefit of individuals. In any case, the terms of the international loans extended to the Latin countries in the past have been notably more severe than those granted to Africa and Asia. The efforts to repay have handicapped Latin America's domestic investment and contributed to the fragile condition of the current Latin economies.

The third charge has a complex background but demands a decisive answer because it will affect us all in a powerful fashion. The Latin Americans (and others) are saying in essence, "You, the developed industrial societies, have now woken up to the dangers of pollution and abuse of the environment but want us, the less developed, to now pay the price of implementing rational policies while you enjoy the short-term benefits of irrationality." It was all right, in other words, for nineteenth-century American timber companies to cut down every tree over a foot thick in Michigan, but it is not all right for twentieth-century Brazilian timber companies to cut down mature mahogany in the Amazon basin. Multiply this example by hundreds, and you will have the position adopted by the Latin Americans and most other leaders of the developing countries in response to the environmental concerns of the developed world.

The developed world then adds salt to the Latin Americans' wounds by paying too little for that mahogany tree compared to the cost of the chain saw that cut the tree or the insurance on the boat that transports the tree to a U.S. mill—both the saw and the insurance, of course, were supplied by the developed world. And further salting comes from the fact that the fine piece of furniture made from the tree will be too expensive to grace an ordinary Latin American home because of the high costs and profits of the U.S. manufacturer. The flight to the cities we have already mentioned in connection with modern Africa is equally strong in Latin America. Towns such as Lima or Bogotá, which were still slumbering in the early twentieth century, have been overwhelmed with peasant migrants in the last thirty years. (For some of the reasons why villagers move into the Latin cities, see the Society and Economy box.) The majority live in shabby barrios or unfinished, do-it-yourself subdivisions that spring up like mushrooms in an ever-widening circle around the older town. Many of the inhabitants of these slums have established a settled, even secure life, but many others are living on a tightrope, balancing petty and sporadic income against constant demands for food and fuel. Much of the urban population seems to be "living on air," hustling up unskilled work on a day-to-day basis or depending on networks of kin and friends to see them through until they can return the favor.

## Rich and Poor

The chasm between rich and poor is deeper and more apparent in Latin American countries than anywhere else. Africa has relatively few very rich and not many people who are well-to-do. In most of Asia, wealth is fairly evenly distributed except in one or two cities in each country. But in South America, the extremes are growing, while the number of those in the middle is more or less stagnant. There are a great many poor and a very small but growing number of rich—and the contrast between them is a powder keg in most Latin American countries. The recent referendum in Venezuela, which saw national voting patterns almost exclusively along lines of social class, is illustrative.

So visible and disturbing is the polarization of Latin American society that the Catholic Church, long the main bastion of conservatism and reaction, has taken the lead in country after country as a voice for the poor. A peculiar combination of Marxist social theory and Catholic humanitarianism has come to life in several countries, notably Brazil, to speak for the common people against a social and economic system that has exploited them for many generations.

Hundreds of priests, nuns, and higher officials of the church have been imprisoned or even murdered by military and civilian reactionaries in the past fifteen years. Archbishop Oscar Romero of El Salvador was shot down while saying mass in his own cathedral for speaking out against the bloody excesses of the military in the civil war in El Salvador in the 1980s. The Romeros of two generations ago would have been blessing the army's guns.

## Changing Styles in Government

Latin America since 1930 has thus tried several different styles of government, including socialism, corporatism, and nationalist populism in an effort to achieve greater social justice and economic prosperity. Most of these have quickly degenerated into dictatorship. All have proved either ineffective or corrupt or were unable to retain their momentum. Castro's Cuba remains the one experiment with scientific socialism, and even its defenders acknowledge that it has failed its people economically in the last ten years.

In the 1960s, it appeared quite possible that Latin American Marxists, inspired by Castro's success, would attempt to seize power in several countries. Economic nationalism was faltering, and little social reform had been effected. Terrorist activity became a menace to the upper classes in Argentina and Brazil, where urban guerrillas operated. The military establishment in country after country pushed aside the ineffectual politicians and governed directly on a platform of law and order. Encouraged

SOCIETY AND ECONOMY

## Mexican Villagers

**IN THE EARLY 1970S,** an American anthropologist stayed for several months in an isolated highlands village in central Mexico. She witnessed the beginnings of the transition of Hueyapan from a quasi-medieval to a twentieth-century society, a phenomenon that was taking place simultaneously throughout Latin America in this epoch:

> During the 1930s, '40s and '50s villagers with a little capital rented large fields from lowlanders. . . . Instead of being paid in money, peons were given corn seed and enough land to plant. In a good year, a man could harvest enough to carry him and a family of six or seven through the year. Although they left their wives and young children at home, men usually took along their older sons and daughters. . . . While the young boys joined the men in the fields, the women and girls worked as corn grinders and cooks. . . . At the end of their stay they received [as their wages] as many liters of unground corn to take back as they had managed to grind for their patrones.
>
> Villagers would spend June, July and August in the lowlands, planting and caring for their vegetables. They would return to Hueyapan until December, at which time they would go down again for another month to harvest the crops.
>
> [In recent years there have been important changes in this pattern, however.] As in the 1950s [corn-grinding] mills started to replace their labor, more and more women began to migrate to Mexico City and Cuernavaca to work as maids. Although a few men left the village to work in factories, the number was negligible compared with that of women. . . . [Also] most of the young people who leave to work in urban centers have settled permanently in the cities. Absorbed into the ever-growing ghettos of the poor, these Hueyapenos return to the village only occasionally to see their families. . . . On their visits, the new migrants take home money and many of the material objects associated with the city. In this way they are contributing to the process that is incorporating Hueyapan into the consumer-oriented economy of Mexico.

Even in this most Indian of all Latin societies, the disadvantage of being an Indian made itself apparent:

> To be Indian in Hueyapan is to have a primarily negative identity. Indian-ness is more a measure of what the villagers are not or do not have vis-à-vis the hispanic [sic] elite than it is of what they have or are. . . . When I visited the homes of people in the village, from the wealthier to the more impoverished, I was often greeted with "Please excuse us, we are only poor little Indians here." . . . Nobody, they assumed, expected an Indian to have either the economic means or the good manners to treat an honored guest properly. . . .
>
> Most villagers responded to their Indian-ness in one of three ways, all of them negative. Some people, mostly the old and illiterate, were fatalistic: such was their unfortunate lot and who could expect more of them? Others believed that although Indians, they could at least try to hide their impoverished cultural condition, so that things would appear "less sad, less poor, less Indian." . . . A third response was to try to lose their Indian identity. . . . When villagers used the word "Indian" it was almost always to insult one another or to make a self-deprecating comment or joke.

### *Analyze and Interpret*

What effects do you think will eventually result from the imbalance of the sexes in Hueyapan, so far as the viability of the village as an independent social unit is concerned? Do you believe the Mexican government has any responsibility to intervene in this transformation? Could it do so effectively?

Source: Adapted slightly from Judith Friedlander, *Being Indian in Hueyapan* (New York: St. Martin's, 1975).

by government policy makers, Western banks loaned huge sums to the Latin American nations. Foreign debt increased by more than twelve times in the 1970s, to a point where with the slightest economic reversal the Latin American nations could not pay even the interest on time.

The 1970s were the low point for constitutional government. At one point in that decade, only three of the twenty Latin American nations were still ruled by elected governments. Everywhere else, the military attempted to meet the increasing demands for social and economic reform by going outside the political process. Almost always these attempts failed or were discarded before they had a chance to take hold. (A wild inflation was the main enemy of the reform plans. At one time, the value of the Argentine peso against the U.S. dollar was dropping at the rate of 10 percent per *day*.)

In the 1980s, the pendulum swung back to civilian rule, and by the end of that decade, only a few countries were still ruled by men in uniform. Argentina and Brazil again led the way. The military in Buenos Aires stepped down in disgrace after foolishly provoking a war with Britain over the Falkland Islands, and a few years later, the Brazilian generals gave up power to the first duly elected government in a quarter-century.

Democratic, constitutional government is still a fragile flower most of the time in most of the continent, but it made some strong gains in the 1980s and 1990s. The ending of the Cold War has had a beneficial effect on U.S.–Latin American relations, as the United States no longer worries that some type of hostile, Soviet puppet regime will be installed in these near neighbors. But the emergence from a century and a half of neocolonialism is a painfully slow process that will continue well into the twenty-first century even in the most hopeful scenarios. Moreover, the relative backwardness of Latin America, as part of the developing world, will cause it to continue to be a breeding ground for social discontent. The continent's future will depend largely on whether and how that discontent is resolved.

## SUMMARY

The twenty nations in Latin and Caribbean America have many overriding similarities, despite some differences. Everywhere, policy makers are concerned with the question of economic development—how to achieve it and how to manage it. Everywhere, the relationship between the United States and the others is vital to the future stability and prosperity of the continent. Various types of economic nationalism, sometimes introduced by the military, have been the Latin American response to their status as poor relations of the more developed nations of the world. Cárdenas in Mexico and Perón in Argentina were perhaps the most noted examples in the past sixty years, but many others have appeared and will continue to do so. Forty years ago, Castro offered a Marxist response to neocolonial status in Cuba, but Marxism has had minimal appeal outside that country, despite initial efforts to spread it. Its future is very dim.

Social problems, especially the maldistribution of wealth and the pressures generated by a high birthrate, haunt the continent south of the Rio Grande. One of the most striking manifestations of these problems is the uncontrollable growth of the cities and their shantytown surroundings. Another is the widespread street crime and law evasion. Despite repeated populist promises of thoroughgoing reform, political solutions have been at best sporadic and partial. Foreign aid has been both sparse and undependable over the longer term. But after the failure of the military regimes of the 1970s, there has been a vigorous recovery in parliamentary government. In the 1990s, some hopeful signs have indicated that constitutional democracy will triumph permanently if the overbearing socioeconomic crises can be mastered.

## IDENTIFICATION TERMS

Test your knowledge of this chapter's key concepts by defining the following terms. If you can't recall the meaning of certain terms, refresh your memory by looking up the boldfaced term in the chapter, turning to the Glossary at the end of the book, or working with the flashcards that are available on the *World Civilizations* Companion Website **http://history.wadsworth.com/adler04**.

Alliance for Progress
banana republics
*descamisados*
Good Neighbor Policy
North American Free Trade Agreement (NAFTA)
Organization of American States (OAS)

## TEST YOUR KNOWLEDGE

Test your knowledge of this chapter by answering the following questions. Complete answers appear at the end of the book. You may also take this quiz interactively and find even more quiz questions on the *World Civilizations* Companion Website: **http://history.wadsworth.com/adler04**.

1. After the Great Depression of the 1930s began, the larger Latin American states
   a. became totally dependent on imported goods.
   b. carried out long-delayed agrarian reforms to favor the peons.
   c. started on a program of economic nationalism.
   d. suffered economic collapse.
   e. joined the Pan American Union and became economically successful.

2. The most socially conscious Mexican president in the twentieth century was
   a. Lázaro Cárdenas.
   b. Porfirio Díaz.
   c. Benito Juarez.
   d. Pancho Villa.
   e. Miguel Hidalgo.
3. The most widely recognized female in recent Latin American history was probably
   a. St. Theresa.
   b. Eva Perón.
   c. Carmen Miranda.
   d. Madonna.
   e. Violeta Chamorro.
4. Juan Perón was forced from power in 1955 by
   a. a mass uprising.
   b. a free election.
   c. U.S. intervention.
   d. a military plot.
   e. ill health.
5. Which of the following countries did *not* experience U.S. military intervention in the twentieth century?
   a. Nicaragua
   b. Chile
   c. Bolivia
   d. Haiti
   e. Cuba
6. President Franklin Roosevelt is responsible for implementing
   a the Good Neighbor Policy.
   b. Dollar Diplomacy.
   c. the United Fruit Company.
   d. the Panama Canal treaty.
   e. the Alliance for Progress.
7. Latin Americans would most accurately be described as viewing American concerns for the environment of Central and South America as
   a. compassionate.
   b. unnecessary.
   c. misguided.
   d. arbitrary.
   e. hypocritical.
8. The strongest voice for the poor in many Latin American countries has been
   a. military strongmen.
   b. the wives of government leaders.
   c. intellectuals.
   d. democratically elected representatives.
   e. the Catholic church.
9. In the 1970s, the government and politics of most Latin American countries experienced
   a. a swing toward the Marxist left.
   b. intervention by military-based reformers.
   c. a swing toward social welfare programs.
   d. a renewal of clerical influence.
   e. a process of democratization.
10. In the later 1980s and 1990s, Latin America has experienced a strong movement toward
   a. democratically elected governments.
   b. military coups d'état.
   c. Marxist dictatorships.
   d. fascist governments.
   e. state capitalism.

## InfoTrac College Edition

Visit the source collections at

**http://infotrac.thomsonlearning.com**

and use the Search function with the following key terms:

Latin America economic aspects

Latin America political aspects

Latin America history

## Wadsworth History Website Resources

Visit the World History Resource Center at **http://history.wadsworth.com/world** for a wealth of general resources, and the *World Civilizations* Companion Website at **http://history.wadsworth.com/adler04** for resources specific to this textbook.

## HistoryNow

Enter *HistoryNow* using the access card that is available for *World Civilizations*. *HistoryNow* will assist you in understanding the content in this chapter with lesson plans generated for your needs. In addition, you can read the following documents, and many more, online:

John F. Kennedy, *On the Alliance for Progress*

Juan Perón, *Justicialism*

Eva Perón, *History of Perónism*

North American Free Trade Agreement

Fidel Castro, *Second Declaration of Havana*

Fidel Castro, *On the Export of Revolution*

*The people of [the Muslim world] sometimes make much more history than they consume locally.*
Saki (H. H. Munro)

# 54 The Reemergence of the Muslim World

The Muslim Countries until World War I

Responses to Muslim Weakness

The Turkish Republic

Palestine

The Return of Islam

The Iranian Revolution

The Oil Weapon
The Gulf War and the Invasion of Iraq

The Muslim Nations Today
The Arabs
The Non-Arabic Nations

| | |
|---|---|
| 1915 | McMahon Letter |
| 1916 | Sykes-Picot Agreement |
| 1917 | Balfour Declaration on Palestine |
| 1920s | Ataturk leads Turkey/Saudi Arabia united by Ibn Saud |
| 1946–1948 | Mandate territories become independent states |
| 1948 | Israel founded and Israeli-Arab War begins |
| 1956 | Suez Canal nationalized by Egypt |
| 1964 | PLO founded to fight Israel |
| 1973 | OPEC oil boycott |
| 1979 | Iranian Revolution/Soviet intervention in Afghanistan |
| 1980–1988 | Iraq–Iran War |
| 1985 | Soviet withdrawal from Afghanistan |
| 1991 | Gulf War against Iraq |
| 1993 | Peace Agreement between Israel and PLO |
| 1999 | Renewed Israeli/Palestinian confrontation |
| 2001 | al-Qaida attack on World Trade Center |
| 2002–Present | U.S. occupation of Afghanistan and Iraq |

For the first time in centuries, the Muslim peoples are at the center of world events and are playing major roles in international affairs. The term *Muslim world* refers to far more than the Middle East or the Arab countries (see Map 54.1). Muslims now number about one-sixth of humanity, and Islam is the dominant religion in thirty-eight countries, reaching from Southeast Asia to the Atlantic coast of Africa. The 148 million Arabs are mostly Muslims, but a great many of the 1 billion Muslims are not Arabs. In this chapter, however, we will focus on the Arab Middle East, because that is where the major events and processes defining the Muslim relationship with the world have taken place in the twentieth century.

One of the most important factors in Middle Eastern history over the last seventy years has been geology. By far the largest known oilfields in the world are located under Saudi Arabia and the other Persian Gulf Muslim

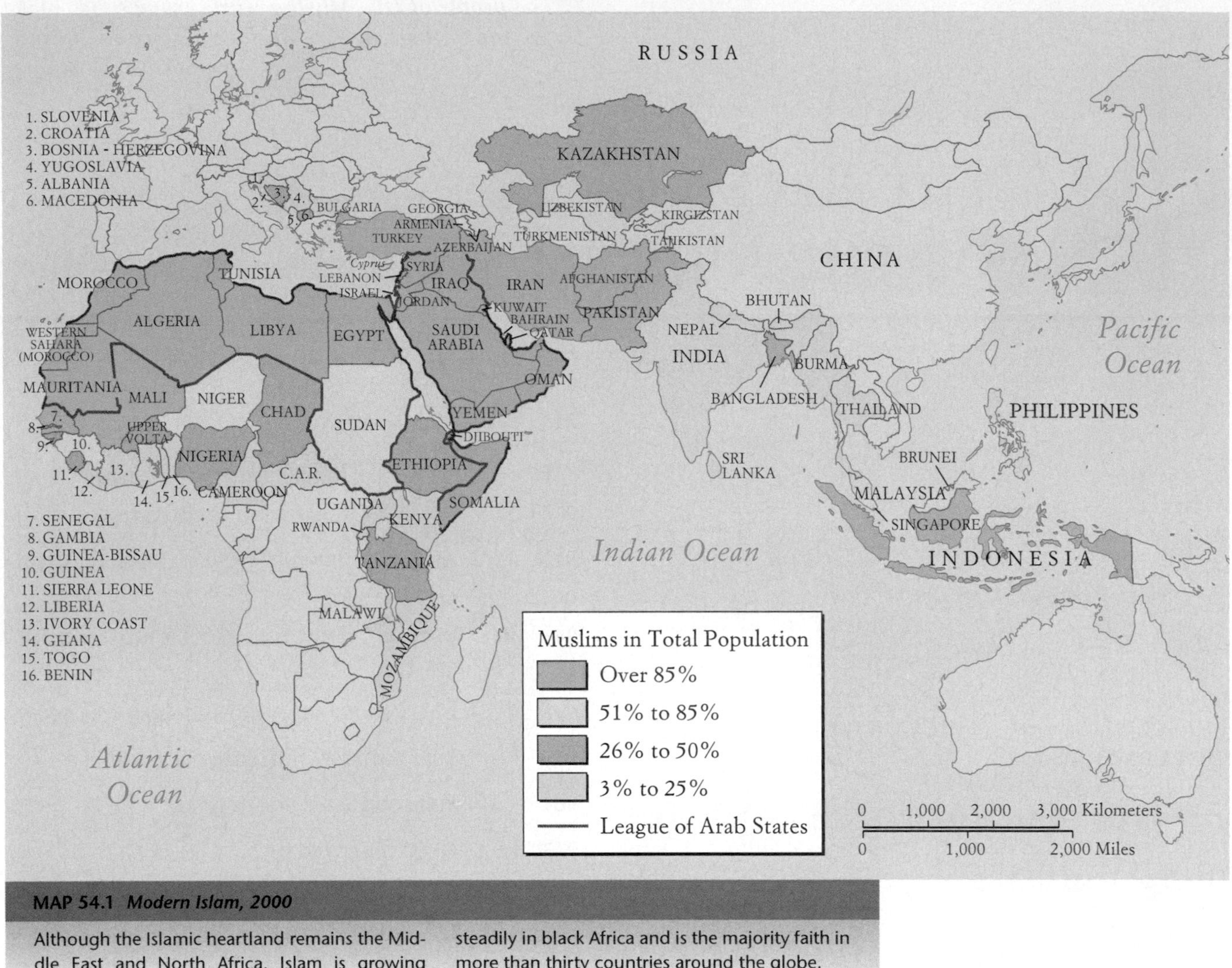


**MAP 54.1** ***Modern Islam, 2000***

Although the Islamic heartland remains the Middle East and North Africa, Islam is growing steadily in black Africa and is the majority faith in more than thirty countries around the globe.

countries. Their development was the key to the massive change in relations between Muslims and non-Muslims in the later twentieth century, particularly since the oil boycott of 1973.

Another major component of modern Middle East history, Arab nationalism, originally was directed against the Turkish overlords, and it had become so strong by the time of World War I that the British found the Arabs willing allies in the fight against their fellow Muslims. The Arabs' reward was supposed to be an independent state, reaching from Egypt to Iraq and headed by the Hashimite family of *shaykhs* in Arabia, who had been among the most prominent of the British allies during the war.

The Arabs' dream of a large, independent state was ended, however, by contradictory wartime diplomatic deals made by the French, British, and Italians in 1916–1917. In effect, Turkish prewar imperial rule was replaced by European rule. The postwar Near Eastern Arab lands were converted into "**mandates**," which were made the legal responsibility of the League of Nations, but placed under the direct administrative rule of the British and French until such time as the Arabs proved their ability to act as responsible sovereign powers. Syria and Lebanon were French mandates from 1919 to 1946, and Jordan, Palestine, and Iraq were British ones. When the Hashimite-led nationalists protested and rebelled, they were put down with decisive military action. Egypt, where the British had had an occupation force since 1882, got a slightly better arrangement. There nationalism was strong enough to induce the British to grant the Egyptians' pro-forma independence in 1922. British troops remained, however, and real independence was withheld until the 1950s because of British concerns about the Suez Canal and their "lifeline to India."

During the 1920s and 1930s, the small gains effected by individual Arab groups gave momentum to the Pan-Arab movement, which tried to get Arabs everywhere to submerge their differences and unite under one political center. The example of Saudi Arabia was held up as a possible model. Under the fundamentalist shaykh Ibn Saud, most of the Arabian peninsula was unified in the 1920s by conquest and voluntary association and turned into a

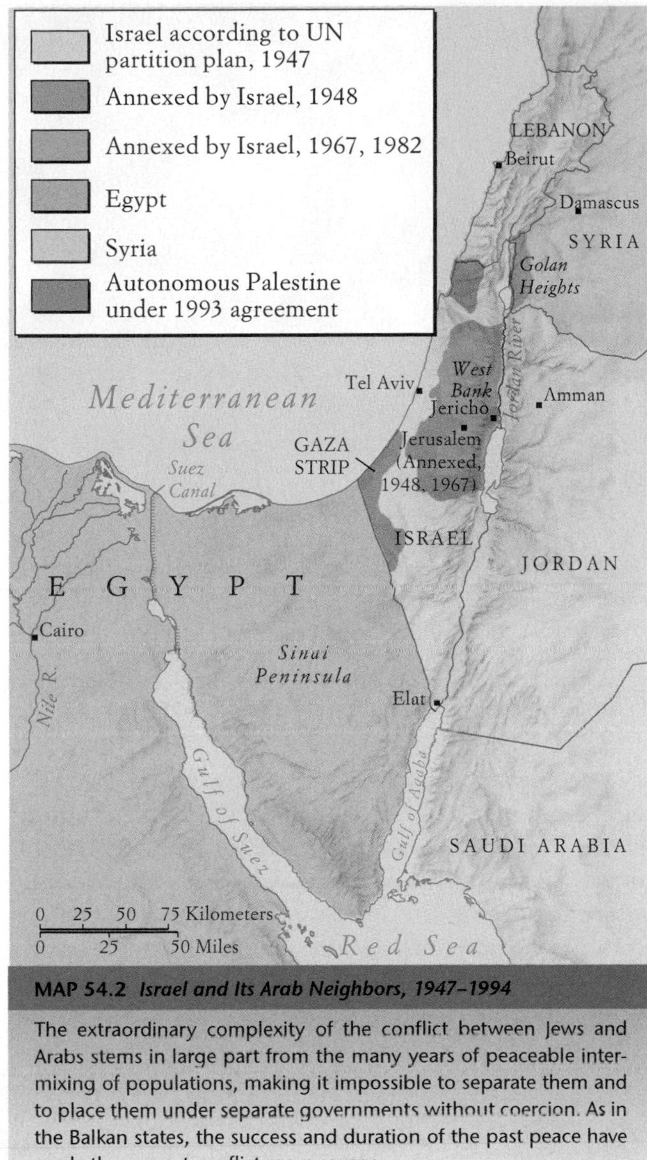


**MAP 54.2** *Israel and Its Arab Neighbors, 1947–1994*

The extraordinary complexity of the conflict between Jews and Arabs stems in large part from the many years of peaceable intermixing of populations, making it impossible to separate them and to place them under separate governments without coercion. As in the Balkan states, the success and duration of the past peace have made the current conflict more savage.

poverty-ridden but sovereign state. But the Pan-Arabists could show few other gains by the time World War II broke out. The colonial grip on individual regions was too strong, and the disunity and jealousies that had plagued Arab politics for a long time showed no sign of abating.

## The Turkish Republic

The exception to the continued subordination of the Muslim states or societies was the new Republic of Turkey. In the aftermath of its defeat as Germany's ally in World War I, the sultan's government had lost all credibility in Turkish eyes. Backed by Great Britain, the Greek government attempted in 1919 to realize the "Great Idea" of restoring the former Byzantine empire and making the interior of Turkey (Anatolia) once more a Greek colony. A Greek army landed on the Turkish coast and began to move inland.

At this critical point, a leader emerged who almost single-handedly brought his people back from the edge of legal annihilation. This was Mustafa Kemal, called **Ataturk** (father of Turkey). Kemal had been a colonel in the Ottoman army. In 1919–1921, he organized the national resistance to the invaders and won a decisive victory against the poorly led Greeks. Alone among the defeated in World War I, Turkey was eventually able to secure a revision of the original peace. The new treaty recognized the full sovereignty of the Turkish state within the borders it now has. The former Arab provinces were abandoned to the Western mandates.

But this was no longer Ottoman Turkey. Kemal was elected the first president (with near dictatorial powers) of the new parliamentary republic. Until his death in 1938, Kemal retained the presidency as he drove Turkey and the Turks to a systematic break with the past. Modernization and Westernization were the twin pillars of Kemal's policies as he focused on separating Turkish civil society from Islamic culture.

In every visible and invisible way Kemal could devise, the citizens of modern Turkey were distinguished from their Islamic ancestors. Western-style dress was introduced and even made mandatory for government workers. The veil was abolished. The Latin alphabet replaced the revered Arabic script. Women were made legally equal to men and could divorce their husbands. Polygamy was forbidden. Western schooling was introduced and made compulsory for both sexes. A new legal code was introduced, which was based on Western models and which allowed no preference for Muslims. The capital was moved from the ethnically half-Greek Istanbul to the more Turkish Ankara.

By the time of his death, Kemal had kept his promise to do for the Turks what Peter the Great had attempted to do for the Russians: to thrust them forward several generations through the abandonment of their Islamic base and through bringing them more into line with twentieth-century Western civilization. Despite intense resistance from conservative Muslim circles, Kemal had managed to turn his people into a superficially secular society in less than twenty years. He had also provided a model that was emulated by other, like-minded reformers all over the non-Western world.

## Palestine

The thorniest of all problems in the Middle East after World War I was the fate of the British mandate of Palestine (later, Israel). Hoping to draw the Arabs into the war against the Turks, the British government began negotiations with one of the principal leaders of the Pan-Arab movement, the Sharif of Mecca, Husayn ibn Ali al-Hashimi (the Hashimites were the clan of the Prophet Muhammad). In 1915, the British High Commissioner of Egypt, acting on behalf of his government, wrote Husayn the **McMahon Letter** in which he promised British support for the creation of an Arab homeland in the region between Iraq and Egypt in return for Arab support. Two years later, in 1917, realizing the political influence of wealthy Jews like Lord Rothschild and seeking support for an American entry into the war, Britain also made promises to the **Zionists**, Jewish nationalists who claimed to represent most European and American Jews. In the **Balfour Declaration**, the British agreed to support a "Jewish national homeland," but this could be achieved only at the expense of the Arab majority. These Arabs had shared Palestine with the biblical Jews and had been the majority people there for nearly 1,800 years. To these Arabs, a "national homeland" sounded like a Jewish-controlled state in which they would be only a tolerated group, and they accordingly did not like the idea. (See Law and Government.)

Esaias Beitel/Liaison/Getty Images

**THE PALESTINIAN *INTIFADA*.** Beginning in 1989 under PLO leadership, the Palestinian Arabs in the Gaza Strip and the West Bank–occupied territories challenged Israeli claims to these areas. Rock-throwing youth rioted in the streets in a persistent *intifada,* or uprising, which forced Israeli countermeasures and gave the Tel Aviv government a black eye in the world press. A second intifada began after the breakdown of the 1993 agreement, the Oslo Accord.

Jewish immigration into Palestine had begun in a minor way as early as the 1880s but had taken on potentially important dimensions only after the founding of the international Zionist movement by the journalist Theodor Herzl at the turn of the twentieth century. Under the well-meaning but muddled British colonial government, Arabs and Jews began to take up hostile positions in Palestinian politics during the 1920s. Soon, this hostility was taking the form of bloody riots, suppressed only with difficulty by the British police. The situation was worsened considerably by the dramatic increase in the number of Jews who immigrated into Palestine immediately after the Balfour Declaration was made public.

Ted Spiegel/Corbis

**WEDDING PROCESSION IN A *KIBBUTZ*.** A tractor is the limousine for the just-married couple in this Israeli *kibbutz.* Tens of thousands of young Jews emigrated to Israel during the 1950s and 1960s to take part in the spartan, communal life on the *kibbutzim,* agrarian settlements on the former wastelands and deserts of the Jewish state.

# The McMahon Letter to the Sharif of Mecca, 1915, and the Balfour Declaration, 1917

**Sir Henry McMahon was the** British High Commissioner in Egypt and Husayn ibn Ali al-Hashimi was the Sharif of Mecca in 1915 when the following letter was written in October 1915. In 1915 and 1916, McMahon wrote Husayn to ask for Arab support against the Ottoman Empire, which was fighting on the side of Germany and Austria against the Allied nations. To get this assistance, Britain had to promise its support for an independent Arab state at the end of the war.

> As for those regions lying within those frontiers wherein Great Britain is free to act without detriment to the interests of her ally, France, I am empowered in the name of the Government of Great Britain to give the following assurances and make the following reply to your letter:
>
> (1) Subject to the above modifications, Great Britain is prepared to recognise and support the independence of the Arabs in all the regions within the limits demanded by the Sherif of Mecca.
>
> (2) Great Britain will guarantee the Holy Places against all external aggression and will recognise their inviolability.
>
> (3) When the situation admits, Great Britain will give to the Arabs her advice and will assist them to establish what may appear to be the most suitable forms of government in those various territories.
>
> (4) On the other hand, it is understood that the Arabs have decided to seek the advice and guidance of Great Britain only, and that such European advisers and officials as may be required for the formation of a sound form of administration will be British.
>
> (5) With regard to the vilayets of Bagdad and Basra, the Arabs will recognise that the established position and interests of Great Britain necessitate special administrative arrangements in order to secure these territories from foreign aggression, to promote the welfare of the local populations and to safeguard our mutual economic interests.
>
> I am convinced that this declaration will assure you beyond all possible doubt of the sympathy of Great Britain towards the aspirations of her friends the Arabs and will result in a firm and lasting alliance, the immediate results of which will be the expulsion of the Turks from the Arab countries and the freeing of the Arab peoples from the Turkish yoke, which for so many years has pressed heavily upon them.

Source: Great Britain. *Parliamentary Papers, 1939, Misc. No. 3,* Cmd. *5957.*

This letter from the British Foreign Secretary to Lord Rothschild was intended to curry Jewish support for the Allies in the First World War:

> Foreign Office
>
> November 2nd, 1917
>
> Dear Lord Rothschild:
>
> I have much pleasure in conveying to you, on behalf of His Majesty's Government, the following declaration of sympathy with Jewish Zionist aspirations which has been submitted to, and approved by, the Cabinet:
>
> His Majesty's Government view with favor the establishment in Palestine of a national home for the Jewish people, and will use their best endeavors to facilitate the achievement of this object, it being clearly understood that nothing shall be done which may prejudice the civil and religious rights of existing non-Jewish communities in Palestine, or the rights and political status enjoyed by Jews in any other country. I should be grateful if you would bring this declaration to the knowledge of the Zionist Federation.
>
> Yours,
>
> Arthur James Balfour

Source: *The Times of London,* November 1917. Taken from the *Internet Modern History Sourcebook*. The Sourcebook is a collection of public domain and copy-permitted texts for introductory-level classes in modern European and World history.

## *Analyze and Interpret*

If you were an Arab, how might you have interpreted the first and third paragraphs of the McMahon Letter? To what extent did the Balfour Declaration conflict with the promises the British had made to the Arab leaders? Why do you suppose the British made these conflicting agreements?

**HistoryNow™**

***To read Balfour's defense of the Palestine mandate, point your browser to the documents area of HistoryNow.***

The British mandate authority did nothing to alleviate the situation until 1939, when belated promises were made to limit immigration. By then, however, the situation was beyond their control. Throughout the 1930s, Jewish immigrants had been pouring into Palestine from Hitler's Germany and eastern Europe, where vicious anti-Semitism had become commonplace. At the outbreak of World War II, perhaps 30 percent of Palestine's inhabitants were Jews.

At the end of the war, the British in Palestine as elsewhere were at the end of their strength and wished to turn over the troublesome Middle East mandates as soon as possible to the United Nations. The pitiful remnants of the Jews of Nazi Europe now defied British attempts to keep them from settling illegally in Palestine. Attempts to get Arabs and Jews to sit down at the negotiating table failed, and the frustrated British announced that they would unilaterally abandon Palestine on May 14, 1948. Faced with this ultimatum, the United Nations eventually (November 1947) came out with a proposal for partitioning the mandate into a Jewish state and an Arab state—a compromise that, needless to say, satisfied neither side. By the time the United Nations proposal was put forth, fighting between irregular Arab and Jewish militias was already under way. Zionist leaders in Palestine immediately proclaimed the creation of the nation of Israel upon British withdrawal in May 1948.

The results of the 1948 war—the first of six armed conflicts in the past half-century between Israel and its Arab neighbors—were strongly favorable to the new Jewish state. Unexpectedly, it held its own and more against its several enemies. But the triumphant Israelis then expelled many hundreds of thousands of Palestinian Arabs from their ancestral lands, creating a reservoir of bitterness that guaranteed hostility for decades to come, with both Palestinian Arabs and Jews making mutually contradictory claims to a "Right of Return."

In 1964, after fifteen years of intra-Arab dissension about how best to deal with the Israeli presence, the **Palestine Liberation Organization (PLO)** was formed by Arab leaders. Its single goal was the destruction of the state of Israel, and both sides pursued their respective goals with bloodshed and intolerance for each other for almost thirty years until 1993. In this effort the PLO was assisted by most of the Arab states, which saw Israel as an enemy that could not be tolerated in their midst. For its part, as a besieged state, Israel used its well-disciplined and largely American-equipped armed forces to repay violence with violence and to continue occupying Palestinian lands. This enmity, like all other conflicts during the Cold War era, became caught up in the general hostility between the United States and the Soviet Union, with the former siding strongly with the Israelis and the latter with the Arabs. (See Map 54.2.)

## The Return of Islam

Westerners have always misunderstood the nature of Islam and have tried to equate it with Christianity in Europe with unfortunate results. Islam is much more than a religion as the West understands that term and is certainly not limited to the private sphere as Christianity has been since the French Revolution. Islamic law, especially, does not recognize the separation of church and state nor of religious belief and civil practice. Rather, for the good Muslim, these concepts are a unity and always have been. They can no more be separated than can the human personality be parted from the body it inhabits.

A leading historian, Bernard Lewis, says, "It was not nation or country that, as in the West, formed the historic basis of identity, but the religio-political community." For this reason, Arab nationalism has never had quite the same meaning or character as American or European nationalism. Muslims felt a higher identity embracing them than the mere fact of being Syrian or Egyptian. For many, "The Fatherland of a Muslim is wherever the Holy Law of Islam prevails." This feeling is not new. Even at the high point of secular nationalism in the Middle East, during the interwar years when the Turkey of Kemal Ataturk was blazing the path, there was a strong undercurrent of religiously based patriotic feeling that rejected secularism as an ideology that had been imposed on Muslim peoples by the West (see Chapter 37).

But only in recent decades have Muslim fundamentalists come into the spotlight in world affairs. In several countries—Afghanistan, Pakistan, Jordan, the Sudan, Yemen, and Libya—they enjoy widespread and vociferous public support to the point of dominating public life and intimidating their civic rivals. In some others—Algeria, Egypt, Saudi Arabia, Syria, and Turkey—they are a minority but seem to be gaining ground against the secularists who still control the governments. In still others—Iran, Indonesia, Morocco—the balance is neatly held and can shift momentarily, but it is evident that fundamentalist Islam is a potentially major determinant of international affairs in the twenty-first century. In recent days, the emergence of al-Qaida, the network of Muslim terrorists headed by the Arab Osama bin Laden and presumed to be responsible for the September 11, 2001, attack on the World Trade Center and the Pentagon, has put a different and much more immediately menacing face on the fundamentalist movement.

## The Iranian Revolution

Three outstanding events or processes in the twentieth century have together defined many of the spiritual and material bases of the Muslim universe. The first was the establishment of the secular Republic of Turkey by Mustafa Kemal Ataturk. The second was the oil boycott of 1973–1974, organized and implemented by the Arab members of the **Organization of Petroleum Exporting Countries (OPEC)**. The third was the Iranian Revolution of 1979, led by the Ayatollah Khomeini.

The modern state of Iran is the successor to the great Persian empires of ancient times. Its inhabitants, who are not Arabs, have been Muslims almost without exception since the Arab conquest in the 640s. In many epochs, the Iranians have been among Islam's most distinguished leaders. Nevertheless, they are separated from the majority of Muslims in one decisive way: they are Shi'ite Muslims and have been that sect's major stronghold for seven centuries.

Modern Iran came into being in the aftermath of World War I, when a military officer named Reza Shah Pahlavi (ruled 1925–1941) seized power from a discredited traditional dynasty and established an authoritarian regime modeled on his Turkish neighbor. His son, Muhammad Reza Shah Pahlavi (ruled 1941–1979) continued his Westernizing and secularizing policies. By the 1970s, considerable progress had been made in the cities, at least. The country had a substantial middle class, technically advanced industry (especially connected with petroleum engineering), an extensive Western educational system, and mechanized agriculture. Its immense oil deposits generated sufficient income to pay for large-scale government projects of every sort, and these proved profitable for a select few contractors and their friends in the bureaucracy.

But the shah had neglected to see to the well-being of much of the urban and most of the rural population. Government corruption was universal, the army and police were all-powerful, and traditional religious values were held in more or less open contempt by the ruling clique. On top of that, many people viewed the shah and his advisers as slavish puppets of the West, who had neither understanding nor respect for the greatness of Islamic Persia.

The upshot was a massive swell of protest, inspired and led by the exiled Ayatollah (Shi'ite theologian) Ruhollah Khomeini. Under the banners of "Back to the Qur'an" and "Iran for the Iranians," Khomeini skillfully led his people into revolution and then returned in 1979 to take the helm of the government that succeeded the bewildered shah. For the next decade, the ayatollah implemented what he had promised Iran from afar: a thoroughly Islamic, uncompromisingly anti-Western, antisecular government. Resistance to this course was brushed aside by his authoritarian attitude that allowed no concessions. The atheistic Soviets were denounced almost as heartily as the Americans, whose long-standing support for the shah as a Cold War counter against the Soviets had earned Khomeini's especial hatred. (For more about Khomeini, see the Patterns of Belief box.)

In the Ayatollah's Iran, Muslim fundamentalism found its most dramatic and forceful exponent so far. But it was by no means a necessarily attractive scenario for other, secular Muslim states, and within a year of the Ayatollah's return, Iran was at war with a Muslim neighbor. In 1980, Iraq attempted to take advantage of the upheaval next door to seize some disputed oil-bearing territory from Iran. The eight-year conflict that followed was one of the bloodiest in recent history, claiming at least 1 million lives (mainly Iranian) and dealing both countries blows from which they have not yet recovered.

With its much smaller population, Iraq would have been defeated early in the war had it not been for the active financial support and armaments supplied by other states. Led by the Saudis, many Arab leaders thought that the Ayatollah's brand of fundamentalism posed a serious threat to all of them and wished to see it contained or defeated. The militant anti-Western positions embraced by Khomeini (notably, the holding of U.S. hostages in 1979–1980) also induced the Western states to support Iraq in various covert ways, actions that they would soon regret.

**Ski Resort, Iran, 1994.** The Muslim women at this ski resort cover their heads somewhat in the traditional fashion. Ayatollah Khomeini's exhortation to recover the pious lifestyle was backed up by public humiliation of those women who defied it and continued to dress in the Western manner.

David Turnley/Corbis

PATTERNS OF BELIEF

## Ayatollah Khomeini (1902–1989)

**Early in 1979, the massive street** demonstrations that had become a daily occurrence in Tehran succeeded in persuading the shah of Iran to leave the country for exile. His place was quickly taken by an unlikely figure: the Ayatollah Ruhollah Khomeini, a blazing-eyed, ramrod-erect man in his seventies, garbed in the long kaftan of a strict Muslim believer. Khomeini had been forced into exile by the shah's police fifteen years earlier. Now the tables had turned, and it would be Khomeini, not the once all-powerful shah, who ruled Iran's 40 million inhabitants until he died.

The *ayatollah* (the word means "theologian") was a member of Iran's leading sect: the Shi'ite Muslims, who make up only about 10 percent of the world's Muslim population but have long been the dominant religious group in Iran. Since the 1960s, conservative Shi'a had opposed the secularizing policies of Muhammad Reza Shah Pahlavi. They believed in a rigid interpretation of the Qur'an, whereby government should be the strong right arm of the religious establishment (the ulama). Not surprisingly, neither the shah nor his close advisers shared this view. Using all of the apparatus of the modern state, including a barbaric secret police, they made the lives of the ayatollah and his followers miserable and assassinated many of them. Among the dead was Khomeini's elder son, who was murdered in Iraq.

Hulton-Deutsch/Corbis

**Ayatollah Khomeini (1902–1989).** A Shi'ite religious scholar who opposed the regime of the Shah of Iran, Khomeini spent many years in exile in Iraq and France. His taped harangues against the Iranian government and its close ties to the United States helped foment the 1979 Iranian Revolution. He remained the "Leader of the Revolution" and supreme head of state of Iran's revolutionary government until he died in 1989.

With the resources of a modern army and police at his command, and with the full support of the U.S. government in his general policies, it seemed unthinkable that the shah's throne was in danger from a small group of unarmed religious fanatics. That was true until the mid-1970s, when it became apparent that the government's initial social reforms—the White Revolution—were failing, thanks in part to massive corruption. Always a country of economic extremes, Iran became the model of a society in which a tiny elite became fantastically wealthy, while the ever-more-numerous poor got the merest crumbs from their table. Surrounded by his elite friends, the shah compounded the bad impression by spending huge sums on personal and familial luxuries.

## The Oil Weapon

What was the number-one history-making event or series of events in the 1970s, in retrospect? Most would now say that it was not the Cold War between the United States and the Soviet Union, or the American adventure in Vietnam, or the rapid steps being taken toward European unity, but rather the worldwide economic crisis precipitated by the OPEC oil boycott. In 1973, the favoritism shown by the West and especially the United States toward Israel was answered during that year's brief Arab-Israeli conflict (sometimes known as the **Yom Kippur War** because it began on that Jewish holiday) by the Arabs' decision to withhold all oil shipments to the United States and its NATO allies. Because the Middle East had long been the dominant supplier of world petroleum markets, the impact was immediate and catastrophic. Prices of crude oil quadrupled within a few months. The economies of the Western nations and Japan were put under great strain. Even the United States, which came closest to oil self-sufficiency of all the affected nations, faced shortages.

A major recession, the worst since the 1930s, with unemployment rates zooming to 13 percent in Western Europe, was one of the results. Soaring energy costs caused consumer prices for practically every necessity of life to spiral upward even as demand decreased. As mass unemployment was accompanied by double-digit inflation in the mid- and late 1970s, a new word came into the vocabulary—*stagflation.* This unlovely compound referred to the worst of all economic worlds, the combination of stagnation and inflation.

The postwar boom, which had lasted a quarter of a century, definitely ended, and most of the West remained in a painful business recession well into the 1980s. Some countries have never entirely recovered from the great oil shock. Their labor markets have been permanently altered by the disappearance of many blue-collar production jobs that depended on cheap energy. (The 1973 shock was

Khomeini had begun denouncing the shah's mistakes in the 1960s. Even in exile he was regarded as the spirit of the opposition in Tehran. He was adept at linking the devout villagers with the urban middle classes and reform-minded intellectuals who were coming to hate the shah's misrule. The police attempt to beat the increasing numbers of street demonstrators into flight only created martyrs for the movement. Thousands were arrested weekly, and new recruits instantly filled their places. The peasant soldiers watched their parents and relatives being beaten, and the army became too unreliable to be used against the demonstrators. From his waiting place in Paris, Khomeini's messengers flew back and forth carrying instructions to the faithful. They boiled down to one demand: the shah and all he stood for must go.

When Khomeini took over, the world knew nothing of him or what he desired. That changed quickly, as he imposed strict Qur'anic standards on every aspect of Iran's constitutional and social affairs. He generally opposed all non-Muslim views but was especially contemptuous of the West and, above all, the Americans. Regarding the U.S. government as the foreign power most responsible for Iran's misery, he cut off all relations and began whipping up crowd hatred of the "Great Satan" in Washington. In November 1979, the demonstrators broke into the U.S. embassy and took fifty-two hostages in an attempt to force the Washington authorities to turn over the ailing shah to revolutionary justice in Tehran. The shah soon died of cancer, but the hostages were held for more than a year until their release was negotiated.

By then, Khomeini (who never took an official post but directed all policy in Tehran) was looked on in the West as a deranged tyrant. His rigid views and his conviction that he had supernatural approval made it next to impossible to approach him with realistic compromises. While the Cold War raged, the West was delighted to see him attack Iran's small Communist Party and to listen to his denunciation of "godless Marxism," but he was equally adamant against the democracies and all they stood for. His own country seemed on the verge of civil war when he died, but the transition of power went smoothly, with clerics of the ayatollah's type gradually giving way to more moderate politicians.

Khomeini's legacies to his people will long be the subject of acrid dispute. Although many regarded him as a saint, his ideas were always opposed by a hard core of secularists, which has grown since his death and the reinstitution of a parliamentary government.

### *Analyze and Interpret*

Do you believe that the ayatollah's attitude toward the U.S. government was justifiable? Is taking hostages from among officials of a foreign country an unheard-of action in modern times? Can you give examples?

**History Now™**

***To read Ayatollah Khomeini's "The Uprising of Khurdad 15," point your browser to the documents area of* HistoryNow.**

later reinforced by events in Iran. Beginning in 1979–1980, international oil prices again quadrupled for several years because of fears of a supply pinch following the Iranian Revolution and the outbreak of the Iran–Iraq War.)

This windfall in Arab oil profits did not last more than a decade, and the OPEC nations were eventually forced to adjust their prices to a diminished world demand. But the brief havoc wreaked in oil supplies—which the West had always thought were shielded from producer-country influence—established a new respect for Arab political potency. What Western consumers knew after 1973 was that a handful of heretofore peripheral and insignificant Middle Eastern and North African kingdoms had risen on a tide of crude oil to become at least transitory major players in world politics. The surge in price made some of the major producers (notably, the largest of all, Saudi Arabia) immensely rich in dollars, and money here, as elsewhere, spelled both economic and political power. No longer could any industrial nation afford to ignore what OPEC was doing or planning. For the first time in at least two centuries, the Muslim East had attained importance through its own initiatives, rather than merely because of what one or another alien group was doing there.

## *The Gulf War and the Invasion of Iraq*

In 1990, the ambitious and bloodstained Iraqi dictator Saddam Hussein (or Husayn), victor in the just-concluded conflict with Iran, believed the time was ripe for a settlement of accounts with Kuwait, his oil-rich neighbor at the head of the Persian Gulf. In an undisguised grab for additional oil revenues, Saddam invaded the tiny country and declared it annexed, thinking that he would present the world with an accomplished fact backed up by a large and well-armed army.

To his surprise, the West reacted violently and was soon joined by most of the non-Western world, including the Soviet Union and most Arabs. These latter feared the effects of opening up the question of the territorial borders derived from the colonial era, and they also rejected Saddam's transparent bid to become the pan-Arab arbiter of the Middle East. Almost all of the United Nations presented Saddam with the most unified front that organization had seen since its inception. The Iraqi dictator refused to back down, however. It took a powerful air and ground attack led by the United States on his forces in 1991 to induce him to withdraw with heavy losses (the Gulf War).

Although a treaty was forced on Saddam that required him to destroy his stockpiles of chemical, biological, and nuclear weapons (weapons of mass destruction), his defiance of his enemies and his efforts to frustrate the work of weapons inspectors caused tensions to continue through the 1990s. Moreover, he proved extremely tenacious in holding on to power. Urgings by President George H. W. Bush that Iraqis remove him from power had only tragic consequences when his administration failed to back up promises of support to Shi'ites in the south of Iraq and Kurds in the north when they rose up against Saddam in 1991–1992. Thousands were killed in gas attacks and air assaults, resulting in further distrust of the United States.

When many of President Bush's advisers returned to power in 2001 under the administration of his son George W. Bush, the "hawks" among them urged the new president to resume the war against Saddam. When Bush and his advisers claimed that Saddam was allied to al-Qaida and was still hiding weapons of mass destruction, the United States invaded Iraq, despite broad international opposition that claimed the invasion was blatant aggression.

Since the invasion, in ways reminiscent of the Vietnam War, the United States has found itself bogged down again in a war that has proven difficult to justify, steadily losing international standing. The invasion has succeeded in removing Saddam from power, but at the price of breeding more Arab hatred of the United States than ever before. Perhaps most ironically, Iraq has become the recruiting grounds for new legions of fundamentalist zealots bent on destroying America in the name of Allah. Sovereignty has been returned to an Iraqi ruling council. As of 2004, it remains to be seen if the country can hold together in the face of fundamentalist radicalism, old ethnic and sectarian rivalries, and opposition from well-armed elements of the old regime that remain opposed to democracy.

## The Muslim Nations Today

The relative importance of the Muslim nations in today's world can be viewed from sharply differing perspectives. Some observers, who focus on the continuing weakness of the domestic political infrastructure and the technological dependency of most Muslim societies on Western nations, tend to dismiss the twentieth-century resurgence as a temporary "blip" that will have no permanent effects on the overall picture of Western world domination.

Others, focusing on such disparate phenomena as the shocking capabilities and determination of the al-Qaida terrorists, the continuance of the Saddam Hussein regime in Iraq and Mu'ammar Qaddafi in Libya, and the sophisticated financial initiatives of the Saudi Arabian government to protect its oil revenues, are of the contrary opinion. They believe that the Muslims have placed themselves firmly and permanently on the world stage. In this view, the West would be making a huge mistake to leave the Islamic peoples out of its calculations on any important international issue. It appears that the latter view is becoming generally accepted.

### *The Arabs*

It is difficult to generalize accurately about the Arab nations. The various Middle East countries inhabited by Arabs are commonly known by their control over much of the world's oil and their enmity with Israel and, because of its support for Israel and the invasion of Iraq, with the United States. But even these supposedly basic facts are subject to sharp variances both over time and

Vahid Slemi/AP Photos

**War and Famine in Afghanistan.** Veiled Afghani women line up for a distribution of wheat in the city of Herat a few days after the anti-Taliban forces of the Northern Alliance took over the city in January 2002. Afghanistan has been wracked by more than twenty years of warfare, beginning with the Soviet army's invasion in 1979 and continuing to the U.S. campaign against the al-Qaida network of Osama bin Laden.

between countries. The oil trade has become much less confrontational and less politicized, but the Arab–Israel hostility seems resistant to any solution. Even the extraordinary diplomatic efforts of U.S. president Bill Clinton in the early 1990s, like those of President Jimmy Carter before him, produced only a mirage of peace, rather than its actuality. In 1993, Clinton was able to induce the government of Israel and the PLO to sign a "path to peace" agreement. But in the past several years, this so-called Oslo Accord has been repeatedly tossed aside by hardliners on both sides, and the bloodshed resumed. At times it has appeared that the ongoing conflict is needed by some of the Arab leadership to divert popular attention from their domestic economic problems, which have persisted despite both oil profit windfalls and international aid. At other times, the Jewish leadership has been deliberately provocative in its assertions of control over Palestinian people and places and its support of new Israeli settlements.

Egypt, with the largest population of the Arab world, is in an especially difficult position. With few resources beyond the fields of the Nile valley, it has become entirely dependent on U.S. and World Bank assistance and migration to rich Saudi Arabia to maintain an even minimal living standard for its people. Economic desperation, especially in contrast to the oil wealth of the Saudis, Iraqis, and others, has added fuel to other resentments, which have given rise to a militant Islamic fundamentalism in Egypt and other nations.

But the potential resolution of the Arab-Israeli conflict also poses the danger that without the common enemy, the Arab nations will be forced to recognize what most leaders already tacitly acknowledge: they lack any mutual policies and goals except for adherence in one degree or another to Islam. And that fact, coupled with the bureaucratic corruption and suppression of their citizens' civil rights common in Third World nations, will almost certainly fuel the rising antipathies between the fundamentalists and the current ruling group of secularist and nationalist politicians. The clash between these two groups focuses on the struggle for the allegiance of the rural majority.

Will the villagers continue to support the urban politicians who have promised them a better life but have delivered on that promise only partially and sporadically since 1945? The secularists include such different past and present personalities as Gamal Abdel Nasser and Anwar Sadat in Egypt, Saddam Hussein in Iraq, Ahmad Ben Bella in Algeria, King Husayn in Jordan, and Hafiz al-Assad in Syria. All of them wanted to lead their nations into a Westernized technology and economy, while giving perhaps only lip service to Western-style political and civil rights.

On the other side of the equation are the Islamic fundamentalists, led by such men as the former associates of Khomeini in Iran, the members of the al-Qaida terrorist network established under Osama bin Laden, and the leaders of the Muslim Brotherhood and the Shi'ite Hizbullah, as well as many others whose names are as yet unknown to the world. They are willing to accept most of the modern world's material and technical achievements, but only if the power of selection remains securely in their own hands, and if it is understood that the society using these achievements must be fully in tune with the words of the Qur'an as interpreted by themselves.

For America and its allies, the extremes to which Osama bin Laden and his al-Qaida followers were willing to go to free the Middle East from America and other "Crusading" states was demonstrated on September 11, 2001. After having failed to destroy the World Trade Center in the early 1990s, al-Qaida terrorists under bin Laden's orders hijacked four American airliners, two of which were flown into the World Trade Center, one into the Pentagon, and one crashed in Pennsylvania, costing thousands of innocent lives. Demands by the United States that the Taliban rulers of Afghanistan turn bin Laden and his lieutenants over to the United States for trial were refused. In an effort to destroy the terrorist network and its Taliban allies, the president and Congress allied themselves with dissident Afghani tribes, under a loose confederation of warlords called the "Northern Alliance." Their goals included toppling the Taliban, capturing bin Laden, and destroying his organization.

As of 2004, the first of these objectives has been achieved. Bin Laden's network has been seriously crippled, although it has found new recruits around the world among those whose hatred of the United States has been fueled by American actions in Iraq. Bin Laden remains at large, believed to be hiding in northern Pakistan.

## *The Non-Arabic Nations*

The Muslim countries of Africa and southern Asia have thus far shown only limited and scattered interest in coordinating their activity, foreign or domestic, with the Arabs despite extensive aid to these nations from Saudi Arabia and Iran. This attitude is partly a result of the circumstances in which Islam was introduced and grew in these parts of the globe. The offspring of converts, who continue to be strongly rooted in their indigenous culture, the African and Asian Muslims have not been quite as single-minded and exclusive as their Arab fellows in religious affairs.

Since attaining independence in 1949, Indonesia, the largest Muslim state and boasting the fourth largest population in the world, has felt its way forward by the technique of "guided democracy." The country was originally guided by the charismatic leader of the anticolonial struggle, Sukarno, and, until 1998, by the secularist General

Suharto. (Guided democracy claims to be more authentic in representing the popular will than the Western parliamentary governments. It purports to reconcile clashing points of view by the benign guidance of a single leader.) Preoccupied with ethnic-religious conflicts and the problems created by a burgeoning population with limited resources (rich oil deposits are by far the most important), the government has shown no interest in forming associations even with nearby Muslim states. In this melting pot of religions, Islamic fundamentalism has produced several movements that seek either the establishment of an Islamic state under Sharia law or total separation.

Pakistan and Bangladesh are the next largest Muslim states. Throughout its short history, Pakistan has been entirely occupied with its recurrently dangerous quarrel with India over Kashmir. Both countries now possess nuclear weapons; both have large populations of minorities who have little identification with the governing groups. In most recent times, the chaos in neighboring Afghanistan has made Pakistan more important in Western eyes, balancing the former tilt toward India. Internally, a series of military takeovers—the latest of which, under American ally General Pervez Musharraf, is now in its sixth year—has prevented any real commitment to democratic politics, which is perhaps impossible given the huge political and economic problems created by events over which the government has comparatively little control (see Chapter 51).

On its side, Bangladesh has been struggling since its creation with abject poverty in an economy that ranks as one of the world's poorest. Lacking any notable human, mineral, or energy resources, both of these countries have remained on the periphery of both Muslim and world affairs and are heavily dependent on aid from foreign sources ranging from China (Pakistan) to the United States (both). Neither has shown any interest in making common policy with other Muslim countries (they could not get along even with one another in an earlier joint state). Secularist generals or their civilian accomplices and puppets have ruled both most of the time since their creation. Fundamentalist Islam is as yet only weakly represented in Bangladesh but is gaining ground in Pakistan, where there are millions of refugees from war-torn Afghanistan who have found allies among its northern tribes.

As a summary labeling, the politics and governments of the Muslim states were still far from democratic in most instances. The monopolistic party with an authority figure at its head was the rule (as random examples, Hosni Mubarak in Egypt, Saddam Hussein in Iraq, and Mu'ammar Qaddafi in Libya). Ethnic minorities and/or religious "deviants" were treated roughly by the central authorities if they showed the slightest resistance. Civil wars, declared and undeclared, raged in several nations, both between competing sections of the Muslim populace and between Muslims and their religious and cultural rivals (Iraq, Sudan, Algeria). Whole regions containing groups unfriendly to the regime were systematically punished, sometimes by armed force, as in Turkey and Iraq.

The domestic economic condition varied from reasonably stable (the oil-blessed Middle East) to very shaky (most of North and West Africa). Indonesia and Malaysia were so badly shaken by recent fiscal and economic miseries as to bring down entrenched dictators, governments, and parties. Even rich Saudi Arabia proved not immune from the worldwide recession of 2001–2002. In most countries, connections with the bureaucracy were usually necessary for successful enterprise, corruption was rampant, and necessary government investments in infrastructure (roads, airports, sewer lines, and the like) were still conspicuous by their absence. All in all, the reentry of Islam into a prominent place in the modern world has not been easy, and the ride ahead promises to be perhaps even rougher, not only for the countries concerned but also for their non-Muslim neighbors.

## Summary

The Muslim world has returned to an important role in world politics and economics during the twentieth century after two or three centuries of insignificance. Making up about one-sixth of the globe's population, Muslims from West Africa to Southeast Asia have been able to reassert themselves into Western consciousness, especially since the oil boycott of the 1970s. The first real change was the creation of the secular Turkish republic after World War I. This state served as a model to many other Muslim thinkers and politicians and fostered the creation of nationalist associations throughout the Middle East and North Africa. The Arab-Israeli struggle over Palestine was a galvanizing force from the 1920s to the present. It was followed by the creation of the Arab-sponsored Organization of Petroleum Exporting Countries, the oil boycott, and the rise of an aggressive Islamic fundamentalism in the 1970s and 1980s. Fueled by a decade of extraordinary profits from oil, some Muslim countries have experienced a tremendous burst of modernization. Others, lacking oil, have remained at or near the bottom of the world prosperity scale.

After a long oblivion, Islamic religious purists have been staging a strong comeback in several countries, notably since the revolution in Iran. Although all previous Pan-Arabic and Pan-Islamic appeals have foundered on sectarian and national rivalries, it is possible that the present surge of fundamentalism could erect and maintain such an alliance. The fundamentalists' uncompromising rejection of Western ideals such as religious toleration and political equality, combined with their appeal to an alienated underclass in poverty-stricken Muslim countries, makes them a potentially dangerous force not only for their secular rivals at home but also for international peace.

## Identification Terms

Test your knowledge of this chapter's key concepts by defining the following terms. If you can't recall the meaning of certain terms, refresh your memory by looking up the boldfaced term in the chapter, turning to the Glossary at the end of the book, or working with the flashcards that are available on the *World Civilizations* Companion Website **http://history.wadsworth.com/adler04**.

Ataturk
Balfour Declaration
mandates
McMahon Letter
Organization of Petroleum Exporting Countries (OPEC)
Palestine Liberation Organization (PLO)
Yom Kippur War
Zionists

## Test Your Knowledge

Test your knowledge of this chapter by answering the following questions. Complete answers appear at the end of the book. You may also take this quiz interactively and find even more quiz questions on the *World Civilizations* Companion Website: **http://history.wadsworth.com/adler04**.

1. After World War I, the chief exception to colonial rule among Muslim countries was
   a. Egypt.
   b. Turkey.
   c. Iraq.
   d. Lebanon.
   e. Iran.
2. The historical movement to unite all Arabs under single political leadership is
   a. Arabs First!
   b. Pan-Arabism.
   c. the Arab Awakening.
   d. Arab Unity.
   e. the Arab Brotherhood.
3. Kemal Ataturk believed that Turks
   a. must remain Muslim to retain a national identity.
   b. must expand beyond their old borders to solve their national woes.
   c. had an obligation to liberate their Muslim comrades in Europe.
   d. must adopt a Western lifestyle.
   e. had a duty to convert all their surrounding neighbors to Islam.
4. The McMahon Letter promised
   a. British support for an Arab state in the Middle East.
   b. allied support for an Arab state in Palestine.
   c. British support for a Jewish homeland in Palestine.
   d. British support for the division of Turkish territories into colonial-like mandates.
5. At the time of the Balfour Declaration on Palestine, that country's population
   a. was in its majority Arabs.
   b. was about half Arab and half Jew.
   c. was almost zero.
   d. was polled on its preferences for the postwar era.
   e. had seen an influx of Muslims in recent years.
6. The state of Israel traces its creation to
   a. an Arab-Jewish pact in World War II.
   b. a United Nations decision to create two states from British Palestine in 1947.
   c. U.S. military intervention after World War II.
   d. a war against Egypt and Syria in 1963.
   e. the success of its Jewish residents in the Yom Kippur War.
7. Perhaps the greatest irritant to Palestinians during the immediate postwar period was
   a. Zionist statements that they desired the creation of a Jewish state in Palestine.
   b. unchecked Jewish immigration into Palestine.
   c. the division of Middle East lands into mandated territories.

d. the failure of the British to deliver on the promises made in the McMahon letter.
e. the strong support given to the Zionists by outside groups.

8. The Iranian Revolution in 1979 was aimed against
a. the shah of Iran and his Soviet backers.
b. the shah and his U.S. backers.
c. the communists who had seized power.
d. the Sunni Muslims who had captured the shah.
e. the shah's inability to deal effectively with the country of Iraq.

9. The trigger for the Arab-sponsored oil boycott in 1973 was
a. the U.S. air raid on Colonel Qaddafi in Libya.
b. the Israeli raid on Yasir Arafat's headquarters in Tunisia.
c. the support given by the West to Israel in the Yom Kippur War.
d. the revenge of Saudi Arabia for the West's support of the shah in Iran.
e. American support for the shah of Iran.

10. The Muslim-majority state with the largest population is
a. Pakistan.
b. Saudi Arabia.
c. Algeria.
d. Iran
e. Indonesia.

## InfoTrac College Edition

Visit the source collections at

**http://infotrac.thomsonlearning.com**

and use the Search function with the following key terms:

Ataturk Palestine Iran

## Wadsworth History Website Resources

Visit the World History Resource Center at **http://history.wadsworth.com/world** for a wealth of general resources and the *World Civilizations* Companion Website at **http://history.wadsworth.com/adler04** for resources specific to this textbook.

## HistoryNow

Enter *HistoryNow* using the access card that is available for *World Civilizations*. *HistoryNow* will assist you in understanding the content in this chapter with lesson plans generated for your needs. In addition, you can read the following documents, and many more, online:

A.J. Balfour, "Defense of the Palestine Mandate"

"Declaration of Israel's Independence"

Ayatollah Khomeini, "The Uprising of Khurdad 15"

*Men have always been mad, and those who think they can cure them are the maddest of all.*
**Voltaire**

# 55 Collapse and Reemergence in Communist Europe

The Immediate Postwar Era
The Communization of Eastern Europe
The Stalinist Regime

From Stalin to Brezhnev
Goulash Communism
Stagnation

The End of Communist Rule
The Breakup of the Soviet Union

Eastern Europe's Revolution of 1989

Problems of the Postcommunist Era

| | |
|---|---|
| 1945–1948 | Eastern Europe comes under Soviet domination |
| 1948–1960 | Stalinist phase in eastern European economies |
| 1953 | Stalin dies |
| 1955–1964 | Khrushchev era |
| 1956 | Hungarian revolt suppressed |
| 1964 | Khrushchev replaced by Brezhnev |
| 1979–1989 | Afghani invasion by USSR |
| 1985–1991 | Gorbachev era |
| 1989–1990 | Eastern Europeans reject communist governments |
| 1991 | Dissolution of USSR |

In 1989, an astounded world watched the spectacle of the impossible happening in eastern Europe: the rapid and complete collapse of the forty-five-year-old communist system. A year later, the doubly impossible happened in the Soviet Union: the peaceable abolition of the Communist Party's control of government. One year after that, the Soviet Union dissolved, and its component ethnic regions became independent states.

Rarely, if ever, has such a totally unexpected and complete reversal of the existing state of international political affairs occurred in such a brief span. The Cold War—which had defined all other international arrangements for a long generation—was abruptly terminated. And an integrated system of political and military controls, governing an economic apparatus that had ruled from fifty to seventy-five years over 300 million people, was simply thrown into the ashcan and the table swept clean. The most memorable Revolution of the Proletariat, so vehemently proclaimed by the followers of Karl Marx, turned out to be the one that ended the reign of Marxism itself.

## The Immediate Postwar Era

As we saw earlier, the Soviet government under Josef Stalin emerged triumphant from the "Great Patriotic War." The Red Army stood in the center of Europe, hailed by some, at least, as the liberator from the Nazi yoke. While the impatient Americans quickly demobilized their forces, Stalin proceeded to reap the fruits of his costly victory over the Nazi enemy.

### *The Communization of Eastern Europe*

Under the Allies' Yalta Agreement of 1945, the Russians were to carry through free, democratic national elections in the eastern European countries as soon as conditions permitted. The divisions among the Big Three (Britain, the Soviet Union, and the United States), which became evident at the war's end, made it impossible to specify more exactly when and how the elections should be held. The Yalta Agreement was in fact a tacit acknowledgment by the West that Stalin and his Red Army would be in control east of the Elbe for at least the immediate postwar years. The best that Washington and London could hope for was the election of governments that would be Soviet-friendly without being outright puppets.

But Stalin, whose suspicion of the Western "capitalist encirclers" had not diminished during the wartime years, was not inclined to accommodate himself to any type of pro-Western or even independent leadership among the eastern Europeans. As early as 1944, in Bulgaria, Yugoslavia, and Albania, communists had seized power through armed resistance movements that had fought the Nazi occupiers and their domestic collaborators. The governments so composed were not yet clearly satellites of Moscow, although communists played leading roles.

In Romania and Hungary, the Soviet-supervised intimidation of the numerous anticommunists took longer. Peasant anticommunist parties held on until 1947, when they were finally eliminated by arresting and executing their leaders. In Greece, however, a wartime agreement resulted in Stalin's abandoning the Greek communists when they attempted to seize power through an uprising. Stalin's failure to support the communists in the civil war (1944–1948) that ensued assured the eventual victory of the royalist side supported by the West.

Alone among the eastern European border states, Czechoslovakia had never had unpleasant experiences with Soviet Russia, and the Czechoslovak Communist Party had sizable popular support. So aided, the communist leaders pulled off a bloodless coup d'état in early 1948. They immediately installed a thoroughly Stalinist regime.

But the vital test case of whether the West would accept Stalin's long-term plans for eastern Europe was Poland. During the war, the Polish government-in-exile had been promised the firm support of the Allies in recovering their country. Many Poles fought bravely in the British Royal Air Force (RAF) and distinguished themselves in the Allied Italian and French campaigns. In 1944, Stalin broke with the Polish exile government over the question of who was responsible for the massacre in the Katyn Forest (thousands of Polish army officers had been murdered in Soviet-occupied Poland in 1940) and then put together a group of Polish communists to act as his cat's-paw in liberated Poland. Despite Western protests, the pro-Soviet group, backed by the Red Army, gradually made political life impossible for their opponents. After a series of highly predictable elections under Soviet "supervision," Poland's decidedly anticommunist and anti-Russian population was forced in 1947 to accept a Soviet satellite regime. The Baltic countries of Estonia, Latvia, and Lithuania received even less consideration. The advancing Red Army simply treated them as recovered provinces of Soviet Russia.

Thus, throughout eastern Europe, a total of about 110 million people from the Baltic to the Adriatic Sea had been forced under Stalinist rule by Soviet puppets. If truly free elections had been held in the area, it is thought that the Communist Party would have received perhaps 10 to 20 percent of the vote, but in the circumstances that fact was irrelevant.

## The Stalinist Regime

The Soviet Union recovered rapidly from the horrendous damage caused by the Nazi invasion, thanks partly to stripping the Soviet Zone of occupied Germany of all industrial goods and also to the forced "cooperation" of the eastern European satellites. For the first several years, the postwar economic policy was a continuation of already familiar Soviet goals and methods. The lion's share of investment went into either new construction or reconstruction of war-ravaged heavy industry and transportation. The first postwar Five-Year Plan reached its goals in considerably less time than planned. By 1950, the Soviet Union was an industrial superpower as well as a military one. It surpassed faltering Britain and still overshadowed recovering Germany, France, and Italy. New Soviet oilfields in central Asia, new metallurgical combines in the Ural Mountains, and new Siberian gas and precious metal deposits were coming on stream constantly.

But in basic consumer goods, the postwar era was even worse than the deprived 1930s. The housing shortage reached crisis proportions in the cities. To have a private bath and kitchen, one had to be either a high party official or an artistic/literary favorite of the day. Personal consumption was held down artificially by every means available to a totalitarian government: low wages, deliberate scarcity, diversion of investment to heavy industry, and constant propaganda stressing the necessity of sacrificing to "build a socialist tomorrow."

In the eastern European communist states, the backward agrarian economies of the prewar era were changed by the same methods employed in the Soviet Union in the 1930s: coercion of the peasantry, forced (and wildly inefficient) industrialization, and the absolute control of the national budget and all public affairs by the single party. The eastern European Communist Parties and their leaders were more or less exact replicas of the Soviet Communist Party and Stalin from the late 1940s until at least the late 1950s. The positive and negative results they obtained resembled those obtained in the Soviet Union fifteen to twenty years earlier, with one important exception: unlike Stalin, who transformed himself into a Russian nationalist when it suited him, the Soviet puppets in eastern Europe were never able during Stalin's lifetime or for years thereafter to appeal for loyalty to the deep-seated nationalism of their own peoples. On the contrary, they bore the burden of being in the general public's eye what they were in fact: minions of a foreign state.

In 1948, Stalin declared the Yugoslav leader Marshal Tito an enemy of communism and undertook a campaign against him that embraced everything but actual war. Tito's crime was that he had objected to the complete subordination of his party and his country to Soviet goals—a process that was well under way everywhere else in eastern Europe.

After a period of hesitation, the United States decided to assist Tito with economic aid. By so doing, Washington allowed the Yugoslav renegade to escape almost certain catastrophe for his country and himself. Tito, still a stalwart Marxist, responded by changing his foreign policies from unquestioning support of the Soviet Union to a prickly neutrality. By 1956, Yugoslavia was busily experimenting with its own brand of social engineering, a peculiar hybrid of capitalism and socialism that for a time seemed to work well enough to attract considerable interest among many African and Asian nations.

## From Stalin to Brezhnev

Tito's heresy was the beginning of the slow breakup of international Marxism into two competing and even hostile camps. The phases of the breakup can best be marked by looking at the Soviet leadership and its policies after the death of Stalin (by a stroke, supposedly) in 1953.

### *Goulash Communism*

Nikita Khrushchev (1894–1974), a longtime member of the Politburo, succeeded to the leadership first of the Communist Party and then of the Soviet state by gradual steps between 1953 and 1955. A son of peasants, Khrushchev was a very different sort of individual than Stalin. Having suffered in fear through the 1930s Stalinist purges himself, Kruschchev was determined that the party, and not the secret police, would be the seat of final power. By 1957, the dreaded KGB had been put back into its cage, and Khrushchev, after a couple of close calls, had succeeded in breaking the Stalinist wing of the party. That wing considered him to be the heedless and ignorant underminer of the system it believed was indefinitely necessary.

Khrushchev's difficulties within the hierarchy of the Communist Party of the Soviet Union (CPSU) sometimes revolved around his crude and volatile personality, but substantive frictions occurred over foreign and domestic policy as well. In foreign policy, Khrushchev allowed the tensions with the Maoist Chinese party to reach a complete break in 1959, splitting the vaunted unity of the world Marxist movement and introducing the unheard-of scandal of competing Marxist governments. In 1961, despite his proclamation of **peaceful coexistence**, he challenged the West and particularly the new U.S. president, John F. Kennedy, by allowing the Soviets' East German satellite to build the **Berlin Wall** in defiance of existing access agreements. Finally, Khrushchev took and lost the huge gamble of the Cuban Missile Crisis of 1962. To save Fidel Castro's vulnerable communist regime in Cuba, the Soviets tried to introduce atomic missiles within ninety miles of Florida (see Chapter 51) and were forced to give way by the United States. All of these initiatives ended in erosion of the Soviet Union's prestige in the Third World, that large group of ex-colonies and neutral nations that sought to avoid being enmeshed in the Cold War.

But Khrushchev ultimately was brought down more by his domestic political innovations than by his foreign policy. Most important by far was his attack on Stalin at the Twentieth Congress of the Party in February 1956. At this highest party meeting, Khrushchev gave a long, supposedly **secret speech** in which he detailed some (although by no means all) of the sins of the dead idol, whom a generation of Russians had been trained to think of as a genius and incomparable savior. Khrushchev's denunciation, which immediately became known outside as well as inside Russia, marked a turning point in international Marxist affairs. Never again would Stalin occupy the same position in the communist pantheon and never again would a European communist leader be looked on as a demigod.

Foreign reactions soon appeared. In the autumn of 1956, first the Poles and then the Hungarians attempted to act on Khrushchev's revelations about Stalin by shaking off Soviet political and military controls. Both were unsuccessful, but the Soviet party would never again have the same iron control over its satellites. Grudgingly, the CPSU had to admit that there were "many roads to socialism" and that each communist party should be allowed to find its own way there.

Secondarily, Khrushchev's "harebrained" attempts to change the structure of the CPSU and to install a mistaken agrarian policy contributed to his political demise. Party leaders came to see him more as a debit than an asset to Russian power and prestige, and in 1964 Khrushchev was unceremoniously ushered into premature retirement by his enemies within the Politburo. He lived out his final years in seclusion, but at least he was not executed by the new authorities—a welcome departure from the Stalinist model.

Khrushchev confidently expected the Soviet system to outproduce the capitalists in the near future and devoted much effort to improving the lot of the Soviet and eastern European consumers during his ten years in office. He coined the telling phrase "goulash communism" to explain what he wanted: a system that put meat in the pot for every table. Some progress was made in this respect in the 1950s and 1960s when consumption of goods and services rose substantially. The tight censorship over the arts and literature imposed by Stalin was also loosened temporarily, but the Khrushchev era was by no means a breakthrough into market economics or political democracy. It was an advance only in comparison to what went before.

## *Stagnation*

Khrushchev was replaced by Leonid Brezhnev (1906–1982), an apparatchik who had climbed the party ladder by sailing close to the prevailing winds. Worried about the long-term effects of the denunciation of Stalin, Brezhnev and his associates presided over a degree of re-Stalinization of Russian life. He cracked down hard on writers who did not follow party guidelines and on the small but important number of dissidents who attempted to evade censorship by *samizdat* (self-publishing). At the same time, he endorsed Khrushchev's policy of increasing consumption. In the 1970s, the living standards of ordinary Russians finally reached upward to levels that had been current in western Europe in the Great Depression of the 1930s.

The hallmark of Brezhnev's foreign policy was a determination to retain what had been gained for world communism without taking excessive or unnecessary risks. The best example of this attitude was the so-called Brezhnev Doctrine applied in Czechoslovakia in 1968. Several months earlier, Alexander Dubcek, a reformer, had been voted into the leadership of the still-Stalinist Czech Communist Party and proceeded to attempt to give his country "socialism with a human face." The Soviet leadership watched this loosening of the reins with intense and increasing concern. The generals warned that Czechoslovakia must not be allowed to escape its satellite status.

In August 1968 Brezhnev acted: Soviet and eastern European army units poured into Czechoslovakia in overwhelming numbers. The Czechs had no alternative but to surrender. Dubcek was forced out, and a faithful puppet was installed in his place. Despite verbal denunciations, the Western countries accepted this resolution of the issue without lifting a hand. As in Hungary twelve years earlier, it was clear that the NATO nations were not prepared to risk a world war on behalf of the freedom of eastern Europeans. Anticommunists in the satellite nations realized that their freedom to act independently could come about only if (1) the Soviet Union gave them leave or (2) the Soviet Union itself radically changed its system of government. Neither prospect seemed likely within a lifetime in 1968.

Brezhnev remained in power (1964–1982) longer than any Soviet leader except Stalin, but his effect on the Soviet state was in no way comparable. Where Stalin had turned the Soviet Union on its head, Brezhnev was intensely conservative. His eighteen years as chief of the state and party were marked by a general loss of morale and momentum in every aspect of Soviet life except the military. Opportunists and career seekers completely dominated the CPSU. Corruption in its top ranks (starting with Brezhnev's own son-in-law) was rampant and went unpunished. Using party connections to obtain personal privileges, such as rights to buy in special stores and permission for foreign travel, was taken for granted. Intellectuals and artists had once considered it an honor to join the party, but now its prestige had degenerated to the point that authentically creative people refused to join.

For a time, the increased emphasis on consumer goods in the 1970s masked what was happening to the **command economy**: the overall productivity of Soviet labor was declining while government investments were being misapplied. Pushed by his generals, Brezhnev went along with a huge increase in the military budget to match the U.S. atomic weaponry. Two forces thus converged to squeeze Soviet consumers from about 1975 onward: increased unproductive investment in military hardware and personnel, and declining civilian gross national product.

The *era of stagnation,* as it was later dubbed, made itself apparent in daily life in different ways. For many people, the most depressing was that Soviet living standards continued to lag far behind the West. Instead of catching up by 1980 as Khrushchev had once rashly predicted, the gap was increasing. After sixty-five years of communist promises, Soviet consumers still faced long lines outside shops selling inferior goods; unexplained shortages of meat, produce, and even bread in the cities; a housing shortage that never seemed to improve; and five-year waits to buy the very expensive but poor-quality domestic automobiles.

The Soviet Union was actually slipping backward, not just compared with the United States and western Europe but also relative to Japan, South Korea, and Taiwan. In fact, the Soviet Union was rapidly becoming a Third World country in every way except military technology and power. The entire postwar communications revolution had bypassed eastern Europe. Even a private telephone was a rarity for all but the higher party ranks and a few favored urbanites. Computers and their electronic spin-offs were few in number and obsolete compared with those in the West. The efficiency and productivity of communist industry and agriculture in both the Soviet Union and the satellites were far below world standards. They showed no signs of improvement as the ailing Brezhnev wheezed on into the 1980s. Had it not been for recently opened Siberian gas and oil resources, the U.S. Central Intelligence Agency estimated that Soviet domestic product would have actually *diminished* in the last years of Brezhnev's era.

**MAP 55.1** *Eastern Europe and Former Soviet Union*

Although in eastern Europe only Yugoslavian borders were changed as an immediate result of the dissolution of the communist regimes, the borders of the Soviet Union were radically rearranged into four independent states and eleven members of a Commonwealth of Independent States (CIS). The Russian Republic is by far the most important of these, followed by Ukraine and Kazakhstan.

## THE END OF COMMUNIST RULE

The problems were not limited to the Soviet Union. By the 1980s, the gerontocracies (rule of the aged) of eastern Europe were also beginning to show signs of doom. Poland, the largest of the Soviet satellites, was the catalyst. The Polish leaders had failed to provide sufficient consumer goods for years and were almost ousted by a nationwide peaceable protest in 1980–1981. This **Solidarity** movement, which was led by shipyard electrician Lech Walesa, was then repressed by a communist general, who tried to rule by martial law for the next several years against massive popular resistance. Although Poland was the most dramatic example, by the mid-1980s, all of the eastern European states were experiencing a rising tide of popular rage at the inability of the leaders to provide a decent standard of living. Yet the leaders insisted on clinging to their obsolete and discredited Marxist ideology while attacking their critics as misinformed or subversive.

In 1985, Mikhail Gorbachev (b. 1931) rose to the leadership of the Soviet Union, promising to reform both the sputtering economy and the CPSU itself. He pushed his program of ***perestroika*** (restructuring) and ***glasnost*** (openness) slowly, however, as it became apparent that both the party and much of the populace were fearful of a future in which the old rules might not hold anymore. Two full generations of Soviet citizens had accustomed themselves to "the system," and they had learned that reforms and reformers tended to disappear in disgrace, while the system went on.

Nevertheless, it became clear that economic restructuring and the regeneration of the tired party could not proceed without basic political reforms that allowed free criticism and initiative. In 1987–1988, Gorbachev took the plunge in this direction, spurred by heroic Soviet dissidents such as the physicist Andrei Sakharov, by his own convictions, and by the necessity of reducing the tremendously costly arms race with the United States. As long as that race went on, the money necessary for productive economic investment would not be available, and the communist world would fall further behind the West.

Gorbachev therefore initiated a rapid winding down of the Cold War, meeting several times with President Ronald Reagan of the United States to sign agreements on arms control and troop reductions in divided Europe. Gorbachev also made gestures of reconciliation to China, and in 1989, he withdrew Russian troops from Afghanistan. They had been engaged there in a highly unpopular war—the Soviet Vietnam—on behalf of Soviet puppet rulers since 1979, while the United States supported the opposing guerrilla forces. Afghanistan proved to be the last of the surrogate wars fought between the two rival systems all over the globe since 1946.

The most remarkable of Gorbachev's domestic initiatives was his drive to separate the Communist Party from the government of the Soviet Union. Between 1988 and 1991, the CPSU first secretary presided over a series of moves that transformed the Soviet state. He initiated a true multiparty democracy with a parliament and a radically revised constitution. The CPSU's seventy-year monopoly on political life was abolished. A Congress of People's Deputies and a Supreme Soviet (a standing parliament) were elected and took office in 1989. Immediately, bitter conflicts arose between the worried communist hard-liners in the parliament and its sizable noncommunist minority.

Gorbachev's cautious moves toward democracy had greatly upset the old guard CPSU activists and bureaucrats, but they had not gone nearly far or fast enough to satisfy the growing numbers of anticommunists and the supporters of thoroughgoing reform. A convinced believer in the possibilities of Marxism, the Soviet Union's last president also knew that real reforms were necessary. Gorbachev was a classic case of the moderate who is criticized by both extremes and cannot bring himself to join either one for survival. The result was his political death in the summer of 1991. An attempted coup by CPSU hard-liners was foiled by the reformers led by Boris Yeltsin, but it simultaneously revealed how naïve Gorbachev had been about his friends and his enemies. He was discredited and was soon pushed aside by Yeltsin.

The failed coup undermined not only Gorbachev's prestige but also the authority of the Communist Party. Yeltsin had already demonstratively resigned from it, and he was now joined by millions of others. Within a few months, the party was declared illegal in Russia (although this decree was later reversed by court action), and its ranks faded to a few hundreds of thousands of embittered and demoralized members. To use Leon Trotsky's cruel words to the anti-Bolsheviks in 1917, it had been "thrown on the ash-heap of history." Its enormous property and financial resources were either taken over by the government of Yeltsin or offered to private hands, in line with a vast "privatization" campaign that was introduced spasmodically, and with great difficulty, into the industrial and consumer economy as a whole. The dismantling of communism in the economic sphere, in fact, was going to prove as challenging as its introduction had been.

## *The Breakup of the Soviet Union*

Gorbachev had failed to recognize the depth of discontent in the Soviet Union. Above all, the fires of nationalism were finding steady fuel from the possibility—for the

Lu-Hovasse Diane/Corbis Sygma

**Boris Yeltsin Defies the Attempted Coup.** In August 1991, Yeltsin, the president of the Russian Republic, mounted a tank drawn up before the Parliament Building to read out his refusal to surrender governmental powers to the hard-liners. At this time, Soviet leader Gorbachev was being held under arrest by the coup participants.

first time in a century of czarist and communist rule—of expressing ethnic discontents openly. Indeed, Glasnost proved to be a tremendous boost to the many peoples in this truly multiethnic union who wished to end their connection with Russia as well as with communism. Among them were Turkic and Mongol Asiatics who were second-class citizens in their own countries, Muslim fundamentalists who rejected Russia and communism with equal passion, and Ukrainian and Baltic nationals who had never accepted their coerced incorporation into the Soviet Union. (See Map 44.2 in Chapter 44.)

Once the reins were loosened, all of the western and southwestern borderlands of the Soviet Union were potential breakaways. Within two years of the initiation of glasnost, Armenians and Azeris were fighting one another over ancient disputes in the far Caucasus Mountains; Russian immigrants were being hunted down by wrathful Kazakhs in the new Kazakhstan; and the three Baltic republics of Latvia, Estonia, and Lithuania were demanding total independence. They were soon joined by Ukraine, Georgia, Moldova, and some of the Muslim provinces along the southern borders of Siberia. By mid-1991, the Soviet political structure of a federation dominated by the huge Russian Republic was in a state of collapse. The final straw came in August with the bungled coup, whose conspirators claimed their goal was to reestablish the union, although their first concern was to restore the rule of the Communist Party.

What eventually emerged from the events of 1991 was the **Commonwealth of Independent States (CIS)**, whose name reflects the difficulty of finding some common ground among its varied members once the lid of Russian communist rule was blown off. Eleven of the fifteen Soviet republics opted to join the commonwealth, while four (the Baltic states and Georgia) refused. The CIS was always a weak confederation—the smaller members would not agree to anything else—and was politically, economically, and territorially dominated by the Russian Republic. In recent years the CIS has become all but meaningless, replaced by bilateral agreements between sovereign states of the former Soviet empire. (See Map 55.1.)

Russia, now led by Yeltsin's successor, Vladimir Putin, is still a politically and economically fragile entity. Putin has managed to walk a fine, and sometimes confusing, line between intimidation or outright repression of his political opponents and the introduction of modern democratic civil life. The economy has been particularly vulnerable to corruption of every type, derived in large part from the too-rapid and helter-skelter distribution of state-owned resources to private parties in the Yeltsin years. Yet on balance foreign observers agree that Russia has made a successful transition into a mainly free-market economy. Agriculture and the isolation of the rural villages remain what they had been under communism: the weakest points of the nation's economic and social life. The bloody, repressive campaign going now into its fifth year against the breakaway Chechen terrorists in the far south has also been a major debit factor in Putin's performance, in both domestic and foreign eyes.

## EASTERN EUROPE'S REVOLUTION OF 1989

In the fantastic fall of 1989, the communist governments of Czechoslovakia, East Germany, Bulgaria, and Romania were thrown out by peaceful protests or more violent means. Earlier, the Hungarian communists had saved themselves temporarily only by agreeing to radical changes, and the Polish Communist Party had in desperation agreed to share political power with Walesa's Solidarity. A bit later, in 1990, the Yugoslav and the Albanian Communist Parties were cast aside. Thus, Soviet-style communism was decisively rejected by all who had had the misfortune to live under it for a long generation in eastern Europe.

As in the Soviet Union, the primary cause of the eastern European **Revolution of 1989** was the failure of the system to deliver on its promises of economic progress. This failure reinforced the nationalist resistance to Russian dominion, which most eastern Europeans traditionally felt but which had been temporarily silenced in the postwar years. When Gorbachev showed that he believed in democratic ideas and was not inclined to keep eastern Europe under communist control by force as his Soviet predecessors had, the cork came flying out of the bottle of discontent. (See the Evidence of the Past box.)

How did the eastern Europeans go about ridding their nations of communism? The means varied from the massive, peaceful protests mounted by the East Germans and Czechs (the "Velvet Revolution" in Prague), to the more gradual pressures brought by a wide spectrum of anti-Marxists in Bulgaria and Albania, to the lethal street fighting in Romania. In all of these countries, the Communist Party attempted to retain some support by renaming itself and participating as a legal party in the free elections held throughout postcommunist Europe in 1990 and 1991. As in Russia, the frictions and disappointments of the transition to a free-market economy and a democratic polity allowed some former party leaders a second chance. Some "reform communists" were able to vindicate themselves in the eyes of their fellow citizens and retained or regained important posts in the Baltics, Hungary, Romania, and other states.

Generally speaking, the discredited old leaders were allowed to retire without being subjected to witch-hunts. There was no attempt to bring any but a handful of the most hated to trial. The most respected of the anticommunist leaders, including Walesa of Poland and Vaclav

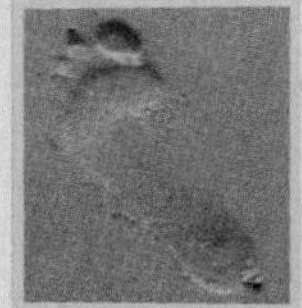

EVIDENCE OF THE PAST

## The End of the Berlin Wall

**The ultimate symbol of the Cold War** between East and West came to be the ten-foot-high concrete line of the Berlin Wall. Erected by the East German government with Soviet approval and assistance in August 1961, it ran along the boundary between East and West Berlin in an attempt to stem the increasing numbers of East Germans who sought asylum in the free and economically prospering West Germany. The "death zones" on the eastern side of the wall were just that: hundreds of people lost their lives attempting to sneak or burst their way across the barrier in the 1960s and 1970s. President John F. Kennedy's "Ich bin ein Berliner" speech at the wall in 1963 committed the Western alliance to the defense of the West Berliners and the eventual removal of the hated barrier to German unity.

The abrupt decision of the tottering East German government in November 1989 to allow free passage across the Berlin boundary signaled the end of the wall and of the Cold War. It heralded the demise of communism in eastern Europe and, a little later, the Soviet Union. On November 9, 1989, the demoralized East German border guards gave up their defense of a collapsing state. The American historian Robert Darnton gives his eyewitness account:

> The destruction of the Wall began in the early evening of Thursday, November 9th, soon after the first wave of East Berliners . . . burst upon the West. A young man with a knapsack on his back somehow hoisted himself upon the Wall . . . he sauntered along the top of it, swinging his arms casually at his sides, a perfect target for bullets that had felled many other Walljumpers . . . border guards took aim, and fired, but only with power waterhoses and without much conviction. The conqueror of the Wall continued his promenade, soaked to the skin, until at last the guards gave up. . . .
>
> A few minutes later hundreds of people . . . were on the Wall, embracing, dancing, exchanging flowers, drinking wine . . . and chipping away at the Wall itself.

Another view comes from an East Berlin woman:

> I was performing with my cabaret group in Cottbus, about three hours' drive away from Berlin, when someone said they'd heard on the radio that the Wall had been opened. We all dismissed that as rumor. But you didn't know what to believe, there were so many rumors going around. About an hour after the performance, we were driving back and heard it on the radio ourselves. When we arrived in Berlin, we immediately drove across into the West. . . . The city center, on Ku'damm, was one big party. After an hour we came back, and my friend dropped me off at my home.
>
> Bert, my husband, was away on a business trip and the kids were already asleep. Thirty minutes later, my friend called me back and said he couldn't sleep. I couldn't, either! so we decided to go back again. It was something like two or three in the morning. . . . I didn't come back till it was time for my kids to get up.
>
> The next weekend Bert and I and the kids went off on a trip to West Germany. People were passing out drinks along the autobahn. There were huge lines. I took a glass of something and thought: what kind of funny lemonade is this? It was champagne!
>
> That first week people were marvelous. There was an openness, a new spirit.

Reuters/Corbis

**The Wall Comes Down.** A horde of willing volunteers turned up on November 9, 1989, and every succeeding day for a month to help smash down the hated wall that had divided Berlin and the Berliners for almost three decades. Here, East German border guards look on from above at the Brandenburg Gate on November 11.

### *Analyze and Interpret*

Where else besides Berlin has a physical barrier been erected to separate people for purely political/ideological reasons? Do you think such separation could be effective in creating permanent ethnic divisions? What was the German experience?

Source: Robert Darnton, *Berlin Journal, 1989–1990* (New York: Norton, 1991), p. 75.

Peter Turnley/Corbis

**VACLAV HAVEL.** After an irresistible wave of public protests brought down the former regime, the playwright and political dissident Vaclav Havel was inaugurated as the first postcommunist president of the Czech Republic in 1990. Because no lives were lost during the uprising, the Czech revolt against the communist government is known as the "Velvet Revolution." Here, a Czechoslovakian student rings a bell and holds a poster of Havel during the Velvet Revolution.

Havel of the Czech Republic, were inclined to put the past behind them as rapidly as possible and to forgive and forget those who had harassed and imprisoned them in the name of the future.

## PROBLEMS OF THE POSTCOMMUNIST ERA

The immediate economic problems of the new governments of eastern Europe and the former Soviet Union were immense. They had to cope with a backward, collectivized agriculture that required far too much of their available labor and produced too little. Markedly inadequate consumer distribution networks and services had been the rule for forty years. Communications and information technology were decades behind current Western practice. The interest payments on the foreign debt accumulated by communist governments seeking popularity in the 1970s were eating up an intolerable percentage of the gross national product. Above all, the industrial sector, packed with superfluous workers by a standard communist policy of maintaining full employment through artificial means, was performing miserably. Most large companies were actually bankrupt, a fact masked by government ownership and subsidies. The biggest plants were almost always antiquated in technology, pollution ridden, and inefficient. Their low-quality output could not be sold in hard-currency markets and had to be forced on the domestic market or other communist countries.

The postcommunist democratic governments had to make the difficult choice between adopting free-market capitalism in one sudden sink-or-swim shift or attempting to achieve a mixed economy less traumatically through a gradual transition from state to private ownership. With the exception of Poland, which introduced basically free markets all at once, the governments opted for the gradual or partial approach. Some, like the Russians and Romanians, have tried to introduce free or freer markets, only to have to back off when they ran into popular resistance.

At the time of this writing, the Poles appear to have been more successful, but all of the countries have had severe difficulties in satisfying the justified demands of their citizenry for decent living standards and a better life. The first fruits of the postcommunist economic order were rapid inflation, endemic corruption, large-scale unemployment at bankrupt state-owned enterprises, and the highly visible division of the new free-market society into haves and have-nots. For many farmers, unskilled workers, and pensioners, the new situation could not be coped with and was a definite worsening of their material status. Although these evils have abated in the past decade, they and similar problems of transition from the communist command economy remain strong enough to generate many negative estimates.

Many citizens, especially the older generation, were embittered at the initially surging crime rates, the appearance of a "mafia" of newly rich and corrupt *biznezmeni,* and other unsavory phenomena of a disoriented and dislocated society. The prolonged inability of the Yeltsin government in Russia (1992–2000) to attain fiscal stability and organize its revenues had injurious repercussions throughout all of eastern Europe, frightening off much potential Western investment that was badly needed.

These economic facts have of course been reflected in the internal political sphere. Russia and most of the eastern European states (Romania was an exception) quickly installed complete personal freedom, honest elections, a free press, and effective justice and security, but these changes were not enough to ward off a certain disillusionment. It should be remembered that the eastern Europeans are laboring under a special handicap. They have never had a prolonged period of political freedom and constitutional government. In most of their countries, the years of parliamentary democracy could be measured on the fingers of both hands (see Chapter 43). The postwar Marxist repression of the educated and the middle classes and its artificially imposed "class solidarity" have made the necessary consensus for parliamentary give-and-take even more difficult to achieve. Worst of all, the violent, negative nationalism that was the curse of the early twentieth century was lying just below the Marxist surface, as the spectacular and tragic disintegration of former Yugoslavia has demonstrated. The eruption in Kosovo between Serbs and Albanians and the bloody repression of the Chechen rebellion in Russia were other severe blows to hopes for an easy transition from communist coercion to democratic harmony.

Clearly, the tasks of establishing effective, responsive, and just government in these multiethnic countries are enormous and will not be solved for many years, if at all. In the international arena, the outlook is currently more promising. Russia under Putin has shown itself committed to reasonable partnership with the West, even to the point of acceding to its former satellites joining the European Union (see Chapter 51) and accepting military and financial aid from the United States—an unthinkable change from Soviet practices. It now seems logical to expect Russia to accept the permanent and authentic sovereignty of the eastern European states. But whether Marxist or free, eastern Europe represents a continuing challenge to a world that seeks mutual and peaceable human development.

## SUMMARY

The astonishingly rapid collapse of the Soviet political and economic dominion in the years 1989–1990 came as a surprise to even the most perspicacious observer. An accumulating discontent with the multiple failures of the communist system to provide freedom or a decent material life for its citizenry joined with the long-standing resentments of non-Russian nationalists under Soviet rule to bring down the Marxist-Leninist regimes like falling dominos. The collapse of the Soviet Union immediately brought forth a series of claims to independence by the peoples along the western and southern borders of the traditional Russian state, claims that had to be recognized, however reluctantly, by the former masters in Moscow. The former Soviet satellites in eastern Europe broke entirely free and began a sometimes painful and halting reintegration into the general European community. Both they and the new Russia found their way into the new millennium laden with inherited difficulties in their economy and in political questions, particularly a rampant nationalism that had survived the communist era.

## IDENTIFICATION TERMS

Test your knowledge of this chapter's key concepts by defining the following terms. If you can't recall the meaning of certain terms, refresh your memory by looking up the boldfaced term in the chapter, turning to the Glossary at the end of the book, or working with the flashcards that are available on the *World Civilizations* Companion Website **http://history.wadsworth.com/adler04**.

August 1968
Berlin Wall
command economy
Commonwealth of Independent States (CIS)
*glasnost*
peaceful coexistence
*perestroika*
Revolution of 1989
secret speech
Solidarity

## TEST YOUR KNOWLEDGE

Test your knowledge of this chapter by answering the following questions. Complete answers appear at the end of the book. You may also take this quiz interactively and find even more quiz questions on the *World Civilizations* Companion Website: **http://history.wadsworth.com/adler04**.

1. Stalin's main objective in eastern Europe in the immediate postwar era was to
   a. hunt down and punish Nazis and their sympathizers.
   b. secure military assistance against a possible Western attack.
   c. generate a better supply of consumer goods.
   d. repair war damage to the Soviet Union and assure communist control.
   e. help eastern European countries become stronger than those in western Europe.

2. Which eastern European country proved that the Western Allies were no longer willing to fight Stalin for control in that region?
   a. Czechoslovakia
   b. Poland
   c. Hungary
   d. Yugoslavia
   e. Germany
3. The Soviet Union controlled the communist governments in every eastern European state *except*
   a. Yugoslavia.
   b. Romania.
   c. Czechoslovakia.
   d. Bulgaria.
   e. Poland.
4. The major reason for Khrushchev's sudden expulsion from leadership of the CPSU in 1964 was his
   a. submission to the Maoists.
   b. embarrassment over the attempt to place missiles in Cuba.
   c. disregard of the mounting pressure for consumer goods.
   d. efforts to emulate Stalin too closely.
   e. attempts to restructure the CPSU and to implement a new farm policy.
5. The creator of the term *goulash communism* was
   a. Gorbachev.
   b. Khrushchev.
   c. Stalin.
   d. Yeltsin.
   e. Tito.
6. The Brezhnev Doctrine
   a. put the world on notice that the Soviet Union was preparing an invasion.
   b. demonstrated that the Soviet Union intended to remain the leader in world Marxism.
   c. forced eastern European states to choose between communism and capitalism.
   d. allowed no existing satellite states to become independent.
   e. claimed all eastern European countries must continue under communism.
7. The only aspect of Soviet life that did not lose momentum under the leadership of Leonid Brezhnev was
   a. religion.
   b. consumer spending.
   c. technology.
   d. the arts.
   e. the military.
8. As the head of the Communist Party in the late 1980s, Gorbachev's fundamental problem
   a. was his inability to see the need for change.
   b. came from foreign affairs such as the Afghan war.
   c. was his indecision about the extent of necessary reforms.
   d. was his continuing belief in the probability of war against the United States.
   e. developed from his need to make friends with Ronald Reagan.
9. After being deposed in 1989, the leaders of the various eastern European Communist Parties generally were
   a. hunted down and accused of crimes against their people.
   b. imprisoned without trial or shot.
   c. allowed to retain their posts.
   d. sent into retirement without being accused of crime.
   e. tried for their crimes but freed in the end.
10. In economics, the postcommunist governments of eastern Europe generally
   a. continued with the Marxist system without change.
   b. introduced a completely free market in a short time.
   c. sought to convert to a free market in gradual steps.
   d. retained the basic idea of a "command economy."
   e. were repulsed by a nervous West when they tried to implement capitalism.

## InfoTrac College Edition

Visit the source collections at

**http://infotrac.thomsonlearning.com**

and use the Search function with the following key terms:

Soviet Union history   Europe Communism   perestroika

## Wadsworth History Website Resources

Visit the World History Resource Center at **http://history.wadsworth.com/world** for a wealth of general resources and the *World Civilizations* Companion Website at **http://history.wadsworth.com/adler04** for resources specific to this textbook.

## History Now

Enter *HistoryNow* using the access card that is available for *World Civilizations*. *HistoryNow* will assist you in understanding the content in this chapter with lesson plans generated for your needs. In addition, you can read the following documents, and many more, online:

Nikita Khrushchev, "The Secret Speech"

Leonid Brezhnev, "The Brezhnev Doctrine"

Gerhard Rempel, "Revolution in Eastern Europe, 1989"

*There is no solution to the problems of birth and death except to enjoy the interval.*
George Santayana

# 56 A New Millennium

A Short and Violent Century behind Us

Technology and Political Culture

The Rich and the Poor: Contrasts

Approaches to Social Reform
Prosperity in the Developed Societies
Losing Ground in the Developing Countries

The Other Half of Humanity

Family and the Individual

Looming Problems
The United Nations and National Sovereignty
Control of Weapons of Mass Destruction
Terrorism
Environmental Deterioration

Choices

| | |
|---|---|
| 1945 | United Nations founded |
| 1948–1973 | Economic boom in West |
| 1950s–1960s | End of Colonial Era |
| 1963 | Nuclear Atmospheric Test Ban |
| 1970 | Widespread recognition of environmental crisis begins |
| 1970s–1980s | Female economic equality drive |
| 1986 | Chernobyl nuclear plant meltdown |
| 1991 | Atmospheric pollution documented over Antarctica |
| 1990s | Global warming demonstrated |
| September 11, 2001 | An Age of Terror begins? |

## A Short and Violent Century behind Us

The commencement of a new millennium is a good point to make a brief survey of current affairs in the world that readers of this book are inheriting. One of the most urgent demands for attention is the sharpening of ethnic hostilities around the world. Simultaneously, the war between social classes that Marx predicted has faded into relative unimportance or has not come about. A notable book* by the historian John Lukacs claims that what we call the twentieth century really lasted only the seventy-five years between the outbreak of world war in 1914 and the collapse of Marxist communism in 1989. According to Professor Lukacs, these two landmarks defined the last century—the first announcing its commencement, the second its end. Leninist communism was a child that was born of chaos in World War I, grew to menacing adulthood in World War II, and died of senility and intellectual poverty in the 1980s. In retrospect, an out-of-control and misguided nationalism, not communism, was the true ideological menace to world stability in the twentieth century and remains so now, Lukacs insists. Since the 1990s, the horrific events in the former Yugoslavia, Rwanda, Armenia, Chechnya, and other places seem to support his thesis. In most recent days the use of politically inspired, indiscriminate terror against civil populations from New York to Baghdad has forced its way into

*John Lukacs, *The End of the Twentieth Century and the End of the Modern Age* (New York: Ticknor & Fields, 1993).

our calculations as well. The twenty-first century's opening has not boded well for a new day of world harmony.

## Technology and Political Culture

It is a shopworn cliché to say that our globe has shrunk incredibly in the last generation. Mass communications and instantaneous transfer of data and ideas from one corner of the Earth to the others have worked a transformation that contemporary human beings have not yet fully grasped. We only dimly understand the dimensions of the problems that have arisen, let alone their solutions.

A chief difficulty is that our technology has far outrun our ethics and our political culture. We can do things that have tremendous power for good or evil in the lives of human beings—our own and those in the future—but we don't know how to determine "good" or "evil" in a consensual fashion. In a world that has become immensely more interdependent, the old chimera of "I win, so you lose" is still being pursued by rivals of all types. This is as true in economic development and environmental protection as it is in international wars and ethnic conflicts. The results are often chaotic and sometimes fatal for whole groups.

One of the noteworthy contradictions of the contemporary world is the fact that, as advances in electronics are making physical distance almost irrelevant to communication, economic and social factors are splitting the human community into pieces that seem to have little to communicate to one another. The Northern Hemisphere abounds in previously unheard-of personal luxuries and social resources of every type, whereas the Southern Hemisphere has few resources and is unable to generate them sufficiently to meet the growing demand. Several countries of the West and North have already experienced a Third Industrial (or Postindustrial) Revolution, but it has not begun in many others of the East and South. Some of these nations have even remained largely untouched by the first two industrial revolutions.

Contemporary society is a kaleidoscope of significant differences, often concealed beneath a thin veneer of similarities that are generated in the West and then adopted worldwide: women apply much the same cosmetics, for exactly the same reasons, throughout the modern world; from Kenyan villages to New York apartments, children play with plastic toys mass-produced in Taiwanese factories; Afghan heroin finds its dark path into Russian seaports as well as Houston nightclubs. But these superficial uniformities of cultural behavior are deceptive. A better acquaintance or the arrival of a crisis lays bare the lasting differences. Many of them are direct reflections of the extreme variations in the economies of the most- and least-developed nations in the world of the twenty-first century.

## The Rich and the Poor: Contrasts

Despite the best efforts of well-meaning individuals in powerful positions, the personal income gradient from the heights of developed countries to the lower slopes of the underdeveloped remains as steep as ever. In the 1990s, the enrichment of the already prosperous was steadily matched by the impoverishment of the already poor. According to the World Bank, in 1950 the average *per capita* income of the developed countries was ten times that of the underdeveloped. In 2000, it was more than forty times! Cash income *per capita* in Ethiopia, in 2000 the poorest nation in the world, was about *1/300th* of that in the United States ($101 versus $32,778, according to the United Nations statistics). And there are a few countries, such as Sweden, Switzerland, and Denmark, in which the per capita income figure exceeds that of the United States.

Both the social interventionists and the supporters of the unrestricted free market have advanced various schemes for improving the living standards of the poor, but in the most poverty-stricken economies, these attempts have failed. Africa, in particular, has sunk deeper into misery. The West, on the other hand, we can now see was on the threshold of the *longest sustained economic advance in modern history,* a quarter-century of burgeoning prosperity for both the owning and the laboring classes, which would result in important social, political, and cultural changes by the century's end. The failure of most of the less-developed nations, particularly in Africa and Latin America, to provide anything like a comparable living standard for their citizens has created a dangerous gap between the two worlds of rich and poor, worlds that can also be characterized as the northern versus the southern hemispheres. Neither the doctrinaire prescriptions of the Marxists nor the "unseen hand" of the free marketeers have halted this sharpening division between haves and have-nots. And despite the hopes of some, the consequences of the increased globalization of world trading patterns show many debatable or downright debilitating features for the have-nots.

## Approaches to Social Reform

The collapse of the Soviet communist bloc in 1989–1991 was the unforeseen end of a system of economics and politics that had haunted the Western democracies for seventy years. In the interwar years and immediately after World War II, communism seemed likely to spread throughout the world either by revolution or by parliamentary procedure. In the underdeveloped lands, many millions saw it as the best hope at a decent material life for them and their children. In some countries such as China and Cuba, communism did bring an initial surge of social and economic justice to the masses and earned their strong support for a generation. They were willing to pay for their better economic prospects by giving up the political and social freedoms they had only minimally and imperfectly enjoyed under the previous, colonial or capitalist system.

But this was not true of the Western countries, including eastern Europe. Here, when the people had a choice, they firmly rejected the political, economic, and intellectual sacrifices demanded by communism. The Western socialist parties severed all connections with Soviet communism during the 1950s and even distanced themselves from many of the long-treasured ideas of Karl Marx. Reformism rather than revolution and gradualism rather than radical change became the order of the day among the social democrats.

What had previously been considered a peculiarly American viewpoint—that the secret of social harmony was in making a bigger pie rather than rearranging the slices—came to prevail in all Western nations. Furthermore, although never clearly admitted, this view came to be the new Soviet orthodoxy after Stalin's death. Revolution in the eyes of Brezhnev or even Khrushchev was reserved for developing countries, where any other means of effecting change was out of the question, and such a revolution was desirable only where it served Soviet foreign policy. By the 1970s, it was fair to say that only Castro in Cuba and Mao in China gave more than lip service to Marx's original doctrines of social and economic egalitarianism. The Marxist dream of the proletariat achieving a universal earthly heaven had been put on the shelf indefinitely.

### Prosperity in the Developed Societies

So long as the economic boom in the West lasted, social changes *did* come as both a reflection and a cause of vast improvement in the workers' living and working conditions. These improvements were what finally nullified the appeal of communism, as the Soviet system proved unable to generate anything like them.

In the 1980s, Western workers (extending "Western" to mean Japan) worked about one-fourth fewer hours weekly to earn wages that purchased about two and a half times as much in real terms as in 1950. They had guarantees of job security, wage or salary increases, vacation and sick time, insurance against accidents and ill health, extended unemployment pay, family leave, and other benefits that would have astounded workers of the 1940s. Under the impact of the higher energy costs after the OPEC oil boycott, increased competitive pressures in world markets since globalization, and outsourcing of jobs to low-wage countries, some of these gains have been curtailed or diluted by governments, but most remain in place.

Higher education is vastly more accessible, with state scholarships or stipends for student living expenses the rule in all countries. Material living conditions have also vastly improved. In the United States, most salaried and about half of the wage-earning people own their homes. In Europe and Japan, where rentals are the urban standard, working-class families can afford more space, and private automobiles have been commonplace for many years even among manual workers. Upward mobility out of the working classes into the technical or professional groups has been extensive everywhere. In these real senses, social and material progress in the West has been consistent and effective since 1945, although it has not been carried out in the name of an ideology or even a set of principles.

### Losing Ground in the Developing Countries

The developing world has unfortunately often shown a contrary pattern. The shift from manual to mental, white-collar work, and from agriculture to technological pursuits, has been slow and halting, at best. Productivity has in some places and job types actually declined, as in much of sub-Saharan family farms. Social mobility has increased, but only a small proportion of persons with access to education and connections have moved upward. In absolute numbers, *downward mobility* has probably been more common than upward in Africa and Latin America, where large groups of previously independent small landowners or tribal community members have been forced out of their traditional niches or impoverished by demographic and economic pressures. The near-total absence of organizations such as independent trade unions or farmers' associations leaves these people vulnerable to changes imposed by modern urban life with no one to help defend their interests. The Latin American peon and African mineworker can rarely improve their economic or social prospects except by migration to the city with its attendant dangers and frequent failure.

## The Other Half of Humanity

In 1964, a French wife and mother had to obtain the written permission of her husband to open a bank account in her own name. Ten years later, after a ferocious verbal battle, the French parliament legalized abortion on the request of the pregnant woman. Twenty years after that, women outnumbered men in the parliament. These three facts are as useful as any to symbolize the changes in the status of women brought about by the struggle for **women's liberation** in the last several decades.

*The Second Sex,* as Simone de Beauvoir's influential book called women, has been steadily closing the vast gap that once stood between them and men in the social and economic arenas of the Western world. Most countries now have laws on the books (sometimes unenforced) that prohibit paying women less than men for the same work, discriminating on the basis of gender for promotions or entry into a profession, refusing credit to women, denying them contractual rights, denying women custody of minors, and so on. In 2000, women made up 56 percent of all U.S. university graduates, up from 20 percent in the 1950s. Forty-six percent of the students entering U.S. law schools are women, a number that has approximately quadrupled since 1980. By 2010, it is estimated that females will be more than one-third of the total number of lawyers.

These indications of rapid change are by no means limited to the economic and labor sectors. The formerly normal status of marriage for young women has been radically questioned. About one-quarter of American women between eighteen and forty-five were single (that is, divorced or unmarried) in 1960, whereas more than half were by 2000. More than half of all first marriages end in divorce. In the United States, one-third of all babies are born to unmarried women, up from about 8 percent forty years earlier. The proportion is higher still for firstborns. Similar or higher numbers are found in other countries, ranging from the villages of Sweden to the city slums of south Asia. Unwed motherhood has become so common in some sectors of the population that it no longer requires comment or explanation. Two generations ago, it would have been grounds for social ostracism.

## Family and the Individual

The dramatic changes in family life over the past generation are evident in several ways. The two-parent, two-generation, male breadwinner and female housewife model, which had been the norm for Western urban families since the mid-nineteenth century, has clearly become but one of several *alternative lifestyles.* With most mothers working at least part-time outside of the home, children under six are commonly cared for by paid employees. The removal of the biological mother from primary responsibility for the young child's welfare during the most impressionable years will presumably have wide-ranging but as-yet-unknowable effects on the importance and permanence of the nuclear family relation.

The increasing numbers of female-headed households and economically independent females in all Western and some non-Western countries have put women into a position of potential political power that has been unparalleled in recent history. But to the dismay of more aggressive feminists, so far this potential has not been realized. Despite the occasional emergence of charismatic political leaders such as Indira Gandhi, Benazir Bhutto, and Golda Meir and a steady upward trend for females in legislative and administrative bodies worldwide, women have shown themselves generally unmoved by appeals to feminism as a political—as contradistinct from a socioeconomic—force. One cogent reason is that informal living

Bisson/Corbis Sygma

**Economic Feminism.** The battle for women's rights shifted during the 1960s and 1970s from a political to an economic and social focus as millions of single and married women entered the Western workforce for the first time. Here, women in Paris march in a street demonstration for women's rights in January 2000.

together supplants formal marriage, and abandonment by the male grows easier and more common, while enforcing legal responsibility for maintenance of spouse or children is difficult, if not impossible. Annually, many millions of women, from the villages of Africa to the ghettos of U.S. cities, find themselves thrown into permanent poverty by the breakup of their living arrangements with a man. Grappling with acute problems of survival, poor women have had little interest and/or energy to organize for longer-term political goals.

A third phenomenon in recent familial history is that the social identification that individuals in the past received from their family has largely become superfluous or is consciously rejected. The individual, not the family or the clan, exercises choice, creates opportunity, accepts responsibility, earns renown, and generally makes his or her mark in the Western world (and increasingly, everywhere else). Although this may be seen as a further large step toward democracy and fair play, it also has definite negative aspects for both individuals and society. The feeling of alienation from others that was mentioned in the chapter on modern cultures is highly stressful. It has been most apparent in those locales where the traditional family has become weakest: the urban, mobile, wealthy West where the individual is an atom among atoms rather than a link in a chain. The degree to which this has become true can be easily demonstrated by a simple question to the reader of these lines: Do you know where you are going to be buried? Probably, you have no idea where this traditionally most sacred rite will be carried out or who will do it—an unthinkable thing to confess until recently in human history.

## Looming Problems

### *The United Nations and National Sovereignty*

One of the touchiest of all topics in the current political discourse has been the degree to which national sovereignty must or should be surrendered to a supranational organization. The United Nations Organization (UN) was founded in 1945 by the victorious Allies to do what its predecessor, the League of Nations, was unable to do: guarantee international peace. Unlike the league, the UN has a potentially powerful executive organ in the Security Council. The council has wide authority, including the power to take air, sea, and land military action against aggression.

The UN General Assembly has no such powers and can only debate issues and recommend action to the Security Council. All states of the world have an equal vote in the General Assembly, which in effect means that the developing countries have a large voice in the UN's nonmilitary aspects, such as labor, cultural affairs, and public health through the International Labor Organization (ILO); the United Nations Educational, Scientific, and Cultural Organization (UNESCO); and the World Health Organization (WHO), respectively. These organs have played an important and positive role in world affairs for the last fifty years, even while the political and military performances of the UN were disappointing to many sympathetic observers.

The reason for their disappointment was that ultimate powers were retained by the sovereign states and not by the UN Secretariat (executive office). When a major state saw that its interests were being threatened by UN intervention of some type, it either exercised its veto in the Security Council or ensured by other means that there would be no effective interference. Throughout the Cold War era, the UN was able to intervene effectively only on the few occasions when both blocs could agree that a given conflict was intolerably dangerous (namely, the Israeli-Arab contest) or when one side chose to boycott the proceedings (namely, the UN decision to defend South Korea in the 1950s). The smaller powers, on the other hand, were frequently forced to conform to Security Council resolutions aimed at controlling their political and military inclinations and initiatives. Thus, the UN's guardianship of the peace was applied on two levels: one for the powerful, when it was dismissable, and other for the less so, when it sometimes was effective.

In the most recent times, the relative collaboration between the United States and Russia in international affairs has given the UN an unprecedented freedom of action in maintaining peace and redressing injustice that might lead to war. The successful coalition against Iraq in the Gulf War of 1991 was an outstanding example of what can be done. Other examples were the universal condemnation of the terrorist acts of the al-Qaida group in 2001 and the support for the antiterrorist campaign in Afghanistan that followed. The limits of such collaboration among the world powers was, however, clearly shown in the international quarrels that marked the United States' unilateral campaign to remove the Iraqi dictator Saddam Hussein shortly thereafter. The facts that there is truly only one superpower and that Cold War maneuvering has ended have by no means proved sufficient to bring harmony or acceptance of that superpower's imposed points of view. Instead, the blunders and frustrations that marked the attempted interventions by NATO and the UN to establish peace in the Yugoslav, Somali, and Rwandan civil wars of the 1990s may be the rule.

### *Control of Weapons of Mass Destruction*

Another pressing problem awaiting solution is the proliferation of nuclear and other weaponry. So long as only the United States, the Soviet Union, Britain, and France

Suhaib Salem/Reuters/Corbis

**The Search for WMD.** An Iraqi soldier (right) uses a stick to make a point while talking to a UN representative in front of the United Nations headquarters in Baghdad on January 26, 2003. Scores of UN weapons inspectors searched Iraqi sites that were suspected of producing weapons of mass destruction on the eve of a crucial UN report that would decide whether Washington would launch a war to disarm the region.

had atomic weapons, the "deadly secret" of creating them could be contained. But in the late 1960s, the Chinese under Mao went ahead with their own research effort, and by the mid-1970s, they had cracked the atomic code. The Israelis and South Africans were next, followed closely by the Indians and Pakistanis. The mushroom cloud is spreading over wider territories and can be set off by more and more hands. At the time of this writing both the North Korean and Iranian governments are suspected of secret attempts to develop atomic weaponry. Much recent diplomatic history, such as the strong support of the Yeltsin and Putin governments in Russia by the United States, is closely linked with the fear that Cold War weapons stocks might be accessed or stolen by terrorists.

The same fears are generated by contemplation of the deadly use of so-called **weapons of mass destruction (WMDs)**, as, for example, in biological warfare through release of epidemic disease germs or poisons into the atmosphere or water supplies (chemical warfare). It is certain that such attempts have already been made. Many think that it is just a matter of time before some terrorist band or desperate government will attempt atomic—or biological—blackmail.

## *Terrorism*

The entire question of terror employed for political or military ends came into sudden focus with the September 11, 2001, airborne attacks on New York City and Washington, D.C., by fanatical Muslims belonging to the worldwide al-Qaida network headed by the Saudi Arabian renegade Osama bin Laden. It was a day of mass death from enemy action, the first time that the United States had ever suffered such an event on its own soil. Whether it will be followed by others, as al-Qaida has repeatedly

Robert McMahan/Bettmann/Corbis

**September 11, 2001.** Members of the Farmingville Fire Department walk along the corner of Fulton and Nassau streets through dust and smoke from the crumbling World Trade Center towers. Hijacked airplanes were used as the instruments of destruction by terrorists who were thought to be members of the al-Qaida international network of Islamic extremists.

stated, cannot be known at this time. In the three years since the 2001 attacks, international surveillance and police collaboration have been able to intercept and render harmless many different plots to destroy lives and property. But al-Qaida or its many similar organizations have succeeded in several other attempts against governments and innocent bystanders, ranging the world from Spain to Indonesia. Most of these attempts have been perpetrated by Muslim fanatics who are waging war on the United States as the "Great Satan" supporting Israel, but some others seem to have had independent aims or have not been acknowledged by any organization.

Much is unclear about this sudden and terrifying outburst. What is certain is that the easy assumption by most of us that malicious violence on a massive scale, for political purposes, was something that happened elsewhere to other people has been shattered, perhaps forever. September 11 was "the day that changed everything."

## Environmental Deterioration

We have all heard so much about the environmental threats to the continued survival of the human race that we may be tempted to throw up our hands and trust to good luck or hope that another habitable planet is found before this one becomes unlivable. Nevertheless, certain environmental dangers are both real and can be addressed effectively, if only we have the will to do so. The most urgent near-term problems facing us in the new millennium seem to be the following:

- *Excessive and unbalanced consumption of nonrenewable energy.* Each year, the average U.S. citizen consumes roughly thirty-five times as much energy (fossil fuel, water, electric) as a person in India and about three times as much as an individual in Italy or France. The tremendous difference between the developed North and the underdeveloped South in global affairs is nowhere more apparent than in energy consumption. The less-developed countries, with about 60 percent of world population, consume only 12 percent of the energy produced in the world; the rest is consumed by the developed countries. And if per capita use remains the same in 2030 as it is today, the world will need to produce 50 percent more energy just to keep pace with population growth.
- *Global warming.* In the past decade what the world's scientific communities had looked upon as a possibility or a probability has become a certainty: the Earth's temperature is going upward at a rate unprecedented in historical times (**global warming**). Debate continues about the rate of increase and the nature of the cause, but no serious scientific body now questions the basic fact. If the speed of change approximates the higher ranges now foreseen for the next twenty years, the world's climate, vegetation, and sea levels will see massive alteration. No one can now accurately predict the extent of some of these changes, but they are liable to cause considerable dislocations and impact most of the world's population.
- *Food production in Africa.* Owing to sharply rising populations and the systematic use of marginal land for agriculture, African food supplies have been actually declining in large areas of the continent. Several countries, including Somalia, Sudan, Chad, and Tanzania,

**Global Warming Dooms Tuvalu Island.** Paani Laupepa, the assistant secretary of the Department of Environment, Energy, and Tourism, faces the incoming swells of the South Pacific ocean, on Funafuti Atoll, Tuvalu Island, in 2002. "The question is not if but when we'll be drowned," says Laupepa, Tuvalu's point man on climate change. Paani says industrialized countries are forcing the entire nation of Tuvalu to leave its homeland.

Matthieu Paley/Corbis

are now permanently dependent on imported food and have become beggars in the world economy. Massive starvation on a periodic scale is the probable future of these nations without a coordinated international attempt to assist them in feeding themselves. One result will be an explosion of civil wars such as the one currently being instigated by the Sudanese government against its own minority citizens.

- *Pollution and radioactive wastes.* Many developing countries are almost entirely ignorant of or choose to disregard the most elementary pollution-control measures. Their industries and mines—frequently controlled by owners in the developed countries—poison the Earth, air, and water on a large scale. The meltdown at the Chernobyl nuclear plant in Ukraine twenty years ago was the most spectacular example of the dangers posed by inadequate or nonexistent policing and protection. Many others might be cited. These potential catastrophes have no respect whatever for national borders, and the long-term, slow effects of pollution may be worse than the occasional explosive event such as Chernobyl.

This list is by no means comprehensive and deals only with what the authors of this book believe to be the problems with the most immediate global repercussions. During the life spans of students reading these lines, the developed world (the United States foremost) will either master the most urgent of these problems or substantially change the hitherto-known environment of human beings from a life *with* nature to a life *against* or *outside* nature. Whether this latter style of life is possible and at the same time humane is an open question.

## Choices

We earthlings live on a small planet, which is only a minor part of a nine-planet solar system, itself one of perhaps hundreds within a still-expanding cosmos. We will soon either succeed (temporarily) or fail (permanently) in our attempt to keep the Earth livable for creatures like ourselves. We have seen that it is possible for humans to damage their habitat so drastically that it will no longer be a fit place for the species. What will be done in these regards in the next decades is largely up to people like yourselves, the educated men and women of a powerful country.

At bottom, there are only two rational approaches to the solution of basic environmental problems: *conservation,* which is the attempt to retain (conserve) existing systems, and *technology,* which is the attempt to discover (develop) superior replacements. The conservationists argue that the Earth's natural systems are the results of eons of slow evolution; that of all earthly beings, humans alone rebel against those systems rather than live with them; and that this rebellion, although it may be successful in the short run, spells ruin in the longer term. The technicians argue that evolution is only one path to an acceptable, sustainable system and that humans can and must try to find other paths when the natural one proves inadequate or has been blocked. The choices that must be made between these differing approaches will largely determine the quality and character of your lives.

Choices of every kind lie before you, as they have before all of your predecessors. Like them, you will often not be sure of what must be or should be done. Like them, you will have to seek guidance from many sources: religion, science, parents, and the study of history. The answers from history especially will often be unclear or cryptic; they may have sections missing or lend themselves to more than one interpretation, but the historical answer will usually be most applicable and most comprehensive: this is what humans, in all their variety, have done successfully to meet and overcome problems somewhat like those you currently encounter. And like all of your predecessors on this Earth, you will have to hope that you have understood correctly and have taken a constructive, viable path as you join the long parade of men and women, moving forward into the infinite future.

## Identification Terms

Test your knowledge of this chapter's key concepts by defining the following terms. If you can't recall the meaning of certain terms, refresh your memory by looking up the boldfaced term in the chapter, turning to the Glossary at the end of the book, or working with the flashcards that are available on the *World Civilizations* Companion Website **http://history.wadsworth.com/adler04**.

global warming

weapons of mass destruction (WMD)

women's liberation

## Test Your Knowledge

Test your knowledge of this chapter by answering the following questions. Complete answers appear at the end of the book. You may also take this quiz interactively and find even more quiz questions on the *World Civilizations* Companion Website: **http://history.wadsworth.com/adler04**.

1. One of the chief problems of today's world is that ethics and the political culture have been outpaced by
   a. education.
   b. longevity.
   c. ambition.
   d. national aspirations.
   e. technology.
2. As of your textbook's printing, the poorest nation in the world was
   a. Ethiopia.
   b. Bangladesh.
   c. Rwanda.
   d. Djibouti.
   e. Eritrea.
3. The Social Democrats found their greatest strength in which of the following places?
   a. Cuba
   b. Soviet Union
   c. Eastern Europe
   d. Western Europe
   e. China
4. In Africa and Latin America, "downward mobility" has often been the lot of
   a. dictators.
   b. those who rejected Christianity.
   c. independent small landowners.
   d. former aristocrats.
   e. almost everyone.
5. Simon de Beauvoir was a strong advocate of
   a. women's rights.
   b. gay rights.
   c. Latino rights.
   d. children's rights.
   e. workers' rights.
6. Which of these statements about social issues in the United States is most accurate?
   a. The percentage of women graduating from universities has almost doubled since 1950.
   b. One in four children is born to an unmarried woman.
   c. The number of women entering law schools has increased about fourfold in two decades.
   d. Estimates are that, by 2010, most lawyers in the United States will be women.
   e. About one-third of American women between the ages of eighteen and forty-five were unmarried in 2000.
7. One of the touchiest subjects for the United Nations has been
   a. an international currency.
   b. national sovereignty.
   c. nuclear proliferation.
   d. poverty eradication.
   e. African dictatorships.
8. The United Nations Security Council voted to defend South Korea in 1950 because of
   a. a unanimous vote by all its members.
   b. the strong support by the United States.
   c. the leadership of U Thant.
   d. the strong fear of communism.
   e. a boycott by one of the council's members.
9. The world's developed countries, with about 40 percent of the Earth's population, consume about what percentage of the energy produced?
   a. 40
   b. 62
   c. 25
   d. 88
   e. 95
10. The Kyoto Conference of 2002 dealt with
    a. nuclear proliferation.
    b. terrorism.
    c. earthquakes and other natural disasters.
    d. global warming.
    e. food production.

## InfoTrac College Edition

Visit the source collections at

**http://infotrac.thomsonlearning.com**

and use the Search function with the following key terms:

wealth redistribution or wealth distribution

feminism social problems

## Wadsworth History Website Resources

Visit the World History Resource Center at **http://history.wadsworth.com/world** for a wealth of general resources, and the *World Civilizations* Companion Website at **http://history.wadsworth.com/adler04** for resources specific to this textbook.

## HistoryNow

Enter *HistoryNow* using the access card that is available for *World Civilizations*. *HistoryNow* will assist you in understanding the content in this chapter with lesson plans generated for your needs. In addition, you can read the following documents, and many more, online:

George W. Bush, "History's Unmarked Grave of Discarded Lies"

# Worldview Six

| |  Law and Government |  Society and Economy |
|---|---|---|
| **Westerners** | The rise of mass democracy in politics creates a new-style party government where money, but no longer birth, plays an important role. Law increasingly reflects popular attitudes, as interpreted by party heads. Property rights are under attack, while civil rights advance. Totalitarian governments appear in some nations after World War I and the ensuing Great Depression of the 1930s. After World War II, a long economic boom allows democratic recovery and stability to occur in the West outside of the Soviet bloc. Soviet communism expands for a generation, but then collapses under internal contradictions. | There are two distinct economic periods: 1920–1945 sees the decline and near collapse of the free market in the West and widespread impoverishment of middle classes and agriculturalists; 1945–present has seen a long boom, interrupted for several years by the oil crisis of the 1970s. Japan emerges as a leading financial power in the 1980s. The European Community becomes an economic reality, whereas the Soviet bloc stagnates and then collapses. The global economy is rapidly forming under Western dominance. |
| **Africans** | The "scramble" for previously independent Africa is completed by the early 1900s. Law and government continue on colonial lines until after World War II. Decolonization brings an unstable mixture of African traditional law and political structures with European models. Western forms are often at odds with precolonial content. Post-independence problems encourage authoritarian, single-party governments. Regionalism, ethnic rivalries, and corruption are major problems. | Increasing emphasis placed on export crops and mining converts some areas to food-deficit regions. Little manufacturing takes place, even after the end of colonial regimes. Increasing international aid is provided in an attempt to overcome declining agricultural productivity and dependency on world markets and imports of all types. Because of large increases in population, many national economies are in crisis by the 1990s. |
| **Muslims** | Minority attempts to introduce modern Western law, education, and politics are made throughout the Muslim world after World War I with only moderate success, except for Turkey. After World War II, a strong reaction favoring various forms of Islamic revival develops, led most recently by Iran. Governments of Islamic countries range from a limited Western constitutionalism to undisguised theocracy. Nationalism and Islam are powerful forces throughout many parts of Africa and Asia. | Middle East oil is the one major export, generating dependence on international customers. Much effort was exerted to avoid this situation by using oil funds for varied domestic investments. Arab states and Indonesia are relatively successful in doing so, but oil production still remains the key to their prosperity. Poor Muslim countries are unstable and still are not constructively integrated into the world economy. |
| **South and East Asians** | Former British possessions have generally retained a Western outlook on law and government. French and Dutch territories are less committed to these ideals. In several nations, Marxist socialism provided a format for combining nationalism with radical reform. Governments currently range from liberal democratic constitutionalism to oppressive dictatorships. China's mutated Marxism is in a category of its own, combining political censorship with economic and social freedoms. | South and East Asia give a mixed picture of economic progress. In Bangladesh, Sri Lanka, and Burma, the traditional agrarian and poverty-stricken economy has barely changed or has worsened as a result of rapid population increases. South Korea, Taiwan, and Malaysia have undergone stunning change in moving toward modern industry and services in the past thirty years. Japan's modified and highly successful free-market example has proven to be influential, but huge China is the X quantity in Asia's economic picture. |
| **Latin Americans** | The fundamental laws continue to be European (Napoleonic codes), and the governmental structures resemble those of the West. The enormous social gap between rich and poor often frustrates the intent of the constitution, however, and makes a segregated legal procedure inevitable. Government often represents only the uppermost minority, although this is slowly changing in most of the continent. | A fully Westernized urban lifestyle is supported for a minority by relatively modern industrial economies. In most of the continent, however, the agrarian and deprived mestizo/mulatto population has made little progress in a century. As in Africa, a rapid population increase prevents substantial or permanent gains from being made by international investments and loans. Most of Latin America continues to be a dependent of the Western nations. |

# Equilibrium Reestablished: The Twentieth-Century World and Beyond, 1920–Present

|  Patterns of Belief |  Arts and Culture |  Science and Technology |
| --- | --- | --- |
| In the "post-Christian era," secularism is elevated to a formal doctrine in most countries, assisted by the rise in influence of Marxism through the 1960s. The failure of Marxism in the 1980s underlines the crisis of sterility in Western philosophical ideas. Concurrently, Western interest in Eastern religion and philosophies rises sharply. | Art and its audience become fragmented. No models or authority are recognized. Much influence is received from non-Western sources. Abstraction in pictorial arts is matched by the rejection of traditional models in all other arts among the avant-garde. Literature and philosophy are either "serious" or popular; there is no middle ground. Mass cultural forms (TV, movies, music, magazines) are often dictated by commercial considerations. | Science becomes the defining reference for knowledge and truth. Social sciences (for example, economics, psychology) rise to prominence. Technology makes enormous strides, removing physical labor as an obstacle to almost any task and enabling an "information revolution" through computers and electronic apparatus. |
| Christian missions make inroads into traditional religions in central and southern regions. Islam dominates the north, west, and eastern coasts. Most Africans blend one or the other formal doctrines with local beliefs and practices. Education for the masses begins after 1950 and increases after decolonization is completed. | Sub-Saharan pictorial and plastic arts become widely recognized for the first time, partly because of increased archaeological finds. Modern African artists blend Western training with native motifs and media. Independence brings much greater opportunities for artists, domestically and internationally. Literature continues to be published mainly in Western languages, hence limited in audience at home, where oral folklore is still the main way of transmitting cultural values. | Physical and social scientists are still relatively few in number and depend on foreign sources for training, financing, and direction. Higher educational facilities remain oriented toward nonscientific programs and degrees, emulating nineteenth-century colonial culture. Technology imported from the West and Japan sometimes has a devastating impact on local cultures and economies. |
| The secularism of some intellectuals and political reformers is sharply opposed by the traditionalists. Only after World War II do the religious revivalists and fundamentalists learn how to propagandize effectively with a nationalist appeal. Islam in their view is combined with a strong rejection of the West's public and private values. | Much-increased literacy results in a revival or first appearance of literature in several Muslim states. The oil wealth of the 1970s provides major governmental patronage of the arts in Arab states. Nationalism is reflected in art forms and a revived interest in folk art. | As in the rest of the non-Western world, the physical and life sciences were dependent on Western training and goal setting. This situation rapidly changed to autonomous science in much of the Muslim world since approximately 1970. An emphasis on science and technology in higher education has apparently been accepted by fundamentalist Muslims as a modern necessity. |
| Asians have retained their religious and cultural independence from the West, even during the colonial era. Buddhism in its several versions is still the most popular of the mass-cults, whereas Islam and Taoism are major competitors in the southeast and China. India remains Hindu, while secular views gain acceptance everywhere among the educated. The superficial cultural phenomena have become increasingly Westernized. | Cultural autonomy in Asia is expressed in the arts now as always. A recognizably non-Western approach is manifested through several regional variations in the fine arts as well as in folklore and artisanry. Literature and philosophy have been deeply affected by Western influences in the last generation, but they remain distinct. Higher education now resembles that in the West, with the same emphases in the advanced countries. | The formerly huge gap between the physical and life sciences in South and East Asia and in the West has almost been closed. Technology still lags, but largely as a result of shortages of investment funds rather than lack of knowledge or willingness. |
| Catholicism has split into a reform-minded and a traditionalist party within the clergy as it gradually loses its automatic acceptance among the masses, which have been touched by modern secularism and Protestant evangelism. The formal link between state and church is nearly gone. Education is still an unmet need in the mestizo and Indian countries, and literacy rates are still low. | Particularly in fiction and poetry, Latin American authors have won world acclaim, and the fine arts, with some exceptions, have also prospered in this century. Formal culture is still restricted to the wealthy and the urban middle class, however. Between them and the rural majority, the cultural chasm still lies open. | The labor-rich and slow-developing economy has only a slight connection with technology. The sciences and technology are still heavily dependent on Western, and particularly American, models and direction. Higher education has been slow in reorienting itself toward a modern curriculum in these fields, while the mainly foreign-owned companies are not research oriented. |

# Glossary

**Abbas the Great** See *Shah Abbas the Great.*

**Abbasid Dynasty** (Ab-BAH-sid) The dynasty of caliphs who governed the Islamic Empire from the 750 until 1258 C.E.

**abbot/abbess** The male/female head of a monastery/nunnery.

**abstract expressionism** A style of modern painting that does not seek to represent external reality but to convey emotional meaning through abstract shape and color.

**abstractionism** A twentieth-century school of painting that rejects traditional representation of external nature and objects.

**Act of Supremacy of 1534** A law enacted by the English Parliament making the monarch the head of the Church of England.

**Actium, Battle of** The decisive 31 B.C.E. battle in the struggle between Octavian Caesar and Mark Anthony, in which Octavian's victory paved the way for the Principate.

**Age of the Barracks Emperors** The period of the Roman Empire in the third century C.E. when the throne was repeatedly usurped by military men.

**Agincourt** The great victory of the English over the French in 1415, during the Hundred Years' War.

**Agricultural Revolution** The substitution of farming for hunting-gathering as the primary source of food by a given people.

**Ain Jalut** (AYN Ja-LOOT) A decisive battle in 1260 during which an Egyptian Mamluk army turned back the Mongols and prevented them from invading North Africa.

**Ajanta** (A-JAN-ta) Caves in central India that are the site of marvelous early frescoes inspired by Buddhism.

**Akbar the Great** (ACK-bar) Best-known of the Shahs of the Mughal Empire of India (r. 1556–1605). He was most famous for his policy of cooperation with his Hindu subjects.

**Akhnaton** Name of a fourteenth century B.C.E. Egyptian ruler who attempted to introduce monotheistic religious practice.

**Al-Afghani, Jamal al-Din** (1838–1897) Early leader of the Islamic reform movement.

**al-Ghazzali** (al-Gaz-ZA-lee) (d. 1111) The "Renewer of Islam," he was an important figure in the development of sufism, Islamic mysticism.

**Allah** (Al-LAAH) Arabic title of the one God.

**Alliance for Progress** The proposal by U.S. president John F. Kennedy in 1961 for large-scale economic assistance to Latin America.

**Alliance of 1778** A diplomatic treaty under which France aided the American revolutionaries in their war against Britain.

**Amerindians** Short for (Native) American Indians.

**Amur River War** 1976 sporadic shooting between Soviet and Chinese troops stationed along the Amur River following tensions that arose on the death of Mao Zedong.

**Anabaptists** Radical Protestant reformers who were condemned by both Lutherans and Catholics.

**anarchism** A political theory that sees all large-scale government as inherently evil and embraces small self-governing communities.

**Anasazi** (A-na-SAA-zee) Term sometimes used to refer to Ancestral Puebloans.

**Ancestral Puebloans** These are the people native to the Four Corners area of the present United States. They built the Chaco Great Houses and cliff dwellings at Mesa Verde.

***ancien régime*** "The old government"; the pre-Revolutionary style of government and society in eighteenth-century France.

**Anghor Wat** (ANG-ghor WAAT) A great Buddhist temple in central Cambodia, dating to the twelfth-century C.E. Khmer Empire.

**Anglo-Egyptian Condominium** Joint British and Egyptian control of the Sudan that followed British occupation of Egypt in 1882.

**Anglo-French Entente** The diplomatic agreement of 1904 that ended British-French enmity and was meant as a warning to Germany.

**Anglo-Russian Agreement** The equivalent to the Anglo-French Entente between Britain and Russia; signed in 1907.

**Angola-to-Brazil trade** A major portion of the trans-Atlantic slave trade.

**animism** A religious belief imputing spirits to natural forces and objects.

***Anschluss*** The German term for the 1938 takeover of Austria by Nazi Germany.

**anthropology** The study of humankind as a particular species.

**Antigonid Kingdom** One of the Hellenistic successor kingdoms to Alexander the Great's empire.

**Anti-Slavery Movement** Faction among mostly British evangelical Christians, which, beginning in the 1790s, was able to pressure Parliament with increasing effectiveness to ban slavery and the slave trade in Britain and throughout the British Empire.

**apartheid** The Afrikaans term for segregation of the races in South Africa.

**appeasement** The policy of trying to avoid war by giving Hitler what he demanded in the 1930s; supported by many in France and Britain.

***Arabian Nights, The*** Also known at *The 1001 Nights.* Medieval collection of tales from the Islamic Middle East which greatly reflect life at the time of the Abbasid caliphs of Baghdad.

**archaeology** The study of cultures through the examination of artifacts.

**Archaic Period** 8000–2000 B.C.E. in Native American history. Period when gathering slowly replaced large-game (megafauna) hunting.

**aristocracy** A social governing class based on birth.

**Ark of the Covenant** The wooden container of the two tablets given to Moses by Yahweh on Mount Sinai (the Ten Commandments); the Jews' most sacred shrine, signifying the contract between God and the Chosen.

**Arthasastra** A compilation of hard-bitten governmental policies supposedly written by Kautilya to guide his master, Chandragupta Maurya, and one of the few literary sources of early India's history and culture.

**Aryans** A nomadic pastoral people from central Asia who invaded the Indus valley in about 1500 B.C.E.

**Ashikaga clan** A noble Japanese family that controlled political power as shoguns from the 1330s to the late 1500s.

**assimilation** The acceptance of the culture and language of an alien majority by an ethnic minority to a degree that effectively blurs the distinctions between those groups.

**Assur** The chief god of the Assyrian people.

**Ataturk, Mustafa Kemal** The "father of the Turks"; a World War I officer who led Turkey into the modern age and replaced the sultanate in the 1920s.

**Audiencía** The colonial council that supervised military and civil government in Latin America.

**August 1991 coup** The attempt by hard-line communists to oust Mikhail Gorbachev and reinstate the Communist Party's monopoly on power in the Soviet Union.

**Ausgleich of 1867** The compromise between the Austro-Germans and Magyars that created the "Dual Monarchy" of Austria-Hungary.

**Austro-Prussian War** The conflict for mastery of the German national drive for political unification, won by the Bismarck-led Prussian Kingdom in 1866.

**Avesta** The holy book of the Zoroastrian religion.

**Avicenna** (A-vi-SEN-na) See *Ibn Sina*.

**Axis Pact** The treaty establishing a military alliance between the governments of Hitler and Mussolini; signed in 1936.

**Axum** (AX-um) The center of the ancient Ethiopian Kingdom.

***ayllu*** (EYE-yu) Quechua name for the clan organization of the Peruvian Indians.

**Ayuthaya** The capital of the Thai Kingdom of early modern southeastern Asia.

**Aztec** Latest of a series of Indian masters of central Mexico before the arrival of the Spanish; developers of the great city of Tenochtitlán (Mexico City).

**Babylon** Most important of the later Mesopotamian urban centers.

**Babylonian Captivity** The transportation of many Jews to exile in Babylon as hostages for the good behavior of the remainder; occurred in the sixth century B.C.E.

**Babylonian Captivity of the papacy** See *Great Schism*.

**Baghdad** (Bag-DAD). Capital of the Islamic Empire under the Abbasid Dynasty. Built by the Caliph al-Mansur *ca.* 763.

***bakufu*** The military-style government of the Japanese shogun.

**Balfour Declaration** The 1917 public statement that Britain was committed to the formation of a "Jewish homeland" in Palestine after World War I.

**banana republics** A dismissive term referring to small Latin American states.

**Bantu** (BAN-too) Related peoples who speak languages that are part of the African language group called Bantu. They are spread through most of subequatorial Africa.

**barbarian** Greek for "incomprehensible speaker"; uncivilized.

**Barracks Emperors** The series of twenty Roman emperors between 235 and 284 who used troop command to force their way into power.

**Battle of the Nations** October 1813 at Leipzig in eastern Germany. Decisive defeat of the army of Napoleon by combined forces of Prussia, Austria, and Russia.

**bedouin** (BEH-doo-in) The nomadic inhabitants of interior Arabia and original converts to Islam.

**Benedictine Rule** The rules of conduct given to his monastic followers by the sixth-century Christian saint Benedict.

**Berbers** Indigenous people of North Africa and the Sahara Desert.

**Beringia** (Beh-RIN-jee-a) A land mass in the region of the Bering Strait over which Ancestral Native Americans migrated to the Western Hemisphere *c.* 30,000 to 10,000 B.C.E.

**Berlin blockade** The 1948–1949 attempt to squeeze the Western allies out of occupied Berlin by the USSR; it failed because of the successful Berlin Airlift of food and supplies.

**Berlin Wall** The ten-foot-high concrete wall and "death zone" erected by the communist East Germans in 1961 to prevent further illegal emigration to the West.

***Bhagavad-Gita*** (BA-ga-vaad GEE-ta) The best-known part of the Mahabharata, detailing the proper relations between the castes and the triumph of the spirit over material creation.

**big bang theory** The theory that the cosmos was created by an enormous explosion of gases billions of years ago.

**Bill of Rights of 1689** A law enacted by Parliament that established certain limits of royal powers and the specific rights of English citizens.

**Black Death** An epidemic of bubonic plague that ravaged most of Europe in the mid-fourteenth century.

**Boers** The Dutch colonists who had been the initial European settlers of South Africa.

**Boer War** South African war between the Boers (people of Dutch descent) and Great Britain. Fought 1899–1902.

**Bolsheviks** The minority of Russian Marxists led by Lenin who seized dictatorial power in the October Revolution of 1917.

**boule** The 500-member council that served as a legislature in ancient Athens.

**bourgeoisie** The urban upper middle class; usually commercial or professional.

**Boxer Rebellion** A desperate revolt by superstitious peasants against the European "foreign devils" who were carving up China in the new imperialism of the 1890s; quickly suppressed.

**Brahman** (BRAH-man) The title of the impersonal spirit responsible for all creation in Hindu theology.

**brahmin** (BRAH-min) The caste of priests, originally limited to the Aryans and later allowed to the Indians, with whom they intermarried.

**bread and circuses** The social policy initiated by Augustus Caesar aimed at gaining the support of the Roman proletariat by freely supplying them with essential food and entertainments.

**Brest-Litovsk Treaty of 1918** The separate peace between the Central Powers and Lenin's government in Russia.

**Bronze Age** The period when bronze tools and weapons replaced stone among a given people; generally about 3000–1000 B.C.E.

**burning of the books** China's Legalist first emperor attempted to eliminate Confucian ethic by destroying the Confucian writings and prohibiting its teaching.

***bushido*** (BOO-shee-do) The code of honor among the samurai.

**Byzantine Empire** The continuation of the Roman imperium in its eastern provinces until its fall to the Muslim Turks in 1453.

**Cahokia** (Ca-HO-kee-a) Large Native American settlement near East St. Louis, Illinois, *c.* 600–1300 C.E. Noteworthy for its enormous ceremonial mounds.

**caliph** (Ka-LEEF) Arabic (*Khalifa*) for "deputy" to the Prophet Muhammad; leader of Islamic community.

**Carthage** Rival in the Mediterranean basin to Rome in the last centuries B.C.E. before ultimate defeat.

***castas*** (CAHS-tas) In colonial Spanish America, free people of color.

**caste** A socioeconomic group that is entered by birth and rarely exitable.

***caudillo*** (Cow-DEE-yo) A chieftain (that is, a local or regional strongman) in Latin America.

**censors** Officials with great powers of surveillance during the Roman republic.

**Chaco phenomenon** (CHA-co) Ancestral Puebloan civilization that centered on the Great Houses of Chaco Canyon, *ca.* 800–1150 B.C.E.

**Chaeronea** The battle in 338 B.C.E. when Philip of Macedon decisively defeated the Greeks and brought them under Macedonian rule.

**Chartists** A British working-class movement of the 1840s that attempted to obtain labor and political reform.

**Chavin** (CHA-vin) Early Peruvian Indian culture.

**Cheka** An abbreviation for the first version of the Soviet secret police.

**Chichén Itzá** (Chee-CHEN Ee-TSA) Site in the Yucatán of Mayan urban development in the tenth to thirteenth centuries.

**Chinghis Khan** (JENG-guhs KHAAN) Mongol conqueror, 1167–1227.
**Civil Code of 1804** Napoleonic law code reforming and centralizing French legal theory and procedures.
**Civil Constitution of the Clergy** 1791 law in revolutionary France attempting to force French Catholics to support the new government and bring clergy into conformity with it.
**civilization** A complex, developed culture.
**Cleisthenes** A sixth century B.C.E. Athenian tyrant who laid the foundations of *polis* democracy.
**Clovis culture** (CLO-vis) The earliest Native American "culture" known to archaeologists. Dated *ca.* 9500–8900 B.C.E., it was largely based on hunting very large game.
**Coloureds** South Africans of mixed European and African descent.
**command economy** The name given to communist economic planning in the Soviet version after 1929.
**Committee of Public Safety** The executive body of the Reign of Terror during the French Revolution.
***Common Sense*** A pamphlet by Thomas Paine that was influential in hastening the American war of independence against Britain.
**Commonwealth of Independent States** (CIS) The loose confederation of eleven of the fifteen former Soviet republics that was formed after the breakup of the Soviet Union in 1991.
***Communist Manifesto*** The 1948 pamphlet by Marx and Engels that announced the formation of a revolutionary party of the proletariat.
**Conciliar Movement** The attempt to substitute councils of church leaders for papal authority in late medieval Christianity.
**Confucius** The fifth century B.C.E. philosopher whose doctrines were permanently influential in Chinese education and culture.
***conquistadores*** Title given to sixteenth-century Spanish explorers/colonizers in the Americas.
**Constance, Council of** The fifteenth century C.E. assembly of Christian officials called to settle the controversy over the papacy and to review and revise the basic doctrines of the church for the first time in a millennium.
**consuls** Chief executives of the Roman republic; chosen annually.
**Coral Sea, Battle of the** Naval engagement in the southwest Pacific during World War II, resulting in the removal of a Japanese invasion threat to Australia.
***Corpus Juris*** (COR-pus JOO-ris) "Body of the law"; the Roman law code, produced under the emperor Justinian in the mid-500s C.E.
**Cortés, Hernan** (Cor-TEZ) Spanish *conquistador* of the Aztec Empire, 1518–1521.
**Counter-Reformation** Series of measures that the Catholic Church took in the 1540s to counterattack against the Protestants, including a thorough examination of doctrines and practices and an emphasis on instruction of the young and of all Christians.
**creationism** A cosmology based on Christian tradition that holds that the universe was created by an intelligent Supreme Being.
**Crecy** Battle in the Hundred Years' War won by the English in 1346.
**Crimean War** Conflict fought in the Crimea between Russia and Britain, France, and Turkey from 1853 to 1856; ended by the Peace of Paris with a severe loss in Russian prestige.
***criollo*** (kree-OH-yo) Creole; term used to refer to whites born in Latin America.
**Cuban Missile Crisis** 1962 crisis created when Soviet Premier Nikita Khrushchev placed nuclear armed missiles in Cuba. America imposed a naval blockade, and a settlement was reached when the missiles were withdrawn in exchange for an American agreement to remove missiles from Turkey.
**cultural relativism** A belief common in the late twentieth-century West that there are no absolute values to measure contrasting cultures.
**culture** The human-created physical and/or mental environment of a group.
**culture system** Dutch method of extracting wealth from Indonesian peasants by paying fixed (and often unfair) prices for their crops.
**cuneiform** Mesopotamian wedge-shaped writing begun by the Sumerians.
**Cuzco** (COOS-co) Capital city of the Inca Empire.
**cynicism** A Hellenistic philosophy stressing poverty and simplicity.
**Dada** A brief but influential European art movement in the early twentieth century that repudiated all obligations to communicate intelligibly to the general public.
**da Gama, Vasco** (duh GAA-ma, VAAS-coo) First Portuguese to sail directly from Portugal to India and back, 1497–1499.
***daimyo*** Japanese nobles who controlled feudal domains under the shogun.
***Dao de Jing*** (DOW de CHING) (Book of Changes) Daoism's major scripture; attributed to Lao Zi.
**Daoism** (Taoism) (DOW-ism) A nature-oriented philosophy/religion of China.
**Dawes Plan** A plan for a dollar loan and refinancing of post–World War I reparation payments that enabled recovery of the German economy.
**D-day** June 6, 1944; the invasion of France from the English Channel by combined British and American forces.
***Declaration of the Rights of Man and Citizen*** The epoch-making manifesto issued by the French Third Estate delegates at Versailles in 1789.
**decolonization** The process by which Europeans withdrew from their colonies in Africa and Asia and restored self-rule.
**deductive reasoning** Arriving at truth by applying a general law or proposition to a specific case.
**De Gaulle, Charles** General who commanded the Free French forces during World War II. Became President of the Fifth Republic, 1958–1968.
**De las Casas, Bartolomé** Spanish Dominican friar who wrote a scathing report in 1522 describing the devastation experienced by Native Americans at the hands of the Spanish.
**Delhi sultanate** (DEH-lee) The government and state erected by the conquering Afghani Muslims after 1500 in North India; immediate predecessor to the Mughal Empire.
**Delian League** An empire of satellite polei under Athens in the fifth century B.C.E.
**deme** The basic political subdivision of the Athenian *polis*.
**demesne** The arable land on a manor that belonged directly to the lord.
**democracy** A system of government in which the majority of voters decides issues and policy.
**demographic transition** The passage of a large group of people from traditional high birthrates to lower ones, induced by changing economic conditions and better survival chances of the children.
**dependency** In the context of national development, the necessity to reckon with other states' powers and pressures in the domestic economy and foreign trade.
***dervish*** (DER-vish) A Turkish term for a sufi. See *Sufi,* below.
***descamisados*** (des-cah-mee-SAH-dos) "Shirtless ones"; the poor working classes in modern Argentina.
***Descent of Man, The*** The 1871 publication by Charles Darwin that applied selective evolution theory to mankind.
**détente** (lit.) (day-tahnt) Relaxation; the term used for the toning down of diplomatic tensions between nations, specifically, the Cold War between the United States and the Soviet Union.

***devshirme*** (duv-SHEER-muh) Ottoman system of recruiting young, Christian boys of the Balkan villages for the Janissary corps.

**dharma** (DAR-mah) A code of morals and conduct prescribed for one's caste in Hinduism.

***dhimmis*** (THIM-mees) "People of the Book": Christians, Jews, and Zoroastrians living under Muslim rule and receiving privileged treatment over other non-Muslims.

**Diaspora** The scattering of the Jews from ancient Palestine.

**Diaz, Bartolomeo** (Dee-YAAS, Bar-to-lo-MAY-oo) Portuguese sea captain, the discoverer the Cape of Good Hope at the southern tip of Africa, 1488.

**diffusion theory** The spread of ideas and technology through human contacts.

**Directory** The five-member executive organ that governed France from 1795 to 1799 after the overthrow of the Jacobins.

***divan*** (di-VAHN) A Turkish form of the Arabic word, *diwan,* meaning a Royal Council which advises the ruler.

**divine right theory** The idea that the legitimate holder of the Crown was designated by divine will to govern; personified by King Louis XIV of France in the seventeenth century.

**Diwan** (Dee-WAHN) A council of Islamic government ministers in Istanbul during the Ottoman Empire.

**Domesday Book** A complete census of landholdings in England ordained by William the Conqueror.

**Dorians** Legendary barbaric invaders of Mycenaean Greece in c. 1200 B.C.E.

***Dream of the Red Chamber, The*** The best known of the eighteenth-century Chinese novels.

**Duce, il** "The Leader"; title of Mussolini, the Italian dictator.

**East India Company** A commercial company founded with government backing to trade with the East and Southeast Asians. The Dutch, English, and French governments sponsored such companies starting in the early seventeenth century.

**economic nationalism** A movement to assert national sovereignty in economic affairs, particularly by establishing freedom from the importation of foreign goods and technology on unfavorable terms.

**Edo** (EH-do) Name of Tokyo before the eighteenth century.

**Eightfold Path** The Buddha's teachings on attaining perfection.

**Ekklesia** The general assembly of citizens in ancient Athens.

**Emir** (Eh-MEER) A provincial official with military duties in Muslim government.

**empirical data** Facts derived from observation of the external world.

**empirical method** Using empirical data to establish scientific truth.

**Empiricist** A school of Hellenistic Greek medical researchers.

**enclosure movement** An eighteenth-century innovation in British agriculture by which formerly communal lands were enclosed by private landlords for their own benefit.

***encomienda*** (en-ko-MYEN-da) The right to organize unpaid native labor by the earliest Spanish colonists in Latin America; revoked in 1565.

***Encyclopédie, The*** The first encyclopedia; produced in mid-eighteenth-century France by the philosophe Diderot.

**Enlightenment** The intellectual reform movement in eighteenth-century Europe that challenged traditional ideas and policies in many areas of theory and practice.

**Epicureanism** A Hellenistic philosophy advocating the pursuit of pleasure (mental) and avoidance of pain as the supreme good.

**equal field system** Agricultural reform favoring the peasants under the Tang Dynasty in China.

**equity** Fairness to contending parties.

**Era of Stagnation** The era of Brezhnev's government in the Soviet Union (1964–1982), when the Soviet society and economy faced increasing troubles.

**Era of the Warring States** The period of Chinese history between c. 500 and 220 B.C.E.; characterized by the breakdown of the central government and feudal war.

***Essay Concerning Human Understanding*** An important philosophical essay by John Locke that underpinned Enlightenment optimism.

**Estates General** The parliament of France; composed of delegates from three social orders: clergy, nobility, and commoners.

**ethnic, ethnicity** The racial, cultural, or linguistic affiliation of an individual or group of human beings.

**Etruscans** The pre-Roman rulers of most of northern and central Italy and cultural models for early Roman civilization.

**European Economic Community** An association of western European nations founded in 1957; now called the European Union, it embraces fifteen countries with several more in candidate status.

**excommunication** The act of being barred from the Roman Catholic community by decree of a bishop or the pope.

**existentialism** Twentieth-century philosophy that was popular after World War II in Europe; insists on the necessity to inject life with meaning by individual decisions.

**Exodus** The Hebrews' flight from the wrath of the Egyptian pharaoh in c. 1250 B.C.E.

**extended family** Parents and children plus several other kin group members such as in-laws, cousins, uncles, and aunts.

**factories** Fortified trading posts that Europeans established along the coast of (mostly West) Africa during the Age of Informal Empire.

**Factory Acts** Laws passed by Parliament in 1819 and 1833 that began the regulation of hours and working conditions in Britain.

**factory system** Massing of labor and material under one roof with a single proprietorship and management of production.

**fallow** Land left uncultivated for a period to recover fertility.

**fascism** A political movement in the twentieth century that embraced totalitarian government policies to achieve a unity of people and leader; first experienced in Mussolini's Italy.

**Fathers of the Church** Leading theologians and explainers of Christian doctrine in the fourth and early fifth centuries.

**Fertile Crescent** A belt of civilized settlements reaching from lower Mesopotamia across Syria, Lebanon, and Israel and into Egypt.

**feudal system** A mode of government based originally on mutual military obligations between lord and vassal; later often extended to civil affairs of all types; generally supported by landowning privileges.

**Final Solution** Name given by the Nazis to the wartime massacres of European Jews.

**First Consul** Title adopted by Napoleon after his coup d'état in 1799 that established him as the ruler of France.

**First Emperor** (Shi Huangdi) The founder of the short-lived Qin Dynasty (221–205 B.C.E.) and creator of China as an imperial state.

**First Five-Year Plan** Introduced in 1929 at Stalin's command to collectivize agriculture and industrialize the economy of the Soviet Union.

**First Industrial Revolution** The initial introduction of machine powered production; began in late eighteenth-century Britain.

**First International** Title of original association of Marxist and other socialists, in 1860s Europe.

**Five Pillars of Islam** Popular term for the basic tenets of Muslim faith. Includes the profession of faith (*shahada*), prayer, fasting, pilgrimage, and giving alms.

**floating world** A term for ordinary human affairs popularized by the novels and stories of eighteenth-century Japan.

**Folsom points** Small, highly notched spear heads used for hunting by Paleoindians.

**Forbidden City** The center of Ming and Qing government in Beijing; entry was forbidden to ordinary citizens.

**"four little tigers"** Singapore, Taiwan, South Korea, and Hong Kong in the 1960s–1980s economic upsurge.

**Four Noble Truths** The Buddha's doctrine on human fate.

**Fourteen Points** The outline for a just peace proposed by Woodrow Wilson in 1918.

**Franco-Prussian War** The 1870–1871 conflict between these two powers resulting in German unification under Prussian leadership.

**Frankfurt Assembly** A German parliament held in 1848 that was unsuccessful in working out a liberal constitution for a united German state.

**Frontier Wars** Territorial wars that resulted when Trekboers (q.v.) encountered Bantu-speaking peoples in the region of the Fish River in the late 1700s.

***Führer, der*** "The Leader" in Nazi Germany—specifically, Hitler.

**Fujiwara clan** Daimyo noble clan controlling the shogunate in ninth- to twelfth-century Japan.

**Gandhi, Indira** Daughter of Jawaharlal Nehru who served as Prime Minister of India 1966–1975 and 1980–1984. Assassinated by Sikh religious extremists.

**Gandhi, Mohandas** (1869–1948) Advocate of non-violent protest against British rule and one of the founders of the modern state of India.

**Gendarme of Europe** Name given by liberals to the Russian imperial government under Czar Nicholas I (1825–1855).

***General Theory of Relativity*** Einstein's theory that introduced the modern era of physics in 1916.

**Gentiles** All non-Jews.

**geocentric** "Earth centered"; theory of the cosmos that erroneously held the Earth to be its center.

**Ghana** (GA-na) The earliest of the extensive empires in the western Sudan; also a modern West African country formed from the colony of Gold Coast when it won independence from Great Britain in 1957.

***ghazis*** (GAA-zee) Muslim "crusaders," or holy warriors who fight against unbelievers.

**ghetto** Italian name for the quarter restricted to Jews.

***Gilgamesh*** One of the earliest epics in world literature, originating in prehistoric Mesopotamia.

***glasnost*** The Russian term for "openness"; along with *perestroika,* employed to describe the reforms instituted by Gorbachev in the late 1980s.

**global warming** The steady warming trend of the planet's temperature in the past century.

**Glorious Revolution of 1688** The English revolt against the unpopular Catholic king James II and the subsequent introduction of certain civil rights restricting monarchic powers.

**Golden Horde** The Russia-based segment of the Mongol world empire.

**golden mean** Greek concept of avoiding the extremes; "truth lies in the middle."

**Good Neighbor Policy** President Franklin D. Roosevelt's attempt to reform previous U.S. policy and honor Latin American sovereignty.

**Gothic style** An artistic style, found notably in architecture, that came into general European usage during the thirteenth century.

**Gracchi brothers** Roman noble brothers who unsuccessfully attempted reform as consuls in the late republican era.

**grand vizier** (Vi-ZEER) Title of the Turkish prime minister during the Ottoman era.

**Great Elector** Frederick William of Prussia (1640–1688); one of the princes who elected the Holy Roman Emperor.

**Great Leap Forward** Mao Zedong's misguided attempt in 1958–1960 to provide China with an instantaneous industrial base rivaling that of more advanced nations.

**Great Proletarian Cultural Revolution** The period from 1966 to 1976 when Mao Zedong inspired Chinese youth to rebel against all authority except his own; caused great damage to the Chinese economy and culture.

**Great Purge** The arrest and banishment of millions of Soviet Communist Party members and ordinary citizens at Stalin's orders in the mid-1930s for fictitious "crimes against the State and Party."

**Great Reforms** (Russia) Decrees affecting several areas of life issued by Czar Alexander II between 1859 and 1874.

**Great Schism** A division in the Roman Catholic Church between 1378 and 1417, when two (and for a brief period, three) popes competed for the allegiance of European Christians; a consequence of the Babylonian Captivity of the papacy in Avignon, southern France.

**Great Trek** The march of the Boers, beginning in 1836, into the northeastern interior of South Africa where they founded the so-called Boer Republics.

**Great Zimbabwe** (Zim-BOB-way) The leading civilization of early southern Africa and exporter of gold to the East African coast.

**Green Revolution** The increased agricultural output in many Third World nations during the 1960s and 1970s that came from introducing high-yield crops and pesticides.

***grossdeutsch* versus *kleindeutsch*** The controversy over the scope and type of the unified German state in the nineteenth century; *kleindeutsch* would exclude multinational Austria, and *grossdeutsch* would include it.

**guild** A medieval urban organization that controlled the production and sale prices of many goods and services.

**Gupta Dynasty** The rulers of most of India in the 300–400s C.E.; the last native dynasty to unify the country.

**Habsburg Dynasty** The family that controlled the Holy Roman Empire after the thirteenth century; based in Vienna, they ruled Austria until 1918.

***hacienda*** (ha-SYEN-da) A Spanish-owned plantation in Latin America that used native or slave labor to produce export crops.

**Hagia Sophia** Greek name ("Holy Wisdom") of the cathedral in Constantinople, later made into a mosque by Ottoman Turkish conquerors.

**Haiku** A type of Japanese poetry always three lines in length. The lines always have five, seven, and five syllables.

***hajj*** (HAAJ) The pilgrimage to the sacred places of Islam.

**Han Dynasty** The dynasty that ruled China from c. 200 B.C.E. to 221 C.E.

**Hangzhou** Capital city of Song dynasty China and probably the largest town in the contemporary world.

**Hanoverian Dynasty** The dynasty of British monarchs after 1714; from the German duchy of Hanover.

**harem** Turkish name for the part of a dwelling reserved for women.

**Harun al-Rashid** (Ha-ROON al-RAH-shid) Abbasid caliph of Baghdad, 786–809 C.E.

**heliocentrism** Opposite of geocentrism; recognizes sun as center of solar system.

**Hellenistic** A blend of Greek and Asiatic cultures; extant in the Mediterranean basin and Middle East between 300 B.C.E. and c. 200 C.E.

**helots** Messenian semislaves of Spartan overlords.

**heresies** Wrong belief in religious doctrines.

**hetairai** High-class female entertainer-prostitutes in ancient Greece.

**hieroglyphics** Egyptian pictographs, beginning as far back as 3000 B.C.E., that could convey either an idea or a phonetic sound.

***Hijra*** (HIJ-ra) Literally, "flight"; Muhammed's forced flight from Mecca in 622 C.E.; it marks the first year of the Muslim calendar.

**Hinayana Buddhism** A stricter, monastic form of Buddhism, claiming closer link with the Buddha's teaching; often called Theravada. Headquartered in Sri Lanka and strong in Southeast Asia.

**historiography** The writing of history so as to interpret it.

**history** Human actions in past time, as recorded and remembered.

**Hittites** An Indo-European people who were prominent in the Near East around 1200 B.C.E.

**Ho Chi Minh** (1890–1969) Communist and nationalist leader in French Indochina who fought against the Japanese in World War II. One of the principal founders of the modern nation of Vietnam, he fought to free his country from French rule, then from American invasion.

**Hohenzollerns** The dynasty that ruled Prussia-Germany until 1918.

**Homer** Legendary author of the two epic poems of ancient Greece, the *Iliad* and the *Odyssey.*

**hominid** A humanlike creature.

**Homo sapiens** "Thinking man"; modern human beings.

**Horus** The falcon-headed god whose earthly, visible form was the reigning pharaoh in ancient Egypt.

**hubris** An unjustified confidence in one's abilities or powers leading to a tragic end.

**Huguenots** French Calvinists, many of whom were forced to emigrate in the seventeenth century.

**humanism** The intellectual movement that sees humans as the sole valid arbiter of their values and purpose.

**Hungarian Revolution** The Hungarians' attempt to free themselves from Soviet control in October 1956; crushed by the Soviets.

**Hussein, Saddam** Iraqi dictator; an American invasion of Iraq in 2003 led to the overthrow of his government and widespread chaos.

**Hyksos** A people who invaded the Nile delta in Egypt and ruled it during the Second Intermediate Period (c. 1650–1570 B.C.E.).

**Ibn Sina** (Ih-bin SEE-na) Well-known Islamic philosopher and physician. (980–1037)

**Ibn Taymiyya, Taqi al-Din** (Ih-bin Tie-MEE-yah) (1263–1328) Ultra-conservative Hanbali legal scholar whose writings are the foundation of the fundamentalist Wahhabi movement.

**ideographs** Written signs conveying entire ideas and not related to the spoken language; used by the Chinese from earliest times.

***Iliad*** The first of the two epics supposedly written by Homer in eighth-century Greece.

**Imperator** Roman title of a temporary dictator given powers by the Senate; later, emperor.

**Impressionists** Members of a Paris-centered school of nineteenth-century painting focusing on light and color.

**Inca** Title of the emperor of the Quechuan-speaking peoples of Peru before arrival of the Spanish.

**indirect rule** The British policy of governing their overseas colonies through "native rulers."

**Indochina, Union of** Official term for the French colonies in Indochina until their dissolution in the 1950s.

**inductive reasoning** Arriving at truth by reasoning from specific cases to a general law or proposition.

***infamia*** Roman term for immoral but not illegal acts.

**Informal Empire** The era in African history that lasted from the 1400s to about 1880, when Europeans remained content to restrict their dealings with Africa primarily to trade.

**Inquisition** Roman Catholic agency that was responsible for censorship of doctrines and books; mainly active in Iberian lands in the fifteenth through seventeenth centuries.

***Institutes of the Christian Religion, The*** John Calvin's major work that established the theology and doctrine of the Calvinist churches; first published in 1536.

**intelligentsia** Russian term for a social group that actively influences the beliefs and actions of others, seeking reforms; generally connected with the professions and media.

***intendants*** The traveling officials appointed originally by Cardinal Richelieu to monitor the honesty and efficiency of provincial French authorities.

**Investiture Controversy** A dispute between the Holy Roman Emperor and the pope in the eleventh and early twelfth centuries about which authority should appoint German bishops.

**Iranian Revolution** The fundamentalist and anti-Western movement led by the Ayatollah Khomeini that seized power from the shah of Iran through massive demonstrations in 1979.

**irredentism** The attempt by members of a nation living outside the national state to link themselves to it politically and/or territorially.

**Isis** A chief Egyptian goddess, represented by the Nile River.

**Jacobins** Radical revolutionaries during the French Revolution; organized in clubs headquartered in Paris.

***Jacquerie*** A French peasant rebellion against noble landlords during the fourteenth century.

**Janissaries** (JA-ni-sayr-rees) From Turkish *yeni cheri,* meaning "new troops"; an elite troop in the Ottoman army; consisted of Christian boys from the Balkans.

**Jesuits** Members of the Society of Jesus, a Catholic religious order founded in 1547 to combat Protestantism.

**Jewish War** A rebellion of Jewish Zealots against Rome in 66–70 C.E.

***jihad*** (Jee-HAAD) Holy war on behalf of the Muslim faith.

**Jihad of Abd al-Qadir** (Abd Al-KAH-deer) Jihad led by the *marabout,* Abd al-Qadir, in the 1840s, against the French invasion of Algeria.

**Jihad of al-Hajj Umar** (al-HAJJ OO-mar) Jihad of the 1840s–1870s which was led by the sufi shaykh, al-Hajj Umar Tal.

**Jihad of Usman dan Fodio** (OOS-man dan FO-dee-oh) Jihad that took place between 1804 and 1817 in the north of what now is Nigeria. It began as a revolt against the "heretical" practices of the Hausa kings, but resulted in the establishment of a Muslim caliphate.

**Judea** One of the two Jewish kingdoms emerging after the death of Solomon when his kingdom was split in two; the other was Samaria.

**July Monarchy** The reign of King Louis Philippe in France (1830–1848); so called because he came to power in July 1830.

***Junkers*** The landowning nobility of Prussia.

***jus gentium*** "Law of peoples"; Roman law governing relations between Romans and others.

**justification by faith** Doctrine held by Martin Luther whereby Christian faith alone, and not good works, could be the path to heavenly bliss.

***ka*** The immortal soul in the religion of ancient Egypt.

***Ka'ba*** (KAH-ba) The original shrine of pagan Arabic religion in Mecca containing the Black Stone; now one of the holiest places of Islam.

**Kabuki** A type of popular Japanese drama depicting heroic and romantic themes and stories.

**Kalidasa** (Ka-li-DA-sa) Hindu philosopher and playwright of the Gupta period; influenced the development of Sanskrit literature.

**Kamakura shogunate** Government by members of a noble Japanese family from the late twelfth to the mid-fourteenth century in the name of the emperor, who was their puppet.

**kami** Shinto spirits in nature.

**Kampuchea** Native name of Cambodia, a state of Southeast Asia bordered by Thailand and Vietnam.

**Karlowitz, Treaty of** (1699) Treaty in which, for the first time, the Ottoman Empire had to cede territory in the Balkans to its Austrian opponent.

**karma** (KAR-mah). The balance of good and evil done in a given incarnation in Hindu belief.

**Karnak** The site of a great temple complex along the Nile River in Egypt.

**Kashmir** A province in northwestern India, largely populated by Muslims, that Pakistan also claims.

**Kellogg-Briand Pact** A formal disavowal of war by sixty nations in 1928.

**KGB** An abbreviation for the Soviet secret police; used after Cheka and NKVD had been discarded.

**Khanate of the Golden Horde** Sub-khanate of the Mongol Empire located in eastern and central Russia.

**Kharijites** (KHA-ri-jites) Like Shi'ites, these are one of the two religious minorities in Islam. Basically, they reject the caliphate, and believe that leadership of the *Umma* (q.v.) rightfully belongs to the most pious, and that authority comes from the community itself.

**Khmers** (KAY-mers) The inhabitants of Cambodia; founders of a large empire in ancient Southeast Asia.

**Khomeini, Ayatollah Ruholla** (1900–1989) Iranian Shi'ite cleric who led the 1979 Iranian revolt against the Shah.

**Khrushchev, Nikita** Succeeded Stalin as First Secretary of the Soviet Communist Party, 1955–1964. Utterly convinced of the eventual triumph of communism in the world, he followed policies that generally were more conciliatory towards the West.

**Kiev, Principality of** The first Russian state; flourished from c. 800 to 1240 when it fell to Mongols.

**Kilwa** (KILL-wa) A Swahili city-state that dominated the gold and ivory trade from East Africa, *c.* 1300–1450 C.E.

**King of Kings** The title of the Persian emperor.

***kleindeutsch*** "Small German"; adjective describing a form of German unification that excluded the multinational Austria; opposite of *grossdeutsch.*

**knights** Type of feudal noble who held title and landed domain only for his lifetime; generally based originally on military service to his overlord.

**Korean War** 1950–1953 war between United Nations, led by the United States, and North Korea; precipitated by the invasion of South Korea.

**Kubilai Khan** (KOOB-lay KHAAN) Mongol Great Khan and founder of the Yuan Dynasty of China.

**Kuomintang** (KMT) The political movement headed by Chiang Kai-shek during the 1930s and 1940s in China.

**Kush** (Kuhsh) Kingdom in northeast Africa that had close relations with Egypt for several centuries in the pre-Christian epoch.

**Kyoto** (KEE-o-to) Ancient capital of the Japanese Empire and seat of the emperor.

**Labour Party** Political party founded in 1906 by British labor unions and others for representation of the working classes.

**Lao Zi** Mythical author of the *Dao de Jing,* or Book of Changes, which has served as the text for various versions of Daoist folklore and philosophy for many centuries in China.

**Late Manzhou Restoration** An attempt by Chinese reformers in the 1870s to restore the power of the central government after the suppression of the Taiping rebellion.

**League of Nations** An international organization founded after World War I to maintain peace and promote amity among nations; the United States did not join.

**Left** The reforming or revolutionary wing of the political spectrum; associated originally with the ideals of the radical French Revolution.

**legalism** A Chinese philosophy of government emphasizing strong authority.

**Legislative Assembly** The second law-making body created during the French Revolution; dominated by the Jacobins, it gave way to the radical Convention.

**Legitimacy** A term adopted by the victors at the Congress of Vienna in 1815 to explain the reimposition of former monarchs and regimes after the Napoleonic wars.

***levée en masse*** General conscription for the army; first occurred in 1793 during the French Revolution.

***Leviathan*** A book by Thomas Hobbes that supported the necessity of the state and, by inference, royal absolutism.

***liberum* veto** Latin for "free veto"; used by Polish nobles to nullify majority will in the Polish parliaments of the eighteenth century.

**lineage** (LIN-ee-age) A technical term for family or clan association.

**little red book** Contained the thoughts of Chairman Mao Zedong on various topics; used as a talisman during the Cultural Revolution by young Chinese.

**Livingstone, David** Medical missionary, explorer, and humanitarian who explored much of sub-equatorial Africa during the period of the 1840s–1860s. He especially advocated "legitimate trade" as a substitute for the slave trade in Africa.

**Locarno Pact** An agreement between France and Germany in 1925.

**Lollards** Name of unknown origin given to the English religious rebels of the 1380s who later protested against the privileges of the clergy and were vigorously persecuted.

**Long March** The 6,000-mile fighting retreat of the Chinese communists under Mao Zedong to Shensi province in 1934–1935.

**Lyric poetry** Poetry that celebrates the poet's emotions.

**Maastricht Treaty** Signed in 1991 by members of the European Community; committed them to closer political-economic ties.

***Machtergreifung*** "Seizure of power;" Nazi term for Hitler's rise to dictatorial powers in Germany.

**Machu Picchu** (MA-choo PEE-choo) Incan city in the high Andes Mountains.

**Magellan, Ferdinand** (Ma-JEL-lan) First man to sail completely around the world, 1519–1522.

**Maghrib** or **Maghreb** (Mag-REEB) Northwest Africa, north of the Atlas Mountains. Usually includes Morocco, Algeria, and Tunisia.

***Mahabharata*** (Ma-hab-ha-RAH-ta) A Hindu epic poem; a favorite in India.

**Mahayana Buddhism** (Mah-hah-YAH-nah) A more liberal, looser form of Buddhism; originating soon after the Buddha's death, it deemphasized the monastic life and abstruse philosophy in favor of prayer to the eternal Buddha and the bodhisattvas who succeeded him.

**Mahdi, The** (MAH-dee) A charismatic Islamic mystic, Muhammad Ahmad, who led a serious rebellion against Egyptian rule in the Sudan, 1881–1885.

**Majapahit** The main town of a maritime empire in fourteenth-century Indonesia.

**Mali** (MA-lee) The West African empire that was the successor to Ghana in the 1300s and 1400s.

**Manchester liberalism** The economic practice of exploiting the laboring poor in the name of the free market.

**Manchuria** Large province of northeastern China, seized in the nineteenth century by Russia and Japan before being retaken by the Maoist government.

**mandarins** Chinese scholar-officials who had been trained in Confucian principles and possessed great class solidarity.

**mandate of heaven** A theory of rule originated by the Zhou Dynasty in China emphasizing the connection between imperial government's rectitude and its right to govern.

**mandates** Britain and France governed several Asian and African peoples after World War I, supposedly as agents of the League of Nations.

**manor** An agricultural estate of varying size normally owned by a noble or the clergy and worked by free and unfree peasants/serfs.

**Mansa Musa** (MAAN-sa MOO-sa) King of Mali, early fourteenth century.

**Manu** Legendary lawgiver in India.

***manus*** "Hand"; Latin term for the legal power of a person over another.

**Manzhou** Originally nomadic tribes living in Manchuria who eventually overcame Ming resistance and established the Qing Dynasty in seventeenth-century China.

**Manzikert, Battle of** (MAN-zi-kert) Battle fought in 1071, which gave victory to the Seljuk Turks over the Byzantines. Made Turkish Muslim entry to Asia Minor possible.

***marabout*** (MA-ra-boot) A leader of a radical sufi brotherhood in North Africa and the Sahara Desert.

**Marathon** The battle in 490 B.C.E. in which the Greeks defeated the Persians, ending the first Persian War.

**March on Rome** A fascist demonstration in 1922 orchestrated by Mussolini as a preliminary step to dictatorship in Italy.

**March Revolution of 1917** The abdication of Czar Nicholas II and the establishment of the Provisional Government in Russia.

**Maritime Expeditions** (China's) Early fifteenth-century explorations of the Indian and South Pacific Oceans ordered by the Chinese emperor.

**Marshall Plan** A program proposed by the U.S. secretary of state George Marshall and implemented from 1947 to 1951 to aid western Europe's recovery from World War II.

**Massacre on Tienanmen Square** See *Tienanmen Square, massacre on.*

**Masscult** The banal culture that some think replaced the traditional elite culture in the twentieth-century West.

**matriarchy** A society in which females are dominant socially and politically.

**matrilineal descent** Attribution of name and inheritance to children via the maternal line.

**Maya** The most advanced of the Amerindian peoples who lived in southern Mexico and Guatemala and created a high urban civilization in the pre-Columbian era.

**May Fourth Movement** A reform movement of young Chinese students and intellectuals in the post–World War I era; Mao Zedong was a member prior to his conversion to Marxism.

**McMahon Letter** British correspondence in 1916 which promised support for the creation of an Arab state in the Middle East in exchange for an Arab alliance in driving Turkey out of the region.

**Medes** An early Indo-European people who, with the Persians, settled in Iran.

**Meiji Restoration** (Mei-JEE) The overthrow of the Tokugawa shogunate and restoration of the emperor to nominal power in Japan in 1867.

***Mein Kampf*** "My Struggle"; Hitler's credo, written while serving a prison term in 1924.

**mercantilism** A theory of national economics popular in the seventeenth and eighteenth centuries; aimed at establishing a favorable trade balance through government control of exports and imports as well as domestic industry.

**meritocracy** The rule of the meritorious (usually determined by examinations).

**Messenian Wars** Conflicts between the neighbors Sparta and Messenia that resulted in Messenia's conquest by Sparta in about 600 B.C.E.

**messiah** A savior-king who would someday lead the Jews to glory.

**mestizo** (mes-TEE-so). A person of mixed Amerindian and European blood.

**metaphor of the cave** Plato's explanation of the difficulties encountered by those who seek philosophical truth and the necessity of a hierarchy of leadership.

**Mexican Revolution** The armed struggle that occurred in Mexico between 1910 and 1920 to install a more socially progressive and populist government.

**Middle Kingdom** The period in Egyptian history from 2100 to 1600 B.C.E.; followed the First Intermediate Period.

**Milan, Edict of** A decree issued by the emperor Constantine in 313 C.E. that legalized Christianity and made it the favored religion in the Roman Empire.

**Minoan** An ancient civilization that was centered on Crete between c. 2000 and c. 1400 B.C.E.

***missi dominici*** Agents of Charlemagne in the provinces of his empire.

**modernism** A philosophy of art of the late nineteenth and early twentieth centuries that rejected classical models and values and sought new expressions and aesthetics.

**Mohenjo-Daro** Site of one of the two chief towns of the ancient Indus valley civilization.

**moksha** The final liberation from bodily existence and reincarnation in Hinduism.

**monarchy** Rule by a single individual, who often claims divine inspiration and protection.

**Mongols** Name for collection of nomadic, savage warriors of Central Asia who conquered most of Eurasia in the thirteenth century.

**Mongol Yoke** A Russian term for the Mongol occupation of Russia, 1240–1480.

**monoculture** Overreliance on one or two crops in a region; an economically precarious system.

**monotheism** A religion having only one god.

**Monroe Doctrine** The announcement in 1823 by U.S. president James Monroe that no European interference in Latin America would be tolerated.

**Mughals** (MOO-guls) A corruption of "Mongol"; refers to the period of Muslim rule in India.

**Muhammad** (Moo-HAA-mad) The prophet of Islam.

**Muhammad Abduh** (Muhammad AHB-doo) (1849–1905). Leading intellectual of the Salafiyya Islamic reform movement in Egypt.

**Muhammad Ali Pasha** (1769–1849) Viceroy of Egypt, 1803–1849, he introduced important reforms to reorganize Egypt and its army and navy along European lines.

**Muhammad Reza Shah Pahlavi** (1919–1980) Son of Shah Reza Pahlavi, he was the Shah of Iran from 1941 until his overthrow by the Iranian Revolution in 1979.

**mulatto** (muh-LOT-to) A person of mixed African and European blood.

**Munich Agreements** The 1938 meetings between Hitler and the British and French prime ministers that allowed Germany to take much of Czechoslovakia; the agreement confirmed Hitler's belief that the democratic governments would not fight German aggression.

**Munich *putsch*** The failed attempt by Hitler to seize power by armed force in 1923.

***municipia*** The basic unit of Roman local government; similar to a present-day municipality.

**Muslim Brotherhoods** Associations of Islamic groups that have strong fundamentalist leanings and practice mutual aid among members.

**Mycenaean** Referring to the history and culture of the earliest known Indo-European inhabitants of the Greek peninsula, between ca. 1600 and ca. 1100 B.C.E.

**mystery religion** One of various Hellenistic cults promising immortal salvation of the individual.

**Nantes, Edict of** A law granting toleration to French Calvinists that was issued in 1598 by King Henry IV to end the religious civil war.

**Napoleonic Settlement** A collective name for the decrees and actions by Napoleon between 1800 and 1808 that legalized and systematized many elements of the French Revolution.

**Nasser, Colonel Gamal Abdel** (1918–1970) Egyptian nationalist leader who was the President of Egypt from 1952. Remembered best for seizing the Suez Canal from Anglo-French control in 1956.

**National Assembly** The first law-making body during the French Revolution; created a moderate constitutional monarchy.

**natural law** The idea, originated by Romans, that all humans, by virtue of their humanity, possess certain rights and duties that all courts must recognize.

**natural selection** The Darwinian doctrine in biology that change in species derives from mechanistic changes induced by the environment.

**Navigation Acts** Laws regulating commerce with the British colonies in North America in favor of Britain.

**Nazism** The German variant of fascism created by Hitler.

**Neanderthal Man** A species of Homo sapiens flourishing between 100,000 and 30,000 years ago and that mysteriously died out; the name comes from the German valley where the first remains were found.

**Negritude** A literary term referring to the self-conscious awareness of African cultural values; popular in areas of Africa formerly under French control.

**Nehru, Jawaharlal** (NAY-roo) (1889–1964) Close associate of Mahatma Gandhi who became Prime Minister of India following Gandhi's death and served in that office for fifteen years until his death in 1964.

**neocolonialism** Literally, "new" colonialism, meaning the control, primarily economic, which the former colonial powers continue to exert over their former colonies in Asia, Africa, and Latin America.

**Neo-Confucianism** An eleventh- and twelfth-century C.E. revival of Confucian thought with special emphasis on love and responsibility toward others.

**Neolithic Age** The period from c. 7000 B.C.E. to the development of metals by a given people.

**New China Movement** An intellectual reform movement in the 1890s that attempted to change and modernize China by modernizing the government.

**New Economic Policy** (NEP) A policy introduced at the conclusion of the civil war that allowed for limited capitalism and private enterprise in the Soviet Union.

**New imperialism** The late nineteenth-century worldwide colonialism of European powers interested in strategic and market advantage.

**New Kingdom or Empire** The period from c. 1550 to 700 B.C.E. in Egyptian history; followed the Second Intermediate Period. The period from 1550 to c. 1200 B.C.E. was the Empire.

**Nicaea, Council of** A fourth-century conclave of bishops that defined essential doctrines of Christianity under the supervision of the emperor Constantine.

**Niger River** The great river draining most of the African bulge.

**Ninety-five Theses** The challenge to church authority publicized by Martin Luther, October 31, 1517.

**Nineveh** The main city and later capital of the Assyrian Empire.

**nirvana** The Buddhist equivalent of the Hindu moksha; the final liberation from suffering and reincarnation.

**NKVD** An abbreviation for the Soviet secret police; used after Cheka but before KGB.

**Nonaggression Pact of 1939** The treaty between Hitler and Stalin in which each agreed to maintain neutrality in any forthcoming war involving the other party.

**North American Free Trade Agreement** (NAFTA) An agreement signed by the United States, Canada, and Mexico in 1993 that provides for much liberalized trade among these nations.

**North Atlantic Treaty Organization** (NATO) An organization founded in 1949 under U.S. aegis as a defense against threatened communist aggression in Europe.

**nuclear family** Composed of parents and children only.

**Nuclear Test Ban** The voluntary cessation of aboveground testing of nuclear weapons by the United States and the Soviet Union; in existence from 1963 to the present.

**Nuremberg Laws** Laws defining racial identity that were aimed against Jews; adopted in 1935 by the German government.

**October Revolution of 1917** The Bolshevik coup d'état in St. Petersburg that ousted the Provisional Government and established a communist state in Russia.

***Odyssey*** Second of the two Homeric epic poems, detailing the adventures of the homeward-bound Ulysses coming from the siege of Troy; see also *Iliad*.

***Oedipus Rex*** Part of a triad of tragedies written by the classical Greek playwright Sophocles concerning the life and death of Oedipus and his daughter, Antigone.

**Oil boycott of 1973** The temporary withholding of oil exports by OPEC members to Western governments friendly to Israel; led to a massive rise in the price of oil and economic dislocation in many countries.

**Old Kingdom** The period of Egyptian history from 3100 to 2200 B.C.E.

**Old Testament** The first portion of the Judeo-Christian Bible; the holy books of the Jews.

**oligarchy** Rule by a few.

**Olmec** The earliest Amerindian civilization in Mexico.

***1001 Nights, The*** See *Arabian Nights, The.*

**Operation Barbarossa** Code name for German invasion of the Soviet Union in 1941.

**Opium Wars** Conflicts that occurred in 1840–1842 on the Chinese coast between the British and the Chinese over the importation of opium into China. The Chinese defeat began eighty years of subordination to foreigners.

**Orange Free State** One of the two political organisms founded after the Boer Great Trek in southern Africa.

**Organization of African Unity** (OAU) The association of sub-Saharan African nations founded in 1963 for mutual aid and, it was hoped, eventually the creation of a "United States of Africa."

**Organization of American States** (OAS) An organization founded in 1948 under U.S. auspices to provide mutual defense and aid; now embraces all countries on the American continents except Cuba.

**Organization of Petroleum Exporting Countries** (OPEC) Oil cartel founded in 1961 by Arab governments and later expanded to include several Latin American and African members.

***Origin of Species, The*** Charles Darwin's book that first enunciated the evolutionary theory in biology; published in 1859.

**Osama bin Laden** (1957–present) Saudi-born Arab who organized the al-Qaida terrorist organization to wage Islamic *jihad* against the Western nations.

**Osiris** A chief Egyptian god, ruler of the underworld.

***Ostpolitik*** German term for Chancellor Brandt's 1960s policy of pursuing normalized relations with West Germany's neighbors to the east.

**Ostracism** In ancient Greece, the expulsion of a citizen from a *polis* for a given period.

**Pagan** Ancient capital of the Burmese Kingdom in southeastern Asia. Destroyed by the invading Mongol army in the thirteenth century C.E.

**Paleoindian Period** 9500–8900 B.C.E. in Native American history.

**Paleolithic Age** The period from the earliest appearance of Homo sapiens to c. 7000 B.C.E., though exact dates vary by area; the Old Stone Age.

**paleontology** The study of prehistoric things.

**Palestine Liberation Organization** (PLO) An organization founded in the 1960s by Palestinians expelled from Israel; until 1994 it aimed at destruction of the state of Israel by any means. Superseded by the autonomous Palestinian Authority created in 1997.

**Pan-Arabism** A movement after World War I to assert supranational Arab unity, aimed eventually at securing a unified Arab state.

**Pantheism** A belief that God exists in all things, living and inanimate.

**Paragraph 231 of the Versailles Treaty** The "war guilt" paragraph, imputing sole responsibility for reparation of all World War I damages to Germany.

**Pariah** An outcast; a person having no acknowledged status.

**Paris Commune** A leftist revolt against the national government after France was defeated by Prussia in 1871; crushed by the conservatives with much bloodshed.

**Parthenon** The classic Greek temple to Athena on the Acropolis in Athens's center.

**patents of nobility** Royal documents conferring nobility.

***patria potestas*** The power of the father over his family in ancient Rome.

**patriarchy** A society in which males have social and political dominance.

**patricians** (patres) The upper governing class in ancient Rome.

**patrilineal descent** Attribution of name and inheritance to children via the paternal line.

***Pax Mongolica*** (POX Mon-GO-li-cah) The "Mongol peace"; between c. 1250 and c. 1350 in most of Eurasia.

***Pax Romana*** The "Roman peace"; the era of Roman control over the Mediterranean basin and much of Europe between c. 31 B.C.E. and 180 C.E. or later.

**peaceful coexistence** The declared policy of Soviet leader Nikita Khrushchev in dealing with the capitalist West after 1956.

**Peace of Augsburg** Pact ending the German religious wars in 1555, dividing the country between Lutheran and Catholic hegemony.

**Peloponnesian War** The great civil war between Athens and Sparta and their respective allies in ancient Greece; fought between 429 and 404 B.C.E. and eventually won by Sparta.

**peonage** (PEE-on-ij) A peasant in semislave status on a hacienda.

***perestroika*** The Russian term for "restructuring," which, with *glasnost,* was used to describe the reforms instituted by Gorbachev in the late 1980s USSR.

**Pericles** The Athenian democratic leader and spokesman who died in the midst of the Peloponnesian War in the fifth century B.C.E.

**Persepolis** With Ecbatana, one of the twin capitals of the Persian Empire in the 500s B.C.E.; destroyed by Alexander the Great.

**Persians** An early Indo-European tribe that, along with the Medes, settled in Iran.

**Persian Wars** The conflict between the Greeks and the Persian Empire in the fifth century B.C.E., fought in two installments and ending with Greek victory.

**Petrine succession** The doctrine of the Roman Catholic Church by which the pope, the bishop of Rome, is the direct successor of St. Peter.

**pharaoh** The title of the god-king of ancient Egypt.

**philosophes** A French term used to refer to the writers and activist intellectuals during the Enlightenment.

**Phonetic alphabet** A system of writing that matches signs with the sounds of the oral language.

**Piedmont** "Foot of the mountains"; the north Italian kingdom that led the unification of Italy in the mid-nineteenth century.

**Plastic arts** Those arts that have three dimensions.

**Platea** The land battle that, along with the naval battle of Salamis, ended the second Persian War with a Greek victory over the Persians.

**plebeians** (plebs) The common people of ancient Rome.

**Pogrom** Mob violence against local Jews.

***polis*** The political and social community of citizens in ancient Greece.

**polytheism** A religion having many gods.

**Popular Front** The coordinated policy of all antifascist parties; inspired by the Soviets in the mid-1930s against Hitler.

**Porte, The** A name for the Ottoman government in Istanbul.

**post-Impressionist** A term for late nineteenth-century painting that emphasizes color and line in a then-revolutionary fashion.

**Praetorian Guard** The imperial bodyguard in the Roman Empire and the only armed force in Italy.

**Precedent** What has previously been accepted in the application of law.

**prehistory** The long period of human activity prior to the writing of history.

**Pre-Socratics** Greek philosophers prior to Socrates who focused on the nature of the material world.

**Primogeniture** A system of inheritance in which the estate passes to the eldest legitimate son.

***princeps*** "The First" or "the Leader" in Latin; title taken by Augustus Caesar.

**Principate** The reign of Augustus Caesar from 27 B.C.E. to 14 C.E.

**proconsuls** Provincial governors and military commanders in ancient Rome.

**proletariat** Poverty-stricken people without skills; also, a Marxist term for the propertyless working classes.

**Provisional Government** A self-appointed parliamentary group exercising power in republican Russia from March to October 1917.

**Psychoanalysis** A psychological technique that employs free associations in the attempt to determine the cause of mental illness.

**Ptolemaic Kingdom of Egypt** The state created by Ptolemy, one of Alexander the Great's generals, in the Hellenistic era.

**Pueblo culture** Name given to the Native American culture that has flourished in the Four Corners region of the U.S., *c.* 400–present.

**Punic Wars** The three conflicts between Rome and Carthage that ended with the destruction of the Carthaginian Empire and the extension of Roman control throughout the western Mediterranean.

***purdah*** (PURR-dah) The segregation of females in Hindu and Muslim society.

**Purgatory** In Catholic belief, the place where the soul is purged after death for past sins and thus becomes fit for Heaven.

**Puritans** The English Calvinists who were dissatisfied by the theology of the Church of England and wished to "purify" it.

**putting-out system** An economic arrangement between individuals or small producers for production of handwork at home and payment by the piece; it was replaced by the factory beginning in late eighteenth-century Britain.

**Pyramid of Khufu** (Cheops) The largest pyramid; stands outside Cairo.

**Qadi** (KAA-dee) An Islamic judge, learned in Islamic theology and law.

**Qing Dynasty** The last Chinese dynasty, which ruled from 1644 until 1911; established by Manzhou invaders after they defeated the Ming rulers.

**Quadruple Alliance** The diplomatic pact to maintain the peace established by the Big Four victors of the Napoleonic Wars (Austria, Britain, Prussia, and Russia); lasted for a decade.

**Quanta** A concept in physics indicating the expenditure of energy.

**Quechua** (KETCH-wa) The spoken language of the Incas of Peru.

**Qur'an** (Koor-AAN) The holy scripture of Islam, thought to be (lit.) the word of God.

**Raison d´état** The idea that the welfare of the state should be supreme in government policy.

**Raja** Turkish for "cattle"; used to refer to non-Muslims.

**Red Guards** The youthful militants who carried out the Cultural Revolution in China during the 1960s.

**Red International** See *Third International.*

**Reform Act of 1832** Brought about a reform of British parliamentary voting and representation that strengthened the middle class and the urbanites.

**Reformation** The sixteenth-century upheaval led by Martin Luther and John Calvin that modified or in some cases rejected altogether some Catholic doctrine and practices; led to the establishment of Protestant churches.

**Reign of Terror** The period (1793–1794) of extreme Jacobin radicalism during the French Revolution.

**Renaissance** The social, artistic, and cultural "rebirth" that arose in Europe in the fourteenth century.

**reparations question** Money and goods that Germany was to pay to the victorious Allies after World War I under the Versailles Treaty.

**Republican government** A form of governing that imitates the Roman *res publica* in its rejection of monarchy.

***Rerum novarum*** An encyclical issued by Pope Leo XIII in 1890 that committed the Roman Catholic church to attempting to achieve social justice for the poor.

**Restoration** (English) The period of the 1660s–1680s when Charles II was called by Parliament to take his throne and was thus restored to power.

**revisionism** (Marxism) The late-nineteenth-century adaptation of Marxist socialism that aimed to introduce basic reform through parliamentary acts rather than through revolution.

**Revolution of 1989** The throwing out of the communist governments in eastern Europe by popular demand and/or armed uprising.

**Rigveda** (Rig VAY-da) The most ancient of the four Vedas, or Hindi religious epics, brought into India by the Aryans.

**Romanov Dynasty** Ruled Russia from 1613 until 1917.

**Romantic movement** The generic name for the trend in literature and the arts of early nineteenth-century Europe away from rationalism and social improvement and toward a celebration of the emotions and individualistic views.

**Rome, Treaty of** The pact signed by six western European nations in 1957 that is the founding document of the European Union.

**Rose Chamber Rescript of 1839** A major component of the Tanzimat; it called for the full equality of all Ottoman subjects, regardless of religion or ethnicity.

***Rubaiyat*** (Roo-BAY-yat) The verses attributed to the twelfth-century Persian poet Omar Khayyam.

**Safavid Empire** (SAAF-a-vid) The dynasty of Shi'ite Muslims that ruled Persia from the 1500s to the 1700s.

**Sahel** The arid belt extending across Africa south of the Sahara; also called the Sudan.

***sakoku*** Japan's self-imposed isolation from the outer world that lasted two centuries until 1854.

**Salafiyya movement** (Sah-lah-FEE-yah) Intellectual movement begun by Muhammad Abduh to try to modernize Islamic law.

**Salamis** The naval battle that, with the battle of Platea, ended the second Persian War with a Greek victory.

**Samaria** One of the two kingdoms into which the Hebrew Kingdom was split after Solomon's death; the other was Judea.

**Samsara** The recurrent reincarnation of the soul; a concept shared by Hinduism and Buddhism.

***samurai*** Japanese warrior-aristocrats of medieval and early modern times.

**Sanhedrin** The Jewish governing council under the overlordship of Rome.

**Sanskrit** The sacred language of ancient India; came originally from the Aryans.

**Sardinia-Piedmont** See *Piedmont.*

**sati** (Su-TEE) In India, the practice in which a widow committed suicide at the death of her husband.

**Satrapy** A province under a governor or *satrap* in the ancient Persian Empire.

**Savanna** The semiarid grasslands where most African civilizations developed.

***Schutzstaffel*** (SS) Hitler's bodyguard; later enlarged to be a subsidiary army and to provide the concentration camp guards.

**scientific method** The method of observation and experiment by which the physical sciences proceed to new knowledge.

**Second Front** The reopening of a war front in the west against the Axis powers in World War II; eventually accomplished by the invasion of Normandy in June 1944.

**Second Industrial Revolution** The second phase of industrialization that occurred in the late 1800s after the introduction of electric power and the internal combustion engine.

**Second International** Association of socialist parties founded in 1889; after the Russian Revolution in 1917, the Second International split into democratic and communist segments.

**secret speech** Premier Nikita Khrushchev of the USSR gave an account in February 1956 of the crimes of Joseph Stalin against his own people that was supposed to remain secret but was soon known internationally.

**secularism** The rejection of supernatural religion as the arbiter of earthly action; emphasis on worldly and humanistic affairs.

**Seleucid Kingdom of Persia** The successor state to the empire of Alexander the Great in most of the Middle East.

**Self-strengthening** The late nineteenth-century attempt by Chinese officials to bring China into the modern world by instituting reforms; failed to achieve its goal.

**Selim III, Sultan** (Se-LEEM) Ottoman sultan, 1792–1807. He introduced the first reforms of the Ottoman Empire, which later became the Tanzimat.

**Seljuks** (Sel-JUCKS) Turkish converts to Islam who seized the Baghdad government from the Abbasids in the eleventh century.

**Semitic** Adjective describing a person or language belonging to one of the most widespread of the western Asian groups; among many others, it embraces Hebrew and Arabic.

**Serfdom** Restriction of personal and economic freedoms associated with medieval European agricultural society.

**Seven Years' War** Fought between France and England, with their allies, around the world, 1756–1763; won by England, with major accessions of territory to the British Empire.

**Shah Abbas the Great** (SHAA Ab-BAAS) Greatest of the Safavid Shahs of Persia (r. 1587–1629). He extended the boundaries of the Safavid Empire to their greatest extent.

**Shaka** King of the Zulu people of South Africa. During the 1810s, he united the Zulu into a powerful, militaristic state in the region of Natal.

**Shang Dynasty** The first historical rulers of China; ruled from c. 1500 to c. 1100 B.C.E.

***Sharia*** (Sha-REE-ya) The sacred law of Islam; based on the Qur'an and the oral traditions (*Sunna*) of the Prophet Muhammad.

**Shaykh** (Shake) An Arabic honorific form of address for a respected elder, leader, or a scholar

**Shaykh al-Islam** (Shake al-Is-LAAM) Highest religious official of the Ottoman Empire.

**Shi'ites** (SHEE-ites) A minority sect of Islam; adherents believe that kinship with Muhammad is necessary to qualify for the caliphate.

***shiki*** Rights attached to parcels of land (*shoen*) in Japan.

**Shinto** Native Japanese animism.

**Shiva** (SHEE-va) A member of the high trinity of Hindu gods; lord of destruction but also of procreation; often pictured dancing.

***shoen*** Parcels of land in Japan with *shiki* (rights) attached to them; could take many forms and have various possessors.

**shogunate** The government of medieval Japan in which the shogun, a military and civil regent, served as the actual leader, while the emperor was the symbolic head of the state and religion.

**show trials** First used for the staged trials of alleged traitors to the Soviet system in 1936–1937; generically, a political trial in which the conviction of the accused is a foregone conclusion.

**Siddhartha Gautama** The proper name of the Buddha.

**Sikhs** (SEEKS) Members of a cult founded in the sixteenth century C.E. who seek a middle way between Islam and Hindu belief; centered on the Punjab region in northern India.

**Sino-Soviet conflict** Differences in the interpretation of Marxism that were accentuated by conflict over proper policy vis-à-vis the United States in the 1950s and 1960s in Moscow and Beijing.

**Sino-Tibetan languages** The family of languages spoken by the Chinese and Tibetan peoples.

**Social Darwinism** The adaptation of Darwinian biology to apply to human society in simplistic terms.

**Social Democrats** Noncommunist socialists who refused to join the Third International and founded independent parties.

**Solidarity** The umbrella organization founded by Lech Walesa and other anticommunist Poles in 1981 to recover Polish freedom; triumphed with new government in 1989.

**Song Dynasty** The dynasty that ruled China from c. 1127 until 1279, when the last ruler was overthrown by the Mongol invaders.

**Songhay Empire** (Song-GEYE) A West African state, centered on the bend of the Niger River, which reached its fullest extent in the sixteenth century before collapsing.

**spinning jenny** A fundamental mechanical improvement over hand-spinning of cotton thread, developed by an English engineer in the 1780s.

***Spirit of the Laws*** One of the basic tracts of the eighteenth-century Enlightenment, written by Baron Montesquieu and adopted by many reformers of government throughout Europe.

**Springtime of the Peoples** The spring and summer of 1848 when popular revolutions in Europe temporarily succeeded.

**Stalingrad** The battle in 1942 that marked the turning point of World War II in Europe.

**Stalinist economy** Involved the transformation of a retarded agrarian economy to an industrialized one through massive reallocation of human and material resources directed by a central plan; imposed on the Soviet Union and then, in the first years after World War II, on eastern Europe.

**Stamp Act of 1765** A law enacted by the British Parliament in 1765 that imposed a fee on legal documents of all types and on all books and newspapers sold in the American colonies.

**state** The term for a territorial, sovereign entity of government.

**Stoicism** A Hellenistic philosophy that emphasized human brotherhood and natural law as guiding principles.

**Structural Adjustment Programs** (SAPs) Programs designed by the World Bank to achieve economic improvement in developing countries; frequently failures.

***stuprum*** A Roman legal term denoting acts that were both immoral and illegal; contrast with *infamia,* which was an immoral but not illegal action.

***Sturmabteilung*** (SA) The street-fighting "bully boys" of the Nazi Party; suppressed after 1934 by Hitler's orders.

**Successor states** Usual term for the several eastern European states that emerged from the Paris treaties of 1919 as successors to the Russian, German, and Austro-Hungarian Empires.

**Sudan** (Soo-DAN) Lit. Arabic for "Blacks," from the Bilad al-Sudan, the "Land of the Blacks" in the arid belt extending across Africa south of the Sahara.

**Sufi** (SOO-fee) Arabic term for a popular form of Islam that emphasizes emotional union with God and mystical powers.

**Sui Dynasty** Ruled China from c. 580 to c. 620 C.E.; ended the disintegration of central government that had existed for the previous 130 years.

***sui juris*** "Of his own law"; Roman term for an individual, especially a female, who was not restricted by the usual laws or customs.

**Suleiman the Magnificent** (SOO-lay-man) Ottoman Sultan, 1520–1566 C.E. Greatest of the Ottoman sultans, his long reign was the high-water mark of the Ottoman Empire.

**Sumerians** The creators of Mesopotamian urban civilization.

***Sunna*** (SOO-nah) Literally, the "way" or example set by the Prophet Muhammad. It is the oral tradition that Muslim legal scholars rely upon to supplement the Qur'an as another source of the Sharia.

**Sunnis** (SOO-nees) The majority group in Islam; adherents believe that the caliphate should go to the most qualified individual and should not necessarily pass to the kin of Muhammad.

**Supremacy, Act of** A law enacted in 1534 by the English Parliament that made the monarch the head of the Church of England.

**suzerain** The superior of a vassal to whom the vassal owed feudal duties.

**Swahili** (Swa-HEE-lee) A hybrid language based on Bantu and Arabic; used extensively in East Africa. Often used to refer to the people and civilization of the East African coast.

**Syndicalism** A doctrine of government that advocates a society organized on the basis of syndicates or unions.

**Taipings** Anti-Manzhou rebels in China in the 1860s.

**Taj Mahal** (TAJ Ma-HAAL) The beautiful tomb built by the seventeenth-century Mughal emperor Jahan for his wife.

***Tale of Genji*** First known novel in Asian, if not world, history; authored by a female courtier about life in the Japanese medieval court.

**Taliban** (Ar. Students) Islamic fundamentalist militants who came to power in Afghanistan in 1995 and were expelled from the country a few years later by American and native forces.

**Tamarlane** (TAA-mar-lane) Turco-Mongolian conqueror and founder of the short-lived Timurid state in the Middle and Near East during the late fourteenth century.

**Tang Dynasty** Ruled China from c. 620 to c. 900 C.E. and began the great age of Chinese artistic and technical advances.

**Tanzimat reforms** (TAN-zi-maat) Lit. "New Order" in Turkish. The state-directed reforms of the Ottoman Empire that lasted from 1839 to 1876.

***tariqa*** (ta-REE-ka) Muslim sufi (popular mystic) brotherhoods, generally all-male.

**Tartars** (TAR-tars) Russian name for the Mongols.

**Tel el Amarna** The site of great temple complexes along the Nile River in Egypt.

**Tenochtitlán** (Te-noch-tit-LAN) Chief city of the Aztec civilization. It probably was built *ca.* 1325, and was conquered by Cortes in 1521. It was renamed Mexico City, and served as the capital of colonial Mexico.

**Teotihuacán** (Tay-o-tee-wa-KAAN) Ancient, classical Mexican city, *ca.* 200 B.C.E–800 C.E.

**Test Act** Seventeenth-century English law barring non-Anglican Church members from government and university positions.

**Tetrarchy** "Rule of four"; a system of monarchic rule established by Roman emperor Diocletian at the end of the third century C.E.; failed to achieve its goals

**theocracy** The rule by gods or their priests.

**Theravada Buddhism** A stricter, monastic form of Buddhism entrenched in Southeast Asia; same as Hinayana Buddhism.

**Thermidorean reaction** The conservative reaction to the Reign of Terror during the French Revolution.

**Third Estate** The great majority of Frenchmen: those neither clerical nor noble.

**Third International** An association of Marxist parties in many nations; inspired by Russian communists and headquartered in Moscow until its dissolution in 1943.

**Third Republic of France** The government of France after the exile of Emperor Napoleon III; lasted from 1871 until 1940.

**Third Rome** A Russian myth that Moscow was ordained to succeed Rome and Constantinople as the center of true Christianity.

**Third World** A term in use after World War II to denote countries and peoples in underdeveloped, formerly colonial areas of Asia, Africa, and Latin America; the First World was the West under U.S. leadership, and the Second World was the communist states under Soviet leadership.

**Tienanmen Square, massacre on** The shooting down of perhaps thousands of Chinese who were peacefully demonstrating for relaxation of political censorship by the communist leaders; occurred in 1989 in Beijing.

**Tilsit, Treaty of** A treaty concluded in 1807 after the French under Napoleon had defeated the Russians; divided Europe/Asia into French and Russian spheres.

**timar** (Ti-MAR) An Ottoman feudal estate held by a member of the Ottoman cavalry.

**Timbuktu** (Tim-buck-TOO) City located on the Niger River in West Africa. One of the principal staging centers of the trans-Saharan caravan trade in the Middle Ages.

**Time of Troubles** A fifteen-year period at the beginning of the seventeenth century in Russia when the state was nearly destroyed by revolts and wars.

**Titoism** The policy of neutrality in foreign policy combined with continued dedication to socialism in domestic policy that was followed by the Yugoslav Marxist leader Tito after his expulsion from the Soviet camp in 1948.

**Toltec** (TOL-tec) An Amerindian civilization centered in the Valley of Mexico; succeeded by the Aztecs.

**Torah** The first five books of the Old Testament; the Jews' fundamental law code.

**Tories** A nickname for British nineteenth-century conservatives; opposite of Whigs.

**totalitarianism** The attempt by a dictatorial government to achieve total control over a society's life and ideas.

**Transvaal** Second of the two independent states set up by the Boer Great Trek in the early nineteenth century in South Africa.

**Trekboers** South African Boer "pioneers" who trekked away from Cape Colony and civilization to settle deep inland on the South African frontier.

**tribunes** The chief representatives of the plebeians during the Roman republic.

**Triple Alliance** A pact concluded in 1882 that united Germany, Austria-Hungary, and Italy against possible attackers; the members were called the Central Powers.

**Triumvirate** "Three-man rule"; the First Triumvirate existed during the 50s B.C.E. and the Second in the 30s B.C.E. during the last decades of the Roman republic.

**Truman Doctrine** The commitment of the U.S. government in 1947 to defend any noncommunist state against attempted communist takeover; proposed by President Harry Truman.

**Tula** Chief city of the Toltec civilization, built around 800 C.E. and located to the northeast of today's Mexico City.

**Twelve Tables** The first written Roman law code; established c. 450 B.C.E.

***ulama*** (oo-la-MAA) Muslim religious scholars, usually specialists in Holy Law (see *Sharia*); sometimes called "mullahs."

**Umayyad Dynasty** (Oo-MA-yad) The caliphs resident in Damascus from 661 to 750 C.E.

***Umma*** (OO-ma) The entire Muslim community, meaning something like the Christian concept of the "Church."

**Uncertainty principle** The modern theory in physics that denies absolute causal relationships of matter and, hence, predictability.

**unequal treaties** Chinese name for the diplomatic and territorial arrangements foisted on the weak Qing Dynasty by European powers in the nineteenth century; also, the commercial treaties forced on just-opened Japan by the same powers and the United States.

**Union of Indochina** Sometimes referred to simply as Indochina. This was the official French name for their colony that included Vietnam, Laos, and Cambodia.

**Upanishads** (Oo-PAH-ni-shads) The ancient Hindu holy epics dealing with morals and philosophy.

**urban migration** A term for the widespread demographic event beginning in Europe in the early nineteenth century that saw millions of people moving into the towns and cities from the countryside.

***Utopia*** "Nowhere"; Greek term used to denote an ideal place or society.

**Utopian socialism** The dismissive label given by Marx to previous theories that aimed at establishing a more just and benevolent society.

**vassal** In medieval Europe, a person, usually a noble, who owed feudal duties to a superior, called a suzerain.

**Vedas** (VAY-das) The four oral epics of the Aryans brought into ancient India.

**Verdun, Treaty of** A treaty concluded in 843 that divided Charlemagne's empire among his three grandsons; established what became the permanent dividing lines between the French and Germans.

**vernacular** The native oral language of a given people.

**Vespucci, Amerigo** (Ves-POO-chee, A-meh-REE-go) Italian geographer who helped map the early discoveries in the New World, and after whom it was named ("America").

**villa** The country estate of a Roman patrician or other wealthy Roman.

**Vishnu** (VISH-noo) One of the high Hindu trinity of gods. The god who preserves the universe and karma.

**vizier** (Vi-ZEER) An official of Muslim government, especially a high Turkish official equivalent to prime minister.

**Wahhabism** (Wah-HOB-ism) Movement begun by Muhammad Abd al-Wahhab in the mid-1700s to impose a fundamentalist, Islamic law on Arabia. It became the foundation of Saudi Arabia as well as contemporary, radical—and sometimes violent—Islamic fundamentalism.

***waqf*** (WAHK-f) An Islamic trust established by the devout to benefit a particular group of people or institution (a mosque, for example). Usually, the *ulama* administer these foundations much as lawyers oversee trusts today.

**wandering of peoples** A term referring to the migrations of various Germanic and Asiatic tribes in the third and fourth centuries C.E. that brought them into conflict with Rome.

**Wannsee Conference** The 1942 meeting of Nazi leaders that determined the "final solution" for the Jews.

**Warsaw Pact** An organization of the Soviet satellite states in Europe; founded under Russian aegis in 1954 to serve as a counterweight to NATO.

**Wars of the Austrian Succession** Two 1740s wars between Prussia and Austria that resulted in important advantages to Prussia and its king, Frederick the Great.

**Wars of the Roses** An English civil war between noble factions over the succession to the throne in the fifteenth century.

**Waterloo** The final defeat of Napoleon in 1815 after his return from Elban exile.

***Wealth of Nations, The*** The short title of the pathbreaking work on national economy by Adam Smith; published in 1776.

**weapons of mass destruction** (WMDs) Deadly nuclear, chemical, or biological weapons.

**Weimar Republic** The popular name for Germany's democratic government between 1919 and the Nazi takeover.

***wergeld*** Under early Germanic law, a fine paid to an injured party or his or her family or lord that was equivalent to the value of the injured individual.

**Westphalia, Treaty of** The treaty that ended the Thirty Years' War in 1648; the first modern peace treaty in that it established strategic and territorial gains as more important than religious or dynastic ones.

**Whigs** A nickname for British nineteenth-century liberals; opposite of Tories.

**white man's burden** A phrase coined by Rudyard Kipling to refer to what he considered the necessity of bringing European civilization to non-Europeans.

**women's liberation** Movement, begun in the 1960s, to improve the economic and social status of women.

**World Bank** A monetary institution founded after World War II by Western nations to assist in the recovery effort and to aid the Third World's economic development.

**Yalta Conference** Conference in 1945 in southern Prussia where Franklin D. Roosevelt, Joseph Stalin, and Winston Churchill (the "Big Three") met to attempt to settle postwar questions, particularly those affecting the future of Europe.

**Yamato state** The earliest known government of Japan; divided into feudal subdivisions ruled by clans and headed by the Yamato family.

**Yin/yang** East Asian philosophical distinction between the male and female characters in terms of active versus passive, warm versus cold, and the like.

**Yom Kippur War** A name for the 1973 conflict between Israel and its Arab neighbors.

**Young Ottomans** A group of Western-educated Turkish intellectuals and journalists who, in the 1870s, supported the transformation of the Ottoman sultanate into a constitutional monarchy.

**Yuan Dynasty** (YOO-an) Official term for the Mongol dynasty of the Great Khans in China, 1279–1368.

**yurts** (YERTS) Tent-like, Mongol dwellings usually made of felt.

**Zama, Battle of** Decisive battle of the Second Punic War; Roman victory in 202 was followed by absorption of most of the Carthaginian Empire in the Mediterranean.

**Zambo** (SAAM-bo) Term for mulattos in Brazil; in colonial Spanish America, offspring of Spanish and Indian.

**Zanzibar Sultanate** Sultanate (Arab government) established in 1832 on the East African island of Zanzibar by the former Sultan of Oman, Sayyid Said bin Sultan al-Busaidi.

**Zarathustra** The mythical founder and chief prophet of the ancient Persian religion known as Zoroastrianism, which influenced Jewish and later Christian belief.

**Zhou Dynasty** The second historical Chinese dynasty; ruled from c. 1100 to c. 400 B.C.E.

***ziggurat*** The stepped and elevated temple structures that the ancient Mesopotamian civilization erected in honor of its gods.

**Zionism** A movement founded by Theodor Herzl in 1896 to establish a Jewish national homeland and to revive the study of Hebrew as a spoken language.

# ANSWERS TO TEST YOUR KNOWLEDGE

**CHAPTER 1**
1. b, 2. e, 3. d, 4. a, 5. c, 6. c, 7. b, 8. b, 9. e, 10. c

**CHAPTER 2**
1. a, 2. b, 3. b, 4. d, 5. b, 6. b, 7. d, 8. c, 9. b, 10. a

**CHAPTER 3**
1. c, 2. c, 3. c, 4. a, 5. e, 6. c, 7. b, 8. a, 9. a, 10. e

**CHAPTER 4**
1. b, 2. d, 3. b, 4. b, 5. c, 6. c, 7. b, 8. a, 9. c, 10. a

**CHAPTER 5**
1. a, 2. b, 3. a, 4. d, 5. d, 6. a, 7. a, 8. c, 9. e, 10. c

**CHAPTER 6**
1. a, 2. b, 3. b, 4. b, 5. a, 6. e, 7. b, 8. d, 9. d, 10. b

**CHAPTER 7**
1. a, 2. b, 3. b, 4. c, 5. b, 6. c, 7. b, 8. a, 9. e, 10. a

**CHAPTER 8**
1. c, 2. c, 3. c, 4. a, 5. a, 6. e, 7. d, 8. d, 9. b, 10. a

**CHAPTER 9**
1. a, 2. b, 3. b, 4. e, 5. d, 6. a, 7. d, 8. a, 9. d, 10. e

**CHAPTER 10**
1. c, 2. b, 3. d, 4. c, 5. a, 6. d, 7. d, 8. a, 9. a, 10. e

**CHAPTER 11**
1. c, 2. a, 3. b, 4. b, 5. e, 6. c, 7. b, 8. d, 9. d, 10. c

**CHAPTER 12**
1. e, 2. c, 3. a, 4. b, 5. a, 6. d, 7. e, 8. d, 9. c, 10. a

**CHAPTER 13**
1. b, 2. a, 3. a, 4. c, 5. b, 6. b, 7. a, 8. d, 9. b, 10. a

**CHAPTER 14**
1. b, 2. c, 3. e, 4. d, 5. b, 6. d, 7. a, 8. e, 9. c, 10. a

**CHAPTER 15**
1. b, 2. b, 3. c, 4. b, 5. b, 6. b, 7. c, 8. c, 9. d, 10. e

**CHAPTER 16**
1. a, 2. c, 3. c, 4. d, 5. b, 6. c, 7. a, 8. a, 9. c, 10. e

**CHAPTER 17**
1. d, 2. d, 3. c, 4. a, 5. a, 6. b, 7. c, 8. a, 9. e, 10. c

**CHAPTER 18**
1. b, 2. a, 3. c, 4. a, 5. d, 6. b, 7. b, 8. c, 9. c, 10. d

**CHAPTER 19**
1. b, 2. a, 3. d, 4. c, 5. c, 6. a, 7. e, 8. a, 9. c, 10. b

**CHAPTER 20**
1. c, 2. b, 3. e, 4. c, 5. a, 6. a, 7. a, 8. d, 9. e, 10. a

**CHAPTER 21**
1. b, 2. d, 3. a, 4. a, 5. c, 6. e, 7. c, 8. b, 9. c, 10. d

**CHAPTER 22**
1. d, 2. e, 3. a, 4. c, 5. b, 6. b, 7. d, 8. a, 9. e, 10. e

**CHAPTER 23**
1.c, 2. a, 3. a, 4. d, 5. b, 6. c, 7. d, 8. c, 9. a, 10. b

**CHAPTER 24**
1. c, 2. b, 3. c, 4. c, 5. c, 6. e, 7. a, 8. b, 9. b, 10. c

**CHAPTER 25**
1. a, 2. b, 3. e, 4. c, 5. a, 6. a, 7. d, 8. a, 9. b, 10. d

**CHAPTER 26**
1. a, 2. b, 3. e, 4. e, 5. b, 6. d, 7 a, 8. b, 9. a, 10. e

**CHAPTER 27**
1. d, 2. b, 3. d, 4. a, 5. b, 6. d, 7. b, 8. c, 9. a, 10. b

**CHAPTER 28**
1. b, 2. d, 3. e, 4. d, 5. d, 6. b, 7. c, 8. b, 9. c, 10. c

**CHAPTER 29**
1. d, 2. a, 3. c, 4. c, 5. b, 6. c, 7. c, 8. b, 9. b, 10. d.

**CHAPTER 30**
1. b, 2. e, 3. c, 4. a, 5. e, 6. d, 7. a, 8. b, 9. b, 10. c

**CHAPTER 31**
1. b, 2. a, 3. b, 4. b, 5. d, 6. b, 7. c, 8. b, 9. a, 10. a

**CHAPTER 32**
1. a, 2. b, 3. d, 4. d, 5. b, 6. e, 7. c, 8. a, 9. c, 10. e

**CHAPTER 33**
1. a, 2. c, 3. d, 4. b, 5. d, 6. b, 7. d, 8. a, 9. b, 10. a

**CHAPTER 34**
1. c, 2. d, 3. b, 4. e, 5. a, 6. a, 7. b, 8. e, 9. b, 10. a

**CHAPTER 35**
1. a, 2. b, 3. c, 4. b, 5. c, 6. a, 7. b, 8. b, 9. b, 10. e

**CHAPTER 36**
1. c, 2. c, 3. a, 4. a, 5. c, 6. a, 7. b, 8. a, 9. c, 10. e

**CHAPTER 37**
1. b, 2. e, 3. d, 4. a, 5. c, 6. e, 7. a, 8. c, 9. d, 10. b

**CHAPTER 38**
1. b, 2. a, 3. e, 4. e, 5. d, 6. c, 7. c, 8. b, 9. d, 10. a

**CHAPTER 39**
1. a, 2. b, 3. c, 4. c, 5. d, 6. c, 7. e, 8. b, 9. b, 10. d

**CHAPTER 40**
1. c, 2. b, 3. d, 4. c, 5. e, 6. c, 7. e, 8. b, 9. d, 10. b

**CHAPTER 41**
1. c, 2. b, 3. e, 4. c, 5. c, 6. d, 7. a, 8. d, 9. e, 10. a

**CHAPTER 42**
1. a, 2. c, 3. d, 4. e, 5. c, 6. a, 7, d, 8. e, 9. e, 10. b

**CHAPTER 43**
1. a, 2. b, 3. b, 4. e, 5. c, 6. c, 7. a, 8. e, 9. a, 10. a

**CHAPTER 44**
1. b, 2. b, 3. c, 4. c, 5. c, 6. b, 7. e, 8. d, 9. b, 10. d

**CHAPTER 45**
1. a, 2. e, 3. a, 4. c, 5. a, 6. d, 7. b, 8. b, 9. c, 10. d

**CHAPTER 46**
1. a, 2. c, 3. c, 4. b, 5. e, 6. e, 7. d, 8. c, 9. a, 10. b

**CHAPTER 47**
1. c, 2. b, 3. b, 4. b, 5. c, 6. b, 7. c, 8. a, 9. d, 10. b

**CHAPTER 48**
1. c, 2. c, 3. c, 4. c, 5. a, 6. d, 7. d, 8. e, 9. b, 10. b

**CHAPTER 49**
1. a, 2. b, 3. e, 4. b, 5. b, 6. a, 7. c, 8. d, 9. c, 10. a

**CHAPTER 50**
1. d, 2. c, 3. e, 4. a, 5. c, 6. e, 7. c, 8. d, 9. a, 10. d

**CHAPTER 51**
1. e, 2. d, 3. c, 4. d, 5. b, 6. e, 7. b, 8. c, 9. a, 10. b

**CHAPTER 52**
1. d, 2. a, 3. b, 4. e, 5. a, 6. d, 7. b, 8. c, 9. d, 10. c

**CHAPTER 53**
1. c, 2. a, 3. b, 4. d, 5. c, 6. a, 7. e, 8. e, 9. b, 10. a

**CHAPTER 54**
1. b, 2. b, 3. d, 4. a, 5. a, 6. b, 7. b, 8. b, 9. c, 10. e

**CHAPTER 55**
1. d, 2. b, 3. a, 4. e, 5. b, 6. d, 7. e, 8. c, 9. d, 10. c

**CHAPTER 56**
1. e, 2. a, 3. c, 4. c, 5. a, 6. c, 7. b, 8. e, 9. d, 10. d

# Index